HANDBOOK OF RESEARCH METHODS IN CLINICAL PSYCHOLOGY

SECOND EDITION

HANDBOOK OF RESEARCH METHODS IN CLINICAL PSYCHOLOGY

SECOND EDITION

Philip C. Kendall
Temple University

James N. Butcher
University of Minnesota

Grayson N. Holmbeck
Loyola University of Chicago

EDITORS

John Wiley & Sons, Inc.
New York • Chichester • Weinheim • Brisbane • Singapore • Toronto

This book is printed on acid-free paper. ∞

Copyright © 1999 by John Wiley & Sons, Inc. All rights reserved.

Published simultaneously in Canada.

This publication is designed to provide accurate and authoritative information in regard to the subject matter covered. It is sold with the understanding that the publisher is not engaged in rendering professional services. If professional advice or other expert assistance is required, the services of a competent professional person should be sought.

ISBN 0-471-29509-4

Printed in the United States of America.

10 9 8 7 6 5 4 3 2 1

We dedicate this volume to the quiet heroes of clinical psychology research: to the mentors and supervisors whose students go forward to add meaningfully to our knowledge base, to the restauranteurs at local eateries who let small groups linger to discuss and design first-rate research programs, and, most importantly, to the manifold participants whose cooperation is essential to our enterprise.

PREFACE

As with this book's first edition, several factors influenced our decision to undertake the present volume. First, we remain convinced that, although clinical psychologists make substantial and important contributions in the professional application of psychological principles, some of the most outstanding contributions have been in, or rooted in, basic clinical research. Examples include the empirically supported psychological therapies and the standardized assessment devices that have, in many ways, moved our field forward. It is to advance the science of clinical psychology, and indirectly the quality of applied professional psychology, that this edition was designed.

Second, it is our conviction that the education of clinical psychologists is optimal when it includes diverse perspectives on the research enterprise. Accordingly, we did not draw theoretical boundaries when gathering contributing authors for this work, but compiled the recognized experts to produce methodological chapters that deal with important topics regardless of theoretical or philosophical biases. It is clear to us that the rewards of research lie in broad-based methodological perspectives.

Third, this edition is intended to fill a gap—a need—for a single text appropriate for a graduate course in research methodology. Courses that emphasize corn yields, economics forecasts, mathematical formulae, or a single theoretical perspective can thwart the development of otherwise blooming scientists. This book presents a detailed discussion of the full range of important topics as well as a sampling of the wide range of more specific topics. Leading researchers in the field of clinical psychology—researchers with diverse interests and areas of expertise—collaborated to bring this text together. Our hope is that it will follow in the path of the first edition and serve as both an encyclopedic arbiter for methodological disputes and a reference guide for the research endeavors themselves.

This handbook reflects the current status of research methodologies employed in the study of human behavior and clinical services. For the volume to be useful for graduate level coursework, we devised a format that reduced the overall length but maintained comprehensive coverage. Specifically, each part begins with chapters that address the most general methodological issues in clinical psychology. Focus chapters follow, briefly addressing more specific topics of interest to clinical psychologists.

The editors express gratitude to their respective staffs, colleagues, graduate students, and family members who cooperated in various ways toward the development and production of this book. Portions of the work were completed while each of the editors was involved in his own research program. Philip C. Kendall is most grateful to the National Institute of Mental Health (MH 44042) and to the John D. and Catherine T. MacArthur Foundation for support of his research. James N. Butcher expresses thanks for support from the University of Minnesota Press. Grayson Holmbeck acknowledges support from the National Institute of Mental Health (MH 50423) and Social and Behavioral Sciences Research Grants (12-FY93-0621; 12-FY95-0496; and 12-FY97-0270) from the March of Dimes Birth Defects Foundation. We acknowledge the assistance of the staff at John Wiley & Sons and Nancy Land at Publications Development Company of Texas, and we extend a special thanks to each of the contributing authors for being a part of this venture.

PHILIP C. KENDALL
JAMES N. BUTCHER
GRAYSON N. HOLMBECK

CONTRIBUTORS————————————

Editors

Philip C. Kendall, Ph.D., ABPP
Professor and Head, Division of
  Clinical Psychology
Temple University
Philadelphia, Pennsylvania

James N. Butcher, Ph.D.
Professor of Psychology
University of Minnesota
Minneapolis, Minnesota

Grayson N. Holmbeck, Ph.D.
Associate Professor of Clinical
  Psychology
Loyola University of Chicago
Chicago, Illinois

Contributors

Lyn Y. Abramson, Ph.D.
Professor of Psychology
University of Wisconsin
Madison, Wisconsin

Lauren B. Alloy, Ph.D.
Professor of Psychology
Temple University
Philadelphia, Pennsylvania

Susan C. Baird, M.A.
Department of Psychology
University of North Carolina at
  Greensboro
Greensboro, North Carolina

David M. Bersoff, Ph.D.
Director, Biogenes Project
Woodbridge, Connecticut

Donald N. Bersoff, J.D., Ph.D.
Professor, Villanova Law School and
  Allegheny University of the Health
  Sciences
Villanova, Pennsylvania

Larry E. Beutler, Ph.D.
Professor, Department of Education,
  Counseling/Clinical/School
  Psychology Program
University of California,
  Santa Barbara
Santa Barbara, California

Daniel D. Blaine, Ph.D.
Department of Psychology
University of Hawaii at Manoa
Honolulu, Hawaii

Andrew Christensen, Ph.D.
Professor of Psychology
University of California, Los Angeles
Los Angeles, California

Dante Cicchetti, Ph.D.
Director, Mt. Hope Family Center
Professor of Psychology, Psychiatry, and
  Pediatrics
University of Rochester
Rochester, New York

John D. Cone, Ph.D.
Professor of Clinical Psychology
Department of Psychology and Family
　　Studies
United States International University
San Diego, California

Jan L. Culbertson, Ph.D.
Professor of Pediatrics
University of Oklahoma Health
　　Sciences Center
Oklahoma City, Oklahoma

John DeLuca, Ph.D.
Associate Professor of Physical
　　Medicine and Rehabilitation,
　　and of Neurosciences
Kessler Medical Rehabilitation Research
　　and Educational Corporation
West Orange, New Jersey

Joseph A. Durlak, Ph.D.
Professor of Psychology
Loyola University of Chicago
Chicago, Illinois

Ilene M. Dyller, M. S.
Department of Psychology
Temple University
Philadelphia, Pennsylvania

Kathleen A. Eldridge, M.A.
Department of Psychology
University of California, Los Angeles
Los Angeles, California

Susan E. Embretson, Ph.D.
Professor of Psychology
University of Kansas
Lawrence, Kansas

Albert D. Farrell, Ph.D.
Professor of Psychology
Virginia Commonwealth University
Richmond, Virginia

Alison Feit, M.A.
Department of Psychology
Harvard University
Cambridge, Massachusetts

Ellen C. Flannery-Schroeder, Ph.D.
Post-Doctoral Research Fellow
Department of Psychology
Temple University
Philadelphia, Pennsylvania

Julian D. Ford, Ph.D.
Director of Behavioral Health
　　Outcomes Research
Department of Psychiatry
University of Connecticut Health Center
Farmington, Connecticut

Scott T. Gaynor, M.A.
Department of Psychology
University of North Carolina at
　　Greensboro
Greensboro, North Carolina

Stephen N. Haynes, Ph.D.
Professor of Psychology
University of Hawaii at Manoa
Honolulu, Hawaii

Lara Honos-Webb, M.A.
Department of Psychology
Miami University
Oxford, Ohio

Miriam L. Jacob, M.S.W.
Research Consultant
V.A. Palo Alto Health Care System
Menlo Park, California

Theodore Jacob, Ph.D.
Research Career Scientist
V.A. Palo Alto Health Care System
Menlo Park, California

Alan E. Kazdin, Ph.D.
Professor and Chair, Department of
　　Psychology
Yale University
New Haven, Connecticut

Lynne M. Knobloch, M.A.
Department of Psychology
Miami University
Oxford, Ohio

Karen S. Kurasaki, Ph.D.
Associate Director, National Research
    Center on Asian American Mental
    Health
Department of Psychology
University of California, Davis
Davis, California

Annette M. La Greca, Ph.D.
Professor of Psychology and Pediatrics
University of Miami
Coral Gables, Florida

Erika Lawrence, M.A.
Department of Psychology
University of California, Los Angeles
Los Angeles, California

Martita Lopez, Ph.D.
Associate Professor, Departments of
    Psychology and Physical Medicine &
    Rehabilitation
Rush Medical College
Chicago, Illinois

Benny Martin, M.A.
Department of Education,
    Counseling/Clinical/School
    Psychology Program
University of California,
    Santa Barbara
Santa Barbara, California

Mary McFarlane, Ph.D.
Behavioral Scientist, Division of STD
    Prevention
Centers for Disease Control and
    Prevention
Atlanta, Georgia

Steven O. Moldin, Ph.D.
Chief, Genetics Research Branch
Division of Basic and Clinical
    Neuroscience Research
National Institute of Mental Health
National Institutes of Health
Rockville, Maryland

Karl Nelson, M.A.
Department of Psychology
University of Hawaii at Manoa
Honolulu, Hawaii

Rosemery O. Nelson-Gray, Ph.D.
Professor of Psychology
University of North Carolina at
    Greensboro
Greensboro, North Carolina

L. Katherine Prenovost, M.A.
Department of Psychology
University of Kansas
Lawrence, Kansas

George P. Prigatano, Ph.D.
Chair, Clinical Neuropsychology
Barrow Neurological Institute
St. Joseph's Hospital and
    Medical Center
Phoenix, Arizona

David Raniere, M.S.
Department of Psychology
Temple University
Philadelphia, Pennsylvania

Fred A. Rogosch, Ph.D.
Associate Professor of Psychology
Mt. Hope Family Center
University of Rochester
Rochester, New York

John M. Ruiz, M.A.
Department of Psychology
University of Utah
Salt Lake City, Utah

Bruce Rybarczyk, Ph.D.
Assistant Professor, Departments of
    Psychology and Physical Medicine &
    Rehabilitation
Rush Medical College
Chicago, Illinois

Janet S. St. Lawrence, Ph.D.
Chief, Behavioral Interventions and
    Research Branch Division of STD
    Prevention
National Center for HIV, STD, and TB
    Prevention
Centers for Disease Control and
    Prevention
Atlanta, Georgia

Wendy B. Schuman, Ph.D.
Assistant Professor of Psychiatry and
    Pediatrics
Children's National Medical Center
George Washington University School of
    Medicine
Washington, District of Columbia

Ruth Ann Seilhamer, Ph.D.
Research Associate
University of Pittsburgh
Pittsburgh, Pennsylvania

Wendy E. Shapera, M.S.
Department of Psychology
Loyola University of Chicago
Chicago, Illinois

Timothy W. Smith, Ph.D.
Professor of Psychology
University of Utah
Salt Lake City, Utah

Shobha Srinivasan, Ph.D.
Statistician, National Research Center on
    Asian American Mental Health
Department of Psychology
University of California, Davis
Davis, California

William B. Stiles, Ph.D.
Professor of Psychology
Miami University
Oxford, Ohio

Stanley Sue, Ph.D.
Professor, Departments of Psychology
    and Psychiatry
Professor and Chair, Asian American
    Studies Program
Director, National Research Center on
    Asian American Mental Health
University of California, Davis
Davis, California

Patrick H. Tolan, Ph.D.
Professor, Department of Psychiatry
Director of Research, Institute for
    Juvenile Research
University of Illinois Medical School
Chicago, Illinois

Andrew Tomarken, Ph.D.
Associate Professor of Psychology
Vanderbilt University
Nashville, Tennessee

Drew Westen, Ph.D.
Associate Professor, Department of
    Psychology
Harvard Medical School and The
    Cambridge Hospital/Cambridge
    Health Alliance
Cambridge, Massachusetts

Carolyn Zittel, M.A.
Department of Psychology
University of Massachusetts
Boston, Massachusetts

CONTENTS

PART ONE

GENERAL ISSUES IN CLINICAL RESEARCH

Chapter 1

OVERVIEW OF RESEARCH DESIGN ISSUES IN CLINICAL PSYCHOLOGY

ALAN E. KAZDIN, PH.D.

In clinical psychology, there are special demands placed on researchers due to the broad range of content areas, populations, and settings that serve as the focus of research. Key content areas include the biological, psychological, social, and cultural influences on adjustment and maladjustment and assessment, diagnosis, treatment, and prevention of clinical dysfunction. These content areas encompass all age groups from infancy through late adulthood. Indeed, in some way, the field extends beyond these age limits by studying processes before birth (e.g., prenatal characteristics of mothers and families that may influence offspring) and after death (e.g., the impact of death on the surviving relatives, treatment of bereavement). Diverse populations are studied, including persons with special experiences (e.g., the homeless, prisoners of prior wars), with psychological or psychiatric impairment (e.g., children, adolescents, or adults with depression, anxiety, posttraumatic stress disorder, autism, schizophrenia), and with medical impairment and disease (e.g., cancer, Acquired Immune Deficiency Syndrome [AIDS], spinal cord injury, diabetes). Persons in contact with special populations are often studied (e.g., children of alcoholics, spouses of depressed patients, siblings of physically handicapped children) and hence also become special populations of interest. The different content areas, age groups, and populations lead to research in diverse settings (e.g., laboratories, day care centers, clinics, hospitals, prisons, schools, industry) and less well-specified "settings" (e.g., homeless families, runaway children).

The diversity and richness of clinical research have direct implications for research methods. Ideal methodological practices (e.g., random assignment, matching of cases to ensure group equivalence) are not always available. Also, special ethical considerations (e.g., withholding treatment) or characteristics of the subject matter (e.g., only small sample sizes available for a particular problem area) limit the researcher's options. The task of the scientist is to draw valid inferences from the situation and to use methodology, design, and statistics toward that end. In clinical psychology, the methodological, design, and data analytic strategies are more diverse than in basic research. The investigator often must engage in innovative strategies and methodological solutions to draw inferences about key phenomena. Clinical research is not in any way soft science; indeed, the processes involved in clinical research reflect science at its best precisely because of the thinking and methodological ingenuity required that forces nature to reveal its secrets.

Multiple methods of study are required to meet the varied conditions in which clinical psychologists work and the special challenges in drawing valid scientific inferences from often complex situations. This chapter discusses key questions and concepts that serve as the impetus of research and the role that methodology plays in addressing these questions. Different types of designs and the conditions under which investigations can be conducted are highlighted. Special methodological challenges in research related to sampling, measurement selection, evaluation of constructs, and statistical evaluation are also presented.

GOALS OF RESEARCH

Key Questions and Concepts That Guide Research

The goals of research are to address substantive questions about the phenomena of interest. Research methods are inextricably related to these questions insofar as selection of the design, sample, measures, and methods of data analyses materially influence the answers. It is not possible to enumerate all of the questions that guide clinical research and their implications for research design. Yet, several key concepts often underlie research in clinical psychology. These concepts convey different levels of understanding phenomena and raise different design issues and strategies.

Table 1.1 presents key questions and concepts that pertain to the relations among variables of interest. At the most basic level of understanding, clinical research often focuses on identifying whether variables are *correlated*. Participants are tested on several measures at a given point in time to relate such variables as symptoms, cognitive processes, personality, stress, social support, family functioning, recall of past experiences (e.g., abuse, attachment), and physical health. The presence of a relation and the magnitude of the relations among such variables can be important for elaborating the nature of a problem and for testing or developing theories about its onset and course.

Establishing that two (or more) events are correlated is a preliminary level of understanding and, of course, does not establish their temporal relation to each other. The notion of *risk factor* represents a deeper level of understanding because the time line is established, namely, that one event or experience (e.g., abuse, prenatal exposure to drugs or alcohol, enriched educational or parenting experiences) is correlated with a later characteristic (e.g., dysfunction at school, marital bliss).[1] The early experience may not be a cause, but we know that the experience, for whatever reason, increases the likelihood of the outcome.

Demonstrating *cause* means, of course, that we have established that the relation is not merely a temporal ordering of events but rather that there is some direct influence of

---

[1] The term risk factor has emerged from epidemiology and public health, where the focus has emphasized adverse antecedents (e.g., exposure to toxins, poor nutrition) and untoward outcomes (e.g., morbidity, mortality). The term is used here more generically, as it has come to be used within clinical research, to denote antecedent factors that increase the likelihood of an outcome (see Chapter 18). The valence, desirability, or focus of either the antecedent or outcome is not critical.

Table 1.1. Sample questions and concepts that serve as the impetus for research

1. What is the relationship between (among) the variables of interest?

    Correlate—The two (or more) variables are associated at a given point in time in which there is no direct evidence that one variable precedes the other.

    Risk factor—A characteristic that is an antecedent to and increases the likelihood of an outcome of interest. A "correlate" in which the time sequence is established.

    Cause—One variable influences, either directly or through other variables, the appearance of the outcome. Changing one variable is shown to lead to a change in another variable (outcome).

2. What factors influence the relationship between variables, that is, the direction or magnitude of the relation?

    Moderator—A variable that influences the relationship of two variables of interest. The relationship between the variables (A and B) changes or is different as a function of some other variable (e.g., sex, age, ethnicity).

    Protective factor—A characteristic that reduces the likelihood of an outcome of interest among individuals identified as at risk. The relation between the risk factor and an outcome is altered by the presence of some other characteristic. Protective factors are moderators but worth distinguishing because of their interest in clinical research.

3. How does the phenomenon work; that is, through what relation or mechanism or process does A lead to B?

    Mediator—The process, mechanism, or means through which a variable produces a particular outcome. Beyond knowing that A may cause B, the mechanism elaborates precisely what happens (e.g., psychologically, biologically) that explains how B results.

4. Can we control or alter the outcome of interest?

    Intervention—Is there something we can do to decrease the likelihood that an undesired outcome will occur (prevention) or decrease or eliminate an undesired outcome that has already occurred (treatment)? Although these questions are usually framed as focusing on some undesirable outcome, they often promote positive, prosocial outcomes to achieve their end.

Note: These terms, the relations they reflect, and diverse research strategies their evaluation entails are detailed elsewhere (see Baron & Kenny, 1986; Holmbeck, 1997; Kazdin, Kraemer, Kessler, Kupfer, & Offord, 1997; Kraemer et al., 1997).

one event on the other. As a rule, several conditions usually need to be satisfied to infer cause, including evidence that the event or agent precedes the outcome, there is a strong association between the event and outcome, the relation is not due to confounding influences, the effects are consistent (replicable) across samples from the same population, and there is a plausible explanation of the mechanisms and processes through which the antecedent and outcome are related (see Haynes, 1992; Hill, 1965; Kenny, 1979; Schlesselman, 1982). No single study is likely to be sufficient to satisfy all of the criteria. From multiple studies, the causal role of the event becomes more plausible and parsimonious, as various competing interpretations are either confirmed or rejected. There are often many causes of a phenomenon of interest so that demonstrating that some event is *a* cause does not mean that the event is *the only* cause. Demonstration of causality is a high level of understanding and a goal of research.

Knowing *the cause* or *a cause* of a phenomenon can reflect different levels of understanding because precision of the knowledge may vary. In the usual case in clinical research, cause refers to knowing how to change a phenomenon. For example, a great deal of research focuses on interventions (treatment, prevention, and educational programs) to reduce clinical dysfunction, to prevent the onset of dysfunction, and to promote well-being or adaptive functioning. These studies focus on causal relations, that is, making a change at the level of the individual, school, or community, for example, will lead to change in the outcome(s) of interest. We may know how to produce change even if we are not sure of the mechanisms involved. For example, successful prevention programs (e.g., for young children at risk for school failure and behavior problems) often rely on multimodal interventions, that is, programs that entail several techniques (e.g., counseling and medical care for the parents, special day care for the child, changes at home for the child such as reading, and others) (see Meisels & Shonkoff, 1990). If such an intervention produces reliable change, we can say that a causal relation was demonstrated, even though we may not know how change was produced, precisely what facet of the intervention produced change, or what intervening steps (e.g., affect, cognition, behavior) led to the change in the target domain.

Research often focuses on *moderators,* which are variables that influence the direction, magnitude, and nature of the relation (Baron & Kenny, 1986; Holmbeck, 1997). For example, early maturation among adolescents is a risk factor for later psychopathology (internalizing and externalizing disorders and suicide attempt) for girls but not for boys (e.g., Graber, Lewinsohn, Seeley, & Brooks-Gunn, 1997). That is, gender moderates the risk-factor outcome relation between early maturation and psychopathology. (For boys, the risk stems from late rather than early maturation.) Identification of moderators is an important advance in understanding because knowing what other factors influence the relation between variables often prompts theory and research to explain why the moderator has an influence. Also, the moderating influence may suggest different causal paths for one group rather than another group.

The study of *protective factors* is an excellent example of the study of moderators. The term "protective factor" has been used in different ways. The first way is to refer to a characteristic in the population that reduces the likelihood of the outcome. In this sense, a protective factor is similar (conceptually) to a risk factor and denotes an antecedent that is associated with a particular outcome. The second and more common use is in the context of a group identified as at risk or high risk for a particular outcome (Rutter, 1987). Among individuals identified as at risk, many may not show the undesired outcome. Characteristics that are associated with a decrease in risk for this group are referred to as protective factors. Stated another way, the relation between two variables is influenced by the presence of another variable, that is, a protective factor. For example, Werner and Smith (1992) found that early influences in childhood, such as parental conflict, alcohol abuse of a parent, and below normal intellectual functioning, placed youths at risk for delinquency in adolescence. The at-risk group that did not become delinquent showed a number of characteristics that seemed to "protect" them from deleterious influences. Those who did not evince delinquency by adolescence were more likely to be firstborn, to be perceived by their mothers as affectionate, to show higher self-esteem and locus of control, and to have alternative caretakers in the family (than the parents) and a supportive same-sex model who played an important role in their development. Stated another way, the relations between several antecedents and delinquency were moderated by these other characteristics.

The focus on *mediators* or *mechanisms* represents a deeper level of understanding beyond the relations noted above, because this means we know *how* the problem unfolds, through what *processes,* and the *ways* in which one variable leads to another (see Holmbeck, 1997). As an example, an association with deviant peers during adolescence is related to subsequent antisocial and delinquent behavior (see Rutter & Giller, 1983; Stoff, Breiling, & Maser, 1997). What mediates this relation or through what mechanisms or processes does one characteristic (association with deviant peers) lead to the other (delinquent behavior)? No doubt there are multiple mechanisms involved; however, evidence suggests that in day-to-day interactions, deviant peers directly reinforce deviant behavior (Dishion & Patterson, 1997). For example, in a delinquent peer group, when the conversation of an individual focuses on rule breaking, there is a positive reaction (e.g., laughter) which serves to reinforce and extend discussion of deviance. In addition, deviant peers tend not to react positively to more normative talk. This evidence suggests that there is a deviance training process in the interactions of delinquent peers and this process leads to escalation of rule-breaking acts. Multiple influences are likely to contribute to and explain the connection between association with deviant peers and delinquent behavior.

Consider another example where the mediator refers to a circumscribed process that explains more precisely the relation of an antecedent and an outcome. Research on the relation of cigarette smoking and lung cancer has spanned the range of concepts included in Table 1.1. That is, both human and animal studies have shown that cigarette smoking is a correlate of, a risk factor for, and a cause of lung cancer. This still leaves open the question of *how* cigarette smoking leads to the disease, that is, through what mechanisms or intervening processes. Recent research has elaborated the mechanism involved in the causal relation. A chemical (benzo[a]pyrene) found in cigarette smoke induces genetic mutation (at specific regions of the gene's DNA) that is identical to the damage evident in lung cancer cells (Denissenko, Pao, Tang, & Pfeifer, 1996). This finding is considered to convey precisely how cigarette smoking leads to cancer at the molecular level. Thus, beyond the demonstration of a causal relation, a fine-grained analysis of mechanisms is important as well. Knowing the mediator of a relation between variables does not require knowing the biological substrates. The mechanism or process through which two variables are related may involve all sorts of psychological constructs.

Our understanding, of course, is optimal when we know all of the above in great detail about a particular phenomenon of interest, that is, correlates, risk factors, moderators, causes, and mechanisms or processes through which outcomes are produced. There are few areas that are so well established. An example that encompasses many of the key concepts is the relation of parenting practices and the development of aggressive and antisocial behavior in children. Research has shown that inept parental discipline practices foster aggressive and antisocial behavior at home (see Dishion, Patterson, & Kavanagh, 1992; Patterson, Reid, & Dishion, 1992). These discipline practices include parental attention to deviant behavior, interactions in which increasingly aggressive child behavior is reinforced, inattention to prosocial behavior, coercive punishment, poor child supervision, and failure to set limits. Initial studies showed that inept discipline practices were correlated with child antisocial behavior, as measured by parent, teacher, and peer ratings, both in community and clinic samples of boys and girls (Dishion et al., 1992; Forgatch, 1991). Further studies helped to establish the time line, namely that inept child-rearing practices preceded child antisocial behavior.

The causal role of parenting practices and antisocial behavior was suggested in *randomized controlled clinical trials* in which parents were randomly assigned to various treatment and control conditions.[2] Those conditions involving direct alteration of parent discipline practices, compared to treatment and control conditions without this focus, led to decreases in child antisocial behavior (Dishion & Andrews, 1995; Dishion et al., 1992). Several controlled studies have shown similar results, namely, changes in parenting skills lead to changes in child behavior (see Kazdin, 1997). From multiple studies, we know that adverse (especially harsh) parenting practices lead to aggressive and antisocial child behavior, even though this does not imply such practices are *the* cause of aggressive behavior, the *only* cause of these behaviors, or even a *necessary or sufficient* cause of the behaviors. Although less well studied, research has identified some of the factors that influence the effectiveness of parent training, including age of the child, severity of child antisocial behavior, socioeconomic disadvantage, stress, and dysfunction in the family (e.g., Kazdin, 1995; Webster-Stratton, 1996). There remains a great deal to learn. The precise mechanisms are not entirely clear. That is, changes in child behavior might result through a number of processes including the direct operation of reinforcement and punishment contingencies and/or improved parental responsiveness to their children (see Wahler & Meginnis, 1997). Yet, from the progression of research we know a great deal about parenting practices, their impact, and what we can do about them.

Importance of Theory

The progression of research from correlation to cause and hence from description to explanation, as described to this point, may inadvertently imply a crass empiricism, that is, one merely tests different types of relations among variables to see what role they play, if any. Underlying the concepts that guide research highlighted in Table 1.1 is the investigator's theory that focuses the research idea. Theory, broadly defined, refers to a conceptualization of the phenomenon of interest. The conceptualization may encompass views about the nature, antecedents, causes, correlates, and consequences of a particular characteristic or aspect of functioning. Also, the theory may specify the relations of various constructs to each other. There are different levels of theory in terms of their breadth, generality, and scope of affect, cognition, and behavior they attempt to encompass. In contemporary work, theories tend to be relatively circumscribed in an effort to explain the relation between selected characteristics and a disorder (e.g., hopelessness and helplessness in relation to depression) and how these characteristics lead to other features of dysfunction. Theories that attempt to explain large segments of functioning

---

[2] A randomized, controlled clinical trial refers to an outcome study in which clients with a particular problem are randomly assigned to various treatment and control conditions.

(e.g., all of clinical depression) are likely to be very general and are very unlikely to adequately account for varied patterns. The focus on segments of a problem, subtypes, and
different developmental periods is more common. Once there is support for a theory
within a narrow domain, it is then likely to be extended.

A goal is to understand human functioning and to accomplish that we do not merely
accumulate facts or empirical findings. Rather, or in addition, we strive to relate these
findings to each other and to other phenomena in a cohesive way. For example, an investigator may demonstrate that there are gender differences regarding a particular
disorder, personality characteristic, or cognitive style. However, such differences are
not necessarily inherently interesting. A theoretical understanding would pose how
this difference develops and what implications the difference may have for understanding biological or psychosocial development. Inevitably, there will be many exceptions to the theory and these will require posing moderators and new lines of work.
From the standpoint of research, theoretical explanations guide further studies and the
data generated by the studies require emendations of the theory. This activity is important because theory moves us to implications beyond the confines of the specific relations that have been demonstrated and the restricted conditions in which these
relations may have been demonstrated.

THE ROLE OF RESEARCH METHODS

Drawing Valid Inferences

The purposes of empirical research are to demonstrate relations among variables, as
highlighted in Table 1.1, and to test theoretical propositions about those relations. Research methods play a central role because most relations of interest cannot be readily
dissected when viewed in their full complexity as they appear in nature. Research design and statistical evaluation help simplify the situation in which the influence of
many variables, often operating simultaneously, can be separated from the variable(s)
of interest to the investigator. Without such simplification and isolation of variables,
many if not an unlimited number of interpretations could explain a particular phenomenon. Among these interpretations is the possibility that in fact there is no relation between the variables of interest, that there is a relation but it is obscured by other
influences, and that there is no relation but one appears to exist in light of other influences that are operating. Research methods make a special contribution by helping to
rule out or make implausible several different factors that might explain the relation
that the investigator wishes to evaluate. An experiment does not necessarily rule out all
possible explanations; the extent to which it is successful in ruling out alternative explanations is a matter of degree. From a methodological standpoint, a well-designed
experiment is one in which competing hypotheses that might explain the results are
made relatively implausible or ruled out.

The purpose of research is to reach well-founded (i.e., valid) conclusions about the
effects of a given intervention, experimental manipulation, or condition. Four types of
experimental validity have been delineated as a useful way to identify major design issues that can emerge and interfere with drawing valid inferences. These consist of internal, external, construct, and statistical conclusion validity (Cook & Campbell,

1979). Table 1.2 lists each type of validity, the methodological question each is designed to address, and sources of influence or threats to validity that can interfere with conclusions the investigator wishes to reach. Research design, methodological practices, and statistical evaluation assist in rendering implausible or less plausible sources of threat that might otherwise explain the results.

Brief Illustrations

The threats to validity and how they interface with substantive questions can be illustrated by considering a few basic experimental arrangements. Consider that an investigator is interested in establishing the effectiveness of a new treatment—in fact, a

Table 1.2.   Types of experimental validity and the issues they raise

Internal validity—To what extent can the intervention, rather than extraneous influences, be considered to account for the results, changes, or group differences?

   Validity is threatened to the extent that the results can be explained by history, maturation, repeated testing, changes in the measure in some way, regression toward the mean, selection differences/biases among groups, attrition, special influences affecting one group but not another, diffusion of treatment, and special treatment or reactions of control participants.

External validity—To what extent can the results be generalized or extended to people, settings, times, measures, and characteristics other than those in this particular experimental arrangement?

   Validity is threatened to the extent that the results are restricted because of special characteristics of the sample, stimulus conditions of the experiment or setting, reactivity (awareness of participating in a study or of the measurement procedures), the way in which the intervention was presented (e.g., in the context of multiple treatments), novelty effects, and test sensitization (the results due in part to the measures that influenced receptivity to the intervention).

Construct validity—Given that the intervention was responsible for change, what specific aspect(s) was the causal agent; that is, what is the conceptual basis (construct) underlying the effect?

   Validity is threatened to the extent that group differences could be explained by differential attention and contact with the subjects, experimenter expectancies, cues of the experimental situation, single operations (e.g., one therapist), and narrow stimulus sampling that cannot be separated from the intervention.

Statistical conclusion validity—To what extent is a relation shown, demonstrated, or evident, and how well can the investigation detect effects if they exist?

   Validity is threatened by low statistical power, variability in the procedures, subject heterogeneity, unreliability of the measures, restrictive or lenient error rates due to multiple tests.

Note: Additional discussion and illustrations of these threats and the issues they raise are provided elsewhere (Kazdin, 1998).

brand new treatment our group has been secretly developing is *ear-movement desensitization.* An investigator may wish to show that this treatment improves a particular clinical problem (i.e., establish a causal relation). An initial demonstration might be reported in which one group is studied. The investigator identifies and treats 20 individuals with the problem. At the end, an evaluation of the measures from pretreatment to posttreatment assessment shows that the group has in fact improved (e.g., statistically significant within-group changes). Without suitable control or comparison groups, it is obvious that the major threats to internal validity, such as historical events, maturational processes, repeated testing, statistical regression, and others (Table 1.2), might well explain the results. Treatment may not have been necessary at all to show improvements. In other words, all sorts of interpretations other than treatment effects can explain the pre- to posttreatment changes; threats to internal validity codify some of the most blatant method problems (see Kazdin, 1998).

Assume that the next study is conducted in which a no-treatment control condition is added to the design. Suppose, for example, that 50 individuals are recruited and assigned randomly to the treatment condition or to a no-treatment control group. All 50 participants complete pre- and posttreatment measures and the results show that the treated cases were better (lower symptom scores) than nontreated cases. Methodologically, this demonstration is a vast improvement insofar as key threats to internal validity are not very plausible. Any influences likely to explain changes from pre- to posttreatment, other than the intervention, probably are similar for treated and nontreated cases. Consequently, we are entitled to say that the intervention is likely to be responsible for change.

There are still other interpretations that loom large in explaining the results of the above study. Among the key issues is construct validity. Although the intervention led to change, what *is* the intervention or what about that intervention is responsible? The investigator wishes to discuss how ear movements and anxiety compete and lead to change, that is, how specific facets of treatment are the key explanatory constructs. However, there are some nontrivial alternative hypotheses. For example, it might well be that treatment was effective because the participants had contact with a therapist, attended regular sessions, worked on their "problems," and expected to improve as a result. That is, even though major threats to internal validity are ruled out or made implausible, interpretation of the findings is not automatically clear.

Undaunted, our investigator next designs a study in which participants ($N = 75$) are randomly assigned to treatment, no-treatment, or attention-placebo groups. The attention-placebo group includes regular sessions in which the therapist and client engage in activities not expected to reduce or eliminate the clinical problem. These activities may consist of discussion of how anxiety came about or other procedures that are not thought to be therapeutic on theoretical grounds but that would provide participants contact with a therapist. This group would make implausible some of the nonspecific or common factors associated with psychotherapy as an explanation of the effects of treatment. Alas, at the end of this study, suppose the findings showed that at posttreatment assessment, the treated cases were better than no-treatment or attention-placebo control cases. This would strongly suggest that some facet of the treatment, other than generic or common influences such as merely coming to any sessions, was responsible. Many threats to construct validity were made less plausible by the demonstration.

These brief illustrations convey some of the key threats that can emerge and how various control conditions can serve to reduce the plausibility of these threats as explanations of the findings. There are varying degrees of plausibility of various threats and also more subtle manifestations of threats than those included in the hypothetical illustrations. For example, even if there were random assignment of participants to treatment, no-treatment, and attention-placebo control conditions, other threats might readily emerge. Suppose the study used one therapist to provide treatment condition and attention-placebo condition. This would raise alternative rival hypotheses in terms of construct validity and external validity. In terms of construct validity, it is possible that it is not the treatment but the treatment-in-combination-with-this-therapist that led to the changes. That is, there may be an interaction in which the therapist effect cannot be separated from the treatment effect. That the therapist was "constant" in both treatment and attention-placebo groups is not helpful because he or she still might administer the conditions in different ways or in ways that could augment the effects of the treatment group, unrelated to the treatment procedures per se. In terms of external validity, it is possible that the effects are not generalizable to any other therapists.

In these illustrations, only a few issues were mentioned. The threats to validity do not usually reflect blatant neglect of influences related to internal validity. More likely, the findings may be restricted to the characteristics of the sample or to the laboratory paradigm in which it was studied (external validity). Also, the reasons why an experimental manipulation or intervention was effective may be unclear (construct validity). In addition, key issues related to the data evaluation such as very low power (e.g., due to small sample size, adjustment of alpha for the number of statistical tests) or excessive variability in the data (e.g., due to heterogeneity of the participants or unreliability of the measures: statistical conclusion validity) can threaten the validity of an experiment. Research, methodology, and statistical evaluation are central tools to optimize the clarity of a demonstration.

General Comments

The challenge of research stems from the fact that no experiment can be perfectly designed to address all threats to validity and potential sources of bias (see Kazdin, 1998). Care and attention to one source of threat to validity may sacrifice another source of validity. For example, randomized controlled trials of psychotherapy are usually conducted under highly controlled conditions, including recruitment of participants who are relatively homogeneous (e.g., in age, social class, education) and whose problems are relatively circumscribed, random assignment of participants to conditions, use of well-trained therapists, monitoring the integrity of treatment, use of manualized treatment, and holding the number of sessions or time in treatment relatively constant. These and other practices reduce several threats to internal and statistical conclusion validity. At the same time, the practices may affect generality (external validity) of the results, that is, raise questions about whether the results apply to persons seen in clinical practice under conditions that are often diametrically opposed to each of the circumstances in research trials. The task in designing a study is to identify the key questions and to arrange conditions so that these particular questions are addressed with minimum ambiguity. This requires making decisions that involve compromises in terms of the priority accorded different types of validity.

The task for clinical psychology is to provide a portfolio of research on a given topic. From the standpoint of the goals of research, the purpose is to uncover the ways in which the construct of interest is manifest and to elaborate the ways in which it operates (e.g., correlates, moderators, and mediators). From the standpoint of methodology, the purpose of multiple studies is to ensure that the findings can be attributed to the key constructs of interest rather than to other influences (e.g., threats to validity). Across a range of studies, it is likely that the various threats to validity will differ. The strength of multiple studies comes from the consistencies of conclusions across a range of methodological conditions.

As part of the research enterprise, replication of findings is critically important. Replication refers to repetition of an investigation. There are many different types of replication that have been distinguished; the types largely vary in the extent to which the study follows the precise conditions of the original investigation (e.g., see Carlsmith, Ellsworth, & Aronson, 1976; Rosenthal, 1991). Replication studies directly test the robustness and generality of a finding. They ask whether the relation holds across changes in conditions of the experiment because not all conditions in the replication study (e.g., who serves as participants) are identical to the original study. If the replication does not support the original research finding, this does not necessarily impugn the original study. Rather, the results may suggest that the relation holds only for a narrow set of conditions or relates to a specific circumscribed set of factors. It is also possible that the original findings were due to "chance" (Type I error) and reflect the 5 out of 100 instances that one would reject the null hypothesis (no difference) when using $p < .05$, if the investigation were repeated an infinite number of times. Replication studies are critically important and serve as the best protection against perpetuating chance findings. When replication studies depart in varying degrees from the original study (e.g., in sample, measures, investigators) and corroborate the original findings, we can be more confident that the relations of interest are reliable and do not depend on very special or narrowly restricted conditions. There are occasions in which we may not be concerned at all about whether the findings are evident only under restricted conditions. In testing very specific theoretical propositions, as in basic laboratory research, the investigator may select a very special paradigm to test a relation of interest. Replication within that paradigm is still important, but the findings might not be evident in any other context.

RESEARCH DESIGN STRATEGIES

Research in clinical psychology relies on a diverse set of design options. Different types of experimental designs, the focus on groups versus individuals, varied conditions of experimentation, and the time frame of research are key dimensions that illustrate the options for addressing the substantive questions of interest and for drawing valid inferences. Key options that are used in clinical psychology are highlighted next.

Types of Designs

Research in clinical psychology actively draws upon three major types of studies: true experiments, quasi-experiments, and observational studies, each with multiple variations (see Kazdin, 1998). *True experiments* consist of investigations in which the arrangement permits maximum control over the independent variable or manipulation of interest. The investigator is able to assign participants to different conditions on a random basis, to vary conditions (e.g., treatment and control conditions) as required by the design, and to control possible sources of bias within the experiment. As mentioned before, when true experiments are conducted in the context of a treatment study, they are referred to as randomized controlled clinical trials. True experiments is the more generic term to apply to studies with an intervention or experimental manipulation and random assignment of participants to conditions. True experiments provide the strongest basis for drawing inferences about the impact of a particular variable. Control of the assignment of participants and of delivery of the intervention permits one to demonstrate a causal relation between the intervention or manipulation and the outcome.

Occasionally, the investigator cannot control all features that characterize true experiments. Some facet of the study such as the assignment of participants to conditions or of conditions to settings cannot be randomized. *Quasi-experiments* refer to those designs in which the conditions of true experiments are approximated (Campbell & Stanley, 1963). For example, an investigator may be asked to evaluate a school-based intervention program designed to prevent drug abuse or teen pregnancy. The investigator wishes to use a nonintervention control group because the passage of time and course of development (e.g., history, maturation, testing, and other internal validity threats) can lead to change. However, for practical reasons, a control condition is not permitted within the school that wishes the program. The investigator seeks other schools that will serve as nonintervention control groups and be tested over time for comparison purposes. These other schools might be similar (e.g., in population, size, and geography). Yet the possibility of selection biases or combination of other threats to internal validity (Table 1.1) may become plausible explanations of the results because the assignment of children or schools to conditions is not random. A host of other factors (e.g., motivation for change among administrators) may differ greatly across conditions. Already the design is less ideal than one would like. Nevertheless, depending on the ingenuity of the investigator in the selection, matching, and assignment of intervention and control conditions, care in the execution of the intervention, and use of statistical evaluation, very strong inferences can be drawn about the impact of the intervention.

True and quasi-experiments refer primarily to studies where an independent variable is manipulated by the investigator. A great deal of clinical research focuses on variables that "nature" has manipulated in some way. *Observational studies* refer to designs in which a variable or set of variables is studied by selecting participants who vary in the characteristic or experience of interest.[3] For example, a commonly used variation of the design is a case-control study in which the investigator might wish to study differences between cigarette smokers and nonsmokers; between marital partners who are in the same occupation versus those who are not; and between individuals who experienced trauma versus those who did not. In the simplest case, the investigator identifies individuals who have the characteristic of interest (cases) and those who

---

[3] Observational studies refer to the design method rather than to the assessments that might be used. Other and overlapping terms for observational studies have included naturalistic, passive-observational, and correlational studies (see Kazdin, 1998).

do not (controls). Groups are compared on other characteristics to test theory or to elaborate novel features of the problem in the past or in the future, depending on the time frame for research.

It is often the case that true experiments, as compared to observational studies, are considered the only firm basis for drawing "causal" inferences in science, a clear demonstration that the independent variable led to the effects on the dependent variable. Yet, observational studies are not merely diluted experiments, invariably flawed, or inherently incapable of yielding causal information. Ingenuity of the investigator in selecting cases and controls, use of prospective designs, statistical analyses (e.g., path analyses, causal modeling, structural equation modeling, cross-lagged panel correlations) often permit strong inferences to be drawn from case-control studies. Many observational studies are prospective, that is, identify one or more groups of participants and then follow them over time. In these variations of research, the time line of events (e.g., risk factors, outcomes), different paths toward an outcome of interest, and the relative contribution of many influences on an outcome can be readily identified (see Kazdin et al., 1997).

Group and Single-Case Designs

The vast majority of studies in clinical psychology, and indeed in psychology in general, consist of *group designs*. With group designs, several subjects are studied and assigned to conditions. Typically, each group receives only one of the conditions (various treatment or control conditions). A between-group design includes at least as many groups as there are experimental conditions. In addition, depending on the precise question or hypothesis of interest, control groups add to the number of groups in the study.

Preliminary assignment of participants to groups is usually determined randomly to produce groups equivalent on factors possibly related to the independent variable (intervention) or that might also account for group differences on the measures (dependent variables). If groups are equivalent on such factors *before* the experimental manipulation or treatment, any differences among groups *after* the manipulation are assumed to result from the effects of different experimental conditions. The effects of different experimental and control conditions across groups are evaluated statistically by comparing groups on the dependent measures. Group designs can be true experiments, quasi-experiments, and observational studies.

Single-case experimental designs are also used in clinical psychology. These designs are characterized by investigation of one or more individuals or a group over time. The underlying goal in between-group and single-case designs is identical, namely, to draw valid inferences about the independent variable or relations among variables. In group research, a large number of subjects usually are assessed on one or two occasions (e.g., pretest and posttest). In single-case research, few participants usually are included but assessment is provided on a large number of occasions. The dependent measures of interest are administered repeatedly over time (e.g., regularly for several days or weeks). The impact of the independent variable is examined in relation to the data pattern for the subject or group of subjects over time. Single-case designs play a special role in clinical work because of the frequent focus on the treatment of individual clients. Single-case designs can be used to evaluate the impact of a given intervention or multiple interventions.

There are many design options that encompass true experiments and quasi-experiments (see Kazdin, 1998). Observational studies that involve only one group might be considered a single-case design. However, typically such designs divide the sample to make critical group comparisons.

Conditions of Experimentation

The conditions under which the investigation is conducted to test the ideas of interest can vary widely. In clinical psychology, the distinction between *laboratory* and *applied conditions* conveys the issues that emerge. In laboratory research, the hypotheses are tested under well-controlled conditions with little or no attempt to address the phenomenon of interest as it might be evident in everyday life. For example, college students may receive instructions designed to alter their mood, perform a task, or evaluate a videotape of another person. The laboratory conditions provide a well-controlled test of a phenomenon. In contrast, research in an applied setting may be at a clinic where patients are seen for treatment. The research may focus on less well-isolated independent variables and under conditions where experimental control is more difficult to exert. Laboratory research is essential for elaborating phenomena, testing theory, and isolating variables of interest through very carefully controlled conditions. At the same time, there is a keen interest in clinical psychology in generating principles and practices that can be applied and are relevant to everyday life.

The generality of findings from one context (e.g., the laboratory) to another (clinic, school, home) invariably is an issue in research and is why the matter is codified as a source of experimental validity (external). The concern is currently voiced in the context of intervention research and is encompassed by the distinction between efficacy and effectiveness research (Hoagwood, Hibbs, Brent, & Jensen, 1995). *Efficacy research* refers to well-controlled, laboratory-based intervention studies. An example is a psychotherapy study that includes several conditions (e.g., homogeneous participants and carefully controlled, monitored, and executed treatments) to optimize experimental control. *Effectiveness research* focuses more on conditions of clinical settings where participants, therapists, and administration of treatment are likely to be much more variable. An example is a psychotherapy study conducted in a service-oriented clinic where therapists and clients in everyday practice participate and where treatment administration is less well controlled. The distinction reflects a frequently discussed theme about the natural tension between rigor and relevance (Ross, 1981). Methodological rigor is likely to be less in clinical settings, but the conditions in which the study is carried out closely resemble or reflect those conditions to which one wants to generalize. Studies can vary widely on a number of dimensions that pertain to conditions of clinical settings, and hence efficacy and effectiveness are bipolar ends of a continuum or multiple continua rather than discrete categories (Kazdin, 1978).

There are hundreds of psychotherapy outcome studies. The conditions in which therapy has been studied place the vast majority of these investigations toward the efficacy side of the continuum. For example, persons recruited in treatment for efficacy studies tend to have more circumscribed, less chronic, and less severe clinical dysfunctions than those who are seen in treatment settings; the therapists who provide treatment and the treatment they provide are carefully monitored in efficacy studies. The question is whether results from therapy in controlled research (efficacy studies) can generalize to therapy in clinical settings (effectiveness). The jury is still out—one meta-analysis suggests that effects are stronger in laboratory-based studies (Weisz, Weiss, & Donenberg, 1992) and another suggests that the effects are similar in both contexts (Shadish et al., 1997).

From the standpoint of research design, it is important to underscore a broader message. Conditions of the investigation or characteristics of the way a phenomenon is studied may well influence the findings. Stated another way, methodological features of the study can serve as *moderators* of the relations that are investigated. These include characteristics of the participants, the specific way in which key constructs are operationalized (i.e., the measures), how and to what extent delivery of experimental conditions is controlled, decisions about the data (e.g., how to handle dropouts, outliers), and the methods of data analysis.

For the individual investigator, the task is to identify at the outset the types of conclusions that he or she wishes to draw and to select the conditions of experimentation in which these are best served. For the field as a whole across multiple investigations, the task may be somewhat different. If characteristics of how a study is completed may moderate the findings, it is important to encourage the use of different approaches (e.g., qualitative, quantitative), design strategies (single case, within group, between subject), types of experiments (e.g., true experiments, case-control designs), and methods of data analyses. Methodological diversity is not an end in its own right but rather a way of revealing different facets of a phenomenon of interest as well as examining the extent to which relations are robust across conditions of investigation.

Generality of findings is not always relevant, important, or an essential criterion for assessing the value of an investigation. In many cases, the goal may be to test a theory or to isolate a phenomenon (e.g., cognitive process) and the conditions on which it depends (e.g., in relation to a specific context) (Mook, 1983). For example, an investigator may wish to show that a particular effect can happen because this would provide an important counterinstance to a theoretical proposition or raise critical questions. One thinks of such effects as only tied to laboratory research and infrahuman studies on basic (e.g., psychophysiological) processes. Yet, in clinical research on critically important issues, the generality of findings is not necessarily essential. For example, research has indicated that some women as adults perceive benefits to having been sexually abused as children (McMillen, Zuravin, & Rideout, 1995). These findings do not gainsay the extensive research indicating that sexual abuse is a risk factor for a variety of deleterious mental and physical health outcomes (see Wyatt & Powell, 1988). Even so, the prospect that there are perceived benefits for some women and that these are associated with adjustment raise provocative theoretical questions about coping mechanisms and potential avenues for intervening among individuals who have been victimized. The finding is important because of the many issues that are raised, whether or not the perceived benefits or reactions of the sample in this study are highly generalizable to very many people.

Time Frame for Research

The bulk of research is conducted in a concurrent time frame in which the independent variables are manipulated and their effect on dependent variables is evaluated within a relatively brief period. At the extreme, a laboratory study may expose participants to experimental conditions and obtain the measures immediately thereafter. *Cross-sectional studies* refer to investigations in which measures are obtained at a single point in time. These stand in contrast to *longitudinal studies* in which measures are obtained over time. At the extreme, the study may involve years or indeed decades. Participants are assessed on separate occasions over time and various groups may be formed at the outset or over the course of the study to make comparisons of interest. Not all longitudinal studies are so protracted. Treatment studies, for example, have a longitudinal perspective but assessment before and after treatment may involve a matter of weeks or months rather than several years.

Cross-sectional and longitudinal studies are not different ways of obtaining the same information. If that were the case, there would be little interest in, need for, or advantage to using longitudinal research. The different time frames can answer quite different questions and also provide different answers to the same questions. For example, many behaviors (e.g., stuttering, anxiety, destroying objects, lying) are common over the course of early child development. The different problems wax and wane, peak at different periods, and among nonclinic samples, usually diminish to a very low rate. The pattern of behavior can be assessed concurrently by evaluating children of different ages (e.g., 4-, 6-, 8-, and 10-year-olds). This would be a cross-sectional study because all children are assessed at a single point in time. If there are patterns across these age groups, the results might *suggest* a developmental pattern, that is, how behaviors change in frequency (or some other characteristic) over time. This is not the same as the yield from a longitudinal study in which a group is identified in infancy or childhood and repeatedly assessed (e.g., every few years) over the course of childhood, adolescence, and adulthood (e.g., Werner & Smith, 1992). The longitudinal study portrays how behaviors actually *change* in a given sample because the same children are studied over time.

One type of study is not inherently superior. Indeed, they have different strengths and limitations. For example, a cross-sectional study may suggest that children show different characteristics at different ages. Yet, there is a possible *cohort effect*. This refers to the possibility that different age groups of participants (cohorts) may have unique characteristics because of their different histories. Thus, for example, when they mature, the 2-year-olds may not have the same pattern of behavior as the 8-year-olds; possibly, something about how the 2-year-olds are growing up (e.g., nutrition, different parenting styles with more or fewer parents in the home) influences their performance in ways not evident in the other group(s) so that in six years, when they are 8 years old, they will not look like the 8-year-olds included in the cross-sectional study.

In a longitudinal study, differential history of the group is controlled because a group or more than one group is followed over time. We know that the 2-year-olds matured into 8-year-olds with a particular pattern. There is a cohort effect as well within the longitudinal study because it is possible that 2-year-olds who were followed over time might differ from other 2-year-olds who were selected at a different point in time (e.g., a decade earlier). Also, in longitudinal studies, it is often difficult to follow the subjects. Attrition or loss of subjects over time can limit the conclusions because of selection biases if the sample is increasingly depleted. Longitudinal and cross-sectional design strategies are often combined by selecting a few groups (e.g., 4-, 6-, and 8-year-olds), assessing them cross-sectionally, and then following them for a few years (e.g., two to four years). The strategy speeds up the design a bit from merely following one sample longitudinally for an extended period and permits one to assess whether cohorts differ when they are at the same age.

Cross-sectional and longitudinal designs often address different questions about a phenomenon of interest. For example, an investigator may be interested in the correlates among children of viewing violence on television, a topic that has received considerable attention. Within a current time perspective, the investigator might compare children who view violent television versus those who watch as much television but who do not view violent programs. Children might be matched on diverse subject (e.g., age, sex, IQ) and demographic characteristics (e.g., socioeconomic status, type of neighborhood). Cross-sectional comparisons might then be made on some other measures such as personality characteristics of the child or parents or perhaps aggressive behavior of the child at home or at school. The purpose would be to elaborate the features associated with television viewing. As an alternative, a more longitudinal focus might include following (assessing) children over time. Among the questions asked might be: What are the correlates of early television viewing later in life; among children who watch violent television, what distinguishes those who become aggressive from those who do not; and among children who do not watch violent television, what distinguishes those who become aggressive from those who do not? Cross-sectional and longitudinal designs play a complementary role in elaborating a phenomenon of interest.

SPECIAL CHALLENGES

Conducting research raises special challenges that derive from decisions the investigator is asked to make about the design of the study. Who will serve as the participants, what measures are to be used, and what conditions are needed to permit inferences to interpret the findings? Challenges raised in addressing these questions and strategies to address these challenges are discussed next.

Sampling Issues

A pervasive concern in research is the restricted range of subject populations that are sampled and the implications that this may have for the findings. The heavy reliance on college students as participants is one source of this concern. Typically, students are recruited to an experiment by receiving credit toward an undergraduate psychology course or monetary incentives or by being solicited as volunteers by experimenters who circulate among psychology classes. An issue is whether the findings obtained with college students will generalize to other samples. For example, psychotherapy research occasionally utilizes student samples whose subject, demographic, and problem-related characteristics (severity, chronicity, and comorbidity) depart from those of persons who are referred for treatment. The generality of findings to clinical samples might plausibly be challenged because many of the characteristics that vary are likely to influence the effectiveness of treatment.

The paucity of studies investigating women, underrepresented minority groups, and persons from different cultures is a second sampling concern. It is quite possible that findings will vary as a function of key sample differences. For example, biological responses to psychotropic medication (e.g., for depression, anxiety) can vary greatly as a function of racial and ethnic differences (Lin, Poland, & Nagasaki, 1993). Such findings underscore the need to sample broadly, to evaluate the moderating role of sample differences, and to pursue mechanisms through which moderating factors may operate.

The use of *samples of convenience* is a third concern. This refers to the selection and use of subjects merely because they are available, whether or not they are particularly well suited to the research question. Selection of college students as subjects is one instance of using a sample of convenience. However, the term is more commonly invoked for the case in which individuals are recruited because of their special characteristics (e.g., seeking help at a special treatment facility or meeting a complex set of inclusion and exclusion criteria). As that study is begun, the original investigators or other investigators realize that the data set can be used to test other hypotheses, even though the original sample may not be the sample that would have been identified originally if the new purposes were the central part of the study. The use of a highly specialized population that is selected merely because it is convenient raises concern. The factors that make the sample special may have implications for generalizing the results. When samples of convenience are used, the onus is on the investigator to evaluate whether unique features of the sample may contribute to the results.

It may be the case that a convenient sample is also one that *is* well suited to a purpose other than the original design. For example, a representative community sample may be recruited to test hypotheses about substance use during pregnancy and its effects on the offspring. Because the data are from a community sample that represents the larger population, the sample may be quite suitable for other purposes (e.g., hypotheses about stress and social support that have nothing to do with substance use).

A fourth sampling issue pertains to the *volunteer status* of the participants. For ethical reasons, most research participants are volunteers in some sense. Informed consent procedures require participants to agree to participate voluntarily, rather than to participate under duress of any kind. Yet, there are degrees of voluntariness, defined in part by how participants are recruited. From a large group (e.g., college students, samples of convenience, community members), participants may be solicited through newspapers, notes posted on kiosks on college campuses, and public radio or television announcements. Some individuals agree to serve (volunteers) and participate in the study; others do not (nonvolunteers). The subjects determine whether they will participate. In some kinds of research in which anonymity is assured (e.g., large-scale surveys or studies of public behavior where the individual cannot be identified), consent procedures may not be administered.

Volunteers may differ in important ways from nonvolunteers and these differences may affect the generality of experimental findings. Indeed, when compared to nonvolunteers, volunteers tend to be better educated, higher in socioeconomic status, less conventional in their behavior, and younger, to mention a few characteristics (e.g., Rosenthal & Rosnow, 1975). Research that randomly samples community members and that makes a special effort to capture as many cases as possible helps to address concerns of generality, though even community samples must volunteer to participate. Yet, a large community sample permits the investigator to examine a wide range of characteristics that might influence the findings.

In selecting a sample for research, the overriding question is clear: Is this specific sample well suited to the goals of the study? The sample cannot be evaluated without considering the goals. Thus, a clinical sample is not inherently better or more desirable and, as already noted, generalizing results from one sample to another is not necessarily a goal of all research. The suitability of the sample to the question ought to be considered in advance of a study in light of the constructs to be studied, the conclusions the investigator wishes to reach, and the extent to which he or she will want to generalize the findings to others.

Not all sampling issues emerge from selection of participants by the investigator. Participants often selectively remove themselves from a research project over the course of the study. Attrition or loss of participants can affect virtually all facets of experimental validity by altering random composition of the groups and group equivalence (internal validity); limiting the generality of findings to a special group (e.g., those subjects who are persistent or especially compliant: external validity); raising the prospect that the intervention, combined with special subject characteristics, accounts for conclusions (external and construct validity); and reducing sample size and power or by systematically changing the variability within the sample (statistical conclusion validity) (see Kazdin, 1998). Showing that dropouts are not different from nondropouts or that dropouts from one group are no different from dropouts from another group is not too helpful in addressing the issues because of small sample sizes among the dropouts in such comparisons.

Attrition is a significant problem in any study in which participants are repeatedly assessed. The longer the time frame of the study, the more difficult it is to retain cases. Understandably, many procedures have been evaluated to reduce the number of cases of dropping out or to handle missing data (see Flick, 1988; Howard, Krause, & Orlinsky, 1986; Kazdin, 1996). As an example, one data analytic strategy is to use existing data (e.g., the last available data point) from cases who drop out as an estimate of any subsequent data point that is needed for the analysis. In this way, missing observations do not require deleting subjects. This strategy preserves the randomness of the sample from the original composition of groups, even if the participant did not complete treatment or repeated assessments during the study. At the same time, on a priori grounds, one assessment (e.g., posttreatment) may or may not be a reasonable estimate of a later assessment (e.g., one-year follow-up, if the rest of the sample shows deterioration during that assessment interval).

Use of Multiple Measures

As a general rule, in research we are interested in concepts or constructs (e.g., depression, attachment, and attributions of control) rather than in measures. Multiple measures usually are needed because most constructs of interest are multifaceted. No single measure is likely to capture these different components adequately. For example, depression is likely to encompass feelings of sadness and loss of interest in activities (self-report), reduced social interaction and activity (overt behavior), and changes in sleep activity (psychophysiology), to mention a few domains. Any evaluation of depression in, say, a test of treatment would be incomplete if change were merely demonstrated in one modality or one measure.

Multiple measures are also needed to ensure that the results are not restricted to the construct as assessed by a particular method and measure. Performance on a given measure is a function of both one's standing on that characteristic (e.g., level of self-esteem) and the precise way (method) the characteristic is measured (e.g., self-report questionnaire, one questionnaire versus another). In other words, the measure itself can contribute to the findings and conclusions. Use of multiple measures permits one to separate the construct from the method of assessment. There is an external validity issue here as well, namely, one often is interested in evaluating the generality of a finding across measures, which includes measures of the same construct and perhaps measures of different constructs.

Although the use of multiple measures is advocated as a general strategy for evaluating a construct, the results may be inconsistent across measures. Some dependent measures may reflect changes or differences in the predicted direction and others may not. Indeed, some measures may even show changes or differences in the opposite direction. The failure of multiple measures to agree in a study is a problem only because of some traditional assumptions about the nature of personality and human behavior and the manner in which independent variables operate. The multifaceted nature of constructs, the contribution of method variance to assessment, the different perspectives of different informants, and differences in rates of change of different aspects of affect, cognition, and behavior are some of the main reasons to expect measures of the same construct not to correspond highly.

As a general rule, multiple measures are essential to represent a given construct. As a guide for research, invariably the recommendation is to include few constructs and multiple measures rather than multiple constructs, each represented by one measure. There are exceptions where multiple measures are not needed. Occasionally, an investigator is interested in highly circumscribed problems (e.g., enuresis, isolated fears, and specific habit disorders), or the goal is expressly focused on a single facet of the problem. In other situations, the measure may be viewed as significant in its own right (a particular type of immune reaction measured by one type of cell reaction) or the single measure is considered to be quite valid and reliable (e.g., death). In such situations, multiple measures may not be critical.

Constructs and Their Interpretation

Constructs that serve as the impetus for studies can vary in their level of specificity. Broad and global variables such as age, sex, social class, ethnicity, and race are examples of constructs studied in clinical research that may be difficult to interpret. Each has multiple components that could readily be distinguished. Interpretation of the findings is facilitated by specificity of the constructs or processes that are studied. To illustrate the point, consider for a moment that we are interested in the impact of socioeconomic status (SES) on mental health. SES is a broad variable that encompasses (is related to) a plethora of other variables. SES has been studied extensively, and from this research we have learned that low social class (as measured by income and educational and occupational status) predicts a very large number of untoward mental and physical health outcomes (e.g., earlier death, greater history of illness, and higher rates of mental illness) (see Adler et al., 1994; Luthar, in press). This research has been extremely important. A limitation of the work is that we know very little about the reasons why these effects occur. The construct is broad and encompasses so many other variables that we now need more specific studies to identify possible bases for the findings.

Some work of this kind has been completed. For example, studies have shown that low SES relates to later psychopathology in children (Dodge, Pettit, & Bates, 1994; Lipman, Offord, & Boyle, 1994). Several factors correlated with SES, including low parent educational attainment, family dysfunction, harsh child-rearing practices, limited parental warmth, single-parent families, peer group instability (e.g., moving to different child care facilities), lack of cognitive stimulation, and exposure to aggressive behavior (e.g., in the home), have been analyzed. Each predicts later psychiatric dysfunction in children and partially accounts for the relation between low SES and clinical dysfunction. Interestingly, even after these factors are taken into account, SES still contributes to the prediction, indicating that other factors are operative. Fine-grained analyses have indicated that some of the above factors are more highly related to the outcomes. For example, harsh discipline practices on the part of the parents are one of the stronger contributors to later aggressive child behavior (Dodge et al., 1994; Patterson et al., 1992). Armed with this finding, we can better theorize about how discipline might be involved in developing aggressive behavior. The specific constructs, compared to SES, permit more focused theory and better understanding of the outcomes of interest.

Ambiguity in the construct and interpretation of the findings can be a problem beyond the focus of subject and demographic variables. In treatment research, the intervention may be multifaceted in ways that do not permit very specific conclusions to be drawn. For example, a treatment-outcome study may compare a cognitive-behavioral treatment with no treatment. At the end of the study, the investigator may wish to discuss why and how the cognitive-behavioral intervention was effective. Yet, group differences could have resulted from intervention subjects attending sessions, expecting to improve, receiving special attention from and contact with a therapist, and other such influences alone or in combination with the influence of the intervention. That is, the construct(s) that might explain the results is not clear. As mentioned previously, if the investigator wished to discuss specific aspects of treatment, other groups (e.g., attention-placebo) would be quite helpful. In addition, the investigator could evaluate processes considered to underlie the cognitive-behavioral treatment and show that these in fact relate to outcome.

As a general guideline, broad constructs may be a useful beginning point for research. Moreover, for a given purpose (e.g., screening, providing targeted preventive interventions), it may be sufficient to know that low SES or that being a male is a risk factor for a particular outcome, even though we may not know precisely what it is about these variables that produces or contributes to risk. Yet, we also want to disaggregate the construct, to identify individual components and their contribution to the outcome, and to understand processes involved that account for the relations (Kazdin et al., 1997). Consequently, it is preferable to identify and to assess specific processes or components of broad constructs that underlie the study, to hypothesize and to specify why the differences or effects would occur, and then to show the relation of these processes to the outcomes or dependent measures. On a continuum from description to explanation, research on components and processes falls more toward the explanatory side and is usually more informative.

Statistical Evaluation

Statistical evaluation refers to the use of quantitative techniques to describe the data and to draw inferences about the effects, that is, whether they are likely to be due to "chance" or to a veridical effect. Current research in psychology and other sciences is based primarily on null hypothesis testing and the search for statistically significant effects. Since the emergence of statistical evaluation, there has been dissatisfaction with the approach of null hypothesis testing. Major sources of dissatisfaction with significance testing include the focus on binary decisions about whether an effect is evident, the absence of information about the strength of the effect, and the notion that significance is more of a measure of sample size than of group differences (i.e., the null hypothesis is probably never true and, with a large enough sample, group differences will be found). The dissatisfaction continues today with recommendations to eliminate tests of statistical significance or, at the very least, to supplement them with other indices (see Kirk, 1996; Schmidt, 1996; Shrout, 1997).

Essentially, in most research, statistical evaluation examines whether groups differing on a particular independent variable (e.g., different conditions) can be distinguished statistically on the dependent measure(s). Statistical evaluation consists of applying a test to assess whether the difference obtained on the dependent measure is likely to have occurred by "chance." A statistically significant difference (e.g., $p < .05$) indicates that if the experiment were completed an infinite number of times, a difference would be likely to occur by chance only 5% of the time if the null hypothesis were true. If the probability obtained in the study were $p \leq .05$, most researchers would reject the null hypothesis and concede that group differences reflect a genuine relation between the independent and dependent variables. To state that a relation in an experiment is statistically significant does not mean that there is necessarily a genuine effect, that is, a relationship exists between the variables or that the effect would be replicated if the study were repeated. Moreover, the obtained probability from the statistical test (e.g., $p < .0001$) does not indicate the likelihood that the null hypothesis is false, that the alternative hypothesis is true, or that the effect is large, strong, or important.

The search for statistical significance raises the issue of power or the extent to which an investigation can detect a difference when one exists. Weak power is the Achilles' heel of psychological research; most studies have insufficient power to detect differences (Cohen, 1992; Rossi, 1990; Sedlmeier & Gigerenzer, 1989). The problem of low power is readily explained by mentioning the concept of effect size. Effect size (ES) is a measure of the strength of effects or differences between groups that result from a study. ES refers to differences in standard deviation units and is computed by the following formula:

$$ES = \frac{m_1 - m_2}{s}$$

where m_1 = the mean of group 1 (e.g., treatment group), m_2 = the mean of group 2 (e.g., no-treatment group), and s = the pooled standard deviation.

Cohen (1988) delineated small, medium, and large effect sizes (.2, .5, and .8, respectively) as a guide to plan the design of studies and to interpret results from completed studies. Reviews cited above indicate that studies frequently have adequate power (e.g., .80, or a 4 out of 5 chance) to detect quite large effects, but low power to detect effects smaller than that. This is not trivial and may lead investigators to reach conclusions that, on methodological grounds, ought to be tempered. For example, studies of psychotherapy often find that treatment and no-treatment are significantly (statistically) different at posttreatment assessment. Relatively large effect sizes (e.g., .70) are commonly found for such comparisons, even though studies, treatments, and results vary. Yet, studies that compare two different treatments obtain much smaller effect sizes (e.g., .4 to .5). In many treatment outcome studies, two different treatments do not differ from each other when compared statistically. A conclusion that treatments are no different, that is, "support" of the null hypothesis, is often interpreted to indicate that treatments are equally effective. Yet, for much of psychotherapy research, weak power is a rival interpretation (threat to statistical conclusion validity) because very small sample sizes are the rule rather than the exception (10–20 cases per group) (see Kazdin & Bass, 1989). For small-to-medium effect sizes, sample sizes would have to be much larger. For example, to detect an effect size of .5 between two treatments (using $p < .05$), a sample of 128 ($n = 64$ in each group) would be needed (for power of .8) (see Cohen, 1988). Relatively few treatment studies include a sufficient sample to test treatment differences with adequate power.

A critical issue for the design of research is to ensure that there is sufficient power to detect differences if they are evident. Power is related to alpha (level of significance), ES (magnitude of the differences between groups), and sample size (N). Adopting power of .8 and alpha of $p = .05$ provides two of the required parameters. As for ES, one can estimate likely effects from prior research, meta-analyses, or on a priori grounds (see Kazdin, 1998). With power, alpha, and an estimate of ES, it is very easy to estimate power before beginning a study. Books and articles (e.g., Cohen, 1988, 1992), as well as computer software (e.g., Gorman, Primavera, & Allison, 1995; Statistical Solutions, 1995), provide all the necessary information. In most cases, an investigator would be surprised to learn before completing the study that the investigation is likely to be underpowered. This is important to learn in advance of the study because many strategies can be deployed to increase power. The usual suggestion is to increase sample size, but there are many other strategies as well, related to selection of the sample, selection of the experimental conditions that are manipulated, selection of the measures, use of multiple assessment occasions, monitoring of the integrity of the experimental manipulation, use of statistical tests (e.g., covariance analyses, directional tests of significance), and others (see Kazdin, 1998).

As mentioned earlier, there is ongoing dissatisfaction with null hypothesis and statistical significance testing. In place of (or in addition to) statistical significance testing, it would be helpful to report some measure of the magnitude or strength of the relation between the independent and dependent variable or the magnitude of the differences between groups. There are many ways to estimate the magnitude of effect or strength of the relation, including ES, as already mentioned, Pearson product-moment correlation *(r, r²)* and in multiple regression (*R* and *R²*), omega² (ω²), eta (η), epsilon² (ε²), and others (see Haase, Ellis, & Ladany, 1989; Kirk, 1996; Rosenthal, 1984; Rosenthal & Rosnow, 1991). ES is the most familiar because of its frequent use in meta-analysis (see Chapter 17). ES reflects the difference between groups in standard deviation units. In a study comparing an intervention and control group, an ES of .70 is readily interpretable in relation to the differences in the distributions between treatment and no-treatment groups. An ES of .70 denotes that the mean of the intervention group is ⁷⁄₁₀ of a standard deviation higher than the mean of the control group.

ES (or some other measure of magnitude of effect) provides a point estimate, that is, a specific value that estimates the population value. Confidence intervals are a useful supplement and reflect the likelihood that the ES in the population falls within a particular range (Kirk, 1996; Schmidt, 1996). Computation of confidence intervals for 95% or 99% provides values that also serve as the usual statistical criteria for alpha of .05 and .01. The formula for computing confidence intervals (CIs) follows:

$$CIs = m \pm z_\alpha s_m$$

where m = the mean score; z_α = the *z* score value (two-tailed) under the normal curve, depending on the confidence level (e.g., *z* = 1.96 and 2.58 for *p* = .05 and *p* = .01, respectively), and s_m is the standard error of measurement (i.e., the standard deviation divided by the square root of *N* [or $s_m = s/\sqrt{N}$]). To provide the lower and upper bound estimates of the confidence interval for the 95% interval, the *z* −1.96 and +1.96 is multiplied by the s_m and subtracted and added, respectively, from the mean.

For individual studies, ESs and confidence intervals provide useful statistics that have been proposed to replace or at the very least supplement tests of statistical significance. The advantage extends beyond the individual study. Meta-analysis is an extension of the use of ES for evaluating multiple studies. Meta-analyses combine many different ESs and many different studies and hence can provide a better estimate of the population parameters. Including ES in individual studies can facilitate the combination of data from several studies.

CONCLUSIONS: METHODOLOGY IN PERSPECTIVE

The goals of research are to test theory and to address specific substantive questions. Methodology reflects a way of thinking about these questions as well as a set of options and practices to obtain the answers. At a general level, one can consider the goals of methodology as addressing the following questions:

1. What is the best available and most feasible way to test the theory, idea, or hypothesis underlying this study?
2. If the study were completed as designed, what would be the salient threats to validity or sources of bias that could interfere with drawing valid inferences?
3. Before, during, and after the study is conducted, what can be done to reduce the plausibility of alternative interpretations of the findings other than those to be tested?

4. Are the purposes (e.g., hypotheses), design, methods of data analysis, and discussion coherent; that is, are they addressing the same key issues, do they speak to the same questions, and are they aligned so that what one says about results can legitimately be stated?

These questions are the critical guideposts for research and underscore the task of the investigator. Sensitivity to methodology is required at each stage of the research. *Before* the study is conducted, the investigator can ensure that threats to internal validity and other types of validity particularly relevant to the study (e.g., construct validity) are addressed, that power is high so that differences can be detected, that the experimental conditions are planned so that if there is an effect it is likely to be evident in this study (e.g., by the conditions or groups that are selected), that the constructs of interest are well represented (e.g., multiple measures), and that the measures are sound in relation to the demands of the study (e.g., are reliable, valid, and sensitive to the predictions). *During* the study, the investigator can ensure that the conditions (e.g., intervention, manipulation) are administered carefully and consistently, that experimenters retain their level of performance (across experimenters and over time for a given experimenter), that subjects are treated in a way that is likely to generate minimally biased data, that loss of subjects is likely to be minimal, and that data are collected with great care to ensure they are complete. *After* the study and when the data are in, the investigator can complete data analyses to address various influences that can be ruled out or made implausible through careful statistical evaluation (e.g., to control for, partial out, and examine the relations of various influences that might interfere with interpretation). These are only some of the strategies, but they convey that methodology is more than a simple set of practices.

In clinical psychology and other areas where research is often conducted outside of the laboratory, grasping the rationale for methodological practices is particularly crucial. Standard practices such as recruiting a large number of participants, maximizing homogeneity of the subjects, randomly assigning participants to conditions, and eliminating attrition are luxuries and not always available. The importance of methodology is to alert one to the range of factors that compete with interpretation of the results and some of the practices that can be used. However, ingenuity in addressing the above questions is more important than any particular methodological practice. Indeed, time-honored practices (e.g., random assignment, significance testing) that are the standard fare of methodology do not guarantee clarity of the outcome or precision in addressing a particular research question or threat to validity. This is not a call to abandon traditional methodology but rather to underscore the fact that methodological practices are designed to address issues, and the issues more than the practices are critical. This chapter has addressed some of the key issues and several of the practices to address them.

REFERENCES

Adler, N. E., Boyce, T., Chesney, M. A., Cohen, S., Folkman, S., Kahn, R. L., & Syme, S. L. (1994). Socioeconomic status and health: The challenge of the gradient. *American Psychologist, 49,* 15–24.

Baron, R. M., & Kenny, D. A. (1986). The moderator-mediator variable distinction in social psychological research: Conceptual, strategic, and statistical considerations. *Journal of Personality and Social Psychology, 51,* 1173–1182.

Campbell, D. T., & Stanley, J. C. (1963). Experimental and quasi-experimental designs for research and teaching. In N. L. Gage (Ed.), *Handbook of research on teaching.* Chicago: Rand McNally.

Carlsmith, J. M., Ellsworth, P. C., & Aronson, E. (1976). *Methods of research in social psychology.* Reading, MA: Addison-Wesley.

Cohen, J. (1988). *Statistical power analysis for the behavioral sciences* (2nd ed.). Hillsdale, NJ: Erlbaum.

Cohen, J. (1992). A power primer. *Psychological Bulletin, 112,* 155–159.

Cook, T. D., & Campbell, D. T. (Eds.). (1979). *Quasi-experimentation: Design and analysis issues for field settings.* Chicago: Rand McNally.

Denissenko, M. F., Pao, A., Tang, M., & Pfeifer, G. P. (1996). Preferential formation of benzo[*a*]pyrene adducts at lung cancer mutational hotspots in *P53. Science, 274.* 430–432.

Dishion, T. J., & Andrews, D. W. (1995). Preventing escalation in problem behaviors with high-risk young adolescents: Immediate and 1-year outcomes. *Journal of Consulting and Clinical Psychology, 63,* 538–548.

Dishion, T. J., & Patterson, G. R. (1997). The timing and severity of antisocial behavior: Three hypotheses within an ecological framework. In D. M. Stoff, J. Breiling, & J. D. Maser (Eds.), *Handbook of antisocial behavior* (pp. 205–217). New York: Wiley.

Dishion, T. J., Patterson, G. R., & Kavanagh, K. A. (1992). An experimental test of the coercion model: Linking theory, measurement, and intervention. In J. McCord & R. E. Tremblay (Eds.), *Preventing antisocial behavior* (pp. 253–282). New York: Guilford Press.

Dodge, K. A., Pettit, G. S., & Bates, J. E. (1994). Socialization mediators of the relation between socioeconomic status and child conduct problems. *Child Development, 65,* 649–655.

Flick, S. N. (1988). Managing attrition in clinical research. *Clinical Psychology Review, 8,* 499–515.

Forgatch, M. S. (1991). The clinical science vortex: A developing theory of antisocial behavior. In D. J. Pepler & K. H. Rubin (Eds.), *The development and treatment of childhood aggression* (pp. 291–315). Hillsdale, NJ: Erlbaum.

Gorman, B. S., Primavera, L. H., & Allison, D. B. (1995). POWPAL: A program for estimating effect sizes, statistical power, and sample sizes. *Educational and Psychological Measurement, 55,* 773–776.

Graber, J. A., Lewinsohn, P. M., Seeley, J. R., & Brooks-Gunn, J. (1997). Is psychopathology associated with the timing of pubertal development? *Journal of the American Academy of Child and Adolescent Psychiatry, 36,* 1768–1776.

Haase, R. F., Ellis, M. V., & Ladany, N. (1989). Multiple criteria for evaluating the magnitude of experimental effects. *Journal of Counseling Psychology, 4,* 511–516.

Haynes, S. N. (1992). *Models of causality in psychopathology: Toward dynamic, synthetic, and nonlinear models of behavior disorders.* Needham Heights, MA: Allyn & Bacon.

Hill, A. B. (1965). The environment and disease: Association or causation? *Proceedings of the Royal Society of Medicine, 58,* 295–300.

Hoagwood, K., Hibbs, E., Brent, D., & Jensen, P. J. (1995). Efficacy and effectiveness in studies of child and adolescent psychotherapy. *Journal of Consulting and Clinical Psychology, 63,* 683–687.

Holmbeck, G. N. (1997). Toward terminological, conceptual, and statistical clarity in the study of mediators and moderators: Examples from the child-clinical and pediatric psychology literatures. *Journal of Consulting and Clinical Psychology, 65,* 599–610.

Howard, K. I., Krause, M. S., & Orlinsky, D. E. (1986). The attrition dilemma: Toward a new strategy for psychotherapy research. *Journal of Consulting and Clinical Psychology, 54,* 106–110.

Kazdin, A. E. (1978). Evaluating the generality of findings in analogue therapy research. *Journal of Consulting and Clinical Psychology, 46,* 673–686.

Kazdin, A. E. (1995). Child, parent, and family dysfunction as predictors of outcome in cognitive-behavioral treatment of antisocial children. *Behaviour Research and Therapy 33,* 271–281.

Kazdin, A. E. (1996). Dropping out of child therapy: Issues for research and implications for practice. *Clinical Child Psychology and Psychiatry, 1,* 133–156.

Kazdin, A. E. (1997). Parent management training: Evidence, outcomes, and issues. *Journal of the American Academy of Child and Adolescent Psychiatry, 36,* 1349–1356.

Kazdin, A. E. (1998). *Research design in clinical psychology* (3rd ed.). Needham Heights, MA: Allyn & Bacon.

Kazdin, A. E., & Bass, D. (1989). Power to detect differences between alternative treatments in comparative psychotherapy outcome research. *Journal of Consulting and Clinical Psychology, 57,* 138–147.

Kazdin, A. E., Kraemer, H. C., Kessler, R. C., Kupfer, D. J., & Offord, D. R. (1997). Contributions of risk-factor research to developmental psychopathology. *Clinical Psychology Review, 17,* 375–406.

Kenny, D. A. (1979). *Correlation and causality.* New York: Wiley.

Kirk, R. E. (1996). Practical significance: A concept whose time has come. *Educational and Psychological Measurement, 56,* 746–759.

Kraemer, H. C., Kazdin, A. E., Offord, D. R., Kessler, R. C., Jensen, P. S., & Kupfer, D. J. (1997). Coming to terms with the terms of risk. *Archives of General Psychiatry, 54,* 337–343.

Lin, K., Poland, R. E., & Nagasaki, G. (Eds.). (1993). *Psychopharmacology and psychobiology of ethnicity.* Washington, DC: American Psychiatric Press.

Lipman, E. L., Offord, D. R., & Boyle, M. H. (1994). Relation between economic disadvantage and psychosocial morbidity in children. *Canadian Medical Association Journal, 151,* 431–437.

Luthar, S. S. (in press). *Children in poverty: Risk and protective forces in adjustment.* Thousand Oaks, CA: Sage.

McMillen, C., Zuravin, S., & Rideout, G. (1995). Perceived benefit from child sexual abuse. *Journal of Consulting and Clinical Psychology, 63,* 1037–1043.

Meisels, S. J., & Shonkoff, J. P. (Eds.). (1990). *Handbook of early childhood intervention.* Cambridge, England: Cambridge University Press.

Mook, D. G. (1983). In defense of external validity. *American Psychologist, 38,* 379–387.

Patterson, G. R., Reid, J. B., & Dishion, T. J. (1992). *Antisocial boys.* Eugene, OR: Castalia Press.

Rosenthal, R. (1984). *Meta-analytic procedures for social research.* Beverly Hills, CA: Sage.

Rosenthal, R. (1991). Replication in behavioral research. In J. W. Neuliep (Ed.), *Replication research in the social sciences* (pp. 1–30). Newbury Park, CA: Sage.

Rosenthal, R., & Rosnow, R. L. (1975). *The volunteer subject.* New York: Wiley.

Rosenthal, R., & Rosnow, R. L. (1991). *Essentials of behavioral research: Methods and data analysis* (2nd ed.). New York: McGraw-Hill.

Ross, A. O. (1981). Of rigor and relevance. *Professional Psychology: Research and Practice, 12,* 318–327.

Rossi, J. S. (1990). Statistical power of psychological research: What have we gained in 20 years? *Journal of Consulting and Clinical Psychology, 58,* 646–656.

Rutter, M. (1987). Psychosocial resilience and protective mechanisms. *American Journal of Orthopsychiatry, 57,* 316–331.

Rutter, M., & Giller, H. (1983). *Juvenile delinquency: Trends and perspectives.* New York: Penguin Books.

Schlesselman, J. J. (1982). *Case-control studies: Design, conduct, analysis.* New York: Oxford University Press.

Schmidt, F. L. (1996). Statistical significance testing and cumulative knowledge in psychology: Implications for training of researchers. *Psychological Methods, 1,* 115–129.

Sedlmeier, P., & Gigerenzer, G. (1989). Do studies of statistical power have an effect on the power of studies? *Psychological Bulletin, 105,* 309–316.

Shadish, W. R., Matt, G. E., Navarro, A. M., Siegle, G., Crisk-Christoph, P., Hazelrigg, M. D., Jorm, A. F., Lyons, L. C., Nietzel, M. T., Prout, H. T., Robinson, L., Smith, M. L., Svartberg, M., & Weiss, B. (1997). Evidence that therapy works in clinically representative conditions. *Journal of Consulting and Clinical Psychology, 65,* 355–365.

Shrout, P. E. (Ed.). (1997). Special series: Should significance testing be banned? Introduction to a special section exploring the pros and cons. *Psychological Science, 8,* 1–20.

Statistical Solutions (1995). *nQuery Advisor*™. Boston: Author.

Stoff, D. M., Breiling, J., & Maser, J. D. (Eds.). (1997). *Handbook of antisocial behavior.* New York: Wiley.

Wahler, R. G., & Meginnis, K. L. (1997). Strengthening child compliance through positive parenting practices: What works? *Journal of Clinical Child Psychology, 26,* 433–440.

Webster-Stratton, C. (1996). Early intervention with videotape modeling: Programs for families of children with oppositional defiant disorder or conduct disorder. In E. D. Hibbs & P. Jensen (Eds.), *Psychosocial treatment research of child and adolescent disorders: Empirically based strategies for clinical practice* (pp. 435–474). Washington, DC: American Psychological Association.

Weisz, J. R., Weiss, B., & Donenberg, G. R. (1992). The lab versus the clinic: Effects of child and adolescent psychotherapy. *American Psychologist, 47,* 1578–1585.

Werner, E. E., & Smith, R. S. (1992). *Overcoming the odds: High risk children from birth to adulthood.* Ithaca, NY: Cornell University Press.

Wyatt, G. E., & Powell, G. J. (Eds.). (1988). *Lasting effects of child abuse.* Newbury Park, CA: Sage.

Chapter 2

ETHICAL PERSPECTIVES IN CLINICAL RESEARCH

DAVID M. BERSOFF, PH.D., and DONALD N. BERSOFF, J.D., PH.D.

Psychologists conduct research competently and with due concern for the dignity and welfare of the participants.
American Psychological Association's Ethics Code (1992)

A group of psychologists working for the military were interested in creating an experimental situation that effectively aroused the fear of death or injury in participants. Using this paradigm, they hoped to identify the determinants of effective performance under the stress of combat. This was the first in the series of experiments they designed and performed as part of their research program.

Sixty-six men ages 18–24 in their first weeks of Army basic training were randomly assigned to one of three groups: an experimental group, a flying control group, and a grounded control group. Subjects in the experimental group boarded a plane for what they were told would be a routine training flight. Once aloft, at 5,000 feet, they completed an irrelevant test then waited for the plane to reach a higher altitude. Suddenly, the aircraft lurched. The passengers saw that one propeller had stopped turning and heard about other malfunctions over the intercom. They were then informed directly that there was an emergency. A simulated pilot-to-tower conversation was provided to the passengers over their earphones to support the deception. As the plane passed within sight of the airfield, the study participants could see fire trucks and ambulances on the airstrip in apparent expectation of a crash landing. After several minutes, the pilot ordered the steward to prepare for ditching in the nearby ocean because the landing gear was not functioning properly.

At this point, the steward distributed to everyone on the plane something called the Emergency Data Form. This was a terribly complicated form the passengers were asked to complete so that the military would know to whom their personal possessions should go in the event of their death. They also were given the Emergency Instructions Test, which asked questions about airborne emergency procedures that the passengers had been required to read before the flight. The supposed purpose of this second form was to furnish proof to insurance companies that emergency precautions had been properly followed. These two sets of forms were to be put in a waterproof container and jettisoned before the aircraft fell to the ocean. After a specified time, the plane made a safe landing at the airport.

The flying control group was taken up for a flight but was not exposed to the fear-of-death-inducing manipulations. The grounded controls never left the ground. All three groups completed the same set of dependent measures. The participants were then debriefed, interviewed about the experience, and asked for a urine sample. (In the case of the experimental group, collecting the urine sample probably entailed simply wringing out their underwear into a beaker.) As expected, the experimental group rated themselves as being more stressed than the control groups, made more errors when filling out the Emergency Data Form and the Emergency Instructions Test, and had more corticosteroids in their urine, a physiological index of stress.

We present the Ditching study (Berkun, Bialek, Kern, & Yagi, 1962) to make three basic, introductory points. The first is that research ethics is fundamentally a methodological issue; each procedural decision a researcher makes has potential ethical implications. As a consequence, ethics should not be an afterthought and attention to ethical considerations must go beyond preparing a consent form and a debriefing. If the Ditching study is unethical, it is in large part because the researchers failed to temper their methodological decision making with empathy for their participants. Their only apparent concession to moral propriety was refraining from actually crashing the plane into the ocean, and that may have been only because one or more of the researchers were on board. This study demonstrates what can happen when scientific goals drive research methodology unchecked by ethical considerations.

The second point is that ethical problems often arise as a result of scientists viewing research participants as objects to be manipulated, as data on the hoof, or as a means to a publication. Apparently, the researchers who performed the Ditching study placed ecological validity and the scientific goals of their research firmly ahead of the emotional welfare of their subjects. The word "subjects" is used here as opposed to the currently preferred "participants" precisely because the men in this study were treated as subjects, as lab rats might be treated, and not as autonomous beings. Participants are people who have graciously given research scientists their time and attention and often their considerable effort; they have a right to expect nonmaleficence and respect in return. Resisting the temptation to objectify the people in their studies is one of the biggest ethical challenges researchers face. As is true with almost all people-oriented professions, it is hard not to come to have a certain degree of contempt for the people one relies on for his or her livelihood. Just as salespeople often view their customers merely as a means to a commission and wait staffs have a certain degree of disdain for restaurant patrons, researchers also may develop a somewhat jaundiced view of the people in their studies especially because research participants often miss appointments, fail to cooperate, and, on occasion, even render data contrary to their hypotheses. Unfortunately, psychologists cannot afford to indulge in objectifying their participants, nor allow their contempt to influence their methodological choices, because psychologists hold far more sway over peoples' well-being than do salesclerks and waiters.

The most important point to remember from this chapter is that you can do damage, that what psychologists say and do to people carries more weight than similar words and deeds on the part of someone who is not a psychologist. If a salesclerk calls a customer an idiot, it is a rude insult. If a psychologist calls a person in a study the equivalent of an idiot (say, in the form of false feedback on a fake intelligence test), it can be construed as a diagnosis based on scientific evidence. Needless to say, the latter is much harder to shrug off than the former, and, at least for a time, the person is actually likely to feel that he or she is of below average intelligence. Especially among college students at competitive universities, such a feeling can be experienced as a significant self-esteem wound.

The third point is that ethical considerations will often require making methodological tradeoffs. This fact may make it seem as though good ethics and good science are often adversaries. As a case in point, there is the Ditching study, a methodological masterpiece. One can imagine the researchers growing more pleased with themselves as each little bit of realism was incorporated into their design. They did not just switch off an engine; they allowed the passengers to hear emergency transmissions between the pilot and tower personnel. As a final touch, they allowed the passengers to see emergency equipment lining the runway. If anyone had the presence of mind to wonder why the passengers had to fill out forms that would be as unlikely to survive a crash as they were, the researchers had the clever idea of introducing the notion of a waterproof canister that could be jettisoned before impact. Every methodological decision the researchers made was in service to convincing their subjects that they were in a life-threatening situation. This was also the heart of the study's ethical problems. It made people suffer the experience of being in fear for their lives. But to the extent that the researchers would have included procedural steps designed to ameliorate this fear, there would have been a cost in terms of the scientific goal of the study—to observe the impact of fear of death on psychological functioning.

In situations such as this, in which good ethics seems to stand in the way of good science, there are several possibilities to consider. The first is that the issue being addressed is unworthy of study. Just because a question can be asked does not mean that it should be asked. A case in point is the notorious Tuskegee study on the disease course of untreated syphilis. Surely, medical science could have done without the information gained in that investigation, especially after a cure for the disease was found partway into the study. Closely related is the possibility that the question being examined is not worth the cost in terms of the suffering required to gain the information sought. The pursuit of knowledge is not humankind's highest virtue; there are considerations that carry more weight. Perhaps knowing how people react in the face of life-threatening situations is less important than abiding by the right people have not to be put in fear of their lives. Although it may be important for the Army to know how their soldiers will react in the face of possible death, more important considerations may mean that this question will have to be left unasked. Deciding to forgo a study, however, is the most drastic and not always the most desirable way of handling a conflict between ethical concerns and research goals.

A less onerous alternative is to consider the possibility of whether there is a different, more ethical, way to operationalize the variable of interest. Perhaps the researchers in the Ditching study could have caused significant fear without making people think that they were about to be in a plane crash. If fear of death is viewed as merely an extreme point on a continuum of fear, then perhaps subjecting people to a lesser fear would still have allowed the researchers to gather the information they wanted. For example, soldiers about to make their first parachute jump could have been used in the experimental group. Surely, such soldiers are harboring some form of fear resembling a fear of death, but they are experiencing this fear by choice, assuming that being a paratrooper is a job one signs up for, and this fear is probably less acute than that generated in the Ditching study.

A final possibility is that instead of examining the question in a manipulation study, perhaps one can take advantage of a naturally occurring situation. Researchers looking for cancer cures do not give people the disease and then try to cure it; they find people who already have cancer. Instead of simulating a plane crash, the Ditching study researchers could have found a war (there is almost always one occurring someplace in the world) and worked with the soldiers at the front who were already in a position to be fearing for their lives.

These last two possibilities point to another link between methodology and ethics. A skilled and creative methodologist can almost always find a way to research an issue in an ethical manner. Conversely, an inferior methodologist is unlikely to do ethical research. Poorly designed, even if otherwise quite benign, research is unethical if for no other reason than that it represents a waste of time, effort, and resources that could have been devoted to research that had the potential to be truly informative (Rosenthal, 1994). Poorly designed research also has a greater likelihood of yielding erroneous or artifact-driven results, which, in turn, can lead to harmful consequences such as misbegotten further research, misinformed policy decisions, and misperceptions on the part of the public (see, e.g., Ernhart, Scarr, & Geneson's 1993 discussion of Herbert Needleman and his research on the effects of low-level lead exposure on children).

Although ethics and psychological research may seem to be in an adversarial relationship, the relationship is actually more like that of the Supreme Court and Congress. The Court's purpose is not to impede the work of Congress but rather to ensure that Congress does not infringe on the basic rights of the people. Though the Court's judgments may seem at times like unwelcome intrusions to the Congress, in the long run they serve to protect Congress and the government as a whole. Our government, as does psychological research, exists only at the pleasure of the people. If either institution comes to be viewed as immoral, exploitative, or insensitive to the values and concerns of society, it will be sanctioned or eliminated. Institutional review boards (IRBs) were mandated into existence in response to perceived abuses by researchers. The more jaundiced a view society comes to have of psychological research, the tighter funding and regulation will become. In the long run, the benefits of good ethical conduct to psychology as a science more than compensate for the constraints it imposes on research methodology.

Unfortunately, even intensive ethics instruction will not prevent bad people from acting in an immoral manner. Thus, this chapter is not aimed at such people (those who are evil by nature might as well skip ahead). It is our belief, though, that most ethical breaches are not the result of bad people acting true to their nature, but rather of good people making bad decisions. As we see it, the biggest culprits in the commission of unethical behavior are lack of information, mindlessness, self-deception, and motivated cognition (the process by which judgment becomes biased by self-interest) (Kunda, 1990). The best defense against these causal factors is education in conjunction with disciplined moral decision making and consultation with colleagues.

There is a substantial and ever growing literature dealing with the ethical issues and dilemmas facing professional and research psychologists. Investigators should become familiar with and keep abreast of this literature in the same way they follow the work being done in their areas of research specialization. A good place to start is with this chapter and a basic text such as D. N. Bersoff (1995) or Koocher and Keith-Spiegel (1998). Monitoring the ethics literature will not only keep researchers informed of the current rules, regulations, and codes governing research and the practice of psychology in general, but it will also sensitize them to the moral implications of what psychologists do, especially in their interactions with research participants, clients, and students.

Disciplined moral decision making means going beyond the immediate, intuitive level of moral thinking and adopting a more critical-evaluative stance (Kitchener, 1984). It means taking out a pencil and paper and documenting one's thought processes step by step as one analyzes the ethical issues involved in a study. There are several models available in the literature for making ethical decisions. We present one model from Koocher and Keith-Spiegel (1998, pp. 12–16) and recommend getting in the habit of using it or one of the others available (see, e.g., The Canadian Psychological Association Committee on Ethics, 1986), especially when one is considering using research procedures or populations with which one has had little or no personal experience.

1. Describe the parameters of the situation. Initially one should obtain information from the parties involved and/or from sources relevant to the matter, such as literature papers or collegial consultation.

2. Define the potential issues involved. From the information assembled from step one, the resulting critical issues should be described.

3. Consult the guidelines, if any, already available that might apply to the resolution of each issue. These guidelines may include the Ethical Principles or other codes or policy statements as well as federal and local laws and regulations. The "right answer" might not necessarily emerge at this point. Nevertheless, this is a critical step to take conscientiously since a disregard for extant policy may well have future consequences.

4. Evaluate the rights, responsibilities, and welfare of all affected parties (including institutions and the general public).

5. Generate the alternative decisions possible for each issue. This phase should be conducted without a focus on whether each option is ethical or feasible, but may include alternatives that the psychologist would consider useless, too risky, or inappropriate. The decision not to make a decision or to do nothing should also be included.

6. Enumerate the consequences of making each decision. Whenever relevant, these consequences should include economic, psychological, and social costs; short-term, ongoing, and long-term effects; the time and effort necessary to effect each decision, including any resource limitations; any other risks, including the violation of individual rights; and any benefits.

7. Present any evidence that the various consequences or benefits resulting from each decision will actually occur. To the extent possible, estimate the probability of such occurrences. Often no evidence exists, because the rapidly changing

discipline is characterized by the frequent emergence of new and not-fully-tested innovative techniques. Lack of evidence must be considered in and of itself a risk, since the decision outcome is not predictable.

8. Make the decision.

In addition to these eight steps, we suggest a ninth:

9. Assume responsibility for the consequences of the action taken, including correction of negative consequences, if any, or re-engaging in the decision-making process if the ethical issue is not resolved (The Canadian Psychological Association, 1986, p. 6E).

It is impossible to stress enough the importance of discussing ethical concerns and issues with colleagues. Most ethical dilemmas involve a preferred resolution. For example, researchers naturally are going to prefer that some interesting and potentially fame-garnering, but perhaps somewhat morally iffy, study that they have designed be considered ethical. Regardless of how objective they may think they are being, there is a good chance that this preference or desire may contaminate their moral judgment in favor of ethical acceptability (D. M. Bersoff, in press; Silver, Sabini, & Miceli, 1989). Even scrupulously following the above decision-making model does not offer sufficient protection from the influence of motivated reasoning (though following a model is significantly more protective than is allowing intuition or a gut feeling to guide one's actions) because the model requires that one make many somewhat speculative judgments regarding risks, benefits, and the likelihood of both good and bad consequences, all of which themselves are prone to contamination by motivated cognition (Kunda, 1990). Consulting with colleagues can help prevent self-deception. It will also force a researcher to explicitly verbalize a moral justification for his or her experimental procedures. Following the steps of a moral-decision-making model can help one form such a justification and can serve as the basis for discussions with colleagues.

In the remainder of the chapter, we address the ethical considerations inherent in specific aspects of research such as subject recruiting, informed consent, methodology choices, debriefing, and the presentation of findings. In the beginning of each section there is a synopsis of the relevant rules and regulations germane to the topic addressed. We then explore the key issues and ethical ambiguities inherent in the topic.

RECRUITMENT OF RESEARCH PARTICIPANTS

Participation in scientific research must be voluntary. When recruiting people for research it is unethical to use undue inducement or any element of force, fraud, deceit, duress, or other form of constraint or coercion (45 C.F.R. 46.103[c], 1983; American Psychological Association [APA] Ethics Code, 1992, section 6.14). The problem is that, short of threats of violence or promises of eternal youth, it is not always easy to recognize coercion and undue inducement. The American Psychological Association (APA) does elaborate to some extent by specifically enjoining teachers from requiring participation in experiments as part of their courses or from offering participation in return for extra credit without making available an equitable alternative activity (APA Ethics Code, 1992, section 6.11 [d]). But even within this more specific guideline, it is quite easy to apply subtle pressure to a class, the members of which are unlikely to want to displease the person holding their grade in his or her hands. In fact, it would not be unreasonable to contend that there is some element of coercion involved in any investigator-participant interaction (Koocher & Keith Spiegel, 1998). Simply being solicited by a person perceived as having prestige and authority can be coercive in itself, especially if the potential participants approached are vulnerable, deferential, starving for attention, desperate for a solution to their psychological problems, or occupy a less powerful position than the solicitor, such as inmates, students, or employees of the organization sponsoring the research. Even if a participation request is not meant to be coercive, it still might be perceived as such by the people solicited.

This is especially likely in institutional settings such as schools, mental hospitals, and prisons. People in such settings are not used to having autonomous choice in everyday matters that influence their lives. They may agree to participate in a study not because they want to but because, within the context of the institution in which their participation was solicited, there is an implicit expectation that official requests are met with compliance (Grisso, 1996). One way around such problems is for investigators to refrain from soliciting individuals directly. Instead, they could advertise passively for participants in newspapers, newsletters, electronic bulletin boards, or with posted sign-up sheets, thus putting potential participants in the position of instigating any contact between themselves and researchers.

Certain inducements to participate in research can also be considered coercive. Examples include offering people in poor neighborhoods cash for participating or allowing their children to participate in unpleasant studies, or offering clinical intervention to people without insurance or other financial resources in need of treatment in return for their participation in an outcome or efficacy study.

Any debate regarding undue inducements entails a conflict between two fundamental moral values: beneficence and the respect for autonomy. To say that offering people who are living in deprivation a relatively large reward for participating in a study is unethical because the reward will cloud their judgment is to assume that the poor cannot make decisions regarding what is in their own best interest. But it would also be grossly naïve to believe that desperation does not affect judgment. At the least, when dealing with studies that involve more than minimal risk, the one put at risk should be the recipient of the benefit. Thus, for example, one should err on the side of beneficence in cases where parents are being compensated for allowing their children to participate in a research project. Among competent adults, the scales are tipped in favor of a respect for autonomy.

Ethical considerations should influence not only how participants are recruited but also who is recruited. By the year 2000, approximately one-third of the U.S. population will be people of color (U.S. Bureau of Census, 1995). Yet historically, psychological research has excluded diverse populations from its participant pool (Hall, 1997). In a study of empirically based articles in six major APA journals between 1970 and 1989, only 3.6% of the studies examined focused on African American participants (Graham, 1992). In another study involving research articles published in the

Journal of Counseling Psychology from 1976 to 1986, only 5.7% had a racial or ethnic minority focus (Ponterotto, 1988).

Western psychology tends to operate from the assumption that research and theories based on the majority population are applicable to all groups (Hall, 1997). Such an assumption is made at a psychologist's own peril in basic research, given mounting evidence of cross-cultural differences involving fundamental psychological concepts such as self-esteem and motivation; but in the realm of diagnostic and treatment-related research, such an assumption is unconscionable and can lead to the misdiagnosis and mistreatment of minority group members (Guthrie, 1976). Clinical research must use demographically diverse samples if it is to be used to make treatment decisions in a multiethnic society.

INFORMED CONSENT

Informed consent is a recognition of people's right to self-determination (Baumrind, 1985), their right to decide for themselves what they are willing to be a part of. It also is, as the name implies, the process by which potential participants in research are informed of exactly what they are being asked to get themselves into. In a sense, it is a contract between the investigator and the participant. Properly crafted consent forms lay out the rights and obligations of each party and give participants all of the relevant information that any reasonable person would want to have before deciding whether or not to participate in a study (APA Ethics Code, 1992, sections 6.10 & 6.11).

Specifically, the elements comprising a proper consent include:

1. An explanation of the purpose, procedures, and duration of the research that is complete enough to allow the potential participant to make an informed, intelligent choice about agreeing to participate. This includes full disclosure of any attendant discomforts and risks reasonably to be expected as well as any benefits reasonably to be expected.
2. Disclosure of any appropriate alternative procedures that might be advantageous to the subject. (This is more germane to treatment-outcome and drug studies than to most basic research.)
3. An offer to answer any inquiries concerning the study procedures.
4. An instruction that the person is free to withdraw consent and to discontinue participating in the project or activity at any time without prejudice.
5. A statement describing the extent, if any, to which the data collected will be kept confidential.
6. Information regarding whom to contact if the person has any concerns regarding the experiment or his or her participation.

Research shows that often subjects barely read let alone understand consent forms (Mann, 1994). When dealing with adults, the temptation is to simply hand them the consent form and stand back waiting for their signature. Researchers, though, have an ethical obligation to make sure consent forms are read and understood. An unread consent form cannot fulfill its ethical purpose. Although it might be easy to lay the blame on the participants for not caring enough about what they are agreeing to do to read the form, a fully informed participant is an ethically desirable goal that one should strive to attain. To this end, we suggest that researchers ask two or three comprehension questions regarding the consent form. Those people who cannot answer these questions appropriately should probably be given a verbal summary of at least the major points in the consent form such as the general procedure and the potential risks and benefits of the study. At a minimum, participants who obviously fail to read the consent form should be told that it contains important information relevant to the study and should be encouraged by the researcher to look it over.

Ideally, every study would employ a truthful and nondeceptive consent. In reality, many studies involve some degree of deception (Adair, Dushenko, & Lindsay, 1985). The ethicality of deception research can and has been debated (for antideception arguments, see Baumrind, 1985; Kelman, 1967; in support of deception, see Fisher & Fyrberg, 1994; Holmes & Bennett, 1974; Milgram, 1964). Our position is that deception is a normative practice, certainly in social psychology (Adair et al., 1985) and probably also in many areas of clinical research, and thus it cannot be ignored. In addition, federal regulations, as does the APA Code of Ethics (1992, section 6.15[a]), permit human subject review boards to approve consent procedures that do not include one or more of the elements listed above or to waive the requirement of informed consent if "the research could not practicably be carried out without the waiver or alteration" (45 C.F.R. 46.110, 1983). Thus, deception is legal and, at least for now, a mainstay of psychological research.

This is not to say that deception should be one's first methodological choice if viable alternatives exist. Every use of deception subverts a person's autonomy and right to self-determination and represents a breach of trust between psychologists and the people they invite to take part in their research. In addition, deceptive consent procedures diminish the consent form as an ethics-enhancing document. In fact, they trade on the document's ethical function in the service of creating a successful subterfuge. One purpose of the consent form is to inform participants of study aims and procedures. In recognition of the fact that participants view its purpose to be such, researchers sometimes use the form as an opportunity to set up certain convenient fictions in the participants' minds. Once consent forms become instruments of manipulation, they cease being ethical safeguards. Furthermore, if repeated exposure to deception experiments creates deception suspicion toward all studies among research participants, then even nondeceptive consent forms will begin to lose their moral worth as subjects will no longer be confident until the end of the study that the information the consent contained was complete and truthful.

The subversion and breach of trust inherent in deception research can be lessened to some degree by (a) withholding information rather than lying outright in consent forms, (b) never withholding risk-related information (withholding such information is in fact a violation of the APA Ethics Code, 1992, section 6.15[b]), and (c) actually informing subjects that they might be deceived sometime during the course of the experiment. This third recommendation can be implemented without specifically saying what that deception will be. If done carefully, such a practice will not necessarily render experimental manipulations less effective (Holmes & Bennett, 1974).

If alerting participants to the possibility of their being deceived is simply unworkable, there is another way to ameliorate the undesirable ethical consequences of this methodology. A primary objection to deception research is that it disempowers research participants. It denies them the opportunity to give or withhold their consent to participate in the actual study and not just the incomplete or fictitious version of the study described in the consent procedure. One can reempower participants to some degree by giving them the opportunity to withdraw their data, in essence to withhold their consent to participate, upon being fully debriefed regarding the experiment (Mills, 1976). This procedure also sets up a system of checks and balances. If a deception is truly central to the research enterprise such that any reasonable person could see why it had to be used, if it is done in a manner that is respectful to the participant, and if participants are thoughtfully and carefully dehoaxed (Holmes, 1976a) and desensitized (Holmes, 1976b) at the end of the study, few if any participants should avail themselves of the opportunity to withdraw their data from a study. Such a sanction is likely to be used only in those cases in which the participants feel abused or wounded, a good indication that the researcher has gone too far and should probably redesign his or her study procedures anyway.

Another, less often mentioned problem with deception research is that participants may end up working harder for their compensation than they bargained. Frequently, people participate in research in return for cash or a couple of extra-credit points. Although they may see $5 or $6 as adequate compensation for an hour spent filling out surveys or engaging in visual discrimination tasks, people may not see that same amount as an equitable recompense for having their self-esteem shaken or their mood lowered or for being forced to face some unpleasant revelation regarding their character. The problem is that deception studies often do not allow people to make an informed decision regarding whether or not the compensation being offered is adequate given what they will be called upon to do and experience. Imagine how someone would feel who signed up for a flight training study at $5 an hour only to end up having to endure the terror of the Ditching study for that same amount. One way of partially redressing this problem is by having unpleasant deception studies offer bonuses to their participants commensurate with how psychologically taxing they are beyond what people were led to believe they would be experiencing. Of course, there is a certain subjectivity in the assessment of psychological taxation beyond how the study was advertised, but a bonus of some sort would at least communicate to participants that the investigator is aware that they may be feeling somewhat exploited.

Some populations, such as children or those with severe mental illness, may not be considered legally competent to give informed consent. In such cases, consent will have to be obtained from a legal guardian. However, unless the potential research participants are very cognitively impaired or extremely young, researchers are required to obtain their assent. Extra care needs to be used in gaining a child's assent. In particular, research has shown that children have trouble understanding the potential benefits and, even more important, the potential risks of participating (Abramovitch, Freedman, Henry, & Brunschot, 1995). In addition, children often fail to appreciate the fact that they can end their participation at any time during the study (Abramovitch et al., 1995). When seeking a minor's assent, these factors need to be emphasized. It should be stressed that gaining assent is not a nicety, it is an ethical obligation (APA, 1992, section 6.11[e]).

METHODS

In evaluating a research proposal, IRBs are mandated to determine that the following conditions are met:

1. Risks to the subjects are minimized. This means that the procedures used are consistent with sound research design and do not unnecessarily expose subjects to risk.
2. Risks to the subjects are reasonable in relation to anticipated benefits, if any, to subjects and in relation to the importance of the knowledge that may reasonably be expected to result.
3. The selection of subjects is equitable.
4. The research plan makes adequate provision for monitoring the data collected to ensure the safety of subjects.

As usual, the devil is in the details. What is the definition of a reasonable risk? How does one determine if a given risk is adequately offset by a benefit? According to whose sensibilities should an adequate risk-benefit trade-off be determined? Perhaps the simplest way to assess the ethical suitability of a study is to ask oneself if one would be willing to submit a beloved family member (or pet, in the case of animal studies) to one's procedures. This, though, is actually a more conservative ethical decision-making criterion than is generally used.

Cost-Benefit Analysis

At the heart of most ethical appraisals of psychological research is a cost-benefit analysis. The key concept here is the ratio of benefits to be obtained from the study relative to the risks involved. Ideally, a study will involve what is known as "minimal risk." Minimal risk means that the risk for harm anticipated in the proposed research is not greater than that ordinarily encountered in daily life or during the performance of routine physical and psychological examinations or tests. Given minimal risk, there is less pressure for a study to result in tangible benefits or in more than an increase in our understanding of basic psychological functioning. But minimal risk does not make poorly designed, quick and dirty research acceptable. Because there is no such thing as zero risk, if for no other reason than that it takes time and an average of $160 to review a research proposal (Ceci, Peters, & Plotkin, 1985) and time and effort to participate in research, potential benefit that asymptotically approaches zero cannot be justified on the basis of a cost-benefit analysis.

Assessing risk means more than determining the potential for bodily harm. In the context of psychological research, common risks include invasion of privacy, loss of self-esteem, negative mood, stress, physical and emotional discomfort, negative reactions to being induced to commit unflattering acts, negative reactions to being deceived, and breach of confidentiality, as well as more collective risks such as the potential that a finding will be misinterpreted or misused by the public to the disadvantage of some group or subpopulation of society (Koocher & Keith-Spiegel, 1998).

Risk assessment can be quite difficult because there is such a variety of ways people may respond to the same stimuli. What one person may find to be anxiety-provoking or stressful, another may experience as exhilarating or exciting, for example, touching a live snake (Koocher & Keith-Spiegel, 1998). In addition, one person's risk may be another person's benefit; for example, placing a woman in an assertiveness training group may make her better able to communicate her needs to her husband, which could be good news for her but bad news for her husband, who may have enjoyed always getting his way.

When calculating the potential costs of a study, it is important to look at the study from the perspective of everyone involved both directly and indirectly. A common mistake in cost analysis is failing to look beyond the research participants to (a) their family and friends, (b) psychology as a science, and (c) society as a whole. Research that solicits, for example, a person's sexual history or family's history of mental illness can be an invasion of the privacy of the people not directly participating in the study but who are nonetheless being discussed. These people's feelings must also be considered, perhaps even more so, given that they have usually not been granted any choice about being an object of study (D. M. Bersoff & Bersoff, in press). In terms of psychology as a discipline, one of the criticisms against deception research is that it makes psychologists look like trickers, a perception that could undermine public support for behavioral science research in general (Baumrind, 1985). Finally, at the societal level, research seeking relationships, for example, between race and IQ or criminality always has the potential to be used to justify racial discrimination. Our aim here is not to instill paralyzing risk paranoia, but rather to encourage people to be more risk sensitive. It is easy to become fixated on the data and overlook the people supplying those data and the people who could potentially be affected by them.

The other side of the risk-benefit equation is the benefit. It, too, must be characterized in assessing the ethicality of a study. Outside the domain of applied research, the potential benefit of most studies is the rather nebulous one of adding to our knowledge of basic psychological functioning, perhaps with an eye toward potential future applications of that knowledge. Given that the major aim of science is to increase our knowledge of the world and how it works, this is not a unimportant benefit. It is, however, a benefit that lacks a certain immediacy, if not to the researcher than to the research participants. This tends not to be a problem in studies involving minimal risk, but it can be a bone of contention in research that places participants at greater than minimal risk. Specifically when it comes to risky research, there is some debate as to whether societal or scientific benefit can compensate for an individual's discomfort or whether cost to the individual can only be balanced by benefit that accrues to that same individual. Of course, it could be argued that the good feeling associated with helping to further science is an individual benefit, but such a feeling is apt to pale in the face of an unpleasant study experience. Our position is that participant fees and other forms of compensation, though not traditionally considered a benefit in a cost-benefit analysis, can at least partially counterbalance a direct cost to the participant that is not matched by a direct benefit. This is one reason why we argue that participants in deception and other potentially jarring studies should receive compensation commensurate with the unpleasantness they experience.

In applied research, the potential benefit is the development or implementation of some technique or intervention that can serve a useful purpose. Here again, though, it is possible that the people directly put at risk by a study may not be the ones most apt to receive the direct benefit, for example, the control group in a treatment-outcome study. This issue will be discussed in more detail below.

The judgment that a study's benefits outweigh its risks is not necessarily objective. This brings up the issue of whose perceptions of risk and benefit should hold sway. For example, Abelson and Miller (1967) performed a study in which people sitting alone on a park bench were approached by an experimenter claiming to represent a survey research organization and were asked if they would be willing to be interviewed. At the beginning of the interview, the experimenter asks a person sitting nearby, who is actually a confederate, if he would mind answering the questions at the same time. The confederate responds with opinions that are clearly opposite those of the subject, and he makes demeaning remarks about the subject's answers.

In a survey of 174 members of the general public, it was found that 52% of the respondents said that they would have minded being a subject in this Abelson and Miller study; 42% felt the study was unethical; and 57% said either "No" or that they were "Not Sure" whether this study was justified by its scientific contribution (Wilson & Donnerstein, 1976). Are these data sufficient to render the judgment that Abelson and Miller acted in an unethical manner by performing this study? Alternatively, in a survey of college students, it was found that most students judged deception studies to be scientifically valuable and valid (Fisher & Fyrberg, 1994). Given that college students are often the participant pool for such research, are these data sufficient to render the judgment that deception experiments, or at least the ones used in the Fisher and Fyrberg study, are ethical? If participants seem to be accepting of the use of deception despite the philosophical objections of some (e.g., Baumrind, 1985), why should psychologists continue to have concerns?

In essence, the question is whether popular opinion is a valid determinant of ethicality. If it is, then studies could be ethically pretested. Researchers would simply have to circulate a detailed description of the proposed study among the population from which their participants will be drawn. The ethical perceptions of these people would then be used to adjudicate potential moral concerns. Of course, this leaves open the question of a decision rule. For example, is a simple majority enough to have a study declared ethical, or should two-thirds approval be required, or perhaps even unanimity?

Although the morality of a practice is almost never considered an empirical question (slavery would be wrong despite any particular survey results to the contrary), that does not mean that ethical problems should not or cannot be informed by data (Gergen, 1973). This is in large part because of the cost-benefit analysis that makes up most moral decision making. Whereas rights do not generally require empirical legitimation, costs can often be empirical matters, especially when those costs involve something fairly easy to measure—the harm and discomfort felt by research participants.

By and large, an empirical or public opinion approach to determining ethicality is not used. Instead, ethical suitability is determined by a small panel of lawyers, researchers, and community members on human subject committees. Nonetheless, we feel that empirical data can be morally relevant and should be used to inform method-ological decision making. Along these same lines, we strongly suggest piloting a study to test for potential ethical problems. This could involve putting a small group of people through the study and questioning them extensively regarding their perceptions and re-actions to their participation.

We encourage such proactive measures in response to the temptation to abdicate all ethical judgment responsibility to the IRB, to equate its acceptance of a proposal with moral acceptability. IRBs, as a rule, do not possess the moral clarity which would make such an abdication desirable. For example, the first author has had the same re-search proposals approved at one institution and rejected at another. At best, IRB ap-proval means only that a study meets the minimum ethical standards required. We encourage people to aim higher, to operate well above reproach. The existence of IRBs is not an excuse to stop policing oneself.

The Obligation to Screen and Intervene

Part of self-policing is refraining from collecting data that one is not equipped to han-dle. We do not feel, for example, that it is ethical for undergraduates and untrained graduate students and even faculty, for that matter, to be collecting information about depression, anxiety, sexuality, and traumatic life experiences without adequate clini-cally or otherwise suitably trained supervision (D. M. Bersoff & Bersoff, in press). When clinically sensitive data are to be collected, plans should be put into place for handling situations in which a participant discloses conduct or a frame of mind that is potentially injurious to the participant, injurious to others, and/or illegal.

In the one study we have found that investigated whether such contingency planning is routinely done, it was quite evident that it is not (Burbach, Farha, & Thorpe, 1986). The reasons given by investigators for a lack of such planning included not expecting to find any at-risk participants in their sample, that their consent forms did not contain provisions for follow-up contacts, and that they did not want to violate confidentiality.

We have very little sympathy for the first excuse. Anyone collecting clinically sen-sitive data should assume that there is always a chance that a distressed person will be identified. But these last two reasons illustrate just how complicated some of the ethi-cal issues associated with collecting clinically sensitive data can be. Although both reasons recognize that children (the studies examined in Burbach et al., 1986, all in-volved children) have a right to privacy and to be treated with fidelity by researchers, they neglect to consider the rights of parents to the care and control of their children, including the right to know about situations that might impair their children's safety or emotional stability. In fact, preserving participant confidentiality in this context leads to an explicit violation of the Society for Research in Child Development's (SRCD) ethical code, which states: "When, in the course of research, information comes to the investigator's attention that may jeopardize the child's well-being, the investigator has a responsibility to discuss the information with the parents or guardians and with those expert in the field in order that they may arrange the necessary assistance for the child" (SRCD, 1990–1991). And though the APA ethical code does not directly man-date that researchers must inform parents in these situations, the code does strongly express the importance of both the principles of fidelity and beneficence, the two competing concerns in this situation.

Predicaments such as this, in which researchers are subject to contradictory ethical considerations, are not uncommon nor easily negotiated (D. N. Bersoff & Koeppl, 1993). Even when working with adults this fidelity/beneficence dilemma is not easily resolved. Imagine how devastating it could be if someone indicated on a survey or questionnaire or in an interview that he or she had a drug problem, was involved in child abuse, or had entertained thoughts of suicide and yet received no follow-up whatsoever. Such people could conclude that their problem or perhaps that they themselves were unimportant even if the consent form did not explicitly contain provisions for follow-up contacts.

In general, although many academic psychologists may consider themselves to be researchers, in the eyes of study participants they may be seen as clinicians, as people in a helping profession. If investigators fail to respond in a caring or concerned manner when someone opens up to them, that can be a very meaningful event in that person's life. This is not to say that a follow-up needs to be invasive, but at a minimum, researchers should screen their data for signs that a participant is in distress and at least offer that person the option of treatment or of referral to an appropriate professional agency. This obligation to screen and intervene is one reason why gathering data beyond one's competence to handle is undesirable. Researchers without proper training are not qualified to intervene themselves and may not even be able to determine when intervention is actually necessary. As a result, nonclinically trained researchers are probably less likely to have a plan in place to identify and respond to at-risk study participants.

Our call for intervention contingency planning is predicated on the presupposition that research participants have the right to expect treatment or at least treatment referrals should they supply information to an investigator indicating that they are potentially in need of services. Although this presupposition may not be popular among those in the research community, it is difficult to defend on ethical grounds ignoring information that a person is potentially in psychological distress simply because the information was gleaned in a research rather than a treatment setting (D. M. Bersoff & Bersoff, in press). If a research physician involved in a medical study of bone fracture healing finds evidence on an X-ray taken as part of the study that one of the participants has a potentially cancerous lesion, one would hope that the physician would follow up with the person even if it entailed breaking the subject number code to obtain that person's name and even though the person was not the physician's patient. There is no reason why the moral expectations should be any different when the investigator is a research psychologist and the potential problem is depression, alcohol abuse, or excessive anxiety.

Because of the problem of socially desirable responding and the difficulty of getting people to discuss openly highly personal and inflammatory topics such as their AIDS status or drug use, research in which participants have total anonymity (i.e., even the primary investigator does not possess the information to crack the code required to match a protocol with a name) is sometimes necessary to increase the likelihood of collecting accurate information. Follow-up interventions for those who manifest clinically troublesome data will, of course, not be possible under these conditions. To help prevent participants from expecting intervention or from misinterpreting a lack of intervention should they reveal clinically significant symptomatology, the investigator's inability to respond to the data provided by individual research participants should be made explicit in the consent form. As an added safeguard, participants in anonymous studies could be invited to approach the investigator with any concerns they may have about their well-being that arise in the course of their study participation. These people could then be offered appropriate referrals to counseling organizations.

These recommendations are ameliorative of some, but not all, of the ethical problems associated with anonymous research. Thus, anonymous research techniques should be used only when the investigator considers them vital to the collection of valid and meaningful data.

Control Groups

Control groups are often a key factor in good experimental methodology. But in clinical research, and in particular in treatment studies, the use of control groups is sometimes contraindicated. In outcome and efficacy studies, the control group is going untreated, often for potentially serious problems such as phobias, eating disorders, or alcoholism. This is perhaps the domain where good science and good ethics seem most directly at odds. This is also an area where cost-benefit equations tend to have high coefficients. The development of an effective treatment can be quite beneficial to people who are suffering, but a lack of treatment can expose individual research participants to significant risk and distress. If no known effective treatment currently exists, then having a control group is less of a problem because people are not being deprived of standard care in the furtherance of research goals. The real problem arises when there is an effective standard of care and participants are being randomized into a no-treatment control group. In such cases, research is altering the lives of these individuals for the worse: They will be doing less well than they would have if they had not participated in the study.

If the study is short term and a lack of treatment will not put participants at high risk, one way to ameliorate the ethical problems is to offer free active treatment to the control group upon completion of the study. Another alternative is to use a wait list control group. These are people who are signed up for a treatment program, but there is currently no space available for them. Thus, these people would mostly likely not have been receiving treatment during the course of the study anyway. In either case, it is quite important that potential participants fully realize that there is a significant possibility that they will be randomized into a condition in which they will receive no or placebic treatment and that as a result their malady will most likely remain the same or perhaps even worsen during the course of the study. In general, though, there is no justification for putting someone at significant long-term risk to have a pure control group when there is a form of effective treatment currently available. In such situations, the current standard of care should be the baseline group rather than a no-treatment control. After all, if a new treatment is not at least as effective as the current regimen, then its utility is probably marginal at best. In addition, if, during the course of a study, it becomes apparent that the experimental treatment is significantly more effective than the baseline or control treatment, one should consider switching the control subjects into the active treatment group before the termination of the study, especially if the study is long term.

CONFIDENTIALITY

When appropriate, researchers have an obligation to take adequate provisions to protect the privacy of subjects and to maintain the confidentiality of data. Such provisions include (a) storing subject-identifying information such as consent forms separately from the actual data, (b) keeping under lock and key data as well as any information that would enable someone to match a name with a particular study, protocol, or data file, and (c) not presenting information that would allow participants to be uniquely identified when promulgating study results.

The investigator's confidentiality guarantee is usually communicated to participants in the consent form with the standard phrasing "all information will be kept strictly confidential except as may be required by law." This disclaimer is certainly adequate for most research, but not for all. In particular, studies that have a high probability of garnering clinically sensitive information such as that about child or elder abuse, drug abuse, AIDS, criminality, or psychopathology require a more elaborate disclaimer. In such cases, it is incumbent upon the researcher to explain to participants the nature of the exceptions required by law, for example, mandatory reporting statutes for child abuse. In addition, minor participants should be informed that if they express suicidal ideation, serious drug use, or signs of other behavior that puts them at risk, their parents are likely to be informed. To do less places the burden on participants (instead of on investigators, where it belongs) to know the disclosure rules in the jurisdiction and context in which the research is being conducted in order for them to fully appreciate the limits of their confidentiality rights (D. M. Bersoff & Bersoff, in press).

A major concern regarding fuller disclosure of the limits of confidentiality is that participants will be less forthcoming with sensitive information or perhaps more hesitant to participate in sensitive research at all. Research evidence does seem to justify this fear (Singer & Frankel, 1982). There are remedies available, though, to this potential problem. In particular, it is possible to obtain a certificate of confidentiality from the secretary of the U.S. Department of Health and Human Services to protect the privacy and identity of research participants (Hoagwood, 1994). Such a certificate provides the investigator with legal protection against being compelled to disclose personal, identifiable information about research participants, including possible exemption from state and local reporting requirements (Hoagwood, 1994). It also assures research participants that identifying information that they provide during a study is protected from disclosure. Such a certificate can allow researchers to study sensitive topics such as sexual practices, drug abuse, and illegal conduct with less fear of losing participants due to confidentiality concerns. It should be noted, however, that the protection offered by these certificates has never been tested in court and that in research involving minors, the certificate does not protect children against the disclosure of information to their parents. In addition, at the present time it is unclear whether other research data, aside from identifying information, are similarly rendered immune from subpoena by the certificate (Hoagwood, 1994). Finally, as always, ultimate moral responsibility lies with the researcher. A certificate of confidentiality does not prevent researchers from voluntarily disclosing to the authorities such problems as child abuse or threats of violence as long as prospective participants are informed of the circumstances under which such disclosures will be made. In other words, a confidentiality certificate does not allow researchers to ignore their moral obligations to screen and intervene.

DEBRIEFING

After gathering data from research participants, it may be tempting to hand them their coats and send them on their way as quickly as possible, but one's responsibility to study participants does not end upon the completion of data collection. Investigators still have the obligation to engage in procedures to detect and alleviate any negative consequences of participation, especially in studies involving deceptions, negative mood manipulations, and the revealing of unpleasant personal characteristics. Psychologists also have an obligation to provide a prompt opportunity for participants to obtain information about the nature, results, and conclusions of the research and to correct any misconceptions participants may have about the design and purpose of a study (APA Ethics Code, 1992, section 6.18[a]). As with most research-related obligations, though, there are exceptions (APA Ethics Code, 1992, section 6.18[b]). Sometimes, the debriefing has the potential to cause more harm than participation in the study itself. This is particularly true if participants were chosen based on their having some deficit or if the behavior being investigated, which they may have unknowingly been observed displaying, is embarrassing or is perceived as undesirable. In such cases, a thorough debriefing may be contraindicated and only very general information about the study need be offered (Sieber, 1982). However, this still does not mean participants can be shooed out the door as quickly as possible. There is always the responsibility to probe for any adverse reactions participants may be experiencing; and in some cases, there is an obligation to educate them about psychology (educational benefit is often the justification for encouraging or requiring participation in experiments as part of psychology courses).

Despite its ethical importance, debriefing is often considered a nuisance, especially among those who do deception-based experiments. It takes time, it does not seem to have a scientific purpose, and it forces researchers to reveal their deceptive manipulations to a potentially loose-lipped stranger who may then go forth and contaminate the participant pool. The fact that participants, especially those who participate just for the money, often would rather get on with their lives than sit through a minilecture on psychology only makes matters worse.

In reality, though, debriefing can serve a scientific purpose, especially in deception experiments. It affords a perfect opportunity to probe participants for suspicion. In addition, it allows one to determine whether the experimental procedures were actually perceived or experienced by the participants as they were intended (Blanck, Bellack, Rosnow, Rotheram-Borus, & Schooler, 1992). Such information can be essential for the accurate interpretation of one's findings. For example, if an investigator is doing a treatment-outcome study and one of the conditions involves a placebo-attention group, it is important to ascertain whether or not the members of this group suspected that their treatment was not real. If such a suspicion is found to be present, then the value of this condition as a control for positive treatment expectancies is called into question, and conclusions based on the data may require modification. Debriefing can also provide leads for future research (Blanck et al., 1992). As participants discuss their feelings and perceptions regarding a study, they may also reveal considerations and perspectives that had not occurred to the investigator. This information can help in the refinement of protocols and even spark ideas for follow-up studies.

While the importance of, and the obligation to provide, a thorough debriefing cannot be overemphasized, it is not an ethical panacea capable of undoing all of the actual and potential harm attendant with participation in a study. First of all, there is some controversy regarding the effectiveness of debriefings in desensitizing participants. Desensitization is the process by which participants' negative reactions to how they behaved in the study or to the experimental manipulations are repaired (Holmes, 1976b). For example, people who fail to respond in bystander intervention (good Samaritan) studies are often told not to think poorly of themselves because most people act as they did in such situations and their behavior says more about the power of certain situational factors than it does about them as caring, empathetic people. People given false feedback about some aspect of themselves are told that the feedback was indeed false and that the information they were given is not necessarily an accurate reflection of their true selves. The problem is that some research has found that people do not always correct their self-perceptions in the manner and degree appropriate to the new information that they have been given during the debriefing (see, e.g., Ross, Lepper, & Hubbard, 1975; Tesch, 1977; Walster, Berscheid, Abrahams, & Aronson, 1967; Wegner, Coulton, & Wenzlaff, 1985). In other words, debriefings do not always reliably ameliorate the psychological damage they are designed to rectify.

In addition, there is some harm that cannot even potentially be reversed by a debriefing. For example, in the Ditching study, being told that the plane's troubles were staged and that they were never really in danger does not change the fact that for a significant period of time the passengers were experiencing fear of death and were forced to think about their families and what they were going to leave to each member should they die. Debriefings are not capable of undoing what participants felt during a study. At best, they can help ensure that participants do not leave the lab with any misconceptions about themselves or the study itself, but often that is only part of what makes a study ethically problematic. Even a good debriefing does not make having had a bad experience go away. This is another reason why ethical considerations must inform study design. One cannot run amok during the study and expect to make everything right with an eloquent debriefing.

PRESENTATION OF FINDINGS

It is one of the few hard and fast rules of research ethics that fabricating data is unacceptable (APA Ethics Code, 1992, section 6.21[a]). Such behavior will often end one's career. Along these same lines, it is unethical to suppress disconfirming data and to fail to report the limitations of one's data. The pressure to publish is immense in academic psychology. That, combined with an emphasis on theory-driven research in which studies are run simply to confirm the researcher's firmly held expectations, makes it quite tempting to play fast and loose with one's data. But trying to get an article or a chapter accepted should not be viewed as analogous to trying to sell the editor a car. It is not up to the editor and the reviewers to find the weak spots in the researcher's data, methodology, and arguments. It is up to the researcher to point them out. This is not a caveat emptor situation.

What is less clear is how to handle significant findings that may have unpleasant social implications. For example, say one's data show that women become more cognitively impaired under stress than men, or that Latinos are more likely to lie to authority figures than European Americans. The potential for such results to be used to discriminate against women and Latinos is obvious. In addition, if one is interested in studying cognitive impairment under stress or even lying behavior, such demographic main effects may not be directly relevant to the arguments one wishes to make. So, do good researchers even look for such effects in the data, and if they find them do they have an obligation to report them?

Researchers do not have an obligation to look at absolutely everything in the data beyond that which is necessary to adequately test and examine their hypotheses (in fact, people who frown upon non-theory-driven mucking about in one's data aptly call this practice data dredging). Data analysis, though, can be like a Pandora's box; the temptation to analyze everything is often irresistible. Unfortunately, once one looks at a variable, one cannot go back again. As to whether one reports the finding, from the point of view of science, the answer is a resounding yes. To function at its best, science requires the free exchange of information. The censorship (either self- or institutionally imposed) of valid findings is antithetical to one of the core values of science. But from the perspective of society, some information may be better left undisseminated, especially if there is a good chance that it will be used to justify prejudice and discrimination.

Psychologists are both scientists and members of society. But caught up in their career and focused on research and the need for publications, it is easy for them to forget that science is not society's (and hopefully not their) most important endeavor or highest value. Protecting people's welfare and human rights should take precedence over the accumulation and dissemination of knowledge when these two goals are in significant conflict. Keeping this ordering of goods in mind while designing research studies would go a long way toward ensuring that psychologists conduct themselves as scientists in an ethical manner.

SUMMARY OF MAIN POINTS

Psychologists can do damage. This damage is often a result of researchers viewing research participants as objects to be manipulated or as a means to a publication. To reduce the chances of engaging in unethical research, the following guidelines should be kept in mind:

1. Participation in scientific research must be voluntary. When recruiting people for research, it is unethical to use undue inducement or any element of force, fraud, deceit, duress, or other form of constraint or coercion.
2. A fully informed participant is an ethically desirable goal that one should strive to attain.

3. Assessing risk means more than determining the potential for bodily harm. In the context of psychological research, common risks that must be considered include invasion of privacy, loss of self-esteem, negative mood, stress, physical and emotional discomfort, negative reactions to being induced to commit unflattering acts, negative reactions to being deceived, and breach of confidentiality, as well as more collective risks such as the potential that a finding will be misinterpreted or misused by the public to the disadvantage of some group or subpopulation of society.

4. When clinically sensitive data are to be collected, plans should be put into place for handling situations in which a participant discloses conduct or a frame of mind that is potentially injurious to the participant, injurious to others, and/or illegal.

5. Researchers should take adequate provisions to protect the privacy of participants and to maintain the confidentiality of data.

6. Investigators should engage in procedures to detect and alleviate any negative consequences of participation, especially in studies involving deceptions, negative mood manipulations, and the revealing of unpleasant personal characteristics. In the end, though, debriefings are not capable of undoing what participants felt during a study. At best, they can help ensure that participants do not leave the lab with any misconceptions about themselves or the study itself, but often that is only part of what makes a study ethically problematic. Even a good debriefing does not make having had a bad experience go away. This is why ethical considerations must inform study design from the beginning.

Ultimately, researchers are responsible for policing themselves. Part of self-policing is becoming familiar with and keeping abreast of the research ethics literature as well as routinely using moral decision-making models and consulting with colleagues, especially when considering the use of research procedures or populations with which one has had little or no personal experience.

Although good research ethics may on occasion be in conflict with expediency, a skilled and creative methodologist can almost always find a way to study an issue in an ethical manner. The eventual cost of failing to act ethically is career damage and the diminution of psychology in the mind of the public. The bottom line—advancing psychology as a science—is supposed to be an avenue for helping people, not a justification for harming them.

REFERENCES

Abelson, R. P., & Miller, J. C. (1967). Negative persuasion via personal insult. *Journal of Experimental Social Psychology, 3,* 321–333.

Abramovitch, R., Freedman, J. L., Henry, K., & Brunschot, M. V. (1995). Children's capacity to agree to psychological research: Knowledge of risks and benefits and voluntariness. *Ethics & Behavior, 5*(1), 25–48.

Adair, J. G., Dushenko, T. W., & Lindsay, R. C. L. (1985). Ethical regulations and their impact on research practice. *American Psychologist, 40*(1), 59–72.

American Psychological Association. (1992). Ethical principles of psychologists and code of conduct. *American Psychologist, 47,* 1597–1611.

Baumrind, D. (1985). Research using intentional deception. *American Psychologist, 40*(2), 165–174.

Berkun, M. M., Bialek, H. M., Kern, R. P., & Yagi, K. (1962). Experimental studies of psychological stress in man. *Psychological Monographs: General and Applied, 76*(15), 1–39.

Bersoff, D. M. (in press). Why good people sometimes do bad things: Motivated reasoning and unethical behavior. *Personality and Social Psychology Bulletin.*

Bersoff, D. M., & Bersoff, D. N. (in press). Ethical issues in the collection of self-report data. In A. Stone, J. Turkkan, C. Bachrach, V. Cain, J. Jobe, & H. Kurtzman (Eds.), *The science of self report: Implications for research and practice.* New York: Erlbaum.

Bersoff, D. N. (1995). *Ethical conflicts in psychology.* Washington, DC: American Psychological Association.

Bersoff, D. N., & Koeppl, P. M. (1993). The relation between ethical codes and moral principles. *Ethics and Behavior, 3,* 345–357.

Blanck, P. D., Bellack, A. S., Rosnow, R. L., Rotheram-Borus, M. J., & Schooler, N. R. (1992). Scientific rewards and conflicts of ethical choices in human subjects research. *American Psychologist, 47*(7), 959–965.

Burbach, D. J., Farha, J. G., & Thorpe, J. S. (1986). Assessing depression in community samples of children using self-report inventories: Ethical considerations. *Journal of Abnormal Child Psychology, 14,* 579–589.

Canadian Psychological Association Committee on Ethics. (1986). Code of ethics. *Highlights, 8*(1), 6E–12E.

Cecil, S. J., Peters, D., & Plotkin, J. (1985). Human subjects review, personal values, and the regulation of social science research. *American Psychologist, 40*(9), 994–1002.

Ernhart, C. B., Scarr, S., & Geneson, D. F. (1993). On being a whistle blower: The Needleman case. *Ethics & Behavior, 3*(1), 73–93.

Fisher, C. B., & Fyrberg, D. (1994). Participant partners: College students weigh the costs and benefits of deceptive research. *American Psychologist, 49,* 417–427.

Gergen, K. J. (1973). The codification of research ethics: Views of a Doubting Thomas. *American Psychologist, 28,* 907–912.

Graham, S. (1992). "Most of the subjects were White and middle class": Trends in published research on African Americans in selected APA journals, 1970–1989. *American Psychologist, 47,* 629–639.

Grisso, T. (1996). Voluntary consent to research participation in the institutional context. In B. H. Stanley, J. E. Sieber, & G. B. Melton (Eds.), *Research ethics: A psychological approach* (pp. 203–224). Lincoln: University of Nebraska Press.

Guthrie, R. (1976). *Even the rat was white.* New York: Harper & Row.

Hall, C. C. I. (1997). Cultural malpractice: The growing obsolescence of psychology with the changing U.S. population. *American Psychologist, 52*(6), 642–651.

Hoagwood, K. (1994). The certificate of confidentiality at the National Institute of Mental Health: Discretionary considerations in its applicability in research on child and adolescent mental disorders. *Ethics & Behavior, 4*(2), 123–131.

Holmes, D. S. (1976a). Debriefing after psychological experiments: I. Effectiveness of postdeception dehoaxing. *American Psychologist, 31,* 858–867.

Holmes, D. S. (1976b). Debriefing after psychological experiments: II. Effectiveness of postexperimental desensitizing. *American Psychologist, 31,* 868–875.

Holmes, D. S., & Bennett, D. H. (1974). Experiments to answer questions raised by the use of deception in psychological research. *Journal of Personality and Social Psychology, 29*(3), 358–367.

Kelman, H. C. (1967). Human use of human subjects: The problem of deception in social psychological experiments. *Psychological Bulletin, 27,* 1–11.

Kitchener, K. S. (1984). Intuition, critical evaluation and ethical principles: The foundation for ethical decision in counseling psychology. *Counseling Psychologist, 12*(3), 43–55.

Koocher, G. P., & Keith-Spiegel, P. (1998). *Ethics in psychology: Professional standards and cases.* New York: Oxford University Press.

Kunda, Z. (1990). The case for motivated reasoning. *Psychological Bulletin, 108*(3), 480–498.

Mann, T. (1994). Informed consent for psychological research: Do subjects comprehend consent forms and understand their legal rights? *Psychological Science, 5,* 140–143.

Milgram, S. (1964). Issues in the study of obedience: A reply to Baumrind. *American Psychologist, 19,* 848–852.

Mills, J. (1976). A procedure for explaining experiments involving deception. *Personality and Social Psychology Bulletin, 2,* 3–13.

Ponterotto, J. (1988). Racial/ethnic minority research in the Journal of Counseling Psychology: A content analysis and methodological critique. *Journal of Counseling Psychology, 35,* 410–418.

Rosenthal, R. (1994). Science and ethics in conducting, analyzing, and reporting psychological research. *Psychological Science, 5,* 127–133.

Ross, L., Lepper, M. R., & Hubbard, M. (1975). Perseverance in self-perception and social perception: Biased attributional processes in the debriefing paradigm. *Journal of Personality and Social Psychology, 32,* 880–892.

Sieber, J. E. (1982). Deception in social research: III. The nature and limits of debriefing. *IRB: A Review of Human Subjects Research, 6,* 1–4.

Silver, M., Sabini, J., & Miceli, M. (1989). On knowing self-deception. *Journal for the Theory of Social Behaviour, 19*(2), 213–227.

Singer, E., & Frankel, M. R. (1982, June). Informed consent procedures in telephone interviews. *American Sociological Review, 47,* 416–427.

Society for Research in Child Development. (1990–1991). Ethical standards for research with children. *Directory of the Society for Research in Child Development,* 337–339.

Tesch, F. E. (1977). Debriefing research participants: Though this be method there is madness to it. *Journal of Personality and Social Psychology, 35,* 217–224.

U.S. Bureau of the Census. (1995). *Statistical abstracts of the U.S.* (115th ed.). Washington, DC: Author.

Walster, E., Berscheid, E., Abrahams, D., & Aronson, V. (1967). Effectiveness of debriefing following deception experiments. *Journal of Personality and Social Psychology, 6,* 371–380.

Wegner, D. M., Coulton, G. F., & Wenzlaff, R. (1985). The transparency of denial: Briefing in the debriefing paradigm. *Journal of Personality and Social Psychology, 49,* 338–346.

Wilson, D. W., & Donnerstein, E. (1976). Legal and ethical aspects of nonreactive social psychological research: An excursion into the public mind. *American Psychologist, 31*(11), 765–773.

Chapter 3

ETHNICITY, GENDER, AND CROSS-CULTURAL ISSUES IN CLINICAL RESEARCH

STANLEY SUE, PH.D., KAREN S. KURASKI, PH.D., and SHOBHA SRINIVASAN, PH.D.

The intent of this chapter is to provide an overview of the challenges we must attend to, and some solutions, to devise, implement, and interpret research in the most bias-free and valid manner possible. Although there are many ways to present these ideas, for heuristic purposes, we have decided to cover the entire research endeavor, from the formulation of research ideas and hypotheses to the interpretation of analyzed data. To some, a discussion of ethnic and gender issues in research may seem like an exercise in political correctness. After all, aren't scientific research designs and methodologies rather objective in nature, free from biases of one sort or another, and applicable to different groups and populations? The answer is "yes" and "no." It is true that hypothesis testing, controlling for extraneous variables in research designs, theory building, and so on, are important for scientific research with any population. However, which hypotheses are formulated, which variables are considered extraneous, how to control variables, and which theory to build are subject to values, priorities, and cultural orientations. Here we discuss the entire research process—formulation of research ideas, definition of variables, selection of measures, selection and sampling of a population, gaining cooperation of research participants, research design, data collection, and interpretation of analyzed data—and show how consideration of ethnicity, gender, and culture are critically important to all research. Rogler (1989) notes that research is made culturally sensitive through a continual process of substantive and methodological insertions and adaptations designed to mesh inquiry with the cultural characteristics of the group being studied. These insertions have to span the entire research process, from the planning of the study to the analysis and interpretation of data.

Our discussion does not cover general principles of research design and methodology or all topics pertinent to ethnicity and gender. Rather, we examine those issues that are more or less specific to properly addressing issues of ethnicity, gender, and culture in clinical research. The guidelines and recommendations we put forth related to ethnic, gender, and cross-cultural clinical research are really those recognized as simply "good" research. Our point is that treating issues of ethnicity, culture, and gender in clinical research as a side issue or as nuisance variables, which are only for those who are specifically investigating questions pertaining to ethnic, cultural, or gender differences, is a serious mistake. Certainly, there are those of us who conduct specifically ethnic, cultural, and gender research and continually grapple with the difficulties of trying to conduct culturally valid, sex-fair, and bias-free research. However, attaining valid research findings and minimizing bias are essential objectives of all good research. For instance, selecting samples that are representative of the population from which the research will be applied, administering measures with metric equivalence for all respondents, and examining variables with conceptual equivalence for all participants are critical whether one is specifically studying ethnic differences in psychiatric symptom manifestation or, more globally, a school-based intervention's impact on children's self-esteem. Furthermore, given the multiethnic nature of society, it is impossible and inadvisable to avoid including research participants or subjects from more than one ethnic or racial group. Ethnicity, culture, gender, and even minority group status influence the entire research endeavor, even if these issues are not intended to be the primary foci of the research investigation.

ASSUMPTIONS UNDERLYING ETHNICITY AND GENDER

Generally, concepts and assumptions concerning ethnicity and gender often are not explicitly stated, and we want to indicate our assumptions from the outset. First, ethnic and gender research can refer to research that is intended to better understand the groups in question (e.g., African Americans or women) or to serve as a comparison group with other groups (e.g., White American men). Second, the use of ethnic or gender terms, such as African Americans, Asian Americans, Hispanic Americans, Native Americans, White Americans, men, and women, are sometimes offensive; in using these terms, we are not suggesting that within-group heterogeneity is minimal. Third, it is important to place ethnic and gender research in the proper context. In the United States, ethnic groups and women often have minority group status; that is, they are frequently underrepresented or disadvantaged in socioeconomic, occupational, and educational mobility. Thus, the study of ethnic minority groups and women in this country can be distinguished from cross-cultural research, in which similarities and differences in individual psychological functioning, as well as the relationships between psychological variables and sociocultural, ecological, and biological variables, are examined (Berry, Poortinga, Segall, & Dasen, 1992). Culture is typically the independent variable. In ethnic minority research, the evaluations and contrasts involve not only people with different cultural origins but also those who have had years of interracial interactions (e.g., African Americans and White Americans). In addition to culture, the history of race/ethnic relations, sexism, prejudice, stereotyping, and discrimination must be taken into account. This history of interactions provides a context that is not identical to the cultural origins of the groups. Therefore, unlike cross-cultural research, ethnic minority and gender research may entail the examination of the main effects of culture and minority group status and the interaction among the variables. Finally, given our diverse society and world, understanding mental health and means to intervene with different groups is important because our knowledge base has largely been acquired on mainstream Americans. Research on these groups can also test the generality of theories or concepts. Thus, ethnic and gender research is good for science.

It is for these reasons that ethnic and gender issues have been combined. Although ethnic and gender issues are not identical—for example, women are not numerically a minority group in the United States or in the world—there are some similarities when it comes to issues of social class and opportunities for upward mobility. There are also similarities between ethnicity and gender in terms of the disproportionate exclusion of ethnic minorities and women in clinical research. It is not only the inclusion of women and ethnic minorities in research that is important but also examining issues that are pertinent to women and looking at issues from women's and the ethnics' perspectives (Reinharz, 1992; Stanley & Wise, 1993). Women have many jeopardies relating to ethnicity/race, gender, and class. Some issues particularly affect women, but there are other factors that have been disproportionately imposed on women due to sociopolitical circumstances, such as the lower status of women of color, the concept of paid work, domestic violence, rape, issues relating to the higher percentage of women below poverty level, women constituting a growing number of HIV-positive and AIDS cases, and so on. Typical clinical research designs, methodologies, and practices, when applied generically to ethnic minority and women samples, are often culturally biased and not sex-fair. Our recommended strategies for increasing the internal and external validity of clinical research reach both of these populations.

PLANNING FOR RESEARCH

Any research that includes different racial/ethnic groups should be conceived and planned from the very outset by investigators who are culturally sensitive. Padilla and Lindholm (1995) argue that careful planning is necessary because a strong Eurocentric paradigm exists. A Eurocentric paradigm is based on a monocultural, male-oriented, and comparative approach, largely Anglo-Saxon or European in nature—an approach that utilizes research instruments and procedures widely employed for a White and generally middle-class group. Moreover, this group frequently serves as a normative population by which to judge other populations. Behaviors or characteristics that deviate from those of the normative population are often considered deviant or deficient. Padilla and Lindholm add that there is nothing wrong with the paradigm if the groups being compared are equivalent in demographic characteristics including social class, cultural background, and proficiency in English. However, in racial/ethnic and gender research, equivalency is difficult to attain.

How can the initial stages of research avoid paradigm problems? There are several steps that can be taken to assist in the planning of research. First, investigators are in a better position to conduct research with internal and external validity if they receive training in research techniques, such as ethnography. Ethnography is a means of data collection that elicits an in-depth analysis of a culture (Bernard, 1995) and covers a wide range of data collection and analytic techniques. Other areas of training should include race relations and ethnic and gender issues. Second, in research involving ethnic minority groups or women, cultural factors and background experiences should be considered in the methodology and design of the study. Some of the experiences include accounting for factors relating to the immigration and limited opportunities and resources for ethnics and women. Third, the research should include the participation of appropriate investigators or collaborators who are familiar with the population to have points of view from cultural insiders.

DEFINITION OF VARIABLES

One growing issue in race/ethnic research is the very definition of "race" and "ethnicity." Race has generally been defined as a subgroup of people who possess certain physical characteristics that are genetically determined and that are more or less distinct from other subgroups. Traditionally, three races have been proposed: Caucasoid, Mongoloid, and Negroid. On the other hand, ethnicity can broadly refer to a religious, racial, national, or cultural group (Gordon, 1978). Ethnicity is used as a social-psychological sense of "peoplehood," in which members of a group share a unique social and cultural heritage that is transmitted from one generation to another. Because culture is a defining characteristic, individuals in a particular ethnic group may share common behavioral patterns, attitudes, and values. Members also feel a consciousness of kind and an interdependence of fate with others in the group (Banks, 1987). Thus, Native Americans, Asian Americans, African Americans, and Latina/os may share with other members of their group beliefs about their fate or common struggles in the United States.

Racial and ethnic designations have raised a number of issues. First, differences in physical characteristics are often a matter of degree. Categorization is often difficult, especially because intermarriage among different races or biologically diverse groups has altered gene pools. In recognition of the complexities of making a racial designation, the U.S. Bureau of the Census now allows individuals multiracial self-designations. The same is true of ethnicity, where members of a particular ethnic group may share varying degrees of culture. Second, it can be argued that the recognition of three races is arbitrary. One can regroup physical characteristics of people to establish that there are only two races or more than three races. Third, psychological researchers rarely use biological markers or physical features to identify individuals from different races. Rather, they typically use social definitions of race, involving self-identification (e.g., individuals are African American if they designate themselves as such). Fourth, members of the same racial group may be different in terms of ethnicity, and members of the same ethnicity may be of different races. For example, Mexicans and White Americans may be considered Caucasian and yet be of different ethnicities. Members of different races may share ethnic identification; for example, acculturated Chinese Americans may consider themselves "American" just as Italian Americans do. Fifth, because of heterogeneity within and between ethnic minority groups, certain racial or ethnic designations may not have much meaning in predicting attitudes or behaviors. In the past, gross distinctions were made, such as between "Whites" and "non-Whites."

These issues in defining race, ethnicity, and culture have pointed to the problems in racial/ethnic research. Sometimes when trying to study race, one may actually be examining ethnicity (or vice versa). Because most psychological researchers rely primarily on self-reported designations, the reliability and validity of the designations depend on the research respondents' definitions. From a conceptual point of view, it is unclear if race or ethnicity is used as a demographic or psychological variable. When used as a demographic variable, race or ethnicity suggests that members of a group may have certain behavioral or attitudinal tendencies. However, membership in a particular group cannot explain phenomena. Rather, the characteristics of a group influence behaviors. For example, knowing that Chinese Americans as an aggregate group are collective rather than individualistic in personality characteristics is less interesting than identifying those social, temperamental, or cultural characteristics that influence collectivism. For instance, socialization with values of interpersonal harmony and maintaining "face" may be important determinants of collectivism, and it just so happens that Chinese Americans are more likely than Caucasians to emphasize these values. It is also apparent that group membership alone may not mean that individuals are exposed to these values. For instance, a Chinese American individual may not be socialized to these values and, hence, not be collectivistic in orientation. Thus, racial or ethnic designations tend to mask the social, temperamental, or cultural heterogeneity that is often found in any group. They are often proxy variables for other variables of interest. Yee, Fairchild, Weizmann, and Wyatt (1993) have called for the establishment of a comprehensive scientific policy on race to guide research. One of their concerns is that studies of race have often been used to portray African Americans in a negative manner, such as research alleging the genetic inferiority of African Americans in intelligence when the very concept of race is problematic.

It should be noted that research on an aggregate, such as Hispanics, might be appropriate to the extent that members of the aggregate share characteristics regardless of other within-group differences. For example, if Mexican Americans, Cuban Americans, and Puerto Ricans tend to be collectivistic in orientation, then combining these groups and comparing them to noncollectivistic groups may be appropriate. This, of course, assumes that within- (Hispanic) group differences do not significantly interact with collectivism.

Because we are faced with problems associated with the definitions of race and ethnicity, we have several suggestions that may be helpful in addressing some of them. First, when racial or ethnic group individuals are included in research, investigators should explicitly state how the groups are defined. If self-report measures are used, was group membership ascertained through an open-ended question or through racial/ethnic categories? If the latter was used, what categories were employed? The question is important in helping to determine the possible limitations that may exist because of the method of defining groups. Second, researchers should try to describe as precisely as possible the characteristics of samples. Here, a number of variables may be important to consider (such as social class and education) that may be confounded with race and ethnicity. To replicate the study's findings, the subject population needs to be described with enough detail. Padilla and Lindholm (1995) have criticized previous studies that merely state that the sample was predominantly White or that the sample was composed of a certain percentage of Whites, African Americans, and so on. It would be helpful to know more detailed information on the subjects: social class, educational level, immigration experiences, the process of acculturation, social and economic stressors, and so on. Third, ideally, when racial or ethnic differences are predicted or observed, the underlying variable accounting for the results should be identified and studied. As mentioned earlier, race and ethnicity are not explanatory variables. Rather, findings from a study can usually be attributed to the characteristics associated with race or ethnicity (often determined by biological or cultural background). For example, the fact that

Asians are concerned about shame and stigma in interpersonal relationships is not attributable to being Asian; rather, Asians may be culturally socialized to values involving "face" that influence feelings of shame and stigma.

There are variables that may be defined differently by men and women, for example, the concept of work. Paid labor is the recognized or measurable economic indicator of economic viability or even in some cases of "independence." However, there are issues relating to housework, which falls under the category of unpaid labor, that are particularly pertinent in Third World rural economies. These activities are predominantly done by women and are crucial for the survival of the family. For example, gathering firewood or fetching water can sometimes take more than half a day to procure. In these situations, it is important to be explicit about the meaning of housework.

SELECTING MEASURES AND ESTABLISHING CROSS-CULTURAL AND LANGUAGE EQUIVALENCY

When selecting or adapting measurement instruments, care must be taken to ensure that the instruments measure meaningful psychological concepts and measure them in ways that produce valid results for the population of interest (Brislin, 1993; Herrera, Delcampo, & Ames, 1993). There are several issues to address when selecting and adapting measures: (a) translation or language equivalence, (b) cultural and socioeconomic equivalence, (c) conceptual equivalence, and (d) metric equivalence. Especially for ethnic minority populations for whom English language proficiency levels may require instruments to be translated, achieving translation or language equivalence is a necessary priority. Language equivalence exists when the descriptors and measures of psychological concepts can be translated well across languages. Cultural and socioeconomic equivalence is related to language equivalence. Translated measures must take into account the cultural and socioeconomic factors of the target population to be understandable to and meaningful for that population. Conceptual equivalence refers to whether the construct being measured exists in the thinking of the target culture and is understood in the same way. For example, cultural variations may exist in the concept of maturity. In the United States, maturity often is associated with autonomy, independence, and wisdom. In more collectivistic societies, maturity may involve the ability to function and work with others to be interdependent rather than independent and autonomous. Needless to say, administering an instrument that taps aspects of maturity in the United States may not provide the most valid assessment of maturity for members of other cultures. Finally, metric or scalar equivalence refers to the analysis of the same concept and the identical measure across cultures, with the assumption that the scale of the measure can be directly compared. For example, one may consider whether an IQ score of 100 on a certain intelligence scale may be truly equivalent to a score of 100 on the translated version of the same intelligence scale.

Herrera et al. (1993) provide step-by-step procedures to achieve reliable and valid instrument translations. Their serial approach consists of essentially three steps: (a) translation into the second language, (b) back-translation to the original language, and (c) field testing for reliability and validity of the two languages. In addition, they make several specific recommendations for carrying out these steps to help prevent some common pitfalls that may result from these conventional translation procedures. Translations that are produced should be not only accurate but also understandable and relevant to the intended population. First, translators should take into account cultural and socioeconomic factors and reading level of the target population. Skilled translators are often well educated and consequently do not always match the education levels of the intended population of study. It is, therefore, beneficial to employ translators who are not only skilled at translating but also have knowledge of which words and topics may not be very easily understood by this target population because of educational, cultural, or class backgrounds. Second, it is recommended to use a small team of translators, at least more than two, who, after completing their translations independently, convene to discuss and resolve any translation differences. Third, to ensure that the translation is relevant and understandable, focus groups or group interviews should be conducted with participants who represent the target population. Using small representative samples, investigators can identify translation and conceptual equivalency problems and make the necessary modifications at that time. Fourth, certain criteria need to be considered in the selection of back-translators. Skilled, bilingual, and well-educated translators make good back-translators. However, ironically, their valuable abilities also increase the risk of their making correct inferences from translations that may in reality be quite poor. To minimize such errors, we agree with Herrera et al.'s suggestion to employ several bilingual persons of different educational backgrounds to perform the back-translation task, or use translators from the target population. Last, when field testing the translated instruments, it is important to select a truly linguistically representative sample. That is, if ultimately the intended population is monolingual, a bilingual sample is not adequate for the field trial. Several researchers have pointed out the flaws in assuming that monolingual and bilingual samples are equivalent (e.g., Diaz, 1988).

For example, to examine the validity of a Mandarin (Chinese) translated instrument that was originally developed in English among a monolingual Mandarin-speaking sample, test-retest reliabilities should be compared to monolingual English- and monolingual Mandarin-speaking samples. High test-retest reliability among the English-speaking sample and low test-retest reliability among the Mandarin-speaking sample would indicate problems in the translated version. However, low test-retest reliability among the English-speaking sample would suggest reliability with the original English instrument itself. Furthermore, to establish the validity of this same Mandarin translated instrument among a bilingual English-Mandarin-speaking sample, two bilingual samples should be tested to control for administration order effects. In other words, one bilingual sample would be administered, the English instrument at pretest and the Mandarin version at posttest; the second bilingual sample would be administered in the reverse order. Low test-retest reliability among the bilingual sample and significant differences between the bilingual and monolingual samples most likely indicate problems with the translation.

In many cases, it is not possible to devise and validate new assessment instruments for particular ethnic populations. This is sometimes due to limited resources and availability of experienced researchers and clinicians who speak the language and understand the culture to develop new instrumentation. If one must use existing measures, see if the test or assessment instrument has been standardized and normed on

the particular group (e.g., African Americans or women) of the client/research participants. If the test has not been standardized and normed on the group:

1. Use caution in interpreting the results.
2. Use multiple measures or multimethod procedures to see if tests provide convergent results.
3. Try to understand the cultural and historical background and present circumstances of the client/participant to put results in the proper context.
4. Enlist the aid of consultants who are familiar with the client's/target population's language and culture.
5. Use tests that can be linguistically understood by the client/target population.
   If one is unsure of the validity of tests for a particular ethnic or gender group,
   use the findings as hypotheses for further testing rather than as conclusive
   evidence.

SELECTION AND SAMPLING OF THE POPULATION

The research principles of selection and sampling of the population are no different for
a cross-cultural or ethnic population than for research in the general population. However, selection of a population and sampling are complicated when conducting research
on ethnically diverse populations, minorities, and women. Researchers studying cross-
cultural and ethnic issues have had a difficult time finding representative and adequate
sample sizes. This is largely due to issues such as the sensitive nature of the topic under
study, unfamiliarity of the respondent with the research process, relative small size of
some ethnic populations, and cultural issues, including necessity to establish rapport,
shame, and loss of face. Given these issues, the ideal of conducting random sampling in
cross-cultural research can be difficult to achieve.

Because finding adequate sample sizes is an issue, researchers sometimes collapse
ethnic categories among the races, which has led to some problems and limitations of
the research conclusions. This is very apparent in the case of the Asian and Pacific Islander American category, which includes all the diverse groups of people from Asia
and the Pacific. There are at least 48 separate Asian and Pacific Islander American ethnic populations in the United States (Asian and Pacific Islander Center for Census
Information and Services, 1993). People from Asia come from very diverse socioeconomic and political histories, languages, cultures, experiences, religions, and economic
and political structures. They have a variety of reasons for migrating to the United
States. Some have immigrated recently, and some can trace their ancestry in the United
States to several generations with very unique and separate histories. For example, the
immigration and exclusion acts of the nineteenth century resulted in Chinese and Japanese women arriving in the United States to work as prostitutes (Hirata, 1982). In the
early 1920s, Japanese and Korean women, the "picture brides," came to marry men of
their own nationalities who were working in the United States and Hawaii (Gee, 1982).
After World War II, with the liberalization of immigration laws in 1965, immigrants
from Asia included those who were well educated in their home countries as well as

people from countries that were affected by U.S. colonialism, war, and neocolonialism, for example, Filipinos, Vietnamese, and other Southeast Asians (Lowe, 1996). Despite these diverse social histories, in most studies in the United States, Asian and Pacific Islander Americans are assessed in research, delivery of services, and policy as a single, homogeneous unit (True & Guillermo, 1996; Wang, 1995). These homogeneous units also do not account for the various types of institutionalized discrimination based on gender, race, ethnicity, and language. All these issues compound the existing socioeconomic factors such as low levels of income and education and the lack of social networks (Mayeno & Hirota, 1994). By considering the Asian and Pacific Islander Americans as a homogeneous group, we ignore sociohistorical, cultural, economic, and political diversity.

Even if we examine one particular group among the Asian American population, the heterogeneity is problematic and not encountered to the same extent by Asians in their homeland. For instance, the Chinese in the United States are more diverse than the Chinese population in overseas parts of the world. Chinese in the United States are composed of both native and foreign-born individuals who come from mainland China, Taiwan, Hong Kong, Singapore, Vietnam, and elsewhere, who speak many dialects and languages, who are exposed to varying degrees to "American" values, and who are members of a minority group. The same is true of nearly all Asian American groups—greater heterogeneity exists for their group in the United States than in their homeland. This means that measures (such as the Minnesota Multiphasic Personality Inventory II) validated with Chinese in China may not have good validity for Chinese in the United States (see Chapter 7).

Given the difficulties in finding adequate samples of certain ethnic minority populations, researchers must often resort to finding convenience samples from quite different sources. For example, the samples may come from lists of ethnic organizations, names suggested by other respondents (the snowballing technique), and universities rather than communities at large.

In some cases, it has been possible to apply sophisticated sampling techniques to study small minority groups, for example, in the Chinese American Epidemiological Study in Los Angeles County (Zheng et al., 1997). Because Chinese Americans constituted less than 3% of the total population in Los Angeles County in 1990, only those geographic areas were selected where Chinese Americans made up at least 6% of the population in a given census tract. This criterion increased the probability of locating a Chinese American household, making the survey more cost effective than conducting a random sample of all census tracts in the county. If the proportion criterion were lowered, it would significantly increase the cost of locating and screening for eligible households. In the final sample, the Chinese population in the selected tracts ranged from 6% to 72.3%. According to the 1990 Census, 149,513 Chinese lived in these tracts, which is approximately 61.1% of the 244,767 Chinese in the county. Although this sample design is the most sophisticated one used for an Asian American group to date, it has a significant limitation. It undersamples people who reside in less ethnically dense areas. These geographic areas are most likely to include wealthier, more native-born, and more long-term residents of the United States. Similar sampling strategies with some variations have been applied to sampling African Americans (Jackson & Hatchett, 1985; Smith, 1993).

Thus, it is possible to devise strategies to find adequate samples of ethnics, though these can be expensive. However, researchers must be aware of the biases and limitations that occur when certain strategies are used.

GAINING COOPERATION FROM RESEARCH PARTICIPANTS

Regardless of the form in which data are collected, there are three basic elements necessary to solicit information from the respondent: empathy, participation, and observation (Gorden, 1980). *Empathy* is understanding how the respondent feels about issues. *Participation* in research is the ability to observe another's activity and response or by way of inference identify and record the respondent's thoughts and feelings. *Observation* is using any sensory ability that helps one to understand human behavior. These three methods are integral to all methods of studying human behavior. As such, interviewing utilizes empathizing, participating, and observing that takes place between the researcher and the researched.

Because the whole process of research can involve power relations between the researcher and the researched, the commitment to conduct research should involve the reduction of this unequal power relationship between the two parties. This may require reframing of research questions to better fit cognitively with the researched. In cross-cultural research, it is also possible that respondents are unfamiliar with the questionnaire process. Recording responses to questions and methods of asking that they do not understand can lead to anxiety among the respondents. This anxiety is heightened by their experiences of government bureaucracy and distrust of governments and by their fear that the information may be used against them. For example, in a study in Tanzania, a demographic survey led to people getting anxious because they were concerned with giving the "right" answers and were afraid of not providing all the "correct" information. In this case, the researchers used the survey as an entry point to the home of the researched and to establish rapport. However, they did not use the information gathered in the survey. Thus, by gaining entry into the homes of the people, they were able to solicit information on issues pertaining to the study by way of a dialogue between the researcher and the researched (Michau, 1998).

While conducting surveys that are sensitive and lengthy and that require in-depth information from the respondent, establishing rapport is imperative. In feminist research, the process becomes a dialogue between the researcher and the researched. As such, an effort is made to examine, explore, and clarify the topic and concepts being discussed. Through this process, rapport is established, making it possible to accomplish lengthy research agendas and explore sensitive topics. Therefore, the process of interviewing is not impersonal, and neither the subjectivity of the researcher nor the researched can be totally eliminated (Acker, Barry, & Esseveld, 1991).

In the research of cross-cultural ethnic populations and women, the interviewing process is not objectified, but there exists a two-way sharing of information. Thus, it has been argued that feminist research involves reciprocity between the researcher and the respondent (Mies, 1991). By this, researchers and those being researched are not in a power relationship but come together to understand and explain the aspects being studied in their totality. This two-way sharing of information leads to a deeper understanding of the research topic. For example, when women's roles in Third World countries are discussed, it is impossible to exclude from the discussion the discrimination faced by women in general, be it that of the researcher or the researched. By exploring issues and experiences common to and different from each other, a new understanding of the subject emerges. Thus, when exploring issues relating to Third World countries, the role of the First World should be discussed. Similarly, when talking of women, men must be included; when exploring issues of poverty, wealth must be understood. Feminist research also emphasizes the role of affect in the creation of knowledge. This is largely an outcome of women's greater familiarity with emotions and feelings and their meanings (Gilligan, 1982).

In conducting research on mental health issues of concern to ethnically diverse populations, respondents may be reticent in answering questions on their feelings or emotions, making the process of collecting data longer than anticipated. Assessing one's emotions is thought to be a luxury in non-Western cultures, and people from those cultures do not easily respond to questions about their emotions and feelings. Offering monetary incentives to answer questionnaires may fail in societies such as India, whereas that approach may be successful in eliciting answers to lengthy questionnaires in the United States. This is largely because participation in a study in societies and cultures like India would be considered a favor to the researcher and cannot be monetarily valued. To gain access to individuals to participate in a study where personal questions are being asked requires the researcher to have a point of reference, which is achieved either by way of a formal introduction or by common knowledge in the community about the researcher. In either situation, money transactions would not be appropriate.

Issues relating to privacy and confidentiality are particularly relevant when interviewing minorities and women. Many live in large families, and extensive periods of contiguous time for an interview or dialogue may be unavailable. Respondents may seem hesitant to discuss issues openly when they fear being overheard by other members of their family and community. Other issues of privacy surround videotaping and photographing, especially when conducting research among traumatized populations cross-culturally. For example, in studies of domestic violence, videotapes or photographs of the women researched should not be used in any community awareness or outreach programs. Other than the ethical issues, there is a potential danger to the woman of being abused further by her partner, as well as feelings of shame and loss of face in the community.

Obtaining consent to participate in the research also varies among cross-cultural and ethnically diverse populations. The standard consent forms used are not always appropriate to administer in these populations. Understanding the consent is related to the respondent's cognizance of aspects such as the research process and also the respondent's language and literacy level. Sometimes, verbal consent may be more appropriate.

Because the goal of feminist and cross-cultural research is the "liberation" of the population or affecting change in the community through the research process, the involvement of people in the community is essential (Mies, 1986; Mobley, 1997). If the community in which the research is being conducted feels an ownership to the research and invested in the outcome, this can significantly increase participation of respondents, further enhancing the research agenda. For example, in her study in India, Mies tried to reconcile the research agenda with the women's movement. Though the research project was mainly to explore the effect of market economic (capitalist) development on poor rural women, the researchers, in this case, lived in the communities and experienced the life of poor rural women. They were able to establish rapport with the women and learn about working hours, exploitation, discrimination, wages, and so on. The researchers also passed on information from their research to the women, which led to existing women's organizations organizing meetings to work on solutions to contend with alcoholism among the men and wife abuse.

RESEARCH DESIGN AND STRATEGIES

As mentioned earlier, mainstream diagnostic concepts, theoretical orientations, and treatment models are laden with values, beliefs, and attitudes representative of the mainstream U.S. culture from which they were derived. Administering mainstream measurement instruments nonselectively across all ethnic and cultural groups in our diverse society has very limited value, and perhaps some notable risks, such as in issues relating to relevance of concepts, translation, and language equivalency.

How, then, do we establish an understanding of relevant concepts and theoretical frameworks across diverse cultures, and how do we ensure that research findings are interpreted within the appropriate cultural context? We would like to discuss two strategies that are helpful in ethnic minority or cross-cultural research: qualitative methods and parallel research. Burton (1997) believes that qualitative and ethnographic methodologies are needed to understand the meanings, patterns, rules, and behaviors that exist in ethnic minority communities. Yet, graduate programs in psychology tend to emphasize quantitative methodology. Qualitative methodology can be of great utility, especially when used in conjunction with quantitative strategies. Although the contribution of qualitative research is by no means limited to ensuring conceptual equivalence, theory development, or interpreting quantitative findings (i.e., it is not simply preliminary or supplemental to quantitative analysis), certainly these strengths are highlighted when it comes to cross-cultural research. Also, it should be noted that use of the global term qualitative research is not intended to simplify the vast number of methodologies that fall within this category. The use of the term here is to emphasize the emic (culture-specific) nature of the approach to research investigation. Nor do we intend to fuel the unproductive debate that pits qualitative research against quantitative methods. Rather, methodological choice involves assessing the level of measurement available and appropriate for a given study (Weisner, 1997). The level of measurement available from qualitative approaches is appropriate for cross-cultural clinical research by which we attempt to better understand indigenous concepts and patterns, and can be quite complementary to other quantitative strategies that are more typically employed by psychologically minded researchers.

Qualitative research encompasses numerous methodologies, too many to be adequately covered here, that have in common an emic approach to understanding human behavior and other phenomena. In conducting cross-cultural clinical research, the use of emic approaches facilitates the discovery of so-called new concepts—that is to say, new to the "outsider" who is conducting the research and indigenous to the culture of interest. There are a number of such emic approaches long known to other social scientists that are becoming more widely accepted by psychological researchers. Two popular techniques are open-ended interviews and focus groups. Both individual interviews and focus groups have gained rapid popularity, most likely because they are efficient, minimally intrusive, and relatively systematic in implementation and data analysis. Interview and focus group techniques are useful because they provide the cross-cultural researcher the tools to explore both emic and etic (culture-general or universal) questions (for a discussion of emic and etic approaches, see Berry, 1969). Their open-ended nature allows the researcher to discover new or indigenous concepts. Yet, their semistructured format allows the researcher to examine a priori research questions as well (e.g., conceptual equivalence of a Western-based diagnostic construct such as depression). In the latter use of these methods, the researcher is using an etic perspective (i.e., does my Western concept of depression have any importance in this other culture?) but applying an emic-oriented approach to the manner of the investigation.

Another important feature of qualitative approaches generally is that qualitative strategies allow the cross-cultural researcher to access "meanings." Semistructured interviews and focus groups, in particular, enable the researcher to understand the meanings of quantitative data; for example, what a response valence of 5 on an item means to a respondent, where 5 is high on a Likert scale of 1–5. Respondents' interpretations may or may not be veridical; however, knowing their interpretation allows the researcher to place responses in a context. These techniques can provide valuable data, but careful effort must be made to ensure that the opinions represented are actually those of the targeted population. For example, if the target population is a low socioeconomic (SES) subgroup within a particular ethnic group, care must be taken to ensure that the opinions represented are not those of the highest SES members within the targeted ethnic group who are most English proficient.

Other techniques have been somewhat slower to gain recognition in the psychology research field. Ethnography, for example, despite its value for cross-cultural research, is not commonly used. Most likely, ethnographic designs are less enticing to psychological researchers due to the time involvement of the required fieldwork, as well as the questions these ethnographic methods raise in terms of objectivity. However, it is important to challenge ourselves to explore beyond our quantitative research training as psychologists. As we respond to the need to better understand diverse cultures and develop culturally responsive clinical interventions, we can greatly benefit from the use of ethnographic strategies.

Another important consideration in our discussion of research methodology is the devising of designs that yield insight into the nature of cultural or group differences. Three approaches can be used in cross-cultural research designs, as discussed by Zane and Sue (1986): (a) point, (b) linear, and (c) parallel. *Point research* refers to isolated group comparisons on one construct or set of constructs derived from one culture. For example, one may want to compare the prevalence of depression among African Americans and White Americans; though this task appears to be rather straightforward, what is unclear is how to interpret findings from this comparison. Care must be exercised in assuming that any observed ethnic or racial differences reflect actual differences according to an assumed construct. For example, Dohrenwend and Dohrenwend (1969) found that Puerto Ricans scored higher than other ethnic groups on a measure of psychopathology, the Midtown Questionnaire. As noted later, the results do not necessarily reflect a greater degree of maladjustment on the part of Puerto Ricans because conceptual equivalence of items on the questionnaire may be lacking across different ethnic groups. In the monocultural approach using monocultural measures, alternative explanations based on cultural differences in values and behaviors are always post hoc. Thus, point research does not allow us to know if the group differences are real or why the differences exist.

To determine if differences are "real" and not simply a measurement problem, a *linear research* model has developed. Linear research involves a series of studies aimed at systematically testing the set of hypotheses predicted by the theory underlying the single construct of interest. As in point research, this construct is usually developed from a monocultural or single perspective. However, rather than one isolated study, there are two or more empirical points of reference on which to compare cultural groups. If the pattern of cultural differences (or similarities) manifests according to the construct's theory, the construct is considered to be a universal that allows for meaningful cultural comparisons.

The use of linear research can be illustrated by examining studies conducted by Dohrenwend and Dohrenwend (1969). The investigators were interested in determining if certain ethnic groups differed in psychopathology. After administering a measure of psychopathology, the Midtown 22-item symptom questionnaire, ethnic differences were found, with Puerto Ricans scoring higher in psychological disturbance than did Jewish, Irish, or African American respondents in New York City. Obviously, at this point the investigators used a point research strategy. But how did they know if the Puerto Ricans were actually more disturbed or if the findings were simply an artifact of the measure? To ascertain whether the differences were valid, patients matched on types of psychiatric disorders from each ethnic group were administered the same questionnaires. Dohrenwend and Dohrenwend assumed that because patients were matched on type and presumable severity of disorders, there should be no differences in psychopathology scores on the symptom questionnaire. However, after administering the symptom questionnaire to the patient groups, Puerto Ricans again scored higher. The investigators concluded that the higher scores for Puerto Ricans probably reflected a response set or a cultural means of expressing distress on the questionnaire rather than actual rates of disturbance.

Thus, linear approaches can help to determine if differences are real or an artifact of the monocultural measurement instrument. The limitation is that once the differences are shown to be real, we still do not know why the differences exit or whether a construct developed from an alternative perspective (e.g., an explanation derived from another culture) can better explain the phenomena under study. Linear studies do not actually balance ethnic perspectives in research. They simply test the adequacy of one perspective in the absence of the other. This is unfortunate because almost all linear research has focused on the cross-cultural applicability of constructs derived from our Western viewpoint.

To truly represent ethnic minority perspectives, research must develop separate but interrelated ways of conceptualizing the behavioral phenomena of interest, one based on a Western conceptualization, the other reflecting an ethnic minority interpretation. Essentially, *parallel research* designs consist of two linear approaches, each based on an alternative cultural viewpoint. In parallel research, it is incumbent upon the researcher to develop a priori two sets of descriptive and explanatory variables. By requiring the concurrent examination of different cultural explanations, the parallel approach fosters divergent and flexible thinking. In the parallel approach, the salience of a construct is empirically tested by comparing it with another equally plausible explanatory concept developed from the ethnic group's host culture. Thus, we should increasingly employ parallel research designs to test Western versus more indigenous explanations for observed ethnic or racial differences.

INTERPRETATION OF FINDINGS AND VALIDITY

When comparisons are made between various ethnic minority groups or between men and women, differences between the groups cannot be routinely assumed to reflect deviance or undesirable characteristics among these groups (i.e., a deficit model interpretation). Similarly, the desirability or undesirability of characteristics is frequently specific to a particular culture, and we should not make the mistake of assuming that others' deviations from one's own norms are necessarily undesirable. This is not to adopt absolute relativism in which there are no standards that cross all groups. Rather, if we have erred, it is typically in the direction of using monocultural standards.

There are other tactics that can be used to improve the ability to make interpretations. Effects of peripheral and extraneous variables (such as immigrant history, social networks, and economic stressors) to the model can be eliminated or controlled through statistical means through the use of regression or covariates. Another method of controlling for unique interpretations is stating the dependent variable as a function of either two or more scores (Berry, Poortinga, Segall, & Dasen, 1992). As noted earlier, if we find certain psychological disorders being much higher than the norm in the samples being studied, this is not necessarily due to higher rates of psychopathology in these populations. It could possibly be attributable to the scale's not being normed for the population being studied or to cultural definitions of certain psychological disorders. We suggest that researchers look at correlations of these symptoms with other pertinent variables. The same is true conversely when extremely low levels of psychological symptoms are identified. This does not mean the absence of a particular psychopathology. Here the pattern of the response of the individuals would provide more information than just the absolute score.

In qualitative research, it is sometimes suggested that the data and the interpretations be taken back to the respondent to be validated. This, it is argued, eliminates the possibility of erroneous inferences and interpretations. In general, researchers should avoid the adoption of a deficit model and use appropriate statistical techniques to control extraneous variables and explanations. Research results should be cautiously interpreted in view of the cultural backgrounds of various groups. Alternative explanations for the outcome of investigations should be considered, including those indigenous to the groups being studied. When problems in the interpretation of findings arise, investigators unfamiliar with a particular population should become aware of the literature on the population and consult with those who have expertise on this population.

In this chapter, we have tried to point to the issues involved in conducting ethnic minority and gender research. It is apparent that ethnic and gender considerations should enter into all phases of the research and that many of our suggestions are simply good general research practice.

RESEARCH TRAINING

To enhance research training on these issues, a number of steps should be taken in training programs. Ponterotto, Alexander, and Grieger (1995) have outlined certain criteria by which training programs can be evaluated for their multicultural emphasis. They include:

1. Recruitment of a critical mass of ethnic minority students, faculty, and staff. At predominantly White campuses, the authors suggest that training programs include about 30% minority representation.
2. Teaching of ethnic and gender courses or integration of ethnic and gender issues into all courses. Programs should experiment with different teaching and evaluation methods to find strategies that are effective.
3. Exposure to clients and supervisors who come from different ethnic groups.
4. Having faculty and students who are engaged in ethnic and gender research and encouragement of such research among students.

We believe that by dealing with ethnic minority and gender issues in research, students will become better researchers because dealing with such issues requires sensitivity, ingenuity, avoidance of ethnocentrism, cultural sophistication, and a thorough knowledge of rigorous research methodology.

REFERENCES

Acker, J., Barry, K., & Esseveld, J. (1991). Objectivity and truth: Problems in doing feminist research. In M. M. Fonow & J. A. Cook (Eds.), *Beyond methodology: Feminist scholarship as lived research*. Bloomington: Indiana University Press.

Asian and Pacific Islander Center for Census Information and Services. (1993). *A profile of Asian and Pacific Islander immigrant populations in California*. San Francisco: Asian/Pacific Islander Data Consortium.

Banks, J. A. (1987). *Teaching strategies for ethnic studies*. Boston: Allyn & Bacon.

Bernard, H. R. (1995). *Research methods in anthropology*. Walnut Creek, CA: AltaMira Press.

Berry, J. W. (1969). On cultural comparability. *International Journal of Psychology, 4,* 119–128.

Berry, J. W., Poortinga, Y. H., Segall, M. H., & Dasen, P. R. (1992). *Cross-cultural psychology: Research and applications*. New York: Cambridge University Press.

Brislin, R. W. (1993). *Understanding culture's influence on behavior,* New York: Harcourt Brace Jovanovich.

Burton, L. M. (1997). Ethnography and the meaning of adolescence in high-risk neighborhoods. *Ethos, 25,* 208–217.

Diaz, J. O. P. (1988). Assessment of Puerto Rican children in bilingual education programs in the United States: A critique of Lloyd M. Dunn's monograph. *Hispanic Journal of Behavioral Sciences, 10,* 237–252.

Dohrenwend, B. P., & Dohrenwend, B. S. (1969). *Social status and psychological disorder.* New York: Wiley.

Gee, E. (1982). Issei women. In N. Tsuchida (Ed.), *Asian and Pacific American experiences: Women's perspectives* (pp. 66–87). Minneapolis, MN: Asian/Pacific American Learning Resource Center.

Gilligan, C. (1982). *In a different voice.* Cambridge, MA: Harvard University Press.

Gordon, M. M. (1978). *Human nature, class, and ethnicity.* New York: Oxford University Press.

Gorden, R. L. (1980). *Interviewing: Strategy, techniques, and tactics.* Homewood, IL: Dorsey Press.

Gynther, M. D. (1972). White norms and black MMPIs: A prescription for discrimination? *Psychological Bulletin, 78,* 386–402.

Herrera, R. S., Delcampo, R. L., & Ames, M. H. (1993). A serial approach for translating family science instrumentation. *Family Relations, 42,* 357–360.

Hirata, L. C. (1982). Chinese immigrant women in nineteenth century California. In N. Tsuchida (Ed.), *Asian and Pacific American experiences: Women's perspectives* (pp. 38–65). Minneapolis, MN: Asian/Pacific American Learning Resource Center.

Jackson, J., & Hatchett, S. (1985). Intergenerational research: Methodological considerations. In N. Data, A. L. Greene, & H. W. Reese (Eds.), *Intergenerational relations.* Hillsdale, NJ: Erlbaum.

Lowe, L. (1996). *Immigrant acts.* Durham, NC: Duke University Press.

Mayeno, L., & Hirota, S. M. (1994). Access to health care. In N. W. S. Zane, D. T. Takeuchi, & K. N. J. Young (Eds.), *Confronting critical health issues of Asian and Pacific Islander Americans.* Thousand Oaks, CA: Sage.

Michau, L. (1998). *Research and action against sexual coercion in Mwanza, Tanzania: The experience of the Jijenge Project.* Paper presented at the International Research Network on Violence Against Women, The Health and Development Policy Project, Washington, DC.

Mies, M. (1986). *Indian women in subsistence and agricultural labor.* Geneva: International Labour Organization.

Mies, M. (1991). Women's research or feminist research? In M. M. Fonow & J. A. Cook (Eds.), *Beyond methodology: Feminist scholarship as lived research.* Bloomington: Indiana University Press.

Mobley, C. (1997). Toward a new definition of accountability: Using applied ethnography as a toll for change in the voluntary sector. *Journal of Contemporary Ethnography, 26*(1), 75–97.

Padilla, A. M., & Lindholm, K. J. (1995). Quantitative educational research with ethnic minorities. In J. A. Banks & C. A. McGee-Banks (Eds.), *Handbook of research on multicultural education* (pp. 97–113). New York: MacMillian.

Ponterotto, J. G., Alexander, C. M., & Grieger, I. (1995). A multicultural competency checklist for counseling training programs. *Journal of Multicultural Counseling and Development, 23,* 11–20.

Reinharz, S. (1992). *Feminist methods in social research.* New York: Oxford University Press.

Rogler, L. H. (1989). The meaning of culturally sensitive research in mental health. *American Journal of Psychiatry, 146,* 296–303.

Smith, W. (1993). Survey research on African Americans: Methodological innovations. In J. Stanfield & R. Dennis (Eds.), *Race and ethnicity in research methods.* Newbury Park, CA: Sage Focus.

Stanley, L., & Wise, S. (1993). *Breaking out again: Feminist ontology and epistemology.* New York: Routledge & Kegan Paul.

Triandis, H. C., & Brislin, R. W. (1984). Cross-cultural psychology. *American Psychologist, 39,* 1006–1016.

True, R. H., & Guillermo, T. (1996). Asian/Pacific Islander American women. In M. Bayne-Smith (Ed.), *Race, gender, and health* (pp. 94–120). Thousand Oaks, CA: Sage.

Wang, G. M. (1995). Health issues for Asian/Pacific Islander women. In D. L. Adams (Ed.), *Health issues for women of color.* Thousand Oaks, CA: Sage.

Weisner, T. S. (1997). The ecocultural project of human development: Why ethnography and its findings matter. *Ethos, 25,* 177–190.

Yee, A. H., Fairchild, H. H., Weizmann, F., & Wyatt, G. E. (1993). Addressing psychology's problems with race. *American Psychologist, 48,* 1132–1140.

Zane, N., & Sue, S. (1986). Reappraisal of ethnic minority issues: Research alternatives. In E. Seidman & J. Rappaport (Eds.), *Redefining social problems* (pp. 289–304). New York: Plenum Press.

Zheng, Y. P., Lin, K. M., Takeuchi, D. T., Kurasaki, K. S., Wang, Y., & Cheung, F. (1997). An epidemiological study of neurasthenia in Chinese-Americans in Los Angeles. *Comprehensive Psychiatry, 38*(5), 249–259.

Chapter 4 —————————————————————

STATISTICAL METHODS IN CLINICAL RESEARCH

Albert D. Farrell, Ph.D.

Numerous exciting developments have occurred in the application of statistical methods to clinical research problems. Models for applying sophisticated statistical tools to a variety of clinical research problems have been presented (e.g., Gottman, 1995; Hoyle, 1994; Newman & Howard, 1991). The advent of increasingly powerful and accessible personal computers has led to user-friendly programs that greatly facilitate the data analysis process. At a more general level, the debate over the merits of null hypothesis significance testing has reemerged and has begun to receive serious attention (e.g., Abelson, 1997; Cohen, 1994; Cortina & Dunlap, 1997; Schmidt, 1996). Although these developments have the potential to improve the quality of clinical research, they have also had some negative consequences.

Many clinical researchers lack sufficient familiarity with some of the newer statistical techniques such that they are not only unable to use them in their own research, but they may have difficulty understanding published research in which these techniques have been used. Keeping up with advances in statistical methods in addition to a substantive research area can be a daunting task, and everyone cannot know everything. I suspect that some researchers find themselves longing for the "old days," when one simply needed a solid grasp of analysis of variance (ANOVA) techniques coupled with a basic understanding of correlational analyses. This may be characteristic not only of researchers who received their training in statistical methods some years ago, but also of recent graduates of doctoral programs. The graduate statistics courses taught in many psychology departments have been slow to incorporate new developments in statistical methods (Aiken, West, Sechrest, & Reno, 1990). Nonetheless, a minimal understanding of a fairly wide array of statistical techniques has become essential for both contributors to and consumers of the research literature in clinical psychology.

Whereas the increasing user-friendliness of statistical software has generally been a positive development, it too has had some negative consequences. Many statistical packages enable individuals with little understanding of statistics (sometimes far too little) to conduct complex data analyses. Such individuals are often able to rely on default settings rather than specifying the model that is most appropriate for their particular research problem (Estes, 1997). Although the default settings may be inappropriate for a given problem, this may not be evident from casual examination of the resulting

72

printout. This situation exemplifies the old adage "A little knowledge can be a dangerous thing." Another negative side effect of these packages is that they can distance the researcher from the data. Growing concern over this problem has led some to argue for a return to the basics, including graphic displays and stem-and-leaf plots that summarize the distribution of individual points in a sample (Cohen, 1990).

Continuing debate over the value of null hypothesis significance testing has created further confusion for some clinical researchers. Although the practice of deciding the outcome of a study based on rejection of a null hypothesis at the $p < .05$ significance level has been controversial since its inception (e.g., see Bakan, 1966; Nunally, 1960; Rozeboom, 1960), most clinical researchers have been well indoctrinated into this practice. Recent challenges to this practice (e.g., Cohen, 1990, 1994; Hunter, 1997; Loftus, 1996; Rosenthal, 1995; Schmidt, 1996) have led to renewed debate. Although this debate has yet to be settled, it has left researchers who are unfamiliar with alternative approaches uncertain how to proceed.

Although advances in statistical methods and computer technology have increased the variety of tools available to clinical researchers, the basic principles that guide the selection of an appropriate statistical procedure and its interpretation remain largely unchanged. Increasing the use of sophisticated statistical techniques will do little to advance the field of clinical research unless these methods are used appropriately. What is needed is a better appreciation of the basic principles that should guide the selection, use, and interpretation of statistics in clinical research.

In this chapter, I discuss some basic principles of statistical analysis with an emphasis on their application to clinical research. Focusing on clinical research problems does little to narrow the focus of this chapter. Clinical researchers address a wide variety of problems representing both experimental and nonexperimental designs and there are a wide range of statistical methods available. Although I describe some specific statistical techniques, these are used primarily as examples. Ideally, interested readers will refer to some of the material referenced in each section to explore some of these procedures in greater depth. My primary focus is on basic strategies for screening data prior to conducting analyses, the considerations that should guide clinical researchers in the selection of a statistical procedure appropriate for their research questions, and factors that influence the interpretation of findings.

GETTING ACQUAINTED WITH YOUR DATA

Because data collection is often a challenging and time-consuming process, researchers are understandably eager to run their primary analyses and determine the fate of their experimental hypotheses. A well-thought-out plan of analysis, however, must always begin with preliminary analyses designed to provide the researcher with a basic understanding of the nature of the observed data. This process includes a thorough examination of the data to determine the pattern of missing data, presence of outliers, distribution properties of the variables, and validity of the measurement model. These preliminary analyses are essential because they may identify problems that need to be addressed before the primary analyses can be conducted. In other cases, they may lead to changes in the analysis plan (Cohen, 1990).

Creating a Data Set

The most tedious and usually least rewarding aspect of the data analysis involves creating the data set and preparing it for analysis. Care at this stage can often save much aggravation later. The specific steps in creating a data set depend on the nature of the data. Researchers increasingly rely on computer applications such as computer-based interviews, observational coding systems, and scanners to record data directly into a computer database (Farrell, 1991). Other clinical applications involve entering data from coding sheets or paper-and-pencil instruments into a computer file by hand. Regardless of the method used, some system should be employed to verify the accuracy of the data. This includes checking some percentage of the original data (e.g., coding sheets or instruments) against the values recorded in the data set. For particularly sensitive and low base-rate data (e.g., sexual abuse or drug use in elementary school children), one incorrect entry can dramatically change the findings. In such circumstances, it may be prudent to verify each recorded occurrence. At a minimum, researchers need to examine the distribution of each variable to determine if the recorded values appear plausible. Are the means and standard deviations in line with expectations? Are all the values within the expected range (i.e., none exceed the maximum possible value)? Are missing data being identified and handled appropriately? Are there patterns of data that indicate random responding (see Farrell, Danish, & Howard, 1991)? Running descriptive analyses that report the means, standard deviations, and minimum and maximum observed values can be useful for examining the data. More generally, a table reporting group means and standard deviations is an essential part of any research report. Such data can help other researchers understand how samples may differ across studies on key variables. These are, however, only summary statistics, and more can be gained by examining stem-and-leaf plots that report all observed values (Cohen, 1990). Researchers should understand the distribution of each variable before they attempt to examine relationships among variables.

Multiple-item measures merit special attention during data entry. In general, it is preferable to enter data from such instruments at the item level and use the computer to do any necessary scoring. When done properly, computer scoring tends to be more accurate. Moreover, entering item-level data makes it possible to conduct item analyses to check the internal consistency of the scales. This also makes it possible to test the researcher's measurement model of the relationships between the items and the constructs they are purported to measure, and to change the scoring if alternative scoring strategies are identified after the data have been entered. In cases where selected items require reverse coding, they can be recoded into new variables that are then used in calculating scores (I add an "r" to the end of the names of such variables to indicate they have been recoded). It is often helpful to calculate item-total correlations for each item on a scale to verify that all the items are positively correlated with the total score. It is important that researchers who use the computer to score their data understand how their software package treats missing data when performing calculations. For example, a researcher using SPSS (Norušis, 1993) might use the *Sum* command within a compute statement to calculate the total score for a 20-item scale. A potential problem is that this command will calculate the total based on however many items are present. For example, if an individual completes only 5 of the 20 items, the total score will be the sum of those 5 items. This can obviously lead to some artificially low scores. One option is to specify that all 20 items must be present to calculate the sum. However, this will cause individuals who are missing only a single item to have the entire scale coded as missing. A generally better option is to estimate or impute missing item values and include the imputed values in the calculations. This topic is addressed in the following section.

How Will You Handle Missing Data?

Missing data is a common occurrence in clinical research. Participants may choose to omit their responses to particular items or give responses that cannot be clearly coded. Some participants may not be able to complete a measure within the allotted time. Observational data may not be available because of equipment malfunctions. Data on some participants may be obtained from parents but not from teachers, or from therapists but not from clients. Absentees or transfers within a school system may result in data from students being available for some time points but not for others. Attrition may result in incomplete follow-up data for clinical trials. Indeed, the collection of a data set in which complete responses are obtained from every participant at each time point would seem to be a relatively rare occurrence. Because of the frequency with which missing data occurs in clinical research, it is important that clinical researchers develop appropriate strategies for addressing this problem.

A key consideration in examining the impact of missing data concerns the extent to which the data are missing at random (Little & Schenker, 1995). If data are missing from a random subsample of participants, the primary effect will be a reduction in the net sample size and a corresponding reduction in the efficiency of the analyses. This may be reflected in larger confidence intervals that result from larger standard errors and in reduced power for significance tests. A more serious problem occurs when participants from whom data are missing differ in some ways from those that provide complete data. In such cases, elimination of these participants will result in biased estimates. This can occur in clinical research. For example, it is to be expected that students with poor school attendance will be less likely to be present at multiple time points in a longitudinal study, that clients with high levels of depression who are assigned to a no-treatment control group will be more likely to seek treatment elsewhere, that participants in a weight reduction program who are not seeing any progress may be more likely to drop out of treatment, and so on. In each of these examples, analysis of cases for whom complete data are available is likely to produce biased results. The most critical factor in developing a strategy for dealing with missing data is the extent to which it minimizes the impact of this bias.

Several commonly used strategies for dealing with missing data involve the deletion of cases with missing data. Analysis of complete cases, sometimes referred to as listwise deletion, eliminates cases with missing data on one or more of the variables included in the analysis (Cohen & Cohen, 1983; Little & Rubin, 1990). This commonly used approach is the default selection for many statistical packages. Although many researchers find this strategy appealing, it has serious drawbacks. Excluding cases missing even a single variable can substantially reduce the sample size and will produce biased results when data are not missing at random (Acock, 1997; Little & Rubin, 1990). A related strategy involves pairwise deletion, or calculating the correlation or covariance between two variables based on all cases that have values for both variables. Covariances reflect the degree of relationship between two variables, but unlike correlation coefficients, they are not adjusted for differences in scale units (i.e., a correlation is essentially the covariance between two variables that have been standardized). A missing-data correlation or covariance matrix based on these coefficients may then be subjected to analysis. This approach is appealing because it appears to make use of all available data (i.e., cases missing only some variables are included in some calculations). However, because each coefficient is based on different subsets of the data, the overall sample size is not clear, and it can result in an overall pattern of coefficients that is mathematically impossible and therefore not amenable to analysis (Cohen & Cohen, 1983). Where analyses of such data are possible the results cannot be generalized to any specific subpopulation. For longitudinal designs, researchers may be able to take advantage of procedures such as hierarchical linear modeling, which estimates parameters based on all available data (Bryk & Raudenbush, 1992; Hedeker & Gibbons, 1997; Nich & Carroll, 1997). Although this approach does not require that all participants be present at every time point, it will also result in biased estimates when data are not missing at random.

Other approaches to handling missing data involve estimating or imputing missing values. One of the most commonly used methods is mean substitution, which involves substituting all missing values for a variable with that variable's mean. The mean represents the best single estimate of a participant's score in the absence of any other information. However, replacing missing values with means will tend to underestimate the population variance because all missing values are placed at the center of the distribution. It will also produce biased estimates of population means if missing cases are not random. Other methods of imputing missing values have been designed to take advantage of whatever data are not missing for an individual case. These include substituting the appropriate subgroup mean rather than the overall mean, or constructing regression estimates in which missing scores are estimated based on all available scores for that individual (i.e., an individual missing a score on 1 variable out of 10 has that score estimated based on his or her scores on the other 9 variables). The success of the regression approach will depend on how well scores on each variable can be predicted from the other variables. This approach can also result in overestimates when correlations are calculated between variables with missing values and the variables used to estimate them. These problems have led to further enhancements in which regression estimates are augmented with an error term based on a randomly selected residual obtained from a complete case or randomly selected residual value from an appropriate distribution (Acock, 1997). A more sophisticated approach, known as expectation maximization, takes this further by conducting an iterative process to improve the prediction of missing values as more and more missing values are imputed (Little & Schenker, 1995). Although several of these approaches require specialized computer programs, standard statistical packages have begun to incorporate these procedures (Acock, 1997).

The best strategy for handling missing data is to do whatever is possible to minimize the problem during the data collection stage. In most clinical research, a certain amount of missing data is inevitable. A reasonable starting point for most researchers is to determine the extent of missing data within their sample and to use whatever data are available to examine differences between individuals with and without missing data (see Cohen & Cohen, 1983, especially Chapter 7, for a discussion of appropriate data analytic strategies). In psychotherapy outcome research, this may involve comparing individuals who complete treatment to those who drop out (e.g., see Kendall, Flannery-Schroeder, & Ford, 1999). When the amount of missing data is small and fairly random, most procedures for handling missing data will produce similar results. In other cases, researchers will need to carefully select an approach most likely to reduce this source of bias. In some instances, it may be informative to compare several different strategies (Flick, 1988).

What Are the Distribution Properties of Your Variables?

Preliminary analyses are also needed to examine the distribution properties of variables. Many statistical techniques are based on assumptions about the underlying distributions of the variables. For example, ANOVA is based on the assumption that the variables are normally distributed. Although it has been established that many methods are fairly robust to some deviations from these assumptions (Keppel, 1982; Kirk, 1982), investigators need to assess the extent to which their data may represent an extreme deviation. In such cases, it may be possible to address this problem by using transformations (Cohen & Cohen, 1983; Tabachnick & Fidell, 1996) or by recoding the data. Another option is to use alternative analyses that make fewer assumptions about the variables' underlying distributions (e.g., Hu, Bentler, & Kano, 1992).

Examining the distribution properties of the data may also identify outliers or cases with extreme high or low values. Outliers are sometimes referred to as influential data points because their presence can produce substantial changes in the findings. For example, in a least squares regression analysis, an extreme score will have a powerful impact on the slope of the regression line because parameters are estimated so as to minimize the sum of squared differences between observed values and predicted values. As a result, the further a case is from the regression line, the more it will influence the slope of the line (i.e., a case 5 points above the regression line will have a squared residual of 25 versus a squared residual of 1 for a case 1 point below the regression line). The identification of outliers must include both univariate and multivariate outliers. Univariate outliers are cases with extreme values on a single variable. The identification of univariate outliers is a straightforward process that involves examining the distribution of each variable using stem-and-leaf plots (Tabachnick & Fidell, 1996). Multivariate outliers represent cases whose scores on any single variable may not be extreme, but that have an unusual pattern of scores. For example, examination of outliers in a recent study of risk and protective factors for adolescent drug use (Farrell & White, 1998) identified an individual who reported a high frequency of peer pressure for drug and alcohol use (e.g., being offered drugs, feeling pressured to drink), but who indicated that none of her friends used alcohol or drugs. Neither score by itself was that extreme, but the combination of scores represented a clearly unusual (and in this case implausible) pattern. Detection of multivariate outliers may be accomplished using a variety of statistical and graphical analyses (see Tabachnick & Fidell, 1996).

The most appropriate procedure for handling an outlier depends on the factors responsible for its occurrence (Tabachnick & Fidell, 1996). Outliers can reflect data entry errors. For example, a 111 is entered instead of a 1. In other instances, outliers can reflect a failure to specify missing value codes for a variable. For example, using 999 to represent missing values for age, but neglecting to screen out these values in the data analysis. Errors of this sort can be common and can be corrected once they are identified. Other reasons for the presence of an outlier may be harder to assess. One possibility is that the individual case is not a member of the population you intended to sample. For example, inclusion of a person with a paranoid thought disorder in a study designed to investigate the relationship between perceived social support and response to stressful life events could result in an extreme pattern of scores that could have a strong influence on the findings. If the researchers did not intend to have their findings generalize to such individuals, they could justify excluding such a case. Some cases with extreme values may be representative of the population of interest, and excluding them from the analysis based on their scores would be inappropriate. Indeed, there are always outliers to some degree and elimination of one extreme data point will inevitably lead to another case being labeled extreme. Tabachnick and Fidell outline procedures that may be followed to reduce the impact of extreme scores in cases where the sample appears to have more extreme scores than would be expected in a normal population. In any case, it is important that researchers specify and justify whatever approaches they used to address outliers in any given study.

Does Your Measurement Model Fit the Data?

Another focus of preliminary analysis is to test the extent to which the researcher's measurement model fits the data. Because most constructs examined in clinical research are not directly observable, the majority of measures assess constructs indirectly, by measuring observable indicators of each construct or latent variable (Hoyle, 1991). For example, a researcher may assess marital satisfaction based on each partner's ratings, social skills by obtaining judges' ratings of responses to a role-play test, school problems by collecting teachers' ratings, and job performance by obtaining supervisors' ratings. Each example assumes a measurement model that specifies a link between the observed variables and the construct of interest. The accuracy of the measurement model is critically important because researchers are generally not interested in making inferences about the specific measures, but rather wish to draw conclusions about the underlying constructs the measures are assumed to measure. For example, a researcher who finds a substantial correlation between a measure of marital satisfaction and a supervisor's ratings of job performance may wish to make inferences about the relationship between marital satisfaction and job performance. The extent to which such inferences are warranted depends on the validity of the underlying measurement model.

Clinical researchers often make implicit assumptions about their measurement models without attempting to verify them. For example, a researcher interested in the relationship between exposure to community violence and frequency of violent behavior among adolescents might examine this relationship by calculating the correlation between scores on self-report measures of both constructs. This implies a measurement model that assumes the existence of two distinct constructs that are each represented by the items included in the observed measures, and that both measures are perfectly reliable. The first assumption is sometimes evaluated by calculating alpha coefficients representing the internal consistency of each measure. Alpha coefficients are not, however, an appropriate index of dimensionality. It is possible for a set of items to reflect several different dimensions, yet have a high alpha coefficient (see Schmitt, 1996). Moreover, two different scales may each have high alpha coefficients, yet not be distinct from each other. For example, two different measures of the same construct could each have high alpha coefficients, but would clearly not be distinct. The assumption of perfect reliability is a consequence of analyzing observed scores and holds true not only for correlation coefficients, but for multiple regression as well (Pedhazur, 1982). In general, unreliability of measurement will attenuate the correlation between two constructs. The impact of unreliability on partial correlations is more complex (see Cohen & Cohen, 1983, pp. 406–413).

Although researchers often neglect to evaluate the fit of their measurement models to the data, analyses are readily available to address this problem. Structural equation modeling provides for a two-step process that begins with an evaluation of the researcher's measurement model and ends with an examination of the structural model representing relationships among the latent variables included in the model (J. C. Anderson & Gerbing, 1988). Figure 4.1 shows a simple two-variable model representing the relationship between two latent variables: exposure to community violence and the frequency of

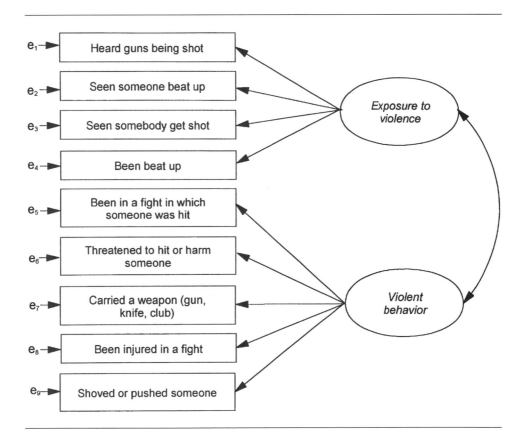

Figure 4.1.   Example of a measurement model. The covariances among test items is represented by two correlated latent variables and measurement error.

violent behavior. Following convention, observed variables in this model are represented by rectangles, and constructs or latent variables are represented by ovals. The one-directional arrows in Figure 4.1 indicate that the variance in each item is accounted for by the latent variable it is purported to measure and measurement error (represented by "e"). The curved, double-headed arrow represents the correlation between the two latent variables. This model attempts to explain the covariances among the observed variables. For example, the covariance between any two items on the same scale is explained by the fact that they load on the same scale. The covariance between two items on different scales is a function of the loading of each variable on its respective scale and the correlation between the two latent variables. The extent to which this model fits the data can be evaluated using a confirmatory factor analysis (see Hoyle, 1991).

The model in Figure 4.1 represents a simplified version of a measurement model that was examined in a study of the impact of exposure to community violence on emotional distress and violent behavior (Farrell & Bruce, 1997). Initial examination of this measurement model indicated that it did not adequately fit the data. Upon further examination, it was evident that, although the two latent variables were considered to be distinct constructs, there was some overlap among the items. For example, the item "been beat up" on the exposure to violence scale was similar to several items on the violent behavior scale, including "been in a fight in which someone was hit." It was concluded that the poor fit of this measurement model was due to overlap in the content of items between the two scales. This led to redefining the construct of "exposure to violence" to focus only on witnessing violence and restricting the items to be consistent with this definition. This modification resulted in a measurement model that adequately fit the data. Had the two original scales simply been correlated without examining the measurement model, it is likely that the overlap in item content would have resulted in an overestimate of the correlation between these two constructs. This example illustrates the value of evaluating the measurement model before examining relationships among constructs. It also underscores the importance of examining the item content of scales, and not just the names of scales. Scale names are often too broad and occasionally not adequately descriptive of the content of a measure.

Confirmatory factor analysis can be used to evaluate a variety of complex measurement models. For example, calculating separate subscales on a test assumes that it measures multiple constructs and that the items are correctly linked to each of these constructs. A confirmatory factor analysis can be used to verify the placement of items into specific subscales and to examine the relationships among subscales (e.g., see Farrell, in press). Sometimes, investigators combine subscales into an overall score. For example, researchers on adolescent problem behavior sometimes construct scales that reflect problem behavior proneness by combining measures of alcohol and drug use, school problems, and delinquent behaviors. Confirmatory factor analysis can be used to determine the extent to which combining these scales into a single construct is consistent with the data (e.g., see Donovan, Jessor, & Costa, 1988). The examples discussed to this point have all involved different measures using the same basic method (i.e., self-report). In most instances, it is preferable to collect data using multiple methods or perspectives (Kendall & Norton-Ford, 1982; Newman & Ciarlo, 1994; Strupp, 1996). In such cases, confirmatory factor analysis can be applied to multitrait multimethod data to examine the extent to which different measures converge on the same constructs and the extent to which the data are influenced by method variance (see Widaman, 1985). Ideally, these analyses can be followed by examining structural relations among the variables as a second step in a structural equation model. Although this is the ideal use of this analysis, researchers can also use a confirmatory factor analysis to confirm their measurement model prior to conducting other analyses of their data.

FITTING THE ANALYSIS TO THE RESEARCH QUESTIONS

One of the most important principles in applying statistical methods to a research problem is that there be a close match between the analytic method and the specific research hypotheses. Wampold, Davis, and Good (1990) discussed this within the context of hypothesis validity, which they defined as "the extent to which research results reflect theoretically derived predictions about the relations between or among constructs" (p. 360). They argued that to assure adequate hypothesis validity, statistical hypotheses need to be congruent with the investigator's research hypotheses and sufficiently specific to determine if the results obtained are similar or dissimilar to the predicted outcome. Wampold et al. discussed various threats to hypothesis validity, including (a) inconsequential research hypotheses that do not differentiate among competing theories, (b) ambiguous research hypotheses that are not adequately specified, (c) noncongruence of research hypotheses and statistical hypotheses, and (d) the use of diffuse statistical hypotheses and tests (e.g., not specifying which groups are expected to differ in an ANOVA). Given the focus of this chapter, I assume that the researcher begins with research questions that are both consequential and unambiguous (see Wampold et al., 1990, for a more detailed discussion of these issues). The focus of this section is on selecting statistical procedures that faithfully address the questions raised by the researcher. This discussion is centered around several specific questions about the nature of the hypotheses and the data used to test them.

What Is the Nature of Your Variables?

Designing an appropriate data analysis plan requires consideration of the nature and scale properties of the variables under investigation. Variables may be classified into two major types of measurement scales: categorical and quantitative (Cohen & Cohen, 1983). Categorical or nominal variables represent sets of objects classified into groups based on common properties (e.g., gender, diagnostic category, treatment condition). When numbers are used to represent such groups, they are simply being used as symbols (e.g., 0 = men, 1 = women). The specific number assigned to an individual takes on greater meaning for a quantitative variable. These numbers represent the degree to which an individual may be said to possess a certain characteristic or attribute (e.g., intelligence, social skills, depressive symptoms). Quantitative variables can be further classified into ordinal, interval, and ratio scales. It has been argued that most quantitative variables in the social sciences represent little more than ordinal-level data, and there has been much debate over the appropriateness of applying parametric statistics to such data (Nunally, 1978). Fortunately, there appears to be consensus that most quantitative measures can be analyzed using statistics developed for interval-level scales without encountering serious problems (Cohen & Cohen, 1983; Kerlinger, 1986; Nunally, 1978).

The distinction between categorical and quantitative scales is important because many analytic techniques limit the types of scales that can be used for independent and/or dependent variables. This sometimes leads researchers to recode variables to fit the assumptions of a particular analytic technique. Rather than transform the data to fit the assumptions of the analysis, the data would be better served by finding an analytic approach that will do justice to the types of variables under investigation. This section presents a sample of the statistical techniques that have been designed to handle categorical and quantitative scales, and techniques designed to handle the special problems associated with assessing change as a variable. This is by no means an exhaustive list, but rather a brief description of some selected strategies. Those interested in learning more about these techniques should refer to the articles referenced in this section.

Quantitative Dependent Variables

A common data analysis problem involves studying the relationship between a set of independent variables and one or more quantitative dependent variables. ANOVA is perhaps the most frequently used approach to analyzing quantitative dependent variables. This can be extended to multivariate ANOVA when there are multiple dependent variables representing the same construct (Huberty & Morris, 1989). Basic training in ANOVA is akin to a rite of passage for most graduate programs in psychology (Aiken et al., 1990), and ANOVA can be a very powerful analytic tool. It is, however, a rather restricted case of the more general linear model. Because it was designed to compare group means, ANOVA requires that the independent variables be categorical, and special methods are needed when the number of cases are not equal across groups. Researchers have sometimes transformed quantitative independent variables into categorical variables using a median split or cutoffs a standard deviation above and below the mean to define high and low groups so that their data could be analyzed using ANOVA. This is usually a bad idea in that such an approach makes limited use of the available data (see Cohen & Cohen, 1983, pp. 309–311). In such situations, comparing means across such groups will typically not provide as clear a picture of the relationship between the independent and dependent variables as a scatterplot or other figure that displays observed or predicted values of the dependent variable across all values of the independent variable, particularly when the relationship is nonlinear.

Use of less restricted applications of the general linear model provides researchers with a flexible set of tools suitable for a variety of problems. Cohen and Cohen (1983), in particular, detail the use of multiple regression as a data analytic technique that can handle categorical and quantitative independent variables, examine nonlinear relationships, and explore interaction effects among independent variables. When the independent variables are categorical, appropriate coding of the data will provide results identical to ANOVA. A thorough grounding in the use of multiple regression should be a basic part of training in statistical methods. In the case of multiple dependent variables, structural equation modeling can be used to broaden this approach further. Such analyses can be applied to path models that specify the hypothesized pattern of relationships among the variables. In cases where multiple dependent variables are viewed as measures of the same construct, structural equation models can be constructed in which the observed dependent variables are represented as indicators of latent variables or constructs and relationships among latent variables are examined (see Bollen, 1989; Byrne, 1994).

Categorical Dependent Variables

Clinical researchers sometimes study categorical variables. Research problems that focus on the relationship between two categorical variables can be addressed by calculation of chi-square statistics (Siegel & Castellan, 1988). Such analyses can be supplemented with a variety of descriptive statistics. For example, researchers assessing the agreement between two sources of data (e.g., interrater agreement on categories, agreement between two diagnostic indicators) can calculate a kappa coefficient that represents the extent to which agreement exceeds what would be expected by chance (Cohen, 1960). Other research problems involve examining the relationship between a set of predictor variables and a categorical dependent variable. For example, a researcher may be interested in identifying the variables associated with successful and unsuccessful response to a particular treatment. One approach to such problems is linear discriminant analysis (see Silva & Stam, 1995; Tabachnick & Fidell, 1996, for description and examples). This analysis forms linear combinations of the independent variables that maximally differentiate between the groups defined by the dependent variables. The statistical significance and magnitude of the weight for each variable (i.e., the discriminant function coefficient) indicates the extent to which that variable differentiates among the groups, and equations can be used to predict group membership based on scores on the independent variables.

A more flexible method of data analysis for categorical dependent variables is provided by logistic regression. Unlike linear discriminant analysis, which requires quantitative independent variables, logistic regression enables the researcher to use both categorical and quantitative independent variables. This approach has the further advantage of making no assumptions regarding the distribution properties of the independent variables (see Darlington, 1990; Tabachnick & Fidell, 1996, for discussion and examples).

Change as a Dependent Variable

Clinical researchers are often interested in the study of change. The analysis of change is a complex topic and a variety of techniques have been developed to investigate different aspects of change (see Collins & Horn, 1991; Gottman, 1995). The most commonly used strategies include repeated measures ANOVA and analysis of covariance. These approaches differ in that the repeated measures approach focuses on changes in raw scores over time, and the analysis of covariance approach focuses on residual change, or the extent to which an individual changes more or less than would be expected based on his or her previous score. Although earlier articles examining the strengths and weaknesses of each of these approaches tended to favor the analysis of covariance approach (e.g., see Cohen & Cohen, 1983, pp. 413–423), more recent articles have suggested that analyses of raw difference scores may have been abandoned prematurely (e.g., see Newman, 1994; Rogosa, 1995).

A variety of techniques can be applied to the study of change. Selection of the most appropriate technique depends on the design of the study and the researcher's assumptions regarding the nature of change. Farrell (1994) described a strategy for applying structural equation models to longitudinal data and illustrated the use of this technique in a study that examined causes and consequences of adolescent alcohol use. Three competing models were tested: one in which the number of peers using alcohol predicted subsequent changes in adolescents' alcohol use (peer influence model), one in which adolescents' alcohol use predicted changes in the number of their peers using alcohol (peer selection model), and a reciprocal model that included both influences. Other approaches have been developed to study variables that show systematic change over time. For example, hierarchical linear models have been used to study individual differences in the growth curves of a variety of variables (Bryk & Raudenbush, 1992). This approach includes a within-person model or growth curve equation that represents each individual's scores on a dependent variable obtained on multiple occasions as a function of initial level and time. Within these equations, change may be represented by a linear or curvilinear trajectory. The parameters (e.g., intercept, slope) within these equations are allowed to differ across individuals (e.g., some individuals may show higher rates of change than others). This analysis also includes a between-person model that uses characteristics of individuals to predict individual differences in the growth curve parameters. For example, this approach could be used to evaluate the extent to which a prevention program resulted in a lower rate of increase in problem behaviors during the course of adolescence. Another method that has been used to study change is latent growth curve analysis, a method that uses structural equation modeling to examine individual growth curves (Willett & Sayer, 1994). This approach may be useful when data are obtained for a group of individuals on three or more occasions, and the number and spacing of the observations is the same for all individuals. Curran, Stice, and Chassin (1997) presented an example of the use of this technique to examine increases in adolescent drug use and peer models of drug use over time. Within their model, an individual's predicted level of alcohol use at a particular time point was expressed as a function of an intercept coefficient representing the initial level of use and a slope parameter that represented the expected degree of change over time. A similar equation was used to represent changes in peer alcohol use. The final model examined the extent to which the initial levels of peer and adolescent alcohol use were related, the extent to which initial levels of one variable predicted changes on the other (e.g., did adolescents with greater initial exposure to peer models show greater increases in alcohol use?), and the extent to which the rates of change for the two variables were related. Curran et al. were also able to examine the extent to which age, gender, and parental alcoholism were related to the rate of change. Statistical methods for studying change over time have also been developed for single-subject data. For example, Crosbie (1993) reviewed the use of statistical methods for examining interrupted time series data. These methods can be applied to single-case designs to determine the extent to which the level and rate of change differs across baseline and intervention phases.

A variety of clinical research questions focus on predicting if and when changes in status occur. Examples include the onset (e.g., initiation of sexual behavior), cessation (e.g., of smoking), and relapse (e.g., of alcohol use) of a behavior. Willett and Singer (1993) described the application of survival analysis to these types of problems and illustrated their description with examples related to the age of first onset of suicidal ideation and depression, and relapse for cocaine addicts following treatment. Survival analysis provides a useful method for determining the extent to which variables can be used to predict time to the occurrence of an event. Techniques have also been developed to study transitions between stages over time. Graham, Collins, Wugalter, Chung, and Hansen (1991), for example, described the use of latent transition analysis and provided an example in which they used this technique to study the impact of a substance use prevention program on transitions across stages of substance use. They showed how students who participated in a prevention program were less likely to move to higher levels of drug use (i.e., from no use, to alcohol or tobacco use, to alcohol and tobacco use, to stages of advanced use).

Are the Research Questions Exploratory or Confirmatory?

A critical consideration in matching the statistical analyses to the research questions concerns the extent to which the research may be considered exploratory or confirmatory. Exploratory studies attempt to discover patterns in data without relying on specific hypotheses (Behrens, 1997). In contrast, confirmatory analyses are designed to test for the presence of specific patterns in the data based on a priori hypotheses. Many studies lie somewhere along the continuum anchored by these two extremes, and both approaches may be used within the same study. Whether a hypothesis is exploratory or confirmatory has clear implications for the selection of data analytic procedures. Exploratory hypotheses are best served by exploratory data analyses designed to discover patterns in the data, rather than making improper use of confirmatory analyses (Behrens, 1997). On the other hand, researchers with specific hypotheses are better served by conducting focused tests using confirmatory techniques than by using exploratory techniques in the hopes that the pattern that emerges from the data will resemble their hypothesized pattern. This is evident from an examination of some frequent practices in the use of ANOVA, multiple regression analysis, and factor analysis.

Example 1: ANOVA

The distinction between exploratory and confirmatory approaches becomes relevant whenever ANOVA techniques are used to examine mean differences among three or more groups. Exploratory analyses are often conducted using omnibus F-tests. Because such tests do not indicate which specific groups differ, significant main effects must be followed by post hoc tests (e.g., Duncan, Scheffe) that compare all possible pairs of group means (e.g., Keppel, 1982). When a large number of significance tests is involved (i.e., m[m − 1]/2 where m = the number of treatment groups), post hoc tests use conservative criteria for significance to avoid a highly inflated Type I error rate (i.e., rejecting the null hypothesis when it is true). This in turn reduces the power of the significance test to detect any differences that may exist.

Researchers with specific hypotheses about group differences can use a more confirmatory approach in which specific group differences are examined using planned comparisons or linear contrasts (Winer, 1971). Typically, the degrees of freedom available for testing the main effect for treatment (m − 1) are partitioned into 1-degree-of-freedom contrasts. Restricting the number of comparisons to a subset that is specified in advance does not result in the same restriction in alpha level and resulting reduction in power associated with post hoc tests. It also gives the researcher flexibility to not only test differences between selected pairs of means, but to employ contrasts that compare different sets of groups. For example, in a four-group design that includes two treatment and two control groups (e.g., an attention-placebo and waiting list control), three contrasts could be used to compare (a) the average effect for the treatment groups to the average effect for the control groups, (b) differences between the two treatment groups, and (c) differences between the two control groups. In spite of the clear advantage of using planned comparisons, it is not difficult to find published studies in which researchers who appear to have fairly specific hypotheses use post hoc tests. In essence, such researchers are reducing the power of the comparisons in which they are most interested by including comparisons in which they may have little interest (Rosnow & Rosenthal, 1988).

Example 2: Multiple Regression

The distinction between exploratory and confirmatory approaches is also relevant to multiple regression analysis. In many such applications, researchers are interested in examining the influence of individual variables or sets of variables. In such instances, they may enter variables into the analysis in separate steps where the order of entry is determined either empirically, based on the data, or rationally, based on the researcher's a priori hypotheses. The ordering of variables is extremely important because the value of a variable is often dependent on the specific step at which it is entered. A variable that would have significantly improved the prediction of the dependent variable at an earlier step may be redundant at a later step after other related variables have been included in the equation. Researchers who pursue an empirical approach can select from a variety of techniques (e.g., forward selection, backward elimination, stepwise, all subsets), all of which are designed to identify a subset of the variables that provides the best estimate of the dependent variable in the sample (see Cohen & Cohen, 1983; Darlington, 1990; Pedhazur, 1982). These empirical approaches may be considered exploratory in that they attempt to find the "best" combination of variables based on the data without regard to any theory or assumptions the researcher may have about the variables under investigation. Cohen and Cohen argued that this approach should not be used except in limited cases when the researcher is interested in prediction rather than explanation. In particular, they note that minor differences across samples can result in dramatic differences in the specific variables selected, and they question the validity of statistical tests based on these approaches.

In contrast to empirical approaches, in which the order of entering variables is determined by the data, hierarchical regression approaches require that the researcher provide an a priori order based on explicit hypotheses. Cohen and Cohen (1983) discussed the relevant factors that should be considered in determining the order of entry. In essence, hierarchical regression analysis provides an ordered partitioning of the variance in the dependent variable in which variables with higher causal priority based on theory are given precedence over other variables. This approach is not likely to provide the empirically optimum subset of predictors at any given step. Its value is that it permits researchers to test specific theories based on the priority of specific variables. Cohen and Cohen noted that researchers may be tempted to employ empirical regression approaches because these relieve them of the responsibility of making often difficult decisions about the logical priority or relevance of each variable. Nonetheless, they argue that "more orderly advance in the behavioral sciences is likely to occur when researchers armed with theories provide a priori hierarchical ordering that reflects causal hypotheses rather than when computers order IVs [independent variables] post and ad hoc for a given sample" (p. 124). This distinction between empirically and rationally driven approaches is relevant not only to multiple regression analyses, but other analyses such as linear discriminant analysis and logistic regression in which variables may be entered in steps (Tabachnick & Fidell, 1996).

Example 3: Factor Analysis

The distinction between exploratory and confirmatory analyses is also of critical importance in factor analysis. Floyd and Widaman (1995) discussed the distinction between exploratory and confirmatory uses. The primary use of exploratory factor analysis is to identify the underlying dimensions or factors assessed by the items in a measure. Identification of items associated with these factors may then be used to form subscales to assess the domain defined by each factor identified in the analysis. Apart from technical issues related to picking a method of factor extraction and rotation, exploratory approaches to factor analysis do not require the investigator to specify anything other than the observed variables to be analyzed. Decisions about the number of factors to be retained are based on the results of an initial analysis of the data, and interpretation of the factors is based on examination of the pattern of relationships between the individual variables and the factors (see Bryant & Yarnold, 1995; Mulaik, 1972). Initial factor solutions are often difficult to interpret because many items will show a moderate degree of relationship to all the factors. Various approaches to rotating factors (e.g., varimax) are typically used to obtain a more readily interpretable factor solution. Because factors can be rotated without changing the total variance accounted for, there are an infinite number of possible solutions to an exploratory factor analysis. Selection of one particular solution is typically based on statistical criteria that identify solutions that can be most readily interpreted. Because the researcher does not specify a particular structure in advance, exploratory approaches are more appropriate for generating theories than for testing them. The researcher may offer a theory to explain the particular pattern of relationships between items and factors, but such post hoc theories are not as compelling as a priori theories that are subsequently supported by data.

Confirmatory approaches to factor analysis are used to test a priori hypotheses about the factor structure of a scale (Floyd & Widaman, 1995; Long, 1983). Confirmatory factor analysis requires that the researcher specify not only the number of factors or latent variables, but also the specific pattern of relationships between the observed variables and the hypothesized factors. In most applications each variable is hypothesized to load on a single factor and the loadings of that variable with all other factors are constrained to zero. Unlike exploratory factor analysis in which factors are generally considered to be orthogonal or uncorrelated, most confirmatory factor analyses assume correlated factors. Confirmatory factor analysis applies the model specified by the researcher to the data and determines the extent to which the researcher's model can account for the observed covariances among variables. Overall fit is assessed by a variety of goodness of fit indices that indicate the extent to which the hypothesized model fits the data. Researchers can also test competing models to determine which provides the best fit to the data. As previously discussed, confirmatory factor analysis can be used to evaluate a researcher's measurement model prior to testing hypotheses about the relationships among the latent variables.

Although confirmatory factor analytic methods have been available for some time (Jöreskog, 1969), it appears that many researchers are not familiar with their advantages for testing specific hypotheses. The literature contains many examples of studies in which a researcher appears to have specific hypotheses about the factor structure of a set of variables, but conducts an exploratory factor analysis to see how closely the empirically derived solution matches the hypothesized structure. There are several problems with this approach. The extent to which the structure identified in an exploratory analysis is consistent with the hypothesized factor structure is subjectively determined. There are no quantitative measures of fit as in a confirmatory analysis. The researcher must instead examine the pattern of relationships between the observed variables and the factors and judge the extent to which it resembles the pattern they hypothesized. Such an examination is often fairly selective. Although each variable is correlated with every factor, researchers typically interpret exploratory solutions based only on the highest correlations between variables and factors. Researchers may even examine several solutions that differ in the number of factors extracted and select the one they find easiest to interpret (i.e., the one most consistent with their hypotheses). A second problem is that rotational approaches used to facilitate the interpretation of the factor solution often constrain the factors to be orthogonal when there may be reason to believe that they are correlated. Finally, even if the results of an exploratory analysis do not resemble the hypothesized factor structure, this does not mean the hypothesized structure does not fit the data. The structure identified in an exploratory analysis is only one of many solutions that will fit the data equally well. As previously noted, exploratory and confirmatory approaches can sometimes be used in combination by using exploratory analyses to generate hypotheses that are then tested in new samples using confirmatory approaches (e.g., see Mueser, Curran, & McHugo, 1997).

Summary and Recommendations

Before designing their data analysis, researchers are wise to consider the extent to which their hypotheses are exploratory or confirmatory. This section discussed several common misuses of exploratory techniques to address confirmatory problems. This was by no means an exhaustive list, nor was it meant to appear critical of exploratory approaches. Exploratory and confirmatory approaches must be properly applied to the types of problems for which they are best suited. For studies where researchers do not have a sufficient body of knowledge to generate specific hypotheses, they may wish to let the data "speak for themselves" and employ exploratory analytic techniques. In such cases, it is important that researchers not interpret the hypotheses generated by such research as though they had been confirmed by the findings. For example, researchers often modify structural equation models to improve their fit to the data and then interpret fit coefficients based on these models (MacCallum, Roznowski, & Necowitz, 1992). Such findings are tentative and should be used to generate theory and provide the basis for confirmatory studies that determine the conditions under which these findings can be replicated. In many cases, researchers begin with fairly explicit hypotheses about the phenomena they are studying. Those comparing group means often have some idea regarding which groups will differ. Those studying sets of variables are likely to have theories about the causal priority of specific variables. It also seems likely that developers of assessment instruments will have some notions regarding the constructs that underlie the items they have written. In such cases, they are better off conducting confirmatory analyses that maximize the hypothesis validity of their study. If these hypotheses are not confirmed, they may wish to go back to exploratory analyses to generate new ideas. More generally, exploratory analyses of the variance not explained by a researcher's model may be particularly fruitful (Behrens, 1997).

What Is Your Model of the Relationships among the Variables?

To match the statistical analyses to the research questions, the researcher needs to begin with clear hypotheses regarding the expected pattern of relationships among the variables under investigation. In some instances, a researcher may simply wish to examine the interrelationships within a set of variables, without making any inferences about the causal nature of these relationships. In other instances, a researcher may wish to examine the relationship between two variables after controlling for the influence of one or more other variables. Researchers may at times wish to test an explicit model that specifies causal relationships among each of the variables under investigation. In some instances, these hypotheses may include moderator effects or nonlinear relationships among the variables. Each situation calls for a different approach to the data analysis. The level of data analysis in turn leads to different interpretations of the results. Several of these approaches can be illustrated using data from a study by Lemmon (1983) that examined the relationships among social skills, dating behavior, loneliness, and postdivorce adjustment in a sample of 84 recently divorced or separated men and women. Figure 4.2 depicts three different models depicting the relationships among these four variables. Each of these models calls for a different approach to the data analysis.

Bivariate Relationships

Model 1 (see Figure 4.2a) specifies zero-order relationships among social skills, dating behavior, loneliness, and postdivorce adjustment. The strength of these relationships is represented by Pearson correlation coefficients (represented by curved, double-headed arrows). This model could be used to address the hypothesis that social skills, dating behavior, and loneliness are each related to postdivorce adjustment. The statistical significance of each correlation can be tested, and confidence intervals for each correlation can be constructed. Several features of this model are important to note. This model does *not* imply anything about the causal nature of the relationships among these variables. In other words, it does not specify whether (a) a high frequency of dating results in good postdivorce adjustment, (b) a good postdivorce adjustment results in more frequent dating, or (c) both variables are the consequence of some third unspecified variable. This model looks at zero-order relationships between pairs of variables without taking any other variables into account. For example, social skills and dating behavior are both significantly related to postdivorce adjustment, and they are also significantly correlated with each other. The correlations in this model provide estimates of the amount of variance shared between social skills and divorce

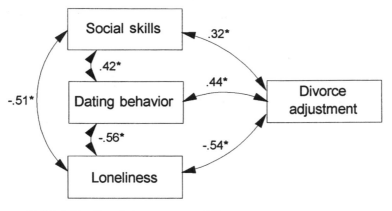

(a) Model 1: Correlations among variables

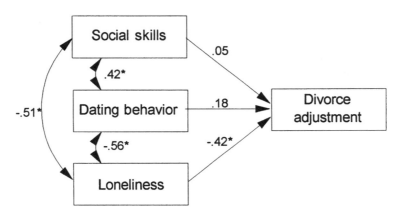

(b) Model 2: Regression model for predicting adjustment

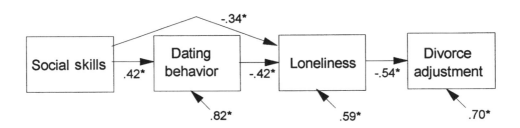

(c) Model 3: Path model of relationships among variables

Figure 4.2.   Examples of three different models for examining the relationships among social skills, dating behavior, loneliness, and postdivorce adjustment.

adjustment (i.e., $r^2 = .10$) and between dating behavior and divorce adjustment ($r^2 = .19$), but they do not indicate the unique contribution of each variable. In this specific example, Pearson correlations were used because both variables were quantitative. Relationships between a categorical variable and a quantitative variable could be examined using a one-way ANOVA. Relationships between two categorical variables could be examined using a two-way table and the associated chi-square test. Each of these analyses focuses on zero-order relationships between a pair of variables.

Partialled Relationships

A more specific model of the relationships among these variables is represented in Model 2 (see Figure 4.2b). Within this model, social skills, dating behavior, and loneliness are represented as predictors of postdivorce adjustment. The relationship of each variable to postdivorce adjustment is represented by a one-directional arrow, and correlations among the three predictors are represented by curved, two-directional arrows. This model could be used to address hypotheses about the unique contribution of each variable to predicting postdivorce adjustment (e.g., what is the relationship between loneliness and postdivorce adjustment after controlling for social skills and dating behavior?), and to determine the total proportion of variance in postdivorce adjustment predicted by all three variables. Unlike Model 1, this model takes correlations among the predictor variables into account. Coefficients reported for this model are standardized partial regression coefficients based on a simultaneous multiple regression analysis in which postdivorce adjustment scores are expressed as a function of a linear combination of social skills, dating behavior, and loneliness. These are referred to as partial coefficients because they represent the relationship between each predictor and the criterion variable after partialing out the influence of the other variables included in the model. Note that these coefficients are smaller in absolute value than corresponding parameters in Model 1, and that two of these parameters are no longer statistically significant. For example, dating behavior is moderately related to postdivorce adjustment, as indicated in Model 1, but the strength of this relationship is reduced dramatically after controlling for the effects of social skills and loneliness. This model also includes a residual or disturbance term that represents the proportion of variance in adjustment not predicted by the variables included in the model (i.e., .68). This term is calculated by taking 1.00 minus the squared multiple correlation representing the variance predicted by the three variables included in the model.

Other analyses may also be used to examine partial relationships. Partial correlation coefficients are sometimes used to examine the relationship between a pair of variables after the variance associated with one or more other variables has been partialled out (e.g., age and gender). Analysis of covariance is sometimes used to compare group differences after adjusting for other variables represented as covariates (e.g., pretreatment differences). Sometimes, researchers examine partialled relationships without being aware of it. For example, unequal cell sizes in an ANOVA result in correlated effects (e.g., in a gender x marital status ANOVA with unequal cell sizes, a person's gender will make him or her more or less likely to be in a particular marital status group). The default approach to handling unequal cell sizes in many statistical packages looks at each independent variable after adjusting for the other independent variables. Researchers must be careful in interpreting the findings of such an analysis. There may be cases where either variable would have produced significant main effects if examined alone, but does not result in significant effects after controlling for the other variable.

Analyses that involve partial coefficients must be interpreted with special care. The interpretation of any partial coefficient must always be done within the context of the other variables included in the analysis. Researchers sometimes appear to lose sight of this in interpreting the results of a regression analysis. For example, examination of Model 2 might lead a researcher to conclude that social skills and dating behavior are not useful predictors of postdivorce adjustment. Examination of their zero-order correlations with postdivorce adjustment indicates that each is a good predictor by itself. Results of the regression analysis simply indicate that each of these variables is redundant when both are combined with loneliness. If different variables had been included in this analysis, either or both of these variables might have retained their value as predictors. One consequence of conducting a simultaneous regression analysis in which all variables are entered into the equation is that none of the variables gets credit for the variance shared by the set of independent variables. This can result in situations where the set of independent variables predicts a significant proportion of the variance in the dependent variable, yet none of the partial coefficients for individual variables is significant. Hierarchical approaches to multiple regression analysis in which variables are entered a step at a time according to a predetermined sequence provide a more elegant and orderly partitioning of variance associated with a set of predictors (see Cohen & Cohen, 1983). This may also be a more fruitful approach to pursuing ANOVA with unequal cell sizes. Because the magnitude of partial coefficients for any given variable is so dependent on that variable's relationship with the other variables included in the analysis, researchers must use special care in ordering the variables in such a way as to provide a faithful test of their hypotheses about that variable.

Path Models

Model 3 (see Figure 4.2c) depicts a path model that represents a further elaboration of the relationships among the four variables examined in this study. This model attempts to account for the covariances among all four variables based on hypothesized relationships among the variables. For example, the relationship between social skills and dating behavior is explained by representing social skills as a cause of dating behavior frequency. This model includes both direct and indirect effects. For example, the relationship between social skills and loneliness is explained by the direct effect of social skills on loneliness and the indirect effect that results from social skills influencing dating behavior, which in turn influences loneliness. Within this model, loneliness mediates the effects of social skills and dating behavior on postdivorce adjustment. A variable functions as a mediator if most of the effect of an independent variable on a dependent variable can be accounted for by an indirect effect that includes the mediating variable (Baron & Kenny, 1986). In other words, dating behavior is related to postdivorce adjustment because it influences loneliness, which in turn influences adjustment. Models such as Model 3 are tested within path analysis by evaluating the extent to which the model adequately explains the covariances among the variables. This involves estimating the strength of each path in the path diagram and evaluating the extent to which these parameters are able to account for the observed relationships among the variables based on actual data. Although regression techniques can be used to analyze path models, these models are well suited to use of structural equation modeling techniques (Klem, 1995). One of the advantages of the latter approach is that it provides an explicit test of how well the model fits the observed data. This approach thus allows researchers to evaluate the extent to which the data are consistent with a specific hypothesized pattern of relationships among the variables. It should be noted, of course, that the fact that the data are consistent with a given model does not mean that that model is the true model or that it is even the best-fitting model (J. G. Anderson, 1987), simply that it is plausible. On the other hand, evidence of poor fit may be sufficient to rule out a model. A further advantage of structural equation models is that they enable researchers who obtain multiple measures of constructs to test their measurement model and to examine relationships among latent variables that take measurement error into account.

Moderator Effects

In addition to the simple additive effects represented by the models in Figure 4.2, investigators may sometimes wish to examine interactions or moderated effects. Baron and Kenny (1986) defined a moderator variable as "a qualitative (e.g., sex, race, class) or quantitative (e.g., level of reward) variable that effects the direction and/or strength of a relation between an independent or predictor variable and a dependent or criterion variable" (p. 1174). Although statistical methods for examining moderator effects are well developed, many researchers appear to have considerable difficulty applying the correct statistical analysis to these problems (Baron & Kenny, 1986). Holmbeck (1997) discussed various terminological, conceptual, and statistical inconsistencies in the study of moderator variables and mediator variables and documented the frequency with which these inconsistencies are evident within the child clinical and pediatric psychology literature. Most of these inconsistencies appear to result from confusion over the distinction between mediator and moderator variables. In contrast to moderator variables, which indicate when certain effects will be evident, mediator variables represent the mechanism through which an effect occurs (Baron & Kenny, 1986). For example, in Figure 4.2c, loneliness represents a mediator of the effects of social skills and dating frequency on postdivorce adjustment. Data analysis options for examining moderator variables depend on whether the independent variables are categorical or quantitative.

Moderator relationships between categorical variables can be examined by testing for significant interactions in ANOVA designs. For example, Farrell and Meyer (1997) conducted a gender x treatment condition (intervention versus control group) analysis of covariance to evaluate the impact of a violence prevention program on reported postintervention levels of violent behavior for a sample of 698 sixth-grade students. Within this analysis, preintervention scores on a violent behavior scale were treated as a covariate to control for any initial differences. The results of this analysis revealed a nonsignificant main effect for treatment, a significant effect for gender, and a significant Gender × Treatment Group interaction. Examination of Figure 4.3a shows the apparent absence of any main effect for treatment; the frequency of violent behavior increased at comparable rates during the sixth grade for students in both the intervention and control groups. Pre- and-postmeans were also plotted separately by gender to examine the Gender × Treatment Group interaction effect (see Figure 4.3b). This figure reveals that the treatment produced very different effects on the boys than on the girls.

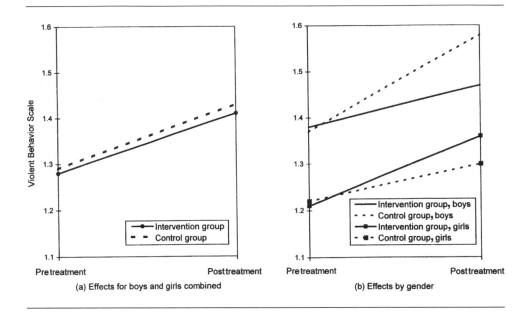

Figure 4.3.   Example of a significant moderator effect for two categorical variables. Results show the absence of treatment effects when means are combined for boys and girls in (a), and the presence of a significant treatment by gender interaction effect in (b).

Participation in the prevention program had the desired effect on the boys in that the intervention group had lower posttest reports of violent behavior relative to the control group. For girls, an opposite trend was found. Girls in the intervention group had higher reports of violent behavior relative to the control group (this difference was not, however, statistically significant). This analysis revealed that the impact of the intervention was moderated by gender, with boys showing different responses than girls. The presence of such an interaction requires careful interpretation. In essence, the impact of the intervention cannot be evaluated without considering the gender of the participant.

Multiple regression techniques provide a flexible model for examining interactions among variables that can be either categorical or quantitative (see Aiken & West, 1991; Jaccard, Turrisi, & Wan, 1990). For example, Palma and Farrell (1997) examined the moderating influence of friends' attitudes toward prosocial behavior on the relationship between peer social support and the use of prosocial responses to conflict situations in a sample of 420 adolescents. These data were analyzed using a hierarchical regression analysis in which the number of prosocial choices in conflict situations was regressed on peer social support, friends' prosocial attitudes, and the Peer Social Support × Friends' Prosocial Attitudes interaction effect (based on taking the product of these two quantitative variables for each participant). Although the relationship between peer social support and number of prosocial responses was not significant (see Figure 4.4a), there was a significant interaction between peer social support and friends' prosocial attitudes. Interpretation of interactions between quantitative variables can be facilitated by plotting regression lines at selected values of the moderator variable. Figure 4.4b depicts the regression lines representing the relationship between level of peer social support and

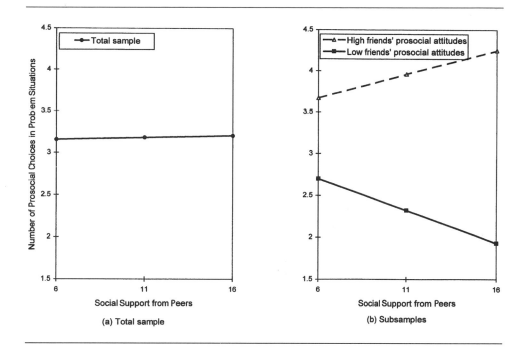

Figure 4.4.   Example of a significant moderator effect for two quantitative variables: (a) regression line reflecting number of prosocial responses in problem situations as a function of peer social support for the full sample, and (b) for subgroups defined by one standard deviation above and below the mean on friends' attitudes toward prosocial behaviors.

number of prosocial responses for adolescents one standard deviation above the mean on friends' prosocial attitudes and for those one standard deviation below. Among adolescents with friends who supported prosocial behavior, higher levels of peer social support were associated with more prosocial responses to conflict situations. Among adolescents with friends who had more negative attitudes toward prosocial behavior, higher levels of peer social support were associated with fewer prosocial responses.

Methods for analyzing more complex interaction effects are also available. Multiple regression analyses can be applied to higher-order interactions such as three-way interactions (see Jaccard et al., 1990). Methods have also been developed to examine interaction effects using structural equation modeling (see Jaccard & Wan, 1996). As with regression analysis, structural equation modeling can examine interactions between variables regardless of whether they are categorical or quantitative. A further advantage is that it enables researchers to construct latent variable models that take measurement error into account.

Summary and Recommendations

This section emphasized the importance of designing the data analysis to reflect the researcher's specific hypotheses about the nature of the relationships among the variables. Within this section, examples were presented of three different approaches to analyzing the same data. All three approaches examined interrelationships among four variables.

Each, however, was based on different assumptions about the nature of the relationships among the variables. Researchers can examine simple relations between two variables using an appropriate bivariate analysis based on zero-order correlations, chi-square analysis, or one-way ANOVA. Analyses such as multiple regression and analysis of co-variance are able to take relationships among independent variables into account by calculating various partial coefficients. Researchers making use of partial coefficients need to exercise special care to ensure that these coefficients accurately reflect their specific hypotheses. Path analysis methods enable researchers to test more comprehensive models about hypothetical cause-and-effect relationships within a set of variables. These methods also rely on partial coefficients that must be interpreted within the context of the specific model. Where there are competing models, each model can be examined and the relative fit of different models compared. Because these models require a high degree of specification, they are best suited to applications where researchers have well-developed theoretical models to test.

This section also discussed the analysis of moderator relationships. Although hypotheses regarding such effects are frequently examined in the clinical literature, the appropriate statistical methods for examining these effects are often not applied (Holmbeck, 1997). The examples included in this section were not meant to represent an exhaustive list. Hypothesized relationships among variables examined in clinical research are often complex and are not restricted to linear relationships (e.g., Howard, Moras, Brill, Martinovich, & Lutz, 1996). The key point of this section is that researchers need to state their hypotheses regarding the expected pattern of relationships among variables as clearly as possible and design their analyses to determine the extent to which these specific hypotheses fit the data.

REPORTING AND INTERPRETING RESULTS

The final stage in the data analysis involves reporting and interpreting the results. The results provide the basis for determining the extent to which the researchers' hypotheses were supported by the data. Results must be reported in sufficient detail to enable other researchers to understand the study's findings and to evaluate for themselves the evidence that confirms or disconfirms the hypotheses. Various rules of evidence have been developed within the field to provide an objective basis for evaluating research findings (Scarr, 1997). In recent years, there has been renewed debate over the value of rules of evidence based on statistical significance tests and the most appropriate approach to presenting and interpreting the findings of individual studies.

The outcome of clinical research studies has typically been determined using a decision rule known as null hypothesis significance testing. Within this approach, hypotheses are not evaluated directly, but rather indirectly by ruling out or nullifying alternative explanations that could account for a study's findings. In most applications, researchers attempt to establish that an effect exists by ruling out the null hypothesis that no effect exists. For example, a researcher who hypothesizes that social skill is related to depression might determine that the correlation between these two variables in a sample of 50 individuals is $r = .28$. To evaluate the hypothesis that these two variables are related in the population, the researcher could conduct a significance test to determine the probability, p, that a sample correlation that large could have been obtained if the true value in the population were zero (i.e., if the null hypothesis were true). For this example, the probability is less than .05. In other words, if the null hypothesis were true, there would be less than a 5% chance of obtaining the observed findings. According to convention, events that occur less then 5% of the time (i.e., at $p < .05$) are considered implausible and provide a basis for ruling out the null hypothesis. Null hypothesis significance tests are a common feature of most statistical analyses in which researchers establish the statistical significance of a particular parameter (e.g., treatment differences in an ANOVA, multiple correlation in a regression analysis, path coefficient in a structural equation model) by determining the probability that the observed results would have been obtained if the parameter were equal to zero in the population.

Although use of null hypothesis significance tests is a well-established part of the training of most clinical researchers (Aiken et al., 1990), the merits of this approach have been the subject of debate for many years (e.g., see Bakan, 1966; Nunally, 1960; Rozeboom, 1960). This debate has received renewed attention with the publication of several recent papers questioning the value of this approach (Cohen, 1990, 1994; Hunter, 1997; Loftus, 1996; Rosenthal, 1995). Schmidt (1996), for example, recently went so far as to suggest that "reliance on statistical significance testing in the analysis and interpretation of research data has systematically retarded the growth of cumulative knowledge in psychology" (p. 115), and some methodologists have called on the American Psychological Association to consider banning the use of significance tests in its journals (Shrout, 1997). Although others have argued that the case against null hypothesis significance tests has been overstated (e.g., Abelson, 1997; Cortina & Dunlap, 1997), there is a growing consensus that such tests are often used and interpreted inappropriately.

One of the problems associated with null hypothesis significance tests is that researchers often misinterpret the meaning of the significance or p-value associated with them. The p-value is a conditional probability that represents the probability of obtaining a sample estimate of a parameter (e.g., mean, correlation) that meets or exceeds a particular value *if the null hypothesis is true*. These p-values play a central role in significance tests. If it falls below a specified cutoff (usually $p < .05$), the researcher concludes that there is little support for the null hypothesis and that it should therefore be rejected; otherwise, the decision is made not to reject the null hypothesis (i.e., no conclusion is reached) (Cohen, 1994). Setting a cutoff for rejecting the null hypothesis establishes the probability of making a Type I error, defined as rejecting the null hypothesis when it is true. The p-value is based on the assumption that the null hypothesis is true. It does not indicate the probability that the null hypothesis is false, nor can it be used to determine the probability that the results would be replicated (see Cohen, 1994). The extent to which individuals persist in misinterpreting p-values is made clear to me each year when I ask students in my graduate-level statistics course to explain what it means to say something is significant at $p < .05$. Invariably, I get a wide range of answers, most of which are incorrect. I go to great lengths to explain the correct interpretation, only to see most of my students select the incorrect interpretation on their exams. Obtaining a statistically significant finding may mean much less than many researchers tend to believe (Cohen, 1994).

Obtaining a statistically significant result will lead us to reject the null hypothesis, which typically states that the effect is equal to zero, but it does not provide any indication of the expected magnitude of the effect. As Rosenthal (1995) pointed out, the results of a significance test are a function of the size of an effect *and* the size of the sample. A "highly significant" effect could reflect a very large effect, a very large sample, or both. This was illustrated by Cohen (1990), who discussed a study that reported a significant correlation between children's height and scores on both intelligence and achievement tests based on a sample of 14,000. He points out that given the sample size, a correlation of $r = .0278$ would be significant at $p < .001$. If this correlation reflected a causal relationship between height and IQ, "raising a child's IQ from 100 to 130 would require giving the child enough growth hormone to increase his or her height by 14 feet" (Cohen, 1990, p. 1309). As this example illustrates, determining that an effect is statistically significant says little about its *theoretical* or *practical* significance. Scarr (1997) observed that researchers often confuse these concepts when they refer to an effect significant at $p < .001$ as "highly significant." She suggests that researchers abandon such uses of the term significance to avoid drawing misleading conclusions about the importance of research findings.

The limited information provided by significance tests has led to frequent calls for researchers to address the "clinical significance" or practical importance of their findings (Kazdin, 1994; Kendall & Norton-Ford, 1982). Such efforts have, however, been complicated by the fact that most psychological measures are based on arbitrary units of measurement (Sechrest, McKnight, & McKnight, 1996). This makes it difficult to interpret the magnitude of effects expressed in terms of raw score units such as differences between treatment means, and unstandardized regression coefficients. Some researchers have advocated the use of a norm-referenced approach to addressing the issue of clinical significance in psychotherapy outcome studies (e.g., Jacobson & Truax, 1991; Kendall & Grove, 1988). This approach represents a particular definition of clinical significance that focuses on how close an individual has moved toward a nonclinical reference sample, rather than on the actual magnitude of the change. At a more general level, Sechrest et al. have called for greater efforts to calibrate measures into units that have inherent meaning. Such efforts would greatly facilitate our ability to evaluate clinical significance. In the absence of meaningful measurement units, most measures of effect size are based on standardized coefficients that represent relationships among variables after they have been converted to standardized scores (i.e., z-scores). Examples include mean differences in standardized scores, correlations, and standardized regression weights (Cohen, 1988). Although standardized coefficients facilitate comparisons of findings across studies where different measures have been used, such coefficients are more sensitive to sample characteristics than unstandardized coefficients (Cohen & Cohen, 1983). More generally, point estimates of effect size and other parameters based on the results of an individual study are only rough approximations of the population parameters they are attempting to estimate. How closely they approximate the actual parameters depends on the degree of sampling error, which is a function of the sample size. For these reasons, researchers have been encouraged to report parameter estimates in the form of confidence intervals. Confidence intervals have been offered as an alternative to null hypothesis significance tests because they provide a clear estimate of error, in that a 95% confidence interval can be expected to include the actual population value 95% of the time (Cohen, 1994; Schmidt, 1996). Their use reflects the degree of accuracy of the sample estimates and demonstrates the increase in accuracy that occurs as the sample size is increased. The same basic approach used to calculate confidence intervals for parameters such as means (e.g., Winer, 1971) and correlations (e.g., Cohen & Cohen,

1983) can be used to estimate other parameters such as factor loadings and path coefficients in a structural equation model.

Null hypothesis significance tests have also been criticized for focusing exclusively on the probability of making a Type I error without addressing the probability of a Type II error (i.e., not rejecting the null hypothesis when it is in fact false) (Cohen, 1990, 1994; Hunter, 1997). Although standards for the probability of making a Type I error have been well established (i.e., $p < .05$) and closely monitored by researchers, journal reviewers, editors, and others, the probability of making a Type II error is rarely even reported. For any given study, the Type II error rate can be determined as a function of three parameters. In particular, it will decrease as the alpha level, effect size, and number of observations increase (Cohen, 1988). In a classic article, Cohen (1962) conducted a power analysis of all studies published in the 1960 volume of the *Journal of Abnormal and Social Psychology* and estimated an average Type II error rate of .52 for medium effect sizes. In other words, a researcher would have a less than 50-50 chance of correctly rejecting the null hypothesis when the effect size in the population was at least medium. A more recent review of articles published in the *Journal of Abnormal Psychology* 24 years later by Sedlmeier and Gigerenzer (1989) indicated that this situation has not improved. Their analysis revealed that the average Type II error rate for medium effects was .56. Consideration of adjustments to reduce experimentwise error rates further increased this error rate to .63. This disparity between Type I and Type II error rates indicates that researchers are unlikely to make errors when the null hypothesis is true (e.g., when there are no effects), but that they have less than a 50-50 chance of making a correct decision when an alternative hypothesis is true (i.e., that there is at least a medium effect present). Critics of significance tests have argued that the null hypothesis that a parameter is equal to zero is almost never true and that the use of such tests therefore results in more incorrect decisions than correct decisions (Cohen, 1994; Hunter, 1997).

One of the more serious criticisms of null hypothesis significance tests is that their use has impeded systematic progress within the field by creating the illusion of inconsistent findings across studies. Schmidt (1996), in particular, has demonstrated how a series of studies that all provide the same estimate of the size of an effect can lead to the appearance of inconsistent findings when the outcome is based on the results of significance tests. Because significance tests are a function of the size of the effect and the size of the sample, comparisons of the results of significance tests for studies that have identical effect sizes, but different sample sizes, may lead to inconsistent conclusions such that some studies have significant results and others do not. If the majority produce nonsignificant results, a case that is likely to occur when the effect size or sample size is small, a reviewer may conclude that there is no support for the presence of an effect. An alternative interpretation may be that a moderator variable or variables are leading to the presence of an effect in some studies but not in others. Schmidt argued that both conclusions may be false and demonstrated how a meta-analysis based on effect size estimates rather than the results of significance tests will lead to the correct interpretation of the findings. A similar point was made by Abelson (1997):

> We act foolishly when we celebrate results with $p = .05$, but wallow in self-pity when $p = .07$. It is more subtly misguided when we lay a "significant" outcome alongside a "nonsignificant" one and make a comparative claim. For example, we might say, "The

experimental effect is significant for wombats but not for dingbats, confirming the hypothesized importance of the bats factor." The error here is easy to understand when results for the wombats reach $p = .05$ and for the dingbats only .07, but the error still applies in less obvious cases. (p. 12)

The area of greatest disagreement between proponents and critics of null hypothesis significance tests concerns the best way to interpret the results of an individual study. Schmidt (1996) has argued that issues should not be decided on the basis of a single study, but that "any individual study must be considered a data point to be contributed to a future meta-analysis" (p. 127). He contends that the pattern of citations in the literature and textbooks has shifted from primary studies to meta-analyses, and that discoveries and advances in cumulative knowledge are more likely to be made by those who do meta-analyses, rather than by those who do primary research studies. Such meta-analyses are based on effect size estimates rather than the results of individual significance tests. A carefully conducted meta-analysis can provide a strong basis for drawing conclusions about a phenomenon that has been well researched. There are, however, many areas that have not been studied in sufficient depth to permit a meta-analysis, and there must be some basis for determining whether a particular line of research merits further study based on a few initial studies (Abelson, 1997). How are the results of an individual study to be interpreted? Schmidt suggested the reporting of effect size estimates with confidence intervals and argues that little can be learned from an individual study. Others, in particular Cortina and Dunlap (1997), find confidence intervals lacking because they do not provide an objective indication of the extent to which the researcher's hypotheses are supported by the data. It is difficult to conceive of a situation where authors of individual studies will not wish to reach some conclusions regarding the degree of support for their theoretical hypothesis, regardless of how tentative these conclusions may be. Although the results of a null hypothesis significance test should not be considered in isolation from considerations of effect size and power, significance tests may be a useful part of a more comprehensive analysis of an individual study (Abelson, 1995). At the more cumulative level, estimated effect sizes will no doubt provide a stronger basis for integrating the findings across studies.

SUMMARY AND CONCLUSIONS

Clinical researchers have access to an increasingly wide variety of sophisticated statistical tools that are well suited to the complex nature of clinical problems. These tools have the potential for improving the quality of clinical research, but only if they are properly used. Proper use requires not only a basic understanding of the procedures themselves, but an appreciation of more general principles that should guide their selection, use, and interpretation. This chapter discussed these principles as they relate to investigating the properties of the data being analyzed, selecting a statistical method, and interpreting the results.

Preliminary analyses are also an essential part of any data analysis plan. Total reliance on summary statistics generated by statistical packages often serves to distance researchers from their data. Fortunately, such packages also have the capability of generating information about individual data points and patterns in the data that can provide researchers with a clearer understanding of their data. This information can be used to help the researcher address important issues related to outliers, patterns of missing data, and distribution properties of each variable. Frequent reliance on indirect measures of constructs also requires careful consideration of the researcher's measurement model and the extent to which it fits the data.

Proper use of statistical techniques requires a close match between the method of analysis and the research questions. The nature of the variables being examined will set certain limits on the most appropriate method of analysis. In designing their data analysis, researchers must also be sensitive to the extent to which their hypotheses are exploratory or confirmatory in nature. Studies in a relatively new research area are often exploratory and are best served by exploratory data analyses designed to discover underlying patterns in the data. The results of such studies may be used to generate theory and form the basis of confirmatory studies that determine the conditions under which these findings can be replicated. For other studies, researchers may have fairly specific hypotheses. These hypotheses may differ in their degree of specificity. In some cases, researchers may simply wish to determine the extent to which one variable can be predicted from a set of other variables. In others, they may have more specific hypotheses that can be represented in a path diagram that specifies hypotheses about the causal relationships within a set of variables. In each case, the hypotheses should be stated as specifically as possible, and the analysis should be designed to provide a clear test of the extent to which the hypotheses fit the data. Exploratory and confirmatory analyses can often be complementary. For example, failure to find support for hypotheses in a confirmatory study may set the stage for exploratory analyses. In either case, it is essential that the data analysis approach reflects the nature of the hypotheses.

Renewed debate over the merits of null hypothesis significance testing has led to a healthy examination of the approach we take to interpreting the results of our studies. It seems clear that there is little value in continuing to interpret findings solely on the basis of whether or not they are statistically significant. At a minimum, this needs to be supplemented with a discussion of the magnitude of effects and their margin of error (i.e., use of confidence intervals). Such estimates of effect sizes and confidence intervals are readily available from most statistical packages across a variety of analytic methods. In cases where findings are not statistically significant, the issue of Type II error rates should also be addressed. Our credibility as a science has clearly been damaged by our tendency to confuse statistical significance with clinical significance or practical importance. Statistical significance will likely remain an important criterion for determining the outcome of an individual study. It is not, however, the only criterion, nor necessarily the most important one. At the more cumulative level, meta-analytic methods based on estimates of effect size appear to provide a stronger basis for integrating the findings of a series of studies.

The types of questions being asked by clinical researchers have become increasingly complex as the field has matured. As our theories become more refined we have become less focused on main effects and more interested in interactions among variables. We have also moved beyond examining simple bivariate relationships to more complex models of the relationships within a set of variables. Further evidence of the increasing complexity of clinical research is provided by the other chapters in this volume. Developments in statistical methods have provided clinical researchers with an impressive array of potential tools that are well suited to many of the types of problems they address. Several of these tools were highlighted in this chapter. An impressive array of tools does not, however, make a good craftsman, nor does it guarantee an excellent finished product. An old adage claims that to someone with a hammer, everything looks like a nail. To carry this metaphor further, many of the sophisticated multivariate procedures available to clinical researchers are more like a power router with a full set of attachments. When such a tool is appropriate for the job and the right attachments are used, it can lead to impressive results. With improper use, the results can be a disaster. On the other hand, sometimes all you need is a really good hammer.

REFERENCES

Abelson, R. P. (1995). *Statistics as principled argument.* Mahwah, NJ: Erlbaum.

Abelson, R. P. (1997). On the surprising longevity of flogged horses: Why there is a case for the significance test. *Psychological Science, 8,* 12–15.

Acock, A. C. (1997). Working with missing values. *Family Science Review, 10,* 76–102.

Aiken, L. S., & West, S. G. (1991). *Multiple regression: Testing and interpreting interactions.* Thousand Oaks, CA: Sage.

Aiken, L. S., West, S. G., Sechrest, L., & Reno, R. R. (1990). Graduate training in statistics, methodology, and measurement in psychology: A survey of PhD programs in North America. *American Psychologist, 45,* 721–734.

Anderson, J. C., & Gerbing, D. W. (1988). Structural equation modeling in practice: A review and recommended two-step approach. *Psychological Bulletin, 103,* 411–423.

Anderson, J. G. (1987). Structural equation models in the social and behavioral sciences: Model building. *Child Development, 58,* 49–64.

Bakan, D. (1966). The test of significance in psychological research. *Psychological Bulletin, 66,* 423–437.

Baron, R. M., & Kenny, D. A. (1986). The moderator-mediator variable distinction in social psychological research: Conceptual, strategic, and statistical considerations. *Journal of Personality and Social Psychology, 51,* 1173–1182.

Behrens, J. T. (1997). Principles and procedures of exploratory data analysis. *Psychological Methods, 2,* 131–160.

Bollen, K. A. (1989). *Structural equations with latent variables.* New York: Wiley.

Bryant, F. B., & Yarnold, P. R. (1995). Principal-components analysis and exploratory and confirmatory factor analysis. In L. G. Grimm & P. R. Yarnold (Eds.), *Reading and understanding multivariate statistics* (pp. 99–136). Washington DC: American Psychological Association.

Bryk, A. S., & Raudenbush, S. W. (1992). *Hierarchical linear models: Applications and data analysis methods.* Newbury Park, CA: Sage.

Byrne, B. (1994). *Structural equation modeling with EQS and EQS/Windows: Basic concepts, applications, and programming.* Thousand Oaks, CA: Sage.

Cohen, J. (1960). A coefficient of agreement for nominal scales. *Educational and Psychological Measurement, 20,* 37–46.

Cohen, J. (1962). The statistical power of abnormal-social psychological research: A review. *Journal of Abnormal and Social Psychology, 65,* 145–153.

Cohen, J. (1988). *Statistical power for the behavioral sciences* (2nd ed.). Hillsdale, NJ: Erlbaum.

Cohen, J. (1990). Things I have learned (so far). *American Psychologist, 45,* 1304–1312.

Cohen, J. (1994). The earth is round (*p* < .05). *American Psychologist, 49,* 997–1003.

Cohen, J., & Cohen, P. (1983). *Applied multiple regression/correlation analysis for the behavior sciences.* Hillsdale, NJ: Erlbaum.

Collins, L. M., &. Horn, J. L. (Eds.). (1991). *Best methods for the analysis of change: Recent advances, unanswered questions, future directions.* Washington, DC: American Psychological Association.

Cortina, J. M., & Dunlap, W. P. (1997). On the logic and purpose of significance testing. *Psychological Methods, 2,* 161–172.

Crosbie, J. (1993). Interrupted time-series analysis with brief single-subject data. *Journal of Consulting and Clinical Psychology, 61,* 966–974.

Curran, P. J., Stice, E., & Chassin, L. (1997). The relation between adolescent alcohol use and peer alcohol use: A longitudinal random coefficients model. *Journal of Consulting and Clinical Psychology, 65,* 130–140.

Darlington, R. B. (1990). *Regression and linear models.* New York: McGraw-Hill.

Donovan, J. E., Jessor, R., & Costa, M. (1988). Syndrome of problem behavior in adolescence: A replication. *Journal of Consulting and Clinical Psychology, 56,* 762–765.

Estes, W. K. (1997). Significance testing in psychological research: Some persisting issues. *Psychological Science, 8,* 18–20.

Farrell, A. D. (1991). Computers and behavioral assessment: Current applications, future possibilities, and obstacles to routine use. *Behavioral Assessment, 13,* 159–179.

Farrell, A. D. (1994). Structural equation modeling with longitudinal data: Strategies for examining group differences and reciprocal relationships. *Journal of Consulting and Clinical Psychology, 62,* 477–487.

Farrell, A. D. (in press). Development and evaluation of problem frequency scales from version 3 of the computerized assessment system for psychotherapy evaluation and research (CASPER). *Journal of Clinical Psychology.*

Farrell, A. D., & Bruce, S. E. (1997). Impact of exposure to community violence on violent behavior and emotional distress among urban adolescents. *Journal of Clinical Child Psychology, 26,* 2–14.

Farrell, A. D., Danish, S. J., & Howard, C. W. (1991). Evaluation of data screening methods in surveys of adolescents' drug use. *Psychological Assessment, 3,* 295–298.

Farrell, A. D., & Meyer, A. L. (1997). The effectiveness of a school-based curriculum for reducing violence among sixth grade students. *American Journal of Public Health, 87,* 979–984.

Farrell, A. D., & White, K. S. (1998). Peer influences and drug use among urban adolescents: Family structure and parent-adolescent relationship as protective factors. *Journal of Consulting and Clinical Psychology, 66,* 248–258.

Flick, S. N. (1988). Managing attrition in clinical research. *Clinical Psychology Review, 8,* 499–515.

Floyd, F. J., & Widaman, J. F. (1995). Factor analysis in the development and refinement of clinical assessment instruments. *Psychological Assessment, 7,* 286–299.

Gottman, J. M. (Ed.). (1995). *The analysis of change.* Mahwah, NJ: Erlbaum.

Graham, J. W., Collins, L. M., Wugalter, S. E., Chung, N. K., & Hansen, W. B. (1991). Modeling transitions in latent stage-sequential processes: A substance use prevention example. *Journal of Consulting and Clinical Psychology, 59,* 48–57.

Hedeker, D., & Gibbons, R. D. (1997). Application of random-effects pattern-mixture models for missing data in longitudinal studies. *Psychological Methods, 2,* 64–78.

Holmbeck, G. N. (1997). Toward terminological, conceptual, and statistical clarity in the study of mediators and moderators: Examples from the child-clinical and pediatric psychology literatures. *Journal of Consulting and Clinical Psychology, 65,* 599–610.

Howard, K. I., Moras, K., Brill, P. L., Martinovich, Z., & Lutz, W. (1996). Evaluation of psychotherapy: Efficacy, effectiveness, and patient progress. *American Psychologist, 51,* 1059–1064.

Hoyle, R. H. (1991). Evaluating measurement models in clinical research: Covariance structure analysis of latent variable models of self conception. *Journal of Consulting and Clinical Psychology, 59,* 67–76.

Hoyle, R. H. (1994). Introduction to the special section: Structural equation modeling in clinical research. *Journal of Consulting and Clinical Psychology, 62,* 427–428.

Hu, L., Bentler, P. M., & Kano, Y. (1992). Can test statistics in covariance structure analysis be trusted? *Psychological Bulletin, 112,* 351–362.

Huberty, C. J., & Morris, J. D. (1989). Multivariate analysis versus multiple univariate analyses. *Psychological Bulletin, 105,* 302–308.

Hunter, J. E. (1997). Needed: A ban on the significance test. *Psychological Science, 8,* 3–7.

Jaccard, J., Turrisi, R., & Wan, C. K. (1990). *Interaction effects in multiple regression.* Thousand Oaks, CA: Sage.

Jaccard, J., & Wan, C. K. (1996). *LISREL approaches to interaction effects in multiple regression.* Thousand Oaks, CA: Sage.

Jacobson, N. S., & Truax, P. (1991). Clinical significance: A statistical approach to defining meaningful change in psychotherapy research. *Journal of Consulting and Clinical Psychology, 59,* 12–19.

Jöreskog, K. G. (1969). A general approach to confirmatory maximum likelihood factor analysis. *Psychometrika, 34,* 183–202.

Kazdin, A. E. (1994). *Research design in clinical psychology* (2nd ed.). New York: Macmillan.

Kendall, P. C., Flannery-Schroeder, E., & Ford, J. D. (1999). Randomized clinical trials. In P. C. Kendall, J. N. Butcher, & G. N. Holmbeck (Eds.), *Handbook of research methods in clinical psychology.* New York: Wiley.

Kendall, P. C., & Grove, W. (1988). Normative comparisons in therapy outcome research. *Behavioral Assessment, 10,* 147–158.

Kendall, P. C., & Norton-Ford, J. D. (1982). Therapy outcome research methods. In P. C. Kendall & J. N. Butcher (Eds.), *Handbook of research methods in clinical psychology* (pp. 429–460). New York: Wiley.

Keppel, G. (1982). *Design and analysis: A researcher's handbook* (2nd ed.). Englewood Cliffs, NJ: Prentice-Hall.

Kerlinger, F. N. (1986). *Foundations of behavioral research* (3rd ed.). New York: Holt, Rinehart and Winston.

Kirk, R. E. (1982). *Experimental design* (2nd ed.). Belmont, CA: Wadsworth.

Klem, L. (1995). Path analysis. In L. G. Grimm & P. R. Yarnold (Eds.), *Reading and understanding multivariate statistics* (pp. 65–97). Washington, DC: American Psychological Association.

Lemmon, G. R. (1983). *Behavioral rehearsal of partner attention: Social skill remediation of loneliness among the separated and divorced.* Unpublished doctoral dissertation, Virginia Commonwealth University.

Little, R. J. A., & Rubin, D. B. (1990). The analysis of social science data with missing values. *Sociological Methods and Research, 18,* 292–326.

Little, R. J. A., & Schenker, N. (1995). Missing data. In G. H. Arminger, C. C. Clogg, & M. E. Sobel (Eds.), *Handbook of statistical modeling for the social and behavioral sciences* (pp. 39–75). New York: Plenum Press.

Loftus, G. R. (1996). Psychology will be a much better science when we change the way we analyze data. *Current Directions in Psychological Science, 5,* 161–171.

Long, J. S. (1983). *Covariance structure models: An introduction to LISREL*. Thousand Oaks, CA: Sage.

MacCallum, R. C., Roznowski, M., & Necowitz, L. B. (1992). Model modifications in covariance structure analysis: The problem of capitalization on chance. *Psychological Bulletin, 111*, 490–504.

Mueser, K. T., Curran, P. J., & McHugo, G. J. (1997). Factor structure of the brief psychiatric rating scale in schizophrenia. *Psychological Assessment, 9*, 196–204.

Mulaik, S. A. (1972). *The foundations of factor analysis*. New York: McGraw-Hill.

Newman, F. L. (1994). Selection of design and statistical procedures for progress and outcome assessment. In M. Maruish (Ed.), *Use of psychological testing for treatment planning and outcome assessment* (pp. 111–134). Hillsdale, NJ: Erlbaum.

Newman, F. L., & Ciarlo, J. A. (1994). Criteria for selection psychological instruments for treatment outcome assessment. In M. Maruish (Ed.), *Use of psychological testing for treatment planning and outcome assessment* (pp. 98–110). Hillsdale, NJ: Erlbaum.

Newman, F. L., & Howard, K. I. (1991). Introduction to the special section on seeking new clinical research methods. *Journal of Consulting and Clinical Psychology, 59*, 8–11.

Nich, C., & Carroll, K. (1997). Now you see it, now you don't: A comparison of traditional versus random-effects regression models in the analysis of longitudinal follow-up data from a clinical trial. *Journal of Consulting and Clinical Psychology, 65*, 252–261.

Norušis, M. J. (1993). *SPSS for Windows: Base system user's guide*. Chicago: SPSS.

Nunally, J. (1960). The place of statistics in psychology. *Educational and Psychological Measurement, 20*, 641–650.

Nunally, J. C. (1978). *Psychometric theory* (2nd ed.). New York: McGraw-Hill.

Palma, T. R., & Farrell, A. D. (1997, November). *Development of the Adolescent Expectations of Peer Support Scale (AEPSS)*. Paper presented at the annual convention of the Association for Advancement of Behavior Therapy, Miami, FL.

Pedhazur, E. J. (1982). *Multiple regression in behavioral research: Explanation and prediction*. New York: Holt, Rinehart and Winston.

Rogosa, D. (1995). Myths and methods: "Myths about longitudinal research" plus supplemental questions. In J. M. Gottman (Ed.), *The analysis of change* (pp. 67–82). Mahwah, NJ: Erlbaum.

Rosenthal, R. (1995). Progress in clinical psychology: Is there any? *Clinical Psychology: Science and Practice, 2*, 133–150.

Rosnow, R. L., & Rosenthal, R. (1988). Focused tests of significance and effect size estimation in counseling psychology. *Journal of Counseling Psychology, 35*, 203–208.

Rozeboom, W. W. (1960). The fallacy of the null-hypothesis significance test. *Psychological Bulletin, 57*, 416–428.

Scarr, S. (1997). Rules of evidence: A larger context for the statistical debate. *Psychological Science, 8*, 16–17.

Schmidt, F. L. (1996). Statistical significance testing and cumulative knowledge in psychology: Implications for training of researchers. *Psychological Methods, 1*, 115–129.

Schmitt, N. (1996). Uses and abuses of coefficient alpha. *Psychological Assessment, 8*, 350–353.

Sechrest, L., McKnight, P., & McKnight, K. (1996). Calibration of measures for psychotherapy outcome studies. *American Psychologist, 51*, 1065–1071.

Sedlmeier, P., & Gigerenzer, G. (1989). Do studies of statistical power have an effect on the power of studies? *Psychological Bulletin, 105*, 309–316.

Shrout, P. E. (1997). Should significance tests be banned? *Psychological Science, 8*, 1–2.

Siegel, S., & Castellan, N. J., Jr. (1988). *Nonparametric statistics for the behavioral sciences* (2nd ed.). New York: McGraw-Hill.

Silva, A. P. D., & Stam, A. (1995). Discriminant analysis. In L. G. Grimm & P. R. Yarnold (Eds.), *Reading and understanding multivariate statistics* (pp. 277–318). Washington, DC: American Psychological Association.

Strupp, H. H. (1996). The tripartite model and the *Consumer Reports* study. *American Psychologist, 51,* 1017–1024.

Tabachnick, B. G., & Fidell, L. S. (1996). *Using multivariate statistics* (3rd ed.). New York: HarperCollins.

Wampold, B. E., Davis, B., & Good, R. H., III. (1990). Hypothesis validity of clinical research. *Journal of Consulting and Clinical Psychology, 58,* 360–367.

Widaman, K. F. (1985). Hierarchically nested covariance structure models for multitrait multimethod data. *Applied Psychological Measurement, 9,* 1–26.

Willett, J. B., & Sayer, A. G. (1994). Using covariance structure analysis to detect correlates and predictors of individual change over time. *Psychological Bulletin, 116,* 363–381.

Willett, J. B., & Singer, J. D. (1993). Investigating onset, cessation, relapse, and recovery: Why you should, and how you can, use discrete-time series analysis to examine event occurrence. *Journal of Consulting and Clinical Psychology, 61,* 952–965.

Winer, B. J. (1971). *Statistical principles in experimental design* (2nd ed.). New York: McGraw-Hill.

Chapter 5

Focus Chapter

PUBLISHING AND COMMUNICATING RESEARCH FINDINGS: SEEKING SCIENTIFIC OBJECTIVITY

Larry E. Beutler, Ph.D., and Benny R. Martin, M.A.

"Publish or perish," the academic scientist's credo, must invoke for many a memory of the well-known *New Yorker* cartoon's countering epitaph: "Published but perished anyway." Embodied in these two truths is the fledgling scientist's dilemma: to publish, but how and at what price?

By its very nature, science is a public process. Publication in science is affected by two counterforces. Scientific journals provide a necessary means of communication among scientists and thereby reduce the likelihood of repeating others' mistakes. But, scientific articles also open the ideas, procedures, and findings of investigators to critique by colleagues. These two processes invoke often opposing forces: the ideals of scientific accuracy, objectivity, and the advancement of knowledge, on one hand, and professional advancement and allotment of grants, on the other. The first exerts pressure to ensure that human bias is removed from the equation that guides the report of scientific findings, but the second exerts pressure to sacrifice objectivity for the sake of personal or political advantages. Sometimes, unfortunately, the latter force wins, as witnessed in reports of scientific fraud. Scientists are aware of this danger and this is why they discourage the distribution of research findings through the mass media, preferring instead the process of peer review to ensure that reasonable levels of objectivity are maintained.

At least some of the factors that pose threats to scientific objectivity can be improved by the use of better procedures, more sophisticated statistical analyses, and more sensitive measurement procedures. A publication can never totally represent the complexity of the research design or the day-to-day research decisions that are made. Authors must select what is presented, and personal blind spots and social biases may be introduced in this process. Some potentially insidious omissions may include the failure to reveal minor breaches of blind controls or violations of randomization. Often, biases may be inserted for "good" social reasons or to avoid conflict with established social beliefs. In many cases, these threats to objectivity are difficult to correct because the solutions strike at favored philosophies, assumptions, and biases both of individual scientists and of a discipline of inquiry.

This chapter explores some of the methodological and sociopolitical forces that affect the nature of published reports, with particular attention to psychotherapy research. We begin with a brief review of some of the forces that can or may affect the transmission of information. Next, we turn to the task of identifying the more general sociopolitical environment of science that threatens the quality of scientific communication.

THREATS TO VALIDITY THAT ARE INTRINSIC TO BEHAVIORAL SCIENCE RESEARCH

Although a discussion of threats to objectivity must necessarily highlight negative aspects of the publication process, we must not lose sight of the many positive aspects of behavioral science methods. The peer review process, for example, has been a major force that has ensured the progression of knowledge. The emergence of peer review boards broadly increased the reliability of reports over that achieved in the pre-WWII "personal" and single-editor journals.

When a scientist or group of scientists have reached a point where they desire to report a finding, they submit a copy (usually from three to four copies) of the report to a professional journal. Table 5.1 outlines the lengthy and time-consuming steps that ensue before the manuscript is published. Journals vary widely in quality, rejection rates, and prestige. Highly sought after journals may publish 30% or fewer of the papers submitted. Others may publish any submission for a fee. It is common for scientists to work their way down the ladder of prestige until they find a publisher who finds their methods acceptable. Because of these variations in quality, any seemingly important research finding must be proven by independent replication. Moreover,

Table 5.1.   Steps taken for manuscript review and publication (1, 5, 8 handled by author; 2–4, 6–7, 9 handled by editor/journal)

1. Author submits manuscript to journal (waits approximately 2 mos.).
2. Editor receives and acknowledges.
3. From 2 to 5 independent and usually anonymous reviewers are asked to critique the paper.
4. Informs author that paper is accepted, rejected, or is invited for resubmission (editor waits about 2 mos.).
5. If manuscript is accepted, author makes changes needed for publication. If manuscript is rejected, author sends to another journal. If invited to resubmit, author *may* revise and resubmit or send to another journal (waits 1–2 mos.).
6. If manuscript is resubmitted, editor may seek additional review or accept; may also ask for one or more revisions.
7. If manuscript goes to print, editor seeks an assurance of accuracy from the author: a signed form. Galley proofs printed and sent to author.
8. Author reviews galley proofs for accuracy and returns (waits 6–9 mos.).
9. Manuscript is published (18 mos. to 2 yrs. after submission).

when judging one another's accomplishments for advancement or recognition, scientists attempt to balance the productivity of an individual with the relative status of the journals in which he or she has published.

The influence of social forces on scientific objectivity does not begin with the submission and peer review of a scientific paper, however. A variety of forces may both positively and negatively affect how a problem is selected for study, how participants are identified, what research procedures are used, and the nature of the analyses long before the influence of peer review is invoked.

The seemingly simple selection of a topic for study is influenced by the priorities of agencies that support the investigator or fund the project, scientific groups that review the proposal for merit, review boards that must approve its being conducted at a specific location, and the professional societies with whom the scientist identifies. At each of these levels, the priorities are made or influenced by other scientists. Because these scientists are people with their own histories and priorities, their advice reflects, to various degrees, extrascientific values. Editors and journal policy boards are the final gatekeepers to scientific communication, but their actions are always reflective of the policies and values of several groups.

In this section, we consider (a) factors that influence the establishment of priorities among research topics, (b) threats to the representativeness of samples, (c) efforts to standardize dependent variables in outcome research, (d) issues in the use of probability testing procedures, and (e) concerns with the peer review process.

Social Influences on Establishing Research Priorities

To a large extent, the priority of research areas is determined at a national level by the agencies that govern and control the distribution of research money. In the behavioral sciences, funding has largely come from the National Science Foundation (NSF) and the National Institutes of Health (NIH). To illustrate the extremes, during the Carter administration, mental health research was targeted for priority in funding, but during the Reagan administration, psychosocial research of any type was discouraged and biological research was highlighted in the Decade of the Brain. Large-scale studies on psychosocial treatments, such as the Treatment of Depression Collaborative Research Program (TDCRP; Elkin, 1994; Elkin, Gibbons, Shea, & Shaw, 1996; Elkin, Parloff, Hadley, & Autry, 1985; Elkin et al., 1989), that survived the priorities of the Reagan administration strongly felt the shift toward biological priorities in the way manuscripts were reviewed and how information was disseminated.

Psychotherapy researchers also felt the influence of biological research priorities in indirect ways. In the 1980s, biological research led to a redefinition of the research designs that earned federal funding. The TDCRP initiated the application of randomized clinical trials (RCT) research designs, which were extrapolated directly from psychopharmacological research programs. This research model has come to be seen as the gold standard for assessing the efficacy of treatments (Kendall, this volume; Klein, 1996; Mann & Kupfer, 1993). Although RCT methods have come under attack as inadequate to the task of accurately assessing psychotherapy as a treatment in the real world (Seligman, 1995), they continue to be accepted as the defining criteria for indexing when a psychotherapy has been adequately validated (Chambless et al., 1996), and a research proposal based on a different design is unlikely to receive federal funding.[1]

Threats to the Representativeness of Samples

The value of treatment research hinges on its ability to be generalized to real-world groups. In turn, generalization depends on whether the samples studied are similar to those treated in conventional clinical practices. Randomizing samples to treatment conditions is one of the major procedures used to ensure representativeness (Shaver, 1993). Recently, however, the assumptions that underlie the use of random assignment in treatment outcome research have been seriously questioned on two grounds: random assignment is seldom random, and problems of institutionalized racial and sexual biases are not addressed in the usual passive methods of reporting participants' demographic qualities.

Howard and colleagues (Howard, Kopta, Krause, & Orlinsky, 1986) have aptly demonstrated that the usual random assignment procedures are subject to considerable influence from nonrandom factors. For example, depending on the restrictiveness and purity of the sample to be used in an RCT study, a large number of people may be screened before finding those who fit the criteria needed for a study. Howard et al. cite examples in which the final sample of randomized participants represent fewer than 20% of those available. In such instances, the samples studied in RCT research cannot be considered to be representative of the patients on whom the treatments are to be practiced. Real-world patients usually have more severe and complicated problems, are more likely to carry multiple diagnoses, and more frequently have chronic personality disturbances than the patients studied in randomized treatment research. Thus, generalization is possibly hazardous, and the treatments developed under controlled conditions may be uninformed and simplistic (Seligman, 1995, 1996). This problem can be intensified because of attrition bias—patients don't drop out of treatment in a random way.

These factors have given rise to renewed emphasis on the use of naturalistic settings, quasi-experimental designs, and effectiveness studies that address clinical utility (Hoagwood, Hibbs, Brent, & Jensen, 1995; Howard, Moras, Brill, Zoran, & Lutz, 1996) as alternatives to RCT (efficacy studies) designs. Whereas efficacy research places great emphasis on the importance of internal validity, it may achieve these ends at the sacrifice of contextual or ecological validity. Effectiveness or clinical utility research, in contrast, is specifically aimed at ensuring generalization of findings by investigating typical groups of patients and contextually feasible treatments (Kazdin, 1992, 1994). These authorities suggest different methods for integrating efficacy and effectiveness research to improve the validity and meaningfulness of subsequent findings. Some journals (e.g., *Journal of Clinical Psychology, Journal of Consulting and Clinical Psychology*) are heeding these concerns and committing some of their resources to publishing studies that address clinical utility.

---

[1] The prestigious *Journal of Consulting and Clinical Psychology* (February, 1998) has recently published a series of articles that explore the strengths and weaknesses of this extrapolation to the definition of "empirically supported treatments."

A second concern in the domain of participant selection is the way that demographic qualities of participants are identified and reported. It is conventional, for example, to report the racial, sexual, and age composition of the sample, ostensibly to allow replication and to account for potential biases in sample selection. The method of obtaining this information is seldom reported, and there are reasons to believe that in the absence of this information, most of these descriptors lack the levels of meaning that are either attributed to or required of them for these purposes (Zuckerman, 1990). Beutler, Brown, Crothers, Booker, and Seabrook (1996) point out that most demographic labels are unreliably determined and of dubious meaning. For example, most individuals are of mixed racial heritage and when asked to self-identify their racial heritage, they must select among their various ancestral histories. When given the opportunity, most refer to themselves as "mixed" or "other" race, and there is as much as 40% disagreement in determining a participant's race as a function of the person offering the designation (Good, 1993).

Similar problems are present with respect to sex and gender determinations. For example, gender refers to one's status with reference to social norms, cultural identity, and sexually related attitudes and preferences, and requires a number of complex judgments. Even biological sex by no means fits nicely within the simple two-category designation that is usually accorded it. Biological sex is determined by a host of factors, including the XX and XY genetic complement, prepartum androgenization of the brain, morphological appearance, and early learning (Bancroft, 1993). Disparities among these various sex-determining conditions are not unusual, but go unnoticed in published demographic descriptors.

A work group of editors convened by the National Institutes of Mental Health (NIMH) have proposed that investigators be asked to describe the methods that were used to measure demographic qualities (e.g., self-report versus observer rating), much as they would be required to do to operationalize any other variable under study (see Beutler, 1996). This recommendation encourages investigators to inspect the effects that these psychological qualities might have on the results of our research.

Threats to the Sensitivity of Dependent Variables

The dependent variables in outcome research are widely varied, reflecting the diversity of theories and preferences that characterize this field and introducing potential bias and error into findings. Lambert (1994) reported that over 40% of the variables considered in published psychotherapy research were based on instruments that had been developed for a specific study. Some (e.g., Kenny & Judd, 1986) have observed that using one sample to both develop a measure and test the theoretical constructs that it is designed to assess introduces idiosyncratic confounds into the measure that limit the generalization of the findings.

Other authors have noted that disparity exists among ratings of improvement made by clinicians, patients, and external observers in treatment-outcome research (Strupp & Hadley, 1977); the unreliability of methods for calculating estimates of change (Beutler & Hamblin, 1986); and the lack of across-study comparability of outcome measures (Lambert, Christensen, & DeJulio, 1983; Waskow & Parloff, 1975) as other factors that limit the sensitivity and specificity of findings. Progress is being made in efforts to reduce sources of error from these factors and to define a standard set of outcome procedures across studies.

Efforts to standardize outcome measures, though originally focused on a specific battery composed of a limited number of particular instruments, have shifted to the selection and prioritization of assessment domains and methods. This procedure both preserves the much needed flexibility in research programs and reduces reliance on old and potentially outmoded tests. Strupp, Horowitz, and Lambert (1997), for example, emphasize the reliance on certain psychometric standards in the selection of instruments and suggest a hierarchy of measurement domains. The first domain would include diagnostic compliance, subjective distress, and functional impairment. These dimensions would derive from different judges—clinician, patient, and a collatoral or external observer, respectively. The second domain of measurement would assess those problems that are specifically targeted for change in a particular treatment or study, and the third level would assess specific, theory-relevant constructs that might advance an understanding of the mechanisms of change or the validity of the guiding theory.

Weaknesses in Probability Testing Procedures

Behavioral science is probabilistic, not exact. Accordingly, it has relied on a statistical estimate that defines the probability of incorrectly concluding that something is true (what is called a Type I error) as a means of assessing the validity of a given finding. This statistical estimate takes into account the unreliability of the outcome measures used and individual differences among those who serve as participants in the study. It does not account for the lack of sample representativeness nor the influence of political forces on the definition of what is important to study. However, there is a growing sentiment that the publication process is too reliant on these indices of statistical significance, and thereby ignores the more important question of the meaningfulness of the findings.

There are several problems with conventional estimates of probability. For example, significance tests indicate the unusualness of findings, not their magnitude or clinical importance (Cohen, 1990). Thus, they are more easily affected by the size of the sample and the reliability of the outcome measure than the size of the difference itself. But, the conventional standard of $p < .05$ indicating that less than a 5% probability that the differences obtained is erroneous is frequently misinterpreted (Cooperschmidt, 1988) as indicating the magnitude of reliable differences. A probability or erroneous finding that is much lower than this conventional value (e.g., $p < .001$) is often inaccurately interpreted as an indication that the difference between the treatments compared is very large and clinically meaningful. A high probability of error (e.g., $p = .60$ or, alternatively, $p > .05$), in contrast, may also be mistaken as an index that two treatments have equivalent effects (this is called a Type II error). Because of imperfections in the instruments that measure outcomes, sometimes very large average differences between treatments are identified as nonsignificant when in fact they are quite meaningful. Although they are not often used, there are methods for assessing the likelihood (probability) that the differences that are observed are reflections of erroneous measurement procedures. Such estimates, however, require information that is not always available and even requires the insertion of arbitrary judgments.

In contrast to estimates of statistical significance, measures of clinical meaningfulness require a direct comparison of treated groups with an index of normal values (Kazdin, 1977). But, nondisturbed, treated control groups are not usually included in outcome studies. As a substitute for normal comparisons, some estimates of clinical meaningfulness use the normative values for the test as a basis for estimating the degree to which treatment returned the patient to a point where his or her scores resemble those of unimpaired individuals. Various methods have been employed to assess this similarity (e.g., Kazdin, 1977; Kendall & Grove, 1988). The most recognized procedures for assessing clinical meaningfulness evaluate the scores typically earned by members of the treated group and statistically estimate whether they are more typical of those who do not seek or need treatment than of those who do (Jacobson & Truax, 1991; Kendall & Grove, 1988).

If the meanings of probability tests are unclear to scientists, they are more so to practitioners, whose familiarity with them is much more limited. Their dissatisfaction is most often expressed as a criticism of the failure of published research to provide information that is relevant to work with the individual patient. The suitability of group statistics for assessing and predicting individual change is still to be determined, though new methods are evolving for applying statistical tests to individual differences (e.g., Kazdin, 1994; Russell, Bryant, & Estrada, 1996).

Confronted with the problems of probability estimates, some have urged the abandonment of probability tests in behavioral publications (e.g., Carver, 1978; Hagan, 1997; Judd, McClelland, & Culhane, 1995). Schmidt (1996) argues for the replacement of significance tests with the use of procedures that provide more direct and exact estimates of predictive accuracy.

Effect size estimates are one way of assessing the magnitude of actual difference between comparison groups and are expressed in standard deviation units. They are relatively independent either of the particular measurement device used or the size of the sample, and thereby allow both estimates of the meaningfulness of findings and comparisons across measures and studies.

In a preliminary report (American Psychological Association, 1996), a task force organized by the American Psychological Association's Science Directorate advocates the computation of effect sizes, complemented by statistics that allow precise estimates of probability and contrasts, such as odds ratios. It also advocates the use of techniques designed to assure that results do not arise from outliers, data abnormalities, or nonrandom influences on missing data, selection, and attrition. Cohen (1990, 1994) points out that these procedures may be insufficient and advocates the use of simplified research designs. He argues for the inclusion of fewer independent and dependent measures in research articles and observes that these procedures, by relying less than is customary on statistics to compensate for weak methods, would lend themselves to easier and simpler data interpretation, including simple visual inspection.

Concerns with Peer Review

The many complicated and contradictory demands of science and politics have been compounded with the advent and advancement of new and quicker ways of communicating research findings. Electronic mail, copiers, fax machines, electronic journals, and

Web sites have all increased the opportunities of both rapid dissemination of information and the probability of premature reports and dissemination of low-quality research. New journals and electronic media increase the speed of science but pose particular problems for quality control in scientific publications (Kassirer, 1992). To maintain adequate review, numerous reviewers are needed, each of whom must have access to expensive equipment to retrieve, print, and protect electronically transmitted information (Flanagin, Glass, & Lundberg, 1992). Obviously, as electronic communication increases, the problems of maintaining the scientific quality of such reports also increase.

Burnham (1990) chronicles the rise of biomedical journals in the nineteenth century, during their often disorderly transition from simple, one-editor productions to the complicated peer review system that evolved in post-WWII America. He points out that early editors searched desperately for enough articles to publish and then published almost every paper submitted. There was no peer review until after 1937, when a federal law was enacted that required that each application for federal cancer funds undergo qualitative review by a panel of experts. Editors suddenly were flooded with papers and had to become selective in what they published. The peer review process was initiated.

Even today, the evolution of low selection rates following qualitative review, as noted by Burnham (1990), has stimulated the development of many new journals of varying quality. This, in turn, threatens the consistency of the peer review process. Burnham contends that contemporary procedures are failing to execute their gatekeeping, quality control, and educational functions. Fisk and Fogg (1990), for example, found that reviewers are at times unreliable, often differ in what attributes they view as constituting strengths and weaknesses, and often disagree about whether to publish a given study.

To protect against the unreliability of reviewers and their potential for biased judgments, many journals have instituted policies for ensuring blind or masked (i.e., anonymous) review, checking reviewer reliabilities against a standard, and programs that train or sensitize reviewers to various problems in the review process. Many journals have implemented these policies. In the midst of these changes, it remains clear that in some form, the peer review process, with all of its problems, is likely to continue. Despite the criticisms, the experience of many authors has been positive, and science has flourished with the use of the peer review process.

PROBLEMS EXTRINSIC TO SCIENTIFIC INQUIRY

There is more to the publication of research papers than the selection of samples and the application of sound statistical methods. The essence of the scientific method is that the procedures used and developed by one group of scientists are shared with others through the processes of peer review. Aside from controlling publication, this procedure provides for cross-validation of findings. Unfortunately, along with these methodological considerations, there is a threat to scientific inquiry from external sources, primarily motivated by political agendas and money (see Table 5.2).

Semir (1996) observes that scientific research often is compromised by social and political pressures, cultural biases, desires for personal aggrandizement, and even by

Table 5.2.   Threats to scientific objectivity

Methodological Threats

1. Social influences on research priorities lead to some topics being ignored or research methods being inappropriate to a given area.
2. Lack of representativeness of samples limits generalization to clinical practice.
3. Lack of standardization in dependent variables introduces error into measures and occludes clear results.
4. Weaknesses in probability testing procedures encourage investigators to overinterpret results and lead to false conclusions.
5. Lack of objectivity in the peer review process results in some important studies being undervalued and inflates the importance of others.

Threats Extrinsic to Scientific Inquiry

1. Promotion policies that link publication to advancement, money, and prestige.
2. The presence of a conflict of interest.
3. The tendency to selectively publish results that support one's prior viewpoints.
4. Redundant and fragmented publication that falsely portrays the importance of certain findings.

the technological revolution. From the policies that govern academic advancement, through pressures that alter the manuscript review process, to those decisions that seek to ensure that publications reflect politically correct decisions, science is becoming decidedly political. These forces threaten to erode the review process and encourage both fraud and misreporting.

Advancement, Money, and Prestige

Neither a science nor a scientist can advance without both money and the support of one's peers. As a result, scientific objectivity can be compromised, at least a little, by the social politics of funding, cultural biases, and struggles for personal aggrandizement (Semir, 1996). Losses of objectivity have been found in a variety of forms, ranging from obvious fraud to premature and unnecessarily fragmented publication. Wilkie (1996) recalls numerous cases of scientific fraud, errors, and mistakes that have blackened the eyes of scientific objectivity, ranging from the fraudulent data of Sir Cyril Burt to those of any number of modern-day aspirants to fame and fortune.

At the level of science, these political pressures and policies dilute the pragmatic and social value of systems that were designed to ensure both that advancement within the scientific community is predicated on the quality of one's achievement and potential, and that scientists are able to communicate with one another (Kassirer, 1992). Universities differ in levels of prestige, largely as a function of the recognition given to the research of their faculties. The academic climate of the Major Research Universities, a formal designation assigned by the Carnegie-Mellon Foundation, is very competitive. Fledgling professors typically have seven years to establish themselves as potential leaders in the field. At the end of that time, it is "up or out." They are either advanced in rank and salary or find their way down the academic track to employment in universities that offer less prestige and lower salaries. The relatively high relationship between the length of one's publication record and the probability of advancement in academia is well known to encourage the proliferation of both meaningful and meaningless research. It is easy to see how one whose research aptitude is being challenged might succumb to the temptations of seeking publication shortcuts to improve the probability of survival in the upper reaches of academia. Publication in weak journals, fragmented or piecemeal publications, falsification of data, and plagiarizing work are only three examples of what can occur to threaten the objectivity of science.

However, it is misleading to think that the pressures to falsify and misrepresent data disappear as one passes the initial hurdles of job retention and academic advancement. Very senior scientists are tempted to find shortcuts to ensure continued funding or to advance their status. In the recent past, the public press has described a former head of NIMH who plagiarized others' work in the rush to publish, well-regarded fertility researchers who deceptively used live sperm from nonspousal donors to improve their published rates of inducing pregnancy, and a psychiatry department chair who diverted funds from pharmaceutical research to a sham corporation for his own use.

Once one's prestige as a scientist has been established, there is considerable pressure to retain such indicators of status as grant support and awards, which are dependent on one's being productive and making new discoveries. Extramural funding for research requires proof that one's previous research demonstrates the need and importance of one's next, to-be-funded proposal. But, applying for grants is a time-consuming process, and frequently one must submit a new proposal before the results of the last project are known and published. In such an environment, where one's livelihood and status are dependent on easily modified data, the ingredients are present for rushing to publication with less than objective support of yet-to-be-analyzed results.

Conflict of Interest and Selective Publication

Another threat to data integrity arises when there are institutionalized restrictions on the use and dissemination of data. Rennie (1997) describes a recent case in which results indicating that a thyroid medication may be dangerous were blocked from publication by a clause in the investigator's contract with the drug company that funded the research. Somewhat related are instances in which research findings can be used to develop products from which the author can financially benefit. Examples of this latter type include physicians who own stock in the company whose products they research and scientists whose patents may come to have value depending on the outcomes of their research. In all of these instances, the scientist is in a situation that poses a conflict of interest. Increasingly, journals require authors to sign assurances that they have no vested interest in the products used in the investigation and will share the data obtained with other scientists.

Wilkie (1996) observes that drug companies are among the most likely to have policies and practices that threaten the validity of science. A common example is the policy, exemplified in the recent tobacco company trials, that disallows further funding to investigators who have failed to find congenial results. It is common practice among pharmaceutical houses to offer honoraria, worldwide travel grants, paid attendance at professional meetings, and professional expenses to investigators who are willing to tell their colleagues of their positive results with various products at these meetings. One can imagine that these threats and incentives may persuade an investigator to alter or selectively report the findings that ensure continued funding.

Redundant and Fragmented Publication

Two popular ways of increasing one's rate of publication is through duplicate and fragmented publication (i.e., redundant publication). Duplicate publication is the presentation of the same paper in two different journals under different titles, a clearly unethical practice that also violates the copyright laws of most states. Fragmented publication is harder to identify and police. It is described as the publication of multiple (but different) articles on minor variations of the problem, all derived from the same set of data (Kassirer & Marcia, 1995).

Identifying when fragmented publication has occurred is complicated by the fact that publishing more than one paper on a given study is often necessary to fully report and understand the findings. Often, for example, a large-scale psychotherapy study is too large and complex to report all findings in a single article. The study may contain information about a number of different but conceptually distinct and interesting outcomes (e.g., depression, sexual functioning, marital relationships), all of which deserve publication. It is neither unethical nor illegal to report these findings separately. It is when the division of these reports is judged to cease advancing understanding by their sequential presentation that fragmented publication is considered to be an issue (Angell & Reiman, 1989). Unless readers know that several different reports have come from the same sample of subjects, they may assume that the different reports are independent replications and, collectively, overemphasize the findings by counting the separate papers as replications.

Various councils of editors, including the Publication Board of the American Psychological Association, have developed guidelines to protect against unnecessary fragmentation and duplication. Among other things, these guidelines mandate that the authors indicate when a paper is reporting information on a project that has been previously described, make the results available to reviewers, and supply the editor of journals with a list of related publications on the same set of data (Beutler, 1994).

SUMMARY AND CONCLUSIONS

This chapter has identified some of the threats to the objectivity of science that may be encountered in the process of publishing scientific research. Some of these problems reflect weaknesses in the methods of behavioral science, others constitute the effects of extrinsic political pressures that may influence the reported results and the ways these results are communicated.

In the final analysis, most research is subject to both intrinsic and extrinsic sources of error, and the published report is likely to be a compromise between the scientific ideal of objectivity and the forces of political expediency, political correctness, and the methodological ignorance of a field of inquiry. At many points in the process of carrying out and reporting research, investigators must balance desires for precision against the feasibility and desirability of the work they are attempting to do. For example, Maher (1978) identifies many of the ideal qualities by which a paper should be assessed, and Kraemer (1981) has pointed to the compromises that are tolerable to balance the desirability of scientific objectivity with the constraints placed on research by real-world settings. She contends that critical, insightful, adaptive, and inventive philosophical designs are required to balance science with external realities. Decisions must reflect acceptability, feasibility, power, and costs. Zwick (1997) has suggested a similarly balanced approach to the issue of probability testing.

The biasing influences of promotion and advancement policies, desires to advance one's prestige, and needs for personal aggrandizement represent more insidious influences than those that arise from methodological considerations. The proliferation of poorly monitored journals, the advent of new technologies through which to communicate, and the increasing specialization of most scientific fields threaten to reduce the quality of scientific information and the accuracy of knowledge available to new scientists. Clearly, there is a need for more definable publication criteria for protection against conflict of interest and for monitoring the quality of individual work. In part, these protections will come by increasing the openness of the research and publication process to public inspection. By letting these processes be more visible to the community of scientists and by instituting more collaborative activity, oversight will be a natural consequence (Kassirer, 1992).

The final protection of publication quality is peer review. It is the best avenue available for providing meaningful feedback to authors and continues to offer hope of improving the quality of science and scientific communication. Though this process consumes large amounts of human and physical resources and sometimes fails tests of objectivity, instituting collaborative review processes, developing criteria-based reviewer training, improving instrumentation for rating quality, and using systematic checks for rater slippage all hold promise for improving the quality of the review process.

With continuing dialogue and openness to oversight, the goals of scientific objectivity remain achievable. Given the forces that work against it, the quality of science in North America is remarkably high and the research enterprise is astonishingly healthy. It may be bent, but it does not appear to be broken.

REFERENCES

American Psychological Association. (1983). *Publication manual of the American psychological association* (3rd ed.). Washington, DC: Author.

American Psychological Association. (1996, December). *Task force on statistical inference: Initial report* (Unpublished memoranda). Washington, DC: Author.

Angell, M., & Reiman, A. S. (1989). Redundant publication. *New England Journal of Medicine, 320,* 1212–1214.

Bancroft, J. (1993). *Human sexuality and its problems* (2nd ed.). London: Churchill Livingstone.

Beutler, L. E. (1994). Fragmented and duplicate publication [Editorial]. *Journal of Consulting and Clinical Psychology, 62,* 3.

Beutler, L. E. (1996). The view from the rear: An editorial. *Journal of Consulting and Clinical Psychology, 64,* 845–847.

Beutler, L. E., Brown, M. T., Crothers, L., Booker, K., & Seabrook, M. K. (1996). The dilemma of factitious demographic distinctions in psychological research. *Journal of Consulting and Clinical Psychology, 64,* 892–902.

Beutler, L. E., & Hamblin, D. L. (1986). Individual outcome measures of internal change: Methodological considerations [Special edition]. *Journal of Consulting and Clinical Psychology, 54,* 48–53.

Bryk, A. S., & Raudenbush, S. W. (1992). *Hierarchical linear models: Applications and data analysis methods.* Newbury Park, CA: Sage.

Burnham, J. C. (1990). The evolution of editorial peer review. *Journal of the American Medical Association, 263,* 1323–1329.

Carver, R. P. (1978). The case against statistical significance testing. *Harvard Educational Review, 48,* 378–399.

Chambless, D. L., Sanderson, W. C., Shoham, V., Johnson, S. B., Pope, K. S., Crits-Christoph, P., Baker, M., Johnson, B., Woody, S. R., Sue, S., Beutler, L. E., Williams, D. A., & McCurry, S. (1996). An update on empirically validated therapies. *Clinical Psychologist, 49*(2), 5–14.

Cohen, J. (1990). The things I have learned (so far). *American Psychologist, 45,* 1304–1312.

Cohen, J. (1994). The earth is round (p < .05). *American Psychologist, 49,* 997–1003.

Cooperschmidt, J. (1988). Improving what is published: A model in search of an editor. *American Psychologist,* 635–641.

Elkin, I. (1994). The NIMH treatment of depression collaborative research program: Where we began and where we are. In A. E. Bergin & S. L. Garfield (Eds.), *Handbook of psychotherapy and behavior change* (4th ed., pp. 114–139). New York: Wiley.

Elkin, I., Gibbons, R. D., Shea, M. T., & Shaw, B. F. (1996). Science is not a trial (but it can sometimes be a tribulation). *Journal of Consulting and Clinical Psychology, 64,* 92–103.

Elkin, I., Parloff, M. B., Hadley, S. W., & Autry, J. H. (1985). NIMH treatment of depression collaborative research program: Background and research plan. *Archives of General Psychiatry, 42,* 305–316.

Elkin, I., Shea, T., Watkins, J. T., Imber, S. D., Sotsky, S. M., Collins, J. F., Glass, D. R., Pilkonis, P. A., Leber, W. R., Docherty, J. P., Feister, S. J., & Parloff, M. B. (1989). National Institute of Mental Health treatment of depression collaborative research program. *Archives of General Psychiatry, 46,* 971–982.

Fisk, D. W., & Fogg, L. (1990). But the reviewers are making different criticisms of my paper: Diversity and uniqueness in reviewer comments. *American Psychologist, 5,* 591–598.

Flanagin, A., Glass, R. M., & Lundberg, G. D. (1992). Electronic journals and duplicate publication: Is a byte a word? *Journal of the American Medical Association, 267,* 2374.

Good, B. J. (1993). Culture, diagnosis and comorbidity. *Culture, Medicine and Psychiatry 16,* 427–446.

Hagan, R. L. (1997). In praise of the null hypothesis statistical test. *American Psychologist, 52,* 15–24.

Hoagwood, K., Hibbs, E., Brent, D., & Jensen, P. (1995). *Journal of Consulting and Clinical Psychology, 63,* 683–687.

Howard, K. I., Cox, W. M., & Saunders, S. M. (1990). Attrition in substance abuse comparative treatment research: The illusion of randomization. In L. Onken & J. Blaine (Eds.), *Psychotherapy and counseling in the treatment of drug abuse* (DHHS Publication No. (ADM) 90-1722, pp. 66–79). Washington, DC: National Institute of Drug Abuse.

Howard, K. I., Kopta, S. M., Krause, M. S., & Orlinsky, D. E. (1986). The dose-effect relationship in psychotherapy. *American Psychologist, 41,* 159–164.

Howard, K. I., Moras, K., Brill, P. L., Zoran, M., & Lutz, W. (1996). Evaluation of psychotherapy: Efficacy, effectiveness, and patient progress. *American Psychologist, 51,* 1059–1064.

Jacobson, N. S., & Truax, P. (1991). Clinical significance: A statistical approach to defining meaningful change in psychotherapy research. *Journal of Consulting and Clinical Psychology, 59,* 12–19.

Judd, C. M., McClelland, G. H., & Culhane, S. E. (1995). Data analysis: Continuing issues in the everyday analysis of psychological data. *Annual Review of Psychology, 46,* 433–465.

Kassirer, J. P. (1992). Journals in bits and bytes, electronic medical journals. *New England Journal of Medicine, 326,* 195–196.

Kassirer, J. P., & Marcia, A. (1995). Redundant publication: A reminder. *New England Journal of Medicine, 333,* 449–450.

Kazdin, A. E. (1977). Assessing the clinical or applied significance of behavior change through social validation. *Behavior Modification, 1,* 427–452.

Kazdin, A. E. (1992). *Research design in clinical psychology* (2nd ed.). Needham Heights, MA: Allyn & Bacon.

Kazdin, A. E. (1994). Methodology, design, and evaluation in psychotherapy research. In A. E. Bergin & S. L. Garfield (Eds.), *Handbook of psychotherapy and behavior change* (4th ed., pp. 19–71). New York: Wiley.

Kendall, P. C., & Grove, W. (1988). Normative comparisons in therapy outcome research. *Behavioral Assessment, 10,* 147–158.

Kenny, D. A., & Judd, C. M. (1986). Consequences of violating the independence assumption in analysis of variance. *Psychological Bulletin, 99,* 422–431.

Klein, D. F. (1996). Preventing hung juries about therapy studies. *Journal of Consulting and Clinical Psychology, 64,* 81–87.

Kraemer, H. C. (1981). Coping strategies in psychiatric clinical research. *Journal of Counseling and Clinical Psychology.* 309–319.

Lambert, M. J. (1994). Use of psychological tests for outcome assessment. In. M. E. Maruish (Ed.), *The use of psychological testing for treatment planning and outcome assessment.* Hillsdale, NJ: Erlbaum.

Lambert, M. J., Christensen, E. R., & DeJulio, S. S. (Eds.). (1983). *The assessment of psychotherapy outcome.* New York: Wiley.

Maher, B. A. (1978). Reports in clinical psychology: A reader's, writer's, and reviewer's guide to assessing research *Journal of Counseling and Clinical Psychology,* 835–838.

Mann, J. J., & Kupfer, D. J. (1993). *Biology of depressive disorders: Part A. A systems perspective.* New York: Plenum.

Rennie, D. (1997). Thyroid storm. *Journal of the American Medical Association, 277,* 1238–1243.

Rogers, J. L., Howard, K. I., & Vessey, J. T. (1993). Using significance tests to evaluate equivalence between two experimental groups. *Psychological Bulletin, 113,* 553–565.

Russell, R. L., Bryant, F. B., & Estrada, A. U. (1996). Confirmatory P-technique analyses of therapist discourse: High- versus low-quality child therapy sessions. *Journal of Consulting and Clinical Psychology, 64,* 1366–1376.

Schmidt, F. L. (1996). Statistical significance testing and cumulative knowledge in psychology: Implications for training of researchers. *Psychological Methods, 1,* 115–129.

Seligman, M. E. P. (1995). The effectiveness of psychotherapy: The *Consumer Reports* study. *American Psychologist, 50,* 965–974.

Seligman, M. E. P. (1996). Science as an ally of practice. *American Psychologist, 51,* 1072–1079.

Semir, V. D. (1996). What is newsworthy? *Lancet, 347,* 1163–1167.

Shaver, J. P. (1993). What statistical significance testing is, and what it is not. *Journal of Experimental Education, 61,* 293–316.

Strupp, H. H., & Hadley, S. W. (1977). A tripartite model of mental health and therapeutic outcomes. *American Psychologist, 32,* 187–196.

Strupp, H. H., Horowitz, L. M., & Lambert, M. J. (1997). *Measuring patient changes in mood, anxiety, and personality disorders: Toward a core battery.* Washington, DC: American Psychological Association.

Waskow, I. E., & Parloff, M. B. (Eds.). (1975). *Psychotherapy change measures* (Publication No. 74-120). Rockville, MD: National Institute of Mental Health.

Wilkie, T. (1996). Sources in science: Who can we trust? *Lancet, 347,* 1308–1312.

Zukerman, M. (1990). Some dubious premises in research and theory on racial differences: Scientific, social, and ethical issues. *American Psychologist, 45,* 1297–1303.

Zwick, R. (1997, March). *Would the abolition of significance testing lead to better science?* Presented in the symposium, "Contemporary Uses of Statistical Significance Testing: Comments from Select Journal Editors and AERA Past Presidents," at the annual meeting of the American Educational Research Association, Chicago, IL.

PART TWO

AREAS OF CLINICAL RESEARCH: ASSESSMENT

Chapter 6

PSYCHOMETRIC ISSUES IN ASSESSMENT RESEARCH

Stephen N. Haynes, Ph.D., Karl Nelson, M.A., and Daniel D. Blaine, Ph.D.

CLINICAL JUDGMENT, PSYCHOLOGICAL ASSESSMENT, AND PSYCHOMETRICS

Many judgments are made during clinical assessment and treatment. Clinical judgments include estimates of the chance that a client will harm himself or herself, psychiatric diagnoses, and the identification of a client's behavior problems. Clinical judgments also include hypotheses about the causes of a client's behavior problems, estimates of a client's behavioral and cognitive competencies, the specification of treatment goals, and the design and evaluation of treatment programs.

A particularly important clinical judgment is the clinical case conceptualization (Eels, 1997; Garb, 1998; Goldstein & Hogarth, 1997), or the functional analysis (Haynes & O'Brien, in press), integrations of lower-order judgments about a client that guide treatment decisions. Judgments made during clinical assessment have important consequences. For example, an estimate of a client's risk of suicide can affect whether he or she is placed in seclusion. A clinician's judgment about the importance of inconsistent parental discipline practices in maintaining a child's oppositional behaviors can affect the focus and type of treatment that the clinician provides for the family.

Clinical judgments are affected by the results of psychological assessment: Data from interviews, questionnaires, and behavioral observations provide the basis for many clinical judgments. Although a clinician can make bad judgments from good assessment measures, the validity of clinical judgments is more often limited by the validity of the measures upon which they are based. For example, if, because of interviewing errors, a clinician underestimates the role of inconsistent parental discipline practices in the oppositional behaviors of a child, the subsequent treatment program may not include a needed component in which parents are trained in effective discipline strategies. Similarly, a clinician may overestimate the importance of depressive symptoms for a client if the clinician uses a depression questionnaire that also includes anxiety items.

There are two guiding tenets to this chapter: (a) clinical judgments are more likely to be valid if based on psychological assessment measures that are valid; (b) psychological assessment instruments can be evaluated on the degree to which they provide valid measures. *Psychometry* (i.e., *psychometrics*) is the science of psychological assessment: the evaluation of measures from psychological assessment instruments and the judgments based on those measures. This evaluation process includes the identification of measurement errors and the errors in judgments based on obtained measures. Psychometry also includes strategies for developing assessment instruments that provide valid measures that facilitate clinical judgments.

Psychometrics is a fundamental element of clinical psychology research: It is the science of measurement, and measurement underlies all clinical psychology research. The proper application of psychometric principles can increase the validity of measures that are acquired in psychological assessment, assist in the development and evaluation of new assessment instruments, and aid the clinician in the interpretation of measures derived from psychological assessment.

Chapter Overview and Principal Ideas

This chapter focuses on the applications of psychometry to the development, refinement, and evaluation of psychological assessment instruments in the context of clinical assessment. We examine the implications of psychometric principles for the clinical application of psychological assessment instruments and for the clinical judgments based on psychological assessment measures. There are multiple dimensions of psychometric evaluation and we also consider the differential applicability and implementation of these evaluative dimensions across methods of assessment: self-report questionnaires, behavioral observation, self-monitoring, interviews, participant reports, and psychophysiological methods of assessment.

An "assessment instrument" is a specific procedure for deriving measures on the behavior of a person, such as a specific questionnaire on depression symptoms or a specific behavioral observation coding system. An "assessment method" is a class of procedures for deriving measures on the behavior of a person or persons (e.g., self-report questionnaires, behavioral observations in the natural environment, interviews). A "measure" refers to the information (e.g., score, ranking, rate of behavior) derived from a psychological assessment instrument, and "measurement" refers to the process of acquiring data and constructing a measure of the targeted construct.

Psychological assessment instruments have other applications, such as the study of personality and development, personnel decisions, achievement testing, and educational placement. Many of these are covered in other chapters in this book and in Anastasi and Urbina (1998), Goldstein and Hersen (1988), and Linn (1993).

The goal of this chapter is to help the reader understand the methods, importance, and utility of psychometrics in psychological assessment research and in clinical assessment contexts. To this end, this chapter emphasizes several ideas that are relevant to the application of psychometric principles to research on clinical applications of psychological assessment:

1. Psychometric properties of psychological assessment instruments can be evaluated on several dimensions (a "dimension" refers to a quantitative attribute of an assessment instrument), and the most appropriate dimensions for estimating

   psychometric properties of an assessment instrument differ across methods of
   assessment.

2. Consistent with this, the utility of *temporal consistency* indices and indices of
   internal consistency of aggregated measures depends on the presumed stability
   and homogeneity, respectively, of the measured variables.

3. Psychometrics provides information on *validity* of measures obtained from a
   psychological assessment instrument. *Construct validity* is the supraordinate
   psychometric evaluative dimension. It encompasses all psychometric evaluative
   dimensions.

4. Estimates of the validity of an assessment instrument are *conditional*. Validity
   estimates for an assessment instrument (e.g., temporal stability and convergent
   validity indices) obtained in one study are not necessarily generalizable to other
   settings, samples/populations, response modes, methods of measurement, and
   assessment contexts, dimensions, and goals.

5. Psychometric evaluative indices are not stable characteristics of an assessment
   instrument. Validity indices reside with the measures and assessment contexts
   and can change across assessment contexts, populations, functions of assessment, and time.

6. The *incremental clinical utility* and *incremental validity* of an assessment instrument must be considered when deciding if a new assessment instrument should
   be developed and if an assessment instrument should be used for a particular
   assessment occasion or purpose.

7. Decisions made about the content of a psychological assessment instrument in
   the early phases of instrument development, the *content validation* phase, are
   particularly important because they set the upper limit for the construct validity
   of the instrument. Errors in the development phase can lead to errors in clinical
   judgments based on measures from the instrument.

8. *Idiographic assessment strategies* are often used in psychological assessment
   and psychometric evaluation can help estimate the validity of the obtained measures and judgments based on those measures.

A number of other ideas are relevant to the application of psychometrics in psychological assessment research and are integrated throughout the chapter. First, the goals
of assessment can differ across assessment occasions, and estimates of the validity of a
psychological assessment instrument are conditional for the goals of the assessment.
An instrument may be valid when used for some purposes and not when used for others. Second, from a functional approach to psychometry, the best methods of estimating psychometric properties of an assessment instrument depend on the judgments that
are to be based on the measures. Third, every assessment method and instrument is associated with multiple and idiosyncratic sources of measurement and inferential error.
Consequently, measurement and inferential errors can often be reduced through the
use of multiple sources of assessment measures (e.g., the use of multiple informants,
assessment methods, and occasions). Fourth, the assessment instruments that target
functional relations are important aids to clinical judgment and are also subject to psychometric evaluation.

DIMENSIONS OF VALIDATION IN PSYCHOLOGICAL ASSESSMENT

The validity of measures obtained from psychological assessment instruments, and the validity of judgments derived from those measures, can be evaluated on several dimensions. These evaluative dimensions have been discussed in many books (e.g., Anastasi & Urbina, 1997; Cronbach, 1988; Linn, 1993; Nunnally & Bernstein, 1994; Suen, 1990; Wainer & Braun, 1988) and are not considered in detail in this chapter.

Table 6.1 delineates some psychometric evaluative dimensions. Several dimensions and aspects of validation that are particularly relevant for clinical applications of psychological assessment are discussed below.

Validation provides information about the *construct validity* of an obtained measure and the validity of clinical judgments based on that measure (Messick, 1995). Construct validity is the degree to which an obtained measure reflects the targeted attribute and the judgments that are permissible from the measure. Construct validity is a meta-judgment: Estimates of construct validity are based on integration of multiple psychometric evaluative dimensions, such as those outlined in Table 6.1. As we discuss below, the contribution of each of the various evaluative dimensions to estimates of the construct validity of an instrument, and the relevance of each evaluative dimension in the validation process, vary as a function of the assessment contexts and goals.

Many multidimensional construct validation studies have been published in *Psychological Assessment.* For example, Kubany et al. (1996) reported six studies on the development and validation of the Trauma-Related Guilt Inventory (TRGI). To increase the relevance and representativeness of the items on the questionnaire, the authors conducted semistructured interviews with 20 trauma survivors about their guilt-related thoughts, behaviors, and feelings relevant to the traumatic event. Potential items were extracted from transcripts of the interviews by trained raters and integrated with items derived from relevant studies and questionnaires. The initial content of the questionnaire, including items, instructions, and the definition of the targeted construct "trauma-related guilt," were quantitatively evaluated by several professionals familiar with trauma and questionnaire development (see discussion of content validation by Haynes, Richard, & Kubany, 1995). A refined version of the questionnaire was administered to an initial sample of several hundred persons who had experienced a traumatic event. Item retention and deletion decisions for the next version were based on item dispersion and factor loadings (see discussion of factor analysis in the development and validation of assessment instruments in Floyd & Widaman, 1995). Subsequent studies focused on replicating the factor structure identified in the first study *(confirmatory factor analysis),* examining the *temporal stability* and *internal consistency* of the scales, and examining covariance with theoretically related measures *(convergent validation)* and theoretically unrelated measures *(discriminant validity),* using several different samples of persons who had experienced traumatic life events. All of the studies contributed to inferences about the *construct validity* of the TRGI—the degree to which it measures the targeted construct.

Construct validity of an assessment instrument (more precisely, of the obtained measures and contingent judgments) affects, and is affected by, clinical assessment judgments and decisions in several ways. First, when selecting the best instrument to

Table 6.1.   Dimensions of psychometric evaluation in psychological assessment

Validity

Validity: An integrated evaluative judgment of the degree to which empirical evidence and theoretical rationales support the adequacy and appropriateness of inferences and actions based on the data acquired from an assessment instrument (Messick, 1993). Close in meaning to "construct validity."

Accuracy: The extent to which observed values approximate the "true" state of nature (Foster & Cone, 1995). Used most often but not exclusively with behavioral observation, when there is something approximating an incontrovertable index of the measured construct.

Construct validity: Comprises the evidence and rationales supporting the trustworthiness of assessment instrument data interpretation in terms of explanatory concepts that account for both the obtained data and relationships with other variables (Messick, 1993). Construct validity refers to all validity evidence bearing on the measure (Kazdin, 1992).

Convergent validity: The extent of covariance between scores from two assessment instruments that measure the same or related constructs. The magnitude of correlation between the measures is expected to vary directly with the degree of expected overlap between the constructs (Campbell & Fiske, 1959).

Content validity: The degree to which elements of an assessment instrument are relevant to and representative of the targeted construct for a particular assessment purpose (Haynes, Richard, & Kubany, 1995).

Criterion-referenced validity: The degree to which measures from an assessment instrument correlate with scores from previously validated instruments that measure the phenomena of interest or with nontest criteria of practical value.

Discriminant (divergent) validity: The degree to which data from an assessment instrument are not related unduly to exemplars of other constructs (Messick, 1993). This evaluative dimension is most useful when applied to alternative constructs that should not, but could, account for variance in the primary measure of interest.

Reliability

Reliability: The part of a test result that is due to permanent, systematic effects and therefore persists from sample to sample (Marriott, 1990).

Temporal stability (test-retest reliability): The stability of obtained scores over a specified time; can be reflected by correlations or degree of agreement between scores obtained at different assessment occasions.

Internal consistency: The degree of consistency of the items or elements within an assessment instrument; can be reflected by split-half reliability, Kuder-Richardson 20 formula, coefficient alpha (Kazdin, 1992).

Internal structure: The degree to which elements of an assessment instrument covary in patterns that are consistent with expectations based on the theory underlying the instrument (e.g., *factor structure*).

Source: Adapted from Haynes & O'Brien, in press.

use in clinical assessment, and when interpreting measures obtained from an assessment instrument, it is important to consider the degree to which the instrument taps the targeted construct. Different methods of measuring the same construct have different sources of measurement error, and the extent of measurement error may differ across instruments.

Consider again potential problems if we make judgments about the magnitude of a client's depressive symptoms from a self-report questionnaire that contains items that tap anxiety. Similarly, in the assessment of family interactions and treatment outcome with aggressive children, it is important to select instruments that help the assessor estimate specific treatment effects (Bank & Patterson, 1992) and important functional relations (i.e., the covariations among target behaviors and other events, such as environmental events and variables manipulated in treatment).

Some assessment instruments may provide valid measures of constructs that are not specific to the targets or goals of assessment. In the example of measuring treatment outcome with aggressive adolescents, intellectual and personality assessment instruments may provide valid measures of many constructs that are only indirectly related to adolescent aggression. Construct validity indices help the assessor select assessment instruments that specifically tap the primary targeted constructs and are congruent with the goals of assessment.

Second, construct validity is the ultimate goal in the development of an assessment instrument, and construct validation guides the instrument development and evaluation process. As we illustrated with the TRGI, the goal of the developer is to maximize the congruence between the measures obtained from the assessment instrument and the domain, facets, parameters, and mode of the targeted attribute.

The best procedures for developing an assessment instrument and for evaluating its validity also depend on the method and focus of assessment (Haynes et al., 1995). The utility of each psychometric evaluative dimension, outlined in Table 6.1, varies depending on whether the instrument involves a self-monitoring method to measure a relatively unstable variable such as mood or heart rate, or a retrospective questionnaire method to measure a more stable variable such as "extroversion" or "conscientiousness."

Measures obtained from psychological assessment should also be consistent with the desired *level of specificity* of the judgments that are to be made. Level of specificity refers to degree of molarity or precision and applies to four components of assessment instruments and the psychological assessment process: (a) the measures obtained from assessment instruments can differ in the diversity and number of elements they subsume (e.g., measures of "trauma" versus measures of "intrusive thoughts about a traumatic experience"); (b) the variables targeted in assessment can differ in the degree to which their dimensions or parameters are specified; (c) obtained measures can vary in the degree to which situational and temporal conditions relevant for the target variable are specified; and (d) clinical judgments based on assessment measures can differ in their level of specificity (Haynes & O'Brien, in press). Specificity has other meanings in other contexts, such as in causal modeling and diagnostic efficacy (see Table 6.2).

Finally, construct validation provides evidence about the validity of a construct as well as of the instrument that measures the construct (Smith & McCarthy, 1995). A failure to confirm expected covariance patterns (e.g., a failure to obtain an expected factor structure or a low magnitude of covariance with criterion measures) across a

Table 6.2. Factors that affect the generalizability of validity estimates for a psychological assessment instrument

Characteristics of a sample/population: An assessment instrument may provide valid measures for Chinese Americans but not African Americans; for younger but not older persons; for college students but not for adults seeking treatment at an outpatient psychiatric center.

Facets of a construct targeted: An assessment instrument may provide valid measures of educational but not emotional facets of social support; for catastrophic thoughts but not automatic thoughts associated with panic episodes.

Assessment context: An observation system may provide valid measures of child oppositional behaviors in the home but not in the classroom; a psychiatric screening interview may be valid when used in outpatient but not community settings.

Response modes: An assessment instrument may provide valid measures of cognitive but not psychophysiological modes of depression; for behavioral but not subjective discomfort modes of anxiety.

Dimensions of measured event: An assessment instrument may provide valid measures of the frequency but not the duration of self-injurious behavior; of the occurrence but not magnitude of migraine headaches.

Goals of assessment: Congruent with a functional approach to construct validation, an assessment instrument may be valid for initial screening of socially anxious individuals but not for a functional analysis of the same client's social anxiety.

Type of validation: An instrument may demonstrate excellent discriminative validity (e.g., ability to discriminate between groups) and poor predictive validity. The importance of different validity indices depends on the intended goal and application of the instrument.

series of studies, with more than one measure of a construct, suggests that the definition, domain, and facets of the construct should be modified (research on the measurement of "social support" [Cohen & Wills, 1985; Coyne & Downey, 1991] illustrates the construct refinement process).

An estimate of the construct validity of an assessment instrument is informed by a pattern of covariance with theoretically related and unrelated constructs (see Table 6.1). The validity of an instrument is most powerfully estimated through *criterion-related validation* (or *accuracy evaluation*)—covariance with previously validated or "gold-standard" measures of the same construct. An example would be correlating a brief IQ measure with a full-scale Wechsler Adult Intelligence Scale–Revised (WAIS-R). Additional evidence can accrue through *convergent validation*—covariance with theoretically related constructs. This is especially useful when criterion measures are unavailable. An example would be correlating a measure of shyness with measures of extroversion and daily social interactions.

It is also important to examine *discriminant validity,* the degree to which measures from an assessment instrument are not related unduly to exemplars of other constructs (Messick, 1993), the degree to which variance in obtained measures reflect only variance in the targeted construct. Discriminant validity can be particularly problematic for psychological assessment instruments. Many psychological constructs are not specifically defined, are defined differently by different investigators, have poorly delineated boundaries with other constructs, and evolve. Additionally, many investigators attend more closely to convergent than to discriminant validity. Of 312 manuscripts submitted to *Psychological Assessment* in 1997, 23% examined convergent validity and only 9% examined discriminant validity (32% examined the factor structure of instruments). Other validation strategies are described in Table 6.1.[1]

There are many sources of inferential error in the construct validation process. For example, the interpretation of patterns of covariance between an assessment instrument and convergent measures is affected by the degree that obtained coefficients of covariance reflect common method variance (Meier, 1994): Strong correlations between two anxiety questionnaires can partially reflect the fact that both are self-report methods, both are paper-and-pencil questionnaires, and both use similar response formats (e.g., both have a 4-point Likert scale).[2] Convergent validity indices can also be inflated by a special form of common method variance: item contamination. If there are similar items on two questionnaires, indices of covariance partially reflect consistency in response to shared items in addition to shared variance with theoretically related but independent measures.

Because of these sources of inferential error, construct validation based on multiple instruments and multiple methods (e.g., correlating a questionnaire measure of aggressive behaviors of a child with observation measures from external observers, parents, and teachers, as well as with questionnaires of related constructs) can often lead to more confident validity inferences (Kane, 1992).

Perhaps the most influential strategy for construct validation has been the multitrait-multimethod approach outlined by Campbell and Fiske (1959) and discussed more recently by Kenny and Kashy (1992) and Meier (1994). Measures from an assessment instrument would be expected to be correlated more highly with measures from instruments that measure identical or theoretically related constructs than with measures from instruments that measure theoretically unrelated constructs. The use of instruments that involve dissimilar methods of assessment reduces the inflation of validity coefficients associated with common method variance. A more recent approach has used confirmatory factor analysis as a general approach to construct validation (Kenny & Kashy, 1992), but its usefulness for estimating construct validity has been questioned (Meier, 1994).

The Conditional Nature of Construct Validation

In studies of the validity of an assessment instrument, many factors affect validity coefficients (e.g., the magnitude of shared variance with convergent measures) and summary

---

[1] Messick (1995, p. 745) proposed six aspects of validity (construct validity): (a) *content* (relevance, representativeness, and technical quality), (b) *substantive* (theoretical rationales for observed consistencies and their underlying mechanisms), (c) *structural* (assessment items and scoring should reflect the internal structure of the construct: structural fidelity), (d) *generalizability* (the degree to which measurements and inferences generalize across groups, settings, and tasks), (e) *external* (convergent and discriminant validity, from multitrait-multimethod comparisons), and (f) *consequential* (the social and policy implications of inferences from measurements).

[2] *Local dependence* is a concept of item response theory (IRT) and refers to the degree that high correlations between items are a function of factors other than variance in common with the targeted construct. Local dependence can occur among groups of questions that are very similar in wording and indicates item redundance (Steinberg & Thissen, 1996).

validity judgments. That is, inferences about the validity of an assessment instrument are conditional: They are not necessarily generalizable across these sources of variance.

Validity indices are particularly affected by the assessment strategies and participants used in the validity study. Some of the factors that affect the generalizability of validity coefficients and judgments include the characteristics of a sample, the facets of a targeted construct, and the context of the assessment. Factors that affect the generalizability of validity estimates for an assessment instrument are outlined in Table 6.2.

In sum, judgments about the validity of an assessment instrument are conditional and are not inherent in the instrument. Validity inferences can vary with the response mode of interest, the methods used in validation, the targeted dimensions, and the goals of assessment.

A functional approach to psychometric evaluation also suggests that strategies to develop and validate an assessment instrument must be appropriate for the intended applications of the instrument. When constructing and evaluating psychological assessment instruments that will be used for clinical assessment, four questions should be considered: For what purposes will an assessment instrument be used? What clinical judgments are to be guided by the obtained measures? For which populations will it be used? and What facets of the construct is the assessment instrument designed to measure? The relevance and generalizability of validity estimates are especially constrained by the functions of the assessment occasion. An assessment instrument that is valid for one assessment purpose may not be valid for others.

The published reliability and validity data for instruments are usually provided without sufficient information about their conditionality. Often, a potential user cannot ascertain if the psychometric indices are valid for the age, ethnicity, sex, context, or purpose with which they will be applied. Thus, reliability and validity are only suggestive that a particular instrument might be valid for the intended application.

Validity Indices Are Unstable

Assessment instruments are developed and evaluated in the context of contemporaneous theories about the domain and facets of the measured construct. In the development of the TRGI discussed earlier, ideas in the early to mid-1990s about the definition and domain of guilt, the facets of guilt such as hindsight bias and personal responsibility for a traumatic event, and ideas about the effects of traumatic life events guided the development of the questionnaire.

Underlying theories can evolve over time with the acquisition of new data, reducing the construct validity of an assessment instrument over time. For example, conceptualizations of posttraumatic stress disorder (PTSD), eating disorders, attention deficit disorders, personality disorders, and marital distress have changed significantly in the past 10 years (see reviews in Turner & Hersen, 1997), reducing the validity of assessment instruments developed in the 1970s and 1980s. The assessment instrument is unlikely to tap new facets of the construct.

There are several implications to instability of construct validity: (a) validity indices from past research may overestimate an instrument's current validity; (b) the construct validity of psychological assessment instruments should be periodically examined and assessment instruments should be revised to reflect revisions in the targeted construct; and (c) inferences about constructs may be in error when they are drawn from assessment instruments that do not reflect contemporaneous ideas about the construct.

The Conditional Nature of Temporal Stability Estimates

In psychological assessment, confidence in the judgments based on a measure often depends on the *reliability* of the obtained measures. Reliability is the proportion of variance in the obtained measure that is due to permanent, systematic effects and, therefore, is presumed to be generalizable across similar assessment conditions (Marriott, 1990). *Temporal stability* (i.e., test-retest reliability) is a dimension of reliability (see discussion of internal consistency below) and refers to the stability over time of obtained measures. Temporal stability is usually estimated by the magnitude of correlation, or the magnitude of agreement, between measures obtained on different assessment occasions.

When measures of presumably stable variables change across a time interval in which no changes in the construct would be expected (e.g., significant changes in scores obtained on an IQ or an "ego strength" test obtained two weeks apart) and under similar assessment conditions, the *precision* of the measure is questionable. In traditional psychometric theory, reliability estimates are used to estimate the standard error of measurement,[3] which is used to estimate confidence boundaries for obtained measures. Indices of temporal stability usually affect the degree of confidence that an obtained measure reflects the targeted construct and the degree of confidence that an obtained measure is generalizable to other assessment occasions.

The degree to which a targeted construct is assumed to be stable affects the utility and interpretation of temporal stability indices. The presumed stability of an obtained measure (and the measured attribute) can vary across attributes, assessment methods and conditions, units of aggregation and analysis, and response modes. In behavioral observation, for example, presumed instability of molecular behaviors (e.g., "interruptions" in marital communication assessment) across time or situations makes it difficult to separate variance associated with measurement error from variance associated with true changes in the measured behavior. Consequently, temporal stability indices are not useful indices of validity when true changes in the measured attribute are expected across sampling intervals.

Consider the difficulties in interpreting differences in the rate of a child's aggressive behavior observed in two identical clinic analog assessment situations, one week apart. On the first assessment occasion, the child is observed to pinch and hit his mother 15 times in a 10-minute observation period, but on the second assessment occasion, he hits and pinches only once during the 10-minute period. Low test-retest agreements may reflect measurement errors (e.g., poorly trained observers, imprecise response definitions) or true differences in the child's behavior.

Regardless of the source of variance, low indices of temporal stability impose restrictions on the judgments that can be drawn from an obtained measure: Judgments about the generalizability of measures across time or situations are diminished with

---

[3] The standard error of measurement is the positive square root of the reliability of a test (r_{tt}) times the standard deviation of the test scores (SD_t): $SD_t(I - r_{tt})^{1/2}$.

temporally unstable measures. It cannot be presumed that measures from a single assessment occasion can accurately predict behavior on other assessment occasions (i.e., in other situations or at other times).

When dynamic phenomena (i.e., phenomena that change over time) are measured, the precision of the obtained measures must be estimated in different ways. In temporal stability studies, concurrently obtained convergent and criterion validity indices are necessary to separate true changes and measurement error when true change in a measured attribute is possible.

With behavioral observation methods, *interobserver agreement* provides an estimate of observer accuracy and the precision (reliability) of a measure. Interobserver agreement indices estimate the degree to which the obtained measures reflect true variance: the degree to which measures can be expected to be replicated across observers. However, interobserver agreement does not provide information about the generalizability of obtained measures across time or situations.

In summary, temporal stability indices of psychological assessment instruments (a) contribute to inferences about the temporal generalizability of obtained measures and judgments, (b) can be helpful in partitioning true from error variance when obtained across intervals in which no change is expected in the targeted construct, and (c) should be obtained in carefully controlled assessment conditions.

The Conditional Utility of Aggregated Measures and Indices of Internal Consistency

Aggregated Measures

Most measures obtained in psychological assessment can be thought of as aggregates, or composites. Assessment data can be aggregated across time samples, questionnaire items, instruments, situations, observers and raters, responses and response modes, and functions (e.g., Buss, 1989). Examples of aggregation include summing several items to arrive at an anxiety score on a self-report questionnaire; summing the number of times a child bites and hits himself during home observations as a measure of self-injury; and averaging the interbeat intervals for two minutes to estimate the heart rate or physiological arousal of a patient with PTSD during laboratory exposure to trauma-related stimuli.

Aggregates are used in psychological assessment for two reasons. First, they are presumed to provide a more reliable estimate of a construct than is provided by the individual elements of the aggregate. For example, if we are observing parent-child interactions in a clinic for 30 minutes, twice, one week apart, the correlation or agreement between measures from two assessment occasions will probably be higher if the measures are based on aggregation across 30 minutes rather than on any 1-minute period (in this case, parent-child interactions are likely to vary considerably across 1-minute observation segments). Similarly, the test-retest correlation coefficients are likely to be higher for the total score of a depression questionnaire than for the individual items within that questionnaire. Estimates of internal consistency, such as coefficient alpha, would also be expected to increase as a function of increasing number of items.

The effect on reliability (i.e., on internal consistency) of increasing or decreasing the number of items in an aggregate can be estimated by means of the Spearman-Brown formula:

$$r_{nn} = \frac{nr_{tt}}{1 + (n-1)r_{tt}}$$

in which r_{nn} = the estimated reliability coefficient, r_{tt} = the obtained coefficient, and n = the number of times the length of the aggregate is increased or decreased (Anastasi & Urbina, 1998). However, estimates of the impact on internal consistency of increasing or decreasing the number of items (Spearman-Brown prophecy formula) hold true only when the additional items tap the same construct.

The estimated reliability of an element of an aggregate would be expected to be lower than the aggregate because each separate element of the aggregate is associated with sources of variance specific to the element. In observation data, elements of a time-sample aggregate (i.e., individual time samples of behavior) are likely to reflect natural variability in behavior. The impact of each specific source of variance would be expected to diminish when multiple elements are combined.

Second, aggregation can strengthen construct validity when measuring a multifaceted construct. Many constructs measured in psychological assessment are higher-order constructs that cannot be captured by single-element measures. For example, a one-item questionnaire on depression would not allow specific assessment of the cognitive, motor, and somatic facets of depression. In general, the number of items or samples must increase proportionately with the number of facets of the targeted construct (however, see exceptions to his principle, discussed later in this chapter).

The relative validity of aggregated and nonaggregated measures of the same construct can be estimated by examining their covariance with other measures of the construct. Extending the Spearman-Brown prophecy regarding the effects of aggregation, we can surmise that an aggregated measure that has been correctly constructed (i.e., given an appropriate magnitude of intercorrelation among the elements and that they are all relevant to a single facet of the targeted construct), correlations with criterion measures, and measures of theoretically related constructs (e.g., convergent validation) will be higher for the aggregated measure than for any subsample of its elements.

Conditional Utility of Aggregated Measures

Aggregation can help or hinder clinical judgments, depending on the function of assessment and the dimensionality of the construct. Although aggregation can increase the reliability of a measure, it can also mask important sources of variance and can introduce new inferential errors. For example, summing items that tap different anxiety response modes (e.g., avoidance of anxiety-arousing situations, anxiety-related thoughts) to derive a composite anxiety score can provide a reliable measure of a multifaceted construct. However, this aggregate score can also mask important differences between anxiety-related thoughts and avoidant aspects of anxiety that may be tapped more specifically by the individual items or smaller subsets of the aggregate.

The goals of assessment affect the appropriateness of aggregation. Aggregation is most useful when it does not mask sources of variance that are important for clinical judgment.

Aggregation and Content Validity

The congruence between aggregation and assessment goals is one aspect of the content validity of an assessment instrument (Haynes et al., 1995). The content validity of the aggregate is the degree to which its dimensions and elements are relevant to and representative of the targeted construct given the goals of assessment. Although traditional psychometric theory suggests that adding items increases reliability, this assumption holds only when the added items are relevant to (isomorphic with) the targeted construct.

For example, content validity would be reduced if a questionnaire measure of PTSD, or a self-monitor measure of panic episodes, included elements that reflected depressed affect or trait anxiety. In these examples, the discriminant validity of the measures would be compromised because they would reflect variance that is not relevant to the targeted construct. More important, clinical judgments based on these measures would also be influenced by irrelevant sources of variance.[4] Steinberg and Thissen (1996) raised similar issues from an IRT perspective in their discussion of the use of "testlets," a small group of homogeneous, correlated items treated as a measurement unit.

The issue of the content validity of assessment instruments and aggregates further illustrates the multidimensional and conditional applicability of psychometric principles to the development and evaluation of clinical assessment instruments (e.g., Messick, 1994, 1995). The importance of each psychometric evaluative dimension depends on the intended applications of an assessment. Assume that a questionnaire is constructed to measure fearful thoughts in clients with panic episodes. The instrument includes items on thoughts of impending death, public embarrassment, and perceived loss of control but erroneously includes many depressive symptom items (e.g., feelings of sadness, hopelessness). The obtained measures could demonstrate (a) excellent discriminative validity (e.g., discriminating between outpatient adults with and without a formal diagnosis of panic disorder would score significantly differently), (b) good convergent validity (e.g., significant covariation with other questionnaire measures of panic, because depressive symptoms often co-occur with panic disorder), (c) excellent temporal stability, but (d) poor content validity because it contains items outside the domain of the targeted construct.

Given these multiple psychometric indices, does this assessment instrument provide a valid and useful measure of panic-related fearful thoughts and can it be used to guide clinical judgments? The questionnaire evidently measures some attribute(s) validly and reliably but does not validly measure the attribute that it is intended to measure. The clinical utility of the instrument depends on the purposes for which it is applied, primarily the specificity of the judgments to be derived. Because some of the items on the questionnaire were outside the domain of the targeted construct, it would be inappropriate to use this instrument to judge the effects of a treatment program on panic-related thoughts. Content validity is more important than temporal stability in judging the validity of the questionnaire for this purpose. However, the instrument could be used with

---

[4] In traditional psychometric theory, there are three sources of variance in obtained scores: (a) common variance (or true variance, due to variance in the targeted construct), (b) systematic error variance (or specific variance—reliable variance that is not due to variance in the targeted construct), and (c) random error variance (unreliable variance).

greater confidence (although it is still not an optimally constructed instrument) as a brief screening instrument to select persons for further assessment. The impact of each type of psychometric validation evidence on our decisions to use an instrument depends on the judgments to be made.

Internal Consistency

Internal consistency is an important evaluative dimension of reliability for many aggregated measures. Internal consistency of an assessment instrument (and of a factor and scale) refers to the magnitude of covariance among its elements (see Table 6.1). Methods of evaluating internal consistency are discussed in Anastasi and Urbina (1998), Brennan (1993), Nunnally and Bernstein (1994), and Suen (1990).

Strategies for evaluating internal consistency of unidimensional measures include Cronbach's alpha, split-half reliability, average interitem correlation, Kuder-Richardson 20 formula, item-total correlations, and item-factor loadings. The term "internal consistency" is sometimes used interchangeably with "homogeneity," which refers to the conceptual integrity of an aggregate. Schmitt (1996) discussed how a high coefficient alpha obtained from a multidimensional aggregate can be misinterpreted as support for the unidimensional nature of the aggregate.

Assuming unidimensionality (i.e., that the aggregate measures a unitary construct), internal consistency is an estimate of reliability. For measures that are intended to tap a unidimensional construct, it is important that all items tap that construct. A low magnitude of covariation among elements of an aggregate suggest that some elements may be poorly constructed, that the aggregate is multidimensional, or that some items are tapping constructs outside of the targeted domain. As noted in the previous section, clinical judgments based on composite measures with low internal consistency may be in error because they are affected by sources of variance extraneous to the targeted construct.

The importance of internal consistency for judging the construct validity of an assessment instrument depends on the assumptions about the interrelationships of its elements. For many assessment instruments (particularly behavioral assessment instruments: see Haynes & O'Brien, in press), covariance among elements is not presumed, aggregation is not appropriate, and internal consistency is an irrelevant psychometric evaluative dimension. Consider the Traumatic Life Events Questionnaire (TLEQ; Kubany, 1998). This is a self-report questionnaire that asks respondents to indicate whether or not they have experienced any of a number of traumatic events, such as rape, auto accidents, sex abuse as a child, and death of a loved one. There is no a priori presumption of covariance among items (e.g., no presumption that self-reports of rape and auto accidents would be correlated). The elements of the TLEQ are not aggregated to measure a higher-order construct, and internal consistency does not contribute to an estimate of its reliability and validity.

Some authors (e.g., Bollen & Lennox, 1991; Foster & Cone, 1995; Smith & McCarthy, 1995) differentiate between *effect indicator* models and *causal indicator* models: whether or not item responses are presumed to reflect the respondent's standing on a trait dimension. Internal consistency is more relevant for instruments based on an effect indicator model than for instruments based on a causal indicator model.

Internal consistency is also important in behavioral observation and in other time-series measurement methods when data collected across different time samples are aggregated. Sometimes, time-series data are aggregated to form a composite measure of a higher-order construct. Examples are summing several behavior codes in marital and family interaction (e.g., "agreement," "compliment") to estimate the higher-order construct "positive dyadic exchange," and summing several negative behaviors from daily recordings by psychiatric staff members (e.g., "verbal aggression," "screaming") to estimate "negative social exchanges" for a hospitalized patient. Internal consistency estimates can indicate the degree to which the aggregated behaviors covary and are reliable elements of the higher-order construct.

Clinical Utility and Incremental Validity

A functional approach to psychometry suggests that construct validity is a necessary but insufficient criterion for deciding if a new assessment instrument should be developed and if an assessment instrument should be used for a particular assessment occasion or purpose. The *incremental clinical utility* (i.e., incremental value to clinical judgments) and *incremental validity* (see definitions in Table 6.3) of an assessment instrument must also be considered (Foster & Cone, 1995).

The estimated incremental clinical utility and validity of a proposed assessment instrument are important considerations when there are extant validated assessment instruments. The enthusiasm of developers of new assessment instruments is sometimes based exclusively on the results of validation studies and is often unbuffered by a comparison of the attributes of the new instrument with those of other instruments that may perform the same functions more quickly, cheaply, or accurately. For example, a 30-item questionnaire may be valid but not useful for community-based substance abuse screening when a 3-item questionnaire is equally valid for that purpose (Sobell, Toneatto, & Sobell, 1994).

Several aspects of incremental utility and validity should be considered during the development and evaluation of a new assessment instrument and when deciding whether or not to use an assessment instrument in a particular clinical application. Will measures from the assessment instrument (a) capture the targeted construct better than available instruments; (b) enhance the validity of clinical case conceptualizations; (c) increase the accuracy of diagnosis, case identification, predictions of risky or dangerous behavior, estimates of real-life performance; and (d) strengthen treatment outcome evaluations? Do the incremental benefits associated with a new instrument outweigh the cost of its development and application? Table 6.3 outlines several interrelated dimensions of incremental utility and validity.

Incremental validity and utility are similar to *cost-effectiveness* evaluations of an assessment instrument. The cost-effectiveness of an assessment instrument depends on the degree to which it contributes information beyond that available from other instruments and the cost of the incremental information. Cost-effectiveness is also an important consideration when constructing assessment batteries: Only instruments that are consistent with the purpose of the assessment battery and contribute new information more cost-effectively than other instruments should be included in an assessment battery.

Table 6.3.   Dimensions of clinical utility of psychological assessment instruments

Treatment utility/validity: The degree to which data from an assessment instrument contribute to clinical case conceptualization and treatment outcome.

Incremental utility/validity: The incremental value of acquired data in clinical judgment. The degree to which acquired assessment data increase the power, sensitivity, specificity, and predictive efficacy of judgments beyond that associated with other assessment data.

Functional analytic utility: The degree to which data from an assessment instrument assist in the identification of functional relationships for a client's behavior problems and treatment goals (i.e., clinical case conceptualization in behavior therapy).

Sensitivity to change: The degree to which data from an assessment instrument reflect small changes in the targeted construct.

Cost-effectiveness: The cost (e.g., in time, financial) of deriving information with an assesment instrument relative to the contrbution of that information to a clinical judgment.

User-friendliness: The ease with which an assessment instrument can be administered and the data obtained and interpreted.

Positive predictive power: The "hit rate" for an assessment instrument score, usually used with binary criteria such as in identifiying persons with a disorder; true positive rate/true positive + false positive rate (e.g., the proportion of individuals identified by an instrument who truly have the disorder/behavior).

Negative predictive power: The true negative for an assessment instrument score, usually used with binary criteria such as in identifying individuals without a disorder; true negative rate/true negative + false negative rate (e.g., the proportion of individuals indicated by an instrument as not having a disorder/behavior who truly do not).

Sensitivity: The probability that a person with a particular attribute will be so identified by a particular assessment instrument.

Specificity: The probability that a person without a particular attribute will be so identified by a particular assessment instrument; the proportion of negative cases so identified by an assessment instrument.

Source: From Haynes & O'Brien, in press.

Summary

Several psychometric evaluative dimensions are particularly relevant to the evaluation of psychological assessment used in clinical assessment. Most validation methods and indices address the construct validity of an obtained measure and of the clinical judgments based on that measure. Construct validity is the degree to which measures from an assessment instrument represent the targeted attributes of the construct and are relevant for the judgments to be drawn.

Many factors can affect obtained validity indices and the interpretation of these indices. Factors include characteristics of a population, facets of a construct targeted, assessment context, response mode, parameters of target event, and the goals of assessment. In addition, the construct validity of some instruments is likely to decrease over time because the targeted constructs change over time.

Confidence in the clinical judgments based on measures from a psychological assessment instrument is affected by indices of its temporal stability and internal consistency.

Temporal stability indices contribute to inferences about the generalizability of obtained measures, help in partialing true from idiosyncratic and error variance in obtained measures, and should be obtained in carefully controlled assessment conditions. The importance of internal consistency in evaluating the construct validity of an assessment instrument depends on the purpose of the instrument and assumptions about the construct that is being measured.

The incremental clinical utility and validity of an assessment instrument is also an important evaluative dimension. There are several facets of incremental utility and validity, including treatment utility/validity, functional analytic utility, sensitivity to change, cost-effectiveness, user-friendliness, positive predictive power, negative predictive power, sensitivity, and specificity.

THE DEVELOPMENT AND REFINEMENT OF PSYCHOLOGICAL ASSESSMENT INSTRUMENTS: AN EMPHASIS ON CONTENT VALIDATION

The construct validity of a psychological assessment instrument is limited by the degree to which its elements were initially constructed to validly measure the targeted construct. Elements of a psychological assessment instrument that affect its validity include items of questionnaires and codes used in behavior observation, response formats, instructions to respondents, the situations sampled in questionnaires and behavioral observation, and strategies used to collect measures (e.g., time-sampling parameters). Decisions made about content in the early phases of instrument development affect the degree to which later studies support the construct validity of the instrument. Errors at the developmental phase—the content validation phase—can lead to errors in clinical judgments when the instrument is used because variance in the obtained measures may not reflect variance in the targeted construct (Clark & Watson, 1995; Foster & Cone, 1995; Haynes et al., 1995; Messick, 1995). Errors during the initial development of an instrument can be remediated only with revision and reevaluation of the instrument. This section reviews psychometric principles of initial instrument development and refinement and emphasizes the conditional and functional nature of content validation. In Butcher, Holmbeck, and Kendall (1998), separate chapters address the development and evaluation of self-report and objective assessment instruments (Butcher, 1998) and observational assessment (Cone, 1998).

Introduction to Content Validation

Content validity is an element of construct validity. It is the degree to which elements of an assessment instrument are relevant to and representative of the targeted construct, for a particular assessment purpose (Haynes et al., 1995). Content validity applies to all elements of the measurement process that can affect the obtained measures. For example, elements of questionnaires that can affect obtained measures include the content of individual items, response formats, instructions, how items are presented on a page, and the technical quality of the questionnaire. The elements of a behavioral observation system include the observation codes, time-sampling parameters, instructions to participants,

and the situations in which observation occurs. The elements of a self-monitoring assessment instrument that can affect obtained measures include instructions, how often
and in what situations recording occurs, the behaviors selected for observation, and data
recording methods (e.g., hand-held computer vs. paper-and-pencil form).

As with other forms of validity, the content validity of an assessment instrument is
conditional for a particular application and may not be generalizable to other applications. For example, a questionnaire measuring symptoms of PTSD may have satisfactory content validity for treatment outcome evaluation but not for clinical case
conceptualization and treatment planning. These two applications may require different
items.

The relevance and representativeness of assessment instrument elements are central
aspects of content validity. The relevance of an assessment instrument is the degree to
which its elements are appropriate for measuring the targeted construct for a given assessment purpose. The representativeness of an assessment instrument is the degree to
which its elements proportionately sample the facets of the targeted construct. It is important to specify the construct that the instrument is intended to tap and to match the
content of the instrument to that construct.

One of the most common errors in the development of psychological assessment instruments is to include elements that tap constructs which are correlated with, but extraneous to, the targeted construct. For example, the relevance of a questionnaire
measure of PTSD would decrease to the degree to which it included items that measured depression or substance use. This error would show up as insufficient discriminant validity in later validation studies.

Another common error in the development of psychological assessment instruments
is a failure to ensure the representativeness of an instrument—failure to include items
that tap all facets of a complex construct (e.g., a questionnaire measure of PTSD without items on avoidance behaviors). In traditional psychometric theory, item content of
an instrument is representative to the degree that the entire domain of the targeted construct can be reproduced (e.g., whether a reading skills test proportionally taps all
facets of reading skills). The representativeness of a particular questionnaire purporting to assess *Diagnostic and Statistical Manual of Mental Disorders,* fourth edition
(DSM-IV) conceptualization of PTSD depends on the degree to which its items are
proportionally distributed across the three major symptom clusters of PTSD as outlined by the *DSM-IV* (American Psychiatric Association [APA], 1994).

Proportionate sampling in content validity refers to the degree to which variance in
aggregate measures of a construct is affected by the facets of a construct, in a proportion appropriate to the role of the facet in the construct. For example, in a measure of
depression in which the total score was calculated by summing 10 somatic items and 5
items from cognitive, emotional, and behavioral facets of depression, the total score
would be disproportionately affected by the somatic facet.

Principles of Initial Assessment Instrument Development

Haynes et al. (1995) outlined 35 qualitative and quantitative strategies to strengthen
the content validity of an assessment instrument during early stages of its development
(see also DeVellis, 1991, and many examples in *Psychological Assessment*). The best

strategies of content validation vary across constructs targeted for assessment and the methods of assessment. The functions of assessment also determine the best strategies for content validation. Content validation will be different for an instrument that will be used for clinical case formulation than for one that will be used for brief screening in the community. Several of these strategies are summarized in Table 6.4. Two of the most important strategies from Table 6.4 are discussed below.

Population Sampling

Population sampling is one of the best and least frequently used ways to strengthen the content validity of an assessment instrument. This usually involves the derivation of items based on qualitative interviews with persons from groups for which the instrument is intended. The use of carefully structured, open-ended interviews with persons or groups from the targeted population (and experts in the area) increases the chance that the important facets of the targeted construct are captured by the instrument. For example, if one is developing an analog observation instrument to assess the verbal and psychophysiological responses of male batterers to provocative interpersonal situations (e.g., videotaped provocations by a female), content development and validation procedures might involve interviews with batterers, battered women, and professionals who work with battering men. The interviews would focus on the situations, provocations,

Table 6.4. Recommended methods of initial instrument development to strengthen the content validity of an assessment instrument

1. Specify the *construct(s)* to be measured (an imprecisely defined and differentiated construct will undermine the validity of the entire assessment instrument).
   a. Specify the domain of the construct (what is to be included and excluded).
   b. Specify the facets and dimensions of the construct (the factors, modes, and temporal parameters).
2. Precisely specify and define the important *contexts* (situations) for the measures (e.g., important situational sources of variance in obtained measures of social anxiety, such as scenarios). This is particularly important in behavioral assessment, which assumes that behavior may differ in important ways across situations.
3. Specify the *intended functions* of the instrument (e.g., brief screening, functional analysis, treatment outcome), and develop an assessment instrument to match the targeted construct and function of assessment.
4. Select and generate *items* (e.g., questionnaire items, individual behavior codes) congruent with decisions in 1–3 above. Sources of item generation include:
   a. Rational deduction (e.g., from discussion among experts)
   b. Clinical experience
   c. Theories relevant to construct
   d. Empirical literature relevant to construct (e.g., studies on construct validity of potential items)
   e. Other assessment instruments (i.e., borrowing items/codes from other instruments that have demonstrated validity)
   f. Suggestions by experts

(Continued)

Table 6.4. *(continued)*

---

   g. *Population sampling:* generating items from suggestions by target population (most important, sample from the population; conduct semistructured interviews with samples from the population that you intend to measure)

5. *Match* items to facets and dimensions (use table of facets of construct and generate multiple items for each facet).

6. Examine *each item* (e.g., its structure, form, topography, content; make sure it is appropriate for its targeted facet, and that items are worded clearly and precisely; remove redundent items).

7. Establish *quantitative parameters* of instrument (e.g., response formats, scales, time-sampling parameters).

8. Develop specific and relevant *instructions* to participants (e.g., on questionnaire, to persons being observed).

9. Have multiple *experts* review all elements of assessment instrument (1–8 above). The review can include quantitative ratings (e.g., 5-point scale) of the precision, relevance, and representativeness of elements as well as qualitative evaluations, such as suggested additions, deletions, or refinements.

10. *Population* review: Have persons from target population review all elements of the assessment instrument. This can involve administration of the instrument to obtain ratings of the quality of the elements.

11. *Rereview* of the assessment instrument by experts and target population sample following refinement.

12. *Pilot test* the instrument.

13. Proceed with additional psychometric evaluation and contingent instrument refinement: criterion-related and convergent validation, reliability evaluation, factor analysis.

Note: The applicability of these strategies will vary across assessment methods.
Source: Haynes et al., 1995; Haynes & O'Brien, in press.

and statements that trigger verbal and physical aggression, as well as the responses of the batterers. This information would help the developer select the best situations to present via video or audiotape.

Expert Review

It is essential that the proposed construct definition, domain, facets, sampling strategies, and elements of an assessment instrument be subjected to quantitative and qualitative review by multiple experts (Messick, 1995). Constructs, facets, and elements should be judged for relevance, representativeness, specificity, technical quality, and clarity. The resulting descriptive statistics and suggestions for refinement can guide judgments about the content validity of the elements. The measures from expert review can assist in the identification of elements of the assessment instrument that require refinement and modification. The optimal number of judges will vary with the consistency of the ratings and practical considerations (e.g., complexity of the construct, instrument length, availability of experts). Both quantitative ratings and qualitative feedback from evaluators can contribute to content validity.

Principles of Assessment Instrument Refinement

The development, evaluation, and refinement of a psychological assessment instrument is ongoing and iterative. There are many strategies for refining an assessment instrument and the relevance of a particular strategy depends on the function of the assessment instrument and its underlying measurement model.

As we discussed earlier, the interpretation and appropriateness of "latent trait" approaches to psychometric evaluation (e.g., Bollen, 1989; Hoyle, 1991), including factor analysis, depend on whether an assessment instrument is based on a causal indicator or an effect indicator model. Similar issues have been raised about whether an obtained measure is considered a sample of a class of behaviors or a sign of a latent trait (e.g., Cone, 1998, this volume; Suen & Ary, 1989). Covariance among items would not be expected for instruments based on causal or sample measurement models (e.g., a questionnaire that inquires about the number and type of traumatic events experienced).

The early content validation stage often results in a pool of items (or scenarios in analog observation, behavior codes in naturalistic observation, psychophysiological measures) larger than that envisioned for the final version of the instrument. The next steps in assessment instrument development involve refinement of the initial version by examining the performance of individual items and their patterns of covariance for the purpose of improving the instrument's construct validity and efficiency (Nunnally & Bernstein, 1994; Smith & McCarthy, 1995).

Depending on assumptions about the targeted construct and the clinical judgments that will be affected by an instrument, decisions about which items to retain, refine, omit, and add (as well as the overall validity and utility of the instrument and scale/factor scores) are affected by several indices: (a) the patterns of covariance (i.e., factor structure) among the elements, (b) the degree of internal consistency of obtained factors/scales or aggregated indices, (c) patterns of item loadings across factors (ideally, an item will load strongly on only one factor), and (d) interitem correlations (to avoid redundancy/colinearity among items).

Following the development of an initial version of an instrument, psychometric evaluation is directed at the establishment of internal consistency of the instrument's unidimensional facets, determination of content homogeneity of each unidimensional facet, inclusion of items that discriminate among participants at the desired level of intensity of the attribute, and replication of the psychometric properties of the measure across independent samples (Comrey & Lee, 1992; Kenny & Kashy, 1992; Reise, Widaman, & Pugh, 1993). Factor and principal components analyses are particularly useful in identifying the internal structure of an instrument and in making item retention and omission decisions. Confirmatory factor analyses can also help estimate the robustness of the obtained factor structure (Cole, 1987).

Instrument development, evaluation, and refinement should be driven by a theoretical model—a clear idea about the targeted construct and the judgments that are to be drawn from the obtained measures. As we introduced earlier, a functional approach to psychometry mandates that the intended application of an instrument be considered when making decisions about instrument modification. The developer should consider the population to which the instrument will be applied, the facets of the construct that are targeted for measurement, the context of the assessment, the response mode and parameters targeted, and the clinical judgments that will be guided by the obtained measures.

Summary

In the early phases of instrument development, decisions about which elements to include will set the upper limits of its construct validity and of associated clinical judgments. Content validity is the degree to which elements of an assessment instrument are relevant to and representative of the targeted construct for a particular assessment purpose.

Content validity is conditional in that it may not be generalizable across applications of an instrument. The relevance of an assessment instrument is the degree to which its elements are appropriate for measuring the targeted construct; the representativeness of an assessment instrument is the degree to which the facets of the targeted construct are proportionately sampled.

There are many strategies to evaluate and strengthen the content validity of an assessment instrument, and the most applicable strategy will depend on which constructs will be targeted, which methods of assessment will be used, and the goals of its application. Two of the most useful but least frequently used are population sampling and expert review. Population sampling usually involves qualitative interviews with persons from targeted groups. Experts can also be used to examine and contribute to the constructs, facets, and elements of an instrument.

Research on a psychological assessment instrument is ongoing and iterative. Following development of an initial form, assessment instrument evaluation often involves examination of the patterns of covariance among the elements, particularly factor analysis. Research on a psychological assessment instrument should be driven by a theoretical model and a clear idea of the intended application of an instrument.

PSYCHOMETRIC PRINCIPLES AND IDIOGRAPHIC ASSESSMENT STRATEGIES

Idiographic and nomothetic approaches to psychological assessment differ in the degree to which (a) the assessment strategies are standardized across clients, (b) inferences from assessment measures depend on comparisons with measures from groups of persons, (c) the assessment strategies focus on groups versus individuals, and (d) inferences are generalizable across persons. Nomothetic assessment instruments are standardized across persons and provide measures on identical dimensions of identical variables across persons. Examples of nomothetic instruments include the Minnesota Multiphasic Personality Inventory-2 (MMPI-2), Rorschach, and WAIS (see review in Parker, Hanson, & Hunsley, 1992). Inferences from a nomothetic measure of a client depend on comparisons with measures obtained from the same instrument with other persons (e.g., in the form of T-scores, scale scores, rankings, classification).

Idiographic assessment strategies involve unstandardized methods, instruments, and/or measures (Haynes & O'Brien, in press). The assessment strategy (e.g., codes and time samples used in an observation instrument, items on a questionnaire) and the measures obtained (i.e., the variables and dimensions measured) are individually designed for each client, although elements of the instrument may be similar across some clients. One example of idiographic assessment is Goal Attainment Scaling (Kiresuk, Smith, & Cardillo, 1994), which involves frequent measurement of the degree to which a client has attained individually selected treatment goals. Self-monitoring methods are usually idiographic in that the events measured and methods of recording are individually tailored for each client (Evans & Sullivan, 1993).

Judgments from the idiographic measures are often based on individually determined criteria rather than on measures from other persons; consequently, the inferences (e.g, regarding treatment effects or estimated functional relations) may not be generalizable across clients. Additionally, measures from idiographic assessment instruments cannot always be aggregated across persons.

The importance of some dimensions of psychometric evaluation is increased with idiographic assessment, whereas the importance of other dimensions is decreased. With idiographic assessment, it is essential that judgments be based on measures that are reliable, accurate, content-valid, and appropriately scaled. The accuracy and construct validity of the idiographic measures are particularly important (Cone, 1988; Suen, 1988). Discriminative validity, the degree to which measures can differentiate individuals in groups formed from independent criteria, is often less important.

An example outlined in Haynes and O'Brien (in press) illustrates psychometric issues in idiographic assessment. The assessment goal was to measure the positive social interactions of a shy client. In addition to standardized interviews and questionnaires on social anxiety and behavior, the client could be asked to respond to weekly idiographic questionnaires about the frequency, type, context, and valence of his or her social interactions. This weekly questionnaire might be used to identify problematic social situations or to identify social contexts that were particularly troublesome for the client, and to estimate the degree to which the weekly treatment goals for social interaction were achieved. Alternatively, we could ask the client to self-monitor social interactions multiple times per day, perhaps using a timer or handheld computer to signal the client to record ongoing social activities.

The methods described in this example are idiographic in that the elements of the assessment instrument and its method of application could differ across clients. Furthermore, clinical judgments about the client drawn from the obtained measures can be derived without reference to measures from other clients.

Although the measurement is idiographic, judgments about the client's social behavior and responses are affected by the validity of the obtained measures, and psychometric evaluative dimensions help us estimate the level of confidence in our judgments that is warranted. In this example, validity will be affected by the accuracy with which the obtained measures reflect the client's social interactions in the natural environment and the sensitivity of the obtained measures to changes in social interactions across time. We are also concerned with the degree to which the instrument adequately samples the domain of interest (its content validity): Does the assessment instrument sample frequency of positive social interactions when the client's main concern is with negative interactions?

ALTERNATIVE STRATEGIES FOR THE DEVELOPMENT AND EVALUATION OF PSYCHOLOGICAL ASSESSMENT INSTRUMENTS

In this section, we examine two additional strategies for instrument development and evaluation: item response theory and generalizability theory. Additional discussions of the impact of recent developments in measurement theory for the development and evaluation of psychological assessment instruments were presented in a special section, "New Rules of Measurement," in *Psychological Assessment* (1996, pp. 341–368) and in a chapter on IRT by Embretson (this volume).

Item Response Theory and Instrument Development

IRT is a collection of statistical methods and models (e.g., Rasch modeling) for interpreting psychometric measures that arise in psychological assessment (Embretson, 1996, 1998; Steinberg & Thissen, 1996). It is designed to facilitate the analysis of the relation between characteristics of an individual (the person's status in relation to the construct measured by a specific instrument) and responses to individual items on an instrument. IRT provides validity estimates that are sometimes more robust across samples and defines difficulty in terms of level of ability needed to answer an item correctly with a given level of probability (or in terms of a person's status in relation to a targeted construct) (Murphy & Davidshofer, 1994).

Item characteristic curves (ICCs) provide the basis for item analysis in IRT. ICCs are a graphical representation of the probability of responding in a particular manner to an item as a function of the level of the construct under examination (e.g., the probability that an individual with a diagnosis of a depressive disorder will answer "true" to an item on a depression symptom questionnaire). ICCs can be seen as a common scale for estimating a respondent's status on a construct, independent of specific items that form a particular assessment instrument (Hambleton & Slater, 1997). As the level of the construct should determine whether an answer is given in a particular manner, difficulty of items or of an obtained measure should not change as a result of the population completing an assessment instrument.

For well-performing items, the probability of providing a "correct" answer to an item (or of indicating a trait presence or behavior occurrence) should increase as the amount of a construct present increases. If an item performs well (i.e., is a good discriminator between those low in a construct and those high in a construct), individuals with a high level of a particular construct dimension will have a higher probability of answering an item correctly (or in a positive direction) when compared to individuals with a low level of the same dimension of the same construct. For example, responses on a well-performing item on a questionnaire designed to measure PTSD status should reflect the individual's PTSD status as judged from another gold standard.

There are many applications of IRT. One application is to use ICCs to identify the level of a construct based on which distractor is selected for a specific item. Another common application of IRT is the construction of computerized, adaptive tests (Hambleton & Slater, 1997). IRT-based testing programs can construct tests that are tailored to determine the ability level of an individual completing an assessment instrument. The ability to compare examinees on the basis of level of construct also allows easy equating to test scores and easy determination of the relative difficulty of individual test items. It also allows for the identification of biased items. If ICCs differ for an item between members of separate groups, then the item is biased because people within similar construct levels will obtain different scores for that particular item. (IRT is discussed further in Chapter 12.)

Generalizability Theory

Generalizability theory (GT) has been developed to help researchers more specifically partition variance in obtained measures. Traditional psychometric theory partitions measures into true score and error variance portions, and the error portion, in turn, is often divided between systematic and random error variance. The usefulness of this partitioning system is based on a researcher's ability to determine what is true score, systematic error, and random error, based on research data (Shavelson, Webb, & Rowley, 1989). However, the error portion of the obtained measures can arise from multiple sources.

GT attempts to identify sources of error and estimate the magnitude of error in measurement from each source or from the interaction between sources. In a GT model, all sources of error are considered individually and simultaneously, rather than lumping all sources of error into one or two categories, as with traditional psychometric theory.

GT focuses on the ability to generalize from one set of obtained measures across time or situations. For example, GT replaces the concept of temporal stability (reliability) with the concept of generalizability across time. The ability to partition error variance allows decision makers to determine what sources of error should be taken into consideration when generalizing from the current results (Shavelson & Webb, 1991).

The identification of specific sources of variance can help to minimize error variance when data are collected for future research. For instance, if fatigue is found to contribute a large portion of the error variance, assessment devices could be administered at a different time of day, or the device itself, if it is the source of the fatigue, could be shortened.

SUMMARY

This chapter presented an overview of the applications of psychometry to the development, refinement, and evaluation of psychological assessment instruments as used in clinical assessment. Several principles were stressed as being particularly important for clinical applications of psychological assessment: (a) the best methods of estimating the psychometric properties of an assessment instrument differ across the methods of assessment; (b) estimates of the validity of an assessment instrument do not reside with the instrument; they are conditional and depend on the goals, settings, samples/populations, response modes, methods of measurement, and the nature of the construct; (c) the validity of an assessment instrument can erode over time; (d) construct validity is the supraordinate psychometric evaluative dimension; it encompasses all methods of estimating reliability and validity; and (e) content validity, incremental validity, and sensitivity to change are particularly important evaluative dimensions for the development and evaluation of clinical assessment instruments.

Validation studies are essential for the development and use of psychological assessment instruments because they provide information about construct validity of an assessment instrument. Construct validity is the degree to which an obtained measure reflects the targeted attribute. Construct validity evidence affects which judgments are permissible from the obtained measure. Estimates of the construct validity of an assessment instrument affect clinical judgments in several ways: (a) they affect judgments about the best instrument to use on a particular assessment occasion; (b) they affect the inferences about a client or group of persons that are drawn from obtained measures; (c) they can suggest the need for refinement of an assessment instrument; and (d) they can provide evidence about the validity of a construct as well as of the instrument that measures the construct.

There are multiple sources of error associated with all assessment instruments. Consequently, clinical judgments are most likely to be valid if based on multiple sources of data. The best strategy for construct validation involves the measurement of multiple traits using multiple methods.

Judgments about the validity of an assessment instrument are conditional. Validity coefficients can help the assessor select potentially useful instruments, but the validity of an instrument can be affected by the response mode of interest, the targeted dimensions of the attribute, and the goals of assessment. An assessment instrument can also be valid for some population, facets of a construct, and assessment contexts, but not others.

Ideas about the domain and facets of a construct can evolve over time as research continues. Consequently, the construct validity of an assessment instrument can erode. Validity estimates derived from past research can overestimate an instrument's current validity, and so the construct validity of psychological assessment instruments should be periodically examined.

Indices of the temporal stability of psychological assessment instruments contribute to inferences about the validity of obtained measures and judgments because they help separate reliable variance from error variance. However, the degree to which a targeted construct is assumed to be stable affects the utility and interpretation of temporal stability indices.

Aggregates are used in psychological assessment to provide a more reliable estimate of a construct and to strengthen construct validity when measuring a multifaceted construct. Aggregation can increase the reliability of a measure, but it can also mask important sources of variance. The degree to which the dimensions and elements of an aggregate are relevant to and representative of the targeted construct is the content validity of the aggregate.

Internal consistency is also an important dimension of aggregated measures. Low internal consistency can suggest that some elements are poorly constructed, that the aggregate is multidimensional, or that some items tap constructs outside the targeted domain.

When evaluating an assessment instrument, its incremental value to clinical judgments and incremental validity in comparison to other instruments should be considered. Several aspects of the incremental utility and validity are relevant. These include treatment utility/validity, functional analytic utility, sensitivity to change, cost-effectiveness, user-friendliness, positive predictive power, negative predictive power, sensitivity, and specificity.

Content validity is an important element of construct validity and refers to the degree to which elements of an assessment instrument are relevant to and representative of the targeted construct for a particular assessment purpose. Relevance is the degree to which an instrument's elements are appropriate for measuring the targeted construct for a given assessment purpose; representativeness is the degree to which its elements proportionately sample the facets of the targeted construct. Both are essential dimensions in the development of an assessment instrument.

The construct being evaluated, the method of assessment, and the functions of assessment determine the best strategies of content validation. Population sampling and expert review are important and frequently omitted strategies of facilitating content validity of an instrument.

Refinement of a psychological assessment instrument should be an ongoing enterprise. Refinement strategies depend on the function of the assessment instrument and its underlying measurement model. The refinement process often involves an examination of the performance of individual items and the pattern of covariance among items. Instrument development, evaluation, and refinement should be driven by a theoretical model and a firm idea of how the instrument will be used.

IRT is a collection of statistical methods and models designed to facilitate the analysis of the relation between characteristics of an individual and responses to individual items on the instrument. ICCs are a graphical representation of the probability of responding in a particular manner to an item as a function of the level of construct under examination and provides the basis for item analysis. GT is a strategy for identifying sources of error and estimating the magnitude of error from each source.

REFERENCES

American Psychiatric Association. (1994). *DSM-IV.* Washington, DC: Author.

Anastasi, A., & Urbina, S. (1998). *Psychological testing.* Englewood Cliffs, NJ: Prentice-Hall.

Bank, L., & Patterson, G. R. (1992). The use of structural equation modeling in combining data from different types of assessment. In J. C. Rosen & P. McReynolds (Eds.), *Advances in psychological assessment* (pp. 4l-74). New York: Plenum Press.

Bollen, K. (1989). *Structural equations with latent variables.* New York: Wiley.

Bollen, K., & Lennox, R. (1991). Conventional wisdom on measurement: A structural equation perspective. *Psychological Bulletin, 110,* 305–314.

Brennan, R. L. (1993). Reliability. In R. L. Linn (Ed.), *Educational measurement* (3rd ed., pp. 105–146). Phoenix, AZ: Oryx Press.

Buss, A. H. (1989). Personality as traits. *American Psychologist, 4,* 1378-1388.

Campbell, D. T., & Fiske, D. (1959). Convergent and discriminant validation by the multitrait-multimethod matrix. *Psychological Bulletin, 56,* 81–105.

Clark, L. A., & Watson, D. (1995). Constructing validity: Basic issues in objective scale development. *Psychological Assessment, 7,* 309–320.

Cohen, S., & Wills, T. A. (1985). Stress, social support, and the buffering hypothesis. *Psychological Bulletin, 98,* 310–357.

Cole, D. A. (1987). Utility of confirmatory factor analysis in test validation research. *Journal of Consulting and Clinical Psychology, 55,* 584–594.

Comrey, A. L., & Lee, H. B. (1992). *A first course in factor analysis* (2nd ed.). Hillsdale, NJ: Erlbaum.

Cone, J. D. (1988). Psychometric considerations and the multiple models of behavioral assessment. In A. S. Bellack & M. Hersen (Eds.), *Behavioral assessment—A practical handbook* (pp. 42–66). New York: Pergamon Press.

Cone, J. D. (1998). Psychometric considerations: Concepts, contents, and methods. In A. S. Bellack & M. Hersen (Eds.), *Behavioral assessment—A practical handbook* (4th ed., pp. 22–46). Needham Heights, MA: Allyn & Bacon.

Coyne, J. C., & Downey, G. (1991). Social factors and psychopathology: Stress, social support, and coping processes. In M. R. Rosenzweig & L. W. Porter (Eds.), *Annual review of psychology* (Vol. 42, pp. 401–426). Palo Alto, CA: Annual Reviews.

Cronbach, L. J. (1988). Five perspectives on validity argument. In H. Wainer & H. I. Braun (Eds.), *Test validity* (pp. 3–17). Hillsdale, NJ: Erlbaum.

DeVellis, R. F. (1991). *Scale development, theory and applications.* Newbury Park, CA: Sage.

Eels, T. (1997). *Handbook of psychotherapy case formulation.* New York: Guilford Press.

Embretson, S. E. (1996). The new rules of measurement. *Psychological Assessment, 8,* 341–349.

Evans, H. L., & Sullivan, M. A. (1993). Children and the use of self-monitoring, self-evaluation, and self-reinforcement. In A. J. Finch, Jr., W. M. Nelson, III, & E. S. Ott (Eds.), *Cognitive-behavioral procedures with children and adolescents—A practical guide* (pp. 67–89). Boston, MA: Allyn & Bacon.

Floyd, F. J., & Widaman, K. F. (1995). Factor analysis in the development and refinement of clinical assessment instruments. *Psychological Assessment, 7,* 286–299.

Foster, S. L., & Cone, J. D. (1995). Validity issues in clinical assessment. *Psychological Assessment, 7,* 248–260.

Garb, H. N. (1998). *Studying the clinician: Judgment research and psychological assessment.* Washington, DC: American Psychological Association.

Goldstein, W. M., & Hersen, M. (Eds.). (1988). *Handbook of psychological assessment* (3rd ed.). New York: Pergamon Press.

Goldstein, W. M., & Hogarth, R. M. (1997). *Research on judgment and decision making: Currents, connections, and controversies.* New York: Cambridge University Press.

Hambleton, R. K., & Slater, S. C. (1997). Item response theory models and testing practices: Current international status and future directions. *European Journal of Psychological Assessment, 13,* 21–28.

Haynes, S. N., & O'Brien. W. O. (in press). *Principles of behavioral assessment: A functional approach to psychological assessment.* New York: Plenum Press.

Haynes, S. N., Richard, D. C. S., & Kubany, E. (1995). Content validity in psychological assessment: A functional approach to concepts and methods. *Psychological Assessment, 7,* 238–247.

Hoyle, R. H. (1991). Evaluating measurement models in clinical research: Covariance structure analysis of latent variable models of self-conception. *Journal of Consulting and Clinical Psychology, 59,* 67–76.

Kane, M. T. (1992). An argument-based approach to validity. *Psychological Bulletin, 112,* 527–535.

Kazdin, A. (1992). *Research design in clinical psychology.* New York: Macmillan.

Kenny, D. A., & Kashy, D. A. (1992). Analysis of the multitrait-multimethod matrix by confirmatory factor analysis. *Psychological Bulletin, 112,* 165–172.

Kiresuk, A., Smith, A., & Cardillo, J. E. (Eds.). (1994). *Goal attainment scaling: Applications, theory, and measurement.* Hillsdale, NJ: Erlbaum.

Kubany, E. (1998). *Development and validation of a brief broad-spectrum measure of trauma exposure: The Traumatic Life Events Questionnaire.* Manuscript submitted for publication.

Kubany, E., Haynes, S. N., Abueg, F. R., Manke, F., Brennan, J., & Stahura, C. (1996). Development and validation of the trauma-related guilt inventory (TRGI). *Psychological Assessment, 8,* 428–444.

Linn, R. L. (Ed.). (1993). *Educational measurement* (3rd ed.). Phoenix, AZ: Oryx Press.

Marriott, F. H. C. (1990). *A dictionary of statistical terms* (5th ed.). New York: Longman Scientific & Technical.

Meier, S. T. (1994). *The chronic crisis in psychological measurement and assessment: A historical survey.* San Diego, CA: Academic Press.

Messick, S. (1993). Validity. In R. L. Linn (Ed.), *Educational measurement* (2nd ed.). Phoenix, AZ: American Council on Education and the Oryx Press.

Messick, S. (1994). Foundations of validity: Meaning and consequences in psychological assessment. *European Journal of Psychological Assessment, 10,* 1-9.

Messick, S. (1995). Validation of inferences from persons' responses and performances as scientific inquiry into score meaning. *American Psychologist, 50,* 741–749.

Murphy, K. R., & Davidshofer, C. O. (1994). *Psychological testing: Principles and applications* (pp. 163–169). Englewood Cliffs, NJ: Prentice-Hall.

Nunnally, J. C., & Bernstein, I. H. (1994). *Psychometric theory* (3rd ed.). New York: McGraw-Hill.

Parker, K. C. H., Hanson, R. K., & Hunsley, J. (1992). MMPI, Rorschach, and WAIS: A meta-analytic comparison of reliability, stability, and validity. In A. E. Kazdin (Ed.), *Methodological issues and strategies in clinical research* (pp. 217–232). Washington, DC: American Psychological Association.

Reise, S. P., Widaman, K. F., & Pugh, R. H. (1993). Confirmatory factor analysis and item response theory: Two approaches for exploring measurement invariance. *Psychological Bulletin, 114,* 552–566.

Schmitt, N. (1996). Uses and abuses of coefficient alpha. *Psychological Assessment, 8,* 350–353.

Shavelson, R. J., & Webb, N. M. (1991). *Generalizability theory: A primer.* Newbury Park, CA: Sage.

Shavelson, R. J., Webb, N. M., & Rowley, G. L. (1989). Generalizability theory. *American Psychologist, 44,* 922–932.

Smith, G. T., & McCarthy, D. M. (1995). Methodological considerations in the refinement of clinical assessment instruments. *Psychological Assessment, 7,* 300–308.

Sobell, L. C., Toneatto, T., & Sobell, M. B. (1994). Behavioral assessment and treatment planning for alcohol, tobacco, and other drug problems: Current status with an emphasis on clinical applications. *Behavior Therapy, 25,* 523–532.

Steinberg, L., & Thissen, D. (1996). Uses of item response theory and the testlet concept in the measurement of psychopathology. *Psychological Methods, 1,* 81–97.

Suen, H. K. (1988). Agreement, reliability, accuracy and validity: Toward a clarification. *Behavioral Assessment, 10,* 343–366.

Suen, H. K. (1990). *Principles of test theories.* Hillsdale, NJ: Erlbaum.

Suen, H. K., & Ary, D. (1989). *Analyzing quantitative observation data.* Hillsdale, NJ: Erlbaum.

Turner, S., & Hersen, M. (Eds.). (1997). *Adult psychopathology and diagnosis* (3rd ed.). New York: Wiley.

Wainer, H., & Braun, H. I. (Eds.). (1988). *Test validity.* Hillsdale, NJ: Erlbaum.

Chapter 7

RESEARCH DESIGN IN OBJECTIVE PERSONALITY ASSESSMENT

James N. Butcher, Ph.D.

Personality appraisal has played a long and vital role in human adaptation. From the beginning of cooperative human efforts, people have appraised their fellow hunters and other associates out of the need to choose the right person(s) for important life activities. Through time, human beings have effectively evolved strategies for appraising others. The formal scientific study of personality evaluation, however, has a substantially briefer history. After some misstarts—such as the phrenology efforts to map character through bumps on the head that was widespread during the early nineteenth century—the scientific study of personality made a more positive leap with the work of Francis Galton at the end of that century. Galton is credited with opening our eyes to the possibility of measuring various human qualities in a scientific fashion, and by the early years of the twentieth century, psychologists were experimenting with methods of appraising personality through several avenues. As we approach the end of the twentieth century, methods of evaluating personality continue to follow in the Galton tradition in having people report on their experiences, with the psychologist employing objective methods to evaluate these reports. This chapter explores contemporary objective procedures for evaluating personality.

Self-report personality assessment is based on a simple assumption that an individual is the best witness to his or her own innermost thoughts, beliefs, and attitudes. After all, who better to provide a window on one's thoughts and personal experiences? This viewpoint is predicated upon the following considerations:

- The person has pertinent information to share.
- The person is able to communicate such information in a form we can process.
- The individual is willing to share those personal experiences and feelings.

This view also assumes that personality assessment researchers:

- Have the means to accurately record and process data from subjective self-reports.
- Have a means of assuring that their shared information is sufficiently credible to warrant attention.

- Have a means of interpreting the information provided and assigning appropriate meaning to it.

THE OBJECTIVE ASSESSMENT TRADITION

Observation and interview have been the primary traditional raw materials upon which personality evaluations are based. However, psychologists have explored other possible approaches to evaluating a subject's performance, for example, on various tasks from which the researcher might infer personality attributes from the respondent's performance on them. Several approaches have emerged that allow the researcher to explore client-shared personality information. The first approach has been described as subjective, projective, or idiographic, and uses client's responses to external stimuli or tasks that are unstructured or projective in origin. The second approach attempts to place these data in a more broad normative perspective (comparing them with data from other people) in a more mechanical manner. This approach has been considered objective in that it requires less in the way of subjective involvement in processing and interpreting the data. In Allport's (1937) personality schema, these data would be referred to as normative or nomothetic, whereas the first approach refers to the individual's own terms as idiographic without comparing them with others'.

This chapter explores issues pertaining to objective and nomothetic personality assessment methods (see Chapter 9 in this volume for a review of projective assessment). The term "objective" has been used in several ways to describe this orientation to personality assessment and has been employed to differentiate the scientific from humanistic approaches to understanding behavior. The term has also been used to describe the structured format in which information is obtained, whereas subjective assessment information is typically acquired through a free-response approach—projective testing or interview. A third way in which the term objective has been employed is to refer to the methods of processing and interpreting results. The more subjective or idiographic approaches tend to require human judgment for interpreting the results, whereas the objective method of personality assessment has been open to interpretation by more automated interpretive strategies (Meehl, 1954). In the objective approach, interpretation best proceeds by actuarial or mechanically combined data rather than by the more clinical interpretation methods that rely on subjective reasoning (Grove & Meehl, 1996). Thus, objective personality assessment methods enable personality researchers to obtain more reliable and replicable data than the use of more subjective methods such as interview or projective techniques and include mechanistically scored and actuarially interpreted data.

ISSUES IN DEVELOPING SELF-REPORT ASSESSMENT DEVICES

Content Validity

A basic concern for personality assessment researchers in employing objective assessment methods is the need to assure that the universe of pertinent variables is contained in the assessment instrument. This concern is often described in terms of the *content validity* of the measures (see this volume). In describing content validity, Haynes, Richard, and Kubany (1995) point out:

> It is the degree to which the elements of an assessment instrument are relevant to and representative of the targeted construct for a particular assessment purpose. Content validation is applicable across assessment methods because it addresses the inferences that are based on the obtained data. Content validity has implications for the prediction of behavior and for causal models of behavior disorders, diagnosis, and estimates of treatment effects. (p. 245)

Content relevance needs to be addressed regardless of whether one is employing verbal (written or spoken) items, visual-graphic stimuli, or real-life video vignettes in the assessment instrument. A sufficiently broad range of content needs to be incorporated in the scale to sample the behavioral variables under study, and content validity requires that the scales on a personality measuring instrument be representative of the personality domain under study. Practically speaking, however, in constructing a personality measure, scale developers need to balance scale length and content coverage of the measure to serve two masters: (a) predictive validity and (b) practical application; a scale usually has a pragmatic limit to the number of items employed.

An essential ingredient in any personality assessment tool is the inclusion of a sufficient range of content that is appropriate to the evaluation. This may seem to be a trite observation; however, all too frequently a personality measure is employed in assessment situations for which relevant content for the evaluation is not representated in the instrument. Haynes et al. (1995) point out: "The use of a content-invalid assessment instrument degrades the clinical inferences derived from the obtained data because variance in obtained scores cannot be explained to a satisfactory degree by the construct" (p. 240). The employment of content-invalid procedures most often occurs when a published instrument is enthusiastically expanded to areas outside the domain of the instrument's development parameters by researchers who want to "see how the test works" with other populations without giving due consideration to the instrument's content limitations. One contemporary example of this situation involves the application of an instrument designed to assess normal range personality attributes (such as the NEO-PI developed by Costa & McCrae, 1992) to evaluate clients with clinical problems (Ben-Porath & Waller, 1992).

Format

The response format for objective recording of self-report responses is another important consideration. The choice of response format can influence both the quality of data obtained in the research and the data processing procedures employed. Several possible objective response formats for structuring the client's responses are open to consideration. The method employed can impact the accuracy of the individual's communication and will determine the ease with which data can be processed. For example, the most common objective recording methods are checklists (e.g., Gough, 1952), rating scales (e.g., Overall & Gorham, 1962), multiple choice ratings (Comrey, 1988), and Likert scales (e.g., Aiken, 1996) and dichotomous format inventories such as true-or-false (T-or-F) responses. Each format requires a different task from the subject, each has its inherent limitations as far as matching the behavior or quality being assessed, and each has its own vulnerabilities with respect to data processing. The choice of format to employ in obtaining self-reported information is important, for with each approach comes a different set of limitations and sources of potential error. For example, the simplest objective rating format is the checklist. With this tool, the participant is instructed to read through the listed items and check those that apply to him or her; however, the task is thought to be very prone to response sets (Bentler, 1969; Green, Goldman, & Salovey, 1993).

Some inventory developers have attempted to circumvent what they consider to be unwanted response sets in dichotomous response inventories by requiring that items be developed with a multiple response format; however, this method can be difficult for subjects and cumbersome in data analyses. Additionally, it often turns out that multiple choice options may actually hinge on only two options anyway. The reader interested in a thorough discussion in the construction and use of checklists and rating scales should consult the recent book published by Aiken (1996). The most widely employed response format for objective personality inventory measurement, and the one described in most detail in this chapter, employs a T-or-F response format.

Scale Construction Strategies

Several approaches to the construction of personality inventories have been explored. In their purest form, they are the rational, the factor analytic, and the empirical or criterion-keying scale construction approaches.

The *rational,* often referred to as the deductive approach, was the earliest method employed by developers of personality and temperament inventories. Early personality inventory developers such as Woodworth (1920) held to the view that people would provide the information needed for an appraisal of personality if the item contents were included in an inventory. Essentially, the rational scale construction method involves generating items based on a theoretical analysis of the construct or variable being assessed and thinking up items that address them. The rational item development approach came under criticism early in the century (Allport, 1921) because the resulting scales were considered too vulnerable to distorted responding owing to the obvious content in the inventory. However, this approach to scale construction was rehabilitated during the 1950s with the thoughtful work of Loevinger (1957).

A great deal of theoretical discussion has taken place with respect to the utility of deductive scale development methods in recent years. The most thorough discussion of the deductive approach to scale construction was provided in the classic monogaph by Loevinger (1957). More recently, Clark and Watson (1995) provide a well-articulated rationale for the use of the deductive approach to item development as a means of assuring substantive validity. Burisch (1984) provided a supporting philosophy for the rational approach to item development.

With appropriate cross-checks, rational deductive scale construction can be effectively employed with safeguards that can be built into an assessment device. Not only can the rational scale construction approach provide a valid source of personality information, but also the measuring instruments can be more easily constructed than can measures developed by empirical or factor analytic methods.

The *empirical* method was developed in reaction to the early discontent with the rational strategy of item selection. Hathaway and McKinley (1940) thought that the rational approach was not the most effective way of originating items for scales because it placed too much responsibility on the test developer to know in advance whether an item actually worked in a valid manner. Instead, the developers of the Minnesota Multiphasic Personality Inventory (MMPI) chose *not* to select items on the basis of a preconceived idea of what content measured but left the task of determining scale membership to empirical reality. They initially selected a broad range of items (symptoms, attitudes, beliefs, etc.) with the idea that they would actually try out the items in a real-world situation and determine which of them actually worked to discriminate well-defined clinical problem groups from a sample of normals. They followed this empirical or criterion-keying approach to form clusters of items into clinical scales—measures that have proven to be very robust and are still in use today, 60 years later!

A comprehensive description of empirical scale development procedures was provided by Butcher and Williams (1992). They summarized this method for developing and improving empirically derived scales:

1. *The personality variable on which the scale is being derived should be well defined.* The construct should be clearly related to personality or symptomatic variables and not attempt to assess nonpersonality factors such as abilities or intellectual variables. The groups being employed to select items (e.g., depressives versus normals) need to be well defined and homogeneous in makeup.

2. *The item pool needs to possess content validity or content relevance to the construct being assessed.* It is not possible, for example, to develop a scale measuring a particular trait if there is insufficient coverage in the item pool.

3. *Cross-validation is critical for empirical scales.* Cross-validation is very important in the development of empirical scales to eliminate items that might be selected on the basis of chance or specific sample characteristics. The sample sizes used for the developmental and the cross-validated studies should be large enough to provide stable test scores and to reduce the possibility of unrelated items being included in the scale.

4. *The resulting empirical scale should possess appropriate statistical properties.* For example, if the scale is proposed as a measure of a unitary dimension, the scale should demonstrate high internal consistency, for example, with an alpha level of .70 or greater, although lower alpha levels can also be valuable in understanding the construct underlying the scale (Schmitt, 1996). If the proposed measure is a multidimensional empirical scale, as are many empirically derived scales, it is not necessary to require homogeneity of items for the entire scale or that the scale possess reliability obtained by such methods as the split-half method. However, the resulting scale should possess an acceptable level of retest reliability.

5. *All empirical scales should have clearly defined empirical relationships or scale correlates.* Any empirical personality scale, or any scale for that matter, needs

to have a clear pattern of external relationships (e.g., correlations with other scales) to assure that it measures what it is supposed to measure.

6. *Practical uses for the scale should be demonstrated.* Research establishing scale predictive power should be available; that is, the scale should possess sufficient sensitivity and specificity in predicting the characteristics it is supposed to assess. It is important to show that the scale classifies relevant cases at the cutoff points recommended.

7. *Construct validity for the scale should be reported.* The initial publication of the empirical scale should present evidence of construct validity (Cronbach & Meehl, 1955). For example, correlations between the proposed scale and other, external behavior should be presented to enable users to compare them.

The *factor analytic approach* to scale development is an item-selection or scale purification method rather than an item-generation technique. Descriptions of the factor analytic method in scale development can be found in several resources (Comrey, 1988; Floyd & Widaman, 1995; Gorsuch, 1983). The most successful application of factor analytic scale development methods can be found in the work of Cattell (1957), who used factor analysis to develop the 16PF Questionnaire (see Cattell, Eber, & Tatsuoka, 1988).

The 16PF was initially developed as a nonclinical measure employing items that described behavior or psychological characteristics referred to as traits. Initially, a pool of items was obtained to represent the characteristics of the proposed traits. Once a universe of item contents had been identified and preliminary data collected, then factor analysis was employed to form likely meaningful scales. The items were found to group into 16 primary personality dimensions that were considered to mark the main elements of personality.

Other Strategies for Item Selection and Refinement: Item Response Theory

A relatively new psychometric approach that can be employed in scale construction involves the item analysis procedure that is referred to as IRT or item response theory. The IRT strategy is based on the idea that responses to test items reflect an underlying dimension such as a trait. Embretson (1996; see also Chapter 12) provides a description of how test construction according to the "new rules" of scale construction (IRT) differs from that of traditional scale construction theory. She postulates that new rules of measurement are fundamentally different from classical test theory and require a different perception of procedures for item selection.

A scale might be developed by reference to the underlying trait by evaluating item characteristic curves that reflect the hypothesized underlying dimension. This relationship of the item properties and the underlying trait can be expressed graphically in the form of an S-shaped curve, referred to as an item characteristic curve (ICC). This curve displays the conditional probabilities of response to an item for different levels of the latent trait to be measured. In general, the higher the theta, the greater the probability of a response in a specified direction (Ellis, Minsel, & Becker, 1989; Weiss & Yoes, 1988).

The three parameters that are involved in this item response function (IRF) are referred to as the a, b, and c parameters of the item—the discrimination, difficulty (or extremity), and pseudo-guessing parameters. The a parameter is an index of item discrimination and is, in many respects, similar to the item-test correlation of classical test theory. Higher values of the a parameter are associated with items that are best able to discriminate among trait values. The difficulty parameter (b) indicates the level of theta necessary for an individual to have a probability of .50 of responding in a given direction to the item. In IRT, high values of item difficulty are associated with items that have low endorsement probabilities. The third parameter (c), pseudo-guessing, represents the probability of keyed response for individuals with very low trait levels. When a test item is described in terms of all three parameters, it is referred to as a three-parameter model. If we assume that the c parameter is zero, and use the a and b parameters to describe the IRF, we are using a two-parameter model. When we describe items only in terms of their item difficulties, we have a one-parameter (Rasch model; Weiss & Yoes, 1988).

IRT requires two specific assumptions before it can be applied to the analysis of item responses: It must be assumed that (a) the item pool is unidimensional, that is, all items assess a single latent trait; and (b) the probabilities of the specified responses at different levels of the underlying trait can be fit adequately by some IRT model. The IRT approach shows promise as an item-selection procedure in constructing personality scales (Hambleton, Swaminathan, & Rogers, 1991; Hulin, Drasgow, & Parsons, 1983; Reise & Waller, 1993), although to date no widely used commercial personality scales have been developed with IRT procedures.

The Relative Effectiveness of Different Scale Construction Methods

Research comparing the performance of the rational, empirical, and factor analytic approaches has not found any of these methods to be superior to the others in overall effectiveness. Research by Hase and Goldberg (1967) and replicated by Burisch (1978) found that the empirical, rational, and factor analytic approaches were equally valid scale development methods. Burisch, in his replication of the Hase and Goldberg study, showed that different test construction methods yield measures with comparable validity. He concluded that because they were equally effective strategies, the deductive, rational approach might be preferable on grounds that it is a more efficient strategy and recommended that test constructors consider using the rational method of developing tests.

Combined Strategies

Today, one is more likely to find a combination of these strategies employed to develop personality scales rather than reliance on a single approach. For example, scale construction might initially follow a deductive or rational approach to develop a provisional item pool; then, with a provisional data set, use factor analytic methods or internal consistency statistics (Alpha coefficient) to purify scales by eliminating low-commonality items; then, after norms are developed, conduct validity studies to determine if the items are predicting behavior in an efficient manner. (For examples, see the development of MMPI-2 content scales in Butcher, Graham, Williams, & Ben-Porath, 1990, and the development of the Treatment Planning Inventory by Butcher, 1998.)

THE RECURRING ISSUE OF RESPONSE DISTORTION IN PERSONALITY ASSESSMENT

Response Sets

Deviant response approaches can intrude into objective personality assessment. They may come as a result of a particular individual's psychopathological need for privacy or may emerge out of the context of the assessment situation itself. For example, parents being assessed in a family custody dispute might have a strong need to appear "highly virtuous" to win custody of their children, or people being evaluated in criminal court may exaggerate mental health symptoms in an effort to convince the court that they were insane at the time of the crime to obtain a softer sentence. Regardless of the underlying motivation and as a first step in understanding their impact, potential invalidating response patterns need to be appraised to assure protocol credibility.

Two earlier response set criticisms aimed at true-false questionnaires, particularly the MMPI, were the social desirability response set (Edwards, 1957) and the acquiescence response set (Cronbach, 1942; Jackson & Messick, 1962). Both of these criticisms were explored extensively during the 1950s and 1960s. The proponents of response set interpretation of objective testing made recommendations for reducing the impact of response sets by such strategies as employing only low socially undesirable items or by balancing scales in terms of true-false responding. However, Block's (1965) critique of the response set interpretation provides the most important statement pertinent to handling the challenge of response sets. Although response sets may be present in different objectively presented materials, they are clearly not the most important determinants of responding. Rather, the extent of external validity is the most important determinant in self-report questionnaires. Block's classic answer to the response set criticisms of Edwards and Jackson and Messick showed that the most important criterion of a scale's worth was whether or not it actually *predicted* and described personality.

One of the most effective ways of dealing with response sets involves measuring them and incorporating this information into the assessment. Although response sets are still occasionally employed to criticize inventory assessment (Jackson, Fraboni, & Helmes, 1997), the critical test of a measuring instrument is its predictive or descriptive power. The final arbiter of response sets is whether they provide useful information themselves if they are operating.

Measures of Invalidating Attitudes

In most clinical assessment situations, response sets such as those noted by Edwards (1957) and Jackson and Messick (1962) are not exerting much influence. People being assessed in mental health contexts are generally up front with their assessment and do not respond in a socially desirable way or simply check yes or no as these response set interpretations imply. Even in a population of convicted felons, the majority of those taking the MMPI-2 responded in an honest manner (Gallagher, Ben-Porath, & Briggs, 1997). It is, of course, important to appraise the possibility of invalidating conditions in any personality assessment; however, once credible self-report is assured, the assessment can proceed as planned.

Historically, MMPI researchers have attempted to deal with the problem of uncooperative responding by assessing known invalidating response approaches to assure the credibility of the protocol. Before the desired personality pattern information is relied on in interpretation, the practitioner must assure that *no* deviant invalidating conditions exist. In the initial publication of the MMPI, the developers were concerned that potentially invalidating conditions could occur if the subject were motivated to distort his or her true picture in their assessment. They published two measures, a "lie" scale and an exaggerated problem presentation scale. Later, Meehl and Hathaway (1946) added a defensiveness scale as a measure of detecting defensive responding not caught by the original lie scale.

A number of methods have been used to detect invalidating conditions that some subjects employ to thwart assessment or to avoid an appraisal of their personality. These strategies can undermine the assessment by producing a protocol that makes no sense. Several of these invalidating conditions in self-report assessment will be described below. All of these potentially invalidating conditions can be effectively assessed and potentially counteracted in the assessment.

Item Omissions

Most personality inventories are developed with the idea that the subject can and will respond to all of the items in the scale. When items are not endorsed, particularly a large number of them, the scores on the inventory can be highly attenuated. It is therefore important to assure compliance with the test instructions or at least obtain an appraisal of the extent to which the individual may have failed to comply with the instructions to complete all the questions. Therefore, an accounting of the omitted responses can provide an important index of noncompliance that needs to be taken into account in evaluating the protocol. Incomplete records can play havoc with data analyses in research studies, thus this variable is important for qualifying records for inclusion. Omitted items can provide clues to motivational sets that could be operating in research. In one study of adolescents, for example, two youngsters completed the one-and-a-half-hour testing session in less than 10 minutes by simply endorsing the first few items on each inventory administered and leaving out the rest. In research studies, participants with incomplete records should be eliminated from the research data pool because missing data would distort and weaken the analyses.

Unusual Pattern Responding

It is a good idea to perform a visual inspection of the answer sheets in group-administered personality research studies. The investigator can often discover some unusual records that might not be evident with machine processing. Some subjects may be insufficiently motivated to participate in self-report studies and may hurry through their responses or simply answer without regard to content by marking answers in a particular pattern. One subject, for example, marked every third item true and the rest false; another person simply responded to every fourth item, leaving those in between blank; another person (who was being tested in late December) marked his item responses on the answer sheet in the shape of a Christmas tree.

All True or All False Responding

Two patterns that are relatively more common among some individuals who do not wish to comply with the testing but wish to mark up the answer sheet as though they have completed the record are the mostly true or mostly false patterns. Inspection of the answer sheet can often discover those uncooperative response patterns. Sometimes, uncooperative research participants will vary this format by engaging in such strategies as responding to the first item as true and the remainder false, or answering one column true and another column false. As noted above, visual inspection of answer sheets will often identify non-content-oriented responding. With respect to the all true or all false pattern, it is important to score these variables and determine for a particular inventory what frequency of true and false would be expected by normal participants. Records can then be evaluated to determine if a particular subject has endorsed an inordinate number of true or false responses.

Random Responding

Another invalidating, non-content-oriented manner of answering personality inventory items is the random response set. In this approach, the subject responds to the items with essentially random checking without reading the content. This situation may occur when the individual, being partially compliant, wants to turn in a completed protocol but does not want to go through the effort of reading and carefully thinking about the content. Random response protocols also are obtained in situations in which the individual gets mixed up in the items or is unable to read and comprehend the items. This invalidating approach to personality items can be detected with several types of control scales. Meehl and Hathaway (1946) developed the F scale of the MMPI, which, if extremely elevated, is sensitive to random responding. On the original MMPI F scale, which contained 64 items, random performances would produce extremely elevated F scale scores: about 32 items would be endorsed. That is, with a 64-item scale and a two-choice format, chances are that the person would endorse about 32 true and 32 false.

Random responding can be detected by the MMPI-2 F scale in a similar manner, although there are slightly fewer items (60). However, there is another effective way of detecting random responding on MMPI-2: the use of a response inconsistency scale.

Inconsistent Responding

Inconsistent responding to personality questionnaire items is a bit more difficult to detect but nevertheless represents a threat to the acquisition of accurate personality information. The best way to obtain an appraisal of inconsistency is to determine, from the individual's protocol, whether he or she has endorsed the content in a consistent manner. To develop an inconsistency measure in a personality questionnaire, it is necessary to have a number of items whose content calls for similar or opposite responding. Perhaps the best example of effective consistency scales is found in the MMPI-2 (Butcher & Williams, 1992). Two scales were developed for this purpose: the VRIN scale and the TRIN scale.

The Variable Response Inconsistency Scale (VRIN) is made up of 67 pairs of items for which one or two of four possible configurations (true-false, false-true, true-true, false-false) represent inconsistent responses. For example, answering true to "I do not tire quickly" and true to "I feel tired a good deal of the time," represents semantically inconsistent responses. The scale is scored by obtaining a total of the number of inconsistent responses.

The True Response Inconsistency Scale (TRIN) was developed to appraise the tendency that some people have to respond in an inconsistent manner to items that, to be consistent, should be endorsed in a particular way. The TRIN scale is made up of 23 pairs of items to which the same response is semantically inconsistent. For example, answering the items "Most of the time I feel blue" and "I am happy most of the time" both true, or both false, is inconsistent. Fourteen of the 23 item pairs are scored as inconsistent only if the client responds *true* to both items. Nine of the item pairs are scored as inconsistent if the client responds *false* to both items. Three additional pairs are scored inconsistent if the client responds either both *true* or both *false*.

Fake Good: Highly Virtuous Self-Presentation

Some people have difficulty self-disclosing personal information and tend to present themselves in an overly favorable light on personality scales. This test-taking strategy is more common in situations such as clinical or forensic settings in which the client has a need to appear well adjusted to gain some benefit or services. For example, applicants for desirable positions tend to present themselves on self-report instruments in a highly favorable and virtuous manner. Some personality inventories, particularly the MMPI and MMPI-2 with the L (lie) scale, contain measures to detect the tendency on the part of some clients to exaggerate their virtues and lay claim to unrealistically higher moral standards than other people.

Fake Good: Problem Denial

Another, somewhat related aspect of presenting a good front on personality inventory items involves problem denial. In this response pattern, the individual is simply checking positive adjustment options and denying problems. The individual does not, as in the situation described immediately above, attempt to claim excessive virtue—he or she only denies problems. This distinction has been described in detail by Lanyon (1993).

Exaggerated Symptom Checking

This invalidating condition has been referred to in several ways in the literature on invalidating response approaches: as faking, exaggerating, plus-getting, malingering, or infrequent responding. This response is commonly found in situations in which the participant feels it is to his or her advantage to appear psychologically disturbed on the testing and approaches the test with an effort designed to claim a lot of symptoms. This invalidating response condition has been more widely studied than any of the other deviant response attitudes (for recent review and discussions, see Baer, Wetter, & Berry, 1992; Berry, 1995; Berry, Baer, & Harris, 1991; Berry et al., 1992; Schretlen, 1988).

This invalidating pattern was initially described by Hathaway and McKinley (1943), who developed an index (the F or infrequency scale) to detect exaggerated responding. The rationale behind this scale is very simple: Persons who attempt to present a more disturbed psychological adjustment than they actually are experiencing tend to claim an *excessive* number of symptoms. Hathaway and McKinley developed the F scale by determining the frequency of response to the MMPI items by the normative sample and chose items that had a low frequency of response, less than 10%. Individuals who were exaggerating their complaint pattern tend to respond to these extreme items in a pathological direction.

More recently, Arbisi and Ben-Porath (1995, 1997) developed another type of infrequency scale for the MMPI-2 that addresses possible malingering of psychological symptoms in a mental health treatment context. This infrequency scale, F(p), provides an estimate of symptom exaggeration based on a psychiatric data set rather than the normative sample as with the original F scale. This measure assesses the extent to which the test taker has responded in a manner that is more extreme than patients in a psychiatric setting.

Unlikely Clinical Picture

One value of having a substantial research base on a personality measure is that the psychologist would have a range of typical performances on the scale to guide usage. Groups of individuals such as depressed patients or police applicants or alcoholics tend to respond more like their own group than not. This, of course, is the underlying basis of MMPI interpretation—that people in various circumstances (e.g., depression) possess many common personality features. That is, the scales have established correlates for various homogeneous populations. A corollary to this general rule is that if an individual from a known, well-established population performs in a manner that is *extremely* different from expectation, then further evaluation of this protocol is needed. One hypothesis is that the individual does not possess the characteristics associated with that prototypal group. Another possibility for interpretation is that the deviant pattern has resulted from an unusual motivational set.

A very substantial literature has grown up around the important task of assessing protocol validity. Any personality scale that is going to be used for making clinical decisions must have a comprehensive set of validity indices. However, some test publishers are still producing new personality measures that do not contain a means of assessing protocol validity. It is important for the practitioner and personality researcher to assure that this critical aspect of self-report is appropriately addressed in assessment instruments that are used.

CULTURAL CONSIDERATIONS IN PERSONALITY SCALE DEVELOPMENT

During the O. J. Simpson trial in 1996, news reporters periodically described public opinion polls that were taken to determine whether citizens believed that the former football player and television celebrity was guilty or not of having murdered his ex-wife and her acquaintance. The results were typically reported by ethnic background, with rather different results depending on the race of the respondent. For example, one national TV poll showed:

African American sample	Not guilty = 66%
White American sample	Not guilty = 33%

This difference is highly significant and is likely to be deeply rooted in American culture and attitudes. If such differences in attitude are so prominent in this situation, are there other cultural differences that could impact other areas in which personal attitudes play a part—in the area of personality assessment? Are personality scales vulnerable to such powerful ethnic differences? If so, what do test developers need to do to account for these differences and modify their procedures, if necessary, to obtain a veridical assessment for everyone?

In the development of a personality scale, researchers need to be aware of potentially biasing effects of culture and, if broad generality is the goal, construct personality measures that will address the problems in question across all ethnic groups (see Chapter 3). Or, if the information collection process is biased, it must be countered by such means as *separate* norms or correction factors to eliminate potential negative results. Publishers of personality scales need to present ethnic group data in test manuals so that potential users will be able to evaluate the possibility of ethnic group differences.

With the original MMPI, questions of ethnic group influence were widely explored (see Dahlstrom, Lachar, & Dahlstrom, 1986). There were several clear reasons why the original MMPI was vulnerable to the criticism of potential bias. Some original item content appeared to pull for differential responding; for example, some items (such as "I like Lincoln better than Washington" or some of the various religion items on the original test) tended to elicit different responses from minority than majority group members. In addition, the original norms for the inventory were overly narrow because only White, middle-class, rural subjects had been incorporated in the original normative sample.

With the revision of the MMPI in 1989, and to eliminate criticisms of ethnic bias, the MMPI Restandardization Committee made great efforts to eliminate potential ethnic and minority group differences in several ways:

1. Items were rewritten to eliminate bias where possible.
2. A new, nationally representative normative sample was collected for the norms.
3. Several studies were conducted to evaluate the potential effects of minority group membership on MMPI-2 scales.

No ethnic bias has been found on the MMPI-2 that would unfairly portray or fail to assess minority group members. The scales appear to address the personality process or structure for minority clients in a manner similar to that for Whites. During the revision of the MMPI, a substantial amount of data was collected to evaluate possible ethnic factors. Moreover, a proportional number of African Americans, American Indians, Asian Americans, and Hispanics was included in the normative sample. On examining these diverse data, the conclusion of the MMPI Restandardization Committee was that no racial bias was operating in groups of normals, consequently only one general norm for all groups was developed. Separate norms for different ethnic groups were not considered necessary. Several studies can be cited to support the view that there is minimal influence of ethnic group membership on MMPI-2 scores (Ben-Porath, Shondrick, & Stafford, 1994; Keefe, Sue, Enomoto, Durvasula, & Chao, 1996; Lucio, Reyes-Lagunes, & Scott, 1994; Timbrook & Graham, 1994; Tinius & Ben-Porath, 1993; Velasquez, 1997).

International Adaptations of Personality Scales

Until fairly recently in human history, people lived in relatively small and generally isolated groups and shared a common language and culture with other people much like themselves. This situation has changed substantially and, with the advent of rapid transportation and instant communication, our national and cultural boundaries have become less rigid. International commerce and relationships have become commonplace, and many countries contain heterogeneous mixes of many subpopulations. It is not unusual, for example, in cities such as Los Angeles, Philadelphia, Chicago, Toronto, London, Paris, and New York (to mention only some of the larger ones), to find large enclaves of very culturally diverse people who, in addition to sharing elements of their new culture, maintain ties to their prior culture. Many reasons can be found for the great population shifts of the nineteenth and twentieth centuries, including economic migrations, refuge from wars, and the search for more acceptable religious and political climates, to name only a few.

The increased heterogeneity of many national populations has made it imperative for nations to develop broader social and scientific perspectives that pay due consideration to cultural diversity (see Chapter 3). In many clinical settings in the United States, for example, it is common for psychology practitioners to be involved in the assessment of clients who come from other countries and speak little English. The science of cross-cultural psychology is devoted to developing an understanding of the influence of cultural factors in human adaptation and behavior. The understanding of human behavior across cultures requires careful weighing of cultural factors and meticulous application of stringent research methods if resultant observations are going to be generalizable.

Ways of viewing psychological adjustment problems have evolved considerably as a result of the greater cultural exchange over the past few decades. We have come to recognize more commonality in human adaptation and maladaptive efforts than we did before and are more aware of the importance of developing procedures that have broad applicability across cultures. There is a great need to incorporate a multicultural perspective in the mental health field today because of the great number of cross-cultural assessments in the United States and the efforts currently being employed to transport psychological assessment technology to other countries. Clinical psychology is no longer a provincial branch of the field that is only oriented toward providing services to a White, middle-class majority. To be used with diverse clients, a personality scale should be culturally permeable when translated.

There has been a long tradition in cross-cultural psychology of studying personality differences between cultural groups as a means of understanding the possible effects of culture on human development. Many psychological tests, particularly projective techniques like the Rorschach and Thematic Apperception Test, were employed in these early studies. It was thought that their ambiguous pictorial stimuli would be relatively culture-free. It was also thought that these measures would provide in-depth information about individuals regardless of cultural background. Unfortunately, this approach to cross-cultural study came under a great deal of criticism for a number of reasons; for example, the interpretation of projective techniques was too subjective (see Lindzey, 1951, for a full discussion of the use of projective techniques in cross-cultural research).

More recent cross-cultural test adaptations have evolved for rather different reasons than the exploration of cultural differences in personality development. Today, personality tests are being widely translated into other languages and cultures as a means of incorporating successful methods of clinical assessment into other cultures. That is, tests are being translated and adapted in other cultures by psychologists and psychiatrists in those countries for use in clinical psychological assessment or research in those countries.

How can a personality scale that was developed in the United States apply in other countries that are linguistically and culturally different? First, it is important to be aware that the manifestation of psychopathology (e.g., schizophrenia) across cultures takes similar forms. The major psychological disorders are typically found to have a common structure across known cultures and language groups (Kendall & Hammen, 1998). This commonality has allowed for the development of effective, reliable psychiatric diagnostic systems such as the *International Classification of Diseases,* 10th edition *(ICD-10)* and the *Diagnostic and Statistical Manual of Mental Disorders,* 4th edition *(DSM-IV)* that can be applied in other countries. Second, the MMPI-2 item pool, a detailed listing of many psychological symptoms, defines many of these psychological disorders. Personality scales such as the MMPI-2 address pertinent diagnostic content that can be translated into other languages and assess psychological problems in other countries (Butcher, 1996). To develop an effective translation of a personality scale, it is important that translators follow rigorous translation procedures (Brislin, 1986; Butcher, 1996):

1. In the initial stages of the translation work, only well-qualified bilingual translators (e.g., those who have lived five or more years in both countries) should be employed to translate the items. The items should be translated by two or more bilingual translators who work together after the initial translations to combine their separate item renderings into agreed upon form.

2. After careful translation, the items should be back-translated into English by a different translator. The back-translation often uncovers a number of items that were not clearly translated in the initial translation. These should be retranslated until an acceptable version is obtained.

3. When an acceptable translation and back-translation have been completed, it is often possible, particularly with a well-established personality measure, to conduct further study of the items to assure equivalence. The translated version and the English version could be administered to a sample of bilingual subjects. The responses to these two administrations can be evaluated in a manner analogous to a test-retest study.

4. Additional field testing of the instrument should be undertaken by administering the final version to known populations in the target culture. For example, studies might be undertaken with clearly diagnosed clinical groups to determine if they respond in a manner similar to patients in the United States.

5. It is also important to conduct research with normals in the target culture to determine if they are responding to the items in a manner similar to those in the original culture. In countries where the normative samples are divergent from the sample on which the original scale was developed, it would be necessary to renorm the scale on samples of normals in the new country to assure appropriate use.

The most widely adapted clinical personality assessment instrument in international contexts is the MMPI. The original MMPI was adapted in many clinical and research settings around the world (Butcher & Pancheri, 1976). Over 150 translations into 46 languages (these were multiple translations in some languages) were completed on this instrument. The cross-national application of the MMPI-2 has increased greatly in recent years as numerous psychologists from other countries have begun to adapt Western psychological tests in their clinical work and research. The recently published *International Adaptations of the MMPI-2* (Butcher, 1996) illustrates broad-based international collaboration in clinical psychology. Fifty-six contributors from 26 countries described their research and clinical efforts to translate and adapt the MMPI-2 in numerous countries.

Several factors account for the broadened application of the MMPI-2 for international uses: It possesses a number of characteristics that make it readily adaptable in other languages; it addresses a wide range of clinical problems that can be found in other cultures; it has an objective-scoring format, making data processing relatively easy; it has demonstrated validity across a range of cultures; it can be a relatively quick and easy instrument to learn; and it is interpreted according to objective rules, reducing subjectivity.

The MMPI-2 items are well suited for international use because their simple language structure and relevance for assessment of important classes of abnormal behavior allow them to be effectively translated into psychopathology measures in other languages. In some languages, the content of some items need to be altered to make them culturally relevant for the target population. Several bilingual retest projects have been reported on MMPI-2 translations to date (Almagor & Nevo, 1996; Deinard, Butcher, Thao, Vang, & Hang, 1996; Konraos, 1996). This research has found that the MMPI-2 scales operate similarly when the inventory is administered to bilinguals in both languages. Many test translators have found that the American norms are applicable in their country because the scale scores in the target country generally fall within the standard error of measurement for the MMPI-2 scales in the U.S. normative population. Many researchers who have developed new norms have typically found that the country-specific *T*-scores fall within the relatively few *T*-score points of the U.S. norms (Almagor & Nevo, 1996; Gillet et al., 1996; Pancheri, Sirigatti, & Biondi, 1996; Sloore, Derksen, de Mey, & Hellenbosch, 1996).

Comparability research on clinical populations has found that the translated MMPI-2 produces similar results in clinical assessment in the new cultures. Moreover, research using discriminant validity evaluations in psychiatric settings in other countries have found results that are congruent with those in the United States. Patients with similar problems in other countries tend to produce similar MMPI-2 patterns, and studies reporting personality ratings have reported behavioral descriptors similar to those in the United States (Ellertsen, Havik, & Skavhellen, 1996; Han, 1996; Lucio & Reyes-Lagunes, 1996; Rissetti, Himmel, & Gonzalez-Moreno, 1996). Factor analyses of MMPI-2 scales in other national research projects have shown comparable factor structures; usually, a four-factor solution emerges when the 10 traditional MMPI standard scales are included in the analysis (Han, 1996; Rissetti et al., 1996; Shiota, Krauss, & Clark, 1996).

In recent cross-cultural research, objective interpretive procedures were shown to have applicability in other countries and interpretations of test protocols based on patients in one country had international generalizability. Practitioners in other countries administer the MMPI-2 to their clients. The test is then computer-interpreted and the narrative report is provided to the clinician, who rates the personality descriptions in terms of relevancy and accuracy (Berah et al., 1993; Gillet et al., 1996). The computer-derived reports, originally developed for patients in the United States, have been rated highly accurate by practitioners in other countries. Recently, Butcher et al. (1998) conducted a study of the Minnesota Report for the MMPI-2 in several countries (Australia, France, Norway, and the United States) and found that the computer-derived reports were highly accurate when applied with patients in those countries.

ASSURING GENERALIZATION VALIDITY

Any personality measure should have a research base that includes a range of demonstrated predictive and descriptive studies. There are a number of standard methods used to demonstrate the effectiveness of a psychometric instrument. Several important features will be described in this section.

The Importance of Up-to-Date Norms

For test scores to be meaningfully interpreted, they must be placed in an appropriate context and compared against a *standard* or reference population. Moreover, to be broadly applied, the reference group for a test needs to be representative of the population on which the instrument is to be employed. With some notable exceptions, most developers of published personality inventories attempt to provide general norms derived on samples of nonpatients obtained from the population at large to serve as a reference population. Two recent exceptions to this traditional normative philosophy are worth describing at this point because the use of these instruments would require a very different approach to understanding the scores than one finds with traditional normative scales.

The first notable exception to sound normative procedures involves the Basic Personality Inventory (BPI) published by Jackson (1989), an instrument devised to assess the clinical domains measured by the MMPI. Jackson employed nonstandard and flawed normative data collection procedures and data analysis methods to develop norms that limit the test's generalizability. For example, the test norms were collected in an unusual manner—by mailing test booklets to potential subjects and inviting them to complete the items. This uncontrolled testing situation leaves potential test users with uncertainty as to who actually completed the items on which the norms are based; in addition, there are questions as to the makeup of the normative sample. No effort was made to assure ethnic balance in the normative sample; the majority of persons participating in the study were White.

Another problem with Jackson's data collection procedures is that people who completed the testing only responded to one-third of the items in the inventory. Thus, few participants responded to the entire item pool in the normative sample, limiting any interpretations from data analyses requiring the use of all of the items in the booklet (such as alpha coefficient) for the scales.

The second variation from the use of standard normative procedures involved the use of a nonstandard normative procedure referred to as "base rate norms" (Millon, 1994) against which to compare scores. The test developer employed a very different normative approach by basing the reference group on patients in treatment rather than persons drawn from the general population. The scale scores provided show the person's standing on the various scales as compared only with other psychiatric patients. There are, of course, some fundamental limitations to the application of the instrument, particularly in situations in which the question of normality might be an important factor to assess. The so-called base rate norms do not allow for the description of normal behavior because there is no normal reference group. Most people taking the test consequently would obtain a fairly pathological picture because they are assumed to be a patient—the test only provides a perspective on *what kind* of patient they are according to their self-description. Thus, the Millon Clinical Multiaxial Inventory (MCMI-III) scales can *not* appropriately be employed for describing or characterizing normal behavior as most other clinically oriented personality tests do. The meaning of scale elevations is more narrowly defined than most personality measures. For example, the MCMI-III should not be employed in forensic assessment (Otto & Butcher, 1995) because it overpathologizes normals and cannot specifically address the question as to *whether* a client is experiencing psychological disorder.

The Question of Separate, Special Norms

The MMPI-2 publisher occasionally receives a request to provide special norms for such groups as police department applicants, child custody litigants, and nuclear power plant employees to provide a "more relevant" comparison group than the standard norms. What is the merit of such suggestions? Is there a downside to the publication of special, alternative norms for a standard measure?

Hathaway (personal communication, March, 1969) staunchly maintained the view that personality scales like the MMPI should have only *one* normative or reference population: "One size fits all. One standard ruler to measure length!" He was opposed to the idea that different populations required the development of separate norms to be useful because "the main goal is to measure personality characteristics against a single, established standard."

The use of multiple standards in evaluating respondents' test scores could create interpretive problems for a standard assessment instrument, but, in situations where a population deviates substantially, specific norm groups might be in order. First, the downside or difficulties of such a suggestion should be noted. Then some mention should be made of several special instances in which a separate test norm has seemed desirable. There are several main problems with developing separate norms for subsegments of the general population:

- The primary value of the normative approach is in having a reference group by which individual scores can be compared: a single standard for the scale. Everyone using the scale knows the makeup of the normative sample and employs the same standard. If multiple norm sets were in use, there would be considerable confusion as to which norm set to employ for a particular situation.

- If alternative norms are developed for adults (e.g., police applicants), then the validity research that has accumulated on the standard set of norms would not apply with the other "special" norms.

- To be meaningful, the instrument would need to be retooled for the new norm group. Additional validity studies would be required and new cut-offs for interpretation would be needed.

When the score distribution of a subpopulation is extremely different from the general normative group and the use of the population norms would result in classification problems, then a separate norm group would need to be given serious consideration. For example, adolescent responses to the MMPI-2 items have been shown to be very different from those of adults. Research on MMPI-based items demonstrated a need to develop specific adolescent norms for individuals between 14 and 18.

Another situation that has prompted the development of separate norms has been found in some foreign language adaptations. In some countries (e.g., China), the responses of normals to the items were sufficiently different on some scales to require a different set of normative *T*-scores for the scales to work properly. In other countries, the responses of normals were essentially no different than those of normals in the United States; however, for political reasons, it was thought imperative to have the scales normed on the indigenous population rather than use the American norms.

Rather than using separate norms for the MMPI-2, an alternative approach for taking population deviations into account has been widely explored: base rate information (Finn & Kamphuis, 1995). That is, researchers have provided empirical information about the scores of various subpopulations by detailing the base rates of well-defined samples. In this way, the standard norms are employed, but special case status is taken into consideration by examining relative frequency of profile scores across various samples (see Butcher, 1996).

RESEARCH DESIGNED TO VERIFY AND EXPLORE MEANINGS OF PERSONALITY SCALES

This section addresses several research strategies that are designed to evaluate the effectiveness of a psychometric measure—its ability to do what it was designed to do. Several types of research are recommended before a new measure can be considered ready for broad use. The types of investigations described in this section are not simply developmental projects to be stashed away after the test has been published. Rather, these can be studies that are devised to contribute to the strength and construct validity of the measure as it is being used.

Exploration of Internal Psychometric Properties

The psychometric properties of a scale help to assure the scale user that the scale is operating properly to address the constructs under study. These studies center on issues of reliability—the extent to which a scale consistently measures what it is designed to measure. There are several approaches to reliability that need to be explored in test construction; each has its place in establishing how well the scale is measuring the constructs it was designed to assess. Specifically, if a person is tested twice, how closely would the scores agree (Cronbach, 1970)? There are several aspects to assessing the reliability of a scale that are important to take into consideration.

The first psychometric property to be considered is scale homogeneity, or the extent to which the scale is measuring a single dimension or is made up of multiple dimensions. The measure that is most frequently employed to assess internal consistency (item homogeneity) is the *alpha coefficient* (Cronbach, 1951; Smith & McCarthy, 1995). In developing any personality scale, it is important to determine the extent to which the intended measure addresses a single trait or underlying dimension or is multifactorial. Recently, Schmitt (1996) called attention to the fact that the alpha coefficient does not provide an appropriate index of homogeneity, noting that it is also important to indicate intercorrelations of the items along with corrected intercorrelations for the alpha coefficient to have meaning.

A second important test characteristic involves a determination of how consistently a measure performs over time. This quality, *retest reliability,* involves the measure's stability or consistency at producing a comparable score if tested on more than one occasion (Cronbach, 1970; Guilford, 1954). The use of retest statistics is one of the most important approaches for test users to review as to whether the scale is likely to result in similar scores if readministered at a later date.

Another important property for evaluating and using a psychometric measure is the standard error of measurement (s.e.m.) or the standard deviation of a set of measures. The s.e.m. for a scale informs us as to how widely measures on the same individual are likely to deviate upon retesting.

Establishment of External Relationships

The extent to which a scale measures the qualities or personality characteristics it is intended to assess is referred to as validity. For many assessment psychologists, this is the most pertinent scale attribute and is considered to be the primary means of determining whether a personality measure can be employed in clinical assessment. Several standard methods of scale validation have been devised.

Content Validity

Earlier in this chapter, the importance of content validity was addressed. The proper selection of item content was considered to be critical to assuring that the scale contained content that reflected the attributes being measured. This approach is one of the earliest methods of assuring scale validity. Content validity is a necessary but not sufficient means of assuring that a test measures what it is supposed to measure.

Concurrent Validity

Concurrent validity was also described earlier in the chapter. It is important that a personality scale be well defined in terms of its relationships with other established measures in use in the field of personality assessment. Concurrent validity studies usually describe the intercorrelations (both positive and negative) between the scale under study and other personality measures. It is important that a scale possess discriminant validity as well as convergent validity. One research method that is widely employed in establishing the power of a scale at discriminating among and between other variables is the multimethod-multitrait method of Campbell and Fiske (1979). It is usually insufficient just to show that a particular scale is associated with one set of variables without also specifying the types of variables with which a scale is not associated.

External or Criterion Validity

Ultimately, the acceptance of a personality measure and its life span in practice will be contingent upon whether it delivers accurate and reliable predictions of behavior in the real world. The ultimate criterion of a personality assessment instrument is its predictive power (predictive criterion-related validity). A scale can be psychometrically elegant and attractive in design, but if it does not perform up to expectation at providing valid and usable personality assessments, it is essentially worthless. By the same token, an instrument that produces valid personality descriptions, even if it is overly long for individuals to take and psychometrically cumbersome for researchers to manage at times, will find a persistent acceptance in the field of clinical decision making as long as it delivers on prediction. One instrument that has been extensively validated in a broad range of samples is the MMPI-2. A number of traditional studies were published on the original MMPI to provide an external correlate database (Gilberstadt & Duker, 1965; Marks, Seeman, & Haller, 1974). The personality descriptors can be automatically applied to obtained MMPI-2 scale scores and indices. Several recent studies have addressed external correlates of the MMPI-2 measures since they underwent revision (Archer, Griffin, & Aiduk, 1995; Butcher, Rouse, & Perry, in press; Williams & Butcher, 1989).

It is important for test developers to explore the operation of the scales and the resulting distribution of scores in the populations for which the scale is intended.

Construct Validity

Another form of scale validation involves exploring the meaning of the construct underlying the scale (Cronbach & Meehl, 1955). Cronbach (1970) pointed out:

> Sooner or later every tester has to go behind the experience table and behind the test content, to say what processes seem to account for the responses observed. Every test is to some degree impure and unlikely to measure exactly what its name implies. Identifying impurities is one part of the process of explanation. (p. 159)

Construct validation involves the task of tying in the empirical observations about a scale with the underlying meaning of the constructs being assessed. The sum total of the validities and the extent to which the scale can be seen to enhance our understanding of the constructs underlying the measures is referred to as construct validity. This type of validation is important in advancing our understanding of the measures in question.

Validation of Cutoff Scores for Personality Scales

A common practice in establishing the utility of a personality scale is to develop appropriate cutoff scores to indicate clinically meaningful elevations. For example, one might employ a scale such as an addiction indicator on the MMPI-2 to suggest potential substance abuse if a raw score is greater than a particular score on the scale.

Butcher, Graham, and Ben-Porath (1995) illustrate this paradigm in establishing MMPI-2 cutoff scores. Researchers often report the various hit rate indices for particular clinical decisions. To develop cutoff points for a scale, a sample of individuals known to have the condition being assessed is compared with others who are known not to have that condition.

The sensitivity and specificity of the tests at detecting the problem under study are of particular interest to personality researchers who want to report the positive and negative predictive power of the scale using the proposed cutoff (see Chapter 7 in this volume). Positive predictive power is the probability that an individual identified by an elevated scale score actually has the condition expected. Negative predictive power is the probability that an individual who does not have an elevated scale score actually does not have the condition being assessed. Positive and negative predictive power are sometimes termed true positive and true negative. A common practice in developing cutoff score research is to present cumulative frequency data on the scale of interest for subjects who have and who do not have the condition of interest. These frequencies are then examined to identify the optimal cutoff score.

A major consideration in the development of hit rates involves the need to assure that the proposed cutoff scores are stable. One of the most effective ways of assuring that cutoff scores will be reliable is to develop them in the context of a cross-validated design. Some shrinkage in results is likely to occur when hit rates are applied in different samples; it is therefore important to report hit rate data that are based on samples different than the one on which the hit rates were initially identified.

Additionally, in evaluating cutoff scores, it is important to consider the validity of the criterion information employed in the development. Clinical criteria such as diagnoses are not infallible, and we should therefore recognize that our hit rate estimates are only as accurate as our criterion data. The accuracy of hit rate estimates in prediction is constrained by the validity of the criterion measures we employ. Are all subjects who we assign to the predicted group in fact members of that group, and are all subjects who are assigned to the nonmembership category absent those characteristics?

Finally, in conducting personality-based cutoff score research, the issue of population base rates needs to be considered. A scale would not have much value or utility if 99% of the target population scored below one standard deviation above the mean of the scale. This situation has occurred with some personality measures, tempting researchers to make predictions based on only slightly deviant scores.

The frequency of a particular phenomenon or the base rates play a vital role in the accuracy of categorical prediction (Finn & Kamphuis, 1995; Meehl & Rosen, 1955). In conducting cutoff research, it is important to use actual base rates or frequencies of the phenomena under study if possible. Researchers sometimes create artificial base rates, for example, by using an equal number of the predicted group and nonpredicted group, producing an artificial base rate of .50. However, because the base rate in a particular clinical setting probably differs from .50, so will the predictive power of the test be affected. An investigation that ignores the issue of base rates and reports only sensitivity and specificity could thus produce highly misleading results and suggest very inaccurate conclusions. Therefore, when conducting personality-based cutoff research, it is essential to design the study such that the base rate in the sample approximates the frequencies found in the clinical setting where the results are to be applied.

Although the strategy of using cutoff scores can provide researchers with a tool for evaluating the performance of a measure, this approach needs to be exercised with considerable caution. Cutoff scores tend to impose an artificial dichotomy that cannot always be justified. Dwyer (1996) recommended that researchers exercise caution in taking cutoff scores as objective psychometric truth. She noted that the use of cutoff scores *always* entails judgment and inherently involves misclassification of cases.

SUMMARY

This chapter explored objective personality assessment using self-report methods. This approach to personality assessment is based on the assumption that an individual is a reliable witness to his or her own innermost thoughts, beliefs, and attitude. The term objective has been used in several ways to describe this orientation to personality assessment, distinguishing this method from more subjective methods such as interview or projective techniques such as the Rorschach, which require more unstructured data collection and subjectivity in interpretation.

One of the most basic concerns of personality assessment researchers in employing objective assessment methods involves the need to assure that the universe of pertinent variables is contained in the assessment instrument, that is, that the measure has content validity. Several objective response formats were described: the rational, the factor analytic, and the empirical, and IRT scale construction approaches. This chapter focused on the most common objective format, the true-or-false inventory of items, because of its relatively simple structure and relatively easy data processing methods.

Two recurring issues with respect to true-false personality questionnaires were described in some detail. Deviant response approaches, referred to as response sets, were noted to possibly intrude into objective personality assessment. Several sources of deviant responding were described and the more common approaches were detailed. The question of potential subcultural influence on personality scales was addressed. The development of the MMPI-2 revision with a focus on making the instrument relevant for all segments of the population by controlling for ethnic bias was discussed. The MMPI-2 has not been shown to unfairly portray minority populations or fail to assess minority group members. Research has shown that the scales appear to address the personality process or structure for minority clients in a manner similar to that for Whites.

The translation and adaptation of personality scales in other languages and cultures was discussed. Extensive test adaptation efforts were noted for one scale (MMPI-2). This instrument is being widely adapted in other countries as a clinical assessment instrument. The recommended procedures for translating and adapting personality tests were discussed.

Finally, several important research strategies that bear on the utility and generalizability of a personality measure were discussed. Test scores are only meaningfully interpreted in the context of a normative or reference population, which is derived on a representative group of the population in which the instrument is to be employed. Three approaches to scale validation were described and the procedure for detailing diagnostic or predictive accuracy was included.

REFERENCES

Aiken, L. R. (1996). *Rating scales and checklists.* New York: Wiley.

Allport, G. W. (1921). Personality and character. *Psychological Bulletin, 18,* 441–455.

Allport, G. W. (1937). *Personality.* New York: Henry Holt.

Almagor, M., & Nevo, B. (1996). The MMPI-2: Translation and first steps in its adaptation. In J. N. Butcher (Ed.), *International adaptation of the MMPI-2* (pp. 487–505). Minneapolis: University of Minnesota Press.

Arbisi, P., & Ben-Porath, Y. S. (1995). An MMPI-2 infrequency scale for use with psychopathological populations: The Infrequency-Psychopathology Scale, F(p). *Psychological Assessment, 7,* 424–431.

Arbisi, P., & Ben-Porath, Y. S. (1997). Characteristics of the MMPI-2 F(p) scale as a function of diagnosis in an inpatient sample of veterans. *Psychological Assessment, 9,* 102–105.

Archer, R. P., Griffin, R., & Aiduk, R. (1995). Clinical correlates for ten common code types. *Journal of Personality Assessment, 65,* 391–408.

Baer, R. A., Wetter, M. W., & Berry, D. T. (1992). Detection of underreporting of psychopathology on the MMPI: A meta-analysis. *Clinical Psychology Review, 12,* 509–525.

Ben-Porath, Y. S., Shondrick, D., & Stafford, K. (1994). MMPI-2 and race in a forensic diagnostic sample. *Criminal Justice and Behavior, 22,* 19–32.

Ben-Porath, Y. S., & Waller, N. (1992). Five big issues in clinical personality assessment: A rejoinder to Costa & McCrae. *Psychological Assessment, 4,* 23–25.

Bentler, P. (1969). Semantic space is (approximately) bipolar. *Journal of Psychology, 71,* 33–40.

Berah, E., Butcher, J. N., Miach, P., Bolza, J., Colman, S., & McAsery, P. (1993, October). *Computer-based interpretation of the MMPI-2: An Australian evaluation of the Minnesota report.* Poster presented at the 28th annual conference of the Australian Psychological Association, Gold Coast.

Berry, D. T. (1995). Detecting distortion in forensic evaluations with the MMPI-2. In Y. S. Ben-Porath, J. R. Graham, G. C. N. Hall, R. D. Hirschman, & M. S. Zaragoza (Eds.), *Forensic applications of the MMPI-2* (pp. 82–103). Thousand Oaks, CA: Sage.

Berry, D. T., Baer, R. A., & Harris, M. J. (1991). Detection of malingering on the MMPI: A meta-analysis. *Clinical Psychology Review, 11,* 585–591.

Berry, D. T., Wetter, M. W., Baer, R. A., Larsen, L., Clark, C., & Monroe, K. (1992). MMPI-2 random responding indices: Validation using a self-report methodology. *Psychological Assessment: A Journal of Consulting and Clinical Psychology, 4,* 340–345.

Block, J. (1965). *Challenge of response sets.* New York: Appleton-Century.

Brislin, R. (1986). The wording and translation of research instruments. In W. J. Lonner & J. W. Berry (Eds.), *Field methods in cross-cultural research* (pp. 137–164). Beverly Hills, CA: Sage.

Burisch, M. (1978). Construction strategies for multiscale personality inventories. *Applied Psychological Measurement, 2,* 97–111.

Burisch, M. (1984). Approaches in personality inventory construction. *American Psychologist, 39,* 214–227.

Butcher, J. N. (1996). *International adaptation of the MMPI-2.* Minneapolis: University of Minnesota Press.

Butcher, J. N. (1997). *Users guide to the Minnesota forensic report for the MMPI-2.* Minneapolis: National Computer Systems.

Butcher, J. N. (1998). *The Butcher Treatment Planning Inventory.* San Antonio, TX: Psychological Corporation.

Butcher, J. N., Berah, E., Ellertsen, B., Miach, P., Lim, J., Nezami, E., Pancheri, P., Derksen, J., & Almagor, M. (1998). Objective personality assessment: Computer-based MMPI-2 interpretation in international clinical settings. In C. Belar (Ed.), *Comprehensive clinical psychology: Sociocultural and individual differences.* New York: Elsevier.

Butcher, J. N., Graham, J. R., & Ben-Porath, Y. S. (1995). Methodological problems and issues in MMPI/MMPI-2/MMPI-A research. *Psychological Assessment, 7,* 320–329.

Butcher, J. N., Graham, J. R., Williams, C. L., & Ben-Porath, Y. S. (1990). *Development and use of the MMPI-2 Content Scales.* Minneapolis: University of Minnesota Press.

Butcher, J. N., & Pancheri, P. (1976). *Cross-national MMPI research.* Minneapolis: University of Minnesota Press.

Butcher, J. N., Rouse, S., & Perry, J. (in press). *MMPI-2 based empirical description of patients in psychological treatment. Foundation sources for the MMPI-2.* Minneapolis: University of Minnesota Press.

Butcher, J. N., & Williams, C. L. (1992). *MMPI-2/MMPI-A: Essentials of interpretation.* Minneapolis: University of Minnesota Press.

Campbell, D. T., & Fiske, D. W. (1979). Convergent and discriminant validation by the multitrait-multiple method matrix. *Psychological Bulletin, 56,* 81–105.

Cattell, R. B. (1957). *Personality and motivation structure and measurement.* Yonkers on Hudson: World Book.

Cattell, R. B., Eber, H., W., & Tatsuoka, M. M. (1988). *Handbook for the sixteen personality factor questionnaire (16PF).* Champaign, IL: Institute for Personality and Ability Testing.

Clark, L. A., & Watson, D. (1995). Constructing validity: Basic issues in objective scale development. *Psychological Assessment, 7,* 309–319.

Comrey, A. (1988). Factor-analytic methods of scale development in personality and clinical psychology. *Journal of Consulting and Clinical Psychology, 45,* 754–761.

Costa, P., & McCrae, R. R. (1992). *Manual for the revised NEO-PI and five factor inventory (NEO-FFI).* Odessa, FL: Psychological Assessment Resources.

Cronbach, L. J. (1942). Studies of acquiescence as a factor in the true-false test. *Journal of Educational Psychology, 33,* 401–415.

Cronbach, L. J. (1951). Coefficient alpha and the internal structure of objective tests. *Psychometrika, 16,* 297–334.

Cronbach, L. J. (1970). *Essentials of psychological testing* (3rd ed.). New York: Harper & Row.

Cronbach, L. J., & Meehl, P. E. (1955). Construct validity in psychological tests. *Psychological Bulletin, 52,* 281–302.

Dahlstrom, W. G., Lachar, D., & Dahlstrom, L. E. (1986). *MMPI patterns of American minorities.* Minneapolis: University of Minnesota Press.

Deinard, A. S., Butcher, J. N., Thao, U. D., Moua Vang, S. H., & Hang, K. (1996). Development of Hmong translation of the MMPI-2. In J. N. Butcher (Ed.), *International adaptation of the MMPI-2* (pp. 194–205). Minneapolis: University of Minnesota Press.

Dwyer, C. A. (1996). Cut scores and testing: Statistics, judgment, truth and error. *Psychological Assessment, 8,* 360–362.

Edwards, A. L. (1957). *The social desirability variable in personality assessment and research.* New York: Holt.

Ellertsen, B., Havik, O. E., & Skavhellen, R. R. (1996). The Norwegian MMPI-2. In J. N. Butcher (Ed.), *International adaptation of the MMPI-2* (pp. 350–367). Minneapolis: University of Minnesota Press.

Ellis, B. B., Minsel, B., & Becker, P. (1989). Evaluation of attitude survey translations: An investigation using item response theory. *International Journal of Psychology, 24,* 665–684.

Embretson, S. E. (1996). The new rules of measurement. *Psychological Assessment, 8,* 341–349.

Finn, S., & Kamphuis, J. H. (1995). What a clinician needs to know about base rates. In J. N. Butcher (Ed.), *Clinical personality assessment: Practical approaches* (pp. 214–235). New York: Oxford University Press.

Floyd, F. J., & Widaman, K. F. (1995). Factor analysis in the development and refinement of clinical assessment instruments. *Psychological Assessment, 7,* 286–299.

Gallagher, R. W., Ben-Porath, Y. S., & Briggs, S. (1997). Inmate views about the purpose and use of the MMPI-2 at the time of correctional intake. *Criminal Justice and Behavior, 24,* 360–369.

Galton, F. (1869). *Hereditary genius.* London: Macmillan.

Gilberstadt, H., & Duker, J. (1965). *A handbook for clinical and actuarial MMPI interpretation.* Philadelphia: Saunders.

Gillet, I., Simon, M., Guelfi, J. D., Brun-Eberentz, A., Monier, C., Seunevel, F., & Svarna, L. (1996). The MMPI-2 in France. In J. N. Butcher (Ed.), *International adaptation of the MMPI-2* (pp. 395–415). Minneapolis: University of Minnesota Press.

Gorsuch, R. I. (1983). *Factor analysis* (2nd ed.). Hillsdale, NJ: LEA Press.

Gough, H. G. (1952). *The adjective checklist manual.* Palo Alto, CA: Consulting Psychologists Press.

Green, D. P., Goldman, S. L., & Salovey, P. (1993). Measurement error masks bipolarity in affect ratings. *Journal of Personality and Social Psychology, 64,* 1029–1041.

Grove, W., & Meehl, P. E. (1996). Comparative efficiency of informal (subjective, impressionistic) and formal (mechanical, algorithmis) predictive procedures: The clinical-actuarial controversy. *Psychology, Public Policy, and the Law, 2*(2), 293–323.

Guilford, J. P. (1954). *Psychometric methods.* New York: McGraw-Hill.

Hambleton, R. K., Swaminathan, H., & Rogers, H. J. (1991). *Fundamentals of item response theory.* Newbury Park, CA: Sage.

Han, K. (1996). The Korean MMPI-2. In J. N. Butcher (Ed.), *International adaptation of the MMPI-2* (pp. 88–136). Minneapolis: University of Minnesota Press.

Hase, H. D., & Goldberg, L. R. (1967). Comparative validity of different strategies of constructing personality inventory scales. *Psychological Bulletin, 67,* 231–248.

Hathaway, S. R., & McKinley, J. C. (1940). A multiphasic personality schedule (Minnesota): I. Construction of the schedule. *Journal of Psychology, 10,* 249–254.

Haynes, S., Richard, D. C., & Kubany, E. S. (1995). Content validity in psychological assessment: A functional approach to concepts and methods. *Psychological Assessment, 7,* 238–247.

Hulin, C. L., Drasgow, F., & Parsons, C. K. (1983). *Item response theory: Application to psychological measurement.* Homewood, IL: Dow Jones Irwin.

Jackson, D. N. (1989). *Basic personality inventory manual.* Goshen, NY: Sigma Assessment Systems.

Jackson, D. N., Fraboni, M., & Helmes, E. (1997). MMPI-2 content scales: How much content do they measure? *Assessment, 4,* 111–117.

Jackson, D. N., & Messick, S. (1962). Acquiescence and desirability as response determinants of the MMPI. *Educational and Psychological Measurement, 22,* 771–790.

Keefe, K., Sue, S., Enomoto, E., Durvasula, R. S., & Chao, R. (1996). Asian American and white college students' performance on the MMPI-2. In J. N. Butcher (Ed.), *International adaptation of the MMPI-2* (pp. 206–220). Minneapolis: University of Minnesota Press.

Kendall, B. C., & Hammen, C. (1998). *Abnormal psychology* (2nd ed.). Boston: Houghton Mifflin.

Konraos, S. (1996). The Icelandic translation of the MMPI-2: Adaptation and validation. In J. N. Butcher (Ed.), *International adaptation of the MMPI-2* (pp. 368–384). Minneapolis: University of Minnesota Press.

Lanyon, R. I. (1993). Development of scales to assess specific deception strategies on the psychological screening inventory. *Psychological Assessment, 5,* 324–329.

Lindzey, G. (1951). *Projective techniques and cross-cultural.* New York: Appleton-Century-Crofts.

Lucio, E., Reyes-Lagunes, I., & Scott, R. L. (1994). MMPI-2 for Mexico: Translation and adaptation. *Journal of Personality Assessment, 63,* 105–116.

Lucio, G. M. E., & Reyes-Lagunes, I. (1996). The Mexican version of the MMPI-2 in Mexico and Nicaragua: Translation, adaptation, and demonstrated equivalency. In J. N. Butcher (Ed.), *International adaptation of the MMPI-2* (pp. 265–284). Minneapolis: University of Minnesota Press.

Loevinger, J. (1957). Objective tests as instruments of psychological theory. *Psychological Reports, 3,* 635–694.

Marks, P., Seeman, W., & Haller, D. (1974). *The actuarial use of the MMPI with adolescents and adults.* Baltimore: Williams & Wilkins.

Meehl, P. E. (1954). *Clinical versus statistical prediction: A theoretical analysis and review of the evidence.* Minneapolis: University of Minnesota Press.

Meehl, P. E., & Hathaway, S. R. (1946). The K factor as a suppressor variable in the MMPI. *Journal of Applied Psychology, 30,* 525–564.

Meehl, P. E., & Rosen, A. (1955). Anteceedent probability and the efficiency of psychometric signs, patterns, or cutting scores. *Psychological Bulletin, 52,* 194–216.

Millon, T. (1994). *MCMI-III: Manual.* Minneapolis: National Computer Systems.

Otto, R., & Butcher, J. N. (1995). Computer-assisted psychological assessment in child custody evaluations. *Family Law Quarterly, 29,* 79–96.

Overall, J. E., & Gorham, D. R. (1962). The brief psychiatric rating scale. *Psychological Reports, 10,* 799–812.

Pancheri, P., Sirigatti, S., & Biondi, M. (1996). Adaptation of the MMPI-2 in Italy. In J. N. Butcher (Ed.), *International adaptation of the MMPI-2* (pp. 416–421). Minneapolis: University of Minnesota Press.

Reise, S. P., & Waller, N. (1993). Traitedness and the assessment of response pattern scalability. *Journal of Personality and Social Psychology, 65,* 143–151.

Rissetti, F. J., Himmel, E., & Gonzalez-Moreno, J. A. (1996). Use of the MMPI-2 in Chile: Translation and adaptation. In J. N. Butcher (Ed.), *International adaptation of the MMPI-2* (pp. 221–251). Minneapolis: University of Minnesota Press.

Schmitt, N. (1996). Uses and abuses of coefficient alpha. *Psychological Assessment, 8,* 350–353.

Schretlen, D. (1988). The use of psychological tests to identify malingered symptoms of mental disorder. *Clinical Psychology Review, 8,* 451–476.

Shiota, N. D., Krauss, S. S., & Clark, L. A. (1996). Adaptation and validation of the Japanese MMPI-2. In J. N. Butcher (Ed.), *International adaptation of the MMPI-2* (pp. 67–87). Minneapolis: University of Minnesota Press.

Sloore, H., Derksen, J., de Mey, H., & Hellenbosch, G. (1996). The Flemish/Dutch version of the MMPI-2: Development of adaptation of the inventory for Belgium and the Netherlands. In J. N. Butcher (Ed.), *International adaptation of the MMPI-2* (pp. 329–349). Minneapolis: University of Minnesota Press.

Smith, G. T., & McCarthy, D. M. (1995). Methodological considerations in the refinement of clinical assessment instruments. *Psychological Assessment, 7,* 300–308.

Tellegen, A., & Ben-Porath, Y. S. (1992). The new uniform T-scores for the MMPI-2: Rationale, derivation, and appraisal. *Psychological Assessment, 4,* 145–155.

Timbrook, R., & Graham, J. R. (1994). Ethnic differences on the MMPI? *Psychological Assessment, 6,* 212–217.

Tinius, T., & Ben-Porath, Y. S. (1993, March). *A comparative study of Native Americans and Caucasian Americans undergoing substance abuse treatment.* Paper given at the 28th annual conference on Recent Developments in the Use of the MMPI/MMPI-2, St. Petersburg, FL.

Velasquez, R., Gonzales, M., Butcher, J. N., Castillo-Canez, I., Apodaca, J. X., & Chavira, D. (1997). Use of the MMPI-2 with Chicanos: Strategies for counselors. *Journal of Multicultural Counseling and Development, 25,* 107–120.

Weiss, D. J., & Yoes, M. E. (1988). Item response theory. In R. K. Hambleton & J. Zaal (Eds.), *New developments in testing: Theory and applications.* North Holland Publishing Company.

Williams, C. L., & Butcher, J. N. (1989). An MMPI study of adolescents: II. Verification and limitations of code type classifications. *Psychological Assessment: A Journal of Consulting and Clinical Psychology, 1,* 260–265.

Woodworth, R. S. (1920). *Personal data sheet.* Chicago: Stoelting.

Chapter 8

OBSERVATIONAL ASSESSMENT: MEASURE DEVELOPMENT AND RESEARCH ISSUES

JOHN D. CONE, PH.D.

At its most basic level, research in clinical psychology deals with the behavior of its participants. Whether studying the interaction patterns of families (e.g., Alexander, Newell, Robbins, & Turner, 1995), the problem behavior of young children (e.g., Eyberg, Bessmer, Newcomb, Edwards, & Robinson, 1994), the pain behavior of accident victims (e.g., Fordyce, 1976), or the independent behavior of elderly persons (e.g., Baltes, Neumann, & Zank, 1994), clinicians are interested in what clients and research participants do. This chapter is about assessment strategies for finding out what they do and the environmental circumstances in which they do it. The focus is on direct measures of behavior, whether cognitive, motor, or physiological. The chapter begins by defining direct observation and distinguishing it from other assessment methods. It next describes types of observational assessment instruments, including distinctions based on who observers are and how observations are collected. Demonstrating the scientific adequacy of observational procedures is then discussed from accuracy, psychometric, and generalizability theory perspectives. Selecting and training observers is described, followed by ethical considerations in using direct observation assessment. Finally, continuing issues in the conceptualization, development, use, and evaluation of observational assessment in clinical psychology are discussed.

WHAT IS DIRECT OBSERVATION?

Two aspects of direct observation assessment can be distinguished: observing and recording (Alexander et al., 1995; Floyd, 1989; Sillars, 1991; Weick, 1985). Events can impinge on our senses (be observed), and they can be noted (recorded) in some form that makes them retrievable and analyzable in the future. Let's take a separate look at each of these two activities.

I wish to thank E. Kent McIntyre for his tireless assistance in preparing this manuscript.

Observing

When behavior is observed, a stimulus-response (S-R) relationship occurs in which that behavior serves as a stimulus for sensations (responses) in the observing person. Verbally expressed impressions or interpretations of sensed events are actually what we mean by observation, rather than the sensory registration itself. Thus, observations are actually the verbal behavior of persons having sensory contact with phenomena. This contact can be direct, in the sense of occurring concomitantly with the phenomena, or it can be delayed, as when observations are made from records (audiotapes, videotapes, transcriptions) of events occurring earlier. Recognizing the inherently verbal nature of observations is helpful because doing so clarifies the potential contributions scientific knowledge of verbal behavior can make to the study of observational methodology. For example, verbally facile individuals might be expected to excel at observations of precisely defined molecular behavior requiring careful distinctions (see Skindrud, 1973). Such a highly refined verbal repertoire might interfere with observing more molar events as the person is stimulated to consider more possibilities (shades of gray) than are necessary to assign the event to a particular coding category.

Another advantage of recognizing the inherently verbal nature of "direct" observation assessment is that it permits more meaningful comparisons with other types of assessment method that are more explicitly verbal (e.g., interviews, self-reports, rating-by-other, and self-monitoring observation). Direct observation is considered more direct than these methods because it comes closest to detecting *the* behavior of clinical interest and doing so at the *time* and *place* of its natural occurrence. Other methods rely more heavily on verbal surrogates of behavior that occurs at some other time and place. Thus, except for electronic or mechanical transducing equipment, direct observation holds the best potential for yielding information of the highest fidelity. Optimizing this fidelity and demonstrating its usefulness is the purpose of research on direct observation methodology.

Recording

Detecting behavior is of limited value unless some notation or record results. Observation coding systems control what the observer does to provide a retrievable notation of the detected behavior. The most commonly used recording formats include narratives, event records, and interval recording.

Narratives

In the earliest stages of studying a phenomenon not much is known, and the job of the scientist is to observe as much of an event and its context as possible and make records of the observations. The records are usually in the form of narratives, written or spoken descriptions of everything the observer sees. Sometimes, the observer writes these observations using a shorthand or abbreviation system. At other times, the observer talks into a tape recorder, describing what is being observed for later transcription into written form. Ethologists have a long history of using narrative types of assessment (Barker & Wright, 1955; Blurton-Jones & Woodson, 1979).

Because narrative forms of observation system are relatively unconstrained, a rich array of events/activities is potentially available for sensing and recording. Unfortunately, being able to sense and record nearly anything comes at a price. The broad band of narrative recordings makes them suitable for initial mapping of a wide range of experience, but the quality of the data they produce is marginal. Their potential for recording a great variety of events is simultaneously their strength and their greatest liability. The low fidelity of narratives is a consequence of their relatively unconstrained and highly flexible nature. It is difficult to establish the objectivity of narrative systems, as the repeatability of observations they produce is nearly impossible to obtain. This is because independent observers describing a particular scene are unlikely to attend to exactly the same events. Indeed, the same person revisiting the scene at a later time is unlikely to notice exactly the same types of events that were noted earlier. This makes it impossible to compute any type of agreement index or to determine the extent to which observers accurately reflected the scene as it actually unfolded. Hartmann and Wood (1990) liken narrative observation to "ad lib sampling" or informal observation and note that it "hardly deserves formal recognition because of its non-rigorous nature" (p. 114).

As repeated observations in a particular context lead to greater familiarity, attention begins to focus on distinct aspects of the context that are of greater interest than others. More frequent events or those occurring with greater intensity are more likely to get noticed. Other noteworthy events are those having importance from a particular theoretical orientation. When attention is narrowed to a limited set of categories, observational coding systems also become more specific.

Event Records

If a notation is made each time a predetermined activity occurs during an observation period, a record of that event is produced. Usually, two types of prior specification are necessary to develop event records. First, behaviors to be observed are defined. Second, some property or dimensional quantity (i.e., frequency, duration, latency, or magnitude) of the behavior is specified (Johnston & Pennypacker, 1993). More will be said about response properties in a later section. When the frequency of events is tracked such that a complete record of occurrences during the observation period results, event and *frequency recording* are synonymous (see Sulzer-Azaroff & Mayer, 1991). Indeed, Barrios (1993) prefers to restrict the term event records to those instances when frequency is being tracked.

An advantage of event records is their relatively complete coverage of the behavior of interest. Each occurrence is noted and the total number of occurrences can be determined at the end of the period. This is easier to accomplish when the number of behaviors is relatively small. A disadvantage of event records is that it is difficult to establish their psychometric adequacy, as point-by-point comparisons between independent observers cannot be made. What can be compared are total counts of events at the end of the period.

These problems can be avoided by recording evens in *real time* (Hartmann & Wood, 1990). Real-time recording involves noting whatever dimensional quantity of behavior is of interest along with the precise time it occurs. Most often, real-time recording is done with electronic or electromechanical recording apparatus such as event recorders (S. Foster, Bell-Dolan, & Burge, 1988) that preserve exact times of onset and offset of each behavior, allowing duration and latency to be determined as well as frequency. For example, Wehby, Symons, and Shores (1995) recorded 28 different interactive behaviors of behaviorally disordered special education children using an electronic event recorder. Rather precise examinations of observer agreement are possible using such equipment. Hartmann and Wood (1990) observed that real-time event recording is the method most often used when frequency responding and conditional probability or transitional analyses are desired (e.g., Bakeman & Gottman, 1997). Unfortunately, the limited availability of technology such as this, along with difficulties encountered when numerous different participants must be observed simultaneously, have restricted the use of real-time recording. More easily implemented observation strategies involve interval procedures.

Interval Recording

To facilitate recording lots of behavior and to provide for easier comparison between observers, time periods for observing are often broken into smaller segments or intervals. Thus, a 15-minute observation session might be divided into 15 1-minute intervals, or it might be divided into 60 15-second intervals.

Subvarieties of interval system can be identified. When frequency of behavior is the response property recorded, *frequency-within-interval* recording is being used. This form of interval system is best suited for observing a small number of responses with relatively discrete onsets and offsets. Continuous recording of frequencies such as this is challenging for observers and limits the number of different responses they can record effectively.

Another variant of interval recording requires a response to occur throughout the entire interval, and is known as *whole interval* recording. To illustrate, if spouses must maintain visual regard of each other for an entire interval to be scored as "engaged," whole interval recording is in effect. *Partial interval* recording requires only that the response occur during some portion of the interval for it to be scored. Finally, if the response must occur at a specific moment in an interval (e.g., at the start or end), *momentary time sampling* is being used.

An example of a partial interval recording system is presented in Figure 8.1. The specific behaviors being observed are identified by codes that are written in each numbered 10-second interval. In this example, each of several children is observed for one minute at a time. Before beginning observations, the names of available children are randomly assigned to minutes and written in the blanks at the left of the sheet. A child could be observed for multiple randomly selected minutes. When observation begins, the observer slashes through each behavior occurring in a 10-second interval. The intervals are numbered, and pacing is facilitated by a tape recorder that plays a number every 10 seconds. The coding sheet could be used as a frequency-within-interval system as well, by instructing observers to slash through the codes each time a behavior is observed in an interval. Likewise, it could serve as a whole interval or momentary time sample coding sheet, depending on the rules for recording specific behavior occurrences.

When behavior duration is of interest, whole interval systems are used. If frequency counts are needed, partial interval, frequency-within-interval, or momentary time sampling systems are more likely to be chosen. With the exception of frequency-within-interval systems, segmenting the observation period into smaller intervals results in compromises in data quality. With partial interval systems, for example, it is

Social Behavior Coding System

Observer: _____ Activity: _____ Sheet # __

Date: _____ Location: _____

Child:	[1] CS PA LE / PW PO UN / PP DS GR	[2] CS PA LE / PW PO UN / PP DS GR	[3] CS PA LE / PW PO UN / PP DS GR	[4] CS PA LE / PW PO UN / PP DS GR	[5] CS PA LE / PW PO UN / PP DS GR	[6] CS PA LE / PW PO UN / PP DS GR
Child:	[7] CS PA LE / PW PO UN / PP DS GR	[8] CS PA LE / PW PO UN / PP DS GR	[9] CS PA LE / PW PO UN / PP DS GR	[10] CS PA LE / PW PO UN / PP DS GR	[11] CS PA LE / PW PO UN / PP DS GR	[12] CS PA LE / PW PO UN / PP DS GR
Child:	[13] CS PA LE / PW PO UN / PP DS GR	[14] CS PA LE / PW PO UN / PP DS GR	[15] CS PA LE / PW PO UN / PP DS GR	[16] CS PA LE / PW PO UN / PP DS GR	[17] CS PA LE / PW PO UN / PP DS GR	[18] CS PA LE / PW PO UN / PP DS GR
Child:	[19] CS PA LE / PW PO UN / PP DS GR	[20] CS PA LE / PW PO UN / PP DS GR	[21] CS PA LE / PW PO UN / PP DS GR	[22] CS PA LE / PW PO UN / PP DS GR	[23] CS PA LE / PW PO UN / PP DS GR	[24] CS PA LE / PW PO UN / PP DS GR
Child:	[25] CS PA LE / PW PO UN / PP DS GR	[26] CS PA LE / PW PO UN / PP DS GR	[27] CS PA LE / PW PO UN / PP DS GR	[28] CS PA LE / PW PO UN / PP DS GR	[29] CS PA LE / PW PO UN / PP DS GR	[30] CS PA LE / PW PO UN / PP DS GR
Child:	[31] CS PA LE / PW PO UN / PP DS GR	[32] CS PA LE / PW PO UN / PP DS GR	[33] CS PA LE / PW PO UN / PP DS GR	[34] CS PA LE / PW PO UN / PP DS GR	[35] CS PA LE / PW PO UN / PP DS GR	[36] CS PA LE / PW PO UN / PP DS GR
Child:	[37] CS PA LE / PW PO UN / PP DS GR	[38] CS PA LE / PW PO UN / PP DS GR	[39] CS PA LE / PW PO UN / PP DS GR	[40] CS PA LE / PW PO UN / PP DS GR	[41] CS PA LE / PW PO UN / PP DS GR	[42] CS PA LE / PW PO UN / PP DS GR
Child:	[43] CS PA LE / PW PO UN / PP DS GR	[44] CS PA LE / PW PO UN / PP DS GR	[45] CS PA LE / PW PO UN / PP DS GR	[46] CS PA LE / PW PO UN / PP DS GR	[47] CS PA LE / PW PO UN / PP DS GR	[48] CS PA LE / PW PO UN / PP DS GR

Codes: **CS**=converses socially,   **PA**=plays alone,   **LE**=leads,
PW=plays with other child, **PO**=passive observation, **UN**=unoccupied,
PP=plays parallel,   **DS**=disrupts,   **GR**=gives reinforcement.

COMMENTS:

Figure 8.1.   An example of a partial interval recoding system used to record children's social behavior.

possible only to estimate the actual frequency of behavior. Data are presented in terms of percentage of intervals observed. Illustrative is Derby et al.'s (1997) recording of toy play and social behavior of preschool-age children and the reinforcing and punishing responses of their parents using a 6-second partial interval system. Individual children's data were presented in terms of percentage of 6-second intervals in which behaviors occurred. Johnston and Pennypacker (1993) refer to interval systems as *discontinuous* because they cannot be used to detect all occurrences of a response during a period of observation. Indeed, research shows that partial interval approaches overestimate behavior frequencies, and whole interval approaches underestimate them (Green & Alverson, 1978; Powell, Martindale, Kulp, Martindale, & Bauman, 1977). Further, Hartmann and Wood (1990) note that the accuracy of partial interval systems can vary with interval length, with long and short intervals tending to under- and overestimate behavior frequencies, respectively. As for duration, partial interval systems are not appropriate, as they tend to overestimate duration. Hartmann and Wood point to the relationship between actual duration of target behaviors and interval length, noting that partial interval systems provide good estimates of response duration only when interval length is short relative to the mean duration of the response.

Thus, interval systems facilitate observing large numbers of behaviors, and they do this at some cost in data quality (Johnston & Pennypacker, 1993), about which more will be said later. Somewhat paradoxically, they facilitate comparisons between observers. This is because segmenting the observation period into small intervals permits interval-by-interval or point-by-point comparison of the observers' entries. This, in turn, allows some confidence that two observers are noting the same behavior when they record it in exactly the same 5-second interval. Methods for assessing agreement between observers are discussed in a later section of this chapter. First, let us address who might be used as observers in the first place.

WHO ARE THE OBSERVERS?

Observers can be outsiders who are inserted into a situation, collect their data, and leave. Or they can be persons indigenous to the situation who are recruited to collect data and stay. The latter are frequently referred to as participant-observers (Bickman, 1976; Hartmann & Wood, 1990; Margolin, 1987). Weiss and Margolin (1986) refer to participant observation as *quasi-observational* or *quasi-behavioral* to emphasize that the observer might be less than optimally objective as a result of personal involvement in the social context being assessed. Another use of this term is described in a later section of this chapter.

Participant-Observers

Among the persons included in this category are parents who observe and record the behavior of their own children (e.g., Forehand, Griest, & Wells, 1979; Patterson, Reid, Jones, & Conger, 1975), spouses who observe and record one another's behavior (e.g., Jacobson, 1979), and teachers who observe and record the behavior of children in their own classrooms (e.g., Kubany & Slodgett, 1973; McLaughlin, 1993). Advantages of participant observation include presumed lower reactivity (although this has not been tested directly), cost savings, access to "private" or infrequent behavior, the potentially greater validity of resulting data, and the completion of functional analyses. Disadvantages include difficulty in training indigenous people to use coding systems reliably and accurately, and the confounding of observation and treatment effects when conducting research on treatment outcomes.

In clinical psychology, the greatest use of participant observation has probably been in marital interaction research. Margolin (1987) identifies two types of participant observation in this context: self-observation and observation by a significant other.[1] She noted that both types can facilitate functional analyses in that antecedent and consequent environmental events can be noted for recurring problem behavior, and controlling variables identified. In addition, participant observation is particularly helpful when affect is being recorded. Margolin described macro- and micro-level forms of observation, noting the former occur more often in the home, the latter more often in the laboratory. With a few exceptions, the examples of macro-level observation might more aptly be viewed as ratings-by-others in that they typically involve retrospective ratings or checkoff of spouse behavior at the end of a day. For example, the Spouse Observation Checklist (Weiss & Perry, 1979) is completed before going to sleep each night and requires each partner to review approximately 400 items and note those that occurred during the previous 24 hours. The Marital Satisfaction Time Lines (Williams, 1979) are closer to direct observation in that data are provided by the partners every 15 minutes throughout the day. The 15-minute data are ratings of the positivity of that time period, however, rather than actual counts of specific behavior.

Laboratory examples of direct observation by participants are more plentiful in the marital interaction area. To illustrate, Margolin (1978) had spouses use handheld electromechanical devices to record instances of "communication helpfulness" while interacting to solve problems in the laboratory. A later refinement involved recording the same behavior from videotapes of the interaction occurring earlier. This had the advantage of avoiding the interruption caused by recording during the problem-solving interchange itself. This videotape reconstruction approach is similar to that of Gottman and Levenson (1985, 1986), who had couples watch videotapes of prior interactions while continuously rating their affect levels. Physiological reactions of the partners also were monitored during the original and reconstructed interactions and were shown to correlate highly. More recently, Foster and colleagues (1997) had couples rate the typicality of their partner's socially supportive and undermining behaviors during immediately preceding videotaped interactions occurring in the home. The goal was to determine the extent to which self-presentational bias exists in the direct observation of couples' interaction. Approximately half of the couples reported their spouse's behavior to be typical (i.e., unbiased). When bias was reported, it was more likely to be in the socially desirable than undesirable direction, confirming the hypothesis that couples attempt to present themselves in socially favorable ways when being observed (D. Foster, Caplan, & Howe, 1997). Powers, Welsh, and Wright (1994) reported a variant of the Gottman and Levenson videotape reconstruction procedure used to assess the subjective experience of adolescents interacting with their parents.

More research is needed on the value of indigenous participant observation methods. Very little is known about the psychometric adequacy of these approaches, for example. Most important, we do not know whether and to what extent they are even accurate. Margolin (1987) reports that differences occur surprisingly often between what spouses report and what non-participant-observers record. It is also well-known that parent reports

---

[1] She actually includes "blend-into-the-woodwork" observation by trained, disinterested observers as a type of participant observation as well, following Wiggins (1973). Participant observation is restricted to data provided by indigenous persons in the present review.

of their children's behavior do not correspond well with those of the children themselves. Indeed, Achenbach, McConaughy, and Howell (1987) report correlations averaging .25 between parents' and children's ratings of the latter's behavior. Whether agreement is even necessary may depend on the purpose of assessment in the first place, however. If an accurate description of the *form* of the behavior is important, agreement might be necessary. If the *function* served by the behavior is more critical, agreement on the *impact* of a behavior might become the focus, with less attention to its precise topography. Relevant here is Gottman's (1979) finding that the *impact* of messages sent by spouses to one another distinguished distressed from nondistressed marriages, whereas the *intent* of the messages did not.

Research on the conduct of functional assessments that rely on data from participant-observers is in its infancy. Carr et al. (1994) involve teachers and others having contact with a referred youngster in the completion of antecedent-behavior-consequent (A-B-C) descriptions. These are provided repeatedly for specific problem behaviors during the descriptive phase of functional assessment. In the interpretive phase, the descriptions are then sorted for possible function by a team of three people. Essentially, hypotheses are formed about the relationship between regularly occurring antecedent and consequent environmental events and the behavior of interest. These are then tested in the verification phase, where mini-experiments are set up to vary the consequences systematically and look for associated changes in the behavior. Carr et al.'s committee approach to identifying possible functions assures greater reliability at the interpretive phase of the process, but what is known about the adequacy of the raw data being deliberated by the committee? Can parents, teachers, spouses, and other participant-observers describe antecedent and consequent environmental events accurately enough to facilitate effective functional analyses? To date, the answer to this question is unknown.

Non-Participant-Observers

Direct observation usually involves trained personnel who are not indigenous to the context in which data are to be collected. In this sense, most direct observation takes the "fly on the wall" or "blend into the woodwork" approach, where observers get in, get their data, and get out. Margolin (1987) refers to this as "objective observation" (p. 391). Among the assumptions underlying the use of trained observers is the inherently greater objectivity they provide. Not being personally invested in the outcomes of interactions among research participants, observers are thought to detect and record events dispassionately and, therefore, to be more under the control of those events. It is interesting to note that, although clear evidence attests to differences in the data of participant- and non-participant-observers, as noted above, there are no studies comparing the impact of such differences. That is, we do not know whether the data from one type of observer or the other result in different treatments being applied and with different outcomes ultimately experienced by clients.

There is some evidence to suggest the importance of observer characteristics in research involving observational assessment, however (cf. Floyd & Markman, 1983). To illustrate, Gonzales, Cauce, and Mason (1996) found differences in the harshness attributed to disciplinary procedures by White and African American coders when observing interaction in African American families. Markman and colleagues note that much of what we know from observational studies of families comes from "young, female, White coders" (Markman, Leber, Cordova, & St. Peters, 1995, p. 376). Would our knowledge be different if our cadres of coders were more diverse? Would we know different things if coders and codees were more often matched on gender, race, age, and other demographic variables? If so, it would be fascinating to know the source of such differences. If it is in changed behavior of the persons being observed, reactivity is an issue and needs specific controls. For instance, unobtrusive procedures (e.g., hidden cameras, tape recorders) could be used. If the source of differences in observer data is in the observers themselves, attention to the definitions of codes, observer training, and ongoing observer quality checking would be important. If differences are a result of interactions between observer and observee characteristics, more complex tactics might be needed. More is said on observers' characteristics related to their effectiveness as transducers in a later section on observer training. First, let us examine some of the factors that go into designing observational coding systems.

VARIABLES TO CONSIDER IN CHOOSING AN OBSERVATIONAL APPROACH

There are a number of important considerations that go into designing coding systems. Nine of these are presented in Table 8.1 and discussed below.

Purpose of Assessment

The most important initial consideration in deciding the form a coding system will take is the reason for making observations in the first place. Numerous authors have provided lists of assessment purposes (Cone, 1995; Evans, 1993; Hawkins, 1979; Mash & Terdal, 1997; Paul, Mariotto, & Redfield, 1986), including to (a) describe/classify, (b) understand, (c) predict, (d) control, and (e) monitor change. If the purpose is broadly descriptive, as in discovering the interactive behaviors that distinguish distressed and nondistressed families (Humphrey, Apple, & Kirschenbaum, 1986) or detailing the ecology of elementary school classrooms (Greenwood, Delquadri, Stanley, Terry, & Hall, 1985) or noting how staff interact with residents in public residential treatment

Table 8.1. Important variables to consider in designing a direct observation coding system

1. Purpose of assessment
2. Place of assessment
3. Restrictions to be imposed on participants
4. Response property
5. Amount of behavior to be observed
6. Size of the behavior to be observed
7. Resources available to accomplish the observations
8. Plans for establishing the scientific adequacy of the system
9. Reactivity

facilities (Zarcone, Iwata, Rodgers, & Vollmer, 1993), we are likely to use a coding system with many categories carefully designed to represent the richness of the behavioral landscape. Breadth of coverage might supersede precision, and interval systems that allow more behaviors to be observed might be preferred over continuous or real-time approaches. If understanding a behavioral construct is our purpose, we might limit our focus to that construct and several others theoretically relevant to it. For example, heterosocial skill might be conceptualized as made up of a relatively small number of discrete interactive behaviors. Socially effective and ineffective persons determined by an independent means could be observed and behaviors examined for their power to discriminate the groups (see Kupke, Calhoun, & Hobbs, 1979; Kupke, Hobbs, & Cheney, 1979). Our understanding of the heterosocial skill construct would be furthered by finding that the groups differed in expected ways. In studying bulimia, Humphrey et al. (1986) found the Marital Interaction Coding System (MICS; Hops, Wills, Weiss, & Patterson, 1972) and the Structural Analysis of Social Behavior (SASB; Benjamin, 1979) to be comparable in terms of distinguishing normal families from those with persons experiencing bulimia. The SASB, however, did a better job providing information theoretically relevant to understanding bulimia.

Suppose the purpose for observing is the straightforwardly practical one of making predictions about the observees. If so, we are likely to use a coding system containing behavior for which there are theoretical or empirical bases for anticipating relationships with a criterion. To illustrate, predicting rate of advancement in an organization is likely to be more accurate if our predictors include behaviors known to impact the judgments of others. Thus, the frequency of positive communicative behavior is more apt to be observed than automatically reinforcing behavior such as smoothing one's mustache or moving hair away from one's eyes. The codes included in such a system might allow for more inference by observers. These inferences might capture some of the impressionistic aspects more likely to be related to the promotability criterion. Similarly, if one is predicting the ratings of clinicians used to determine treatment effectiveness, higher levels of accuracy might stem from using codes that permit more inference. Or greater accuracy might result from using precisely defined codes that can easily be combined into higher-order categories (e.g., "total aversive behavior"; Patterson et al., 1975).

Now, consider that the purpose for assessing is to determine variables controlling behavior. This would be the case when directly verifying hypotheses derived in the interpretive phase of functional analyses (Cone, 1997). For such a purpose, precisely defined codes are likely to be included with a view toward showing systematic covariation between molecular behavior and carefully identified environmental events. Real-time recording of the frequency of behavior will provide the most sensitive measure of changes in the behavior as antecedent and consequent stimuli are manipulated systematically. When monitoring change, the last of our five assessment purposes, real-time recording of molecular behavior frequencies is again likely to be preferable. Unfortunately, the high levels of precision possible with real-time recording might not be realistic for many clinical applications of direct observation.

Place of Assessment

In addition to purpose, a closely related consideration in choosing an observational system is the location in which behavior is to be observed. Two major types of setting are analog or contrived, and natural (Hartmann & Wood, 1990). Whenever possible, clinical psychologists observe in the natural context because in vivo observation provides the potential for obtaining the highest quality data. Cost and resource considerations lead more often to observations in analog contexts, however. Observing in contrived settings has many advantages, including the provision of a more sensitive type of measurement (Hartmann & Wood, 1990), greater convenience, and more control over variables likely to be related to the behavior of both observees and observers. Other advantages include being able to create situations in which low-frequency behavior is more likely to occur. Baskett (1985) found, for instance, that over a third of the observations of nonproblem families did not even involve mutual interaction. Further advantages include being able to observe behavior that is difficult to view in the natural context (e.g., alcohol consumption, sexual activity) and arranging the setting to permit the use of sophisticated observing and recording apparatus. S. Foster, Inderbitzen, and Nangle (1993) describe advantages and disadvantages of analog observation, and Hughes and Haynes (1978) discuss laboratory observation of parent-child interaction, specifically.

Among the disadvantages associated with analog observation are concerns with the generalizability of the data to the natural environment (Mash & Terdal, 1997). Sillars (1991) refers to the "moonscape qualities" (p. 205) typical of university laboratories and urges "naturalizing" these settings to enhance their resemblance to real-life home environments. An early study comparing data from home and laboratory settings found families to be more positive during decision-making tasks undertaken at home (O'Rourke, 1963). At the same time, marital interaction was more emotional in the home setting, consistent with Gottman's (1979, 1980) finding of greater negativity at home. Zangwill and Kniskern (1982) found higher rates of behavior for mothers and children observed in clinic settings compared with homes. Belsky (cited in Jacob, Tennenbaum, & Krahn, 1987) reported mothers of infants to be more active and responsive to their children in the laboratory than at home, whereas the infants themselves appeared unaffected. This finding parallels earlier research showing mothers to be less interactive, less helpful, and more restrictive at home (Moustakas, Sigel, & Schalock, 1956).

Jacob et al. (1987) summarize analog versus natural context observational differences, noting that effects appear related to the ages of the participants, with adults showing greater cross-setting differences than children, especially infants (unless they are deliberately stressed). Adults are more apt to show "constrained and socially desirable behavior" (Sillars, 1991) in the laboratory than at home. With respect to marital interaction, Jacob et al. observe, reassuringly, that results obtained in one setting do not appear contradictory to those obtained in another. At the same time, they point to findings by Lytton (1974) in which observational data collected in situ were more supportive of theoretical predictions than those collected in the laboratory. Webster-Stratton (1985) observed that the comparability between home- and clinic-collected observational data may depend on the structure imposed. Her data suggest greater similarity between settings when the clinic is relatively unstructured.

At this point, definite conclusions with respect to the impact of setting on data quality would be premature. Order effects (observing in home first, followed by laboratory [e.g., O'Rourke, 1963]) and method-setting confounds (e.g., audiotaping at home vs. videotaping in the laboratory [Burggraf & Sillars, 1987]) are among methodological concerns with research to date. Moreover, there have been too few studies directly exploring the issue for definitive conclusions to be drawn at this time. Mash and Terdal

(1997) warn against assuming that failure to generalize from clinic to home settings inevitably suggests that clinic observations are unrepresentative. There would need to be independent verification of the representativeness of the home observations before this conclusion would be tenable.

Restrictions Imposed on Participants

A third consideration in choosing an observation system is whether and what type of restrictions will be imposed on observees. Three types of restriction have been used. In behavioral role plays, participants play several different roles during the presentation of a number of vignettes (Bellack, 1979). Unfortunately, generalization of role-played behavior to the natural environment has been limited, as has its concurrent validity (Kazdin, Matson, & Esveldt-Dawson, 1984). S. Foster et al. (1993) also note the relatively little attention given the social validity of behavioral role-play assessment.

A second type of restriction involves having participants work on certain tasks. For example, Eyberg and Robinson (1983) instruct parents to let their child play with whatever he or she wants, to take the lead, while the parent just follows along (child-directed interaction). Eyberg's Dyadic Parent-Child Interaction Coding System (DPICS-II; Eyberg et al., 1994) is similar to the system used extensively by Forehand and McMahon (1981), in which clinic observations of parent-child pairs include 5-minute "child's game" and "parent's game" conditions. A less complex form of this system has been developed for home observations (McMahon & Estes, 1993). Marital couples and families also have been observed under restrictions imposed by certain tasks (e.g., Gottman, Markman, & Notarius, 1977). For example, Henggeler and colleagues (Henggeler, Borduin, Rodick, & Tavormina, 1979) observed parents and their adolescent child under instructions to plan where they might go on vacation. Another task required them to discuss the family's biggest problem. Interestingly, more conflict was noted when discussing the instrumental (Plan a vacation) than the expressive (What's the problem?) topic. Jacob, Seilhamer, and Jacob (Chapter 28, this volume) draw some preliminary conclusions concerning the benefits of constraining participants by assigning them tasks to perform. First, structuring observational assessment in this way seems to afford enhanced opportunities for behavior of particular theoretical or practical interest to emerge (e.g., Mash & Johnston, 1982). Second, tasks providing a context more salient to the participants are more likely to produce relevant data than those less salient. Third, objective observational methods reveal reasonable consistency in the structure of families across tasks.

A third way in which the behavioral variability of participants has been limited by imposing restrictions is most often associated with observations conducted in the home. These involve requirements that all family members be present during the observation session, that they restrict themselves to two adjacent rooms, that the television and radio be off, that there be no outgoing telephone calls, and that incoming ones be terminated quickly (see Maerov, Brummett, & Reid, 1978). The impact of such restrictions on data quality is yet to be documented.

Response Property of Interest

A fourth variable to consider when designing observational assessment systems is the characteristic of the behavior that is of most interest. Johnston and Pennypacker (1993) describe individual dimensional quantities (e.g., countability, duration, latency, interresponse time interval) and combinations of them. Others (e.g., Gelfand & Hartmann, 1984) list the response properties of frequency, latency, duration, intensity, and direction as important. Consistent with Skinner's (1938) view of the importance of rate is a strong argument for observing cycles of behavior that, by definition, involve movement or countability (Barrett, Johnston, & Pennypacker, 1986). Indeed, Lindsley (cited in Johnston & Pennypacker, 1993) proposed the "Dead Man's Test" as a criterion for determining whether a behavior was worth observing in the first place. If a dead man could do it, it was a behavior without a movement cycle and therefore not worth observing. For instance, a teacher concerned with improving comportment in a third-grade class might use momentary time sampling to record the number of children on task at 15-minute intervals. If on task is defined as "in assigned seat, at least one foot on floor, eyes oriented within a 90-degree arc of the material or the teacher, and vocalizing only if called upon," it would not pass the dead man's test. A dead person could be propped into position and "appear" to be engaging in this behavior. There is no definable movement cycle for the response. It might be preferable for the teacher to record copying words from a spelling list on the board, completing problems on a math sheet, or raising one's hand to be recognized. Another example comes from assessing the social competence of withdrawn children. Isolate behavior or time spent alone suggests duration as the dimensional quantity of most relevance. This behavior does not pass the dead man's test, however, and might be replaced with "initiates contact with other children," for which countability and frequency are relevant properties and movement cycles can be defined.

Event recording, real-time recording, or frequency-within-interval recording are likely choices for behavior involving movement cycles. Practical considerations sometimes require compromises, however. In the classroom example, the teacher might lack the resources to observe and record the specific movement cycles involved in completing academic tasks for each child. Thus, real-time recording and other methods providing direct accounts of behavior might be less feasible than an interval recording system of the momentary time sampling variety. The teacher can observe easily the number of children on task when signaled periodically and required merely to note the number meeting the definition (see Kubany & Slodgett, 1973). Improvements in on task percentages might be sufficient evidence to convince the teacher of the effectiveness of the intervention selected to improve class comportment.

Which response property or dimensional quantity to emphasize in defining behavior depends on a number of factors in addition to the issue of feasibility. When observing children, for example, developmental status is important. Barrios (1993) notes that *duration* of crying when teased by peers is likely to be more important when observing very young children, whereas its *frequency* is likely to be of more value when observing adolescents. The purpose of assessing and the audience for the data are additional factors of importance. Suppose the teacher in the above example is under review for retention by the school district. The teacher might choose to focus on improving the frequency of problems completed correctly and not care particularly whether the children stand up, blurt out, or otherwise disrupt the calm and quiet so long as they are learning their math. The audience for data on the teacher's class is the district's administration. The district happens to be a fairly conservative one in which order and decorum are highly valued classroom characteristics. For it, time on task (i.e., duration) is likely to be the more relevant dimensional quantity to observe. System design should consider who is to be convinced by the data, an issue closely related to social validity (Kazdin, 1977; Wolf, 1978). S. Foster et al. (1993) discuss social validity as an important consideration when observational assessment is used to evaluate treatment impact.

Amount of Behavior

A fifth factor impacting the form of the observation system is the size of the observational task, or observer load. The teacher with a number of children to observe simultaneously can have a daunting responsibility noting one or more behaviors of the children and recording them consistently. Real-time and event record approaches are unlikely to produce accurate data because the teacher simply cannot track the start times and stop times of a large number of behaviors concurrently. The challenge can be even greater when multiple characteristics of each behavior must be recorded. For example, the Interpersonal Process Code (IPC; Rusby, Estes, & Dishion, 1991) requires noting the activity, content, and affect of each response recorded. The Home Observation Assessment Method (HOAM; Steinglass, 1979) requires noting specific aspects of the behavior of family members (e.g., whether it involves positive or negative physical contact) as well as the context of the behavior, who initiates it, the type of interaction (e.g., information exchange), and the outcome from the perspective of the person observed. In addition, affect level is rated on a 7-point scale.

Systems with extensive observer requirements such as these demand long hours of observer training and must have coding sheets or other data entry mechanisms that can be used reliably. When multiple judgments are required for each behavior, observation at any moment is likely to be limited to a single family member or dyad. It is unrealistic to expect all members of a class to be observed simultaneously and have fine discriminations made about their behavior as are called for in complex systems.

Size of Behavior

Related to the amount of behavior being recorded is the precision with which a behavior unit is defined. "Hits sister" is a much more specific discrimination for an observer than "aggressive toward sister." How molar versus molecular a behavior category should be has been the topic of extensive discussion in the literature (Alexander et al., 1995; Cairns & Green, 1979; Floyd, 1989; S. Foster & Cone, 1995; Margolin, 1987; Mash & Terdal, 1997). Indeed, how to use both general and specific categories in the same system has been evaluated (Bales & Cohen, 1979; Benjamin, 1979, 1993).

The specificity of the behaviors to be observed may depend on the theoretical orientation of the investigator. This, in turn, influences the nature of the subject matter being studied. If behavior per se is the subject of interest, more molecular categories are likely to be preferred. This is because the investigator is interested in the behavior observed as it represents more of the same. That is, observed responses are viewed as representing samples of a larger population of identical or very similar behavior. When behavior per se is not the subject of interest, but is used merely as a window on something else, as a "sign" of an underlying disposition or trait (Goodenough, 1949), more molar categories are likely.

As an illustration, Abikoff and colleagues (Abikoff, Gittelman, & Klein, 1980; Abikoff, Gittelman-Klein, & Klein, 1977) observed hyperactivity in elementary school children. One of the 13 categories originally included in their observation code was "interference." This was scored whenever calling out, clowning, or interruption of the work of others occurred. These three behaviors were viewed as interchangeable indicators of interference. Another category, "physical aggression," included hitting, pushing, throwing objects, and destruction of materials. Similarly, Alexander (1973) observed "supportive communication" in families and included spontaneous problem solving, genuine information seeking and giving, equality, and empathic understanding as interchangeable indicators of this construct.

The size of the response observed can be distinguished from the complexity of the behavior required of the observer upon detecting it (Floyd, 1989). "Smiles" are relatively small bits of behavior that can be detected easily. If the observer needs merely to note their occurrence, recording is relatively straightforward. If, however, the observer must infer something about the smile (e.g., that it indicates positive affect), the task is more complex. Again, the nature of the subject matter and the theoretical context of the observations seem key. When behavior is the focus, inference is likely to be low and the observer's task relatively simple. When dispositions or traits are the focus, inference is likely to be higher and more than simple observation is required. Indeed, the process is now more appropriately viewed as rating, and, as Cairns and Green (1979) noted, a "rater is assumed to be a competent personality theorist, methodologist, *observer,* and psychometrician" (p. 212; emphasis added).

Even when observers make judgments about molecular events, there is an inevitable interest in what those events might mean. This interest can be served by combining the events or summarizing them in some way. One means of producing summaries of observational data involves the use of higher-order systems. In these, less expensive, global inferential ratings substitute for costlier, molecular observations. Justification for the substitution comes from correlations between the two types of data. Higher-order systems can be extremely efficient in clinical assessment for screening out nonproblem areas and identifying ones in need of further information. Thus, a child might be rated average with respect to compliance with adult requests, self-help skills, and communication, but lower than average in terms of social interaction. Further analysis might reveal higher than average ratings on physical aggression. Specific intervention can be preceded by direct observations of social interactions using a code with a category for physically aggressive behavior. If the molecular observations confirm there is a problem as identified by the molar ratings, intervention can be initiated and monitored for effectiveness with the direct observation code. Periodically, molar ratings can be used to confirm that progress is being made.

An approach similar to this has been reported by Borduin and colleagues (1995), who found global inferential constructs (supportiveness, conflict/hostility) that were composed of specific molecular behaviors changed in predictable ways following family intervention. Hops, Davis, and Longoria (1995) have recently reported a multilevel system in which a few superordinate content and affect categories are composed of a larger number of more molecular responses. They found "micro socially" observed behaviors correlated with more global ratings provided by both trained observers and family members themselves.

Resources Available

More exotic coding system formats can be used when extensive resources are available to the researcher. Observers are the most obvious resource, though others include time and equipment. If a cadre of observers is available more or less continuously and they use palm-top computers, a complex and comprehensive observational code can be employed. It will take time to train them, however. Rueter and Conger (1995) trained observers for 200 hours over a 10-week period, for example. Reid and colleagues report 10 to 15 hours of training on videotaped examples before exposing observers to field experience (Maerov et al., 1978). Careful observing and recording of many behaviors takes time, especially if representative data are necessary. If time is plentiful, real-time recording of onsets and offsets of multiple responses is possible. If time is short, compromises are needed, and interval recording of the momentary time sampling variety might be the best that can be expected. The availability of observational equipment also permits more complex systems to be used. Such equipment includes timing devices, event recorders, audio and video recording machines, one-way mirrors, time-lapse photography, handheld or palm-top computers for data entry and interim data storage (cf. Dugan et al., 1995), and desktop computers and associated software for analyzing data. Hartmann and Wood (1990) describe these technological aids and others and provide a table of technology types and references to their use.

How Scientific Adequacy Is to Be Established

Foresight with respect to the psychometric qualities needed for the instrument will also influence the design of the system. When behavior is the subject matter, it is assumed that observations of a sample of the behavior will generalize to a larger population of the behavior. In such cases, observer accuracy is important. Real-time and event records permit accuracy determinations more readily than interval recording systems or narrative ones. If behavior is viewed as a sign of an underlying trait or disposition, accuracy is not relevant, and systems estimating occurrences rather than recording each one can suffice. From such a perspective, however, internal consistency and temporal stability become relevant and one would need to design a system to permit their calculation. For instance, data on the individual behaviors said to indicate "shyness" would be collected and a coefficient alpha calculated to document their equivalence or interchangeability. The system would be designed in such a way as to permit occurrences of the individual behaviors to be recorded separately from one another.

Reactivity

The ninth and final variable to consider in choosing a system is the impact observing is likely to have on the participants. If observing the behavior is likely to affect its occurrence, the system can take this reactivity into account and attempt to minimize it. For example, live observations can be forgone in favor of hidden cameras or microphones that allow for video- and audiotaped records of the behavior that can be observed later (see Bernal, Gibson, Williams, & Pesses, 1971). Jacob and colleagues (Jacob, Tennenbaum, Seilhamer, Bargiel, & Sharon, 1994) recently tape recorded the dinnertime conversation of families under conditions varying in obtrusiveness to examine reactivity. In the most obtrusive condition, one tape recorder was placed in the home in the dining area, and the family activated it immediately prior to beginning the evening meal. In a less obtrusive condition, three tape recorders in suitcase-like containers were placed in the home, one in the dining area and two elsewhere. The family was led to believe a timer would automatically activate the recorder at random times throughout the day. Actually, only the dining area tape recorder was active, and it was set to turn on for the same hour each day. Extensive analyses revealed relatively little reactivity.

Tape records can be insensitive to some types of behavior, however, providing inappropriate substitutes for live observations. Observing talking from videotapes can be difficult, for example, and audiotape recording prohibits observing facial expression, postures, and other visually sensed responses. Fortunately, the impact of live observers can be minimized in several ways. One of these is to use coding systems and data entry mechanisms that are relatively unobtrusive. For example, pressing and holding keys on a handheld data entry device that is kept out of sight under a coat or in a lap under a table can minimize reactivity. An approach of this sort will have to be kept simple, however, with few behaviors being tracked, or observers will need extensive training to use a more complex system consistently. (For additional considerations of ways to minimize reactivity, see Haynes and Horn, 1982.)

EVALUATING THE SCIENTIFIC ADEQUACY OF DIRECT OBSERVATION SYSTEMS

Barrios (1993) describes three general approaches for establishing the quality of direct observation data: (a) the psychometric model, (b) the generalizability model, and (c) the accuracy model. Hartmann and Wood (1990) discuss reliability and validity concerns, subsuming generalizability under the former and accuracy under both. In the previous edition of this text, Cone and Foster (1982) treated data quality in terms of accuracy and generalizability across universes of observer, time, setting, behavior, and method. Conceptually, the primary concern with data from any assessment instrument is the extent to which they generalize. That is, we want to argue convincingly that the data mean something (Kane, 1992). The more scores generalize, the more they have meaning.

When evaluating assessment instruments, it is customary to focus first on reliability. The primacy of reliability stems from the limits it sets on validity. A validity coefficient cannot exceed the square root of the product of the individual reliabilities of two things being correlated (Kaplan & Saccuzzo, 1997). Thus, unless scores are consistent or reliable, they will not be valid. When a latent trait or classical measurement perspective is taken, this logic is compelling. If observations are undertaken to document behavior per se, however, the primary concern is with accuracy. This is because of the need to know our instrument is measuring what we intend it to measure before looking at the relationship between its scores and those from instruments tapping other variables. Viewed in this way, accuracy is synonymous with validity, at least the simplest form of validity defined as "the extent to which a score measures what it is intended to measure" (Hartmann & Wood, 1990). Validity is much more than this, of course. It has to do with the entire network of relationships entered into by scores on a measure (see

Foster & Cone, 1995; Haynes, Richard, & Kubany, 1995; Messick, 1995). Accuracy can be seen as one aspect of validity—a very important aspect to be sure, but not all there is to validation.

Accuracy

Observational measures can be said to produce accurate scores when those scores are controlled by the phenomenon being observed and not something else. Establishing accuracy requires two things: an incontrovertible index of what is being assessed, and rules for using the assessment instrument (Cone, 1981). Whether one is using the observed behavior to generalize to a larger universe of unobserved behavior or as a sign of a latent variable, it is important to know how well the behavior of interest is actually being sensed by the instrument. A person smokes a cigarette or does not. A child talks back to parents or does not. A husband stays engaged in a conversation with his wife or does not. Each of these behaviors can be observed with greater or lesser accuracy depending on the system being used. The accuracy of an observational code should be established before the code is used to obtain information about behavior (Cone, 1981). This is a logical requirement to have confidence that we are measuring what we think we are. Though seldom done in the behavioral sciences, the prior establishment of instrument accuracy is the rule in the physical sciences, where phenomena are studied with microscopes and other instruments whose power and resolution are known. Under these circumstances, failure to detect a particular molecule can be taken to indicate its absence. The investigator need not worry that the microscope was insufficiently powerful and might have missed it.

In the behavioral sciences, prior calibration of instruments before using them to obtain information about behavior can lead to increased clarity as well. Without the calibration step, failure to detect specific behavior can lead to ambiguity. Was the behavior truly absent, or was the instrument merely too inaccurate to detect it? To be sure, calibration is a challenging process that involves careful selection of criteria and specification of the procedures for using the instrument. There will be no criterion of absolute truth, but there can be criteria that are generally agreed to represent the behavior of interest. To illustrate, scripts can be written to portray interchanges between adolescents and parents. The scripts can be prepared so as to represent behaviors with predetermined frequencies. Reviews of the scripts can verify the frequencies. Observations of actors following the scripts can lead to behavior counts that agree with those programmed into the script if the observation code is accurate. The limits of this accuracy can be predetermined in a calibration phase of instrument development. Subsequent users of the system can have confidence in the accuracy of their data to the extent they use it in ways that are consistent with the rules worked out in the calibration phase.

System accuracy can be differentiated from observer accuracy. Even the most precise microscope will yield inaccurate data if used improperly. Likewise, an observational code found to be accurate in calibration conditions can retain its accuracy only if used appropriately. Calibration procedures determine whether and to what extent an instrument is *capable* of being controlled by the phenomenon it is assessing. Whether it actually is, depends on user behavior. That is, accurate instruments may or may not be used in ways that result in accurate data. In classical psychometrics, appropriate use of instruments is most closely related to the concept of scorer reliability, one of several reliability concepts that are treated next.

Reliability

There are different views of reliability depending on the theoretical orientation of the investigator and subject matter of interest. Traditional measurement theory interprets reliability in terms of absence of error. In this view, reliability is seen as the ratio of true score variance to observed score variance that includes true score and error variance. Because of the random nature of error, its existence limits relationships into which scores can enter, that is, the extent of usefulness or validity they can be shown to have.

From a behavioral perspective, Johnston and Pennypacker (1993) define reliability as "the extent to which the measurement procedure yields the same value when brought into repeated contact with the same state of nature" (p. 138). In this view, a scale consistently giving weights two pounds lower than the actual weight of objects is seen as highly reliable even though it is consistently inaccurate.

Latent trait and behavioral perspectives are not that far apart, given the reliance on consistency in determining absence of error in the traditional sense. That is, a highly reliable measure of a latent variable is one whose indicators are interchangeable. In other words, measures with high degrees of internal consistency are reliable because their indicators or items are determined equivalently by the latent variable underlying them. If items are seen as ways of contacting a "state of nature," multiple items represent multiple such contacts. If different items produce the same value or information, the instrument they constitute must be reliable. This is not the place to elaborate the nuances of contrasting perspectives on measurement theory, however, and interested readers are directed to available treatments of this subject by others (e.g., Johnston & Pennypacker, 1993; Silva, 1993).

Scorer Reliability

Traditionally, one speaks of scorer reliability to refer to the extent to which data produced by different users of an instrument agree with one another. This type of reliability is fundamental because its absence limits further study of both reliability and validity. A measure that cannot be scored consistently produces scores that are themselves inconsistent and therefore incapable of relating to themselves or to scores from other devices assessing other variables. It should be clear that users of a measure may do so consistently, that is, be reliable, while not being accurate. Differences between reliability and accuracy have been recognized for some time (Gewirtz & Gewirtz, 1969; Johnson & Bolstad, 1973; Johnston & Pennypacker, 1993; Kazdin, 1973, 1977), and these differences are not unique to observational measurement.

Recognizing the importance of scorer reliability or agreement among independent observers, users of direct observation systems have focused extensive attention on ways of documenting it (Berk, 1979; S. Foster & Cone, 1986; Hartmann, 1977; Hollenbeck, 1978; Jacob et al., 1987; Kelly, 1977; Mitchell, 1979; Suen & Ary, 1989). In addition, much research has addressed variables influencing such agreement (Barrios,

1993; Reid, 1982). Some of the more common ways of reporting interobserver agreement are described next. Interested readers are directed to references above for more extensive treatments.

Percentage Agreement Measures   The simplest, most frequently used, and most controversial approaches to representing agreement between observers involve calculating percentages. Popular when interval recording systems are used, percentage agreement requires defining what constitutes an agreement and then dividing the number of agreements by the number of agreements and disagreements combined. *Overall percentage agreement* defines agreement as both observers noting that a behavior did occur in a particular interval and both observers noting that it did not occur in others. In other words, both occurrences and nonoccurrences are considered. Because of the likelihood that this approach capitalizes on chance when behaviors occur in most or a few of the intervals, more conservative percentage agreements based on occurrence or nonoccurrence have been used. Thus, a behavior that occurs frequently could easily produce high chance agreement on its occurrence, whereas agreement that it did not occur would be more difficult to achieve by chance. In this case, *agreement on nonoccurrence* is the more conservative approach. Conversely, when a behavior occurs in few of the intervals, it is relatively easy to agree that it did not occur, so *agreement on occurrence* would be the more conservative approach.

Whether one uses overall, occurrence, or nonoccurrence forms of percentage agreement, all are subject to inflation by chance. This is also true of so-called *total agreement,* in which the smaller total of two observers' data is divided by the larger. Thus, Observer A sees 12 occurrences of a behavior in a 15-minute period while Observer B sees 10. Dividing 12 into 10 gives an agreement percentage of 83%. Total agreement is sometimes used when it is not possible or necessary to identify individual occurrences of a behavior. For example, Hayes and Cone (1977) counted the number of persons walking through a park in an environmentally destructive manner under different stimulus conditions. Agreement on total persons staying on or venturing off paths was of interest, whereas agreement on each individual person was not. Likewise, when latency or duration of the behavior is recorded, agreement on the passage of time is of greatest interest. Dividing the shorter mean duration or latency by the larger produces an easily interpretable measure of interobserver agreement.

Kappa   Cohen (1960) reported a chi-square-like statistic for assessing agreement on categorical data that improves on the simple percentage agreement measures by controlling for chance. The formula for kappa is:

$$K = \frac{p_o - p_c}{1 - p_c}$$

where p_o is the proportion of agreements for the two observers, and p_c is the proportion of chance agreements. It can be seen that both the numerator and denominator are corrected for chance. Kappa takes values ranging from −1 to 1, with −1 indicating less than chance agreement, 0 indicating that observed agreement and chance agreement are the same, and 1 indicating no disagreement (given that both observers show some variation in scoring categories). An example of how kappa is calculated is provided in Table 8.2.

In addition to controlling for chance, kappa has the advantage of a known sampling theory and statistical properties allowing further statistical examination to be conducted (Jacob et al., 1987). It has been shown that kappa is sensitive to base rates of behavior, however, decreasing as base rate increases. This can lead to high levels of apparent agreement for low base rate behaviors. Langenbucher, Labouvie, and Morgenstern (1996) discuss this problem and some of the alternative statistics proposed to subvert it. Kappa remains less controversial than simple percentage agreement and is widely applicable to different types of data, making it the "interobserver agreement index of choice" (Suen & Ary, 1989, p. 113).

Correlational Procedures   When observers record sums of behaviors within intervals, it is virtually impossible to establish point-by-point agreement, or agreement on each specific occurrence of a behavior. When totals, or sums, or amounts of time are the basic datum, it is possible to use total agreement, as described above. A more statistically satisfactory approach is to correlate totals (sums or amounts) between observers across intervals. Product-moment correlations can be computed for data that are continuous, and these values have all the interpretative and statistical implications of the usual correlation coefficient. For dichotomous data (as when interval recording of the whole or partial interval variety is being used) the phi coefficient is available. As noted by Hartmann (1977), phi and kappa are effectively identical when the two

Table 8.2.   An example of the use of kappa to calculate agreement between two observers

	Observer 1	
	Occurrence of Target Behavior	Nonoccurrence of Target Behavior
Observer 2		
Occurrence of Target Behavior	A 40	C 10
Nonoccurrence of Target Behavior	B 20	D 30

$Kappa\ (K) = (p_o - p_c) / (1 - p_c)$

$\quad p_o = (A + D) / 100$

$\qquad = (40 + 30) / 100 = .70$

$\quad p_c = [(A + B)(B + D) / N^2] + [(A + C)(C + D)/N^2]$

$\qquad = [(40 + 10)(10 + 30) / 100^2] + [(40 + 20)(20 + 30)/100^2]$

$\qquad = [(50 \times 40) / 100^2] + [(60 \times 50) / 100^2$

Therefore,

$\quad Kappa = (.70 - .50) / (1 - .50)$

$\qquad = .40$

observers being compared report approximately equal occurrences of the behavior. Thus, under these circumstances, phi, just as kappa, can be viewed as a chance-corrected percentage agreement measure.

Although correlational approaches share with kappa their known statistical properties and the fact that they have an underlying defined distribution, there are important limitations to their use. Because level is eliminated in the calculation of correlations, the resulting values are insensitive to it. This means that one observer can systematically record more data than another and the product-moment correlation will still be high. Another difficulty can occur when global agreement is being calculated between observers over multiple behavior codes. An example is a situation in which 12 different behaviors are observed, and frequencies for each are correlated between observers over an entire observation period. As noted by Jacob et al. (1987), a high correlation would inevitably result because of the different base rates of the behaviors being observed. It is unlikely such a global approach would be taken, however, as most uses of observational assessment will involve examination of the rates of individual behavior codes. To do this, agreement must be established at the individual code level rather than for all codes taken as a group.

Intraclass Correlation   When multiple observers code the behavior of multiple persons, it is possible to treat the data in analysis of variance terms and identify different sources of variability. In such a case, total variance might be decomposed into variance attributable to observers, persons, and error. Dividing variance due to persons by that variance plus error variance results in the intraclass reliability coefficient (Brennan, 1983). If between-person variance is large relative to that between observers and error, the observational system can be said to be reliable. If the observer main effect is large, the system is not reliable, systematic differences between observers having been established.

Bakeman and Gottman (1986) observed similarities between intraclass correlations and Cronbach's coefficient alpha, showing how the latter can be estimated from the former. As noted by Suen and Ary (1989), however, the use of alpha in this way estimates the reliability of an average score when multiple observers are used. If one intends always to use the same number of observers in future studies, this approach can be helpful. If the intention is the more common one of using a single observer, however, the intraclass correlation is more appropriate.

Intraclass correlational procedures have had a long history, but the exposition of generalizability theory by Cronbach and colleagues (Cronbach, Gleser, Nanda, & Rajaratnam, 1972) in the 1970s focused more attention on them. Although conceptually appealing, there are important limitations to routine use of intraclass correlations for evaluating the adequacy of observation systems. As Jacob et al. (1987) point out, the analysis of variance is calculated on aggregate data from several observers, precluding point-by-point comparisons. Moreover, to identify particular observers who might need additional training, pairs of observers from within the pool of all observers need to be compared. Another difficulty is the amount of data needed to conduct satisfactory analyses. This is much more than typically collected to assess interobserver agreement (Jacob et al., 1987). Furthermore, the intraclass correlation is calculated after the data have been amassed. It is not practical to conduct interim agreement checks along the way (Frick & Semmel, 1978). Thus, such an approach is not appropriate for time-series data collected across multiple phases of an intervention study. In such designs, it is imperative to know the quality of observational data on an ongoing basis to inform decisions regarding the timing of phase changes.

Another consideration is the insensitivity of correlational approaches to level or amount of behavior, as discussed above. As Suen and Ary (1989) note, this can be a problem when criterion-referenced interpretations of scores are used because absolute levels of performance are critical to such interpretations. Finally, Mitchell (1979) raised concerns about the practicality of the intraclass correlation approach given the need for relatively large variance components for subjects. A restricted range of scores can make it difficult to obtain a correlation of any magnitude. These caveats notwithstanding, several recent studies (Ge, Best, Conger, & Simons, 1996; Gordis, Margolin, & John, 1997) report intraclass correlation coefficients, and interested readers are encouraged to consult them.

Factors Affecting Scorer Reliability

Considerable research has investigated the extent to which agreement between observers is affected by such variables as the training they receive (Reid, 1982), the complexity of the code (Reid, 1982), whether they receive feedback and the type of feedback they receive on their performance (DeMaster, Reid, & Twentyman, 1977), their knowledge that agreement is being checked (Romanczyk, Kent, Diament, & O'Leary, 1973; Taplin & Reid, 1973), whether they receive periodic retraining (Johnson & Bolstad, 1973; Kazdin, 1977), overall motivation of the observers (Dancer et al., 1978; Guttman, Spector, Sigal, Rakoff, & Epstein, 1971), including contingencies for declining performance and incentives for maintaining agreement (Reid, 1982), and recalibration throughout the data collection period (Johnson & Bolstad, 1973; Kazdin, 1977). In addition, Mash and McElwee (1974) found observers to be affected by whether they were trained on behavior patterns that were similar to those subsequently encountered. It is also known that observers working in pairs agree more with one another than with observers from other pairs concurrently observing the same phenomenon (Hawkins & Dobes, 1977; Kent, O'Leary, Diament, & Dietz, 1974; Wildman, Erickson, & Kent, 1975).

Recommendations emanating from these studies include:

1. Overtrain observers before starting data collection.
2. Keep codes simple.
3. Provide continuous (or at least frequent) feedback on observer performance.
4. Communicate that agreement could be checked at any time.
5. Provide periodic retraining, even when performance appears to remain high.
6. Maintain observer motivation.
7. Avoid pairing the same observers for long periods.
8. Conduct periodic recalibration checks and vary the criterion protocols used in these checks to avoid memorization of the protocols.
9. Train on samples of behavior comparable to those likely to be encountered in the field.

10. Have someone other than the observers calculate agreement, at least periodically.

11. Use an agreement index that is unaffected by chance.

Beyond Scorer Reliability

Establishing that scores can be obtained reliably from assessment devices is but the first step in showing their scientific adequacy. In generalizability theory terms, this means that the data do not depend on the scorer—that scorers are interchangeable within a universe of all possible scorers. As noted elsewhere, there are other important facets of generalizability to be established once scorer reliability is known (Cone, 1977; Hartmann & Wood, 1990; Melby, Conger, Ge, & Warner, 1995). The extent to which scores generalize across behaviors within a category, over time, and to other settings will be of more or less interest depending on the purposes of the assessment. Hartmann and Wood observed that these other facets have not been addressed extensively by researchers interested in observational methodology. In the years since their review, these facets have continued to be ignored (Melby et al., 1995).

In keeping with the present analysis, the highest priority when establishing the scientific adequacy of observation systems would go to accuracy, then reliability. Data from even one observer can provide confidence that a distinct phenomenon is being observed if there is evidence of that observer's accuracy. The accurate observer can deteriorate over time, to be sure, and intraobserver measures as suggested by Weick (1985) can be used to assess whether this has occurred. Consistency within an observational session is necessary for accuracy to be maintained, for example, and low internal consistency values for an observer will serve as a sign that accuracy is compromised. High interobserver agreement will not, however, and can mask the fact that neither observer is accurate.

Validity

Reviewers of direct observation methodology have opined the relative neglect of validity concerns (Hartmann & Wood, 1990; Weick, 1985). As Weick noted, this neglect appears related to the view that observations are perforce valid, and that "to be in the field is to guarantee validity" (p. 604). Elsewhere (Cone, 1995; S. Foster & Cone, 1995), it was argued that validity is best understood in terms of representational validation and elaborative validation. Space does not allow revisiting the complete logic for this distinction here, but a brief treatment follows. The first concern of purveyors of a new measurement procedure of any type is the extent to which it represents the phenomenon of interest. Once shown to represent something adequately, attention can turn to whether that representation is of any use. In other words, do scores on the measure enter into relationships that are practically and/or theoretically valuable? The usefulness of a measure shown to represent a phenomenon faithfully is elaborated in studies exploring such relationships.

The priority is given representational validity evidence because without it, negative findings from studies attempting to elaborate the meaning of scores on a measure are difficult to interpret. Do they mean the theory is flawed and there is no relationship? Or was the design of the study inadequate to test the relationship? Finally, was one or more of the measures involved deficient in some way? When the meaning of scores is elaborated only after they have been shown to represent the phenomenon of interest, at least the third of these possibilities can be eliminated.

Representational validity evidence can come from traditional content analyses (Haynes et al., 1995) and from convergent and discriminant analyses (Campbell & Fiske, 1959) addressing whether multiple methods of representing the same thing agree, and whether measures of unrelated things do not. With direct observation assessment, a limited amount of research has addressed convergent validation issues. An illustrative study by Yarrow and Waxler (1979) examined the extent to which direct observations, interviews, and ratings by others converged to provide comparable information when assessing interactions between mothers and their preschool children. A total of four hours of data was obtained from observations in the home on two different occasions. In general, assessment information from the different methods was "not in close association" (p. 54).

More recently, Hops et al. (1995) found significant relationships between observational frequencies and ratings by observers of parent and adolescent behaviors. Northup, Jones, Broussard, and George (1995) compared self-report, forced choice self-report, and observation of time spent interacting with reinforcing toys/games, and found the different assessment methods disagreed more than they agreed. Floyd, O'Farrell, and Goldberg (1987) found little convergence between two different observational measures designed to assess positive and negative communication in marital interaction. This was true even though the definitions for the behaviors in one system were taken largely from the same criteria used in the other. In an ethnographic analysis of time use in an Egyptian village, Ricci et al. (1995) compared participants' recall of activities engaged in the previous day with observers' records of these activities. Recall errors were substantial (total recall error = 56%), making it unreasonable to rely on self-report for accurate time use information.

More encouraging results were reported by West, French, Kemp, and Elander (1993), who studied the correspondence between self-reports and direct observations of driving in adult automobile drivers in Britain. Correspondence varied substantially across different driver behaviors, being highest for speed, calmness, and carefulness. Interestingly, direct observations of speed correlated positively (.37 to .47) with self-reports of accidents during the previous three years.

Jacob et al. (1987) reviewed observational studies of family interaction and addressed the issue of convergent validation. In general, they were impressed by the low correspondence among self-report, rating-by-other, and direct observation data. Noting that integrating different research findings in family research is difficult without studies of such correspondence, Jacob et al. urged more rigorous and systematic efforts in this area. Taking up the challenge, Melby et al. (1995) reported the use of structural equation modeling (SEM) to examine correspondence among direct observations, self-reports, and spouse reports of hostility in marital interactions. The greatest convergence was between self- and spouse reports (validity coefficients of .51 and .61 for husbands' and wives' behavior, respectively). When observer data were involved in comparisons, convergence was less impressive (.32 and .36 for husbands and wives, spouse vs. observers; and .38 and .40 for husbands and wives, self vs. observer). Noting limitations of traditional multitrait-multimethod approaches to studying convergence, Melby et al. argue the advantages of SEM. Although SEM can be valuable, it is unlikely to be used extensively for this purpose, given its requirements of relatively large sample sizes and the need for data from multiple observers. Moreover, the approach does not seem suitable for data from interaction studies involving sequences of behavior.

Elaborative validity evidence comes from analyses traditionally labeled criterion-related or construct validity studies. When sufficient representational validity evidence is available to indicate what the observational system does and does not measure, it makes sense to examine whether the data it produces are useful. In exploring the meaning of direct observations of couples' interactions, for example, a principal interest has been discriminative validation evidence. That is, can the system satisfactorily distinguish happily from unhappily married couples (Markman & Notarius, 1987)? D. Foster et al. (1997) examined relationships between the amounts of emotional validation/invalidation partners were observed to receive and their perceptions of support, undermining, and dyadic adjustment. They found higher levels of emotional validation in couples reporting high social support, good adjustment, and low undermining. Gordis et al. (1997) observed children's anxiety, withdrawal, and distraction during laboratory interactions with their parents. These behaviors were shown to be correlated with parents' reports of physical aggression in their marriage during the past year.

Summary

The scientific adequacy of observational assessment methods is argued in essentially the same way as for any other assessment method. First, show the measure represents the thing being assessed as it is supposed to and that it does this consistently. When behavior per se is the subject matter, this means demonstrate accuracy. When a hypothetical construct is the subject matter, this means demonstrate reliability in the classical sense initially, and then convergent and discriminant validity afterwards. After showing a coding system to be accurate and/or reliable in initial derivation or calibration conditions, continue monitoring this during applications of the system. Document scorer reliability using chance-corrected indices (e.g., kappa). Move into the elaborative validation phase when representational validity evidence is sufficient, and avoid seeking both types of information from the same data.

ETHICAL CONSIDERATIONS

Direct observation is the least obtrusive of the array of assessment methods available to social scientists (Adler & Adler, 1994). This characteristic is at once the most and least important reason for its potential misuse. With obtrusive methods (e.g., self-report, interview), the person being studied knows data are being collected. With direct observation used unobtrusively, this knowledge need not be available. In other words, one's privacy can more easily be invaded with observational measures than with other types of assessment.

Much has been written about the extent to which a researcher should call attention to the data collection process and obtain the informed consent of participants before observations are made (Adler & Adler, 1994; Barrios, 1993; Bussell, 1994; Pepler & Craig, 1995). Even in so-called public settings, there is disagreement as to whether observees should be informed. As noted by Adler and Adler, there is also variation in how one defines public, further complicating the issue.

Space does not permit lengthy discussion of the ethics of direct observation assessment here. An extensive treatment of ethical issues in clinical research can be found in Bersoff and Bersoff (Chapter 2, this volume). If clinical research is conducted at institutions receiving at least partial support from the federal government, it must conform to the regulations of institutional review boards (IRBs). Observation involving public behavior requires IRB approval (Adler & Adler, 1994). This approval is more likely when the observees cannot be personally identified, the data do not place the subject at risk of criminal or civil liability, and the subjects' behavior does not involve sensitive content such as illegal conduct, drug use, sexual activity, or the use of alcohol. Where the public behavior of children is at issue, the consent of IRBs is normally pro forma so long as the observer does not participate in the activities being observed. When nonpublic behavior is being observed, or the observer is participating in activities along with children who are being observed, IRBs require the informed consent of participants. If children are the observees, the consent of their legal guardians is necessary. Further, the assent (preferably in writing) of the child must be obtained (West Virginia University, 1986).

Informed consent requires telling potential participants what specific behaviors will be observed, who will be observing them, and under what conditions (Barrios, 1993). In addition, potential participants should be told the specific steps that will be taken to protect the anonymity of their data. Unfortunately, by informing participants that they will be observed, the process becomes reactive and the external validity of the data can be compromised. Barrios notes several ways to deal with this problem, including replacing human observers with mechanical or electronic transducers (Johnston & Pennypacker, 1993). The use of such devices, including hodometers (Bechtel, 1967) or actometers (Tryon, 1991), will be less and more reactive, respectively, and not without ethical implications of its own. Another solution to the reactivity problem is to carry out observations over such long periods that adaptation or habituation to the process occurs. Tactics for making observations less obtrusively have shown some promise also (Bernal et al., 1971; Jacob et al., 1994; Pepler & Craig, 1995).

ISSUES IN THE USE OF DIRECT OBSERVATION ASSESSMENT

Since the publication of the first edition of this handbook, direct observation has remained the most effective way of obtaining ecologically valid information on behavior (Barkley, 1997). Its use is extensive in clinical psychology research as well as related fields. Elliott and colleagues (Elliott, Miltenberger, Kaster-Bundgaard, & Lumley, 1996) document its substantial application among behavior therapists, for example, and Bennion (cited in Melby et al., 1995) noted a 300% proportional increase in studies appearing in *Developmental Psychology* between 1970 and 1990 that used observational methods. Similarly, Jacob and colleagues (Jacob et al., 1994) note a "move toward direct observation" (p. 354) in the family, marital, and parent-child in-teraction areas. Unfortunately, it is underused in treatment-outcome research in clinical psychology, though scattered examples can be found (e.g., Kendall, 1994).

Notwithstanding the present viability of systematic direct observation as an assess-ment method, a number of important issues challenge its future. These are discussed briefly in this section.

Conceptual Issues

Literature on the development and evaluation of observational assessment methodol-ogy historically has been insular and has not benefited from theoretical conceptualiza-tions in apparently related areas of research. Hartmann and Wood (1990) complained of the paucity of conceptual analysis in their review, and conditions do not appear to have changed in the interim. Surely, significant gains can be achieved by borrowing from rather extensive literature on vigilance, for one (see Ballard, 1996), and eyewit-ness accuracy, for another (see Deffenbacher, 1991; Martin-Miller & Fremouw, 1995). Hartmann and Wood (1990) noted the failure to apply information processing theory and basic instruction theory to issues of observer training and implied that the insular-ity of the area has stifled improvements over the past 50 years.

Lower- and Higher-Order Observation Systems

Markman and colleagues (1995) point to the common practice of using direct observa-tion to note and record large numbers of individual behaviors, which are then combined in various ways for analysis at an aggregated level. Aggregation facilitates the manage-ment, analysis, and interpretation of large amounts of data and is especially useful when dealing with low-frequency behaviors for which reliable recording is challenging. Markman et al. note the advantage of being able to return to the larger data set and con-struct new summary codes as research results and changes in theory dictate.

The expense of direct observation, especially when a large number of behaviors is in-volved, provides part of the rationale for bypassing the method altogether and relying on more global measures such as rating scales. This becomes even more defensible if sum-mary codes are used anyway. Why not purchase the improved efficiency of global mea-sures by rating the dimensions represented by the codes directly (Markman et al., 1995)? Indeed, some researchers have attempted to obtain the advantages of direct observation and rating methods by developing hybrid systems combining both (Bales & Cohen, 1979; Benjamin, 1979, 1993; Blaske, Borduin, Henggeler, & Mann, 1989; Forgatch, Patterson, & Ray, 1996; Tuteur, Ewigman, Peterson, & Hosokawa, 1995). Mash and Terdal (1997) suggest that part of the rationale for relying on global ratings is efficiency and the view that global ratings provide an "equivalent integrative summary of the molecular re-sponses" (p. 44).

There are dangers inherent in such combinations, however. As Cairns and Green (1979) emphasize, direct observations and ratings assess different things and are used for different purposes. They are not interchangeable. Similar sentiments are offered by Floyd (1989), noting that micro- and macrosystems provide different information about social interaction. Observations of molecular responses provide data that are sensitive to moment-by-moment changes in context, observer, and observee. Ratings tap stable characteristics of the observee, eliminating the momentary events as error contributing to unreliability. To understand the mechanisms of social interaction, for example, observations are key. To understand the longer-term effects of these on stable characteristics of the person, ratings become important. Cairns and Green suggest using direct observations to assess the "processes by which social patterns arise" (p. 224), and ratings to describe more stable outcomes of development. Employing their suggestion in clinical psychology, observations can be used to assess progress toward instrumental treatment goals, and ratings are used to assess ultimate treatment outcomes (Rosen & Proctor, 1981). Markman et al. (1995) made a similar suggestion, observing that macroanalytic systems aimed at larger constructs might be used to assess clinical outcomes. As counterpoint, Alexander and Turner (1995) urge us not to abandon microanalytic approaches.

Assessing Affect

Related to interest in more global, inferential, clinically meaningful observational assessment is increased focus on the emotional qualities of social interaction. This is perhaps most noteworthy in marital interaction and family research arenas where, as Gottman (1994) notes, affect, power, and problem solving have been the primary foci of research. The basis for interest in affect appears to be the realization that there are important qualitative aspects of social interactions that are not represented in frequency counts of specific motor acts. For example, Hops and colleagues (Hops, Biglan, Sherman, Friedman, & Osteen, 1987) found the affect codes of the Living in Familial Environments (LIFE) discriminated between the interactions of families with depressed and nondepressed mothers. In addition, families with aggressive adolescents show more negative affect than those with nonaggressive adolescents when discussing problems (McColloch, Gilbert, & Johnson, 1990).

For observers to sense positive and negative qualities of the behavior they are coding, they must react to some overt behavior. This is clear in Gottman's Specific Affect Coding System (SPAFF; Gottman & Levenson, 1985), where codes are based on "a gestalt consisting of verbal content, voice tone, context, facial expression, gestures, and body movement" (p. 153). The SPAFF is used to supplement observations of specific facial muscles using the Emotion Facial Action Coding System (EMFACS) developed by Ekman and Friesen (1978).

Whereas an interest in global, macroanalytic observation systems is often motivated by economies of time and other resources, coding affect reliably does not always serve such ends. Although simple ratings of positivity-negativity or cheerful-angry can show discriminative validity, there are many questions unanswered about their meaning. What is it, afterall, in the behavior of observees that leads to judgments of positivity? Serious scientific interest in the concept of affect addresses such questions, and with considerable expense. Gottman and Levenson (1985) report two observers spending two years to code 30 couples, for example. Far from being an easy way of distinguishing participants based on qualitative judgments, full understanding of affect will come from objective counts of its constituents at the microanalytic level.

Sequential Analyses in Assessing Interaction

When direct observation is used to assess interaction between people, system design and data analytic procedures appropriate for documenting contingent relationships must be considered. It is not enough to record the frequency with which social interactive behaviors occur in the repertoires of the individual participants. This is especially apparent if one adopts Duncan's (1995) view that "the defining characteristic of interaction is sequential dependency in the respective actions of the participants" (p. 241). Without data on sequences, there can be no meaningful information about social interaction from Duncan's perspective.

Users of direct observation to assess interaction have long appreciated the importance of designing coding systems to permit sequences of behavior to be recorded (e.g., Bales, 1950; Mash, Terdal, & Anderson, 1973; Patterson, Reid, & Maerov, 1978). Indeed, the sine qua non of behavior analysis is the assessment of contingent relationships between environmental events and behavior. A substantial proportion of the important environmental events is the social behavior of others (Guerin, 1994). An illustration of how social contingencies might be recorded is the Response Class Matrix of Mash and colleagues (1973). It involves arranging a 6 (consequent) × 7 (antecedent) matrix for recording a child's responses to someone else's behavior, and a 7 (consequent) × 6 (antecedent) matrix for recording the other person's responses to the child. One observer notes a mother's antecedent behavior while another simultaneously notes the child's consequent behavior. For example, mother "commands," child "complies."

Gottman and Roy (1990) provide a lucid description of the analytic steps to use with observational data representing the contingent social behaviors of dyads such as mother-child or husband-wife. Attending to just two of the codes, one might start with a string such as AABABABABAABBA showing the occurrences of A and B sequentially. The sequence could be described nonsequentially in terms of the sums of the two behaviors (e.g., 7 As, 5 Bs), or it could be described in terms of probabilities. For the latter, the unconditional probability of A in this example is $\frac{7}{12}$ or .58, and that of B is .42. What is of most interest, however, is the conditional probability of A given B *(p[A/B])*, or of B given A. In this example, the conditional probability of B given A is found by counting the times A immediately precedes B. This happens four times. Thus, the conditional probability of B given A is $\frac{4}{7}$ or .57. The predictability of B is improved somewhat, knowing the prior occurrence of A.

Gottman and Roy (1990) warn that it is not enough to report conditional probabilities when analyzing behavior sequences. Our interest is in reducing the uncertainty of predicting a particular behavior given the occurrence of other behavior. Whether and by how much that uncertainty has been reduced requires comparisons with appropriate base rates. The same conditional probability value can mean vastly different things when compared with greatly differing base rates. Gottman and Roy and Bakeman and Gottman (1997) provide more appropriate analytic procedures when data are sequential, as well as indices to assess whether the uncertainty reduced by the analyses is statistically significant. Data analysis is not the focus of the present chapter, however, and interested readers should consult these sources for more thorough exposition. It is enough to leave the topic of sequential analysis with the observation that even a few behaviors of two participants can lead to extensive data sets when examined for interactions. Bakeman (1991), noting that a simple 5×5 matrix can yield 25 transitions (e.g., AB, AC), recommends limiting investigative questions to a few and representing each of them with a 2×2 contingency table. This will provoke careful thought about theoretically or practically relevant sequences in advance and reduce the likelihood of becoming overwhelmed by a mass of data.

Emerging Quasi-Observational Methodology

Efforts to produce the high-quality data of direct observation while minimizing its cost have led to the emergence of "quasi-observational" (S. Foster & Robin, 1997, p. 675) assessment approaches. Examples include telephone interview procedures such as the Parent Daily Report (PDR; Chamberlain & Reid, 1987; Patterson, 1974), in which parents are phoned at frequent intervals (e.g., three times a week) and asked to report the occurrence/nonoccurrence of specific problem behaviors during the past 24 hours.

Other quasi-observational approaches include the use of self-observation cued remotely to occur at random times during the day (Csikszentmihalyi & Larson, 1987; Larson, 1989). The Experience Sampling Method (ESM) used by Larson requires observees to carry a pager and make entries on a form whenever the pager is beeped. Entries include location, mood rating, activity, and companions. A similar momentary time sampling approach was used by Kubany and Slodgett (1973) to prompt teachers to record student behavior. It would be interesting to compare data from this approach and the PDR. Given the retrospective nature of the PDR, one might expect higher convergence between ESM-type assessment and direct observations than Chamberlain and Reid (1987) found for the PDR. Another quasi-observational tactic involves putting tape recorders in unobtrusive places in a home and equipping them with timers to turn on at random or prespecified times (Bernal et al., 1971; Johnson, Christensen, & Bellamy, 1976). Comparisons of data from these procedures and ESM and PDR approaches against direct observations would be useful in advancing observational methodology.

Final Concerns and Conclusions

The high fidelity associated with direct observation assessment data does not come cheaply, as previous sections have shown. Partly for this reason, many studies using it contain small numbers of participants and obtain relatively small behavior samples from them. At the same time, the absence of normative data hinders interpretations of direct observation scores. Barkley (1997) recently called for more use of yoked controls as a partial solution to this problem, noting that the very sensitivity of observations to contextual changes makes it unlikely that normative data collected in one setting would have much applicability to another. Echoing an earlier suggestion (Mash & Barkley, 1986), Barkley reissues a call for establishing regional assessment centers similar to MRI laboratories, which would have the resources to conduct comprehensive evaluations using standard protocols and could archive data to produce local norms.

Another concern is the proliferation of different coding systems. These will often have categories with similar-sounding names. Mash and Dalby (1979) point out that similarly labeled categories can be defined quite differently, reminding us of Kelley's

(1927) warning of the jingle fallacy, that is, that things *named* the same may not necessarily *be* the same. It is unlikely much standardization will occur given the common rational basis (Mash & Terdal, 1997) on which categories are selected, however. That is, systems frequently get developed to contribute data relevant to solving a particular problem. Spousal abuse in one context may be characterized differently than in another, leading to different definitions of categories such as "verbal threats." A remedy for this lack of consistency would be to produce systems more directly based in theory. Presumably, the theory would not be situation-bound, leading to more general applicability of its codes.

The use of technology in direct observation assessment promises to lower the cost of applying it in both research and applied settings. Observers can be trained more efficiently using virtual subjects (Colle & Green, 1996). Greater numbers of observations can be recorded more accurately and reliably using handheld computers (e.g., Hops et al., 1995; Wehby et al., 1995) or bar code technology (Fradenburg, Harrison, & Baer, 1995). And quasi-observational methodology can be expanded, as exemplified by Taylor, Fried, and Kenardy's (1990) use of real-time computer diaries. Interested readers are referred to the recent review of computerized observation systems by Kahng and Iwata (1998) for an excellent description of a variety of options.

Finally, as S. Foster and Robin (1997) point out, the codes of most existing systems are likely to reflect a Eurocentric bias. If so, they may not have the same functional equivalence when used with persons of other backgrounds. For example, a particular parent behavior in Hispanic families might have different correlations with child-relevant outcomes than the same behavior in Caucasian or African American families. It was noted earlier that the same behavior can be viewed differently by observers of different races (Gonzales et al., 1996). The development and evaluation of direct observation systems will benefit from increased cultural and ethnic sensitivity, and research with these systems will help identify when differences are important and when they are not.

Direct observation continues to be the assessment method of choice when data of the highest quality are sought in clinical research and practice. Its development and use has been slower than desirable for the advancement of clinical psychology, but as this chapter has shown, significant progress has been made. It can be expected that the continued evolution of psychological science and the rapid changes being experienced in health care delivery systems will accelerate this progress in the near future.

REFERENCES

Abikoff, H., Gittelman, R., & Klein, D. F. (1980). Classroom observation code for hyperactive children: A replication of validity. *Journal of Consulting and Clinical Psychology, 48,* 555–565.

Abikoff, H., Gittelman-Klein, R., & Klein, D. F. (1977). Validation of the classroom observation code for hyperactive children. *Journal of Consulting and Clinical Psychology, 45,* 772–783.

Achenbach, T. M., McConaughy, S. H., & Howell, C. T. (1987). Child/adolescent behavioral and emotional problems: Implications of cross-informant correlations for situational specificity. *Psychological Bulletin, 101,* 213–232.

Adler, P. A., & Adler, P. (1994). Observational techniques. In N. K. Denzin & Y. S. Lincoln (Eds.), *Handbook of qualitative research* (pp. 377–392). Thousand Oaks, CA: Sage.

Alexander, J. F. (1973). Defensive and supportive communications in normal and deviant families. *Journal of Consulting and Clinical Psychology, 40,* 223–231.

Alexander, J. F., Newell, R. M., Robbins, M. S., & Turner, C. W. (1995). Observational coding in family therapy process research. *Journal of Family Psychology, 9,* 355–365.

Alexander, J. F., & Turner, C. W. (1995). The creative dialectic tension of coding strategies. *Journal of Family Psychology, 9,* 380–384.

Bakeman, R. (1991). Analyzing categorical data. In B. Montgomery & S. Duck (Eds.), *Studying interpersonal interaction* (pp. 255–274). New York: Guilford Press.

Bakeman, R., & Gottman, J. M. (1986). *Observing interaction: An introduction to sequential analysis.* New York: Cambridge University Press.

Bakeman, R., & Gottman, J. M. (1997). *Observing interaction: An introduction to sequential analysis* (2nd ed.). New York: Cambridge University Press.

Bales, R. F. (1950). *Interaction process analysis.* Cambridge, MA: Addison Wesley.

Bales, R. F., & Cohen, S. P. (1979). *SYMLOG: A system for multiple level observation in groups.* New York: Free Press.

Ballard, J. C. (1996). Computerized assessment of sustained attention: A review of factors affecting vigilance performance. *Journal of Clinical and Experimental Neuropsychology, 18,* 843–863.

Baltes, M. M., Neumann, E., & Zank, S. (1994). Maintenance and rehabilitation of independence in old age: An intervention program for staff. *Psychology and Aging, 9,* 179–188.

Barker, R. G., & Wright, H. F. (1955). *Midwest and its children: The psychological ecology of an American town.* New York: Harper & Row.

Barkley, R. A. (1997). Attention-deficit/hyperactivity disorder. In E. J. Mash & L. G. Terdal (Eds.), *Assessment of childhood disorders* (3rd ed., pp. 71–129). New York: Guilford Press.

Barrett, B. H., Johnston, J. M., & Pennypacker, H. S. (1986). Behavior: Its units, dimensions, and measurement. In R. O. Nelson & S. C. Hayes (Eds.), *Conceptual foundations of behavioral assessment* (pp. 156–200). New York: Guilford Press.

Barrios, B. A. (1993). Direct observation. In T. H. Ollendick & M. Hersen (Eds.), *Handbook of child and adolescent assessment* (pp. 140–164). Boston: Allyn & Bacon.

Baskett, L. M. (1985). Understanding family interactions: Most probable reactions by parents and siblings. *Child and Family Behavior Therapy, 7,* 41–50.

Bechtel, R. B. (1967). The study of man: Human movement and architecture. *Transaction, 4,* 53–56.

Bellack, A. S. (1979). Behavioral assessment of social skills. In A. S. Bellack & M. Hersen (Eds.), *Research and practice in social skills training* (pp. 75–104). New York: Plenum Press.

Benjamin, L. S. (1979). Structural analysis of differentiation failure. *Psychiatry, 42,* 1–23.

Benjamin, L. S. (1993). *Interpersonal diagnosis and treatment of personality disorders.* New York: Guilford Press.

Berk, R. A. (1979). Generalizability of behavioral observations: A clarification of interobserver agreement and interobserver reliability. *American Journal of Mental Deficiency, 83,* 460–472.

Bernal, M. E., Gibson, D. M., Williams, D. E., & Pesses, D. I. (1971). A device for automatic audio tape recording. *Journal of Applied Behavior Analysis, 4,* 151–156.

Bickman, L. (1976). Observational methods. In C. Selltiz, L. S. Wrightsman, & S. W. Cook (Eds.), *Research methods in social relations.* New York: Holt, Rinehart and Winston.

Blaske, D. M., Borduin, C. M., Henggeler, S. W., & Mann, B. J. (1989). Individual, family, and peer characteristics of adolescent sex offenders and assaultive offenders. *Developmental Psychology, 25,* 846–855.

Blurton-Jones, N. G., & Woodson, R. H. (1979). Describing behavior: The ethologist's perspective. In M. E. Lamb, S. J. Suomi, & G. R. Stephenson (Eds.), *Social interaction analysis: Methodological issues.* Madison: University of Wisconsin Press.

Borduin, C. M., Mann, B. J., Cone, L. T., Henggeler, S. W., Fucci, B. R., Blaske, D. M., & Williams, R. A. (1995). Multisystemic treatment of juvenile offenders: Long-term prevention of criminality and violence. *Journal of Consulting and Clinical Psychology, 63,* 569–578.

Brennan, R. L. (1983). *Elements of generalizability theory.* Iowa City: ACT.

Burggraf, C. S., & Sillars, A. L. (1987). A critical examination of sex differences in marital communication. *Communication Monographs, 54,* 276–294.

Bussell, D. A. (1994). Ethical issues in observational family research. *Family Process, 33,* 361–376.

Cairns, R. B., & Green, J. A. (1979). How to assess personality and social patterns: Observations or ratings? In R. B. Cairns (Ed.), *The analysis of social interaction: Methods, issues, and illustrations* (pp. 209–226). New York: Erlbaum.

Campbell, D. T., & Fiske, D. (1959). Convergent and discriminant validation by the multitrait-multimethod matrix. *Psychological Bulletin, 56,* 81–105.

Carr, E. G., Levin, L., McConnachie, G., Carlson, J. I., Kemp, D. C., & Smith, C. E. (1994). *Communication-based intervention for problem behavior. A user's guide for producing positive change.* Baltimore: Brookes.

Chamberlain, P., & Reid, J. B. (1987). Parent observation and report of child symptoms. *Behavioral Assessment, 9,* 97–109.

Cohen, J. (1960). A coefficient of agreement for nominal scales. *Educational and Psychological Measurement, 20,* 37–46.

Colle, H. A., & Green, R. F. (1996). Introductory psychology laboratories using graphic simulations of virtual subjects. *Behavior Research Methods, Instruments & Computers, 28,* 331–335.

Cone, J. D. (1977). The relevance of reliability and validity for behavioral assessment. *Behavior Therapy, 8,* 411–426.

Cone, J. D. (1981). Psychometric considerations. In M. Hersen & A. Bellack (Eds.), *Behavioral assessment: A practical handbook* (2nd ed., pp. 38–68). New York: Pergamon Press.

Cone, J. D. (1995). Assessment practice standards. In S. C. Hayes, V. M. Follette, R. M. Dawes, & K. E. Grady (Eds.), *Scientific standards of psychological practice: Issues and recommendations* (pp. 201–224). Reno, NV: Context Press.

Cone, J. D. (1997). Issues in functional analysis in behavioral assessment. *Behaviour Research and Therapy, 35,* 259–275.

Cone, J. D., & Foster, S. L. (1982). Direct observation in clinical psychology. In P. C. Kendall & J. N. Butcher (Eds.), *Handbook of research methods in clinical psychology.* New York: Wiley.

Cronbach, L. J., Gleser, G. C., Nanda, H., & Rajaratnam, N. (1972). *The dependability of behavioral measurements: Theory of generalizability for scores and profiles.* New York: Wiley.

Csikszentmihalyi, M., & Larson, R. (1987). Validity and reliability of the experience-sampling method. *Journal of Nervous and Mental Disease, 175,* 526–536.

Dancer, D. D., Braukmann, C. J., Schumaker, J. B., Kirigin, K. A., Willner, A. G., & Wolf, M. M. (1978). The training and validation of behavior observation and description skills. *Behavior Modification, 2,* 113–134.

Deffenbacher, K. A. (1991). A maturing of research on the behavior of eyewitnesses. *Applied Cognitive Psychology, 5,* 377–402.

DeMaster, B., Reid, J., & Twentyman, C. (1977). The effects of different amounts of feedback on observer's reliability. *Behavior Therapy, 8,* 317–329.

Derby, K. M., Wacker, D. P., Berg, W., DeRaad, A., Ulrich, S., Asmus, J., Harding, J., Prouty, A., Laffey, P., & Stoner, E. A. (1997). The long-term effects of functional communication training in home settings. *Journal of Applied Behavior Analysis, 30,* 507–531.

Dugan, E., Kamps, D., Leonard, B., Watkins, N., Rheinberger, A., & Stackhaus, J. (1995). Effects of cooperative learning groups during social studies for students with autism and fourth-grade peers. *Journal of Applied Behavior Analysis, 28,* 175–188.

Duncan, S., Jr. (1995). Individual differences in face-to-face interaction. In P. E. Shrout & S. T. Fiske (Eds.), *Personality research, methods, and theory: A festschrift honoring Donald W. Fiske* (pp. 241–256). Hillsdale, NJ: Erlbaum.

Ekman, P., & Friesen, W. V. (1978). *Facial action coding system.* Palo Alto, CA: Consulting Psychologists Press.

Elliott, A. J., Miltenberger, R. G., Kaster-Bundgaard, J., & Lumley, V. (1996). A national survey of assessment and therapy techniques used by behavior therapists. *Cognitive and Behavioral Practice, 3,* 107–125.

Evans, I. M. (1993). Dynamic response relationships: The challenge for behavioral assessment. *European Journal of Psychological Assessment, 9,* 206–212.

Eyberg, S. M., Bessmer, J., Newcomb, K., Edwards, D., & Robinson, E. (1994). *Dyadic parent-child interaction coding system: II. A manual.* Unpublished manuscript, University of Florida.

Eyberg, S. M., & Robinson, E. A. (1983). Dyadic parent-child interaction coding system (DPICS): A manual. *Psychological Documents, 13*(2), 24.

Floyd, F. (1989). Segmenting interactions: Coding units for assessing marital and family behaviors. *Behavioral Assessment, 11,* 23–29.

Floyd, F. J., & Markman, H. J. (1983). Observational biases in spouse observation: Toward a cognitive/behavioral model of marriage. *Journal of Consulting and Clinical Psychology, 51,* 450–457.

Floyd, F. J., O'Farrell, T. J., & Goldberg, M. (1987). Comparison of marital observational measures: The marital interaction coding system and the communication skills test. *Journal of Consulting and Clinical Psychology, 55,* 423–429.

Fordyce, W. E. (1976). *Behavioral methods for chronic pain and illness.* St. Louis: Mosby.

Forehand, R., Griest, D., & Wells, K. C. (1979). Parent behavioral training: An analysis of the relationship among multiple outcome measures. *Journal of Abnormal Child Psychology, 7,* 229–242.

Forehand, R., & McMahon, R. J. (1981). *Helping the noncompliant child: A clinician's guide to parent training.* New York: Guilford Press.

Forgatch, M. S., Patterson, G. R., & Ray, J. A. (1996). Divorce and boys' adjustment problems: Two paths with a single model. In E. M. Hetherington & E. A. Blechman (Eds.), *Stress, coping and resiliency in children and the family.* Hillsdale, NJ: Erlbaum.

Foster, D. A., Caplan, R. D., & Howe, G. W. (1997). Representativeness of observed couple interaction: Couples can tell, and it does make a difference. *Psychological Assessment, 9,* 285–294.

Foster, S. L., Bell-Dolan, D. J., & Burge, D. A. (1988). Behavioral observation. In A. S. Bellack & M. Hersen (Eds.), *Behavioral assessment: A practical handbook* (3rd ed., pp. 119–160). New York: Pergamon Press.

Foster, S. L., & Cone, J. D. (1986). Design and use of direct observation systems. In A. Ciminero, K. S. Calhoun, & H. E. Adams (Eds.), *Handbook of behavioral assessment* (2nd ed., pp. 253–324). New York: Wiley.

Foster, S. L., & Cone, J. D. (1995). Validity issues in clinical assessment. *Psychological Assessment, 7,* 248–260.

Foster, S. L., Inderbitzen, H. M., & Nangle, D. W. (1993). Assessing acceptance and social skills with peers in childhood: Current issues. *Behavior Modification, 17,* 255–286.

Foster, S. L., & Robin, A. L. (1997). Family conflict and communication in adolescence. In E. J. Mash & L. G. Terdal (Eds.), *Assessment of childhood disorders* (3rd ed., pp. 627–682). New York: Guilford Press.

Fradenburg, L. A., Harrison, R. J., & Baer, D. M. (1995). The effect of some environmental factors on interobserver agreement. *Behaviour Research and Therapy, 16,* 425–437.

Frick, T., & Semmel, M. I. (1978). Observer agreement and reliabilities of classroom observational measures. *Review of Educational Research, 48,* 157–184.

Ge, X., Best, K. M., Conger, R. D., & Simons, R. L. (1996). Parenting behaviors and the occurrence and co-occurrence of adolescent depressive symptoms and conduct problems. *Developmental Psychology, 32,* 717–731.

Gelfand, D. M., & Hartmann, D. P. (1984). *Child behavior analysis and therapy* (2nd ed.). New York: Pergamon Press.

Gewirtz, H. B., & Gewirtz, J. L. (1969). Caretaking settings, background events and behavior differences in four Israeli child-rearing environments: Some preliminary trends. In B. M. Foss (Ed.), *Determinants of infant behaviour* (Vol. 4, pp. 229–295). London: Methuen.

Gonzales, N. A., Cauce, A. M., & Mason, C. A. (1996). Interobserver agreement in the assessment of parental behavior and parent-adolescent conflict: African-American mothers, daughters, and independent observers. *Child Development, 67,* 1483–1498.

Goodenough, F. L. (1949). *Mental testing: Its history, principles and applications.* New York: Rinehart.

Gordis, E. B., Margolin, G., & John, R. S. (1997). Marital aggression, observed parental hostility, and child behavior during triadic family interactions. *Journal of Family Psychology, 11,* 76–89.

Gottman, J. M. (1979). *Marital interactions: Experimental investigations.* New York: Academic Press.

Gottman, J. M. (1980). Consistency of nonverbal affect and affect reciprocity in marital interaction. *Journal of Consulting and Clinical Psychology, 48,* 711–717.

Gottman, J. M. (1994). *What predicts divorce?* Hillsdale, NJ: Erlbaum.

Gottman, J. M., & Levenson, R. W. (1985). A valid measure for assessing self-report of affect in marriage. *Journal of Consulting and Clinical Psychology, 53,* 151–160.

Gottman, J. M., & Levenson, R. W. (1986). Assessing the role of emotion in marriage. *Behavioral Assessment, 9,* 31–48.

Gottman, J. M., Markman, H. J., & Notarius, C. I. (1977). The topography of marital conflict: A sequential analysis of verbal and nonverbal behavior. *Journal of Marriage and the Family, 39,* 461–477.

Gottman, J. M., & Roy, A. K. (1990). *Sequential analysis: A guide for behavioral researchers.* New York: Cambridge University Press.

Green, S. B., & Alverson, L. G. (1978). A comparison of indirect measures for long-duration behaviors. *Journal of Applied Behavior Analysis, 11,* 530.

Greenwood, C. R., Delquadri, J. C., Stanley, S. O., Terry, B., & Hall, R. V. (1985). Assessment of ecobehavioral interaction in school settings. *Behavioral Assessment, 7,* 331–348.

Guerin, B. (1994). *Analyzing social behavior.* Reno, NV: Context Press.

Guttman, H. A., Spector, R. M., Sigal, J. J., Rakoff, V., & Epstein, W. B. (1971). Reliability of coding affective communications in family therapy sessions: Problems of measurement and interpretation. *Journal of Consulting and Clinical Psychology, 37,* 397–402.

Hartmann, D. P. (1977). Considerations in the choice of interobserver reliability estimates. *Journal of Applied Behavior Analysis, 10,* 103–116.

Hartmann, D. P., & Wood, D. D. (1990). Observational methods. In A. S. Bellack, M. Hersen, & A. E. Kazdin (Eds.), *International handbook of behavior modification and therapy* (2nd ed., pp. 109–138). New York: Plenum Press.

Hawkins, R. P. (1979). The functions of assessment: Implications for selection and development of devices for assessing repertoires in clinical, educational, and other settings. *Journal of Applied Behavior Analysis, 12,* 501–516.

Hawkins, R. P., & Dobes, R. W. (1977). Behavioral definitions in applied behavior analysis: Explicit or implicit. In B. C. Etzel, J. M. LeBlanc, & D. M. Baer (Eds.), *New developments in behavioral research: Theory, methods, and applications. In honor of Sidney W. Bijou.* New York: Erlbaum.

Hayes, S. C., & Cone, J. D. (1977). Decelerating environmentally destructive lawn-walking. *Environment and Behavior, 9,* 511–534.

Haynes, S. N., & Horn, W. F. (1982). Reactivity in behavioral observation: A review. *Behavioral Assessment, 4,* 369–385.

Haynes, S. N., Richard, D. C. S., & Kubany, E. S. (1995). Content validity in psychological assessment: A functional approach to concepts and methods. *Journal of Consulting and Clinical Psychology, 7,* 238–247.

Henggeler, S. W., Borduin, C. M., Rodick, J. D., & Tavormina, J. D. (1979). Importance of task content for family interaction research. *Developmental Psychology, 15,* 660–661.

Hollenbeck, A. R. (1978). Problems of reliability in observational research. In G. P. Sackett (Ed.), *Observing behavior: Vol. II. Data collection and analysis methods* (pp. 79–98). Baltimore: University Park Press.

Hops, H., Biglan, A., Sherman, J., Friedman, L., & Osteen, V. (1987). Home observations of family interactions of depressed women. *Journal of Consulting and Clinical Psychology, 55,* 341–346.

Hops, H., Davis, B., & Longoria, N. (1995). Methodological issues in direct observation: Illustrations with the living in familial environments (LIFE) coding system. *Journal of Clinical Child Psychology, 24,* 193–203.

Hops, H., Wills, T. A., Weiss, R. L., & Patterson, G. R. (1972). *Marital interaction coding system.* Eugene: University of Oregon and Oregon Research Institute.

Hughes, H. H., & Haynes, S. N. (1978). Structured laboratory observation in the behavioral assessment of parent-child interactions: A methodological critique. *Behavior Therapy, 9,* 428–447.

Humphrey, L. L., Apple, R. F., & Kirschenbaum, D. S. (1986). Differentiating bulimic-anorectic from normal families using interpersonal and behavioral observational systems. *Journal of Consulting and Clinical Psychology, 54,* 190–195.

Jacob, T., Tennenbaum, D. L., & Krahn, G. (1987). Factors influencing the reliability and validity of observation data. In T. Jacob (Ed.), *Family interaction and psychopathology: Theories, methods, and findings* (pp. 297–328). New York: Plenum Press.

Jacob, T., Tennenbaum, D., Seilhamer, R. A., Bargiel, K., & Sharon, T. (1994). Reactivity effects during naturalistic observation of distressed and nondistressed families. *Journal of Family Psychology, 8,* 354–363.

Jacobson, N. S. (1979). Increasing positive behavior in severely distressed marital relationships: The effects of problem-solving training. *Behavior Therapy, 10,* 311–326.

Johnson, S. M., & Bolstad, O. D. (1973). Methodological issues in naturalistic observation: Some problems and solutions for field research. In L. A. Hamerlynck, L. C. Handy, & E. J. Mash (Eds.), *Behavior change: Methodology, concepts, and practice* (pp. 7–67). Champaign, IL: Research Press.

Johnson, S. M., Christensen, A., & Bellamy, G. T. (1976). Evaluation of family intervention through unobtrusive audio recordings: Experiences in "bugging" children. *Journal of Applied Behavior Analysis, 9,* 213–219.

Johnston, J. M., & Pennypacker, H. S. (1993). *Strategies and tactics of behavioral research* (2nd ed.). Hillsdale, NJ: Erlbaum.

Kahng, S., & Iwata, B. A. (1998). Computerized systems for collecting real-time observational data. *Journal of Applied Behavior Analysis, 31,* 253–261.

Kane, M. T. (1992). An argument-based approach to validity. *Psychological Bulletin, 112,* 527–535.

Kaplan, R. M., & Saccuzzo, D. P. (1997). *Psychological testing: Principles, applications, and issues* (4th ed.). Pacific Grove, CA: Brooks/Cole.

Kazdin, A. E. (1973). Methodological and assessment considerations in evaluating reinforcement programs in applied settings. *Journal of Applied Behavior Analysis, 6,* 517–531.

Kazdin, A. E. (1977). Artifact, bias, and complexity of assessment: The ABCs of reliability. *Journal of Applied Behavior Analysis, 10,* 141–150.

Kazdin, A. E., Matson, J. L., & Esveldt-Dawson, K. (1984). The relationship of role-play assessment of children's social skills to multiple measures of social competence. *Behaviour Research and Therapy, 22,* 129–139.

Kelley, T. L. (1927). *Interpretation of educational measurements.* Yonkers-on-Hudson, NY: World Book.

Kelly, M. B. (1977). A review of the observational data-collection and reliability procedures reported in the *Journal of Applied Behavior Analysis. Journal of Applied Behavior Analysis, 10,* 97–101.

Kendall, P. C. (1994). Treating anxiety disorders in children: Results of a randomized clinical trial. *Journal of Consulting and Clinical Psychology, 62,* 100–110.

Kent, R. N., O'Leary, K. D., Diament, C., & Dietz, A. (1974). Expectation biases in observational evaluation of therapeutic change. *Journal of Consulting and Clinical Psychology, 42,* 774–780.

Kubany, E. S., & Slodgett, B. B. (1973). Coding procedure for teachers. *Journal of Applied Behavior Analysis, 6,* 339–344.

Kupke, T. E., Calhoun, K. S., & Hobbs, S. A. (1979). Selection of heterosocial skills: II. Experimental validity. *Behavior Therapy, 10,* 336–346.

Kupke, T. E., Hobbs, S. A., & Cheney, T. H. (1979). Selection of heterosocial skills: I. Criterion-related validity. *Behavior Therapy, 10,* 327–335.

Langenbucher, J., Labouvie, E., & Morgenstern, J. (1996). Measuring diagnostic agreement. *Journal of Consulting and Clinical Psychology, 64,* 1285–1289.

Larson, R. (1989). Beeping children and adolescents: A method for studying time use and daily experience. *Journal of Youth and Adolescence, 18,* 511–530.

Lytton, H. (1974). Comparative yield of three data sources in the study of parent-child interaction. *Merrill-Palmer Quarterly, 20,* 53–64.

Maerov, S. L., Brummett, B., & Reid, J. B. (1978). Procedures for training observers. In J. B. Reid (Ed.), *A social learning approach to family intervention: Vol. II. Observation in home settings* (pp. 37–42). Eugene, OR: Castalia Press.

Margolin, G. (1978). A multilevel approach to the assessment of communication positiveness in distressed marital couples. *International Journal of Family Counseling, 6,* 81–89.

Margolin, G. (1987). Participant observation procedures in marital and family assessment. In T. Jacob (Ed.), *Family interaction and psychopathology: Theories, methods, and findings* (pp. 391–426). New York: Plenum Press.

Markman, H. J., Leber, B. D., Cordova, A. D., & St. Peters, M. (1995). Behavioral observation and family psychology—strange bedfellows or happy marriage? Comment on Alexander et al. (1995). *Journal of Family Psychology, 9,* 371–379.

Markman, H. J., & Notarius, C. I. (1987). Coding marital and family interaction: Current status. In T. Jacob (Ed.), *Family interaction and psychopathology: Theories, methods, and findings* (pp. 329–390). New York: Plenum Press.

Martin-Miller, C., & Fremouw, W. J. (1995). Improving the accuracy of adult eyewitness testimony: Implications for children. *Clinical Psychology Review, 15,* 631–645.

Mash, E. J., & Barkley, R. A. (1986). Assessment of family interaction with the response class matrix. In R. Prinz (Ed.), *Advances in behavioral assessment of children and families* (Vol. 2, pp. 29–67). Greenwich, CT: JAI Press.

Mash, E. J., & Dalby, J. T. (1979). Behavioral interventions for hyperactivity. In R. L. Trites (Ed.), *Hyperactivity in children: Etiology, measurement, and treatment implications* (pp. 161–216). Baltimore: University Park Press.

Mash, E. J., & Johnston, C. (1982). A comparison of mother-child interactions of younger and older hyperactive and normal children. *Child Development, 53,* 1371–1381.

Mash, E. J., & McElwee, J. D. (1974). Situational effects on observer accuracy: Behavioral predictability, prior experience, complexity of coding categories. *Child Development, 45,* 367–377.

Mash, E. J., & Terdal, L. G. (1997). *Assessment of childhood disorders* (3rd ed.). New York: Guilford Press.

Mash, E. J., Terdal, L. G., & Anderson, K. (1973). The response class matrix: A procedure for recording parent-child interactions. *Journal of Consulting and Clinical Psychology, 40,* 163–164.

McColloch, M. A., Gilbert, D. A., & Johnson, S. (1990). Effects of situational variables on the interpersonal behavior of families with an aggressive adolescent. *Personality and Individual Differences, 11,* 1–11.

McLaughlin, T. F. (1993). An analysis and evaluation of educator selected data collection procedures in actual school settings: A brief report. *Child and Family Behavior Therapy, 15,* 61–64.

McMahon, R. J., & Estes, A. (1993). *Fast track parent-child interaction task: Observational data collection manuals.* Unpublished manuscript, University of Washington.

Melby, J. N., Conger, R. D., Ge, X., & Warner, T. D. (1995). The use of structural equation modeling in assessing the quality of marital observations. *Journal of Family Psychology, 9,* 280–293.

Messick, S. (1995). Validity of psychological assessment: Validation of inferences from persons' responses and performances as scientific inquiry into score meaning. *American Psychologist, 50,* 741–749.

Mitchell, S. K. (1979). Interobserver agreement, reliability, and generalizability of data collected in observational studies. *Psychological Bulletin, 86,* 376–390.

Moustakas, C. E., Sigel, I. E., & Schalock, M. D. (1956). An objective method for the measurement and analysis of child-adult interaction. *Child Development, 27,* 109–134.

Northup, J., Jones, K., Broussard, C., & George, T. (1995). A preliminary comparison of reinforcer preference assessment methods for children with attention deficit hyperactivity disorder. *Journal of Applied Behavior Analysis, 28,* 99–100.

O'Rourke, J. F. (1963). Field and laboratory: The decision-making behavior or family groups in two experimental conditions. *Sociometry, 26,* 422–435.

Patterson, G. R. (1974). Retraining of aggressive boys by their parents: Review of recent literature and follow-up evaluation. *Canadian Psychiatric Association Journal, 19,* 142–161.

Patterson, G. R., Reid, J. B., Jones, R. R., & Conger, R. E. (1975). *A social learning approach to family intervention: Vol. l. Families with aggressive children.* Eugene, OR: Castalia Press.

Patterson, G. R., Reid, J. B., & Maerov, S. L. (1978). Development of the family interaction coding system (FICS). In J. B. Reid (Ed.), *A social learning approach to family intervention: Vol. II. Observation in home settings* (pp. 3–19). Eugene, OR: Castalia Press.

Paul, G. L., Mariotto, M. J., & Redfield, J. P. (1986). Assessment purposes, domains, and utility for decision making. In G. L. Paul (Ed.), *Assessment in residential treatment settings* (pp. 1–25). Champaign, IL: Research Press.

Pepler, D. J., & Craig, W. M. (1995). A peek behind the fence: Naturalistic observations of aggressive children with remote audiovisual recording. *Developmental Psychology, 31,* 548–553.

Powell, J., Martindale, B., Kulp, S., Martindale, A., & Bauman, R. (1977). Taking a closer look: Time sampling and measurement error. *Journal of Applied Behavior Analysis, 10,* 325–332.

Powers, S. I., Welsh, D. P., & Wright, V. (1994). Adolescents' affective experience of family behaviors: The role of subjective understanding. *Journal of Research on Adolescence, 4,* 585–600.

Reid, J. B. (1982). Observer training in naturalistic research. In D. P. Hartmann (Ed.), *Using observers to study behavior: New directions for methodology of social and behavioral science* (pp. 37–50). San Francisco: Jossey-Bass.

Ricci, J. A., Jerome, N. W., Megally, N., Galal, O., Harrison, G. G., & Kirksey, A. (1995). Assessing the validity of information recall: Results of a time use pilot study in peri-urban Egypt. *Human Organization, 54,* 304–308.

Romanczyk, R. G., Kent, R. N., Diament, C., & O'Leary, K. D. (1973). Measuring the reliability of observational data: A reactive process. *Journal of Applied Behavior Analysis, 6,* 175–184.

Rosen, A., & Proctor, E. K. (1981). Distinctions between treatment outcomes and their implications for treatment evaluation. *Journal of Consulting and Clinical Psychology, 49,* 418–425.

Rueter, M. A., & Conger, R. D. (1995). Antecedents of parent-adolescent disagreements. *Journal of Marriage and the Family, 57,* 435–448.

Rusby, J. C., Estes, A., & Dishion, T. (1991). *The interpersonal process code (IPC)* (Unpublished manuscript). Eugene: Oregon Social Learning Center.

Sillars, A. L. (1991). Behavioral observation. In B. Montgomery & S. Duck (Eds.), *Studying interpersonal interaction.* New York: Guilford Press.

Silva, F. (1993). *Psychometric foundations and behavioral assessment.* Newbury Park, CA: Sage.

Skindrud, K. (1973). Field evaluation of observer bias under overt and covert monitoring. In L. A. Hamerlynck, L. C. Handy, & E. J. Mash (Eds.), *Behavior change: Methodology, concepts, and practice* (pp. 97–118). Champaign, IL: Research Press.

Skinner, B. F. (1938). *The behavior of organisms.* New York: Appleton-Century-Crofts.

Steinglass, P. (1979). The home observation assessment method (HOAM): Real time observations of families in their homes. *Family Process, 18,* 337–354.

Suen, H. K., & Ary, D. (1989). *Analyzing quantitative behavioral observation data.* Hillsdale, NJ: Erlbaum.

Sulzer-Azaroff, B., & Mayer, G. R. (1991). *Behavior analysis for lasting change.* Fort Worth, TX: Holt, Rinehart and Winston.

Taplin, P. S., & Reid, J. B. (1973). Effects of instructional set and experimental influences on observer reliability. *Child Development, 44,* 547–554.

Taylor, C. B., Fried, L., & Kenardy, J. (1990). The use of a real-time computer diary for data acquisition and processing. *Behaviour Research and Therapy, 21,* 93–97.

Tryon, W. W. (1991). *Activity measurement in psychology and medicine.* New York: Plenum Press.

Tuteur, J. M., Ewigman, B. E., Peterson, L., & Hosokawa, M. C. (1995). The maternal observation matrix and the mother-child interaction scale: Brief observational screening instruments for physically abusive mothers. *Journal of Clinical Child Psychology, 24,* 55–62.

Webster-Stratton, C. (1985). Comparisons of behavior transactions between conduct-disordered children and their mothers in the clinic and at home. *Journal of Abnormal Child Psychology, 13,* 169–184.

Wehby, J. H., Symons, F. J., & Shores, R. E. (1995). A descriptive analysis of aggressive behavior in classrooms for children with emotional and behavioral disorders. *Behavioral Disorders, 20,* 87–105.

Weick, K. E. (1985). Systematic observational methods. In G. Lindzey & E. Aronson (Eds.), *The handbook of social psychology* (Vol. 1, 3rd ed., pp. 567–634). Menlo Park, CA: Addison-Wesley.

Weiss, R. L., & Margolin, G. (1986). Assessment of marital conflict and accord. In A. Ciminero, K. S. Calhoun, & H. E. Adams (Eds.), *Handbook of behavioral assessment* (2nd ed., pp. 561–600). New York: Wiley.

Weiss, R. L., & Perry, B. A. (1979). *Assessment and treatment of marital dysfunction* (Unpublished manuscript). Eugene: University of Oregon, Marital Studies Program.

West, R., French, D., Kemp, R., & Elander, J. (1993). Direct observation of driving, self reports of driver behaviour, and accident involvement. *Ergonomics, 36,* 557–567.

West Virginia University. (1986). *Institutional review board guidelines.* Morgantown: West Virginia University.

Wiggins, J. S. (1973). *Prediction and personality: Principles of personality assessment.* Reading, MA: Addison-Wesley.

Wildman, B. G., Erickson, M. T., & Kent, R. N. (1975). The effect of two training procedures on observer agreement and variability of behavior ratings. *Child Development, 46,* 520–524.

Williams, A. M. (1979). The quantity and quality of marital interaction related to marital satisfaction: A behavioral analysis. *Journal of Applied Behavior Analysis, 12,* 665–678.

Wolf, M. M. (1978). Social validity: The case for subjective measurement or how applied behavior analysis is finding its heart. *Journal of Applied Behavior Analysis, 11,* 203–214.

Yarrow, M. R., & Waxler, C. Z. (1979). Observing interaction: A confrontation with methodology. In R. B. Cairns (Ed.), *The analysis of social interaction: Methods, issues, and illustrations.* New York: Erlbaum.

Zangwill, W. M., & Kniskern, J. R. (1982). Comparison of problem families in the clinic and at home. *Behavior Therapy, 13,* 145–152.

Zarcone, J. R., Iwata, B. A., Rodgers, T. A., & Vollmer, T. R. (1993). Direct observation of quality of care in residential settings. *Behavioral Residential Treatment, 8,* 97–110.

Chapter 9

Focus Chapter

METHODOLOGICAL ISSUES IN RESEARCH USING PROJECTIVE METHODS

DREW WESTEN, PH.D., ALISON FEIT, M.A., and CAROLYN ZITTEL, M.A.

Researchers and clinicians traditionally have relied primarily on two methods of assessing individual differences in personality and psychopathology: asking people directly, and trying to make inferences from their narratives and actions. The former tradition has typically been called "objective testing," whereas the latter has been referred to as "projective." A central argument of this chapter is that "projective" need not be synonymous with "subjective"—that projective techniques can be useful in both research and clinical practice, but that their use requires the same attention to psychometrics as the construction and application of self-report instruments.

We begin by defining projective tests and describing a range of existing instruments that may be useful for assessing personality and psychopathology. Next we describe why projective tests may be important in clinical research and assessment. As we will argue, developments in cognitive neuroscience suggest that such methods are fundamental to assessment because they tap implicit processes, that is, mental processes expressed in behavior but not available to introspection or accessible to conscious awareness. We then examine the applicability of psychometric principles of reliability and validity to projective measures. We conclude by considering future directions for the use of projective techniques in clinical research.

WHAT ARE PROJECTIVE TESTS? A CONTEMPORARY VIEW

Projective testing had its origins in the psychoanalytic assumption that people express their characteristic patterns of thought, feeling, and motivation in almost everything they do. Freud turned to free association and interpretation as therapeutic techniques because of his belief that (a) thoughts, feelings, and motives are organized along networks of association that are unconscious, and (b) people are often unaware of important aspects of their personalities and the meanings of their symptoms because awareness would lead to unpleasant feelings. Freud did not clearly distinguish between unconscious networks of association that are unconscious by virtue of cognitive architecture and unconscious processes that are unconscious because their consciousness would be painful, but in either case, the implication of the psychoanalytic position is that many meaningful psychological processes cannot be readily assessed by asking people directly to describe them.

Projective techniques essentially developed as adjuncts to free association; some, such as word association tests, were in fact little more than elaborations of it. The assumption that unconscious processes play a pervasive role in mental life and behavior, and the correlative use of techniques designed to bypass introspective reports, are no longer exclusive to psychodynamic psychologists. Perhaps the most important new data supporting the use of projective methods in clinical assessment and research come not from psychoanalytic clinical observation or even studies of traditional projective tests but from cognitive neuroscience. A substantial body of evidence now suggests that most mental processes—including cognitive, affective, and motivational processes as well as behavioral skills—are implicit, that is, activated and expressed outside of awareness and typically beyond conscious volitional control (Bargh & Barndollar, 1996; Reber, 1992; Schacter, 1992; Seger, 1994; Westen, 1998a, in press). Indeed, much research in contemporary cognitive science is predicated on one of the same hypotheses that led to projective methods: that mental contents are represented along associative networks, and that these networks can only be assessed using indirect measures.

Consider research on repetition priming, in which participants are exposed to a stimulus (called the "prime") to see how it will affect later behavior. For example, in word completion tasks, experimental participants are given a word stem (e.g., *ca__* for *calf*) or word fragment (e.g., *_ill__* for *pillow*) and are instructed to complete it with the first word that comes to mind. Individuals tend to complete such phrases with words to which they have been recently exposed (or semantically related words), even if they have no explicit (conscious) memory of having been exposed to the prime (Graf, Mandler, & Haden, 1982; Tulving, Schacter, & Stark, 1982). The same findings apply whether their lack of explicit memory of the prime reflects simple forgetting, subliminal exposure to the prime (so that they were never consciously aware of it), or brain damage to the medial temporal memory system that underlies explicit memory. The underlying assumption of this research is that the strength of implicit (unconscious) associations can be assessed indirectly using dependent variables such as item content (whether participants complete word fragments with words related to the prime) or response latency (how quickly, for example, they recognize the word *robin* after having been exposed to the prime *bird*).

This assumption is identical to the assumption behind projective testing, and indeed, many of the methods are identical, such as word association tasks that are used to assess the strength of associative links in neural networks, except for one difference: Projective tests assess individual differences in associative networks (e.g., the tendency of patients with borderline personality disorder to associate people seen on the Rorschach with malevolent intent; Stuart et al., 1990), whereas cognitive research has focused instead on normative associative connections (e.g., between *bird* and *robin*). In recent years, however, cognitive researchers have begun looking at group differences using these and similar techniques, such as the emotional Stroop task, to measure automatic, implicit processes, such as attentional interference from words associated with threat or sadness in anxious and depressed patients (e.g., Mathews, Richards, & Eysenck, 1989; Mineka & Sutton, 1992). Researchers are now beginning to discover that such methods can be used to assess individual differences in associational networks (e.g., Fazio, Jackson, Dunton,

& Williams, 1995; Stacy, 1997), and we suspect that within a few years, the field will see a reemergence of the study of individual differences in implicit processes such as networks of association and affect-regulatory strategies that are activated even when the person has no awareness of the affect (Westen, Muderrisoglu, Fowler, Shedler, & Koren, 1997).

Shorn of commitments to a particular theoretical language, then, *projective techniques* can be defined as *methods for assessing individual differences in personality or psychopathology that (a) involve the interpretation of patterns of thought, feeling, or motivation expressed in narrative or verbal behavior or in response to standardized stimuli, and (b) are designed to assess implicit processes that are unavailable to conscious introspection.*

THE RANGE OF PROJECTIVE TESTS

Psychodynamically informed clinicians tend to use a range of projective tests for clinical assessment, such as the Rorschach Inkblot Test, the Thematic Apperception Test (TAT), and various forms of sentence completion tests, early memories tests, and so forth. They also frequently use less structured responses from the Wechsler Adult Intelligence Scale III (WAIS-III) as projective stimuli, such as verbalizations on the Comprehension subtest, or responses to the Picture Arrangement task when patients are asked to tell the story they had in mind when they arranged the cards, to assess thought disorder and object relations (i.e., the enduring patterns of thought, feeling, motivation, and behavior involved in close relationships).

Because patients differ in infinite ways in the structure of their associational networks (i.e., in the idiosyncratic ways they associate thoughts, feelings, motives, ways of regulating affect, and behaviors), clinicians often can and, we believe, should go beyond standardized scoring techniques in interpreting projective material, although their general interpretations should be moored in scores from psychometrically sound instruments applied to projective responses. For research purposes, researchers can use a number of existing, well-validated instruments, although they can also develop procedures for specific tasks using projective methodologies if they pay careful attention to psychometric issues (described later) that make projective tests objective tests.

Here, we briefly describe a range of existing, well-validated tests, which we use as examples throughout this chapter to discuss issues of reliability, validity, and so forth. In each case, the measure is theory-driven and assesses a particular construct or set of constructs, such as thought disorder or object relations. For research purposes, specific measures of this sort tend to be more useful than global batteries because they provide answers to specific questions.

The Thought Disorder Index (TDI; Johnston & Holzman, 1979) is a multidimensional system for classifying and measuring disordered thinking both quantitatively and qualitatively. The TDI can be applied to proverbs and other verbal productions (such as responses to items from verbal subtests of the WAIS-III), although it has been most widely used with Rorschach responses, and for good reason: The perceptual nature of the task and the ambiguity of the stimulus appear to be particularly useful for assessing thought disorder, especially for patients who may be motivated to conceal thought disorder or who may be frightened that they are "going crazy" or being treated as if they were crazy. The TDI was an outgrowth of the work of Rapaport, Gill, and Schafer (1945/1968), who developed a series of scoring classifications to identify cognitive disturbances. The TDI is comprised of 23 qualitative categories of thought disturbance (e.g., vagueness, peculiar verbalization) that are weighted along a continuum of severity.

Loevinger's Sentence Completion Test (SCT; Hy & Loevinger, 1996; Locvinger & Wessler, 1970) was designed for the purpose of assessing "ego development," a construct roughly corresponding to psychological maturity (see Hauser, 1976; Loevinger, 1979, 1993; Westenberg, Blasi, & Cohn, 1998). Participants complete sentence stems, such as "As a woman . . . ," and their responses are scored for qualities such as the complexity with which they think about themselves and others and the extent to which they seem to weigh their own and others' needs. Based on participants' responses to 36 items, the SCT yields an overall developmental score, placing them at one of eight developmental stages, which have been revised over several decades based on data from hundreds of studies. As described later, Loevinger and others have demonstrated, using developmental samples, that these stages do indeed form a developmental sequence and that they also distinguish various normal and pathological groups.

Influenced by the ego psychology of the 1950s and 1960s, which provided one of the first attempts to blend psychoanalytic theory with empirical approaches to cognitive development, Blatt and his colleagues (see Blatt, Auerbach, & Levy, 1997) have been working for several decades on a set of measures that integrate object relations theory with Piagetian and Wernerian concepts of differentiation and integration to assess the developmental level of object representations (i.e., representations of people). Although they initially began coding qualities such as accuracy, articulation (description of details of the person), and malevolence-benevolence of human responses to the Rorschach (Blatt, Brenneis, Schimek, & Glick, 1976), since that time they have been moving toward increasing use of this measurement approach with open-ended descriptions of significant others, particularly parents (Blatt, Wein, Chevron, & Quinlan, 1979).

Blatt's measure of representations of significant others assesses several dimensions, perhaps the most important of which is conceptual level of the representation, which assesses complexity, integration, and differentiation of representations as well as the extent to which the individual takes a need-gratifying versus a more mature emotional stance toward significant others. At the lowest levels, participants describe their parents (or other significant others) in relatively simple ways, in terms of the gratifications they provide. At the highest levels, the participant demonstrates an understanding of the complexities of the significant other's personality, viewing the individual as an independent actor with complex traits and a personality that changes and develops over time. Other scales measure the extent to which participants' responses indicate boundary confusion (i.e., confusing one person's attributes with another's), a benevolent or malevolent view of the person, the ambivalence of the representation, and several other aspects of the content of representations.

The Social Cognition and Object Relations Scales (SCORS; Westen, 1991, 1998b) is a system that can be applied to TAT responses, early memories, or open-ended interpersonal interviews such as the Adult Attachment Interview (Main, Kaplan, & Cassidy, 1985) that ask people to describe a series of interpersonal interactions with significant others. Like Blatt's program of research, the research of Westen and colleagues has increasingly focused on measuring implicit aspects of patients' personality functioning less from responses to the more traditional projective stimuli (Rorschach and TAT) than from open-ended interviews with more obvious ecological validity. Derived from both object relations theory and research on the development of social cognition in children, the latest version of the instrument has six scales: complexity of representations, affect-tone of relationship schemas (the extent to which the person views relationships as malevolent or enriching), emotional investment in relationships (the extent to which the person is capable of mature, intimate interdependence or views people in terms of what they can provide him or her), emotional investment in values and moral standards, understanding of social causality (the extent to which the person can provide logical and compelling narratives about why people do what they do), and dominant interpersonal concerns (themes expressed in interpersonal narratives). In addition, the interview version of the instrument now includes two more scales: self-esteem and management of aggression (which cannot be readily coded from TAT responses but *can* be coded from interviews).

To use the SCORS, researchers elicit from participants a series of narratives, vignettes, or "stories" (e.g., in response to TAT cards or to instructions to describe an important experience with a significant other), and each response is coded on each dimension. With the exception of dominant interpersonal concerns, which involve ranking each of roughly 50 themes for the extent to which they are salient in the entire protocol (using a Q-sort procedure), the other scales involve making 1–7 ratings on each response on each dimension and then taking the mean response for each scale. Like Blatt's (Blatt et al., 1979) measure, the SCORS distinguishes children at different ages (Westen et al., 1991) as well as adults and adolescents with various forms of psychopathology (Westen, Lohr, Silk, Gold, & Kerber, 1990) and has been used successfully to predict treatment response (Ford, Fisher, & Larson, 1997).

The final instrument briefly described is a new measure that, like other projective tests, assesses implicit processes participants may not be able to report. However, unlike other measures, the data are close to the data of clinical observation: standard clinical interviews or a loosely structured clinical research interview (Westen, 1996) that asks people to tell a series of vignettes about their history, symptoms, significant relationships, and stressful experiences. The instrument, called the Shedler–Westen Assessment Procedure–200 (SWAP–200), provides an MMPI-like (Minnesota Multiphasic Personality Inventory) profile of a patient's personality pathology and dynamics based on the observations of a skilled observer using a 200-item Q-sort that covers a range of healthy and pathological personality processes and attributes (Shedler & Westen, 1998; Westen & Shedler, in press-a, in press-b).

Current Axis II instruments rely on patients' direct reports of their pathology on questionnaires or interviews. Recent findings suggest, however, that experienced clinicians of all theoretical orientations diagnose personality pathology primarily by listening to the narratives they tell about significant interpersonal events rather than by asking them direct questions about socially undesirable personality traits (Westen, 1997). Thus, after spending several clinical sessions with a patient (for clinical purposes) or conducting an extensive interview (for research purposes), the clinician arranges the 200 items that constitute the SWAP–200 according to the extent to which they describe the patient, that is, in order of their diagnosticity. (On the logic of Q-sort techniques, see Block, 1978.) The SWAP–200 can yield Axis II *T*-scores (standard scores with a mean of 50 and standard deviation of 10, like the MMPI-II); scale scores based on the match between the patient's profile and criterion groups of interest (such as different types of batterers); or a narrative description of the patient based on items placed in the "most descriptive" categories of the Q-sort (ranked 5, 6, or 7 in a 0 to 7 distribution, where 1 = not descriptive at all of the patient, and 7 = defining of the patient's personality).

The aim of the SWAP–200 is to use the same psychometric procedures employed in the development of sophisticated self-report instruments such as the MMPI-2 to harness the observations and inferences of skilled clinical observers. Although the SWAP–200 is the least classically projective of the measures we have described thus far, what it shares with these techniques is the assessment of implicit processes and the assumption that people may not be able to self-report important aspects of their personality and psychopathology that they may nevertheless reveal indirectly. Figure 9.1 describes a patient diagnosed with borderline personality disorder from a recent $N = 797$ study of patients with personality disorders. *T*-scores reflect the degree of match between the patient's profile and criterion prototypes of each of the current Axis II disorders (plus a high-functioning prototype). As can be seen from the figure, the patient would be diagnosed with borderline personality disorder with histrionic features.

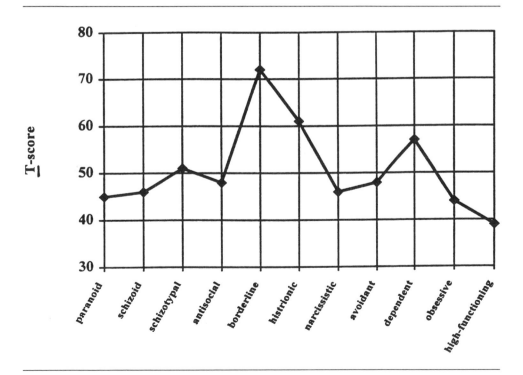

Figure 9.1.   SWAP-200 profile of a patient with borderline personality disorder.
Source: From Westen & Shedler (in press-a).

WHY USE PROJECTIVE TECHNIQUES?

Having described five projective measures, we now address the question of why we believe they should be routinely incorporated into research on personality, psychopathology, treatment outcome, and the range of phenomena studied by clinical researchers. Self-report questionnaires and structured interviews are clearly much easier and less expensive to use because they do not require extensive coding, and a rich psychometric tradition guides their development and application. So why should researchers complicate their lives with projective instruments?

Projective instruments can be useful and even essential, particularly in combination with self-reports and structured interviews, for several reasons (see Westen, 1995). First, projective methods do not depend on people to know themselves well. They presume that experts who have spent years studying a phenomenon are likely to make discriminations and notice phenomena that lay people may not recognize, even about themselves. Physicians rely on self-reports in medicine to direct their attention to relevant symptoms, but they do not rely on factor analyses of patient checklists to make diagnoses. Patients do not typically have the training to make sophisticated enough observations to distinguish, for example, benign from malignant growths; the same may be true for personality patterns and pathology.

Second, although patients can (and frequently do) protect themselves against self-disclosure by providing sparse answers to stimuli such as the Rorschach, projective methods tend to be less vulnerable than self-reports to defensive biases. Indeed, the aim of many such methods is to assess precisely these processes (Cramer, 1996; Westen et al., 1997). Defensive reporting is particularly problematic in assessing personality pathology, which is, by definition, socially undesirable.

A considerable body of research documents the pervasiveness of defensive biases when people self-report aspects of their personality or psychopathology (for a review, see Westen, in press). For example, social psychologists have long demonstrated self-serving biases in attributions, inferences, memory, and so forth. More recently, researchers studying *individual differences* in self-serving biases have found them systematically related to the personality traits of narcissism (John & Robins, 1994) and avoidance of negative affect (Dozier & Kobak, 1992; Shedler, Mayman, & Manis, 1993; Weinberger, 1990). Studies from several different research traditions converge on the finding that psychophysiological indices such as heart rate and skin conductance can detect individuals who report low negative affectivity but show evidence of defensive emotional avoidance. Of particular importance is the research of Shedler and colleagues (1993, 1994), who showed that individuals with "illusory mental health," who report minimal anxiety while spiking on psychophysiological indices, can be detected by a projective method but not by self-report lie and validity scales.

Indirect measures of this sort are not only valuable for assessing personality and psychopathology cross-sectionally but also for assessing change in psychotherapy outcome studies. Assessing the impact of psychotherapy for depression using self-report questionnaires and structured interviews that rely on self-reports is the norm in outcome research and is certainly essential for a comprehensive assessment. However, any patient who completes 12 sessions of therapy as part of a research protocol for depression and still reports feeling stupid or incompetent is probably angry at his or her therapist. Particularly given the recent and now replicated finding that the effects of most short-term treatments for depression tend to dissipate by two years (e.g., Shea et al., 1992), the use of more indirect measures might prove useful in distinguishing those patients who show not only temporary symptomatic change but change in the cognitive-affective schemas, affect regulation strategies, conflicts, and so on that different theories hypothesize create the underlying vulnerability to depression. Of relevance is research by Peterson and Ulrey (1994) finding that measures of pessimistic explanatory style assessed by self-report and by TAT both correlate with depression but do not correlate with each other (Peterson & Ulrey, 1994). This suggests, as did research reported years ago by Beck (1967) on the continued presence of depressive themes in the dreams of remitted depressed patients, that explicit and implicit processes that contribute to depression may be at least partially independent. From a cognitive neuroscience perspective, this makes sense, given the relatively slow nature of change in associative networks relative to conscious beliefs.

A third reason projective techniques may be useful is that they attempt to provide a *functional assessment* of personality, a concept shared by behavioral and psychodynamic clinicians. When we assess intelligence, we do not ask people how smart they think they are; we assess their intellectual abilities on a number of tasks and judge their abilities ourselves. When we administer a mental status examination, we do not ask patients what they believe about their capacity for abstract reasoning or how well they think they would do on a proverbs test; we ask them the meanings of some proverbs and make a functional assessment. Similarly, for personality variables relevant to psychopathology, if we want to assess how empathic, emotionally constricted, depressed, or hostile a person is, a functional approach suggests that we observe how much the person expresses these attributes in his or her *behavior.* In assessing personality pathology, this is, empirically, what practitioners actually do, *regardless of theoretical orientation:* They tend to observe the patient's behavior in the consulting room and listen to the patient's narratives about significant interpersonal events, rather than relying solely on self-reports or responses to direct questions about their personality and symptomatology (Westen, 1997).

Fourth, as we have seen, a considerable body of recent research now suggests the importance of distinguishing between implicit and explicit processes in perception, memory, thought, affect, and motivation. To the extent that implicit and explicit processes have distinct psychological and neuroanatomical properties, and that people can only imperfectly report on implicit processes (by making the same kinds of inferences about regularities in their behavior made by observers), then these two kinds of processes should be assessed using methods uniquely suited to their attributes.

Finally, a property of solid research in psychology is the use of multiple measures. For example, psychotherapy researchers (see Kendall, Flannery-Schroeder, & Ford, this volume) no longer rely on single outcome measures because each measure, no matter how well developed and how well validated, has built into it some substantial error component. Using both a questionnaire and a structured interview for assessing dimensions or diagnoses such as depression or personality disorders is clearly a substantial improvement, but this does not address the extent of shared error variance in questionnaires and structured interviews, because both rely on self-reports filtered through the same cognitive biases and activated self-schemas. Coding qualities such as depression from TAT responses, word stems, open-ended self-descriptions, or descriptions of salient interpersonal encounters with significant others may minimize the problem of method variance shared by variants of self-reports.

RELIABILITY AND VALIDITY IN PROJECTIVE ASSESSMENT

We have suggested here that *projective tests should be objective tests*—that is, that assessing implicit processes from narratives is not inherently subjective, although qualitative interpretation can certainly be useful in fleshing out the meaning of quantitative findings and pointing to directions for future research. Many of the issues of reliability and validity that apply to what are typically called objective tests (self-reports) apply to projective tests as well. Other issues, however, are unique to projective techniques, some of which may have reciprocal implications for objective tests.

Reliability

Many issues of reliability are the same for projective as for self-report measures. Loevinger's SCT provides an excellent example. Studies of the reliability of the SCT (see Hauser, 1976; Loevinger, 1979) indicate strong retest reliability, interrater reliability (generally between $r = .80$ and $r = .90$), and internal consistency (coefficient alpha in the range of .85). The SCT includes 36 sentence stems, and responses to each stem are scored for level of ego development. Together, the items are used to reach an overall ego development score, using multiple methods, including simple means and a more complicated algorithm.

As with self-report questionnaires, projective measures such as the SCT need to include a sufficient number of items to produce an internally consistent test. The "items" on most projective tests refer to the number of independent scores assessing the same construct. In research applying the SCORS to TAT responses, for example, a participant receives one score per story on each of four to six scales measuring different dimensions of social cognition and object relations. For some scales, such as complexity of representations of people, as few as four cards are required to achieve an acceptable coefficient of internal consistency; empirically, people do not vary tremendously in their level of social-cognitive complexity, although some people are more vulnerable to developmentally simplistic thinking when strong negative affect is aroused. In contrast, the more affective dimensions of the SCORS require 8 to 10 observations per subject (that is, 8 to 10 TAT cards) to converge on a reliable measure of central tendency because the affective quality of stories varies depending on the stimulus.

An important issue in evaluating projective measures is whether the same standards of reliability are appropriate as for self-reports, particularly for retest reliability (temporal stability). Relative to projective tests, estimates of retest reliability for self-reports can be inflated by the fact that the same person is responding to precisely the same stimuli (items) with precisely the same highly constrained set of response choices (e.g., a 1–7 rating scale). The situation is very different for projective measures. Consider assessment of achievement motivation by self-report and TAT. One would expect a person whose self-concept has a reasonable degree of stability over time to respond to an item such as "It is very important to me that I succeed" within one or two scale points on a 7-point scale on two different occasions separated by only a few weeks. In contrast, when the same person tells stories to 10 TAT cards twice over a two-month interval, he or she will tell different stories, and each will be coded by an imperfect rater, which further attenuates reliability. Whether this means that projective techniques are less reliable than self-reports or that estimates of reliability of self-reports are inflated by characteristics of that method is an open question.

A similar issue pertains to the issue of interrater reliability. The interrater reliability of all of the projective measures described earlier has typically been above $r = .80$ in published studies. There is no comparable statistic for self-report measures, which obviously have no interrater reliability. Recent data suggest, however, that the aggregated description of an individual by two independent informants, even informants without any particular expertise in personality assessment (e.g., friends of the target person), is better than self-reports in predicting the way the individual actually *behaves* when coded from videotapes (Kolar, Funder, & Colvin, 1996). This suggests that the true variance explained by self-reports may actually be attenuated by unreliability in comparison with observer reports that can be aggregated (as in research with projective tests using multiple raters, which is the norm).

Validity

Projective tests establish convergent and discriminant validity the same way self-report instruments do. For example, Blatt's measure of parental representations, the SCORS for TAT and narrative data, and Loevinger's SCT for ego development all claim to reflect developmental dimensions. To test this, all three have been applied to normal developmental samples and in all cases have shown age differences in children and adolescents where predicted (see, e.g., Blatt, Auerbach, & Levy, 1997; Westen et al., 1991). In addition, Loevinger's SCT has shown substantial correlations with other measures of developmental stages, such as a correlation of $r = .60$ with Kohlberg's test of moral judgment, even after partialing out age (Sullivan, McCullough, & Stager, 1970).

To continue with the example of the SCT, validity studies have shown that scores from the sentence completion measure correlate around $r = .80$ with ego development assessed from TAT stories (Sutton & Swensen, 1983) and predict external behavioral patterns such as altruism (Cox, 1974), responsibility taking (Blasi, 1976), conformity (Hoppe & Loevinger, 1977), and delinquent behavior such as fighting in adolescents. Particularly noteworthy about the SCT is the effort researchers have taken to assess its ability to predict actual *behavior,* as too many measures of personality and psychopathology have established validity primarily by predicting scores on other measures. In two decades of research on personality disorders, for example, we are unaware of any validity study of any structured interview or questionnaire that has used variables such as observed behavior in the waiting room or affective lability as assessed using beeper methods as criterion variables.

As with reliability, some distinctive aspects of validity of projective measures deserve mention. Once again, the size of validity coefficients may be suppressed relative to self-reports, particularly when other self-reports are criterion variables. A correlation of $r = .50$ between two self-report measures is likely to contain a substantial amount of method variance because, as with retest reliability, responses to both measures (or in retest reliability, on both occasions) are filtered through the same self-concept and response biases. Further, validity coefficients in questionnaire research are frequently inflated by shared item content, as when researchers correlate one depression scale with another. These problems disappear when the criterion is behavioral, such as history of suicide attempts or psychiatric hospitalizations, or when informant data are used to validate a measure. In these cases, the same standards should apply to projective and self-report measures.

An important issue with respect to validation of projective measures that has only recently been appreciated is that failure to predict self-report measures of the same construct may not be evidence against the validity of a projective measure. One example comes from TAT measures of motivation, which predict long-term behavioral outcomes such as entrepreneurial success but are completely uncorrelated with self-report measures (McClelland, Koestner, & Weinberger, 1989). Self-reported achievement motivation predicts achievement behavior when achievement motives are explicitly activated with instructions such as "It is important that you do well on this test" but not otherwise.

A similar situation can be seen in the attachment literature, where self-report and narrative-based assessments of adult attachment show only moderate convergence (Brennan, Clark, & Shaver, 1998), even though both are highly predictive of a number of other variables with which one would expect them to correlate. For example, adults' attachment status vis-à-vis their own parents assessed using the Adult Attachment Interview (a narrative measure) is strongly associated with the attachment status of their own children, even when adult attachment is assessed before the child's birth (Fonagy, Steele, & Steele, 1991). In a recent study using an adult community sample, Calabrese (1998) found no correlation between attachment assessed by self-report and dimensions of object relations assessed from interpersonal narratives using the SCORS. Narrative assessment using the SCORS, but not attachment assessed by questionnaire, predicted whether participants were in a long-term love relationship as well as whether their own parents' marriage was still intact. Different findings emerged in a study using Blatt's measure of parental representations, which found expected correlations between attachment assessed by self-report and descriptions of parents assessed from open-ended descriptions (Levy, Blatt, & Shaver, 1998). This suggests that asking people directly to provide a description of their parents may be closer to self-report methods than to narrative methods asking them to describe interpersonal vignettes, because the latter are designed to bypass conscious, explicit, semantic (generic) representations. Further research is needed to determine when self-report and projective measures should be expected to converge and diverge.

What has become clear, however, is that the same distinction between implicit and explicit processes seen in research on memory and cognition is equally true of affect and motivation (Westen, in press). Thus, we would do well to assess both the person's explicit beliefs, feelings, and goals, as well as the implicit beliefs, feelings, and goals that direct behavior when people's limited conscious attentional resources are focused elsewhere. Individual differences in the *discrepancies* between self-reported and projective indices of various dispositions (such as anxiety or depression) are an important area for future research (see Shedler et al., 1993).

Projective Stimuli Are neither Valid nor Invalid

A crucial point to note about the validity of projective measures is that validity is always relative to the purpose for which a measure is constructed. If the Hypochondriasis scale of the MMPI-2 does not distinguish bipolar from unipolar depressives, this does not bear on the validity of the instrument; distinguishing these two types of mood disorder is not the aim of the scale, and there is no theoretical reason to believe that it would. Similarly, the common claim that "the Rorschach has no validity" reflects a misunderstanding of the difference between a stimulus and a measure.

The Rorschach is neither valid nor invalid, any more than questionnaires as a source of data are either valid or invalid. Specific scales show varying degrees of validity. For example, the TDI, which is used to assess thought disorder, is highly reliable and valid when applied to Rorschach and WAIS-III responses. Numerous studies have utilized the TDI to discriminate very subtle aspects of thought disturbance that distinguish manic, schizoaffective, and schizophrenic patients (Shenton, Solovay, & Holzman, 1987; Solovay, Shenton, & Holzman, 1987). The TDI can also distinguish children at risk for schizophrenia and bipolar disorder from normal comparison subjects (Arboleda & Holzman, 1985) and can detect subtle peculiarities of thought in first-degree relatives of patients with schizophrenia (Coleman, Levy, Lenzenweger, & Holzman, 1996).

A major question in the use of projective techniques is the extent to which researchers should employ theory-driven measures such as those described above or more strictly empirical measures such as Exner's (1991) system for scoring Rorschach responses. Exner's system assesses characteristics such as the subject's use of color and shading, dimensions on which individuals clearly differ but whose presumed meaning has largely been derived empirically through dozens of studies.

The jury is still out on the broader uses of the Rorschach as an all-purpose stimulus to which Exner's (1991, 1993) Comprehensive System for Rorschach administration, scoring, and interpretation can be applied. Wood, Nezworski, and Stejskal (1996a, 1996b, 1997) have leveled some substantial criticisms at Exner's system, arguing that interrater reliability has been calculated inappropriately in many studies and that the validity of widely used scores and indices (such as the egocentricity index, depression index, and suicide constellation) have been inadequately supported. On the other hand, Meyer (1997a, 1997b), among others, has offered compelling responses to many of these critiques, and meta-analyses have been largely supportive of the utility of Exner's system for many diagnostic purposes (Parker, Hanson, & Hunsley, 1988; Shontz & Green, 1992).

In the hands of competent researchers, interrater reliability is not a problem with Exner's system, and several dimensions included in the Comprehensive System are indeed predictive of subtle aspects of personality and psychopathology. For example, Hilsenroth, Fowler, Padawer, and Handler (1997) found reliably coded reflection, pair, personalization, and idealization scores, as well as the egocentricity index, to differentiate patients with narcissistic personality disorder not only from a nonclinical sample but from patients with other personality disorders, including other Axis II Cluster B (erratic cluster) disorders, which structured interviews for personality disorders have had difficulty doing as cleanly. The number of reflection and idealization responses also positively correlated with the number of *Diagnostic and Statistical Manual of Mental Disorders,* 4th edition *(DSM-IV)* narcissistic criteria, providing a strong test of the ability of variables reliably coded from responses to inkblots to predict personality traits—certainly not an obvious or intuitive prediction, and hence a rigorous test.

These findings demonstrate that at least some of the variables assessed by Exner's system, when theoretically selected for their relevance to a given hypothesis, can be useful in prediction. On the other hand, Wood and colleagues (1996a, 1996b, 1997) have, at the very least, called attention to the importance of maintaining higher psychometric standards in Rorschach research than has often been the case.

CONCLUSION

We are at a paradoxical place in clinical psychology. Projective techniques, along with psychodynamic approaches to treatment and psychopathology more generally, are gradually disappearing from the curriculum in clinical psychology programs just as research in cognitive neuroscience and a range of other subfields in psychology has come to document the importance of implicit processes that guide thought, feeling, and behavior. It would be unfortunate if empirically-minded researchers were to dismiss projective methods as unreliable and invalid without reading the empirical literature and considering the implications of developments in cognitive neuroscience for the scientific assessment of personality and psychopathology. The available data suggest that (a) projective data can be coded reliably; (b) carefully designed scales using projective techniques can predict subtle and important criterion variables; and (c) many of the processes underlying human behavior are unconscious or implicit and can be assessed indirectly through methods that tap associational processes.

We conclude with two suggestions for future research using projective techniques. First, appropriate use and development of projective methods requires a thorough understanding of psychometrics and test construction, because many of the same principles apply to projective as to objective tests. Indeed, the utility of a projective measure lies in its ability to harness the inferential skills of a trained observer in psychometrically rigorous ways.

Second, the stimuli used for projective assessment should, like all methods employed in research, be selected to match the hypothesis being tested. Stimuli and procedures should not be selected based on tradition. Inkblots, ambiguous interpersonal drawings, sentence stems, and the like may be perfectly appropriate for particular purposes, but they are not for all purposes. In clinical research, we would do well not to default to any method of data collection—whether asking people to answer questions about themselves, make up stories, or respond to inkblots—but should instead think carefully about what we are trying to measure, the optimal ways to measure it, and the limits to the methods we are considering employing.

REFERENCES

Arboleda, C., & Holzman, P. S. (1985). Thought disorder in children at risk for psychosis. *Archives of General Psychiatry, 42,* 1004–1013.

Bargh, J., & Barndollar, K. (1996). Automaticity in action: The unconscious as repository of chronic goals and motives. In P. M. Gollwitzer & J. Bargh (Eds.), *The psychology of action: Linking cognition and motivation to behavior* (pp. 457–481). New York: Guilford Press.

Beck, A. T. (1967). *Cognitive therapy and the emotional disorders.* New York: International Universities Press.

Blasi, A. (1976). Personal responsibility and ego development. In R. deCharms (Ed.), *Enhancing Motivation: Change in the Classroom* (pp. 177–199). New York: Irvington.

Blatt, S., Auerbach, J., & Levy, K. (1997). Mental representations in personality development, psychopathology, and the therapeutic process. *Review of General Psychology, 1,* 351–374.

Blatt, S., Brenneis, C. B., Schimek, J. G., & Glick, M. (1976). Normal development and psychopathological impairment of the concept of the object on the Rorschach. *Journal of Abnormal Psychology, 85,* 364–373.

Blatt, S., Wein, S., Chevron, E., & Quinlan, D. (1979). Parental representations and depression in normal young adults. *Journal of Abnormal Psychology, 78,* 388–397.

Block, J. (1978). *The Q-sort method in personality assessment and psychiatric research.* Palo Alto, CA: Consulting Psychologists Press.

Brennan, K. A., Clark, C. L., & Shaver, P. (1998). Self-report measurement of adult romantic attachment: An integrative overview. In J. A. Simpson & W. S. Rholes (Eds.), *Attachment theory and close relationships* (pp. 46–76). New York: Guilford Press.

Calabrese, M. (1998). *Object representations as they relate to adult attachment, intimacy and self-esteem.* Unpublished doctoral dissertation, Columbia University.

Coleman, M. J., Levy, D. L., Lenzenweger, M. F., & Holzman, P. S. (1996). Thought disorder, perceptual aberrations, and schizotypy. *Journal of Abnormal Psychology, 105,* 469–473.

Cox, N. (1974). Prior help, ego development, and helping behavior. *Child Development, 45,* 594–603.

Cramer, P. (1996). *Story-telling, narrative, and the Thematic Apperception Test.* New York: Guilford Press.

Dozier, M., & Kobak, R. (1992). Psychophysiology in attachment interviews: Converging evidence for deactivating strategies. *Child Development, 63,* 1473–1480.

Exner, J. (1991). *The Rorschach: A comprehensive system: Vol. 2. Current research and advanced interpretation.* New York: Wiley.

Exner, J. (1993). *The Rorschach: A comprehensive system: Vol. 1. Basic foundations* (3rd ed.). New York: Wiley.

Fazio, R., Jackson, J. R., Dunton, B., & Williams, C. J. (1995). Variability in automatic activation as an unobtrusive measure of racial attitudes: A bona fide pipeline? *Journal of Personality and Social Psychology, 69,* 1013–1027.

Fonagy, P., Steele, H., & Steele, M. (1991). Maternal representations of attachment during pregnancy predict the organization of infant-mother attachment at one year of age. *Child Development, 62,* 891–905.

Ford, J. D., Fisher, P., & Larson, L. (1997). Object relations as a predictor of treatment outcome with chronic posttraumatic stress disorder. *Journal of Consulting and Clinical Psychology, 65,* 547–559.

Graf, P., Mandler, G., & Haden, P. (1982). Simulating amnesic symptoms in normal subjects. *Science, 218,* 1243–1244.

Hauser, S. T. (1976). Loevinger's model and measure of ego development: A critical review. *Psychological Bulletin, 83,* 928–955.

Hilsenroth, M., Fowler, C., Padawer, J., & Handler, L. (1997). Narcissism in the Rorschach revisited: Some reflections on empirical data. *Psychological Assessment, 9,* 113–121.

Hoppe, C. F., & Loevinger, J. (1977). Ego development and conformity: A construct validity study of the Washington University Sentence Completion Test. *Journal of Personality Assessment, 41,* 497–504.

Hy, L. X., & Loevinger, J. (1996). *Measuring ego development* (Rev. ed.). Mahwah, NJ: Erlbaum.

John, O., & Robins, R. W. (1994). Accuracy and bias in self-perception: Individual differences in self-enhancement and the role narcissism. *Journal of Personality and Social Psychology, 66,* 206–219.

Johnston, M. H., & Holzman, P. S. (1979). *Assessing schizophrenic thinking.* San Francisco: Jossey-Bass.

Kolar, D. W., Funder, D. C., & Colvin, C. (1996). Comparing the accuracy of personality judgments by the self and knowledgeable others. *Journal of Personality, 64,* 311–337.

Levy, K. N., Blatt, S. J., & Shaver, P. (1998). Attachment styles and parental representations. *Journal of Personality and Social Psychology, 74,* 407–419.

Loevinger, J. (1979). Construct validity for the Sentence Completion Test for ego development. *Applied Psychological Measurement, 3,* 281–311.

Loevinger, J. (1993). Measurement of personality: True or false? *Psychological Inquiry, 4,* 1–16.

Loevinger, J., & Wessler, R. (1970). *Measuring ego development: Construction and use of a Sentence Completion Test* (Vol. 1). San Francisco: Jossey-Bass.

Main, M., Kaplan, N., & Cassidy, J. (1985). Security in infancy, childhood, and adulthood: A move to the level of representation. In I. Bretherton & E. Waters (Eds.), Growing points of attachment theory and research. *Monographs of the Society for Research in Child Development, 50*(No. 1/2), 67–104.

Mathews, A., Richards, A., & Eysenck, M. (1989). Interpretation of homophones related to treatment in anxiety states. *Journal of Abnormal Psychology, 98,* 31–34.

McClelland, D. C., Koestner, R., & Weinberger, J. (1989). How do self-attributed and implicit motives differ? *Psychological Review, 96,* 690–702.

Meyer, G. J. (1997a). Assessing reliability: Critical corrections for a critical examination of the Rorschach Comprehensive System. *Psychological Assessment, 9,* 480–489.

Meyer, G. J. (1997b). Thinking clearly about reliability: More critical corrections regarding the Rorschach Comprehensive System. *Psychological Assessment, 9,* 495–498.

Mineka, S., & Sutton, S. K. (1992). Cognitive biases and the emotional disorders. *Psychological Science, 3,* 65–69.

Parker, K. C. H., Hanson, R. K., & Hunsley, J. (1988). MMPI, Rorschach, and WAIS: A meta-analytic comparison of reliability, stability, and validity. *Psychological Bulletin, 103,* 367–373.

Peterson, C., & Ulrey, L. (1994). Can explanatory style be scored from TAT protocols? *Personality and Social Psychology Bulletin, 20,* 102–106.

Rapaport, D., Gill, M. M., & Schafer, R. (1968). The Rorschach test. In R. Holt (Ed.), *Diagnostic psychological testing* (pp. 268–463). New York: International Universities Press. (Original work published 1945)

Reber, A. (1992). The cognitive unconscious: An evolutionary perspective. *Consciousness and Cognition, 1,* 93–133.

Schacter, D. L. (1992). Understanding implicit memory: A cognitive neuroscience approach. *American Psychologist, 47,* 559–569.

Seger, C. A. (1994). Implicit learning. *Psychological Bulletin, 115,* 163–196.

Shea, M. T., Elkin, I., Imber, S., Sotsky, S., et al. (1992). Course of depressive symptoms over follow-up: Findings from the National Institute of Mental Health Treatment of Depression Collaborative Research Program. *American Journal of Psychiatry, 49,* 782–787.

Shedler, J., Mayman, M., & Manis, M. (1993). The illusion of mental health. *American Psychologist, 48,* 1117–1131.

Shedler, J., Mayman, M., & Manis, M. (1994). More illusions. *American Psychologist, 49,* 974–976.

Shedler, J., & Westen, D. (1998). Refining the measurement of Axis II: A Q-sort procedure for assessing personality pathology. *Assessment, 5,* 335–355.

Shenton, M. E., Solovay, M. R., & Holzman, P. S. (1987). Comparative studies of thought disorders: II. Schizoaffective disorder. *Archives of General Psychiatry, 44,* 21–30.

Shontz, F. C., & Green, P. (1992). Trends in research on the Rorschach: Review and recommendations. *Applied and Preventative Psychology, 1,* 146–149.

Solovay, M. R., Shenton, M. E., & Holzman, P. S. (1987). Comparative studies of thought disorders: I. Mania and schizophrenia. *Archives of General Psychiatry, 44,* 13–20.

Stacy, A. W. (1997). Memory activation and expectancy as prospective predictors of alcohol and marijuana use. *Journal of Abnormal Psychology, 106,* 61–73.

Stuart, J., Westen, D., Lohr, N. E., Silk, K. R., Becker, S., Vorus, N., & Benjamin, J. (1990). Object relations in borderlines, depressives, and normals: Analysis of human responses on the Rorschach. *Journal of Personality Assessment, 55,* 296–314.

Sullivan, E. V., McCullough, G., & Stager, M. (1970). A developmental study of the relationship between conceptual, ego, and moral development. *Child Development, 41,* 399–411.

Sutton, P. M., & Swensen, C. H. (1983). The reliability and concurrent validity of alternative methods for assessing ego development. *Journal of Personality Assessment, 47,* 468–475.

Tulving, E., Schacter, D. L., & Stark, H. A. (1982). Priming effects in word-fragment completion are independent of recognition memory. *Journal of Experimental Psychology: Learning, Memory, and Cognition, 8,* 336–342.

Weinberger, D. (1990). The construct validity of the repressive coping style. In J. Singer (Ed.), *Repression and dissociation: Defense mechanisms and personality styles: Current theory and research.* Chicago: University of Chicago Press.

Westen, D. (1991). Social cognition and object relations. *Psychological Bulletin, 109,* 429–455.

Westen, D. (1995). A clinical-empirical model of personality: Life after the Mischelian ice age and the NEO-lithic era. *Journal of Personality, 63,* 495–524.

Westen, D. (1996). *Personality diagnostic interview.* Unpublished manual, Harvard Medical School.

Westen, D. (1997). Divergences between clinical and research methods for assessing personality disorders: Implications for research and the evolution of Axis II. *American Journal of Psychiatry, 154,* 895–903.

Westen, D. (1998a). Implicit cognition, affect, and motivation: The end of a century-long debate. In R. Bornstein & J. Masling (Eds.), *Empirical studies of unconscious processes.* Washington, DC: American Psychological Association Press.

Westen, D. (1998b). *Social Cognition and Object Relations Scales (SCORS) for narrative data and projective stories.* Unpublished manual, Harvard Medical School.

Westen, D. (in press). The scientific legacy of Sigmund Freud: Toward a psychodynamically informed psychological science. *Psychological Bulletin.*

Westen, D., Klepser, J., Ruffins, S., Silverman, M., Lifton, N., & Boekamp, J. (1991). Object relations in childhood and adolescence: The development of working representations. *Journal of Consulting and Clinical Psychology, 59,* 400–409.

Westen, D., Lohr, N., Silk, K., Gold, L., & Kerber, K. (1990). Object relations and social cognition in borderlines, major depressives, and normals: A TAT analysis. *Psychological Assessment: A Journal of Consulting and Clinical Psychology, 2,* 355–364.

Westen, D., Muderrisoglu, S., Fowler, C., Shedler, J., & Koren, D. (1997). Affect regulation and affective experience: Individual differences, group differences, and measurement using a Q-sort procedure. *Journal of Consulting and Clinical Psychology, 65,* 429–439.

Westen, D., & Shedler, J. (in press-a). Revising and assessing Axis II: I. Developing a clinically and empirically valid method. *American Journal of Psychiatry.*

Westen, D., & Shedler, J. (in press-b). Revising and assessing Axis II: II. Toward an empirically and clinically sensible taxonomy of personality disorders. *American Journal of Psychiatry.*

Westenberg, P. M., Blasi, A., & Cohn L. D. (1998). *Personality development: Theoretical, empirical, and clinical investigations of Loevinger's conception of ego development* (pp. 297–313). Mahwah, NJ: Erlbaum.

Wood, J. M., Nezworski, M. T., & Stejskal, W. J. (1996a). The Comprehensive System for the Rorschach: A critical examination. *Psychological Science, 7,* 3–10.

Wood, J. M., Nezworski, M. T., & Stejskal, W. J. (1996b). Thinking critically about the Comprehensive System for the Rorschach: A reply to Exner. *Psychological Science, 7,* 14–17.

Wood, J. M., Nezworski, M. T., & Stejskal, W. J. (1997). The reliability of the Comprehensive System for the Rorschach: A comment on Meyer (1997). *Psychological Assessment, 9,* 490–494.

Chapter 10

Focus Chapter

METHODOLOGICAL ISSUES IN RESEARCH ON NEUROPSYCHOLOGICAL AND INTELLECTUAL ASSESSMENT

GEORGE P. PRIGATANO, PH.D., and JOHN DELUCA, PH.D.

Neuropsychological assessment, which often includes the assessment of intellectual function, has grown tremendously over the past 25 years (Lezak, 1995). It is now recognized as an established and useful service by the neurological community (Subcommittee of American Academy of Neurology, 1996). Clinical psychologists can meaningfully contribute to neuropsychological research and assessment by attending to both specific and general methodological issues when assessing (or studying) individuals with known or suspected brain disorders. This chapter highlights some of the relevant issues using research and clinical examples. For more extensive discussion of the topic, the reader is referred to Parsons and Prigatano (1978); Peyser, Rao, LaRocca, and Kaplan (1990); and Prigatano, Parsons, and Bortz (1995).

GENERAL METHODOLOGICAL ISSUES

Four general methodological issues deserve consideration when examining experimental and clinical studies related to neuropsychological and intellectual assessment. First, a research strategy that considers all of the variables that permit controlled observation and the replication of findings must be developed (see Table 10.1): clear definition of the problem to be investigated, procedures, sampling technique, sample size, and appropriate control groups.

Second, the use of new technology, when appropriate, can expand our knowledge base. New technology that clinical psychologists and neuropsychologists can use to investigate assessment has exploded in the neurosciences. Patients can be studied with computed tomography (CT), magnetic resonance (MR) imaging, functional MR imaging, positron emission tomography, and a host of other procedures, including genetic testing. The use of these new technologies in conjunction with psychological studies raises the third issue: The investigator should determine if the research question can be answered given the research strategy and the technology employed. In some instances, the answer is yes; in others, it may be no. For any given investigation,

Table 10.1.   Factors and questions to consider in clinical neuropsychological research

Common Generic Areas of Study

Prevalence of a neuropsychological disturbance in a given patient group

Nature and severity of the disturbance(s)

Natural history of the disturbance(s) (the need for controlled, prospective studies)

Clinicopathologic correlates of the disturbance(s)

Impact of the disturbance(s) on daily life (i.e., is the effect both statistically reliable and clinically relevant?)

Development of time-efficient assessment procedures

Impact of interventions on the disturbance(s)

Common Methodological Questions

Are hypotheses and methods of testing hypotheses clearly stated?

Are diagnostic criteria explicit?

Are sampling problems addressed?

Does the sample size adequately represent the population under investigation?

Are there selection biases? If so, how are they controlled statistically or experimentally?

Is comorbidity of problems in a given sample considered (i.e., history of traumatic brain injury and history of alcohol abuse in the same participant group)?

Is the rationale for specific control groups clear?

How are various moderator variables, inherent in research with human participants, controlled in the research investigation (e.g., age, education, gender, handedness, socioeconomic status, cultural influences, language disturbances, and motivation to perform)?

Common Statistical Questions

Are statistical procedures applied appropriately?

Are multivariate statistics used when multiple outcomes are measured?

Are appropriate correction factors used to reject the null hypothesis when multiple statistical tests are calculated?

What is the justification for using a given scale (i.e., ratio vs. interval, ordinal or categorical data); are the appropriate statistical analyses used with these different types of data?

Are results interpreted parsimoniously?

Are the implications and limitations of the findings explained?

How do the findings relate to the existing literature?

Source: This list describes issues that researchers should consider to improve the quality of their clinical neuropsychological research (adapted and modified from Parsons & Prigatano, 1978; Peyser, Rao, LaRocca, & Kaplan, 1990).

experienced clinical researchers can clarify whether the strategy and technology employed will actually answer the research question.

Fourth, the investigator must consider whether the question asked by a given research study is not only interesting but worthwhile. This question may be the most difficult dimension in which to train clinical researchers. Numerous questions can be asked. Limited resources, however, demand that target questions not only be answerable but that the answers provide useful information related to the delivery of services and the development of a scientific database.

METHODOLOGICAL ISSUES REFLECTED BY SPECIFIC RESEARCH QUESTIONS

The four general issues discussed above are now considered from the perspective of specific research issues that raise specific methodological problems.

What Controls Are Needed to Determine if Confabulation after Brain Injury Is a "General" Effect of Disorientation or Related to Specific Brain Pathology?

During their clinical neuropsychological examination, some acute brain dysfunctional patients may confabulate. Confabulation can be defined as statements in a patient's discourse that distort actual events, represent fabricated events, or represent real events displaced in temporal context. Patients do not intend to deceive, but the content of their discourse is incorrect. Does confabulation result from an acute confusional state, or is it part of a more specific brain disorder that persists beyond the acute stage? Does confabulation occur during diffuse cerebral dysfunction, or is there a specific underlying deficit (i.e., frontal lobe involvement)?

To answer these questions, DeLuca and Cicerone (1991) studied two patient groups. The first group consisted of patients with an aneurysm of the anterior communicating artery (ACoA), a group known to exhibit some behavior specifically related to pathology of the mesial basal frontal lobe. The second group consisted of patients who suffered a cerebral hemorrhage but who had no specific damage to the same regions as the ACoA group (e.g., posterior, diffuse, or dorsolateral frontal pathology). To determine whether the confusional state was related to acuteness of brain injury, the researchers studied confabulation in two naturally occurring conditions: when subjects were disoriented to person, place, and time and when their orientation had returned to normal. Confabulation occurred more often in the ACoA group (100% vs. 41%) during the disoriented phase than in the other group. When orientation recovered, confabulation was almost exclusively restricted to the ACoA subjects (100% vs. 6%).

This study illustrates the importance of two control conditions, one related to lesion location and the other to time since lesion onset. The research design permitted the identification of confabulation as specifically related to frontal lobe pathology. This finding helps clinicians to recognize that such patients may not intend to deceive but represent information in a way that reflects their cognitive confusion. Such information can be important in planning their rehabilitation.

Does Performance on the Wechsler Adult Intelligence Scale Relate to Specific Structural Changes in the Brain after Traumatic Brain Injury?

Wilson et al. (1988) used MR imaging and CT to study 25 patients with a history of closed head injury 5 and 18 months after their injury. They found that performance on this neuropsychological test showed little relationship to early findings on CT or MR imaging. One to 1.5 years after injury, however, test performance was strongly correlated with the findings on MR imaging. Ventricular enlargement, a finding consistent with cerebral atrophy, related to test performance. The performance subtests of the

Wechsler Adult Intelligence Scale (WAIS) strongly correlated with ventricular enlargement. Poor performance on the block design and digit symbol tests was especially related to this anatomical finding.

Johnson, Bigler, Burr, and Blatter (1994) replicated and extended these findings. Based on MR imaging, they constructed a ventricle-to-brain ratio score. This score significantly correlated with performance IQ. Males ($r = -.48$, $p = .006$), but not females ($r = -.27$, $p = .19$), exhibited a strong negative correlation between their digit symbol scores and the ventricle-to-brain ratio. This study is important for neuropsychological assessment and the measurement of intelligence because it suggests that performance IQ can be sensitive to structural changes in the brain. Gender, however, is an important moderator variable. This raises important questions about how gender differences affect not only performance on IQ tests but differential responses to brain injury. Other studies, for example, suggest that females may recover from a brain injury better than males (Kertesz, 1993; Prigatano, Wong, Williams, & Plenge, 1997).

Together, these two studies illustrate some of the main methodological concerns listed earlier. Each study was conducted in a manner that could easily be replicated. Both studies used new technology to expand the existing knowledge database. The questions asked were clearly answerable by the methodology, and the answers were worth knowing (e.g., the degree of estimated cerebral atrophy is strongly related to speed of performance measures, but there may be gender differences).

Does Performance on Tests Such as the Wechsler Adult Intelligence Scale Provide the Same Information as Other Neuropsychological Tests?

An important question for practicing clinicians involved in assessment is whether different psychological tests provide different information about individuals with known or suspected brain damage. Hebb (1939, 1941) was one of the first psychologists to note that patients could have extensive damage to the frontal lobes and still perform normally on standard IQ measures. Halstead (1947) developed a battery of neuropsychological tests purportedly sensitive to functions not measured by standard IQ measures. His earlier work suggested that patients with significant frontal pathology would perform poorly on the Halstead Neuropsychological Test Battery but not necessarily on the Wechsler Bellview Scale. The question therefore becomes what these different tests measure in common and what they measure differently.

Although it is beyond the present scope to discuss this question in detail, Reitan (1956) studied the relationship between "psychometric" and "biological" intelligence, establishing the prototype for research conducted in this area since then. Reitan examined 50 patients with documented brain dysfunction and 50 individuals without brain dysfunction. Subjects were matched in pairs on the basis of race, gender, age, and years of formal education, important variables to control when measuring the effects of brain damage on neuropsychological or intelligence tests (Table 10.1). Reitan found that verbal and performance IQ measures correlated with the Halstead Impairment Index score (the overall score indicating impairment on the Halstead Neuropsychological Test Battery). The correlations ranged between .50 and .60, accounting for 25% to 36% of the shared variance. These results indicated that, to some degree, the tests measured different cognitive constructs. Interestingly, certain subtests of the battery, which relate to severity of brain injury (e.g., the Halstead Finger Tapping Test), did not strongly correlate with the IQ measures. Such data provide important insights about how different neuropsychological measures can reflect different phenomena.

For example, a series of studies have shown that speed of finger tapping may be related to recovery following stroke (Prigatano & Wong, 1997) and impaired self-awareness after traumatic brain injury across cultures (e.g., Prigatano & Altman, 1990; Prigatano, Ogano, & Amakusa, 1997). It has been observed that patients who have dorsal lateral frontal lobe injuries may be especially slow in terms of speed of finger tapping. A proportion of these individuals consistently overestimate their behavioral competencies following brain injury. Patients with orbital frontal injuries may not show this pattern (Prigatano, in press). Thus, by exploring the pattern of neuropsychological functions, one is able to determine what specific neurobehavioral problem may be related to specific neuropsychological and intellectual test performance.

How Can Modifications in the Administration of Neuropsychological Tests Lead to a Better Understanding of Underlying Cognitive Deficits after Brain Damage?

Standardized tests offer significant clinical benefits such as reliable test administration and appropriate norms matched to appropriate procedures. However, using neuropsychological instruments rigidly can constrain our understanding of the precise cognitive factors underlying the test scores obtained. Diamond, DeLuca, and Kelley (1997) illustrated how slight modifications to existing tests can yield important, clinically relevant information.

Diamond et al. (1997) were interested in understanding the precise mechanism responsible for amnesia in patients with an aneurysm of the ACoA. It is well established that ACoA amnesiacs display significant impairment of visual memory on the Rey Complex Figure, a standardized test of visual memory (DeLuca & Diamond, 1995). However, the standardized administration of the test (i.e., first copying the figure, then obtaining both an immediate and delayed recall of the figure) precluded obtaining answers to certain clinically relevant questions. Namely, are amnesiacs impaired on this memory task because encoding related to executive functions is impaired? (Executive dysfunction is a common finding in ACoA patients because of their frontal lobe damage.) Or is performance a result of compromised factors related to memory (i.e., retrieval failure or accelerated rate of forgetting)? If the deficient encoding hypothesis was correct, then ACoA amnesiacs should show normal retrieval and forgetting if initial learning could be improved. In contrast, if memory factors were the primary reason for poor performance on the test, improving initial learning should not affect performance.

Consequently, the researchers altered the standard administration slightly to perform an experiment to address this question. First, amnesic and nonamnesic ACoA subjects (all with documented frontal lobe pathology) were administered the standard copy and immediate recall trials of the Rey Complex Figure. Next, a procedure was developed to help the patients organize the complex figural design (in essence, to serve as the patients' "frontal lobes"). This organizational procedure was repeatedly presented to amnesiacs until their immediate recall was within (or close to) the performance level of the nonamnesic ACoA control subjects. Their recall was retested 30 minutes after the learning session. The amnesic patients then recalled the information as well as the nonamnesic ACoA control subjects. Impaired performance on the visual memory test thus appears to be related to encoding of information rather than to memory-specific factors of recall and forgetting.

This study illustrates an important point in neuropsychological assessment: Often, standardized tests tell us *what* is happening (e.g., there is memory impairment), but few have the sensitivity to tell us *why*. Thoughtful and controlled modifications to standardized administration of neuropsychological tests can be powerful research tools for answering important, clinical neuropsychology questions, as the Diamond et al. (1997) study demonstrates.

PERFORMING POORLY ON STANDARD IQ TESTS FOR DIFFERENT REASONS

There is growing recognition that the human brain is susceptible to various forms of disease and injury throughout life (Spreen, Risser, & Edgell, 1995). Disturbed psychological functioning is highly dependent on factors such as age at time of injury (Levin et al., 1994), the nature of the pathological process (Anderson, Damasio, & Tranel, 1990), and the location and size of the brain insult (Heilman & Valenstein, 1993). An individual's stage of psychosocial development and premorbid functioning also seem to influence the behavior expressed after brain injury (Birch, 1964).

Consequently, patients may perform poorly on standard measures of intelligence for different reasons. For example, one brain-injured patient may have impaired visuospatial and perceptual problem-solving difficulties related to a right parietal injury. As a result of the visuospatial disturbance, the patient may perform extremely poorly on measures such as the Block Design subtest. Another brain dysfunctional patient, however, may have difficulties with executive functions. The abilities to plan, problem solve, and benefit from one's errors may no longer function normally. This impairment would also result in poor performance on the Block Design subtest. Indeed, Luria (1966) also noted that patients can perform poorly on the Block Design subtest for different reasons. His observation helped stimulate the work of Edith Kaplan, who has attempted to develop the Wechsler scales as a neuropsychological instrument (Kaplan, Fein, Morris, & Delis, 1991).

THOUGHTS ON CONCEPTUALIZING HUMAN INTELLIGENCE

IQ measures sample a small set of functions related to real-world intelligence. Sternberg (1990) and Gardner (1983) have both eloquently described the limitations of standardized IQ tests. IQ tests, such as the WAIS-R and the WAIS-III, measure only a few broad areas of functioning. They typically focus on verbal and nonverbal problem-solving skills. Important intellectual abilities reflected in artistic, musical, mathematical and scientific, and practical social and emotional skills are not sampled by these IQ measures. Therefore, highly gifted people can be misclassified if tested only by standard IQ measures.

Standard IQ tests have remained an important part of neuropsychological assessment probably because they are loaded heavily on what Spearman (1904) identified as a general or "g factor" in intelligence. That is, IQ measures seem to reflect an underlying central factor that integrates various components of intelligent behavior.

Many alternative and often contradictory models of intellectual functioning have been proposed. While Spearman (1904) suggested the g factor, Guilford (1967) identified more than 100 subcomponents of intelligence. Recently, Neisser et al. (1996) also proposed that there are many forms of intelligence. Neuropsychologists still struggle with this issue, and there is no consensus as to what is the actual nature of intellectual functioning.

Reductionistic approaches to intelligence have tried to provide a conceptual model to explain individual differences in intelligence by identifying subcomponents of intelligence (Deary & Stought, 1996). This approach has shown that speed of information processing is one of the cognitive constructs that consistently contributes most to explaining the variances associated with IQ performance. Speed of information processing can correlate as high as .40 and .50 with intelligence tests (Dreary & Stought, 1996). In general, therefore, people with high scores on intelligence tests tend to apprehend, scan, retrieve, and respond to stimuli more quickly than those who score lower (Neisser et al., 1996, p. 83). Brain damage can adversely affect speed of information processing but not necessarily affect overall intelligence. Resolving this difficult issue will require an ongoing dialogue between theorists of intelligence and those involved in the clinical assessment of individuals with brain disorder.

CLINICAL NEUROPSYCHOLOGICAL QUESTIONS INVOLVING IQ MEASURES

In the course of clinical practice, questions that highlight important methodological issues involved in analyzing performances on neuropsychological tests and how they relate to measures on standard IQ tests naturally emerge. Four cases are discussed to highlight these issues.

Case 1

An 80-year-old attorney nationally and internationally recognized for his legal expertise had a verbal IQ score of 130 and a performance IQ score of 109, yielding a full-scale IQ of 124 based on present norms. His performance on various memory tests varied, ranging from the 5th to the 82nd percentile. When given the Rey Auditory Verbal Learning Test, he could not recall more than 10 words by the fifth trial. After a brief distraction, he could recall 6 words; 20 minutes later, he could recall 5 of 15 words. His scores on the memory tests are clearly impaired and appear to be a measure of function not sampled by the standard IQ measures.

Case 2

A 36-year-old woman who had eight years of education was never able to obtain gainful employment. Her background was culturally deprived and she was on public assistance. She was referred for testing to determine if she exhibited objective evidence of a progressive brain disorder that would progress to dementia. Her standard IQ scores revealed a verbal IQ score of 73 and a performance IQ score of 74. All scale scores ranged between 3 and 5, except for three measures (digit span = 8; similarities = 8; digit symbol = 7). This pattern of findings is atypical of progressive dementia and more compatible with an individual with long-standing subnormal IQ values (at least as measured by the Wechsler Scale). Formal language assessment revealed no true aphasic errors. The IQ test scores were helpful because they supported that her condition reflected only a long-standing pattern of subnormal intelligence. Other causes for her complaints of "declining ability" could then be explored.

Case 3

A 19-year-old female suffered a traumatic brain injury with unequivocal damage to the frontal lobes. About four months after her brain injury, she had a verbal IQ score of 97 and a performance IQ score of 110. These scores are within the normal range and compatible with her educational background. Yet, there were indications that her intelligence was above average before her brain injury. For example, her WAIS-R block design score was 16. On tests that required speed of finger tapping (Halstead Finger Tapping Test) and abstract reasoning (Halstead Category Test), her performances were below average. An unknowledgeable examiner who considered only her normal IQ scores might question why she should receive medical disability. The answer is that she has impairments in judgment and abstract reasoning not reflected by her IQ scores.

Case 4

A 62-year-old physician who teaches at a major university was discovered to have a hydrocephalic condition. He and his neurosurgeon agonized over whether he needed a shunt. Before making the decision, the patient underwent IQ testing. His verbal IQ was 132, his performance IQ score was 97, and his full-scale IQ score was 119. His performance IQ score was lower than would normally be expected given the patient's history. His digit symbol subtest score was 10, his block design score was 12, and his similarities score was 15. Other tests revealed subtle problems with memory and verbal learning. The patient underwent placement of a shunt. His IQ scores did not change substantially, but his performance on memory tests did improve substantially. This case highlights that IQ values provide some information relevant to clinical questions but may be inadequate as the basis for a complicated clinical decision.

CONCLUSIONS

This chapter strove to alert clinical psychologists to several important methodological issues involved in research in neuropsychological and intellectual assessment. Because

IQ measures are often used by clinical psychologists, we have focused heavily on the strengths and limitations of using these standard tests to assess patients with brain dysfunction. Although the standardized IQ (e.g., the Wechsler Bellview, the WAIS, the WAIS-R, and the WAIS-III) measures have been revised and restandardized, these measures fail to sample many cognitive functions adequately. If clinical psychologists or clinical neuropsychologists administer measures of intelligence and conduct neuropsychological research with these tests, they must recognize how the scores obtained can be influenced by a variety of variables (e.g., age, education, gender). It is also important to determine how test performance relates to neurological factors (i.e., location of brain damage, nature of brain damage). We have attempted to highlight some of the important considerations involved in conducting research in this area of assessment. The continued development of methodologically and theoretically sound neuropsychological research will improve our profession and enhance the services we can offer individuals who suffer brain dysfunction.

REFERENCES

Anderson, S., Damasio, H., & Tranel, D. (1990). Neuropsychological impairments associated with lesions caused by tumor or stroke. *Archives of Neurology, 47,* 397–405.

Birch, H. (1964). *Brain damage in children: The biological and social aspects.* New York: Williams & Wilkins.

Deary, I. J., & Stought, C. (1996). Intelligence and inspection time: Achievements, prospects and problems. *American Psychologist, 51,* 599–608.

DeLuca, J., & Cicerone, K. D. (1991). Confabulation following aneurysm of the anterior communicating artery. *Cortex, 27,* 417–423.

DeLuca, J., & Diamond, B. J. (1995). Aneurysm of the anterior communicating artery: A review of neuroanatomical and neurobehavioral sequelae. *Journal of Clinical and Experimental Neuropsychology, 17,* 100–121.

Diamond, B. J., DeLuca, J., & Kelley, S. M. (1997). Memory and executive functions in amnesic and non-amnesic patients with aneurysms of the anterior communicating artery. *Brain, 120,* 1015–1025.

Gardner, H. (1983). *Frames of mind.* New York: Basic Books.

Guilford, J. P. (1967). *The nature of human intelligence.* New York: McGraw-Hill.

Halstead, W. C. (1947). *Brain and intelligence: A quantitative study of the frontal lobes.* Chicago: University of Chicago.

Hebb, D. O. (1939). Intelligence in man after large removals of cerebral tissue: Report of four left frontal lobe cases. *Journal of General Psychology, 21,* 73–87.

Hebb, D. O. (1941). Human intelligence after removal of cerebral tissue from the right frontal lobe. *Journal of General Psychology, 25,* 257–265.

Heilman, K. M., & Valenstein, E. (1993). *Clinical neuropsychology* (3rd ed.). New York: Oxford University Press.

Johnson, S. C., Bigler, E. D., Burr, R. B., & Blatter, D. (1994). White matter atrophy, ventricular dilation, and intellectual functioning following traumatic brain injury. *Neuropsychology, 8,* 307–315.

Kaplan, E., Fein, D., Morris, R., & Delis, D. (1991). *WAIS-R as a neuropsychological instrument.* San Antonio, TX: The Psychological Corporation.

Kertesz, A. (1993). Recovery and treatment. In K. M. Heilman & E. Valenstein (Eds.), *Clinical neuropsychology* (3rd ed., pp. 647–674). New York: Oxford University Press.

Levin, H. S., Mendelsohn, D., Lilly, M. A., Fletcher, J. M., Culhane, K. A., Chapman, S. B., Harvard, H., Cyanuric, L., Bruce, D., & Eisenberg, H. M. (1994). Tower of London performance in relation to magnetic resonance imaging following closed head injury in children. *Neuropsychology, 8,* 171–179.

Lezak, M. (1995). *Neuropsychological assessment* (3rd ed.). New York: Oxford University Press.

Luria, A. R. (1966). *Higher cerebral functions in man.* New York: Basic Books.

Neisser, U., Boodoo, G., Bouchard, T. J., Boykin, A. W., Brody, N., Ceci, S. J., Halpern, D. F., Loehlin, J. C., Perloff, R., Sternberg, R. J., & Urbina, S. (1996). Intelligence: Knowns and unknowns. *American Psychologist, 51,* 77–101.

Parsons, O. A., & Prigatano, G. P. (1978). Methodological considerations in clinical neuropsychological research. *Journal of Consulting and Clinical Psychology, 46,* 608–619.

Peyser, J. M., Rao, S. M., LaRocca, N. G., & Kaplan, E. (1990). Guidelines for neuropsychological research in multiple sclerosis. *Archives of Neurology, 47,* 94–97.

Prigatano, G. P. (in press). Disorders of behavior and self-awareness. In P. Azouzi & B. Bussel (Eds.), *Prefrontal dysfunctions: Assessment and rehabilitation.* Paris: Arnette.

Prigatano, G. P., & Altman, I. M. (1990). Impaired awareness of behavioral limitations after traumatic brain injury. *Archives of Physical Medicine and Rehabilitation, 71,* 1058–1063.

Prigatano, G. P., Ogano, M., & Amakusa, B. (1997). A cross-cultural study on impaired self-awareness in Japanese patients with brain dysfunction. *Neuropsychiatry, Neuropsychology, and Behavioral Neurology, 10,* 135–143.

Prigatano, G. P., Parsons, O. A., & Bortz, J. J. (1995). Methodological considerations in clinical neuropsychological research: 17 years later. *Psychological Assessment, 7,* 396–403.

Prigatano, G. P., & Wong, J. (1997). Speed of finger tapping and goal attainment after unilateral cerebral vascular accident. *Archives of Physical Medicine and Rehabilitation, 78,* 847–852.

Prigatano, G. P., Wong, J. L., Williams, C., & Plenge, K. L. (1997). Prescribed versus actual length of stay and inpatient neurorehabilitation outcome for brain dysfunctional patients. *Archives of Physical Medicine Rehabilitation, 78,* 621–629.

Reitan, R. M. (1956). Investigation of relationships between "psychometric" and "biological" intelligence. *Journal of Nervous and Mental Disease, 123,* 536–541.

Spearman, C. (1904). General intelligence, objectively determined and measured. *American Journal of Psychology, 15,* 201–293.

Spreen, O., Risser, A. H., & Edgell, D. (1995). *Developmental neuropsychology.* New York: Oxford University Press.

Sternberg, R. J. (1990). *Metaphors of mind: Conceptions of the nature of intelligence.* Cambridge, England: Cambridge University Press.

Subcommittee of the American Academy of Neurology. (1996). Report of the therapeutics and technology assessments. Assessment: Neuropsychological testing of adults. Considerations for neurologist. *Neurology, 47,* 592–599.

Wilson, J. T. L., Wiedmann, K. D., Hadley, D. M., Conden, B., Teasdale, G., & Brooks, D. N. (1988). Early and late magnetic resonance imaging and neuropsychological outcome after head injury. *Journal of Neurology, Neurosurgery, Psychiatry, 51,* 391–396.

Chapter 11

Focus Chapter

METHODOLOGICAL ISSUES IN PSYCHOPHYSIOLOGICAL RESEARCH

Andrew J. Tomarken, Ph.D.

The term "psychophysiology" denotes that branch of research in which electrodes or other devices placed on the surface of the body are used to measure activity in the brain, in the autonomic nervous system (ANS), or in the skelotomotor system. For example, psychophysiologists record event-related potentials (ERPs) from electrodes placed on the scalp to assess changes in the electrical activity of the brain that occur in response to experimental stimuli. Such changes reflect neurophysiological processes implicated in perception, cognition, emotion, or motor responding. Examples of autonomic measures are the electrocardiogram (ECG), used to measure heart rate, and electrodermal activity (often referred to as skin conductance and formerly referred to as the galvanic skin response), a measure of the sweat responses in the hand or other regions. Such measures have been linked to a variety of processes (e.g., attending to novel or important stimuli) and individual differences. An example of the measurement of skeletomotor activity is the recording of muscle potentials from electrodes placed on the face to assess the facial expression of emotion. An additional skelotomotor measure is the startle eyeblink reflex that is elicited by a brief loud noise. The size of the startle blink can vary according to the individual's focus of attention and emotional state.

In the section below, I present some examples of how psychophysiological measures have contributed to research programs in several different areas of relevance to clinical psychologists. In subsequent sections, I discuss some of the methodological advantages of psychophysiological measures and some of their methodological constraints and potential limitations.

Preparation of this manuscript was supported by NIMH grant MH-49759. Correspondence concerning this chapter should be addressed to Andrew J. Tomarken, Department of Psychology, 301 Wilson Psychology Building, Vanderbilt University, Nashville, TN 37240.

SOME EXAMPLES OF THE USE OF PSYCHOPHYSIOLOGICAL MEASURES IN CLINICAL RESEARCH

Relevance to Psychopathology

Psychophysiological measures have proven useful in addressing a variety of scientific questions of interest to psychopathologists. Researchers have used psychophysiological measures to test hypotheses concerning the pathophysiology of and vulnerability to specific disorders (e.g., Braff & Geyer, 1990; Patrick, 1994; Tomarken & Keener, 1998). In the process, such measures have often served to link more molar, cognitive, behavioral, or descriptive perspectives on psychopathology to more molecular genetic or neurobiological levels of analysis (M. Dawson, 1990).

For example, one long-standing perspective on the cognitive deficits associated with schizophrenia is that they reflect an inability to filter out or inhibit the processing of stimulus information when such filtering is adaptive. Psychophysiological measures have been used to test the hypothesis that schizophrenics demonstrate deficits in such gating or filtering mechanisms (Braff & Geyer, 1990). One such measure is conditioned suppression of the P50 ERP. In this paradigm, experimental participants are exposed to a series of trials. On each trial, participants hear two very brief auditory clicks that are separated by a very short interval of time (e.g., 500 milliseconds). The first click typically generates a change in electrical activity, recorded from electrodes placed on the scalp, that occurs approximately 50 milliseconds after the occurrence of the click. This change in electrical activity reflects processing of the auditory features of the stimulus by specific brain regions. The second click typically elicits a change in brain activity that is markedly lower in amplitude than the change induced by the first click. It has been argued that this lowering of amplitude reflects inhibitory or gating mechanisms that serve to "protect" the processing of the first click from interference by the second click.

The difference in responses to the two clicks is shown by the two tracings on the left side of Figure 11.1, which is reprinted from Braff and Geyer (1990). These two tracings show the responses of a normal subject to the first click (top panel) and to the second click (bottom panel). The abscissa in this figure is time and the ordinate is the amount of electrical activity. The hatched areas denote the amplitude of the P50 ERP. Note how these areas occur between 25 and 75 milliseconds after exposure to the clicks. As indicated by a comparison of the two panels, the normal subject's P50 response to the second click is notably lower than the response to the first click.

This pattern contrasts sharply with the responses of a schizophrenic patient shown on the right side of Figure 11.1. In this case, the response to the second click does not appear at all diminished relative to the response to the first click. That schizophrenic patients often fail to demonstrate a decrease in amplitude to the second click has been interpreted as evidence that schizophrenia is often associated with deficits in sensorimotor gating. Note also the extremely short time durations involved (e.g., 50 milliseconds) in this paradigm. As will be noted below, psychophysiological measures can be particularly useful for assessing very brief processes that are inaccessible via other methods.

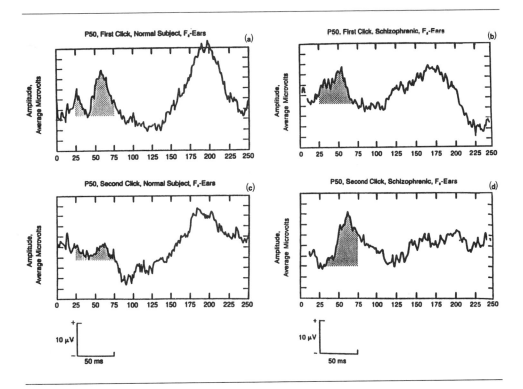

Figure 11.1.   A comparison of P50 conditioned suppression in normal and schizophrenic subjects. As the hatched areas in the left panels indicate, the normal subject's P50 response to the second click (c) is notably lower than the P50 response to the first click (a). In contrast, the schizophrenic subject's response to the second click (d) is not smaller than the response to the first click (b). The undiminished P50 to the second click indicates deficits in sensorimotor grating.

Source: Braff, D.L., & Geyer, M.A. (1990). Sensorimotor grating and schizophrenia: Human and animal model studies. *Archives of General Psychiatry, 47,* pp. 181–188. Copyright © 1990 by the American Medical Association. Reprinted with permission.

Psychophysiological measures have also proven useful to researchers who are interested in uncovering markers of vulnerability to psychopathology among at-risk populations. For example, several studies using electroencephalographic (EEG) methods have shown that, relative to normal control subjects, depressed patients demonstrate decreased activation in specific regions of the left hemisphere frontal cortex (e.g., Henriques & Davidson, 1991). It has been argued that the decrease in left frontal activation linked to depression reflects deficits in an "approach system" that mediates responses to rewards and other positive affective stimuli. In a recent study, we assessed whether left frontal hypoactivation might be a marker of vulnerability to depression among children and adolescents (Tomarken, Simien, Garber, & Dichter, 1998; see also Tomarken & Keener, 1998). We assessed EEG asymmetry in two groups of young adolescents: children known to be at heightened risk for depression because their mothers had a positive lifetime history of depression, and low-risk children for whom neither parent had ever met diagnostic criteria for depression. Despite the fact that these two groups failed to differ in current depressive symptoms, the high-risk group demonstrated decreased relative left frontal activation when compared to the low-risk group. Other studies have found that infants of currently depressed mothers demonstrate relative left frontal hypoactivation (e.g., Field, Fox, Pickens, & Nawrocki, 1995). Thus, EEG methods may reveal a pattern of enduring vulnerability to depression. There are a number of other examples of the use of psychophysiological measures to assess differential vulnerability to psychopathology (e.g., Clementz, Grove, Iacono, & Sweeney, 1992; Polich, Pollock, & Bloom, 1994; Raine, Venables, & Williams, 1990).

Psychophysiological measures have proven useful in several other respects to psychopathology researchers. First, although not typically incorporated into formal diagnostic criteria, they can contribute to the classification of subtypes. For example, schizophrenics who are consistently underresponsive on electrodermal measures appear to differ in significant respects (e.g., symptoms, metabolic activity in the brain) from those schizophrenic patients who are hyperresponsive on such measures (e.g., M. Dawson, 1990).

Psychophysiological measures have also contributed in important ways to the prediction of course and outcome. In a particularly striking example, Levenson and Gottman (1983, 1985) recorded heart rate, skin conductance, and several other psychophysiological measures from both members of a married couple during naturalistic interactions. They found that measures of physiological activation and/or "physiological linkage" (indicating the degree to which the physiological responses of marital partners are concordant) accounted for over 60% of the variance in current marital satisfaction. In addition, such measures subsequently predicted long-term marital satisfaction assessed three years later. In these studies, psychophysiological measures typically afforded better prediction of marital satisfaction than self-report or behavioral measures. This point underscores the importance of incorporating psychophysiological measures into multimethod assessments of behavioral and psychological problems.

Psychophysiological measures have also proven useful to researchers interested in studying processes and outcomes associated with the treatment of psychopathology. For example, in one line of research, Klorman and his colleagues (e.g., Klorman, Brumaghim, Fitzpatrick, Borgstedt, & Strauss, 1994) have used ERP measures of brain responses during cognitive tasks to assess the effects of pharmacological interventions on the cognitive functioning of children who suffer from attention deficit disorder (ADD). Similarly, psychophysiological measures such as heart rate and blood pressure have regularly been incorporated into studies assessing processes and outcomes associated with the treatment of anxiety disorders and sexual disorders.

In some cases, psychophysiological measures have been used to optimally match patients and treatments. For example, Öst, Jerremalm, and Johansson (1981) divided social phobics into two groups on the basis of responses to a social interaction test: those who predominantly responded with expressive or behavioral signs of anxiety (e.g., speech disturbances) and those who predominantly responded physiologically (with increases in heart rate). Subjects in each group were then randomly assigned to a behaviorally focused treatment (social skills training) or to a physiologically focused treatment (applied relaxation). As hypothesized, physiologically reactive subjects generally benefited more from the applied relaxation treatment, and behaviorally reactive subjects generally responded better to social skills training.

Relevance to Neuropsychology

Psychophysiological measures have also been used to clarify the specific perceptual, cognitive, or motor processes that are compromised by brain damage. In the process, they have contributed to knowledge about the specific functions of particular brain regions or neural circuits. For example, prospagnosia is a neurological disorder that can occur when a particular region of the brain (the medial occiptotemporal cortex) is damaged. A classic feature of this disorder is the patient's inability to recognize familiar faces, such as those of family members or famous people. Tranel and Damasio (1985) showed, however, that, even when the verbal reports of prospagnosics indicate an inability to recognize familiar or famous faces, they show enhanced electrodermal skin conductance responses to such faces. These findings suggest that some early stages of the process of recognizing a stimulus are preserved among prospagnosics, but that the results of such operations are not made available to consciousness. Note how the incorporation of a psychophysiological measure helps clarify what processes are and are not preserved among prospagnosics.

Just as psychophysiological measures can predict the later onset of psychopathology, they can predict cognitive development or the onset of developmental disabilities. For example, using ERP measures, Molfese and Molfese (1997) showed that the brain responses of newborn infants to consonant-vowel syllables predicted their later development of language skills by the age of 5 years.

Relevance to Behavioral Medicine

Psychophysiological measures have also played an important role in behavioral medicine. For example, there are a number of ongoing research programs that focus on cardiovascular reactivity as a factor in the onset of hypertension and coronary heart disease. Such research reflects the assumption that there are individual differences in cardiovascular responses to a variety of situations or stimuli, and that, in interaction with other factors, the predisposition for heightened cardiovascular responses may constitute a risk factor for the later onset of disease (e.g., Fredrikson & Matthews, 1990). Heart rate, blood pressure, and other cardiovascular measures are among the most frequently employed psychophysiological measures. Thus, it is not surprising that psychophysiologists have played a leading role in the study of cardiovascular risk factors. Psychophysiological measures have also proven useful in several other areas of research (e.g., chronic pain, headache disorders) falling under the broad rubric of behavioral medicine. Because psychophysiological measures also assess several physiological systems (e.g., the sympathetic nervous system) known to mediate the effects of stressors, such measures have also played a leading role in studies of the effects of stress on health and disease outcomes (e.g., Sgoutas-Emch et al., 1994).

In short, psychophysiological measures have proven useful in a number of different areas of research that are of interest to clinical psychologists. Despite the utility of psychophysiological measures, nonspecialists are often unfamiliar with the salient methodological and conceptual issues raised by their use. Below, I discuss some of the advantages afforded by the use of psychophysiological measures relative to other types of measures (e.g., self-report, observational) commonly used by clinical researchers.

METHODOLOGICAL ADVANTAGES ASSOCIATED WITH PSYCHOPHYSIOLOGICAL RESEARCH

Psychophysiological measures can assess unique processes that are not tapped by other measures. Even when the same processes are targeted by psychophysiological and other measures, the former often allow more sensitive measurement. Five more specific benefits are nested under these two general advantages: decreased reliance on the individual's capacity for accurate verbal reports; sensitivity to processes that are not accessible to consciousness; sensitivity to motor or response processes that are below the threshold for observable behavior; sensitivity to inhibitory processes; and the ability to reveal the temporal sequencing or chronometry of psychological and physiological processes.

Decreased Reliance on the Capacity for Accurate Verbal Reports

Relative to self-report measures, psychophysiological measures are less dependent on the capacity or willingness of the individual to make accurate self-reports about his or her experience. Psychophysiological measures can index processes that are not reflected in self-reports due to intentional deception, self-presentational tendencies, or other factors. For example, psychophysiological measures are routinely used in studies of "lie detection." Although lie detection is a controversial topic, it is clear that specific psychophysiological measures can reveal attempts to deceive under specific conditions (e.g., Bashore & Rapp, 1993).

Similarly, psychophysiological studies have been used to identify those individuals whose self-reports may be inaccurate due to introspective limitations or a cognitive style characterized by the denial or avoidance of negative affective states. One set of experiments has compared groups defined as "high anxious," "low anxious," and "repressors" (e.g., Tomarken & Davidson, 1994; Weinberger, Schwartz, & Davidson, 1979; for review, see Weinberger, 1990; see also Shedler, Mayman, & Manis, 1993). The key comparison in these studies is between low-anxious individuals and repressors. Subjects in both of these groups report low levels of trait anxiety. However, on the basis of their elevated responses on the Marlowe-Crowne Inventory (Crowne & Marlowe, 1964), it has been hypothesized that repressors are more likely to avoid or defensively deny anxiety. To test this hypothesis, several studies have compared the psychophysiological responses of repressors and low-anxious subjects to laboratory stressors (e.g., a free-association task involving exposure to phrases with sexual or aggressive content). Although both repressors and low-anxious subjects have typically reported low levels of anxiety when exposed to stressors, repressors have demonstrated significantly greater autonomic and neuroendocrine responses. Some caution is necessary because such effects have not been observed in all contexts and because there are alternative interpretations of the heightened psychophysiological reactions demonstrated by repressors (e.g., see Brown et al., 1996). Nevertheless, these results do suggest that psychophysiological measures can play an important role in the assessment of individual differences in personality. In many circumstances, multimethod assessment strategies involving both self-report and psychophysiological measures are likely optimal.

It is also often difficult or impossible to obtain valid self-reports from infants or children. Psychophysiological methods have proven to be one important means for assessing both cognitive (e.g., Molfese & Molfese, 1997; Nelson, 1994) and emotional (e.g., G. Dawson, 1994; Kagan, Reznick, & Snidman, 1988) processes in such populations. One example is the research program conducted by Kagan and his collaborators that compares behaviorally inhibited and behaviorally uninhibited infants and children (for reviews, see Kagan et al., 1988; Snidman, Kagan, Riordan, & Shannon, 1995). These two groups are classified on the basis of their responses to novel stimuli. Inhibited children withdraw from novel stimuli, whereas uninhibited children approach such stimuli. Kagan and his collaborators have proposed that behaviorally inhibited children have a unique physiological profile that reflects a lowered threshold for reactivity in brain regions that mediate responses to novel or fearful stimuli. Across several studies, behaviorally inhibited and uninhibited groups have differed on psychophysiological measures such as heart rate and blood pressure. Such differences have been observed both under resting conditions and in response to laboratory stressors (e.g., a loud noise that induces a startle response). These results have served to validate the behavioral inhibition construct and the notion that this temperamental dimension has stable physiological correlates. There are several other excellent examples of the use of psychophysiological measures to assess biologically based temperamental dimensions among infants and children (e.g., Fox, 1991).

Sensitivity to Unconscious or Preconscious Processes

One common limitation of self-report methods is that they predominantly reflect those processes and experiences that gain access to consciousness. As indicated by the distinction between explicit and implicit processes among cognitive psychologists (e.g., Kihlstrom, 1987) and by the emphasis on unconscious or preconscious processing in several theories of emotion (e.g., LeDoux, 1987; Zajonc, 1980), many cognitive, behavioral, and affective processes of interest are not accessible to consciousness. It is particularly difficult for individuals to discriminate processes that are relatively short in duration and that occur soon after exposure to a stimulus (e.g., within 500 msec). Such processes include early stages of the perception or recognition of a stimulus. ERPs have the temporal resolution to allow researchers to assess such processes (for review, see Coles, Gratton, & Fabiani, 1990). As noted above, ERPs indicate changes in the electrical activity of the brain that are time-locked to the occurrence of significant stimuli. Such electrical changes often reflect perceptual, cognitive, and motor processes of interest (e.g., detection of a mismatch between the current stimulus and previous stimuli). Many such processes are not accessible to consciousness.

Other psychophysiological measures have proven similarly sensitive to unconscious processes. For example, as noted above, Tranel and Damasio (1985) found that prospagnosics demonstrated enhanced electrodermal skin conductance responses to familiar faces that they could not consciously recognize. Similarly, Öhman and Soares (1994) showed that snake phobics demonstrate enhanced electrodermal responding to pictures of snakes even when such pictures were exposed so briefly that experimental participants could not consciously recognize them. Both sets of findings are consistent with the proposal that electrodermal responding can tap preattentional or preconscious processes (e.g., Öhman, 1979).

Sensitivity to Subthreshold Response Processes

Just as psychophysiological measures can index perceptual and cognitive processes that are below the threshold for conscious experience, they can reveal subthreshold response processes that are below the threshold for observable behavior (e.g., Coles, Gratton, Bashore, Eriksen, & Donchin, 1985). For example, subtle changes in facial muscle activity that may not be evident to an observer can be recorded from electrodes placed on regions of the face known to reflect emotional expressivity. Such electromyographic (EMG) measures can assess very minute changes in muscle activity (e.g., Cacioppo, Martzke, Petty, & Tassinary, 1988). The ability to dissociate observable and nonobservable components of facial expressivity may be relevant to the study of psychopathology. For example, Kring and her collaborators have shown that, though schizophrenics demonstrate less overt emotional expressivity when observational ratings are used (e.g., Kring & Neale, 1996), they demonstrate reliable facial EMG changes in response to emotional stimuli (e.g., Earnst et al., 1996). Although the precise reasons for this discrepancy across measures of expressivity are unclear, this pattern suggests several intriguing possibilities. For example, perhaps due to early aversive experiences, schizophrenics have learned to inhibit their overt responding to emotional stimuli.

When experimental paradigms are used that require an overt response to task stimuli, several psychophysiological measures (ERPs, EMG, heart rate) can be used to assess attentional and motor processes that are linked to *preparation* for responses (e.g., Brunia, 1993). Because such preparatory or anticipatory responses may not be expressed by overt behavioral changes, they may be difficult to assess by behavioral methods. Dysfunction in such preparatory processes appears linked to vulnerability to psychopathology (e.g., Simons, Macmillan, & Ireland, 1982; Yee & Miller, 1988).

Sensitivity to Inhibitory Processes

Psychophysiological measures can be sensitive to the *inhibition* of thought or behavior. For example, autonomic changes are observed when individuals are instructed to inhibit the experience or expression of emotion (e.g., Gross & Levenson, 1993). Such changes may reflect physiological activity that mediates the detrimental effects of emotional inhibition on health outcomes (e.g., Esterling, Antoni, Kumar, & Schneiderman, 1993). Specific ERP measures are also linked to the inhibition of responsivity in task paradigms (e.g., Pfefferbaum Ford, Weller, & Kopell, 1985).

Ability to Reveal the Chronometry of Complex Processes

A focus on the temporal sequencing or *chronometry* of behavior has been a characteristic of several areas of psychological research. Cognitive and perceptual psychologists often focus on the sequencing and interrelation of the component processes that underlie what might superficially appear to be even relatively simple phenomena such as "recognition of a sound" or "recognition of a familiar face." For example, among the processes required for recognition of a face are perception of a variety of lower-level component features (e.g., color, shape, texture), integration of such features into a composite image, and comparison of such an image to a template stored in memory.

Such processes occur over the course of time, with the output of early processes made available to subsequent processes.

Similarly, several models of emotion stipulate that emotional processing reflects the buildup of processes that unfold over the course of time. For example, Cacioppo et al. (1988) have proposed a "continuous flow" model of affective expressivity. According to this model, very early facial-expressive responses to the first appearance of an emotional stimulus are typically small in amplitude and reflect only broad evaluative dimensions of emotion (e.g., good vs. bad, positive vs. negative). With a buildup of intensity over time, facial-expressive responses become observable and more clearly differentiated into patterns of muscle activity that are linked to specific discrete emotions (e.g., anger vs. fear vs. disgust). Note the emphasis on the temporal course (i.e., chronometry) of facial expressivity over time. Several other models of emotion also focus explicitly on the temporal sequence of emotion-related processes (e.g., Lang, Bradley, & Cuthbert, in press; Lazarus, 1966; Solomon & Corbit, 1974).

The study of temporal patterning is also important in studies of stress, coping, and disease onset. In some cases, individual differences in coping and in behavioral or health outcomes are best captured by measures that take into account the overall patterning of responsivity to stressors over time (for reviews, see Dienstbier, 1989; Haynes, Gannon, Orimoto, O'Brien, & Brandt, 1991; Sapolsky, 1990). For example, in some contexts, those human and nonhuman organisms who appear to cope better with stressors do not necessarily demonstrate a lowered response in physiological systems that respond to stress (e.g., the hypothalamic-pituitary-adrenal axis). Rather, such individuals often demonstrate a brisk initial response to the onset of the stressor that rapidly declines at stressor offset. In contrast, individuals who have worse outcomes ("poor copers") sometimes demonstrate a sluggish response at stressor onset and a markedly delayed return to prestressor levels after stressor offset. Note that what primarily differentiates these two groups is the overall patterning (i.e., chronometry) of responding over time.

Despite evidence concerning the importance of temporal patterning, many studies conducted by clinical scientists do not sufficiently focus on the temporal course of the processes of interest and do not use measures that are capable of resolving such processes. A major methodological advantage of psychophysiological measures is their ability to assess the temporal patterning of cognitive, affective, or behavioral processes. As a tool for capturing the temporal course of a phenomenon, psychophysiological measures have several desirable features. The first is temporal resolution, which denotes the ability of a measure to discriminate changes in physiological activity that can occur within specific units of time (e.g., minutes, seconds, milliseconds). Several of the most commonly used psychophysiological measures can resolve changes that occur over the course of 1 to 2 seconds, and some measures have temporal resolution on the order of milliseconds (e.g., ERP). Such temporal resolution is critical when it is considered that many experimental paradigms in studies of cognition or emotion focus on processes that occur in the millisecond to second range.

A second advantage is that psychophysiological measures often allow for repeated data collection over time in a relatively unobtrusive manner. For these reasons, a researcher could, for example, continuously record the ECG or other measures while participants are viewing a film clip designed to induce emotion. Consider the dilemma for a researcher relying on self-report measures. He or she could obtain continuous self-reports during the film clip, but the rating task itself would certainly be distracting to subjects and thus weaken or otherwise alter emotional responses. The more common alternative, of course, would be to obtain self-reports immediately after the film clip is completed. However, this approach fails to assess the temporal course of affective responsivity. Furthermore, retrospective self-reports may not even be particularly accurate indices of average responsivity over time (e.g., Fredrickson & Kahneman, 1993).

Because of their temporal resolution, psychophysiological measures can parse complex processes that unfold over time into their constituent parts. One example is provided by a comparison of reaction time (RT) and ERP measures of cognitive processing. Many cognitive studies use measures of RT to assess the amount of time required for cognitive processing of a stimulus to be completed. In such experiments, differences in RT across experimental conditions are often used to infer differences in the number and/or complexity of the component processes required for successful task performance. However, RT effects are often difficult to interpret because RT is a summary index that reflects contributions from virtually every stage of processing that occurs between the onset of a stimulus and the response to that stimulus. Such stages include those pertaining to the perception, identification, and categorization of task stimuli and those pertaining to response selection and execution processes.

For example, consider a task in which experimental participants are exposed to a series of words across trials. Some of the words on any given trial are the names of people (e.g., Nancy), and some are words that are not names. Suppose further that on any given trial, participants are instructed to respond by pressing a button on a response box (e.g., the left button) when a female name appears on a computer screen and to press a different button (e.g., the right button) when a male name appears on the screen. Further, suppose that the specific buttons associated with male and female names vary across trials. The time required to categorize a word as male, female, or a nonname would be considered the duration of stimulus categorization processes. The time required to make a decision concerning whether to press a button and, if so, to press the right button or the left button would be considered the duration of response selection processes. RT is a summary measure that reflects the combined effects of both processes.

In some experimental protocols, response selection and execution processes may have an appreciable duration. In such cases, the P300 ERP is likely to provide a more sensitive measure of the effects of experimental manipulations on stimulus categorization processes than RT. The P300 ERP is a change in the electrical activity of the brain that occurs between 300 and 800 milliseconds after exposure to task stimuli. The P300 can index several interrelated cognitive processes (for reviews, see Coles et al., 1990; Johnson, 1993). Of prime relevance to the present context is the evidence that (a) the latency of the P300 ERP is a sensitive index of the amount of time required to categorize stimuli; and (b) P300 latency is relatively *independent* of the duration of response selection and execution processes (e.g., Coles et al., 1990; Luck, 1998; McCarthy & Donchin, 1981). Perhaps not surprisingly, then, in some studies P300 has proven to be a more sensitive index than RT measures of the cognitive dysfunction linked to psychopathology (e.g., Yee & Miller, 1994).

METHODOLOGICAL CONSTRAINTS AND LIMITATIONS ASSOCIATED WITH PSYCHOPHYSIOLOGICAL RESEARCH

Although psychophysiological measures are associated with a number of advantages, this area of research has stiff methodological requirements for the presentation of experimental stimuli and the accurate recording and quantification of responses to such stimuli. Following a brief discussion of such requirements, I consider some potential methodological limitations or costs associated with psychophysiological research. I particularly emphasize what I consider to be the most critical methodological and conceptual issue associated with psychophysiological research: the establishment of linkages between psychophysiological measures and psychologically meaningful processes.

Technical and Methodological Requirements for Psychophysiological Recording and Analysis

The reader is referred to several excellent books (e.g., Cacioppo & Tassinary, 1990b; Coles, Donchin, & Porges, 1986) and articles (e.g., Fowles et al., 1981; Fridlund & Cacioppo, 1986; Pivik et al., 1993) for an extensive discussion of technical issues pertaining to psychophysiological recording and analysis. Several general points will suffice to convey to the nonspecialist the most salient general issues. First, psychophysiologists use electrodes to record electrical activity that originates within the human body. Electrodes are placed on the body at locations known to be optimal for recording the signals of interest. In some cases, transducers are used to convert biological activity from other physical forms into an electrical form. Unfortunately, the signals of interest are typically small in amplitude (e.g., in the microvolt or millivolt range) and subject to contamination from both environmental sources (e.g., electrical devices in the laboratory environment) and biological sources (e.g., electrical activity associated with eye movements confounds EEG recordings). Such artifacts can potentially be much higher in amplitude than the signals of interest. As a result, psychophysiological recording requires the capabilities to enhance the critical signal of interest and minimize the contaminating effects of other electrical signals. Differential amplifiers and filters are commonly used for this purpose. EEG researchers, for example, amplify and filter scalp-recorded electrical activity to accentuate signal frequencies (1–40 Hz) that reflect the electrical activity of the brain and minimize higher frequencies that reflect muscle tension or other sources of noise. Researchers also need to ensure that other features of the laboratory environment limit the effects of electrical noise or other sources of artifact.

After amplification, filtering, or other forms of signal conditioning, the biological signals of interest are typically sampled and digitized by an analog-to-digital converter or similar device that converts electrical units (i.e., voltage) into counts or numbers that can be stored by a computer. Researchers need to ensure that the rate of sampling is appropriate for the specific measure recorded and the analytic procedures that will later be performed. In subsequent steps, researchers typically perform computerized analyses to further condition and quantify the digitized data. For example, using computer algorithms and statistical routines, researchers may correct the EEG from the contaminating effects of eye movements or blinks. As another example, researchers may run computer programs that average ERP responses over a large number of trials. Consistent with basic principles of signal averaging, though the ERP components of interest may not be evident on an examination of individual trials, such components are typically evident when data are averaged across trials.

As this brief summary indicates, optimal recording and analysis of psychophysiological signals typically requires a variety of hardware and software capabilities. In addition, it requires researchers who are knowledgeable about both general principles of bioelectrical measurement and more specific principles relevant to the particular measures and paradigms used. Psychophysiological research is also labor and time intensive. For example, it typically requires extensive pilot testing and troubleshooting, particularly when new measures and/or paradigms are used.

Methodological Issues Associated with Stimulus Presentation and Control

Although there is a variety of experimental paradigms used by psychophysiologists (e.g., Cacioppo & Tassinary, 1990c), the prototypical experiment involves an assessment of psychophysiological responses to experimentally manipulated stimuli. For example, many contemporary studies in the area of emotion assess psychophysiological responses to pictorial slides or film clips selected to elicit specific emotions. In this context, the slides or film clips are considered to be the experimental stimuli. In the P300 example described above, the words (male name, female name, nonname) used on each trial are the experimental stimuli that elicit ERP responses. In laboratory stress studies, a variety of experimental stimuli have been used, including the anticipation of a public speaking task or a difficult mental arithmetic task.

Although there are a variety of specialized issues pertaining to the presentation and control of experimental stimuli in psychophysiological studies, there are several general points of relevance to nonspecialists. First, psychophysiological research typically requires that stimulus control be highly precise. There are various facets of precision. For example, when the focus is on processes that are short in duration, as in ERP research, precise timing of the onset and offset of experimental stimuli is critical. When visual, auditory, or tactile stimuli are used, it is important that researchers precisely specify the perceptual features of stimuli. For example, many psychophysiological studies assess responses to auditory stimuli, such as clicks, tones, or loud noises. Psychophysiological responses to such acoustic stimuli can vary notably depending on several parameters, including the loudness (intensity), pitch (frequency), time required for the stimulus to reach peak loudness (rise time), and duration (e.g., Blumenthal, 1988; Griffith, Hoffer, Adler, Zerbe, & Freedman, 1995). Variations in such parameters can determine the precise psychological processes and neurobiological systems that are recruited.

Many psychophysiological studies manipulate multiple stimuli, each of which is linked to a specific level of an experimental factor. In such cases, in accord with basic principles of experimental design, researchers need to ensure that the stimuli differ on the dimensions of interest and not extraneous dimensions that could confound interpretation of results. For example, there have been a number of studies that have assessed whether verbal (e.g., word finding) and nonverbal (e.g., visual search) tasks elicit different patterns of brain activation. In such cases, it is essential that the verbal and nonverbal tasks be matched on difficulty level. In the absence of such task matching, it is difficult to ascertain whether differences in brain activation reflect regional specialization for verbal and nonverbal processing versus the effects of task difficulty on brain activation (e.g., Davidson, Chapman, Chapman, & Henriques, 1990).

As another example, a number of studies have assessed whether discrete emotions such as anger, sadness, and happiness differ in their psychophysiological patterning. In such studies, subjects are typically exposed to several different emotional stimuli (e.g., several imagery scripts), each of which is intended to recruit a target emotion. To ensure that any differences on psychophysiological measures are linked to differences among emotions versus extraneous factors, researchers conducting such studies need to follow several methodological guidelines that have been outlined by Davidson and Tomarken (1989). Such guidelines include matching experimental stimuli on the overall intensity of the target emotion elicited, verifying that each experimental stimulus clearly elicits one dominant emotion, and using more than one stimulus exemplar per emotion category.

Researchers also need to be careful about the precise instructional set that subjects receive. For example, a number of psychophysiological studies assess orienting responses using electrodermal activity, heart rate, or other measures. An orienting response indicates the degree to which an individual is allocating attention to a novel or significant stimulus. Results in orienting (e.g., Iacono & Lykken, 1979) and related (e.g., Guterman, Josiassen, & Bashore, 1992) paradigms can vary significantly depending on several instructional factors, including whether or not subjects are specifically told beforehand to pay attention to experimental stimuli and/or to respond to such stimuli in the context of an ongoing task. Researchers also must be sensitive to the broader socioenvironmental context. Psychophysiological responses can change when subjects believe that they are being observed (Cacioppo, Rourke, Marshall-Goodell, Tassinary, & Baron, 1990). In addition, a psychophysiological laboratory may be a novel environment, and many psychophysiological measures are responsive to novelty per se.

A related issue is the fact that the great majority of psychophysiological studies take place in a laboratory environment rather than naturalistic contexts. Two major reasons are the reliance on equipment that is not easily portable and the fact that stimulus control and psychophysiological recording typically require a well-controlled environment. In this respect, psychophysiological measures offer less flexibility than self-report measures and, in some contexts, observational measures. The reliance on a laboratory context may be associated with limitations in generalizability to naturalistic contexts. For example, on several dimensions (e.g., severity, duration), the stressors that can be reasonably manipulated in laboratory environments may differ significantly from naturalistic stressors that have been linked to the onset of psychopathology or other biomedical disorders. Similarly, although naturalistic responses to stressors occur over the course of days and weeks, psychophysiological assessments are typically conducted on a much shorter timescale (e.g., seconds or minutes). In recent years, devices have been developed for the ambulatory assessment of specific psychophysiological measures in naturalistic contexts (e.g., heart rate, blood pressure). Unfortunately, studies that have assessed whether autonomic and hormonal responses to laboratory stressors predict naturalistic levels or responses have generally yielded equivocal results (for review, see van Doornen & van Blokland, 1992).

Psychometric Issues: Reliability and Temporal Stability

Psychophysiological measures should fulfill the same criteria of reliability and temporal stability that are applicable to other types of measures (Tomarken, 1995). It is relevant, for example, to assess the internal consistency reliability of cardiovascular responses across the trials of a mental arithmetic task. The temporal stability of psychophysiological measures is particularly relevant when such measures are treated as markers of stable individual differences. It is a well-known psychometric principle that reliability and stability can constrain the magnitude of the relations that can be observed with external measures (e.g., Nunnally, 1978).

Unfortunately, the reliability and stability of psychophysiological measures are often not assessed (Tomarken, 1995). When they have been assessed, the results have been mixed. Internal consistency assessments of within-session reliability have generally indicated acceptable levels of reliability (e.g., reliabilities of .8 or above) (Tomarken, 1995). The test-retest stability of psychophysiological measures of putative individual differences has proven more variable. The stability of several measures frequently used by clinical researchers is adequate (i.e., test-retest rs in the .6 to .8 range) (e.g., Gooding, Iacono, & Beiser, 1994; Segalowitz & Barnes, 1993; Tomarken, Davidson, Wheeler, & Kinney, 1992). In other cases, the stability values are below those that would be deemed acceptable for cognitive or personality measures (e.g., Kamarck, 1992; Smith, Boutros, & Schwarzkopf, 1994; see also Cardenas, Gerson, & Fein, 1993).

Given the evident importance of reliability and stability, particularly for trait markers of vulnerability or other individual difference constructs, it is important that psychophysiologists assess these psychometric properties and incorporate procedures that can maximize the values yielded. For example, as predicted by psychometric theory, aggregation across trials or occasions of measurement can increase the temporal stability of psychophysiological measures (e.g., Tomarken, Keener, & Neubauer, 1994). See Tomarken (1995) for a discussion of several additional psychometric issues related to the use of psychophysiological measures.

Psychometric Issues: The Problem of Construct Validity

As several commentators have noted, the establishment of the construct validity of psychophysiological measures is among the most critical methodological problems facing researchers in this area (Cacioppo & Tassinary, 1990a, 1990c; Tomarken, 1995). Although construct validity is a broad term, I am referring specifically to the attempt to link psychophysiological measures to psychologically meaningful processes or to the specific biological substrates of such processes. One indication of the importance of this issue is the frequent response of nonspecialists to findings yielded by psychophysiological studies: What does it mean? In the context of psychopathology research, this response might translate into the following more specific types of questions: What precisely does electrodermal nonresponsivity tell us about schizophrenia? Why is lowered P300 amplitude linked to familial risk for alcoholism? Among adolescents, why does lowered heart rate predict the later onset of antisocial behavior?

These are excellent questions that reflect the fact that there is sometimes no immediately evident theoretical or conceptual explanation for the linkage between psychophysiological measures and either normal or pathological processes. In the absence of such a theoretical account, it may be unclear whether such measures actually are linked to important descriptive, pathophysiological, or etiological features of psychopathological and other disorders. It should be emphasized that not all psychophysiological studies are subject to interpretive problems. In addition, the great majority of psychophysiologists are acutely aware of the potential interpretive ambiguities associated with their measures. Even given these points, there are several reasons why the psychological meaning and functional significance of psychophysiological measures are sometimes ambiguous.

One source of difficulty is the fact that most psychophysiological measures are linked to at least several psychological processes and can be influenced by different types of experimental stimuli (Cacioppo & Tassinary, 1990a, 1990b; Tomarken, 1995). For example, it is well-known that electrodermal activity is linked to a variety of processes, including orienting and defensive responding, preattentive processing, the arousal dimension of emotional responding, ruminative thinking about "current concerns," and the inhibition of thoughts and behavior (e.g., M. Dawson, Schell, & Filion, 1990). As another example, the amplitude of the P300 ERP can reflect the interactive effects of several cognitive processes or stimulus attributes, each of which has multiple subcategories (e.g., Johnson, 1993). Such several-to-one or many-to-one relations between psychological processes and psychophysiological measures can make it difficult to understand the psychological significance of any given measure in any given experiment (Cacioppo & Tassinary, 1990a; Tomarken, 1995). In turn, such ambiguity makes linkages to core features of psychopathological or other disorders difficult to establish.

Biological factors can also muddy up the attempt to link psychophysiological measures to psychological or neurobiological processes. Just as psychophysiological measures are influenced by a variety of psychologically meaningful stimuli, they typically have multiple physiological influences. For example, the spatial resolution of traditional methods for measuring EEG and ERPs is limited. As a result, it is possible that a highly focalized change in activation occurring in the cerebral cortex could be measured at the scalp as a much more diffuse, nonfocalized pattern of activation. This "smearing" effect makes it difficult to localize EEG and ERP signals in the brain. As a result, any given pattern of activity recorded from scalp sites could conceivably reflect multiple underlying patterns of neural excitation and inhibition.

Similarly, the fact that heart rate is influenced both by the sympathetic nervous system (SNS) and the parasympathetic nervous system can introduce ambiguity into the interpretation of effects involving this measure (Berntson, Cacioppo, & Quigley, 1991). Such ambiguity can make it more difficult to delineate the neurobiological substrates of psychopathology. For example, markedly increased heart rate is a classic feature of a panic attack. Some commentators have attributed such increases in heart rate to heightened activation of the sympathetic nervous system (SNS). Such a conclusion would be consistent with traditional linkages between SNS activation and what has been termed "flight-or-fight motivation." However, as Tomarken and Hollon (1992) noted, several sources of evidence suggest that the increases in heart rate that occur during panic attacks may actually be a more direct reflection of impaired parasympathetic regulation of the heart.

Such ambiguity concerning the biological sources of psychophysiological activation reflects the fact that many psychophysiological measures tap physiological systems that are rather far "downstream" from the brain structures and circuits that mediate the psychological processes of greatest interest to many researchers. This conclusion is especially applicable to some of the most commonly used psychophysiological measures such as electrodermal activity and heart rate. Such ambiguity also reflects the fact that, for ethical and other reasons, psychophysiologists typically do not directly manipulate the physiological systems of interest. The ability to directly manipulate physiological systems is a major methodological advantage of biological research that uses nonhuman animals.

In addition to the fact that psychophysiological measures can reflect multiple psychological and biological processes, they are also affected by a variety of nuisance factors and irrelevant individual differences. Many nuisance factors are biomedical in nature (e.g., medication status, circadian and menstrual variations, aerobic fitness, handedness, smoking and drug use). Researchers often deal with such factors by the use of strict inclusion and exclusion criteria (e.g., using only right-handers in electrophysiological studies), although at the potential cost of generalizability. In other cases, specific design features or statistical techniques need to be used. For example, within-subjects designs and range-correction procedures are often used to derive measures that are free of the effects of irrelevant individual differences in response magnitude. However, not all nuisance factors and irrelevant individual differences can be corrected. When such factors are operative, they can weaken relations between psychophysiological measures and measures of psychological constructs because they introduce construct-irrelevant variability.

Clarifying Linkages between Psychophysiological Measures and Psychological Processes

It is important that researchers using psychophysiological methods take steps to establish linkages between their measures and psychologically meaningful processes and/or the biological substrates of such processes. Any approach to this problem should reflect one overriding principle that is consistent with basic notions of construct validity (e.g., Cronbach & Meehl, 1955). Researchers should design experiments that not only use psychophysiological measures to test substantive hypotheses. Such experiments should also directly test hypotheses concerning the meaning and/or functional significance of the relevant psychophysiological measures. There are two major methodological approaches that researchers can use when designing experiments to test hypotheses about the psychological significance of psychophysiological measures. One approach focuses on the experimental manipulations used (i.e., the independent variables), and the other focuses on the psychophysiological response measures that are typically the dependent variables. Optimally, both approaches should be used in any given experiment.

Concerning the first of these approaches, researchers can test alternative hypotheses about the psychological processes linked to psychophysiological measures by (a) manipulating experimental factors or levels of factors that differentially recruit the alternative processes under consideration; and (b) assessing the effects on the psychophysiological measures of interest. One excellent example of this approach is a set of studies conducted by Bradley, Cuthbert, and Lang (1990, 1993) that were designed to test alternative hypotheses concerning the psychological processes linked to modulation of the startle blink reflex by emotional stimuli. These studies are pertinent because the startle reflex has been used in a number of studies to index attentional and emotional processes that are relevant to psychopathology.

Prior studies had demonstrated that the amplitude of the eyeblink startle reflex to a brief burst of white noise is increased when the individual is viewing unpleasant pictures that elicit negative affect. As Bradley et al. (1990) noted, this finding is subject to two alternative interpretations. An "affective valence interpretation" is based on the argument that (a) negative affective stimuli potentiate a defensive-protective set to withdraw from aversive stimuli that is consistent with the defensive-protective nature of the startle reflex; and (b) reflexes with the same valence as an ongoing emotional state are augmented or potentiated by that state. An "attentional interpretation" is based on the following reasoning: (a) when confronted with an aversive visual stimulus, attentional resources are withdrawn from the visual modality and are then available to other perceptual modalities; and (b) increased attentional resources allocated to a given modality (e.g., auditory) serve to enhance the startle reflex elicited by a probe (e.g., a loud noise) that is processed by that modality.

In their first study, Bradley et al. (1990) tested these competing accounts. In addition to pairing emotional and nonemotional pictorial slides with an auditory startle probe (i.e., loud noise) as in previous studies, they added an experimental condition in which slides were paired with a visual startle probe (bursts of strobe lights). The affective valence interpretation would predict that exposure to negative affective slides would potentiate the startle reflex across both probe conditions. The attentional hypothesis would predict potentiation of startle in the acoustic probe condition but inhibition of startle in the visual probe condition. Such inhibition would presumably occur because of the withdrawal of attentional resources from the visual modality. As indicated by Figure 11.2, however, their findings indicated that negative affective pictures were associated with an enhanced startle reflex in both the auditory and visual startle probe conditions. Thus, their results support the affective valence interpretation

Prior evidence also suggested, however, that the relative priority of attentional versus affective processes might be conditional on how soon the startle probe occurred relative to the onset of the pictorial slide. Manipulating this factor in a second experiment, Bradley et al. (1993) found that blink modulation effects assessed soon after slide onset (e.g., 300 msec) appeared to reflect attentional factors, whereas modulation effects assessed at later points in time (e.g., 1,300 and 3,800 ms after onset) appeared to reflect emotional modulation. These two studies are an excellent example of the systematic manipulation of experimental factors to clarify the specific psychological constructs linked to psychophysiological measures and the conditions under which such linkages hold.

In most experiments, psychophysiological measures serve as dependent variables rather than independent variables that are directly manipulated. When feasible, more direct physiological manipulations can be an especially valuable way to clarify functional linkages between psychophysiological and psychological processes of interest to clinical scientists. For example, in a series of studies, Elbert and collaborators have studied the effects of changes in blood pressure by experimentally varying the pressure

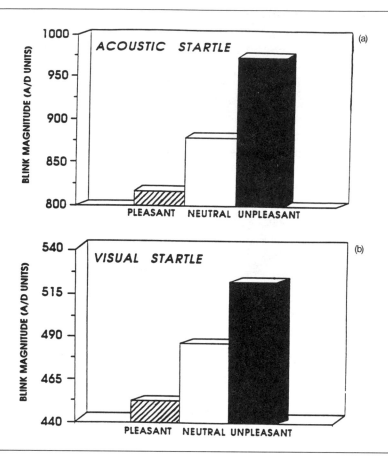

Figure 11.2.   Startle reflex magnitudes for acoustic (a) and visual (b) probes during viewing of pleasant, neutral, and unpleasant slides. The data show the same pattern of reflex modulation by emotional valence, independent of probe stimulus modality.

Source: Bradley, M.M, Cuthbert, B.N., & Lang, P.J. (1990). Startle reflex modification: Emotion or attention? *Psychophysiology, 27,* pp. 513–522. Reprinted with permission.

in a cervical cuff placed around the neck (e.g., Rau, Elbert, Geiger, & Lutzenberger, 1992). Changes in cuff pressure produce effects that are similar to those produced by naturally occurring changes in blood pressure. Using this device, these authors have shown whereas borderline hypertensives respond to cuff-stimulated increases in blood pressure with increased pain tolerance, normotensives demonstrate the opposite effect (Elbert et al., 1988). This finding suggests that, among hypertensives, increases in blood pressure may functionally serve to attenuate the effects of painful stimuli. Note how direct manipulation of a physiological system helps clarify one of the functions of that system in psychologically meaningful terms.

When psychophysiological measures are primarily the dependent variables in experiments, there are several approaches that researchers can use to clarify psychological significance. As Cacioppo and Tassinary (1990a, 1990c) have pointed out, by including multiple dependent variables and by assessing the patterning of responses over time, psychophysiologists can clarify the psychological processes linked to psychophysiological measures. For example, orienting, startle, and defensive responding may all be linked to increases in electrodermal activity. However, when heart rate is also measured and the patterning of responsivity over time is assessed, each of these three constructs is associated with a unique response profile.

The research of Bernstein and his collaborators (1988) on orienting deficits among schizophrenic and depressed patients is an excellent example of the use of multiple dependent measures to clarify the meaning of psychophysiological measures. As noted above, an orienting response is an indication that the individual is allocating attention to novel or significant stimuli in the immediate environment. Orienting deficits have sometimes been linked to psychopathology. For example, relative to normal control groups, both depressed patients and schizophrenic patients demonstrate decreased electrodermal skin conductance responses to novel tones or other stimuli commonly used in orienting paradigms. Although such decreased responsivity may indicate deficits in the psychological process of orienting, they could also reflect a more circumscribed dysfunction in the electrodermal system.

To test these alternative hypotheses, Bernstein et al. (1988) used two psychophysiological measures of orienting: electrodermal activity (EDA) and finger-pulse volume constriction (FPV). Interestingly, schizophrenics tended to demonstrate decreased responsivity across both psychophysiological measures, and depressed individuals demonstrated deficits only on electrodermal measures. Bernstein et al. concluded that schizophrenics have a true orienting deficit that is evident across multiple measures of orienting, whereas depressed individuals may have a more specific deficit in electrodermal responding. The authors speculated that this latter deficit may reflect dysfunction in peripheral systems that are innervated by the neurotransmitter acetylcholine. Consistent with this speculation is the evidence that (a) EDA is cholinergically mediated; and (b) depressed individuals show diminished activity in other physiological measures (e.g., salivation) that are also cholinergically mediated but that do not necessarily reflect orienting processes. Note how an analysis of the patterns of convergence and divergence among multiple physiological measures helps clarify the pathophysiological processes that are linked to two disorders. Such an analysis is consistent with basic principles of construct validity.

The approach used by Bernstein et al. (1988) also suggests that researchers need to focus on the broader biological systems in which psychophysiological measures are embedded. One characteristic feature shared by the most seminal contributions to the field of psychophysiology is that they all embed psychophysiological measures in broader biological and behavioral systems (e.g., Fowles, 1980; Lacey & Lacey, 1970; Obrist, 1975). Unfortunately, it is not uncommon to read studies in which no reference is made to higher-order control of a given measure, to the effects downstream of changes in a measure, or to the broader physiological systems in which a measure is embedded. Further, when hypotheses about relations to psychological processes focus on higher-order neural influences or systems, psychophysiologists should incorporate measures that more directly reflect the activity of the systems of interest. For example, impedance cardiography (Sherwood et al., 1990), a more direct measure of sympathetic innervation, or respiratory sinus arrhythmia (Porges, 1986), a more direct measure of parasympathetic innervation, may be preferable to measures of heart rate in studies of the central and autonomic substrates of psychopathological or other disorders.

As noted above, psychophysiological measures are often of interest because they shed light on processes (e.g., orienting) that are mediated by the brain. However, some measures such as EDA and heart rate are relatively far downstream from the neural processes of interest. For this reason, researchers should consider the use of EEG and ERP measures as a more direct window on brain processes. As noted above, a traditional limitation of such measures has been their relatively coarse spatial resolution. However, more recently developed methods that involve recording from large numbers of electrodes promise improvements in the ability to localize activity in specific brain regions or neural networks (e.g., Gevins et al., 1994).

In addition, in recent years, there have been major steps in the development of neuroimaging procedures that are capable of assessing the activity of the human brain (for reviews, see Andreasen, 1989; Binder & Rao, 1994; Cohen, Noll, & Schneider, 1993). Functional magnetic resonance imaging (FMRI) is a particularly promising technique because it is noninvasive (i.e., does not involve injections of radioactive agents) and has excellent spatial resolution that is superior to that offered by EEG and ERP methods. For example, FMRI can potentially discriminate differences in brain activation that encompass an area as small as 1 to 3 millimeters. FMRI also has excellent temporal resolution (on the order of seconds), although ERPs are superior in this regard (temporal resolution on the order of milliseconds). As this brief comparison indicates, different methods for assessing brain activation have differing strengths and weaknesses. FMRI has already been used in basic research studies to map out perceptual, cognitive, motor, and affective processes (e.g., Binder, Frost, Hammeke, Cox, Rao, & Prieto, 1997; Cohen et al., 1997; Irwin et al., 1996). In the future, FMRI will almost certainly become an important tool for elucidating neurobiological dysfunction linked to psychopathology.

SUMMARY AND CONCLUSIONS

Psychophysiological methods have several strengths that account for their ability to contribute significantly to our understanding of psychopathological and other disorders. However, for psychophysiological measures to yield maximal benefit, researchers have to surmount several methodological and conceptual problems. The most serious is the establishment of linkages between psychophysiological activity and psychologically meaningful processes. To clarify such linkages, researchers should incorporate an explicit hypothesis-testing approach to their measures, manipulate experimental stimuli and factors in such a way as to test alternative hypotheses, assess patterning across multiple psychophysiological measures and over time, adopt a broader focus on neurobiological systems, and use measures that most directly and sensitively assess the physiological systems of interest. Such procedures will further increase the usefulness of psychophysiological approaches to the study of both basic and clinical phenomena.

REFERENCES

Andreasen, N. C. (1989). *Brain imaging: Applications in psychiatry.* Washington, DC: American Psychiatric Press.

Bashore, T. R., & Rapp, P. E. (1993). Are there alternatives to traditional polygraph procedures? *Psychological Bulletin, 113,* 3–22.

Bernstein, A. S., Riedel, J. A., Graae, F., Seidman, D., Steele, H., Connolly, J., & Lubowsky, J. (1988). Schizophrenia is associated with altered orienting activity: Depression with electrodermal (cholinergic?) deficit and normal orienting response. *Journal of Abnormal Psychology, 97,* 3–12.

Berntson, G. G., Cacioppo, J. T., & Quigley, K. S. (1991). Autonomic determinism: The modes of autonomic control, the doctrine of autonomic space, and the laws of autonomic constraint. *Psychological Review, 98,* 459–487.

Binder, J. R., Frost, J. A., Hammeke, T. A., Cox, R. W., Rao, S. M., & Prieto, T. (1997). Human brain language areas identified by functional magnetic resonance imaging. *Journal of Neuroscience, 17*(1), 353–362.

Binder, J. R., & Rao, S. M. (1994). Human brain mapping with functional magnetic resonance imaging. In A. Kertesz (Ed.), *Localization and neuroimaging in neuropsychology* (pp. 185–212). New York: Academic Press.

Blumenthal, T. D. (1988). The startle response to acoustic stimuli near startle threshold: Effects of stimulus rise and fall time, duration, and intensity. *Psychophysiology, 25,* 607–611.

Bradley, M. M., Cuthbert, B. N., & Lang, P. J. (1990). Startle reflex modification: Emotion or attention? *Psychophysiology, 27,* 513–522.

Bradley, M. M., Cuthbert, B. N., & Lang, P. J. (1993). Pictures as prepulse: Attention and emotion in startle modification. *Psychophysiology, 30,* 541–545.

Braff, D. L., & Geyer, M. A. (1990). Sensorimotor gating and schizophrenia: Human and animal model studies. *Archives of General Psychiatry, 47,* 181–188.

Brown, L. L., Tomarken, A. J., Orth, D. N., Loosen, P. T., Kalin, N. H., & Davidson, R. J. (1996). Individual differences in repressive-defensiveness predict basal salivary cortisol levels. *Journal of Personality and Social Psychology, 70,* 362–371.

Brunia, C. H. M. (1993). Waiting in readiness: Gating in attention and motor preparation. *Psychophysiology, 30,* 327–339.

Cacioppo, J. T., Martzke, J. S., Petty, R. E., & Tassinary, L. G. (1988). Specific forms of facial EMG response index emotions during an interview: From Darwin to the continuous flow hypothesis of affect-laden information processing. *Journal of Personality and Social Psychology, 54,* 592–604.

Cacioppo, J. T., Rourke, P. A., Marshall-Goodell, B. S., Tassinary, L. G., & Baron, R. S. (1990). Rudimentary physiological effects of mere observation. *Psychophysiology, 27,* 177–186.

Cacioppo, J. T., & Tassinary, L. G. (1990a). Inferring psychological significance from physiological signals. *American Psychologist, 45,* 16–28.

Cacioppo, J. T., & Tassinary, L. G. (1990b). *Principles of psychophysiology: Physical, social, and inferential elements.* New York: Cambridge University Press.

Cacioppo, J. T., & Tassinary, L. G. (1990c). Psychophysiology and psychophysiological inference. In J. T. Cacioppo & L. G. Tassinary (Eds.), *Principles of psychophysiology: Physical, social, and inferential elements* (pp. 3–33). New York: Cambridge University Press.

Cardenas, V. A., Gerson, J., & Fein, G. (1993). The reliability of P50 suppression as measured by the conditioning/testing ratio is vastly improved by dipole modeling. *Biological Psychiatry, 33,* 335–344.

Clementz, B. A., Grove, W. M., Iacono, W. G., & Sweeney, J. A. (1992). Smooth-pursuit eye movement dysfunction and liability for schizophrenia: Implications for genetic modeling. *Journal of Abnormal Psychology, 101,* 117–129.

Cohen, J. D., Noll, D. G., & Schneider, W. (1993). Functional magnetic resonance imaging: Overview and methods for psychological research. *Behavior Research Methods, Instruments, & Computers, 25,* 101–113.

Cohen, J. D., Perlstein, W. M., Braver, T. S., Nystrom, L. E., Noll, D. C., Jonides, J., & Smith, E. E. (1997). Temporal dynamics of brain activation during a working memory task. *Nature, 386,* 604–607.

Coles, M. G. H., Donchin, E., & Porges, S. W. (1986). *Psychophysiology: Systems, processes, and applications.* New York: Guilford Press.

Coles, M. G. H., Gratton, G., Bashore, T. R., Eriksen, C. W., & Donchin, E. (1985). A psychophysiological investigation of the continuous flow model of human information processing. *Journal of Experimental Psychology: Human Perception and Performance, 11,* 529–553.

Coles, M. G. H., Gratton, G., & Fabiani, M. (1990). Event-related brain potentials. In J. T. Cacioppo & L. G. Tassinary (Eds.), *Principles of psychophysiology: Physical, social, and inferential elements* (pp. 413–455). New York: Cambridge University Press.

Cronbach, L. J., & Meehl, P. E. (1955). Construct validity in psychological tests. *Psychological Bulletin, 52,* 281–302.

Crowne, D. P., & Marlowe, D. (1964). *The approval motive: Studies in evaluative dependence.* New York: Wiley.

Davidson, R. J., Chapman, J. P., Chapman, L. J., & Henriques, J. B. (1990). Asymmetrical brain electrical activity discriminates between psychometrically matched verbal and spatial cognitive tasks. *Psychophysiology, 27,* 528–543.

Davidson, R. J., & Tomarken, A. J. (1989). Laterality and emotion: An electrophysiological approach. In F. Boller & J. Grafman (Eds.), *Handbook of neuropsychology* (pp. 419–441). Amsterdam, The Netherlands: Elsevier.

Dawson, G. (1994). Development of emotional expression and emotion regulation in infancy: Contributions of the frontal lobe. In G. Dawson & K. W. Fischer (Eds.), *Human behavior and the developing brain* (pp. 346–379). New York: Guilford Press.

Dawson, M. E. (1990). Psychophysiology at the interface of clinical science, cognitive science, and neuroscience. *Psychophysiology, 27,* 243–255.

Dawson, M. E., Schell, A. M., & Filion, D. L. (1990). The electrodermal system. In J. T. Cacioppo & L. G. Tassinary (Eds.), *Principles of psychophysiology: Physical, social, and inferential elements* (pp. 295–324). New York: Cambridge University Press.

Dienstbier, R. A. (1989). Arousal and physiological toughness: Implications for mental and physical health. *Psychological Review, 96,* 84–100.

Earnst, K. S., Kring, A. M., Kadar, M. A., Salem, J. E., Shepard, D. A., & Loosen, P. T. (1996). Facial expression in schizophrenia. *Biological Psychiatry, 40,* 556–558.

Elbert, T., Rockstroh, B., Lutzenberger, W., Kessler, M., Pietrowsky, R., & Birbaumer, N. (1988). Baroreceptor stimulation alters pain sensation depending on tonic blood pressure. *Psychophysiology, 25,* 25–29.

Esterling, B. A., Antoni, M. H., Kumar, M., & Schneiderman, N. (1993). Defensiveness, trait anxiety, and Epstein-Barr viral capsid antigen antibody titers in healthy college students. *Health Psychology, 12,* 132–139.

Field, T., Fox, N. A., Pickens, J., & Nawrocki, T. (1995). Relative right frontal EEG activation in 3- to 6-month-old infants of "depressed" mothers. *Developmental Psychology, 31,* 358–363.

Fowles, D. C. (1980). The three arousal model: Implications of Gray's two-factor theory for heart rate, electrodermal activity, and psychopathy. *Psychophysiology, 17,* 87–104.

Fowles, D. C., Christie, M. J., Edelberg, R., Grings, W. W., Lykken, D. T., & Venables, P. H. (1981). Publication recommendations for electrodermal measurements. *Psychophysiology, 18,* 232–239.

Fox, N. A. (1991). If it's not left, it's right. *American Psychologist, 46,* 863–872.

Fredrickson, B. L., & Kahneman, D. (1993). Duration neglect in retrospective evaluations of affective episodes. *Journal of Personality and Social Psychology, 65,* 45–55.

Fredrikson, M. (1991). Physiological responses to stressors: Implications for clinical assessment. *Psychological Assessment, 3,* 350–355.

Fredrikson, M., & Matthews, K. A. (1990). Cardiovascular responses to behavioral stress and hypertension: A meta-analytic review. *Annals of Behavioral Medicine, 12,* 30–39.

Fridlund, A. J., & Cacioppo, J. T. (1986). Guidelines for human electromyographic research. *Psychophysiology, 23,* 567–589.

Gevins, A., Le, J., Martin, N. K., Brickett, P., Desmond, J., & Reutter, B. (1994). High resolution EEG: 124-channel recording, spatial deblurring and MRI integration methods. *Electroencephalography and Clinical Neurophysiology, 90,* 337–358.

Gooding, D. C., Iacono, W. G., & Beiser, M. (1994). Temporal stability of smooth-pursuit eye tracking in first-episode psychosis. *Psychophysiology, 31,* 62–67.

Griffith, J., Hoffer, L. D., Adler, L. E., Zerbe, G. O., & Freedman, R. (1995). Effects of sound intensity on a midlatency evoked response to repeated auditory stimuli in schizophrenic and normal subjects. *Psychophysiology, 32,* 460–466.

Gross, J. J., & Levenson, R. W. (1993). Emotional suppression: Physiology, self-report, and expressive behavior. *Journal of Personality and Social Psychology, 64,* 970–986.

Guterman, Y., Josiassen, R. C., & Bashore, T. R. (1992). Attentional influence on the P50 component of the auditory event-related brain potential. *International Journal of Psychophysiology, 12,* 197–200.

Haynes, S. N., Gannon, L. R., Orimoto, L., O'Brien, W. H., & Brandt, M. (1991). Psychophysiological assessment of poststress recovery. *Psychological Assessment, 3,* 356–365.

Henriques, J. B., & Davidson, R. J. (1991). Left frontal hypoactivation in depression. *Journal of Abnormal Psychology, 100,* 535–545.

Iacono, W. G., & Lykken, D. T. (1979). The orienting response: Importance of instructions. *Schizophrenia Bulletin, 5,* 11–14.

Irwin, W., Davidson, R. J., Lowe, M. J., Mock, B. J., Sorenson, J. A., & Turski, P. A. (1996). Human amygdala activation detected with echo-planar functional magnetic resonance imaging. *NeuroReport, 29,* 1765–1769.

Johnson, R., Jr. (1993). On the neural generators of the P300 component of the event-related potential. *Psychophysiology, 30,* 90–97.

Kagan, J., Reznick, J. S., & Snidman, N. (1988). Biological bases of childhood shyness. *Science, 240,* 167–173.

Kamarck, T. W. (1992). Recent developments in the study of cardiovascular reactivity: Contributions from psychometric theory and social psychology. *Psychophysiology, 29,* 491–503.

Kihlstrom, J. F. (1987). The cognitive unconscious. *Science, 237,* 1445–1452.

Klorman, R., Brumaghim, J. T., Fitzpatrick, P. A., Borgstedt, A. D., & Strauss, J. (1994). Clinical and cognitive effects of methylphenidate on children with Attention Deficit Disorder as a function of aggression/oppositionality and age. *Journal of Abnormal Psychology, 103,* 206–221.

Kring, A. M., & Neale, J. M. (1996). Do schizophrenic patients show a disjunctive relationship among expressive, experiential, and psychophysiological components of emotion? *Journal of Abnormal Psychology, 105,* 249–257.

Lacey, J. I., & Lacey, B. C. (1970). Some autonomic-central nervous system inter-relationships. In P. Black (Ed.), *Physiological correlates of emotion.* New York: Academic Press.

Lang, P. J., Bradley, M. M., & Cuthbert, B. N. (1990). Emotion, attention, and the startle reflex. *Psychological Review, 97,* 377–395.

Lang, P. J., Bradley, M. M., & Cuthbert, B. N. (in press). Motivated attention: Affect, activation, and action. In P. J. Lang, R. F. Simons, & M. Balaban (Eds.), *Attention and orienting: Sensory and motivational processes.* Hillsdale, NJ: Erlbaum.

Lazarus, R. S. (1966). *Psychological stress and the coping process.* New York: McGraw-Hill.

LeDoux, J. E. (1987). Emotion. In V. B. Mountcastle & F. Plum (Eds.), *Handbook of physiology: The nervous system V* (pp. 419–459). Bethesda, MD: American Physiological Society.

Levenson, R. W., & Gottman, J. M. (1983). Marital interaction: Physiological linkage and affective exchange. *Journal of Personality and Social Psychology, 45,* 587–597.

Levenson, R. W., & Gottman, J. M. (1985). Physiological and affective predictors of change in relationship satisfaction. *Journal of Personality and Social Psychology, 49,* 85–94.

Luck, S. J. (1998). Sources of dual-task interference: Evidence from human electrophysiology. *Psychological Science, 9,* 223–227.

McCarthy, G., & Donchin, E. (1981). A metric for thought: A comparison of P300 latency and reaction time. *Science, 211,* 77–80.

Molfese, D. L., & Molfese, V. J. (1997). Discrimination of language skills at five years of age using event-related potentials recorded at birth. *Developmental Neuropsychology, 13,* 135–156.

Nelson, C. A. (1994). Neural correlates of recognition memory in the first postnatal year. In G. Dawson & K. W. Fischer (Eds.), *Human behavior and the developing brain* (pp. 269–313). New York: Guilford Press.

Nunnally, J. C. (1978). *Psychometric theory.* New York: McGraw-Hill.

Obrist, P. A. (1975). The cardiovascular-behavioral interaction-as it appears today. *Psychophysiology, 13,* 95–107.

Öhman, A. (1979). The orienting response, attention and learning: An information processing perspective. In H. D. Kimmel, E. H. van Olst, & J. F. Orlebeke (Eds.), *The orienting reflex in humans* (pp. 443–471). Hillsdale, NJ: Erlbaum.

Öhman, A., & Soares, J. J. F. (1994). "Unconscious anxiety": Phobic responses to masked stimuli. *Journal of Abnormal Psychology, 103,* 231–240.

Öst, L.-G., Jerremalm, A., & Johansson, J. (1981). Individual response patterns and the effects of different behavioral methods in the treatment of social phobia. *Behaviour Research and Therapy, 12,* 1–16.

Patrick, C. J. (1994). Emotion and psychopathy: Startling new insights. *Psychophysiology, 31,* 319–330.

Pennebaker, J. W., & Chew, C. H. (1985). Behavioral inhibition and electrodermal activity during deception. *Journal of Personality and Social Psychology, 49,* 1427–1433.

Pfefferbaum, A., Ford, J. M., Weller, B. J., & Kopell, B. S. (1985). ERP's to response production and inhibition. *Electroencephalography and Clinical Neurophysiology, 60,* 423–434.

Pivik, R. T., Broughton, R. J., Coppola, R., Davidson, R. J., Fox, N., & Nuwer, M. R. (1993). Guidelines for the recording and quantitative analysis of electroencephalographic activity in research contexts. *Psychophysiology, 30,* 547–558.

Polich, J., Pollock, V. E., & Bloom, F. E. (1994). Meta-analysis of P300 amplitude from males at risk for alcoholism. *Psychological Bulletin, 115,* 55–73.

Porges, S. W. (1986). Respiratory sinus arrhythmia: Physiological basis, quantitative methods, and clinical implications. In P. Grossman, K. H. L. Jansen, & D. Vaitl (Eds.), *Cardiorespiratory and cardiosomatic psychophysiology* (pp. 101–115). New York: Plenum Press.

Raine, A., Venables, P. H., & Williams, M. (1990). Relationships between central and autonomic measures of arousal at age 15 years and criminality at age 24 years. *Archives of General Psychiatry, 47,* 1003–1007.

Rau, H., Elbert, T., Geiger, B., & Lutzenberger, W. (1992). PRES: The controlled noninvasive stimulation of the carotid baroreceptors in humans. *Psychophysiology, 29,* 165–172.

Sapolsky, R. M. (1990). Stress in the wild. *Scientific American,* 116–123.

Segalowitz, S. J., & Barnes, K. L. (1993). The reliability of ERP components in the auditory oddball paradigm. *Psychophysiology, 30,* 451–459.

Sgoutas-Emch, S., Cacioppo, J. T., Uchino, B. N., Malarkey, W., Pearl, D., Kiecolt-Glaser, J. K., & Glaser, R. (1994). The effects of an acute psychological stressor on cardiovascular, endocrine, and cellular immune response: A prospective study of individuals high and low in heart rate reactivity. *Psychophysiology, 31,* 264–271.

Shedler, J., Mayman, J., & Manis, M. (1993). The illusion of mental health. *American Psychologist, 48,* 1117–1131.

Sherwood, A., Allen, M. T., Fahrenberg, J., Kelsey, R. M., Lovallo, W. A., & van Doornen, L. J. P. (1990). Methodological guidelines for impedance cardiography. *Psychophysiology, 27,* 1–23.

Simons, R. F., Macmillan, III, F. W., & Ireland, F. B. (1982). Anticipatory pleasure deficit in subjects reporting physical anhedonia: Slow cortical evidence. *Biological Psychology, 14,* 297–310.

Smith, D. A., Boutros, N. N., & Schwarzkopf, S. B. (1994). Reliability of P50 auditory event-related potential indices of sensory gating. *Psychophysiology, 31,* 495–502.

Snidman, N., Kagan, J., Riordan, L., & Shannon, D. C. (1995). Cardiac function and behavioral reactivity during infancy. *Psychophysiology, 32,* 199–207.

Solomon, R. L., & Corbit, J. D. (1974). An opponent-process theory of motivation: I. Temporal dynamics of affect. *Psychological Review, 81,* 119–145.

Tomarken, A. J. (1995). A psychometric perspective on psychophysiological measures. *Psychological Assessment, 7,* 387–395.

Tomarken, A. J., & Davidson, R. J. (1994). Frontal brain activation in repressors and nonrepressors. *Journal of Abnormal Psychology, 103,* 339–349.

Tomarken, A. J., Davidson, R. J., Wheeler, R. E., & Kinney, L. (1992). Psychometric properties of resting anterior EEG asymmetry: Temporal stability and internal consistency. *Psychophysiology, 29,* 576–592.

Tomarken, A. J., & Hollon, S. D. (1992). Disorders of emotion: Questions about clarity and integration. *Psychological Inquiry, 2,* 94–96.

Tomarken, A. J., & Keener, A. M. (1998). Frontal brain asymmetry and depression: A self-regulatory perspective. *Cognition and Emotion, 12,* 387–420.

Tomarken, A. J., Keener, A., & Neubauer, D. L. (1994). Long-term stability of frontal brain asymmetry: It helps to aggregate. *Psychophysiology, 31,* s97.

Tomarken, A. J., Simien, C., Garber, J., & Dichter, G. S. (1998). *Resting frontal brain asymmetry and differential risk for depression among adolescents: Linkages and moderators.* Manuscript in preparation.

Tranel, A. R., & Damasio, D. (1985). Knowledge without awareness: An autonomic index of facial recognition by prospagnosics. *Science, 228,* 1453–1454.

van Doornen, L. J. P., & van Blokland, R. W. V. (1992). Relationship between cardiovascular and catecholamine reactions to laboratory and real-life stress. *Psychophysiology, 29,* 173–181.

Weinberger, D. A. (1990). The construct validity of the repressive coping style. In J. L. Singer (Ed.), *Repression and dissociation: Implications for personality theory, psychopathology, and health* (pp. 337–386). Chicago: University of Chicago Press.

Weinberger, D. A., Schwartz, G. E., & Davidson, R. J. (1979). Low-anxious, high-anxious, and repressive coping styles: Psychometric patterns and behavioral and physiological responses to stress. *Journal of Abnormal Psychology, 88,* 369–380.

Yee, C. M., & Miller, G. A. (1988). Emotional information processing: Modulation of fear in normal and dysthymic subjects. *Journal of Abnormal Psychology, 97,* 54–63.

Yee, C. M., & Miller, G. A. (1994). A dual-task analysis of resource allocation in dysthymia and anhedonia. *Journal of Abnormal Psychology, 103,* 625–636.

Zajonc, R. B. (1980). Feeling and thinking: Preferences need no inferences. *American Psychologist, 35,* 151–175.

Chapter 12

Focus Chapter

ITEM RESPONSE THEORY IN ASSESSMENT RESEARCH

SUSAN E. EMBRETSON, PH.D., and L. KATHERINE PRENOVOST, M.A.

Item response theory (IRT) is rapidly emerging as the major psychometric basis of testing. IRT has many advantages over classical test theory (CTT); for example, IRT makes adaptive testing feasible because scores can be equated across any subset of calibrated items. It is well-known that several large-scale tests, such as the Graduate Record Examination (GRE) and the Armed Forces Qualification Test (AFQT), are now based on IRT. The GRE and AFQT are administered by computer using adaptive testing, in which items are selected to be optimally informative about the person's ability.

Less well-known is the trend toward IRT utilization in tests routinely used in clinical assessment. Many individually administered intelligence tests are now partially based on IRT to equate scores that result from clinically adaptive testing procedures, which often include basal and ceiling stop rules. For example, the Differential Ability Scales (DAS) use IRT-based results not only to facilitate test equating across ability levels, but also to guide the test selection process for particular clinical populations. Research on applying IRT to affective tests, such as psychopathology, personality, attitudes, and behavioral rating scales, has increased dramatically as well. Although IRT is not yet applied routinely on affective tests, the research basis for such applications is rapidly accumulating.

This chapter describes clinical assessment research in which IRT has been applied to solve important psychometric issues in construct definition and scale development. In a short chapter, the research review cannot be comprehensive or exhaustive. Instead, we focus on a few key issues and show how IRT is employed to address the issues. In the presentations, IRT's conceptual advantages will be emphasized rather than its principles explained. For clarification, we begin with a short section on IRT. Because IRT principles differ substantially from CTT (see Embretson, 1996, for some contrasts), an extended discussion is not possible in a short chapter. Two recent textbooks that require only knowledge of CTT provide an introduction to IRT (Embretson & Reise, in press; Hambleton, Swaminathan, & Rogers, 1991).

BASICS IN ITEM RESPONSE THEORY

IRT predicts the response of a person to a specific item. The prediction is given by a model that contains both the characteristics of the item and the trait level (i.e., "score") of the person. The item properties include difficulty level (analogous to proportion passing in CTT), item discrimination (analogous to CTT correlation of item to total score, such as in biserial correlations), and guessing (probability of passing item with a random response). IRT models vary in both the number of item parameters and the number of traits that are estimated for each person. IRT models also differ in mathematical functions. Currently, the logistic function is most prevalent; it is an exponential model in which a dichotomous response is predicted from a linear combination of person and item parameters. For the two-parameter logistic model (2PL), item responses, X_{ij}, are predicted with item difficulty, b_i, item discrimination, a_i, and a person's trait level, θ_j, as follows:

$$P(X_{ij} = 1) = \frac{\text{Exp}(a_i(\theta_j - b_i))}{1 + \text{Exp}(a_i(\theta_j - b_i))} \quad (1).$$

The item parameters in IRT correspond to various indices in CTT. That is, item difficulty is related to p value, item discrimination is related to the biserial correlation with total score, and trait level is related to a weighted sum of the items (weighted by item discrimination). Unlike CTT, however, the IRT item indices are invariant over populations (which may differ in performance levels) and IRT trait levels are invariant over the items that are administered (which may differ in difficulty and discrimination). This invariance property is accomplished by estimating person and item parameters jointly in the model—also unlike CTT. Hence, the estimates are implicitly controlled for varying item or person properties (see Embretson & Reise, 1997, for a more complete explanation).

It should be noted that item or category characteristics curves are typically employed to illustrate the predicted probabilities for responses to an item. Figure 12.1 shows an item characteristics curve in which success on a dichotomous item is predicted over varying trait levels. In many applications, the magnitude of trait level is similar to z scores.

ISSUES IN TEST DEVELOPMENT

IRT has important applications for both construct validity and reliability. The following sections consider several types of applications in each area:

Elaborating Construct Validity

The initial empirical tryouts of items can provide important information for establishing construct validity. Construct validity concerns not only the quality of a particular item set but also the plausibility of the postulated latent trait that underlies the item responses. Item analysis concerns how the latent trait influences responses on specific items. Construct definition is especially facilitated by having a strong theory to guide item specifications. The theory not only guides item development, but also provides a framework for interpreting item tryout results.

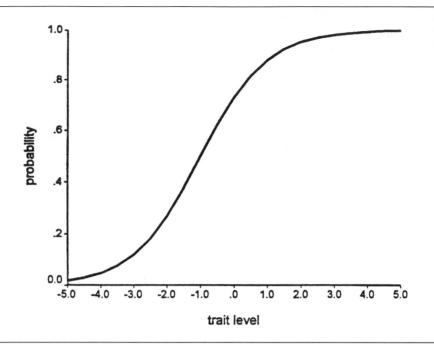

Figure 12.1.   An item characteristics curve from IRT.

IRT provides some diagnostic information for construct development that is not well elaborated by CTT. These areas include diagnostic information about (a) the appropriate number of latent traits (i.e., dimensionality assessment), (b) the trait level represented by various item responses (i.e., item difficulty scaling), (c) the impact of item design features on item difficulty, (d) the informativeness of the item response categories for the latent trait, and (e) constancy of the trait across populations.

Dimensionality Assessment

Test development typically begins with specifying a target trait to be studied and measuring domain items or behaviors that indicate the trait. Explicating the number of latent traits involved in responding to the items is an important aspect of construct definition. Linear factor analysis methods, such as principal factor analysis or principal component analysis, often are applied to assess the number of latent traits or dimensions that underlie an item set. However, linear factor analysis results can be misleading for items with a limited number of response categories (two to seven item response categories are typical in assessment). Linear factor analysis methods assume that the variables (items) are continuous and normally distributed. When these assumptions are violated (e.g., as occurs with a limited number of response categories), the results from linear factor analysis will be confounded by item difficulty levels. For example, if items have only two response categories (e.g., "pass" versus "fail," "yes" versus "no"), correlations are restricted by the match of their difficulty levels. Factor analysis of such items leads to overestimating the number of common dimensions and to underestimating the factor loadings on the latent trait (see Gibbons, Clarke, VonAmmon-Cavanaugh, & Davis, 1985). Similar problems can arise with factor analysis of rating scale items as well.

Applying linear factor analysis methods to personality and psychopathology tests has led to inconsistency about the number and the nature of the underlying dimensions. For example, Waller (in press) shows how difficulty factors have influenced various proposed factor structures for the Minnesota Multiphasic Personality Inventory (MMPI). In fact, the nonreplicability and uninterpretability of the MMPI factors has led to recommendations that attempts to explicate the MMPI factor structure be abandoned.

A multidimensional IRT model (Bock, Gibbons, & Muraki, 1988; Muraki & Engelhard, 1985) has been developed to appropriately assess the dimensionality for dichotomous items. Multidimensional IRT models provide full-information factor analysis because the frequencies within specific response categories are predicted. The items are factored by applying the multidimensional IRT model repeatedly, with a successively increasing number of dimensions. Dimensions are extracted until the data are well predicted by the model. Recently, a multidimensional IRT model for full-information factor analysis of rating scale formats has been developed (Muraki & Carlson, 1995).

Some recent examples of full-information factor analysis in assessment research includes Haviland and Reise (1996) and Hendryx, Haviland, Gibbon, and Clark's (1992) studies of the dimensionality of the Toronto Alexithymia Scale. The results suggested that the scale is multidimensional; hence, a single global score is not adequate to describe the measure. Similarly, Waller (in press) applied nonlinear factor analysis and IRT methods to identify a replicable and interpretable structure of the MMPI.

Item Difficulty Scaling

If a single latent trait underlies the item domain, IRT scaling of item difficulty levels provides important information about the construct. Examining the content of items with high and low difficulty levels helps elaborate the construct because item difficulty directly reflects trait level. For example, Bell, Low, Jackson, and Dudgeon (1994) scaled symptoms as indicators of schizophrenia. An inspection of item difficulty levels would show which symptoms are likely only for persons exhibiting high levels of schizophrenic behavior. Kirisci, Moss, and Tarter (1996) scaled an instrument to assess self-efficacy in drinking situations. Again, an inspection of item difficulty levels provides important information about the role of specific situations in self-efficacy. Several researchers have scaled everyday living skills (Bode & Heinemann, 1997; Ludlow & Haley, 1996) and general motor skills (Ludlow, Haley, & Gans, 1992). Item scaling for these measures has important implications for skills that are readily lost in handicapped or elderly populations.

Bode and Heinemann's (1997) analysis of the Functional Independence Measure (FIM) illustrates how IRT scaling results aid construct definition. Elderly individuals were rated for possession of specific everyday behaviors, such as shown in Figure 12.2. The results from an IRT analysis of the behavioral rating are relevant to two major issues. First, the results supported a consistent progression of skill loss in the population. This progression is supported by fit of a unidimensional IRT model (i.e., the Rasch model, in this case) to item responses. Because the behaviors are appropriately scaled on a single continuum, behaviors with high difficulties are unlikely to be possessed by anyone who lacks behaviors with lower difficulties. Second, the item difficulty levels of the behaviors defines the progression of skill loss. So, from Figure 12.2, the scaling implies that a person who has difficulty with upper dressing has a low probability of bathing without assistance, for example:

Impact of Item Design Features on Difficulty Level

Some IRT models can be used to examine the impact of item design features on item difficulty. Such features could include item content categories, postulated involvement of particular underlying processes or skills, knowledge level, and so forth. The linear logistic latent trait model (LLTM; Fischer, 1973) estimates the impact of stimulus content features on item difficulty. To apply it, each item must be scored on the features. LLTM not only estimates the relative weights of the features in item difficulty but also can decompose the source of difficulty for each item.

Several cognitive ability test items have been studied in experimental research to characterize the processes that underlie their solution. For example, applications of LLTM have supported spatial visualization items as involving a series of processes, of which the spatial analogue processes were the most important (see Embretson, 1994). Further, the LLTM results can be applied to select items for specific sources of processing difficulty.

A recent study shows that personality self-report measures also can be developed and results interpreted from a precise item design framework. Roskam and Broers (1996) applied a facet design to generate items to measure proneness to lonesomeness. The facets classified descriptions of social interactions in a 2 (direction) × 3 (focus) × 3 (partner) × 2 (mode) × 2 (locus) design. Roskam and Broers applied LLTM to estimate the impact of each facet, and possible interactions, on item difficulty (here, endorsability). The findings were interpreted with respect to the lonesomeness construct.

Informativeness of Item Response Categories

Rating scales are prevalent in personality and psychopathology assessment. To operationalize a rating scale, both the number of response categories and some category anchors must be specified. Fitting IRT models to polytomous data, such as rating scales,

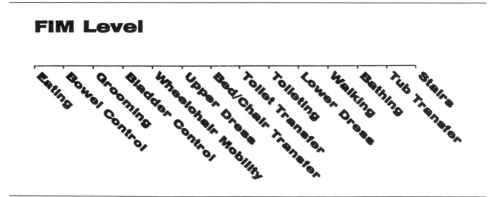

Figure 12.2.   A scaling of the Functional Independence Measure (FIM).

provides some new insights about the usefulness of the various response categories. Polytomous IRT models that are appropriate for rating scales include the graded response model (Samejima, 1969), Rasch rating scales (Andrich, 1978), the partial credit model (Masters, 1982; Muraki, 1993), and nonparametric IRT models (Ramsay, 1991).

For example, Santor, Ramsay, and Zuroff (1994) applied IRT to examine the relative effectiveness of the items and the appropriateness of the response option weights in the Beck Depression Inventory. Importantly, fitting nonparametric IRT models indicated that increasing endorsement levels did not involve more of the latent trait for some items. In this case, increasing total score from this item (with increasing item endorsement level) led to an inefficient estimate of a person's depression level.

To illustrate how IRT assesses the usefulness of various response categories, Figure 12.3 shows results from fitting the partial credit model to Thayer's Energetic Arousal scale on a sample of about 700 young adults. The Energetic Arousal items are adjectives that are rated on a 4-point scale (rating categories from 0 to 3). Figure 12.3 presents the category characteristics curves for two items. These figures give the probability of endorsing each category for a person at a particular trait level. The higher the trait level, the more likely the person is to endorse the higher-level categories. In the upper panel, for example, a person with a trait level of 0.0 has the highest probability of endorsing Category 1 (Rarely Characteristic) and the lowest probability of endorsing Category 3 (Very Characteristic). For a person with a trait level of 3.0, the highest probability is for endorsing Category 3.

The item in the upper panel has well-ordered rating categories. Each category has a range on the latent trait for which it is the most likely response. The item in the lower panel is not well ordered. One response category (Category 1) is never the most likely category. If several items function like the one in the lower panel, reducing the number of rating categories or changing the anchoring statements is indicated.

Trait Constancy across Classes

For some traits, populations with qualitatively different approaches to the items exist. Because these populations differ on (typically) unobservable qualities, they are referred to as *latent classes* of respondents. These distinct latent classes vary in what construct is represented in responses to the items. Although the classes may be related to overt demographic classifications (e.g., gender, race, age), they are generally only detected through characteristic response patterns across items on a scale. Membership in a class depends on the probability that the person's response pattern would occur in that class. Although a multidimensional IRT model could provide improved fit to such data, an IRT model that includes two or more latent classes would be more appropriate.

Latent class models that utilize IRT are mixture distribution models. In these models (e.g., Rost, 1992), the presence of qualitatively distinct classes of people are identified based on characteristic response patterns on the scale. If distinct classes do exist, it is important to consider class membership in score interpretations. Recall that respondents from different classes are interpreting the scale differently, hence different constructs drive item responses. In other words, when latent classes are detected, two people with the same total score may belong to different classes, which means they are *not being assessed on the same trait*. It becomes clear that not accounting for population membership in assessment can lead to misclassification of

Ex003 I003:   Locn = 0.455   Resid = 5.278   ChiSqProb = 0.000

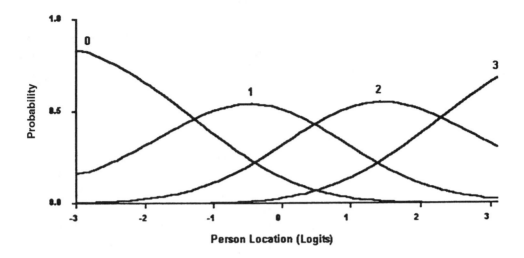

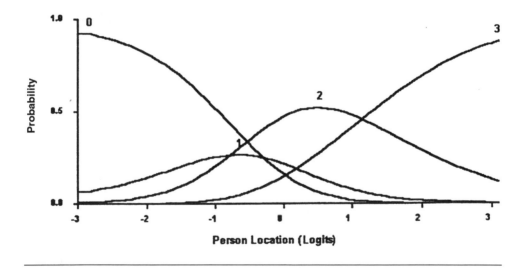

Figure 12.3.   Category characteristics curves for two items from the Energetic Arousal scale.

respondent. Personality and clinical research particularly must be mindful of such possibilities.

To illustrate, consider Prenovost's (1996) analysis of a dietary restraint scale (Herman & Mack, 1975) that yielded two substantively distinct classes and a random class of respondents. Figure 12.4 shows the average item *easiness* for the two substantive (as opposed to random) classes on each of the 10 items of the scale. Note that item easiness, as opposed to difficulty, is estimated by the computer program MIRA (Rost, 1992). Figure 12.4 summarizes each item easiness for each of the latent classes. For example, on average, it is easier for a respondent in class 2 than in class 1 to endorse higher values on the item that asks about dieting frequency. Based on response patterns and other reference tests, class 1 could be conceptualized as representing a population that experiences some degree of negative cognitions toward eating and food, does not identify with fluctuations in weight, and does not frequently diet. Class 2 may be seen as coming from a population that does diet and experiences weight fluctuations but does not have many negative cognitions toward eating. Interestingly, although the response patterns to the items of the scale differ across classes, no *mean difference in total scores* was observed (means were 17.3 and 17.0, respectively).

An implication of this finding is that total score alone leads to incorrect conclusions. Although neither class reported frequent dieting or bingeing behaviors, notable differences in patterns can be seen. It was easier for class 1 than for class 2 to report giving too much time and thought to food and having more guilt feelings after overeating. Class 1 also tended to report being more conscious of what they eat, yet tended to report fewer weight fluctuations. Class 2 tended to not report cognitive or affective ties to eating (e.g., guilt feelings, thinking excessively about food), yet they did report more weight fluctuation than class 1 members. Had only total score been considered and used to diagnose restrained eating behavior, the relationship of the construct to the person would be misunderstood.

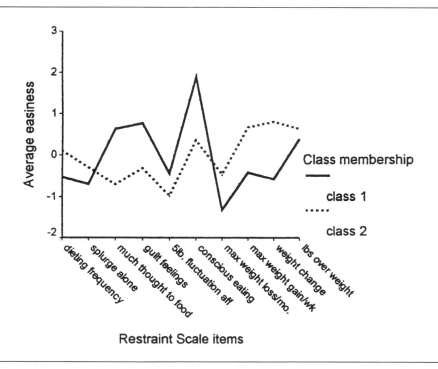

Figure 12.4.   Class differences in IRT item easiness for the restraint scale.

An example from the cognitive domain is McCollam and Embretson's (1995) study on spatial visualization ability. They identified two qualitatively different processing strategies by applying MIRA: verbal-analytic processing and spatial analogue processing. Typically, it is assumed that spatial tests do indeed measure spatial processing; however, these results identify a substantial class of persons who solve the items with verbal-analytic processing. Thus, the meaning of the trait depends on the population to which the person belongs.

Another example is Reise and Gomel's (1995) study on the Positive Interpersonal Engagement Scale. Two classes of respondents were identified: agenics and communals. The former class consisted of people who felt more efficacious in social situations; the latter felt more comfortable with interpersonal closeness. Reise and Gomel hypothesize that qualitative classes of people occur most in personality typically along psychological lines rather than on overt demographic dimensions (e.g., sex, race, age).

Further, latent class IRT can be useful in situations where distinct types of clinical disorders exist. For example, it is thought that different types of depressions exist (Reise & Gomel, 1995). Perhaps these can be assessed by characteristic response patterns.

Maximizing Reliability in Scale Construction

IRT may be employed in several aspects of scale construction to maximize reliability for individuals and for groups. The results typically differ from classical theory approaches. The topics to be covered here include (a) item selection, (b) assessing item bias, (c) optimal weighting of item information to estimate trait level, (d) equating trait levels from varying item sets (i.e., due to stopping rules, alternative forms or adaptive testing, (e) anchoring and interpreting trait levels, and (f) assessing person fit.

Item Selection

Although the IRT item parameters are related to CTT indices, item selection is much more precise in IRT. Specifically, items can be selected to target measurement precision at particular trait levels. In IRT, the standard error of measurement differs between trait levels, depending on the difficulty and discrimination of the items administered. In general, the standard error is low for a particular trait level when the test contains many highly discriminating items with item difficulty levels closely matched to the trait level. Test and item information curves are plotted over trait levels. In most applications, it is more convenient to utilize test information (the reciprocal of the standard error) to guide item selection. Then, items can be selected to maximize measurement precision for (a) a range of trait levels, (b) a particular trait level (such as a cutline), or (c) a particular person, using fully adaptive testing.

To give some examples, items were selected for the Woodcock-Johnson Psycho-Educational Battery to provide equal precision over a range of trait levels (Woodcock, 1978). In the DAS, a clinically adaptive test, items were selected into subsets to minimize measurement error over the trait level distribution within an age level (see Daniel, in press). Items were selected for a short form of the Eysenck Personality Questionnaire to minimize measurement error over a range of trait levels (Grayson, 1986).

Minimize Item Bias for Diverse Populations

Another aspect of item selection is to minimize item bias across demographic groups. Bias assessment is useful when developing equivalent tests across language, gender, racial, or other groups. As used in this sense, bias refers to differential item functioning (DIF), wherein a particular population's performance on a test item differs even when trait level is controlled. DIF is detected when persons *at the same trait level* differ in item probabilities, depending on group membership. For example, consider an item from a depression scale that inquires about the amount of treatment sought for the person's depressive episodes. As it has been known that the acceptance and acknowledgment of depression or other mental illnesses differ among ethnic groups, it could be ethnic group membership that drives how much treatment is sought for a person *rather than actual depression severity*. Consequently, this problem of DIF occurs if two people from vastly different ethnic backgrounds (e.g., Italian and British), yet having the same level of depression, respond differently to the above item. On average, the Italian respondent will tend to endorse the higher anchors than the British respondent.

Contrary to a common view, items with different *p* values, or proportion of positive endorsements, across demographic groups are not necessarily biased. In the CTT framework, however, a dependence exists between proportion of people endorsing an item (*p* value) and total score distribution. The mean total score for a distribution is the sum of item *p* values (endorsabilities) across items on a test. Thus, if group means differ, then at least some *p* values will differ among groups as well, indicating bias.

In the IRT framework, the relationship between endorsabilities and item score is different than in CTT. DIF can be detected by examining the item characteristic curves (ICC). These plots contain trace lines for an item that illustrates the relationship between probability of endorsement of the item as a function of trait level as opposed to test score. DIF is reflected by either disparate item discrimination parameters (i.e., the slope of the item characteristic curve) among groups or by disparate item difficulties among groups.

Differential discrimination means that the item provides more information about the trait in one group than in another. Figure 12.5 illustrates differential discriminability for an item across two groups. The item provides less information for the group with the flatter slope. This may be seen, for example, in an item that assesses the degree of social support by asking about number of regular social contacts. Assume the response anchors consist of the following categories: *0–1 contacts, 2–3, greater than 3*. Because women tend to have greater numbers of contacts than men, an item allowing for only the lower ends of the continuum will not discriminate among the levels of the construct of support as well for women as for men. This is an example where an item is capable of more cleanly identifying trait level for one population than for another.

Further, *differential item difficulties* indicate that an item is generally more easily endorsed for one group than for another. In Figure 12.6, the item has a higher probability of endorsement at most trait levels for one group. An unbiased item (i.e., free of DIF) would have both equal item discriminations and equal item difficulties *regardless* of demographic group (for more technical explorations, see Budgell, Raju, & Quartetti, 1995; Fischer, 1993; Potenza & Dorans, 1995; Zwick, 1990, 1997). To illustrate, consider

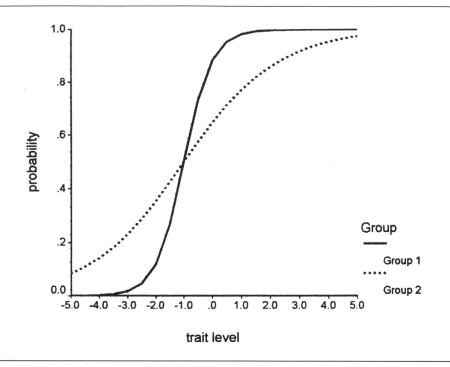

Figure 12.5.   Two items with differential item functioning due to IRT discrimination parameters.

again the above hypothetical social support item, except now imagine the anchors are *0–3 contacts, 4–6 contacts,* and *greater than 6.* Also assume that men and women differ in number of regular social contacts; a man with two regular contacts may feel *equally* as socially supported as a woman having twice that number. In terms of this example, a man endorsing the first response category actually lies higher on the latent continuum than a woman who endorses the same category. Hence, score on this item carries different locations of person on the social support construct depending on whether the respondent is a man or a woman.

DIF has been an active area in assessment research. Ellis, Minsel, and Becker (1989) assessed DIF for an attitudes toward mental health survey across French and German respondents. Both language and cultural differences between respondent groups may led to different interpretations of items. Results showed that, based on ICCs, 8 of 80 items had DIF. After removal of the biased items, French and German group mean differences were reduced. This serves as a clear example of a case where misleading interpretations are made if biased items are included on a test. Drasgow and Hulin (1987) also presented relevant psychometric issues inherent in developing language-fair instruments.

Beyond language and cultural groups, assessment instruments are often used to identify clinical conditions in varying contexts, such as in clinical, subclinical, and nonclinical groups. For example, DIF was assessed for a measure of psychopathic personality disorder (PCL-R) across North American subsamples (Cooke & Michie, 1997). They

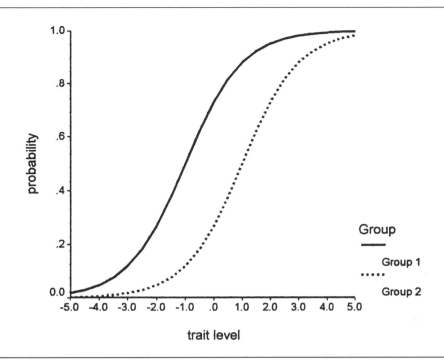

Figure 12.6.   Two items with differential item functioning due to IRT difficulty parameters.

concluded that the PCL-R, based on IRT techniques, showed robust item consistency across different settings (hospital, psychiatric units, outpatient clinics, and prisons) and cultural groups (White and Black prisoners). Other examples in the literature that have utilized IRT in DIF assessment include the detection of differential item functioning for gender groups in the Beck Depression Inventory (BDI; Santor et al., 1994); clinical versus nonclinical DIF of the BDI (Hammond, 1995); DIF as a function of lower versus higher levels of hopelessness (Young, Halper, Clark, & Scheftner, 1992); gender DIF for a Drug Use Screening Inventory (DUSI; Kirisci, Tarter, & Hsu, 1994); and analysis of DIF in language proficiency tests for English and Spanish populations (Woodcock & Munoz-Sandoval, 1993).

Optimal Weights for Relating Item Responses to Trait Level

A third important aspect of scale construction is estimating appropriate item and person parameters to maximize fit of the observed data to the model. In contrast, in CTT, trait level is estimated by summing performance across items. This approach does not utilize item response information efficiently. When items differ in discrimination, the same total score may result from different trait levels, depending on which items are passed or endorsed. In general, endorsing a highly discriminating item implies a higher trait level than endorsing a poorly discriminating item. Thus, employing an IRT model with item discrimination parameters, such as the 2PL in the equation at the beginning of this chapter, will more effectively discriminate between persons.

For rating scale items, an additional problem in optimal weighting may exist. That is, the psychological distance between the rating categories may depend on the specific item. For example, for a Likert-type rating scale, the distance between 1 and 2 may depend on whether the item represents a moderate or an extreme behavior. Employing a polytomous model such as the partial credit model allows for optimal spacing of category distances on the latent trait, and hence more efficient measurement of trait level.

Equating vs. Varying Item Sets

Many individually administered tests employ stopping rules (e.g., basal and ceiling rules) to minimize testing time and to maintain the examinee's motivation. Thus, a person is not given items that are either much too easy or much too hard. Stopping rules are provided to determine when some items can be omitted. Under CTT, equating scores and analyzing psychometric properties required implausible assumptions about the items that were not administered, namely, that the easy items were all passed and that the hard items were all failed. Daniel (in press) notes how such assumptions provide an underestimation of measurement error for the test. IRT is increasingly employed on individually administered tests to equate scores when different item subsets are given. In IRT, trait level is estimated in the context of a model that includes the properties of the items that were actually administered. Thus, differences in the number or difficulty of items administered will be controlled. More extended discussions of trait estimation are given in Hambleton et al. (1991) and Embretson and Reise (1997).

Anchoring and Interpreting Scores

A major principle of testing is that raw scores rarely have meaning. A person's test score, such as number correct or a sum of item ratings, is uninterpretable unless anchored to a standard of comparison. It is nearly axiomatic that the comparison standard is an appropriate norm group. Thus, raw scores are converted to standard scores that reflect relative positions in the distribution of a target population. The normative comparison standard is so prevalent that many psychologists are not aware of alternative comparison standards.

Interestingly, an alternative standard for interpreting scores existed very early in testing; namely, a score obtains meaning by comparisons to items or behaviors. E. L. Thorndike and collaborators (Thorndike, Bregman, Cobb, & Woodyard, 1926) scaled various behaviors and item responses for their intellectual requirements and scaled individuals on a continuum as well. However, the scale values attached to items involved judgments about behavior that soon seemed implausible, so the item or behavior referenced standard was abandoned.

In IRT, items are located on the continuum by the response probabilities for persons at various trait levels. Items and persons are jointly scaled on the latent trait, such as shown in the equation at the beginning of the chapter.

The item-referenced standard has meaning if the items are well ordered on the latent trait; that is, the IRT model fits the item response data. Good fit to a unidimensional IRT model requires that item difficulties are ordered in the same way across persons in the population. In general, persons should endorse items that fall below their trait level and not endorse items that are much above their trait level. Response patterns in which a person endorses difficult items and does not endorse easy items should be quite infrequent. A test that has high internal consistency from CTT indices has constant item difficulty ordering (see Hoyt, 1941).

To illustrate the difference between norm-referenced and item-referenced score interpretations, consider again the FIM scaling shown in Figure 12.2. Suppose that the goal is to assess the everyday living skills of four elderly persons. Figure 12.7 provides a norm-referenced interpretation of scores; the four persons are located in a distribution of appropriate elderly persons aged from 80 to 89. Notice that Anna scores below the mean, Paul is at the mean, and Mary and Vera score above the mean. Unfortunately, although Anna scores below the mean, this comparison standard gives no information about which everyday living skills she has lost and which ones she still possesses. Figure 12.8 provides an item-referenced interpretation; the four persons are located on the scaling of items from Figure 12.2. Behaviors that fall at the person's level are as likely to be successful as to fail, whereas behaviors above their position are much less likely to be accomplished. Thus, Anna's grooming is as often poor as good, whereas successfully dressing the upper body is very unlikely for her. Similarly, the everyday living skills of the other four individuals may be readily interpreted with this item-referenced standard of the item scale.

Some promising applications of IRT models with potential for item- or behavior-referenced comparison standards are appearing in the assessment literature. In psychopathology assessment, Maier and Philipp (1986) scaled six different operational systems for diagnosing depression on a single continuum of severity. They suggest that the person's scale location assesses the decisiveness of the diagnosis. For another example, Bell

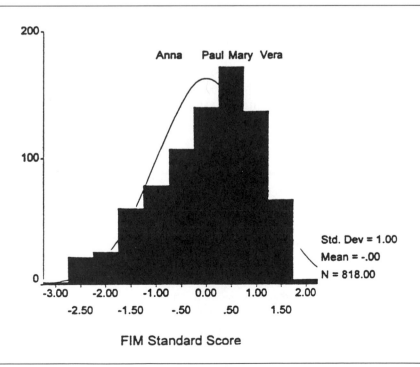

Figure 12.7.   Norm-referenced interpretations for four scores on FIM.

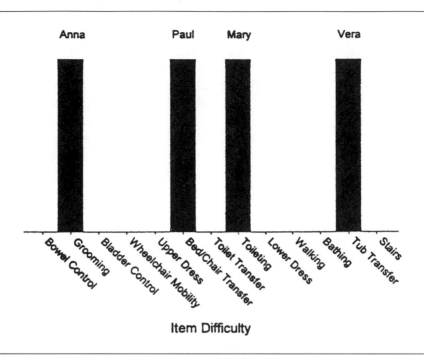

Figure 12.8. Behavior-referenced interpretations for four scores on FIM.

et al. (1994) scaled schizophrenic symptoms by a polytomous IRT model and patients were positioned on the continuum of positive and negative symptoms. In the cognitive domain, early work by Woodcock (1978) using Rasch IRT scaling of abilities and achievement provided interpretations of scores directly in terms of skills. More recently, Embretson (1994) shows how an IRT scaling of a person's change over remedial instruction can be interpreted directly by task performance. Sheridan and Puhl (1996) show that scaling of items and tasks on literacy can provide a behaviorally based standard to interpret a person's skills.

Assessing Person Fit

Our final consideration in scale construction is the estimation of how well a respondent's trait is detected by the items of a scale; or rather, persons may differ in how well a trait level describes their responses to the items. This research area has been alternatively described as "test appropriateness," "traitedness," "aberrant response patterns," and "person fit." A person's response pattern can fail to fit for various reasons, including guessing, inconsistent testing conditions, physical handicaps, misinterpretations of items, response styles, and so forth. Or, more globally, the individual may have an idiosyncratic trait structure.

In IRT, person misfit is detected by the likelihood of a response pattern, given the item parameters and the estimated trait level. Figure 12.9 illustrates responses to four items measured with a 5-point Likert scale format. Persons 1, 2, and 4 are consistent in their responses, although the magnitude of their endorsement differs. Person 4 gives high rating to the items, and Person 1 gives low ratings. Relatively speaking, for all these

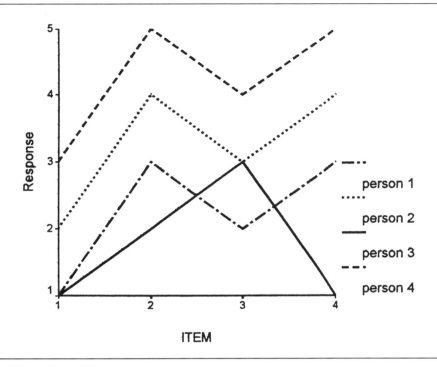

Figure 12.9.   Consistent and inconsistent response patterns.

items, Item 2 and Item 4 are given higher ratings. In contrast, Person 3's response pattern differs qualitatively. Person 3 rates Item 3 relatively higher than the other items. This pattern would be unlikely if most people have response patterns that are like the other three. IRT-based indices of person misfit can assess the appropriateness of a test score for describing the person on the trait. Numerous indices of person fit have been proposed (Reise, 1990, 1995; Reise & Waller, 1993; Tatsuoka & Linn, 1983); however, a detailed discussion is beyond the scope of this chapter. Routine assessment of person fit could provide important information about score meaning.

SUMMARY

This chapter has examined the role of IRT in developing measures that are used in assessment contexts. It was shown that IRT provides important information for both elaborating construct validity and maximizing reliability in scale construction. These results are more adequately given by IRT than by CTT. Examples of current assessment research were given to illustrate the type of problems that IRT addresses.

Beyond the scope of this chapter, but no less important, is using IRT-based indices to guide test use. That is, IRT-based indices are available to handle diverse clinical problems. For example, selecting tests for special clinical populations is optimally handled by using IRT-based test information functions, such as described above. Further, the test administration process for clinical populations can also be guided by individual response patterns. A clinically administered adaptive test (with the examiner using a computer) can help select items to provide maximal information and to assess person fit. For another example, score interpretations may utilize special reference standards. The IRT-based item-referenced scale interpretations described above can be combined with normative anchoring. Thus, an individual's score can be linked to the substantive aspects of item responses for different clinical groups.

Although this chapter has summarized the emerging impact of IRT in two areas of assessment research, the potential scope of impact is potentially much greater.

REFERENCES

Andrich, D. (1978). A rating formulation for ordered response categories. *Psychometrika, 43,* 357–374.

Bell, R. C., Low, L. H., Jackson, H. J., & Dudgeon, P. L. (1994). Latent trait modeling of symptoms of schizophrenia. *Psychological Medicine, 24,* 335–345.

Bock, R. D., Gibbons, R., & Muraki, E. (1988). Full-information item factor analysis. *Applied Psychological Measurement, 12,* 261–280.

Bode, R. K., & Heinemann, A. W. (1997, March). *Inter-disciplinary ratings of FIM motor items.* Paper presented at ninth international Objective Measurement Workshop, Chicago, IL.

Budgell, G. R., Raju, N. S., & Quartetti, D. A. (1995). Analysis of differential item functioning in translated assessment instruments. *Applied Psychological Measurement, 19,* 309–321.

Cooke, D. J., & Michie, C. (1997). An item response theory analysis of the Hare Psychopathy Checklist–Revised. *Psychological Assessment, 9,* 3–14.

Daniel, M. (in press). Behind the scenes: Using new measurement methods on the DAS and KAIT. In S. E. Embretson & S. Hershberger (Eds.), *The new rules of measurement: What every psychologist and educator should know.* Mahwah, NJ: Erlbaum.

Drasgow, F., & Hulin, C. L. (1987). Cross-cultural measurement. *InterAmerican Journal of Psychology, 21,* 1–24.

Ellis, B. B., Minsel, B., & Becker, P. (1989). Evaluation of attitude survey translations: An investigation using item response theory. *International Journal of Psychology, 24,* 665–684.

Embretson, S. E. (1996). The new rules of measurement. *Psychological Assessment, 8,* 341–349.

Embretson, S. E. (1994). Applications of cognitive design systems to test development. In C. R. Reynolds (Ed.), *Cognitive assessment: A multidisciplinary perspective* (pp. 107–136). New York: Plenum Press.

Embretson, S. E., & Reise, S. P. (1997). *Item response theory for psychologists.* Hillsdale, NJ: Erlbaum.

Fischer, G. H. (1973). The linear logistic test model as an instrument in educational research. *Acta Psychologica, 37,* 359–374.

Fischer, G. H. (1993). Notes on the Mantel-Haenszel procedure and another chi-squared test for the assessment of DIF. *Methodika, 7,* 88–100.

Gibbons, R. D., Clarke, D. C., VonAmmon-Cavanaugh, S., & Davis, J. M. (1985). Application of modern psychometric theory in psychiatric research. *Journal of Psychiatric Research, 19,* 43–55.

Grayson, D. A. (1986). Latent trait analysis of the Eysenck personality questionnaire. *Journal of Psychiatric Research, 20,* 217–235.

Hambleton, R. K., Swaminathan, H., & Rogers, H. J. (1991). *Fundamentals of item response theory.* Newbury Park, CA: Sage.

Hammond, S. M. (1995). An IRT investigation of the validity of non-patient analogue research using the Beck Depression Inventory. *European Journal of Psychological Assessment, 11,* 14–20.

Haviland, M. G., & Reise, S. P. (1996). Structure of the twenty-item Toronto Alexthymia Scale. *Journal of Personality Assessment, 66,* 116–125.

Hendryx, M. S., Haviland, M. G., Gibbons, R. D., & Clark, D. C. (1992). An application of item response theory to alexithymia assessment among abstinent alcoholics. *Journal of Personality Assessment, 58,* 506–515.

Herman, C. P., & Mack, D. (1975). Restrained and unrestrained eating. *Journal of Personality, 43,* 647–660.

Hoyt, C. (1941).Test reliability estimated by analysis of variance. *Psychometrika, 6,* 153–160.

Kirisci, L., Moss, H. B., & Tarter, R. E. (1996). Psychometric evaluation of the situational confidence questionnaire in adolescents: Fitting a graded item response model. *Addictive Behaviors, 21,* 303–317.

Kirisci, L., Tarter, R. E., & Hsu, T. (1994). Fitting a two-parameter logistic item response model to clarify the psychometric properties of the drug use screening inventory for adolescent alcohol and drug abusers. *Alcoholism Clinical and Experimental Research, 18,* 1335–1341.

Ludlow, L. H., & Haley, S. M. (1996). Displaying change in functional performance. In G. Engelhard & M. Wilson (Eds.), *Objective measurement: Theory into practice* (Vol. 3). Norwood, NJ: ABLEX.

Ludlow, L. H., Haley, S. M., & Gans, B. M. (1992). A hierarchical model of functional performance in rehabilitation medicine: The Tufts assessment of motor performance. *Evaluation and the Health Professions, 15,* 59–74.

Maier, W., & Philipp, M. (1986). A polydiagnostic scale for dimensional classification of endogenous depression: Derivation and validation. *Acta-Psychiatrica-Scandinavica, 74,* 152–160.

Masters, G. N. (1982). A Rasch model for partial credit scoring. *Psychometrika, 47,* 149–174.

McCollam, K. M., & Embretson, S. E. (1995, August). *A mixed Rasch model defining strategies for spatial folding.* Paper presented at the annual meeting of the American Psychological Association, New York.

Muraki, E. (1993). Information functions of the generalized partial credit model. *Applied Psychological Measurement, 17,* 351–363.

Muraki, E., & Carlson, J. E. (1995). Full-information factor analysis for polytomous item responses: Polytomous item response theory [Special issue]. *Applied Psychological Measurement, 19,* 73–90.

Muraki, E., & Engelhard, G. (1985). Full-information item factor analysis: Applications of EAP scores. *Applied Psychological Measurement, 9,* 417–430.

Potenza, M. T., & Dorans, N. J. (1995). DIF assessment for polytomously scored items: A framework for classification and evaluation. *Applied Psychological Measurement, 19,* 23–37.

Prenovost, L. K. (1996, June). *Applying mixed Rasch models to separate classes with disordered versus normal dieting behaviors.* Paper presented at the meeting of the Psychometric Society, Banff, Canada.

Ramsay, J. O. (1991). Kernel smoothing approaches to nonparametric item characteristic curve estimation. *Psychometrika, 56,* 611–630.

Reise, S. P. (1990). A comparison of item- and person-fit methods of assessing model-data fit in IRT. *Applied Psychological Measurement, 14,* 127–137.

Reise, S. P. (1995). Scoring method and the detection of person misfit in a personality assessment context. *Applied Psychological Measurement, 19,* 213–229.

Reise, S. P., & Gomel, J. N. (1995). Modeling qualitative variation within latent trait dimensions: Application of mixed-measurement to personality assessment. *Multivariate Behavioral Research, 30,* 341–358.

Reise, S. P., & Waller, N. G. (1993). Traitedness and the assessment of response pattern scalability. *Journal of Personality and Social Psychology, 65,* 143–151.

Roskam, E. E., & Broers, N. (1996). Constructing questionnaires: An application of facet design and item response theory to the study of lonesomeness. In G. Engelhard & M. Wilson (Eds.), *Objective measurement: Theory into practice* (Vol. 3). Norwood, NJ: ABLEX.

Rost, J. (1992). *MIRA: A PC-program for the mixed Rasch model—user manual.* Kiel, Germany: Institute for Science Education.

Samejima, F. (1969). Estimation of latent ability using a response pattern of graded scores. *Psychometrika Monograph Supplement, 34,* 100.

Santor, D. A., Ramsay, J. O., & Zuroff, D. C. (1994). Nonparametric item analyses of the Beck depression inventory: Evaluating gender item bias and response option weights. *Psychological Assessment, 6,* 255–270.

Sheridan, B., & Puhl, L. (1996). Evaluating an indirect measure of student literacy competencies in higher education using Rasch measurement. In G. Engelhard & M. Wilson (Eds.), *Objective measurement: Theory into practice* (Vol. 3). Norwood, NJ: ABLEX.

Snyder, S., & Sheehan, R. (1992). The Rasch measurement model: An introduction. *Journal of Early Intervention, 16,* 87–95.

Tatsuoka, K. K., & Linn, R. L. (1983). Indicies for detecting unusual patterns: Links between two general approaches and potential applications. *Applied Psychological Measurement, 7,* 81–96.

Thorndike, E. L., Bregman, E. O., Cobb, M. V., & Woodyard, E. (1926). *The measurement of intelligence.* New York: Teachers College Bureau of Publications.

Vale, C. D. (1986). Linking item parameters onto a common scale. *Applied Psychological Measurement, 10,* 333–344.

Waller, N. (in press). Searching for structure in the MMPI. In S. E. Embretson & S. Hershberger (Eds.), *The new rules of measurement: What every psychologist and educator should know.* Mahwah, NJ: Erlbaum.

Woodcock, R. W. (1978). *Development and standardization of the Woodcock-Johnson psychoeducational battery.* Itasca, IL: Riverside.

Woodcock, R. W., & Munoz-Sandoval, A. F. (1993). An IRT approach to cross-language test equating and interpretation: Behavioral assessment [Special issue]. *European Journal of Psychological Assessment, 9,* 233–241.

Young, M. A., Halper, I. S., Clark, D. C., & Scheftner, W. A. (1992). An item-response theory evaluation of the Beck hopelessness scale. *Cognitive Therapy and Research, 16,* 579–587.

Zwick, R. (1990). When do item response functions and Mantel-Haenszel definitions of differential item functioning coincide? *Journal of Educational Statistics, 15,* 185–197.

Zwick, R. (1997). The effect of adaptive administration on the variability of the Mantel-Haenszel measure of differential item functioning. *Educational and Psychological Measurement, 57,* 412–421.

PART THREE

AREAS OF CLINICAL RESEARCH: TREATMENT

Chapter 13

APPLICATION OF TIME-SERIES (SINGLE-SUBJECT) DESIGNS IN CLINICAL PSYCHOLOGY

SCOTT T. GAYNOR, M.A., SUSAN C. BAIRD, M.A., and ROSEMERY O. NELSON-GRAY, PH.D.

A gulf exists between research and practice in clinical psychology (Rice, 1997). It has been suggested that researchers are not sufficiently guided by clinical discoveries, and that practitioners, though valuing research findings, do not access these from traditional research journals (Beutler, Williams, Wakefield, & Entwistle, 1995). Reflecting on the centennial of clinical psychology, Meehl (1997) commented on the fallibility of anecdotal evidence (i.e., clinical experience) and the need for quantitative research. Practitioners, however, often struggle to generalize from large-scale, quantitative research findings, where results are reported as probabilities of efficacy across groups, to the unique situation of an individual client (Stricker & Trierweiler, 1995). Thus, Stricker and Trierweiler call for a local clinical scientist model, whereby practitioners apply not only general research findings, but also employ a scientific attitude, or scientific thinking, in individualizing treatment for specific clients in the local setting.

The issues introduced above could be addressed if a methodology existed that is pragmatic and useful for the practicing clinician, more scientifically rigorous than anecdotal impressions, and sensitive to the individual nature of clinical cases. We argue that time-series (i.e., single-subject) designs are such a methodology.[1] This chapter explores the major reasons to use these designs, the fundamental information needed for their application, and the different component elements of which they are comprised. Where possible, examples from the clinical literature are employed. This chapter is written to highlight the basic knowledge needed to implement single-subject designs and to provide numerous examples of their use. As such, space does not allow for an exhaustive account of all the methodological subtleties involved in single-subject designs. The interested reader is directed to books by Barlow and Hersen (1984), Hayes, Barlow, and Nelson-Gray (in press), and Kratochwill (1978) for more exhaustive analyses.

---

[1] Time-series and single-subject will be used interchangeably in this chapter. The former is somewhat preferable as it places the focus on the design rather than the number of subjects involved, as time-series designs often involve more than one subject.

WHY USE TIME-SERIES METHODOLOGY?

The reasons to employ time-series methods include both the practical and the empirical. Practically, demonstrating accountability and cost-effectiveness of treatment is becoming increasingly necessary in the current managed care environment (Giles, 1991). Time-series methods can enhance clinicians' ability to demonstrate the effectiveness of their interventions without a great deal of additional effort. Practitioners, in their clinical decision making, likely use a similar rationale to that recommended in time-series designs (Hayes, 1981). For instance, initial sessions with the client are likely to focus on assessment (i.e., determining the frequency, intensity, duration, and historical context of the client's difficulties). This is the baseline against which the intervention will be judged. The outcome of this initial assessment is a case conceptualization, sometimes called a functional analysis, which points (implicitly or explicitly) toward the critical dependent variables that will be the focus of treatment. The subsequent treatment is the independent variable. Broadly speaking, time-series designs simply involve more systematic delineation of these aspects of clinical intervention.

As well as being consistent with the rationale of routine clinical practice, time-series designs may actually enhance clinical practice. The systematic nature of time-series designs may increase precision in making assessment and treatment decisions. For instance, frequent objective measures provide feedback for the clinician that allows for the potential alteration of ineffective interventions and the continuation of effective ones.

Empirically, time-series designs can address many of the scientifically important questions raised in the clinical environment (e.g., Does a treatment work? Which of two treatments is most effective? Are they both effective? What are the "active" components of a treatment?) (Hayes, Barlow, & Nelson-Gray, in press). In addition, time-series designs seem to provide a direct mechanism for the integration of research and practice. On the one hand, researchers often use large numbers of homogeneous subjects to demonstrate the efficacy of interventions. The generality of these efficacious treatments, however, is often less well established (Seligman, 1995). This is where practicing clinicians could make important contributions, using more idiographic and flexible, yet rigorous, time-series designs (Hayes et al., in press). On the other hand, clinicians, especially those of a psychodynamic orientation, find that "the traditional case report remains our most compelling means of communicating clinical findings" (Spence, 1993, p. 37). Logically, however, to go from a traditional case study to a more scientifically rigorous time-series design simply involves increased quantification of the dependent variable and greater specification of the independent variable, which is increasingly becoming recognized by psychodynamically oriented researchers and clinicians (e.g., Fonagy & Moran, 1993). Finally, the implementation of time-series designs may help increase the likelihood that researchers are informed and influenced by the expertise of practicing clinicians.

FUNDAMENTALS OF TIME-SERIES METHODOLOGY

The objective when using time-series methodology, like any experimental methodology, is to distinguish the effects that result from a given intervention (i.e., the independent variable) from effects that may be caused by unrelated variables (extraneous variability or error in measurement). In short, the objective is to rule out threats to internal validity. When the effects can clearly be attributed to the independent variable, the experiment is internally valid (Kazdin, 1980). In this broad sense, time-series methodology is no different from group comparison approaches. The major distinction between time-series and group designs is that in the former, the effects are analyzed at the level of the individual. This requires that data be collected in a fashion that facilitates the making of valid inferences at the idiographic level (Kazdin, 1981). In this section, we highlight some of the major issues and design characteristics influencing the likelihood that valid inferences can be drawn. These are also summarized in Table 13.1.

Type of Dependent Measures

Time-series designs require the use of objective dependent measures that accurately and sensitively measure the important units of behavior targeted for change (e.g., as determined in the initial assessment and conceptualization of a clinical case). The clinically important units may include client actions, or overt behavior; cognition, or verbal behavior; and/or physiological responses (Nelson, 1981). For instance, Ferguson and Rodway (1994), in a study of cognitive-behavioral treatment for perfectionism, measured both perfectionistic thoughts (via two questionnaires) and instances of perfectionistic behaviors (agreed upon by the therapist and the client).

The collecting of dependent measures should begin early in therapy, possibly before the first session with the client. For instance, Beck, Rush, Shaw, and Emery (1979) mailed initial assessment measures to clients to bring completed to the first session. In many clinical settings, clients spend a period of time on a waiting list, time that could

Table 13.1. Characteristics of the design and major threats to internal validity to be considered in drawing inferences from time-series data

Characteristics of the Design

Objective data

Continuous assessment

Stability of problem

Immediate and marked effects

Replication with multiple subjects or reversals

Major Threats to Internal Validity

Coincidental external/extraneous events

Maturation/learning (gradual biological or psychological processes occurring within a person over time)

Testing/assessment (reactivity; potential changes as the result of assessment)

Statistical regression (regression to the mean)

Variability

Multiple intervention interference (order effects, carryover effects, alternation effects)

Source: Adapted from Kazdin, 1981; Hayes et al., in press.

be used for assessment. Taking measures early allows for an adequate baseline to be established while not unnecessarily delaying treatment.

In addition to beginning data collection early, multiple measures that are both global and specific should be taken initially. The use of a broad range of measures early in the course of therapy is consistent with the general clinical practice of using the first sessions for initial assessment and information gathering. Taking multiple measures may appear cumbersome as some measures are lengthy and time consuming. However, there are several remedies for this. First, after the initial assessment, some areas that are not targeted for treatment will no longer need to be assessed. Second, more practical measures can be utilized more frequently and global, lengthier, or more difficult measures less often. In a study combining cognitive therapy and interpersonal therapy for depression, Jensen (1994) had subjects complete the 21-item Beck Depression Inventory (BDI; Beck et al., 1979) weekly, whereas the more global Social Adjustment Scale (SAS; Weissman & Paykel, 1974) was completed only at pre- and posttreatment.

The Jensen (1994) study highlights another critical point: Measures need to be taken repeatedly over the course of the initial assessment, during treatment, and, ideally, at follow-up after treatment. The quality of the measure as well as its practical utility should be considered in determining which measures to use most often (see Fischer & Corcoran, 1994, for actual questionnaire measures covering a wide range of clinical symptoms and for use with adults, children, couples, and families; see also Nelson, 1981, for discussion of a broad range of realistic dependent measures involving self-monitoring, direct observation, self-ratings, and self-report).

The final point regarding the taking of dependent measures relates to the situation specificity of behavior (Mischel, 1968). Because a client's responding may be situationally determined, the conditions under which dependent measures are taken should be similar across measurement instances to the extent possible. For instance, Ferguson and Rodway (1994) asked clients to complete each weekly measurement package in the same location and at the same time during the day.

There are several cautions in order when taking repeated measures with the same instrument. Many of these cautions apply any time dependent measures are taken and are not unique to repeated measures. In general, the concerns described below involve alternative explanations for observed changes and are thus threats to internal validity (see Table 13.1). One potential problem involves reactivity to the measurement process. Reactivity is defined as behavioral change that results simply from the awareness that one's behavior is being monitored. As this change in behavior is not the result of the intervention, but may appear as such, it is a threat to internal validity. However, as reactivity to measurement generally occurs at the onset of measurement, the collection of a careful baseline provides a protection against attributing such effects to the intervention. It is also important to reduce demand characteristics that may be associated with assessment. That is, clients may report positive therapeutic effects when in fact such results are absent. For instance, after several weeks of treatment, a client may feel obligated to report some positive changes for reasons such as feeling warmly toward the therapist, wanting to please the therapist, or because he or she is paying for the service rather than because improvement has actually occurred. Taking multiple measures of different types (e.g., global and specific as well as self-report and direct observation) and discussing the measurement process, including the client's reaction to and experience of it, may reduce the likelihood that demand characteristics significantly impact the results. A final concern results from the tendency for extreme scores to revert toward the mean without intervention. Such an effect is called regression to the mean. For instance, clients presenting to therapy in extreme distress may report a reduction in symptoms over the course of treatment that may be better accounted for by a return to previous levels of functioning as opposed to effective treatment. A constant-series control (see below) may provide some protection against statistical regression. The use of a constant-series control allows for a between-series comparison of treatment versus no-treatment, controlling for regression to the mean, which should have a comparable impact in both series. Also, establishing a relatively stable preintervention baseline provides some protection against regression to the mean. That is, the more similar the baseline scores within a series, the more unlikely it is that they are simply transient extreme scores, which would subsequently regress to the mean. It is to the topic of establishing a preintervention baseline that we now turn.

Establishing a Preintervention Baseline or A Phase

Measurement typically begins prior to intervention, and this is called the baseline or A phase (Barlow & Hersen, 1984). The baseline provides the basis with which the intervention (B phase) will be evaluated. That is, the baseline involves repeated measures of the client's behavior as it is maintained in the absence of intervention. The rationale is that without intervention the baseline should continue and, therefore, provide a prediction of what would occur in the absence of treatment.

An ideal baseline allows for the assessment of level, trend, and variability (Hayes et al., in press). Level is essentially some measure of the magnitude of the dependent variable, such as a BDI score of 30 (BDI scores between 0 and 9 are considered normal, 10 to 20 mild depression, 20 to 30 moderate depression, and greater than 30 severe depression [Kendall, Hollon, Beck, Hammen, & Ingram, 1987]). Trend refers to the pattern of the dependent variable during baseline and is analogous to slope. For instance, BDI scores of 20 and 40 over two consecutive weeks of baseline would suggest a trend toward increasing symptoms of depression (a steep slope). However, BDI scores of 32, 27, and 31 suggest very little trend in the data (a shallow slope). Variability in the dependent measures collected influences our confidence in the estimates of the level and trend of the behavior. For instance, a client with baseline BDI scores of 32, 27, and 31 provides a more stable baseline than a client with BDI scores of 20, 40, and 30.

The minimum number of data points needed for an assessment of level, trend, and variability is three (although level can be assessed with one data point and trend with two) (Hayes et al., in press). The more data the better, as this provides a comprehensive picture of what is occurring in the absence of treatment and is used as a predictor of future client functioning with which treatment results will be compared. The clinical environment often limits the amount of baseline data that can be gathered. That is, in some clinical situations, such as with a client expressing suicidal ideation, immediate treatment is required. At a minimum, the level, trend, and variability in baseline must allow for an effect to be seen if it occurs. Assessment of baseline functioning can serve clinically and scientifically useful purposes. If the level of a client's responding to the BDI, for example, is repeatedly in the normal range, an intervention targeting depression may not be warranted practically and effects may not be visible. Similarly, if the trend in the baseline data is in the direction expected by the intervention, it makes it more difficult to determine treatment effects. The top panel of Figure 13.1, adapted from Ferguson and Rodway's (1994) study of the treatment of perfectionism with cognitive-behavioral therapy, illustrates such a case. Notice how the major decrease in irrational values occurs prior to the initiation of treatment. A substantial additional decrease would be needed to demonstrate a treatment effect. One is also left wondering what was occurring during the first two assessment periods for this client. It is possible the individual had several particularly difficult days (possibly due to some coincidental events) that temporarily elevated the scores, which subsequently decreased to reflect the individual's more average functioning (regression to the mean) throughout the remainder of baseline.

The middle panel of Figure 13.1 demonstrates a highly variable baseline that stabilizes when treatment begins and decreases in Week 7. Confidence in the treatment effect is bolstered because the latter data points fall clearly outside the range of the variable baseline. However, the potential effect of extraneous events occurring in Week 7 needs to be ruled out as an explanation for the abrupt decrease at that time. Ideally, the abrupt decrease would occur earlier in treatment. This point emphasizes the tendency to place more confidence in effects that are large in magnitude and occur immediately when the intervention is implemented. The effects pursued in clinical work are often more gradual, however. In addition, some treatments are presented over several sessions, and, therefore, an immediate effect would not be expected. In these cases, other strategies (e.g., replication) are available to bolster confidence that the intervention produced the gradual or delayed effects.

There is no one solution to dealing with excessively variable baseline data. Hayes et al. (in press) make four recommendations: analyze potential sources of variation, continue baseline, evaluate the level/unit of analysis being used, and proceed with the intervention anyway. Notice, in the middle portion of Figure 13.1, that Ferguson and Rodway (1994) decided to proceed with the intervention despite the variability. This decision may have been made because they thought that even with the variability an acceptable treatment effect could be demonstrated if it occurred, and/or they felt an ethical responsibility to begin treatment. Interestingly, Ferguson and Rodway took baseline data every three days and intervention data weekly, thus using somewhat different units across the conditions. Blocking (or "chunking") data in baseline so that the unit is now a weekly composite reduces the variability significantly and reveals a moderate downward trend (see bottom of Figure 13.1). Altering the unit of analysis is not a trick to turn poor data into good data. A rationale should always be provided. In this case, the rationale was that different units were being compared across conditions and that the additional measures taken in baseline may have increased the likelihood that extraneous daily factors were included in these data that would be less likely to be included in a weekly measure.

Implementing the Intervention or B Phase

As discussed previously, the goal of time-series designs is to rule out threats to internal validity, thereby strengthening confidence that any effects noted are the product of the intervention (i.e., independent variable). Thus, it is important that only one independent variable be introduced at a time (Hayes, 1981). If two or more independent variables are

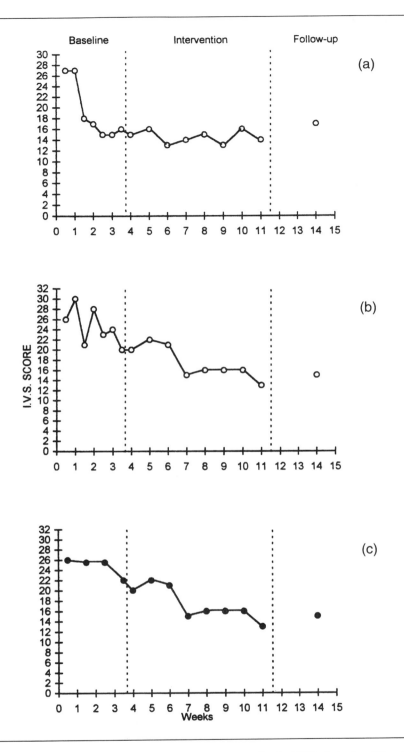

Figure 13.1. A graphic display of the Irrational Values Scale (IVS) data for Client 6 is shown in (a). It demonstrates a trend in the baseline data in the direction expected of treatment. The graphic display of the IVS data for Client 3 is shown in (b); it demonstrates a highly variable baseline. The same data for Client 3 is presented in (c) but with the baseline data blocked, or chunked, by the current authors to create a weekly composite of data points during baseline, as a weekly measure was used during treatment.

Source: Panels (a) and (b) modified from Ferguson, K.L., & Rodway, M.R. (1994). Cognitive behavioral treatment of perfectionism: Initial evaluation studies. *Research on Social Work Practice, 4,* pp. 294, 297. Copyright © 1994 by Sage Publication, Inc. Reprinted with permission.

introduced simultaneously, their effects are confounded and inseparable. Note, however, that a single intervention may involve multiple pieces (e.g., in-session hypothesis testing, homework assignments) but can still be conceptualized as a single independent variable if it is the effect of the entire treatment package that is being analyzed. If different components of a treatment package are to be analyzed, then they would have to be introduced separately.

It is also desirable to keep phase lengths as similar as possible. When phase lengths are extremely discrepant, the chances for extraneous events to occur increases in the lengthier phase. As noted earlier, it would be rare in clinical situations to have a lengthier baseline than intervention. Avoiding overly lengthy baselines is defensible for ethical reasons; however, it does increase the chances for the introduction of uncontrolled sources of variation during intervention. Potential solutions include collecting as much baseline data as a reasonable assessment period allows and utilizing additional controls (e.g., replication) to strengthen conclusions.

The impact of the intervention is evaluated relative to the baseline. That is, it is assumed that without the intervention, the baseline would proceed along a course similar to that which has been established. Deviation from baseline, at the point of or during the course of the intervention, is attributed to the intervention if the threats to internal validity listed in Table 13.1 are adequately addressed. Earlier, we discussed establishing estimates of level, trend, and variability in baseline. When assessing for intervention effects, the focus is generally on changes in level or trend that occur during the intervention phase compared to the level and trend established during baseline. (Note: This is not to suggest that variability is unimportant, as the data must be stable enough that an effect can be noticed if it occurs; however, clinical interventions are generally not designed with a goal of reducing or increasing variability.)

Figure 13.2 uses hypothetical data to clearly demonstrate patterns of change in level or trend (i.e., slope) from baseline to intervention (Kazdin, 1984). A change in level between baseline and intervention is noted by an immediate change when the intervention is introduced (see panels a, c, and f in Figure 13.2). A change in trend following the introduction of the intervention is noted by a change in the slope, or angle, of the data points relative to baseline (see panels c, d, e, and f in Figure 13.2) (Kazdin, 1984). Finally, notice that changes in level and trend are not necessarily indicative of changes in the mean (or average) performance across phases (see panels d and f) (Kazdin, 1984).

The hypothetical functions shown in Figure 13.2 illustrate the difference between changes in level and trend. In addition, the functions are designed such that changes across phases in level and trend, or the lack thereof, are easy to discriminate visually. In fact, visual analysis of data is the most common interpretive technique for time-series data. Visual analysis is accomplished by graphing the data with the abscissa (X-axis) of the graph generally representing time (e.g., session number, day, week) and the ordinate (Y-axis) providing an index of the dependent measure. Phase changes, or any other alteration of conditions, are also indicated on the graph (see the vertical lines in Figure 13.1 marking the onset and conclusion of treatment). For a thorough discussion of graphing, see Krishef (1991). The reliance on visual analysis of graphed data highlights the importance placed in time-series methodology on large effects visible at the level of the individual. The graphical presentation of data points over time allows for these changes to be evaluated. This is in contrast to between-group research designs where outcome is

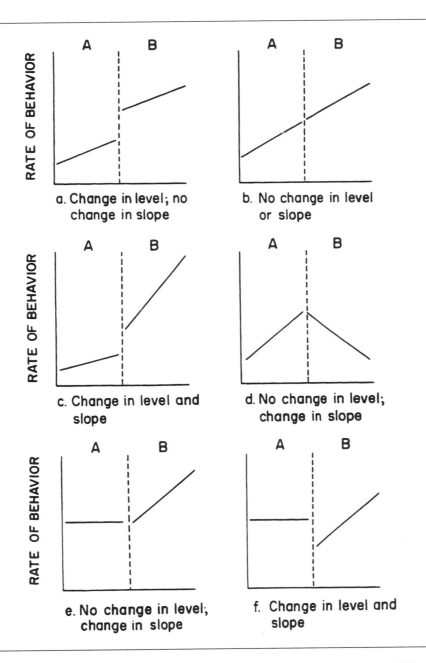

Figure 13.2.   Examples of selected patters of data over two phases (A and B), illustrating changes in level and/or trend.

Source: Kazdin, A.E. (1984). Statistical analyses for single-case experimental designs. In D.H. Barlow & M. Hersen (Eds.), Single case experimental designs: Strategies for studying behavior change (2nd ed., p. 298). Copyright © 1984 by Simon & Schuster. Reprinted with permission of the author.

typically judged by comparing pre- and posttreatment using statistical analyses. These issues are discussed in more detail in the section below entitled "Issues in Analyzing Time-Series."

In communicating the results of a time-series design, it is important that the researcher/practitioner specify the intervention that is used. This specification should be as detailed as possible, such that other competent professionals can employ the intervention and replicate the results. It is also beneficial to report any attempt made to assess treatment integrity—that treatment occurred as specified—which may involve recording sessions to be analyzed later for the presence of critical therapy components (Nelson-Gray, 1994; see also Waltz, Addis, Koerner, & Jacobson, 1993, for a review of strategies for assessing treatment integrity). The growing body of treatment manuals available to clinicians provides a model of the type of specification possible (Wilson, 1996, 1997). Also, these manuals provide a ready description of interventions waiting to be evaluated in the local clinical setting.

In addition to detailing the intervention, the defining characteristics of the clients should be described as objectively as possible. This might include a description of the presenting problem, *Diagnostic and Statistical Manual of Mental Disorders,* 4th edition *(DSM-IV)* diagnosis, case formulation developed, and other relevant background information (Hayes et al., in press). For example, in his treatment of four adolescents with panic disorder with agoraphobia, Ollendick (1995) indicated each subject's age, race, gender, *DSM* diagnoses, history of the problem, degree of severity, and course of the disorder.

Replication

In the preceding sections, several comments have been made about the need to strike a balance between research design and clinical reality. Specifically, in the clinical setting, baselines may not be as long or stable as desirable and effects may be gradual and cumulative rather than large and immediate. These realities point to the critical importance of replicating results. Time-series methodology relies heavily on the assumption that it is unlikely that similar effects across successive interventions are due to coincidence (Hayes, 1981; Hayes et al., in press). The rationale is that each replication of an intervention diminishes the odds that extraneous coincidence produced the results.

Replications can be arranged to occur across subjects (as in A-B replication series or multiple baseline designs across individuals) or within a particular subject (as in A-B-A-B designs or multiple baseline designs across behaviors). Replications across and within clients help increase confidence in the effectiveness of the intervention. Furthermore, replication across subjects is critical for determining the external validity (or generalizability) of the intervention.

The type of replication pursued depends on the situation. For instance, many clinical interventions, if effective, cannot be replicated in the same client. For instance, many treatments are designed to be prophylactic, such that effective therapy reduces the likelihood of relapse after termination. A greater understanding of the available design strategies and their strengths and weaknesses will help in determining which designs best fit a given situation. The following sections describe the major design elements.

TIME-SERIES ELEMENTS

Consistent with Hayes (1981), Hayes et al. (in press), and Kratochwill (1992), we categorize the time-series elements based on the kind of inferences that each type of element allows. Table 13.2 presents the three major design elements along with a brief description of their defining characteristics.

Within-Series Elements

In within-series design elements, inferences are drawn from the intraseries changes that occur following a phase change. A phase is defined as all the measures taken in one stimulus condition or level of the independent variable (e.g., A phase and B phase), and each phase is evaluated relative to the preceding and succeeding phases (i.e., across time) (Hayes et al., in press).

Simple Phase Changes

A simple phase change begins with the establishment of an estimate of the level, trend, and variability in the data series (baseline). The independent variable (intervention) is

Table 13.2.   Three major time-series designs and their associated characteristics

Design Type	Representative Example(s)	Characteristics
Within-series elements	Simple phase change (e.g., A/B, A/B/A, A/B/A/B) Complex phase change (e.g., interaction element: B/B+C/B; combined simple-phase changes: A/B/A/C/A)	In these design elements, estimates of variability, level, and trend within a data series are assessed under similar conditions; the independent variable is introduced; and concomitant changes are assessed in the stability, level, and trend across phases of a single series.
Between-series elements	Alternating treatments design	In these design elements, estimates of variability, level, and trend in a data series are measured within a specific condition and across time. Outcome is assessed by comparing the series from two or more specific conditions.
Combined-series elements	Multiple baseline (e.g., across subjects, behaviors, settings)	In these design elements, comparisons are made both between and within a data series. Repetitions of an A/B simple phase change are arranged (across subjects, behaviors, or settings) such that the length and timing of the phases differ across repetitions.

Source: Adapted from Hayes, 1981; Kratochwill, 1992.

then manipulated, while measurement procedures remain constant, creating the phase change. An effect of the phase change is noted when the intervention produces significant changes in the level or trend of the data series compared to the preceding phase. As mentioned earlier, the significance of the change must be evaluated in reference to the amount of variability in the series.

A/B Design   An A/B design involves two phases: a baseline phase and the intervention phase. Without replication, an effect demonstrated using this design has no internal validity because other causes of change (other than the intervention) cannot be ruled out. However, a series of A/B designs across clients has both internal and external (i.e., generalizability) validity.

Jensen (1994) treated nine women meeting *DSM-III-R* criteria for major depressive disorder. The clients were randomly assigned to no baseline or baseline lengths of 3, 4, or 5 weeks (the waiting list at the community mental health center was approximately 10 weeks), followed by eight sessions of integrated cognitive and interpersonal therapy. The results, shown in Figure 13.3, are compelling. All clients began therapy with BDI scores in the moderately severe or extremely severe range and by the conclusion of treatment were in the normal range. These results allow Jensen to demonstrate accountability and also allow for causal statements to be made about the results. In essence, nine independent replications are provided, and this, in combination with the known efficacy of cognitive and interpersonal approaches in the treatment of depression (Dobson, 1989; Elkin et al., 1989), make the most parsimonious explanation that the results were caused by the treatment. Furthermore, the clients were self-referred to a community mental health center for treatment. This allows statements to be made about the generalizability of the treatment to an outpatient clinical environment.

Also, consider the changes in terms of level and trend. Examine the data of Subjects 3, 6, and 7 in Figure 13.3. Comparing the intervention to the baseline data, there appears to be no change in level, but there is a change in trend, as the slope of the intervention points is steeper than the baseline slope. Contrast this with the data from Subject 5, where there is a change in both level and trend from baseline to intervention. Subjects 2, 8, and 9 show what might be interpreted as small changes in level and a rather large change in slope comparing baseline and intervention phases. These data suggest that the integrated cognitive-behavioral and interpersonal therapy often did not produce an immediate change in depressive symptoms during the first session. Instead, a steady decrease in symptoms across the treatment was observed.

Not all treatments are going to be as effective as that demonstrated by Jensen (1994). However, failure to demonstrate an effect of treatment can provide important insights into the limitations of the treatment. If a client is showing limited or no improvement, there are at least three options: (a) wait; (b) try an entirely new treatment, thus concluding that A = B and creating an A = B/C design; or (c) adjust the current treatment, possibly adding or subtracting portions, creating an A = B/B + C design. Worse than no improvement, it is possible a client will show a deterioration in functioning. In this case, it is critical to determine what is producing the deterioration. Withdrawing treatment allows for some assessment of the role of the treatment in producing the deterioration (Hayes et al., in press).

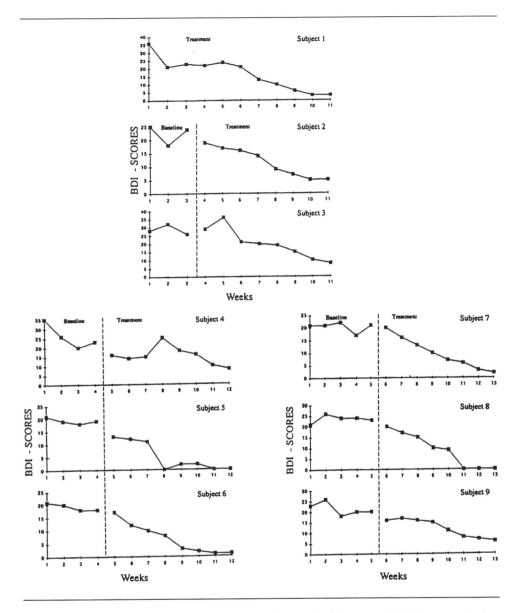

Figure 13.3.   The top column displays Beck Depression Inventory (BDI) scores during 11 weeks of treatment for Clients 1 through 3. The bottom left column displays BDI scores during 12 weeks of treatment for Clients 4 through 6. The bottom right column displays BDI scores during 13 weeks of treatment for Clients 7 through 9.

Source: From Jensen, C. (1994). Psychosocial treatment of depression in women: Nine single-subject evaluations. *Research on Social Work Practice, 4,* pp. 277–279. Copyright © 1994 by Sage Publication, Inc. Reprinted with permission.

A/B/A and A/B/A/B Designs   These designs involve the withdrawal of treatment in the second A phase (A/B/A) and then the reintroduction in the second B phase (A/B/A/B). The second A phase is often called a return to baseline; however, intervention-related changes may persist (and in the clinical setting, interventions are usually designed with this as a goal), such that a true return to baseline is not possible. This is somewhat problematic because from a scientific perspective, the goal of the second A phase is to demonstrate that the dependent measure tracks the changing conditions (Barlow & Hersen, 1984). However, from a clinical perspective, the goal is to maintain therapeutic gains despite the change in conditions, an outcome that weakens the internal validity of the design. As well, deliberately removing a successful intervention is ethically questionable. Again, a balance must be achieved between research ideals and clinical reality. For instance, therapy is often time-limited, and if a client has completed an entire course of therapy for which there is a rationale for expecting gains to be maintained, the second A phase can provide data to support this belief. In this case, a minimum second A phase consists of a single follow-up measure taken after the conclusion of treatment and often at a specified interval (e.g., 1 month, 3 months, 1 year). As always, the more data that can be collected, the better.

Some interventions may not be expected to persist, however. For instance, if a client diagnosed with obsessive-compulsive disorder (OCD) receives several sessions of exposure and response prevention therapy (e.g., Hiss, Foa, & Kozak, 1994), initial improvement may be noted. If the client then misses several therapy sessions, these initial gains may not be expected to persist. A natural withdrawal design has been created. In addition, the reintroduction of therapy provides the opportunity for an A/B/A/B reversal to be demonstrated. This hypothetical (but common) therapy situation points out how these designs can be modified to accommodate unanticipated circumstances, as well as be used in an a priori fashion as outlined earlier. The A/B/A/B design is more ethically defensible than the A/B/A design in that the final phase consists of the intervention (Barlow & Hersen, 1984). This does not obviate collecting subsequent follow-up measures, as mentioned above, to determine the maintenance of therapeutic gains.

Bulik, Epstein, and Kaye (1990) provide an example of the utilization of an A/B/A/B design in the treatment of laxative abuse with a female inpatient diagnosed with bulimia. The client was allowed to self-administer up to six doses of either an active drug laxative or a placebo in alternating phases. The outcome measures consisted of both overt behavior, the actual number of daily doses administered, as well as self-reports of subjective cravings for the laxative. As shown in Figure 13.4, the number of doses administered was high and steady during the active drug phase and decreased during the placebo phase. This rate increased when the active drug was reintroduced and, finally, decreased substantially in the final phase. A similar pattern was noted for subjective reports of craving. The change in the rate of self-administered doses and subjective cravings for the laxative followed the change in conditions providing evidence for internal validity. There is limited evidence for external validity as only one subject was used; replication is needed to generalize from these findings. This study demonstrates through the use of an A/B/A/B design that the presentation of stimulus cues associated with laxative use (placebo) without the accompanying reinforcer (active drug) led to the extinction of subjective reports of cravings for the drug, as well as

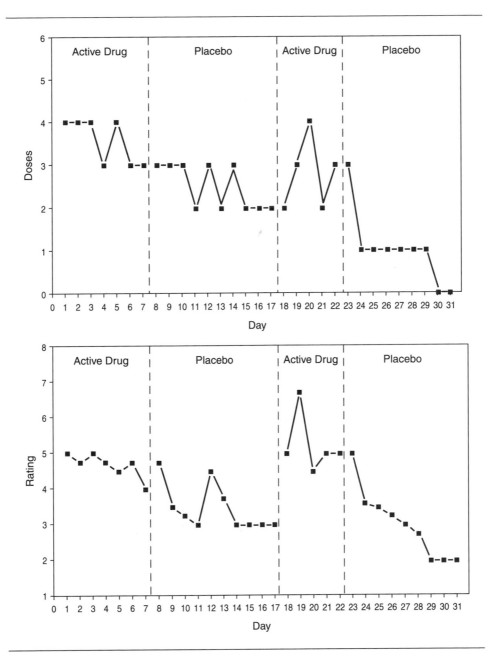

Figure 13.4.   The top panel is a graphic display of the daily doses of laxative or placebo self-administered. The bottom panel is a graphic display of the mean daily cravings (average of four daily postmeal ratings).

Source: From Bulik, C.M., Epstein, L.H., & Kaye, W. (1990). Treatment of laxative abuse in a female with bulimia nervosa using an operant extinction paradigm. *Journal of Substance Abuse, 2,* pp. 384–385. Copyright © 1994 by Ablex Publishing Corporation. Reprinted with permission.

a decrease in the rate of self-administration. See also Himadi and Curran (1995) for an additional example of an A/B/A/B design examining a treatment for the reduction of auditory hallucinations.

Complex Phase Changes

As a within-series design element, inferences from complex phase change designs are based on comparing a subsequent phase to a preceding phase (see Table 13.2). What complex phase changes add is the ability to assess the interaction of different portions of an intervention or to determine if two treatments are both effective (Hayes et al., in press).

Interaction Element   The interaction element allows for an assessment of the additive effects of treatment. This might be used when a component is to be added to (or subtracted from) a treatment that is known to be efficacious (possibly because the known efficacious treatment is not providing maximal results in a given case). Kohlenberg and Tsai (1994) provide a relevant example. They hypothesized that adding functional analytic psychotherapy (FAP) might increase the effectiveness of cognitive therapy (CT) with a depressed male client. Initially, CT was employed (without a no-treatment baseline phase), followed by an integration of FAP and CT creating a B/B + C design (see Figure 13.5). This is logically analogous to an A/B design (which could be written A/A + B), and all the weaknesses of an A/B design apply (Hayes, 1981). Kohlenberg and Tsai's data suggest that for this subject, adding FAP to CT resulted in a greater response to treatment. However, the design could be strengthened in several ways. The internal validity could be strengthened by adding a second B phase (e.g., B/B + C/B) and/or by providing replication across clients using the same and different sequences (e.g., B/B + C, B + C/B, B + C/B/B + C). Such replication would also help to control for the possibility of multiple intervention interference (e.g., order effects, carryover effects), that is, the possibility that within this series one treatment (i.e., CT) is influencing another treatment (i.e., FAP). Finally, external validity also waits on replication, as results from only one client were presented.

   Ollendick, Hagopian, and Huntzinger (1991) treated the nighttime fearfulness of two children meeting *DSM* criteria for separation anxiety disorder. Initial baseline data were collected (A phase) on the number of nights per week the children slept in their own bed and the children's subjective reports of anxiety regarding sleeping in their own bed (using the State form of the State-Trait Anxiety Inventory for Children: STAIC). Baseline was followed by self-control training for both the children and their parents (B phase). The interaction effects of providing the children with direct reinforcement for sleeping in their own beds along with continued self-control training was then assessed (B + C phase). The outcome as assessed by the STAIC scores is shown in Figure 13.6 and suggests the addition of direct reinforcement led to an enhanced treatment response. Note that the most meaningful evaluation of the B + C phase is relative to the B phase and not the A phase, because the B and B + C phases are temporally contiguous. The design used by Ollendick et al. (1991) was strengthened by the addition of a baseline phase, the replication across subjects, and the multiple baseline format (which is described in detail in a later section and also illustrates how design elements can be combined). The design might have been further strengthened by the

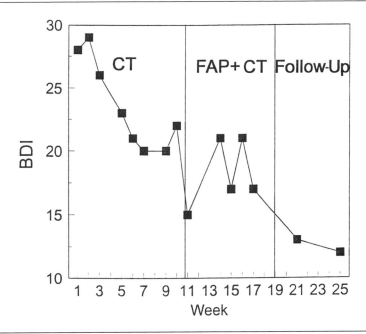

Figure 13.5.   BDI scores obtained at the beginning of each of the 13 treatments and two follow-up sessions during standard cognitive therapy (CT), FAP-enhanced cognitive therapy (CT + FAP), and follow-up that occurred over a 25-week period.
Source: From Kohlenberg, R.J., & Tsai, M. (1994). Improving cognitive therapy for depression with functional analytic psychotherapy: Theory and case study. *The Behavior Analyst, 17,* p. 314. Reprinted with permission of the author.

addition of an A/B + C design (which is essentially an A/B simple phase change, where B is the package of both self-control training and direct reinforcement), which would address concerns about the potential importance of the sequence in which the treatment was employed (e.g., influence of order effects, carryover effects). Finally, the one- and two-year follow-up data may be influenced by physical and social maturational processes, which may also result in a reduction in the children's nighttime fearfulness.

Combining Simple Phase Changes to Create a Complex Phase Change   An A/B/A/C/A design combines two simple phase changes (A/B and A/C) and allows for comparison of treatment effects relative to baseline (B to A and C to A) and some comparison of the two different interventions (B to C). If the client's behavior tracks the withdrawal and initiation of the intervention, then confidence is increased that the intervention is responsible for the changes. In essence, a reversal (A/B/A/B) has been demonstrated with two interventions. The B to C comparison is weak, however, because of potential order effects (Hayes et al., in press). As mentioned earlier, it is preferable to compare contiguous phases. One solution is to replicate using the opposite order (A/C/A/B/A).

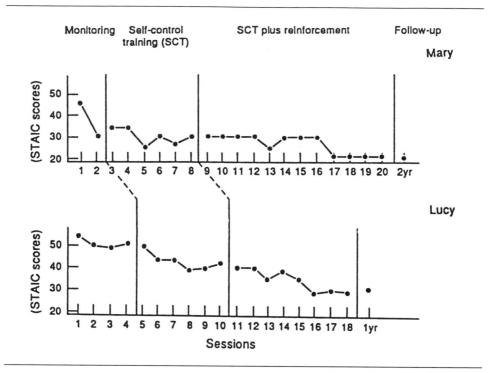

Figure 13.6.   State Trait Anxiety Inventory for Children (STAIC) scores across baseline (monitoring), self-control training (SCT), and SCT plus reinforcement. A follow-up assessment was also made two years after the final treatment session for Mary and one year after the final treatment session for Lucy.

Source: From Ollendick, T.H., Hagopian, L.P., & Huntzinger, R.M. (1991). Cognitive-behavior therapy with nighttime fearful children. *Journal of Behavior Therapy and Experimental Psychiatry, 22*(2), p. 118. Copyright © 1991 with kind permission from Elsevier Science Ltd., The Boulevard, Langford Lane, Kidlington OX5 1GB, UK.

Harmon, Nelson, and Hayes (1980) combined two simple phase changes to examine the differential impact of self-monitoring activity level and subjective mood states on the self-reports of engagement in pleasant activities and the experience of depressed affect. Initially, baseline data on mood and activity level were obtained for all clients. Three clients then experienced the following sequence: self-monitoring activity level, baseline-two, self-monitoring mood, and baseline-three (i.e., A/B/A/C/A). Three additional clients received a counterbalanced sequence: self-monitoring of mood, baseline-two, self-monitoring of activity level, and baseline-three (i.e., A/C/A/B/A).

This design, shown in Figure 13.7, allowed for several interesting conclusions. First, self-monitoring of either mood or activity led to increases in pleasant activities and decreases in depressed mood as compared to baseline conditions (A to B and A to C comparisons). That is, throughout the sequence of phases, the changes in self-reports of mood and activity level tracked the implementation and removal of the intervention, demonstrating the internal validity of the results. Second, self-monitoring of activity was more effective than self-monitoring of mood in increasing reports of engagement in pleasant activities. As this result was consistent across both sequences of the design,

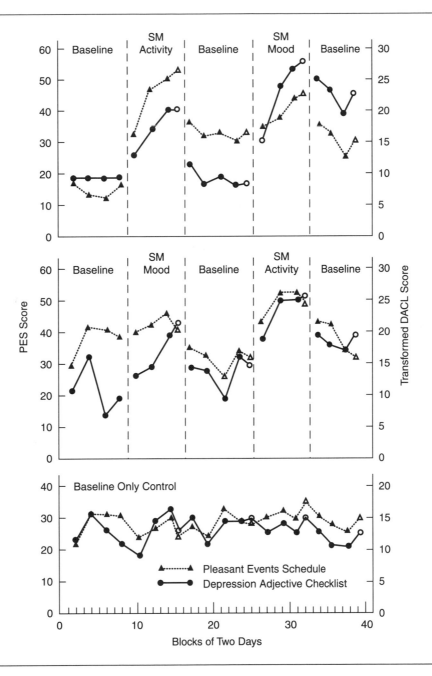

Figure 13.7.   Variations in mean scores on the Pleasant Events Schedule (PES) and the Depression Adjective Check List (DACL) for the two experimental groups and the control group across the five experimental conditions. (Solid points represent the mean of two days' data, whereas open points represent one day's data; SM = self-monitoring.)

Source: From Harmon, T.M., Nelson, R.O., & Hayes, S.C. (1980). Self-monitoring of mood versus activity by depressed clients. *Journal of Consulting and Clinical Psychology, 48,* p. 34. Copyright © 1980 by the American Psychological Association. Reprinted with permission.

it cannot easily be attributed to order effects. However, across both sequences, greater improvements in mood were demonstrated in the second intervention phase, thus failing to rule out the effect of sequence on mood (Harmon et al., 1980).

Between-Series Elements

When using within-series elements, the critical comparisons are the changes in level, trend, or variability in the series across phases. Between-series elements differ in that the critical comparison is across two series (i.e., interventions). Because comparisons are made across series, between-series elements do not require phases. However, this design does not preclude the use of phases (e.g., adding a baseline phase prior to the interventions). Between-series elements are often used to compare the effectiveness of two interventions within the same individual. In addition, as mentioned above, the design can be easily altered to add a baseline phase, allowing for both interventions to be assessed relative to baseline (Hayes et al., in press).

A common between-series design is the alternating treatments design (ATD). In this design, each client is exposed to two interventions or conditions that alternate randomly or semirandomly across some meaningful interval of time (e.g., across sessions). Because treatment alternation occurs regularly and the data are compared across series, there is no need for a stability criterion and no need for treatment withdrawal. The effects are assessed by direct comparison between the two series.

McKnight, Nelson, Hayes, and Jarrett (1984) treated nine depressed women with both social skills and CT. Based on their initial assessment, McKnight et al. determined that three of the women had predominantly social skills deficits, three had predominantly irrational cognitions, and three had problems in both areas. Over eight sessions, each woman was randomly assigned to receive four sessions each of CT and social skills training. Figure 13.8 shows the results. Notice that the data points are connected separately based on condition. Scores on the Depression Adjective Checklist (DACL) collected prior to sessions of CT are separate from those collected prior to sessions of social skills training. The degree to which the two lines separate indicates the relative effectiveness of one treatment over the other for each client. In short, the more distinct the two lines, the more confidence there is in the differential effectiveness of the treatments. The more overlap in the two lines, the less confidence. In addition to comparisons between the treatments, McKnight et al., because of the use of a pretreatment baseline, also allow for a comparison of the effectiveness of both treatments relative to baseline (a within-series comparison).

The random (or semirandom) assignment of treatment sessions by McKnight et al. (1984) is an important feature in ATDs, providing a protection against coincidental events external to the treatment producing the effects. Also, consistent with minimum guidelines offered by Hayes et al. (in press), four measures were collected in each intervention condition. Finally, the use of an ATD alleviated the need for a withdrawal of treatment phase, an important consideration in the clinical environment.

The major weakness of the ATD is that the interventions may combine or interact to create the effects. This may occur due to the sequencing of conditions (despite random or semirandom alternation) or carry over from one session to the next. In addition, it

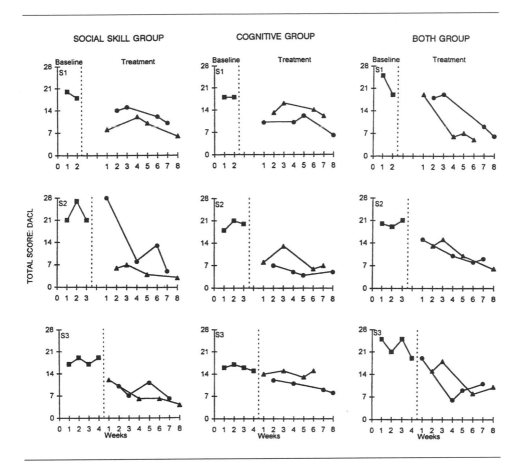

Figure 13.8.   **The effects of cognitive treatment (circles) and social skills treatment (tri-angles) as measured by the total score on the Lubin Depression Adjective Checklist (DACL). The left column depicts the three subjects experiencing difficulties in social skills. The middle column depicts the three subjects experiencing difficulties in irrational cognitions. The right column depicts the three subjects experiencing difficulties in both social skills and irrational cognitions.**

Source: From McKnight, D.L., Nelson, R.O., Hayes, S.C., and Jarrett, R.B. (1984). Importance of treating individually assessed response classes in the amelioration of depression. *Behavior Therapy, 15,* pp. 324, 326, 329. Copyright © 1984 by the Association for Advancement of Behavior Therapy. Adapted with permission.

may not be feasible to switch back and forth between treatments on a session-to-session basis.

For additional examples of the use of ATDs, see studies examining the effects of per drink alcohol content on total alcohol intake (Van Houten, Van Houten, & Malenfant, 1994), the moment-to-moment impact of therapist behavior on clients' ability to generate solutions to problems in family therapy (Sternberg & Bry, 1994), and the impact of cognitive coping statements on the speed of progression through desensitization hierarchies (Hayes, Hussian, Turner, Anderson, & Grubb, 1983).

Combined Design Elements

These designs, as their title suggests, are arranged to allow both within- and between-series comparisons to be made.

Multiple Baseline Design

Multiple baseline designs involve the introduction of a single intervention at different points in time. The intervention may be introduced across different subjects with similar clinical problems, across different problem areas within a single individual, or across different situations with a single individual and a single problem. In short, the designs are applicable across subjects, behaviors, and settings (Hayes, 1981; Hayes et al., in press; Barlow & Hersen, 1984). In essence, multiple baseline designs are a series of simultaneous A/B designs in which the length of the A phase is varied. This design feature allows for both within-series and between-series comparisons. Within-series comparisons are identical to those made with the standard A/B phase change; that is, interventions are evaluated in terms of the intraseries changes in trend or level from baseline. Between-series comparisons involve evaluating a series in which an intervention has been introduced relative to a separate series in which an intervention has yet to be introduced (baseline) (Hayes et al., in press).

Ollendick (1995) employed a multiple baseline design across subjects in treating four adolescents, seen at an outpatient clinic, who qualified for the diagnosis of panic disorder with agoraphobia. As can be seen in Figure 13.9, there is an absence of some desirable methodological features. In several cases, the baseline data do not allow for an estimate of trend or variability and only a limited assessment of level (Clients 1 and 2), treatment effects were often not instantaneous, and subsequent phase changes were instituted before data had stabilized from the phase change in the previous series.

Nevertheless, the data are still compelling for several reasons. At intake, the four adolescent clients reported experiencing panic attacks for the prior six months, two years, six years, and six years, respectively, suggesting the presence of a long-standing problem. However, all showed a decline in panic attacks during treatment, such that in the last two weeks of treatment, no panic attacks were endorsed by any client. In addition, the effect was maintained at a six-month follow-up for all clients. These results suggest that the magnitude of the effects were clinically significant. As well, by virtue of his use of a multiple baseline design across subjects, Ollendick (1995) presents four independent replications of the effects, decreasing the likelihood that extraneous external events produced the changes. For additional recent clinical examples of the use of multiple baseline designs across subjects, see Ladouceur, Freeston, Gagnon, Thibodeau, and Dumont's (1995) treatment of obsessions; Chadwick and Lowe's (1990) modification of delusional beliefs; and Bird, Alexopoulos, and Adamowicz's (1995) interventions to reduce behavior problems in clients with senile dementia.

Acierno and Last (1995) used a multiple baseline design across behaviors to assess the effectiveness of response prevention and exposure-based treatment in reducing six compulsions of a client diagnosed with OCD. Following a baseline period, Acierno and Last operationalized performance goals and directed the initial intervention at the least anxiety-producing target (see Figure 13.10). The other compulsions remained in baseline and, as shown in Figure 13.10, remained unchanged despite the immediate and

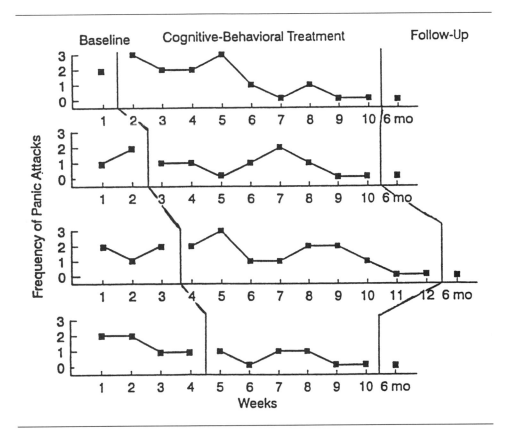

Figure 13.9.   Frequency of weekly panic attacks for Clients 1 through 4, listed from top to bottom.

Source: From Ollendick, T.H. (1995). Cognitive behavioral treatment of panic disorder with agoraphobia in adolescents: A multiple baseline design analysis. *Behavior Therapy, 26,* p. 524. Copyright © 1995 by the Association for Advancement of Behavior Therapy. Reprinted with permission.

large increase in goal attainment with respect to toothbrushing (i.e., a reduction in compulsive toothbrushing). This provides evidence that the compulsions targeted for change are independent. Dependence (or generalization) would be noted if improvements in a targeted compulsion resulted in improvements in other nontargeted compulsions. The remaining five compulsions were targeted sequentially and only after effects had been demonstrated for the previous compulsion. For three of the six behaviors (i.e., toothbrushing, hair washing, and ear hair cutting), changes in level but not trend were evident. However, for three other behaviors (i.e., use of the scale, hemorrhoidal cream use, and cortisone cream use), both changes in level and trend were observed. Notice also the stable and lengthy baselines (established by obtaining pretherapy retrospective and current preintervention baseline measures), the immediate and substantial effects of intervention, and the implementation of the intervention across each series until all the phase changes occurred.

Many clinical interventions are not going to involve large, immediate intervention effects, nor will all the methodologically preferred design characteristics be practical

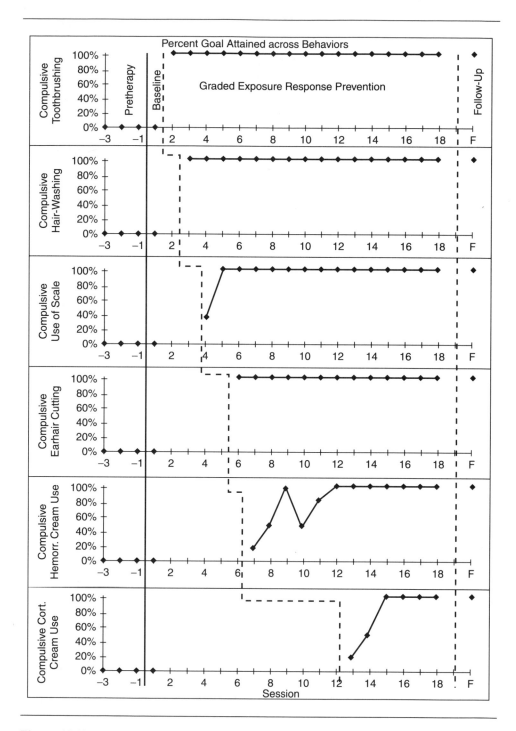

Figure 13.10.   Behavioral gains reported as percentages of predetermined performance goals for each compulsive area during graduated exposure-response prevention treatment.

Source: From Acierno, R., & Last, C.G. (1995). Outpatient treatment of obsessive compulsive disorder by self-directed graded exposure and response prevention. *Psychotherapy in Private Practice, 14*(3), p. 8. Copyright © 1995 by the Haworth Press, Inc. Reprinted with permission.

in every case (e.g., collecting lengthy baseline data, waiting for the intervention to have its full effect before instituting the intervention on the next series). As stated throughout this chapter, a balance needs to be achieved between the research tools and clinical realities, and, despite the need for this balance, useful, informative, and compelling data can still be collected.

The strengths of the multiple baseline design for clinicians include the relatively simple design strategy (A/B phase changes) and the lack of need for withdrawal of the intervention as in an A/B/A/B design. The strongest internal validity in a multiple baseline design is demonstrated when the series are shown to be independent. That is, effects are noticed only after the intervention is introduced for a series, and introducing the intervention for a prior series had no effect (as demonstrated in Figure 13.10). In some cases, if two behaviors or settings are thought to be functionally similar, generalization might be expected. This is often not known a priori, however, and in these cases, the multiple baseline design can serve as a generalization test (Hayes et al., in press).

Using a multiple baseline across settings design, Paniagua, Morrison, and Black (1990) examined the effect of correspondence training (i.e., reinforcing the correspondence between how one says one will behave and how one then behaves) on the inattention, overactivity, and conduct of a child diagnosed with attention-deficit hyperactivity disorder and conduct disorder. The inattention data across the three settings (shown in Figure 13.11) suggest that when correspondence was reinforced in the classroom, inattention decreased in that setting but not in the simulated classroom or treatment room. However, when the intervention was introduced in the simulated classroom, the effects generalized to the treatment room. Confidence in the internal validity of the design is maintained by the independence of the classroom setting. In addition, a theoretically based interpretation in terms of training of sufficient exemplars (cf. Paniagua et al., 1990; Stokes & Baer, 1977) provides a possible mechanism to account for how the observed generalization could have been produced by the intervention rather than extraneous factors. These results, as do any based on only one client, need to be replicated.

In the above examples, the dependent measures were collected simultaneously in time across series, with only the phase changes separated in time. This provides the most rigorous protection of internal validity. However, one of the most convenient designs for clinical practice involves collecting data on several similar clients for which the same intervention was employed but over different time periods (e.g., sequentially). The data presented in Figure 13.3 provide an example (see also Besa, 1994). This type of clinical replication series creates what has been termed a natural, or nonconcurrent, multiple baseline across clients (Hayes, 1981, 1985; Watson & Workman, 1981). However, some have disagreed with calling such temporally separated series a multiple baseline and have preferred to view these as replicated simple phase changes (Harris & Jenson, 1985a, 1985b). Regardless, such clinical replication series are a powerful tool for clinicians to demonstrate the effects of their interventions and inform clinical science.

Constant-Series Control

The constant-series control involves the use of a series for which conditions remain similar across time. Constant series are used in conjunction with other design elements and are a relatively easy way to provide additional interpretive power. The rationale for using a constant-series control is similar to that provided by the extended A phases of

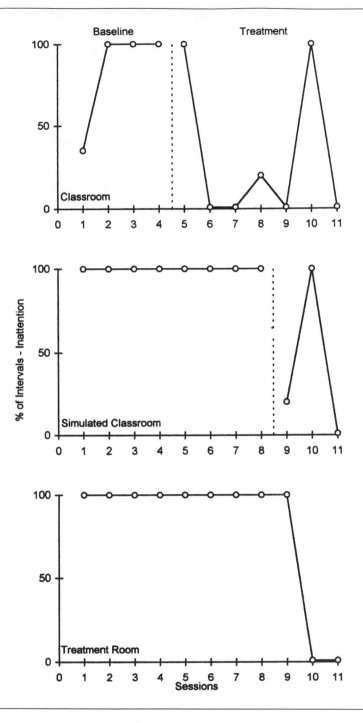

Figure 13.11. **Daily percentages of inattention during baseline and treatment across a classroom and a simulated classroom setting. In the third setting (treatment room), a decrease in target behaviors is noted in the absence of training when the treatment is introduced in the simulated classroom.**

Source: From Paniagua, F.A., Morrison, P.B., & Black, S.A. (1990). Management of a hyperactive-conduct disordered child through correspondence training: A preliminary study. *Journal of Behavior Therapy and Experimental Psychiatry, 21*(1), p. 66. Copyright © 1990 with kind permission from Elsevier Science Ltd., The Boulevard, Langford Lane, Kidlington OX5 1GB, UK.

multiple baseline designs. Specifically, if changes in other series coincide with changes in the introduction, and possibly withdrawal, of the intervention while the control series is essentially unchanged, it reduces that likelihood that external events are producing the changes. Thus, the constant-series control is conceptually similar to a no-treatment control group, which is often used in traditional between-group research designs.

Harmon et al. (1980) added a baseline (A/A/A/A/A) control group to the complex phase change design described earlier (see bottom panel of Figure 13.7). The two subjects in the baseline control group showed fairly stable depression and activity level across time. The changes noted during intervention phases for the individuals receiving treatment, in comparison with the limited changes in the control subjects (a between-series comparison), provides additional confidence in the internal validity of these results. In addition, the two subjects Harmon et al. used in the baseline-only group had initial levels of depression similar to those of the other subjects, who received the interventions, on objective measures of depression. This, again, increases confidence that the results were due to the intervention and not, for example, to the cyclical nature of depression. As Hayes et al. (in press) point out, the control series must be one for which it is reasonable to expect change to be evident if external sources are responsible for the change noted in the intervention.

Baseline controls can raise ethical dilemmas in clinical practice and may need to be avoided if it requires the complete withholding of treatment. When a client presents with several problem areas, however, an area that is not the initial focus of treatment could serve as a nontreatment control series. The multiple baseline design or ATD is beneficial in cases where a baseline control series is not feasible as they do not require the removal or complete withholding of intervention. Another possibility is an intervention-only constant series, such as that employed by Jensen (1994), which can be used alone or in conjunction with a baseline-only control series.

ISSUES IN ANALYZING TIME-SERIES

The analysis of time-series data remains a debated issue. In general, when analyzing time-series data, the effect of a given intervention is evaluated relative to the preintervention baseline. As mentioned earlier, the focus when assessing intervention effects is generally on changes in level or trend that occur during the intervention phase compared to the level and trend established during baseline. Visual inspection of graphed data is the most common interpretive method, which can be accurate in recognizing changes in level or trend that follow stable baselines. However, in situations where the intervention change is smaller, the data are serially dependent, and/or there is a large amount of variability in the data, visual analysis may be less reliable in recognizing intervention effects (Jones, Vaught, & Weinrott, 1977; Jones, Weinrott, & Vaught, 1978). The potential for visual inspection to be unreliable has led visual analysis to be supplemented by statistical analysis (Busk & Marascuilo, 1992; Edgington, 1992). Others, however, suggest that there is no statistical gold standard and that reliability among different statistical analyses is also questionable (Parsonson & Baer, 1992).

Both visual inspection and statistical analyses attempt to protect against Type I and Type II errors. Type I errors involve falsely concluding that the intervention produced an effect when the results are due to sampling error; Type II errors involve falsely concluding that the intervention was not responsible for the effects when in fact it was (Baer, 1977; Kazdin, 1984). The error rates are inversely related, such that the more conservative is in protecting against Type I errors, the more likely are Type II errors and vice versa. Statistical procedures provide protection against these errors by setting a standard probability level (often $p < .05$). If the likelihood that the results occurred via sampling variability alone is lower than .05, then the result is attributed to the independent variable (statistically significant). No such "objective" marker equivalent to a probability level is possible for visual analysis. However, in clinical situations, other information is available to aid in evaluation. For instance, subjective ratings by the client (e.g., reporting no panic attacks) or ratings obtained from others in the client's environment (e.g., a spouse) may directly speak to the social validity of the effects (Kazdin, 1977). In addition, normative data related to the dependent measure can be used as a benchmark against which treatment effects can be judged (Jacobson, Follette, & Revenstorf, 1984; Kendall & Grove, 1988). For example, treated individuals' depression scores could be compared to scores obtained from a normative sample to determine the extent of the decrease in depressive symptoms from baseline to posttreatment. In such cases, meeting a therapeutic criterion (clinical significance) adds to statistical confirmation. In fact, the reliance of visual inspection on large and meaningful effects makes it a generally conservative method (Kazdin, 1984; Parsonson & Baer, 1992). However, recent innovations in statistical methods for assessing clinically significant change at the level of the individual have been offered. Jacobson and Truax (1991) propose a statistical approach for defining clinically meaningful change, termed a reliable change index, that is consistent with the use of normative data mentioned above. That is, it is based on the extent to which treatment moves a client out of the dysfunctional range or into the functional range on the dependent measure. Calculation of the reliable change index, however, only makes use of pre- and posttreatment measures and is not a time-series analysis.

Statistical Analyses

Commonly used parametric statistics (ANOVAs and t tests) cannot be used with time-series data due to serial dependency (autoregression) in the observations (each observation is more like, or correlated with, the score prior to it than the mean of the series). When the observations are serially dependent, the assumption of independence of the observations is violated. One method for analyzing serially dependent data is called a time-series analysis (Box & Jenkins, 1970; cf. Krishef, 1991). Time-series analysis fits a model to the stochastic (error) component of the data to factor out the nonrandom portion of the error, thereby removing the serial dependency (prewhitening). The residuals (what is left) can then be analyzed using common parametric techniques. Analyses consider differences in level and trend across baseline and intervention phases. However, this model is quite complicated and requires a great deal of expertise to ensure an appropriate fit to the data. Also, it is recommended that there be 50 to 100 data points in each phase (Crosbie, 1993), making it quite impractical.

Crosbie (1993) offers a time-series analysis (ITSACORR) for brief time-series data which is a modified version of the analysis just described. This analysis is designed to provide control of Type I error rates for brief data with serial dependency. In addition, it is suggested that ITSACORR can be used with as few as five scores per phase. The output specifies whether there is a change in intercept or slope, gives the exact probabilities for F and $t,$ and graphs the data with steady-state trend lines (Crosbie, 1993).

In addition, nonparametric procedures have also been proposed, the most common of which are randomization tests (Busk & Marascuilo, 1992; Edgington, 1987, 1992). Randomization tests fit most easily with the logic of an ATD. Two treatments are assigned randomly to an equal number of sessions so that, for example, each treatment is applied on four random occasions across eight sessions of treatment. Summary statistics (e.g., means) for both treatments can then be calculated and the means compared to generate a test statistic (e.g., $t,$ $F,$ or difference in means). At this point, the data are randomly reshuffled. With eight sessions and two treatments, there are 70 potential sequences. The random reshuffling may involve all 70 possible reshufflings (systematic procedure) or a random sample of reshufflings (random procedure) (Edgington, 1992). The proportion of random reshufflings that are of the magnitude of the test statistic used to compare the means (e.g., $t,$ $F,$ or the difference in means) provides the probability level (p value). For instance, if three reshufflings produce a difference in means larger than that obtained, the result is a p value of 0.043 (3/70). Alterations of the basic rationale above have been employed to apply randomization tests to A/B, A/B/A/B, and multiple baseline across behavior designs (Busk & Marascuilo, 1992; Edgington, 1987, 1992, 1996; Ferron & Ware, 1994).

Randomization tests have several limitations for clinical work. A major tenet of time-series designs is their flexibility in application, which allows for alteration of the design in response to the data. However, randomization tests usually require a priori planning of the intervention (randomizing) and thereby limit the flexibility (Kazdin, 1984; see also Ferron & Ware, 1994, for an attempt to make randomization tests more responsive). Similarly, phases of equal length, or immediate treatment reversibility (needed for use of ATD), are often not possible in clinical interventions.

A final aid for discriminating change in time-series data is to plot a trend line to the data in each phase. Two techniques have been suggested: split-middle and least squares (for a more complete description, see Kazdin, 1984; Krishef, 1991; Parsonson & Baer, 1992). A major goal in plotting a trend line is to facilitate a visual inspection so that it is easier to discriminate changes in trend or slope between phases. However, with brief time-series data, trend lines can be unduly influenced by one or two variable points. Thus, when trend lines are used, the amount of variance accounted for by the trend line (R^2) should also be reported.

Combining Analyses

As mentioned earlier, traditional parametric statistics cannot be used with time-series data due to the serial dependency in the data, produced by the frequent measurements taken. However, in the discussion of types of dependent measures, both global and specific measures are recommended. Global or lengthier measures are often taken only at preintervention, postintervention, and, possibly, follow-up, which can be summed across subjects and allow for more routine statistical analyses (e.g, repeated measures of

ANOVA). In this fashion, the more traditional approach to outcome studies where only preintervention and postintervention data are compared can be combined with time-series methodology. This combination allows for both an overall assessment of group efficacy, as well as a more fine-grained analysis of the process of individual change.

In summary, statistical analyses of time-series data may facilitate the recognition of reliable smaller-scale changes that would be missed by visual analysis (Kazdin, 1984). However, these analyses often impose structure on the design, somewhat reducing the flexibility that makes time-series designs so applicable to the clinical environment. Taking dependent measures that facilitate evaluation at the level of the individual and the group allows for a combination of analyses.

CONCLUSION

Time-series methodology provides a tool for clinicians to report their treatment successes, and failures, in a manner that can advance clinical science and thereby begin to address the gulf between research and practice that currently exists in clinical psychology. Time-series approaches are consistent with the logic of and can enhance clinical intervention, while also addressing most, if not all, scientifically important questions that arise in the clinical environment (Hayes et al., in press). Time-series approaches, despite their evolution in the experimental analysis of behavior and applied behavior analysis, are not bound to a particular theoretical orientation but can be used by any willing clinician. This chapter has provided examples of the use of these designs in evaluating treatments of depression, eating disorders, obsessive-compulsive disorder, panic disorder with agoraphobia, parent-child conflict, separation anxiety disorder, perfectionism, delusions, and hallucinations, demonstrating their applicability to a range of clinical phenomena across a range of clinical questions. Armed with this research methodology, it is our belief that the breadth and depth of the clinical phenomena studied, and the clinical questions addressed, can be greatly expanded to the benefit of both clinical science and clinical practice.

REFERENCES

Acierno, R., & Last, C. G. (1995). Outpatient treatment of obsessive compulsive disorder by self-directed graded exposure and response prevention. *Psychotherapy in Private Practice, 14*(3), 1–11.

Baer, D. M. (1977). Perhaps it would be better not to know everything. *Journal of Applied Behavior Analysis, 10,* 167–172.

Barlow, D. H., & Hersen, M. (Eds). (1984). *Single case experimental designs: Strategies for studying behavior change* (2nd ed.). New York: Pergamon Press.

Beck, A. T., Rush, A. J., Shaw, F. B., & Emery, G. (1979). *The cognitive therapy of depression.* New York: Guilford Press.

Besa, D. (1994). Evaluating narrative family therapy using single-system research designs. *Research on Social Work Practice, 4*(3), 309–324.

Beutler, L. E., Williams, R. E., Wakefield, P. J., & Entwistle, S. R. (1995). Bridging scientist and practitioner perspectives in clinical psychology. *American Psychologist, 50*(12), 984–994.

Bird, M., Alexopoulos, P., & Adamowicz, J. (1995). Success and failure in five case studies: Use of cued recall to ameliorate behaviour problems in senile dementia. *International Journal of Geriatric Psychiatry, 10*, 305–311.

Box, G. E. P., & Jenkins, G. M. (1970). *Time series analysis: Forecasting and control*. San Francisco: Holden-Day.

Bulik, C. M., Epstein, L. H., & Kaye, W. (1990). Treatment of laxative abuse in a female with bulimia nervosa using an operant extinction paradigm. *Journal of Substance Abuse, 2*, 381–388.

Busk, P. L., & Marascuilo, L. A. (1992). Statistical analysis in single-case research: Issues, procedures, and recommendations, with applications to multiple behaviors. In T. R. Kratochwell & J. R. Levin (Eds.), *Single-case research design and analysis* (pp. 159–185). Hillsdale, NJ: Erlbaum.

Chadwick, P. D. J., & Lowe, C. F. (1990). Measurement and modification of delusional beliefs. *Journal of Consulting and Clinical Psychology, 58*(2), 225–232.

Crosbie, J. (1993). Interrupted time-series analysis with brief single-subject data. *Journal of Consulting and Clinical Psychology, 61*(6), 966–974.

Dobson, K. S. (1989). A meta-analysis of the efficacy of cognitive therapy for depression. *Journal of Consulting and Clinical Psychology, 57*(3), 414–419.

Edgington, E. S. (1987). *Randomization tests* (2nd ed.). New York: Marcel Dekker.

Edgington, E. S. (1992). Nonparametric tests for single-case experiments. In T. R. Kratochwell & J. R. Levin (Eds.), *Single-case research design and analysis* (pp. 133–157). Hillsdale, NJ: Erlbaum.

Edgington, E. S. (1996). Randomized single-subject experimental designs. *Behaviour Research and Therapy, 34*(7), 567–574.

Elkin, I., Shea, T., Watkins, J. T., Imber, S. C., Sotsky, S. M., Collins, J. F., Glass, D. R., Pilkonis, P. A., Leber, W. R., Fiester, S. J., Docherty, J., & Parloff, M. B. (1989). NIMH treatment of depression collaborative research program. *Archives of General Psychiatry, 46*, 971–982.

Ferguson, K. L., & Rodway, M. R. (1994). Cognitive behavioral treatment of perfectionism: Initial evaluation studies. *Research on Social Work Practice, 4*(3), 283–308.

Ferron, J., & Ware, W. (1994). Using randomization tests with responsive single-case designs. *Behaviour Research and Therapy, 32*(7), 787–791.

Fischer, J., & Corcoran, K. (1994). *Measures for clinical practice: A sourcebook* (2nd ed.). New York: Free Press.

Fonagy, P., & Moran, G. (1993). Selecting single case research designs for clinicians. In N. E. Miller, L. Luborsky, J. P. Barber, & J. P. Docherty (Eds.), *Psychodynamic treatment research: A handbook for clinical practice* (pp. 62–95). New York: Basic Books.

Giles, T. R. (1991). Managed mental health care and effective psychotherapy: A step in the right direction. *Journal of Behavior Therapy and Experimental Psychiatry, 22*(2), 83–86.

Harmon, T. M., Nelson, R. O., & Hayes, S. C. (1980). Self-monitoring of mood versus activity by depressed clients. *Journal of Consulting and Clinical Psychology, 48*(1), 30–38.

Harris, F. N., & Jenson, W. R. (1985a). AB designs with replication: A reply to Hayes. *Behavioral Assessment, 7*, 133–135.

Harris, F. N., & Jenson, W. R. (1985b). Comparisons of multiple-baseline across persons designs and AB designs with replication: Issues and confusions. *Behavioral Assessment, 7*, 121–127.

Hayes, S. C. (1981). Single case experimental design and empirical clinical research. *Journal of Consulting and Clinical Psychology, 49*, 193–211.

Hayes, S. C. (1985). Natural multiple baselines across persons: A reply to Harris and Jenson. *Behavioral Assessment, 7*, 129–132.

Hayes, S. C., Barlow, D. H., & Nelson-Gray, R. O. (in press). *The scientist practitioner* (2nd ed.). Boston: Allyn & Bacon.

Hayes, S. C., Hussian, R. A., Turner, A. E., Anderson, N. B., & Grubb, T. D. (1983). The effect of coping statements on progress through desensitization hierarchy. *Journal of Behavior Therapy and Experimental Psychiatry, 14*(2), 117–129.

Himadi, B., & Curran, J. P. (1995). The modification of auditory hallucinations. *Behavioral Interventions, 10*(1), 33–47.

Hiss, H., Foa, E. B., & Kozak, M. J. (1994). Relapse prevention program for treatment of obsessive-compulsive disorder. *Journal of Consulting and Clinical Psychology, 62*(4), 801–808.

Jacobson, N. S., Follette, W. C., & Revenstorf, D. (1984). Psychotherapy outcome research: Methods for reporting variability and evaluating clinical significance. *Behavior Therapy, 15,* 336–352.

Jacobson, N. S., & Traux, P. (1991). Clinical significance: A statistical approach to defining meaningful change in psychotherapy research. *Journal of Consulting and Clinical Psychology, 59,* 12–19.

Jensen, C. (1994). Psychosocial treatment of depression in women: Nine single-subject evaluations. *Research on Social Work Practice, 4*(3), 267–282.

Jones, R. R., Vaught, R. S., & Weinrott, M. R. (1977). Time-series analysis and operant research. *Journal of Applied Behavior Analysis, 10,* 151–166.

Jones, R. R., Weinrott, M. R., & Vaught, R. S. (1978). Effects of serial dependency on the agreement between visual and statistical inference. *Journal of Applied Behavior Analysis, 11,* 277–283.

Kazdin, A. E. (1977). Assessing the clinical or applied significance of behavior change through social validation. *Behavior Modification, 1,* 427–453.

Kazdin, A. E. (1980). *Research design in clinical psychology.* New York: Harper & Row.

Kazdin, A. E. (1981). Drawing valid inferences for case studies. *Journal of Consulting and Clinical Psychology, 49,* 183–192.

Kazdin, A. E. (1984). Statistical analyses for single-case experimental designs. In D. H. Barlow & M. Hersen (Eds.), *Single case experimental designs: Strategies for studying behavior change* (2nd ed., pp. 285–324). New York: Pergamon Press.

Kendall, P. C., & Grove, W. M. (1988). Normative comparisons in therapy outcome. *Behavioral Assessment, 10,* 147–158.

Kendall, P. C., Hollon, S. D., Beck, A. T., Hammen, C. L., & Ingram, R. E. (1987). Issues and recommendations regarding use of the Beck Depression Inventory. *Cognitive Therapy and Research, 11*(3), 289–299.

Kohlenberg, R. J., & Tsai, M. (1994). Improving cognitive therapy for depression with functional analytic psychotherapy: Theory and case study. *Behavior Analyst, 17,* 305–319.

Kratochwill, T. F. (1978). *Single subject research: Strategies for evaluating change.* New York: Academic Press.

Kratochwill, T. F. (1992). Single-case research design and analysis: An overview. In T. F. Kratochwill & J. R. Levin (Eds.), *Single-case research design and analysis* (pp. 1–14). Hillsdale, NJ: Erlbaum.

Krishef, C. H. (1991). *Fundamental approaches to single subject design and analysis.* Malabar, FL: Krieger.

Ladouceur, R., Freeston, M. H., Gagnon, F., Thibodeau, N., & Dumont, J. (1995). Cognitive-behavioral treatment of obsessions. *Behavior Modification, 19*(2), 247–257.

McKnight, D. L., Nelson, R. O., Hayes, S. C., & Jarrett, R. B. (1984). Importance of treating individually assessed response classes in the amelioration of depression. *Behavior Therapy, 15,* 315–335.

Meehl, P. E. (1997). Credentialed persons, credentialed knowledge. *Clinical Psychology Science and Practice, 4,* 91–98.

Mischel, W. (1968). *Personality and assessment.* New York: Wiley.

Nelson, R. O. (1981). Realistic dependent measures for clinical use. *Journal of Consulting and Clinical Psychology, 49,* 168–182.

Nelson-Gray, R. O. (1994). The scientist-practitioner model revisited: Strategies for implementation. *Behaviour Change, 11*(2), 61–75.

Ollendick, T. H. (1995). Cognitive behavioral treatment of panic disorder with agoraphobia in adolescents: A multiple baseline design analysis. *Behavior Therapy, 26,* 517–531.

Ollendick, T. H., Hagopian, L. P., & Huntzinger, R. M. (1991). Cognitive-behavior therapy with nighttime fearful children. *Journal of Behavior Therapy and Experimental Psychiatry, 22*(2), 113–121.

Paniagua, F. A., Morrison, P. B., & Black, S. A. (1990). Management of a hyperactive-conduct disordered child through correspondence training: A preliminary study. *Journal of Behavior Therapy and Experimental Psychiatry, 21*(1), 63–68.

Parsonson, B. S., & Baer, D. M. (1992). The visual analysis of data, and current research into the stimuli controlling it. In T. F. Kratochwill & J. R. Levin (Eds.), *Single-case research design and analysis* (pp. 15–40). Hillsdale, NJ: Erlbaum.

Rice, C. E. (1997). Scenarios: The scientist-practitioner split and the future of psychology. *American Psychologist, 52*(11), 1173–1181.

Seligman, M. E. P. (1995). The effectiveness of psychotherapy: The consumer reports study. *American Psychologist, 50*(12), 965–974.

Spence, D. P. (1993). Traditional case studies and prescriptions for improving them. In N. E. Miller, L. Luborsky, J. P. Barber, & J. P. Docherty (Eds.), *Psychodynamic treatment research: A handbook for clinical practice* (pp. 37–52). New York: Basic Books.

Sternberg, J. A., & Bry, B. H. (1994). Solution generation and family conflict over time in problem-solving therapy with families of adolescents: The impact of therapist behavior. *Child and Family Behavior Therapy, 16*(4), 1–23.

Stokes, T. B., & Baer, D. M. (1977). An implicit technology of generalization. *Journal of Applied Behavior Analysis, 10,* 349–367.

Stricker, G., & Trierweiler, S. J. (1995). The local clinical scientist: A bridge between science and practice. *American Psychologist, 50*(12), 995–1002.

Van Houten, R., Van Houten, J., & Malenfant, J. (1994). The effects of low alcohol beverages on alcohol consumption and impairment. *Behavior Modification, 18*(4), 505–513.

Waltz, J., Addis, M. E., Koerner, K., & Jacobson, N. S. (1993). Testing the integrity of a psychotherapy protocol: Assessment of adherence and competence. *Journal of Consulting and Clinical Psychology, 61*(4), 620–630.

Watson, P. J., & Workman, E. A. (1981). Non-concurrent multiple-baseline across individuals design: An extension of the traditional multiple-baseline design. *Journal of Behavior Therapy and Experimental Psychiatry, 12,* 257–259.

Weissman, M. M., & Paykel, E. S. (1974). *The depressed woman: A study of social relationships.* Chicago: University of Chicago Press.

Wilson, G. T. (1996). Manual-based treatments: The clinical application of research findings. *Behaviour Research and Therapy, 34*(4), 295–314.

Wilson, G. T. (1997). Treatment manuals in clinical practice. *Behaviour Research and Therapy, 35*(3), 205–210.

Chapter 14 ————————————————————

THERAPY OUTCOME RESEARCH METHODS

Philip C. Kendall, Ph.D., Ellen C. Flannery-Schroeder, Ph.D., and Julian D. Ford, Ph.D.

Clinical psychologists are central both in the provision of clinical services and the conduct of research to evaluate the outcome of therapeutic intervention. For several decades, controlled studies have been conducted and published, and clinical psychology has matured as a discipline guided by the scientific practitioner model.

To provide for the continuous improvement of the clinical services offered to thousands of clients, clinical psychologists have adopted and refined the methods and guidelines of science. Although the initial formulation of effective therapeutic strategies may result from activities other than rigorous research, such as careful observation or theoretical extrapolations, empirical evaluation of the efficacy and effectiveness of therapy is considered necessary before widespread utilization can be sanctioned. As a result, clinical psychologists have evolved a sophisticated array of research methods for the evaluation of the outcome of therapeutic intervention.

The development of therapy outcome research methods within clinical psychology has stemmed largely from the fundamental commitment of clinical psychologists to a scientist-practitioner model for training and professional practice (Shakow, 1976). Therefore, we begin with a brief discussion of this model, its implications for research evaluations of therapy, and the empirical-clinical model of clinical practice and research that has developed as an operationalization of this guiding philosophy. In the second section, we describe and define the issues that are addressed by therapy outcome research and discuss questions concerning those treatments that have been evaluated. Specific methods for scientifically addressing these issues are described in the third section. In addition, we consider the methodological problems that make definitive clinical outcome research difficult and discuss the tactics evolved by clinical researchers to handle these challenges. Finally, the methods for cumulative analyses of therapy outcome studies are reviewed.

The authors thank Helena Chmura Kraemer for her comments. Preparation of this manuscript was facilitated by research support provided by NIMH (MH4042) and the John D. and Catherine T. MacArthur Foundation.

SCIENTIST-PRACTITIONER MODEL OF CLINICAL RESEARCH AND INTERVENTION

Clinical psychologists, trained in APA-approved programs, are typically trained to fill the dual role of scientist/researcher and practitioner/clinician. Though the feasibility of such an ambitious role has been questioned, a succession of national conferences has reaffirmed the position first stated by the American Psychological Association Commission on Training in Clinical Psychology (1947): Clinical psychologists are scientists who evaluate their work and their theories with rigor and practitioners who utilize a research-based understanding of human behavior in social contexts to aid people in resolving psychological dysfunctions and enhancing their lives (Hoch, Ross, & Winder, 1966; Korman, 1974; Raimy, 1950; Strother, 1957). In practice, the scientist-practitioner model is not intended to create professional split personalities but rather to train clinical psychologists to be both service providers who evaluate their interventions scientifically and researchers who study applied questions and interpret their findings with an understanding of the richness and complexity of human experience (Kendall & Norton-Ford, 1982). Shakow (1976), whose career exemplified such a scientist-practitioner integration, offered this observation:

> The scientific-professional [is] a person who, on the basis of systematic knowledge about persons obtained primarily in real-life situations, has integrated this knowledge with psychological theory, and has then consistently regarded it with the questioning attitude of the scientist. . . . Thus, what defines the "scientist/professional" is the combination of the skilled acquisition of reality-based psychological understanding and the attitude of constant inquiry toward this knowledge. (p. 554)

If results are to be meaningful, an immediate implication for clinical research on the outcome of therapy is that it must reflect both the guidelines of science and an understanding of the subtleties of human experience and behavior change. Finely controlled investigations that are distant from the realities of human living and the therapeutic experience may offer only limited conclusions. Studies of therapeutic results that fail to pinpoint the effects that can be accurately attributed to therapy provide at most speculative knowledge. Clinical psychologists continue to develop a variety of methods for studying meaningful therapeutic interventions and outcomes in a scientific fashion. Indeed, the commitment to the scientist-practitioner is evident when we ask and answer the question "What if we did not seek empirical evaluation of the efficacy of therapy?" (Beutler, 1998; Kendall, 1998).

At the heart of the methods used to evaluate therapy is an *empirical-clinical* principle. This principle is a set of guidelines designed to enable practicing clinicians to be scientific and clinical researchers to achieve ecological validity. In the former case, each client is handled as a participant in what Thorne (1947) described more than 50 years ago as:

> [A] single well-controlled experiment. The treatment may be carefully controlled by utilizing single therapeutic factors, observing and recording results systematically, and checking through the use of appropriate quantitative laboratory studies. . . . Individual

clinicians are encouraged to apply experimental and statistical methods in the analysis of case results, and larger scale analyses are made of the experience of a whole clinic over a period of years. (pp. 159, 166)

Behavior therapists provided the major impetus for the development of single-subject methods for clinical practitioners (see Barlow & Hersen, 1984; Gaynor, Baird, & Nelson-Gray, this volume), but the empirical-clinical methodology that spawned these methods is shared by many clinical psychologists of diverse theoretical orientations. Clinical researchers also have an integral role in operationalizing the empirical-clinical methodology. This operationalism can take place in many ways, such as research projects designed to scientifically evaluate the efficacy of the treatment that involve clients receiving the therapeutic intervention with others receiving a control or comparison condition, or program evaluation studies in which the outcomes achieved by clients being treated in clinical settings can be assessed and experimentally compared to appropriate control conditions. The scientist-practitioner model and the empirical-clinical methodology are an established nucleus for clinical psychology.

Although individual therapeutic efforts contribute more reliable information when the precautions of the single-subject experimental designs are used, and research studies provide more definitive evaluations when true-to-life clinical interventions are provided, neither approach to the investigation of the result of the therapy is entirely sufficient. A continuous dialectic of science and practice is needed to produce meaningful research capable of evaluating the efficacy and effectiveness of therapy.

This chapter focuses on the issues to be considered and the methods to be employed when undertaking scientific comparisons in the study of the efficacy and effectiveness of therapy. Researchers may also wish to consult other sources that consider additional and related approaches (e.g., Barlow & Hersen, 1984; Basham, 1986; Beutler & Hamblin, 1986; Durlak, Wells, Cotten, Johnson, 1995; Gaynor et al., this volume; Kazdin, 1998; Stiles & Shapiro, 1994).

GENERAL ISSUES TO CONSIDER

Over the past two decades, the application of research methods to clinical treatment outcome has amassed a sizable literature. There have been discussions of appropriate research designs, treatment procedures, and adequate control conditions, among other important topics. The resolutions to these issues remain in place and the amassed research is consistent in suggesting that psychological treatments confer benefit to clients. Generalized conclusions about the efficacy of treatment (based on findings from controlled studies) and effectiveness of treatment (based on findings from studies using clinical practitioners in mental health systems) have been reached via the use of box score tallies and, more recently, meta-analyses (see also Durlak, this volume). Even more recently, the field has begun to develop a set of criteria to be used when reviewing the cumulative literature on the outcomes of therapy, criteria to make determinations of whether or not a treatment can be said to have been "empirically supported."

Empirically supported treatments may be defined as treatments shown to be efficacious in randomized clinical research trials with given populations (see American Psychological Association Task Force on Promotion and Dissemination of Psychological Procedures, 1995; Chambless & Hollon, 1998). There exists a multitude of perspectives on the utility of defining and delineating validated treatments, and the topic has been much debated in recent years (e.g., Clinical Psychology: Science and Practice). Although the majority see the necessity of the evaluation of treatments, not all agree on the methods to use to identify these treatments (Kazdin, 1996).

The operational definition of empirically supported treatments focuses on the accumulated data on the efficacy of a psychological therapy (see Table 14.1). These demonstrations of treatment efficacy often involve a randomized clinical trial in which an intervention is applied to diagnosed cases and compared to a comparison condition (e.g., wait list, alternative treatment) to determine the degree or relative degree of beneficial change associated with treatment. The evidence that is accumulated comes from studies the purposes of which were to establish the presence (or absence) of a treatment effect (Jacobson & Christensen, 1996). However, even if a treatment has been supported empirically, the transport of the treatment from one setting (research clinic) to another (service clinic) represents a separate issue. One then considers the

Table 14.1. Summary of criteria for empirically supported psychological therapies

- Comparison with a no-treatment control group, alternative treatment group, or placebo (a) in a randomized control trial, controlled single-case experiment, or equivalent time-samples design and (b) in which the EST* is statistically significantly superior to no-treatment, placebo, or alternative treatments or in which the EST is equivalent to a treatment already established in efficacy, and power is sufficient to detect moderate differences.

- These studies must have been conducted with (a) a treatment manual or its logical equivalent; (b) a population, treated for specified problems, for whom inclusion criteria have been delineated in a reliable, valid manner; (c) reliable and valid outcome assessment measures, at minimum tapping the problems targeted for change; and (d) appropriate data analysis.

- For a designation of efficacious, the superiority of the EST must have been shown in at least two independent research settings (sample size of three or more at each site in the case of single-case experiments). If there is conflicting evidence, the preponderance of the well-controlled data must support the EST's efficacy.

- For a designation of possibly efficacious, one study (sample size of three or more in the case of single-case experiments) suffices in the absence of conflicting evidence.

- For a designation of efficacious and specific, the EST must have been shown to be statistically significantly superior to pill or psychological placebo or to an alternative bona fide treatment in at least two independent research settings. If there is conflicting evidence, the preponderance of the well-controlled data must support the EST's efficacy and specificity.

*EST = empirically supported therapy.
Source: From "Defining Empirically Supported Therapies," by D. L. Chambless and S. D. Hollon, 1998, *Journal of Consulting and Clinical Psychology, 66,* p. 18. Copyright 1998 by the American Psychological Association. Reprinted with permission.

effectiveness of the treatment (e.g., Hoagwood, Hibbs, Brent, & Jensen, 1995). The effectiveness of a treatment has to do with the generalizability, feasibility, and cost-effectiveness of the therapeutic procedures. The investigation of treatment effectiveness necessarily grows out of studies on treatment efficacy, and it seems reasonable to assert that randomized clinical trials are useful to address both questions of efficacy and effectiveness. Some have argued (e.g., Garfield, 1996; Seligman, 1995), however, that the efficacy study is insufficient in answering questions pertaining to effectiveness because it overlooks features of therapy conducted in the field. For example, Seligman argued that therapy in a clinical setting differs from the randomized clinical trial in a research clinic in the following ways: (a) therapy is often of long duration; (b) psychotherapeutic strategies can be changed throughout the therapy; (c) patients frequently actively select a therapist and style of treatment; (d) patients are most frequently comorbid with multiple disorders; and (e) therapy tends to focus on improvements in general functioning rather than improvements on specific symptoms or amelioration of disorders. The counterarguments are that although each of these issues is important, quite a few randomized clinical trials include cases with comorbid conditions, include measures of general functioning, and are not of short duration. Moreover, the methods of a randomized clinical trial can accommodate variations in the issues raised such that they can be directly manipulated and evaluated. The evaluator of treatment outcome needs to make informed decisions with regard to both the internal and external validity of the study in question.

One of the major forces affecting the field of mental health is the managed care revolution. What role will treatment outcome research play in the future of mental health services vis-à-vis managed care? Although it is not the thrust of this chapter to fully address managed care, it does appear to be the case that the treatment outcome literature is now receiving a much more widespread readership; parties involved in the payments for psychological treatment are paying increased attention to the data that inform us about the outcomes associated with types of treatment. For better or worse, the future of treatment outcome research is likely to prosper in part as a means to distill the preferred interventions from the larger number of practiced treatments. Treatment outcome research that integrates the finely honed results of randomized clinical trials (efficacy) with the nuanced complexities found by clinicians operating in the trenches (effectiveness) is essential to the development of optimal mental health services.

METHODOLOGICAL ISSUES

Research evaluations of the efficacy and effectiveness of therapeutic interventions have evolved from less rigorous estimations of the percentage improved to multimethod experimental investigations of carefully defined treatments (or treatment components) applied to genuine clients. Although all of the ideals outlined in the present chapter are not often achieved in a single study, they serve as exemplars nonetheless. Consistent attempts to incorporate these ideals into research designs must be made, although there is recognition that, due to ethical, financial, and logistical constraints, not all studies achieve complete methodological rigor. This section of the chapter identifies and addresses three domains relevant to treatment outcome research: matters of design, matters of procedure, and the measurement of change over time.

Matters of Design

To adequately assess the causal impact of the therapeutic intervention, control procedures derived from experimental science have been adapted by clinical researchers. The objective is to separate the effects of the therapy per se from the changes that result from other factors (e.g., expectancy, the passage of time, attention, repeated assessments, regression to the mean). These extraneous factors must be "controlled." In this section, we discuss several matters of design: selection of control conditions, random assignment, posttreatment and follow-up evaluations, and between-group treatment comparisons.

Selection of Control Conditions

Comparisons of persons randomly assigned to different conditions are required to ensure the control of the effects of factors other than the treatment. Comparable persons are randomly placed into either the control condition or the treatment condition, and by comparing the changes evidenced by the members of both conditions, the efficacy of therapy over and above the outcome produced by the extraneous factors can be determined. The decision about the nature of the control condition, however, is not easy. Researchers have the difficult job of deciding which type of control condition (e.g., no-treatment, wait list, attention-placebo, standard treatment) to employ (see Table 14.2 for recent examples).

Clients who are assigned to a no-treatment control condition are administered the assessments on repeated occasions, separated by an interval of time equal to the length of the therapy provided to those in the treatment condition. Any changes seen in the treated clients are compared to the changes seen in the nontreated clients. When treated clients evidence significantly superior improvements over nontreated clients, the treatment is credited with producing the changes. This control procedure has desirable features and eliminates several rival hypotheses (e.g., spontaneous remission, historical effects, maturation, regression to the mean). However, a no-treatment control condition does not guard against other potentially confounding factors, including client anticipation of treatment, client expectancy for change, and the act of seeing a therapist—independent of what treatment the therapist actually provided.

A variant of a no-treatment procedure, the wait list condition, provides for some additional control. For example, clients in a wait list control condition have made the step of initiating treatment and may anticipate change due to therapy. The changes that occur for wait-listed clients are evaluated exactly as are those of the clients who received therapy. Assuming the clients in the wait list and the treatment conditions are comparable in terms of variables such as gender, age, ethnicity, severity of presenting problem, and motivation, the researcher can make inferences that the changes over and above those manifested by the wait list clients are likely to have been due to the intervention rather than to any extraneous factors that were operative for both the treated and the wait list cases. The important demographic and other data are

Table 14.2.   Types of control conditions in therapy outcome research

Control Condition	Definition	Examples	
		Description	Reference
No-treatment control	Clients are administered assessments on repeated occasions, separated by an interval of time equal to the length of treatment.	Homeless persons were randomly assigned to an intensive case management intervention or a control condition. Individuals in the control condition received no treatment but were assessed on repeated occasions.	Freeston et al., 1997
Wait list control	Clients are assessed before and after a designated duration of time, but receive the treatment following the waiting period. They may anticipate change due to therapy.	Clients with obsessive-compulsive disorder who did not have overt compulsions were randomly assigned to a cognitive-behavioral treatment for obsessive thoughts or a 16-week wait list control condition.	Toro et al., 1997
Attention-placebo/ nonspecific control	Clients receive a treatment that involves nonspecific factors (e.g., attention, contact with a therapist).	Patients hospitalized for severe burns were randomly assigned to a hypnotic analgesic intervention or a control condition in which they received attention, information, and brief relaxation instructions.	Patterson & Ptacek, 1997
Standard treatment/ routine care control	Clients receive an intervention that is the current practice for treatment of the problem under study.	Juvenile offenders and their families were randomly assigned to multisystemic therapy or usual juvenile justice services.	Henggeler et al., 1997
Neutral/counter-demand expectancy control	Clients are provided with no basis for expecting change or are induced to expect not to change for a given period of time.	No example of this type of control condition was found.	

Note: All examples were drawn from a single year in a major peer-reviewed journal.

gathered so that statistical comparisons can be conducted to determine condition comparability.

A potential problem with wait list controls is that a wait list client might experience a life crisis that forces immediate professional attention. It is recommended that each control client's status be monitored informally but frequently. Independent of pressing distress, wait list clients are offered the therapy, or an acceptable and effective substitute, as soon as possible after the wait list is completed. The withholding of treatment has been raised as a concern regarding clients assigned to wait list and no-treatment control conditions. Consider the following: It is preferable in treatment outcome studies that the duration of the control condition is the same as the duration of the treatment condition(s). The comparable durations help to ensure that any differential changes between the conditions would not be due to the passage of time. However, this design has several potential problems. For example, if a treatment is provided in 16 sessions (that take four to five months to accomplish), then clients in the control condition would have to wait four to five months before beginning treatment. Do ethical restraints prohibit such wait periods (see also Bersoff & Bersoff, this volume)? Also, with long wait list durations, the probability of differential attrition rises, a situation that could have a compromising effect on the study results. If rates of attrition from a wait list condition are high, the sample in the control condition may be rendered sufficiently different from the treatment condition to be no longer representative of the larger sample. Control conditions are essential to demonstrate the efficacy of treatment, but may not be required once a treatment has, on several occasions, been found to be more effective than wait list conditions (Kendall & Flannery-Schroeder, 1998). Once established as efficacious, a treatment may then serve as a comparison condition for the evaluation of other interventions.

Attention-placebo, or nonspecific treatment, control conditions are an alternative to the wait list control that not only rules out threats to internal validity but also controls for the effects that might be due simply to meeting with a therapist. Participants in attention-placebo conditions have contact with and receive attention from a therapist. In addition, these participants receive a description of the treatment rationale (a statement of purpose and explanation of the treatment procedures offered at the beginning of the intervention). The rationale provided to attention-placebo clients is intended to mobilize an *expectancy* of positive gains. These nonspecific elements in the therapy (elements separate from the identified treatment strategies) may account for client change, just as medication placebos and psychological placebos have been found effective in some situations (see Hollon & DeRubeis, 1981; Jacobson & Hollon, 1996a, 1996b; A. Shapiro & Morris, 1978). Attention-placebo conditions enable clinical researchers to identify the changes produced by specific therapeutic strategies over and above the effects of nonspecific factors.

Despite their advantages, attention-placebo controls are not without limitations (Parloff, 1986). When long-term therapy is being evaluated, it is questionable from an ethical standpoint to offer some clients contact (placebo) that does not deal directly with the problems for which they have sought therapy. Attention-placebos must be "theoretically inert" while nevertheless providing professional contact and attention and instilling positive expectancies in clients. To offer such an intervention in the guise of effective therapy is acceptable only when clients are fully informed in advance and sign informed consent acknowledging their willingness to take a chance on receiving either a placebo or a therapy intervention. In the absence of data to justify the provision of a treatment, clinical researchers accept the ethical mandate to conduct scientifically rigorous evaluations to examine the efficacy of practiced therapies—and this may require controlling for nonspecific effects. Of course, following proper evaluations of and positive results from interventions, there is no longer the need for researchers to ask clients (some of whom may have immediate needs) to consent to the possibility of placebo treatment.

Methodologically, it is difficult to ensure that the therapists who conduct attention-placebo conditions have the same degree of positive expectancy for client gains as do therapists conducting specific interventions (O'Leary & Borkovec, 1978). Demand characteristics suggest that when therapists predict a favorable outcome, clients will tend to improve accordingly (Kazdin, 1998). Thus, therapist expectancies may not be equated in therapy versus placebo conditions, and this could produce a confounding factor. Similarly, even if clients in an attention-placebo condition have high expectations at the start, they may grow disenchanted when no specific changes are emerging. When the results suggest that the therapy condition evidenced significantly better outcomes than the attention-placebo control condition, it is essential that the researcher conduct and evaluate clients' perceptions of the credibility of the treatment rationale and their expectations for change (e.g., manipulation checks) to confirm that clients in the attention-placebo control condition perceived the treatment to be credible and expected to improve. Otherwise, differences in treatment outcome are confounded by differences in the credibility of the condition or the expectations for outcomes.

Conceptually, it is difficult to select procedures believed to be inert yet still likely to be credible to clients. Having been involved in the design of attention-placebo control conditions, we found that each credible rationale was indeed someone else's form of therapy! A credible treatment rationale used in therapy outcome research as an attention-placebo control tends to have a short life span:

> If one finds placebo effects, the determinants of the effects should soon be isolated and documented. As determinants of the placebo become known, conceptualizations of the control procedure are relabeled. What was originally labeled a placebo procedure might be relabeled as demand stimuli for improved posttest behavior, implicit or explicit instructional sets to establish the expectation of benefit from the particular treatment procedures, confidence in the therapist, response to societal or community expectations of benefit from a treatment, or desire to please the therapist who spends many hours with the patient. (O'Leary & Borkovec, 1978, p. 823)

Thus, nonspecific effects tend to be specified and redefined as components of effective therapy when they show a consistent robust effect. The factors that cause client change in attention-placebo conditions merit delineation and inclusion in therapeutic intervention, rather that being left vague and mysterious.

Standard treatment (or routine care) controls involve replacing attention-placebo intervention with the intervention that is currently being applied for treatment of the problems and clients involved in the therapy being evaluated. If it is demonstrated that the standard care intervention and the therapy under study are equated for nonspecific factors—for example, duration of treatment or client and therapist expectancies—this approach enables the researcher to test the relative efficacy of one type of intervention against its major contemporary competitor. It is of course important that researchers ensure that both the standard (routine) treatment and the new treatment are implemented in a high-quality fashion (Kendall & Hollon, 1983) and use standard treatment comparisons only after the standard treatment has itself been shown to be superior to conditions that control for alternative explanations of outcome. One distinct advantage arises via use of the standard treatment control condition: the ethical concerns that arise from the use of no-treatment controls are quelled, given that quality care is provided to all participants in the study; attrition is likely to be kept to a minimum as all participants receive genuine treatment procedures; and nonspecific factors are likely to be equated (Kazdin, 1998).

O'Leary and Borkovec (1978) described "neutral" or "counterdemand expectancy" controls that involve, respectively, providing clients with no basis for expecting therapeutic improvement, and inducing clients to actually expect *not* to change for a stated length of time. Neutral expectancy control conditions would be expected to show change only if the specific therapy intervention has an impact over and above placebo effects. However, several problems appear inescapable with this method: (a) although expectancy effects may be controlled, other placebo factors such as therapist attention are not ruled out; (b) once clients begin to receive the intervention, it is doubtful that they would fail to generate positive expectancies simply because they can see that help is being provided; and (c) ethically, it is a violation of informed consent to involve a client in therapy without forewarning him or her of the therapy's possible and likely effects.

The counterdemand procedure suffers from these limitations as well. In addition, it requires that the researcher have a solid basis for predicting the time interval required before change will occur due to the intervention. If change does begin to occur during the time that clients are instructed not to expect it, a host of positive and negative expectancies may be engendered, thus confounding the control procedure. Furthermore, the counterdemand instructions are remarkably similar to an intervention widely used by systems-oriented family therapists: "paradox" or "prescribing the symptom" (Haley, 1976). Although experimental support for this intervention is not fully developed (see DeRubeis & Crits-Christoph, 1998), an extensive theoretical rationale (Watzlawick, Weakland, & Fisch, 1974) and clinical case literature (Watzlawick, 1978) offer support for paradoxical intervention. Thus, rather than providing an expectancy-minimizing and inert control condition, the counterdemand procedure may in fact be a type of therapeutic intervention meriting evaluation in its own right!

Random Assignment

Following the design of the comparison condition(s), consideration turns to the procedures for assigning participants to conditions. *Random assignment* of participants to the therapy or control conditions as well as random assignment of participants to therapists is essential to strive to achieve initial comparability between the two conditions. For instance, random assignment of clients would likely eliminate the unwanted effects of age or socioeconomic status, because in most cases random assignment would not result in one condition being older or more wealthy and educated than another condition. Following random assignment, because randomization does not guarantee comparability, appropriate statistical tests are applied to examine condition comparability.

Randomization may be accomplished by any procedure that gives every participant an equal chance of being assigned to either the control or treatment condition (e.g., assignment by a coin toss). There can be problems when random assignment is not applied; consider the situation when the first 30 clients are assigned to therapy, and the next 30 clients are placed on the wait list. Such assignment is not truly random and may hide subtle selection biases. Perhaps the first 30 clients sought therapy more quickly due to stronger motivation than the next 30. Perhaps the first 30 clients were exposed to a temporary environmental stress that was no longer a factor when the next 30 clients applied for aid.

Although random assignment does not absolutely assure comparability of the control and therapy conditions on all measures, it does maximize the likelihood that this will occur. An alternative procedure, randomized blocks (or matched-pair) assignment, or assignment by stratified blocks, involves matching prospective clients in subgroups that (a) each contain clients that are highly comparable on key dimensions (e.g., initial severity) and (b) contain the same number of clients as the number of conditions. For example, if the study requires a control condition and one treatment condition, clients could be paired off so that each pair is highly comparable. The members in each subgroup are then randomly assigned to either the treatment or control condition, thus increasing the likelihood that each condition will contain mirror-image participants while retaining the randomization factor. Randomized blocks assignment of clients to conditions (e.g., Kendall & Wilcox, 1980), often using initial severity as the blocking factor, is a recommended research methodology. Use of this design feature requires that the stratification be used in the data analysis as well.

Posttreatment, Follow-up, and Intratreatment Evaluations

Assessments of clients at posttreatment are essential to examine the comparative efficacy of treatment versus control conditions to produce beneficial change. However, any evidence of treatment efficacy immediately upon therapy completion may not be indicative of more long-term success (maintenance). Treatment outcome may be appreciable at posttreatment but fail to exhibit maintenance of the effects. It is highly recommended that treatment outcome studies include in their design a follow-up assessment. Follow-up assessments (e.g., six months, one year) are a signpost of methodological rigor, expected by research journals and deemed necessary in the demonstration of treatment efficacy. For evidence of maintenance, the treatment must have produced results at the follow-up assessment that are comparable to those evident at posttreatment (improvements from pretreatment and an absence of detrimental change since posttreatment).

Follow-up evaluations can identify late effects resulting from the treatment. For example, the effects of two different treatments may be favorable and comparable at the end of treatment, but one treatment may be more effective in the prevention of relapse (see Greenhouse, Stangl, & Bromberg, 1989, for discussion of survival analysis). When two treatments are deemed comparable at the posttreatment evaluation, yet one is associated with higher relapse, the knowledge gained from the follow-up evaluation is a valuable rationale for the selection of one treatment over another (see Figure 14.1 for an example).

Follow-up evaluations also may detect continued improvement associated with a treatment because the benefits of some therapeutic interventions may accumulate rather than lag over time. In follow-up evaluations, it is important, moreover, to determine if participants have sought or received additional treatment services subsequent to

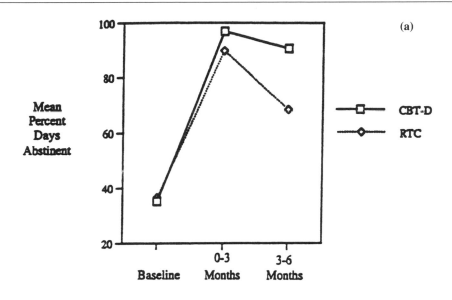

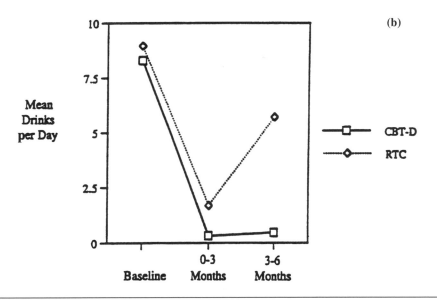

Figure 14.1.   Drinking frequency and quantity at follow-up by treatment condition and time. CBT-D = cognitive-behavioral treatment for depression; RTC = relaxation training control.

Source: Brown, R., et al. (1997). Cognitive-behavioral treatment for depression in alcoholism. *Journal of Consulting and Clinical Psychology, 65,* p. 722. Copyright © 1997 by the American Psychological Association. Reprinted with permission.

the study's intervention. Interpretation of these data requires care, because additional treatment may be viewed either as a success (i.e., increased access to needed care) or a problem (e.g., increased costs to health care systems). In any event, treatment outcome can include not only reduced symptoms and improved psychological functioning, but also enhanced use of health care systems.

Follow-up evaluations are labor intensive and costly, and some have argued that these evaluations may not be necessary (Nicholson & Berman, 1983). Others, however (and we would agree), find the literature to support the need for follow-up evaluations (e.g., Goldstein, Lopez, & Greenleaf, 1979; Nich & Carroll, 1997; Ollendick, 1986; D. Shapiro & Shapiro, 1982; Smith, Glass, & Miller, 1980), and the current expectation is that an evaluation of treatment will include a follow-up (e.g., Chambless & Hollon, 1998).

Researchers increasingly are operationalizing Kiesler's (1973) view of psychotherapy process and outcome as intertwined phenomena, such as by assessing change during treatment (i.e., intratreatment) as well as at posttreatment and follow-up. Repeated assessment of client symptoms and functional change suggest that the first several sessions of treatment constitute the period of most rapid positive change (K. Howard, Lueger, Maling, & Martinovich, 1993). Change across several domains of functioning tends to be phasic, however, and may require more extended treatment (K. Howard et al., 1993). Intratreatment assessments not only permit a fine-grained mapping of the course of change in therapy, but also provide important clues (e.g., Jaycox, Foa, & Morral, 1998) to identify mediators of positive or adverse outcomes.

Comparing Alternative Treatments

The methods described thus far are typically employed in the evaluation of the effects of a single treatment. To determine the comparative efficacy and effectiveness of therapeutic interventions, between-groups designs with more than one treatment condition must be applied (Kiesler, 1966)—a direct comparison of one treatment and one or more alternative treatments (akin to the standard intervention comparison). Several additional precautions are necessary in such investigations. For example, sample size considerations are influenced by whether the comparison is between a treatment and a control condition or one treatment versus another treatment (Kazdin & Bass, 1989).

As in all between-group comparisons, it is optimal when each client is randomly assigned to receive one and only one kind of therapy and the assignment of clients to conditions results in the comparability of the clients receiving each intervention. As previously mentioned, a randomized block procedure, with participants blocked on an important variable (e.g., pretreatment severity), is a desirable design characteristic. It is also wise to check the comparability of the clients in the different treatment conditions on other important variables (e.g., age, socioeconomic status, prior therapy experience) before concluding the evaluation of the intervention. If all participants are not available at the outset of treatment, such as when participants come from successive clients entering a clinic, then the comparability of conditions can be checked at several intervals as the therapy outcome study progresses toward completion.

It is important for the comparison of different treatments that the therapists conducting each type of treatment are comparable with regard to potentially influential factors as (a) training background, (b) length and type of professional and clinical experience, (c) expertise in conducting the particular intervention, (d) allegiance with one or the other of the treatments, and (e) expectancy that the intervention is effective. As one way to control for (and possibly also rigorously delineate) these therapist effects, researchers have often had each therapist conduct each type of intervention with at least one client per intervention, or utilized a stratified blocking procedure to assure that each intervention is conducted by several comparable therapists. The first method enables an experimental examination of the effects of differing therapists, but this evaluation is valid only if therapists are equally expert and positively oriented toward each intervention. For example, it would be an invalid test to ask a group of cognitive-behavioral therapists to conduct both a cognitive-behavioral therapy (in which their expertise is high) and an existential therapy (in which their expertise is minimal). The second method, although therapist comparability requires documentation, enables the researcher to examine the effect of a variety of therapists in one intervention with the effect of a variety of therapists in an alternative intervention.

Treatment comparisons also require that the intervention procedures be equated for salient variables such as (a) duration; (b) length, intensity, and frequency of therapist contacts with client; (c) credibility and impact of the rationale; (d) setting; and (e) involvement of persons significant to the client. In some cases, these factors may be the basis for two alternative therapies (e.g., conjoint vs. individual marital therapy), in which case, the variable becomes part of the experimental contrast rather than a matter for control.

The assessment measures used for evaluation when different types of intervention are compared must (a) cover the range of psychosocial functioning that is a target for therapeutic change, (b) include measures that tap the costs and possible negative side effects of the interventions, and (c) be unbiased with respect to the alternative kinds of intervention. The last precaution is necessary because the outcome of a comparison of therapies may be misleading if the assessments are not equally sensitive to the types of changes that are most likely caused by each of the types of intervention.

A potentially important issue often ignored in comparative therapy studies pertains to the level of efficacy of each individual therapeutic approach in relation to the "expected efficacy" of each therapy based on prior studies. For example, two treatments are compared, and therapy A is found superior to therapy B. The question arises, was therapy A superior, or did therapy B fail to be efficacious in this instance? It would be desirable in demonstrating the efficacy of therapy A if the results due to therapy B reflected the level of efficacy found in earlier demonstrations of therapy B's efficacy. Interpretations of the results of comparative studies are dependent on the level of efficacy of each of the therapies in relation to their expected (or standard) efficacy. Effect sizes are useful in making these comparisons and reaching sound conclusions.

Last, although the issues discussed nevertheless apply, comparisons of psychological therapy with medications (psychopharmacology) present special issues for consideration. For example, how and when should placebo medications be used with psychological therapy? How best to address expectancy effects? How should differential attrition be handled? Follow-ups become especially important: After the active treatments are discontinued, are the effects maintained? This question is especially pertinent given that psychological treatment effects may persist after treatment, whereas the effects of medications may not persist when the medications are discontinued. (Readers interested in discussions of these issues are referred to Hollon, 1996; Hollon & DeRubeis, 1981; Jacobson & Hollon, 1996a, 1996b.)

Matters of Procedure

Procedural issues must be considered in the development of treatments and the evaluation of their outcomes. Procedural matters such as the use of manual-based treatments, the use of fidelity or integrity checks, and the issue of the transportability of treatments, as well as factors important in sample selection (e.g., use of analogue versus clinical samples, ethnic diversity of clients) will be considered.

Manual-Based Treatments

To replicate an evaluation of treatment, it is essential that the treatment can be implemented by others. Accordingly, there is increasing interest in and need for the development and use of treatment manuals in therapy outcome research. Treatment manuals offer a number of advantages, such as enhancing internal validity and treatment integrity. They allow the comparison of the treatments across contexts and formats while eliminating often potential confounds (e.g., differences in the amount of contact between therapist and client, type and amount of training required prior to implementation of the treatment, time between therapy sessions; Dobson & Shaw, 1988). Therapist manuals facilitate training and contribute meaningfully to the soundness of the replication of therapy outcome studies (Dobson & Shaw, 1988). Using our work with anxiety disordered youth as an example, there are manuals to operationalize therapy for individual (e.g., Kendall, Kane, Howard, & Siqueland, 1990; March & Mulle, 1996), family (Howard & Kendall, 1996), and group (Flannery-Schroeder & Kendall, 1996) treatment.

Debate has ensued regarding the use of manual-based treatment versus the individualized approach typically found in practice. Those who discuss the limits of manualization (e.g., Garfield, 1996; Havik & VandenBos, 1996) have suggested that manuals limit therapist creativity (for other discussion, see Davison & Lazarus, 1995; Wilson, 1996) and place restrictions on the individualization that the therapy can undergo (for other discussion, see Waltz, Addis, Koerner, & Jacobson, 1993; Wilson, 1995). Although more work needs to be done, the issues facing the application of manual-based treatments can be stated in testable terms and can be examined empirically (Kendall, 1998). In at least one evaluation, use of a manual-based treatment did not restrict therapist flexibility (Kendall & Chu, 1999).

Fidelity or Integrity Checks

Evaluators of therapy recognize that simply because a manual is written and is said to guide an intervention does not mean that the therapy provided was the therapy described in the manual. For example, it does not appear to be the case that professionals can become proficient in the administration of therapy simply by reading a manual. Effective use of manual-based treatments must be preceded by adequate training (Barlow, 1989). A therapist may strictly adhere to the manual yet fail to administer the therapy in an otherwise competent manner, or he or she may competently administer therapy while significantly deviating from the manual. In both cases, the operational definition of the independent variable (i.e., the treatment manual) has been violated, treatment integrity impaired, and replication rendered impossible (Dobson & Shaw, 1988). In addition, the use of manual-based treatments does not eliminate the potential for differential therapist effects; rather, the researcher could examine those therapist variables (e.g., warmth, therapeutic relationship) that might be related to treatment outcome. Evaluations of treatment include checks on the integrity of the treatment, documenting that the treatment as described was indeed the treatment provided.

Integrity checks are needed, but they are not a complete solution. Although manuals foster the integrity of the independent variable, there remains the need to study potential variations in treatment outcome that are associated with differences in the *quality* of the treatment provided (Garfield, 1998; Kendall & Hollon, 1983). Expert judges would be needed to make determinations of differential quality prior to the examination of differential outcomes for high- versus low-quality therapy implementations (for further discussion of evaluating treatment integrity, see Waltz et al., 1993).

Manual-based treatments are preferred for the advancement of the evaluation of the outcomes of treatment. However, the proper use of manual-based therapy requires flexible application and ongoing supervision. For example, contemporary treatment manuals allow for the therapist to attend to each client's specific needs/concerns and comorbid conditions without deviating from the manual. The goal may be described as one that includes the provision of a standardized implementation of therapy while utilizing a personalized case formulation (Kendall, Chu, Gifford, Hayes, & Nauta, 1998).

Simply put, a quality research project includes a check on the manipulated variable. In controlled therapy outcome evaluations, the manipulated variable is typically treatment or a characteristic of treatment. For example, the researcher may design the study so that different treatments will be provided for clients who are assigned to the different conditions. By design, all clients are not treated the same. However, simply because the study has been so designed does not guarantee that the independent variable has been manipulated as intended.

Steps to help assure that the treatments (independent variable) are indeed manipulated as designed include requiring that a treatment plan be followed, training therapists carefully, employing therapy manuals, and supervising and monitoring the treatment. Even though these steps are helpful, it is worthwhile for the researcher to conduct an independent check of the manipulation. For example, requiring that therapy sessions be audiotaped allows for an independent rater to listen to the tapes and conduct a manipulation check. Quantifiable judgments regarding characteristics of the treatment provide the necessary manipulation check. In addition, audiotapes are inexpensive, can be used for subsequent training, and can be analyzed for other research purposes.

Tape recordings of the therapy sessions evaluated by outcome studies not only provide a check on the treatment within each separate study but also can allow for a check on the comparability of treatments provided across studies. That is, the therapy provided as cognitive-behavioral therapy in one clinician's study could be checked to determine its comparability to other clinician-researchers' cognitive-behavioral therapy. Moreover, as discussed, the *quality* (Kendall & Hollon, 1983) of the therapy can be examined. Treatment manuals that describe the general therapy procedures and some specific details are needed for researchers to conduct and evaluate comparable types of intervention, but independent checks alone can document treatment comparability and examine treatment quality.

Analogue versus Clinical Samples

Debate exists over the appropriateness of samples for treatment outcome research. An analogue sample refers to a sample of participants who approximate clinically disordered individuals. Clinical trials, by contrast, apply and evaluate treatments with actual clients who are seeking clinical services. Consider a study investigating the effects of treatment X on depression: It might use (a) a sample consisting of clinically depressed clients diagnosed via structured interviews (clinical) or (b) a sample consisting of a group of college students who undergo a procedure to induce dysphoric mood (analogue). The latter participants may or may not meet diagnostic criteria for depression. Those who argue for the use of analogue samples cite a greater ability to control various conditions and minimize sources of internal invalidity. On the other hand, those critical of analogue samples argue that external validity is compromised if there exists a lack of continuity between the construct as experienced by clinical versus analogue participants. With respect to depression, for instance, there is controversy as to whether depression in clinical populations is significantly different from that found in college student samples (e.g., Coyne & Gotlib, 1983; Gotlib, 1984; Krupnick, Shea, & Elkin, 1986; Tennen, Hall, & Affleck, 1995; Vredenburg, Flett, & Krames, 1993).

Although exceptions exist, it appears that the use of analogue samples, though not ideal, may be acceptable when (a) the sample size and power would otherwise be quite small and (b) only those analogue participants who are shown to have measurable characteristics relevant to the disorder in question (e.g., depressive symptoms) are included. Reflection on the nature of the particular study and how the results will be used is imperative in the decision of whether to use a clinical or analogue sample.

Transporting Treatments

To determine the efficacy and effectiveness of treatments, their outcomes must be evaluated scientifically. But it is not sufficient to demonstrate treatment efficacy within a narrowly defined sample in a highly selective setting (e.g., an analogue situation); unless the evaluation was conducted with actual diagnosed cases receiving real treatment in a genuine clinic, the question of whether or not the treatment can be transported to other settings requires independent evaluation. In many instances, treatment outcome evaluations are conducted within research-oriented (as compared to clinical service–oriented) settings. The results of investigations conducted at research centers are valuable but may or may not be transportable into clinical practice. One cannot assume that the treatment will be as efficacious within the clinical service setting as in the research setting (see Weisz, Donenberg, Han, & Weiss, 1995; Weisz, Weiss, & Donenberg, 1992). Some initial research, where panic disordered clients were treated in a service clinic using a manual-based treatment developed in a research clinic (Wade, Treat, & Stuart, 1998), suggests that the amount of beneficial change seen in the service clinic was comparable to that produced in the research clinic. Although much more applied research is needed, this initial study suggests that at least some types of treatment (e.g., cognitive-behavioral) may be transported across contexts. Closing the gap between clinical research and clinical practice requires effort to further transport and evaluate treatments (getting "what works" into practice) and additional research into those factors (e.g., client, therapist, researcher, service delivery setting; Kendall & Southam-Gerow, 1995) that may be involved in successful transportation.

Client Diversity

The literature indicates ethnic and other differences in perceptions of mental health service providers and that some minorities may underutilize these services (e.g., Homma-True, Greene, Lopez, & Trimble, 1993; Neal & Turner, 1991; Neighbors, 1985, 1988; Sue, Kurasaki, & Srinivasan, this volume). Investigations have also addressed the potential for bias in diagnoses and in the provision of mental health services (e.g., Flaherty & Meaer, 1980; Homma-True et al., 1993; Lopez, 1989; Simon, Fleiss, Gurland, Stiller, & Sharpe, 1973).

Despite the increased research attention given to ethnocultural diversity, surprisingly few studies have investigated the role of ethnicity as it relates to outcome. Research samples may unwittingly include an underrepresentation of certain groups and contribute to misleading conclusions (see Alvidrez, Azocar, & Miranda, 1996; Beutler, 1996; Miranda, 1996). It is imperative that research samples accurately reflect the population to which the results will be generalized. Outreach efforts may be needed to inform ethnic minorities of available services. Once diversity within the sample is accomplished, statistical analyses can examine potential differential treatment outcomes (see Beutler, Brown, Crothers, Booker, & Seabrook, 1996; Treadwell, Flannery-Schroeder, & Kendall 1994). Coding research participants by ethnic status is one, although simplistic, approach—simplistic because it fails to address variations in an individual's identity. It may be the degree to which an individual identifies with and is enculturated in any of what may be several ethnocultural groups or communities or an ethnicity, not simply the ethnicity itself, that potentially moderates treatment outcome.

In addition, service providers should be trained in multicultural perspectives to decrease the likelihood of misunderstanding (Homma-True et al., 1993; Miranda, Azocar, Organista, Munoz, & Lieberman, 1996; Thompson, Neighbors, Munday, & Jackson, 1996). Mandatory multicultural training could minimize the cultural gaps that may be responsible, in part, for the underinclusion of ethnic minorities in research studies. Inclusion of ethnic minorities may enhance generalizability and also provide an opportunity to examine between-group differences.

Measuring Change over Time

No single measure of the outcome of therapeutic intervention possesses either the reliability or the comprehensiveness to serve as the sole indicator of clients' gains (or setbacks). A variety of methods, measures, data sources, and sampling domains (e.g., symptomatic distress, functional impairment, quality of life) is necessary to fully assess treatment outcomes. With reference to their contributions to the assessment of changes over time, we consider assessment measures, examining the intent-to-treat sample, reporting clinical significance, and testing for mediators and moderators of outcomes.

Assessment Measures

It should be standard that a contemporary study of the effects of therapy uses a variety of measures of outcome that tap a variety of sources. The list of sources for therapy outcome data include, but are not limited to, assessments of client self-report (Butcher, this volume), client test (or task) performance, therapist judgments and ratings, archival or documentary records (e.g., health care visits and costs, work and school records), observations by trained, unbiased, blind observers (Cone, this volume), ratings by significant people in the client's life, and independent judgments by professionals (see also Butcher, 1997). Outcomes are more impactful when seen by independent (blind) judges than when based solely on client self-reports. In addition, the developmental level of the clients requires consideration; for instance, measures appropriate for adults are not always appropriate for adolescents or for children.

In addition to the multiple sources available for gathering outcome data, multiple targets of assessment must be considered. For example, one can measure overall psychological/psychosocial adjustment, specific interpersonal skills, the presence of a diagnosis, self-reported mood, cognitive functioning, or dimensions of personality, life environment, vocational status, or quality of interpersonal relationships. No one target captures all of the potential benefits of treatment. The use of the multiple targets facilitates an examination of positive therapeutic changes when they occur as well as the absence of change when interventions are not successful. Although we have focused on assessments as a source of pre- and post-treatment data for use in the evaluation of outcomes, assessments have also been developed for use at pretreatment—to make decisions about the nature and type of treatment that may be best for individual clients (e.g., Perry & Butcher, in press).

Multimethod assessment permits an evaluation of therapy-induced change on two different levels: the specifying level and the impact level (Kendall, Pellegrini, & Urbain, 1981). The *specifying level* refers to the exact skills, cognitive or emotional processes, or behaviors that have been modified during treatment (e.g, examining the number of coping self-statements generated during a specific task). In contrast, the *impact level* refers to the general level of functioning of the client (e.g., absence of a diagnosis, sociometric status of the client). A compelling demonstration of beneficial treatment would include change that occurs at both the level of specific discrete skills and behaviors as well as at the impact level of generalized functioning in which the client interacts differently within the larger environmental context.

Intent-to-Treat Analyses

Not all clients who are assigned to treatment complete their participation in the study. In clinical outcome studies, a loss of research participants may occur prior to completion (i.e., prior to posttreatment) or during the follow-up interval and is generally referred to as attrition. Attrition can be problematic for the analysis of outcomes, such as when there is a large number of noncompleters, or when attrition varies across conditions (see K. Howard, Krause, & Orlinsky, 1986). To address this matter, two sets of analyses can be conducted: analysis of outcomes for the treatment completers, and analyses of outcomes for all clients who were included at the time of randomization. Analyses of treatment completers involves the evaluation of only those who completed treatment: What are the effects when someone completes treatment? Treatment dropouts, treatment refusers, and clients who fail to adhere to treatment procedures would not be included in outcome analyses. These analyses provide researchers with an estimate of treatment efficacy (Kendall & Sugarman, 1997). Intent-to-treat analyses, a more conservative approach requires evaluating the outcomes for all participants involved at the point of randomization and provides an estimate of treatment effectiveness: What are the effects for people who present with this problem? Both approaches can be recommended as steps toward a more clear determination of outcome.

Intent-to-treat analyses can be (a) end-point or "last value" analyses, (b) analyses at completion of the therapy, or (c) analyses of pretreatment scores substituted as posttreatment scores. End-point analyses involve evaluating participants at the point they drop out of the study; analyses at completion involve evaluating participants at the end of the treatment program regardless of when they dropped out. The use of pretreatment scores as posttreatment scores simply has the pretreatment score reappear as the treatment outcome score.

Analyses of treatment completers result in the least conservative estimate of the efficacy of treatment outcome. Reports of treatment outcome may be somewhat high because they represent the results for only those who adhered to and completed the protocol. End-point analyses and analyses at the completion of treatment present a problem for those studies in which data collection is not continuous or that take place at set intervals across time. It is likely that participants who drop out, for example, may not have completed a data collection point for a considerable amount of time (e.g., weeks or months). Thus, the last data collection point cannot be considered representative of the participant's progress or lack of progress at the time of the dropout. Moreover, end-point analyses fail to control for the passage of time. In addition, participants who withdrew from the study, regardless of the reason, may be unwilling to complete an assessment at that point in time. Willingness to participate in the treatment protocol and willingness to complete measurement procedures are highly correlated (Lavori, 1992). Even if participants are recontacted and agree to participate in an evaluation at the end of the treatment protocol, the evaluation may be confounded if the client sought an alternative treatment during the intervening period. When conducting end-point analyses, it is important to evaluate the comparability of not only pretreatment scores but also pre- to posttreatment change levels for the study completers versus the dropouts. For example, Marks, Lowell, Noshirvani, Livanou, and Thrasher (1998) found that noncompleters in exposure-based cognitive-behavioral therapy for posttraumatic stress disorder (PTSD), although not significantly different at pretreatment from completers, were significantly less improved at posttreatment than completers. Accordingly, the apparent superiority at follow-up of the exposure-based treatments over a cognitively focused therapy may have been an artifact of differential attrition.

Use of pretreatment scores as posttreatment scores is also not devoid of problems. For example, although not likely or expected, it is possible that a treatment is somewhat detrimental to participants (or to participants with certain characteristics). The use of pretreatment scores in outcome analyses when the participant actually developed more severe psychological disturbance could result in an inflated estimate of treatment effects.

Although there is no currently agreed upon solution to these problems, several strategies can be advanced. When assessing the outcomes of a treatment that is considered "probably efficacious" or "well established" (see Chambless & Hollon, 1998), using pretreatment scores as posttreatment scores is probably the most conservative method to assess treatment gains. Because of its very conservative nature, it is probably best when paired with reports of the outcome evaluations using treatment completers.

If it is possible for noncompleting participants to be contacted and evaluated at the time when the treatment protocol would have ended, then perhaps the best strategy is to include these data in the analyses. This method controls for the passage of time such that both dropouts and treatment completers are evaluated over time periods of the same duration. If this method is used, however, it is extremely important to determine whether or not dropouts sought and/or received alternative treatments in the time between dropout and return for assessment.

Clinical Significance

The data produced by research projects designed to evaluate the efficacy or effectiveness of therapy are submitted to statistical tests of significance. Condition means are compared, the within-group and between-group variability is considered, and the analysis produces a numerical figure, which is then checked against critical values. An outcome achieves statistical significance if the magnitude of the mean difference is beyond what could have resulted by chance alone. Statistical analyses and statistical significance are essential for therapy evaluation, but they alone do not provide evidence of *clinical significance.*

Generally speaking, clinical significance refers to the meaningfulness of the magnitude of change, the remediation of the presenting problem to the point that it is no longer troublesome (Kendall & Grove, 1988). In a depressive disorder, for example, changes in depression would have to be of the magnitude that, after therapy, the person no longer suffers from debilitating depression. Specifically, this can be made operational as changes on a measure of the presenting problem (e.g., depression) that result in the client's being within normal limits on that measure.

Accordingly, clinically significant improvement can be identified using normative comparisons (Kendall & Grove, 1988), a method for operationalizing clinical significance testing (see also Kendall, Marrs-Garcia, Nath, & Sheldrick, 1999). National normative data are available for certain dependent measures (e.g., Beck Depression Inventory, BDI; Child Behavior Checklist, CBCL) and local norms are available for others, and these norms can be used to help assess clinical significance (see Figure 14.2 for an example). Sole reliance on statistical significance can lead to perceived differences (i.e., treatment gains) as potent, when in fact they may be clinically *in*significant. For example, imagine that results of a treatment outcome study demonstrate that mean BDI scores are significantly lower at posttreatment than pretreatment. An examination of the means, however, reveals a shift from a mean of 29 to a mean of 24. Given large sample sizes, this difference may well be statistically significant, yet perhaps be of limited practical significance. At both pre- and post-treatment, the scores are within the range that is considered indicative of clinical levels of distress (Kendall, Hollon, Beck, Hammen, & Ingram, 1987).

Both clinical and statistical significance are of great importance in the assessment of treatment outcomes. Given the complex nature of change, it is essential to evaluate

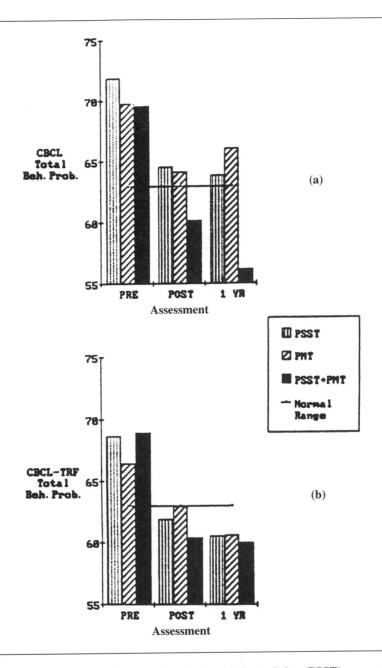

Figure 14.2.   Mean T scores for problem-solving skills training (PSST), parent management training (PMT), and PSST + PMT combined for the Total Behavior Problem scales of the (a) parent-completed Child Behavior Checklist (CBCL) and (b) teacher-completed CBCL. The horizontal line reflects the upper limit of the nonclinical (normal) range of children of the same age and sex. The T scores below this line were within the normal range.

Source: Kazdin, A.E., Siegel, T.C., & Bass, D. (1992). Cognitive-problem-solving skills training and parent management training in the treatment of antisocial behavior in children. *Journal of Consulting and Clinical Psychology, 60,* p. 744. Copyright © 1992 by the American Psychological Association. Reprinted with permission.

treatment with consideration of both approaches. Statistically significant improvements are not equivalent to "cures," and clinical significance is an additional, not a substitute, evaluative strategy. Statistical significance is required to document that changes were beyond those due to chance alone, yet it is useful to also consider if the changes returned dysfunctional clients to within normative limits. For example, to be considered clinically significant, improvement beyond a minimum criterion could be set for dependent measures (e.g., within 1.5 standard deviations from the normative mean).

Other approaches to the examination of clinically significant change include the Reliable Change Index (RCI; Jacobson, Follette, & Revenstorf, 1984; Jacobson & Truax, 1991). This method involves calculation of the number of clients moving from a dysfunctional to a normative range. The RCI is a calculation of a difference score (posttreatment minus pretreatment) divided by the standard error of measurement (calculated based on the reliability of the measure). The RCI is influenced by the magnitude of change and the reliability of the measure (for a reconsideration of the interpretation of RCI, see Hsu, 1996).

Clinical significance can be examined by means of social validation (see Kazdin, 1977). Social validation may involve social comparisons or subjective evaluation. Social comparison involves comparing the posttreatment behavior of the client to the behavior of a normative peer group. It is hoped that the posttreatment behavior will be indistinguishable from the behavior of the nondeviant peer group. Subjective evaluation involves an assessment by significant others as to whether or not the treatment-induced change is able to be detected. Individuals who interact closely with the client make qualitative judgments about behavior.

Clinical significance is an important addition to the evaluation of psychological therapies. Although the methods vary, the centralizing issue is the emphasis on the clinical meaningfulness of the change in addition to the fact that the change occurred at a level that is beyond chance.

Mediators and Moderators

Attempts to clarify the varying effects of psychological treatments for different persons has emphasized the need to be clear when using the terms "moderator" and "mediator" (e.g., Baron & Kenny, 1986; Holmbeck, 1997; James & Brett, 1984). A *moderator* is a variable that influences either the direction or the strength of a relationship between an independent (predictor) variable and a dependent (criterion) variable. The nature of the effect of the independent variable on the dependent variable varies depending on the value or level of the moderator (such as in an interaction). Thus, the relationship between the variables is influenced by or is a function of some third variable with a moderating effect (Kazdin, 1998). A *mediator,* on the other hand, is that variable that specifies the process or mechanism by which a particular outcome is produced. The mediating effect elucidates precisely the mechanism by which the independent variable is related to the outcome variable. In the words of Baron and Kenny (1986, Fig. 14.3, p. 1176), "Whereas moderator variables specify when certain effects will hold, mediators speak to how or why such effects occur." (See Figure 14.3 for a graphic representation.)

Illustrative examples are in order. With regard to moderating effects, consider the report by Fauber, Forehand, Thomas, and Wierson (1990). These researchers studied

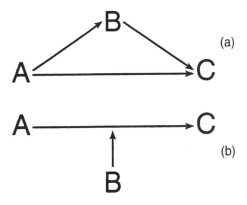

Figure 14.3.   Models of mediated and moderated effects. In (a), B mediates the relationship between A and C. In (b), B moderates the relationship between A and C.

Source: Holmbeck, G.N. (1997). Toward terminological, conceptual, and statistical clarity in the study of mediators and moderators: Examples from the child-clinical and pediatric psychology literatures. *Journal of Consulting and Clinical Psychology, 65,* p. 600. Baron, R.M., & Kenny, D.A. in the mediator-moderator variable distinction in social psychological research. Conceptual, strategic, and statistical considerations. *Journal of Personality and Social Psychology, 51,* 1173–1182. Copyright © 1997 by the American Psychological Association. Reprinted with permission.

the relationship between marital conflict and adjustment in intact and divorced families. They hypothesized that marital conflict would negatively affect quality of parenting, which would then result in changes in adolescent adjustment. Parenting quality serves as an example of a mediator—a variable that helps to describe the mechanism by which differential child adjustments are produced. However, if the researchers were to examine the relationship between conflict and adjustment in intact versus divorced families, then family composition (intact/divorced) could serve as a moderating variable—a variable that increases or decreases the strength of the association between conflict and adjustment.

With regard to mediating treatment effects, consider the following question: Within a treatment for anxiety disorders in youth that is considered empirically supported, what changes within the clients mediate the positive outcomes? Treadwell and Kendall (1996) reported that changes in negative self-talk (but not positive self-talk) mediated treatment gains. To test for mediation, Treadwell and Kendall computed three regression equations for each dependent variable. In the first, the mediating variable was regressed on the independent variable. The second equation regressed the dependent variable on the independent variable. In the third equation, the dependent variable was regressed on the mediating and independent variable. For mediation, the independent variable must predict the mediator variable, the mediator variable must predict the dependent variable, and the independent variable must predict the dependent variable. If the mediating hypothesis is correct, the effects of the independent variable (treatment) on the dependent variable (improvement) would be less in the third equation (with the mediator) than in the second equation (no mediation). The results confirmed the mediational hypothesis: Change in negative self-talk (not positive self-talk) was a mediating variable.

The identification of moderating and mediating effects will further enable the treatment outcome researcher and the practicing clinician to develop a better understanding of the causal mechanisms occurring between the application of therapy and the accrual of beneficial outcomes. Caution is needed in the interpretation of the literature on mediating and moderating effects, as these terms are not always used consistently (for discussion, see Holmbeck, 1997). Nevertheless, we second and underscore Holmbeck's plea for greater consistency in and increased frequency of the appropriate use of moderators and mediators.

CUMULATIVE OUTCOME ANALYSES

Beginning with Eysenck's (1952) limited yet provocative review of the therapy outcome research that was available prior to 1951, several major cumulative analyses have undertaken the challenging task of reviewing and reaching conclusions with regard to the effects of psychological therapy. Some of these examinations have used tabulations of the number of studies favoring one type of intervention versus competitors (e.g., Beutler, 1979; Luborsky, Singer, & Luborsky, 1975), whereas others have developed multidimensional multivariate analyses of the impact of potential causal factors on therapy outcome: meta-analysis (Smith & Glass, 1977). Most recently, the evaluation of therapy has taken a "meet criteria" approach. That is, a set of criteria that define empirically supported treatments have been proposed (APA Task Force Report, 1995; Chambless & Hollon, 1998), and authors have reviewed the published works to determine if specific treatments for specific disorders do or do not meet the criteria.

Several difficult choices confront the would-be reviewer of a body of research as diverse in quality, methodology, theoretical orientation, target issues and variables, and number of studies as that of the evaluation of therapy. First, should studies of inferior methodological quality be included or omitted in a review of outcomes? It is easy to agree with the comment "garbage in, garbage out" (Eysenck, 1978; Luborsky et al., 1975). However, others take the position that the vagaries of individual studies will cancel out in favor of truly meaningful trends and conclusions, if a substantial body of research is tapped, much as individual differences in clients are presumed to be unimportant if a large enough sample is utilized (Smith & Glass, 1977). The "quality selection" approach provides a reviewer with studies in which unexpected extraneous variables have the least chance of distorting results. Yet in doing so, the number of available investigations is often sufficiently reduced that it becomes difficult to assess whether or not the findings are replicated. Nevertheless, quality research is needed to answer the important questions, and additional quality research will resolve this problem.

Once a sample of studies is obtained, the next issue concerns the method by which the findings are combined and analyzed. At one end of the continuum, reviewers have tallied or eyeballed the separate analyses from each study to produce a "box score" (Beutler, 1979; Luborsky et al., 1975). In contrast, others use each study's correlation (e.g., Berman, 1979) or analysis of variance (e.g., Smith & Glass, 1977) data to calculate "effect sizes" in terms of either *standard deviation scores* or *percentages of variance.* Effect sizes in terms of standard deviation scores involve subtracting the mean score for one therapy condition from that from a competing therapy condition, and dividing the difference by either or both conditions' standard deviations. The percentage of variance method involves calculating expected mean squares from the analyses of variance effect data.

Although the box score method can be criticized as an oversimplification, the more sophisticated analytic techniques have been said to be capable of producing almost contradictory conclusions depending on the type of effect size calculated (Durlak, this volume; Gallo, 1978). To date, however, authors of cumulative analyses have generally drawn similar conclusions; essentially, it appears that several therapies help most clients to improve the average level of adjustment over wait list control clients. And, with some greater specificity, some treatments have been found to be better than others in producing certain target improvements.

Meta-analyses have begun to go beyond a general comparison of intervention modalities to search for optimal matching of disorders (clients) and interventions (types of treatments) (e.g., Kiesler, 1966). In the beginning, Smith and Glass (1977) incorporated several client variables, such as diagnosis and intelligence, and therapist variables, such as experience, into regression equations to attempt to predict the effect of these factors on outcome in psychodynamic versus behavioral therapies. The majority of treatment outcome research conducted since the Smith and Glass report has focused on comparisons of alternative treatment protocols as well as treatment techniques specific to particular symptoms and/or disorders (VandenBos, 1996), and though some writers point to methodological problems and considerations (e.g., Rachman & G. T. Wilson, 1980), the field does seem to have accepted the supportive conclusions (e.g., Lambert & Bergin, 1994; Lipsey & D. B. Wilson, 1993).

The merits of integration and summation of the results of related outcome studies are recognized, yet some cautions must be exercised in any meta-analysis. First, as noted earlier, one must check on the quality of the studies, eliminating those that cannot contribute meaningful findings due to basic inadequacies (Kendall & Maruyama, 1985; Kraemer, Gardner, Brooks, & Yesavage, 1998). Consider the following: Would you accept the recommendation that one treatment approach is superior to another if the recommendation was based on *inadequate* research? Probably not. Would you accept this same evidence to refute the recommendation? Again, probably not. If the research evidence is methodologically unsound, it is inadequate as to be insufficient evidence for a recommendation, it remains inadequate as a basis for either supporting or refuting treatment recommendations, and therefore should not be included in cumulative analyses. If a study is methodologically sound, then regardless of the outcome, it must be included.

Second, the studies that are assembled into groups for drawing conclusions about effect sizes must be comparable. Assembling groups of studies in which clients were diagnosed by different procedures, where therapists were markedly diverse, and where the length of treatment varied enormously will not necessarily clear the picture. Initial groupings must be homogeneous. Subsequently, the generality of the conclusions can be assessed with more heterogeneous groups of studies, and the relationships between diagnostic or therapist diversity can be examined in relation to outcome.

Caution is paramount in meta-analyses in which various studies are said to provide evidence that treatment is superior to controls. The exact nature of the control condition in each specific treatment outcome study must be examined, especially in the case of attention-placebo control conditions. This caution arises from the indefinite definition of attention-placebo control conditions. As noted earlier, one researcher's attention-placebo control condition may be serving as another researcher's therapy condition! Meta-analyzers cannot tabulate the number of studies in which treatment was found to be efficacious in relation to controls without examining the nature of the control condition.

In addition to comparing the outcomes of therapy, research has addressed the process of psychotherapy (Kiesler, 1973). Process analyses permit the mapping of the tasks and critical incidents facing clients and therapists as they develop and implement the treatment plan over the course of therapy (see Stiles et al., this volume). For instance, across the range of behavioral (e.g., Ford, 1978), interpersonal (Ford, Fisher, & Larson, 1997), and dynamic (Russell & Orlinsky, 1996) therapies, relational aspects of the client's experience can be predictive of treatment outcomes.

Currently, there are major efforts to identify and examine those psychological treatments that can be considered empirically supported (Kendall, 1998). These efforts take a set of "criteria" that have been proposed as required for a treatment to be considered empirically supported (see Table 14.1) and review the reported research literature in search of studies that can be used to meet the criteria. A series of such reviews (e.g., Baucom, Shoham, Mueser, Daiuto, & Stickle, 1998; Compas, Haaga, Keefe, Leitenberg, & Williams, 1998; DeRubeis & Crits-Christoph, 1998; Kazdin & Weisz, 1998) and reactions to the approach (e.g., Beutler, 1998; Borkovec & Castonguay, 1998; Calhoun, Moras, Pilkonis, & Rehm, 1998; Davison, 1998; Garfield, 1998; Goldfried & Wolfe, 1998; Persons & Silberschatz, 1998) document not only that this approach is being applied, but also that there are treatments that meet the criterion of having been supported by empirical research.

CONCLUSIONS

We have reviewed methodological considerations pertinent to treatment outcome research and offered guidelines and recommendations for a continued accumulation of empirical findings. The criteria for determining empirically supported treatments have been proposed and the quest for identification of such treatments has begun. The goal is for the research to be rigorous, with the end goal that the most promising procedures serve professional practice. Therapy outcome research also plays a vital role in facilitating a dialogue between treatment providers and outcome researchers, as well as between scientist-practitioners and the public and private sector (e.g., Department of Health and Human Services, insurance payors, policymakers). Outcome research increasingly is examined by both managed care organizations and professional associations with the intent of formulating practice guidelines for cost-effective psychological care. There is the risk that psychological science and practice will be co-opted and exploited in the service only of cost containment and profitability: Therapy outcome research must retain scientific rigor while enhancing the ability of practitioners to deliver effective procedures to individuals in need.

REFERENCES

Alvidrez, J., Azocar, F., & Miranda, J. (1996). Demystifying the concept of ethnicity for psychotherapy researchers. *Journal of Consulting and Clinical Psychology, 64,* 903–908.

American Psychological Association Commission on Training in Clinical Psychology. (1947). Recommended graduate training program in clinical psychology. *American Psychologist, 2,* 539–558.

American Psychological Association Task Force on Promotion and Dissemination of Psychological Procedures. (1995). Training in and dissemination of empirically-validated psychological treatments: Report and recommendations. *Clinical Psychologist, 48,* 3–23.

Barlow, D. H. (1989). Treatment outcome evaluation methodology with anxiety disorders: Strengths and key issues. *Advances in Behavior Research and Therapy, 11,* 121–132.

Barlow, D. H., & Hersen, M. (1984). *Single case experimental designs: Strategies for studying behavior change* (2nd ed.). New York: Pergamon Press.

Baron, R. M., & Kenny, D. A. (1986). The mediator-moderator variable distinction in social psychological research: Conceptual, strategic, and statistical considerations. *Journal of Personality and Social Psychology, 51,* 1173–1182.

Basham, R. B. (1986). Scientific and practical advantages of comparative design in psychotherapy outcome research. *Journal of Consulting and Clinical Psychology, 54,* 88–94.

Baucom, D., Shoham, V., Mueser, K., Daiuto, A., & Stickle, T. (1998). Empirically supported couple and family interventions for marital distress and adult mental health problems. *Journal of Consulting and Clinical Psychology, 66,* 53–88.

Berman, J. (1979). *Therapeutic expectancies and treatment outcome: A quantitative review.* Paper presented at the American Psychological Association Annual Convention, New York.

Beutler, L. E. (1979). Toward specific psychological therapies for specific conditions. *Journal of Consulting and Clinical Psychology, 47,* 882–897.

Beutler, L. E. (1996). The view from the rear: An editorial. *Journal of Consulting and Clinical Psychology, 64,* 845–847.

Beutler, L. E. (1998). Identifying empirically supported treatments: What if we didn't? *Journal of Consulting and Clinical Psychology, 66,* 37–52.

Beutler, L. E., Brown, M. T., Crothers, L., Booker, K., & Seabrook, M. K. (1996). The dilemma of factitious demographic distinctions in psychological research. *Journal of Consulting and Clinical Psychology.*

Beutler, L. E., & Hamblin, D. L. (1986). Individualized outcome measures of internal change: Methodological considerations. *Journal of Consulting and Clinical Psychology, 54,* 48–53.

Borkovec, T., & Castonguay, L. (1998). What is the scientific meaning of empirically supported therapy? *Journal of Consulting and Clinical Psychology, 66,* 136–142.

Brown, R. A., Evans, M., Miller, I., Burgess, E., & Mueller, T. (1997). Cognitive-behavioral treatment for depression in alcoholism. *Journal of Consulting and Clinical Psychology, 65,* 715–726.

Butcher, J. (1997). *Personality assessment in managed care: Using the MMPI-2 in treatment planning.* New York: Oxford University Press.

Calhoun, K., Moras, K., Pilkonis, P., & Rehm, L. (1998). Empirically supported treatments: Implications for training. *Journal of Consulting and Clinical Psychology, 66,* 151–162.

Chambless, D. L., & Hollon, S. D. (1998). Defining empirically supported therapies. *Journal of Consulting and Clinical Psychology, 66,* 7–18.

Compas, B., Haaga, D., Keefe, F., Leitenberg, H., & Williams, D. (1998). Sampling of empirically supported psychological treatments from health psychology: Smoking, chronic pain, cancer, and bulimia nervosa. *Journal of Consulting and Clinical Psychology, 66,* 89–112.

Coyne, J. C., & Gotlib, I. H. (1983). The role of cognition in depression: A critical appraisal. *Psychological Bulletin, 94,* 472–505.

Davison, G. (1998). Being bolder with the Boulder model: The challenge of education and training in empirically supported treatments. *Journal of Consulting and Clinical Psychology, 66,* 163–167.

Davison, G. C., & Lazarus, A. A. (1995). The dialectics of science and practice. In S. C. Hayes, V. M. Follette, R. D. Dawes, & K. Grady (Eds.), *Scientific standards of psychological practice: Issues and recommendations* (pp. 95–120). Reno, NV: Context Press.

DeRubeis, R., & Crits-Christoph, P. (1998). Empirically supported individual and group psychological treatments for adult mental disorders. *Journal of Consulting and Clinical Psychology, 66,* 37–52.

Dobson, K., & Shaw, B. (1988). The use of treatment manuals in cognitive therapy: Experience and issues. *Journal of Consulting and Clinical Psychology, 56,* 673–682.

Durlak, J. A., Wells, A. M., Cotten, J. K., & Johnson, S. (1995). Analysis of selected methodological issues in child psychotherapy research. *Journal of Clinical Child Psychology, 24,* 141–148.

Eysenck, H. J. (1952). The effects of psychotherapy: An evaluation. *Journal of Consulting Psychology, 16,* 319–324.

Eysenck, H. J. (1978). An exercise in mega-silliness. *American Psychologist, 33,* 517.

Fauber, R., Forehand, R., Thomas, A., & Wierson, M. (1990). A mediational model of the impact of marital conflict on adolescent adjustment in intact and divorced families: The role of disrupted parenting. *Child Development, 61,* 1112–1123.

Flaherty, J. A., & Meaer, R. (1980). Measuring racial bias in inpatient treatment. *American Journal of Psychiatry, 137,* 679–682.

Flannery-Schroeder, E., & Kendall, P. C. (1996). *Cognitive-behavioral therapy for anxious children: Therapist manual for group treatment.* Ardmore, PA: Workbook Publishing.

Ford, J. D. (1978). Process and outcome in behavior therapy. *Journal of Consulting and Clinical Psychology, 46,* 1302–1314.

Ford, J. D., Fisher, P., & Larson, L. (1997). Object relations as a predictor of outcome with chronic posttraumatic stress disorder. *Journal of Consulting and Clinical Psychology, 65,* 547–559.

Freeston, M., Ladouceur, R., Gagnon, F., Thibodeau, N., Rheaume, J., Letarte, H., & Bujold, A. (1997). Cognitive-behavioral treatment of obsessive thoughts: A controlled study. *Journal of Consulting and Clinical Psychology, 65,* 405–413.

Gallo, P. S., Jr. (1978). Meta-analysis—A mixed metaphor? *American Psychologist, 33,* 515–517.

Garfield, S. (1996). Some problems associated with "Validated" forms of psychotherapy. *Clinical Psychology: Science and Practice, 3,* 218–229.

Garfield, S. (1998). Some comments on empirically supported psychological treatments. *Journal of Consulting and Clinical Psychology, 66,* 121–125.

Goldfried, M., & Wolfe, B. (1998). Toward a more clinically valid approach to therapy research. *Journal of Consulting and Clinical Psychology, 66,* 143–150.

Goldstein, A. P., Lopez, M., & Greenleaf, D. O. (1979). Introduction. In A. P. Goldstein & F. H. Kanfer (Eds.), *Maximizing treatment gains: Transfer enhancement in psychotherapy.* New York: Academic Press.

Gotlib, I. H. (1984). Depression and general psychopathology in university students. *Journal of Abnormal Psychology, 93,* 19–30.

Greenhouse, J., Stangl, D., & Bromberg, J. (1989). An introduction to survival analysis: Statistical methods for analysis of clinical trial data. *Journal of Consulting and Clinical Psychology, 57,* 536–544.

Haley, J. (1976). *Problem solving therapy.* San Francisco: Jossey-Bass.

Havik, O. E., & VandenBos, G. R. (1996). Limitations of manualized psychotherapy for everyday clinical practice. *Clinical Psychology: Science and Practice, 3*(3), 264–267.

Henggeler, S. W., Melton, G., Brondino, M., Scherer, D., & Hanley, J. (1997). Multisystemic therapy with violent and chronic juvenile offenders and their families: The role of treatment fidelity in successful dissemination. *Journal of Consulting and Clinical Psychology, 65,* 821–833.

Hoagwood, K., Hibbs, E., Brent, D., & Jensen, P. (1995). Introduction to the special section: Efficacy and effectiveness in studies of child and adolescent psychotherapy. *Journal of Consulting and Clinical Psychology, 63,* 683–687.

Hoch, E. L., Ross, A. O., & Winder, C. L. (Eds.). (1966). *Professional preparation of clinical psychologists.* Washington, DC: American Psychological Association.

Hollon, S. D. (1996). The efficacy and effectiveness of psychotherapy relative to medications. *American Psychologist, 51,* 1025–1030.

Hollon, S. D., & DeRubeis, R. J. (1981). Placebo-psychotherapy combinations: Inappropriate representations of psychotherapy in drug-psychotherapy comparative trials. *Psychological Bulletin, 90,* 467–477.

Holmbeck, G. N. (1997). Toward terminological, conceptual, and statistical clarity in the study of mediators and moderators: Examples from the child-clinical and pediatric psychology literatures. *Journal of Consulting and Clinical Psychology, 65,* 599–610.

Homma-True, R., Greene, B., Lopez, S. R., & Trimble, J. E. (1993). Ethnocultural diversity in clinical psychology. *Clinical Psychologist, 46,* 50–63.

Howard, B., & Kendall, P. C. (1996). *Cognitive-behavioral family therapy for anxious children: Therapist manual.* Ardmore, PA: Workbook Publishing.

Howard, K. I., Krause, M. S., & Orlinsky, D. E. (1986). The attrition dilemma: Toward a new strategy for psychotherapy research. *Journal of Consulting and Clinical Psychology, 54,* 106–110.

Howard, K. I., Lueger, R., Maling, M., & Martinovich, Z. (1993). A phase model of psychotherapy. *Journal of Consulting and Clinical Psychology, 61,* 678–685.

Hsu, L. (1996). On the identification of clinically significant changes: Reinterpretation of Jacobson's cut scores. *Journal of Psychopathology and Behavioral Assessment, 18,* 371–386.

Jacobson, N. S., & Christensen, A. (1996). Studying the effectiveness of psychotherapy: How well can clinical trials do the job? *American Psychologist, 51,* 1031–1039.

Jacobson, N. S., Follette, W. C., & Revenstorf, D. (1984). Psychotherapy outcome research: Methods for reporting variability and evaluating clinical significance. *Behavior Therapy, 15,* 336–352.

Jacobson, N. S., & Hollon, S. D. (1996a). Cognitive-behavior therapy versus pharmacotherapy: Now that the jury's returned its verdict, it's time to present the rest of the evidence. *Journal of Consulting and Clinical Psychology, 64,* 74–80.

Jacobson, N. S., & Hollon, S. D. (1996b). Prospects for future comparisons between drugs and psychotherapy: Lessons from the CBT-versus-pharmacotherapy exchange. *Journal of Consulting and Clinical Psychology, 64,* 104–108.

Jacobson, N. S., & Truax, P. (1991). Clinical significance: A statistic approach to defining meaningful change in psychotherapy research. *Journal of Consulting and Clinical Psychology, 59,* 12–19.

James, L. R., & Brett, J. M. (1984). Mediators, moderators, and test for mediation. *Journal of Applied Psychology, 69,* 307–321.

Jaycox, L., Foa, E., & Morral, A. (1998). Influence of emotional engagement and habituation on exposure therapy for PTSD. *Journal of Consulting and Clinical Psychology, 66,* 185–192.

Kazdin, A. E. (1977). Assessing the clinical or applied importance of behavior change through social validation. *Behavior Modification, 1,* 427–451.

Kazdin, A. E. (1986). Comparative outcome studies of psychotherapy: Methodological issues and strategies. *Journal of Consulting and Clinical Psychology, 54,* 95–105.

Kazdin, A. E. (1996). Validated treatments: Multiple perspectives and issues—Introduction to the series. *Clinical Psychology: Science and Practice, 3,* 216–217.

Kazdin, A. E. (1998). *Research design in clinical psychology* (3rd ed.). Boston, MA: Allyn & Bacon.

Kazdin, A. E., & Bass, D. (1989). Power to detect differences between alternative treatments in comparative psychotherapy outcome research. *Journal of Consulting and Clinical Psychology, 57,* 138–147.

Kazdin, A. E., Siegel, T., & Bass, D. (1992). Cognitive behavioral problem solving skills training and parent management training in the treatment of antisocial behavior in children. *Journal of Consulting and Clinical Psychology, 60,* 733–747.

Kazdin, A. E., & Weisz, J. R. (1998). Identifying and developing empirically supported child and adolescent treatments. *Journal of Consulting and Clinical Psychology, 66,* 19–36.

Kendall, P. C. (1998). Empirically supported psychological therapies. *Journal of Consulting and Clinical Psychology, 66,* 1–4.

Kendall, P. C., & Chu, B. (1999). Retrospective self-reports of therapist flexibility in a manual-based treatment for youths with anxiety disorders. *Journal of Clinical Child Psychology,* in revision.

Kendall, P. C., Chu, B., Gifford, A., Hayes, C., & Nauta, M. (1998). Breathing life into a manual. *Cognitive and Behavioral Practice,* in press.

Kendall, P. C., & Flannery-Schroeder, E. C. (1998). Methodological issues in treatment research for anxiety disorders in youth. *Journal of Abnormal Child Psychology, 26,* 27–38.

Kendall, P. C., & Grove, W. (1988). Normative comparisons in therapy outcome. *Behavioral Assessment, 10,* 147–158.

Kendall, P. C., & Hollon, S. D. (1983). Calibrating therapy: Collaborative archiving of tape samples from therapy outcome trials. *Cognitive Therapy and Research, 7,* 199–204.

Kendall, P. C., Hollon, S., Beck, A. T., Hammen, C., & Ingram, R. (1987). Issues and recommendations regarding use of the Beck Depression Inventory. *Cognitive Therapy and Research, 11,* 289–299.

Kendall, P. C., Kane, M., Howard, B., & Siqueland, L. (1990). *Cognitive–behavioral therapy for anxious children: Treatment manual.* Ardmore, PA: Workbook Publishing.

Kendall, P. C., Marrs-Garcia, A., Nath, S. R., & Sheldrick, R. C. (1999). Normative comparisons for the evaluation of clinical significance. *Journal of Consulting and Clinical Psychology,* in press.

Kendall, P. C., & Maruyama, G. (1985). Meta-analysis: On the road to synthesis of knowledge? *Clinical Psychology Review, 5,* 79–89.

Kendall, P. C., & Norton-Ford, J. D. (1982). *Clinical psychology: Scientific and professional dimensions.* New York: Wiley.

Kendall, P. C., Pellegrini, D. S., & Urbain, E. S. (1981). Approaches to assessment for cognitive-behavioral interventions with children. In P. C. Kendall & S. D. Hollon (Eds.), *Assessment strategies for cognitive-behavioral interventions.* New York: Academic Press.

Kendall, P. C., & Southam-Gerow, M. A. (1995). Issues in the transportability of treatment: The case of anxiety disorders in youth. *Journal of Consulting and Clinical Psychology, 63,* 702–708.

Kendall, P. C., & Sugarman, A. (1997). Attrition in the treatment of childhood anxiety disorders. *Journal of Consulting and Clinical Psychology, 65,* 883–888.

Kendall, P. C., & Wilcox, L. E. (1980). A cognitive-behavioral treatment for impulsivity: Concrete versus conceptual training with non-self-controlled problem children. *Journal of Consulting and Clinical Psychology, 48,* 80–91.

Kiesler, D. J. (1966). Some myths of psychotherapy research and the search for a paradigm. *Psychological Bulletin, 65,* 110–136.

Kiesler, D. J. (1973). *The process of psychotherapy.* Chicago: Aldine.

Korman, M. (1974). National conference on levels and patterns of professional training in psychology: The major themes. *American Psychologist, 29,* 441–449.

Kraemer, H. C., Gardner, C., Brooks, J., & Yesavage, J. (1998). Advantages of excluding underpowered studies in meta-analysis: Inclusionist versus exclusionist viewpoints. *Psychological Methods, 3,* 23–31.

Krupnick, J., Shea, T., & Elkin, I. (1986). Generalizability of treatment studies utilizing solicited patients. *Journal of Consulting and Clinical Psychology, 54,* 68–78.

Lambert, M. J., & Bergin, A. E. (1994). The effectiveness of psychotherapy. In A. E. Bergin & S. L. Garfield (Eds.), *Handbook of psychotherapy and behavioral change* (4th ed., pp. 143–189). New York: Wiley.

Lavori, P. W. (1992). Clinical trials in psychiatry: Should protocol deviation censor patient data? *Neuropsychopharmacology, 6,* 39–48.

Lipsey, M. W., & Wilson, D. B. (1993). The efficacy of psychological, educational, and behavioral treatment: Confirmation from meta-analysis. *American Psychologist, 48,* 1181–1209.

Lopez, S. R. (1989). Patient variable biases in clinical judgement: Conceptual overview and methodological considerations. *Psychological Bulletin, 106,* 184–204.

Luborsky, L., Singer, B., & Luborsky, L. (1975). Comparative studies of psychotherapy. *Archives of General Psychiatry, 32,* 995–1008.

March, J., & Mulle, K. (1996). *Cognitive-behavioral psychotherapy for obsessive–compulsive disorder.* Unpublished manuscript, Duke University Medical Center, Durham, NC.

Marks, I., Lowell, Noshirvani, H., Livanou, M., & Thrasher, S. (1998). Treatment of posttraumatic stress disorder by exposure and/or cognitive restructuring. *Archives of General Psychiatry, 55,* 317–325.

Miranda, J. (1996). Introduction to the special section on recruiting and retaining minorities in psychotherapy research. *Journal of Consulting and Clinical Psychology, 64*(5), 848–850.

Miranda, J., Azocar, F., Organista, K. C., Munoz, R. F., & Lieberman, A. (1996). Recruiting and retaining low-income Latinos in psychotherapy research. *Journal of Consulting and Clinical Psychology, 64,* 868–874.

Neal, A. M., & Turner, S. M. (1991). Anxiety disorders research with African Americans: Current status. *Psychological Bulletin, 109,* 400–410.

Neighbors, H. W. (1985). Seeking help for personal problems: Black Americans' use of health and mental health services. *Community Mental Health Journal, 21,* 156–166.

Neighbors, H. W. (1988). The help-seeking behavior of Black Americans. *Journal of the National Medical Association, 80,* 1009–1012.

Nich, C., & Carroll, K. (1997). Now you see it, now you don't: A comparison of traditional versus random-effects regression models in the analysis of longitudinal follow-up data from a clinical trial. *Journal of Consulting and Clinical Psychology, 65,* 252–261.

Nicholson, R. A., & Berman, J. S. (1983). Is follow-up necessary in evaluating psychotherapy? *Psychological Bulletin, 93,* 261–278.

O'Leary, K. D., & Borkovec, T. D. (1978). Conceptual, methodological, and ethical problems of placebo groups in psychotherapy research. *American Psychologist, 33,* 821–830.

Ollendick, T. H. (1986). Behavior therapy with children and adolescents. In S. L. Garfield & A. E. Bergin (Eds.), *Handbook of psychotherapy and behavior change* (3rd ed., pp. 525–565). New York: Wiley.

Parloff, M. B. (1986). Placebo controls in psychotherapy research: A sine qua non or a placebo for research problems? *Journal of Consulting and Clinical Psychology, 54,* 79–87.

Patterson, D., & Ptacek, J. (1997). Baseline pain as a moderator of hypnotic analgesia for burn injury treatment. *Journal of Consulting and Clinical Psychology, 65,* 60–67.

Perry, J. N., & Butcher, J. (in press). The Butcher treatment planning inventory (BTPI): An objective guide to treatment planning. In M. Maruish (Ed.), *Use of psychological testing for treatment planning and outcome assessment* (2nd ed.). Hillsdale, NJ: Erlbaum.

Persons, J., & Silberschatz, G. (1998). Are results of randomized controlled trials useful to psychotherapists? *Journal of Consulting and Clinical Psychology, 66,* 126–135.

Rachman, S. J., & Wilson, G. T. (1980). *The effects of psychological therapy* (2nd ed.). New York: Pergamon Press.

Raimy, V. C. (Ed.). (1950). *Training in clinical psychology.* New York: Prentice-Hall.

Rosenthal, R. (1995). Progress in clinical psychology: Is there any? *Clinical Psychology: Science and Practice, 2,* 133–150.

Russell, R., & Orlinsky, D. (1996). Psychotherapy research in historical perspective. *Archives of General Psychiatry, 53,* 708–715.

Seligman, M. (1995). The effectiveness of psychotherapy: The Consumer Reports study. *American Psychologist, 50,* 965–974.

Shakow, D. (1976). What is clinical psychology? *American Psychologist, 31,* 553–560.

Shapiro, A. K., & Morris, L. A. (1978). The placebo effect in medical and psychological therapies. In S. L. Garfield & A. E. Bergin (Eds.), *Handbook of psychotherapy and behavior change: An empirical analysis* (2nd ed.). New York: Wiley.

Shapiro, D. A., & Shapiro, D. (1982). Meta-analysis of comparative therapy outcome studies: A replication and refinement. *Psychological Bulletin, 92,* 581–604.

Simon, R., Fleiss, J., Gurland, B., Stiller, P., & Sharpe, L. (1973). Depression and schizophrenia in hospitalized Black and White mental patients. *Archives of General Psychiatry, 28,* 509–512.

Smith, M. L., & Glass, G. V. (1977). Meta-analysis of psychotherapy outcome studies. *American Psychologist, 32,* 752–760.

Smith, M. L., Glass, G. V., & Miller, T. I. (1980). *The benefits of psychotherapy.* Baltimore: Johns Hopkins University Press.

Stiles, W. B., & Shapiro, D. A. (1994). Disabuse of the drug metaphor: Psychotherapy process-outcome correlations. *Journal of Consulting and Clinical Psychology, 62,* 942–948.

Strother, C. R. (Ed.). (1957). *Psychology and mental health.* Washington, DC: American Psychological Association.

Tennen, H., Hall, J. A., & Affleck, G. (1995). Depression research methodologies in the *Journal of Personality and Social Psychology*: A review and critique. *Journal of Personality and Social Psychology, 68,* 870–884.

Thompson, E. E., Neighbors, H. W., Munday, C., & Jackson, J. S. (1996). Recruitment and retention of African American patients for clinical research: An exploration of response rates in an urban psychiatric hospital. *Journal of Consulting and Clinical Psychology, 64,* 861–867.

Thorne, F. C. (1947). The clinical method in science. *American Psychologist, 2,* 159–166.

Toro, P., Passero-Rabideau, J., Bellavia, C., Daeschler, C., Wall, D., Thomas, D., & Smith, S. J. (1997). Evaluating an intervention for homeless persons: Results of a field experiment. *Journal of Consulting and Clinical Psychology, 65,* 476–484.

Treadwell, K., Flannery-Schroeder, E. C., & Kendall, P. C. (1994). Ethnicity and gender in a sample of clinic-referred anxious children: Adaptive functioning, diagnostic status, and treatment outcome. *Journal of Anxiety Disorders, 9,* 373–384.

Treadwell, K., & Kendall, P. C. (1996). Self-talk in youth with anxiety disorders: States of mind, content specificity, and treatment outcome. *Journal of Consulting and Clinical Psychology, 64,* 941–950.

VandenBos, G. R. (1996). Outcome assessment of psychotherapy. *American Psychologist, 51,* 1005–1006.

Vredenburg, K., Flett, G. L., & Krames, L. (1993). Analogue versus clinical depression: A critical reappraisal. *Psychological Bulletin, 113,* 327–344.

Wade, W., Treat, T., & Stuart, G. (1998). Transporting an empirically-supported treatment for panic disorder to a service setting: A benchmarking strategy. *Journal of Consulting and Clinical Psychology, 66,* 231–239.

Waltz, J., Addis, M. E., Koerner, K., & Jacobson, N. S. (1993). Testing the integrity of a psychotherapy protocol: Assessment of adherence and competence. *Journal of Consulting and Clinical Psychology, 61,* 620–630.

Watzlawick, P. (1978). *The language of change.* New York: Norton.

Watzlawick, P., Weakland, J., & Fisch, R. (1974). *Change.* New York: Norton.

Weisz, J. R., Donenberg, G. R., Han, S. S., & Weiss, B. (1995). Bridging the gap between laboratory and clinic in child and adolescent psychotherapy. *Journal of Consulting and Clinical Psychology, 63,* 688–701.

Weisz, J. R., Weiss, B., & Donenberg, G. R. (1992). The lab versus the clinic: Effects of child and adolescent psychotherapy. *American Psychologist, 47,* 1578–1585.

Wilson, G. T. (1995). Empirically validated treatments as a basis for clinical practice: Problems and prospects. In S. C. Hayes, V. M. Follette, R. D. Dawes, & K. Grady (Eds.), *Scientific standards of psychological practice: Issues and recommendations* (pp. 163–196). Reno, NV: Context Press.

Wilson, G. T. (1996). Treatment of bulimia nervosa: When CBT fails. *Behaviour Research and Therapy, 34,* 197–212.

Chapter 15

TREATMENT PROCESS RESEARCH METHODS

WILLIAM B. STILES, PH.D., LARA HONOS-WEBB, M.A., and LYNNE M. KNOBLOCH, M.A.

What happens in psychotherapy? How do therapies differ? How do clients act and think differently? What are the common factors across different therapies? Which are the effective ingredients? What happens as clients improve? We have organized this chapter around this series of questions and we have used illustrative studies to focus on the methods psychotherapy researchers have used to address them.

The questions are interesting because of the answers to two prior questions. The first question people usually ask about psychotherapy is, Does it work? The consensus answer to this question is now clearly Yes—usually (e.g., Kendall & Chambless, 1998; Lambert & Bergin, 1994; Lipsey & Wilson, 1993; Seligman, 1995; M. L. Smith, Glass, & Miller, 1980). Methods of addressing this question are described in other chapters in this volume (e.g., Kendall, Flannery-Schroeder, & Ford, this volume). The broadly positive answer is crucial for process research because it suggests that what happens in therapy is worth studying.

The second prior question arises because there are so many psychotherapies. Approaches to adult individual psychotherapy include psychoanalytic, psychodynamic, cognitive, behavioral, interpersonal, client-centered, gestalt, archetypal, personal construct, process-experiential, reality, and solution-focused, each of which has multiple subtypes. There are also many varieties of child, couples, family, and group therapies. Counts of alternatives run into the hundreds (Herink, 1980; Kazdin, 1986). The differences are not merely technical; the theories underlying the alternatives differ in their understanding of the nature of personality, psychopathology, client change, preferred intervention strategies, and the scope, length, and depth of the therapeutic enterprise.

The second prior question is, then, Which psychotherapy is best? The surprising, though controversial, answer is the Dodo verdict, from *Alice's Adventures in Wonderland: "Everybody* has won, and *all* must have prizes" (Carroll, 1865/1946, p. 28, italics in original; first quoted in this context by Rozenzweig, 1936, p. 412, and frequently repeated by reviewers and critics, e.g., Beutler, 1991, p. 165; Frank, 1973, p. 1; Grencavage & Norcross, 1990, p. 372; Luborsky, Singer, & Luborsky, 1975, p. 995; Stiles, Shapiro, & Elliott, 1986, p. 165; Wampold et al., 1997). Reviews of outcome research (e.g., Lambert & Bergin, 1994; Lipsey & Wilson, 1993; Luborsky et al., 1975; Smith et al., 1980; Wampold et al., 1997, p. 203) and major comparisons of contrasting psychotherapeutic approaches (e.g., Elkin, 1994; Elkin et al., 1989; Greenberg & Watson, 1998; Shapiro et al., 1994; Strupp & Hadley, 1979) have reported that most therapies tend to yield more or less equivalent positive changes in clients. This widely replicated result has been described as the *equivalence paradox*—the equivalence of outcomes despite the apparent nonequivalence of theory and the treatment process (Stiles et al., 1986).

Of course, no two psychological procedures have exactly equivalent effects (the null hypothesis is never really true; Meehl, 1978), the degree of equivalence of outcomes remains controversial (e.g., Beutler, 1991; Crits-Christoph, 1997; Howard, Krause, Saunders, & Kopta, 1997; Norcross, 1995), and there may be exceptions (e.g., Emmelkamp, 1994, made a strong case for the superiority of in vivo exposure methods over other behavioral techniques for treating phobias). Nevertheless, the failure to yield differences in effectiveness of a magnitude comparable to the theoretical differences among treatments has been a continuing puzzle.

Process researchers have responded vigorously to the equivalence paradox. Investigators have asked whether the therapies really differ as much as the theories suggest: If the differences were only theoretical, the outcome equivalence would not be paradoxical. They have asked whether there are systematic differences among clients: Interactions with client differences might obscure differences in treatment effectiveness. They have asked what factors are common across apparently different therapies: The outcome equivalence might reflect common effective ingredients that override superficial differences. In this chapter, we consider how investigators have addressed each of these questions. We begin, however, with a more descriptive treatment process question.

WHAT HAPPENS IN PSYCHOTHERAPY?

Logically and historically, treatment process research begins with naming, describing, classifying, and counting what therapists and clients do. That is, researchers must begin by developing measures. They have done this with great energy. One of the most salient features of treatment process research is the profusion of measures. Researchers have developed thousands of categories and scales, and they have organized these into hundreds of measuring instruments and systems of classification. We have space to mention only a few of them as illustrations in this chapter. More extensive descriptions of some of the better-constructed process instruments and systems have been collected in volumes edited by Kiesler (1973), Greenberg and Pinsof (1986b), and A. P. Beck and Lewis (in press).

So many systems of process classification have been developed that there is even a literature on *meta-classification*—that is, classification of classifications (Elliott, 1991; Elliott & Anderson, 1994; Greenberg, 1986; Greenberg & Pinsof, 1986a; Lambert & Hill, 1994; Russell, 1988; Russell & Staszewski, 1988; Russell & Stiles, 1979). To convey an idea of the variety of ways treatment process has been described, we list some meta-classificatory principles, ways in which process categories and measures differ:

1. *Size of the scoring unit* (e.g., single words or gestures; phrases, clauses, sentences; speaking turns; topic episodes; timed intervals of various durations,

whole sessions; phases of treatment, whole treatments, series of treatments). Measures that target whole sessions are sometimes described as *session impact* measures (Stiles, 1980); measures that target whole treatments may be considered outcome measures. Kiesler (1973) distinguished the *scoring unit* (the material to which the measure is directly applied) from the *contextual unit* (the material that coders or raters are told to consider when assigning the score, which may be considerably larger) and from the *summarizing unit* (the material over which scores are aggregated). For example, for the category "interpretation," the scoring unit might be a single sentence, the contextual unit might include the preceding speech (or some larger context), and the summarizing unit might be the session (or some segment of the session), in which a percentage of interpretations is calculated.

2. *Perspective.* Whose viewpoint is used (therapist, client, external observers, or judges)? Perhaps not surprisingly, the process often looks different from the inside than from the outside and from the perspective of clients than of therapists (e.g., Dill-Standiford, Stiles, & Rorer, 1988).

3. *Data format and access strategy.* What materials from the treatment are studied (e.g., transcripts, session notes, audiotape, videotape, current experience, post-session recall, long-term recall)? How are the materials observed (e.g., observation, self-report, tape-assisted recall)? Tape-assisted recall is a procedure in which audio- or videotape recordings of therapy sessions are replayed for participants, who code, rate, or describe the experience they were having at the time of the recording (e.g., Elliott, 1986; Kagan, 1975).

4. *Measure format* (e.g., coding, rating, verbal description, Q-sort, questionnaire). Coding refers to classifications into nominal categories. Rating refers to placement on an (at least) ordinal scale. Q-sort refers to a procedure in which descriptors are sorted according to how well they characterize the target (e.g., Ablon & Jones, 1998; Jones & Pulos, 1993).

5. *Level of inference.* Marsden (1971), following Berelson (1952), distinguished the *classical strategy,* in which only observable behavior is coded or rated by judges, from the *pragmatic strategy,* in which the coders or raters make inferences about the speaker's thoughts, feelings, intentions, or motivations based on the observed behavior. The classical strategy generally yields higher reliability, but pragmatic schemes may allow raters to integrate and weigh clinically relevant information not encompassed by classical categories.

6. *Theoretical orientation* (e.g., psychoanalytic, experiential, cognitive, behavioral, interpersonal). Some measures aim to assess therapy within particular schools, whereas others claim broader applicability.

7. *Treatment modality* (e.g., individual adult, child, family, group therapy).

8. *Target person(s):* the focus of the measurement (therapist, client, dyad, family, group).

9. *Communication channel* (e.g., verbal, paralinguistic, kinesic).

10. *Aspect/attribute/feature/dimension.* Among the verbal coding measures, *content categories,* which deal with semantic meaning, have been distinguished from

speech act categories, which concern what is done when someone says something. For example, the utterance "What about the situation made you frightened?" might be coded as concerning the content "fear" but the speech act "question." *Paralinguistic measures* concern behaviors that are not verbal but accompany speech (hesitations, dysfluencies, emphasis, tonal qualities). Evaluative ratings (which require some judgment of quality or competence) can be distinguished from descriptive ratings.

Why are there so many measures? In 1973, Kiesler complained that many process measures were developed and then never used again, with many reinvented by researchers who were uninformed of the previous work. Researchers' awareness of previous work now seems to have improved; however, the proliferation of measures has continued. Using standard instruments would offer the advantages of continuity and comparability across studies, to say nothing of saving the effort of developing new measures. On the other hand, replicating results using different measures of the same theoretical concepts can contribute a great deal to confidence in the theory. We presume that informed researchers continue to develop new measures mainly because the old measures have failed to answer their questions and because they believe that some important aspect of the process remains unassessed.

Some beginning researchers may attempt to locate the best or most comprehensive measure of the treatment process. We think that this is impossible. Instead, we suggest, the choice of measure depends on the specific hypothesis, question, or topic being investigated. The examples in this chapter illustrate how investigators choose or design their measures to address each study's specific purposes.

After the measures have been applied, they can be reported directly, as in case studies or intensive analyses of brief segments. More often, measures are aggregated across some stretch of treatment (the summarizing unit), for example, the frequency or percentage of a category in each session, or the average of a rating across a whole treatment. Or the process may be described by using the measures in multivariate or sequential analyses (e.g., Czogalik & Russell, 1995; Luborsky, 1995; Russell, 1995; Russell & Trull, 1986; Stiles & Shapiro, 1995; Stinson, Milbrath, & Horowitz, 1995). The examples in this chapter illustrate some of the alternatives.

DO THERAPIES DIFFER?

One way to resolve the equivalence paradox is to challenge the assumption that the treatments are different. At one time, some influential authors believed that, despite theoretical differences, the behavior of therapists was much the same across many therapies (e.g., London, 1964). However, process researchers have repeatedly identified systematic differences in therapists' techniques across different orientations (e.g., Brunink & Schroeder, 1979; DeRubeis, Hollon, Evans, & Bemis, 1982; Elliott et al., 1987; Hill, O'Grady, & Elkin, 1992; Hill, Thames, & Rardin, 1979; Startup & Shapiro, 1993; Stiles, 1979; Stiles, Shapiro, & Firth-Cozens, 1988; Strupp, 1955, 1957). The empirically demonstrated process differences have generally been consistent with the theoretical differences between treatments.

To assess differences in treatment processes, investigators have applied process measures to contrasting treatments and compared the results. To illustrate this straightforward logic, we have summarized a few studies that have used different sorts of measures, including verbal category systems, adherence rating scales, and intensive qualitative comparison.

Treatment Differences in Participants' Verbal Behavior

Verbal response modes (speech act categories, e.g., reflections, interpretations, questions, self-disclosures) have probably been the most widely studied therapist process variable (Elliott et al., 1987; Hill, 1986; Stiles, 1986). In terms of the meta-classification principles, verbal response modes are speech act categories; the scoring units are sentences or clauses; and they are usually coded (into nominal categories) from tapes or transcripts from a trained coder's (i.e., an external observer's) perspective. Most response mode systems are applicable across theoretical orientations and treatment modalities.

Illustrative Study 1

Stiles et al. (1988) investigated both clients' and therapists' verbal response mode profiles in two different treatment conditions, interpersonal-psychodynamic therapy and cognitive-behavioral therapy. Clients ($N = 39$) were randomly assigned to receive eight weekly sessions of one treatment condition, followed by eight additional weekly sessions in the other treatment condition in a crossover research design that permitted within-subjects comparisons of verbal processes across the two treatments.

Therapists' and clients' verbal behavior was measured using a verbal response modes taxonomy in which each utterance (simple sentence or independent clause) was coded twice, once for its grammatical form (literal meaning) and once for its communicative intent (pragmatic meaning). Utterances were coded into one of eight mutually exclusive categories: disclosure, edification, question, acknowledgment, advisement, confirmation, interpretation, and reflection (Stiles, 1992). To illustrate, "Could you tell me how you felt?" is coded question in form but advisement in intent (i.e., the utterance was apparently meant as a directive, "Tell me how you felt," rather than a question about the client's ability). For each client, four complete sessions of each treatment condition (eight sessions in all) were coded by five coders, who worked directly from audiotape recordings. Coders received 40 to 60 hours of training, and throughout the coding period, they met weekly with investigators to receive feedback and prevent coder drift (the tendency of a coder's standards to change over time). Eighty-four sessions, or approximately one-fourth of all sessions, were coded independently by two coders. This was done to assess intercoder reliabilities of the category percentages. The reliabilities were measured by the intraclass correlation coefficient (Shrout & Fleiss, 1979).

Consistent with cognitive-behavioral therapy's active, directive, and educational stance, therapists averaged 50% more utterances per session in cognitive-behavioral than in interpersonal-psychodynamic therapy, while using higher percentages of questions, edifications (informational statements), and general advisements (directives concerning behavior outside the therapy session). Focusing on client experience and interpersonal relations, the therapists used higher percentages of interpretations and reflections in interpersonal-psychodynamic therapy. Clients used more acknowledgments (e.g., "mm-hm," "yeah") in prescriptive therapy, and more disclosure in interpersonal-psychodynamic therapy, although these client differences between treatments were much smaller than the therapists' differences. The most common client mode in both treatments was disclosure, consistent with the client role of revealing thoughts and feelings.

Illustrative Study 2

As part of a larger components analysis of cognitive-behavioral self-control therapy with children, Braswell, Kendall, Braith, Carey, and Vye (1985) examined client and therapist verbal behaviors in three treatment conditions. Children ($N = 27$) in grades 3 through 6 were referred by their teachers for having displayed non-self-controlled behavior. Nine students each were assigned to the three treatments, which consisted of 12 45–55 minute sessions over seven weeks. The cognitive-behavioral treatment consisted of verbal self-instruction via modeling with a response-cost contingency for promoting appropriate task performance and self-instruction. The behavioral treatment used modeling and behavioral contingencies, and the attention-control treatment used the same tasks and materials but did not receive either self-instructional training or behavioral contingencies. Each session was audiotaped, and sessions 1, 2, 3, 10, 11, and 12 were analyzed.

The coding system, developed for the study, included 15 categories: five for children's behaviors (self-disclosure, suggested change in task or procedure, evaluative statement about own performance, statements unrelated to task at hand, and duration of the verbal behavior unrelated to the task), nine for therapist behaviors (self-disclosure, emphasizing feelings, correcting the child regarding use of self-instructions, rate of speed or attentiveness, verbal positive reinforcement, asking for feedback on task difficulty or level of enjoyment, frequency of statements unrelated to the task at hand, and duration of verbal behavior unrelated to the task), and one joint therapist-child behavior (duration of task-related activity). The coding unit was the statement or utterance.

Fourteen undergraduate coders were split into three coding groups and were trained for a total of 24 hours in biweekly sessions. When coders achieved 85% agreement on codes, they began coding the study data. Mean reliabilities for each code ranged from 89% to 100% agreement.

Comparisons among treatments indicated that in-session verbal behavior was consistent with treatment style. Cognitive-behavioral and behavior treatment groups showed higher levels of child positive statements about performance, therapist corrections of child performance, and on-task duration. The three groups did not differ in the frequency of therapist encouragement or confirmation. Additional analyses linked the children's active and positive involvement with better outcomes.

Treatment Differences in Adherence Ratings

To ensure treatment integrity in clinical trials comparing different treatments, researchers have tried to standardize the treatments using detailed treatment manuals (DeRubeis et al., 1982; Luborsky, Woody, McLellan, O'Brien, & Rosenzweig, 1982). This step has led researchers to assess therapists' adherence to therapeutic protocols.

The logic is that if treatments are to be compared, they must be delivered according to protocol. If an adherence check were to show that the therapists were not following the manual, the treatment was not being delivered correctly and the clinical trial could not be interpreted.

Illustrative Study 3

Hill et al. (1992) tested therapists' adherence to their respective treatment approaches in the National Institutes of Mental Health Treatment of Depression Collaborative Research Program (TDCRP; Elkin, 1994; Elkin et al., 1989). Clients ($N = 180$) diagnosed with major depression were randomly assigned to three treatment conditions: either cognitive-behavioral therapy (A. T. Beck, Rush, Shaw, & Emery, 1979), interpersonal therapy (Klerman, Weissman, Rounsaville, & Chevron, 1984), or clinical management treatments, which were characterized by drug- or placebo-management strategies (Fawcett, Epstein, Fiester, Elkin, & Autry, 1987).

The 96-item Collaborative Study Psychotherapy Rating Scale–Version 6 (CSPRS; Hollon et al., 1988) was used to assess therapist adherence. Adherence was defined as therapists being rated as scoring higher on scales designed to tap essential behaviors of their treatment approach and, conversely, scoring lower on behaviors essential to other approaches. The CSPRS was designed to study specific components of the TDCRP's treatment conditions: cognitive-behavioral therapy, interpersonal therapy, and clinical management. For example, subscales on the CSPRS measuring essential behavior in cognitive-behavioral therapy included evaluating and changing beliefs, homework, and behavioral focus; interpersonal therapy was measured by such subscales as focus on feelings, assessing interpersonal relationships and tendencies, and role transitions; clinical management was marked by symptom and illness focus. To apply the CSPRS, a rater first listens to a whole therapy session on tape, making notes as needed, and then completes the 96 items.

The CSPPRS was applied to four sessions (1, 4, 7, or 8, and 14, 15, or the last session) of each client by eight advanced doctoral students in counseling and clinical psychology. Raters participated in 50 hours of training and calibrated their coding after independently rating 30 audiotapes of training/pilot phase sessions. Two coders were randomly assigned to each audiotape using a balanced incomplete block design. Raters met periodically with the trainer to discuss rating and prevent drift. Intraclass correlations were used to assess intercoder reliability.

The CSPRS discriminated among the three different treatments very well. Therapists used more techniques consistent with their respective treatment modality and fewer techniques appropriate to the other treatments. That is, the therapists were doing different things in different therapies and the differences were consistent with the differences in the underlying theories.

Comment on Adherence Rating Scales

Adherence should be distinguished from competence and quality of treatment (e.g., Waltz, Addis, Koerner, & Jacobson, 1993). Adherence refers to how much therapists used the specified techniques (and avoided other techniques), whereas competence refers to how well techniques were applied. High scores on adherence scales tend to reflect the diversity and intensity of techniques used in the session; they do not indicate whether a session was more effective, more competently conducted, or even if a specific intervention was appropriately used. At times, using only one technique (or even remaining silent) may be appropriate, whereas use of many techniques (gaining a high adherence score) may reflect floundering. Assessing therapist competence and quality of treatment appear to require more sophisticated judgments (see proposals by Hoffart, 1997; Kendall & Hollon, 1983).

Qualitative Research on Treatment Differences

Rating scales offer a common metric that can be applied across cases, but, by the same token, they may obscure important context and details. Qualitative research, such as intensive case study, allows "thick" description that incorporates the context and detail—albeit at some cost in generality. Qualitative researchers have had to develop procedures for ensuring and assessing trustworthiness that differ from the procedures used for assessing reliability and validity in statistical hypothesis-testing research (Stiles, 1993).

Illustrative Study 4

Insight has been identified as an important treatment variable by many psychotherapy theorists, starting with Freud. Elliott et al. (1994) investigated six significant insight events (three each from interpersonal-psychodynamic therapy and cognitive-behavioral therapy) as part of the First Sheffield Psychotherapy Project (Shapiro & Firth, 1987). Insight events—moments in therapy when clients felt they gained a new perspective—were identified using a combination of procedures, including identification by the therapist, client, and outside observers. These events were analyzed using the Comprehensive Process Analysis technique (CPA), a qualitative and interpretive method used to examine significant therapeutic events.

CPA is a complex procedure during which researchers systematically attend to three domains: context (factors that lead up to the event, including background, presession context, session context, and episode context), key responses (client or therapist utterances, including action, content, style, and quality or skillfulness), and effects (sequence of consequences of an event.) Analysts were trained and followed the steps for CPA (Elliott, 1989, 1993). Each analyst applied the CPA framework to selected passages using transcripts and session tapes. Then they convened to develop a consensus interpretation for each significant insight event, considering the key responses, the effects of these responses, and the context in which they occurred.

Results indicated that insight events (moments in which new understanding was achieved) in both therapies involved therapist interpretations of clients' recent difficulties delivered firmly but in ways that encouraged interaction. Interpersonal-psychodynamic therapy insight events typically included two-part significant events and distinctive key words. They had links to important themes discussed in previous sessions, which led to awareness of painful emotions. Cognitive-behavioral insight events were distinguished by the role of context in transforming small therapy events into more significant events, and by externalizing reattributions provided to distressed clients. For example, in one client's cognitive-behavioral therapy, her tentative judgment about a problematic person ("He is a pain") was amplified and reinforced by the therapist's assurance that her assessment of him was "justified." This externalizing attribution moved the focus of the problematic behavior from the client to an external other.

Commentary

Each approach to assessing how therapies differ has advantages and disadvantages. Illustrative study 1 (Stiles et al., 1988) applied a general-purpose verbal response modes coding system designed to describe any type of verbal communication. Illustrative study 2 (Braswell et al., 1985) applied a system developed to display differences among that study's treatment conditions. Illustrative study 3 (Hill et al., 1992) applied systems of adherence ratings constructed as manipulation checks for specific manualized treatments. The first strategy had the virtue of a common metric, allowing any therapy to be compared with another or with other sorts of interpersonal encounters; the latter ones had the virtue of assessing each treatment in its own theoretical terms. Whereas the verbal response modes and adherence measures yield frequencies or ratings of set categories (e.g., interpretations), illustrative study 4's qualitative CPA approach (Elliott et al., 1994) can incorporate important contextual features that were not anticipated before the study began. By implication, however, CPA analyses of additional cases might reveal further features. Thus, the qualitative approach's greater clinical richness and realism may be balanced by a lesser generality of the conclusions.

ARE THERE SYSTEMATIC DIFFERENCES AMONG CLIENTS?

Kiesler (1966) argued that a myth of "patient uniformity" underlay much of psychotherapy research. Patient uniformity is the implicit assumption that all patients—or at least patients with the same diagnosed disorder—compose a homogeneous group. This assumption certainly appears false. Kiesler argued for incorporating patient heterogeneity into research designs.

Of course, people differ in all sorts of ways that may be manifested in the therapeutic process. We here consider four prominent approaches: (a) content analysis based on frequencies of word use, (b) the Core Conflictual Relationship Theme (CCRT) approach, (c) cognitive style approaches, and (d) interpersonal style approaches based on circumplex models.

Client Differences in Semantic Content

Computer-based analysis of the text of psychotherapy sessions has become increasingly sophisticated and accessible, making it relatively easy to measure how often clients use particular words, phrases, or categories in verbatim transcripts of sessions. Computer-aided analyses of vocabulary characteristics tend to be highly reliable and reduce or eliminate the need for intensive training of coders.

Illustrative Study 5

Hölzer, Mergenthaler, Pokorny, Kächele, and Luborsky (1996) sought features of therapist and client speech that indicated therapeutic change was occurring. They developed measures of vocabulary and applied these to 10 of the most successful cases and the 10 least successful cases of psychodynamic therapy in the Penn Psychotherapy Project (Luborsky, Crits-Christoph, Mintz, & Auerbach, 1988), based on clients' residual gain and rated benefit scores on several measures, including the Minnesota Multiphasic Personality Inventory (MMPI), Health Sickness Rating Scale, and the Prognostic Index Interview. Median treatment length was 61 weeks for the most improved group and 43 weeks for the least improved group. Sessions were audiotaped and transcribed, and four segments (the first 20 minutes of a session) were sampled, two from the initial sessions and two from the final phase of treatment.

Hölzer et al. (1996) used computer-aided strategies to identify the following vocabulary characteristics: (a) verbal activity of therapist and client, (b) the size of the private versus shared vocabularies of therapist and client, and (c) the presence of regressive imagery. Specifically, they measured (a) the total number of words spoken by each participant, (b) the number of different words each used (vocabulary), and (c) psychodynamic regression toward primary process thinking, measured using the Regressive Imagery Dictionary (RID; Martindale, 1975). The RID is a computerized method of content analysis that measures primary process, secondary process, and emotion. Primary process, or regression, is defined by psychodynamic theory as containing words that reference such constructs as drives ("sex," "orality"); sensation ("touch," "taste"); regressive cognition ("unknown," "timelessness," "narcissism"); Icarian imagery ("fire," "water," "falling"); and defensive symbols ("voyage," "diffusion," "chaos"). Secondary process was defined as abstract thought and behavior ("moral behavior," "order," "restraint"). Emotions were classified by words such as "anxiety," "sadness," or "aggression." The Ulm version of the RID, used in this study, classifies a total of more than 5,000 words into 43 mutually exclusive categories.

Results indicated that across both outcome groups, the mean ratio of client-to-therapist verbal activity was 3.5 to 1. In terms of the primary process category as measured by the RID, the improved group of patients were more likely to show an increase in Icarian imagery. Both the successful and unsuccessful clients showed a significant drop in secondary process, which was attributed to the decreased reliance on abstract thought (Hölzer et al., 1996).

Client Differences in Core Conflictual Relationship Theme

Based on the psychoanalytic tenet that client transference is central to psychotherapy, the CCRT method (Luborsky, 1976) has been developed to assess transference reliably. The method examines spontaneous client narratives in psychotherapy, which commonly focus on interactions with other people in the client's life, including the therapist. It identifies three main components in the patterns and relationship conflicts in these interactions: wishes toward others, responses of others, and responses of the self (Luborsky, Barber, & Crits-Christoph, 1990). The CCRT is identified as the combination of the types with the highest frequency within each component across all relationship narratives.

Illustrative Study 6

Barber, Luborsky, Crits-Christoph, and Diguer (1995) compared the traditional method for formulating CCRTs, in which the core theme is extracted from relationship episodes in transcripts of early sessions of brief dynamic therapy, with a pretreatment structured interview method. In the Relationship Anecdotes Paradigm interview method, a researcher asks the client to relate 10 incidents or events describing an interaction with another person. The study addressed the criticism that because CCRTs are extracted from psychotherapy sessions they may reflect mainly the therapist's influence rather than core structures internal to the client.

After the episodes had been selected, either from the transcripts or from the relationship anecdotes interviews, independent judges read the selected episodes and identified the three components of the CCRT: wishes, responses from others (ROs), and responses of self (RSs). Judges then identified the theme that occurred most frequently for each of the three components across all of the episodes. The judge returned to the original episodes to determine if the preliminary CCRT formulation fit the best. The judges' themes were translated into standard categories, yielding 35 wishes, 30 ROs, and 31 RSs (e.g., wish to be understood; rejecting; and opposing).

Interjudge agreement was assessed using a weighted kappa and ratings were in the acceptable range for both the CCRT determined from transcripts (.60–.68) and from the interview method (.64–.81). In comparing CCRTs derived from the relationship anecdotes interviews with those derived from therapy sessions, a moderate-to-good level of correspondence using weighted kappas was found (.52 for wishes, 1.0 for ROs, .40 for RSs). The similarity between CCRTs elicited from the pretherapy interview and those elicited from therapy suggested that CCRTs are not unduly influenced by therapist processes.

Client Differences in Cognitive Style

In research on cognitive therapy, the term "treatment process" often refers to the client's cognitive processes rather than to in-session behaviors, such as the therapist's use of techniques. Cognitive theorists have hypothesized that negative beliefs and maladaptive information processing play a key role in major psychological disorders and that cognitive therapy reduces symptoms by changing cognitive processes. Researchers interested in depression, for example, have emphasized such components of cognition as causal attributions (Abramson, Seligman, & Teasdale, 1978; Peterson & Seligman, 1984) and depressive schemata—knowledge structures that contain undesirable biases (A. T. Beck, 1967).

Illustrative Study 7

DeRubeis et al. (1990) examined the role of client cognitive processes in the change fostered by cognitive therapy and imipramine pharmacotherapy. Adult outpatients ($N = 112$) were screened for major depressive disorder and randomly assigned to one of four 12-week treatments: cognitive therapy alone, imipramine pharmacotherapy alone, combined cognitive therapy and imipramine pharmacotherapy, and imipramine therapy for 12 weeks combined with a year of maintenance imipramine therapy. Four cognitive therapists delivered psychotherapy; three were clinical social workers, and one was a clinical psychologist.

Measures of cognition and depression were obtained before treatment, during the 6th week of treatment, and after the 12th week of treatment. Four cognitive self-report measures were used. The 30-item Automatic Thoughts Questionnaire (ATQ; Hollon &

Kendall, 1980) examines the frequency with which patients experience 30 negative self-statements (e.g., "I'm no good," "I'll never make it"). The Hopelessness Scale (HS; Beck, Weissman, Lester, & Trexler, 1974) is a 20-item true-false measure that assesses the degree of the respondent's general pessimism. The Dysfunctional Attitudes Scale, Form A (DAS; A. Weissman & Beck, 1978) is a 40-item series of depressotypic "underlying assumptions" that subjects endorse on a 7-point Likert scale. The Attributional Styles Questionnaire (ASQ; Seligman, Abramson, Semmel, & von Baeyer, 1979) asks subjects to rate the degree to which six positive and six negative causes for life events are internal, stable, and global. Depression was assessed before and after treatment using a composite of three clinical rating measures.

Significant improvement from pretreatment to midtreatment was demonstrated by all four treatment groups on all four cognitive measures. That is, cognitive therapy did not uniquely produce changes on cognitive measures by midtreatment. However, midtreatment to posttreatment change in depression was predicted by early change (change occurring in the first six weeks of treatment on the ASQ, DAS, and HS) in the cognitive therapy groups. In the no-cognitive-therapy groups, none of these predictive relationships were observed. The authors concluded that improvement is influenced by different causal processes for cognitive therapy and pharmacotherapy.

Client Differences in Interpersonal Behavior: Circumplex Models

Interpersonal theorists, building on the pioneering work of Harry Stack Sullivan (1953), focused attention on the ways in which interpersonal experiences contribute to the development of personality and psychopathology. Interpersonal researchers, following Kiesler (1982, 1996), have argued that interpersonal transactions should be considered the fundamental unit of analysis in psychotherapy process research. In this view, client attributes, therapist techniques, and the relationship are not distinct but are intertwined in the interpersonal interactions of therapy.

Leary (1957) argued that interpersonal behavior rather than symptoms should be used in psychological diagnosis. He explained personality using a circumplex: a circle of interpersonal characteristics defined by two dimensions. The horizontal axis, affiliation, is a continuum ranging from hate to love, and the vertical axis dimension, control, ranges from submission to dominance. The Structural Analysis of Social Behavior (SASB; Benjamin, 1974, 1982, 1996; Henry, 1996) is an elaboration of Leary's concepts. SASB uses a more complex circumplex coding scheme, in which three underlying dimensions (dominance, affiliation, and individuation) are used to describe clients' interactions with self and others.

Illustrative Study 8

Henry, Schacht, and Strupp (1986) sought process variables that would distinguish between good and poor outcomes of brief psychodynamic therapy. Four psychotherapists were each rated on two cases, one with a poor and one with a good outcome ($N = 8$). Patients were single men, ages 18–25, who presented with complaints of anxiety, depression, and social withdrawal. Outcomes were measured by pre-post change in MMPI profiles and by ratings of target complaints and global change by clients, therapists, and nonparticipant clinicians.

SASB (Benjamin, 1974, 1982) was used to code segments of each client's third therapy session. SASB ratings reflect clusters of behaviors (which have evocative descriptors) and are understood as reflecting unique combinations on the dimensions of affiliation-disaffiliation and independence-interdependence. Examples of behavioral clusters include "helping and protecting," "affirming and understanding," "blaming and belittling," "disclosing and expressing," "walling off and avoiding," and "trusting and relying." Coding followed procedures outlined in the SASB manual (Benjamin, Giat, & Estroff, 1981). Coders were blind to case outcome and used both transcripts and audiotapes. They classified the first 150 thought units of each session (15–20 minutes) into SASB dimensions and clusters. Interrater agreement in SASB cluster assignment was assessed by Cohen's kappa (Cohen, 1960), and disagreements were resolved through discussion and mutual consent.

In an analysis of the interpersonal variables that distinguished better outcomes, higher levels of "helping and protecting" and "affirming and understanding" and lower levels of "blaming and belittling" differentiated good outcomes from the poor ones. At the level of patient behaviors, greater frequencies of "disclosing and expressing" were exhibited in good-outcome cases, whereas "walling off and avoiding" and "trusting and relying" were more frequent in poor-outcome cases. Negative complementarity (hostile or controlling interactions, marked by reciprocity on the dominance dimension and congruence on the affiliation dimension) was associated with poor-outcome cases.

Commentary

The studies reviewed in this section highlight ways in which investigators' assumptions about the nature of people and psychopathology determine their approach to treatment process research. At first glance, illustrative study 5 (Hölzer et al., 1996) may seem to have taken a strictly empirical approach, using computers to classify and count spoken words in successful and unsuccessful cases. The authors' theory appeared in their construction of the dictionary, whose categories (dealing with regressive imagery) seem strongly driven by a psychodynamic conceptualization. Illustrative study 6's CCRT methodology (Barber et al., 1995) was even more clearly based on psychodynamic principles. The development of the CCRT into a reliable tool has demonstrated that such seemingly elusive and idiosyncratic phenomena as clients' transference patterns can be measured and studied empirically. Illustrative study 7 (DeRubeis et al., 1990) was driven by cognitive assumptions about personality and psychopathology, and it measured cognitive process variables, such as automatic thoughts and attributions. Finally, illustrative study 8 (Henry et al., 1986) was driven by interpersonal assumptions; the SASB scales describe interpersonal attitudes and actions (e.g., "helping and protecting," "affirming and understanding," "blaming and belittling," "walling off and avoiding").

WHAT ARE THE COMMON FACTORS?

One possible resolution to the equivalence paradox runs as follows: Yes, psychotherapies differ in their theories and techniques, but these factors are not the important ones. There are many features that all psychotherapies have in common, and some of these common factors may be responsible for different treatments' equivalent effectiveness. Early impetus was given to the search for common factors by Fiedler's (1950a, 1950b, 1951) finding that therapists and clients from different theoretical orientations agreed in their ratings of the ideal therapy with respect to such global aspects as warmth and overall quality of the therapeutic relationship. In global terms, the desirable characteristics of divergent theoretical orientations sounded alike. Process research on common factors has looked at (a) therapist-provided common factors, (b) client-provided common factors, and (c) the therapeutic alliance or the interaction between the therapist and the client.

Therapist Common Factors

The common factors offered by therapists across divergent theoretical backgrounds can be considered in terms of two broad categories: warm involvement with the client, and the communication of a new perspective on the client's person and situation (Goldfried, 1980; Stiles et al., 1986). We focus here on warm involvement, which was elaborated by Rogers (1957), who delineated three "facilitative conditions" ideally offered by the therapist: accurate empathy, unconditional positive regard, and genuineness or congruence. Rogers argued that these three conditions were necessary and sufficient to promote significant change in the client. Process researchers designed measures of Rogerian Therapist-Offered Conditions from the therapist's perspective, the client's perspective, or an observer's perspective. They found correlations suggesting that high levels of Therapist-Offered Conditions were associated with successful therapeutic outcome (Barrett-Lennard, 1985, 1986), though the generality of the association has been questioned (e.g., Lambert, DeJulio, & Stein, 1978).

Illustrative Study 9

Truax and Carkhuff (1965) experimentally tested the client-centered hypothesis that the therapist's levels of empathic understanding, unconditional positive regard, and genuineness are key ingredients of effective psychotherapy. Clients were three female patients, ages 21–55, recently admitted to a state hospital with tentative diagnoses of schizophrenic reaction. The therapist sought to convey high levels of accurate empathy and unconditional positive regard during the first 20 minutes of an initial client-centered therapeutic interview to establish a baseline of patient depth of interpersonal exploration. Next, the therapist deliberately introduced moderately low levels of the facilitative conditions for the next 20 minutes, followed by a return to providing high conditions for the last 20 minutes of the interview.

The three segments of the interview were divided into five three-minute time periods, resulting in a total of 45 samples across the three patients studied. The 45 samples were then randomly assigned to trained raters. Four raters rated the clients' speech on the 10-point Depth of Interpersonal Exploration Scale, which measures the patient's active exploration of personal feelings, values, perceptions of others, relationships, fears, turmoil, and life choices. Three separate groups of three coders each rated accurate empathy, unconditional positive regard, and therapist genuineness. The 9-point Accurate Empathy Scale specifies stages along a continuum according to the therapist's responsiveness to the patient's emotional content. The Unconditional Positive Regard Scale defines five stages in regard to the therapist's nonpossessive and nondemanding warmth. Finally, the 5-point therapist Self-Congruence Scale measures the degree to which the therapist is free to be himself or herself, is open to experience, and is nondefensive. Intercoder reliability ranged from .68 to .83 across the four measures.

Results indicated that accurate empathy and unconditional positive regard did drop significantly during the middle portion of the interview. However, the therapist was not instructed to lower the level of genuineness, and this construct was actually measured as greater during the period of lowered facilitative conditions (tentatively explained by the authors as a compensation for the lowered levels of the other conditions). The clients' depth of interpersonal exploration declined during the middle portion of the interview and returned to the previously established higher baseline level when greater levels of facilitative conditions were restored.

In contrasting the Rogerian conception of facilitative conditions with the broader construct of therapeutic alliance, Horvath and Luborsky (1993) noted a degree of one-sidedness:

> Although client-centered theory is often regarded as a quintessentially humanistic position emphasizing the "I and Thou" aspect of therapy, Rogers' propositions do not address the possibility of variations in the clients' ability and motivation to respond to the offer of such a relationship. There is a presumption of a fated response to the correct attitude of the therapist. (p. 562)

Client Common Factors

In contrast to the effort to locate the common ingredients of successful therapy in the therapist, some theorists have proposed that the essential ingredients are to be located within the client. Two related client processes that have received attention in process research are client self-disclosure (e.g., Stiles, 1995) and client focusing or experiencing (Gendlin, 1964, 1981; Klein, Mathieu, Gendlin, & Kiesler, 1970; Klein, Mathieu-Coughlan, & Kiesler, 1986).

Patient and Therapist Experiencing Scales were constructed to measure the depth and immediacy of experiencing (Klein et al., 1970, 1986). A client or therapist capable of focusing on a felt bodily referent, attending to the ongoing flow of experience, and symbolizing these things would be rated high on experiencing. Some reviewers have concluded that the Experiencing Scale robustly predicts outcome (Greenberg, Elliott, & Lietaer, 1994).

Illustrative Study 10

Kiesler (1971) studied experiencing in the first 30 sessions of client-centered therapy with 12 hospitalized schizophrenic clients and 26 psychoneurotic outpatients. The Experiencing Scale ranges from 1, at which the client does not express any feelings or relate any private information, to 7, at which the client can easily express feelings and the significance and meaning of those feelings. Four-minute segments were randomly selected from each of the first 30 sessions and were rated by four trained judges. The reliability of the four judges' ratings was .76 for the schizophrenic sample and .79 for the psychoneurotic sample (using Ebel intraclass reliabilities). The primary dependent variable was the means of the four judges' ratings for the 360 segments from the schizophrenic clients and the 780 segments from the psychoneurotic clients. Clients in each group were divided into successful and unsuccessful outcome clients. Outcome for the psychoneurotic clients was measured by the therapists' global judgment of improvement. The MMPI was used to assess outcome for the schizophrenic clients.

Results suggested that neurotic clients functioned at higher levels of experiencing than schizophrenic clients in psychotherapy and that more successful clients in each sample scored higher on experiencing than unsuccessful clients.

Common Factors in the Relationship: The Alliance

The alliance construct (sometimes called the therapeutic alliance, the working alliance, or the helping alliance) locates the common change factors in the relationship between the psychotherapist and the client rather than trying to localize the common factors in one or the other. The alliance is a multidimensional concept, which includes attachment components (therapist-client bond) and collaborative components (including a willingness to invest in the therapy process) (Horvath & Luborsky, 1993). Perhaps because the strength of the alliance has been found to be correlated with outcome more often than have other process variables (Beutler, Machado, & Neufeldt, 1994; Horvath & Luborsky, 1993; Horvath & Symonds, 1991; Orlinsky, Grawe, & Parks, 1994), there has been a proliferation of alliance measures, including the California Psychotherapy Alliance Scales (Gaston, 1991; Gaston & Ring, 1992; Marmar, Weiss, & Gaston, 1989), the Penn Helping Alliance Scales (Alexander & Luborsky, 1987; Luborsky, 1976), the Therapeutic Alliance Scale (Marziali, 1984), the Vanderbilt Therapeutic Alliance Scale (Hartley & Strupp, 1983), the Working Alliance Inventory (Horvath & Greenberg, 1989), and the Agnew Relationship Measure (Agnew-Davies, Stiles, Hardy, Barkham, & Shapiro, 1998). Most of these instruments have separate self-report forms for clients and therapists, and some include rating instruments that can be applied by raters listening to tape recordings.

Illustrative Study 11

Mallinckrodt (1993) hypothesized that session impact and working alliance have a reciprocal, interactive relationship with each other that mutually influences therapy outcome. He collected data from 61 clients and 41 therapists who participated in individual psychotherapy dyads over a two-year period at a psychotherapy training clinic. The therapists were first-year master's and first-year doctoral students.

At intake, clients completed the Brief Symptom Inventory (BSI), a shortened version of the Symptom Checklist-90-R (Derogatis, 1983), as a global indicator of psychological functioning. After the third or fourth session, therapists and clients completed the Working Alliance Inventory (WAI; Horvath & Greenberg, 1989). Parallel forms of the 36-item WAI for therapist and client included three subscales measuring dimensions of the working alliance, including bond, tasks, and goals (although only the total scale score was used in this study). After each of the first 12 sessions, therapists and clients provided Session Evaluation Questionnaire ratings (SEQ; Stiles & Snow, 1984a, 1984b). The SEQ is a measure of session impact, which includes participants' postsession mood and evaluation of immediate session effects. It contains 24 bipolar semantic differential items rated on 7-point scales. Four subscales, depth, smoothness, positivity, and arousal, are scored. Depth refers to the session's value and power; smoothness measures perceived comfort, safety, and personal distress; positivity refers to postsession moods of confidence and happiness, as well as a lack of anger and fear; arousal measures feelings of activity and excitement versus calmness and quietness. At termination, clients completed a second set of measures, including the BSI and the WAI, and therapists also completed the WAI. To assess therapeutic outcome, therapists and clients both were asked to evaluate the degree of change in the client's target concerns. Because of attrition, only 40 clients of the original 61 completed termination measures, although Mallinckrodt (1993) found no significant differences between the 40 who completed posttest data and the 21 who did not.

Results indicated that evaluations of sessions in the early treatment phase were related to early client working alliance ratings, with significant linear and curvilinear effects for clients. This relationship was not significant for therapists, however. Positive early alliance ratings were significantly correlated with subsequent session evaluations for client-rated depth and positivity. Session evaluations, summed over the course of therapy, were significant predictors of termination alliance for both therapists and clients. Session evaluations of depth and smoothness and working alliance were significantly and uniquely related to outcome for client ratings, and showed both linear and curvilinear effects. However, only alliance uniquely predicted outcome for therapist ratings. Therapist and client early ratings of working alliance were not significantly correlated, replicating the frequent observation that therapists and clients evaluate their encounters differently (Dill-Standiford et al., 1988).

Common Factors as Evaluative

The common factors that are predictive of positive outcome tend to be global and evaluative rather than specific and descriptive. Evaluative measures include the alliance, therapist-offered conditions, therapist competence (Waltz et al., 1993), and session impact (Orlinsky & Howard, 1986; Stiles, 1980). Such measures reflect respondents' expert judgments or an integration of their affective or empathic personal reactions, rather than being based on explicit behavioral criteria. For example, achieving a strong alliance is not a matter of simply increasing the frequency or intensity of particular behaviors, but of responding appropriately to clients' requirements as they emerge in the context of treatment.

Evaluative process judgments may incorporate elements of early outcome. That is, in a therapy that is on its way to being successful, therapists may be judged relatively competent and the alliance may be judged relatively strong. Indeed, by definition, using an intervention skillfully or having a strong alliance seems to imply that the intervention or relationship was therapeutically productive. Thus, there may be some circularity in the link of outcomes with evaluative judgments of treatment processes. Because of this concern, correlations of outcome with the strength of the alliance, therapist competence, or other evaluative measures may be better understood not as reflecting cause-effect relations, but rather as a step in unpacking the complex process of outcome.

WHICH ARE THE EFFECTIVE INGREDIENTS?

In a widely cited article, Yeaton and Sechrest (1981; see also Norcross & Beutler, 1997) urged therapists and investigators to attend to the strength, integrity, and effectiveness of treatment. Effective treatments, they argued, should contain large amounts of helpful change ingredients (strength) and should be delivered in a pure manner (integrity). If the theory underlying the treatment is correct, then delivering interventions with strength and integrity should be effective in producing client change. This view of process-outcome relations has been called the drug metaphor (Stiles & Shapiro, 1989, 1994).

The drug metaphor strategy used in much process-outcome research has been to assess the relationship of process ingredients with outcome by correlating the process and outcome measures across clients. It has been assumed that this method would allow researchers to determine which process components are the active ingredients (which should be positively correlated with outcome) and which are merely inert flavors and fillers (uncorrelated with outcome). Later in this section, however, we suggest that this reasoning may be seriously misleading (cf. Stiles, 1988, 1994, 1996).

In their comprehensive review of the process-outcome literature, Orlinsky et al. (1994) concluded that there was evidence for differential effectiveness of some therapeutic operations, including interpretation (along with paradoxical intention and experiential confrontation). A review of psychodynamic approaches in the same volume by Henry, Strupp, Schacht, and Gaston (1994), however, concluded that "[t]ransference interpretations do not elicit differentially greater affective response or necessarily increase depth of experiencing when compared to nontransference interpretations or other interventions" (p. 475). It may be noted that transference interpretations are not equivalent to interpretations, but insofar as the former are a subset of the latter, the contrasting conclusions were striking.

Interpretations Pro and Con

To highlight some of the issues that may underlie the contrasting conclusions, we consider two studies that attempted to assess the impact of interpretations on treatment outcome: one that suggested a negative impact and one that suggested a positive impact. In addition to their different conclusions, the way they measured interpretation differed sharply. Whereas one considered transference interpretations in conjunction with client traits in a naturalistic setting (Piper, Azim, Joyce, & McCallum, 1991), the other focused on the specific characteristics of the interpretation itself in an experimental analogue study (i.e., based on students put in a situation analogous to therapy, rather than on actual therapy; J. T. Beck & Strong, 1982). The juxtaposition of these two studies illustrates how differences in operationalizing process components make generalizations difficult.

Illustrative Study 12

Piper et al. (1991) measured the proportion of transference interpretations provided by therapists in a naturalistic setting. Clients ($N = 64$) were seen in short-term dynamic psychotherapy in a walk-in clinic for an average of 18.8 sessions. Therapists' interventions were categorized by raters using the Therapist Intervention Rating System (Piper, Debbane, de Carufel, & Bienvenu, 1987). A transference interpretation was defined as an interpretation that included a reference to the therapist. The average percentage of perfect agreement on transference interpretations was 89%, supporting the reliability of this measure. The investigators also sought to assess clients' quality of object relations (QOR)—their lifelong pattern of interpersonal relations to significant others—as a variable thought to mediate the effectiveness of transference interpretations. Clients' QOR was assessed through a two-hour interview. On the basis of the interview, clients were assessed on five levels (mature, triangular, controlling, searching, and primitive), which, taken together, yielded a QOR score ranging from 1 to 9, with higher scores indicating higher quality of relationships. The intraclass correlation coefficient for the 9-point rating scale was a marginal .50.

Results suggested that for clients with a high QOR, a high proportion of transference interpretations was significantly associated with *poorer* outcomes and alliances—a paradoxical result that seemed to contradict the theory.

Illustrative Study 13

J. T. Beck and Strong (1982) conducted an experimental analogue study in which students were recruited to undergo a treatment intervention of two sessions. Students were assigned to one of two treatment groups or to a control group. The two treatment groups differed in whether the interpretations offered had a positive or negative connotation. The treatment intervention consisted of two 30-minute sessions in which the therapist delivered three prepared interpretations verbatim at 5-minute intervals during the last 17 minutes. In the negative connotation condition, the interpretations attributed negative qualities to the depressed client (e.g., "Feeling sad and down is a passive-aggressive way of punishing others and trying to make them feel guilty"). In the positive connotation treatment, therapists attributed positive qualities to the client for being depressed (e.g., "You are fortunate to be so aware of your feelings and emotions and to be so completely aware of being alive"). In this way, the process component was not measured but was manipulated experimentally. The study found that clients in both treatment conditions improved on self-report measures of depression, but that clients in the negative connotation condition experienced symptom relapse following treatment.

Commentary

These two studies illustrate the extent of variation in methods for measuring what is described as a single variable, interpretation. In illustrative study 12, Piper et al. (1987) understood interpretations within a psychodynamic perspective and studied them as they occurred naturally in ongoing therapy, whereas in illustrative study 13, J. T. Beck and Strong (1982) viewed interpretations as more akin to the cognitive-behavioral technique of reframing and were experimentally manipulated in an artificial setting.

Responsiveness Critique of the Drug Metaphor

The drug metaphor approach to process-outcome relations uses a linear logic; it assumes that the cause-effect relations of process and outcome variables run in a single direction (i.e., that process variables cause outcome variables). However, this reasoning neglects therapists' and clients' appropriate *responsiveness*—the tendency of both therapists and clients to make appropriate adjustments in their behavior as a result of ongoing changes in their own and each other's requirements (Stiles, Honos-Webb, & Surko, 1998). In human interaction, participants are responsive to each other's behavior on time scales that range down to a few tens of milliseconds (Elliott et al., 1994; Goodwin, 1981). If therapists respond appropriately to varying client requirements, rather than emitting a process component randomly or ballistically (i.e., at some predetermined level), then the level (e.g., frequency, intensity) of that component will tend to be near its optimum level in each client's treatment. To the extent that treatment is appropriately responsive to a client or therapist variable, the outcome will tend to be constant insofar as it depends on that variable. A greater intensity or frequency of a process component is unlikely to be helpful if clients are already getting enough. For this reason, the correlation coefficient or any other linear statistical description of process-outcome relations can be a misleading criterion for judging the value of a psychotherapy process component (Stiles, 1988).

To illustrate, Henry et al. (1994) suggested that the negative correlation of transference interpretations with outcome indicated a potential for interpretations to be damaging. The responsiveness critique suggests an alternative interpretation: that the more resistant or severely disturbed clients required interpretations to be repeated, whereas clients who were improving rapidly caught on quickly and required fewer interventions. The therapists responded appropriately and offered more interpretations to the former clients, who were less likely to improve or make as much progress. That is, clients who do not show as much improvement (poor outcome) receive more interpretations (process), resulting in a negative correlation. Something of this sort may have happened among the high QOR clients in the Piper et al. (1987) study.

The responsiveness logic also applies to client behavior. The fever model of self-disclosure (Stiles, 1987) offered a responsiveness-based account of the paradoxical finding that client disclosure has not been found to be consistently correlated with outcome, even though disclosure accounts for a majority of what clients do in therapy and high-disclosing passages are rated as reflecting good process (e.g., high experiencing; Stiles, McDaniel, & McGaughey, 1979):

> The fever model suggests that clients normally disclose at optimum levels; those who are more distressed tend to disclose more and therefore are (appropriately) judged by experts as making good use of the setting. However, the more distressed clients do not necessarily have better outcomes. Indeed, one might expect clients who are initially more dysfunctional to have worse outcomes. Moreover, as clients improve, they presumably feel less distressed, and their rate of disclosure should decrease; so their average level (across many sessions) may be lower than the level for clients who fail to improve. (Stiles, 1987, pp. 268–269)

The important general conclusion is that a process component can be an active ingredient in successful psychotherapy despite its lack of linear correlation with outcome measures. Demonstrating this, however, may require alternative and innovative methods, particularly insofar as the responsiveness may occur on time scales that range from several months down to several tens of milliseconds (Stiles et al., 1998; see also discussion of mediation by Holmbeck, 1997).

Experimental studies do not escape the responsiveness critique insofar as manipulating one process component may be compensated by responsive adjustments in others. For example, an interviewer told to decrease question asking may compensate by using more evocative reflections or remaining silent, giving clients more space to talk.

Cox, Holbrook, and Rutter (1981; Cox, Rutter, & Holbrook, 1981) observed such compensation when they experimentally manipulated interviewer style in diagnostic interviews with mothers of referred children. Interviewers using four contrasting styles (directive vs. nondirective crossed with active vs. passive) elicited very similar levels of information and feeling, but by different paths, as participants responsively adjusted to the experimental manipulations.

The responsiveness critique does not imply that linear statistical results of process-outcome studies should be ignored. On the contrary, nonchance findings usually have some interesting explanation. The critique suggests, however, that simple linear cause-effect interpretations should be viewed with caution and skepticism. Recursive, responsive relationships among variables should be carefully considered in interpreting any positive or null result.

Client-Level Responsiveness: Aptitude-Treatment Interactions

Responsiveness at the client level consists in selecting treatments or techniques that are appropriate for each client. One client's active ingredient may be another client's inert filler. Dimensions of client individual differences that contribute to the change process may be considered moderator variables (Holmbeck, 1997) or "aptitudes" for particular treatments (Shoham-Salomon, 1991; B. Smith & Sechrest, 1991; Snow, 1991). Efforts to investigate how such contributions interact with the treatment process to produce different outcomes have thus been called aptitude-treatment interactions (ATIs).

Illustrative Study 14

Shoham-Salomon, Avner, and Neeman's (1989) analogue research, often cited as illustrating the possible importance of ATIs, concerned the differing impact of paradoxical interventions on clients high or low in psychological reactance. In a paradoxical intervention, a therapist attempts to facilitate change by seemingly discouraging it; for example, prescribing the symptom the client came to therapy to alleviate. Reactance is a state of mind in which individuals are motivated to achieve self-direction when they perceive their freedom is being impinged upon. A student might be advised, paradoxically, to intentionally procrastinate rather than working toward an elimination of the procrastination. Theoretically, if reactant clients are advised to procrastinate, they will be motivated to regain their freedom by contradicting the injunction placed on them by not procrastinating.

In two studies of undergraduate Israeli students who complained of problems with procrastination, recruited from introductory psychology classes, Shoham-Salomon et al. (1989) measured reactance, first as a personological trait component and second as an experimentally manipulated (situationally aroused) state. The students were randomly assigned to two half-hour sessions of either a paradoxical intervention treatment or a self-control treatment. In the first study, reactance was measured using ratings of tone of voice with the content filtered out. Four judges achieved interjudge effective reliability of .77 (Rosenthal & Rosnow, 1984). The measure of reactance was construct validated by having clinical psychologists rate the content of the speech for reactance. In the second study, reactance was manipulated experimentally. Clients were asked to choose which type of therapeutic intervention of two they preferred to be assigned to. Clients assigned to the reactant condition were led to believe that they were not being given the type of intervention they had asked for. Both studies found that reactant clients were more likely than nonreactant clients to experience symptom reduction when assigned to the paradoxical intervention condition. This seemed to represent an ATI—an interaction of reactance (an aptitude, both as a personality trait and a situationally induced state) with response to paradoxical interventions (the treatment).

Despite the apparent promise of ATIs, however, most attempts to identify client variables that are predictive of differential treatment responsiveness have been disappointing (Dance & Neufeld, 1988; Shoham-Salomon, 1991; B. Smith & Sechrest, 1991). Reviewers have attributed this to various methodological faults in published ATI research, to the lack of a guiding theoretical basis for investigating client variables, or to insufficient power to detect significant differences across client groups (B. Smith & Sechrest, 1991; Snow, 1991).

Episode-Level Responsiveness: Plan Compatibility and Affective Reactions

Responsiveness has also been incorporated into process research at the level of therapeutic episodes within sessions. That is, classes of interventions have been studied in relation to ongoing processes within the session. For example, Weiss, Sampson, and the Mount Zion Research Group (1986) conceptualized accuracy of interpretation as "plan compatibility." According to their theory, clients have pathogenic beliefs learned from their childhood and families of origin, and they enter therapy with a plan to disconfirm these beliefs.

Illustrative Study 15

Silberschatz, Fretter, and Curtis (1986) identified interpretations in psychoanalytic therapy transcripts and assessed each one's plan compatibility: whether an interpretation fit or did not fit the patient's plan. Plan formulations were constructed from initial interviews by five expert clinicians. The plan formulation was made up of four components: (a) the client's goals for therapy, (b) the pathogenic beliefs or obstacles preventing the attainment of goals, (c) the plan to test the therapist, to disconfirm the pathogenic beliefs, and (d) the insights that would be helpful to the patient. Reliabilities were determined by intraclass correlations and achieved levels of .89 for goals, .90 for obstructions, .82 for tests, and .86 for insights. The plan compatibility of specific interpretations was determined using the Plan Compatibility of Interventions Scale (PCIS; Caston, 1986), which is a 7-point Likert scale ranging from −3 (strongly anti-plan) to +3 (strongly pro-plan). Reliability of the PCIS was assessed using intraclass correlations and ranged from .85 to .89 across the three cases to which the measure was applied. The three minutes prior to and following the interpretation were rated for depth of experiencing on the Experiencing Scale (Klein et al., 1986). PCIS ratings were then compared to patient change in experiencing from immediately before to immediately following the interpretation.

A significant positive correlation was found between the change in depth of experiencing and the plan compatibility of the interpretation. That is, the value of the interpretation seemed to depend on its appropriate responsiveness to the patient's requirements. In contrast, the type of interpretation (assessed as transference vs. nontransference) did not correlate with patient productivity.

Illustrative Study 16

McCullough et al. (1991) sought to incorporate responsiveness at the episode level by taking into account patient reactions to therapist interventions. They studied four sessions from each of 16 completed short-term psychodynamic therapies (which ranged from 27 to 53 sessions). Their process coding system included measures of therapist interventions and of patient process in the three minutes following the therapist intervention. They focused on therapist interventions that were coded as clarification, interpretations of the patient-therapist relationship, or interpretations of relationships with significant others. Patient process was coded for either defensive responding or affective responding in the three minutes following the therapist's intervention. Defensive responding was coded when clients showed evidence of avoidance or efforts to resist painful topics addressed in the therapist's interpretation or clarification. Affective responding by the patient was coded when clear expression of emotion was evident.

Each session was coded by three judges on a moment-to-moment basis from videotape. The pool of 13 judges was trained for three months and achieved intercoder reliability for intraclass correlations of $r = .75$ for therapist activity and $r = .68$ for patient activity. Two coders had to agree on the presence of a process component in the same minute for it to be coded. The intercoder reliability for the six "interactive episodes" ranged from .62 to .93.

Using the process codes, McCullough et al. (1991) distinguished interactive episodes from noninteractive episodes. Interactive episodes were defined as the client's affective responding in each minute of the three minutes following the therapist's intervention. They tested two different hypotheses: that interactive episodes would correlate with outcome, and that noninteractive episodes would not correlate with outcome. Thus, the codes were separate from each other, measuring the same material.

Treatment outcome was measured using the Social Adjustment Scale (Weissman & Bothwell, 1976) and three Target Complaints (Battle et al., 1966). Outcome measures were analyzed using analysis of covariance (ANCOVA) with the admission scores as the covariate. The resulting outcome scores reflected each patient's residual gain from admission to termination. Outcome scores were determined using ANCOVA, which were then compared with the episode types. Briefly, results suggested that patient-therapist interpretations followed by patient affect were significantly related to positive outcome. Any intervention followed by client defensiveness was negatively correlated with outcome. The frequency of noninteractive variables was not significantly correlated with outcome.

Commentary

Illustrative studies 14, 15, and 16 can be considered alternative attempts to study the effects of appropriate responsiveness on the process and outcome of therapy. In illustrative study 14 (Shoham-Salomon et al., 1989), experimental methods (including random assignment to conditions) were used to assess the potential effectiveness of therapist responsiveness to reactance, a client personality characteristic. In illustrative study 15

(Silberschatz et al., 1986), the changes in experiencing (presumed to be a desirable consequence) following plan-compatible interventions (appropriately responsive, according to the theory) were compared with changes following plan-incompatible interventions. Illustrative study 16 (McCullough et al., 1991) studied client responsiveness to therapists' interpretive interventions, reasoning that interventions that evoked affect would be therapeutic, whereas those that evoked defensiveness would not. The interesting findings of all three studies show the potential productiveness of studying responsiveness.

Future studies of responsiveness, however, should be cognizant of multiple time scales. Because responsiveness occurs at time scales down to a few tens of milliseconds, apparent unresponsiveness at one level might be compensated by responsiveness at lower levels or vice versa. For example, one might imagine offering a plan-compatible interpretation in a crude and insensitive manner that overrides the apparent compatibility. Thus, again, failure to find simple linear links of outcome with process indices that incorporate responsiveness need not impugn those indices. The failure may reflect compensating responsiveness or unresponsiveness on other time scales (Stiles et al., 1998).

Dismantling

Dismantling studies employ experimental methods to identify which components of a treatment package are responsible for facilitating change. Two or more treatment groups that vary in only one or a few of the treatment's techniques are compared. One group typically receives a complete treatment, whereas other groups receive only a portion of the treatment.

Illustrative Study 17

Nezu and Perri (1989) compared problem-solving therapy with an abbreviated version of problem-solving therapy and a wait list control group. They investigated which techniques in the treatment package were necessary and sufficient for producing relief in unipolar depression, measured by standard self-report inventories. The process element of interest—training in problem orientation—was isolated by using two separate treatment groups and comparing them to a control group. Training in problem orientation is a technique aimed to motivate clients to apply the other elements of the training program and make them feel that they will be successful in implementing the treatment package. Clients were assigned to either a group that received the full treatment, a group that received the treatment without the training in problem orientation component (called abbreviated problem-solving treatment), or a control group. In this way, the process component was not measured but was experimentally manipulated. After attrition, there were 39 clients, with 14 in each treatment condition and 11 in a wait list control condition. Results suggested that clients were more likely to obtain clinically significant relief from unipolar depression in the overall treatment condition than in the abbreviated treatment condition.

Commentary

Dismantling studies represent a valuable tool, but interpreting them requires caution. They assume that components are self-contained modules that can be added and removed independently. However, as illustrated by studies described earlier (Cox, Holbrook, et al., 1981; Cox, Rutter, et al., 1981), therapists and clients may compensate for restrictions by making different or more extensive use of the tools they are allowed, thus confounding experimental manipulations.

WHAT HAPPENS AS CLIENTS IMPROVE?

The difficulties in establishing linear links between process and outcome have revived interest in more descriptive studies, including qualitative studies, of what has been called the process of outcome or change process research. Researchers have tried to study sessions or episodes in which it appears that change is occurring and describe what they believe to be good therapeutic process:

> A focus on process of change serves to transcend the dichotomy between process and outcome that has previously hindered the field. . . . With processes of change as the focus of investigation, the emphasis is not on studying what is going on in therapy (process research) nor only on the comparison of two measurement points before and after therapy (efficacy research) but rather on identifying, describing, explaining, and predicting the effects of the processes that bring about therapeutic change over the entire course of therapy. (Greenberg, 1986, p. 4)

Events Paradigm and Task Analysis

The *events paradigm* (Rice & Greenberg, 1984) focuses on the intensive analysis of significant events in psychotherapy: recurring categories of events that have a common structure and are important for change. Brief passages sharing some specified common feature are collected and examined using microanalytic techniques and close attention to the context.

Task analysis is one method for studying a particular type of significant event in therapy (a task) and describing the process of change. Rice and Greenberg (1984) described a rational-empirical strategy for analyzing therapeutic tasks. The rational aspect is the use of clinical knowledge to construct an initial model of a change event—an ideal occurrence and resolution. The empirical aspect is collecting transcripts of many events, comparing theory with data, and repeated cycling between revising the theory and checking further data. Typically, each event in such a collection includes (a) a client marker of the problem, (b) the therapist's initiation of a task, (c) the client's performance, and (d) the immediate in-session outcome (Greenberg, 1986).

Rice and Saperia (1984) illustrated task analysis with their description of a problematic reaction point (PRP) as a significant event in therapy. The marker of a PRP is a statement by the client of finding his or her own behavior problematic (e.g., "I overreacted but I don't know why; it was unlike me"). The therapist's task at a PRP is systematic evocative unfolding (Rice, 1974). The therapist directs the client to reenter the scene of the original stimulus situation vividly and to explore his or her own understanding of the situation at the time of the problematic reaction. The therapist tries to get the client to focus on either the stimulus or the inner reaction, but not on both at the same time. According to Rice and Saperia, a marker of a PRP followed by therapist use of systematic evocative unfolding led to a resolution more frequently than if the therapist responded with empathic caring.

Illustrative Study 18

Joyce, Duncan, and Piper (1995) conducted a task analysis of patient responses to dynamic interpretation in short-term individual psychotherapy. They developed a model distinguishing "working" (i.e., successful interpretation) from "nonworking" (i.e., unsuccessful interpretation episode) client responses. This study illustrated the early stages of task analysis in which the goal is development of a descriptive model, prior to the construction of a reliable measure of the event type.

Three process measures were used to identify working episodes. The Therapist Intervention Rating System (Piper et al., 1987) was used to ensure that the interpretation addressed only a single dynamic component, that is, a wish, a fear, a defensive process, or an expression linking affects, thoughts, and behavior. The second measure was a rating of the client's response as either a working or nonworking episode. Three criteria were required to qualify a response as working: Client maintains focus on (a) self and (b) the meaning of the interpretation and (c) adds something to the interpretation. If these criteria were not all met, the client's response was rated as nonworking. Raters' agreement on the work-nonwork dimension averaged 70% (kappa = .38). The third measure was the Experiencing Scale (Klein et al., 1986). A 1 standard deviation change in experiencing was required for an episode to be counted as working.

The measures were applied to 10 working episodes in the first stage of the research, 10 working episodes in the second stage, and 10 nonworking episodes in the third stage. Raters were given a transcript of the event, including five minutes before and after each interpretation. By cycling between the data and the evolving model, the researchers developed a model to differentiate between working and nonworking responses to therapist interpretation. Briefly, the model suggested that the client's state of readiness, as signaled by an "invitation to interpret," was more important in determining impact than the accuracy of the interpretation. That is, responsiveness to the client's state of readiness appeared crucial.

Referential Activity and FRAMES

Two related lines of psychoanalytically oriented process research aimed at describing change processes concern referential activity (Bucci, 1997) and Fundamental Repetitive and Maladaptive Emotion Structures, or FRAMES (Dahl, 1988; Hölzer & Dahl, 1996). According to Bucci's multiple code model, people have nonverbal emotional structures that determine how they feel and act. Referential activity refers to the degree of connection and verbalization of these emotional structures. High referential activity is characterized by concreteness, specificity, and clarity of expression. It marks effective analytic work and greater emotional expressiveness. FRAMES refer to repetitive, invariant, and therefore neurotic structures within the client, which are represented in the narratives told by the client under instructions to free-associate. An assumption underlying these approaches is that not all process is the same, and the measures of referential activity or FRAMES allow one to identify and describe significant processes within sessions.

Illustrative Study 19

Bucci (1988) coded the level of referential activity in 10 previously classified "work" hours of psychoanalytic therapy and 10 previously classified "resistance" hours of therapy. Her approach sought to distinguish between the detection of structures (which is the goal of process research) and the construction of structures (judges imposing their own frames of reference, which is a potential risk in measuring unconscious processes). To make this distinction, she used a multistage, multijudge methodology for measuring nonverbal emotional structures. The decomposition of the task into separate stages was intended to prevent judges from using their clinical intuition to construct a structure rather than detect one. One set of judges segmented the transcripts into specified units. The idea units were then randomized, taken out of context, and presented to a second set of judges, who translated these sentences into themes. A third set of judges looked for repetitions in the themes and developed a more generalized description of a nonverbal emotional structure. Reliability was assessed at each stage and was determined to be satisfactory. Results indicated that, as expected, the level of referential activity was higher in work hours than in resistance hours.

Illustrative Study 20

The goal of FRAMES analysis is to represent the emotional logic of a client's story and thereby explicate key emotional structures implicated in the client's neuroses. Hölzer and Dahl (1996) described a five-step methodology for finding FRAMES: (a) select session, (b) classify emotions, (c) select segments, (d) analyze sequence, and (e) construct FRAMES and look for repetitions in other text. The first step includes selection of the data to which the measure will be applied. Different strategies were suggested depending on the goal of the investigation. For example, they recommend random sampling of therapy transcripts if the goal is to characterize a particular population. The second step involves classifying the emotions in the selected sessions. Emotions are classified using three orthogonal dimensions: orientation ("it" or "me"), valence (attraction or repulsion in relation to "it" and positive or negative in relation to "me"), and activity (active or passive). The third step entails selection of significant segments, and the construction of an object map that details the significant others talked about in the selected sessions and highlights passages in which FRAMES are found. In the fourth step, researchers determine the narrative structure of the client's identified segments. Raters characterize the client's wishes and beliefs, actions carried out in service of the wishes, and information concerning the fulfillment or nonfulfillment of the wishes. In the fifth step, the same researchers construct prototypes of FRAMES and look for instantiations. An example of an instantiation of critical-friendly FRAMES included a series of acts in which the client thought of friendship, felt inferior, and became critical as a way of overcoming her inferiority. This allowed her to fulfill her wish to be friendly.

Commentary

Inferential process measures demand a rigorous methodology. In studying unconscious processes, the authors of illustrative studies 19 and 20 went to great lengths to ensure that the proposed unconscious structures were detected in the clients and not constructed by the researchers. Illustrative study 19 (Bucci, 1988) used different judges at different stages of the research to prevent contamination. The five-step methodology developed to detect FRAMES in illustrative study 20, with the constraints on classification of themes (orientation, valence, activity), also aimed to ensure that clinical inferences were grounded in the material itself.

Assimilation Analysis

Assimilation analysis is an intensive qualitative approach to understanding the process of outcome in single cases. According to the assimilation model, therapeutic progress consists of the assimilation of problematic experiences into the client's schemata (Stiles et al., 1990). In successful therapy, assimilation of a problematic experience is proposed to proceed through part or all of a sequence of eight stages: warded off; unwanted thoughts; vague awareness/emergence; problem statement/clarification; understanding/insight; working through/application; problem solution; and mastery.

Illustrative Study 21

Honos-Webb, Stiles, Greenberg, and Goldman (1998) conducted an assimilation analysis on two cases of process-experiential psychotherapy for depression: one successful case and one unsuccessful case, according to conventional criteria (change on standard symptom intensity measures). Verbatim transcripts of all of each client's sessions ($N = 15$ and 19, respectively) were read and reread by the primary investigator, whose analysis was subject to audit (review and revision) by the coinvestigators. The four steps of assimilation analysis included (a) cataloguing the transcripts (listing all topics mentioned), (b) identifying and describing insights or common themes, (c) excerpting passages that concerned the targeted themes, and (d) applying the Assimilation of Problematic Experiences Scale (APES; Stiles et al., 1991) to the selected passages. Differences in interpretations were discussed among investigators and resolved by consensus or by compromises acceptable to all. This process of consensus replaced measures of reliability. Results suggested that the unsuccessful case made some progress in assimilation but terminated when central problems were at stages characterized by negative affect (unwanted thoughts, vague awareness). In contrast, the successful client showed progress to a stage of assimilation characterized by positive affect and a resolution of central conflicts (understanding/insight).

Discourse Analysis

Discourse analysis (Labov & Fanshel, 1977; Potter & Wetherell, 1987) is an intensive qualitative approach in which the process of change is understood as related to negotiation of sociocultural meanings. The psychotherapeutic process is thus set in a larger sociohistorical context. Like many other qualitative approaches, discourse analysis entails an intensive engagement with transcripts of psychotherapy and a multidimensional, detailed analysis of the text (Stiles, 1993). The intended yield of discourse analysis is a richly descriptive understanding of particular processes rather than a generalizable finding based on a large sample of different cases.

Illustrative Study 22

Discourse analysis was applied to a successful case of brief psychodynamic-interpersonal psychotherapy by Madill and Barkham (1997). Raters identified passages related to the theme selected for analysis: the client's efforts to care for herself. The discourse analysis itself was carried out by the first author and was subject to audit by the case therapist, a weekly research group, and other discursive psychologists. Such intensive auditing procedures substituted for measures of interrater reliability.

Once passages were selected, the analyst read the text intensively, in an effort to go beyond the information conveyed to determine how the information was constructed. She looked for inconsistencies in the client's account as a starting point for unraveling the rationale for the construction of a particular account. Finally, she interpreted the function that the particular construction served. Validity was assessed by coherence, participant's orientation, new problems, and fruitfulness. Madill and Barkham (1997) showed how the key change moment in one woman's therapy was related to cultural norms rather than intrapsychic processes. The client changed because the therapist affirmed her efforts to fulfill her own needs first, which contradicted cultural roles of women as dutiful caretakers.

Although the conclusions are necessarily tentative because they were based on a single case, Madill and Barkham's (1997) discourse analysis points to the relevance of even the broadest sociocultural context. The cultural norms dictating the roles of women seemed relevant to a full understanding of the client's struggles to honor her own needs above those of her aging mother. Thus, the change process imperative to contextualize psychotherapeutic process may extend beyond the confines of the case itself into the wider social context in which the case is set.

Commentary

The illustrative studies in this section (18–22) involved detailed, intensive examination of therapeutic discourse. In studying what happens as clients improve, investigators sought a systematic, deep, and broad exposure to the participants' in-session behavior (mainly verbal behavior). They seemed to assume that an understanding of the treatment process would not yield to quick, simple measures or manipulations. To a large extent, they followed a pragmatic strategy (Berelson, 1952; Marsden, 1971), allowing investigators to bring to bear clinical skills and judgment as well as knowledge of the classification system.

Several of these studies used qualitative methods. They did not reject precise quantitative measurement—most used explicit measures and numbers in some way—rather, they adopted a different relation to theory. The goal of a qualitative, descriptive study is often to elaborate a theory rather than to test a particular consequence. For example, the goal of task analysis is often explained as the development of a model of psychotherapeutic change. This gives qualitative studies a greater openness to new information, but their conclusions are correspondingly more tentative than those of hypothesis-testing research (Stiles, 1993).

CONCLUSION

We have tried to convey what psychotherapy process researchers have done, how they have done it, and why they have done it, using examples of process studies. Our focus has been on method, and we have not attempted to summarize the substantive achievements of treatment process research; this has been done by others (e.g., Hill & Corbett, 1993; Orlinsky et al., 1994; Orlinsky & Howard, 1986; Stiles & Shapiro, 1989). Like all research, process research requires continuing invention; each study addresses a new question and requires creativity in the development of new methods. We suggest that new researchers can hone their creativity by understanding the what, how, and why of previous research.

The process of therapy is the process of outcome; it is not separate from outcome. Rather than considering treatment as a black box with inputs and outputs, treatment process research looks inside the box. Because people are responsive to each other and to events that emerge during treatment, a treatment's outputs are not easily predictable from its inputs. An understanding of treatment effectiveness, we suggest, requires an understanding of the process.

REFERENCES

Ablon, J. S., & Jones, E. E. (1998). How expert clinicians' prototypes of an ideal treatment correlate with outcome in psychodynamic and cognitive-behavioral therapy. *Psychotherapy Research, 8,* 71–83.

Abramson, L. Y., Seligman, M. E. P., & Teasdale, J. D. (1978). Learned helplessness in humans: Critique and reformulation. *Journal of Abnormal Psychology, 84,* 49–74.

Agnew-Davies, R., Stiles, W. B., Hardy, G. E., Barkham, M., & Shapiro, D. A. (1998). Alliance structure assessed by the Agnew relationship measure (ARM). *British Journal of Clinical Psychology, 37,* 155–172.

Alexander, L. B., & Luborsky, L. (1987). The Penn helping alliance scales. In L. S. Greenberg & W. M. Pinsof (Eds.), *The psychotherapeutic process: A research handbook* (pp. 325–366). New York: Guilford Press.

Barber, J. P., Luborsky, L., Crits-Christoph, P., & Diguer, L. (1995). A comparison of core conflictual relationship themes before psychotherapy and during early sessions. *Journal of Consulting and Clinical Psychology, 63,* 145–148.

Barrett-Lennard, G. T. (1985). The helping relationship: Crisis and advance in theory and research. *Counseling Psychologist, 13,* 278–294.

Barrett-Lennard, G. T. (1986). The relationship inventory now: Issues and advances in theory, method and use. In L. S. Greenberg & W. M. Pinsof (Eds.), *The psychotherapeutic process: A research handbook* (pp. 439–476). New York: Guilford Press.

Battle, C., Imber, S., Hoehn-Saric, R., Stone, A., Nash, E., & Frank, J. (1966). Target complaints: A criterion of improvement. *American Journal of Psychotherapy, 20,* 184–192.

Beck, A. P., & Lewis, C. M. (Eds.). (in press). *Process in therapeutic groups: A handbook of systems of analysis.* Washington, DC: APA Books.

Beck, A. T. (1967). *Depression: Causes and treatment.* Philadelphia, PA: University of Philadelphia Press.

Beck, A. T., Rush, A. J., Shaw, B. F., & Emery, G. (1979). *Cognitive therapy for depression.* New York: Wiley.

Beck, A. T., Weissman, A., Lester, D., & Trexler, L. (1974). The measurement of pessimism: The hopelessness scale. *Journal of Consulting and Clinical Psychology, 42,* 861–865.

Beck, J. T., & Strong, S. R. (1982). Stimulating therapeutic change with interpretations: A comparison of positive and negative connotation. *Journal of Counseling Psychology, 29,* 551–559.

Benjamin, L. S. (1974). Structural analysis of social behavior. *Psychological Review, 81,* 392–425.

Benjamin, L. S. (1982). Use of structural analysis of social behavior (SASB) to guide intervention in psychotherapy. In J. C. Anchin & D. J. Kiesler (Eds.), *Handbook of interpersonal psychotherapy* (pp. 190–212). New York: Pergamon Press.

Benjamin, L. S. (1996). *Interpersonal diagnosis and treatment of personality disorders* (2nd ed.). New York: Guilford Press.

Benjamin, L. S., Giat, L., & Estroff, S. (1981). *Coding manual for structural analysis of social behavior (SASB).* Unpublished manuscript, University of Wisconsin, Department of Psychiatry, Madison.

Berelson, B. (1952). *Content analysis in communication research.* Glencoe, IL: Free Press.

Beutler, L. E. (1991). Have all won and must all have prizes? Revisiting Luborsky et al.'s verdict. *Journal of Consulting and Clinical Psychology, 59,* 226–232.

Beutler, L. E., Machado, P. P. P., & Neufeldt, S. A. (1994). Therapist variables. In A. E. Bergin & S. L. Garfield (Eds.), *Handbook of psychotherapy and behavior change* (4th ed., pp. 229–269). New York: Wiley.

Braswell, L., Kendall, P. C., Braith, J., Carey, M. P., & Vye, C. S. (1985). "Involvement" in cognitive-behavioral therapy with children: Process and its relationship to outcome. *Cognitive Therapy and Research, 9,* 611–630.

Brunink, S. A., & Schroeder, H. E. (1979). Verbal therapeutic behavior of expert psychoanalytically oriented, gestalt, and behavior therapists. *Journal of Consulting and Clinical Psychology, 47,* 567–574.

Bucci, W. (1988). Converging evidence for emotional structures: Theory and method. In H. Dahl, H. Kächele, & H. Thomä (Eds.), *Psychoanalytic process research strategies* (pp. 29–50). New York: Springer-Verlag.

Bucci, W. (1997). *Psychoanalysis and cognitive science: A multiple code theory.* New York: Guilford Press.

Carroll, L. (1946). *Alice's adventures in wonderland.* New York: Random House. (Original work published 1865)

Caston, J. (1986). The reliability of the diagnosis of the patient's unconscious plan. In J. Weiss, H. Sampson, & The Mount Zion Psychotherapy Research Group (Eds.), *The psychoanalytic process: Theory, clinical observation, and empirical research.* New York: Guilford Press.

Cohen, J. (1960). A coefficient of agreement for nominal scales. *Educational and Psychological Measurement, 20,* 37–46.

Cox, A., Holbrook, D., & Rutter, M. (1981). Psychiatric interviewing techniques: VI. Experimental study: Eliciting feelings. *British Journal of Psychiatry, 139,* 144–152.

Cox, A., Rutter, M., & Holbrook, D. (1981). Psychiatric interviewing techniques: V. Experimental study: Eliciting factual information. *British Journal of Psychiatry, 139,* 29–37.

Crits-Christoph, P. (1997). Limitations of the Dodo Bird verdict and the role of clinical trials in psychotherapy research: Comment on Wampold et al. (1997). *Psychological Bulletin, 122,* 216–220.

Czogalik, D., & Russell, R. L. (1995). Interactional structures of therapist and client participation in adult psychotherapy: P technique and chronography. *Journal of Consulting and Clinical Psychology, 63,* 28–36.

Dahl, H. (1988). Frames of mind. In H. Dahl, H. Kächele, & H. Thomä (Eds.), *Psychoanalytic research strategies* (pp. 51–66). New York: Springer-Verlag.

Dance, K. A., & Neufeld, W. J. (1988). Aptitude-treatment interaction research in the clinical setting: A review of attempts to dispel the "patient uniformity" myth. *Psychological Bulletin, 104,* 192–213.

Derogatis, L. R. (1983). *The SCL-90-R: Administration, scoring and procedures–manual II.* Towson, MD: Clinical Psychometric Research.

DeRubeis, R. J., Evans, M. D., Hollon, S. D., Garvey, M. J., Grove, W. M., & Tuason, V. B. (1990). How does cognitive therapy work? Cognitive change and symptom change in cognitive therapy and pharmacotherapy for depression. *Journal of Consulting and Clinical Psychology, 58,* 862–869.

DeRubeis, R. J., Hollon, S., Evans, M., & Bemis, K. (1982). Can psychotherapies for depression be discriminated? A systematic investigation of cognitive therapy and interpersonal therapy. *Journal of Consulting & Clinical Psychology, 50,* 744–756.

Dill-Standiford, T. J., Stiles, W. B., & Rorer, L. G. (1988). Counselor-client agreement on session impact. *Journal of Counseling Psychology, 35,* 47–55.

Elkin, I. (1994). The NIMH treatment of depression collaborative research program: Where we began and where we are. In A. E. Bergin & S. L. Garfield (Eds.), *Handbook of psychotherapy and behavior change* (4th ed., pp. 114–139). New York: Wiley.

Elkin, I., Shea, M. T., Watkins, J. T., Imber, S. D., Sotsky, S. M., Collins, J. F., Glass, D. R., Pilkonis, P. A., Leber, W. R., Docherty, J. P., Fiester, S. J., & Parloff, M. B. (1989). National institute of mental health treatment of depression collaborative research program: General effectiveness of treatments. *Archives of General Psychiatry, 46,* 971–982.

Elliott, R. (1986). Interpersonal process recall (IPR) as a psychotherapy process research method. In L. S. Greenberg & W. M. Pinsof (Eds.), *The psychotherapeutic process: A research handbook* (pp. 503–527). New York: Guilford Press.

Elliott, R. (1989). Comprehensive process analysis: Understanding the change process in significant therapy events. In M. J. Packer & R. B. Addison (Eds.), *Entering the circle: Hermeneutic investigation in psychology* (pp. 165–184). Albany: State University of New York Press.

Elliott, R. (1991). Five dimensions of psychotherapy process. *Psychotherapy Research, 1,* 92–103.

Elliott, R. (1993). *Comprehensive process analysis: Mapping the change process in psychotherapy.* Unpublished research manual. (Available from author, Department of Psychology, University of Toledo, Toledo, OH 43606).

Elliott, R., & Anderson, C. (1994). Simplicity and complexity in psychotherapy research. In R. L. Russell (Ed.), *Reassessing psychotherapy research* (pp. 65–113). New York: Guilford Press.

Elliott, R., Hill, C. E., Stiles, W. B., Friedlander, M. L., Mahrer, A. R., & Margison, F. R. (1987). Primary therapist response modes: Comparison of six rating systems. *Journal of Consulting and Clinical Psychology, 55,* 218–223.

Elliott, R., Shapiro, D. A., Firth-Cozens, J., Stiles, W. B., Hardy, G. E., Llewelyn, S. P., & Margison, F. R. (1994). Comprehensive process analysis of insight events in cognitive-behavioral and psychodynamic-interpersonal psychotherapies. *Journal of Counseling Psychology, 41,* 449–463.

Emmelkamp, P. M. G. (1994). Behavior therapy with adults. In A. E. Bergin & S. L. Garfield (Eds.), *Handbook of psychotherapy and behavior change* (4th ed., pp. 379–427). New York: Wiley.

Fawcett, J., Epstein, P., Fiester, S. J., Elkin, I., & Autry, J. H. (1987). Clinical management—imipramine—placebo adminstration manual: NIMH treatment of depression collaborative research program. *Psychopharmacology Bulletin, 23,* 309–324.

Fiedler, F. E. (1950a). A comparison of therapeutic relationships in psycho-analytic, nondirective, and Adlerian therapy. *Journal of Consulting Psychology, 14,* 436–445.

Fiedler, F. E. (1950b). The concept of an ideal therapeutic relationship. *Journal of Consulting Psychology, 14,* 239–245.

Fiedler, F. E. (1951). Factor analysis of psychoanalytic, non-directive, and Adlerian therapeutic relationships. *Journal of Consulting Psychology, 15,* 32–38.

Frank, J. D. (1973). *Persuasion and healing: A comparative study of psychotherapy* (Rev. ed.). Baltimore: Johns Hopkins University Press.

Gaston, L. (1991). Reliability and criterion-related validity of the California psychotherapy alliance scales-patient version. *Psychological Assessment, 3,* 68–74.

Gaston, L., & Ring, J. M. (1992). Preliminary results on the inventory of therapeutic strategies. *Journal of Psychotherapy Research and Practice, 1,* 1–13.

Gendlin, E. T. (1964). A theory of personality change. In Y. T. Hart & T. M. Tomlinson (Eds.), *New directions in client-centered psychotherapy* (pp. 129–173). Boston: Houghton Mifflin.

Gendlin, E. T. (1981). *Focusing.* New York: Bantam Books.

Goldfried, M. R. (1980). Toward the delineation of therapeutic change principles. *American Psychologist, 35,* 991–999.

Goodwin, C. (1981). *Conversational organization: Interaction between speakers and hearers.* New York: Academic Press.

Greenberg, L. S. (1986). Change process research. *Journal of Consulting and Clinical Psychology, 54,* 4–9.

Greenberg, L. S., Elliott, R., & Lietaer, G. (1994). Research on experiential psychotherapies. In A. E. Bergin & S. L. Garfield (Eds.), *Handbook of psychotherapy and behavior change* (4th ed., pp. 509–539). New York: Wiley.

Greenberg, L. S., & Pinsof, W. M. (1986a). Preface. In L. S. Greenberg & W. M. Pinsof (Eds.), *The psychotherapeutic process: A research handbook* (pp. xiii–xvii). New York: Guilford Press.

Greenberg, L. S., & Pinsof, W. M. (Eds.). (1986b). *The psychotherapeutic process: A research handbook.* New York: Guilford Press.

Greenberg, L. S., & Watson, J. (1998). Experiential therapy of depression: Differential effects of client centered relationship conditions and process experiential interventions. *Psychotherapy Research, 8,* 210–224.

Grencavage, L. M., & Norcross, J. C. (1990). Where are the commonalities among the therapeutic common factors? *Professional Psychology: Research and Practice, 21,* 372–378.

Hartley, D. E., & Strupp, H. H. (1983). The therapeutic alliance: Its relationship to outcome in brief psychotherapy. In J. Masling (Ed.), *Empirical studies in analytic theories* (pp. 1–37). Hillside, NJ: Erlbaum.

Henry, W. P. (1996). Structural analysis of social behavior as a common metric for programmatic psychopathology and psychotherapy research. *Journal of Consulting and Clinical Psychology, 64,* 1263–1275.

Henry, W. P., Schacht, T. E., & Strupp, H. H. (1986). Structural analysis of social behavior: Application to a study of interpersonal process in differential psychotherapeutic outcome. *Journal of Consulting and Clinical Psychology, 54,* 27–31.

Henry, W. P., Strupp, H. H., Schacht, T. E., & Gaston, L. (1994). Psychodynamic approaches. In A. E. Bergin & S. L. Garfield (Eds.), *Handbook of psychotherapy and behavior change* (4th ed., pp. 467–508). New York: Wiley.

Herink, R. (Ed.). (1980). *The psychotherapy handbook: The A to Z guide to more than 250 different therapies in use today.* New York: New American Library.

Hill, C. E. (1986). An overview of the Hill counselor and client verbal response modes category systems. In L. S. Greenberg & W. M. Pinsof (Eds.), *The psychotherapeutic process: A research handbook* (pp. 131–160). New York: Guilford Press.

Hill, C. E., & Corbett, M. M. (1993). A perspective on the history of process and outcome research in counseling psychology. *Journal of Counseling Psychology, 40,* 3–24.

Hill, C. E., O'Grady, K. E., & Elkin, I. (1992). Applying the collaborative study psychotherapy rating scale to rate therapist adherence in cognitive-behavioral therapy, interpersonal therapy, and clinical management. *Journal of Consulting and Clinical Psychology, 60,* 73–79.

Hill, C. E., Thames, T. B., & Rardin, D. K. (1979). Comparison of Rogers, Perls, and Ellis on the Hill counselor verbal response category system. *Journal of Counseling Psychology, 26,* 198–203.

Hoffart, A. (1997). A schema model for examining the integrity of psychotherapy: A theoretical contribution. *Psychotherapy Research, 7,* 127–143.

Hollon, S. D., Evans, M. D., Auerbach, A., DeRubeis, R. J., Elkin, I., Lowery, A., Kriss, M., Grove, W., Tuason, V. B., & Piasecki, J. (1988). *Development of a system for rating therapies for depression: Differentiating cognitive therapy, interpersonal therapy, and clinical management.* Unpublished manuscript, University of Minnesota, Minneapolis.

Hollon, S. D., & Kendall, P. C. (1980). Cognitive self-statements in depression: Development of an automatic thoughts questionnaire. *Cognitive Therapy and Research, 4,* 383–396.

Holmbeck, G. N. (1997). Toward terminological, conceptual, and statistical clarity in the study of mediators and moderators: Examples from the child-clinical and pediatric psychology literatures. *Journal of Consulting and Clinical Psychology, 65,* 599–610.

Hölzer, M., & Dahl, H. (1996). How to find frames. *Psychotherapy Research, 6,* 177–197.

Hölzer, M., Mergenthaler, E., Pokorny, D., Kächele, H., & Luborsky, L. (1996). Vocabulary measures for the evaluation of therapy outcome: Re-studying transcripts from the Penn psychotherapy project. *Psychotherapy Research, 6,* 95–108.

Honos-Webb, L., Stiles, W. B., Greenberg, L. S., & Goldman, R. (1998). Assimilation analysis of process-experiential psychotherapy: A comparison of two cases. *Psychotherapy Research, 8,* 264–286.

Horvath, A. O., & Greenberg, L. S. (1989). Development and validation of the working alliance inventory. *Journal of Counseling Psychology, 36,* 223–233.

Horvath, A. O., & Luborsky, L. (1993). The role of the therapeutic alliance in psychotherapy. *Journal of Consulting and Clinical Psychology, 61,* 561–573.

Horvath A. O., & Symonds, B. D. (1991). Relation between working alliance and outcome in psychotherapy: A meta-analysis. *Journal of Counseling Psychology, 38,* 139–149.

Howard, K. I., Krause, M. S., Saunders, S. M., & Kopta, S. M. (1997). Trials and tribulations in the meta-analysis of treatment differences: Comment on Wampold et al. (1997). *Psychological Bulletin, 122,* 221–225.

Jones, E. E., & Pulos, S. M. (1993). Comparing the process in psychodynamic and cognitive-behavioral therapies. *Journal of Consulting and Clinical Psychology, 61,* 306–313.

Joyce, A. S., Duncan, S. C., & Piper, W. E. (1995). Task analysis of "working through" responses to dynamic interpretation in short-term individual psychotherapy. *Psychotherapy Research, 5,* 49–62.

Kagan, N. (1975). *Interpersonal process recall: A method of influencing human interaction.* Unpublished manuscript, College of Education, Michigan State University, East Lansing.

Kazdin, A. E. (1986). Comparative outcome studies of psychotherapy: Methodological issues and strategies. *Journal of Consulting and Clinical Psychology, 54,* 95–105.

Kendall, P. C., & Chambless, D. L. (Eds.). (1998). Special section: Empirically supported psychological therapies. *Journal of Consulting and Clinical Psychology, 66,* 3–167.

Kendall, P. C., & Hollon, S. D. (1983). Calibrating the quality of therapy: Collaborative archiving of tape samples from therapy outcome trials. *Cognitive Therapy and Research, 7,* 199–204.

Kiesler, D. J. (1966). Some myths of psychotherapy research and the search for a paradigm. *Psychological Bulletin, 65,* 110–136.

Kiesler, D. J. (1971). Patient experiencing and successful outcome in individual psychotherapy of schizophrenics and psychoneurotics. *Journal of Consulting and Clinical Psychology, 39,* 370–385.

Kiesler, D. J. (1973). *The process of psychotherapy: Empirical foundations and systems of analysis.* Chicago: Aldine.

Kiesler, D. J. (1982). Interpersonal theory for personality and psychotherapy. In J. C. Anchin & D. J. Kiesler (Eds.), *Handbook of interpersonal psychotherapy* (pp. 3–24). New York: Pergamon Press.

Kiesler, D. J. (1996). *Contemporary interpersonal theory and research: Personality, psychopathology, and psychotherapy.* New York: Wiley.

Klein, M. H., Mathieu, P. L., Gendlin, E. T., & Kiesler, D. J. (1970). *The experiencing scale: A research and training manual.* Madison: Wisconsin Psychiatric Institute.

Klein, M. H., Mathieu-Coughlan, P., & Kiesler, D. J. (1986). The experiencing scales. In L. S. Greenberg & W. M. Pinsof (Eds.), *The psychotherapeutic process: A research handbook* (pp. 21–71). New York: Guilford Press.

Klerman, G. L., Weissman, M. M., Rounsaville, B. J., & Chevron, E. S. (1984). *Interpersonal psychotherapy of depression.* New York: Basic Books.

Labov, W., & Fanshel, D. (1977). *Therapeutic discourse: Psychotherapy as conversation.* New York: Academic Press.

Lambert, M. J., & Bergin, A. E. (1994). The effectiveness of psychotherapy. In A. E. Bergin & S. L. Garfield (Eds.), *Handbook of psychotherapy and behavior change* (4th ed., pp. 143–189). New York: Wiley.

Lambert, M. J., DeJulio, S. S., & Stein, D. M. (1978). Therapist interpersonal skills: Process, outcome, methodological considerations, and recommendations for future research. *Psychological Bulletin, 85,* 467–489.

Lambert, M. J., & Hill, C. E. (1994). Methodological issues in studying psychotherapy process and outcome. In A. E. Bergin & S. L. Garfield (Eds.), *Handbook of psychotherapy and behavior change* (4th ed., pp. 72–113). New York: Wiley.

Leary, T. (1957). *Interpersonal diagnosis of personality: A functional theory and methodology for personality evaluation.* New York: Ronald Press.

Lipsey, M. W., & Wilson, D. B. (1993). The efficacy of psychological, educational, and behavioral treatment: Confirmation from meta-analysis. *American Psychologist, 48,* 1181–1209.

London, P. (1964). *The modes and morals of psychotherapy.* New York: Holt, Rinehart, & Winston.

Luborsky, L. (1976). Helping alliances in psychotherapy. In J. L. Cleghhorn (Ed.), *Successful psychotherapy* (pp. 92–116). New York: Brunner/Mazel.

Luborsky, L. (1995). The first trial of the p-technique in psychotherapy research—a still-lively legacy. *Journal of Consulting and Clinical Psychology, 63,* 6–14.

Luborsky, L., Barber, J. P., & Crits-Christoph, P. (1990). Theory-based research for understanding the process of dynamic psychotherapy. *Journal of Consulting and Clinical Psychology, 58,* 281–287.

Luborsky, L., Crits-Christoph, P., Mintz, J., & Auerbach, A. (1988). *Who will benefit from psychotherapy? Predicting therapeutic outcomes.* New York: Basic Books.

Luborsky, L., Singer, B., & Luborsky, L. (1975). Comparative studies of psychotherapies: Is it true that "Everyone has won and all must have prizes"? *Archives of General Psychiatry, 32,* 995–1008.

Luborsky, L., Woody, G. E., McLellan, A. T., O'Brien, C. P., & Rosenzweig, J. (1982). Can independent judges recognize different psychotherapies? An experience with manual-guided therapies. *Journal of Consulting and Clinical Psychology, 49*, 49–62.

Madill, A., & Barkham, M. (1997). Discourse analysis of a theme in one successful case of brief psychodynamic-interpersonal psychotherapy. *Journal of Counseling Psychology, 44*, 232–244.

Mallinckrodt, B. (1993). Session impact, working alliance, and treatment outcome in brief counseling. *Journal of Counseling Psychology, 40*, 25 32.

Marmar, C., Weiss, D. S., & Gaston, L. (1989). Toward the validation of the California therapeutic alliance rating system. *Psychological Assessment, 1*, 46–52.

Marsden, G. (1971). Content analysis studies of therapeutic interviews: 1954 to 1968. In A. E. Bergin & S. L. Garfield (Eds.), *Handbook of psychotherapy and behavior change* (pp. 345–407). New York: Wiley.

Martindale, C. (1975). *Romantic progression. The psychology of literary history.* Washington, DC: Hemisphere.

Marziali, E. (1984). Prediction of outcome of brief psychotherapy from therapist interpretive interventions. *Archives of General Psychiatry, 41*, 301–305.

McCullough, L., Winston, A., Farber, B. A., Porter, F., Pollack, J., Laikin, M., Vingiano, W., & Trujillo, M. (1991). The relationship of patient-therapist interaction to outcome in brief psychotherapy. *Psychotherapy, 28*, 525–533.

Meehl, P. E. (1978). Theoretical risks and tabular asterisks: Sir Karl, Sir Ronald, and the slow progress of soft psychology. *Journal of Consulting and Clinical Psychology, 46*, 806–834.

Nezu, A. M., & Perri, M. G. (1989). Social problem-solving therapy for unipolar depression: An initial dismantling investigation. *Journal of Consulting and Clinical Psychology, 57*, 408–413.

Norcross, J. C. (1995). Dispelling the dodo bird verdict and the exclusivity myth in psychotherapy. *Psychotherapy, 32*, 500–504.

Norcross, J. C., & Beutler, L. E. (1997). Determining the therapeutic relationship of choice in brief therapy. In J. N. Butcher (Ed.), *Personality assessment in managed health care: Using the MMPI-2 in treatment planning.* New York: Oxford University Press.

Orlinsky, D. E., Grawe, K., & Parks, B. K. (1994). Process and outcome in psychotherapy—Noch einmal. In A. E. Bergin & S. L. Garfield (Eds.), *Handbook of psychotherapy and behavior change* (4th ed., pp. 270–376). New York: Wiley.

Orlinsky, D. E., & Howard, K. I. (1986). The psychological interior of psychotherapy: Explorations with the therapy session reports. In L. S. Greenberg & W. M. Pinsof (Eds.), *The psychotherapeutic process: A research handbook* (pp. 477–501). New York: Guilford Press.

Peterson, C., & Seligman, M. E. P. (1984). Causal explanations as a risk factor for depression: Theory and evidence. *Psychological Review, 91*, 347–374.

Piper, W. E., Azim, H. F. A., Joyce, A. S., & McCallum, M. (1991). Transference interpretations, therapeutic alliance, and outcome in short-term individual psychotherapy. *Archives of General Psychiatry, 48*, 946–953.

Piper, W. E., Debbane, E. G., de Carufel, F. L., & Bienvenu, J. P. (1987). A system for differentiating therapist interpretations and other interventions. *Bulletin of the Menninger Clinic, 51*, 532–550.

Potter, J., & Wetherell, M. (1987). *Discourse and social psychology: Beyond attitudes and behaviour.* London: Sage.

Rice, L. N. (1974). The evocative function of the therapist. In D. A. Wexler & L. N. Rice (Eds.), *Innovations in client-centered therapy* (pp. 289–311). New York: Wiley.

Rice, L. N., & Greenberg, L. S. (1984). *Patterns of change.* New York: Guilford Press.

Rice, L. N., & Saperia, E. P. (1984). Task analysis and the resolution of problematic reactions. In L. N. Rice & L. S. Greenberg (Eds.), *Patterns of change* (pp. 29–66). New York: Guilford Press.

Rogers, C. R. (1957). The necessary and sufficient conditions of therapeutic personality change. *Journal of Consulting Psychology, 21,* 95–103.

Rosenthal, R., & Rosnow, R. L. (1984). *Essentials of behavioral research: Methods and data analysis.* New York: McGraw-Hill.

Rosenzweig, S. (1936). Some implicit common factors in diverse methods of psychotherapy. *American Journal of Orthopsychiatry, 6,* 412–415.

Russell, R. L. (1988). A new classification scheme for studies of verbal behavior in psychotherapy. *Psychotherapy, 25,* 51–58.

Russell, R. L. (1995). Introduction to the special section on multivariate psychotherapy process research: Structure and change in the talking cure. *Journal of Consulting and Clinical Psychology, 63,* 3–5.

Russell, R. L., & Staszewski, C. (1988). The unit problem: Some systematic distinctions and critical dilemmas for psychotherapy process research. *Psychotherapy, 25,* 191–200.

Russell, R. L., & Stiles, W. B. (1979). Categories for classifying language in psychotherapy. *Psychological Bulletin, 86,* 404–419.

Russell, R. L., & Trull, T. J. (1986). Sequential analysis of language variables in psychotherapy process research. *Journal of Consulting and Clinical Psychology, 54,* 16–21.

Seligman, M. E. P. (1995). The effectiveness of psychotherapy: The *Consumer Reports* study. *American Psychologist, 50,* 965–974.

Seligman, M. E. P., Abramson, L. Y., Semmel, A., & von Baeyer, C. (1979). Depressive attributional style. *Journal of Abnormal Psychology, 88,* 242–247.

Shapiro, D. A., Barkham, M., Rees, A., Hardy, G. E., Reynolds, S., & Startup, M. (1994). Effects of treatment duration and severity of depression on the effectiveness of cognitive/behavioral and psychodynamic/interpersonal psychotherapy. *Journal of Consulting and Clinical Psychology, 62,* 522–534.

Shapiro, D. A., & Firth, J. (1987). Prescriptive vs. exploratory psychotherapy: Outcomes of the Sheffield psychotherapy project. *British Journal of Psychiatry, 151,* 790–799.

Shoham-Salomon, V. (1991). Introduction to special section on client-therapy interaction research. *Journal of Consulting and Clinical Psychology, 59,* 203–204.

Shoham-Salomon, V., Avner, R., & Neeman, R. (1989). You're changed if you do and changed if you don't: Mechanisms underlying paradoxical interventions. *Journal of Consulting and Clinical Psychology, 57,* 590–598.

Shrout, P. E., & Fleiss, J. L. (1979). Intraclass correlations: Uses in assessing rater reliability. *Psychological Bulletin, 86,* 420–428.

Silberschatz, G., Fretter, P. B., & Curtis, J. T. (1986). How do interpretations influence the process of psychotherapy? *Journal of Consulting and Clinical Psychology, 54,* 646–652.

Smith, B., & Sechrest, L. (1991). Treatment of aptitude x treatment interactions. *Journal of Consulting and Clinical Psychology, 59,* 233–244.

Smith, M. L., Glass, G. V., & Miller, T. I. (1980). *The benefits of psychotherapy.* Baltimore: Johns Hopkins University Press.

Snow, R. E. (1991). Aptitude-treatment interaction as a framework for research on individual differences in psychotherapy. *Journal of Consulting and Clinical Psychology, 59,* 205–216.

Startup, M. J., & Shapiro, D. A. (1993). Therapist treatment fidelity in prescriptive vs. exploratory psychotherapy. *British Journal of Clinical Psychology, 32,* 443–456.

Stiles, W. B. (1979). Verbal response modes and psychotherapeutic technique. *Psychiatry, 42,* 49–62.

Stiles, W. B. (1980). Measurement of the impact of psychotherapy sessions. *Journal of Consulting and Clinical Psychology, 48,* 176–185.

Stiles, W. B. (1986). Development of taxonomy of verbal response modes. In L. S. Greenberg & W. M. Pinsof (Eds.), *The psychotherapeutic process: A research handbook* (pp. 161–199). New York: Guilford Press.

Stiles, W. B. (1987). "I have to talk to somebody." A fever model of disclosure. In V. J. Derlega & J. H. Berg (Eds.), *Self-disclosure: Theory, research, and therapy* (pp. 257–282). New York: Plenum Press.

Stiles, W. B. (1988). Psychotherapy process-outcome correlations may be misleading. *Psychotherapy, 25,* 27–35.

Stiles, W. B. (1992). *Describing talk: A taxonomy of verbal response modes.* Newbury Park, CA: Sage.

Stiles, W. B. (1993). Quality control in qualitative research. *Clinical Psychology Review, 13,* 593–618.

Stiles, W. B. (1994). Drugs, recipes, babies, bathwater, and psychotherapy process-outcome relations. *Journal of Consulting and Clinical Psychology, 62,* 955–959.

Stiles, W. B. (1995). Disclosure as a speech act: Is it psychotherapeutic to disclose? In J. W. Pennebaker (Ed.), *Emotion, disclosure, and health* (pp. 71–91). Washington, DC: American Psychological Association.

Stiles, W. B. (1996). When more of a good thing is better: Reply to Hayes et al. (1996). *Journal of Consulting and Clinical Psychology, 64,* 915–918.

Stiles, W. B., Elliott, R., Llewelyn, S. P., Firth-Cozens, J. A., Margison, F. R., Shapiro, D. A., & Hardy, G. (1990). Assimilation of problematic experiences by clients in psychotherapy. *Psychotherapy, 27,* 411–420.

Stiles, W. B., Honos-Webb, L., & Surko, M. (1998). Responsiveness in psychotherapy. *Clinical Psychology: Science and Practice, 5,* 439–458.

Stiles, W. B., McDaniel, S. H., & McGaughey, K. (1979). Verbal response mode correlates of experiencing. *Journal of Consulting and Clinical Psychology, 47,* 795–797.

Stiles, W. B., Morrison, L. A., Haw, S. K., Harper, H., Shapiro, D. A., & Firth-Cozens, J. (1991). Longitudinal study of assimilation in exploratory psychotherapy. *Psychotherapy, 28,* 195–206.

Stiles, W. B., & Shapiro, D. A. (1989). Abuse of the drug metaphor in psychotherapy process-outcome research. *Clinical Psychology Review, 9,* 521–543.

Stiles, W. B., & Shapiro, D. A. (1994). Disabuse of the drug metaphor: Psychotherapy process-outcome correlations. *Journal of Consulting and Clinical Psychology, 62,* 942–948.

Stiles, W. B., & Shapiro, D. A. (1995). Verbal exchange structure of brief psychodynamic-interpersonal and cognitive-behavioral psychotherapy. *Journal of Consulting and Clinical Psychology, 63,* 15–27.

Stiles, W. B., Shapiro, D. A., & Elliott, R. (1986). Are all psychotherapies equivalent? *American Psychologist, 41,* 165–180.

Stiles, W. B., Shapiro, D. A., & Firth-Cozens, J. A. (1988). Verbal response mode use in contrasting psychotherapies: A within-subjects comparison. *Journal of Consulting and Clinical Psychology, 56,* 727–733.

Stiles, W. B., & Snow, J. S. (1984a). Counseling session impact as viewed by novice counselors and their clients. *Journal of Counseling Psychology, 31,* 3–12.

Stiles, W. B., & Snow, J. S. (1984b). Dimensions of psychotherapy session impact across sessions and across clients. *British Journal of Clinical Psychology, 23,* 59–63.

Stinson, C. H., Milbrath, C., & Horowitz, M. J. (1995). Dysfluency and topic orientation in bereaved individuals: Bridging individual and group studies. *Journal of Consulting and Clinical Psychology, 63,* 37–45.

Strupp, H. H. (1955). An objective comparison of Rogerian and psychoanalytic techniques. *Journal of Consulting Psychology, 19,* 1–7.

Strupp, H. H. (1957). A multidimensional comparison of therapists in analytic and client-centered therapy. *Journal of Consulting Psychology, 21,* 301–308.

Strupp, H. H., & Hadley, S. W. (1979). Specific versus nonspecific factors in psychotherapy: A controlled study of outcome. *Archives of General Psychiatry, 36,* 1125–1136.

Sullivan, H. S. (1953). *The interpersonal theory of psychiatry.* New York: Norton.

Treadwell, K. R. H., & Kendall, P. C. (1996). Self-talk in youth with anxiety disorders: States of mind, content specificity, and treatment outcome. *Journal of Consulting and Clinical Psychology, 64,* 941–950.

Truax, C. B., & Carkhuff, R. R. (1965). Experimental manipulation of therapeutic conditions. *Journal of Consulting Psychology, 29*(2), 119–124.

Waltz, J., Addis, M. E., Koerner, K., & Jacobson, N. S. (1993). Testing the integrity of a psychotherapy protocol: Assessment of adherence and competence. *Journal of Consulting and Clinical Psychology, 61,* 620–630.

Wampold, B. E., Mondin, G. W., Moody, M., Stich, F., Benson, K., & Ahn, H. N. (1997). A meta-analysis of outcome studies comparing bona fide psychotherapies: Empirically, "all must have prizes." *Psychological Bulletin, 122,* 203–215.

Weiss, J., Sampson, H., & the Mount Zion Research Group. (Eds.). (1986). *The psychoanalytic process: Theory, clinical observation, and empirical research.* New York: Guilford Press.

Weissman, A., & Beck, A. T. (1978, November). *Development and validation of the dysfunctional attitudes scale: A preliminary investigation.* Presented at the annual meeting of the American Educational Research Association, Toronto, Ontario, Canada.

Weissman, J. J., & Bothwell, S. (1976). Assessment of social adjustment by patient self-report. *Archives of General Psychiatry, 33,* 1111–1115.

Yeaton, W. H., & Sechrest, L. (1981). Critical dimensions in the choice and maintenance of successful treatments: Strength, integrity, and effectiveness. *Journal of Consulting and Clinical Psychology, 49,* 156–167.

Chapter 16

Focus Chapter

RESEARCH METHODS IN COMMUNITY-BASED TREATMENT AND PREVENTION

PATRICK H. TOLAN, PH.D.

This chapter addresses issues of clinical methodology in prevention and community-based interventions. Community-based and prevention interventions are related but distinct variations of traditional clinical interventions. Both areas of investigation developed as attempts to address and overcome some of the limitations in external validity that have been noted for individually focused and clinic-based treatments (Tolan, Keys, Jason, & Chertok 1990; Weissberg & Greenberg, 1998). Both community-based and prevention interventions expanded the focus of efficacy research to include the setting and the relation of impact to normal development. These areas of investigation also share a common orientation to psychopathology and intervention that is derived from an epidemiological perspective based in public health (Afifi & Breslow, 1994). This mutual history and the extent to which primary prevention has a community-level focus have linked these areas within clinical research (Institute of Medicine, 1994).

However, community-based and prevention interventions are not synonymous. A community-based intervention may or may not be preventive, and prevention may or may not be community-based. Although there are methodological issues that overlap, there are also increasing areas of distinction for each field as the sophistication of research questions increases. For example, methodological issues are emerging in community-based services due to service delivery issues such as measuring the interaction of client and delivery system characteristics as determinants of intervention effect. Methodological issues occupying the most attention in prevention research, however, are derived from the strain on existing clinical trial methodologies when one attempts

Correspondences should be sent to Patrick H. Tolan Ph.D. Professor, Dept. Of Psychiatry, Institute for Juvenile Research, University of Illinois at Chicago, 907 S. Wolcott, Chicago, IL 60612. E-mail address is Tolan@uic.edu. Preparation of this chapter was supported in part by NIMH grants R1848034 and RO148248, NICHD grant HS35415, CDC grant R49/CCR512739, SAMHSA Grants 2-5-24675 and 2-5-24683, and NSF grant SPR-9601157. Also, the author has benefited from numerous discussions over the past eight years with Ray Lorion, David Henry, Rowell Huesmann, Hendricks Brown, Robert Gibbons, Deborah Gorman-Smith, and numerous others about this topic. In their patient attempts to help me understand these issues, they have aided the quality of the rendering provided here. However, they and the funding agencies listed above are not responsible for any views and statements presented here.

to estimate prevention effects (Brown, 1993b; Lorion, Price, & Eaton, 1989). Full explication of all of the methodological issues in each area requires more space than available here. Fortunately, there are several comprehensive guides that can be consulted in regard to prevention methodology (Brown, 1993b; Kraemer & Kraemer, 1994; West, Aiken, & Todd, 1993) and community-based interventions (Connell, Kubisch, Schorr, & Weiss, 1995; Seidman, 1983; Tolan & Brown, 1997). This chapter will efficiently summarize several major methodology issues affecting preventive interventions, including community-based interventions.[1] As will be evident, many of these issues are incumbent concerns for all community-based interventions and, in fact, are integral to good clinical trials (Tolan, 1996; Tolan, Kendall, & Beidel, 1997).

Prevention research is distinguished most basically from other clinical intervention studies by its focus on "before-the-fact" intervention to reduce the prevalence of the problem. This means that intervention is intended to alter patterns of prevalence and incidence by targeting theoretically and empirically suggested predictors (Coie et al., 1993; Kellam, 1990; Kraemer & Kraemer, 1994). These targets can be developmental precursors (e.g., early oppositional behavior predicting conduct disorder) or correlates implicated in developmental processes leading to the undesirable outcome (e.g., parental management of normal oppositional behavior of a toddler). These statistical predictors and their variation in prevalence for defined populations also indicate who should be included, which differs from the treatment research interest defining the population by presence of a specified set of symptoms. It should be noted that by definition, risk factors do not perfectly predict outcome; all prevention trials will include some participants who would not realize the undesirable outcome, even without intervention. Variation in impact among the intervened within a group is expectable. Outcome is measured as the resultant *lack* or *lower rate* of the problem than would occur without the prevention effort (Brown, 1993b; Lorion, Price, & Eaton, 1989). In prevention, the interest is not in change for each individual per se but in change in rates of the studied population(s) (Brown & Liao, in press; Kraemer & Kraemer, 1994; Lorion, et al., 1989; Tolan, in press). These are fundamentally different emphases from that of traditional clinical trials, in which the target is to reduce or eliminate something that is already present and where the usual measure is average reduction across the sample.

These basic features suggest four methodological issues that should be of concern to every prevention researcher and inform research design: (a) assumptions about sampling; (b) the centrality of developmental and ecological thinking in defining and measuring prevention effects; (c) issues of measurement of outcomes; and (d) the

---

[1] Community-based intervention is most basically distinguished by its specification of location of services (Connell et al., 1995; Koepsell et al., 1992). In some cases, the primary methodologic differences from other treatment studies is in the interest in service delivery issues (e.g., access to services in community vs. same services in a clinic). In other instances, when the interest is in community-focused intervention, the methodological concerns are driven much more by practical limitations in making such comparisons (e.g., difficulty in testing an intervention in a large enough number of communities needed to permit random assignment assumptions to hold, the problem in controlling community-level intervention processes enough to approximate normal standards of fidelity for clinical intervention trials, and the problem of assuming comparability/homogeneity of communities used in comparisons). This chapter will not focus on these topics apart from prevention methodology. Readers are referred to other volumes for fuller discussion of these and other design and measurement questions arising in regard to community-based intervention (see Connell et al., 1995; Tolan & Brown, 1997).

importance and expansion of the focus of assessing processes and components of intervention effects.

ASSUMPTIONS ABOUT SAMPLES AND SAMPLING

Epidemiological versus Random Sampling

Prevention's epidemiological approach imposes a different assumption from traditional clinical trials (Rothman, 1986). Treatment samples are presumed to be composed of interchangeable and randomly selected representatives of the defined homogeneous group they represent. In most cases, samples are selected based on exhibiting the same symptom picture. In contrast, for prevention, samples are selected to be representative of demographically or epidemiologically defined populations (e.g., children living in lower-socioeconomic-status communities or children showing early aggression, which is statistically predictive of later antisocial behavior; Kellam, 1990). However, the sample is not expected to be homogeneous and may, in fact, be assembled to represent distinct variation in risk and likely benefit from the intervention (Brown, 1993a, 1993b; Kellam, 1990). In other words, the goal is to have proportional representation that is diverse enough to represent the distinguishable risk-related segments of the population rather than attempting to ensure that each participant is another instance of randomly sampling a homogeneous population (Hsu, 1989; Rothman, 1986). For example, although one may apply a social competence prevention effort to a whole school to reduce prevalence of later antisocial behavior, it is recognized that there is variation in risk for this behavior among those included and that most included have relatively low risk (Weissberg et al., 1981). The question of interest is the impact on the epidemiologically defined population, not just on individuals with risk. In addition, as risk assessment and its prediction of outcome are, by definition, probability statements with inherent error, even those with the same score on a risk assessment may vary substantially in actual risk. Thus, it is presumed there will be a range of risk levels and amount of change in benefit among participants. In fact, because the variation in impact among participants should depend on risk level or other characteristics (e.g., demographics, protective factors), this relation can itself be a major focus of prevention efficacy analyses (Brown, 1993a; Kellam, 1990).

Heterogeneity in risk and risk-related characteristics is a primary reason that the samples for prevention studies often need to be much larger than required for treatment studies (Kraemer & Kraemer, 1994; Muthen & Curran, 1997). The extent of impact (effect size) will be a function of not only the impact of the intervention, but also the predictive power (i.e., the correlation of predictor to outcome) and specificity (i.e., the rate of accurate prediction of outcome based on the given predictor[s]) of risk factors targeted in relation to the undesirable outcome, and the precision of inclusion criteria (i.e., the extent to which those participating are only those at risk) (Lorion et al., 1989; Mayer & Warsi, 1996). A preventive intervention will affect the prevalence of a problem to the extent that the occurrence of the problem is under the control of targeted mediating risk factor(s), the extent to which the risk factor(s) is/are prevalent across those participating, and the extent to which the intervention modifies the mediating risk factor(s) (MacKinnon & Dwyer, 1993).

Differentiating Types of Prevention

The relation of risk distribution in the population and the strength of the relation of the risk factor to the undesirable outcome are basic dimensions along which types of prevention are differentiated (Institute of Medicine, 1994; Lorion et al., 1989). In some cases, risk is relatively small but is widespread (e.g., social stress effects on depression), whereas in others, it is concentrated in a small segment but may be substantially related to outcome for that group (e.g., early aggression and later serious criminality). Prevention as originally defined in biomedical public health is distinguished as primary (meant to prevent the incidence of a generally risky disease), secondary (meant to reduce the prevalence of a disease affecting specific segments), and tertiary (meant to stem the harm of a disease of those afflicted) (Caplan, 1964). Each type of prevention suggests different strategies and differential individual-risk relations. However, when applied to behavioral research and psychopathology, these distinctions were less clear, especially how risk distribution relates to inclusion as prevention targets. The importance of these features and, therefore, what portion of the population should be targeted has driven recent reorganization of prevention in regard to mental health outcomes into universal, selective, and indicated prevention efforts (Lorion et al., 1989; Mrazek & Haggerty, 1994).

Universal prevention efforts are those meant to affect the whole population. This focus is based on the presumption that risk is spread across the population and that prevalence rates can be reduced best by including the whole population or sampling without regard to risk. Peer mediation programs to improve the methods used to solve interpersonal programs are universal prevention programs for antisocial behavior (Hawkins, Catalano, & Miller, 1992). *Selective* interventions focus on the portion of the population sampled that has elevated risk, as it is assumed that targeting this portion is the most efficient method to reduce risk. A program focused on children showing below average social-problem-solving skills or above average early aggression is an example of a selective intervention to prevent later antisocial behavior (Tolan & Guerra, 1994). *Indicated* interventions assume prevention is best realized through targeting those who already show early symptoms or powerful risk factors. An example of an indicated prevention program is a multicomponent support and habilitation program for children in first grade who have several behavioral problem incidents to prevent the growth of such problems into serious antisocial behavior or conduct disorder (Coie & Dodge, 1996).

Each of these types of prevention has different criteria for determining efficacy/effectiveness and attendant variation in evaluation design (Brown & Liao, in press; Tolan, in press; Tolan & Brown, 1997). More detailed explanations about the implications of universal versus selective and indicated interventions can be found elsewhere (Lorion et al., 1989; Mrazek & Haggerty, 1994; Tolan, in press). Figure 16.1 summarizes some major design distinctions among the types of prevention. Also illustrated there are the implications these differences have for the statistical judgment about proximal and distal outcomes and the clinical or practical criteria usually applied. In

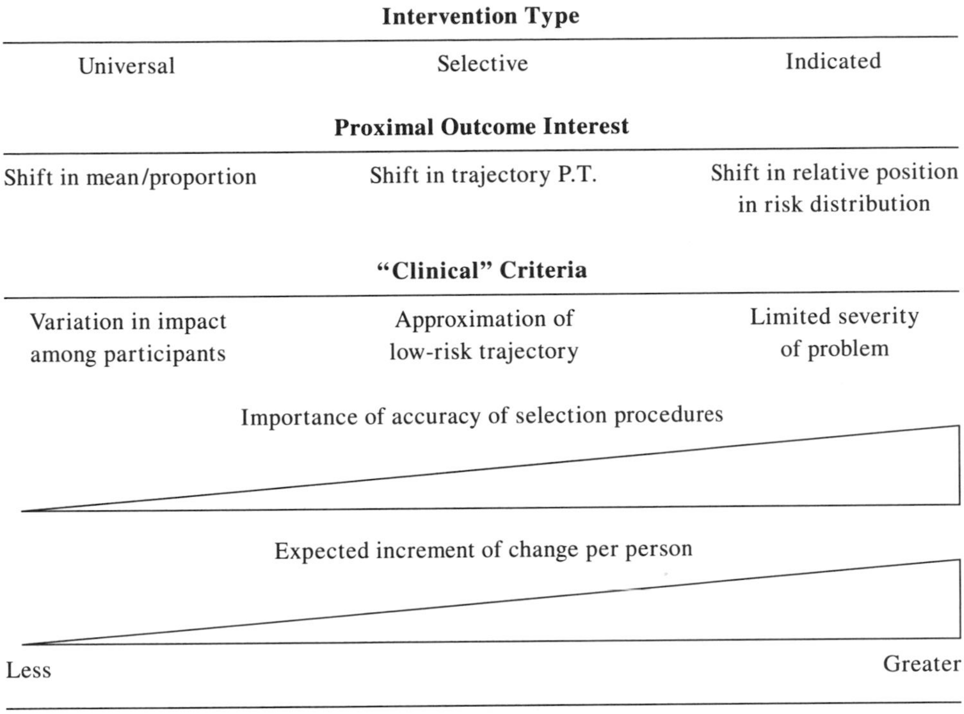

Intervention Type		
Universal	Selective	Indicated
Proximal Outcome Interest		
Shift in mean/proportion	Shift in trajectory P.T.	Shift in relative position in risk distribution
"Clinical" Criteria		
Variation in impact among participants	Approximation of low-risk trajectory	Limited severity of problem

Importance of accuracy of selection procedures

Expected increment of change per person

Less   Greater

Figure 16.1. Prevention design characteristics.

addition, this figure shows the related role of accuracy of selection procedures to the type of prevention and how effects size should relate to expected increment of change per participant. The general principle is that the more concentrated the risk, the more intensive the intervention and the more careful and specific selection should be.

THE CENTRALITY OF THE DEVELOPMENTAL/LONGITUDINAL PERSPECTIVE

Prevention is ultimately focused on effects that are not evident until some time after the completion of intervention (distal/ultimate outcomes). There is interest in proximal effects or outcomes evident at intervention completion but primarily as part of the causal chain between risk and the ultimate outcome (Curran & Muthen, 1996; Kellam, 1990). Depending on the theoretical contention, it may be that proximal effects are expected to be maintained over time and therefore lessen risk for the distal outcome(s), or it may be that the intervention is thought to work via another theoretical link between proximal effects on intervention targets and distal benefits (e.g., changing family behavior management will lessen later susceptibility to peer influences thought to proximally precipitate delinquency; Dishion & Andrews, 1995). These relations represent developmental hypotheses. Thus, all prevention trials are inherently longitudinal and can be expressed as developmental models (Coie et al., 1993; Kellman, 1990; Muthen & Curran, 1997). As noted by Lorion et al. (1989), the proximal targets of preventive interventions should therefore be developmental processes rather than specific behaviors or symptoms (Sroufe, 1997). It follows, then, that any preventive trial can be understood as a test of a developmental theory (Coie et al., 1993; Weissberg & Greenberg, 1998). It is quite possible, and unfortunately too frequently the case, that the longitudinal nature of the test is not articulated and the developmental theory not expressed. However, this does not obviate the influence these features have on design and analyses (e.g., autocorrelation of measures, potential developmental shifts in measurement reliability and validity, threats due to attrition bias and level; see Brown & Liao, in press; Muthen & Curran, 1997).

Given the centrality of developmental theory, prevention analyses must be able to model and test variation in growth over time (Brown, 1993b; Brown & Liao, in press; Burchinal & Applebaum, 1991). Specifically, preventive interventions are most readily understood through growth modeling. Variations in development by condition and epidemiologically relevant characteristics are the most pertinent evidence of effects. These growth models can be latent or measured (Muthen & Curran, 1997). This analytic approach is a basic shift from a covariance model emphasizing pre-post comparisons as the primary efficacy measurement. It should be noted, however, that the covariance model is too often the single test of prevention trials. Traditional covariance models are quite vulnerable to bias and misestimation of intervention effects longitudinally and so may misdirect understanding of prevention trials (see Burchinal & Appelbaum, 1991). Growth modeling techniques are also more able to incorporate nonlinear relations and make use of new methods for estimating missing data (Brown, 1993a, 1993b; Little & Rubin, 1987). The primary advantage, however, is greater precision and sensitivity for evaluating differences in change patterns over time along with comparisons of variation from initial condition (e.g., comparing slopes as well as intercept differences). Also, because repeated measures over several points are employed, growth models can fully exploit the power of a sample (Muthen & Curran, 1997; Tolan, Kendall, et al., 1997).

Expansion to a Developmental-Ecological Model

In addition to the centrality of developmental thinking and its implications for prevention trials as longitudinal data, there has been increasing recognition that the impact of prevention efforts also are dependent on the social ecology in which development occurs and the intervention is provided (Tolan, Guerra, & Kendall, 1995). Inclusion of contextual indicators is an important aspect of accurately modeling development and, therefore, preventive effects (Muehrer & Koretz, 1992).[2] What were once considered nuisance variables to be controlled through randomization or covariance are, from this perspective, considered integral components in evaluating the validity of prevention efforts (e.g., socioeconomic status; Tolan et al., 1995). The implication for analysis is to move from attempting to show no difference in social ecological factors by condition and no relation to outcome, to testing hypotheses about the relation of outcome to these variables by systematically modeling the variation in effects attributable to such

---

[2] The need for construct and measurement development in this area cannot be overestimated (Tolan et al., 1996; Tolan & Guerra, 1994).

variables (Kendall et al., this volume). For example, one sees an increasing interest in how classroom, school, neighborhood, and other "larger system" characteristics relate to effects.[3, 4] Prevention and related risk modeling efforts have brought out the recognition of the need to include such "nesting" variables in analyses (Shinn, 1990; Tolan, Kendall, et al., 1997; Weissberg & Greenberg, 1998). These theoretical requirements impose a heavy conceptual and analytic burden on prevention efficacy trials. The assessment of interventions effects in these models depends on a multivariate and multilevel model of developmental processes, specification of the variations in those processes that produce psychopathology or other clinical and social problems, and modeling of variation of normal and pathological processes by social settings (Brown & Liao, in press).

Recognition of Multilevel Influences on Development and Intervention

In addition, there has been a parallel interest in developing analytic models that can distinguish variance attributable to individuals from that related to larger shared characteristics (e.g., classroom) (Bryk & Raudenbush, 1992; Gibbons et al., 1993; Laird & Ware, 1982). Because many prevention efforts are implemented with assignment to condition based on units larger than the individual (e.g., school attended), models are now being applied to examine variation in impact by these higher-level influences (Bryk & Raudenbush, 1992; Gibbons et al., 1993). This has generated a great deal of effort to produce methods robust enough to test the complex developmental-ecological and multilevel models guiding the interventions (Curran & Muthen, 1996). This issue is examined in more detail below in regard to outcome assessment.

Viewing Intervention as an Interaction with Development

A third implication for methodology of the centrality of the developmental perspective in prevention is the shift from viewing intervention as a main effect with relatively equal impact across participants and one that is primarily evident at posttest. When a developmental-ecological approach is articulated, the intervention is an *interaction* with the developmental processes and pathway (Brown, 1993b; West et al., 1993). The time of the intervention is understood as one segment of a longitudinal assessment (Rogosa & Willett, 1985). This shift means that intervention effects are modeled as variation in growth over time and by variation in circumstances, rather than as average differences between treatment and control. Results are interpreted against the reference to epidemiologically defined normal and pathological development (Kellam, 1990). The implications of these shifts have prompted substantial conceptual and empirical developments in measuring prevention outcome.

---

[3] Readers are referred to Shinn (1990), Gibbons et al. (1993), and Bryk and Raudenbush (1992) for trenchant discussions of the conceptual and statistical issues related to multiple-level variables in intervention research.

[4] This interest in how contextual variables constrain and mediate intervention effects is a central focus of much of the services research methodology developments that are influencing community-based intervention research and multisite clinical trials, as well as prevention trials (Gibbons et al., 1993).

MEASURING PREVENTION OUTCOME EFFECTS

Measuring prevention outcome seems at first glance quite straightforward. The ultimate interest is in the proportion of the targeted group that are absent the disorder at some later point or within some postintervention time period in comparison to their nonparticipating counterparts (Kraemer & Kraemer, 1994). Thus, one can argue that because the interest is in proportion affected (e.g., prevalence), chi-square or logistic regression comparisons of participants and controls should be adequate. This seems readily calculated and easily interpreted. However, in fact, it is rare that such a comparison is plausible and rarer still that it is adequate. When the estimation is longitudinal with outcome at a point beyond the completion of the intervention the effects depend on more than simply contrasting intervention exposure to no exposure. The complicating features are numerous. Primary examples are: (a) measuring effects as prevalence within a given time period; (b) measuring developmental effects among initial risk, the end of intervention, and the time of the outcome effects measurement; (c) issues in modeling multilevel influences; (d) the relation of the type of comparison to the type of prevention (universal, selective, indicated); (e) importance of specifying the expected relation between the proximal and distal outcomes; (f) the effects of sample size on power; and (g) the evaluation of small to moderate effect sizes.

Measuring Eventual Prevalence

Hazard rates and other forms of survival analyses are central to distal outcome analyses. Hazard analyses compare the rate of succumbing to a disorder, mortality, or other undesirable outcome at a given point in time or over a given period of time (Cox & Oakes, 1984). This and associated analytic models permit evaluation of what proportion of the compared groups show the to-be-prevented outcome by what point (e.g., usually expressed as years postintervention or by a given age). For example, one might demonstrate the value of a prevention program for adolescent illegal drug use with hazard rate comparisons that show fewer youth in the prevention program use illegal drugs by age 18 and that there is a later onset of such use among those who do start (Biglan, Duncan, Black, & Smolkowski, 1998). Thus, the interest is in the time of succumbing as well as the absolute prevalence at a certain point in time. In this example, delay of onset is valuable because likelihood of serious and chronic use is related to onset age (Coie et al., 1993).

Measuring Developmental Effects between Initial Risk and Proximal and Distal Outcomes

Measuring outcome is complicated in most prevention studies by the need to understand effects as a function of influences across time, with variation in distal effects depending on variations in initial risk among participants, proximal effects (immediate postintervention), and interim developmental influences that can mediate the proximal-distal relation (Kellam, 1990). The first consideration refers to the expected heterogeneity of risk among participants at the outset of the program. If, as expected, programs affect those most at risk, then there will be a change in the distribution among the target population postintervention, such that higher-risk participants will show more change in risk status than lower-risk groups. For example, those with the greatest reliance on self-blaming attributes may benefit most from a depression prevention program targeting these. There can also be an interaction between initial risk and maintenance of proximal risk reduction. Thus, although a depression prevention program reduces vulnerability in cognitive styles related to depression risk, it may be that those most at risk are also most susceptible to "relapse" to such cognition in the face of major loss such as death of a parent. Similarly, there may be events or conditions that moderate the relation between proximal effects and distal effects and these may be related to initial risk. An example is that the risk for eventual drug use may be greater in schools where such use is more common. However, children with greater preintervention risk may be more likely to attend such schools, or within such schools this risk elevation may apply only to children with higher risk (e.g., those with parents who approve of drug use; Biglan et al., 1998). Therefore, the ultimate impact is dependent on the initial risk apart from proximal prevention effects. This initial risk-effects relation must be incorporated in outcome assessment (Brown, 1993a, 1993b).

This example also illustrates the second type of potential interaction effect. In the time between completion of the intervention and the ultimate outcome across prevention efforts, developmental influences are ongoing and can act as mediators (partial or full) between status at proximal and distal time points. In this depression prevention example, the relapse to depression risk depends not only on initial vulnerability but also on the misfortune of loss of a parent. Thus, it is likely that there will be variation in effect among the participants in the prevention program as a function of initial risk and of other developmental influences. A sample focus on main effects will be misleading about the value of the program (Brown, 1993b).

Multilevel Modeling

From an ecological perspective, influences on development, including prevention, can be from several levels of social organization: from the individual to microsystems such as the family and small group, to larger macrosystem focus such as institutions and social and cultural values (Bronfenbrenner, 1979; see Tolan et al., 1995; Tolan & Guerra, 1994, for discussion of application of these principles to violence prevention). In regard to analyses of development (and intervention as a specific example of the general issues for developmental analyses), this requires recognition that individuals' scores on measures correlate because of these shared memberships or influences and that variation in these scores may reflect these larger level, shared characteristics as much as individual differences (Bryk & Raudenbush, 1992; Gibbons et al., 1993, provide extensive primary discussions of these issues and attendant analytic issues). These considerations complicate design and analysis, primarily by requiring sampling plans that are sensitive to group memberships and analyses that can accurately calculate and distinguish effects of these levels. For example, the impact of a school-based behavior management program's impact must consider the fact that children are "nested" within classrooms and these classrooms are "nested" within schools; partialing variance in individuals' outcome scores appropriately is necessary to account for this nesting and the associated shared characteristics as well as individual-level variation (Brown, 1993b; Bryk & Raudenbush, 1992).

All of these likely interactions require statistical modeling that can evaluate differences in growth patterns (slopes) as well as average differences in level (intercepts). Random regression models (Gibbons et al., 1993), additive models (Brown, 1993a), and latent growth models (Muthen & Curran, 1997) are all approaches that have adequate sensitivity and robustness to model these effects. More importantly, many of the traditional and most accepted statistical models (e.g., ANCOVAs, general linear model regressions) are unlikely to adequately estimate actual effects because they are not designed to consider multiple-level models, variation in effects among participants, and the impact of repeated measurements on statistical calculations (Laird & Ware, 1982; Smith & Sechrest, 1991). The recent advances in statistical modeling and applications to prevention enable due consideration of these many design features (Brown & Liao, in press; Kraemer & Kraemer, 1994; Muthen & Curran, 1997). However, even these methods can be strained by prevention studies, especially community-level interventions (Biglan et al., 1998; Weissberg & Greenberg, 1998). Thus, robust evaluation methodology to capture the long-term and complex manner of prevention programs is still emerging.

The Relation of Type of Prevention to Analysis

As indicated in Figure 16.1, the type of statistical comparison may vary by the type of prevention. For universal interventions, the overall effect for the whole population is usually the primary interest (average or proposition, depending on scaling), whereas for selective interventions, it is the extent to which high-risk participants approximate normal development of others living within similar contexts. For indicated interventions, proximal effects are measured by the reduction in level of behavioral precursors among the participants and the eventual prevalence. The intent in indicated interventions is to attenuate disparity between developmental status of the high-risk participants and low-risk members of the same social ecology. These differentiations of theoretical interests and related statistical comparisons do not obviate the goal of any prevention effort: to eradicate the problem for all that may be of risk. However, these differences suggest meaningful variation in which efficacy tests are most appropriate.

Also, the reference group may vary depending on the basis for inclusion in the selective or universal intervention. For example, risk can be identified by social setting (e.g., all children living within gang-dominated neighborhoods) instead of by individual or family characteristics. The comparison for persons designated as high risk by setting or circumstance should be persons with similar personal characteristics but in a setting or under circumstances that are absent the risk factor(s) implicated in the intervention trial (e.g., if gang presence is the risk factor for greater antisocial behavior, the comparison to youth from a socioeconomically comparable urban community without gangs would be appropriate). One alternative to attempting to find matching communities is to randomly assign within the setting, but this assumes that protective factors or other theoretical mediators of the community-related risk can be located within families or individuals (Tolan & Brown, 1997). One is assuming that risk can be reduced by affecting these mediators, even if risk is assigned based on setting. This may require community-level comparison, which can require very large samples of communities to permit randomization (30 or more) although relatively few persons per community (e.g., 10–15). Otherwise matched pairs or other less powerful comparison methods must be used (Koepsell et al., 1992). In any case, organizing and maintaining adequate scientific control over such sampling can be difficult (Biglan et al., 1998).

The Importance of the Theorized Relation of Proximal Effects to Developmental Processes and the Distal Outcome

Because the ultimate interest in prevention trials is in lower prevalence at some later point, the theorized relation between status immediately posttest (proximal effects) and distal risk is an important part of designing and evaluating prevention trials and affects the type of analysis that should be applied. This is a theoretical as well as a statistical issue. Unlike treatment studies, where proximal effects are of most interest (e.g., decrease or eradicate symptoms), and interest in the distal status is about maintenance of initial benefits, in prevention proximal effects (e.g., reduced aggression or aggressive beliefs) are of interest in how they theoretically relate to the distal outcome (e.g., less delinquency). Therefore, any preventive test should be based on and permit testing of the theorized developmental relation. This means that there is not only a need to determine if there is long-term effect, but if the effect occurs in accordance with the theorized relation between the proximal and distal. For example, there is a need to decide if the proximal benefits are a main effect on the distal or will only occur under certain conditions (as an interaction with other influences on the distal outcome). Similarly, it is important to decide if distal benefits will only be evident in those participants showing a required level of effects at posttest. For example, it can be theorized that aggression leading to delinquency will be stemmed only for those youth in families that have parents who demonstrate consistent discipline techniques and adequate monitoring by posttest (Tolan et al., 1997). In that case, one would expect distal effects only for those who had met this proximal criterion. Thus, demonstration of the theoretical relation of proximal intervention effects to distal outcome is an important aspect of prevention evaluation.

The Effects on Power of Sample Size

One of the most commonly noted limitations in treatment as well as prevention reviews is that many studies are vastly underpowered to detect the expectable effect sizes (Cohen, 1988). This issue is complicated in prevention, in which the power of the sample size is also constrained by the expected prevalence of the problem (Mayer & Warsi, 1996). The lower the prevalence, the larger the sample size needed to ensure inclusion of adequate numbers of at-risk subjects to permit detection of any effects that might occur. Of course, a useful strategy is to enrich the base rate in the sample by screening and carefully targeting subjects with elevated risk (thus the basis for selective and indicated prevention). Nevertheless, even among carefully selected samples, prevention trials can require quite large numbers of participants to have adequate power (Curran

& Muthen, 1996). For example, if one has a risk factor present in 50% of the sample and this factor has a 0.6 predictive relation to the problem, one must have a sample size three times the number needed to detect the same effect size if the prevalence rate was 100%, as is the case for treatment samples.

Power for prevention studies is also threatened by the need to calculate attrition over longer periods of time. For example, if one has attrition of only 0.2% per year, at a 10-year follow-up, one would have only 82% of the original sample. This additional reduction must be calculated into sample size for initial intervention. One must also consider potential bias in attrition related to long-term effects (Koepsell et al., 1992; McGuigan, Ellickson, Hays, & Bell, 1997).

Issue of Moderate Effect Sizes

It is quite common for prevention trials to show small to moderate effect sizes (e.g. less than 0.3 standard deviation [SD] units). There is much room for debate about whether these effect sizes are clinically meaningful (Mayer & Warsi, 1996). However, there are two considerations that lend support to the contention that even small effect sizes from preventive efforts can be important. The first is that a small-size effect on a population can translate into substantial public health benefits (Mayer & Warsi, 1996). Assume one has a depression prevention program for school-age children that has an effect size of 0.15 SD, which is approximate to reducing the prevalence 15%. If the approximate prevalence rate for depression among children is about 10%, this could reduce it only to 8.5%. However, if such a program was offered to the approximately 8 million school-age children at risk for depression, this would translate to 1.2 million fewer children being depressed! The value may also be evidenced by then comparing the cost of this service to the cost of treating these children. One can see that what may appear to be a "weak" prevention effort may be more effective than a "potent" treatment.

Second, the meaning of effect sizes should be informed by recognition that prevention efforts should affect risk only to the extent that the targeted risk factors explain risk. The predictive correlation between the targeted risk factor(s) and the outcome is the limit of potential effect size of the intervention. Termed the "preventive fraction" attributable to a given intervention, this ceiling provides a criterion by which to measure the relative value of a given prevention effort (Mayer & Warsi, 1996). The preventive fraction possible for a given intervention is dependent on the prevalence of the risk characteristic(s) among those included, the specificity of the presence of that/those characteristic(s) to the outcome, and the ability of the intervention to change or remove the risk factor(s). In addition, it can also be influenced by the interrelation of the targeted risk factor(s) with other outcome influences (Mayer & Warsi, 1996). Therefore, one methodological issue in assessing outcome of prevention (and determining power) is to determine the preventive fraction and to measure impact against that ceiling.

SPECIFYING PROCESSES OF EFFECTS

Although not specific to prevention, process effects are important foci in prevention research. How an intervention works, which components are essential, the processes by which intervention components build on one another, and for whom the trial works are all critical aspects. Each can be tested using variations to how they are tested in traditional clinical trials (MacKinnon & Dwyer, 1993; Tolan et al., 1997; West et al., 1993). Given the assumption of variation in risk and that many prevention trials are conducted across sites or with systematic variation in service delivery settings, these process issues become more central in outcome analyses than they have been historically in treatment studies. In fact, it may be that how and for whom the trial is beneficial may be more important than some summary judgment of efficacy (Kellam, 1990). For that reason, Brown (1993b) suggests that prevention trials should be designed to determine not only if the intervention had an effect but also how the effect occurred, to liberally explore for whom and under what conditions the effect was found, and to inform knowledge about normative and pathogenic development.

The emergence of the developmental-ecological understanding of prevention has blurred the traditional boundaries between process during intervention and follow-up posttest. The activity within and implementation of the intervention are one level of processes of development that is affected by the preventive effort. However, process questions of "For whom does the intervention work?" and "What are the key components and processes?" can be applied in a general fashion to the entire longitudinal model employed: How does the intervention impact vary depending on other developmental influences?

This area of prevention science is just developing (MacKinnon & Dwyer, 1993; West et al., 1993). Currently, common practice is to borrow methods from treatment process research (Tolan et al., 1997) and mediational models intended to specify component contributions (MacKinnon & Dwyer, 1993; West et al., 1993). However, the application of these to longitudinal models is not likely to be straightforward. Thus, although some useful models are available and some exciting developments are emerging, this is an area in need of methodological development.

SUMMARY AND CONCLUSIONS

This chapter summarized some key methodological issues in prevention and community research. These comments are provided with some contrasting of prevention research from traditional clinical trials. For example, there are important differences in assumptions about the population and how outcomes are estimated; prevention assumes meaningful heterogeneity in sample and counts prevalence as outcome effects. A perspective is taken that prevention research is inherently longitudinal modeling of developmental processes and trajectories and that incorporation of circumstantial and setting influences are critical to adequate modeling. This developmental-ecological perspective models the intervention as part of a complex chain of influences on the trajectories over time and with interest in how these trajectories vary systematically by social ecology and demography basic to evaluating the preventive value (Coie et al., 1993; Kellam, 1990; Lorion et al., 1989; Tolan et al., 1995). From this perspective, prevention research is not a special case of treatment design or the antithesis of clinical trials. Instead, the view is that methodological issues that arise in prevention research are general to intervention. The result is to bring a more sophisticated understanding to interventions trials (including treatment). This should produce better understanding of treatment program effects than can be gained from simple treatment-control comparisons of variance because it permits understanding of how intervention, whether prevention or treatment, affects the persons within the social contexts and developmental trajectories that influence ultimate benefit (Tolan, 1996, in press). These prevention methods are emerging in response to real limits of existing methods to model the phenomenon of interest adequately (Brown, 1993a, 1993b; Muehrer & Koretz, 1992; Muthen & Curran, 1997), limitations that are often influential on treatment trials, although they may not be figural impediments or may be dismissed as trivial influences. However, as these analytic models are developed and applied more broadly, they can permit a reconnection of prevention and treatment research. A likely major avenue will be through the influence of these on services research that identifies how community and other setting characteristics modify and mediate clinical intervention effects. This perspective is therefore also one that can connect the emerging centrality of mental health services research in understanding treatment with the issues of community-based services and prevention sciences. Thus, although discussed here as prevention and community-based services issues, these analytic concerns have a more general implication of widening the lens to consider context and functioning over time in testing intervention effects.

REFERENCES

Afifi, A. A., & Breslow, L. (1994). The maturing paradigm of public health. *Annual Review of Public Health, 15,* 223–235.

Biglan, A., Ary, D. V., Duncan, T. E., Black, C., & Smolkowski, K. (1998). *A randomized control trial of a community intervention to prevent adolescent tobacco use.* Eugene: Oregon Research Institute.

Bronfenbrenner, U. (1979). *The ecology of human development: Experiments by nature and design.* Cambridge, MA: Harvard University Press.

Brown, C. H. (1993a). Analyzing preventive trials with generalized additive models. *American Journal of Community Psychology, 21,* 635–664.

Brown, C. H. (1993b). Statistical methods for preventive trials in mental health. *Statistics in Medicine, 12,* 289–300.

Brown, C. H., & Liao, J. (in press). Principles for designing randomized preventive trials in mental health: An emerging developmental epidemiologic paradigm. *American Journal of Community Psychology.*

Bryk, A. S., & Raudenbush, S. W. (1992). *Hierarchical linear models: Applications and data analysis methods.* Newbury Park, CA: Sage.

Burchinal, M., & Appelbaum, M. I. (1991). Estimating individual developmental functions: Methods and their assumptions. *Child Development, 62,* 23–43.

Caplan, G. (1964). *Principles of preventive psychiatry.* New York: Basic Books.

Cohen, J. (1988). *Statistical power analysis for the behavioral sciences* (2nd ed.). Hillsdale, NJ: Erlbaum.

Coie, J. D., & Dodge, K. A. (1996). Aggression and antisocial behavior. In W. Damon (Series Ed.) & N. Eisenberg (Vol. Ed.), *Handbook of child psychology: Vol. 3. Social, emotional, and personality development* (5th ed., pp. 779–862). New York: Wiley.

Coie, J. D., Watt, N. F., West, S. G., Hawkins, J. D., Asarnow, J. R., Markham, H. J., Ramey, S. L., Shure, M. B., & Long, B. (1993). The science of prevention: A conceptual framework and some directions for a national research program. *American Psychologist,* *4,* 261–273.

Connell, J. P., Kubisch, A. C., Schorr, L. B., & Weiss, C. H. (1995). *New approaches to evaluating community initiatives: Concepts, methods, and contexts.* Washington, DC: The Aspen Institute.

Cox, D. R., & Oakes, D. (1984). *Survival analysis.* London: Chapman and Hall.

Curran, P., & Muthen, B. O. (1996). *Testing developmental theories in intervention research: Latent growth analysis and power estimation.* Submitted for publication.

Dishion, T. J., & Andrews, D. W. (1995). Preventing escalation in problem behaviors with high-risk young adolescents: Intermediate and 1-year outcomes. *Journal of Consulting and Clinical Psychology, 63,* 538–548.

Gibbons, R. D., Hedeker, D. R., Elkin, I., Waternaux, C., Kraemer, H. C., Greenhouse, J. B., Shea, M. T., Imber, S. D., Sotsky, S. M., & Watkins, J. T. (1993). Some conceptual and statistical issues in analysis of longitudinal psychiatric data. *Archives of General Psychiatry, 50,* 739–750.

Hawkins, J. D., Catalano, R. F., & Miller, J. Y. (1992). Risk and protective factors for alcohol and other drug problems in adolescence and early adulthood: Implications for substance abuse prevention. *Psychological Bulletin, 112,* 64–105.

Hsu, L. M. (1989). Random sampling, randomization, and equivalence of contrasted groups in psychotherapy outcome research. *Journal of Consulting and Clinical Psychology, 57,* 131–137.

Institute of Medicine. (1994). *Reducing risks for mental disorders: Frontiers for preventive intervention research.* Washington, DC: National Academy Press.

Kellam, S. G. (1990). Developmental epidemiological framework for family research on depression and aggression. In G. R. Paterson (Ed.), *Depression and aggression in family interaction* (pp. 11–48). Hillsdale, NJ: Erlbaum.

Koepsell, T. D., Wagner, E. H., Cheadle, A. C., Patrick, D. C., Martin, P. H., & Diehr, B. (1992). Selected methodological issues in evaluating community-based health promotion and disease prevention programs. *Annual Review of Public Health, 13,* 31–57.

Kraemer, H. C., & Kraemer, K. L. (1994). Design and analysis issues for trial of prevention programs in mental health research. In *Reducing risks for mental Disorders: Frontiers for preventive intervention research* (pp. 129–156). Washington, DC: Institute of Medicine.

Laird, N. M., & Ware, J. H. (1982). Random effects models for longitudinal data. *Biometrics, 38,* 963–974.

Little, R. J. A., & Rubin, D. B. (1987). *Statistical analysis with missing data.* New York: Wiley.

Lorion, R. P., Price, R. H., & Eaton, W. W. (1989). The prevention of child and adolescent disorders: From theory to research. In D. Shaffer, I. Philips, & W. W. Silverman (Eds.), *Prevention of mental disorders, alcohol and other drug use in children and adolescents* (pp. 55–96). Rockville, MD: Office for Substance Abuse Prevention.

MacKinnon, D. P., & Dwyer, J. H. (1993). Estimating mediated effects in prevention studies. *Evaluation Review, 17*(2), 144–158.

Mayer, L., & Warsi, G. (1996). *Attributable risks & prevented fractions in a proximal distal impact model.* Manuscript submitted for publication.

McGuigan, K., Ellickson, P., Hays, R., & Bell, R. (1997). Adjusting for attrition in school based samples. *Evaluation Review, 5,* 554–567.

Muehrer, P., & Koretz, D. S. (1992). Issues in preventive intervention research. *Current Directions, 3,* 109–112.

Muthen, B. O., & Curran, P. (1997). General growth modeling in experimental designs: A latent variable framework for analysis and power estimation. *Psychological Methods, 2,* 371–402.

Mrazek, P. J., & Haggerty, R. J. (1994). Reducing risks for mental disorders: Frontiers for preventive intervention research. Washington, DC: National Academy Press.

Rogosa, D. R., & Willett, J. B. (1985). Understanding correlates of change by modeling individual differences in growth. *Psychometrika, 50,* 203–228.

Rothman, K. J. (1986). *Modern epidemiology.* Boston: Little Brown.

Seidman, E. (1983). *Handbook of Social Intervention.* London: Sage.

Shinn, M. (1990). Mixing and matching: Levels of conceptualization, measurement, and statistical analysis in community research. In P. H. Tolan, C. Keys, F. Chertok, & L. Jason (Eds.), *Research community psychology: Issues of theory and methods* (pp. 111–126). Washington, DC: American Psychological Association.

Smith, B., & Sechrest, L. (1991). Treatment of aptitude x treatment interactions. *Journal of Consulting and Clinical Psychology, 59,* 233–244.

Sroufe, L. A. (1997). Psychopathology as an outcome of development. *Development and Psychopathology, 9,* 251–268.

Tolan, P. H. (1996). Characteristics shared by exemplary child clinical interventions for indicated populations. In M. C. Roberts (Ed.), *Model programs in service delivery in child and family mental health* (pp. 91–107). Hillsdale, NJ: Erlbaum.

Tolan, P. H. (in press). Family-focused prevention research: Tough but tender family intervention research. In H. Liddle, J. Bray, D. Santesban, & R. Levant (Eds.), *Family psychology intervention science.* Washington, DC: American Psychological Association.

Tolan, P. H., & Brown, C. H. (1997). Methods for evaluating intervention and prevention efforts. In P. K. Trickett & C. Schellenbach (Eds.), *Violence against children in the family and the community* (pp. 439–464). Washington, DC: American Psychological Association.

Tolan, P. H., Gorman-Smith, D., Zilli, A., & Huesmann, L. R. (1996). Assessment of family relationship characteristics: A measure to explain risk for antisocial behavior and depression in youth. *Psychological Assessment, 9,* 212–223.

Tolan, P. H., & Guerra, N. (1994). *What works in reducing adolescent violence: An empirical review of the field.* Monograph prepared for the Center for the Study and Prevention of Youth Violence. Boulder: University of Colorado.

Tolan, P. H., Guerra, N., & Kendall, P. C. (1995). A developmental-ecological perspective on antisocial behavior in children and adolescents: Towards a unified risk and intervention framework. *Journal of Consulting and Clinical Psychology, 63,* 579–584.

Tolan, P. H., Kendall, P. C., & Beidel, D. C. (1997). *A case for treatment comparison studies of child and adolescent interventions.*

Tolan, P. H., Keys, C., Jason, L., & Chertok, F. (1990). Conversing about theories, methods, and community research. In P. H. Tolan, C. Keys, F. Chertok, & L. Jason (Eds.), *Researching community psychology: The integration of theories and methods* (pp. 3–8). Washington, DC: American Psychological Association.

Weissberg, R. P., Gesten, E. L., Rapkin, B. D., Cowen, E. L., Davidson, E., Flores de Apodaca, R., & McKim, B. J. (1981). Evaluation of a social problem solving training for suburban and inner-city third-grade children. *Journal of Consulting and Clinical Psychology, 49,* 251–261.

Weissberg, R. P., & Greenberg, M. T. (1998). School and Community competence-enhancement and prevention programs. In W. Damon (Series Ed.) & I. E. Sigel & K. A. Renninger (Vol. Eds.), *Handbook of child psychology: Vol. 4. Child psychology in practice* (5th ed., pp. 877–954). New York: Wiley.

West, S. G., Aiken, L. S., & Todd, M. (1993). Probing the effects of individual components in multiple component prevention programs. *American Journal of Community Psychology, 21,* 571–605.

Chapter 17

Focus Chapter

META-ANALYTIC RESEARCH METHODS

JOSEPH A. DURLAK, PH.D.

This chapter cannot tell you all you need to know about how to do a meta-analysis; it can, however, inform you about *when* to do one. This slightly different orientation permits discussion of several critical issues useful for those who initiate their own meta-analysis as well as those who want more information about how to evaluate meta-analyses that appear in the literature. If your knowledge of meta-analysis is rudimentary, see Light and Pillemer's (1984) excellent nontechnical introduction to meta-analysis and Rosenthal's (1995) highly readable piece on how to write a meta-analytic report. Explanations of the most common technical and procedural aspects of meta-analysis with plenty of helpful examples are available in several other sources (Cooper & Hedges, 1994; Durlak, 1995; Durlak & Lipsey, 1991; Hedges & Olkin, 1985; Hunter & Schmidt, 1990; Wolf, 1986). The first and last three of these sources are texts devoted to meta-analysis.

Before we proceed, note that some researchers would answer the question "When should one do a meta-analysis?" with an emphatic "Never!" Although an estimated 1,500 meta-analyses have appeared in print and approximately 100 new meta-analyses appear each year in the social sciences, controversy still swirls around the technique.

Sharpe (1997) offers a good commentary on the pro and con arguments about meta-analysis. Well done reviews are extremely helpful in synthesizing past research and highlighting potentially fruitful directions for new work. Poorly done reviews, however, can be harmful if they offer misleading information and unjustified conclusions that might close off inquiry in some aspects of a field prematurely or misdirect researchers to the wrong issues and variables. It is true that meta-analysis can be misused and misinterpreted, but so can any research method and statistical technique. This chapter is written from the perspective that, in principle, meta-analysis is an appropriate research strategy, although in practice, meta-analyses definitely vary in their quality, utility, and overall value.

Perhaps the most common misperception of meta-analysis, which is generated by its statistical features (after all, numbers don't lie, do they?), is that meta-analysis is a highly structured objective strategy with clear decision rules for each important step. Actually, there is no one standardized approach in meta-analysis. Several advances in meta-analytic techniques have occurred since Smith and Glass (1977) popularized the use of meta-analysis within the social sciences with their review of psychotherapy research. Moreover, many decisions are required while conducting a meta-analysis. It is extremely important that these decision points be made explicit so that the quality of a

419

meta-analysis can be judged. Some of these judgment calls are discussed here, and further information is available in several sources (Matt, 1989; Nurius & Yeaton, 1987; Wanous, Sullivan, & Malinak, 1989).

WHAT IS META-ANALYSIS?

Meta-analysis is an approach to research synthesis whereby the results of different studies are transformed into a common metric, the effect size, which is then pooled or aggregated across studies. Meta-analysts usually report the overall mean effect obtained from all reviewed studies and for important subcategories of studies and then attempt to explain these outcomes by searching for moderators. Studies always vary in their outcomes; if every investigation obtained similar results, there would be little need for a review in the first place. In other words, a major question in most meta-analyses is: What accounts for the variability of obtained effects?

There are two main types of effect sizes (ESs): product-moment correlations and standardized mean effects. Because meta-analyses of treatment studies usually use ESs, this chapter only discusses these types of effects, which are also referred to as $d, d+,$ or g. However, product-moment correlations can be used effectively for reviewing clinical research, as demonstrated in Reid and Crisafulli's (1990) meta-analysis. Across 33 studies, there was an average r of 0.16 between the extent of marital discord present in the home and the level of boys' externalizing problems. An r of 0.16 corresponds to a mean ES of 0.32.

In most treatment meta-analyses, an ES is calculated within each study by subtracting the posttreatment mean of the control group from the posttreatment mean of the treatment group and then dividing by the pooled standard deviation (Cooper & Hedges, 1994). The ESs from each study are then averaged to produce mean ESs.

How to Judge Mean Effects

Table 17.1 presents the distribution of mean ESs obtained in a meta-analysis of 156 meta-analyses of behavioral, psychological, and educational treatments (Lipsey & Wilson, 1993). These data indicate the magnitude of ESs typically obtained in the social

Table 17.1.   Effect sizes obtained from 156 meta-analyses of behavioral, psychological, and educational treatments

Proportion of Meta-Analyses with Certain Effects	Magnitude of Effect
Mean of all meta-analyses	0.48
68% of all meta-analyses	0.19 to 0.75
16% of meta-analyses	> 0.75
16% of meta-analyses	< 0.19
5% of meta-analyses	> 1.00
0.006% of meta-analyses	< 0.00

Note: Data are drawn from Lipsey and Wilson (1993), Figure 7, and are based on treatment versus control group designs.

sciences and education. The mean ES drawn from all 156 meta-analyses was 0.48: in one-sixth of the reviews, the mean ES was greater than 0.75; in another one-sixth, the mean was less than 0.19; and only one meta-analysis reported a negative mean effect, which indicated that the control group did better than the treatment group over time. Lipsey and Wilson's (1993) data are consistent with Cohen's (1977) initial suggestions, offered before meta-analysis became popular, that mean ESs of 0.20, 0.50, and 0.80 should be considered small, moderate, and large in magnitude, respectively.

However, the magnitude of an ES does not necessarily reflect its practical significance. Much depends on what the outcomes are. In some cases, "small" ESs can have substantial practical value if they are based on such outcomes as the presence or absence of a clinical diagnosis, graduation from school, arrest rates, or serious antisocial behavior (Lösel, 1995). If the outcome is a matter of life and death, as it sometimes is in medical trials, ESs as low as 0.07 can nevertheless represent a highly successful intervention (Rosenthal, 1991). There are now several ways to calculate the clinical or practical significance of ESs (see Baucom & Hoffman, 1986; Durlak, Fuhrman, & Lampman, 1991).

ESs can also be calculated from single-subject designs (Busk & Serlin, 1992; see also Gaynor, Baird, & Nelson-Gray, this volume), from one-group-only designs (Lipsey & Wilson, 1993), and in studies comparing two or more treatments but lacking a control group. However, ESs should not be combined across these categories. Compared to ESs obtained from treatment versus control situations, ESs from single-subject designs are based on within- rather than between-group data, one-group-only designs are often much higher in magnitude, and treatment versus treatment comparisons are much lower in magnitude. In the second case, there is no control group that can change positively over time, and in the third case, another treatment should have more positive impact than a no-treatment condition.

Major Steps in a Meta-Analysis

There are six major steps in a meta-analysis, which are listed in Table 17.2. The steps include (1) formulating the research question(s), (2) doing a literature search, (3) coding studies, (4) making decisions regarding the calculation of effects, (5) conducting statistical analyses, and, finally, (6) offering conclusions and interpretations. Each step has several major parts that are described in detail elsewhere (Durlak & Lipsey, 1991). Step 4, for instance, involves such issues as dealing with multiple treatment

Table 17.2.   Major steps in a meta-analysis

1. Formulate the research question(s)
2. Do an adequate literature search
3. Code relevant studies
4. Make decisions on calculating effects
5. Conduct statistical analyses
6. Offer conclusions and interpretations

Note: See Durlak and Lipsey (1991) for extended discussion of each step.

groups and outcome measures in individual studies, appropriate weighting procedures, and adjusting ESs based on small sample sizes.

This chapter focuses on five issues to consider in deciding when to do a meta-analysis that relate to four of the six steps. These issues are offered as questions to ask when planning a meta-analysis: Do you have specific hypotheses (Step 1)? Are there enough studies to code? How will you obtain representative studies? (Both are related to Step 2.) How will you code studies (Step 3)? How will you rule out rival explanations (Step 5)?

Do You Have Specific Hypotheses?

You should do a meta-analysis when you have specific hypotheses about a research literature that can be tested. Just as in an individual experiment, it is better to start with specific hypotheses concerning what you hope to find rather than embark on a fishing expedition that analyzes every possible variable and relationship. In the latter case, as long as you keep doing analyses, something is bound to come out significant. Unfortunately, there are examples of meta-analyses in which multiple analyses were conducted without any hypotheses to guide them (and without any control of Type I error), and in which authors have attached undue importance to a few significant results that appeared among the many analyses that were attempted.

An important requirement in doing a useful meta-analysis, which many do not realize, is the need for adequate working knowledge of the relevant research, including its major theories and procedures *prior to doing the review*. This step is important to formulate the best a priori hypotheses. For example, what controversies exist in the field? Can you identify certain conceptual, theoretical, or procedural issues that might account for disparities in research findings? Have new theories been developed or introduced that might be applied to past studies or research from another area? Are there new findings from well done investigations that suggest which variables might be most important? These are the types of issues that generate interesting hypotheses.

Are There Enough Studies to Review?

Suppose, in an individual study, we wanted to analyze the differences between a treatment and control group on an outcome measure using a *t*-test. The power of the statistical analysis in this case is determined by a combination of three factors: the effect size (which often has to be estimated), the probability level of the statistic being used, and the number of subjects in the two groups. If the population effect size were 0.50, the chosen probability level were 0.05, and a two-tailed test were conducted, we would need 64 subjects *per group* to have 80% statistical power, which in most cases would be sufficient.

In treatment effectiveness meta-analyses, mean ESs generated by group studies are often compared. For instance, the mean effects produced by one type of treatment are compared to the mean produced by another type of treatment. In this case, power is determined by the same first two factors (the effect size and probability level) and by the number of *studies* that are being compared, not by the number of subjects in these studies. If we used a *t*-test to compare group ESs, we would need 64 *studies* of each type of treatment to reach 80% power. Meta-analyses rarely have this degree of power throughout all their analyses.

Sufficient statistical power has been an important limitation in many meta-analyses and may be one explanation for the sometimes surprising finding that the type of treatment makes no difference in outcome, that clients with all types of problems improve equally with intervention, and so on. It is not unusual to have some analyses conducted on fewer than 10 studies per group. In our above example, 10 studies translates into less than 20% power. We cannot reach very strong conclusions under such limiting conditions.

How many studies are needed for a meta-analysis? This question can only be answered in reference to the specific aims of the meta-analysis. Although 128 studies, for example, would seem sufficient, it may not be once studies are subdivided to examine specific research questions. For instance, suppose one predicts that behavioral treatment will produce significantly higher ESs than dynamic treatment when specific measures of problem behavior are collected, but dynamic treatment will yield significantly better outcomes on measures of self-esteem and personality functioning *at follow-up but not at posttreatment.* The latter prediction might be made based on the logical premise that gains from dynamic treatment consolidate slowly and it is only some time after treatment ends that the true effects of treatment will be realized.

The above hypothesis would be impossible to assess in the child therapy literature. One can probably find 50 studies of behavioral treatment measuring outcomes on specific problems and on self-esteem at posttreatment, but there are not 50 behavioral studies with follow-up data on both these measures, and there are only a handful of dynamically oriented child therapy studies at all, much less ones with follow-up data. In other words, there is no point in attempting to do the impossible in a meta-analysis. The necessary data are sometimes unavailable.

Typically, the only way to discern if a meta-analysis is possible, or which hypotheses can be tested, is to do a lengthy and time-consuming literature search and then code the studies (see below) to determine if there are sufficient data for analysis.

How Will You Obtain Representative Studies?

Although power considerations suggest that one should collect as many studies as possible, there are two possible complications. First, decisions have to be made about what studies to include and exclude. Second, reliable methods must be used to find relevant reports. There is no such thing as an exhaustive search of the literature; there are simply too many studies in too many published and unpublished sources to identify every study done on any topic. The major issue is *representativeness.* How will you obtain a nonbiased representative sample of studies for review?

Identifying Relevant Studies   The domain of eligible research must be described by explicit inclusionary and exclusionary criteria that operationalize exactly what research is being reviewed, the minimal requirements for sample inclusion, and the basis for excluding studies. For instance, in an attempt to describe several characteristics of child therapy outcome research, we searched for all studies "in which some form of psychotherapy for maladapting children (ages ≤ 13) was compared with a control group" (Durlak, Wells, Cotten, & Johnson, 1995). We went on to define what was meant by psychotherapy and excluded drug treatments, peer counseling, and family therapy.

The inclusionary and exclusionary criteria are guided by the meta-analyst's specific research questions. If one were interested only in the effects of treatment on children with certain types of problems, problems that reach a specific level of clinical severity, or clients treated only by professional therapists, then the search criteria would reflect these specific aims.

Finding Relevant Studies Do *not* depend solely on computer searches to secure an adequate sample of studies because such searches are notoriously unreliable in terms of their true positive hit rate. Computer searches tend to identify high numbers of irrelevant studies and frequently miss relevant reports. This is because the indexing system for computer searches rarely corresponds precisely to a reviewer's interests, no database is comprehensive, and some subjectivity is involved when each individual study is indexed.

Therefore, computer searches are not as simple as using a few terms to capture all relevant studies. In some cases, computer searches have captured less than 6% of the relevant literature (Lösel, 1991), or identified more than 10 times as many studies than eventually qualify for a review (Weisz, Weiss, Alicke, & Klotz, 1987). The Cooper and Hedges (1994) volume offers several helpful suggestions about literature searches.

Three search strategies are combined in many well done meta-analyses and these include computer searches, manual searches of journals that typically publish articles in the research area, and inspection of the reference lists of included studies and previous research reviews. This three-pronged approach is much more likely to yield a representative group of studies.

Publication Bias Meta-analysts must deal with the issue of publication bias, which refers to the reluctance of editors and reviewers to accept for publication studies with nonsignificant results coupled with, and this is frequently overlooked, the hesitation on the part of authors to submit their nonsignificant findings for possible publication. Basically, this means that published studies are more likely to produce higher ESs than unpublished reports, a phenomenon that is quite common in the social and medical sciences (Dickersin, 1997).

Unfortunately, unpublished studies are particularly difficult to track down because they may consist of dissertations, convention papers, technical reports, and studies lurking in investigators' file drawers. Researchers vary in their willingness to send in copies of their unpublished work, so there can be many "fugitive" studies that are never obtained for scrutiny.

Although they do not represent all of the unpublished literature, selecting dissertations for analysis is an appropriate strategy. Databases targeting dissertations and volumes of *Dissertations Abstracts* can be searched to estimate the population of relevant studies, and dissertations can be obtained from most institutions through interlibrary loan. In addition, dissertations often contain more procedural details than published studies.

The importance of clear inclusionary and exclusionary criteria and a careful search for representative studies is underscored when one compares different reviews of ostensibly the same literature. For instance, no single study appeared in each of four reviews of school-based drug prevention (Hansen, 1992) or in each of six reviews of student evaluations of teachers' effectiveness (Abrami, Cohen, & d'Apollonia, 1988). If reviewers are not examining the same literature, it is no wonder that the findings from meta-analyses do not always agree.

How Will You Code Studies?

A meta-analysis can only examine variables that are captured in coding. Which variables should be coded? Basically, one should code those substantive and methodological variables and study artifacts that might influence outcome. A priori hypotheses and prior working knowledge of the research literature direct meta-analysts to the most critical variables in each area. Coding is tedious and time-consuming, and usually multiple revisions of a coding system are required to achieve high interjudge agreement and to settle on a satisfactory way to abstract the needed information from different studies. Levels of interjudge agreement should always be checked and reported in a meta-analysis. Yeaton and Wortman (1993) and Hartmann (1982) offer helpful advice about coding.

Nurius and Yeaton (1987) offer these words of wisdom: "A likely scenario with applied social science data is that there will be many studies from which one can glean some of the desired data, a moderate number from which one can retrieve most of the data, and only a few from which one can obtain virtually all of the data" (pp. 701–702). Therefore, coding systems should contain codes for "missing" or "uncertain" data, and this information should be clearly communicated to the reader. Recognizing the lack of potentially important data is essential when evaluating the results of a meta-analysis and can also be extremely helpful in influencing future research. The best meta-analyses emphasize the limitations of the current database and how investigators can correct these deficiencies (see also Beutler & Martin, this volume).

How Will You Rule Out Rival Explanations?

In treatment effectiveness meta-analyses, the information that is often of prime interest surrounds variables that have theoretical or clinical importance. For example, is this treatment effective? Or better than another one? Which problems can be treated most effectively? How long do the effects of treatment last? These variables are often called substantive variables. Before jumping to conclusions about substantive variables, however, it is essential that rival explanations for the findings are ruled out.

In addition to substantive variables, the results might be due, at least in part, to four other possibilities: (a) sampling error, (b) study artifacts, (c) methodological features, and (d) confounded study features. Each of these possibilities should be examined. For example, Lipsey (1992) found that 89% of the variance in the outcomes from 397 delinquency studies could be explained: 27% was attributed to sampling error; 15% to study artifacts; 25% to method variables, and 22% to the characteristics of treatment. In other words, treatment was important but so were other factors.

Sampling Error There are different methods to estimate the impact of sampling error, which is affected by the number of participants in each study. The degree of sampling error can be calculated (Hunter & Schmidt, 1990), and homogeneity tests can be used to determine if the variability in ESs produced by a group of studies is likely due to sampling error (Hedges & Olkin, 1985). Several examples of meta-analyses using these techniques are available (Durlak et al., 1991; Lipsey, 1992; Shadish et al., 1993). It is important to check for sampling error in some way because if most of the variability in outcomes is traceable to this rival explanation, then there is not much variance left for substantive variables to explain.

Study Artifacts   Hunter and Schmidt (1990) describe at least 11 different types of study artifacts, which in general refer to error that is introduced into studies from such sources as unreliable outcome measures, or failure to implement treatments faithfully. It is not always possible to control or correct for study artifacts, but coding systems can at least estimate their possible occurrence. For example, how many studies made a careful attempt at ensuring faithful treatment implementation?

Methodological Features   Every meta-analyst should attempt to estimate the impact of methodology on outcomes. Some reviewers only include studies that meet certain methodological standards. Two treatments may differ in their outcomes because the individual studies employing these treatments varied in experimental quality. Two issues are often prominent with respect to methodology. First, there is no "gold standard" when it comes to methodology. Which features should be examined (see Kazdin, this volume, for a review of methodological issues in treatment research)? Second, there is the question of how to deal with multiple-design features. Should one assess their impact individually, in interaction with each other, or by combining several variables to create groups of studies that vary in their experimental quality (e.g., high, medium, and low)? No hard-and-fast rules are possible except to say that it is important not to misinterpret outcomes as solely attributable to substantive variables without considering the way studies were designed and evaluated. There are several good examples of different ways that meta-analysts have examined the impact of design features (Lipsey, 1992; Lösel, 1991; Shadish et al., 1993; see also Kazdin, this volume).

Surprisingly, the impact of methodological features on outcomes has not been consistent. For example, sometimes studies employing randomized designs yield higher effects than quasi-experimental designs (Shadish & Ragsdale, 1996), sometimes the reverse is true (Serketich & Dumas, 1996), and sometimes there is no difference (Durlak & Wells, 1997). The results of such analyses can be misinterpreted. When findings suggest that quasi-experimental designs do not differ in their outcomes from randomized trials, this is *not* a justification for more quasi-experimental studies. It merely means that assignment to conditions did not significantly influence the effects obtained in a particular meta-analysis. Most social scientists would argue for randomized experiments except in cases where they are truly impractical or ethically improper, as, for example, in the case of serious suicidal risk (see also Kendall, Flannery-Schroeder, & Ford, this volume).

Finally, the general experimental quality of reviewed studies is important. If most studies suffer from serious design flaws, the ESs they produce are not to be trusted no matter how high the effects or how many studies there are. Quantity is no substitute for quality.

Confounded Variables   Many confounds can exist among reviewed studies. There could be confounds among methodological variables, substantive variables, and study artifacts, and between all three of these categories in the same review. For example, the results of two treatments may differ because one type of treatment is less well implemented, because different outcomes have been used to assess treatment impact, or because one treatment is restricted to a limited range of presenting problems. Before any generalizations are made about different treatments, the most plausible rival explanations for outcomes need to be examined. This is usually done by comparing studies of interest on different variables such as design feature, outcome measures, and the like (see Cooper & Hedges, 1994; Hunter & Schmidt, 1990). Power becomes critical in such comparisons, however, if study groups must be subdivided several times to assess multiple possible confounds.

SUMMARY

This chapter examined five primary issues to consider when planning a meta-analysis as a way to highlight some important features of this research strategy. Other sources contain helpful information on additional aspects of meta-analysis, such as calculating ESs based on limited details, determining how to combine multiple ESs from individual studies, different types of statistical analyses, presentation of findings, and interpreting results (Cooper & Hedges, 1994; Durlak & Lipsey, 1991; Hunter & Schmidt, 1990; Wolf, 1986).

Hopefully, the reader will not be discouraged by some of the comments offered here about the difficulties and time-consuming nature of doing a meta-analysis. The intent is to encourage high-quality meta-analyses that can make important contributions to science by accurately summarizing past research, highlighting its strengths and limitations, and directing investigators to critical areas for further work. Despite controversy about its benefits, meta-analysis remains popular and meta-analyses will continue to appear in the literature. Therefore, to be an informed consumer if not an active practitioner of the technique, it is important to be acquainted with its basic features.

REFERENCES

Abrami, P. C., Cohen, P. A., & d'Apollonia, S. (1988). Implementation problems in meta-analysis. *Review of Educational Research, 58,* 151–179.

Baucom, D. H., & Hoffman, J. A. (1986). The effectiveness of marital therapy: Current status and application to the clinical setting. In N. Jacobson & A. Gurman (Eds.), *Clinical handbook of marital therapy* (pp. 597–620). New York: Guilford Press.

Busk, P. L., & Serlin, R. C. (1992). Meta-analysis for single-case research. In T. R. Kratochwill & J. R. Levin (Eds.), *Single-case research design and analysis* (pp. 187–212). Hillsdale, NJ: Erlbaum.

Cohen, J. (1977). *Statistical power analysis for the behavioral sciences* (Rev. ed.). New York: Academic Press.

Cooper, H., & Hedges, L. V. (Eds.). (1994). *Handbook of research synthesis.* New York: Russell-Sage Foundation.

Dickersin, K. (1997). How important is publication bias? A synthesis of available data. *AIDS Education and Prevention, 9,* 15–21.

Durlak, J. A. (1995). Understanding meta-analysis. In L. G. Grimm & P. R. Yarnold (Eds.), *Reading and understanding multivariate statistics* (pp. 319–352). Washington, DC: American Psychological Association.

Durlak, J. A., Fuhrman, T., & Lampman, C. (1991). Effectiveness of cognitive-behavior therapy for maladapting children: A meta-analysis. *Psychological Bulletin, 110* 204–214.

Durlak, J. A., & Lipsey, M. W. (1991). A practitioner's guide to meta-analysis. *American Journal of Community Psychology, 19,* 291–332.

Durlak, J. A., & Wells, A. M. (1997). Primary mental health programs for children and adolescents: A meta-analytic review. *American Journal of Community Psychology, 25,* 115–152.

Durlak, J. A., Wells, A. M., Cotten, J. K., & Johnson, S. (1995). Analysis of selected methodological issues in child psychotherapy research. *Journal of Clinical Child Psychology, 24,* 141–148.

Hansen, W. B. (1992). School-based substance abuse prevention: A review of the state of the art in curriculum, 1980–1990. *Health Education Research, 7,* 403–430.

Hartmann, D. P. (Ed.). (1982). *Using observers to study behavior: New directions for methodology of social and behavioral sciences.* San Francisco: Jossey-Bass.

Hedges, L. V., & Olkin, I. (1985). *Statistical methods for meta-analysis.* New York: Academic Press.

Hunter, J. E., & Schmidt, F. L. (1990). *Methods of meta-analysis: Correcting error and bias in research findings.* Newbury Park, CA: Sage.

Light, R. J., & Pillemer, D. B. (1984). *Summing up: The science of reviewing research.* Cambridge, MA: Harvard University Press.

Lipsey, M. W. (1992). Juvenile delinquency treatment: A meta-analytic inquiry into variability of effects. In T. D. Cook, H. Cooper, D. S. Cordray, H. Hartmann, L. V. Hedges, R. L. Light, T. A. Louis, & F. Mosteller (Eds.), *Meta-analysis for explanation* (pp. 83–127). New York: Russell-Sage Foundation.

Lipsey, M. W., & Wilson, D. B. (1993). The efficacy of psychological, educational, and behavioral treatment: Confirmation from meta-analysis. *American Psychologist, 48,* 1181–1209.

Lösel, F. (1991). Meta-analysis and social prevention: Evaluation and a study on the family—Hypothesis in developmental psychopathology. In G. Albrecht & H. Otto (Eds.), *Social prevention and the social sciences: Theoretical controversies, research problems, and evaluation strategies* (pp. 305–332). Berlin: Walter de Gruyter.

Lösel, F. (1995). Increasing consensus in the evaluation of offender rehabilitation? Lessons from recent research syntheses. *Psychology, Crime and Law, 2,* 19–39.

Matt, G. E. (1989). Decision rules for selecting effect sizes in meta-analysis: A review and reanalysis of psychotherapy outcome studies. *Psychological Bulletin, 105,* 106–115.

Nurius, P. S., & Yeaton, W. H. (1987). Research synthesis reviews: An illustrated critique of "hidden" judgments, choices, and compromises. *Clinical Psychology Review, 7,* 695–714.

Reid, W. J., & Crisafulli, A. (1990). Marital discord and child behavior problems: A meta-analysis. *Journal of Abnormal Child Psychology, 18,* 105–117.

Rosenthal, R. (1991). *Meta-analytic procedures for social research* (Rev. ed.). Newbury Park, CA: Sage.

Rosenthal, R. (1995). Writing meta-analytic reviews. *Psychological Bulletin, 118,* 183–192.

Serketich, W. J., & Dumas, J. E. (1996). The effectiveness of behavioral parent training to modify antisocial behavior in children: A meta-analysis. *Behavior Therapy, 27,* 171–186.

Shadish, W. R., Montgomery, L. M., Wilson, P., Wilson, M. R., Bright, I., & Okwumabua, T. (1993). Effects of family and marital psychotherapies: A meta-analysis. *Journal of Consulting and Clinical Psychology, 61,* 992–1002.

Shadish, W. R., & Ragsdale, K. (1996). Random versus nonrandom assignment in controlled experiments: Do you get the same answer? *Journal of Consulting and Clinical Psychology, 64,* 1290–1305.

Sharpe, D. (1997). Of apples and oranges, file drawers and garbage: Why validity issues in meta-analysis will not go away. *Clinical Psychology Review, 17,* 881–901.

Smith, M. L., & Glass, G. V. (1977). Meta-analysis of psychotherapy outcome studies. *American Psychologist, 32,* 752–760.

Wanous, J. P., Sullivan, S. E., & Malinak, J. (1989). The role of judgment calls in meta-analysis. *Journal of Applied Psychology, 74,* 259–264.

Weisz, J. R., Weiss, B., Alicke, M. D., & Klotz, M. L. (1987). Effectiveness of psychotherapy with children and adolescents: A meta-analysis for clinicians. *Journal of Consulting and Clinical Psychology, 55,* 542–549.

Wolf, F. M. (1986). *Meta-analysis: Quantitative methods for research synthesis.* Beverly Hills, CA: Sage.

Yeaton, W. H., & Wortman, P. M. (1993). On the reliability of meta-analytic reviews. *Evaluation Review, 17,* 292–309.

PART FOUR

AREAS OF CLINICAL RESEARCH: PSYCHOPATHOLOGY AND HEALTH

Chapter 18 —————————————————————————————

CONCEPTUAL AND METHODOLOGICAL ISSUES IN DEVELOPMENTAL PSYCHOPATHOLOGY RESEARCH

DANTE CICCHETTI, PH.D., and FRED A. ROGOSCH, PH.D.

Developmental psychopathology is an evolving interdisciplinary scientific perspective whose overarching focus is elucidating the interplay among the biological, psychological, and social-contextual aspects of normal and abnormal development across the life course (Cicchetti, 1993; Cicchetti & Toth, 1998b; Rutter, 1996b; Zigler & Glick, 1986). In one of the early statements concerning its goals, Cicchetti (1990) asserted:

> Developmental psychopathology . . . should bridge fields of study, span the life cycle, and aid in the discovery of important new truths about the processes underlying adaptation and maladaptation, as well as the best means of preventing or ameliorating psychopathology. Moreover, this discipline should contribute greatly to reducing the dualisms that exist between the clinical study of and research into childhood and adult disorders, between the behavioral and biological sciences, between developmental psychology and psychopathology, and between basic and applied science. (p. 20)

Indeed, during the quarter century that has elapsed since its emergence, theory and research in the field of developmental psychopathology have contributed to dramatic knowledge gains in the multiple domains of child and adult development (see Cicchetti & Cohen, 1995a, 1995b). In particular, there has been an emphasis on increasingly specific process-level models of normal and abnormal development, an acknowledgment that multiple pathways exist to the same outcome and that the effects of one component's value may vary in different systems, and an intensification of interest in biological and genetic factors, as well as in social and contextual factors related to the development of maladaptation and psychopathology.

In recognition of this young field's scientific achievements, the Steering Committee of the Institute of Medicine (1989) adopted the principles of developmental psychopathology as the organizing framework for its report entitled *Research on Children and Adolescents with Mental, Behavioral, and Developmental Disorders.* Likewise, the National Institute of Mental Health's *National Plan for Research on Child and Adolescent Mental*

Our work on this chapter was supported, in part, by grants from the William T. Grant Foundation, the National Center on Child Abuse and Neglect, the National Institute of Mental Health (MH45027), and the Spunk Fund, Inc.

Disorders (National Advisory Mental Health Council, 1990), an outgrowth of the work of the Institute of Medicine's report, embraced developmental psychopathology as its overarching paradigm for organizing future research priorities. Furthermore, the Institute of Medicine (1994) highlighted developmental psychopathology as one of four core sciences considered to be essential to expand the frontiers of prevention and intervention efforts into reducing the risk factors for mental disorders and their sequelae throughout the life course.

Prior to its relatively recent crystallization as an integrative framework for examining the links between the study of psychopathology and the study of normal development, the field of developmental psychopathology must acknowledge a long ancestry dating back to the beginning of Western thought (Cicchetti, 1990; Kaplan, 1967; Overton & Horowitz, 1991). Specifically, developmental psychopathology owes its emergence and coalescence to many historically based endeavors within a variety of disciplines, including cultural anthropology, embryology, epidemiology, genetics, the neurosciences, philosophy, psychiatry, psychoanalysis, psychobiology, clinical, developmental, and experimental psychology, and sociology (see Cicchetti, 1990, for a review of these historical forces). Notably, a number of the major theoretical systematizers in these diverse scientific fields conceptualized psychopathology as a distortion or exaggeration of the normal condition and reasoned that the study of normal biological, psychological, and social processes could be more clearly understood through the investigation of pathological phenomena (Cicchetti & Cohen, 1995c).

Although the field of developmental psychopathology first came into ascendance during the 1970s, predominantly through being highlighted as an important perspective by researchers who were conducting prospective longitudinal studies of children at risk for becoming schizophrenic (Garmezy & Streitman, 1974; Watt, Anthony, Wynne, & Rolf, 1984), it wasn't until the 1980s that the field of developmental psychopathology began to exert a major impact on the manner in which researchers investigated the mental disorders and high-risk conditions of children and adults (see, e.g., Cicchetti, 1984a, 1984b; Rutter, 1986; Rutter & Garmezy, 1983; Zigler & Glick, 1986). Conceptualizations of the nature of mental disorder, etiological models of risk and pathology, the scientific questions that were posed, and the sampling, design, measurement, and data analytic strategies utilized in traditional research on psychopathology were reexamined, challenged, and cast into a new light by developmental psychopathologists (e.g., Cicchetti & Richters, 1997; Richters, 1997; Richters & Cicchetti, 1993; Sameroff & Chandler, 1975; Sroufe, 1990; Sroufe & Rutter, 1984; Wakefield, 1997).

In this chapter, we define the parameters of the field of developmental psychopathology and review some of the organizing principles that have implications for informing research investigations conceptualized within a developmental psychopathology framework. We offer examples from research in the field as illustrations of these principles. Subsequently, we describe representative research designs and methods that can be used to guide investigations conducted within developmental psychopathology.

WHAT IS DEVELOPMENTAL PSYCHOPATHOLOGY?

Sroufe and Rutter (1984) originally defined developmental psychopathology as "*the study of the origins and course of individual patterns of behavioral maladaptation,* whatever the causes, whatever the transformations in behavioral manifestation, and however the course of the developmental pattern may be" (p. 18; italics in original). The authors of the Institute of Medicine (1989) report on child and adolescent behavioral and mental disorders elaborated on this definition and stated that the developmental psychopathology perspective should incorporate "the emerging behavioral repertoire, cognitive and language functions, social and emotional processes, and changes occurring in anatomical structures and physiological processes of the brain" (p. 14).

Theorists and researchers in the field of developmental psychopathology seek to unify, within a life span framework, the many contributions to the study of high-risk and disordered individuals (cf. Magnusson & Cairns's, 1996, call for an integrated developmental science). Developmental psychopathologists strive to engage in a comprehensive evaluation of biological, psychological, and social factors and to ascertain how these multiple levels of functioning may influence individual differences, the continuity or discontinuity of adaptive or maladaptive behavioral patterns, and the pathways by which the same developmental outcomes may be achieved. In practice, this entails a comprehension of and an appreciation for the developmental transformations and reorganizations that occur in neurobiological, cognitive, socioemotional, linguistic, and representational development over time, an analysis of the risk and protective factors operating in the individual and his or her environment, the investigation of how emergent functions, competencies, and developmental tasks modify the expression of a disorder or lead to new symptoms and difficulties, and the recognition that a particular stressor, set of stressful circumstances, or underlying mechanism may result in different biological and psychological problems, depending on when in the developmental period they occur (Cicchetti & Aber, 1986; Institute of Medicine, 1989; Rutter, 1987). Moreover, various difficulties will constitute different meanings for an individual depending on cultural considerations, as well as an individual's current level of psychological and biological functioning. The interpretation of the experience, in turn, will affect the adaptation or maladaptation that ensues.

Developmental psychopathologists stress that disordered individuals may move between pathological and nonpathological forms of functioning (cf. Zigler & Glick, 1986). Moreover, even in the midst of pathology, patients may display adaptive coping mechanisms. It is only through the consideration of both adaptive and maladaptive processes that it becomes possible to delimit the presence, nature, and boundaries of the underlying psychopathology. Furthermore, developmental psychopathology is a perspective that is especially applicable to the investigation of critical transitional turning points in development across the life span. With respect to the emergence of psychopathology, all periods of life are consequential in that the developmental process may take a pernicious turn toward mental disorder at any phase. Developmental psychopathologists acknowledge that disorders may appear at any point in the life span (Cicchetti, 1993; Rutter, 1996a) and advocate the importance of examining the course of disorders once manifest, including their phases and sequelae (Post et al., 1996; Zigler & Glick, 1986). Rutter (1990) has theorized that key life turning points may be times when the presence of protective mechanisms could help individuals redirect themselves from a risk trajectory onto a more adaptive developmental pathway. In contrast to the often dichotomous world of mental disorder/nondisorder in psychiatry, a developmental psychopathology perspective recognizes that normality often fades into abnormality, adaptive and maladaptive may take on differing definitions depending on whether one's time referent is immediate circumstance or long-term development, and that processes within the individual can be characterized as having shades or degrees of psychopathology.

Accordingly, the field of developmental psychopathology transcends traditional disciplinary boundaries and provides fertile ground for moving beyond descriptive facts to a process-level comprehension of normal and abnormal developmental trajectories. Rather than competing with existing theories and facts, the developmental psychopathology perspective provides a broad, integrative framework within which the contributions of separate disciplines can be fully realized in the broader context of understanding individual development and functioning. The research armamentarium of developmental psychopathologists is drawn from existing techniques in an array of disciplines and subdisciplines (Achenbach, 1990; Cicchetti, 1990; Rutter, 1996b). Because the goals of developmental psychopathology are broad and integrative, seeking to understand adaptation and maladaptation across the life course, diverse methodological strategies are applicable to address multilevel questions of interest to the field. Many research designs and data analytic procedures currently used by developmental psychopathologists are not unique to the discipline. However, the assumptions that guide a developmental psychopathology perspective call for the utilization of these research methods to address questions of developmental process explicitly, a goal that may not be central to other disciplines. Because of the breadth of the field's foci, no single developmental psychopathologist will possess competence in all areas of conceptual and methodological expertise thought to be essential to comprehending the complex interplay among biological, psychological, and social processes in the development of normality and pathology. However, a commitment to the principles of the field should characterize research conducted by developmental psychopathologists to elucidate the pathways to adaptive and maladaptive development, as well as to enhance the understanding of the links between normal and psychopathological processes. Multidisciplinary collaborations of developmentalists knowledgeable in the various aspects of the field, as well as integrative syntheses of the extant literature, are two means by which the fuller goals of a developmental psychopathology perspective can be achieved. Further, new research paradigms will need to be developed to enable developmental psychopathologists to attain greater fidelity between the principles that guide their theories and research and the procedures used to examine and elucidate those perspectives (Cicchetti & Richters, 1997; Richters, 1997).

PRINCIPLES OF DEVELOPMENTAL PSYCHOPATHOLOGY

To elaborate more completely the principles that undergird the field of developmental psychopathology, we turn next to an explication of its tenets. Our delimitation of the principles is not presented in any presumed order of importance, nor is it meant to be an all-inclusive list. Rather, we describe those underlying principles that we view as especially relevant to the overarching goal of this handbook.

Normal and Abnormal

A focus on the boundary between normal and abnormal development is central to a developmental psychopathology perspective. Such a viewpoint emphasizes not only how knowledge from the study of normal development can inform the study of high-risk conditions and psychopathological disorders, but also how the investigation of risk and pathology can enhance our comprehension of normal development. Even before a psychopathological disorder emerges, certain pathways signify adaptational failures in normal development that probabilistically forebode subsequent maladaptation and psychopathology (Cicchetti & Rogosch, 1996a; Sroufe, 1989). Similarly, information obtained from investigating psychopathology can augment the comprehension of normal development.

Defining categories of disturbance (i.e., syndromes and diagnoses) requires the ability to derive discrete groups of individuals who share similar patterns of dysfunction. The natural categories of such diagnostic entities currently are by no means firmly established. In addition to defining psychopathology, either quantitatively as an extreme on a continuum or qualitatively as a discrete diagnostic category, developmental psychopathologists also seek to understand variation in the nonpathological range. In particular, because of interest in the evolution and emergence of psychopathology, focus on subclinical vulnerabilities also is important for elucidating early precursor states to later dysfunction. For example, the study of schizotypal personality features in late adolescence may provide insights into the emergence of schizophrenia among a subgroup with this personality organization (Meehl, 1964, 1990).

The central focus of developmental psychopathology involves the elucidation of developmental processes and how they function as indicated and elaborated by the examinations of extremes in the distribution (i.e., individuals with psychopathology). Developmental psychopathologists also direct attention toward variations in the continuum between the mean and the extremes. These variations may represent individuals who are currently not divergent enough to be considered disordered but who may progress to further extremes as development continues. Such individuals may be vulnerable to developing future disordered outcomes, or developmental deviations may, for some individuals, reflect either the earliest signs of an emerging dysfunction or an already existing dysfunction that is partially compensated for by other processes within or outside the individual.

Because of the interrelations between the investigation of normal and abnormal development, developmental psychopathologists must be cognizant of normal pathways of development within a given cultural context (Garcia Coll et al., 1996), uncover deviations from these pathways, articulate the developmental transformations that occur as individuals progress through these deviant developmental courses, and identify the processes and mechanisms that may divert an individual from a particular pathway and onto a more or less adaptive course (Cicchetti & Aber, 1986; Cicchetti & Rogosch, 1996b; Sroufe, 1989).

As an example of how research can elucidate the interplay between normal and abnormal development, if an investigator were interested in understanding the nature of the relation between cognitive and emotional development in infancy, then there would be limitations inherent to the study of a sample comprising solely normal infants. Specifically, in the rapidly developing normal infant, the simultaneous emergence of affective and cognitive competencies may be coincidental, thereby compromising the ability to tease apart the way in which affect and cognition interrelate. However, if in the study one also were to include a group of infants born with a chromosomal anomaly that is commonly associated with varying degrees of mental retardation, such as is the case with infants with Down syndrome, then it would be possible to ascertain true convergences and discontinuities in the relation between these two domains (see Cicchetti & Sroufe, 1976). When extrapolating from atypical populations with the goal of informing developmental theory, however, it is important that a range of populations and conditions be considered. The study of a single psychopathological or risk process, such as Down syndrome in the example provided, may result in spurious conclusions if generalizations to normal development are based solely on that condition or disorder. However, if we were to examine a question (such as the nature of the relation between cognitive and emotional development) in the light of an entire spectrum of atypical or disordered modifications (e.g., autistic youngsters, infant offspring of caregivers with a major depressive or schizophrenic disorder), then we may be able to gain significant insight into the processes of development not generally achieved through sole reliance on studies of relatively homogeneous nondisordered populations.

The study of child maltreatment provides another example of how study of atypical populations can inform the understanding of normative development. Because of the extremes of dysfunction in parenting experienced by maltreated children, a broader range of psychological maladaptation is observed, emphasizing the criticality of more adaptive parenting practices in the attainment of adjustment in normative populations (Cicchetti, 1989). Moreover, an expansion of appreciation of developmental diversity may be achieved. For example, the study of attachment relationships in young maltreated children revealed a predominance of a new form of attachment organization, Type D or disorganized/disoriented attachment (Carlson, Cicchetti, Barnett, & Braunwald, 1989); this pattern of attachment organization, not articulated in normative populations, nevertheless led to reevaluations of how attachment in normative, as well as other atypical populations, has been studied (Main & Solomon, 1990).

Conversely, knowledge of normal developmental constraints that children of differing ages possess in the areas of cognition, social cognition, emotion and self-understanding, language, memory, and the like are critical to intervention efforts (Kendall, Lerner, & Craighead, 1984; Shirk & Russell, 1996; Toth & Cicchetti, in press). An inadequate understanding of children's developmental organization can result in the provision of interventions and/or the interpretation of child functioning that may result in faulty conclusions about the kinds of intervention to utilize or may misjudge children's abilities to derive benefit from a chosen intervention (Toth & Cicchetti, in press).

Diversity in Process and Outcome

Diversity in process and outcome are hallmarks of the developmental psychopathology perspective. With the acquisition of more knowledge about diversity in development, it has become increasingly recognized that the same rules of normal development do not necessarily exist for or apply to all children and families (e.g., Baldwin, Baldwin, & Cole, 1990). In this regard, the principles of equifinality and multifinality, derived from general systems theory, are relevant (Cicchetti & Rogosch, 1996a; von Bertanlanffy, 1968). Equifinality refers to the observation that a diversity of paths may lead to the same outcome (Sroufe, 1989). Accordingly, the breakdown, as well as the maintenance, of a system's function can occur in many ways, especially when taking into account environment-organism interactions and transactions. As such, instead of a singular primary pathway, a variety of developmental progressions may eventuate in a given disorder. In contrast, multifinality suggests that single pathways can lead to multiple outcomes. Thus, a particular adverse event should not necessarily be seen as contributing to the same psychopathological or nonpsychopathological outcome in every individual.

To provide an illustration, Sroufe (1989) reported that there are multiple pathways to attention-deficit/hyperactivity disorder (ADHD), one predominantly biological, the other largely attributable to insensitive caregiving. Similarly, Walker et al. (1996) found that there are a variety of developmental pathways that can precede the onset of schizophrenia in early adulthood.

With regard to multifinality, a major reason for the finding that any given pathway will eventuate in an array of outcomes rather than in a single linear endpoint is the concept of differentiation in development (Werner, 1957). Thus, as Robins (1966) reported, children diagnosed with conduct disorder may, as adults, develop antisocial personality, alcoholism, depression, or schizophrenia, or manifest normal functioning. Likewise, investigations of the correlates and consequences of maltreatment in childhood have consistently revealed diversity in process and outcome, despite similarities in the occurrence of abuse (Cicchetti & Toth, 1995). In discussing depressive disorder in childhood, Harrington, Rutter, and Fombonne (1996) concluded that there are several different kinds of depressive syndromes in children, with some being related to depressive disorders in adulthood and others better conceptualized as components of another psychopathological disorder.

Self-Organization

Although more distal historical factors and current influences are seen as important to the process of development, the individual is not merely a passive recipient of environmental input. Rather, active individual choice and self-organization increasingly have been viewed as exerting critical influences on development (Cicchetti & Tucker, 1994). The concept of self-organization, drawn from nonlinear dynamic systems theory, entails how individuals maintain continuity despite changing environmental circumstances, as well as how new features of the self, that appear discontinous with prior adaptation, may emerge (Schore, 1997). Early experience and prior levels of adaptation neither doom the individual to continued maladaptive functioning nor inoculate the individual from future problems in functioning. Moreover, because it has been demonstrated that not only can biological factors impact on psychological processes, but also that psychological experiences can modify brain structure, functioning, and organization (Cicchetti & Tucker, 1994; Eisenberg, 1995; Nelson & Bloom, 1997), across the life course developmental plasticity can take place through both biological and psychological self-organization. Thus, for example, Cicchetti and Rogosch's (1997a) finding that, over time, most maltreated children evidence at least some self-righting tendencies in the face of the extreme adversity experienced in their lives, attests to the strong biological/genetic and psychological self-strivings toward resilience that virtually all humans possess (Cicchetti & Rogosch, 1997b; Waddington, 1957). In contrast, the absence of such resilient self-strivings in a not insignificant number of maltreated children attests to the deleterious and pernicious impact that traumatic experiences can exert on the biological and psychological processes of self-organization (Cicchetti & Rogosch, 1997a).

Resilience

Developmental psychopathologists are as interested in individuals at high risk for the development of pathology who do not manifest it over time, as they are in individuals who develop an actual disorder (Sroufe & Rutter, 1984). Relatedly, developmental psychopathologists also are committed to understanding pathways to competent adaptation despite exposure to conditions of adversity (Cicchetti & Garmezy, 1993; Masten, Best, & Garmezy, 1990; Masten & Coatsworth, 1998; Rutter, 1990; Skuse, 1984). In addition, developmental psychopathologists emphasize the need to understand the functioning of individuals who, after having diverged onto deviant developmental pathways, resume more positive functioning and achieve adequate adaptation (Cicchetti & Richters, 1993).

Resilience has been operationalized as the individual's capacity for adapting successfully and functioning competently despite experiencing chronic adversity, or following exposure to prolonged or severe trauma (Masten et al., 1990). The roots of work on resilience can be traced back to prior research in diverse areas, including investigations of individuals with schizophrenia and their offspring, studies of the effects of persistent poverty, and work on coping with acute and chronic stressors (Cicchetti & Garmezy, 1993). By uncovering the mechanisms and processes that lead to competent adaptation despite the presence of adversity, developmental psychopathologists have helped to enhance the understanding of both normal development and psychopathology. Along with Rutter (1990), we concur that resilience does not exist statically in the "psychological chemistry of the moment" (p. 210). It is a dynamic process, and both biological and psychological processes of self-organization exert a vital role in how individuals fare when they are exposed to adversity.

Within this perspective, it is important that resilient functioning not be conceptualized as a static or traitlike condition, but as being in dynamic transaction with intra- and extraorganismic forces (Cicchetti, Rogosch, Lynch, & Holt, 1993; Egeland, Carlson, & Sroufe, 1993). Furthermore, research on the processes leading to resilient outcomes offers great promise as an avenue for facilitating the development of prevention and intervention strategies (Cicchetti & Toth, 1992; Toth & Cicchetti, in press). Through the examination of the proximal and distal processes and mechanisms that contribute to positive adaptation in situations that more typically eventuate in maladaptation, researchers and clinicians will be better prepared to devise ways of promoting competent outcomes in high-risk populations.

Contextual Influences

Developmental psychopathologists are devoting increasing attention toward contextual issues (see Boyce et al., 1998; Cicchetti & Aber, 1998). Despite the fact that there is growing awareness that contextual factors play an important role in defining phenomena as "psychopathological" (Richters & Cicchetti, 1993), there are vast differences in how the contexts for human development are conceptualized. To date, researchers interested in context tend to examine contextual influences at one (or perhaps two) levels of analysis, usually within the family. In charting children's and adults' trajectories along various developmental pathways, it is necessary to examine their functioning in multiple domains of development and across multiple settings (Luthar, 1991). Consequently, community-, institutional-, and societal-level influences on individual development are now beginning to be examined systematically.

As an illustration, Luthar and McMahon (1996) discovered that inner-city youth whose peer reputations were aggressive nonetheless were popular with their peers. Thus, in addition to the more typical pathway to peer popularity (e.g., prosocial behaviors, academic success), Luthar and McMahon identified a less typical pathway characterized by disruptive and aggressive behaviors and poor academic functioning. Congruent with Richters and Cicchetti's (1993) theoretical position, Luthar and McMahon hypothesized that within the crime-, violence-, and poverty-laden disenfranchised communities where these youth reside, aggressive behaviors that are viewed as deviant by the mainstream may be associated with prestige and high status among particular sociocultural groups.

Relatedly, empirical work demonstrates that social-contextual experiences can affect neurobiological structure and functioning (Cicchetti & Tucker, 1994; Eisenberg, 1995). For example, a number of investigators have demonstrated that a mother's emotional condition and, implicitly, her interactions with her infant may impact developing patterns of brain organization in the early years of life when sensitive periods for neurobiological growth most likely exist (Cicchetti & Tucker, 1994; Dawson, Grofer Klinger, Panagiotides, Hill, & Spieker, 1992; Edelman, 1987; Nelson & Bloom, 1997). Infants of depressed mothers have been shown to exhibit frontal lobe EEG asymmetries, suggestive of an emerging propensity toward greater negative affectivity (Field, Fox, Pickens, & Nawrocki, 1995), and quality of attachment among 14-month-old offspring of mothers with depressive symptomalogy also has been related to hemispheric activation asymmetries (Dawson et al., 1992). Similarly, among adults, exposure to severe trauma has been shown to influence brain structure, as evidenced by altered hippocampal volume in patients with combat-related posttraumatic stress disorder (Bremner et al., 1995).

DESIGN ISSUES

The aforementioned explication of selected principles of developmental psychopathology guide the conceptualization and conduct of empirical work in this field. We next survey some of the representative research designs and methodological/measurement issues that are utilized by developmental psychopathologists as they embark on investigations that address the questions that are central to the goals of the field.

Given the broad and integrative features of the developmental psychopathology perspective, encompassing transactions among multiple domains from diverse disciplines over the life course, no one study can capture completely the complexity involved in specifying the developmental process in its entirety. As a result, explicit choices must be made by researchers regarding the specific questions they wish to address, the processes that they seek to investigate, the assessment and measurement of those processes particularly over time, and the adequacy of strategies utilized to analyze their data. Employing up-front precision and parsimony of design to address specific questions will most likely yield more straightforward findings than reliance on statistical procedures to control for extraneous or confounding challenges to interpretation.

Ideally, research should be grounded solidly in a strong theoretical conceptualization. In turn, there must be fidelity between the theory the researcher is attempting to evaluate and the research methods and analyses employed in the study design. Research designs will be particularly strong if alternative theoretical predictions can be pitted against each other in the same study. Care must be taken that both positions are adequately conceptualized and measured for this comparison to be meaningful. Given the multiple systems involved in development and the emergence of psychopathology, it also is beneficial for research to incorporate more than one level of analysis into the study design. Exclusive focus within one domain or developmental system does not allow for an examination of how development may be affected across domains. For example, attention to phenomena at the cognitive level alone, without consideration of affective processes, may result in an incomplete appraisal of the phenomena under study (Cicchetti, Rogosch, Toth, & Spagnola, 1997; Cicchetti & Sroufe, 1976; Schneider-Rosen & Cicchetti, 1991). Research incorporating assessment at both the psychological and the biological level is particularly important. Understanding the biological effects of psychological experience or the psychological impact of biological processes will result in a more integrated perspective of development (Cicchetti & Tucker, 1994; Nelson & Bloom, 1997).

Developmental psychopathology research must be concerned with differentiating variation over time that results from development versus variation that is due to emerging individual differences. Ascertainment of disturbances in functioning needs to be considered within the context of what is normative for individuals within different developmental periods. Measures need to be appropriate for assessment within the developmental periods of interest; some measures may lose their usefulness as children progress to more advanced levels, and researchers need to plan for how comparable, developmentally appropriate measurements will be obtained across the time span under study.

Understanding continuity and discontinuity in development is of critical concern in developmental psychopathology, and conceptualizing how change and continuity are expected to be manifested in developmental investigations is centrally important. Developmental change occurs both quantitatively as well as qualitatively. Continuity in development needs to be considered not only from the levels of particular behavior observed but also from the meaning of that behavior, given the developmental level of the individual. Homotypic continuity, involving the same behavioral presentation of an underlying developmental process at subsequent age periods, may indeed be rare (Kagan, 1971). For example, toileting problems in a 2-year-old versus a 16-year-old represent very different phenomena. Alternatively, continuity of developmental process may in fact be represented by very different behavioral manifestations, that is, heterotypic continuity. The concept of coherence in development (Sroufe, 1979) suggests that there may be heterotypic continuity in terms of persistence in the meaning and organization of behavior despite changing behavioral manifestations. For example, Sroufe (1997) illustrates that children with avoidant attachments in infancy, exhibiting withdrawal from caregivers and a muting of affective expression, might be expected to be withdrawn and affectless later in development. In contrast, these infants with insecure avoidant attachments to their caregivers tend to be aggressive and bullying later in childhood. Continuity in terms of alienation and lack of empathic connection is observed rather than similarity of behavioral expression. For infants with resistant attachments to their caregivers, who tend to express angry rejection toward mothers and have difficulty being comforted, a later pattern of anxiety problems rather than oppositional and defiant behavior is observed. Coherence and continuity in developmental process is indicated by chronic vigilance and uncertainty regarding environmental and interpersonal expectancies, although the behavioral manifestation is of a different form than observed previously. Thus, because of the potential for heterotypic continuity, developmental psychopathology researchers must be able to formulate explicitly how continuities and discontinuities in development will be exhibited.

Within the framework of these various developmental research designs, developmental psychopathologists are interested in learning from developmental variations that ensue from children who are exposed to different adverse conditions. Because there are limits to experimental manipulation that can be invoked with humans, true experimental designs with random assignment of individuals to different risk exposures (e.g., lead levels) cannot be conducted. Therefore, so-called experiments of nature in which risk exposure occurs by accident or circumstance, not by design, are useful for elucidating the understanding of developmental processes and mechanisms. These natural experiments are important for differentiating among possible mechanisms that offer alternative accounts of a particular array of outcomes. Because pathological conditions such as brain injury, mental disorder, catastrophes, and being reared in a malignant home environment enable scientists to isolate the components of the integrated system, their investigation sheds light on the normal structure of the system. Often, the investigation of a system in its smoothly operating normal or healthy state does not afford the opportunity to comprehend the interrelations among its component subsystems (Chomsky, 1968).

RESEARCH DESIGNS

Because those conducting research in developmental psychopathology are centrally interested in the manifestations of psychopathology at different periods across the life course, as well as the processes that lead to those outcomes, research designs that address developmental variation over time are of special significance. Each type of research design that incorporates contrasts across developmental periods has inherent strengths and limitations, yet each is valuable depending on the questions being addressed and the stage of research that those questions entail. In studying time and the effects of development over time, developmentalists are confronted with what has been called the "age, period, cohort" problem (Mason & Feinberg, 1985; Schaie, 1965). This problem involves the confidence with which the researcher is able to attribute observed changes to developmental change. In some circumstances, rather than variation being due to development, it may be more a consequence of the age cohort to which a child belongs. Differences in performance between children born in 1980 versus 1990 may result from different experiences encountered by the two cohorts in historical time (e.g., different teaching methods utilized during the early school years for the two cohorts; access to computers). Further, period effects also may confound interpretation of developmental effects. Period effects result from different relations being obtained in the specific year in which data are obtained. These may result from secular differences at varying periods of assessment. For example, differential availability of drugs in different years as a result of variation in interdiction efforts or due to changing popularity of different substances could result in differences in usage levels depending on the year in which assessments are made. Although developmentalists are eager to ascribe developmental interpretations to differences involving age, cohort and period effects can diminish the confidence with which these conclusions can be made. Different developmental research designs encounter varying degrees of ability to differentiate age, period, and cohort effects, as discussed with the following types of developmental research designs.

Cross-Sectional Designs

Cross-sectional research designs involve assessment of groups of individuals and processes of interest at discrete ages or developmental periods. For example, a study might examine the relations between family conflict and oppositional-defiant behavior among groups of children at different ages to determine the extent to which family conflict differentially may relate to oppositional behavior at progressive developmental periods. During early phases of investigation, cross-sectional studies may be informative in revealing age-related patterns of variation in the processes under examination. The advantages of cross-sectional designs at early phases in a research program are that results are obtained quickly compared to longitudinal investigations and are less costly in terms of time commitment and resources. However, with cross-sectional studies it is not possible to examine developmental change within individuals, which is a primary interest of developmental psychopathologists. Moreover, it also is not possible to differentiate cohort and period effects from developmental effects in cross-sectional designs.

Prospective Longitudinal Designs

Perhaps the most powerful developmental design involves the prospective longitudinal design in which groups of individuals are studied repeatedly as they progress through subsequent periods of development. This design allows for the examination of continuity and change within individuals over time, rather than having to infer developmental changes from age-group comparisons.

The drawbacks of prospective longitudinal designs are that substantial resources are necessary to follow and track individuals over many years of development. Depending on the span of development under consideration, the studies will necessarily last as long as it takes for participants to age through the years being studied. For example, to investigate developmental processes from first grade to high school graduation, one would need to devote a 12-year time interval to data collection, expending considerable time and resources before the questions one set out to answer could be addressed. In the ensuing period, the questions of interest may change and the measurement strategies may become obsolete. Despite the level of information that longitudinal studies provide, problems with cohort and period effects remain. Because a single cohort is being followed, one cannot be certain whether patterns of change and continuity are generalizable to other age cohorts or whether they characterize the specific cohort under study. In terms of period effects, data are collected for specific ages in specific years, and it cannot be ruled out that there are particular relations obtained because of the year of measurement. Moreover, if the form of psychopathology under investigation is rare or does not have a typical onset until later periods of development (e.g., schizophrenia), the main outcome of interest may occur too seldom despite the major investment of time and resources (see, e.g., Sameroff, Seifer, & Zax, 1982). Thus, prospective longitudinal studies must be carefully planned and executed. Despite the demands of this research design, prospective longitudinal studies are essential for evaluating the long-term course of development and the unfolding of diversity in outcomes.

Follow-Up Studies

To circumvent the time requirements of prospective longitudinal studies, follow-up studies may have the potential to yield valuable information on developmental processes. Follow-up studies involve assessment at the current time of a group of individuals for whom prior data are available from earlier periods of development. For example, records of children seen in treatment may be used to establish early patterns of functioning, and these children can be assessed currently to determine patterns of continuity and change from the data attained at an earlier period in development (Robins, 1966).

Follow-up research will be meaningful if the earlier records available are uniform and consistent in terms of the information they contain, if all or most children in the original pool are available for later follow-up, if biases in the record data can be made explicit, and if it is possible to determine intervening circumstances of the life course (e.g., history of schooling, subsequent periods of disorder, quality of relationships) between the period of record data and current assessment. Unfortunately, meeting these requirements is difficult and the research has little ability to rectify problems in the original data source, particularly because these records are likely not to have been established with stringent research requirements in mind.

Follow-Back Studies

These studies also strive to gain a longitudinal perspective by reducing the time demands of prospective studies. Individuals of a specified group, for example, a sample of persons diagnosed with schizophrenia, are delineated, and efforts to obtain earlier record data on these individuals and appropriate comparison groups are undertaken. Representativeness of the target sample, as well as of the comparisons, is a critical concern that may bias any potential findings. Also, all of the problems potentially detracting from follow-up studies apply for follow-back studies. Nonetheless, follow-back studies may provide important insights that may be difficult to obtain with other approaches. Walker and her colleagues (Walker, Savoie, & Davis, 1994) utilized a follow-back design for patients diagnosed with schizophrenia. Home movies made of these individuals in childhood were sought long before evidence of schizophrenia was discernible. Walker and her colleagues were able to identify an array of subtle neurodevelopmental anomalies (e.g., dystonic posturing, spontaneous movement abnormalities) observable in the childhood home movies of the schizophrenic adults that suggested early developmental aberrations that were potential precursors to later schizophrenia. Despite a range of potential limitations in this follow-back study (e.g., lack of home movies for all patients, potential socioeconomic bias determining which patients' parents made home movies), this approach allowed for a window on early development in a clinical group that would not have been readily attained in prospective research because of the low base rate of schizophrenia that would ensue in any sample targeted in childhood, unless the sample were prohibitively large (also see Garmezy & Streitman, 1974).

Accelerated Longitudinal Designs

Also known as cohort-sequential designs, accelerated longitudinal studies are designed to reduce the time required for prospective longitudinal studies by examining different age groups for short-term prospective periods (Anderson, 1995). For example, four age cohorts of children ages 5 to 8 years at baseline could be seen for three subsequent annual assessments, thereby ending with data for the youngest group at age 8 and for the oldest group at age 11. Thus, data are obtained covering the age periods from 5 through 11, a six-year span but requiring three years of data collection. Comparison of data for the different cohorts at the age of 8 allows for the determination of cohort effects; in the absence of cohort effects, developmental differences can be attributed, although period effects are not ruled out. Further elaboration of this design to incorporate a second wave of baseline data collection and subsequent follow-up beginning at a later point in time would allow the researcher to determine whether period effects were operative. Thus, these types of accelerated longitudinal designs are advantageous for differentiating age, cohort, and period effects that are variously confounded in other research designs.

High-Risk Designs

Similar to studies of children exposed to toxic or traumatic experiences, studies of children in "high-risk" groups, contrasting them with children who are not exposed to the risk factors, also provide naturally occurring circumstances for examining how various environmental/experiential and biological factors influence the course of development. The study of child maltreatment is one such example. In this research, children who have experienced abuse and/or neglect are compared with children who have not been maltreated but who have experienced similar levels of social adversity. Thus, the extreme and adverse parent-child relationships experienced by maltreated children provide an opportunity to examine how disturbed parent-child relationships thwart optimal development and contribute to psychopathological outcomes (Emery & Laumann-Billings, 1998; Rogosch, Cicchetti, Shields, & Toth, 1995). The effects of aberrant family experiences on biological processes also can be investigated (Hart, Gunnar, & Cicchetti, 1996; Pollak, Cicchetti, Klorman, & Brumaghim, 1997). Children who have experienced other forms of family disruption such as parental unemployment or divorce also provide important insights into environmental factors in the emergence of behavioral disturbance.

Another prominent area of high-risk studies includes investigations of the development of offspring of parents with different forms of psychopathology, for example, schizophrenia, manic-depressive illness, major depressive disorder, alcoholism, substance abuse, and/or personality disorders. Children in such families are at increased likelihood (risk) of being exposed to aberrations in normative child-rearing experiences and relationships; these children also face heightened genetic risk for the disorders evidenced by their parents. Studying the development of offspring of parents with mental disorders can elucidate intrafamilial processes that may contribute to psychopathological outcomes in these children. Such divergences in normative child-rearing experiences and their linkages to emergent psychopathology may represent processes contributing to negative outcomes for children generally, but more prominently in families of parents with psychopathology because of the increased likelihood in such families of the adverse familial process under consideration. For example, marital conflict or parenting inconsistency may be intensified in families with depressed or alcoholic parents, and although these family factors are more prominent in families with disordered parents, they constitute family processes that are not specific to the parental disorder (Downey & Coyne, 1990). In this way, offspring studies can contribute to an understanding of development in both normative and atypical populations. Alternatively, some adverse family processes that are evident in families with disturbed parents may constitute unique conditions that occur primarily in these atypical families (e.g., communication deviance in families with schizophrenic parents; Wynne & Singer, 1963) and contribute to dysfunction in the offspring. Moreover, aberrant intrafamilial processes in these high-risk families (e.g., high negative expressed emotion in schizophrenic families; Vaughn & Leff, 1976) may constitute the environmental conditions in which genetic liabilities for disorder are actualized.

Studies of the offspring of parents with psychopathology also can be informative in terms of understanding psychobiological and genetic components of disorder. Identification of trait markers of disorder (atypicalities that are present before as well as during episodes of disorder versus those that are only present during episodes of disorder, i.e., state markers; Puig-Antich, 1986) in offspring of disordered parents constitute an important contribution to understanding potential genetic contributions to disorder. For example, detection of possible trait markers, such as altered patterns of alcohol metabolism in offspring of alcoholic parents or anomalies in sleep architecture or cortisol regulation in children of depressed parents, particularly before the emergence of disorder in the offspring, would provide valuable information about how genetic vulnerability for disorder may be transmitted. Differentiation of offspring who did and did not exhibit the marker and subsequent examination of differential risks for disordered outcomes also would help to specify which offspring were in fact at heightened genetic risk. Thus, studies of the offspring of parents with mental disorders provide many opportunities for examining the complex interplay of environmental and genetic processes in the emergence of psychopathology.

Behavior-Genetic Designs

Genetic and environmental factors are ubiquitously involved in behavioral development generally. Consequently, understanding the role of genetics and environment and their intricate transactions in the development of psychopathology are crucial concerns for developmental psychopathologists. Behavior-genetic designs offer strategies to disaggregate genetic and environmental contributions to psychopathological development at the etiologic level, and investigation of both sources of influence conjointly contributes to a more powerful means of delineating processes of pathogenesis (Moldin, this volume). These designs capitalize on contrasts of different family contexts in which varying degrees of genetic similarity and/or environmental similarity can be compared. For example, in adoption studies, the development of siblings (who share 50% of their genetic makeup) who are reared in different families are contrasted with siblings reared in the same family. Contrasts in similarity between those siblings reared apart versus those reared together allow for differentiation of the degree of heritable versus environmental contributions to behavioral outcomes. Families of remarried parents with children from prior partnerships provide another family situation in which contrasts can be made of similarities and differences between genetically unrelated stepsiblings versus full siblings raised in the same family environment. Cross-fostering designs involve adoption of children of parents with a specified psychopathology into families in which parents do not have the disorder under study, and examining whether the adoptees have the same degree of risk for pathological development as offspring reared by parents with the disorder.

Twin studies utilize the difference in degree of shared genetic makeup between monozygotic (MZ, 100%) and dizygotic (DZ, 50%) twins to contrast these twin groups in terms of similarities and differences in the development of behavioral characteristics and psychopathological outcomes. Given the same rearing environments, greater similarity between MZ twins as compared to DZ twins implies greater genetic influence. Behavior-genetic designs using twin samples contrast correlations between MZ and DZ twins to establish heritability estimates, as well as estimates of the degree of environmental influence.

The partitioning of genetic and environmental contributions to variance in outcomes is only a beginning step to understanding the complex interplay of genetics and environment in the development of psychopathology (Rende & Plomin, 1995; Rutter et al., 1997). For example, there has been growing recognition of nonshared environmental effects experienced by siblings despite growing up in the same family. These nonshared environmental effects may involve unique experiences of individual siblings that are not experienced by other siblings (e.g., different stressors, different experiences in extrafamilial contexts) and intrafamilial processes that tend to emphasize and encourage differentiation between sibling pairs rather than similarities, thereby contributing to sibling differences (Plomin & Daniels, 1987). Moreover, genetic and environmental effects often are not independent (Scarr & McCartney, 1983). Gene-environment correlations and gene-environment interactions are cases in point. With gene-environment correlations, genes influence the types of environments the individual experiences. For example, with passive gene-environment correlations, genes influence the type of environment experienced; that is, parental genes (shared with offspring) may influence the types of rearing environments the parents provide. For example, a more intellectually stimulating learning environment in part may be determined by parents whose genes contribute to their greater intelligence. Evocative gene-environment correlations involve genetically determined characteristics contributing to the types of responses an individual elicits from others. For example, an impulsive, energetic child will evoke different types of responses from others than a shy, inhibited child. The differential responses from others will contribute an environmental effect on ongoing development. With active gene-environmental correlations, the environment experienced is in part determined by actions and selection of the individual. As one illustration, individuals high in sensation seeking will likely select activities and similar individuals consistent with high stimulation. The environments thus selected will in turn promote differential experiences and interpersonal relationships.

Gene-environment interactions involve another sort of interplay between genetics and environment. Certain environments may provide the necessary conditions in which a genetic propensity can be realized. If the particular environment is not experienced, then the genetic tendency is not actualized. For example, phenylketonuria (PKU), a genetic disorder typically resulting in mental retardation, only becomes manifested based on diet. If children with this genetic condition are restricted to low phenylalanine diets, retardation does not occur.

Quantitative genetics provides an important approach for differentiating whether psychopathology constitutes an extreme mode of functioning on a normal distribution or a disordered condition that is discontinuous from normal variation in adapation. For example, is clinical depression an extreme of normal sadness or a distinct disease entity? If quantitative (dimensional) data are obtained on probands, probands' relatives, and the population at large, then it is possible to assess the extent to which the genetic and environmental etiologies of abnormality differ from the genetic and environmental etiologies of normality. If group familiality differs from individual familiality, then this would provide strong evidence that the etiology of the disorder in question differs from the etiology of the normal distribution of variability. If, on the other hand, the two types of familiality are similar, then the results would be consistent with the hypothesis that psychopathology is etiologically part of the normal distribution (see Plomin, Rende, & Rutter, 1991; Rende & Plomin, 1995, for an elaboration).

Prevention and Intervention Designs

Efforts to prevent the emergence of psychopathology or to ameliorate its effects also can be informative for understanding processes involved in psychopathological development (Cicchetti & Toth, 1992; Kellam & Rebok, 1992; Koretz, 1991; Tolan, this volume). For example, if the developmental course is altered as a result of the implementation of preventive interventions and risk for negative outcomes is reduced, then prevention research helps to specify processes that are involved in the emergence of psychopathology or other negative developmental outcomes. As such, prevention research can be conceptualized as true experiments in altering the course of development, thereby providing insight into etiology and pathogenesis of disordered outcomes. Prevention research is based on theoretical models of how risk conditions are related to adverse outcomes, positing processes that link the risk condition to the negative outcome. For example, poverty and single and teenage parenthood constitute risks for adverse family functioning, that is, child abuse and neglect, increased negative developmental outcomes, and welfare dependence (Coley & Chase-Lansdale, 1998; McLoyd, 1998). Olds and his colleagues (Olds et al., 1997) posited that maternal isolation, lack of parenting skills, and poor understanding of child development were processes mediating or linking the risk conditions to negative outcomes. A pre- and postnatal home visitation program was implemented to reduce these intervening processes, and the long-term effects of the intervention have been studied. The effectiveness of the intervention helps to establish the importance of the specified mediators as processes explaining how the risk factors contribute to negative outcomes. Kellam and colleagues (Kellam, Rebok, Ialongo, et al., 1994; Kellam, Rebok, Mayer, et al., 1994), in studying risk for negative outcomes among predominately poor urban children, identified early disruptive classroom behavior as a process contributing to school failure and conduct disorder, and poor achievement (specifically, in reading) as a factor contributing to heightened depressive symptomatology. Interventions were implemented to decrease classroom disruptive behavior and to improve reading skills, with the goal of reducing conduct disorder and depression symptomatology, respectively. In summary, prevention research cannot only lead to support or lack of support for theoretical formulations accounting for the development of psychopathology, but also can contribute to the knowledge base of strategies that can be implemented to reduce psychopathology and promote positive adaptation.

Intervention studies also can be informative for understanding the developmental contributions to psychopathology. Interventions that are designed to alter processes that are theoretically conceptualized to relate to the disorder or dysfunction under investigation can shed light on the etiological processes that have contributed to the development of the psychopathology (see Gaynor, Baird, & Nelson-Gray, this volume; Kendall, Flannery-Schroeder, & Ford, this volume; Stiles, Honos-Webb, & Knobloch, this volume). Comparisons of treated individuals to normative groups on diverse aspects of normative functioning provide a stringent test of treatment effectiveness, beyond symptom remission, and knowledge of normative variation on various indicators of adaptation is vital for informing such evaluations (Kendall & Grove, 1988). Moreover, knowledge of developmental norms, appreciation of how developmental level may vary within the same age group, attention to the effects of developmental transitions and reorganizations, and understanding of the factors that are influential within different developmental periods are essential features to incorporate into the design and implementation of treatment studies, to enhance the potential for optimal treatment effectiveness (Holmbeck & Kendall, 1991; Holmbeck & Updegrove, 1995; Kendall, 1991; Toth & Cicchetti, in press).

Variable-Centered versus Person-Centered Designs

Much research in developmental psychopathology has involved designs contrasting groups of individuals at the level of the variable. Differences in the mean levels of functioning for groups and investigation of processes influencing the group-level differences are traditionally the major focus of research. Although this standard approach is important for revealing general developmental phenomena that apply to the population broadly, it does not reveal specific information about the development of individuals. Concentration on average level performance of groups as a means to understanding functioning of individuals tends to regard divergences from the norm as error variance. However, the principles of equifinality and multifinality in developmental psychopathology necessitate an appreciation that the same outcome can be derived from different pathways and that there are multiple outcomes that may eventuate from a common origin (Cicchetti & Rogosch, 1996a). Differentiation of the unique and diverse pathways involved in the development of psychopathology increasingly calls for different approaches to research design and analysis that move beyond examination of average patterns across a group to characterize individual functioning. Specifically, designs that incorporate an emphasis on tracking development within individuals, rather than concentrating on the average of group members, are likely to allow for greater precision in delineating alternative pathways and processes involved in psychopathological development.

Examination of subgroup differences within a larger outcome group constitutes one way that capturing diversity in process and outcome can be incorporated into research strategies. For example, comorbidity between diagnostic categories of child psychopathology is a common finding. Brady and Kendall (1992) review studies on the comorbidity of childhood anxiety and depressive disorders, noting comorbidty rates ranging from 0.8% to 61.9%. Children who were comorbid for anxiety and depression tended to be older and to have anxiety symptoms precede depressive symptoms. Lack of attention to the diagnostic heterogeneity that exists in, for instance, a sample of adolescents with conduct disorder may obscure important findings. Adolescents who are comorbid for conduct disorder and depression may be very different in terms of the processes contributing to their presentation than other adolescents who have conduct disorder alone (Cicchetti & Toth, 1998a). Analyses of profiles for individuals across multiple dimensions or domains of functioning are likely to be informative for delineating different developmental pathways that may be obscured when group variables are averaged or considered in isolation. To illustrate, Stattin and Magnusson (1996) draw attention to the phenomenon of problem aggregation in predicting adult criminality. At the variable-centered level, a variety of factors were found to predict later disturbance. However, in utilizing an approach to cluster together individuals with similar profiles across multiple features of risk, it was shown that the individuals who were truly in jeopardy of future disturbance had numerous risk factors in common. Any risk factor in isolation was a poor predictor of outcome. Thus, aggregation of many problems in a relatively small group of individuals can result in group-level differences that are misleading, as well as obscure the variation in developmental pathways exhibited by different subgroups of individuals. Consequently, developmental psychopathologists increasingly are interested in designing their research anticipating diversity in process and outcome and, in so doing, attending more explicitly to patterns of individual growth and development.

SAMPLING ISSUES

Developmental psychopathologists need to be keenly aware of sampling issues and how decisions made may impact upon the results obtained. The choices made in the samples recruited will affect the extent to which findings from a study are generalizable and to which groups they are generalizable. Numerous selection factors can operate to restrict the extent to which findings are applicable to other groups. For example, samples relying on subjects to self-identify for participation (rather than utilization of recruitment efforts to contact individuals in the population who specified sample criteria) may be biased in terms of factors that contribute to individuals volunteering for participation. For risk groups (e.g., depressed mothers, substance abusers), selection factors may operate such that less impaired individuals in the overall group targeted may be more likely to present for participation in research, whereas more impaired individuals within the risk group, feeling more overwhelmed, may be disinclined to participate. Obtained samples will thus not include the range of variation existing in the larger population of interest. Studies using high school students also illustrate this problem. Students who have dropped out of school or who are institutionalized because of mental health or delinquency problems will not be included in such samples relying on high school attendance for inclusion. As a result, individuals who may be of particular interest because of their negative developmental outcomes will not be included in the obtained sample. Other sampling strategies that rely, for example, on contacting participants by telephone will overlook families who do not have a telephone, thereby failing to include a group that may be extremely impoverished and/or socially isolated. Similar biases may emerge in recruitment of nonrisk comparison control groups. Reliance on volunteers may introduce bias in terms of who volunteers. This may include only individuals who are better functioning, thus providing an inadequate basis for comparison. Alternatively, some individuals who are in need of help may volunteer in an effort to make a connection with psychological researchers whom they may perceive as being able to offer assistance. Other samples of convenience, such as college students, represent a narrow segment of the population and thus are likely to provide a very selective sample with restriction in range on many attributes compared to the population at large.

Incorporation of epidemiological procedures for recruitment of research samples is an effective way to reduce selection bias and obtain more representative samples. Such strategies require more active effort on the part of researchers to seek out their samples rather than rely on samples of convenience. For example, using birth records of all children born in a geographic area as a source to identify a study population and randomly selecting from this pool would be a strategy to ensure a more representative sample. For risk conditions, other procedures to identify targeted cases more broadly could be used. For example, in studying the effects of parental alcoholism, rather than relying on volunteer samples, recruitment of families with a high likelihood of parental alcoholism through utilizing arrests for driving while intoxicated would be an active strategy by the researcher to obtain a broader community sample of families with an alcoholic parent (Chassin, Rogosch, & Barrera, 1991; Zucker & Fitzgerald, 1991). Representativeness of this sample could be ascertained through determination of refusal rates of targeted families, with some provision for thus determining factors that could contribute to selective recruitment of participants. In addition, incorporation of epidemiological approaches for recruiting nonrisk comparison cases is equally important. Efforts to recruit comparison cases from the same neighborhoods with similar intrafamilial and socioeconomic composition will help to reduce biases that contextual variation may have on the subsequent differences between groups that will be examined.

Developmental psychopathologists are explicitly interested in the effects of context on development, and contextual considerations are critically important in deriving sampling plans. Contextual issues may influence the patterns of relations that are obtained among process variables and outcomes. For example, effectiveness of parenting styles and their relation to child competence and maladjustment varies depending on the socioeconomic/sociocultural context; authoritative parenting styles valued in middle-class samples have been shown not to be optimal among low-income families (Baldwin et al., 1990). Thus, researchers must be aware of contextual influences operating in samples that are selected and the impact of context on the generalizations that may be made from findings obtained (see papers in Cicchetti & Aber, 1998).

MEASUREMENT ISSUES

Continuous versus Categorical Approaches

Conceptualizing psychopathology historically has taken two different approaches. Psychiatry, drawing from a disease model, has emphasized distinct categories of psychopathology in the form of psychiatric diagnoses. These diagnostic categories are regarded as discrete in content and organization from normal modes of functioning. A clear discontinuity between normal and abnormal is thus posited. Diagnoses have the advantage of describing relatively uniform groups of individuals who share similar constellations of symptoms. As a result, diagnostic approaches can contribute to precision in how researchers specify distinct problems under investigation. In contrast, clinical psychology has emphasized the normal distribution of characteristics and has conceptualized psychopathology in terms of extreme deviation on a continuum of individual differences. As such, this approach recognizes gradations in functioning between mental health and psychopathology. Cut points on such continua can be established to demarcate normal from abnormal levels of functioning. Continuous approaches are better able to delineate patterns of adaptation across multiple dimensions, resulting in a more complex depiction of individual strengths and weaknesses in functioning than is possible with a presence versus absence categorical system. Both the categorical and continuous approaches provide complementary levels of information, and, depending on the questions of interest, the different approaches may be more or less well suited to the problem at hand.

In studying the development of psychopathology in children, and particularly in very young children, obtaining direct and comprehensive information from the child on his or her functioning is marked by considerable difficulty. Children are less able than adults to report on their symptoms because they lack the cognitive capacities to abstract and characterize their patterns of functioning, particularly over time (Achenbach, 1991). Moreover, children may not have a recognition of disturbance in their functioning, although such difficulties may be apparent to adults. Additionally, adults, rather than children themselves, usually are the source of identification of child problems and the agents to initiate mental health evaluation and treatment. Consequently, researchers cannot solely rely on child self-report of symptomatology, particularly with young children, and they must look to other methods of assessment.

Parents and teachers, because they have the opportunity to observe and interact with children in varied contexts over time, constitute invaluable sources for gaining broad assessments of child functioning. Standardized questionnaire measures, notably the Child Behavior Checklist (CBCL/4–18) (Achenbach, 1991) with comparable forms for parents and teachers (as well as for preadolescent and older youth), provide a means to evaluate broad dimensions of child maladaptation and psychopathology. Such measures are based on a continuous conceptualization of child mental health and psychopathology, and normative data from general and treatment populations allow for the establishment of criteria for clinical levels of disturbance. The perspectives of mothers, fathers, teachers, and older youth can provide a differentiated appraisal of adaptation across contexts of functioning and relationships.

In contrast to dimensional approaches to psychopathology, semistructured interviews also have been developed to evaluate whether children meet diagnostic criteria for diverse psychiatric diagnoses. Examples of such interviews include the Child and Adolescent Psychiatric Assessment (CAPA; Angold et al., 1995), the Diagnostic Interview Schedule for Children (DISC; Shaffer et al., 1996), the Diagnostic Interview for Children and Adolescents (DICA; Reich & Welner, 1988), the Schedule for Affective Disorders and Schizophrenia–Child version (K-SADS; Puig-Antich & Chambers, 1986), the Child Assessment Schedule (CAS; Hodges, 1993), and the Anxiety Disorders Interview Schedule for Children (ADIS-C, Silverman & Nelles, 1988). These measures rely on interviewing parents and/or older children, and structured questions inquire about the presence/absence of symptoms required for *Diagnostic and Statistical Manual of Mental Disorders (DSM)* diagnoses, including duration and impairment criteria. Thus, these interviews provide researchers with standardized tools to ascertain categorical appraisals of whether children meet diagnostic criteria for a spectrum of diverse mental disorders.

These continuous and categorical approaches relying on parental report provide one level of information on child functioning. Adult observers have more ready access to overt, externalizing symptoms (e.g., hyperactivity, oppositional behavior), but may have less certainty regarding aspects of children's internal experience (e.g., depression, anxiety) (Loeber, Green, Lahey, & Stouthamer-Loeber, 1989). In contrast, the older child can reveal more about internalizing symptoms, but be more reluctant to acknowledge or recognize his or her own conduct difficulties. Thus, it is advantageous for researchers to incorporate multiple informants and measurement strategies to attain a comprehensive appraisal of child psychopathology.

Observational methods also can be valuable in the determination of more discrete forms of behavioral disturbance. There is a long tradition of classroom behavioral observation, particularly for hyperactive, impulsive, and aggressive behaviors. This level of information can be valuable to contrast with information reported by adult observers, particularly when there may be bias or distortion by observers based on conflictual relationships with the child.

In addition to methods for assessing psychopathology, developmental psychopathologists utilize a spectrum of other measurement strategies from the psychological, biological, and sociological arenas to investigate specific processes of interest in relation to psychopathology. As with the limitations of self-report in the ascertainment of psychopathology, methods for investigations involving young children must employ innovative measurement strategies to capture constructs of interest. Although parental report data on such topics as family relations, temperament, and child experiences can provide one level of information, the researcher must be aware of potential biases in parental report, particularly if parents also provide the source of data on child functioning. Relations among constructs may result from consistency in the constructions of the reporter (i.e., common method variance) rather than the phenomena themselves. Thus, observational and experimental procedures are valuable in developmental

psychopathology research for gaining access to independent measurements of constructs of interest. Videotaped observations of interactions between mothers and their
young children can be coded for a variety of constructs (e.g., parenting behaviors,
mother-child communication, child affect regulation, and conflict resolution, to name
a few). Such interactional tasks can be structured to facilitate capturing specific issues
of interest.

Measurement Equivalence

Within a developmental perspective, evaluation of measurement equivalence at different stages of development is critical, particularly in longitudinal investigations. If the
manifestation of a construct of interest changes over the course of development, utilizing the same measurement strategy at successive periods of development would not
adequately capture the phenomenon under consideration. For example, the Strange Situation procedure (Ainsworth, Blehar, Waters, & Wall, 1978) involves a specified sequence of maternal and infant separations and reunions, designed to activate the child's
attachment system. Coding of videotapes of infants and young children in the Strange
Situation to assess individual differences in attachment has resulted in a wealth of information about early child emotional organization and development (Sroufe, 1996).
The developmental appropriateness of the Strange Situation also is noteworthy. The
coding of the Strange Situation is closely tied to the child's age. As children progress
from infancy through toddlerhood and the preschool years, the meaning of specific behaviors observed in the Strange Situation changes. Consequently, coding systems to assess quality of attachment organization beyond infancy needed to be developed to
accurately capture these newly emerging behavioral strategies (Cassidy & Marvin,
1992; Crittenden, 1992). Later in childhood, the Strange Situation does not effectively
activate the attachment system, and thus is no longer as useful for assessing attachment
organization. Longer separation-reunion procedures, child self-report measures, and attachment interviews have been developed and validated to assess attachment organization at later developmental periods (Cicchetti, Toth, & Lynch, 1995). The use of the
Strange Situation procedure highlights the importance of evaluating the developmental
appropriateness of measures, and the changing utility of measurement strategies necessary to assess the same constructs at different stages of development.

DATA ANALYTIC PROCEDURES

Researchers in developmental psychopathology typically utilize traditional multivariate statistics to analyze their data sets (see Farrell, this volume). Path analysis and
structural equation modeling have increasingly been employed, particularly in longitudinal designs, and these techniques have many advantages in terms of their sophistication for handling measurement error and testing models of complex interrelations
among multiple constructs. Nevertheless, these techniques are primarily variable
oriented. In structural equation modeling, for example, the object of study becomes
covariance matrices and relations among variables. The person and individual patterns of adaptation over time can become lost, and, despite their elegance, the meaning

of findings for different individuals, as opposed to an idealized average individual, can become obscure. Structural equation models do not address the individual-level processes that contribute to relations among variables (Rogosa, 1995). Moreover, Richters (1997) has criticized many of the underlying assumptions of statistical inference in developmental psychopathology and in psychology more broadly (see also, Cohen, 1990; Meehl, 1978). Research and data analytic approaches that retain a focus on the individual are needed. Person-centered approaches are less well developed than variable-oriented approaches. However, future development in this area holds promise for increasing the fidelity between developmental theory and research method. We next highlight a few exemplars of person-oriented approaches and how these strategies have particular relevance for developmental psychopathology.

Cluster and Pattern Approaches

Variable-oriented statistical strategies tend to examine variables in isolation, rather than how individuals vary across multiple dimensions. In so doing, the diversity of patterns of adaptation and maladaptation within individuals may not be realized. Moreover, attention to individuals who do not conform to mean group patterns may be particularly informative for developmental psychopathology and not merely nuisance outliers resulting from measurement error. Cluster analytic techniques have potential value for identifying different patterns of adaptation among individuals across multiple domains, thereby revealing differential patterns of organization of component constructs (Bergman & Magnusson, 1997). Individuals who share similar profiles across constructs are clustered together, and then comparisons of the different pattern groups that emerge may be critically important for understanding diversity in the processes leading to these different patterns of organization. Delineation of distinct patterns of adaptation across multiple dimensions may provide insight into differential modes of adaptation that result from the operation of dynamic systems over time. With developmental data collected over time, grouping similar individuals together who share common characteristics can be approached in two ways. First, the longitudinal pattern or trajectory across multiple variables and time points can be the basis of classification to derive developmental types. Alternatively, individuals can be clustered based on similar features at each point in a longitudinal assessment, and then linkages between the derived types over time can be examined in terms of continuity and discontinuity. A variety of cluster analytic approaches are available. Some approaches allow overlap between clusters or a residual group that does not classify everyone, allowing for a small group that is not adequately force classified. Various approaches can incorporate both continuous and categorical measures.

Configurational frequency analysis (CFA) is a newer, promising approach that identifies all possible configurations across domains of interest. For example, with three dichotomous variables (i.e., presence or absence of three risk variables), eight potential combinations of these constructs are possible. Based on the expected and observed frequencies of the constructs, CFA identifies configurations that occur more often than chance, known as *types*. Additionally, *antitypes* are identified as cases that occur less often than expected by chance. Identification of types can be useful in discerning patterns that emerge with regularity, suggesting a convergence of influences frequently eventuating in such outcomes. In contrast, antitypes reveal unusual outcomes that emerge from a different, more atypical constellation of determinants. An example of an application of this approach is provided by Zucker and his colleagues (Zucker, Ellis, Fitzgerald, Bingham, & Sanford, 1996), who used CFA to differentiate divergent life course patterns of alcoholism and antisociality, linking the resulting pattern of types and antitypes to differential social adaptational and psychopathological outcomes. The results illustrate the more complex and rich understanding that can be achieved with a more person-centered approach.

Latent Growth Curve Modeling

For longitudinal studies in developmental psychopathology, latent growth curve modeling represents an approach that combines the power of structural modeling techniques with the retention of a focus on tracking within-individual patterns of developmental change over time (Stoolmiller, 1995). Thus, latent growth curve techniques are able to address concerns of a more person-centered data analytic strategy (Willett, Singer, & Martin, 1998). In this method, parameters are estimated for each case in a longitudinal repeated measures data set to specify the intercept (or starting point of a trajectory) and the slope of the trajectory over time. More numerous assessments will allow for a better delineation of individual growth curves. Through this approach, differential developmental patterns can be delineated. For example, if antisocial behavior were examined over time, different individuals who exhibit growth or acceleration of antisocial behavior can be isolated, contrasting with individuals who exhibit stability in antisocial behavior over time or declines in antisociality as they develop. Thus, rather than revealing overall group trends, this type of analysis can allow for illumination of differential patterns of growth within a sample under investigation. Moreover, individual differences factors can be incorporated into the estimation procedures to examine processes that contribute to the variation in growth curves that are delineated. Stable characteristics, such as gender or history of paternal alcoholism, can be utilized in the modeling procedures to examine differences in the types of developmental trajectories for boys versus girls or children with and without alcoholic fathers. Additionally, factors that vary over time also may be incorporated into the statistical model. For example, repeated measurements of family conflict or violence in the community could be modeled, thereby allowing for an understanding of how these processes influence the developmental trajectories exhibited. Through examination of these constructs in latent growth curve models, the research is thus able to assess how these factors operate to influence the developmental trajectories observed. Thus, latent growth curve modeling techniques offer many advantages for data analysis in developmental psychopathology research through their ability to articulate individual patterns of development and assess the contribution of developmental processes to the patterns of growth exhibited by differing individuals.

Survival Analysis

Survival analysis, or hazard modeling, constitutes another strategy that has potential applications in developmental psychopathology (Willett & Singer, 1995). With this approach, the risk for or probability of an event occurrence over time is modeled. This has particular relevance for developmental psychopathology in understanding when and for whom events occur, such as the onset of a disorder (see Willett et al., 1998). For example, the occurrence of failing a school grade, the onset of a depressive episode, or the initiation of drug use are events that may occur within a study population. A unique feature handled by survival analysis (but not well addressed by more traditional approaches) is that it addresses the fact that not all individuals in the study sample will evidence the targeted event occurrence. Further, over time, the number of individuals who "survive" and do not experience the specified outcome progressively decreases. This approach establishes a survival function (based on the progressive probability of event nonoccurrence) as well as a hazard function (based on the probability of event occurrence). Evaluating when (e.g., at what developmental period) the risks for the event occurrence are greatest and for whom are critical questions addressed by this approach. Additionally, similar to linear and logistic regression, different predictors may be assessed to determine their impact on the survival and hazard functions. Time-invariant (e.g., gender, ethnicity) and time-variant (e.g., occurrence of life event stressors, changes in living situation) influences can be evaluated for their impact on the onset of disorder or other developmental outcomes. In so doing, this approach should be valuable for developmental psychopathologists in elucidating different developmental pathways that emerge over time (i.e., early versus late versus no onset of disorder) and processes over time that contribute to such variation among individuals.

SUMMARY AND CONCLUSIONS

Although progress has occurred in the research designs and methodologies used in developmental psychopathology, considerable reliance on established scientific procedures from various disciplines has continued. Investigators interested in a developmental psychopathology approach continue to evaluate the appropriateness and utility of methodological strategies, as well as devise innovative scientific approaches for addressing the complex interplay of biological, psychological, and social processes inherent to the field of developmental psychopathology (Richters, 1997).

Because a developmental psychopathology perspective requires multidomain, prospective assessments, it is clear that progress toward a process-level understanding of individuals with high-risk conditions and psychopathological disorders will require longitudinal research designs. Thus, assessments of the changing integration and organization of the domains of psychological development need to occur in the context of age-appropriate measurements of the major stage-salient developmental issues, in concert with concomitant evaluation of functioning at the biological level for developmental psychopathologists to achieve the unique goals of the discipline: to explain the development of individual patterns of adaptation and maladaptation.

To realize the potential of the developmental psychopathology perspective, investigators strive to attain enhanced fidelity between the elegance and complexity of the existing theoretical models and the measurement and data analytic strategies employed. The existence of equifinality and multifinality in development requires that researchers strive to demonstrate the multiplicity of processes and outcomes that may be anticipated at the individual, person-oriented level as opposed to the prevailing variable-oriented strategies that dominate the field (Bergman & Magnusson, 1997). In the future, research will benefit as investigators begin to conceptualize and design their research with these differential pathways concepts in mind (Cicchetti & Rogosch, 1997a). The continued elaboration and refinement of research methods in developmental psychopathology will contribute significantly to advancing the understanding of risk, disorder, and adaptation across the life course.

REFERENCES

Achenbach, T. M. (1990). What is "developmental" about developmental psychopathology? In J. Rolf, A. Masten, D. Cicchetti, K. Nuechterlein, & S. Weintraub (Eds.), *Risk and protective factors in the development of psychopathology* (pp. 29–48). New York: Cambridge University Press.

Achenbach, T. M. (1991). *Integrative guide for the 1991 CBCL/4-18, YSR, and TRF profiles.* Burlington: University of Vermont Department of Psychiatry.

Ainsworth, M. D. S., Blehar, M., Waters, E., & Wall, S. (1978). *Patterns of attachment: A psychological study of the Strange Situation.* Hillsdale, NJ: Erlbaum.

Anderson, E. R. (1995). Accelerating and maximizing information from short-term longitudinal research. In J. M. Gottman (Ed.), *The analysis of change* (pp. 139–163). Malwah, NJ: Erlbaum.

Angold, A., Prendergast, M., Cox, A., Harrington, R., Simonoff, E., & Rutter, M. (1995). The child and adolescent psychiatric assessment (CAPA). *Psychology Medicine, 25,* 739–753.

Baldwin, A., Baldwin, C., & Cole, R. (1990). Stress-resistant families and stress-resistant children. In J. Rolf, A. Masten, D. Cicchetti, K. Nuechterlein, & S. Weintraub (Eds.), *Risk and protective factors in the development of psychopathology* (pp. 257–280). New York: Cambridge University Press.

Bergman, L. R., & Magnusson, D. (1997). A person-oriented approach in research on developmental psychopathology. *Development and Psychopathology, 9,* 291–319.

Bertanlanffy, L., von (1968). *General system theory.* New York: Braziller.

Boyce, W. T., Frank, E., Jensen, P. S., Kessler, R. C., Nelson, C. A., & Steinberg, L. (1998). Social context in developmental psychopathology: Recommendations for future research from the MacArthur network on psychopathology and development. In D. Cicchetti & J. L. Aber (Eds.), Contextualism and developmental psychopathology [Special issue]. *Development and Psychopathology, 10*(2), 143–164.

Brady, E. U., & Kendall, P. C. (1992). Comorbidity of anxiety and depression in children and adolescents. *Psychological Bulletin, 111,* 244–255.

Bremner, J. D., Randall, P., Scott, M., Bronen, R., Seibel, J., Southwick, S., Delaney, R., McCarthy, G., Charney, D., & Innis, R. (1995). MRI-based measurement of hippocampal volume in patients with combat-related post traumatic stress disorder. *American Journal of Psychiatry, 152,* 973–981.

Carlson, V., Cicchetti, D., Barnett, D., & Braunwald, K. (1989). Disorganized/disoriented attachment relationships in maltreated infants. *Developmental Psychology, 25,* 525–531.

Cassidy, J., & Marvin, R. S. (1992). *Attachment organization in three- and four-year-olds: Procedures and coding manual.* Unpublished coding manual. (Available from the author at University of Maryland.)

Chassin, L., Rogosch, F. A., & Barrera, M. (1991). Substance abuse and symptomatology among adolescent children of alcoholics. *Journal of Abnormal Psychology, 100,* 449–463.

Chomsky, N. (1968). *Language and mind.* New York: Harcourt Brace Janovich.

Cicchetti, D. (Ed.). (1984a). *Developmental psychopathology.* Chicago: University of Chicago Press.

Cicchetti, D. (1984b). The emergence of developmental psychopathology. *Child Development, 55,* 1–7.

Cicchetti, D. (1989). How research on child maltreatment has informed the study of child development: Perspectives from developmental psychopathology. In D. Cicchetti & V. Carlson (Eds.), *Child maltreatment: Theory and research on the causes and consequences of child abuse and neglect* (pp. 377–431). New York: Cambridge University Press.

Cicchetti, D. (1990). An historical perspective on the discipline of developmental psychopathology. In J. Rolf, A. Masten, D. Cicchetti, K. Nuechterlein, & S. Weintraub (Eds.), *Risk and protective factors in the development of psychopathology* (pp. 2–28). New York: Cambridge University Press.

Cicchetti, D. (1993). Developmental psychopathology: Reactions, reflections, projections. *Developmental Review, 13,* 471–502.

Cicchetti, D., & Aber, J. L. (1986). Early precursors to later depression: An organizational perspective. In L. Lipsitt & C. Rovee-Collier (Eds.), *Advances in infancy* (Vol. 4, pp. 81–137). Norwood, NJ: ABLEX.

Cicchetti, D., & Aber, J. L. (Eds.). (1998). Contextualism and developmental psychopathology [Special issue]. *Development and Psychopathology, 10*(2), 137–426.

Cicchetti, D., & Cohen, D. (Eds.). (1995a). *Developmental psychopathology: Vol. 1. Theory and method.* New York: Wiley.

Cicchetti, D., & Cohen, D. (Eds.). (1995b). *Developmental psychopathology: Vol. 2. Risk, disorder, and adaptation.* New York: Wiley.

Cicchetti, D., & Cohen, D. (1995c). Perspectives on developmental psychopathology. In D. Cicchetti & D. Cohen (Eds.), *Developmental psychopathology: Vol. 1. Theory and method* (pp. 3–20). New York: Wiley.

Cicchetti, D., & Garmezy, N. (1993). Prospects and promises in the study of resilience. *Development and Psychopathology, 5,* 497–502.

Cicchetti, D., & Richters, J. E. (1993). Developmental considerations in the investigation of conduct disorder. *Development and Psychopathology, 5,* 331–344.

Cicchetti, D., & Richters, J. E. (Eds.). (1997). The conceptual and scientific underpinnings of research in developmental psychopathology [Special issue]. *Development and Psychopathology, 9*(2), 189–471.

Cicchetti, D., & Rogosch, F. A. (Eds.). (1996a). Developmental pathways [Special issue]. *Development and Psychopathology, 8*(4) 597–896.

Cicchetti, D., & Rogosch, F. A. (1996b). Equifinality and multifinality in developmental psychopathology. *Development and Psychopathology, 8,* 597–600.

Cicchetti, D., & Rogosch, F. A. (1997a). The role of self-organization in the promotion of resilience in maltreated children. *Development and Psychopathology, 9*(4), 799–817.

Cicchetti, D., & Rogosch, F. A. (Eds.). (1997b). Self-organization [Special issue]. *Development and Psychopathology, 9*(4), 595–942.

Cicchetti, D., Rogosch, F. A., Lynch, M., & Holt, K. (1993). Resilience in maltreated children: Processes leading to adaptive outcome. *Development and Psychopathology, 5,* 629–647.

Cicchetti, D., Rogosch, F. A., Toth, S. L., & Spagnola, M. (1997). Affect, cognition, and the emergence of self-knowledge in the toddler offspring of depressed mothers. *Journal of Experimental Child Psychology, 67,* 338–362.

Cicchetti, D., & Sroufe, L. A. (1976). The relationship between affective and cognitive development in Down's syndrome infants. *Child Development, 47,* 920–929.

Cicchetti, D., & Toth, S. L. (1992). The role of developmental theory in prevention and intervention. *Development and Psychopathology, 4,* 489–493.

Cicchetti, D., & Toth, S. L. (1995). A developmental psychopathology perspective on child abuse and neglect. *Journal of the American Academy of Child and Adolescent Psychiatry, 34,* 541–565.

Cicchetti, D., & Toth, S. L. (1998a). The development of depression in children and adolescents. *American Psychologist, 53,* 221–241.

Cicchetti, D., & Toth, S. L. (1998b). Perspectives on research and practice in developmental psychopathology. In W. Damon (Series Ed.), *Handbook of child psychology* (5th ed., pp. 479–583). New York: Wiley.

Cicchetti, D., Toth, S. L., & Lynch, M. (1995). Bowlby's dream comes full circle: The application of attachment theory to risk and psychopathology. In T. Ollendick & R. Prinz (Eds.), *Advances in clinical child psychology* (Vol. 17, pp. 1–75). New York: Plenum Press.

Cicchetti, D., & Tucker, D. (1994). Development and self-regulatory structures of the mind. *Development and Psychopathology, 6,* 533–549.

Cohen, J. (1990). Things I have learned so far. *American Psychologist, 45,* 1304–1312.

Coley, R. L., & Chase-Lansdale, P. L. (1998). Adolescent pregnancy and parenthood: Recent evidence and future directions. *American Psychologist, 53,* 152–166.

Crittenden, P. M. (1992). Quality of attachment in the preschool years. *Development and Psychopathology, 4,* 209–241.

Dawson, G., Grofer Klinger, L., Panagiotides, H., Hill, D., & Spieker, S. (1992). Frontal lobe activity and affective behavior of infants of mothers with depressive symptoms. *Child Development, 63,* 725–737.

Downey, G., & Coyne, J. C. (1990). Children of depressed parents: An integrative review. *Psychological Bulletin, 108,* 50–76.

Edleman, G. (1987). *Neural Darwinism.* New York: Basic Books.

Egeland, B., Carlson, E., & Sroufe, L. A. (1993). Resilience as process. *Development and Psychopathology, 5,* 517–528.

Eisenberg, L. (1995). The social construction of the human brain. *American Journal of Psychiatry, 152,* 1563–1575.

Emery, R., & Laumann-Billings, L. (1998). An overview of the nature, causes, and consequences of abusive family relationships: Toward differentiating maltreatment and violence. *American Psychologist, 53,* 121–135.

Field, T., Fox, N., Pickens, J., & Nawrocki, T. (1995). Relative right frontal EEG activation in 3- to 6-month old infants of "depressed" mothers. *Developmental Psychology, 31,* 358–363.

Garcia Coll, C., Crnic, K., Lamberty, G., Wasik, B., Jenkins, R., Garcia, H., & McAdoo, H. (1996). An integrative model for the study of developmental competencies in minority children. *Child Development, 67,* 1891–1914.

Garmezy, N., & Streitman, S. (1974). Children at risk: The search for the antecedents of schizophrenia. *Schizophrenia Bulletin, 8,* 14–90.

Hart, J., Gunnar, M., & Cicchetti, D. (1996). Altered neuroendocrine activity in maltreated children related to depression. *Development and Psychopathology, 8,* 201–214.

Harrington, R., Rutter, M., & Fombonne, E. (1996). Developmental pathways in depression: Multiple meanings, antecedents, and endpoints. *Development and Psychopathology, 8,* 601–616.

Hodges, K. (1993). Structured interviews for assessing children. *Journal of Child Psychology and Psychiatry, 34,* 49–68.

Holmbeck, G. N., & Kendall, P. C. (1991). Clinical-childhood-development interface: Implications for treatment. In P. Martin (Ed.), *Handbook of behavior therapy and psychological science: An integrative approach* (pp. 73–99). Elmsford, NY: Pergamon Press.

Holmbeck, G. N., & Updegrove, A. L. (1995). Clinical-developmental interface: Implications of developmental research for adolescent psychotherapy. *Psychotherapy, 32,* 16–33.

Institute of Medicine. (1989). *Research on children and adolescents with mental, behavioral, and developmental disorders.* Washington, DC: National Academy Press.

Institute of Medicine. (1994). *Reducing risks for mental disorders: Frontiers for preventive intervention research.* Washington, DC: National Academy Press.

Kagan, J. (1971). *Change and continuity in infancy.* New York: Wiley.

Kaplan, B. (1967). Meditations on genesis. *Human Development, 10,* 65–87.

Kellam, S. G., & Rebok, G. W. (1992). Building developmental and etiological theory through epidemiologically based preventive intervention trials. In J. McCord & R. E. Tremblay (Eds.), *Preventing antisocial behavior: Interventions from birth through adolescence* (pp. 162–195). New York: Guilford Press.

Kellam, S. G., Rebok, G. W., Ialongo, N., & Mayer, L. S. (1994). The course and malleability of aggressive behavior from early first grade into middle school: Results of a developmental epidemiologically-based preventive trials. *Journal of Child Psychology and Psychiatry, 35,* 259–281.

Kellam, S. G., Rebok, G. W., Mayer, L. S., Ialongo, N., & Kalonder, C. R. (1994). Depressive symptoms over first grade and their responsiveness to a preventive trial aimed at improving achievement. *Development and Psychopathology, 6,* 463–481.

Kendall, P. C. (1991). *Child and adolescent therapy: Cognitive-behavioral procedures.* New York: Guilford Press.

Kendall, P. C., & Grove, W. M. (1988). Normative comparisons in therapy outcome. *Behavioral Assessment, 10,* 147–158.

Kendall, P. C., Lerner, R., & Craighead, W. E. (1984). Human development and intervention in childhood psychopathology. *Child Development, 55,* 71–82.

Koretz, D. (1991). Prevention-centered science in mental health. *American Journal of Community Psychology, 19,* 453–458.

Loeber, R., Green, S., Lahey, B., & Stouthamer-Loeber, M. (1989). Optimal informants on childhood disruptive behaviors. *Development and Psychopathology, 1,* 317–337.

Luthar, S. S. (1991). Vulnerability and resilience: A study of high-risk adolescents. *Child Development, 62*(3), 600–616.

Luthar, S. S., & McMahon, T. (1996). Peer reputation among inner city adolescents: Structure and correlates. *Journal of Research on Adolescence, 6,* 581–603.

Magnusson, D., & Cairns, R. B. (1996). Developmental science: Toward a unified framework. In R. B. Cairns, G. H. Elder, & E. J. Costello (Eds.), *Developmental science* (pp. 7–30). New York: Cambridge University Press.

Main, M., & Solomon, J. (1990). Procedures for identifying infants as disorganized/disoriented during the Ainsworth Strange Situation. In M. Greenberg, D. Cicchetti, & E. M. Cummings (Eds.), *Attachment in the preschool years* (pp. 121–160). Chicago: University of Chicago Press.

Mason, W., & Feinberg, S. E. (1985). *Cohort analysis in social research: Beyond the identification problems.* New York: Springer-Verlag.

Masten, A., & Coatsworth, J. D. (1998). The development of competence in favorable and unfavorable environments: Lessons from research on successful children. *American Psychologist, 53,* 205–220.

Masten, A., Best, K., & Garmezy, N. (1990). Resilience and development: Contributions from the study of children who overcome adversity. *Development and Psychopathology, 2,* 425–444.

McLoyd, V. (1998). Socioeconomic disadvantage and child development. *American Psychologist, 53,* 185–204.

Meehl, P. E. (1964). *Manual for use with checklist of schizotypic signs.* Unpublished manuscript, University of Minnesota. (Available from the author.)

Meehl, P. E. (1978). Theoretical risks and tabular asterisks: Sir Karl, Sir Ronald, and the slow progress of soft psychology. *Journal of Consulting and Clinical Psychology, 46,* 1–42.

Meehl, P. E. (1990). Toward an integrated theory of schizotaxia, schizotypy, and schizophrenia. *Journal of Personality Disorders, 4,* 1–99.

National Advisory Mental Health Council. (1990). *National plan for research on child and adolescent mental disorders* (Publication 90-1683). Rockville, MD: U.S. Department of Health and Human Services.

Nelson, C. A., & Bloom, F. E. (1997). Child development and neuroscience. *Child Development, 68,* 970–987.

Olds, D., Eckenrode, J., Henderson, C., Kitzman, H., Powers, J., Cole, R., Sidora, K., Morris, P., Pettitt, L., & Luckey, D. (1997). Long-term effects of home visitation on maternal life course and child abuse and neglect: Fifteen-year follow-up of a randomized trial. *Journal of the American Medical Association, 278,* 637–643.

Overton, W., & Horowitz, H. (1991). Developmental psychopathology: Integration and differentiations. In D. Cicchetti & S. L. Toth (Eds.), *Rochester Symposium on Developmental Psychopathology: Vol. 3. Models and integrations* (pp. 1–42). Rochester, NY: University of Rochester Press.

Plomin, R., & Daniels, D. (1987). Why are children in the same family so different from one another? *Behavioral and Brain Sciences, 10,* 1–15.

Plomin, R., Rende, R., & Rutter, M. (1991). Quantitative genetics and developmental psychopathology. In D. Cicchetti & S. L. Toth (Eds.), *Rochester Symposium on Developmental Psychopathology: Vol. 2. Internalizing and externalizing expressions of dysfunction* (pp. 155–202). Hillsdale, NJ: Erlbaum.

Pollak, S., Cicchetti, D., Klorman, R., & Brumaghim, J. (1997). Cognitive brain event-related potentials and emotion processing in maltreated children. *Child Development, 68,* 773–787.

Post, R., Weiss, S., Leverich, G., George, M., Frye, M., & Ketter, T. (1996). Developmental neurobiology of cyclic affective illness: Implications for early therapeutic interventions. *Development and Psychopathology, 8,* 273–305.

Puig-Antich, J. (1986). Psychobiological markers: Effects of age and puberty. In M. Rutter, C. Izard, & P. Read (Eds.), *Depression in young people* (pp. 341–382). New York: Guilford Press.

Puig-Antich, J., & Chambers, W. (1986). *Kiddie schedule for affective disorders and schizophrenia, present state version.* Pittsburgh: Western Psychiatric Institute and Clinic.

Reich, W., & Welner, Z. (1988). *Revised version of the diagnostic interview for children and adolescents (DICA-R).* St. Louis, MO: Department of Psychiatry, Washington University School of Medicine.

Rende, R., & Plomin, R. (1995). Nature, nurture, and the development of psychopathology. In D. Cicchetti & D. J. Cohen (Eds.), *Developmental psychopathology: Vol. 1. Theory and methods* (pp. 291–314). New York: Wiley.

Richters, J. E. (1997). The Hubble hypothesis and the developmentalist's dilemma. *Development and Psychopathology, 9*(2), 193–229.

Richters, J. E., & Cicchetti, D. (1993). Mark Twain meets DSM-III-R: Conduct disorder, development, and the concept of harmful dysfunction. *Development and Psychopathology, 5,* 5–29.

Robins, L. (1966). *Deviant children grown up.* Baltimore: Williams & Wilkins.

Rogosa, D. (1995). Myths and methods: "Myths about longitudinal research" plus supplemental questions. In J. M. Gottman (Ed.), *The analysis of change* (pp. 3–66). Malwah, NJ: Erlbaum.

Rogosch, F. A., Cicchetti, D., Shields, A., & Toth, S. L. (1995). Parenting dysfunction in child maltreatment. In M. H. Bornstein (Ed.), *Handbook of parenting* (Vol. 4, pp. 127–159). Hillsdale, NJ: Erlbaum.

Rutter, M. (1985). Resilience in the face of adversity: Protective factors and resistance to psychiatric disorder. *British Journal of Psychiatry, 147,* 598–611.

Rutter, M. (1986). Child psychiatry: The interface between clinical and developmental research. *Psychological Medicine, 16,* 151–160.

Rutter, M. (1987). Psychosocial resilience and protective mechanisms. *American Journal of Orthopsychiatry, 57,* 316–331.

Rutter, M. (1989). Age as an ambiguous variable in developmental research: Some epidemiological considerations from developmental psychopathology. *International Journal of Behavioral Development, 12,* 1–34.

Rutter, M. (1990). Psychosocial resilience and protective mechanisms. In J. Rolf, A. S. Masten, D. Cicchetti, K. H. Nuechterlein, & S. Weintraub (Eds.), *Risk and protective factors in the development of psychopathology* (pp. 181–214). New York: Cambridge University Press.

Rutter, M. (1996a). Developmental psychopathology: Concepts and prospects. In M. F. Lenzenweger & J. J. Haugaard (Eds.), *Frontiers of developmental psychopathology* (pp. 209–237). New York: Oxford University Press.

Rutter, M. (1996b). Developmental psychopathology as an organizing research construct. In D. Magnusson (Ed.), *The lifespan development of individuals: Behavioral neurobiological, and psychosocial perspectives* (pp. 394–413). New York: Cambridge University Press.

Rutter, M., Dunn, J., Plomin, R., Simonoff, E., Pickles, A., Maughan, B., Ormel, J., Meyer, J., & Eaves, L. (1997). Integrating nature and nurture: Implications of person-environment correlations and interactions for developmental psychopathology. *Development and Psychopathology, 9,* 335–364.

Rutter, M., & Garmezy, N. (1983). Developmental psychopathology. In P. Mussen (Series Ed.) & E. M. Hetherington (Volume Ed.), *Handbook of child psychology* (4th ed.) (Vol. 4, pp. 774–911). New York: Wiley.

Sameroff, A. J., & Chandler, M. J. (1975). Reproductive risk and the continuum of caretaking casualty. In F. D. Horowitz (Ed.), *Review of child development research* (Vol. 4, pp. 187–244). Chicago: University of Chicago Press.

Sameroff, A. J., Seifer, R., & Zax, M. (1982). Early development of children at risk for emotional disorder. *Monographs for the Society for Research in Child Development, 47*(Serial No. 199).

Scarr, S., & McCartney, K. (1983). How people make their own environments: A theory of genotype-environment effects. *Child Development, 54,* 424–435.

Schaie, K. W. (1965). A general model for the study of developmental problems. *Psychological Bulletin, 64,* 92–107.

Schneider-Rosen, K., & Cicchetti, D. (1991). Early self-knowledge and emotional development: Visual self-recognition and affective reactions to mirror self-image in maltreated and nonmaltreated toddlers. *Developmental Psychology, 27,* 481–488.

Schore, A. N. (1997). Early organization of the nonlinear right brain and the development of a predisposition to psychiatric disorders. *Development and Psychopathology, 9,* 595–631.

Shaffer, D., Fisher, P., Dulcan, M. K., Davies, M., Piacentini, J., Schwab-Stone, M. E., Lahey, B. B., Bourdon, K., Jensen, P. S., Bird, H. R., Canino, E., & Regier, D. A. (1996). The NIMH diagnostic interview schedule for children version 2.3 (DISC-2.3): Description, acceptability, prevalence rates, and performance in the MECA study. *Journal of the American Academy of Child and Adolescent Psychiatry, 35,* 865–877.

Shirk, S., & Russell, R. (1996). *Change processes in child psychotherapy.* New York: Guilford Press.

Silverman, W. K., & Nelles, W. B. (1988). The anxiety disorders interview schedule for children. *Journal of the American Academy of Child and Adolescent Psychiatry, 27,* 772–778.

Skuse, D. (1984). Extreme deprivation in early childhood: II. Theoretical issues and comparative review. *Journal of Child Psychology and Psychiatry, 25,* 543–572.

Sroufe, L. A. (1979). The coherence of individual development. *American Psychologist, 34,* 834–841.

Sroufe, L. A. (1989). Pathways to adaptation and maladaptation: Psychopathology as developmental deviation. In D. Cicchetti (Ed.), *Rochester Symposium on Developmental Psychopathology: Vol. 1. The emergence of a discipline* (pp. 13–40). Hillsdale, NJ: Erlbaum.

Sroufe, L. A. (1990). An organizational perspective on the self. In D. Cicchetti & M. Beeghly (Eds.), *The self in transition: Infancy to childhood* (pp. 281–307). Chicago: University of Chicago Press.

Sroufe, L. A. (1996). *Emotional development: The organization of emotional life in the early years.* New York: Cambridge University Press.

Sroufe, L. A. (1997). Psychopathology as an outcome of development. *Development and Psychopathology, 2*(9), 251–268.

Sroufe, L. A., & Rutter, M. (1984). The domain of developmental psychopathology. *Child Development, 55,* 17–29.

Stattin, H., & Magnusson, D. (1996). Antisocial development: A holistic approach. *Development and Psychopathology, 8,* 617–645.

Stoolmiller, M. (1995). Using latent growth curve models to study developmental processes. In J. M. Gottman (Ed.), *The analysis of change* (pp. 103–138). Malwah, NJ: Erlbaum.

Toth, S. L., & Cicchetti, D. (in press). Developmental psychopathology and child psychotherapy. In S. Russ & T. Ollendick (Eds.), *Handbook of psychotherapies with children and families* New York: Plenum Press.

Vaughn, C., & Leff, J. (1976). The influence of family and social factors in the course of psychiatric illness. *British Journal of Psychiatry, 129,* 125–137.

Waddington, C. H. (1957). *The strategy of genes.* London: Allen & Unwin.

Wakefield, J. (1997). When is development disordered? Developmental psychopathology and the harmful dysfunction analysis of mental disorder. *Development and Psychopathology, 9,* 269–290.

Walker, E., Neumann, G. C., Baum, K., Davis, D. M., DiForio, D., & Bergman, A. (1996). The developmental pathways to schizophrenia: Potential moderating effects of stress. *Development and Psychopathology, 8,* 647–665.

Walker, E., Savoie, T., & Davis, D. (1994). Neuromotor precursors of schizophrenia. *Schizophrenia Bulletin, 20,* 441–451.

Watt, N., Anthony, E. J., Wynne, L., & Rolf, J. (Eds.). (1984). *Children at risk for schizophrenia: A longitudinal perspective.* New York: Cambridge University Press.

Werner, H. (1957). The concept of development from a comparative and organismic point of view. In D. B. Harris (Ed.), *The concept of development* (pp. 125–148). Minneapolis: University of Minnesota Press.

Willett, J. B., & Singer, J. D. (1995). Investigating onset, cessation, relapse, and recovery: Using discrete-time survival analysis to examine the occurrence and timing of critical events. In J. M. Gottman (Ed.), *The analysis of change* (pp. 203–259). Malwah, NJ: Erlbaum.

Willett, J. B., Singer, J. D., & Martin, N. C. (1998). The design and analysis of longitudinal studies of development and psychopathology in context: Statistical models and methodological recommendations. *Development and Psychopathology, 10.*

Wynne, L., & Singer, M. (1963). Thought disorder and family relations of schizophrenics: I. A research strategy. *Archives of General Psychiatry, 9,* 191–198.

Zigler, E., & Glick, M. (1986). *A developmental approach to adult psychopathology.* New York: Wiley.

Zucker, R. A., Ellis, D. A., Fitzgerald, H. E., Bingham, C. R., & Sanford, K. (1996). Other evidence for at least two alcoholisms: II. Life course variation in antisociality and heterogeneity of alcoholic outcome. *Development and Psychopathology, 8,* 831–848.

Zucker, R. A., & Fitzgerald, H. E. (1991). Early developmental factors and risk for alcohol problems. *Alcoholic Health and Research World, 15,* 18–24.

Chapter 19

RESEARCH METHODS IN ADULT PSYCHOPATHOLOGY

Lauren B. Alloy, Ph.D., Lyn Y. Abramson, Ph.D., David Raniere, M.S., and Ilene M. Dyller, M.S.

A VULNERABILITY-STRESS FRAMEWORK FOR PSYCHOPATHOLOGY RESEARCH

Why does an individual develop a particular psychological disorder? Historically, researchers and theorists sought the causes of psychopathology either in factors internal to the person or in factors found in the external environment. However, the majority of current psychopathology researchers have adopted a *vulnerability-stress model* in which it is acknowledged that most psychological disorders are caused by a combination of constitutional and environmental factors. It is recognized that various environmental insults, such as stressful life events, early childhood traumas, brain injuries, viruses, and poor parenting can precipitate the development of behavioral disorders in some individuals. But not everyone succumbs to such stress in the same way; because of genetic, personality, cognitive, biological, or behavioral predispositions, "risk factors," or "diatheses," some people are more vulnerable to developing a psychological disorder when confronted with the same environmental stress than others (see Kraemer et al., 1997, for a discussion of the definitions and types of risk factors). Thus, the guiding principle of the vulnerability-stress model of psychopathology is that environmental stress triggers a predisposed person's vulnerability, such that the vulnerability is converted into psychopathology (e.g., Abramson, Metalsky, & Alloy, 1989; Meehl, 1962; Monroe & Simons, 1991; Zubin & Spring, 1977).

Most current theories of psychopathology adopt a vulnerability-stress framework either explicitly or implicitly. For example, since the classic publications of Meehl (1962) and Rosenthal (1970), vulnerability-stress theories in which a genetic predisposition to schizophrenia is transformed via environmental stress into schizophrenia itself have dominated the field for the past 30 years. More recent vulnerability-stress models of schizophrenia (e.g., Walker & Diforio, 1997; Weinberger, 1987) have focused on the neural mechanisms by which stressful life events, prenatal injuries, and birth complications

Preparation of this chapter was supported by National Institute of Mental Health Grants MH 48216 to Lauren B. Alloy and MH 43866 to Lyn Y. Abramson.

convert the genetic diathesis for schizophrenia into the full-blown disorder. In depression research, aside from genetic diathesis-stress models (e.g., Kendler et al., 1995), recent psychological theories have emphasized the role of negative cognitive styles, personality characteristics, or interpersonal strategies as vulnerability factors that increase individuals' risk for developing depression when they encounter stressful life events (e.g., Abramson et al., 1989; Beck, 1987; Blatt & Zuroff, 1992; Joiner, 1995). Theories of panic attacks and panic disorder also have included diathesis-stress models in which anxiety sensitivity, the disposition to believe that autonomic arousal has harmful consequences, is hypothesized to make people vulnerable to developing panic attacks when confronted with stressful life events (e.g., Schmidt, Lerew, & Jackson, 1997). Even posttraumatic stress disorder (PTSD), originally conceptualized in the *Diagnostic and Statistical Manual of Mental Disorders,* 3rd edition (*DSM-III;* American Psychiatric Association, 1980) as a normative response to extreme environmental stress, is now recognized to require personal vulnerability (e.g., genetic risk, particular personality traits) for its occurrence as well (Yehuda & McFarlane, 1995). Similar vulnerability-stress approaches abound in research on alcoholism and drug use, dissociative, somatoform, eating, and other anxiety disorders (Alloy, Jacobson, & Acocella, 1998).

Consequently, in this chapter, we use a vulnerability-stress framework to guide our discussion of methods in psychopathology research. In the sections that follow, we first discuss the crucial role of theory in determining the choice of appropriate designs for research studies, including the need to be cognizant of the hypothesized causal relations among vulnerabilities, stressors, mediators, moderators, and disorder outcomes in the psychopathology models to be tested. Next, we describe an "ideal" design for testing vulnerability-stress models, as well as the practical and ethical problems associated with such an ideal design. We then review actual research designs used in psychopathology research, including experimental and quasi-experimental designs and correlational designs that are either cross-sectional, retrospective, longitudinal, prospective, or involve high-risk strategies. We evaluate the adequacy of these various designs for testing vulnerability-stress models and the kinds of inferences that may legitimately be drawn from them. We end with a discussion of difficult conceptual and methodological issues (e.g., the interdependence of the vulnerability, stress, and disorder, the stability of the vulnerability, disorder subtypes) that must be addressed in the design of studies to evaluate vulnerability-stress models of psychopathology.

THE ROLE OF THEORY IN THE CHOICE OF RESEARCH DESIGN

Although some psychopathology research is purely exploratory, in general, most research efforts are guided by theory or, at least, by some empirically testable hypothesis. Indeed, in the absence of theory, investigators are left to conduct "fishing expeditions" in which even a strong observed association between some variable and an abnormal behavior of interest is potentially uninterpretable. For example, the recent finding that the course of schizophrenia is more benign in developing countries than in westernized countries (Jablensky et al., 1992) is difficult to understand without some hypotheses about the factors (e.g., family structure, culture, treatment response) that influence the

maintenance versus remission of schizophrenic symptoms. Popper (1963) described the
necessity of theory well:

> The belief that we can start with pure observation alone, without anything in the nature of
> a theory is absurd. . . . Twenty-five years ago I tried to bring home the same point to a
> group of physics students in Vienna by beginning a lecture with the following instructions:
> Take a pencil and paper; carefully observe, and write down what you have observed. They
> asked of course, *what* [italics in original] I wanted them to observe. . . . Observation is al-
> ways selection. It needs a chosen object, a definite task, an interest, a point of view, a
> problem. (p. 46; quoted in Follette & Houts, 1996, p. 1122)

Theory and research influence one another reciprocally (Follette & Houts, 1996;
Skinner, 1981). Theory guides the selection of research design and the interpretation
of any obtained empirical findings. In turn, research findings may lead to the further
elaboration, modification, or abandonment of particular theories. For our present purposes, it is important to emphasize that the theory specifies the hypotheses to be tested
and determines the optimal research designs so that the research study affords a fair
opportunity to subject the theory to "grave danger of refutation" (Meehl, 1978; Popper, 1963, 1972). In particular, with respect to vulnerability-stress models of psychopathology, investigators must appreciate the kinds of causal relations specified in
particular theories and use these hypothesized causal relations to guide their choice of
optimal research strategies (Abramson, Metalsky, & Alloy, 1988; Alloy, Hartlage, &
Abramson, 1988).

Hypothesized Causal Relations in Vulnerability-Stress
Models of Psychopathology

In vulnerability-stress models, the hypothesized logical and temporal relations between
proposed causes and the disorder of interest influence the choice of research design to
test the model. Are the hypothesized vulnerability and stress necessary, sufficient, or
contributory causes of the disorder? Do they exert their causal effects close in time to
the onset of disorder or in the more distant past? Do they combine additively or do they
interact synergistically to increase the likelihood of disorder?

A *necessary cause* of a disorder is an etiological factor (E) that must be present or
have occurred for the disorder (D) to occur; or, mathematically speaking, Probability
$(E/D) = 1.00$.[1] The disorder cannot occur if the etiological factor did not occur. However,
the disorder is not required to occur when the necessary cause has occurred (i.e., the
cause is necessary but not sufficient). A *sufficient cause* of a disorder is an etiological
factor whose occurrence guarantees the occurrence of the disorder; or, mathematically
speaking, Probability $(D/E) = 1.00$. If the disorder does not occur, then the etiological
factor must not have occurred. However, the disorder may occur in the absence of a sufficient cause (i.e., the cause is sufficient but not necessary). A *contributory cause* of a
disorder is an etiological factor that increases the likelihood that the disorder will occur,

---

[1] This conditional probability should read: "The probability of the presence (or occurrence) of the etiological factor given the presence (or occurrence) of the disorder is equal to 1.00."

but is neither necessary nor sufficient for its occurrence (Abramson et al., 1988, 1989). Mathematically speaking, Probability (D/E) > Probability (D/not E), where Probability (E/D) < 1.00 (i.e., not necessary) and Probability (D/E) < 1.00 (i.e., not sufficient).

Consider the effect of the hypothesized logical relations between causes and disorder on the choice of research strategy. As an example, in genetic vulnerability-stress theories of alcoholism (e.g., Finn & Pihl, 1987; Levenson, Oyama, & Meek, 1987), ingestion of alcohol (the stress) is considered to be a necessary, but not a sufficient, cause of the development of alcoholism among genetically predisposed persons. Consequently, a study that compared alcoholics and nonalcoholics on their likelihood of exposure to alcohol prior to the onset of their disorder would be an appropriate test of these theories. In contrast, a study that compared the likelihood of alcoholism in people exposed versus nonexposed to alcohol would not provide an adequate test of these theories because alcohol exposure is not a sufficient cause of alcoholism in these theories and, therefore, some people exposed to alcohol are not expected to become alcoholic. Alternatively, in the hopelessness theory of depression (Abramson et al., 1989), hopelessness is viewed as a sufficient, but not a necessary, cause of depression. Thus, a prospective study that compared people who were hopeless versus hopeful on their likelihood of becoming depressed would be an appropriate research design to test this aspect of the theory, whereas a comparison of depressed versus nondepressed individuals on their likelihood of exhibiting hopelessness would not be appropriate because hopelessness is not a necessary cause of depression, and, therefore, some depressed persons may not be hopeless.

In addition to varying in their logical relation to the occurrence of a disorder, causes also may vary in their temporal relation to the occurrence of the disorder. In a sequence of events leading to the occurrence of a disorder, some causes *(distal causes)* operate toward the beginning of the sequence, distant from the occurrence of the disorder, whereas others operate toward the end of the sequence, proximate to the occurrence of the disorder (*proximal causes;* Abramson et al., 1988, 1989). For example, in some recent vulnerability-stress models of schizophrenia (e.g., Bracha, Torrey, Gottesman, Bigelow, & Cunniff, 1992; Mednick, Machon, Huttunen, & Bonett, 1988), prenatal exposure to viral infection or other brain-injuring trauma is conceptualized to be a stressor that leads to the development of schizophrenia in young adulthood in genetically predisposed individuals. Thus, prenatal viral exposure is a very distal hypothesized cause of schizophrenia. An appropriate research design to test this hypothesis might include a retrospective, follow-back study of adult schizophrenics and normal comparison participants to examine their mothers' exposure to viral infection while the participants were in utero, or better yet, a prospective study of infants exposed and not exposed to viral infection while in utero followed longitudinally through the age of risk for the onset of schizophrenia. However, given the distal nature of this hypothesized cause, a cross-sectional, retrospective, or prospective research design that assessed viral exposure in schizophrenics versus normal controls in childhood or adulthood would not be an adequate test of this model. In contrast, most vulnerability-stress theories of depression hypothesize that negative life events that occur proximal to the onset of depression serve as the stress that triggers the onset of the depressive episode. Consequently, studies that examine the association between recent, but not distant, negative events and depression onset would be required to test these theories.

Given that vulnerability-stress models hypothesize that a combination of personal predispositions and environmental inputs causes disorder, an adequate research design would involve the manipulation or assessment of both vulnerability and stress in the same study. However, the exact nature of the vulnerability-stress combination featured in particular models is an important consideration as well (Abramson, Alloy, & Hogan, 1997; Monroe & Simons, 1991). In some models, the vulnerability and stress are conceptualized as combining in an additive fashion according to a "titration" model, such that the degree of vulnerability and the degree of stress summate, with either combinations of low vulnerability compensated for by high stress or low stress compensated for by high vulnerability leading to disorder, as seen in Figure 19.1. Alternatively, vulnerability and stress may be postulated as truly interacting, so that the two have a synergism beyond their separate effects, with only combinations of high vulnerability and high stress leading to disorder, as shown in Figure 19.2. Whether the vulnerability-stress model is additive or interactive has implications for the levels (high, low, or both) of predisposition and stress that must be sampled or manipulated in research to test the model, as well as for the statistical procedures used to analyze the obtained data.

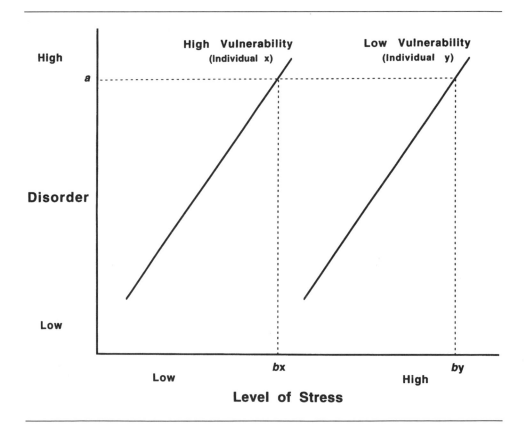

Figure 19.1.   Additive model of vulnerability-stress interaction. In an additive model, levels of vulnerability and stress summate to increase the likelihood of disorder, such that either a combination of low vulnerability compensated for by high stress or low stress compensated for by high vulnerability leads to disorder.

Source of data: Monroe & Simons, 1991, p. 414.

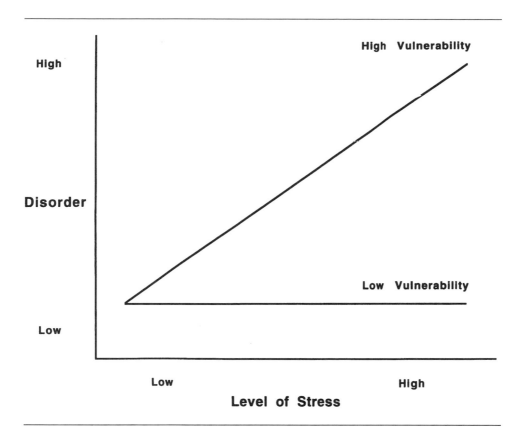

Figure 19.2.   Interactive model of vulnerability-stress interaction. In an interactive model, levels of vulnerability and stress have a synergistic effect, such that only a combination of high vulnerability and high stress leads to disorder.
Source of data: Monroe & Simons, 1991, p. 414.

Mediators versus Moderators in Vulnerability-Stress Models of Psychopathology

The presence of third variables that act as either moderators or mediators in vulnerability-stress models is also an important consideration in research strategy and the choice of statistical analysis (Baron & Kenny, 1986; Holmbeck, 1997). A *moderator* is a third variable that affects the relationship between the independent variable (i.e., the vulnerability or stress or both) and the dependent variable (disorder). In essence, a moderator interacts with the vulnerability or stress (or both) and affects the direction or strength of the relationship between the vulnerability-stress combination and disorder (see Figure 19.3, bottom). For example, some recent schizophrenia research has shown that men are one and a half times more likely than women to develop schizophrenia (Iacono & Beiser, 1992a, 1992b). Thus, a person's sex may be a moderator of the vulnerability and stress effects on schizophrenia. To the extent that a psychopathology theory proposes a moderator of the vulnerability/stress – disorder relation, it is crucial to include either a manipulation of the hypothesized moderator or an assessment of the vulnerability/stress – disorder association across different sampled levels of the moderator in one's research

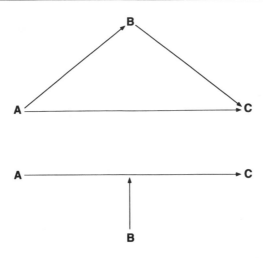

Figure 19.3.   Models of mediated and moderated effects. In the top model, B mediates the relationship between A and C, meaning that B is the mechanism or psychological process by which A leads to C. In the bottom model, B moderates the relationship between A and C, meaning that B affects the direction and/or strength of the relationship between A and C.

Source of data: Holmbeck, 1997, p. 600.

design. In our current example, one would need to examine the genetic risk/birth complication prediction of schizophrenia in men and women separately. (The reader is referred to Farrell, and Holmbeck & Shapera, both in this volume, for the appropriate statistical procedures for testing moderators and mediators.)

Alternatively, a *mediator* is a third variable that accounts for the relation between an independent variable (vulnerability, stress, or their combination) and the dependent variable (disorder). The mediator is the mechanism or psychological process by which the vulnerability-stress combination causes the disorder (see Figure 19.3, top). Whereas moderators specify the conditions under which a vulnerability-stress combination will lead to disorder, mediators specify how or why the vulnerability-stress combination leads to disorder (Baron & Kenny, 1986; Holmbeck, 1997). To continue with the schizophrenia example, Walker and Diforio (1997) propose that damage to the hippocampus brought about by prenatal or birth injuries (the stress) in individuals with an inherited abnormality in dopamine receptors (the genetic vulnerability) leads to a dopaminergic hypersensitivity to the cortisol release that occurs in response to stressful life events, which, in turn, leads to the symptoms of schizophrenia. Here, the dopaminergic hypersensitivity to stress serves as the mediator or mechanism by which the combination of genetic predisposition and early brain injury causes schizophrenia. Ideally, research studies designed to test vulnerability-stress models containing mediators require multiple independent and converging measures of the proposed mediator (Baron & Kenny, 1986; Campbell & Fiske, 1959) as well as appropriate statistical procedures for testing mediation (see Baron & Kenny, 1986; Holmbeck, 1997, for statistical strategies).

An "Ideal" Research Design for Testing Vulnerability-Stress Models of Psychopathology

Every psychologist designing a research study hopes to find the perfect design to test his or her hypotheses. Unfortunately, due to ethical, practical, or financial constraints, the perfect design is often impossible to implement. What might an example of an "ideal" design for testing a vulnerability-stress model look like?

Imagine you are a researcher interested in testing Walker and Diforio's (1997) model of schizophrenia. As noted above, the diathesis in this model is a genetic vulnerability that, in combination with prenatal or birth injuries, may lead to dopaminergic hypersensitivity to cortisol. This neurochemical problem, which is activated by stressful life events, brings on the symptoms of schizophrenia.

What would be the "ideal" design to test this model? To begin with, you would need two groups: a genetic high-risk (one or both parents with schizophrenia) and a genetic low-risk (no family history of schizophrenia) group. In the not too distant future, with the completion of the human genome mapping project and the advent of genetic engineering, it might be possible to actually manipulate participants' genetic vulnerability by giving one group "schizophrenia genes" and the other group "normal genes." The hypothesized stress in the model occurs before or during the birth process; therefore, you would need to identify your participants before their birth. You would then need to assign participants from both groups randomly to either a prenatal or birth trauma experimental condition or a nontrauma control condition. Participants in the experimental condition would be exposed to traumatic prenatal experiences (such as the influenza virus) or to injurious birth conditions, and participants in the control condition would be shielded from these experiences. To control for the possible effects of nongenetic family factors in schizophrenia, it would be helpful to pair each high-risk participant with a low-risk participant who experienced similar prenatal and birth conditions aside from the manipulated trauma, and to raise pairs together in the same family. Finally, as they approached the typical age-at-onset of schizophrenia, some of the pairs of participants (chosen at random, of course) would be exposed to stressful life events, and other pairs would be protected from all life stress.

Your statistical analyses would be designed to determine whether high-risk participants who experienced both prenatal or birth trauma and later life stressors were more likely than their low-risk counterparts to develop schizophrenia; whether high-risk participants who experienced early injury developed schizophrenia more often than high-risk participants who did not have this experience; and whether experiencing later life stress put high-risk, early trauma participants in greater danger of developing schizophrenia. Moreover, you would assess the integrity and sensitivity of each participant's dopaminergic system shortly after birth and again near the age-at-risk for schizophrenia (both baseline and in response to neurochemical and stressful life event challenges) and conduct analyses to examine whether dopaminergic hypersensitivity mediated the effects of the combination of genetic risk, prenatal/birth trauma, and stressful life events on the likelihood of onset of schizophrenia.

Thus, the "ideal" design for testing the causal hypotheses of a vulnerability-stress model of a disorder is one that experimentally manipulates both the hypothesized vulnerability and the stress, such as our example above. However, it should be obvious that such a design cannot and should not be used. Not only is it impossible to implement, but the ethical, legal, and financial considerations are staggering. Although this example may be somewhat extreme, similar issues arise in every psychopathology study. Ideal designs are unrealistic in research where real people are used as participants. All we can do is try to create a solid design that minimizes alternative interpretations and confounding factors, while staying within practical and ethical boundaries (Bersoff & Bersoff, this volume). The remainder of this chapter is devoted to that endeavor.

EXPERIMENTAL AND QUASI-EXPERIMENTAL DESIGNS IN PSYCHOPATHOLOGY RESEARCH

There are two basic types of research designs used in clinical psychology: correlational or passive observational designs, and experiments (Kazdin, this volume). *Correlational* or *observational designs* are those in which the researcher systematically studies relationships among variables without trying to manipulate these relationships. Correlational designs will be discussed more fully below. *Experiments* are those studies in which the researcher actively manipulates at least one variable and measures the effect of this manipulation on another variable. Therapy-outcome studies (see Kendall, Flannery-Schroeder, & Ford, this volume) are a good example of experimental designs in clinical psychology; the researcher actively provides treatment (the manipulation) to research participants and then measures the effects of this treatment on psychopathology (the dependent variable). In psychopathology research, experiments are typically designed either to induce psychopathological states or milder analogues of disorder or to reduce or mitigate such states via manipulation of vulnerability, stress, or both.

Of course, even if a researcher has developed a carefully designed manipulation, he or she cannot assume that the manipulation "worked" as expected. Thus, an important component of a well-designed experiment is a *manipulation check* or a measurement of the effectiveness of the manipulation. For example, an investigator interested in the effect of exposure to threat (e.g., a live cobra) on memory for stimuli in the environmental context might check on the effectiveness of the manipulation by assessing subjective, behavioral, and physiological indices of anxiety before and after the threat exposure. It is only by knowing the degree of effectiveness of the manipulation that the researcher can interpret any obtained difference or lack of difference in contextual memory between the experimental (exposed to threat) and control (no exposure to threat) groups.

Experimental designs come in two varieties: true experiments and quasi-experiments. In a *true experiment,* research participants are assigned at random to the different conditions (e.g., experimental and control groups). Each participant has an equal likelihood of being assigned to any of the groups. An essential characteristic of a true experiment is a control group that is equivalent to the treatment group on all dimensions except for the one being manipulated (see below for more discussion of control groups). True experiments provide the researcher with better control over the independent variable than any other research design, and for this reason, many researchers view the true experiment as the preferred design for making strong inferences regarding the causal role of vulnerability and stress in disorder. Our "ideal" design above is an example of a true experiment. However, frequently, a true experiment is not possible. Often, researchers who study vulnerability-stress models of psychopathology want to compare high-risk (vulnerable) and low-risk (nonvulnerable) individuals to help determine whether and how vulnerability contributes to the development of disorder. These investigators may not be able to assign participants to high- and low-risk conditions for ethical or practical reasons; thus, random assignment is impossible. In cases such as this, researchers resort to using quasi-experimental designs. A *quasi-experiment* is identical to a true experiment except that assignment of participants to groups is not done randomly, but is instead conducted in a systematic way based on participants' a priori characteristics. For example, the investigator may select participants with and without panic disorder, rather than randomly assigning normal participants to a panic-induction versus a control condition. However, even when there are no obvious confounding differences between the pathological and control groups, there is no guarantee that the groups are equivalent with the exception of the presence of disorder.

Issues of Participant Selection

Researchers study subgroups of people. These subgroups are called *samples,* and the job of the researcher is to use statistical techniques to make inferences from samples to the entire population of individuals they are interested in understanding. The extent to which the investigator is safely able to make these inferences is called *external validity.* To maximize external validity, experimenters may use random selection of research participants from a population. *Random selection* is a strategy for choosing participants in which each member of the population is equally likely to be included in the sample. For example, in a study of genetic predisposition to generalized anxiety disorder, every person with the genetic vulnerability would have an equal likelihood of ending up in the study.

Where random selection is possible, it enables researchers to use small samples and still make valid inferences about the population. However, random selection is often impossible to achieve. In the above example, random selection would require that the researchers include at-risk people of all ages, nationalities, and language groups. Participants would have to come from all parts of the world, and people without telephones or mailing addresses would have to be contacted and chosen to participate. Needless to say, this would be prohibitively expensive if not completely impossible. For this reason, researchers often use convenience samples rather than random samples. A *convenience sample* is a group of research participants chosen, at least in part, because the researcher has access to them. Many psychopathology studies, for example, use samples of university students because many researchers work at universities.

Most psychopathology research utilizes convenience samples, and this often does not pose problems. However, some questions are worth asking before one decides to settle for an easily selected, local sample. If a college sample is being used, are college-age individuals, or individuals with the intellectual and financial resources to go to college, as likely as others to exhibit the signs of a particular disorder? If the study is being conducted in an urban setting, are the relevant stresses similar in urban and rural environments? Are people who are willing to participate in the study meaningfully different from those who are unwilling? Most generally, do the factors that make particular individuals convenient members of the sample also affect their vulnerability, exposure to stress, or likelihood of exhibiting the disorder? If so, then findings obtained from the study may not lead to valid inferences about the population.

Participant Matching

One problem psychopathology researchers sometimes encounter is that the hypothe-sized causes of disorder (vulnerability, stress) that they are interested in studying may themselves be correlated with other variables. This situation is not problematic in all cases, but it poses serious difficulties when the correlated "third variables" actually predict the disorder of interest. For example, depression is more common among women than men (Nolen-Hoeksema, 1987). A researcher interested in testing the in-terpersonal theory of depression (e.g., Coyne, 1976; Joiner, 1995) may run into prob-lems if it turns out that a reassurance-seeking or negative feedback-seeking style (the hypothesized vulnerabilities) is more common among women than men. If this were the case, the finding that people with the negative interpersonal style are more likely to become depressed than those without this style may be due to gender differences, rather than to the interpersonal strategies per se.

One way to combat this problem is to use *participant matching*. In this technique, the study groups are equated on potential "third variables." Matching can be carried out on either a samplewide or individual basis. In samplewide matching, the investiga-tor ensures that the study groups as a whole are equated on potentially confounding variables (after the study, groups are compared and found not to differ). For example, in a study on interpersonal aspects of depression, high and low reassurance-seeking groups can be equated on gender, ethnic group, and so on. In individual matching, each participant in one group is paired (matched) on a case-by-case basis with a par-ticipant from another group who has similar characteristics. For example, each female participant high on reassurance-seeking may be paired with a female participant low on reassurance-seeking with whom she shares similar ethnic and class backgrounds. The same may then be done with the male participants. With individual matching, specific research designs may be used, but with either type of matching, the investi-gator strives to ensure that the high- and low-risk groups are balanced in terms of gen-der, class, and ethnicity. Under these circumstances, differences in the rates of depression between the two groups are more likely to be due to differences in inter-personal style than to differences in any of these other potentially confounding fac-tors. It is important to consider, however, that matching may create as many problems as it remedies if one or both of the groups become unrepresentative of the population from which they were drawn in order to achieve matching (Huesmann, 1982). As an illustration, to match a schizophrenic and normal control group on IQ, it may be nec-essary to select high-IQ schizophrenics or low-IQ normals, leaving one or the other group unrepresentative of its corresponding population.

Internal and External Validity

To draw valid inferences and clearly demonstrate a particular relationship among vulnerability, stress, and resultant disorder, investigators must operationalize these constructs by defining them in specific, quantifiable terms. This simplification and isolation of variables is essential to minimizing the ambiguity of research findings; without it, confounding variables enable a variety of alternative interpretations that could explain an observed relation among vulnerability, stress, and disorder. *Internal validity,* a crucial facet of well-conducted research, refers to the extent to which a study rules out alternative explanations of the findings. This type of experimental validity is addressed by the question: To what extent can the specific variable of interest (e.g., vulnerability, stress, and their combination), rather than extraneous influences, be considered to account for the results (Kazdin, 1998)? One of the best ways to ensure internal validity is to include appropriate control groups in the study design. We discuss control groups in the next section.

Factors other than the independent variables (vulnerability and stress) that could explain research results are referred to as *threats to internal validity.* Although numerous threats to internal validity have been identified (Cook & Campbell, 1979; Kazdin, 1998), several are particularly relevant to psychopathology research. *Testing* refers to the effects of repeated testing or assessment in which task performance or symptom endorsement may be influenced by practice or familiarity. *Instrumentation* involves changes in measurement instruments or procedures over time and is especially relevant to longitudinal data. *Statistical regression* refers to the tendency for extreme scores to revert toward the mean of a distribution with repeated administration of a measure. The threat of *attrition* involves the differential loss of participants across conditions within a study that may influence group score. Finally, *maturation* refers to processes within the participant that change over time (e.g., remission of disorder, aging, fatigue). Note that maturation is not necessarily a threat to internal validity; in fact, it may be the focus of study, particularly in certain quasi-experimental designs in which there is no treatment group or experimental condition.

External validity refers to the extent to which research findings generalize beyond the specific conditions of a study to other populations, settings, conditions, and so on. This dimension of experimental validity is addressed by the question: To what extent can these results be extended or generalized to people, settings, measures, and/or characteristics other than those used in this particular study (Kazdin, 1998)? Threats to external validity indicate the boundaries of a research finding, the parameters that constrain a demonstrated relationship among vulnerability, stress, and disorder.

Of the various threats to external validity that have been identified, two are particularly relevant to vulnerability-stress models. *Reactivity of assessment* involves limitations to generalizability that occur when a participant's awareness of being assessed influences his or her responses. *Timing of measurement* refers to the contingency of results on the point in time when assessment instruments were administered. For example, as described earlier in our discussion of distal versus proximal causes, assessment of life events two years before onset of disorder as the relevant stress in a study designed to test a vulnerability-stress model that features recent life events would provide misleading findings with regard to the validity of the model.

An important issue related to external validity is the discrepancy among researchers' methods of operationalizing constructs of study. Differences in operational definitions can lead to different conclusions about vulnerability-stress disorder relations and impede comparability with other findings. For example, the study of childhood depression has commonly involved child self-report of depressive symptoms, parents' ratings of the child's depression, and interview-based psychiatric diagnosis. Kazdin (1989) found that when all three methods are compared for the same sample, there is little overlap among the children identified as depressed.

A natural tension exists between internal and external validity, such that greater control over threats to internal validity generally result in decreased generalizability of the findings. The trade-offs between emphasizing internal versus external validity must be considered within the context of the specific hypotheses of a given vulnerability-stress model. Given that one must first obtain an unambiguous finding before one can generalize about it, internal validity often takes logical precedence over external validity. However, highly controlled experimental conditions rarely approximate the real-life environment in which disorders actually occur. Further, the failure to generalize inspires further theoretical elaboration and empirical research to clarify these emerging facets of psychological disorders.

Control Groups

If an investigator were interested in examining the role of perfectionism as a vulnerability for obsessive-compulsive disorder (Frost & Gross, 1993; Frost, Steketee, Cohn, & Griess, 1994), he or she might expose a group of participants to unsolvable problems in the laboratory (guaranteeing that they would make errors) and examine the effect of this treatment on their level of obsessive-compulsive symptoms. Imagine that the researcher found that the participants showed an average of three symptoms following unsolvable problems. How could he or she determine whether this is different from what would have happened if they had not made errors on unsolvable problems? To answer this question, the researcher would need to compare this group to another group of people who had not been exposed to the unsolvable problems. This second group would be the control group. In an experimental design, a *control group* is a group of research participants who do not receive the experimental manipulation and whose outcomes can be compared to those of the experimental group. In a correlational study, a control group is a group of participants who differ from the group of interest and whose outcomes can serve as a comparison. For example, in a correlational study of the impact of an alcoholic parent on family functioning, the control group might consist of families in which there is no alcoholic parent. Ideally, a control group should be similar to the experimental group on all dimensions except for the experimental manipulation.

There are many different kinds of control groups, and the type to use depends largely on the research questions being asked. In studies testing vulnerability-stress models, the choice of appropriate control groups can be quite complex. Two examples will illustrate why selection of control groups can be a tricky but important question for researchers.

Imagine a researcher who is interested in studying anxiety sensitivity as a vulnerability factor for the development of panic attacks (Schmidt et al., 1997). He or she conducts a prospective study (see below) to determine whether individuals who measure high on anxiety sensitivity but have not yet had a panic attack are more likely to develop panic than other individuals. What other individuals should be included in the study? One possibility is that the investigator could compare high-anxiety-sensitivity participants to people whose anxiety sensitivity is unusually low. An advantage to this approach is that the statistical power will be good; in other words, if there are differences in development of panic between high- and low-anxiety-sensitivity individuals, the researcher will more likely be able to detect those differences than if he or she had used a randomly selected control group. However, what the researcher gains in increased power is paid for in loss of external validity. Knowing that high-anxiety-sensitivity people develop panic more often than low-anxiety-sensitivity people tells us nothing about how high-sensitivity people compare to the average individual. Perhaps high-anxiety-sensitivity people are not actually at increased risk compared to the average person, but instead, low-anxiety-sensitivity people are especially unlikely to develop panic.

One way the researcher could combat this problem is to sample individuals at random and treat anxiety sensitivity as a continuous variable. In other words, he or she might simply measure the correlation between anxiety sensitivity and panic without dividing people into groups. The advantage of this approach is that the results are generalizable to the population at large. However, the researcher runs the risk of not having many participants with high enough vulnerability to lead to development of panic, or of needing a prohibitively large sample to achieve an appropriate statistical conclusion.

Which of these approaches is better? The answer lies in the model for how anxiety sensitivity increases risk for panic. Does vulnerability increase in a continuous fashion, with most people experiencing at least a little risk but some experiencing substantially more vulnerability? If this is what the theory states, then tests should reflect this by treating risk as continuous rather than grouping people by risk status. On the other hand, if the theory holds that there is a threshold beyond which anxiety sensitivity becomes a vulnerability factor, then it is appropriate to include a high-risk group and a low-risk comparison group.

Different issues can arise in tests of vulnerability-stress models. Imagine, for example, that an investigator wants to test whether people with schizophrenia are more likely to have experienced birth complications than nonschizophrenic individuals (Cannon et al., 1993). To whom should the researcher compare the schizophrenic group? If the investigator includes a nonpathological group only, he or she can determine whether birth complications are associated with psychopathology but cannot be certain that they are associated with schizophrenia more than with another disorder. For this reason, it may be wise to include a *specificity control group,* a group of people with another disorder. Once again, the hypothesis to be tested should guide the design. If the theory states that birth complications contribute to schizophrenia but not other disorders, a specificity control group may be necessary. If the theory states that schizophrenia is one of various disorders caused, in part, by birth complications, then a nonpathological control group may be sufficient.

Posttest-Only versus Pretest-Posttest Designs

In experimental designs, another important choice the investigator must make is whether or not to include a pretest prior to the experimental manipulation. The *posttest-only* design, although not the most common, is the most basic experimental design. Generally, participants from a single population are assigned randomly to the various conditions of the independent variable(s) under study (i.e., procedures or interventions) and measured after these conditions are applied. This design may be quite adequate in certain research contexts in which a pretest is not necessary (e.g., brief laboratory experiments using random assignment and a large sample size), not feasible (because of practical or ethical reasons), or undesirable (where pretest sensitization may influence the effects of the independent variable; Kazdin, 1998). A major drawback of this design is that without a pretest, potentially critical information about participants (e.g., traits, demographics, level of functioning) prior to the experiment remains unknown and cannot be used to match participants on relevant dimensions to equalize the groups and rule out alternative interpretations, to predict differential response to an intervention, or to examine differential attrition across groups. A second limitation of posttest-only designs is that one cannot assess change in behavior as a function of the intervention or manipulation.

Consequently, psychopathology researchers often utilize *pretest-posttest designs* to overcome these limitations. Participants who meet particular levels of disorder or vulnerability to disorder are selected prior to the delivery of the independent variable(s) and pretest measurement is used to establish group equivalence. Additionally, the use of a pretest confers statistical advantages by allowing within-subject error variance to be estimated separately from between-subject variance, thereby yielding more powerful statistical tests of the effects of the independent variable (Farrell, this volume). Further, more precise predictions can be examined because pretest data enables the investigator to move beyond simply establishing group differences in the direction of examining the unique impact of independent variables. As mentioned above, the major limitation of this design is the potential effect of the pretest in sensitizing the participant to the conditions of the independent variable.

Analogue Research Designs

Analogue research in psychopathology involves studies of situations that are analogous to real life and, thus, provide a model of how disorders may develop. Analogue designs may employ any of four methods: studies of subclinical phenomena among individuals exhibiting various degrees of psychological symptoms that do not reach diagnostic threshold; the experimental induction of pathological states in normals; animal models of psychopathology; and computer simulation techniques (for review, see Sher & Trull, 1996). An advantage of analogue studies is that the investigator can manipulate potential causal variables (e.g., vulnerability or stress) that could not be manipulated ethically with actually disordered individuals. Whereas analogue designs generally involve controlled experimental or quasi-experimental designs that maximize internal validity, the generalizability of findings from subclinical to clinical populations, from temporarily induced pathological states in normals to naturally occurring disorders, and from animals to humans (see Suomi, this volume) is a fundamental issue.

Given the virtual impossibility of completely modeling human behavior using laboratory analogues, researchers have argued that certain criteria must be established to validate analogue models. For example, Abramson and Seligman (1977) suggested four criteria essential to the validity of human or animal laboratory analogues of psychopathology: (a) a thorough description of the disorder's essential features, including the causes, symptoms, prevention, and treatment; (b) a demonstrated similarity between the analogue model and the actual disorder; (c) an adequate demonstration of the similarity of physiology, cause, prevention, and cure; and (d) specificity of the laboratory analogue in describing a particular disorder rather than others.

CORRELATIONAL DESIGNS IN PSYCHOPATHOLOGY RESEARCH

Correlational or observational designs are those in which the researcher systematically studies relationships (correlations) among variables without manipulating the relationships. In correlational studies, the investigator examines relationships that have occurred naturally. For example, if a researcher wanted to test the hypothesis that early parental loss creates a vulnerability to depression, he or she could not ethically manipulate the death of participants' parents. Instead, the investigator could examine the association between the age of participants when one of their parents happened to die with the likelihood of developing depression by age 50 in a correlational design. Correlational studies may be conducted in either a cross-sectional or longitudinal fashion. *Cross-sectional* studies involve observation of the relationships among independent and dependent variables (e.g., vulnerability, stress, and disorder) measured at one point in time, whereas *longitudinal* studies involve observation of relationships among variables measured at multiple points over time.

Cross-Sectional Case-Control Designs

One type of correlational design used frequently in psychopathology research is the *case-control design,* in which people with a disorder (cases) are compared with people who do not have the disorder in question (controls) on variables of interest (e.g., vulnerability, stress). Cross-sectional correlational designs are popular in part because they are relatively easy and inexpensive to conduct. Compared to experimental designs, however, cross-sectional case-control studies provide a weak basis for drawing causal inferences. This weakness is because they can establish only one of the three conditions for causal inference (covariation of causes and outcomes, temporal precedence of causes, and elimination of plausible alternative causes), namely, covariation of potential causes (vulnerability, stress) with outcomes (disorder). Even if one observes a correlation between potential vulnerability factors or stressors and disorder, cross-sectional case-control studies cannot establish whether the vulnerability and/or stress temporally preceded disorder and are less able to rule out plausible alternative causes.

One strategy employed by many investigators of vulnerability-stress models is to try to establish cross-sectional relationships between the presence of disorder and vulnerability or stress through the use of correlational designs first, before testing the theory with more difficult and expensive experimental or longitudinal designs that permit stronger causal inferences. However, this strategy can mislead an investigator about a theory's validity. For example, if the hypothesized vulnerability or stressor occurs prior to onset of the disorder and does not overlap in time with the disorder, then use of this strategy may lead the researcher to reject the model when, in fact, an appropriate longitudinal design would have supported the model. Thus, as discussed earlier, it is crucial to take into account the logical and temporal relations between hypothesized causes and disorder in choosing a suitable research design for testing a vulnerability-stress theory.

Longitudinal Designs

Correlational studies that are longitudinal allow the researcher to specify the time-order relationship among vulnerability, stress, and disorder because the same participants are studied on more than one occasion over time. Longitudinal designs can be *retrospective,* looking backward in time, or *prospective,* looking forward in time.

Retrospective and Follow-Back Studies

In a typical retrospective study, disordered cases and nondisordered controls are selected and asked to recall information about past stress or past vulnerability factors. Although such studies may suggest that posited vulnerabilities and stressors are related to disorder and, possibly, preceded disorder in time, a major shortcoming is that retrospective recall is subject to forgetting as well as systematic biases based on the participants' knowledge of their current disorder status. As an example, people with social phobia may recall more humiliating experiences in their past in an effort to explain their current social anxiety, a bias called "effort after meaning" (G. W. Brown & Harris, 1978), than will nonsocially phobic controls. Even temporal precedence of vulnerability and stress factors is more difficult to establish with retrospective designs because it is not possible to distinguish with certainty between the hypothesis that past vulnerability or stress contributed to the present disorder or that early signs of the disorder in the past contributed to the past occurrence of vulnerability or stress (Alloy, Lipman, & Abramson, 1992).

In *follow-back* studies, cases and controls are identified and then preexisting records (e.g., doctors' records, school records) of their experiences or characteristics are located, rather than risking the possibility of recall biases by having the participants or other informants recall the relevant past history. However, even preexisting records may contain systematic biases related to participants' current disorder status, as, for example, when school records are incomplete for currently disordered participants because of school truancy, which, in turn, may be related to their adult outcome (Achenbach, 1982). Thus, in sum, retrospective studies can provide useful information but they are not optimal, as a rule, for testing vulnerability-stress models of disorder.

Remitted Disorder Studies

In *remitted disorder* or *postmorbid studies,* individuals who have recovered or remitted from a disorder are compared to currently symptomatic cases and normal controls. This comparison can be made in a cross-sectional version of the design or, more commonly, in a longitudinal version. In longitudinal versions of the design, disordered cases are compared to nondisordered controls both when the cases are symptomatic and then, after follow-up, when the cases' symptoms have remitted. In addition, longitudinal within-subject comparisons are also usually conducted of cases in the symptomatic versus the remitted states. In psychopathology research, remitted disorder studies are most commonly used to test whether certain variables act as vulnerability factors for the disorder in question (e.g., Barnett & Gotlib, 1988; Cornblatt & Keilp, 1994). The logic is that if some biological or psychological characteristic is a vulnerability factor for a disorder, then this characteristic should be highly stable and persist beyond remission of a current episode of the disorder. On the other hand, if the characteristic is a symptom or concomitant of the disorder, then it should be present during the episode of the disorder but dissipate upon remission of the episode (Alloy, Abramson, & Just, 1995; Alloy et al., 1992; Just, Abramson, & Alloy, in press). For example, if attentional dysfunction is a vulnerability factor for schizophrenia, as some theories have suggested (e.g., Cornblatt & Keilp, 1994), then attentional problems should be present both when a schizophrenic is actively symptomatic as well as when his or her symptoms have abated.

Remitted disorder designs may be one of the research strategies of choice for testing whether vulnerabilities or stressors worsen or otherwise change as a consequence of experiencing an episode of disorder. They may also be extremely useful in determining whether vulnerabilities and stressors that are present following an episode of a disorder (regardless of whether they were present prior to the initial onset of the disorder) predict relapses or recurrences of the disorder. However, Just et al. (in press; Alloy et al., 1995) provided four reasons why remitted designs are problematic for testing whether certain characteristics act as vulnerabilities for onset of a disorder. Here, we discuss two of these reasons with broadest applicability to a range of disorders. The first, and most telling, reason why remitted disorder studies are nonoptimal is that they cannot distinguish whether a particular characteristic is a vulnerability factor or a consequence of disorder. Even if remitted disorder studies found that a hypothesized vulnerability factor was present during the remitted state, such results would still leave uncertain whether the characteristic was present before the episode and contributed to its onset or, instead, developed as a result of the disorder. If remitted disorder studies do not permit inferences about the validity of vulnerability hypotheses regardless of what results are obtained, then they are not optimal designs for testing these hypotheses.

A second problem with remitted disorder designs is that they are based on the assumption that the hypothesized vulnerability is an immutable (unchanging) trait and, thus, should be exhibited in the remitted as well as the symptomatic state. Although this may be appropriate for theories that propose genetic diatheses for disorder, not all vulnerability-stress models feature an immutable trait as the vulnerability. Thus, if a particular vulnerability-stress model features a vulnerability factor that may change over time, remitted disorder designs would not provide an appropriate test of the vulnerability hypothesis of such a model (Alloy et al., 1995; Just et al., in press). We discuss the methodological implications of the relative stability of hypothesized vulnerabilities further in the section "Stability."

Prospective Studies

A *prospective study* is a specific kind of longitudinal design in which the hypothesized causes of a disorder (vulnerabilities, stressors) are assessed (in a correlational version of the design) or manipulated (in an experimental version of the design) prior to the measurement of the dependent variable (the disorder) at some later point in time. Prospective studies, even if they do not include an experimental manipulation, are one of the best designs for testing vulnerability-stress models of disorder because they not only can establish covariation between hypothesized causes and disorder but also allow for the relatively unambiguous determination that the hypothesized causes preceded the occurrence of disorder (two of the conditions necessary for establishing causality). However, even in prospective studies, plausible alternative causes ("third variables") must still be ruled out either by assessing the potential alternative causes and controlling for them statistically, by matching participants on potential alternative causes, or by manipulating the potential alternative causes and observing their effects on disorder. Prospective studies may involve a single follow-up of participants who vary initially on vulnerability and stress, but they provide better tests of vulnerability-stress models when they include repeated assessments of vulnerability, stress, and disorder over time.

Prospective studies have several advantages over other research designs (e.g., Cannon & Mednick, 1993). First, the participants have not yet experienced confounding effects of the relevant disorder such as medication, hospitalization, or symptoms that could, in turn, affect the measurement of vulnerability or stress. Second, much bias is eliminated from the assessments of vulnerability and stress because neither the participant, other informants, nor the researcher knows who will develop the disorder. Finally, information from the assessments of vulnerability and stress is current and does not depend on the participants' or other informants' recollection.

High-Risk Studies

One of the most powerful forms of prospective, longitudinal research in psychopathology is the high-risk design. *High-risk designs* involve the prospective, longitudinal study of people who have a high probability of developing a disorder of interest in the future because they possess the hypothesized vulnerability for the disorder. In *genetic high-risk studies,* used to test genetic vulnerability-stress models of disorder, participants (usually children) who do not initially have the disorder of interest but who are at risk for developing the disorder because they have a parent, twin, or other first-degree relative with the disorder are followed prospectively along with a comparison group of participants with normal first-degree relatives who are at hypothesized low genetic risk for the disorder (e.g., Cannon & Mednick, 1993; Mednick & Silverton, 1988; see Moldin, this volume). Another type of high-risk design that has been used increasingly in recent years is the *behavioral high-risk design* (e.g., Alloy et al., 1992; Chapman, Chapman, Kwapil, Eckblad, & Zinser, 1994; Depue et al., 1981). In this paradigm, nondisordered participants are chosen not because of genetic risk, but because they possess some behavioral characteristic hypothesized to make them vulnerable to developing a particular disorder in the future and are followed prospectively, along with a comparison group of individuals who score low on the hypothesized behavioral vulnerability.

In addition to all of the general advantages of prospective studies, high-risk designs have the additional feature that they have two built-in control groups: low-risk participants and high-risk participants who do not develop the disorder. The latter comparison group allows the investigator to study the role of stress as a factor that determines which high-risk participants develop the disorder as well as the role of potential moderating variables that serve to protect some high-risk participants from developing the disorder.

DIFFICULT CONCEPTUAL/METHODOLOGICAL ISSUES IN PSYCHOPATHOLOGY RESEARCH

In addition to choosing an appropriate research design from among the options reviewed above, an investigator who wishes to test hypotheses derived from a vulnerability-stress model also must confront several difficult conceptual issues with important methodological implications that complicate the implementation of these designs. Although there are many conceptual/methodological issues to be considered in vulnerability-stress re search, we discuss some of the most important ones here.

Interdependence of Vulnerability, Stress, and Disorder

It is often assumed that the hypothesized vulnerability, stress, and resultant disorder are independent of one another. That is, the predisposition to a disorder is assumed to lie dormant until activated by independent environmental inputs, and then the interaction of these constitutional and environmental factors is thought to lead to the development of the disorder. In reality, however, this situation rarely occurs. Instead, vulnerability, stress, and disorder are typically interdependent in ways that greatly complicate researchers' ability to test such models of psychopathology (Monroe & Simons, 1991). We examine some of these interdependencies in turn.

Effects of Vulnerability on Stress

Hypothesized vulnerabilities, whether genetic, biological, behavioral, or cognitive in nature, may influence either the measurement or the actual occurrence of hypothesized stressors. For example, the assessment of hypothesized stressors such as poor parenting or stressful life events may be affected by perceptual or reporting biases engendered by cognitive or personality diatheses. To illustrate further, the predispositions featured in cognitive vulnerability-stress models of depression (e.g., Abramson et al., 1989; Beck, 1987) involve a style to perceive and interpret life experiences negatively. Individuals who exhibit such negative cognitive styles may be more likely than those who do not possess this vulnerability to report relatively benign experiences as negative events and to perceive negative life events that do occur as especially aversive or "stressful" (Monroe & Simons, 1991). Thus, in general, the attempt to measure the featured stressors in vulnerability-stress models and to test the stressors' contribution to the development of disorder may be confounded by vulnerability-based perceptual or reporting biases. Such confounding could lead to statistical interactions between diathesis and stress that do not actually provide support for the vulnerability-stress model because the vulnerability is counted twice, once in the measure of vulnerability and again in the measure of stress (Cohen & Wills, 1985; Monroe & Simons, 1991; Thoits, 1982).

The potential confounding effects of vulnerabilities are not limited to the measurement of stress; vulnerabilities may affect the occurrence of the hypothesized stressors as well. Many stressors featured in various vulnerability-stress models of disorder are at least partially under people's control. Individual differences in vulnerability may influence the environments to which people expose themselves as well as actually contribute to the production of some stressors. Consider, as examples, that someone high in perfectionism, a hypothesized diathesis for obsessive-compulsive disorder in one theory (Frost & Gross, 1993; Frost et al., 1994), may tend to expose himself or herself to situations in which mistakes (a triggering stressor for OCD) are inevitable, or that someone high in dependency, a hypothesized predisposition to depression in some interpersonal theories (Blatt & Zuroff, 1992; Hirschfeld et al., 1989), may engage in excessive reassurance-seeking that eventuates in his or her rejection (a triggering stressor for depression) by significant others (e.g., Coyne, 1976; Joiner, 1995). Even stressors that occur early in life may be affected by vulnerability. A schizophrenic woman may not only pass on her genetic vulnerability to her offspring, but her genetic risk may also lead her to behave in ways (e.g., poor prenatal care) that increase the chances her offspring will be exposed to birth complications (a hypothesized stressor for schizophrenia) as well. In sum, exposure to stress may not be random but, rather, may be systematically influenced by a person's vulnerability (Monroe & Simons, 1991).

How is an investigator to cope with the potential effects of vulnerability on stress? There are no easy solutions, but psychopathology researchers have suggested several useful procedures. One recommendation to increase the degree of independence between vulnerability and measured stress is to utilize investigator-based rather than respondent-based assessment procedures (e.g., G. W. Brown & Harris, 1986; Dohrenwend, Link, Kern, Shrout, & Markowitz, 1990), whereby hypothesized stressors such as poor parenting or stressful life events are assessed via direct observation or the investigator's ratings, respectively, rather than the person's self-report. To begin to address the potential impact of vulnerability on the actual generation of stress, researchers suggest two approaches. First, high- versus low-vulnerable persons can be compared on their exposure to stress (measured according to investigator ratings) prior to the onset of disorder to determine whether differences in vulnerability-driven stress generation must be included as additional pathways in the vulnerability-stress model of a disorder (Monroe & Simons, 1991). Second, investigators can rate the degree to which stress is independent of versus dependent on the person's behavior or vulnerability and include only independent stressors (e.g., uncontrollable or fateful stressors) in their tests of vulnerability-stress predictions (G. W. Brown & Harris, 1986; Shrout et al., 1989).

Effects of Disorder on Stress

Not only can vulnerability influence the measurement and occurrence of stress, but disorder, too, may be confounded with stress in these same two ways. The disorder itself or early subsyndromal symptoms of the disorder may affect stressor measurement, as in the case of an individual with paranoid symptoms who perceives and reports the benign comments of others as hostile communications. Behavioral manifestations of disorder also can generate stress that, in turn, further exacerbates the disorder (Hammen, 1991). Consider, for example, a socially phobic individual whose blushing and trembling during a speech interferes with her performance and, thus, increases her anxiety further (Schneier, 1991; Uhde, Tancer, Black, & Brown, 1991). The potential contamination of stress by disorder may be addressed methodologically with the same procedures described above for the confounding of stress by vulnerability. In addition, however, the potential contaminating effects of disorder on stress call for the use of prospective, longitudinal designs in which stress is assessed prior to the onset of disorder and, therefore, is unconfounded by disorder.

Effects of Disorder on Vulnerability

The occurrence of disorder or subsyndromal early manifestations of disorder can also influence a person's level of vulnerability. Specifically, vulnerability may initially develop or preexisting vulnerability may be exacerbated as a consequence of disorder, similar to the manner in which a physical injury may leave a scar (e.g., Rohde, Lewinsohn, & Seeley, 1990; Zeiss & Lewinsohn, 1988). As an example, the experience of a panic attack may worsen an individual's anxiety sensitivity (a hypothesized vulnerability factor for panic disorder; Schmidt et al., 1997) or may create anxiety sensitivity where it did not previously exist.

Investigators have utilized two approaches to deal with the potential effects of disorder on vulnerability. The first, and preferred, approach is to adopt a prospective, longitudinal design in which participants who vary in their levels of vulnerability but who do not currently have the disorder of interest are followed through a period of risk to examine the likelihood of disorder onset (Alloy et al., 1995; Just et al., in press). A further issue with this solution, however, is whether one should select currently nondisordered participants or, even more stringently, never disordered participants. Never disordered participants provide perhaps the cleanest test of vulnerability effects on the likelihood of disorder onset, uncontaminated by "scars" from prior occurrences of the disorder. However, by selecting participants who have no prior history of the disorder, one might be left with an unrepresentative group of high-risk participants who, despite being vulnerable to the disorder, have been protected by unknown factors from actually developing the disorder (Alloy et al., 1995). This would lead to an overly conservative test of a vulnerability hypothesis.

The second approach for dealing with possible confounding effects of current or past disorder on vulnerability is to control for disorder statistically by including measures of current or past disorder as a covariate in analyses predicting future disorder from vulnerability (and stress). However, the covariate approach also provides a very conservative test of the vulnerability hypothesis. The problem is that any variance in future disorder onset that is shared between vulnerability and current or past disorder is allocated to current or past disorder rather than to vulnerability, even though the vulnerability hypothesis predicts that such shared variance should exist (assuming that the sample is experiencing some stress). In such a case, an obtained relationship between vulnerability and future disorder onset may vanish when measures of current or past disorder are used as covariates, even when the vulnerability hypothesis is, in fact, correct. Use of this covariate approach, then, may lead to pseudofalsification of a valid vulnerability hypothesis (see Meehl, 1971). Thus, whether to select out or control statistically for past or current disorder in tests of vulnerability-stress models remains a very thorny question.

Issues in the Assessment of Vulnerability

A powerful test of any vulnerability-stress model requires adequate measurement of the hypothesized vulnerability factor. Although many issues arise in measuring vulnerability (e.g., internal consistency), we discuss two that are particularly important in a theory-based approach: priming and stability.

Priming

Just as researchers of physical health problems have discovered that some biological vulnerabilities to physical disorders cannot be detected easily when a person is in a baseline or resting state, psychopathologists (e.g., Depue & Monroe, 1983) have suggested that some vulnerabilities to various mental disorders lie "latent" until activated by appropriate stimuli. For example, in Beck's (1967, 1987) theory, the negative self-schema, a hypothesized cognitive vulnerability factor for depression, is characterized as latent until activated by the occurrence of a life event that is relevant to the content embodied in the self-schema. More recently, several theorists (e.g., Persons & Miranda, 1992; Segal & Ingram, 1994) have further proposed that a negative mood state also may activate or prime cognitive vulnerabilities for depression.

Adequate measurement of a hypothesized latent vulnerability requires a *challenge protocol* in which the relevant biological or psychological system is primed environmentally, pharmacologically, or in some other way (Depue & Monroe, 1983). To be useful, a theory featuring a latent vulnerability factor must specify the prime(s) hypothesized to activate the vulnerability. Thus, to continue with the depression example, a researcher wishing to test Beck's (1967, 1987) vulnerability-stress model would need to prime negative self-schemata with negative events or mood to provide a measure of vulnerability with high theoretical fidelity. Currently, controversy surrounds Beck's priming hypothesis because some prospective (e.g., Alloy et al., in press; Alloy, Abramson, Murray, Whitehouse, & Hogan, 1997; G. P. Brown, Hammen, Craske, & Wickens, 1995) and laboratory (Dykman, 1997) studies have found that even when measured in an unprimed state, cognitive vulnerabilities still predict depression onset and/or increases. Future research is needed to determine which hypothesized vulnerabilities for various disorders actually do require priming for adequate measurement.

Stability

Another important measurement issue is the stability of the hypothesized vulnerability factor. Different measurement strategies are required for vulnerabilities that do not change over time compared to those that may change. Historically, psychopathologists often have inferred, incorrectly we would argue, that to qualify as a vulnerability factor, a variable must possess traitlike stability. Perhaps this assumption arose from adoption of the term diathesis, which nicely denotes an individual difference variable but, unfortunately, also may connote traitlike stability given that this term sometimes is used in medicine to refer to a fixed characteristic providing risk for a disorder. Consequently, we prefer the term vulnerability to diathesis because the former is less likely to connote stability than the latter.

An example from medicine illuminates that an individual difference vulnerability factor for disease need not necessarily show traitlike stability and, instead, may show transient or long-term fluctuations. Consider the role the immune system plays in vulnerability to disease. A person's vulnerability to various diseases is in part a function of the integrity of the various arms of his or her immune system. Marked immune suppression increases vulnerability for a host of diseases, from influenza at the mild end to cancer at the severe end of the continuum. Yet, the integrity of the various branches of a person's immune system can change over time (e.g., Coe, 1994; Schindler, 1991).

Similarly, it is possible that at least some vulnerabilities for various psychopathologies may change over time. Consistent with this view, some schizophrenia researchers have begun to suggest that vulnerability for schizophrenia may vary over time within a given individual as well as across individuals (see Gooding & Iacono, 1995, for an excellent discussion of the evolution of the concept of vulnerability in the field of schizophrenia). For example, Prescott and Gottesman (1993) have entertained the possibility that schizogenes can switch on and off in a given person over time.

The possibility that some vulnerabilities may not be immutable or unchanging over time has critical implications for the design of longitudinal studies. One cannot assume that someone at hypothesized high risk for the relevant disorder at the outset of the study also will be at high risk later in the study or that a low-risk person will remain at low risk. Therefore, an ideal longitudinal study would include assessment of vulnerability at multiple times throughout the follow-up period along with corresponding assessment of disorder to determine whether changing levels of vulnerability predicted expected increases and decreases in the likelihood of disorder. A powerful theory of a given disorder would describe the conditions under which vulnerability is hypothesized to change and thereby specify the optimal times for reassessing vulnerability and consequent disorder during the study.

Issues in the Assessment of Stress

Although vulnerability-stress models of psychopathology rest on the simple premise that stress activates and transforms a preexistent predisposition into disorder, the multifaceted nature of stress and its complex interrelations with disorder and vulnerability introduce formidable challenges to its assessment. Given that many vulnerability-stress models of disorder focus on life events as the hypothesized stressor, this section outlines basic conceptual and methodological issues encountered by prominent approaches to life-stress assessment and highlights current methods to standardize measurement.

Respondent- versus Investigator-Based Approaches

Numerous biological and psychosocial constructs have been employed in the study of stressful life experiences. Although there is no consensus as to a single definition of stress, the construct is generally viewed as a transaction between an individual and his or her environment (Monroe & Roberts, 1990). For psychosocial models in particular, the nature of this transaction—the individual's subjective experience in the context of an objective environment—is a fundamental source of theoretical and methodological problems that are represented by two major approaches to stress measurement. *Respondent-based* approaches adopt a subjective reference point by utilizing the self-report of the individual experiencing the stressor. This approach regards respondents as the most qualified with respect to evaluating stressful circumstances in their own lives and, consequently, relies extensively on the individual's perception and interpretation of an event. In contrast, *investigator-based* approaches are anchored in objective characteristics of a stressor and the environmental context in which events occur. Here, the goal is to assess the nature and magnitude of an event without the contaminating influence of an individual's idiosyncratic perceptual tendencies (G. W. Brown, 1981). To illustrate the difference between the two approaches, consider two participants who each indicate on a life events checklist that they experienced the stressor of "a serious illness in the family" in the past month. One participant is referring to her mother's diagnosis of cancer and the other to his cousin's earache. In a respondent-based approach to the measure of stress, the participant's subjective report would be accepted as his or her level of stress. In an investigator-based approach, a set of a priori criteria would be developed for deciding whether the participant's actual experience (mother's cancer or cousin's earache) qualified as an example of "a serious illness in the family."

Although respondent-based methods and the use of self-report measures are most commonly used in life-stress research, the interdependence of vulnerability, stress, and disorder discussed earlier renders this approach quite problematic for vulnerability-stress models. The potential fusion of independent (stress, vulnerability) and dependent (disorder) variables that accompanies respondent-based methods has motivated researchers to examine the stressor and diathesis components separately to more clearly examine their relations to disorder. It is worth emphasizing that the focus of investigator-based methods on environmental facets of stress in no way diminishes the significance of subjective perception. On the contrary, vulnerability-stress models that adopt the investigator-based measurement approach often view perceptions as extremely important in mediating the effect of objective characteristics of the environment on the onset, course, and remission of disorder. In fact, by separating these potentially confounded components, investigators have begun to demonstrate, for example, that participants' cognitive styles influence the generation of life events, the threshold for reporting life events, and the rating of their severity (Dohrenwend et al., 1990; Simons, Angell, Monroe, & Thase, 1993). Investigator-based approaches simply maintain that the effects of individual differences in vulnerability can only be examined meaningfully within a system of measurement that clearly distinguishes between objective characteristics of stress and an individual's perceptions of it (Monroe & Roberts, 1990).

Definitional and Procedural Issues in Operationalizing Stress

To distinguish between diathesis and stressor components, studies designed to test vulnerability-stress models must establish a set of procedures and operational criteria for assessing stressful events. To address the most fundamental issue of what constitutes an event, researchers must utilize several strategies. First, definitional criteria for life events must be specified to set a threshold for what environmental conditions qualify as stressors. Then, threshold conditions that distinguish events according to their magnitude (e.g., major events, minor events, hassles, chronic difficulties) must be established. The extensive work of G. W. Brown and Harris (1978, 1989) in the development of the Bedford College Life Events and Difficulties Schedule (LEDS) and rating system exemplifies efforts to standardize event definitions. Based on the notion of contextual threat and the average expectable impact of a stressor given an individual's specific biographical circumstances, the LEDS system controls for individual differences in perception by utilizing consensually derived definitions and ratings of stress.

A related issue that arises in the operationalization of stress involves how to go about representing the complexity of stressful circumstances. In other words, at what point should different aspects of a stressful encounter be considered separate events? Again, a set of clear guidelines and procedures must be established. To date, such guidelines have focused on the determination of whether various facets of an experience involve distinct implications with respect to coping, threat, or consequences. Temporal features of the event occurrence can also guide the appropriate partitioning of complex experiences. For example, researchers assessing life events may adopt a "one-day rule" for those cases that could be recorded as single or multiple events. That is, if the events occurred within the same day (e.g., broken leg and contusions) and do not pose significantly distinct demands on the individual with respect to coping or consequences, they may be represented as a single event (e.g., an accident).

Issues in the Assessment of Disorder

Formidable conceptual issues with important methodological implications also surround the assessment of disorder in vulnerability-stress models. We consider two of the most relevant issues here: the continuity versus discontinuity of disorder and disorder subtypes.

Continuity versus Discontinuity of Disorder

Among clinical researchers, there is much debate about whether psychopathological disorders are continuous or discontinuous with milder psychological distress or dysfunction. The essence of the *continuity issue* is whether mild and moderate distress or dysfunction differ quantitatively (in degree) or qualitatively (in kind) from syndromal disorder that meets diagnostic criteria (Coyne, 1994; Flett, Vredenburg, & Krames, 1997). Are milder forms of dysfunction distributed throughout the normal population linearly related to diagnosed cases of disorder, or are diagnosed cases distinct entities? The continuity debate is relevant to most forms of psychopathology, including depression (Compas, Ey, & Grant, 1993; Coyne, 1994; Flett et al., 1997), bipolar disorder (Depue et al., 1981), schizophrenia (Lenzenweger & Korfine, 1992), panic disorder (Norton, Cox, & Malan, 1992), social phobia (Davidson, Hughes, George, & Blazer, 1994), obsessive-compulsive disorder (Gibbs, 1996), eating disorders (Shisslak, Crago, & Estes, 1995), and personality disorders (Widiger & Costa, 1994), to name a few. The reader is referred to these references for the current empirical status of the debate for each of these disorders. It is important to distinguish the continuity issue from the comparability issue (Flett et al., 1997; Kendall & Flannery-Schroeder, 1995). Whereas continuity concerns the degree of similarity among various levels of dysfunction within a sample, comparability concerns the generalizability of findings across samples (e.g., between college student and clinical samples), a form of external validity.

The continuity issue has important implications for selection of optimal samples and measurement procedures in psychopathology research. In guiding their choice of research sample and assessment instruments, researchers who wish to test particular vulnerability-stress models of disorder need to carefully consider whether the model in question hypothesizes explicitly or assumes implicitly continuity or discontinuity between subsyndromal forms of the disorder and cases that meet diagnostic threshold. If the model hypothesizes continuity, then studies could appropriately include nonclinical or clinical samples and optimally would use dimensional assessment procedures, whether self-report, observational, or interviewer-rated, that allow for measurement of the full range of severity along the continuum of disturbance. Alternatively, models that assume discontinuity require the use of measurement tools that allow for decisions about diagnostic "caseness," such as semistructured diagnostic interviews (e.g., Schedule for Affective Disorders and Schizophrenia [SADS], Endicott & Spitzer, 1978; Structured Clinical Interview for *DSM-IV* [SCID], Spitzer & Endicott, 1995).

Subtypes of Disorder

A second important consideration in assessing disorder is whether the disorder in question is unitary or is heterogeneous with one or more subtypes. Clinicians and re-searchers alike have long suggested that several different forms of psychopathology, including depression (e.g., Craighead, 1980), schizophrenia (Crow, Cross, Johnstone, & Owen, 1982; Kraepelin, 1923), obsessive-compulsive disorder (Rachman & Hodg-son, 1980), and alcoholism (Cloninger, Bohman, & Sigvardsson, 1981), to name a few, are actually heterogeneous entities. Some vulnerability-stress models specify etiolog-ical pathways hypothesized to lead to the development of a subtype of a heterogeneous disorder; for example, the hopelessness theory (Abramson et al., 1989) predicts the development of the subtype of "hopelessness depression" rather than depression in general, and Cloninger and colleagues' (Cloninger et al., 1981) genetic model predicts a familial subtype of male alcoholism rather than alcoholism in general. Even when a particular vulnerability-stress model does not predict explicitly to a disorder subtype, the possibility that a disorder may, in fact, be heterogeneous with multiple subtypes has important implications for research designed to test the model.

First, research designs (whether cross-sectional, retrospective, or prospective) that compare the likelihood of exhibiting the hypothesized vulnerability or stress in indi-viduals with the general disorder versus nondisordered controls may frequently yield negative results, despite the fact that the vulnerability-stress model is correct, when the general disorder contains subtypes (Abramson et al., 1988; Alloy et al., 1988). This is because not all members of the general disorder category (e.g., schizophrenia) will show the relevant vulnerability or stress if the vulnerability-stress model only predicts to a subtype of the general disorder (e.g., paranoid schizophrenia). Given that some schizophrenics (e.g., catatonic and disorganized types) would not be expected to show the paranoia-relevant vulnerability or stress, whether one obtains differences between a heterogeneous group of schizophrenics and nonschizophrenics on vulnera-bility or stress depends on the prevalence of the relevant subtype (i.e., paranoid type) in the particular sample of general schizophrenics. Moreover, the failure to recognize and assess subtypes of the general disorder can lead to the inability to replicate re-search findings. This is because the magnitude and consistency of vulnerability or stress differences between disordered and nondisordered participants will vary across studies, depending on the base rate of the relevant subtype in each study sample of participants with the heterogeneous, general disorder (Abramson et al., 1988; Buchs-baum & Rieder, 1979). Finally, even prospective studies designed to test whether the interaction of hypothesized vulnerability and stress leads to the future development of a disorder can lead to inappropriate rejection of the theoretical model if the model predicts a subtype of the heterogeneous disorder and the researcher has failed to as-sess the subtype specifically.

CONCLUSION

In reading through this chapter, one might become overwhelmed by the difficult choices of research design and the challenging conceptual and methodological issues an investigator faces in conducting psychopathology research. However, if the reader keeps several general points in mind, the task may not seem so daunting; indeed, it can be fun. First and foremost, as we began this chapter, we end by emphasizing that the choice of research design and the strategies for tackling conceptual and methodological challenges should be guided by the theory or hypothesis to be tested. Second, at present, it is not possible to conduct the "ideal" study, so all research studies are bound to have some shortcomings. By conducting a program of research, an investigator can overcome the limitations of any individual study and gather a body of evidence that leads to valid conclusions. Finally, the excitement and importance of discovering and validating potential risk factors, triggering agents, potentiating and protective factors, and mediating mechanisms for psychopathological disorders can frequently promote elegant and sophisticated solutions to the research design issues covered herein.

REFERENCES

Abramson, L. Y., Alloy, L. B., & Hogan, M. E. (1997). Cognitive/personality subtypes of depression: Theories in search of disorders. *Cognitive Therapy and Research, 21,* 247–265.

Abramson, L. Y., Metalsky, G. I., & Alloy, L. B. (1988). The hopelessness theory of depression: Does the research test the theory? In L. Y. Abramson (Ed.), *Social cognition and clinical psychology: A synthesis* (pp. 33–65). New York: Guilford Press.

Abramson, L. Y., Metalsky, G. I., & Alloy, L. B. (1989). Hopelessness depression: A theory-based subtype of depression. *Psychological Review, 96,* 358–372.

Abramson, L. Y., & Seligman, M. E. P. (1977). Modeling psychopathology in the laboratory: History and rationale. In J. D. Maser & M. E. P. Seligman (Eds.), *Psychopathology: Experimental models.* San Francisco: Freeman.

Achenbach, T. M. (1982). Research methods in developmental psychopathology. In P. C. Kendall & J. N. Butcher (Eds.), *Handbook of research methods in clinical psychology* (1st ed., pp. 569–589). New York: Wiley.

Alloy, L. B., Abramson, L. Y., & Just, N. (1995, November). *Testing the cognitive vulnerability hypotheses of depression onset: Issues of research design.* Paper presented at the Association for the Advancement of Behavior Therapy Meeting, Washington, DC.

Alloy, L. B., Abramson, L. Y., Murray, L. A., Whitehouse, W. G., & Hogan, M. E. (1997). Self-referent information-processing in individuals at high and low cognitive risk for depression. *Cognition and Emotion, 11,* 539–568.

Alloy, L. B., Abramson, L. Y., Whitehouse, W. G., Hogan, M E., Tashman, N. A., Steinberg, D. L., Rose, D. T., & Donovan, P. (in press). Depressogenic cognitive styles: Predictive validity, information processing and personality characteristics, and developmental origins. *Behaviour Research and Therapy.*

Alloy, L. B., Hartlage, S., & Abramson, L. Y. (1988). Testing the cognitive diathesis-stress theories of depression: Issues of research design, conceptualization, and assessment. In L. B. Alloy (Ed.), *Cognitive processes in depression* (pp. 31–73). New York: Guilford Press.

Alloy, L. B., Jacobson, N., & Acocella, J. (1998). *Abnormal psychology: Current perspectives* (8th ed.). New York: McGraw-Hill.

Alloy, L. B., Lipman, A. J., & Abramson, L. Y. (1992). Attributional style as a vulnerability factor for depression: Validation by past history of mood disorders. *Cognitive Therapy and Research, 16,* 391–407.

American Psychiatric Association. (1980). *Diagnostic and statistical manual of mental disorders* (3rd ed.). Washington, DC: Author.

Barnett, P. A., & Gotlib, I. H. (1988). Psychosocial functioning and depression: Distinguishing among antecedents, concomitants, and consequences. *Psychological Bulletin, 104,* 97–126.

Baron, R. M., & Kenny, D. A. (1986). The moderator-mediator variable distinction in social psychological research: Conceptual, strategic, and statistical considerations. *Journal of Personality and Social Psychology, 51,* 1173–1182.

Beck, A. T. (1967). *Depression: Clinical, experimental, and theoretical aspects.* New York: Harper & Row.

Beck, A. T. (1987). Cognitive models of depression. *Journal of Cognitive Psychotherapy: An International Quarterly, 1,* 5–37.

Blatt, S. J., & Zuroff, D. C. (1992). Interpersonal relatedness and self-definition: Two prototypes for depression. *Clinical Psychology Review, 12,* 527–562.

Bracha, H. S., Torrey, E. F., Gottesman, I. I., Bigelow, L. B., & Cunniff, C. (1992). Second-trimester markers of fetal size in schizophrenia: A study of monozygotic twins. *American Journal of Psychiatry, 149,* 1355–1361.

Brown, G. P., Hammen, C. L., Craske, M. G., & Wickens, T. D. (1995). Dimensions of dysfunctional attitudes as vulnerabilities to depressive symptoms. *Journal of Abnormal Psychology, 104,* 431–435.

Brown, G. W. (1981). Life events, psychiatric disorder, and physical illness. *Journal of Psychosomatic Research, 25,* 461–473.

Brown, G. W., & Harris, T. O. (1978). *Social origins of depression: A study of psychiatric disorder in women.* New York: Free Press.

Brown, G. W., & Harris, T. O. (1986). Establishing causal links: The Bedford College studies of depression. In H. Katschnig (Ed.), *Life events and psychiatric disorders: Controversial issues* (pp. 107–187). Cambridge, England: Cambridge University Press.

Brown, G. W., & Harris, T. O. (Eds.). (1989). *Life events and illness.* New York: Guilford Press.

Buchsbaum, M., & Rieder, R. (1979). Biologic heterogeneity and psychiatric research. *Archives of General Psychiatry, 36,* 1163–1169.

Campbell, D. T., & Fiske, D. W. (1959). Convergent and discriminant validation by the multitrait-multimethod matrix. *Psychological Bulletin, 56,* 81–105.

Cannon, T. D., & Mednick, S. A. (1993). The schizophrenia high-risk project in Copenhagen: Three decades of progress. *Acta Psychiatrica Scandinavica,* (Suppl. 370), 33–47.

Cannon, T. D., Mednick, S. A., Parnas, J., Schulsinger, F., Praestholm, J., & Vestergaard, A. (1993). Developmental brain abnormalities in the offspring of schizophrenic mothers: I. Contributions of genetic and perinatal factors. *Archives of General Psychiatry, 50,* 551–564.

Chapman, L. J., Chapman, J. P., Kwapil, T. R., Eckblad, M., & Zinser, M. C. (1994). Putatively psychosis-prone subjects 10 years later. *Journal of Abnormal Psychology, 103,* 171–183.

Cloninger, C. R., Bohman, M., & Sigvardsson, S. (1981). Inheritance of alcohol abuse: Cross-fostering analysis of adopted men. *Archives of General Psychiatry, 38,* 861–868.

Coe, C. L. (1994). Implications of psychoneuroimmunology for allergy and asthma. In E. Middleton, C. E. Reed, E. F. Ellis, N. F. Adkinson, J. W. Yunginger, & W. W. Busse (Eds.), *Allergy: Principles and practice* (4th ed., pp. 1–15). St Louis: Mosby Yearbook.

Cohen, S., & Wills, T. A. (1985). Stress, social support, and the buffering hypothesis. *Psychological Bulletin, 98,* 310–357.

Compas, B. E., Ey, S., & Grant, K. E. (1993). Taxonomy, assessment, and diagnosis of depression during adolescence. *Psychological Bulletin, 114,* 323–344.

Cook, T. D., & Campbell, D. T. (1979). *Quasi-experimentation: Design and analysis issues for field settings.* Chicago: Rand McNally.

Cornblatt, B. A., & Keilp, J. G. (1994). Impaired attention, genetics, and the pathophysiology of schizophrenia. *Schizophrenia Bulletin, 20,* 31–46.

Coyne, J. C. (1976). Toward an interactional description of depression. *Psychiatry, 39,* 14–27.

Coyne, J. C. (1994). Self-reported distress: Analog or ersatz depression? *Psychological Bulletin, 116,* 29–45.

Craighead, W. E. (1980). Away from a unitary model of depression. *Behavior Therapy, 11,* 122–128.

Crow, T. J., Cross, A. J., Johnstone, E. C., & Owen, F. (1982). Two syndromes in schizophrenia and their pathogenesis. In F. A. Henn & H. A. Nasrallah (Eds.), *Schizophrenia as a brain disease.* New York: Oxford University Press.

Davidson, J. R. T., Hughes, D. C., George, L. K., & Blazer, D. G. (1994). The boundary of social phobia: Exploring the threshold. *Archives of General Psychiatry, 51,* 975–983.

Depue, R. A., & Monroe, S. M. (1983). Psychopathology research. In M. Hersen, A. E. Kazdin, & A. S. Bellack (Eds.), *The clinical psychology handbook* (pp. 239–264). New York: Pergamon Press.

Depue, R. A., Slater, J., Wolfstetter-Kausch, H., Klein, D., Goplerud, E., & Farr, D. (1981). A behavioral paradigm for identifying persons at risk for bipolar depressive disorder: A conceptual framework and five validation studies. *Journal of Abnormal Psychology, 90,* 381–438.

Dohrenwend, B. P., Link, B. G., Kern, R., Shrout, P. E., & Markowitz, J. (1990). Measuring life events: The problem of variability within event categories. *Stress Medicine, 6,* 179–187.

Dykman, B. M. (1997). A test of whether negative emotional priming facilitates access to latent dysfunctional attitudes. *Cognition and Emotion, 11,* 197–222.

Endicott, J., & Spitzer, R. L. (1978). A diagnostic interview: The schedule for affective disorders and schizophrenia. *Archives of General Psychiatry, 35,* 837–844.

Finn, P. R., & Pihl, R. O. (1987). Men at high risk for alcoholism: The effect of alcohol on cardiovascular response to unavoidable shock. *Journal of Abnormal Psychology, 96,* 230–236.

Flett, G. L., Vredenburg, K., & Krames, L. (1997). The continuity of depression in clinical and nonclinical samples. *Psychological Bulletin, 121,* 395–416.

Follette, W. C., & Houts, A. C. (1996). Models of scientific progress and the role of theory in taxonomy development: A case study of the *DSM. Journal of Consulting and Clinical Psychology, 64,* 1120–1132.

Frost, R. O., & Gross, R. C. (1993). The hoarding of possessions. *Behaviour Research and Therapy, 31,* 367–381.

Frost, R. O., Steketee, G., Cohn, L., & Griess, K. (1994). Personality traits in subclinical and non-obsessive-compulsive volunteers and their parents. *Behaviour Research and Therapy, 32,* 47–56.

Gibbs, N. A. (1996). Nonclinical populations in research on obsessive-compulsive disorder: A critical review. *Clinical Psychology Review, 16,* 729–773.

Gooding, D. C., & Iacono, W. G. (1995). Schizophrenia through the lens of a developmental psychopathology perspective. In D. Cicchetti & D. J. Cohen (Eds.), *Manual of developmental psychopathology: Vol. II. Risk, disorder, and adaptation* (pp. 535–580). New York: Wiley.

Hammen, C. (1991). Generation of stress in the course of unipolar depression. *Journal of Abnormal Psychology, 100,* 555–561.

Hirschfeld, R. M. A., Klerman, L. L., Lavori, P., Keller, M. B., Griffith, P., & Coryell, W. (1989). Premorbid personality assessments of major depression. *Archives of General Psychiatry, 46,* 610–618.

Holmbeck, G. N. (1997). Toward terminological, conceptual, and statistical clarity in the study of mediators and moderators: Examples from the child-clinical and pediatric psychology literatures. *Journal of Consulting and Clinical Psychology, 65,* 599–610.

Huesmann, L. R. (1982). Experimental methods in research in psychopathology. In P. C. Kendall & J. N. Butcher (Eds.), *Handbook of research methods in clinical psychology* (1st ed., pp. 223–248). New York: Wiley.

Iacono, W. G., & Beiser, M. (1992a). Are males more likely than females to develop schizophrenia? *American Journal of Psychiatry, 149,* 1070–1074.

Iacono, W. G., & Beiser, M. (1992b). Where are the women in the first-episode studies of schizophrenia? *Schizophrenia Bulletin, 18,* 471–480.

Jablensky, A., Sartorius, N., Ernberg, G., Anker, M., Korten, A., Cooper, J. E., Day, R., & Bertelsen, A. (1992). Schizophrenia: Manifestations, incidence and course in different cultures—A World Health Organization ten-country study. *Psychological Medicine, Monograph Supplement 20,* 1–97.

Joiner, T. E., Jr. (1995). The price of soliciting and receiving negative feedback: Self-verification theory as a vulnerability to depression theory. *Journal of Abnormal Psychology, 104,* 364–372.

Just, N., Abramson, L. Y., & Alloy, L. B. (in press). Remitted depression paradigms as tests of the cognitive vulnerability hypotheses of depression onset: A critique and conceptual analysis. *Clinical Psychology Review.*

Kazdin, A. E. (1989). Identifying depression in children: A comparison of alternative selection criteria. *Journal of Abnormal Child Psychology, 17,* 437–455.

Kazdin, A. E. (1998). *Research design in clinical psychology* (3rd ed.). Boston: Allyn & Bacon.

Kendall, P. C., & Flannery-Schroeder, E. C. (1995). Rigor, but not rigor mortis, in depression research. *Journal of Personality and Social Psychology, 68,* 892–894.

Kendler, K. S., Kessler, R. C., Walters, E. E., MacLean, C., Neale, M. C., Heath, A. C., & Eaves, L. J. (1995). Stressful life events, genetic liability, and onset of an episode of major depression in women. *American Journal of Psychiatry, 152,* 833–842.

Kraemer, H. C., Kazdin, A. E., Offord, D. R., Kessler, R. C., Jensen, P. S., & Kupfer, D. J. (1997). Coming to terms with the terms of risk. *Archives of General Psychiatry, 54,* 337–343.

Kraepelin, E. (1923). *Textbook of psychiatry.* New York: Macmillan. (Original work published 1883)

Lenzenweger, M. F., & Korfine, L. (1992). Confirming the latent structure and base rate of schizotypy: A taxometric analysis. *Journal of Abnormal Psychology, 101,* 567–571.

Levenson, R. W., Oyama, O. N., & Meek, P. S. (1987). Greater reinforcement from alcohol for those at risk: Parental risk, personality risk, and sex. *Journal of Abnormal Psychology, 96,* 242–253.

Mednick, S. A., Machon, R. A., Huttunen, M. O., & Bonett, D. (1988). Adult schizophrenia following prenatal exposure to an influenza epidemic. *Archives of General Psychiatry, 45,* 189–192.

Mednick, S. A., & Silverton, L. (1988). High-risk studies of the etiology of schizophrenia. In H. A. Nasrallah, M. T. Tsuang, & J. C. Simpson (Eds.), *Handbook of schizophrenia: Vol. 3. Nosology, epidemiology, and genetics of schizophrenia* (pp. 543–562). New York: Elsevier.

Meehl, P. E. (1962). Schizotaxia, schizotypy, schizophrenia. *American Psychologist, 17,* 827–838.

Meehl, P. E. (1971). High school yearbooks: A reply to Schwarz. *Journal of Abnormal Psychology, 77,* 143–148.

Meehl, P. E. (1978). Theoretical risks and tabular asterisks: Sir Karl, Sir Ronald, and the slow progress of soft psychology. *Journal of Consulting and Clinical Psychology, 46,* 806–834.

Monroe, S. M., & Roberts, J. R. (1990). Definitional and conceptual issues in the measurement of life stress: Problems, principles, procedures, progress. *Stress Medicine, 6,* 209–216.

Monroe, S. M., & Simons, A. D. (1991). Diathesis-stress theories in the context of life stress research: Implications for the depressive disorders. *Psychological Bulletin, 110,* 406–425.

Nolen-Hoeksema, S. (1987). Sex differences in unipolar depression: Evidence and theory. *Psychological Bulletin, 101,* 259–282.

Norton, G. R., Cox, B. J., & Malan, J. (1992). Nonclinical panickers: A critical review. *Clinical Psychology Review, 12,* 121–139.

Persons, J. B., & Miranda, J. (1992). Cognitive theories of vulnerability to depression: Reconciling negative evidence. *Cognitive Therapy and Research, 16,* 485–502.

Popper, K. R. (1963). *Conjectures and refutations: The growth of scientific knowledge.* New York: Harper & Row.

Popper, K. R. (1972). *Objective knowledge.* Oxford, England: Oxford University Press.

Prescott, C. A., & Gottesman, I. I. (1993). Genetically mediated vulnerability to schizophrenia. *Psychiatric Clinics of North America, 16,* 245–267.

Rachman, S. J., & Hodgson, R. J. (1980). *Obsessions and compulsions.* Englewood Cliffs, NJ: Prentice-Hall.

Rohde, P., Lewinsohn, P. M., & Seeley, J. R. (1990). Are people changed by the experience of having an episode of depression? A further test of the scar hypothesis. *Journal of Abnormal Psychology, 99,* 264–271.

Rosenthal, D. (1970). *Genetic theory and abnormal behavior.* New York: McGraw-Hill.

Schindler, L. W. (1991). *Understanding the immune system* (NIH Publication No. 92-529). U.S. Department of Health and Human Services, Public Health Service, National Institutes of Health.

Schmidt, N. B., Lerew, D. R., & Jackson, R. J. (1997). The role of anxiety sensitivity in the pathogenesis of panic: Prospective evaluation of spontaneous panic attacks during acute stress. *Journal of Abnormal Psychology, 106,* 355–364.

Schneier, F. R. (1991). Social phobia. *Psychiatric Annals, 21,* 349–353.

Segal, Z. V., & Ingram, R. E. (1994). Mood priming and construct activation in tests of cognitive vulnerability to unipolar depression. *Clinical Psychology Review, 14,* 663–695.

Sher, K. J., & Trull, T. J. (1996). Methodological issues in psychopathology research. *Annual Review of Psychology, 47,* 371–400.

Shisslak, C. M., Crago, M., & Estes, L. S. (1995). The spectrum of eating disturbances. *International Journal of Eating Disorders, 18,* 209–219.

Shrout, P. E., Link, B. G., Dohrenwend, B. P., Skodol, A. E., Stueve, A., & Mirotznik, J. (1989). Characterizing life events as risk factors for depression: The role of fateful loss events. *Journal of Abnormal Psychology, 98,* 460–467.

Simons, A. D., Angell, K. L., Monroe, S. M., & Thase, M. E. (1993). Cognition and life stress in depression: Cognitive factors and the definition, rating, and generation of negative life events. *Journal of Abnormal Psychology, 102,* 584–591.

Skinner, H. A. (1981). Toward the integration of classification theory and methods. *Journal of Abnormal Psychology, 90,* 68–87.

Spitzer, R. L., & Endicott, J. E. (1995). *The structured clinical interview for DSM-IV.* Washington, DC: American Psychiatric Press.

Thoits, P. A. (1982). Conceptual, methodological, and theoretical problems in studying social support as a buffer against life stress. *Journal of Health and Social Behavior, 23,* 145–159.

Uhde, T. W., Tancer, M. E., Black, B., & Brown, T. M. (1991). Phenomenology and neurobiology of social phobia: Comparison with panic disorder. *Journal of Clinical Psychiatry, 52,* 31–40.

Walker, E. F., & Diforio, D. (1997). Schizophrenia: A neural diathesis-stress model. *Psychological Review, 104,* 667–685.

Weinberger, D. (1987). Implications of normal brain development for the pathogenesis of schizophrenia. *Archives of General Psychiatry, 44,* 660–669.

Widiger, T. A., & Costa, P. T., Jr. (1994). Personality and personality disorders. *Journal of Abnormal Psychology, 103,* 78–91.

Yehuda, R., & McFarlane, A. C. (1995). Conflict between current knowledge about posttraumatic stress disorder and its original conceptual basis. *American Journal of Psychiatry, 152,* 1705–1713.

Zeiss, A. M., & Lewinsohn, P. M. (1988). Enduring deficits after remissions of depression: A test of the scar hypothesis. *Behaviour Research and Therapy, 26,* 151–158.

Zubin, J., & Spring, B. (1977). Vulnerability—new view of schizophrenia. *Journal of Abnormal Psychology, 86,* 103–126.

Chapter 20

METHODOLOGICAL ISSUES IN ADULT HEALTH PSYCHOLOGY

Timothy W. Smith, Ph.D., and John M. Ruiz, M.A.

Health psychology has grown considerably over the past two decades (G. Stone, Cohen, & Adler, 1979). Clinical research addresses an ever-growing array of medical conditions and health-relevant behavior, and this progress has been accompanied by the development and application of increasingly sophisticated methodologies. Just as the content of the field lies at the intersection of several different biomedical, behavioral, and social sciences, research in health psychology has incorporated a variety of methodological and quantitative approaches. An exhaustive review of all of the research methods in this diverse field is beyond the scope of this chapter. Instead, we provide an illustrative overview of several critical methodological issues in each of the major aspects of the field.

Methodological decisions in planning research and evaluations of the strengths and weaknesses of specific studies in health psychology depend—at least in part—on the specific focus of the investigation. Thus, the plurality of methodological issues and strategies necessitated by the broad range of topics in the field poses a significant challenge to both producers and consumers of health psychology research. Certainly, general principles of sound methodology are as essential in health psychology as in other areas of psychological research. Basic issues of measurement, design, analysis, and critical interpretation discussed elsewhere in this volume are an essential foundation for the field. Health psychology research has benefitted from decades of methodological refinements in psychological and behavioral assessment, treatment process and outcome research, psychophysiology, and several other areas. However, there are unique conceptual and methodological challenges when these general principles are applied to problems of physical health. The relative importance of these principles and nuances of their application depend on the nature of specific diseases and health threats, their distribution across segments of the population, and the traditional medical approach to treatment.

In organizing the specific methodological issues, health psychology can be segmented into three broad research areas. The first—health behavior and risk reduction—focuses on the determinants of behaviors that influence risk of disease (e.g., smoking, diet, physical activity levels), and the efficacy of interventions intended to prevent disease through the modification of these behaviors. The second area—stress and illness, or psychosomatics—focuses on more direct psychobiologic influences on illness. Psychological stress, related emotions, and personality traits (e.g., anger, depression), and features of the social environment (e.g., job demands, social support) are presumed to influence disease by way of their direct psychophysiological consequences. The third area—the psychosocial impact and management of medical illness—focuses on the emotional and social consequences of illness and health care, as well as interventions intended to improve adjustment and augment the effects of traditional medical care. Examples would include the effects of patient–physician interactions on adherence to medical regimens, psychological preparations for stressful medical and surgical care, and the psychosocial management of chronic physical illness.

We first provide an overview of general methodological issues as they appear in health psychology research. We then discuss the most critical methodological problems in the three general research areas described. Finally, we discuss the methodological challenges posed by changes underway in medical research.

GENERAL METHODOLOGICAL CONSIDERATIONS

The Importance of Conceptual Models

Clear conceptualizations of hypothetical constructs and the relationships among them are an essential element in the design of psychological research (Cook & Campbell, 1979; Meehl, 1978). This is certainly true for research in health psychology, yet in several areas, conceptual ambiguities surrounding psychological constructs and the theoretical models in which they are embedded are the source of recurring problems (Coyne & DeLongis, 1986; Coyne & Gottlieb, 1996; Smith, 1994; Weinstein, 1993). Conceptual clarity is made both more important and more difficult, however, by the fact that these psychological constructs and models are embedded in a biological or medical context.

The biopsychosocial model (Engel, 1977) provides the conceptual foundation for the field. At a general level, this perspective maintains that health and disease result from the interactions among biologic, psychologic, and social processes. Thus, any conceptual model of psychological influences on health and disease must be integrated with viable biological and social models as well. The biological aspects of conceptual models in health psychology are often far less developed than the other levels of analysis, placing limitations on their ultimate contribution. At a specific level, the importance of research questions and the appropriateness of many features of measurement, design, and analysis depend on nonpsychological, biological, or medical considerations. For example, before studying the psychological causes or consequences of a specific disease, investigators must become familiar with the pathophysiology of the condition and current medical approaches to its management. Given the complexity of these issues, multidisciplinary research teams have become common in health psychology.

Measurement

Research in health psychology often suffers from inadequate measurement of key psychological constructs. The quality of research in many areas could be improved through the rigorous application of basic principles of measurement development and evaluation. Evaluation and refinement of commonly used measurement techniques have been overlooked in at least some areas within each of the major content areas of health psychology, and as a result these literatures contain unfortunate—and in many cases unnecessary—interpretive limitations.

Inadequate demonstration of construct validity—specifically, convergent *and* divergent validity—is a common measurement limitation. Scales are often created for individual studies and may be successfully used to predict important health outcomes. Yet, insufficient information about what the scale measures limits the value of the observation. The limitations of self-report and the interpretive ambiguities created by over-reliance on this method are related concerns. The ease of this method comes at the cost of important threats to construct validity, such as the accuracy of recall and reporting, social desirability, and inflation of associations due to common method variance. Thus, basic measurement issues with a long history in clinical psychology research are critical in health psychology.

Measurement considerations become more complex as physiological and medical variables are added to research protocols. Most physiological systems and disease processes of interest to health psychologists are complex, and considerable sophistication is required for the identification of key variables and methods of assessment. The appropriateness and feasibility of individual measures depends on the specific medical context. Many areas of biomedical measurement have established criteria for evaluating reliability and validity. Furthermore, the assessment procedures are often technologically complex and beyond the expertise of psychologists, again creating the need for collaboration.

Design

Many research questions in health psychology require observational rather than experimental designs. It may not be feasible to manipulate the purported causal factors, or the costs of such manipulations must first be justified by supportive correlational findings. In such cases, cross-sectional designs are useful. However, cross-sectional findings in health psychology are often subject to alternative interpretations involving the direction of causality. For example, a concurrent association between depression and the presence or severity of disease could reflect either (or both) a psychosomatic influence on disease or an emotional reaction to illness and its limitations (S. Cohen & Rodriguez, 1995). Third variables pose another familiar class of alternative explanations in observational designs. In the preceding example, medication side effects could account for the apparent association between disease and mood.

Prospective studies have obvious advantages over cross-sectional designs. However, the third variable issue remains a concern. In health psychology studies, the array of third variables to be considered must be expanded to include relevant aspects of the disease and its medical management. In implementing a prospective design, careful consideration must be given to the appropriate time course. For example, some psychological influences on the development of coronary disease take place over decades, as in the case of negative emotions, problematic social relations, or unhealthy lifestyles contributing to the slow, progressive narrowing of the coronary arteries (Kamarck & Jennings, 1991).

Other psychological influences on the occurrence of this disease unfold over minutes or hours, as when a specific episode of anger precipitates a heart attack (Gullette, Blumenthal, & Babyak, 1997; Ironson, Taylor, & Boltwood, 1992; Kamarck & Jennings, 1991). Thus, the selection of time frames in prospective studies must be consistent with biologically plausible models of the association between behavior and disease.

Experimental designs provide invaluable inferential power in studies of health and behavior and are the primary approach for evaluating the health benefits of psychological interventions. Decisions about the specific experimental conditions to be compared depend on the state of a given literature. In cases of new applications of psychological interventions, simple comparisons between standard medical care controls and standard care plus intervention are an appropriate design for initial questions about treatment effectiveness. However, many areas of intervention research have advanced to the point that questions about relative effectiveness of interventions, active ingredients of multicomponent interventions, or moderators of treatment effects are important. These situations require different comparison groups and analytic strategies, but the extensive related literature in clinical psychology can provide useful guidance (Chambless & Hollon, 1998; Kendall & Norton-Ford, 1982; Kendall et al., this volume). Expectancy, attention, and placebo effects have a long and well-documented history in medical intervention research (i.e., Turner, Deyo, & Loweser, 1994). Thus, even initial attempts to evaluate the effectiveness of psychological interventions should consider the need to control these alternative explanations of treatment effects (Compas, Haaga, Keefe, Leitenberger, & Williams, 1998). Evaluations of the reliability of implementation of the independent variable are as important for intervention studies in health psychology as they are in other areas of clinical psychology. Thus, procedures to evaluate the integrity of intervention protocols (Waltz, Addis, Koerner, & Jacobson, 1993) should be included.

Sampling

The selection of appropriate samples and the implications of sampling procedures for the interpretation of results are often underemphasized in health psychology research. The prevalence of most serious adult illnesses increases with age, and these illnesses are associated with reduced life expectancy. Thus, the age of a sample can influence the presence, magnitude, and even direction of associations between behavioral variables and health. For example, behavioral risk factors may not be related to health early in young adulthood because the effects on disease emerge later. Similarly, the same risk factor may not predict life expectancy among older adults because the individuals for whom the risk factor will reduce life expectancy are missing from the sample due to their premature death.

Samples used in clinical studies pose interpretive problems because of the complex process through which patients become available for inclusion (Turk & Rudy, 1990). Access to health care services, physician referral patterns, response to prior medical interventions, and other factors have an impact on who is available for participation in such studies. Difficulty describing with any certainty the population such samples represent poses limitations on the interpretation and generalization of study findings.

Much of medical research has been appropriately criticized for its lack of diversity. Studies of white, middle, and upper-class men predominant in many aspects of the literature (N. Anderson, 1989; N. Anderson & Armstead, 1995; Stanton, 1995). Race, ethnicity, socioeconomic status, and sex are all related to health and illness in systematic ways. Threats to health and the biological, psychological, and social influences on disease vary as a function of these demographic characteristics. In addition to attention to diversity in the design of research, interpretation of prior research findings must consider the potential interpretive limitations resulting from sampling. Attention to this problem has grown in recent years (Park, Adams, & Lynch, 1998), but much more work is needed.

Analysis

Some research in medicine and related disciplines (e.g., epidemiology) employs quantitative techniques that are unfamiliar to psychologists (e.g., logistic regression, survival analysis), and these statistical analyses are often used in health psychology research. Nonetheless, many of the techniques are familiar to behavioral researchers, and in all cases familiar issues arise. For example, a close correspondence between clearly drawn conceptual questions and focused statistical tests is highly desirable but often lacking (J. Cohen, 1990; Wampold, Davis, & Good, 1990; Weinstein, 1993). Given that many statistical relationships in the field are small, low power is often a plausible explanation of null results (J. Cohen, 1992). Finally, violations of test assumptions raise concerns about the validity of statistical conclusions.

The presence of any association between a psychological variable and a health outcome has considerable conceptual importance. Nonetheless, the issue of the magnitude, practical importance, or clinical significance (Cook & Campbell, 1979; Jacobson & Traux, 1991) of effects is relevant in all areas of health psychology research. However, evaluations of this aspect of research findings depend on a variety of issues unique to the specific research area and the surrounding biomedical and even health economic context. Even small effects have practical significance in the case of prevalent and costly conditions such as coronary heart disease (Smith & Leon, 1992).

HEALTH BEHAVIOR AND RISK REDUCTION

Daily habits influence the risk of developing and dying from each of the major health threats. Decades of epidemiologic research has produced compelling evidence that tobacco use, a diet high in saturated fat, and low levels of regular physical activity increase risk for coronary heart disease, stroke, and cancer (Adler & Matthews, 1994). These behaviors also increase the risk of physical conditions that themselves confer additional risk of serious illness and premature mortality, such as high blood pressure, elevated blood glucose, and obesity. High risk behaviors are now the primary mechanisms through which HIV infection is spread, making behavioral risk reduction the key to preventing AIDS (e.g., St. Lawrence & McFarlane, this volume). Behaviors also profoundly influence risk of accidental injury and death, such as seat belt use and driving under the influence of alcohol. The early detection of life threatening illness is influenced by behavior, as when women practice breast self-examination or individuals participate in medical screening for high blood pressure. The identification of these and other modifiable behavioral contributions to the leading causes of morbidity and mortality was a driving force in the rapid development of health psychology (Matarazzo, 1980). Because certain behaviors influence many of our most troubling and expensive health problems, identification of the determinants of those behaviors and the consequent development and evaluation of behavioral risk reduction interventions have been critical concerns of the field.

Operationalizing Outcomes in Health Behavior Research

An important initial step in research on health behavior and risk reduction is the use of reliable and valid assessments. Individual health behaviors are *not* closely correlated with each other, nor are they highly stable over time (Norris, 1997). For example, people who exercise regularly may or may not use a seat belt regularly, and their exercise habits are likely to change. Thus, it is not appropriate to base measurement decisions on a notion of a general, stable lifestyle characterized by more or less healthy behavior. Rather, specificity across behaviors and time must guide measurement decisions.

Given the straightforward nature of some of the specific target behaviors, an obvious approach to measurement is to ask research participants about their health risk behaviors. Although sometimes unavoidable, self-report methods of assessment contain serious drawbacks. All of the typical limitations of self-report assessments are a threat to the reliability and construct validity of self-reports of risk behaviors, such as limitations in recall memory. However, because many of the target behaviors are clearly valenced, social desirability threatens the use of this approach. More—rather than less—physically active lifestyles, less—rather than more—tobacco use, fewer—rather than more—calories consumed, are all well-established as "socially desirable" habits. This creates a clear advantage for the use of behavioral observations, reports from significant others, and various mechanical (e.g., activity monitors) or biochemical (e.g., carbon monoxide validation of smoking status) indicators in studies of health behavior.

In some instances, these more complex and time-consuming assessment procedures are not feasible, such as in large epidemiological studies of the prevalence, correlates, or consequences of health behavior in which thousands of participants are surveyed. Such studies are invaluable in health psychology, because they provide the power to detect important but small effects, permit generalization to large and varied segments of the population, and can identify important variations in the magnitude of effects as a function of other demographic, behavioral, or medical factors. Nonetheless, the role of social desirability and other limitations in self-report methods must always be considered in the critical evaluation of research findings. For example, if participation in organized religious activities is generally considered socially desirable, then an association between this psychosocial characteristic and self-reports of positive health behaviors could be influenced by this methodological artifact. That is, the third variable of individual differences in the tendency to present oneself in a socially desirable light could account for—at least in part—the association between self-reported religious activity and self-reported health behavior.

Recent research has identified another such threat in studies in which participants already know that they have or are at high risk of a specific disease. If a given health behavior is known to influence that illness, then biased or hypothesis-driven recall and reporting can lead the individual to overestimate the extent to which they engaged in that high-risk behavior (Croyle & Loftus, 1993). Thus, covariation between known high-risk status or diagnosed disease and self-reports of current or past risk behavior could reflect the operation of this cognitive artifact, rather than an actual association between illness and behavior. As a result, all cross-sectional studies of behavioral risks for medical conditions contain this interpretive caution.

The limitations of self-reports are even greater in the context of treatment outcome research (Kendall et al., this volume). Risk reduction interventions communicate a strong demand for socially-desirable behavior changes. Structured interventions to stop smoking, lose weight, or increase regular physical exercise all convey a strong implicit message that socially desirable behavior changes are possible and expected. Self-report assessments of treatment outcomes can therefore produce a significant overestimate of treatment efficacy. In cases where objective assessment of behavioral changes are not feasible (e.g., large scale, community trials), this interpretive caution must be carefully considered. Because of the universality of these problems in health behavior research, advanced assessment methods have been developed and evaluated for virtually all of the established behavioral risk behaviors, including smoking (Glasgow et al., 1993; Patrick et al., 1994; Velicer, Prochaska, Rossi, & Snow, 1992) diet and weight loss (Brownell & Wadden, 1992), exercise (Dubbert, 1992), and participation in health risk screenings (Champion & Miller, 1997). Investigators and consumers of health behavior research in a particular area would be well-advised to become familiar with developments in measurement research in their area of interest.

Testing Models of Health Behavior

One of the strengths of health behavior research is that it is often guided by clearly articulated models of the determinants of health behavior, the process of change, and the influences on the maintenance of health behavior changes (Weinstein, 1993; Weinstein, Rothman, & Sutton, 1998). The Health Beliefs Model (Janz & Becker, 1984), Self-Efficacy Theory (Bandura, 1977), the Relapse Prevention Model (Marlatt & Gordon, 1985), and the Transtheoretical or Stages of Change Model (Prochaska & DiClemente, 1984) have all had important and continuing impacts on the field. These models are the source of theory-driven research, an invaluable asset in the development of cummulative psychological knowledge (Meehl, 1978). Unfortunately, the translation of these models into testable hypotheses and specific operations is sometimes limited.

Measurement of key model components can be a problem in this area of research. Care must be taken to insure that measures—often developed for specific studies—are reliable and valid. In many studies, no independent evidence is provided of the construct validity of measures of key variables. Other than the associations with other constructs specified by the research hypotheses, there may not be independent evidence that a measure of health beliefs or self-efficacy, for example, actually assesses the intended construct. Demonstrations of validity must establish not only convergent validity but divergent or discriminant validity as well, as many competing constructs in this area of research have similar conceptual definitions (Weinstein, 1993).

Even when well-validated assessments are used to measure the key components of theory-driven research questions, studies in this area may be limited by other aspects of their design and analysis. The models in the area typically include statements concerning variables through which a determinant of health behavior exerts its effect, or describe conditions under which the influence operates to a greater or lesser extent. Despite the availability of several clear discussions of the conceptual and analytic distinctions between mediating and moderating variables (Baron & Kenny, 1986; Holmbeck, 1997), these features of models of health behavior are often inaccurately conceptualized, described, and analyzed (Weinstein, 1993). Thus, the conceptual distinctions among mediating and moderating variables, as well as the appropriate analytic strategies for their evaluation, are critical in studies of health behavior and risk reduction.

Occasionally, models of health behavior specify time-linked processes that are not incorporated adequately in research designs. For example, stage models imply discrete categories of health behavior change that occur in a specific sequence. Cross-sectional studies provide a highly limited test of the assumptions underlying stage models, yet they are a common design choice in the field (Miller, 1994; Weinstein et al., 1998). Both the discreteness and sequence of stages can be artificially supported in cross-sectional designs. Longitudinal designs have many advantages in testing stage and other causal models of health behavior and related behavior change, but the timing of assessments must match the underlying model. For example, the Relapse Prevention Model (Marlatt & Gordon, 1985) describes some factors that influence the probability of relapse over long periods of time (e.g., self-management skills), but other factors influence maintenance versus relapse of health behavior change on a moment-to-moment basis (e.g., urges, exposure to high risk situations). The latter types of associations are not tested well in longitudinal designs that assess participants only every few months or even less frequently. Recent developments in the design and analysis of daily diary or momentary experience studies have provided valuable opportunities to test time-linked models that specify critical but brief causal sequences (Shiffman et al., 1994, 1997; Shiffman, Paty, Gnys, Kassel, & Hickox, 1996). Thus, the timing of assessments in longitudinal designs must reflect the time frames specified by the underlying conceptual model.

Increasingly, health behavior and health behavior change are conceptualized as biopsychosocial phenomena. For example, conceptual models and empirical studies of smoking cessation must take into account the biology of nicotine addiction (Kleges, Ward, & DeBon, 1996) and related processes (Lerman et al., 1998). Similarly, behavioral approaches to obesity and weight regulation must take into account a variety of interdependent biological factors, such as genetic susceptibility, physiologic differences between obesity developing early versus later in life, energy expenditure, and the metabolic effects of behavior change (Brownell & Wadden, 1992). The same behavioral risk factor displayed by two individuals may have differing biologic determinants or consequences, and these factors can moderate the effectiveness and even importance of behavioral interventions. Traditional medical research and practice has been accurately criticized for ignoring psychologic and social processes, but health psychology research will fall short of its potential if biologic processes are ignored. Thus, samples must be carefully described using relevant biological variables, and their role in mediating or moderating the effects of behavioral risk factors must be considered.

Finally, the importance, prevalence, correlates, and determinants of health behavior vary considerably across the life-span and as a function of sex, race, socioeconomic status, and other demographic factors. Thus, the generalizability or external validity of health behavior research findings is a critical but understudied consideration. For example, the threats to health and related behavioral risks for young urban minorities are likely quite different from those for older, suburban Caucasian groups. Similarly, the determinants of a given behavioral risk (e.g., low levels of physical activity, smoking) may differ widely across such demographic variables, creating the need for active evaluation of the generalization of research findings. Regular physical exercise is easier to accomplish in environments that provide convenient access to safe, open spaces and moderate weather conditions. Such access is not evenly distributed across the populations that would benefit from increased physical activity levels and, as a result, the relative importance of the determinants of activity levels will vary across such groups.

Evaluating Behavioral Risk Reduction Interventions

Several issues discussed above are critical in the evaluation of interventions intended to reduce risk of disease and premature mortality by changing behavior, such as adequate assessment of health behaviors and attention to generalizability of outcomes. Other issues common to all clinical intervention research are important as well, such as the integrity of intervention protocols (Waltz et al., 1993) and control of nonspecific factors (Chambless & Hollon, 1998). The translation of these issues into the specific context of health behavior change research can sometimes require careful consideration, as when interventions are brief and delivered by physicians or other members of the health care team during otherwise routine contacts with the health care system. In most areas of research of this type, several other problems are common; for example, many people do not maintain positive health behavior changes (Brownell, Marlott, Lichtenstein, & Wilson, 1986). In some instances, such as smoking cessation, failure to maintain a positive change may be the most common long-term outcome (Curry & McBride, 1994; Fisher, Lichtenstein, Haire-Joshu, Morgan, & Rehberg, 1993).

This unfortunate natural history of health behavior change creates the necessity for long follow-ups after the conclusion of formal intervention and the statistical management of treatment dropouts. Early in the development of the field, researchers identified the need for follow-ups of one year or more in evaluations of weight loss interventions (Wilson, 1978), exercise programs (Martin & Dubbert, 1982), and smoking cessation treatments (McFall, 1978). Although many relapses occur soon after treatment ends, maintenance continues to be a significant problem for months and years. In some cases, such as weight loss, maintenance is at least as important a research issue as the magnitude of initial change. Thus, appropriate follow-up periods must be included in treatment studies.

Attrition is common in such studies with dropout rates as high as 50% in some cases. Attrition is often unequal across study groups and may be more common among individuals failing to achieve or maintain desired behavioral changes. Therefore, attrition is a common threat to the internal validity of intervention studies. If participants drop out because they fail and if drop-outs are more common in some groups than others, apparent group differences can be misleading. For example, if more participants drop out of an active treatment group than a wait-list control, then the apparent benefits of treatment will reflect differential attrition. If follow-up information is not available on dropouts, the conservative strategy for managing this problem is the analysis of the intent-to-treat sample, in which all participants randomized are included in the analysis and initial, pretreatment status on the outcome variable is substituted for missing posttest or follow-up assessments (Flick, 1988; Kendall et al., this volume).

Although the intention-to-treat approach typically offers appropriate, conservative protection against the overestimation of treatment effects, it can lead to an underestimation of efficacy in some cases. If dropouts make some improvements in targeted behaviors, then inclusion of their pretreatment status in analyses of outcome can produce an underestimation of group differences. Quantitative alternatives to the intent-to-treat approach have been described (Little & Yau, 1998; Shadish, Hu, Glaser, Kownacki, & Wong, 1998). These procedures estimate the likelihood of a variety of treatment effects, based on varying assumptions about the fate of dropouts. The optimal solution is to obtain outcome data on as many randomized participants as possible. In evaluating health behavior change, the degree of attrition, its causes, its differential distribution across groups, and the possible consequences for the statistical and internal validity of conclusions about outcome must be carefully considered.

Health behavior change interventions are often delivered to groups of individuals, rather than individual patients, as in many psychological intervention studies. In some important instances, these groups involve whole communities and large public health interventions (Hancock, Sanson-Fisher, & Redman, 1997). Such community-based behavior change programs pose multifaceted challenges in design and analysis, and even the most methodologically sophisticated studies do not achieve the level of control and consequent inferential power of smaller trials. Rather, they provide invaluable information about large-scale feasibility and impact at the expense of experimental control, and are often appropriately considered quasi-experimental designs (Cook & Campbell, 1979).

For psychologists, the more common intervention approach are small group treatments or interventions for couples or families. Such approaches permit true experimental control, but because treatment is delivered simultaneously to several individuals, the analytic assumption of independent observations is violated. Unique features of any individual group—such as the degree to which group interactions are positive versus negative—can influence the degree of behavior change, independent of the specific intervention or control condition elements (Etringer, Gregory, & Lando, 1984). If individual treatment or control groups vary systematically in their behavior change, this dependency in observations across individuals can create misleading statistical conclusions, usually in the direction of an overestimation of treatment differences (Rooney & Murray, 1996). Thus, in designing and evaluating health behavior change research, the impact of intervention format (i.e., group vs. individual) on statistical analyses must be considered. This unit-of-analysis problem is well-known in other areas of clinical intervention research (e.g., Crits-Christoph & Mintz, 1991).

Research on health behavior change interventions addresses a pressing practical concern—the prevention of serious illness, injury, or death. Thus, many decisions about the design and analysis of such studies should be directed toward maximizing the likelihood of valid conclusions about efficacy. However, studies based on at least one theoretical model of the determinants of health behavior or the process of change provide a unique opportunity to test or even compare theories, rather than simply evaluate outcomes. Measurement of key process variables and tests of conceptual models of the mediation of treatment effects can produce valuable information. That is, treatment studies can be expanded easily to provide an evaluation not only of whether a treatment works but how it works, as well. Regrettably, many treatment studies fail to take advantage of the opportunity for theory testing.

Finally, a common concern in the evaluation of psychological interventions is the clinical or practical significance—as opposed to statistical significance—of treatment effects (e.g., Jacobson & Traux, 1991; Kendall & Norton-Ford, 1982). In health behavior change research, it is important to evaluate the importance of statistically significant intervention effects. Some targets, such as smoking cessation, provide a clear indicator of significance. Smoking cessation is best considered a dichotomous outcome, and it has remarkable clinical significance in terms of disease risk and life expectancy. Thus, the benefits of successful interventions are obvious. Most other areas do not provide such clear indicators of the clinical significance or importance of behavioral risk reduction. For example, increasing activity levels should produce a reduced likelihood of disease, but it is difficult to determine the importance of a given degree of change in activity level. Epidemiological studies can describe the levels of risk associated with specific activity levels, but this information provides only an indirect suggestion of the importance of changes observed in intervention research. The same is true of reductions in dietary fat, adoption of protective behaviors such as breast self-examination, and other desirable behaviors. Comparisons to normative groups, an approach to clinical significance evaluation used in other areas in clinical psychology (Jacobson & Traux, 1991; Kendall & Grove, 1988), may be less applicable in certain health areas such as dietary fat intake or physical activity, where the normative level might not be desirable. For others, such as weight loss goals for the obese, normal levels might not be feasible or even medically appropriate (Brownell & Wadden, 1992).

It can be argued that morbidity and mortality are the twin gold standards for evaluating the importance of health behavior changes. Some very large trials have attempted to evaluate health behavior change interventions by examination of subsequent death and disease, often with disappointing results (Hancock et al., 1997). It is important to recognize that the associations between behavior and subsequent disease are probabilistic, as illustrated by the smoker who lives to be eighty or even ninety years old. This probabilistic association between behavior and health limits the health benefits of even the most successful health behavior change interventions (R. Kaplan, 1984).

In addition to clinical significance of these interventions, a public policy perspective raises the issue of cost effectiveness. Are the benefits of a successful health behavior change program sufficient to justify the cost of that program, especially in a health economic environment in which services compete for financing? In evaluating the cost effectiveness of such treatments, benefits such as improved quality of life, reductions in morbidity and mortality and reduced health care expenditures are weighed against the multiple costs in changing behavior and shifting causes of morbidity and mortality from one disease to another (R. Friedman, Subel, Meyers, Caudill, & Benson, 1995; R. Kaplan, 1994; Yates, 1994). Ultimately, the most attainable and important benefit of behavioral risk reduction may not be the postponement of mortality, but the compression of morbidity into the last few months and years of life. Thus, the improvement of functional activity or quality of life, postponement of age-related declines in this construct, and the associated protection of individual economic productivity and savings in health care expenditures are increasingly recognized as a central outcome in health behavior change research (R. Kaplan, 1994). Evaluations of health behavior change ultimately must be informed by the perspective of public health expenditures and health economics.

STRESS AND DISEASE

The effects of psychological stress on the development and course of physical illness have been a central focus of the field of health psychology since its inception. The basic model guiding this component of the field begins with the hypothesis that environmental threats and demands evoke physiological arousal in the individual, typically mediated by the sympathetic nervous system (Lovallo, 1997). If sufficiently severe or prolonged, this physiological arousal can initiate and exacerbate physical illness. Further, characteristics of the individual, such as personality traits, and features of the social environment can moderate the effects of environmental stressors on physiological response and subsequent disease. That is, some individuals are more susceptible to the health-damaging effects of stress, because of the personality traits or the social conditions they experience (Adler & Matthews, 1994).

Personality traits and aspects of the social environment can contribute to disease by way of their effects on the health behaviors just described. For example, high levels of the trait of sensation seeking might be a risk factor for premature death, because of its association with risk-taking. Similarly, low levels of social support might confer increased risk of heart disease and cancer because isolated individuals are more likely to smoke, consume a diet high in fat, and lead sedentary lives. However, these indirect, behavioral connections between psychosocial risk factors and disease are conceptually quite distinct from the more direct psychobiological connection (F. Cohen, 1979; S. Cohen & Rodriguez, 1995; Smith & Gallo, 1998).

Research and theory on the health effects of stress are most advanced in the case of cardiovascular disease (i.e., hypertension and coronary heart disease) and illnesses influenced by the immune system, such as infectious disease and cancer. Measures of sources of stress, moderators of its effects, and the related psychophysiological mechanisms have been developed and refined through decades of research (S. Cohen, Kessler, & Gordon, 1995). A variety of research strategies are brought to bear on this area of study, and they have specific goals and complementary strengths. Psychosocial epidemiology attempts to identify psychological and social characteristics associated with the subsequent development and course of physical illness. This type of research examines large numbers of people over long periods of time and is essential for the initial identification of potential influences on disease. Animal research permits the experimental manipulation of psychosocial risk factors, such as stress, testing their effects on the development and course of disease, and also providing an opportunity for experimental tests of the psychobiologic mechanisms through which those risk factors exert their effects on the disease process. Experimental tests in which risk of disease is purposely created through manipulations of psychosocial characteristics are, of course, unethical in human research. Thus, animal research provides an important complement to the observational or correlational approach in epidemiology. Human mechanism research typically involves experimental manipulation of stress or observations of naturally occurring stressors and assessment of the impact on the psychophysiological processes (i.e., mechanisms) believed to link psychosocial risk factors to subsequent disease. Finally, intervention research examines the impact of stress-reducing treatments on illness. Each of these research strategies makes useful contributions to our understanding of psychosomatics, and each contains unique methodological considerations.

Psychosocial Epidemiology

A primary concern in psychosocial epidemiology is the nature of the outcome variable. A key distinction that is sometimes obscured in this type of work is that between actual illness and illness behavior (F. Cohen, 1979; Smith & Rhodewalt, 1992; Watson & Pennebaker, 1989). Medical diagnoses of disease based on medical tests and physical examinations are often accompanied by self-reports of symptoms and increased health care utilization. That is, people who are ill behave in ways that are a result of their illness, as when the patient suffering from documented coronary artery disease complains of chest pain during physical exertion. However, objective indications of illness are much less ambiguous than are complaints and other behavioral indicators. Symptom reports, sick days, and health care visits typically do reflect actual illness, and self-reported physical symptoms have been found to predict subsequent mortality (G. Kaplan & Camacho, 1983). However, these associations are far from perfect, and the variance in illness behavior that is independent of actual illness may be reliably associated with psychosocial variables. For example, individuals high in the trait of neuroticism or negative affectivity report and act on physical symptoms that are not accounted for by actual illness (Costa & McCrae, 1987; S. Stone & Costa, 1990; Watson & Pennebaker, 1989). They also report more frequent and distressing life circumstances (Depue & Monroe, 1986). Thus, an association between a psychosocial risk factor (e.g., marital distress) and the later development of self-reported health problems (e.g., chest pain) could reflect the influence of stress on actual disease or the effects of the third variable of negative affectivity (S. Stone & Costa, 1990). Given the current status of research in this area, self-reports or other indicators influenced by behavior (e.g., sick days) are not acceptable operational definitions of health and disease, and diagnoses based largely on symptom reports (e.g., angina as an indication of coronary heart disease) must be viewed with more caution than medical endpoints that are established through objective tests (e.g., myocardial infarction as a coronary endpoint).

In several research areas, the pathophysiology of specific diseases is well understood. The mechanisms through which psychosocial factors could plausibly influence disease are identified, at least to some extent, and the changing role of these mechanisms over the course of the disease has been outlined. For example, coronary heart disease begins with the development of fatty deposits at the site of microscopic injuries to the lining of the coronary arteries. Later stages of the disease involve the growth of these lesions, to the point where they disrupt the blood supply to the heart tissue. Psychobiological influences on the early stages of the initiation and progression of coronary artery disease are quite different from those of the later stages involving chest pain, heart attack, and sudden death (S. Cohen, Kaplan, & Manuck, 1994; Kamarck & Jennings, 1991). A similar heterogeneity of psychobiological mechanisms may characterize psychosocial influences on the initial growth of malignancies versus their later metastasis and the progression of cancer (B. Andersen, Kiecolt-Glaser, & Glaser, 1994). The end result of this advancing understanding of connections between the mind and body is that research on psychosocial predictors of disease should be guided by medically plausible hypotheses about the nature of such influences on pathophysiology across the natural history of disease. Further, it must be recognized that associations between a psychosocial predictor and the diagnosis of or death from a specific disease could reflect an influence at any of several points in the pathophysiology.

In the history of the field, replicated statistical associations between personality traits or aspects of the social environment and later disease have represented central contributions, even though they were not based on detailed psychobiological models. Such observations established the potential importance of the field. In the case of newly proposed or understudied psychosocial predictors of disease, simple associations between a personality trait or characteristic of the social environment may still be important observations. However, once the predictive utility of a particular psychosocial characteristic has been documented, psychosocial epidemiological research should be guided by more fully articulated, psychobiological conceptualizations.

The assessment of psychosocial predictors in this type of research has also posed problems. Measures of personality traits or aspects of the social environment are often used in epidemiological research without adequate evaluation of their construct validity (Smith & Rhodewalt, 1992). As a result, it is sometimes difficult to determine if the statistical association demonstrated actually involves the personality or social construct of interest, or some conceptually irrelevant factor. Demonstrations of predictive relations between personality or social characteristics measured at one time and death several decades later are dramatic and central to the field. Such demonstrations are often undermined by the lack of independent evidence establishing the construct validity of the key psychosocial measure (Smith, 1994).

A related problem in psychosocial epidemiology is the unintegrated proliferation of traits and the associated measures. Not only are measures of traits or aspects of the social environment often included and interpreted without sufficient evidence of their convergent and discriminant validity, but research in this area is continuously at risk of studying overlapping psychosocial predictors under new and differing names (Smith, Pope, Rhodewalt, & Poulton, 1989). The process of construct validation can productively include the empirical location of new measures in known nomological nets, as when personality traits are related to established taxonomies such as the Five-Factor Model (Smith & Williams, 1992). Although not without its critics (e.g., Block, 1995), this taxonomy is increasingly recommended as an adequate representation of broad individual differences in normal personality (Digman, 1990; John, 1990). The systematic organization of health relevant personality traits through reference to the Five-Factor Model could provide much needed integration in the study of personality and health, and reduce the likelihood that investigators will reinvent old risk factors under new names. Similar frameworks are available for the integration of social risk factors and the concurrent evaluation of personality and social characteristics (Gallo & Smith, 1998). Even if this specific taxonomy is not used, empirical investigations of the similarities and differences among personality scales used to predict health outcomes is valuable in constructing a more systematic and integrated literature.

Psychosocial epidemiology suffers other interpretive limitations due to its inherently correlational approach. Even when valid measures are employed, it is rarely clear that the characteristic of interest is conferring the increased risk of disease, as opposed to something closely related to that construct. For example, social support and social integration are considered well-established risk factors for premature mortality and a variety of serious diseases (Adler & Matthews, 1994), and several plausible psychobiological mechanisms underlying this association have been identified (Uchino, Cacioppo, & Kiecolt-Glaser, 1996). Yet, the effects of low social support or social isolation on health could actually reflect the effects of social conflict (Coyne & DeLongis, 1986), a conceptually distinct feature of the social environment that often accompanies isolation and low support but is rarely assessed. One critical use of epidemiological research is as a guide to the development of preventive interventions. Interventions to facilitate social support might differ in important ways from those intended to reduce conflict. Thus, the use of psychosocial epidemiological research to guide design of risk-reducing interventions requires the articulation and evaluation of competing explanations of observed associations. Third variables pose a constant interpretive caution.

On many occasions, these third variables are well-known and the issue arises as to their optimal management. Unhealthy personality traits or aspects of the social environment are often associated with unhealthy behavior. For example, hostile people are more likely to develop serious illnesses and to die at an earlier age than their more agreeable counterparts (Miller et al., 1996). Hostile people are also more likely to smoke (Siegler, 1994). Thus, the third variable of negative health behavior poses a conceptually distinct account of the relationship between personality and health than the psychobiological model (F. Cohen, 1979; Smith & Gallo, 1998). That is, rather than through physiological correlates of the personality trait, such as more pronounced sympathetic nervous system responses to daily stressors, hostile persons may be prone to disease simply because they smoke. In these cases, the association between hostility and health can be tested with and without statistical control of smoking, in essence testing a model in which smoking mediates the effects of hostility on health. Because the health behavior and psychosomatic models are so conceptually distinct, this approach to the third variable problem is appropriate. If negative health behaviors accounted for the health effects of a social or personality characteristic, the conceptual and practical implications would be quite different than those of the psychosomatic model.

However, in many cases, the appropriateness of separating correlated risk factors is not so obvious. For example, unhealthy personality traits and aspects of the social environment are often interrelated, as in the case of depression and perturbed social functioning (Davila, Bradbury, Cohan, & Torhluk, 1997; Johnson & Jacob, 1997). Both confer increased risk of death following a heart attack (Frasure-Smith, Lesperance, & Talajic, 1993; Williams et al., 1992). The traditional approach to this situation is the statistical control of correlated risk factors in an attempt to evaluate their independent effects (Frasure-Smith, Lesperance, & Talajic, 1995). Quantitatively, this approach is potentially limited by the fact that the apparent relative independent contributions of correlated risk factors can vary artifactually as a function of random features of the sample. The resulting instability of conclusions regarding independence and relative importance of effects increases as a function of the magnitude of the association between the predictors (i.e., multicolinearity). However, forced distinctions between correlated risk factors have conceptual limitations as well. Statistical control in the case of depression and social support, for example, produces an artificial situation (i.e., counterfactual; Meehl, 1970) in which depressed and nondepressed groups are created with equivalent social functioning. Statistical tests of predictors that do not exist in nature must also be interpreted with caution.

Sometimes the effects of personality and social-environmental risk factors are statistically separated on the basis of the underlying assumption that the former reflect aspects of the individual whereas the latter reflect a distinct category of phenomena— external factors. Research suggests that this distinction is overdrawn, as personality traits are clearly involved in reciprocal causal relations with the social environment (Davila et al., 1997) and aspects of the social environment can actually reflect stable, possibly genetically influenced characteristics of the person (Kendler, 1997). Importantly, the processes through which these personality and social factors influence disease might involve their interrelation. For example, depression and social isolation may both predict poor prognosis following heart attack because they are key elements of a physiologically taxing transactional process through which the patient's emotional state and his or her family context exacerbate each other. Depressed patients place strains on their families and strained family members retreat from or even criticize the patient (Coyne & Smith, 1994). The physiological effects of this process could contribute to the expression of disease. By forcing an artificial independence, statistical separation of depression and social support in studying the psychosocial predictors of coronary prognosis fails to capture this dynamic risk process.

Even traditional risk factors are correlated. Smokers often get less exercise than nonsmokers, and it is useful to know if both behaviors confer risk of heart disease. Statistical control as a solution to this problem in epidemiology has proven to be invaluable. However, decisions about the management of correlated risk factors in psychosocial epidemiology should be driven by theory rather than an automatic attempt to parse the natural confounding of people's personalities, their social experiences, and the environments they inhabit. Construction of a useful psychosocial epidemiology of everyday life requires that the elements of risk must be considered both separately and in their natural, interconnected state.

Sampling is often a problem in psychosocial epidemiology. Large samples are required to provide sensitive tests of risk factors, and they must be followed for long periods of time to permit the development of a sufficient number of affected cases. Occasionally, smaller samples of convenience are used to circumvent these practical impediments to research. For example, a group of medical students who underwent personality testing many years ago as part of the admission process might be contacted again to determine their current health status. This permits the prospective testing of psychosocial epidemiological hypotheses that would otherwise take decades to evaluate in an original prospective study designed specifically for that purpose. Psychosocial epidemiology includes many such studies, and they have provided valuable opportunities for rapid advancement in the field. Nonetheless, the samples are clearly not random and population based, and generalizations must be tentative as a result.

Other interpretive qualifications arise when clinical samples are employed. Questions about the psychosocial predictors of the course or prognosis of established disease require the use of medical samples. However, entry into such samples is certainly not a random process representative of the general population who might suffer from the condition, and consequently appropriate care must be taken in the interpretation of such research. Further, studies of psychosocial predictors of the course of established disease are clearly distinct from those evaluating the role of the same predictors in the initial development of illness. Potential risk factors may appear to have quite different effects on disease in these two types of investigations. If a risk factor exerts a significant effect on the initial development of disease, there are at least two methodological reasons why it might not predict the course of established disease (Miller, Turner, Tindale, Posavac, & Dugoni, 1991). First, in studies of prognosis, only cases of established disease are selected. Therefore, the range of both the predictor and outcome variables will be restricted, making it more difficult to detect an effect. Second, cases for which the risk factor resulted in death will be missing from the sample, leaving an unrepresentative group of more resilient individuals. Thus, sampling differences between studies of initially healthy individuals versus those already suffering from a disease can produce dramatically different conclusions about the importance of a risk factor. As described, there may be substantive differences in the pathophysiology across stages of the disease process that alter the role of risk factors. Thus, studies of predictors of disease course in medical samples contain all of the potential limitations of general psychosocial epidemiological research, and those resulting from the selection processes inherent in entry into an identified medical population.

Statistically significant associations between psychosocial variables and later, objective indicators of morbidity or mortality have obvious conceptual significance for psychosomatic models. However, the clinical significance or importance of such associations must be evaluated as well. The results of the logistic regression analyses most common in epidemiological research express the magnitude of association in terms of odds ratios or relative risk—the degree to which the presence of a risk (or protective) factor multiplies an individual's chances of developing an illness or dying during the follow-up period. Survival analysis is a variant of this approach that also takes into account the outcome of time to the development of the endpoint (i.e., disease onset or death). These indices of effect size will be unfamiliar to many behavioral researchers, and when they are converted to more familiar indices of effect size, the associations may appear small. Comparisons with other risk factors (e.g., smoking) are useful in evaluating the results of investigations in psychosocial epidemiology, as are extrapolations of the risk ratios to population-based estimates of disease incidence. Even small effects can suggest that thousands of cases could be prevented each year through successful modification of risk factors.

Animal Research

Given the interpretive ambiguities inherent in the observational or correlational nature of human psychosocial epidemiology, true experiments based on animal models are an invaluable, complementary research strategy. Initially equivalent animals can be randomly assigned to experience differing levels of a psychosocial variable believed to influence disease. The life span—and as a result, time course of disease—is typically compressed in animal models, providing another advantage. Further, surgical or pharmacologic procedures can be used to manipulate the biological mechanisms through which psychosocial factors influence disease, thereby providing comprehensive tests of the underlying conceptual model.

Despite the important advantages, animal models have obvious limitations in health psychology. As in animal models of psychopathology and social-emotional development, generalizations to humans must be made cautiously. A critical first concern in evaluating the appropriateness of such generalizations is the similarity of the animal and human physiological system or disease of interest. There are important differences in stress physiology, the cardiovascular and immune systems, and susceptibility to cardiovascular and other diseases, even among species of primates. Even if the specific pathophysiology can be roughly equated, the relevance of experimental manipulations of psychosocial risk factors in animal models to the human experience is a key concern.

Despite such threats to generalizability, animal models of stress and disease have considerable potential. For example, the cynomolgus macaque model of psychosocial influences on coronary disease developed by J. Kaplan and Manuck (1998; Manuck, Marsland, Kaplan, & Williams, 1995) has permitted experimental tests of the effects of chronic social stress on the development of atherosclerosis. Disease in these animals is histologically very similar to that observed in humans, and it is exacerbated by similar factors, such as a high fat diet. The model permits the manipulation of aspects of the social environment that have parallels in the human psychosocial epidemiological literature, such as isolation and conflict. It also permits the evaluation of individual differences that have close parallels in the human literature, such as autonomic nervous system reactivity, social dominance, and aggressiveness. The model permits the manipulation of basic mechanisms linking stress and disease (e.g., beta-adrenergic blockade) and detailed examination of stages in the atherosclerotic process in which stress may play a role (i.e., initiation of endothelial injury vs. plaque growth). Finally, this model has documented important sex differences in the psychosocial influences on disease, as well as the underlying neuroendocrine mechanisms.

When animal models are developed and evaluated thoroughly, they can provide invaluable information about basic psychosomatic hypotheses. However, far less well-developed animal models are occasionally presented as relevant to the understanding of psychosocial influences on human disease. In those cases, the sources of threats to generalizability described above must be considered carefully.

Human Mechanism Research

In nearly all conceptual models of direct psychosocial influences on disease, various aspects of the endocrine and autonomic nervous systems are identified as the link between risk factors and pathophysiology (Lovallo, 1997). Through autonomic neural innervation or through endocrine responses, stress has physiological effects which if sufficiently pronounced, prolonged, or frequent can initiate or hasten the development of disease. As in the case of psychosocial epidemiological research, the effects of health behavior and stress must be separated in mechanism research. For example, a recent study indicated that some of the effect of stress on the immune system may be accounted for by the fact that stress disrupts sleep, and disrupted sleep—rather than the psychobiologic correlates of stress itself—may suppress the immune system (Hall et al., 1998). Thus, these recurring conceptual and empirical distinctions are important in mechanism research, as well.

The models and supporting bodies of research are most clearly developed in the case of cardiovascular disease and diseases otherwise controlled by the immune system—notably infectious disease and cancer. In the case of both cardiovascular and immune mechanisms, the systems influenced by stress are complex. Simple responses such as increased heart rate and blood pressure during the stress of public speaking reflect a mosaic of autonomic influences, such as sympathetic stimulation of the heart, parasympathetic withdrawal, and increases in peripheral vascular resistance (Lovallo, 1997). Current technology in cardiovascular psychophysiology permits all of these variables to be assessed simultaneously. Stress effects on the multiple components of the immune system are similarly complex (Uchino, Kiecolt-Glaser, & Glaser, 1998), and most studies of stress and immune response assess many immune parameters and perhaps related physiological events (e.g., endocrine responses).

The interdependent effects pose conceptual and analytic problems. With multiple dependent variables, inattention to experiment-wise Type 1 error rates can produce misleading results. However, an atheoretical approach to the control of this problem (e.g., Bonferroni corrections) both ignores what is known about the structure of such responses and precludes tests of related conceptual models. A more appropriate approach is a conceptually-driven organization and prioritization of dependent variables, or the interpretation of multivariate outcomes (Huberty & Morris, 1989). Thus, physiological theory should guide the treatment of the large and growing array of dependent variables examined in human stress mechanism research.

Incomplete articulation of the underlying conceptual model poses a threat to other aspects of human mechanism research. For example, autonomic responses are involved in two distinct but often confused conceptualizations (Smith et al., 1997). In the first, autonomic responsiveness is seen as an individual difference dimension that itself is a risk factor for disease. Individuals with characteristically large autonomic responses to stress are believed to be at greater risk of disease, whereas less reactive individuals are at less risk. In the second conceptualization, physiological reactivity is a mediating variable—the link between psychosocial risk factors and the development of disease. Job stress, for example, is believed to contribute to cardiovascular disease via its effects on recurring, daily increases in blood pressure and circulating catecholamines. These two conceptualizations have distinct implications for research design. The development of reliable and valid assessments of individual differences in stress reactivity is an essential component of evaluation of the first model. Physiological responses to laboratory stressors can be inconsistent across specific tasks, settings, and time, and they have weak relationships with stress responses assessed during daily activities (Gerin, Rosofsky, Pieper, & Pickering, 1994). This raises multiple concerns about the nature of this individual difference and its predictive utility. Research based on psychometric theory has resulted in better assessments of individual differences in cardiovascular stress responses (Kamarck, Jennings, Pogue-Geiler, & Manuck, 1994), and even more limited assessments have been found to predict cardiovascular disease endpoints (Manuck, 1994). However, tests of the individual difference model must address potential limitations in the assessment of this key construct.

Mediating models pose other challenges. Psychosocial variables such as social support and chronic hostility are believed to contribute to disease through their effects on physiological responses. As an initial step in evaluating this model, the psychosocial risk factors must be measured or manipulated and their effects on psychophysiological responses assessed. The most clearly established risk factors involve social interactions or relationships (Adler & Matthews, 1994). Yet, the majority of studies of psychophysiological reactivity have employed nonsocial stressors, such as reaction time tasks, mental arithmetic, or other easily standardized and controlled cognitive challenges (Smith et al., 1997). Although such research has produced important information about the nature and consequences of stress responses, it has only indirect implications for the mediational model. The task of counting backwards from 1,000 by 13s reliably evokes a large increase in blood pressure, but this cardiovascular response by itself tells us little about the effect of social conflict or support on the purported pathophysiological mechanism that links the interpersonal environment to subsequent cardiovascular disease. More appropriate tests of the mediational model require a social psychophysiological approach in which features of the social situation are measured or manipulated, along with relevant individual differences (e.g., personality traits), and related to physiological responses. That is, tests of the mediational model require more ecologically valid or generalizable stressors. This social psychophysiological approach contains its own challenges and drawbacks, as social interactions are less easily standardized and can contain artifacts, such as the effects of speech on physiological response. These problems are not insurmountable, however. Careful attention to methodological detail can provide an adequate level control and still adequately represent psychosocial risk constructs. Further, reliable and valid interpersonal assessments can provide independent information about the extent to which the intended social processes were modeled effectively (Smith, Gallo, Goble, Ngu, & Stark, 1998; Smith, Limon, Gallo, & Ngu, 1996). This laboratory-based approach has been combined with current medical imaging technology to demonstrate that social stressors evoke myocardial ischemia in patients with coronary artery disease (Ironson et al., 1992). Thus, social psychophysiological research can test basic hypotheses about the effects of psychosocial risk factors on putative mechanisms in healthy individuals, as well as hypotheses about the effects of stress on the expression or course of established disease.

Even when psychosocial risk factors are successfully modeled, laboratory-based assessments of physiological stress responses still may lack ecological validity. To address this problem, at least two avenues are available. In the first, members of established relationships can be studied in the laboratory, and conceptually important features of their interaction measured or manipulated in order to assess the impact of realistic social processes on stress responses. Studies of married couples, for example, have provided important evidence of the impact of stressful interactions on cardiovascular (Ewart, Taylor, Kraemer, & Agras, 1991; Smith & Brown, 1991; Smith et al., 1998), neuroendocrine, and immunologic responses (Kiecolt-Glaser et al., 1997). This laboratory-based approach demonstrates that psychosocial risk factors (e.g., supportive vs. conflictual interactions) have the expected impact on physiology in the context of established relationships.

Ambulatory studies provide a second way to extend the ecological validity of stress mechanism research. Advances in ambulatory assessments of physiological functioning can be combined with daily diary assessments of experiences related to psychosocial risk factors, such as social support, conflict, or anger. Using appropriate quantitative techniques (Jaccard & Wan, 1993; J. Schwartz & Stone, 1998), covariation between experience and physiology in the natural environment can be tested. This approach to evaluating mediational hypotheses has been used in the study of a variety of psychosocial risk factors (e.g., Guyll & Contrada, 1998; Kamarck et al., 1998). Although external and ecological validity are strengths of this approach, it is not without limitations. The independent variable is typically some measured aspect of the participant's experience. The conditions of assessment and sampling frame must be carefully designed to insure that this psychosocial construct occurs a sufficient number of times and to a sufficient extent to provide an adequate operationalization of the independent variable. In addition, the daily diary assessment must be carefully evaluated to assess its psychometric properties. As with laboratory-based research, the ambulatory methodology has also been combined successfully with advanced medical monitoring to document an association between stress and ischemia during the daily activities of heart patients (e.g., Gullette et al., 1997). Thus, this approach to stress mechanism research can also be used to study effects on later stages of disease.

In evaluations of the mediational model of stress and disease, it is rare that the entire model is evaluated. The results of psychosocial epidemiological studies can document an association to be explained, as is the case for social support, hostility, and other risk factors. The aggregate results of laboratory, ambulatory, and clinical research demonstrating that these risk factors have the hypothesized effects on physiological mediating mechanisms are certainly consistent with the model, and the absence of such effects would be strong disconfirming evidence. However, a complete test would require the assessment of psychosocial predictors and the stress mechanism, as well as appropriate mediational analyses. Despite the widespread influence of this general model, such studies are quite rare (Krantz & Hedges, 1987). In the few cases in which they have been attempted, the mediational model may not be supported. For example, S. Cohen and his colleagues (Cohen, Tyrell, & Smith, 1991) reported that self-reported stress was associated with increased susceptibility to infection following experimental exposure to a cold virus, but the hypothesized intervening association between stress and suppressed immune functioning did not account for the effect. It may be that complete tests of the mediational model in humans are not feasible in many of the areas where they guide research.

In the absence of complete tests, several basic questions must be asked in evaluating the implications of human mechanism research (S. Cohen & Rabin, 1998). First, are the physiological responses observed of the *type* that could plausibly influence the development of a specific disease? Second, if plausible, are they of sufficient *magnitude?* Finally, are these responses *frequent* enough to influence disease? In many cases, the answers to these questions will compel cautious interpretation of findings in human mechanism research.

Implications for Intervention Research

Understanding the effects of stress on disease is itself a worthy scientific goal. However, in most cases this work is guided by the ultimate goal of preventing or treating disease. The psychosocial risk factors for major physical illness (e.g., problematic social relations, anger, and aggressive behavior) are similar to many identified as predictors of emotional and social adjustment difficulties and substance abuse among adolescents and young adults. Some important stress-related medical conditions begin to emerge during this same period, such as high blood pressure. Thus, specific interventions and associated methodology in traditional areas of prevention research could be usefully applied to the prevention of the health-damaging effects of stress.

The much more common application of research on psychosocial risk factors, stress, and disease is as an intervention for individuals already suffering from illness. Given evidence that stress and related psychosocial processes can influence their development, stress reduction has been studied as an ancillary treatment for coronary heart disease (Blumenthal, Jiang, Babyak, & Krantz, 1997; Linden et al., 1996), cancer (Fawzy et al., 1993; Spiegel, Bloom, Kraemer, Gottheil, 1989), and a variety of other serious chronic medical conditions (Parker, 1995). In this type of research, all of the design and analysis considerations in treatment outcome research in other areas of psychological interventions are relevant (Chambless & Hollon, 1998; Compas et al., 1998; Kendall et al., this volume). The most important of these include thorough description of sampling and recruitment procedures; enrollment of an adequate sample size; randomization and evaluation of initial group equivalence; assessment and control of expectancies and other non-specific factors; evaluation of therapist adherence to clearly specified intervention protocols; inclusion of reliable and valid outcome measures; evaluation of the effects of attrition; appropriate analyses of change; and inclusion of an adequate follow-up period for the evaluation of maintenance of treatment effects. Given the specific context of evaluating the effects of psychosocial interventions on medical disease, some of these issues require additional consideration.

As described earlier, patients with diagnosed disease are available for inclusion in this type of clinical intervention research after a complex process of seeking medical attention, medical evaluation, referral, and prior treatment (Turk & Rudy, 1990). The representativeness of the sample is difficult to assess. At a minimum, the procedures for recruiting the sample and relevant medical and demographic information should be thoroughly described. In this way, results can be generalized in an informed manner.

The issues of outcome variables and samples sizes are closely related. In the case of some psychosocial interventions designed to impact disease, recurrence and even survival are relevant outcomes, as in the case of cancer or coronary disease. These are central medical outcomes and the focus of evaluations of medical and surgical treatments. Therefore, significant effects of psychosocial outcomes on these outcomes is of major importance. Some of the most widely reported treatment studies in the field have found that psychological therapies reduce the recurrence of disease or extend life among seriously ill patients (Fawzy et al., 1993; Friedman, Thoresen, & Gill, 1986; Spiegel et al., 1989). The effects of psychosocial interventions on these objective, major endpoints would reasonably be expected to be small or moderate in size. Yet, there are many studies with small sample sizes. An a-priori power analysis would likely suggest the necessity of a much larger sample in order to detect effects on these outcomes. Therefore, even when dramatic results are reported, small studies must be considered tentative. The design of necessary replications should be guided by careful consideration of likely effect sizes. In some instances, more sensitive but still medically relevant outcome variables can be used, such as changes in blood pressure or the frequency and duration of myocardial ischemia during ambulatory assessment of heart patients (Blumenthal et al., 1997).

Even in carefully randomized studies, initial equivalence of groups on key medical variables must be assessed. The components of the typical medical evaluation for a specific illness can identify the set of characteristics to be considered. Minor differences across groups in the site or staging of cancer, the extent of prior cardiac disease, or the severity of hypertension or type of pharmacologic treatment could contribute to apparent treatment effects. An additional advantage of such thorough pretreatment assessments is opportunity to examine the moderation of the effects of psychosocial interventions by clinical features of the medical condition. The results of such analyses could have substantial practical and scientific benefits.

Placebo effects are well-documented in the medical and surgical treatment of physical symptoms and serious illnesses (e.g., Turner, Deyo, & Loweser, 1994). Therefore, no-treatment or usual care control groups can be expected to overestimate the benefits of psychosocial treatments, as such interventions are likely to create clear expectations for improvement. Improved outcome over usual medical care conditions suggests an important practical benefit of the intervention, but leaves the question of the responsible causes unanswered (Compas et al., 1998; Schwartz et al., 1997).

Finally, the choice of follow-up periods should be guided by what is known about the natural history of the disease and the effects of traditional medical and surgical treatment. In the case of some severe conditions, treatment benefits can be expected to appear within a few weeks or months but not persist beyond a year or two, simply because of the brief life expectancy associated with the condition. In other cases of serious but less dire prognoses, longer follow-up periods will be necessary to evaluate the extent and maintenance of treatment effects.

PSYCHOSOCIAL IMPACT AND MANAGEMENT OF ILLNESS

Our third major component of health psychology is the study of psychosocial aspects of acute and chronic medical illness and its treatment. Acute illness and the associated medical or surgical treatment are often the source of considerable physical and emotional distress, and can create severe adaptive demands. This is true not only in the case of unwelcome medical events, such as surgery (Anderson, 1987) and invasive medical tests (Kendall et al., 1979), but even largely desirable events, such as pregnancy and childbirth (Stanton & Danoff-Burg, 1995). Individuals vary in how well they cope with these stressors, and the outcome of their efforts can have a major impact on their subsequent quality of life. Chronic medical conditions such as diabetes or heart disease can pose even greater challenges, as the adaptive demands can be not only more prolonged but more extensive, as well. Both the disease and its treatment can impact many areas of the patient's life, such social and vocational functioning (Smith & Nicassio, 1995). Research in this area has two major goals. First, many studies attempt to identify the nature and determinants of the impact of medical illness and care. Influences on this impact include characteristics of the individual, such as coping style; aspects of the social environment, such as the level of support from family members; and features of the medical setting, such as the nature of interactions with health care professional (Auerbach, 1989). Second, other research uses this information to guide the development and evaluation of interventions intended to improve adjustment and augment traditional care. Examples of this type of research include evaluations of: psychological preparations for stressful medical procedures (Suls & Wan, 1989); interventions intended to facilitate compliance with medical regimens (Dunbar-Jacob et al., 1995); and psychosocial treatments designed to augment standard medical care through symptom reduction, management of treatment side effects, or improvement of emotional adjustment (Parker, 1995; Turk & Salovey, 1995). Some interventions of this type are directed at the needs of family members and caregivers, rather than patients themselves (Schulz & Quittner, 1998).

Adjustment to Illness and Stressful Medical Care

For researchers to accurately describe the psychosocial impact of medical conditions or illnesses, they must understand the specific symptoms, underlying pathophysiology, prognosis, and standard diagnostic and treatment procedures. Attention to the specific illness and treatment context is essential, because it is a far-reaching determinant of the patient's experience (Belar & Deardorff, 1995; Smith & Nicassio, 1995). Key dependent variables (e.g., pain, adherence to treatment, emotional adjustment, sexual functioning, treatment side effects), potentially relevant predictor variables (e.g., marital support, coping strategies), and appropriate time frames for assessment can be identified in this manner. For example, the site and staging of cancer have clear implications of the nature and severity of psychosocial impacts of the disease (Andersen, 1992), because these variables determine symptoms, prognosis, the type of treatment, and related side effects. This is also the case for the location and extent of underlying coronary artery disease and cardiac damage for patients suffering myocardial infarction (Smith & Leon, 1992). Any attempt to identify the important features and determinants of adjustment to these conditions will be incomplete at best—and quite possibly misleading—if the research protocol is not based on a clear understanding of the medical situation and the patient's likely experience of it.

For most acute and chronic medical conditions, researchers have described the key assessment targets resulting from this contextual perspective, and reliable and valid measures of several important constructs are available for use in the context of specific illnesses or medical procedures (see Belar & Deardorff, 1995; Derogatis, Fleming, Sudler, & DellaPietra, 1995; Turk & Melzack, 1992, for reviews). In choosing measures for specific research applications and evaluating research findings, it is essential to consider both the appropriateness of a measure given the medical context and the available independent evidence of its reliability and construct validity in that context.

Despite the need for context-specific decisions about methodology, research in this area does confront recurring general issues. The assessment of emotional adjustment is a central concern. Most medical conditions have at least temporary effects on the patient's mood, and in some cases the effects are prolonged and severe. Research on this aspect of patient functioning often suffers methodological limitations stemming from measurement models and procedures. First, many studies in this area utilize measurement procedures developed for the assessment of emotional adjustment in psychiatric or other mental health populations. Because the medically ill often experience depressive symptoms, widely used measures of depression (e.g., Beck Depression Inventory, MMPI Depression Scale) often serve as indices of medical patient adjustment. A serious threat to the validity of these scales in studies of the medically ill is the meaning of somatic symptoms depression, such as fatigue, changes in appetite, and concerns about physical appearance (McDaniel, Mussleman, Porter, Reed, & Nemeroff, 1995; Mohr et al., 1997; O'Donnell & Chung, 1997). Although these symptoms are typically highly diagnostic in the case of depression in the absence of physical disease, they can be the source of false positive diagnoses of affective disorder or the overestimation of the severity of depressive symptoms in medical populations (Clark, Cook, & Snow, 1998). Patients with a variety of illnesses can score at least in the mildly depressed range simply by accurately reporting their physical symptoms or treatment side effects. Elimination of the somatic content of these scales can improve their construct validity in medical populations (Peck, Smith, Ward, & Milano, 1989).

A more basic issue in the assessment of emotional adjustment in physical illness is the appropriateness of the underlying conceptual model. In most studies, emotional adjustment is conceptualized as varying degrees of maladjustment or disorder, as in the case of depression. However, the most common emotional impacts of serious medical disease or disorder fall short of clinically diagnosable levels. The interpretation of continuous depression scores below levels associated with diagnosable disorder has been the source of considerable debate for many years (Coyne, 1994; Flett, Vredenburg, & Krames, 1997; Kendall, Hollon, Beck, Hammen, & Ingram, 1987), mostly because of skepticism about the assumption that information of this sort informs our understanding of depressive disorders. This issue is equally relevant in the case of medical illness (Coyne & Schwenk, 1997), but appropriateness of maladjustment as the underlying conceptual approach is also questionable. Models of the structure and determinants of normal emotional experience might be more appropriate in assessing the impact of illness, or at least serve as a useful complement to the traditional clinically-oriented approach. One such model is the two-dimensional model proposed by Watson and Tellegen (1985). Normal mood varies along the independent (or at least minimally correlated) dimensions of negative and positive affect. Measures of depression combine these dimensions, as depression consists of high negative and low positive affect (Watson et al., 1995). Use of the single dimension of depression can lead to a loss of information, because in chronic illness populations negative and positive affect have distinct correlates (Smith & Christensen, 1996; Zautra et al., 1995). Thus, a more complete and specific description of the emotional impact of illness can be obtained with the two-dimensional model. Although the medically ill may be at increased risk of diagnosable emotional disorders, in most cases their emotional adjustment is well within the normal range. Nonetheless, their physical condition can have important emotional consequences. These illnesses can be the source of negative affect, but also can detract from the patient's quality of life through the reduction of positive emotional experiences. Assessment procedures must be designed or selected appropriately.

Self-reports are the most commonly used assessment method across the principle domains of the psychosocial impact of medical illness—emotional adjustment, functional activity levels (vs. disability), pain and other symptoms, and social functioning. Although psychometrically sound self-report instruments are available in each of these areas, over-reliance on this modality may create interpretive problems. Artifacts inherent in self-reports, such as social desirability, can inflate estimates of covariation among these domains of adjustment, as can the inclusion of similarly worded items on measures intended to assess distinct constructs. For example, a large correlation between measures of pain and depression can reflect (a) a substantive association between these constructs, (b) the influence of individual differences in the willingness to report negative experiences, or (c) inclusion of affective wording in items on the pain scale or somatic wording of depression items. Thus, multimethod approaches are as desirable in this research area as they are in much of clinical psychology (Auerbach, 1989). In several areas, the multimethod approach has been guiding assessment work for many years. For example, reliable and valid behavioral assessments of pain and activity levels can be combined with self-reports and significant other ratings to provide a comprehensive assessment of chronic pain (Turk & Melzack, 1992).

This problem of reliance on self-reports is even more worrisome in the study of potential determinants of adjustment to medical conditions. Cognitive models of adjustment to illness are perhaps the predominant perspective in the field (Smith, 1992). The key constructs studied as predictors of emotional and behavioral response to illness such as coping strategies, attributions, cognitive distortions, self-efficacy beliefs, helplessness, are most commonly assessed via self-report scales. Cognitive assessment has long struggled with the question of the extent to which important cognitive influences on emotion and behavior are accessible for accurate self-report (Coyne & Gotlib, 1983). For example, several recent studies have raised concerns about the accuracy of widely-used self-report coping checklists (Coyne & Gottlieb, 1996; A. Stone et al., 1998). However, self-reports of cognitive influences on response to illness contain a more mundane interpretive caution inherent to self-report measures of cognitive influences on adjustment (Smith, 1989); the items in these scales may contain wording reflecting the emotional distress and functional limitations that the cognitive constructs are hypothesized to influence. Associations between cognitive variables and emotional or functional outcomes may partially or fully reflect the "thinly veiled tautology" (Coyne & Gotlib, 1983) caused by this particular source of common method variance. This makes comprehensive evaluations of convergent and discriminant validity an important initial step in testing models of adjustment to physical illness. Structural equation modeling techniques can be used to evaluate both measurement models and conceptual models to manage this methodological problem, but multimethod approaches remain highly desirable.

Just as in the case of personality predictors of disease in psychosomatics, the proliferation of insufficiently validated individual difference measures has been problematic in this area of research. Often a new influence on adjustment is proposed, a scale is created to assess it, and it is used in a study predicting some aspect of the impact of illness. More thorough validation and empirical evaluation of associations with established constructs and measures would help produce a more integrated and informative literature on the topic. Further, many studies based on a cognitive model of adjustment to chronic illness do not examine the social context of the cognitive predictors. A patient's sense of helplessness in the face of serious illness, for example, may be a consequence or cause of dysfunctional family interactions. Thus, inclusion of individual and interpersonal predictors of adjustment in the same study may lead to a more complete description of the impact of disease (Coyne & Smith, 1994; Manne & Zautra, 1989).

Many studies of the impact of illness and medical care employ cross-sectional, correlational designs. In the initial stage of measurement development and theory testing, this approach may be appropriate. However, it is ultimately an inadequate approach to explicating what are likely to be complex, reciprocal influences among illness, the individual's emotional and behavioral response, and the surrounding social context (Depue & Monroe, 1986). Longitudinal designs have an obvious advantage, as a result, but as discussed earlier the time frame selected for assessments must be consistent with the phenomenon under investigation. Longer periods between assessments are appropriate for adjustment processes that change slowly, such as changes in chronic pain, disability, or significant levels of emotional distress. However, important aspects of the impact of illness fluctuate much more rapidly. Daily monitoring studies and the associated hierarchical linear modeling techniques used in studies of health behavior and stress physiology as discussed above have been recently used with success in studies of the determinants of pain and other effects of chronic illness (Affleck, Tennen, Urrows, & Higgins, 1992; Affleck et al., 1998). This application of new research technology could facilitate a much more complete and nuanced understanding of the adjustment process. In both long- and short-term time frames, growth curve modeling techniques have the potential to identify important relationships with the shape, pattern, or trajectory of adjustment over time, rather than simply the degree of change (Frank et al., 1998).

Evaluating Adjunctive Treatments

Psychological interventions have been developed as adjuncts to medical and surgical care for a great variety of acute and chronic conditions. Some brief interventions are intended to reduce the physical discomfort and emotional distress associated with specific procedures, such as childbirth, surgery, or invasive medical tests, as well as reduce the likelihood of complications. For many chronic conditions (e.g., headache, arthritis, back pain, irritable bowel syndrome), pain reduction and increased functional activity levels are the primary targets of psychosocial interventions, and include the secondary goal of reduced reliance on pain reducing medication (Keefe, Dunsmore, & Burnett, 1992; Wilson & Gil, 1996). In other cases, such as diabetes, renal disease, and hypertension, compliance with primary medical treatments is a critical behavioral goal. Despite the fact that noncompliance can have life threatening consequences, many patients display a significant problem in this area. Finally, in the cases of some conditions, such as cancer (Andersen, 1992; Fawzy, Fawzy, Arndt, & Pasnau, 1995) and heart disease (Linden et al., 1996; Smith & Leon, 1992), psychosocial treatments often address one or more of the multiple impacts of the illness, including symptom management, changes in diet or exercise, management of treatment side effects, and emotional adjustment.

The guidelines for the design and evaluation of this type of intervention research can be gleaned from much of the preceding discussion. The selection of outcome measures must be informed by a careful consideration of the specific medical context. For example, in studies of acute medical treatments or procedures, transient physical and emotional distress can be assessed with self-reports, psychophysiological measures, observer ratings, medication administered, and the duration and extent of complications in the procedure. This type of multimethod approach has been used in the evaluation of interventions intended to facilitate adjustment to invasive medical procedures, surgery, and childbirth (Auerbach, 1989; Suls & Wan, 1989).

In the case of many chronic diseases and conditions, well-established, clinically-relevant outcome measures are available (e.g., Meyer & Mark, 1995; Smith & Leon, 1992; Turk & Melzack, 1992), and they have often been demonstrated to be sensitive to the effects of psychosocial interventions (e.g., Parker et al., 1995). Self-report methodologies are not only acceptable but actually essential in many of these situations, because the primary complaint is a subjective experience, such as pain, nausea, or anxiety. However, sole reliance on self-reports poses a problem, because as discussed earlier, psychosocial intervention protocols convey strong demands or expectancies for improvement. Thus, as in the case of acute conditions and procedures, multimodal assessment is an important feature of evaluations of psychosocial interventions for chronic medical conditions.

The primary features of the experimental design in these cases must also be determined by the specific medical context. The nature, timing, and duration of interventions will vary widely, from brief informational or coping interventions prior to surgery (e.g., E. Anderson, 1987) to multisession treatments for the management of chronic conditions (Blumenthal et al., 1997; Spiegel et al., 1989). The necessary length of follow-up assessment similarly depends on the context. Hours or days are sufficient for many acute situations, whereas months or even years are necessary in some chronic conditions. As noted in our discussion of general methodological issues, the selection of comparison or control groups depends on the nature of questions relevant to the given state of a specific research area, but also is influenced by aspects of the medical problem and treatment context (Auerbach, 1989; Compas et al., 1998). For new treatments or new applications, no-treatment or waiting list controls are appropriate. However, given the likelihood of demand and expectancy effects in reports of pain or other symptoms (Turner et al., 1994), subsequent studies must include appropriate controls. Regrettably, some types of controls are not plausible, feasible, or ethical in many medical applications (Compas et al., 1998), creating difficult and likely imperfect choices in this aspect of design. The assessment of expectancies and nonspecific factors is therefore an important feature of these research protocols.

The clinical significance of treatment effects has been discussed in areas of adjunctive psychological interventions, and guidelines have been proposed in some cases. For example, a 50% reduction in the frequency of episodes is often expressed as a clinically significant outcome in episodic pain disorders (Blanchard & Malamood, 1996; Blanchard & Schwartz, 1988). The use of standardized measures of pain (Jensen, Turner, Turner, & Romano, 1996), distress (Derogatis et al., 1995), and functional activity (Bergner et al., 1981) can permit comparisons with both normative groups and results of related studies.

In light of developments in managed care, medical costs are increasingly relevant in intervention trials. Intervention and related costs (Friedman et al., 1995) must be considered along with treatment benefits. This perspective also encourages assessment of the impacts on subsequent health care utilization, as well as the quantification of outcomes in units that permit comparisons across a variety of behavioral and medical/surgical approaches (cf. R. Kaplan, 1994). Often, decisions about funding for adjunctive care are made in comparison to other treatments or services. The opportunity to compare benefits and costs of diverse services with common metrics can facilitate such decisions.

CONCLUSIONS

Well-known strengths and weaknesses of psychological research are relevant to the design and evaluation of health psychology research. However, the biopsychosocial model (Engel, 1977) that guides health psychology and the specific context of medical problems and services necessitate care and creativity in application of traditional methods. The need for thoughtful translation will continue as medical technology advances at an increasing rate. These changes will pose new psychological questions about the impact of medical procedures, as in the case of genetic testing (Lerman, 1997). These advances will also provide new methodologic opportunities, as developments in medical imaging and instrumentation, genetics, and biochemistry continuously extend and refine our ability to study the association between psychological and physiological events.

The nature of the connection between psychological events and disease has been a captivating question for centuries, and advanced medical and behavioral research methods currently provide the opportunity to address these questions with unprecedented precision and thoroughness. Yet, at the same time, pressing public health problems and growing scrutiny of health expenditures demand that health psychology research attend to practical concerns. Thus, balancing the importance of theory-driven research on long-standing, basic questions about the connections between health and behavior with the obvious value of applying behavioral methods to current health needs is at present an overarching challenge in the field. Some of the most valuable contributions in the history of health psychology have come from this tension between basic and applied science.

REFERENCES

Adler, N., Boyce, W. T., Chesney, M., Folkman, S., & Syme, S. L. (1993). Socioeconomic inequalities in health. *Journal of the American Medical Association, 269,* 3140–3145.

Adler, N., & Matthews, K. (1994). Health psychology: Why do some people get sick and some stay well? *Annual Review of Psychology, 45,* 229–259.

Affleck, G., Tennen, H., Urrows, S., Hall, C., Higgins, P., Abeles, M., Karoly, P., & Newton, C. (1998). Fibromyalgia and women's pursuit of personal goals: A daily process study. *Health Psychology, 17,* 40–47.

Affleck, G., Tennen, H., Urrows, S., & Higgins, P. (1992). Neuroticism and the pain-mood relation in rheumatoid arthritis: Insights from a prospective daily study. *Journal of Consulting and Clinical Psychology, 60,* 119–126.

Andersen, B. L. (1992). Psychosocial interventions for cancer patients to enhance quality of life. *Journal of Consulting and Clinical Psychology, 60,* 552–568.

Andersen, B. L., Kiecolt-Glaser, J. K., & Glaser, R. (1994). A biobehavioral model of cancer stress and disease course. *American Psychologist, 49,* 389–404.

Anderson, E. (1987). Preoperative preparation facilitates recovery, reduces psychological distress, and reduces the incidence of acute postoperative hypertension. *Journal of Consulting and Clinical Psychology, 55,* 513–520.

Anderson, N. B. (1989). Racial differences in stress-induced cardiovascular reactivity and hypertension: Current status and substantive issues. *Psychological Bulletin, 105,* 89–105.

Anderson, N. B., & Armstead, C. A. (1995). Toward understanding the association of socioeconomic status and health: A new challenge for the biopsychosocial approach. *Psychosomatic Medicine, 57,* 213–225.

Auerbach, S. M. (1989). Stress management and coping research in the health care setting: An overview and methodological commentary. *Journal of Consulting and Clinical Psychology, 57,* 388–395.

Bandura, A. (1977). Self-efficacy: Toward a unifying theory of behavioral change. *Psychological Review, 84,* 191–215.

Baron, R. M., & Kenny, D. A. (1986). The moderator-mediator variable distinction in social psychological research: Conceptual, strategic, and statistical considerations. *Journal of Personality and Social Psychology, 51,* 1173–1182.

Belar, C. D., & Deardorff, W. W. (1995). *Clinical health psychology in medical settings.* Washington, DC: American Psychological Association.

Bergner, M., Bobbit, R. A., Carter, W. B., & Gilson, B. S. (1981). The sickness impact profile: Validation of a health status measure. *Medical Care, 14,* 57–67.

Blanchard, E. B., & Malamood, H. S. (1996). Psychological treatment of irritable bowel syndrome. *Professional Psychology: Research and Practice, 27,* 241–244.

Blanchard, E. B., & Schwartz, S. P. (1988). Clinically significant changes in behavioral medicine. *Behavioral Assessment, 10,* 171–188.

Block, J. (1995). A contrarian view of the five-factor approach to personality description. *Psychological Bulletin, 117,* 182–215.

Blumenthal, J. A., Jiang, W., Babyak, M. A., & Krantz, D. S. (1997). Stress management and exercise training in cardiac patients with myocardial ischemia. *Archives of Internal Medicine, 157,* 2213–2223.

Bolger, N., & Zuckerman, A. (1995). A framework for studying personality in the stress process. *Journal of Personality and Social Psychology, 69,* 890–902.

Brownell, K. D., Marlatt, G. A., Lichtenstein, E., & Wilson, G. T. (1986). Understanding and preventing relapse. *American Psychologist, 41,* 765–782.

Brownell, K. D., & Wadden, T. A. (1992). Etiology and treatment of obesity: Understanding a serious, prevalent, and refractory disorder. *Journal of Consulting and Clinical Psychology, 60,* 505–518.

Chambless, D. L., & Hollon, S. D. (1998). Defining empirically supported therapies. *Journal of Consulting and Clinical Psychology, 66,* 7–18.

Champion, V. L., & Miller, A. (1997). Adherence to mammography and breast self-examination regimens. In D. S. Gochman (Ed.), *Handbook of health behavior research* (Vol. 2, pp. 245 268). New York: Plenum Press.

Clark, D. A., Cook, A., & Snow, D. (1998). Depressive symptom differences in hospitalized, medically ill, depressed psychiatric inpatients, and nonmedical controls. *Journal of Abnormal Psychology, 107,* 38–48.

Cohen, F. (1979). Personality, stress, and the development of physical illness. In G. Stone, F. Cohen, & N. Adler (Eds.), *Health psychology* (pp. 77–111). San Francisco: Jossey-Bass.

Cohen, J. (1990). Things I have learned so far. *American Psychologist, 45,* 1304–1312.

Cohen, J. (1992). A power primer. *Psychological Bulletin, 112,* 155–159.

Cohen, S., Kaplan, J., & Manuck, S. (1994). Social support and coronary heart disease: Underlying psychological and biological mechanisms. In S. Schumaker & S. Czajkowski (Eds.), *Social support and cardiovascular disease* (pp. 195–222). New York: Plenum Press.

Cohen, S., Kessler, R. C., & Gordon, L. U. (1995). *Measuring stress.* New York: Oxford University Press.

Cohen, S., & Rabin, B. S. (1998). Psychologic stress, immunity, and cancer. *Journal of the National Cancer Institute, 90,* 3–4.

Cohen, S., & Rodriguez, M. (1995). Pathways linking affective disturbances and physical disorders. *Health Psychology, 14,* 374–380.

Cohen, S., Tyrell, D. A. J., & Smith, A. P. (1991). Psychological stress and susceptibility to the common cold. *New England Journal of Medicine, 325,* 606–612.

Compas, B. E., Haaga, D. A., Keefe, F. J., Leitenberg, H., & Williams, D. A. (1998). Sampling of empirically supported psychological treatments from health psychology: Smoking, chronic pain, cancer, and bulimia nervosa. *Journal of Consulting and Clinical Psychology, 66,* 89–112.

Cook, T. D., & Campbell, D. T. (1979). *Quasi-experimentation: Design and analysis issues for field settings.* Chicago: Rand McNally.

Costa, P. T., Jr., & McCrae, R. R. (1987). Neuroticism, somatic complaints, and disease: Is the bark worse than the bite? *Journal of Personality, 55,* 299–316.

Coyne, J. C. (1994). Self-reported distress: Analog or ersatz depression? *Psychological Bulletin, 116,* 29–45.

Coyne, J. C., & DeLongis, A. (1986). Going beyond social support: The role of social relationships in adaptation. *Journal of Consulting and Clinical Psychology, 54,* 454–460.

Coyne, J. C., & Gotlib, I. (1983). The role of cognition in depression: A critical review. *Psychological Bulletin, 94,* 472–505.

Coyne, J. C., & Gottlieb, B. H. (1996). The mismeasure of coping by checklist. *Journal of Personality, 64,* 959–991.

Coyne, J. C., & Schwenk, T. L. (1997). The relationship of distress to mood disturbance in primary care and psychiatric populations. *Journal of Consulting and Clinical Psychology, 65,* 161–168.

Coyne, J. C., & Smith, D. A. (1994). Couples coping with myocardial infarction: Contextual perspective on patient self-efficacy. *Journal of Family Psychology, 8,* 43–54.

Crits-Christoph, P., & Mintz, J. (1991). Implications of therapist effects for the design and analysis of comparative studies of psychotherapies. *Journal of Consulting and Clinical Psychology, 59,* 20–26.

Croyle, R. T., & Loftus, E. F. (1993). Recollection in the kingdom of AIDS. In D. G. Ostrow & R. Kessler (Eds.), *Methodological issues in AIDS behavioral research* (pp. 163–180). New York: Plenum Press.

Curry, S. J., & McBride, C. M. (1994). Relapse prevention for smoking cessation: Review and evaluation of concepts and interventions. *Annual Review of Public Health, 15,* 345–366.

Davila, J., Bradbury, T. N., Cohan, C. L., & Tochluk, S. (1997). Marital functioning and depressive symptoms: Evidence for a stress generation model. *Journal of Personality and Social Psychology, 73,* 849–861.

Depue, R. A., & Monroe, S. M. (1986). Conceptualization and measurement of human disorder in life stress research. The problem of chronic disturbance. *Psychological Bulletin, 99,* 36–51.

Derogatis, L. R., Fleming, M. P., Sudler, N. C., & DellaPietra, L. (1995). Psychological assessment. In P. M. Nicassio & T. W. Smith (Eds.), *Managing chronic illness: A biopsychosocial perspective* (pp. 59–116).Washington, DC: American Psychological Association.

Digman, J. (1990). Personality structure: Emergence of the five-factor model. *Annual Review of Psychology, 41,* 417–440.

Dubbert, P. M. (1992). Exercise in behavioral medicine. *Journal of Consulting and Clinical Psychology, 60,* 613–618.

Dunbar-Jacobs, J., Burke, L. E., & Puczynski, S. (1995). Clinical assessment and management of adherence to medical regimens. In P. M. Nicassio & T. W. Smith (Eds.), *Managing chronic illness: A biopsychosocial perspective* (pp. 313–350). Washington, DC: American Psychological Association.

Engel, G. L. (1977). The need for a new medical model: A challenge for biomedicine. *Science, 196,* 129–136.

Etringer, B. D., Gregory, V. R., & Lando, H. A. (1984). Influence of group cohesion on the behavioral treatment of smoking. *Journal of Consulting and Clinical Psychology, 52,* 1080–1086.

Ewart, C. K., Taylor, L. B., Kraemer, H. C., & Agras, W. S. (1991). High blood pressure and marital discord: Not being nasty matters more than being nice. *Health Psychology, 10,* 155–163.

Fawzy, F. I., Fawzy, N. W., Arndt, L. A., & Pasnau, R. O. (1995). Critical review of psychological interventions in cancer care. *Archives of General Psychiatry, 52,* 100–113.

Fawzy, F. I., Fawzy, N. W., Hyun, C. S., Elashoff, R., Gutheire, D., Fahey, J. L., & Morton, D. (1993). Malignant melanoma: Effects of an early structured psychiatric intervention, coping, and affective state on recurrence and survival 6 years later. *Archives of General Psychiatry, 52,* 100–113.

Fisher, E. B., Jr., Lichtenstein, E., Haire-Joshu, D., Morgan, G. D., & Rehberg, H. R. (1993). Methods, successes, and failures of smoking cessation programs. *Annual Review of Medicine, 44,* 481–513.

Flett, G. L., Vredenburg, K., & Krames, L. (1997). The continuity of depression in clinical and nonclinical samples. *Psychological Bulletin, 121,* 395–416.

Flick, S. N. (1988). Managing attrition in clinical research. *Clinical Psychology Review, 8,* 499–515.

Frank, R. G., Thayer, J. F., Hagglund, K. J., Vieth, A. Z., Schopp, L. H., Beck, N. C., Hashani, J. H., Goldstein, D. E., Cassidy, J. T., Clay, D. L., Chaney, J. M., Hewett, J. E., & Johnson, J. C. (1998). Trajectories of adaptation in pediatric chronic illness: The importance of the individual. *Journal of Consulting and Clinical Psychology, 66,* 521–532.

Frasure-Smith, N., Lesperance, F., & Talajic, M. (1993). Depression following myocardial infarction: Impact on 6-month survival. *Journal of the American Medical Association, 270,* 1819–1825.

Frasure-Smith, N., Lesperance, F., & Talajic, M. (1995). The impact of negative emotions on prognosis following myocardial infarction: Is it more than depression? *Health Psychology, 14,* 388–398.

Friedman, M., Thoresen, C. E., & Gill, J. J. (1986). Alteration of type A behavior and its effects on cardiac recurrences in post myocardial infarction patients: Summary results of the recurrent coronary prevention project. *American Heart Journal, 112,* 653–665.

Friedman, R., Subel, D., Meyers, P., Caudill, M., & Benson, H. (1995). Behavioral medicine, clinical health psychology, and cost offset. *Health Psychology, 14,* 509–518.

Gallo, L. C., & Smith, T. W. (1998). Construct validation of health-relevant personality traits: Interpersonal circumplex and five-factor model analyses of the aggression questionnaire. *International Journal of Behavioral Medicine, 5,* 129–147.

Gerin, W., Rosofsky, M., Pieper, C., & Pickering, T. (1994). A test of generalizability of cardiovascular reactivity using a controlled ambulatory procedure. *Psychosomatic Medicine, 56,* 360–368.

Glasgow, R. E., Mullooly, J. P., Vogt, T. M., Stevens, V. J., Lichetenstein, E., Hollis, J. F., Lando, H. A., Severson, H., Pearson, K., & Vogt, M. (1993). Biochemical validation of smoking status in public health settings: Pros, cons, and data from four low-intensity intervention trials. *Addictive Behaviors, 18,* 511–527.

Gullette, E. C. D., Blumenthal, J. A., & Babyak, M. (1997). Mental stress triggers myocardial ischemia during daily life. *Journal of the American Medical Association, 277,* 1521–1526.

Guyll, M., & Contrada, R. C. (1998). Trait hostility and ambulatory cardiovascular reactivity: Responses to social interaction. *Health Psychology, 17,* 30–39.

Hall, M., Baum, A., Buysse, D. J., Prigerson, H. G., Kupfer, D. J., & Reynolds, C. F. (1998). Sleep as a mediator of the stress-immune relationship. *Psychosomatic Medicine, 60,* 48–51.

Hancock, L., Sanson-Fisher, R. W., & Redman, S. (1997). Community action for health promotion: A review of methods and outcomes 1990–1995. *American Journal of Preventive Medicine, 13,* 229–239.

Holmbeck, G. N. (1997). Toward terminological, conceptual, and statistical clarity in the study of mediators and moderators: Examples from the child-clinical and pediatric psychology literatures. *Journal of Consulting and Clinical Psychology, 65,* 599–610.

Huberty, C. J., & Morris, J. D. (1989). Multivariate analysis versus multiple univariate analyses. *Psychological Bulletin, 105,* 302–308.

Ironson, G., Taylor, C. B., & Boltwood, M. (1992). Effects of anger on left ventricular ejection fraction in coronary artery disease. *American Journal of Cardiology, 70,* 281–285.

Jaccard, J., & Wan, C. K. (1993). Statistical analysis of temporal data with many observations: Issues for behavioral medicine data. *Annals of Behavioral Medicine, 15,* 41–50.

Jacobson, N. S., & Traux, P. (1991). Clinical significance: A statistical approach to defining meaningful change in psychotherapy research. *Journal of Consulting and Clinical Psychology, 59,* 12–19.

Janz, N. W., & Becker, J. H. (1984). The health belief model: A decade later. *Health Education Quarterly, 11,* 1–47.

Jensen, M., Turner, L., Turner, J., & Romano, J. (1996). The use of multiple-item scales for pain intensity measurement in chronic pain patients. *Pain, 67,* 35–40.

John, O. P. (1990). The "Big Five" factor taxonomy: Dimensions of personality in the natural language and in questionnaires. In L. Pervin (Ed.), *Handbook of personality: Theory and research* (pp. 66–100). New York: Clifford Press.

Johnson, S. L., & Jacob, T. (1997). Marital interactions of depressed men and women. *Journal of Consulting and Clinical Psychology, 65,* 15–23.

Kaplan, G. A., & Camacho, T. (1983). Perceived health and mortality: A nine year follow-up of the human population laboratory cohort. *American Journal of Epidemiology, 117,* 292–304.

Kaplan, J. R., & Manuck, S. B. (1998). Monkeys, aggression, and the pathobiology of atherosclerosis. *Aggressive Behavior, 24,* 323–334.

Kaplan, R. M. (1984). The connection between clinical health promotion and health status: A critical overview. *American Psychologist, 39,* 755–765.

Kaplan, R. M. (1994). The Ziggy theorem: Toward an outcomes-focused health psychology. *Health Psychology, 13,* 451–460.

Kamarck, T. W., & Jennings, J. J. (1991). Biobehavioral factors in sudden cardiac death. *Psychological Bulletin, 109,* 42–75.

Kamarck, T. W., Jennings, J. J., Pogue-Geile, M., & Manuck, S. B. (1994). A multidimensional measurement model for cardiovascular reactivity: Stability, and cross-validation in two adult samples. *Health Psychology, 13,* 471–478.

Kamarck, T. W., Shiffman, S. M., Smithline, L., Goodie, J. L., Paty, J. A., Gnys, M., & Jong, J. Y. K. (1998). Effects of task strain, social conflict, and emotional activation on ambulatory cardiovascular activity: Daily life consequences of recurring stress in a multiethnic adult sample. *Health Psychology, 17,* 17–29.

Keefe, F. J., Dunsmore, J., & Burnett, R. (1992). Behavioral and cognitive-behavioral approaches to chronic pain: Recent advances and future directions. *Journal of Consulting and Clinical Psychology, 60,* 528–536.

Kendall, P. C., & Grove, W. (1988). Normative comparisons in therapy outcome. *Behavioral Assessment, 10,* 147–158.

Kendall, P. C., Hollon, S. D., Beck, A. T., Hammen, C. L., & Ingram, R. E. (1987). Issues and recommendations regarding use of the Beck Depression Inventory. *Cognitive Therapy and Research, 11,* 289–300.

Kendall, P. C., & Norton-Ford, J. D. (1982). Therapy outcome research methods. In P. C. Kendall & J. N. Butcher (Eds.), *Handbook of research methods in clinical psychology* (pp. 429–460). New York: Wiley

Kendall, P. C., Williams, L., Pechacek, T. F., Graham, L. E., Shisslak, C., & Herzoff, N. (1979). Cognitive-behavioral and patient education interventions in cardiac catheterization procedures: The Palo Alto Medical Psychology Project. *Journal of Consulting and Clinical Psychology, 47,* 49–58.

Kendler, K. S. (1997). Social support: A genetic-epidemiologic analysis. *American Journal of Psychiatry, 154,* 1398–1404.

Kiecolt-Glaser, J. K., Glaser, R., Cacioppo, J. T., MacCallum, R. C., Snydersmith, M., Kim, C., & Malarkey, W. B. (1997). Marital conflict in older adults: Endocrinological and immunological correlates. *Psychosomatic Medicine, 59,* 339–349.

Kleges, R. C., Ward, K. D., & DeBon, M. (1996). Smoking cessation: A successful behavioral/pharmacologic interface. *Clinical Psychology Review, 16,* 479–496.

Krantz, D. S., & Hedges, S. M. (1987). Some cautions for research on personality and health. *Journal of Personality, 55,* 351–357.

Lichtenstein, E., & Glasgow, R. E. (1992). Smoking cessation: What have we learned over the past decade? *Journal of Consulting and Clinical Psychology, 60,* 518–527.

Lerman, C. (1997). Psychological aspects of genetic testing. *Health Psychology, 16,* 3–7.

Lerman, C., Caporaso, N., Main, D., Audrain, J., Boyd, N. R., Bowman, E. D., & Shields, P. G. (1998). Depression and self-medication with nicotine: The modifying influence of the dopamine D4 receptor gene. *Health Psychology, 17,* 56–62.

Linden, W., Stossel, C., & Maurice, J. (1996). Psychosocial interventions for patients with coronary artery disease: A meta-analysis. *Archives of Internal Medicine, 156,* 745–752.

Little, R. J., & Yau, L. H. Y. (1998). Statistical techniques for analyzing data from prevention trials: Treatment no-shows using Rubin's causal model. *Psychological Methods, 3,* 147–159.

Lovallo, W. (1997). *Stress and health.* Thousand Oaks, CA: Sage.

Manne, S., & Zautra, A. (1989). Spouse criticism and support: Their association with coping and psychological distress among women with rheumatoid arthritis. *Journal of Personality and Social Psychology, 56,* 608–617.

Manuck, S. B. (1994). Cardiovascular reactivity in cardiovascular disease: "Once more unto the breach." *International Journal of Behavioral Medicine, 1,* 4–31.

Manuck, S. B., Marsland, A. L., Kaplan, J. J., & Williams, J. K. (1995). The pathogenicity of behavior and its neuroendocrine mediation: An example from coronary artery disease. *Psychosomatic Medicine, 57,* 275–283.

Marlatt, G. A., & Gordon, J. J. (1985). *Relapse prevention.* New York: Guilford Press.

Martin, J. E., & Dubbert, P. M. (1982). Exercise applications and promotion in behavioral medicine: Current status and future directions. *Journal of Consulting and Clinical Psychology, 50,* 1004–1017.

Matarazzo, J. D. (1980). Behavioral health and behavioral medicine: Frontiers for a new health psychology. *American Psychologist, 35,* 807–817.

McDaniel, J. S., Mussleman, D. L., Porter, M. R., Reed, D. A., & Nemeroff, C. B. (1995). Depression in patients with cancer: Diagnosis, biology, and treatment. *Archives of General Psychiatry, 52,* 89–99.

McFall, R. M. (1978). Smoking cessation research. *Journal of Consulting and Clinical Psychology, 46,* 703–712.

Meehl, P. E. (1970). Nuisance variables and the ex post facto design. In M. Radner & S. Winokur (Eds.), *Minnesota studies in the philosophy of science: Vol. IV. Analyses of theories and methods of physics and psychology* (pp. 373–402). Minneapolis: University of Minnesota Press.

Meehl, P. E. (1978). Theoretical risks and tabular asterisks: Sir Karl, Sir Ronald, and the slow progress of soft psychology. *Journal of Consulting and Clinical Psychology, 46,* 806–834.

Meyer, T. J., & Mark, M. (1995). Effects of psychosocial interventions with adult cancer patients: A meta-analysis of randomized experiments. *Health Psychology, 14,* 101–108.

Miller, T. Q. (1994). A test of alternative explanations for the stage-like progression of adolescent substance use in four national samples. *Addictive Behaviors, 19,* 287–293.

Miller, T. Q., Smith, T. W., Turner, C. W., Guijarro, M. L., & Hallett, A. J. (1996). A meta-analytic review of research on hostility and physical health. *Psychological Bulletin, 119,* 322–348.

Miller, T. Q., Turner, C., Tindale, R., Posavac, E., & Dugoni, B. L. (1991). Reasons for the trend toward null findings in research on the Type A behavior pattern. *Psychological Bulletin, 110,* 469–485.

Mohr, D. C., Goodkin, D. E., Likosky, W., Beutler, L., Gatto, N., & Langan, M. K. (1997). Identification of Beck Depression Inventory items related to multiple sclerosis. *Journal of Behavioral Medicine, 20,* 407–414.

Norris, F. H. (1997). Frequency and structure of precautionary behavior in the domains of hazard preparedness, crime prevention, vehicular safety, and health maintenance. *Health Psychology, 16,* 566–575.

O'Donnell, K., & Chung, J. Y. (1997). The diagnosis of major depression in end-stage renal disease. *Psychotherapy and Psychosomatics, 66,* 38–43.

Park, T. L., Adams, S. G., & Lynch, J. (1998). Sociodemographic factors in health psychology research: 12 years in review. *Health Psychology, 17,* 381–383.

Parker, J. C. (1995). Stress management. In P. M. Nicassio & T. W. Smith (Eds.), *Managing chronic illness: A biopsychosocial perspective* (pp. 285–312). Washington, DC: American Psychological Association.

Parker, J. C., Smarr, K. L., Buckelew, S. P., Stucky-Ropp, R. C., Hewett, J. E., Johnson, J. C., Wright, G. E., Irvin, W. S., & Walker, S. E. (1995). Effects of stress management on clinical outcomes in rheumatoid arthritis. *Arthritis and Rheumatism, 38,* 1807–1818.

Patrick, D. L., Cheadle, A., Thompson, D. C., Diehr, P., Koepsell, T., & Kinne, S. (1994). The validity of self-reported smoking: A review and meta-analysis. *American Journal of Public Health, 84,* 1086–1093.

Peck, J., Smith, T. W., Ward, J. J., & Milano, R. (1989). Disability and depression in rheumatoid arthritis: A multi-trait, multi-method investigation. *Arthritis and Rheumatism, 32,* 1100–1106.

Prochaska, J. O., & DiClemente, C. C. (1984). *The transtheoretical approach: Crossing traditional boundaries of change.* Homewood, IL: Irwin.

Rooney, B. L., & Murray, D. M. (1996). A meta-analysis of smoking prevention programs after adjustment for errors in the unit of analysis. *Health Education Quarterly, 23,* 48–64.

Schulz, R., & Quittner, A. L. (1998). Caregiving for children and adults with chronic conditions: Introduction to the special issue. *Health Psychology, 17,* 107–111.

Schwartz, C. E., Chesney, M. A., Irvine, J., & Keefe, F. J. (1997). The control group dilemma in clinical research: Applications for psychosocial and behavioral medicine trials. *Psychosomatic Medicine, 59,* 362–371.

Schwartz, J. E., & Stone, A. A. (1998). Strategies for analyzing ecological momentary assessment data. *Health Psychology, 17,* 6–16.

Shadish, W. R., Hu, X., Glaser, R. R., Kownacki, R., & Wong, S. (1998). A method for exploring the effects of attrition in randomized experiments with dichotomous outcomes. *Psychological Methods, 3*, 3–22.

Shiffman, S., Fisher, L. A., Paty, J. A., Gnys, M., Kassel, J. D., Hickox, M., & Perez, W. (1994). Drinking and smoking: A filed study of their association. *Annals of Behavioral Medicine, 16*, 203–209.

Shiffman, S., Hufford, M., Hickox, M., Paty, J. A., Gnys, M., & Kassel, J. (1997). Remember that? A comparison of real-time versus retrospective recall of smoking lapses. *Journal of Consulting and Clinical Psychology, 65*, 292–300.

Shiffman, S., Paty, J. A., Gnys, M., Kassel, J. D., & Hickox, M. (1996). First lapses to smoking: Within subject analysis of real-time reports. *Journal of Consulting and Clinical Psychology, 64*, 366–379.

Siegler, I. C. (1994). Hostility and risk: Demographic and lifestyle variables. In A. W. Siegman & T. W. Smith (Eds.), *Anger, hostility, and the heart* (pp. 199–214). Hillsdale, NJ: Erlbaum.

Smith, T. W. (1989). Assessment in rational-emotive therapy: Empirical access to the ABCD model. In M. E. Bernard & R. DiGiusseppe (Eds.), *Inside rational-emotive therapy* (pp. 135–152). New York: Academic Press.

Smith, T. W. (1992). Mind and body: Cognitive perspectives in health psychology. *Cognitive Therapy and Research, 16*, 97–98.

Smith, T. W. (1994). Concepts and methods in the study of anger, hostility, and health. In A. W. Siegman & T. W. Smith (Eds.), *Anger, hostility, and the heart* (pp. 23–42). Hillsdale, NJ: Erlbaum.

Smith, T. W., & Brown, P. (1991). Cynical hostility, attempts to exert social control, and cardiovascular reactivity in married couples. *Journal of Behavioral Medicine, 14*, 579–590.

Smith, T. W., & Christensen, A. J. (1996). Positive and negative affect in rheumatoid arthritis: Increased specificity in the assessment of emotional adjustment. *Annals of Behavioral Medicine, 18*, 75–78.

Smith, T. W., & Gallo, L. C. (1998). Personality traits as risk factors for physical illness. In A. Baum, T. Revenson, & J. Singer (Eds.), *Handbook of health psychology*. Hillsdale, NJ: Erlbaum.

Smith, T. W., Gallo, L. C., Goble, L., Ngu, L. Q., & Stark, K. A. (1998). Agency, communion, and cardiovascular reactivity during marital interaction. *Health Psychology*.

Smith, T. W., & Leon, A. S. (1992). *Coronary heart disease: A behavioral perspective.* Champaign–Urbana, IL: Research Press.

Smith, T. W., Limon, J., Gallo, L. C., & Ngu, L. Q. (1996). Interpersonal control and cardiovascular reactivity: Goals, behavioral expression, and the moderating effects of sex. *Journal of Personality and Social Psychology, 70*, 1012–1024.

Smith, T. W., Nealy, J. B., Kircher, J. C., & Limon, J. P. (1997). Social determinants of cardiovascular reactivity: Effects of incentive to exert influence and evaluative threat. *Psychophysiology, 34*, 65–73.

Smith, T. W., & Nicassio, P. (1995). Psychosocial practice in chronic medical illness: Clinical application of the biopsychosocial model. In P. C. Nicassio & T. W. Smith (Eds.), *Managing chronic illness: A biopsychosocial perspective* (pp. 1–32). Washington, DC: American Psychological Association.

Smith, T. W., Pope, M. K., Rhodewalt, F., & Poulton, J. L. (1989). Optimism, neuroticism, coping, and symptom reports: An alternative interpretation of the Life Orientation Test. *Journal of Personality and Social Psychology, 56*, 640–648.

Smith, T. W., & Rhodewalt, F. (1992). Methodological challenges at the social/clinical interface. In C. R. Snyder & D. F. Forsyth (Eds.), *Handbook of social and clinical psychology* (pp. 739–756). New York: Pergamon Press.

Smith, T. W., & Williams, P. G. (1992). Personality and health: Advantages and limitations of the five factor model. *Journal of Personality, 60,* 395–423.

Spiegel, D., Bloom, J., Kraemer, H. C., & Gottheil, E. (1989). Effect of psychosocial treatment on survival of patients with metastatic breast cancer. *Lancet, 2,* 888–891.

Stanton, A. (1995). Psychology of women's health: Barriers and pathways to knowledge. In A. L. Stanton & S. J. Gallant (Eds.), *The psychology of women's health* (pp. 3–21). Washington, DC: American Psychological Association.

Stanton, A., & Danoff-Burg, S. (1995). Selected issues in women's reproductive health. In A. L. Stanton & S. J. Gallant (Eds.), *The psychology of women's health* (pp. 261–305). Washington, DC: American Psychological Association.

Stone, A. A., Schwartz, J. E., Neale, J. M., Shiffman, S., Marco, C., Hickox, M., Paty, J., Porter, L., & Cruise, L. (1998). A comparison of coping assessed by ecological momentary assessment and retrospective recall. *Journal of Personality and Social Psychology, 74,* 1670–1680.

Stone, G. C., Cohen, F., & Adler, N. E. (1979). *Health psychology.* San Francisco: Jossey-Bass.

Stone, S. V., & Costa, P. T., Jr. (1990). Disease-prone personality or distress-prone personality? The role of neuroticism in coronary heart disease. In H. S. Friedman (Ed.), *Personality and disease* (pp. 178–200). New York: Wiley.

Suls, J., & Wan, C. K. (1989). Effects of sensory and procedural information on coping with stressful medical procedures and pain: A meta-analysis. *Journal of Consulting and Clinical Psychology, 57,* 372–379.

Turner, J. A., Deyo, R. A., Loweser, J. D. (1994). The importance of placebo effects in pain treatment and research. *Journal of the American Medical Association, 271,* 1609–1614.

Turk, D. C., & Melzack, R. (Eds.). (1992). *Handbook of pain assessment.* New York: Guilford Press.

Turk, D. C., & Rudy, T. E. (1990). Neglected factors in chronic pain treatment outcome studies—Referral patterns, failure to enter treatment, and attrition. *Pain, 43,* 7–21.

Turk, D. C., & Salovey, P. (1995). Cognitive-behavioral treatment of illness behavior. In P. M. Nicassio & T. W. Smith (Eds.), *Managing chronic illness: A biopsychosocial perspective* (pp. 245–284). Washington, DC: American Psychological Association.

Uchino, B. N., Cacioppo, J. T., & Kiecoly-Glaser, J. K. (1996). The relationship between social support and the physiological processes: A review with emphasis on underlying mechanisms and implications for health. *Psychological Bulletin, 119,* 488–531.

Uchino, B. N., Kiecolt-Glaser, J. K., & Glaser, R. (1998). Psychological modulation of cellular immunity. In J. T. Cacioppo, L. G. Tassinary, & G. C. Berntson (Eds.), *Handbook of psychophysiology.* Cambridge, England: Cambridge University Press.

Velicer, W. F., Prochaska, J. O., Rossi, J. S., & Snow, M. (1992). Assessing outcome in smoking cessation studies. *Psychological Bulletin, 111,* 23–41.

Waltz, J., Addis, M. E., Koerner, K., & Jacobson, N. S. (1993). Testing the integrity of a psychotherapy protocol: Assessment of adherence and competence. *Journal of Consulting and Clinical Psychology, 61,* 620–630.

Wampold, B. E., Davis, B., & Good, R. (1990). Hypothesis validity of clinical research. *Journal of Consulting and Clinical Psychology, 58,* 360–367.

Watson, D., & Pennebaker, J. W. (1989). Health complaints, stress, and distress: Exploring the central role of negative affectivity. *Psychological Review, 96,* 234–254.

Watson, D., & Tellegen, A. (1985). Toward a consensual structure of mood. *Psychological Bulletin, 98,* 219–235.

Watson, D., Weber, K., Assenheimer, J. S., Clark, L. A., Strauss, M. E., & McCormick, R. A. (1995). Testing a tripartite model: I. Evaluating the convergent and discriminant validity of anxiety and depression symptom scales. *Journal of Abnormal Psychology, 104,* 3–14.

Weinstein, N. D. (1993). Testing four competing theories of health-protective behavior. *Health Psychology, 12,* 324–333.

Weinstein, N. D., Rothman, A. J., & Sutton, S. R. (1998). Stage theories of health behavior: Conceptual and methodological issues. *Health Psychology, 17,* 211–213.

Williams, R. B., Barefoot, J. C., Califf, R. M., Haney, T. L., Saunders, W. B., Pryor, D. B., Hlatky, M. A., Siegler, I. C., & Mark, D. B. (1992). Prognostic importance of social and economic resources among medically treated patients with angiographically documented coronary artery disease. *Journal of the American Medical Association, 267,* 520–524.

Wilson, G. T. (1978). Methodological considerations in treatment outcome research on obesity. *Journal of Consulting and Clinical Psychology, 46,* 687–702.

Wilson, J. J., & Gil, K. M. (1996). The efficacy of psychological and pharmacological interventions for the treatment of chronic disease-related and non-disease-related pain. *Clinical Psychology Review, 16,* 573–597.

Yates, B. T. (1994). Toward the incorporation of costs, cost-effectiveness analysis, and cost-benefit analysis into clinical research. *Journal of Consulting and Clinical Psychology, 62,* 729–736.

Zautra, A., Burleson, M., Smith, C., Blalock, S., Wallston, K., DeVellis, R., DeVellis, B., & Smith, T. W. (1995). Arthritis and perceptions of quality of life: An examination of positive and negative affect in rheumatoid arthritis patients. *Health Psychology, 14,* 399–408.

Chapter 21

Focus Chapter

RESEARCH METHODS IN PEDIATRIC PSYCHOLOGY

Annette M. La Greca, Ph.D., and Wendy B. Schuman, Ph.D.

Pediatric psychology is an interdisciplinary field that covers a broad range of issues and topics. Specifically, pediatric psychology addresses the developmental, physical, cognitive, social, and emotional aspects of functioning as they relate to health and illness issues in children, adolescents, and families (Society of Pediatric Psychology, 1998). As such, research in pediatric psychology, broadly construed, focuses on:

> [T]he interrelationship between psychological and physical well-being of children, adolescents, and families, including: psychosocial and developmental factors contributing to the etiology, course, treatment, and outcome of pediatric conditions; assessment and treatment of behavioral and concomitants of disease, illness, and developmental disorders; the role of psychology in health care settings; behavioral aspects of pediatric medicine; the promotion of health and health-related behaviors; the prevention of illness and injury among children and youth; and issues related to the training of pediatric psychologists. (Society of Pediatric Psychology, 1998)

Although many aspects of research in pediatric psychology are similar to issues that emerge in clinical child psychological research (e.g., Kazdin, 1988; also see chapters by Ciccetti and Rogosch, and Culbertson, this volume), there are a number of unique challenges that face researchers in pediatric psychology. One concerns the difficulties of recruiting a sufficient number of subjects to adequately evaluate the research question of interest. Many pediatric conditions have low base rates, making the accrual of large subject samples a difficult and sometimes impossible task. Efforts to work collaboratively across medical centers may help to increase sample size and enhance generalizability of findings (Drotar, 1994), although multisite studies often present other logistic challenges (Armstrong, 1995).

Time constraints represent another challenge to research protocols (La Greca & Lemanek, 1996). In many instances, behavioral or psychosocial measures are incorporated into larger protocols that involve other medical tests and procedures; in fact, psychosocial assessments may take a backseat to medical variables of interest (Glasgow & Anderson, 1995). In other cases, participants may be recruited as they are waiting to receive medical treatment, and the investigator may need to tailor the protocol to the narrow window of time that is available.

Developing research protocols that are culturally sensitive and not overly demanding of participants' reading and language competence is yet another common challenge for pediatric researchers. There is tremendous interest in developing culturally sensitive medical treatments (Tarnowski & Rohrbeck, 1993); yet, studies of minority health issues must be sensitive to the different and varied cultural and language backgrounds of the participants (see Sue et al., this volume).

The above represent but a few of the varied issues that researchers in pediatric psychology encounter. In the sections below, we describe the research designs most commonly used in pediatric psychology research and highlight several conceptual and methodological issues in this field of research. We also consider future research directions in pediatric psychology. Given the focused nature of the chapter, the review is necessarily selective. However, whenever possible, reference materials are cited to guide the reader to more detailed coverage of important research issues.

TYPICAL PEDIATRIC PSYCHOLOGY RESEARCH QUESTIONS, METHODS, AND RELATED PROBLEMS

Descriptive and Explicative Research

Much of the research in pediatric psychology has been referred to as descriptive or explicative (La Greca, 1997; Roberts, 1992), in that it seeks to provide information about the characteristics of children with various medical conditions and their families. Specifically, researchers have been interested in examining various aspects of psychosocial functioning among pediatric populations, such as social adjustment, family adjustment, psychological symptoms including depression and anxiety, and cognitive and academic skills (e.g., Daniels, Moos, Billings, & Miller, 1987; Lavigne & Faier-Routman, 1992; R. Thompson, Hodges, & Hamlett, 1990). Recently, however, research has moved beyond studying simple associations between disease and adjustment, and increasingly has emphasized the use of complex conceptual models that incorporate medical, behavioral, and psychosocial variables. For example, Varni and colleagues (Varni, Blount, Waldron, & Smith, 1995) described a biobehavioral model of factors that predict pediatric pain, and Wallander and Thompson (1995) reviewed several models of stress and coping in the prediction of children's adaptation to chronic disease. This shift in research focus, from simple description and association to that of more complex linkages and prediction between health and behavior, is reflected in the change from between-group research designs to more complex multivariate, within-group research strategies.

Group Comparison Design

Questions about how children with pediatric conditions fare in terms of their psychosocial functioning primarily have relied on between-group comparison designs. Specifically, children with pediatric conditions have been compared to healthy (nonill) children, such as classmates, siblings, or children not receiving medical treatment, on a variety of psychosocial measures (e.g., Daniels et al., 1987; R. Thompson et al., 1990). In some studies, children with pediatric conditions have been compared to normative samples or population statistics (see Bennett, 1994; Lavigne & Faier-Routman, 1992).

Investigations have addressed such questions as, "Are adolescents with diabetes more depressed than healthy adolescents?", "Do children with cystic fibrosis perceive their families to be less cohesive than healthy children?", and "Are children who receive bone marrow transplantation at increased risk of having a learning disability?"

Group comparison designs are extremely valuable for understanding the behavioral and psychosocial characteristics of children with pediatric conditions and are often used in initial studies of a particular pediatric condition or treatment. Moreover, group comparisons can help to identify special vulnerabilities and strengths associated with pediatric treatments or conditions and can stimulate further research linking the strengths/vulnerabilities with aspects of the disease process. For example, Johnson (1980) reviewed studies of youth with diabetes (mostly group comparison designs), concluding that children and adolescents with diabetes do not have more psychological problems than comparison youth, but do appear to have more social difficulties. This finding identified a special area of vulnerability for youth with diabetes and hinted that the difficulties of managing such a complex disease could interfere with youngsters' social functioning. As a result, more recent within-group studies have focused on youngsters' social functioning as it relates to their diabetes management and control (e.g., Hanson, Henggeler, & Burghen, 1987; La Greca, Auslander, et al., 1995).

Group comparison approaches with pediatric populations present some special challenges. One is the difficulty of determining an appropriate comparison group (Lemanek, 1994). Siblings, when available, may differ in gender and age from the ill child and may be affected by the illness of their sibling in a manner that affects the variables of interest (e.g., stress levels may be elevated in all family members when a child in the family has a serious disease). On the other hand, it may be difficult to recruit classmates or other comparison children, as their parents may have little motivation to allow their children to participate in research concerning medical conditions that do not affect them. Such children may also differ from the physically ill youth in many ways other than the presence or absence of a particular medical diagnosis. For example, children with a chronic illness may be absent from school more, undergo painful treatment, have an altered appearance, be restricted from certain activities, or experience greater family stress than their peers (e.g., see Creer & Bender, 1995; Johnson, 1995; La Greca & Schuman, 1995; Powers, Vannatta, Noll, Cool, & Stehbens, 1995). Further, finding behavioral or psychosocial differences between children with a pediatric illness and nonill youth may do little to identify the specific features of the illness that contribute to the obtained group differences and that may be important targets for pediatric interventions.

Another challenge to between-group research is the significant heterogeneity found among children with any given physical illness. Difficulties recruiting participants for pediatric research often result in samples that vary substantially in terms of age range and socioeconomic status, as well as in disease and treatment status (Drotar, 1994; La Greca & Lemanek, 1996; Lemanek, 1994). Moreover, there may be considerable variability in the behavioral or psychosocial variables of interest. For example, children with a physical illness might report higher levels of depressive symptoms than nonill children overall, yet there may be a great range of depressive symptoms among the children, with some reporting extremely low levels (see Bennett, 1994). Explaining this variability and determining the demographic, disease, or other factors that put *some* children with pediatric conditions at risk for depression (but not others) requires that investigators move beyond between-group research designs. Furthermore, group comparisons are not suitable for investigating the specific psychological implications of disease-related experiences, or for identifying the most effective strategies for coping with difficult treatment regimens (Kazak, 1993).

Within-Group Designs

A growing sophistication in the research on children with acute and chronic pediatric conditions has led investigators to ask questions that require the use of within-group research designs. Within-group designs are especially useful for understanding the behavioral, family, social, and medical factors that *predict* positive and negative health outcomes. Examples include studies designed to predict treatment adherence among children with chronic disease (La Greca & Schuman, 1995) or positive outcomes within a chronic disease population (e.g., Murphy, Thompson, & Morris, 1997; Weissberg-Benchell & Glasgow, 1997). Within-group studies have also been used for identifying *risk and protective factors* in pediatric populations (see Wallander & Thompson, 1995). This type of research has drawn increasingly on the use of conceptual models that evaluate linkages among behavioral, psychological, and medical variables (e.g., Varni et al., 1995; Wallander & Thompson, 1995). Studies that use within-group research strategies can help to explain differences in adjustment among children and families affected by a given disease or its treatment, thereby identifying specific risk factors for poor outcome and highlighting potential areas for intervention. Specifically, within-group designs have enabled investigators to address questions such as "Is social support from friends or family members associated with better treatment adherence among adolescents with a chronic disease?" and "Does family cohesion lessen the negative impact of chemotherapy for children with cancer?"

Essentially, within-group designs measure various behavioral, medical, or psychosocial parameters among a sample of children with a given medical condition, and try to establish linkages or to predict pathways of connection among the variables. For the most part, within-group designs have been correlational and rely on data analytic approaches such as multiple regression and correlation (e.g., Gil, Williams, Thompson, & Kinney, 1991; La Greca, Auslander, et al., 1995). However, correlations that do not consider factors such as gender, age, socioeconomic status, and so on may not be very informative (Glasgow & Anderson, 1995).

With an increasing emphasis on theory-driven research (Wallander, 1992), investigators are turning toward more complex models of linkages among the variables, and consequently are using more sophisticated multivariate statistical techniques, such as path analyses (Peyrot, 1996), logistic regression (Hosmer & Lemeshow, 1989), and structural equation modeling (e.g., Johnson, Tomer, Cunningham, & Henretta, 1990; Veger & Liang, 1986; see also Farrell, this volume). In particular, hierarchical analyses, which allow researchers to consider the effects of sociodemographic variables before considering behavioral and psychological measures, are becoming essential to pediatric research (e.g., see Hanson, De Guire, Schinkel, Henggeler, & Burghen, 1992; Johnson et al., 1990).

Furthermore, as models of predictor-adjustment relationships become more complex, it becomes critical for pediatric investigators to understand the role of mediated and moderated effects and to know how best to evaluate these effects (see Holmbeck,

1997, for a detailed discussion). Essentially, a *moderator* variable affects the relationship between two other variables. For example, gender may moderate the linkage between depressive symptoms and poor metabolic control for adolescents with diabetes, in that girls who report depression have poor metabolic control, but for boys, depression and metabolic control appear to be unrelated (La Greca, Swales, Klemp, Madigan, & Skyler, 1995). In contrast, a *mediator* helps to explain or account for the relation between two variables. For instance, the association between shorter disease duration and better treatment adherence in children with chronic disease might be mediated by family support (which is typically greater in newly diagnosed youth). In this case, family support mediates (explains) why shorter disease duration is linked with better treatment adherence. Multiple regression and structural equation modeling are essential analytic tools for evaluating moderating and mediating effects in pediatric psychology research (see Holmbeck, 1997; Peyrot, 1996).

Intervention Research

Although pediatric psychologists are conducting interventions and providing training in this area (La Greca, Stone, Drotar, & Maddux, 1988), less effort has been devoted to systematically evaluating intervention efforts. A small percentage (less than 15%) of the articles published over the past 10 years in the *Journal of Pediatric Psychology*, the primary scientific journal of the Society of Pediatric Psychology, have focused on intervention research (La Greca, 1997; Roberts, 1992). These low figures undoubtedly reflect the difficulties of conducting treatment-outcome studies in pediatric psychology.

In many respects, this situation reflects a broader concern regarding the quantity and quality of child and adolescent psychotherapy research (Kazdin, Bass, Ayers, & Rodgers, 1990). Only a few of the more than 200 different forms of therapy used with children and adolescents have been evaluated empirically (Kazdin, 1988). Furthermore, numerous methodological problems have beset child treatment research, including the absence of suitable control groups; the use of global outcome measures; failure to monitor treatment integrity; small sample sizes; and limited follow-up periods (Kazdin et al., 1990; also see chapters by Kazdin and by Kendall et al., this volume). These criticisms also apply to intervention research in pediatric psychology.

Pediatric intervention studies fall primarily into one of four areas: (a) evaluating the impact of behavioral and psychosocial interventions on youngsters' medical status, treatment adherence, health outcomes, or quality of life; (b) evaluating the impact of medical treatments on psychological functioning; (c) evaluating efforts to promote health and health-related behaviors; and (d) preventing injury among children and youth. Perhaps the greatest focus has been on efforts to improve youngsters' medical status, treatment adherence, and health outcomes, such as by evaluating family interventions for improving the metabolic control of adolescents with diabetes (Satin, La Greca, Zigo, & Skyler, 1989); promoting social competence in children newly diagnosed with cancer (Varni, Katz, Colegrove, & Dolgin, 1993); or evaluating strategies for improving adherence to appointment keeping in primary care allergy clinics (Finney, Lemanek, Brophy, & Cataldo, 1990).

As with child psychotherapy research (Kazdin, 1993; Kazdin et al., 1990), pediatric psychology intervention research has focused primarily on the effectiveness of variations of a given treatment approach. Evaluations of the combination of different types of treatment or combinations of psychological and medical treatments are relatively rare, as are efforts to match participants to the type of treatment received (La Greca & Varni, 1993). Moreover, important questions regarding the factors that predict or influence treatment outcome, and the processes by which change occurs, have been seriously neglected (La Greca & Varni, 1993).

Despite some of its challenges, pediatric intervention research represents an important and growing area. In an era of managed care, efforts to document treatment effectiveness are critical, as witnessed by the recent dissemination of empirically supported treatments for adults and children (see Kendall & Chambless, 1998; Lonigan, Elbert, & Johnson, 1998). Efforts to disseminate empirically supported interventions in the pediatric psychology area also appear to be forthcoming (A. E. Kazak, personal communication, January 1998).

Common Research Strategies

The most common research design used in pediatric intervention research is the *randomized clinical trial* (i.e., pre-post between-group comparisons, with random assignment to treatment conditions) (e.g., Black, Dubowitz, Hutcheson, Berenson-Howard, & Starr, 1995; Delamater et al., 1990; Satin et al., 1989; see also Cook & Campbell, 1979). Although less common, *single-subject case designs* have also been used (Epstein et al., 1981; Mindell & Durand, 1993; see also Gaynor et al., this volume). To a lesser extent, well-documented *case studies* have also advanced our intervention knowledge base (e.g., Boggs, Geffken, Johnson, & Silverstein, 1992; Stark, Bowen, Tyc, Evans, & Passero, 1990; for more details, see Drotar, 1997; Drotar, La Greca, Lemanek, & Kazak, 1995).

Another research strategy, used in medical research but rarely in pediatric psychology research, is a *crossover design* (e.g., Seigler, La Greca, Citrin, Reeves, & Skyler, 1982). In a crossover design, participants may be randomly assigned to two treatment conditions following a baseline (no-treatment) period; after the initial treatment period, subjects are "crossed over" to the alternate treatment condition. Advantages of this design are that all participants receive treatment and also serve as their own controls. When using this design, however, the effects of the initial treatment can carry over to the next study phase. Thus, investigators must allow for "washout" periods between treatments to ensure uncontaminated treatment effects.

Pediatric psychologists who work in settings in which center- or clinic-based interventions are implemented for most or all patients with a given condition (e.g., hospital preparation programs, pain management programs, interdisciplinary team approach to diabetes care) have yet another strategy available for intervention research: *within-group research designs*. If all children and adolescents are receiving the same type of medical/psychosocial care, studies of individual differences among those receiving treatment may be of considerable interest. Which children and families profit most from these interventions? What processes or mechanisms account for treatment success? This type of information can prove invaluable in refining intervention services.

Treatment Integrity

Treatment integrity is an often neglected methodological issue in pediatric intervention research, yet it is critical for determining treatment efficacy (La Greca & Varni, 1993).

If a treatment was not delivered as intended, then the results will reveal little about its efficacy. Researchers should ask: Was the intervention administered in a standard or uniform manner to all participants? Can it be replicated accurately? What safeguards were taken to ensure that the treatment was carried out as intended?

Treatment integrity is enhanced by the use of treatment manuals or films (Kazdin et al., 1990; also see Kendall et al., this volume); an important advantage of developing specific treatment materials is that they facilitate further research on a particular intervention approach, as others can replicate the intervention procedures (Kazdin, 1988, 1992). Other strategies for enhancing treatment integrity include providing explicit training for those who are conducting the intervention and including systematic efforts to monitor, check, or evaluate the intervention sessions (Kazdin, 1988). Although very few investigations in pediatric psychology report this type of information (La Greca & Varni, 1993), much greater attention to this issue is needed.

Moderators of Treatment Outcome

Because pediatric populations are typically diverse with respect to behavioral and psychological functioning, it is extremely unlikely that one type of intervention will be effective for all children or adolescents with a given pediatric condition. Rather, a host of child, parent, and family variables may affect treatment outcome (Kazdin, 1988, 1993). Thus, the study of moderators of treatment outcome is essential to the advancement of practice (Drotar, 1997; La Greca & Varni, 1993).

What moderating variables are of interest to study? Child demographic characteristics (age, sex, ethnicity) as well as disease status (e.g., duration and severity) represent important variables for consideration. For example, Osterhaus et al. (1993) examined the effects of a combined behavioral/psychophysiological treatment for migraine among adolescents and found that several pretreatment parameters were related to outcome: gender, migraine history, age, and breadth of somatic complaints. Girls profited more from training than boys, as did those with a shorter history of migraine. Older adolescents, and those with fewer somatic complaints prior to intervention, also profited more from training than younger adolescents and those with more extensive somatic symptoms. These moderating variables can aid pediatric psychologists in selecting appropriate candidates for certain interventions.

Child and family variables that have been suggested as important for child psychotherapy research may also be relevant moderators for pediatric interventions. Such variables include comorbidity with other conditions/problems; the child's and family's experience of distress; coping strategies used by the child; degree of parental involvement in treatment; degree of parental cooperation; absence of parental dysfunction; and the presence of a stable home life (Kazdin et al., 1990).

Evaluating the Process of Change: Mediating Variables

When an intervention is successful, we often have little information regarding the mechanisms responsible for the therapeutic effect. For example, Satin et al. (1989) found that a family-based intervention led to improvements in glycemic control among adolescents with diabetes. However, because potential mediating variables were not included in the study design, it was not clear what processes (e.g., better treatment adherence? greater family support? less family stress?) specifically explained or accounted for this positive change in glycemic control. Greater efforts are needed to evaluate the process of change in pediatric psychology interventions (La Greca & Varni, 1993).

Because of the experimental designs typically used in treatment-outcome research, the study of treatment process can be illuminating even when an intervention does not turn out as expected. For example, Boardway, Delamater, Tomakowsky, and Gutai, (1993) found that a stress management program for adolescents with diabetes reduced diabetes-related distress; however, stress reduction did not lead to improvements in adolescents' treatment adherence or metabolic control. These findings call into question the role of stress in diabetes management and suggest the need for studying individual differences (i.e., moderators) in the impact of stress on glycemic control.

In general, it is most desirable to study process factors (i.e., mediators) after there is evidence of a treatment's efficacy. However, smart investigators should always be considering what potential mechanisms or factors might account for treatment effects and plan to assess such factors, even if only in an exploratory manner. In this regard, the study of treatment process is one area where the use of multivariate conceptual models can be extremely useful, as they provide a basis for examining how and why behaviors are related (Kazdin, 1993). Moreover, treatment-outcome research will, in turn, help to further refine our conceptual models of psychosocial adaptation and disease (see Drotar, 1994; Glasgow & Anderson, 1995; La Greca & Varni, 1993; Wallander, 1992; see Stiles et al., this volume, for a detailed discussion of treatment process research).

Longitudinal Research

An important trend in pediatric psychology research has been an increased emphasis on longitudinal research (La Greca, 1997). Investigators have recognized that for most medically ill children, particularly those with a chronic illness, their condition is not static, but rather a process that varies over time with changes in symptoms, treatment course, age, and developmental level (Drotar, 1994). Longitudinal designs, therefore, have become critical to understanding the complex interplay between health and adjustment. For example, one longitudinal study found that rates of adjustment in children with cystic fibrosis were steady over a 12-month period, although the types of behavior problems changed over time (R. Thompson, Gustafson, George, & Spock, 1994). In another investigation, Northam and colleagues (Northam, Anderson, Adler, Werther, & Warne, 1996) found that symptoms of psychological distress observed among youngsters with newly diagnosed diabetes were largely resolved by a 12-month follow-up.

Prospective longitudinal designs are also essential for evaluating the interplay between health behavioral and disease status. For example, specific linkages between children's adherence behavior and their glucose control can best be understood by using prospective research designs (e.g., Johnson et al., 1992) rather than more typical cross-sectional, correlational designs. Longitudinal approaches have also been employed to examine the long-term impact of both medical and psychosocial interventions. For example, Larsson and Carlsson (1996) demonstrated that children with chronic tension-type headaches who received a relaxation training intervention experienced a significant reduction in headaches that was maintained six months postintervention. Another example is an ongoing investigation into the long-term impact of bone marrow transplantation on children's cognitive and behavioral functioning, which includes assessments at regular intervals posttransplant (McCabe et al., 1997).

In any context, longitudinal studies are difficult to conduct, but this is especially true in pediatric settings. Often, the timing of the follow-up assessment is not entirely under the investigator's control, but rather determined by the participants' schedule for medical care and their ability to keep medical appointments (La Greca & Lemanek, 1996). Other factors, such as the family's relationship with the treatment team, the degree to which study participation is limited to regular medical appointments, demographic and socioeconomic factors, as well parental well-being, have been shown to influence willingness to participate in a pediatric longitudinal study (Janus & Goldberg, 1997).

Moreover, repeated measurements present a variety of additional problems, in that practice effects as well as participants' boredom and fatigue must be taken into account. Youngsters who miss one or more follow-up points in the course of a longitudinal investigation also present challenges for repeated-measures statistical designs and may have to be eliminated, thereby limiting sample size. Fortunately, newer statistical procedures, such as hierarchical linear modeling (HLM) and, to some extent, growth curve analysis, can circumvent the problems associated with occasional missing data points (Bryk & Raudenbush, 1987, 1992; Burchinal & Appelbaum, 1991; Willett, Singer, & Martin, 1998). Further, with HLM, one need not be as concerned that all of the participants are exactly the same age at each data collection point. Finally, structural equation modeling can also be a useful tool for longitudinal data (Farrell, 1994; also see Farrell, this volume). These newer procedures, however, have not yet made their way into the mainstream of pediatric psychology research.

SELECTED CONCEPTUAL AND METHODOLOGICAL ISSUES IN PEDIATRIC PSYCHOLOGY RESEARCH

Although the types of research questions that engage pediatric psychologists vary considerably, there are several conceptual and methodological issues that pediatric researchers commonly encounter. In the sections below, several selected conceptual and methodological issues are highlighted.

Participant Issues

Recruitment/Selection Bias

Most pediatric psychology researchers would agree that recruiting representative samples of youngsters with pediatric conditions is one of their biggest challenges (Drotar, 1994; Glasgow & Anderson, 1995; La Greca & Lemanek, 1996; Taylor & Fletcher, 1995). In fact, many pediatric studies have relied on convenience samples, which often yield relatively small, nonrepresentative samples (Glasgow & Anderson, 1995). As Drotar notes, children with identical medical conditions who are recruited from different settings may have very different rates or types of problems; in general, those recruited from ambulatory care settings have less severe problems than those recruited from inpatient, hospital settings. Further, those who are the least adherent with medical treatments may not even be seen in a medical setting and are therefore not likely to be recruited for a research study (La Greca & Schuman, 1995). The use of national, state, or countywide registries, when available, may help to address this problem (Glasgow & Anderson, 1995).

In addition to contextual factors, selection bias will also affect the representativeness of the sample recruited (Drotar, 1994). Not all children and families will consent to participate in research. Recruiting study participants can be extremely difficult and is often determined by the course of youngsters' medical treatment. Although many investigators try to recruit participants during regularly scheduled medical appointments (e.g., clinic-based studies), medical appointments can be time-consuming and stressful, making youngsters and families less amenable to research participation. Several other factors may also affect a family's willingness to participate. Some children may already be participating in research protocols related to their medical treatment, such as medication trials, that require extra visits and tests; therefore, they may be less willing to commit to yet another study. Parents of young patients with chronic conditions, such as HIV or cancer, may express concern that, as a participant in multiple studies, their child is being "overused" for research (Sherwen & Boland, 1994). In addition, parents may not recognize the value of research or be reluctant to disclose personal information, especially when the researcher is on the medical team and already a part of their lives. Finally, when the research focuses on areas of difficulty, such as depressive symptoms or cognitive impairments, parents may be reluctant to identify yet another problem area when their children already face many medical challenges.

Researchers have identified a number of strategies for successful subject recruitment. First, enlisting the support of the medical treatment team is essential (Gans & Brindis, 1995; N. J. Peterson, personal communication, May 8, 1998). Staff members, including nurses and social workers, often have established successful working relationships with families and are in a position to encourage participation (keeping in mind that the youngster's and family's decision whether or not to participate must in no way affect the care they receive). Similarly, investigators may also have more success in recruitment when they are familiar with the participants. Second, recruitment and retention in a study can be enhanced by designing a protocol that will be seen as relevant and important to children and families. Oftentimes, this can be accomplished by the use of focus groups, prior to study initiation, to ensure that the measures, procedures, and study presentation fit well with the target population (see Vaughn, Schumm, & Sinagub, 1996). Third, providing incentives for participation, such as monetary payment, lunch or transportation vouchers, and feedback or reports summarizing relevant information, can greatly increase research participation (Stevens-Simon, Dolgan, Kelly, & Singer, 1997). Such incentives represent recognition and appreciation of the participants' time and effort. Fourth, investigators often must go beyond convenient, accessible settings to recruit more representative samples of children, youth, and families (Jemmott, 1997). Mailing questionnaires directly to potential participants and making home visits will facilitate the inclusion of children and families in research protocols who do not keep regular medical appointments for a variety of reasons (e.g., family stress, lack of transportation, noncompliance). Similarly, keeping in touch with participants through birthday cards, phone contacts, newsletters, and so on can be critical to maintaining participation in longitudinal investigations. Finally, a limited, focused protocol, rather than a large battery of measures, decreases the time commitment for subjects, reducing boredom and fatigue and often increasing willingness to participate (La Greca & Lemanek, 1996).

Small Sample Size

Related to the above, recruiting sufficiently large samples of children, youth, or families to test hypotheses of interest represents a serious challenge. Many pediatric conditions have very low base rates. For instance, although diabetes is the most common endocrine disorder of childhood, it affects only about 1.8 children per 1,000 (LaPorte & Tajima, 1985). Attention to developmental issues may further restrict the available pool of participants if only preschoolers or early adolescents are to be studied. Too often, null findings in pediatric research result from an inadequate sample size.

Specifically, statistical power is a function of the *sample size, alpha level* (usually .05), and *effect size* (Cohen, 1988). Many pediatric researchers are dealing with phenomena that might yield only a small or moderate effect size; thus, relatively large samples may be needed to achieve statistical significance. For example, comparisons of alternative treatments or variations of a given treatment typically yield small to medium effect sizes (Kazdin et al., 1990). In such cases, treatment effects would not be detected with a typical pediatric sample of 30 subjects across two or three conditions.

One potential strategy for dealing with the difficulties of recruiting large pediatric samples is the use of *multicenter studies,* which involve the collaboration of multiple investigators at different sites. This strategy has been used effectively in childhood cancer clinical trials (e.g., Pediatric Oncology Group), and has facilitated the development of new biomedical treatments for childhood cancer, even with extremely low prevalence rates for the disease (see Armstrong, 1995; Drotar, 1994; Glasgow & Anderson, 1995; La Greca & Varni, 1993).

Measurement/Assessment Issues

Assessment in pediatric psychology always begins with a question (or hypothesis) that will determine what kind of research design is needed and which measures are appropriate to use (La Greca, 1994; La Greca & Lemanek, 1996). At a minimum, the assessment process involves choosing suitable informants; selecting methods that are feasible and appropriate; deciding on the best timing for the assessment; evaluating instruments' psychometric qualities, strengths, and limitations; and balancing the practical demands of a medical setting (e.g., time constraints) with the desire to obtain the best information possible. Decisions made during this process will determine the kinds of conclusions that can be drawn from the data obtained.

Problems in assessment often begin with poorly framed, imprecise questions. A typical research question may be "What is the family functioning (or peer relations) of children with diabetes like?" However, this question is too broad. Rather, the researcher should consider what is meant by family functioning (or peer relations); with whom children with diabetes are being compared; and whether age or gender is a consideration. An improved research question would be "Do school-aged children with diabetes perceive their families to be more cohesive and supportive than children with other chronic conditions or than healthy youngsters?" With a more specific question, the pediatric researcher can begin to design an appropriate assessment.

How does one develop good questions? It is our bias that questions should be theory-driven yet sensitive to clinical needs. Research questions based on a conceptual framework or theory have the best chance of yielding information about psychological processes that affect children's health and well-being (see Drotar, 1994; La Greca & Lemanek, 1996; Wallander, 1992). Moreover, the practical relevance of the question for clinical applications is also paramount (La Greca & Varni, 1993; Roberts & McNeal, 1995). Below are several important considerations that may help researchers to improve the quality and focus of their assessments.

Choosing the Best Informant: Whom to Assess?

Researchers should always identify the "best" informant for the problem at hand, that is, the person (or persons) who can provide the most valid, accurate picture of the problem or area of functioning. Identifying the "best" informant is often difficult, as this varies as a function of the child's developmental level and the type of problem studied (see La Greca & Lemanek, 1996).

In general, the best informant for one type of problem/area is not necessarily the best informant for another. In pediatric research, parents (especially mothers) often serve as the sole informant (e.g., Manne et al., 1995; Stein & Newcomb, 1994). Although parent reports are valuable for assessing observable behaviors, they are less adequate for assessing children's internal states (e.g., pain, anxiety) or social competence. For example, Gragg and colleagues (1996) found that youngsters, parents, and physicians provided very different perspectives on children's pain experiences. Furthermore, parents' estimates of their children's social competence and peer relations have often been found to be at odds with teachers' or children's reports (e.g., Colegrove & Huntzinger, 1994; Lemanek, Horowitz, & Ohene-Frempong, 1994). Thus, researchers should not rely solely on parental reports, especially when youngsters' subjective distress or level of social competencies are the targets of assessment.

In terms of developmental considerations (see La Greca & Lemanek, 1996), as a general rule, for children under 6 years of age, the parents or primary caretakers are the best informants, although child care providers may also be useful for children who spend considerable time in child care. Parents, teachers, and the children themselves are likely to represent the best informants for preadolescents, depending on the construct of interest. By early to midadolescence, however, teachers have much more limited contact with students; adolescents and parents are more valuable informants at this point. In fact, for certain areas (e.g., internal feelings; deviant behaviors; alcohol and drug use), adolescents are the best informant source (see Loeber, Green, & Lahey, 1990).

In addition to developmental changes, the best informants also vary as a function of the type of problem or area that is being assessed. For externalizing problems that are readily observable (e.g., noncompliance), adults (parents, teachers, or health care providers) may be in the best position to evaluate children (e.g., Barkley, 1988; McMahon & Forehand, 1988). In contrast, for internalizing behaviors (e.g., anxiety, depression) or subjective phenomena such as pain, the children/adolescents themselves may be the best informants (see Dahlquist, 1990; Kazdin, 1990; Stone & Lemanek, 1990), although parents are often a valuable secondary source. Teachers, on the other hand, are less useful informants for subjective feelings (Loeber et al., 1990), especially with older children and adolescents. For reports of health care behaviors, such as adherence to a treatment regimen, the parent and the child/adolescent will be the best informants, with relatively greater emphasis on the parent for children under 12 years and on the adolescent for teens (Dahlquist, 1990; Johnson, 1995; La Greca, Follansbee, & Skyler, 1990). Finally, for assessments of peer relations and social competence, the child and/or peers represent the best informant source at any age (Landau & Milich, 1990).

Several implications can be drawn from this discussion. First, *multiple informants* will be necessary to adequately answer certain research questions in pediatric psychology. At a minimum, it is desirable to have the "best" informant for each of the constructs being assessed. Second, it will often be necessary to use *multiple methods* of assessment (e.g., questionnaires, observations) to reduce the bias inherent in any one type of assessment method. And, third, efforts should be made to study more *cohesive developmental groupings,* such as middle elementary school-aged children or early adolescents. Informant issues make it extremely difficult to include diverse age groups in the same study and obtain an adequate assessment.

Timing of the Assessment

The temporal course of the pediatric disease or condition is important to consider, as this will determine the timing of the assessment (see Drotar, 1994). For instance, investigators should determine whether they are most interested in processes that occur at disease onset, in the period following initial diagnosis, during the course of treatment, or after certain complications arise. Cancer-related stressors, for example, may be more salient to children soon after their initial diagnosis than after their treatment is completed (Bull as cited by Drotar, 1994). On the other hand, adherence to medical treatments for chronic pediatric conditions appears to decline substantially over time (see La Greca & Schuman, 1995), so that efforts to understand nonadherence may be more critical after the initial "honeymoon" period.

Investigators should also be mindful of important developmental transitions when planning the timing of an assessment. In some cases, developmental transitions represent good opportunities for research. For example, the marked physical, cognitive, and social changes that accompany the onset and course of puberty can complicate the management of a chronic disease (La Greca & Skyler, 1995), making this developmental transition an important one for pediatric research. On the other hand, an investigator who is interested in the stress levels of youngsters who are newly diagnosed with a life-threatening disease (e.g., cancer) may find it difficult to isolate disease effects if the participants are also undergoing a typically stressful developmental transition, such as starting elementary or middle school.

Generalizability of Measures

In an effort to evaluate the psychological, behavioral, and emotional functioning of children with illness, pediatric investigators have obtained reports from parents, teachers, and children using measures that have been designed to assess child psychopathology (La Greca, 1994). Instruments such as the Child Behavior Checklist (CBCL; Achenbach & Edelbrock, 1991), the Youth Self-Report (YSR; Achenbach & Edelbrock, 1987), and the Child Depression Inventory (CDI; Kovacs, 1979) have been used in pediatric research; they assess symptoms of psychopathology, are based on large standardization samples, have established reliability and validity, are widely recognized, and are easy to administer, score, and interpret. However, they were not designed for use with physically ill children and have limitations when used in that context. For example, the CBCL and YSR contain items regarding physical symptoms, which were included to screen for somatic complaints (not based on medical cause). However, informants (parent, child) may endorse symptoms attributable to the child's illness and inadvertently inflate the behavior problems score (Perrin, Stein, & Drotar, 1991). Similarly, the CDI contains items, such as loss of appetite, energy, and sleep, and decrease in school performance, which may be due to the child's illness rather than depression per se. Thus, it can be difficult to distinguish true depressive symptoms from the symptoms of a chronic illness. Another consideration to keep in mind when using instruments designed to assess child psychopathology is that they are less effective at describing the subtle or mild behavioral difficulties, within the range of normal functioning, that appear to be common among chronically ill children (La Greca, 1994; Perrin et al., 1991). In response to these limitations, researchers are increasingly turning to the development of disease-specific measures.

Generic vs. Disease-Specific Measures

Pediatric researchers are often confronted with the decision of whether to use generic versus disease-specific measures (La Greca & Lemanek, 1996). For the most part, this decision depends on the research question, as either or both types of measures may be useful and appropriate.

Disease-specific measures will be increasingly important as research agendas focus on within-group factors that are predictive of coping and disease adaptation, or health outcomes, among youth with pediatric conditions. As an example, recent investigations have examined whether disease-specific social support from family and friends is predictive of health outcomes for adolescents with diabetes (e.g., La Greca, Auslander, et al., 1995; La Greca & Thompson, 1998; K. Thompson & La Greca, 1998). These investigators found that family support for diabetes care is predictive of better treatment adherence for adolescents (La Greca, Auslander et al., 1995) and that peer support is predictive of better metabolic control, particularly among African American adolescents (K. Thompson & La Greca, 1998). In this context, the Diabetes Social Support Interview, a disease-specific measure of family and friend support, was essential to the assessment process and helped to provide clinically useful information that could also be used to develop supportive treatments for adolescents with diabetes.

Disease-specific measures are also useful when studying the effects of pediatric interventions. For example, Satin et al. (1989) evaluated the impact of a multifamily intervention on the metabolic control and family adjustment of adolescents with diabetes. Although the intervention improved youngsters' metabolic functioning, it had little demonstrated impact on overall family functioning (assessed by the Family Environment Scale; Moos & Moos, 1981). However, it is possible that this disease-specific intervention might have improved the way the families managed their adolescents' disease, although this was not measured. In this specific instance, both disease-specific and generic measures of family functioning would have been desirable, as together they may have better elucidated the processes underlying the intervention's impact than would either type of measure alone.

Because of the growing importance of disease-specific measures in pediatric psychological research, the development of such measures represents a growth area in pediatric research (see studies by Peterson, Saldana, & Heilblum, 1996; Quittner et al., 1996; Spieth & Harris, 1996). When developing disease-specific measures, however, investigators should examine the linkages between these new measures and their more generic counterparts, so that other investigators can relate the new measures to more general levels of functioning. For example, families who provide more diabetes-specific support should also be perceived as providing more social/emotional support overall (La Greca, Auslander, et al., 1995). Without these kinds of linkages to establish the validity of the disease-specific measures, it will be difficult to draw generalizations about children's psychosocial functioning and adaptation from pediatric psychological research (see Drotar, 1994; Van Dongen-Melman, De Groot, Hahlen, & Verhulst, 1996).

Content Overlap

Pediatric researchers should be careful to consider potential overlap of content between measures, and especially between measures that represent the predictor and outcome variables in a study. Perhaps the study of stress and disease best illustrates the problems that can arise. Measures of stressful life events often contain "illness" items (e.g., serious illness or injury, hospitalization), which can inflate the observed relationship between stress and illness. Another example is the study of depression and metabolic control among youth with diabetes; some of the physiological symptoms of depression (e.g., irritability, trouble concentrating) are also signs of poor metabolic control. In such cases, investigators may need to reanalyze data after removing the overlapping items or deliberately select measures that do not confound the variables of interest.

Considering Diverse Aspects of the Construct

When planning a measurement strategy, researchers should consider the various characteristics or aspects of the construct. Many constructs of interest in pediatric psychology, like adherence or stress, are multifaceted (Johnson, 1992). For instance, if an investigator wants to know whether stress leads to problems in diabetes management, it will be important to clarify what is meant by stress. Stressors can be acute (e.g., car accident) or chronic (e.g., parental separation and divorce); stressors can be brief and highly impactful (e.g., experiencing an earthquake or major natural disaster) or ongoing and moderately irritating (e.g., daily hassles, such as having a long commute to work or school). Further, the investigator should consider whether he or she is interested in youngsters' appraisal of the stressors or simply the occurrence of verifiable life events. These aspects of stress need to be specified before proceeding further with the study design and measurement strategy.

IMPORTANT FUTURE DIRECTIONS FOR PEDIATRIC PSYCHOLOGY RESEARCH

Despite the challenges of pediatric psychological research, it is an important and growing field. Advances in medical treatments, the need for effective and cost-efficient medical services, and the recognition of the contributions of behavior and quality of life to health outcomes for children and adolescents have provided new avenues for pediatric research. In closing, we highlight several areas that represent important growth areas for pediatric psychological research (also see La Greca, 1997).

Role of Behavior in Health Care: Treatment Adherence and Disease Prevention

With recent medical advances, there is a corresponding emphasis on the role of *behavior* in the management of disease (see Kaplan, 1990; Kazak, 1993) and the prevention of disease (McGinnis, 1993). These trends should provide many opportunities for psychologists, especially in the areas of improving adherence to increasingly difficult and demanding pediatric treatment protocols, and preventing chronic diseases associated with high morbidity and mortality (e.g., cancer, heart disease), which have behavioral risk factors that *begin* in childhood or adolescence (e.g., tobacco and alcohol use, sedentary lifestyle, improper diet). These trends should provide opportunities for psychological service providers to develop and implement effective preventive services for children, youth, and their families.

The role of behavior in the *management* of pediatric chronic disease is well illustrated by the findings of the Diabetes Control and Complications Trial (1993), which demonstrated that intensive diabetes management led to better metabolic control and substantially reduced morbidity (e.g., retinopathy, nephropathy, and neuropathy) relative to conventional diabetes treatment. Yet, conventional management is already complex and demanding for children and families (Johnson, 1995). If intensive management is widely adopted as the medical treatment of choice for youth with diabetes, it will increase the focus on behavioral factors in diabetes care. How can such demanding medical interventions be implemented? How do we motivate children, youth, and families to maintain complex, intensive regimens over long time periods?

Similarly, the advent of new, sophisticated antiretroviral drug treatments for HIV infection typically include three or four drugs given in combination. The drugs must be administered on a fixed schedule, without missing doses. Any variation from this complicated regimen may limit the effectiveness of the drugs and increase the risk of developing viral resistance and treatment failure (Condra, Holder, & Schleis, 1996). Thus, although new drugs offer the potential promise of dramatic improvement in health status and prolonged life, if patient adherence is inconsistent, the treatment becomes ineffective and may never be effective for that individual again. Given the potential benefits of the new treatments and the risks of poor adherence, interventions to improve adherence are crucial.

Similarly, there is ample evidence to support the role of behavior in the *prevention* of chronic diseases that typically have their onset in adulthood and that are associated with high morbidity, mortality, and medical costs. For example, in 1990, heart disease was the leading cause of death in the United States and was associated with over $75 billion in medical costs (McGinnis, 1993). At the same time, the primary risk factors for heart disease—tobacco use, obesity, elevated blood pressure and cholesterol, and a sedentary lifestyle—are largely based on behaviors that begin in childhood or adolescence (McGinnis, 1993). Efforts to develop effective programs to reduce or prevent the development of heart disease, and other chronic conditions, will require the input of pediatric researchers, and represents an important new avenue for pediatric research and practice.

Financial Accountability

Accountability is another issue that demands serious consideration in pediatric research. In an era of managed care, it is critical to document the cost-effectiveness and potential cost savings of psychological interventions (Drotar, 1997; La Greca, 1997). Do children with medical problems who receive psychological services have fewer medical needs, reduced hospital stays, and fewer outpatient visits? Pediatric psychologists are often in the position of having to justify the cost benefits of the behavioral and mental health services they provide, yet data of this kind are seriously lacking (see Roberts & Hurley, 1997).

One way of evaluating the cost benefit of pediatric psychological services is by documenting "medical offset," or the amount "saved" in medical services and expenses by the provision of psychological services. Pediatric psychologists could use medical offset data to document their value to the health care system. For example, Rosen and Wiens (1979) studied the medical impact of providing psychological evaluation and treatment services to children in a medical setting. They found that pediatric patients who received psychological services decreased their medical usage by 41%, significantly reduced their number of prescriptions, and were substantially less likely to be hospitalized. Using these data, one could calculate the cost of providing psychological services to these pediatric patients, which would substantially offset the much higher cost of outpatient medical visits, prescriptions, and inpatient care. Similarly, Finney and colleagues (Finney, Riley, & Cataldo, 1991) reported that providing psychological consultation services in a pediatric outpatient setting (at a large HMO) resulted in significant medical offset. Specifically, the provision of brief, targeted treatments for behavioral and emotional problems led to significant reductions in medical visits. Pediatric psychologists would do the field a tremendous service by systematically collecting data of this type (see work by Newacheck et al., 1996; Pinto & Hollandsworth, 1989).

Primary Care Settings

Health care systems can generally be divided into two levels of care: primary and tertiary. Primary care is the first line of medical care the patient receives, including both general health maintenance as well as intervention for health problems. For children, this care is provided by general pediatricians, family practitioners, general internists, and pediatric nurse practitioners, and is typically delivered in office-based settings (Kelleher & Long, 1994). Tertiary care is the specialized level of care provided to patients with more serious or complex conditions or any health concern requiring the attention of a specially trained practitioner. Examples include endocrinology, gastroenterology, and neurology, among many others.

Since the early development of pediatric psychology, emphasis has been placed on tertiary care settings and has encouraged specialization within pediatric areas (e.g., pediatric hematology/oncology or pediatric endocrinology). Only recently has attention has been directed toward the integration of pediatric psychology into primary care settings (Holden & Schuman, 1995). This increasing focus on primary care has grown out of research revealing the high prevalence of underdetected and undertreated emotional and behavioral disorders in primary care settings (Costello et al., 1988; Lavigne et al., 1993). Moreover, this change in focus is being fueled by recent health care reform, as secondary payors attempt to reverse the trend toward overspecialization and fragmented care by increasing the number of primary care providers and bolstering primary care medical services so they can become the foundation for a more effective and cost-efficient health care system (Cartland & Yudkowsky, 1992; Miranda, Hohmann, Atkinson, & Larson, 1994).

As a result, pediatric psychologists have been increasing their presence in primary care settings, establishing programs in which their evaluation, treatment, and management services are used to augment primary care (Finney, Riley, Cataldo, 1991; Kanoy & Schroeder, 1985). Incorporating psychological services into primary care settings should improve the detection of emotional and behavioral disorders, reduce barriers to intervention with and management of these disorders, decrease the need for referral to tertiary care services, and encourage pediatricians to become more aware of behavioral disorders and more comfortable managing them.

Future investigations are needed to evaluate the impact of augmented primary care services and determine the effectiveness, and cost-effectiveness, of this model. Of particular interest will be an exploration of the efficacy of mental health service provision in the context of pediatric primary care within lower-socioeconomic-status, disadvantaged, inner-city populations (Tarnowski & Rohrbeck, 1993) as children from these populations are at increased risk for problems due to their exposure to multiple environmental and biological etiological factors.

CONCLUSION

This chapter has highlighted the special challenges and potential rewards that researchers in pediatric psychology encounter. Reflecting its interdisciplinary nature, research in pediatric psychology covers a broad range of issues and topics. Although many research issues are similar to those that emerge in clinical child psychological research, there are a number of unique challenges that face researchers who work in the interface between psychology and medicine, and these were highlighted in this chapter.

At the present time, most of the research in pediatric psychology has been descriptive in nature, but recent years have witnessed growing sophistication in the types of research questions that are asked and in the methodology used. Greater emphasis on theory-driven research, on complex models of linkages between adjustment and health, and on evaluating the efficacy of pediatric interventions has been evident. Moreover, the twenty-first century should be a productive time for pediatric researchers as well. Throughout the chapter, critical areas for future research were highlighted. These include the need for prospective, longitudinal studies of the interplay between health behavioral and disease status; evaluations of the effectiveness and financial cost benefits of pediatric interventions; studies of the prevention of adult-onset chronic and debilitating diseases, which have their behavioral roots in child and adolescent health behaviors; and psychological research in primary care settings. Pediatric psychologists will have a full research agenda. The twenty-first century is almost upon us; are we up to the challenge?

REFERENCES

Achenbach, T. M., & Edelbrock, C. (1987). *Manual for the youth self-report.* Burlington: Department of Psychiatry, University of Vermont.

Achenbach, T. M., & Edelbrock, C. (1991). *Manual for the child behavior checklist and revised child behavior profile.* Burlington: Department of Psychiatry, University of Vermont.

Anderson, B. J., Wolf, F. M., Burkhart, M. T., Cornell, R. G., & Bacon, G. E. (1989). Metabolic effects of a peer-group intervention with adolescents with IDDM: A randomized controlled study in an outpatient setting. *Diabetes Care, 12,* 179–183.

Armstrong, F. D. (1995). Commentary: Childhood cancer. *Journal of Pediatric Psychology, 20,* 417–421.

Barkley, R. A. (1988). Attention deficit disorder with hyperactivity. In E. J. Mash & L. G. Terdal (Eds.), *Behavioral assessment of childhood disorders* (3rd ed., pp. 69–104). New York: Guilford Press.

Bennett, D. S. (1994). Depression among children with chronic medical problems: A meta-analysis. *Journal of Pediatric Psychology, 19,* 149–170.

Black, M., Dubowitz, H., Hutcheson, J., Berenson-Howard, J., & Starr, R. H. (1995). A randomized clinical trial of home intervention for children with failure to thrive. *Pediatrics, 95,* 807–814.

Boardway, R. H., Delamater, A. M., Tomakowsky, J., & Gutai, J. P. (1993). Stress management training for adolescents with diabetes. *Journal of Pediatric Psychology, 18,* 29–45.

Boggs, S. R., Geffken, G. R., Johnson, S. B., & Silverstein, J. (1992). Behavioral treatment of nocturnal enuresis in children with insulin-dependent diabetes mellitus. *Journal of Pediatric Psychology, 17,* 111–118.

Bryk, A. S., & Raudenbush, S. W. (1987). Application of hierarchical linear models to assessing change. *Psychological Bulletin, 101,* 147–158.

Bryk, A. S., & Raudenbush, S. W. (1992). *Hierarchical linear models: Applications and data analysis methods.* Newbury Park, CA: Sage.

Burchinal, M., & Appelbaum, M. I. (1991). Estimating individual developmental functions: Methods and their assumptions. *Child Development, 62,* 23–43.

Cartland, J. D., & Yudkowsky, B. K. (1992). Barriers to referral in managed care systems. *Pediatrics, 89,* 183–192.

Cohen, J. (1988). *Statistical power for the behavioral sciences* (2nd ed.). Hillsdale, NJ: Erlbaum.

Colegrove, R. W., & Huntzinger, R. M. (1994). Academic, behavioral, and social adaptation of boys with hemophilia/HIV disease. *Journal of Pediatric Psychology, 19,* 457–473.

Condra, J. H., Holder, D. J., & Schleis, W. A. (1996). *Bi-directional inhibition of HIV-1 drug resistance selection by combination therapy with Indinavir and reverse transcriptase inhibitors.* Abstracts of the XIth International Conference on AIDS. Abstract number #Th.B.932. Vancouver, Canada.

Cook, T. D., & Campbell, D. T. (1979). *Quasi-experimentation design and analysis issues for field settings.* Chicago: Rand McNally.

Costello, E. J., Burns, B. J., Costello, A. J., Edelbrock, C., Dulcan, M., & Brent, D. (1988). Service utilization and psychiatric diagnosis in pediatric primary care: The role of the gatekeeper. *Pediatrics, 82,* 435–441.

Creer, T. L., & Bender, B. G. (1995). Pediatric asthma. In M. C. Roberts (Ed.), *Handbook of pediatric psychology* (2nd ed., pp. 219–240). New York: Guilford Press.

Dahlquist, L. M. (1990). Obtaining child reports in health care settings. In A. M. La Greca (Ed.), *Through the eyes of the child: Obtaining self-reports from children and adolescents* (pp. 395–439). Boston: Allyn & Bacon.

Daniels, D., Moos, R. H., Billings, A. G., & Miller, J. J., III. (1987). Psychosocial risk and resistance factors among children with chronic illness, healthy siblings, and healthy controls. *Journal of Abnormal Child Psychology, 15,* 295–308.

Delamater, A. M., Bubb, J., Davis, S. G., Smith, J. A., Schmidt, L., White, N. H., & Santiago, J. V. (1990). Randomized prospective study of self-management training with newly diagnosed diabetic children. *Diabetes Care, 13,* 492–498.

Diabetes Control and Complications Trial Research Group. (1993). The effect of intensive treatment of diabetes on the development and progression of long-term complications in insulin-dependent diabetes mellitus. *New England Journal of Medicine, 329,* 977–986.

Drotar, D. (1994). Psychological research with pediatric conditions: If we specialize, can we generalize? *Journal of Pediatric Psychology, 19,* 403–414.

Drotar, D. (1997). Intervention research: Pushing back the frontiers of pediatric psychology. *Journal of Pediatric Psychology, 22,* 593–606.

Drotar, D., La Greca, A. M., Lemanek, K. L., & Kazak, A. (1995). Case reports in pediatric psychology: Uses and guidelines for authors and reviewers. *Journal of Pediatric Psychology, 20,* 549–566.

Epstein, L. H., Beck, S., Figueroa, I., Farkas, G., Kazdin, A. E., Daneman, D., & Becker, D. (1981). The effects of targeting improvements in urine glucose on metabolic control in children with insulin dependent diabetes. *Journal of Applied Behavior Analysis, 14,* 365–375.

Farrell, A. D. (1994). Structural equation modeling with longitudinal data: Strategies for examining group differences and reciprocal relationships. *Journal of Consulting and Clinical Psychology, 62,* 477–486.

Finney, J. W., Lemanek, K. L., Brophy, C. J., & Cataldo, M. F. (1990). Pediatric appointment keeping: Improving adherence in a primary care allergy clinic. *Journal of Pediatric Psychology, 15,* 571–579.

Finney, J. W., Riley, A. W., & Cataldo, M. F. (1991). Psychology in primary care health: Effects of brief targeted therapy on children's medical care utilization. *Journal of Pediatric Psychology, 16,* 447–462.

Gans, J. E., & Brindis, C. D. (1995). Choice of research setting in understanding adolescent health problems. *Journal of Adolescent Health, 17,* 306–313.

Gil, K. M., Williams, D. A., Thompson, R. J., & Kinney, T. R. (1991). Sickle cell disease in children and adolescents: The relation of child and parent pain coping strategies to adjustment. *Journal of Pediatric Psychology, 16,* 643–664.

Glasgow, R. E., & Anderson, B. J. (1995). Future directions for research on pediatric chronic disease management: Lessons from diabetes. *Journal of Pediatric Psychology, 20,* 389–402.

Gragg, R. A., Rapoff, M. A., Danovsky, M. B., Lindsley, C. B., Varni, J. W., Waldron, S. A., & Bernstein, B. H. (1996). Assessing chronic musculoskeletal pain associated with rheumatic disease: Further validation of the Pediatric Pain Questionnaire. *Journal of Pediatric Psychology, 21,* 235–250.

Hanson, C. L., De Guire, M. J., Schinkel, A. M., Henggeler, S. W., & Burghen, G. A. (1992). Comparing social learning and family systems correlates of adaptation in youths with IDDM. *Journal of Pediatric Psychology, 17,* 555–572.

Hanson, C. L., Henggeler, S. W., & Burghen, G. A. (1987). Social competence and parental support as mediators of the link between stress and metabolic control in adolescents with insulin-dependent diabetes. *Journal of Consulting and Clinical Psychology, 55,* 529–533.

Holden, E. W., & Schuman, W. B. (1995). The detection and management of mental health disorders in pediatric primary care. *Journal of Clinical Psychology in Medical Settings, 2,* 71–87.

Holmbeck, G. N. (1997). Toward terminological, conceptual, and statistical clarity in the study of mediators and moderators: Examples from the child-clinical and pediatric psychology literatures. *Journal of Consulting and Clinical Psychology, 65,* 599–610.

Hosmer, D. W., Jr., & Lemeshow, S. (1989). *Applied logistic regression.* New York: Wiley.

Janus, M., & Goldberg, S. (1997). Factors influencing family participation in a longitudinal study: Comparison of pediatric and healthy samples. *Journal of Pediatric Psychology, 22,* 245–262.

Jemmott, L. S. (1997, July). *Mothers and sons strengthening the bonds: Health promotion strategies to reduce HIV-risk behavior.* Paper presented at the fifth annual conference on the Role of Families in Preventing and Adapting to HIV/AIDS, Baltimore.

Johnson, S. B. (1980). Psychosocial factors in juvenile diabetes: A review. *Journal of Behavioral Medicine, 3,* 95–116.

Johnson, S. B. (1992). Methodological issues in diabetes research: Measuring adherence. *Diabetes Care, 15,* 1658–1667.

Johnson, S. B. (1994). Health behavior and health status: Concepts, methods, and applications. *Journal of Pediatric Psychology, 19,* 129–142.

Johnson, S. B. (1995). Insulin-dependent diabetes mellitus in childhood. In M. C. Roberts (Ed.), *Handbook of pediatric psychology* (2nd ed., pp. 263–285). New York: Guilford Press.

Johnson, S. B., Kelly, M., Henretta, J., Cunningham, W., Tomer, A., & Silverstain, J. (1992). A longitudinal analysis of adherence and health status in childhood diabetes. *Journal of Pediatric Psychology, 17,* 537–553.

Johnson, S. B., Tomer, A., Cunningham, W., & Henretta, J. (1990). Adherence in childhood diabetes: Results of a confirmatory factory analysis. *Health Psychology, 9,* 493–501.

Kanoy, K. W., & Schroeder, C. S. (1985). Suggestions to parents about common behavior problems in a pediatric primary care office: Five years of follow-up. *Journal of Pediatric Psychology, 10,* 15–30.

Kaplan, R. M.. (1990). Behavior as the central outcome in health care. *American Psychologist, 45,* 1211–1220.

Kazak, A. (1993). Psychological research in pediatric oncology. *Journal of Pediatric Psychology, 18,* 313–318.

Kazdin, A. E. (1988). *Child psychotherapy: Developing and identifying effective treatments.* New York: Pergamon Press.

Kazdin, A. E. (1990). Assessment of childhood depression. In A. M. La Greca (Ed.), *Through the eyes of the child: Obtaining self-reports from children and adolescents* (pp. 189–233). Boston: Allyn & Bacon.

Kazdin, A. E. (1992). *Research design in clinical psychology.* Boston: Allyn & Bacon.

Kazdin, A. E. (1993). Adolescent mental health: Prevention and treatment programs. *American Psychologist, 48,* 127–141.

Kazdin, A. E., Bass, D., Ayers, W. A., & Rodgers, A. (1990). Empirical and clinical focus of child and adolescent psychotherapy research. *Journal of Clinical Psychology, 57,* 138–147.

Kelleher, K. J., & Long. N. (1994). Barriers and new directions in mental health services research in the primary care setting. *Journal of Clinical Child Psychology, 23,* 133–142.

Kendall, P. C., & Chambless, D. L. (Eds.). (1998). Empirically-supported psychological therapies [Special issue]. *Journal of Consulting and Clinical Psychology, 66*(1).

Kovacs, M. (1979). *Children's depression inventory*. Pittsburgh: University of Pittsburgh.

La Greca, A. M. (1994). Assessment in pediatric psychology: What's a researcher to do? *Journal of Pediatric Psychology, 19*, 283–290.

La Greca, A. M. (1997). Reflections and perspectives on pediatric psychology: Editor's vale dictum. *Journal of Pediatric Psychology, 22*, 759–770..

La Greca, A. M., Auslander, W. F., Greco, P., Spetter, D., Fisher, E. B., Jr., & Santiago, J. V. (1995). I get by with a little help from my family and friends: Adolescents' support for diabetes care. *Journal of Pediatric Psychology, 20*, 449–476.

La Greca, A. M., Follansbee, D., & Skyler, J. S. (1990). Developmental and behavioral aspects of diabetes management in youngsters. *Children's Health Care, 19*, 132–137.

La Greca, A. M., & Lemanek, K. L. (1996). Assessment as a process in pediatric psychology. *Journal of Pediatric Psychology, 21*, 137–151.

La Greca, A. M., & Schuman, W. B. (1995). Adherence to prescribed medical regimens. In M. C. Roberts (Ed.), *Handbook of pediatric psychology* (2nd ed., pp. 55–83). New York: Guilford Press.

La Greca, A. M., & Skyler, J. S. (1995). Psychological management of diabetes. In C. J. H. Kelnar (Ed.), *Childhood and adolescent diabetes* (pp. 295–310.) London: Chapman Hall.

La Greca, A. M., Stone, W. L., Drotar, D., & Maddux, J. E. (1988). Training in pediatric psychology: Survey results and recommendations. *Journal of Pediatric Psychology, 13*, 121–140.

La Greca, A. M., Swales, T., Klemp, S., Madigan, S., & Skyler, J. S. (1995). Adolescents with diabetes: Gender differences in psychosocial functioning and glycemic control. *Children's Health Care, 24*, 61–78.

La Greca, A. M., & Thompson, K. (1998). Family and friend support for adolescents with diabetes. *Analise Psicologica, 1*, 101–113.

La Greca, A. M., & Varni, J. W. (1993). Interventions in pediatric psychology: A look toward the future. *Journal of Pediatric Psychology, 18*, 667–680.

Landau, S., & Milich, R. (1990). Assessment of children's social status and peer relations. In A. M. La Greca (Ed.), *Through the eyes of the child: Obtaining self-reports from children and adolescents* (pp. 259–291). Boston: Allyn & Bacon.

LaPorte, R., & Tajima, N. (1985). Prevalence of insulin-dependent diabetes. In M. Harris & R. Hamman (Eds.), *Diabetes in America* (NIH Publication No. 95-1468, pp. V: 1–8) Bethesda, MD: National Institutes of Health.

Larsson, B., & Carlsson, J. (1996). A school-based, nurse-administered relaxation training for children with chronic tension-type headache. *Journal of Pediatric Psychology, 21*, 603–614.

Lavigne, J. V., Christoffel, K. K., Binns, H. J., Rosenbaum, D., Arend, R., Smith, K., & Hayford, J. R. (1993). Behavioral and emotional problems among preschool children in pediatric primary care: Prevalence and pediatricians' recognition. *Pediatrics, 91*, 649–655.

Lavigne, J. V., & Faier-Routman, J. (1992). Psychological adjustment to pediatric physical disorders: A meta-analytic review. *Journal of Pediatric Psychology, 17*, 133–157.

Lemanek, K. L. (1994). Research on pediatric chronic illness: New directions and recurrent confounds. *Journal of Pediatric Psychology, 19*, 143–148.

Lemanek, K. L., Horowitz, W., & Ohene-Frempong, K. (1994). A multiperspective investigation of social competence in children with sickle cell disease. *Journal of Pediatric Psychology, 19*, 443–456.

Loeber, R., Green, S., & Lahey, B. B. (1990). Mental health professionals' perception of the utility of children, mothers, and teachers as informants on child psychopathology. *Journal of Clinical Child Psychology, 19*, 136–143.

Lonigan, C. J., Elbert, J. C., & Johnson, S. B. (1998). Empirically supported psychosocial interventions for children: An overview. *Journal of Clinical Child Psychology, 27,* 138–147.

Manne, S. L., Lesanics, D., Meyers, P., Wollner, N., Steinherz, P., & Redd, W. (1995). Predictors of depressive symptomatology among parents of newly diagnosed children with cancer. *Journal of Pediatric Psychology, 20,* 491–510.

McCabe, M. A., Shimoda, K. C., Crowe, H. P., Schuman, W. B., Pfeil, C. U., & Dinndorf, P. A. (1997, April). *Prospective neurocognitive assessment following bone marrow transplantation: Part I. Long term follow-up of cognitive and academic outcome with children.* Paper presented at the annual meeting of the Society for Research on Child Development, Washington, DC.

McGinnis, J. M. (1993). The role of behavioral research in national health policy. In S. J. Blumenthal, K. Matthews, & S. M. Weiss (Eds.), *New research frontiers in behavioral medicine: Proceedings from the national conference* (pp. 217–222). Washington, DC: US Government Printing Office.

McMahon, R. J., & Forehand, R. (1988). Conduct disorders. In E. J. Mash & L. G. Terdal (Eds.), *Behavioral assessment of childhood disorders* (3rd ed., pp. 105–153). New York: Guilford Press.

Mindell, J. A., & Durand, V. M. (1993). Treatment of childhood sleep disorders: Generalization across disorders and effects on family members. *Journal of Pediatric Psychology, 18,* 731–750.

Miranda, J., Hohmann, A. A., Atkinson, C. C., & Larson, D. B. (Eds.). (1994). *Mental disorders in primary care.* San Francisco: Jossey-Bass.

Moos, R., & Moos, B. (1981). *Family environment scale manual.* Palo Alto, CA: Consulting Psychologists.

Murphy, L. M. B., Thompson, R. J., Jr., & Morris, M. A. (1997). Adherence behaviors among adolescents with Type I insulin dependent diabetes mellitus: The role of cognitive appraisal processes. *Journal of Pediatric Psychology, 22,* 811–825.

Newacheck, P. W., Stein, R. E. K., Walker, D. K., Gortmaker, S. L., Kurthau, K., & Perrin, J. H. (1996). Monitoring and evaluating managed care for children with chronic illnesses and disabilities. *Pediatrics, 98,* 952–958.

Northam, E., Anderson, P., Adler, R., Werther, G., & Warne, G. (1996). Psychosocial and family functioning in children with insulin-dependent diabetes at diagnosis and one year later. *Journal of Pediatric Psychology, 21,* 699–717.

Osterhaus, S. O. L., Passchier, J., van der Helm-Hylkema, H., de Jong, K. T., Orlebeke, J. F., de Grauw, A. J. C., & Dekker, P. H. (1993). Effects of behavioral psychophysiological treatment on school children with migraine in a nonclinical setting: Predictors and process variables. *Journal of Pediatric Psychology, 18,* 697–715.

Perrin, E. C., Stein, R. E. K., & Drotar, D. (1991). Cautions in using the Child Behavior Checklist: Observations based on research about children with a chronic illness. *Journal of Pediatric Psychology, 16,* 411–421.

Peterson, L., Saldana, L., & Heilblum, N. (1996). Quantifying tissue damage from childhood injury: The minor injury severity scale. *Journal of Pediatric Psychology, 21,* 251–267.

Peyrot, M. (1996). Causal analysis: Theory and application. *Journal of Pediatric Psychology, 21,* 3–24.

Pinto, R., & Hollandsworth, J. (1989). Using videotape modeling to prepare children psychologically for surgery: Influence of parents and costs versus benefits of providing preparation services. *Health Psychology, 1,* 75–79.

Powers, S. W., Vannatta, K., Noll, R. B., Cool, V. A., & Stehbens, J. A. (1995). Leukemia and other childhood cancers. In M. C. Roberts (Ed.), *Handbook of pediatric psychology* (2nd ed., pp. 310–326). New York: Guilford Press.

Quittner, A. L., Tolbert, V. E., Regoli, K. J., Orenstein, D. M., Hollingsworth, J. L., & Eigen, H. (1996). Development of the role play inventory of situations and coping strategies for parents of children with cystic fibrosis. *Journal of Pediatric Psychology, 21,* 209–235.

Roberts, M. C. (1992). Vale dictum: An editor's view of the field of pediatric psychology and its journal. *Journal of Pediatric Psychology, 17,* 785–805.

Roberts, M. C., & Hurley, L. K. (1997). *Managing managed care.* New York: Plenum Press.

Roberts, M. C., & McNeal, R. E. (1995). Historical and conceptual foundations of pediatric psychology. In M. C. Roberts (Ed.), *Handbook of pediatric psychology* (2nd ed., pp. 3–18). New York: Guilford Press.

Rosen, J. C., & Wiens, A. N. (1979). Changes in medical problems and use of medical services following psychological interventions. *American Psychologist, 34,* 420–431.

Satin, W., La Greca, A. M., Zigo, M. A., & Skyler, J. S. (1989). Diabetes in adolescence: Effects of multifamily group intervention and parent simulation of diabetes. *Journal of Pediatric Psychology, 14,* 259–276.

Seigler, D. E., La Greca, A. M., Citrin, W. S., Reeves, M. L., & Skyler, J. S. (1982). Psychological effects of intensification of diabetic control. *Diabetes Care, 5*(Suppl.), 19–23.

Sherwen, L. N., & Boland, M. (1994). Overview of psychosocial research concerning pediatric human immunodeficiency virus infection. *Developmental and Behavioral Pediatrics, 15,* S5–S11.

Society of Pediatric Psychology. (1998). Statement of purpose. *Journal of Pediatric Psychology, 23,* back cover.

Spieth, I. F., & Harris, C. V. (1996). Assessment of health-related quality of life in children and adolescents: An integrative review. *Journal of Pediatric Psychology, 21,* 175–194.

Stark, L. J., Bowen, A. M., Tyc, V. L., Evans, S., & Passero, M. A. (1990). A behavioral approach to increasing calorie consumption in children with cystic fibrosis. *Journal of Pediatric Psychology, 15,* 309–326.

Stark, L. J., Owens-Stively, J., Spirito, A., Lewis, A., & Guevermort, D. (1990). Group behavioral treatment of retentive encopresis. *Journal of Pediatric Psychology, 15,* 659–671.

Stein, J. A., & Newcomb, M. D. (1994). Children's internalizing and externalizing behaviors and maternal health problems. *Journal of Pediatric Psychology, 19,* 571–594.

Stevens-Simon, C., Dolgan, J. I., Kelly, L., & Singer, D. (1997). The effect of monetary incentives and peer support groups on repeat adolescent pregnancies. *Journal of the American Medical Association, 277,* 977–982.

Stone, W. L., & Lemanek, K. L. (1990). Developmental issues in children's self-reports. In A. M. La Greca (Ed.), *Through the eyes of the child: Obtaining self-reports from children and adolescents* (pp. 18–56). Boston: Allyn & Bacon.

Tarnowski, K., & Rohrbeck, C. A. (1993). Disadvantaged children and families. In T. H. Ollendick & R. J. Prinz (Eds.), *Advances in clinical child psychology* (Vol. 15, pp. 41–79). New York: Plenum Press.

Taylor, H. G., & Fletcher, J. M. (1995). Progress in pediatric neuropsychology. *Journal of Pediatric Psychology, 20,* 695–701.

Thompson, K., & La Greca, A. M. (1998). *Family and friend support for diabetes care, among low-income, ethnically diverse adolescents.* Manuscript submitted for publication.

Thompson, R. J., Jr., Gil, K. M., Burbach, D. J., Keith, B., & Kinney, T. R. (1993). The role of child and maternal processes in the psychological adjustment of children with sickle cell disease. *Journal of Consulting and Clinical Psychology, 61,* 468–474.

Thompson, R. J., Jr., Gustafson, K. E., George, L. K., & Spock, A. (1994). Change over a 12-month period in the psychological adjustment of children and adolescents with cystic fibrosis. *Journal of Pediatric Psychology, 19,* 189–204.

Thompson, R. J., Jr., Hodges, K., & Hamlett, K. W. (1990). A matched comparison of adjustment in children with cystic fibrosis and psychiatrically referred and nonreferred children. *Journal of Pediatric Psychology, 15,* 745–759.

Van Dongen-Melman, J. E. W. M., De Groot, A., Hahlen, K., & Verhulst, F. C. (1996). Potential pitfalls of using illness-specific measures. *Journal of Pediatric Psychology, 21,* 103–106.

Varni, J. W., Blount, R. L., Waldron, S. A., & Smith, A. J. (1995). Management of pain and distress. In M. C. Roberts (Ed.), *Handbook of pediatric psychology* (2nd ed., pp. 105–123). New York: Guilford Press.

Varni, J. W., Katz, E. R., Colegrove, R., Jr., & Dolgin, M. (1993). The impact of social skills training on the adjustment of children with newly diagnosed cancer. *Journal of Pediatric Psychology, 18,* 751–768.

Vaughn, S., Schumm, J. S., & Sinagub, J. (1996). *Focus group interviews in education and psychology.* Thousand Oaks, CA: Sage.

Veger, S. L., & Liang, K. Y. (1986). The analysis of discrete and continuous longitudinal data. *Biometry, 42,* 121–130.

Wallander, J. L. (1992). Theory-driven research in pediatric psychology: A little bit on why and how. *Journal of Pediatric Psychology, 17,* 521–536.

Wallander, J. L., & Thompson, R. J., Jr. (1995). Psychosocial adjustment of children with chronic physical conditions. In M. C. Roberts (Ed.), *Handbook of pediatric psychology* (2nd ed., pp. 124–141). New York: Guilford Press.

Weissberg-Benchell, J., & Glasgow, A. (1997). The role of temperament in children with insulin-dependent diabetes mellitus. *Journal of Pediatric Psychology, 22,* 795–809.

Willett, J. B., Singer, J. D., & Martin, N. C. (1998). The design and analysis of longitudinal studies of development and psychopathology in context: Statistical models and methological recommendations. *Development and Psychopathology, 10,* 395–426.

Chapter 22

Focus Chapter

RESEARCH METHODS IN BEHAVIORAL GENETICS

Steven O. Moldin, Ph.D.

HISTORICAL PERSPECTIVE

The field of behavioral genetics offers theory and methods to consider both genetic and nongenetic influences as interactive sources of behavioral differences among individual organisms. Its fundamental underlying principle is that both heredity and environment are necessary to understand the complexity of behavior.

A major influence on human behavioral genetics has been the nineteenth-century work of Galton (1865), who used biometrical methods to analyze behaviors like talent and character. These methods formed the basis for the discipline of quantitative genetics, which draws inferences on the inheritance of a behavioral trait from mathematical analyses of information collected from related individuals. Another influential paradigm developing at this time relied on the work of Mendel (1865), whose experiments in plants led to our understanding that genes are fundamental and discrete units of inheritance that follow predictable patterns of transmission across generations. Mendel's work formed the basis for the discipline of molecular genetics, which is concerned with the biology of genes and gene action. Over time, the Galtonian and Mendelian paradigms have converged in application. Modern behavioral genetics now employs the extended methods and analytic tools of both in order to understand the genetic and environmental underpinnings of complex behavior in humans and animals.

SCOPE OF BEHAVIORAL GENETICS

The principles, methods, and technologies of behavioral genetics have been applied to the study of complex behavioral traits like intelligence and sociability, and to the study of complex behavioral disorders like schizophrenia, bipolar disorder, and autism. Several scientific disciplines of genetics are encompassed within modern behavioral genetics, and these include *molecular genetics,* which applies the tools and technologies of molecular and cellular biology to the study of genes; *population genetics,* which focuses on factors that affect the distribution of genes in the population; *quantitative genetics,* which focuses on the partitioning of variation in observed characteristics into its genetic and environmental components; and *genetic epidemiology,* which explicitly focuses on understanding the genetic and environmental causes, distribution, and control of human diseases in families and in populations.

DNA STRUCTURE AND FUNCTION

Genetic information is stored in *deoxyribonucleic acid* (DNA) molecules, which are used to synthesize *ribonucleic acid* (RNA) molecules and also to permit the synthesis of the polypeptides that make up proteins. The structure of DNA is an antiparallel (i.e., running in opposite directions) double helix in which two DNA molecules (strands) are held together to form a duplex. Bonds form between pairs of laterally opposed bases (nitrogenous compounds), of which four variants occur in DNA. A sugar with an attached base and phosphate group constitutes a *nucleotide,* the basic linear sequence of simple repeating units of a DNA strand. Short, single-stranded pieces of DNA (typically 15–50 nucleotides) are called *oligonucleotides.*

DNA is contained in very large, linear structures called *chromosomes,* whose number and DNA content can vary considerably among species. Generally, the size of the *genome*—the total genetic information, or DNA content, in cells—parallels the complexity of the organism. Humans have a genome contained in 23 pairs of chromosomes that consist of one pair of chromosomes that determine sex and 22 remaining pairs of identical chromosomes *(autosomes).* On these chromosomes are an estimated total of 50,000 to 100,000 human genes (Fields, Adams, White, & Venter, 1994), of which perhaps 40,000 to 50,000 have been identified to date (Rowen, Mahairas, & Hood, 1997; Schuler et al., 1996).

GENETIC MAPS

Central to the description of an organism's genome is a comprehensive catalogue of the sequence and location of all its genes. Mapping is a critical tool to many different areas of biological research that can be used to dissect the heritable and nonheritable components of complex behavioral traits and to identify the mechanisms by which they interact.

Genetic map construction requires the identification of strips of DNA whose sequence is highly variable. These *polymorphic genetic markers* have at least two *alleles,* or alternate forms of a gene differing in DNA sequence, at significant frequencies in the population and are not necessarily related to disease or to gene action. As long as the markers segregated in families and were polymorphic enough, a map could be constructed. Prior to the 1980s, the idea of constructing human genetic maps was considered unobtainable because of the very limited number of suitable polymorphic markers available at that time.

The scientific community became aware of the existence of a level of enormous genetic variation that naturally occurs in humans. Botstein and colleagues (Botstein, White, Skolnick, & Davies, 1980) proposed to treat differences in the DNA sequence like allelic variants of a gene and use them as genetic markers for mapping. Based on a molecular technique described by Southern (1975), these differences can be made visible by the use of restriction enzymes, which cut DNA fragments of various lengths. Polymorphisms obtained in this fashion are called *restriction fragment length polymorphisms* (RFLPs), and presumably are anonymous markers (i.e., sequences of DNA that have no known biologic function).

These and other types of genetic markers are placed via different methods on two distinct types of maps that can be derived for each chromosome in the genome. *Linkage* and *physical maps* are distinguished by the methods by which they are derived and the metric used for measuring distances on them. In theory, these maps should provide the same information on chromosomal assignment and the ordering of genes. The linkage map assigns the relative order of specific positions on a chromosome, or *loci,* and the distances that separate them in units of measurement called *centimorgans* (cM). Linkage maps have been enormously valuable in assigning genes that cause rare human diseases to relatively small areas on chromosomes.

Physical maps are based on the direct analysis of DNA. Physical distances between and within loci are measured in terms of DNA base pairs. The entire human genome is 3 billion base pairs. After localization to a chromosome for a complex trait or disorder is established using markers on the linkage map, the next step is to examine the region in more detail to identify the precise location within that region of a gene that influences that trait or disorder; high-resolution physical maps are needed to accomplish this.

Human Genome Project

The Human Genome Project is an international effort whose ultimate aim is to obtain a comprehensive description of the human genome by determining the complete human DNA sequence. This multibillion-dollar, multiyear effort began in the 1980s and was planned in the United States by the federal government's Department of Energy and the National Institutes of Health. Major goals include: (a) construction of a high-resolution linkage map (Schuler et al., 1996); (b) construction of a high-resolution physical map (Rowen et al., 1997); and (c) determination of the complete DNA sequence of the human genome, expected by 2005. The impact of having a complete sequence will be profound; the human organism's genetic capacity will become entirely known and researchers will have the opportunity to find and study every genetic element. About 60 million base pairs (2% of the human genome) have been sequenced to date (Rowen et al., 1997). The goal of a complete human DNA sequence may be obtained sooner, given recent plans by private industry to make a large-scale contribution to this effort (Wade, 1998).

MODELS OF FAMILIAL TRANSMISSION

A fundamental distinction in behavioral genetics is between the *genotype,* an inferred set of genes, and the *phenotype,* an observed effect of those genes. Phenotypes of interest in behavioral genetics include quantitative traits that are measured on a continuous scale (e.g., attention impairments, eye-tracking dysfunction, cognitive ability, and novelty seeking) and behavioral disorders that are measured on a categorical scale as affected or unaffected (e.g., schizophrenia and autism). For the remainder of this chapter, "complex trait" will refer to both quantitative traits and behavioral disorders. Although molecular methods permit direct study of an organism's genotype, mathematical models are required in behavioral genetics to represent the ways in which the genotype and the environment interact to form complex phenotypes that are transmitted within families (Table 22.1).

Single Major Locus Model

The single major locus model assumes that all relevant genetic variation is due to the presence of alleles of a gene at a single locus and that environmental variation is unique to an individual. Human disorders transmitted through a single major locus are referred to as *Mendelian diseases,* since the pattern of inheritance in families follows the rules of Mendelian segregation and can usually be recognized through visual inspection of pedigrees. Characteristic single major locus disorders include Duchenne muscular dystrophy, phenylketonuria, Huntington disease, and cystic fibrosis.

Multilocus Models

The complex traits studied in behavioral genetics do not follow simple Mendelian patterns in families, and the relationship between genotype and phenotype is obscured (Gottesman, 1994; Lander & Schork, 1994; Moldin, 1997b; Moldin & Gottesman, 1997; Plomin, Owen, & McGuffin, 1994; Risch, 1990a, 1990b; Risch & Merikangas, 1996; Vogel & Motulsky, 1997; Weeks & Lathrop, 1995). The more likely model of inheritance includes the effects of multiple loci, with or without contributions from environment factors (Risch, 1990a). It is useful to distinguish *familial (common) environmental effects* from *individual-specific (idiosyncratic) environmental effects.* The latter refer to environmental experiences unique to the individual and not shared among family members; this is also called the within-family environment. The former refer to environmental influences that are common to, or shared by, family members; this is also called the between-family environment.

Genetic influences in multilocus models may arise from the effects of genes of major effect versus genes of minor effect. The former refer to genes that make a large

Table 22.1. Models of familial transmission for complex behavioral traits

Model	Source of Familial Resemblance			
	Genes of Relatively Major Effect (Number)	Genes of Minor Effect	Common Environment	Individual-Specific Environment
Single major locus	Yes (1)	No	No	Yes
Multilocus models				
Multifactorial	No	Yes	Yes	Yes
Mixed	Yes (1)	Yes	Yes	Yes
General multilocus	Yes (>1)	Yes	Yes	Yes

relative contribution to the total variance in the disease attributable to genetic influences; the latter refer to genes that each make a small relative contribution to the total variance attributable to genetic factors. The distinction between genes of major versus minor effect refers exclusively to the relative degree of influence that they have on the final behavioral outcome. Multilocus models may be distinguished in regard to the number (if any) of loci that exert a larger influence on the phenotype, relative to the influence of other genes.

Multifactorial Model

The multifactorial model originally conceptualized by Falconer (1965, 1967, 1989) assumes that all genetic variance is attributable to genes that each exert a small relative effect *(polygenes)*. All relevant genetic and environmental contributions to variation can be combined into a normally distributed continuous variable termed liability. Familial inheritance is modeled through correlations among family members. The multifactorial model assumes that relevant genes act additively and are each of small effect in relation to the total variation, and that environmental contributions are due to many events whose effects are additive. When all transmissible effects are genetic (i.e., common environment exerts no influence), this is the classic polygenic model. Quantitative traits likely inherited in this fashion include intelligence, stature, skin color, total dermal ridge count, and blood pressure. When the observed phenotype is categorical (i.e., presence or absence of disorder), an underlying, unobservable continuous liability distribution is assumed.

Mixed Model

The mixed model is a marriage of the single major locus model and the multifactorial model (Lalouel, Rao, Morton, & Elston, 1983; Morton & MacLean, 1974; Morton, Rao, & Lalouel, 1983). A distribution of liability is determined by the effects of a major locus, a multifactorial transmissible background (polygenes or common environmental factors), and residual individual-specific environmental factors. The mixed model differs from the multifactorial model regarding the presence of a single locus of major effect.

General Multilocus Models

The general multilocus model differs from the mixed model by the specification of more than one locus of relative major effect (Risch, 1990a, 1990b). The major assumption is that the marginal effects of these genes are detectable and separable from the background effects of loci of minor effect or environmental contributors. Complex interactions among loci of major or minor effect *(epistasis)* may occur. The general multilocus model is a comprehensive and realistic transmission model for the familial transmission of most complex traits; the phenotype is likely influenced by major and minor genetic effects and by common environment. When multiple loci of small relative effect influence a phenotype measured on a continuous scale in humans or animals, they are commonly referred to as *quantitative trait loci* (QTLs).

Models of Gene-Environment Interaction

Many complex behavioral traits likely depend on the interaction between genetic and environmental factors. Understanding this interaction is important to accurately determine the familial mode of inheritance (Tiret, Abel, & Rakotovao, 1993) and to estimate gene effects (Eaves, 1984). The two traditional approaches used to examine gene-environment interactions are to stratify pedigrees into groups based on one of the factors (e.g., environmental exposure vs. no exposure) and then analyze the relationship between the gene and the trait in each group; or to directly model gene-environment interactions in segregation analysis (Konigsberg, Blangero, Kammerer, & Mott, 1991; Moldin & Van Eerdewegh, 1995).

BEHAVIORAL GENETIC RESEARCH DESIGNS

To investigate genetic and environmental factors that influence complex traits, several research designs are employed in humans and animals (Table 22.2). These designs help establish the genetic factors involved and ultimately provide approaches from which a specific gene(s) can be identified and studied in the laboratory.

Family Studies

Studying families permits the determination of correlations among relatives on quantitative traits of interest, and the determination of whether behavioral disorders aggregate among relatives. High familial correlations or increased familial aggregation are necessary, but not sufficient, to implicate a genetic mechanism for the complex trait of interest.

For the analysis of behavioral disorders, family studies compare the frequency of the disorder in the relatives of affected index cases, or *probands,* with the frequency in a sample of individuals drawn from the general or control population. An increased frequency of the disorder in the relatives of probands is evidence of the familial aggregation

Table 22.2. Study designs for behavioral genetic research

Study	Unit of Analysis	Goal
Family	Pedigrees	Establish familial resemblance
Twin	Monozygotic and dizygotic twins	Distinguish genetic from environmental effects
Adoption	Adoptees; adoptive and biologic relatives of adoptees	Distinguish genetic from environmental effects
Association	Unrelated affected individuals and controls	Identify a specific gene that confers susceptibility to a behavioral disorder
Discordant sibling	Pairs of sibs sampled on the basis of a high and low quantitative trait value	Establish chromosomal location of a gene
Transgenic	Animals in which selected foreign genetic material has been introduced into gametes (egg and sperm)	Study gene expression and function

of that disorder. Family studies are also useful to establish a familial relationship between the disorder of interest and other behavioral disorders or traits. Such a familial relationship may indirectly implicate genetic factors that the disorders share in common.

A classic family study is the Roscommon Family Study (Kendler et al., 1993a, 1996). The study was formed from the standardized assessment of families containing multiple individuals affected with schizophrenia, and the families were drawn from psychiatric facilities covering over 90% of the population in Ireland and Northern Ireland. Diagnostic, clinical, and other information was gathered from 277 pedigrees containing 1,770 affected and unaffected individuals, as well as relatives of individuals affected with affective disorders and normal controls. Results showed that a significantly greater rate of schizophrenia occurred among the relatives of schizophrenic probands versus the relatives of controls and of probands with affective disorders. In addition, significantly elevated rates of other disorders (poor outcome schizoaffective disorder, schizophreniform disorder, delusional disorder, atypical psychosis, schizotypal personality disorder, paranoid personality disorder, schizoid personality disorder) were found in the families of individuals with schizophrenia (Kendler et al., 1993a, 1993b, 1993c). The presence of a familial relationship between schizophrenia and these disorders may be indicative of a shared familial liability. This information is important for future genetic studies of schizophrenia, in which individuals with these disorders may be considered as having increased genetic liability for schizophrenia.

Twin Studies

A limitation of family studies is that increased resemblance among relatives on a complex trait could be caused by the shared familial environment and not by genetic factors. The twin method has been a popular research design to refute this hypothesis and implicate genetic factors as influencing a complex trait (Bouchard & Propping, 1993; Gottesman, 1997). Classic studies of identical (monozygotic [MZ] or one-egg) and fraternal (dizygotic [DZ] or two-egg) twins reared together test whether or not genes are the cause of the familiality. MZ twins share 100% of their genes, whereas DZ twins on average share 50% of their genes. If shared environment is of primary importance in causing a disorder or trait, all cotwins (regardless of zygosity) would be similar. Because MZ twins have identical genotypes, any dissimilarity between pair members must be due to the action of the prenatal or postnatal environment. Consequently, anything less than 100% concordance among MZ pairs living through the period of risk excludes genetic factors as a sufficient determinant of that trait.

A classic twin study of a behavioral disorder was conducted in Denmark by Bertelsen and colleagues (Bertelsen, Harvald, & Hauge, 1977). A set of twins with manic-depressive illness was identified through the Danish Psychiatric Twin Register and personally interviewed. The MZ concordance rate (67%) was more than three times higher than the corresponding DZ rate (20%), thus implicating genetic factors. The MZ concordance rate less than 100% also showed environmental factors to be of importance. An interesting subsequent finding was that the offspring of the normal MZ cotwins have a risk of affective disorder of 25%, which was very similar to the 21% risk in the offspring of the affected probands (McGuffin, Owen, O'Donovan, Thapar, & Gottesman,

1994). This result suggests that the unaffected MZ cotwins of individuals with a manic-depressive illness have an unexpressed genotype that is passed on to their offspring. The most common explanation of why the discordant twins did not become affected is that they avoided exposure to the environmental factor that their affected cotwins (and affected offspring) unfortunately were not able to avoid.

Critics of the twin method have argued that MZ pairs share more similar environments than DZ pairs, and that this is responsible for the higher MZ concordance rates for behavioral disorders. No conclusive evidence exists that this has substantially or consistently biased the results of twin studies of complex traits (Kendler, 1995).

Adoption Studies

Adoption studies have been conducted to circumvent the potential biases of similar environments in studies of twins reared together. Whereas twin studies endeavor to hold the family environment constant to compare the resemblances between persons with the same and different genotypes, adoption studies permit the comparison of the effects of different types of rearing on groups who are assumed to be similar in their genetic predispositions. Adoption studies attempt to separate the effects of genes and the familial environment by capitalizing on the adoption process, in which children receive their environment and their genes from different sources. The ability to draw inferences from an adoption study is strongest when the adopted children are separated from their biological parents at birth.

A classic adoption study of a behavioral disorder was started in the 1960s by Kety and his colleagues to study schizophrenia in Denmark (Kety, Rosenthal, Wender, & Schulsinger, 1968). The researchers started with a national register of all 14,500 adoptions in Denmark between 1924 and 1927. The results showed that schizophrenia was found exclusively in the biological relatives of adoptees who later developed schizophrenia (Kety, 1987; Kety & Ingraham, 1992; Kety et al., 1968, 1994). In addition, the prevalence of a spectrum of psychopathology, defined as latent schizophrenia in the original studies and as paranoid and schizotypal personality disorders in later work, was greater in the biological relatives of schizophrenic adoptees than in the relatives of control adoptees (Kendler & Gruenberg, 1984; Kety et al., 1994). Major accomplishments of the project have been to rule out an alleged environmental factor (being reared by a schizophrenic parent) as either necessary or sufficient for the development of schizophrenia in the offspring of schizophrenic parents, and to confirm the validity of previous family and twin studies of schizophrenia in implicating the etiological role of genes. The data have held up remarkably well, even after probands and relatives were reclassified with modern diagnostic criteria (Kendler & Gruenberg, 1984; Kendler, Gruenberg, & Strauss, 1981a, 1981b) and after data were analyzed in samples of adoptees from Copenhagen and from the rest of Denmark (Kendler, Gruenberg, & Kinney, 1994; Kety et al., 1994).

Association Studies

One approach to mapping genes for behavioral disorders is to look for statistical associations in the general population between the disorder and a gene. Association analysis implicates a specific gene by assuming a relationship between a disorder and alleles at a specific locus. Population associations can generally arise for three reasons:

1. The implicated locus is itself a disease susceptibility locus; possession of the particular allele associated with the disease is neither necessary not sufficient, but increases the likelihood of becoming ill.

2. A disease locus and the associated marker locus are tightly linked, that is, physically very close to each other. The nonrandom association of alleles at tightly linked loci is commonly called *linkage disequilibrium.* Linkage disequilibrium can persist for many generations as a function of the physical distance between the disease locus and the marker locus.

3. People with the disease and those without may be genetically different subsets of the population which coincidently differ in allele frequencies (population stratification); in this case, the implicated locus is unrelated to the disorder.

Classic disease-marker studies have been conducted by studying a sample of unrelated affected persons and comparing the frequency of a particular marker allele in the affected group with its frequency in a control sample *(population-based case-control study).* Such studies have been difficult to replicate or interpret in the study of behavioral disorders because problems with selections of controls lead to difficulties in distinguishing true linkage disequilibrium from population stratification (Gelernter, Goldman, & Risch, 1993), and inadequate statistical correction for the testing of associations at many loci may have led to an increased Type I error rate. Methods have been developed to largely circumvent the difficulties in finding suitable controls for association studies. *Family-based association studies* use disease and marker data within families (Ewens & Spielman, 1995; Falk & Rubinstein, 1987; Hodge, 1993; Spielman & Ewens, 1996; Spielman, McGinnis, & Ewens, 1993). Comparisons are made by comparing genetic material from a sample of individuals with a behavioral disorder to genetic material obtained from their two parents.

One recent example of an association study of a behavioral disorder involved the use of a family-based association test (Spielman et al., 1993) to identify an association between attention-deficit/hyperactivity disorder (ADHD) and a specific allele at the dopamine transporter gene on chromosome 5 (Cook et al., 1995). A greater frequency of this allele was found in individuals affected with ADHD than in their parents. However, given that the number of other association tests conducted was not specified, the statistical meaning of this result is unclear.

Discordant Sibling Studies

Behavioral genetics is frequently concerned with the study of quantitative traits. In addition, several quantitative traits observed in humans may either directly underlie a behavioral disorder or may function as a risk factor for the disorder. A problem in studying quantitative traits in humans is the low power to detect loci contributing to the trait when unselected samples of subjects are employed. Haseman and Elston's (1972) sibling (sib) pair method is a commonly employed linkage approach that has been extended to pedigree relationships other than sibs (Amos & Elston, 1989). However, for sib pairs selected at random, the power of this approach is low unless the proportion of variance due to a single contributing locus is large (Blackwelder & Elston, 1982). When sib pairs are selected through individuals with extreme values, the power is increased but still remains low under many circumstances (Carey & Williamson, 1991). Sibships where one member has a high and the other a low quantitative trait (*extreme discordant sib pairs,* or EDSPs) have substantial power and may be the design of choice to map QTLs underlying complex traits in humans (Eaves & Meyer, 1994; Gu & Rao, 1997a, 1997b; Risch & Zhang, 1995, 1996). A variant of EDSP sampling has been proposed, in which sibships are sampled if they contained an individual affected with a complex disease and at least one unaffected sib with a score in the lower end of the distribution for a quantitative trait correlated with disease (Moldin, 1997a). Discordant sibling studies of real data have yet to be conducted in which a specific chromosomal region or gene is implicated in the etiology of a behavioral disorder or trait.

Transgenic Studies in Model Organisms

An alternative approach for identifying genes for complex human traits is to first identify such genes from studies of an analogous trait in a model organism, like the mouse or rat, and then to attempt mapping studies in humans by examining chromosomal regions of homology (Risch, Ghosh, & Todd, 1993). Although the genes that influence a given behavior in a model organism may not be the same as those for the human, the genetic model (e.g., number of genes, interaction effects) may be similar between the two species. Most important, genetic dissection of complex behaviors in experimental organisms may provide insights into physiological mechanisms that underlie the human trait. Such insights into pathophysiology would be especially relevant in the study of human behavioral disorders.

The breeding of one genetically distinct strain with another, an *experimental cross,* is a traditional setting for the genetic dissection of complex behaviors in mammals (Silver, 1995). Such experiments recently have led to the chromosomal localization in mice of QTLs influencing contextual fear conditioning (Caldarone et al., 1997; Wehner et al., 1997) and may serve as a model for elucidating genes that regulate individual differences in learning and emotion (LaBar, LeDoux, Spencer, & Phelps, 1995; LeDoux, 1992).

Advances in molecular biology now permit new strategies for identifying QTLs. A foreign gene, or *transgene,* can be inserted and studied in a variety of different cellular environments in a whole animal. Although transgenes often integrate into the host chromosomes without affecting gene expression, sometimes this results in a recognizable phenotype. Molecular technologies have been developed to permit selective modification of a sequence of a predetermined gene. Known as *gene targeting* or *targeted mutagenesis,* this is a powerful methodology that can be used to produce experimental organisms with a mutation in a predetermined gene. The mutation may result in inactivation of gene expression (a *knock-out* mutation). Gene targeting in mice is typically used for producing artificial mouse models of human disease and complex behavior, and provides a powerful general method to study gene function. A recent study employed gene targeting to produce mice deficient for a gene that influences cell development (Lijam et al., 1997) and found that these mice exhibited a variety of behavioral abnormalities, such as reduced social interaction and abnormal sensorimotor gating. Such abnormalities have been observed in human behavioral disorders like schizophrenia, and the investigators proposed that their mice may provide a genetic animal model to understand the homologous human behaviors.

Procedures for gene targeting are complex, labor-intensive, and time-consuming. A new approach, called *random mutagenesis,* has been developed to make alterations randomly throughout the mouse genome and use specific behavioral tests to screen for behavioral abnormalities.

ANALYTIC METHODS

Data collected through the research designs described above typically can be analyzed by using sophisticated mathematical models and high-speed computers. The methods most commonly used in the study of genetic factors are presented in Table 22.3.

Path Analysis

Path analysis is applied to explain the interrelations among variables by analyzing their correlational structure, and to evaluate the relative importance of varying causes that influence a certain variable. The primary application of path analysis in behavioral genetics is to distinguish genetic effects from common environmental effects that contribute to the familial transmission of a complex trait. The path analysis of phenotypic data collected in family, twin, and adoption studies permits estimation of the proportion of variance attributable to genetic differences, or *heritability.* Familial correlations are estimated through *maximum likelihood techniques,* statistical procedures for estimating parameters, such that the best-fitting estimates are those that maximize the probability of the observations. Comparisons of competing models are made by fitting a general model and alternative submodels.

Contemporary path analytic methods for analyzing twin data are implemented through structural equation modeling or linear and logistic regression techniques to

Table 22.3.   Analytic methods of behavioral genetic analysis

Method	Data Source	Goal
Path analysis	Twin, adoption	Distinguish transmissible environment from polygenes
Segregation analysis	Pedigree	Distinguish a major locus from polygenes or transmissible environment
Linkage analysis	Pedigree	Establish chromosomal localization of a locus
Association analysis	Unrelated affecteds, controls	Implicate a specific gene as a disease susceptibility locus, given linkage disequilibrium

estimate and evaluate the significance of genetic and environmental contributions to the variance of a complex trait (DeFries & Fulker, 1985; Neale & Cardon, 1992; Sham et al., 1994). Several standard computer packages, such as LISREL (Joreskog & Sorbom, 1989) and MX (Neale, 1994), can be used to apply structural equation models to variance-covariance matrices derived from twin data. These methods are particularly suited to the analysis of quantitative traits and can be extended to dichotomous and ordinal twin data (Ramakrishnan, Meyer, Goldberg, & Henderson, 1996). A classic application of path analysis to the study of a behavioral disorder was presented by McGue and colleagues (McGue, Gottesman, & Rao, 1983, 1985, 1986). The analysis of pooled twin and family data from multiple Western European studies resulted in a heritiability estimate for schizophrenia of over 80%; idiosyncratic environmental factors were nongenetic contributors.

Segregation Analysis

Segregation analysis is applied to resolve a single major locus effect and is conducted by collecting phenotypic information from families. The primary goal is to statistically assess evidence for the segregation of a major gene in the presence of other sources of familial resemblance. A variety of sophisticated computer programs implement segregation analysis and permit the testing of multifactorial versus single locus models (Hasstedt, 1989; Morton & MacLean, 1974; "Statistical Analysis for Genetic Epidemiology" [SAGE], 1994). Unfortunately, segregation analyses have not been unambiguously successful in resolving single effects in the genetic analysis of behavioral traits or disorders.

Linkage Analysis

Linkage analysis is a statistical procedure by which pedigree data are examined to determine whether a complex trait is cosegregating with a genetic marker of known chromosomal location. Linkage analysis allows an investigator to infer that two loci (a genetic marker locus and a putative locus influencing a complex trait) are located close enough together on the same chromosome that their alleles tend to be transmitted together from parent to child more frequently than would occur by random assortment. The demonstration of linkage between a putative complex trait locus and one or more genetic markers thus determines on which chromosomal region that putative complex trait locus lies. Chromosomal localization through linkage analysis is the first essential step in the process of identifying, isolating, and cloning a specific gene. Linkage analyses are conducted by collecting from probands and their relatives phenotypic information (e.g., the presence or absence of a behavioral disorder) and blood samples. The latter are used to determine genotypic information, that is, which alleles occur at multiple genetic markers. The most informative families for linkage typically are those in which there are multiple affected individuals.

When two loci are together through families by virtue of the physical distance between them, alleles at these different loci appear to be genetically coupled. That is called *genetic linkage*. Two analytical strategies are used to search for genetic linkage to complex traits: parametric maximum likelihood methods, as applied to small or extended pedigrees, and nonparametric methods, as applied to study allele sharing among sib or other relative pairs. Numerous linkage studies of complex traits have been published, but unambiguous identification and replication of a chromosomal region of interest has not been forthcoming (Moldin, 1997b; Risch & Botstein, 1996).

Parametric Methods

These methods permit calculation of the recombination fraction, which is the probability that a *haplotype,* a specific combination of linked alleles, inherited from a parent represents a *recombinant event* (i.e., recombination between two genes means that two different grandparents each contributed one allele at each of the two genes to the haplotype). Because recombination events can be recognized only on the basis of haplotypes passed from parents to children, linkage analysis requires phenotypic observations on pedigree members.

Estimating the recombination fraction is carried out by using the method of maximum likelihood, which also permits calculation of a *lod score* (Morton, 1955). The lod score serves as a statistical measure of the weight of the data in favor of the hypothesis of linkage. A critical value of 3 is generally adhered to as the criterion for significant evidence for linkage of autosomal loci to Mendelian diseases with unambiguously determined phenotypes and established modes of transmission (Ott, 1991). The one-sided Type I error rate associated with this value is 0.0001 when the recombination fraction is the only estimated parameter (i.e., the mode of transmission is known) and when the linkage test is conducted in large samples at a single marker. Appropriate lod score criteria for the analysis of complex traits in which linkage results are evaluated using multiple markers that span the entire genome are described below.

The major difficulty with traditional lod score methods is computational. To extract the full information in a pedigree, a dense set of genetic markers is required. Such *multipoint analyses* are infeasible for more than a handful of loci because of the inherent constraints of the mathematical approach used to calculate the likelihood of a set of pedigree data (Elston & Stewart, 1971). The problem has been circumvented for certain pedigree structures (Kruglyak & Lander, 1995b; Lander & Green, 1987; Lathrop, Lalouel, & White, 1986), and recent work promises to make multipoint analysis with a limited number of loci more rapid and practical (O'Connell & Weeks, 1995).

Allele-Sharing Methods

In the analysis of behavioral disorders, it is assumed that a locus conferring susceptibility can be identified given that a pair of affected relatives—typically a sib pair *(affected sib pair)*—will tend to inherit the same allele more often than expected under random Mendelian assortment. Each pair shares either 2, 1, or 0 alleles identical by descent (IBD) at a given locus (i.e., the allele is actually inherited from a common ancestor), and the *allele-sharing proportion* is defined as the proportion of affected relative pairs that share a single allele IBD at that locus.

Tracing the inheritance pattern in the affected sib pair method uses perturbations in the distribution of IBD scores at a marker locus to detect the presence of a linked locus. In the absence of linkage, the probability that two siblings share neither, one, or both marker haplotypes IBD is independent of their disease phenotypes, and the allele-sharing proportion for sib pairs is 50%. When a disease locus is linked to a marker locus and pairs of affected sibs are studied, there is a perturbation in the IBD score distribution at that marker locus such that the allele-sharing proportion is greater than 50%. Allele-sharing methods may also be applied in the linkage analysis of quantitative traits (Amos & Elston, 1989; Haseman & Elston, 1972; Sage, 1994).

The specific advantages of affected sib pair methods in the study of behavioral disorders are the following: (a) specification of complex, non-Mendelian modes of transmission, which is necessary in parametric analysis, is not required; (b) the practice of testing for linkage under several transmission models, which necessitates some downward correction to the linkage statistic to prevent inflation in the Type I error rate for testing across multiple disease transmission models (Risch, 1991), is unnecessary; and (c) large, multigenerational families with many affected members, which are typically difficult to locate and study, are not required.

Association Analysis

Parametric and allele-sharing linkage methods may require very large sample sizes to detect the modest gene effects most likely operative in most complex behavioral disorders. In addition, isolation of a specific gene knowing only its subchromosomal location *(positional cloning)* depends on high-resolution mapping of the chromosomal regions detected through linkage analysis. With current technologies, a gene must be localized to a region of about 1 million base pairs before it is practical to identify it. Given the magnitude of the genetic effects found in behavioral disorders, localization to regions of this size may require over 1,000 affected sib pairs (Kruglyak & Lander, 1995a).

The initial detection and positional cloning of genes of modest effect may occur through association analysis. Falk and Rubinstein (1987) proposed the haplotype relative risk method as a family-based test of association. The control sample is the alleles at different loci received from one parent not present in the affected person, which represents a random sample of haplotype pairs from the same genetic population. Spielman and colleagues (Spielman & Ewens, 1996, 1998; Spielman et al., 1993) developed a related method—the transmission/disequilibrium test—as a test for linkage between a complex disease and a marker given an established disease-marker association (linkage disequilibrium). The transmission/disequilibrium test employs the alleles not transmitted by parents to an affected offspring as the controls. Thus, DNA needs to be collected from unrelated affected subjects and their two biological parents. A simple 2 x 2 contingency table can be constructed given a marker with two alleles.

Statistical Criteria for Declaring Linkage in Behavioral Genetics

It is crucial in the genetic investigation of complex traits that a sufficiently stringent standard is adopted for the declaration of linkage to maintain a high likelihood that the assertion will be true and stand the test of time. As discussed above, the lod score criterion for declaring a linkage is 3 in the study of classical Mendelian diseases with known modes of familial transmission.

Ever-evolving genetic methods and technologies now permit systematic screening of the entire human genome. The increased number of markers being tested inflate the

Table 22.4.   Criteria for evaluating reports of linkage to complex behavioral traits

Linkage Method	Nominal P Value	Genome-Wide P Value	Number of Random Occurrences per Genome Scan	Equivalent Lod Score	Decision Classification
Lod score analysis	1.70×10^{-3}	0.632	1.000	1.86	Suggestive
	4.88×10^{-5}	0.049	0.050	3.30	Significant
	6.37×10^{-7}	0.001	0.001	5.10	Highly significant
Allele-sharing methods	7.36×10^{-4}	0.632	1.000	2.20	Suggestive
	2.25×10^{-5}	0.049	0.050	3.61	Significant
	3.02×10^{-7}	0.001	0.001	5.41	Highly significant

Note: Lod score analysis refers to methods in which lod scores are determined in whole pedigrees; allele-sharing methods refer to the analysis of pairs of relatives (thresholds shown are for sibling pairs); an "equivalent" lod score associated with the comparable nominal and genome-wide P value is also shown.
Source: Adapted from Lander & Kruglyak, 1995.

Type I error rate. Lander and Kruglyak (1995) proposed a set of guidelines for interpreting linkage results of complex traits. They distinguish the *nominal* significance level, which is the probability of encountering a linkage statistic of a given magnitude at one specific locus, from the *genome-wide* significance level, which is the probability that one would encounter such a deviation somewhere in a whole-genome scan. A given linkage statistic like a lod score has a corresponding nominal P value and a genome-wide P value.

Lander and Kruglyak (1995) further proposed that genome-wide P values be interpreted to evaluate the magnitude of linkage evidence and classify it as "suggestive," "significant," or "highly significant." Suggestive linkage reports will often reflect chance findings and will often be wrong, but are worth reporting as tentative findings. Table 22.4 shows equivalent lod score values and associated nominal and genome-wide P values for these categories. A more stringent lod score criterion (3.3 for lod score methods; 3.6 for allele-sharing methods) than the traditional value of 3 is required to claim significant linkage evidence in the analysis of behavioral disorders and other complex traits. Linkage confirmation requires a two-step process: significant linkage evidence is found in at least one study, and evidence of linkage to the same region is obtained by an independent investigator in an new, independent sample.

NEW MOLECULAR AND STATISTICAL TOOLS

The next paradigmatic advance in genetic analysis is currently occurring and involves the marriage between methods routinely used in the semiconductor industry and in the standard chemical synthesis of oligonucleotides. High-density silicon DNA arrays, or *DNA microchips,* the size of a thumbnail are the result (Chee et al., 1996; Fodor, 1997; Lockhart et al., 1996). Potentially hundreds of thousands of oligonucleotides can be synthesized on a single chip. This technology will revolutionize genotyping, DNA sequencing, and mutation analysis as applied to the genetic analysis of complex behavioral traits and will permit a full understanding of subtleties in the expression, function, and regulation of all human genes under various conditions. The utility of DNA microchip arrays in screening individuals for mutations and in studying expression patterns in breast cancer has been demonstrated (DeRisi et al., 1996; Hacia, Brody, Chee, Fodor, & Collins, 1996).

Single nucleotide polymorphisms, or SNPs, are strips of DNA that vary at a single base pair. SNPs are the most common DNA sequence variations found in the human genome (Collins, Guyer, & Chakravarti, 1997; Lander, 1996; Risch and Merikangas, 1996), and will form the basis of a new map of genetic markers currently being developed for extensive use in future genetic analyses (Wang et al., 1996, 1998). A dense panel of SNPs from such a map can be used to identify associations and narrow chromosomal regions across the genome that may contain a locus influencing susceptibility to a behavioral disorder.

A variety of new statistical methods has been developed for application in behavioral genetics. The intense computations required when calculating multipoint likelihoods in parametric linkage analysis may be lessened through the use of new mathematical techniques (Guo & Thompson, 1992; Thompson, 1994a, 1994b). New allele-sharing linkage techniques have been developed to rapidly extract inheritance information provided by many genetic markers and to permit estimation of gene location in small families, for continuous (Kruglyak & Lander, 1995b) or qualitative (Hauser, Boehnke, Guo, & Risch, 1996; Risch, 1993) traits, and in pedigrees of arbitrary size (Kruglyak, Daly, Reeve-Daly, & Lander, 1996). Other new allele-sharing linkage methods have been developed to permit estimation of the variance contributed by each of multiple loci (Almasy & Blangero, 1998). New path analytic approaches for analyzing categorical variables have been proposed (Ramakrishnan et al., 1996; Sham et al., 1994). Recent extensions of family-based association analysis permit analyses of multiallelic markers (Cleves, Olson, & Jacobs, 1997) and also consideration of marker data from unaffected sibs instead of parents (Spielman & Ewens, 1998). Full genomic screens of SNPs via family-based association methods have been advocated, with the intriguing possibility presented of eventually testing all human genes for disease associations (Risch & Merikangas, 1996).

Table 22.5 lists a variety of World Wide Web resources related to new advances in quantitative genetics, molecular genetics, and behavioral genetics, which expand upon the information provided in this chapter.

CONCLUSION

Complex human behaviors and behavioral disorders are undoubtedly influenced by the interaction among multiple genes and environmental factors. Behavioral genetics may incorporate a variety of state-of-the-art statistical tools and molecular technologies that have tremendous potential for the genetic dissection of these complex traits. Gene discovery will lead to renewed avenues of research to explore the effects of the environment and gene-environment interactions on developing genotypes. This will have profound implications for understanding the genetic basis of behavioral disorders, which are then expected to revolutionize diagnosis, treatment, and prevention.

Table 22.5.   Scientific resources related to behavioral genetics on the World Wide Web

Electronic Address	Description
http://genetics.nature.com	*Nature Genetics*
http://www.faseb.org/genetics/ashg/ jou-ashg.htm	*American Journal of Human Genetics*
http://www.faseb.org/genetics/ashg/ ashgmenu.htm	American Society of Human Genetics
http://www.bga.org	Behavior Genetics Association
http://darwin.cwru.edu/iges.html	International Genetic Epidemiology Society
http://biology.ncsa.uiuc.edu/	NCSA Biology Workbench
http://www.sph.umich.edu/group/statgen/	Statistical genetics at the University of Michigan
http://www.sfbr.org/online/departments/ genetics/population.html	SFBR Population Genetics Laboratory
http://lotka.stanford.edu	Stanford University Human Population Genetics Laboratory
http://www.mc.duke.edu/depts/genetics/course	Genetic analysis methods course at Duke University
http://www.hgmp.mrc.ac.uk/Public/human-gen-db.html	Human genome databases
http://www.ornl.gov/TechResources/Human_ Genome/home.html	Human Genome Project
http://linkage.rockefeller.edu/soft/list.html	Linkage analysis software
http://nitro.biosci.arizona.edu/zbook/book.html	*Fundamentals of Quantitative Genetics*
http://www3.ncbi.nlm.nih.gov/omim	*Online Mendelian Inheritance in Man*
http://www-grb.nimh.nih.gov	Genetics Research Branch at the NIMH

REFERENCES

Almasy, L., & Blangero, J. (1998). Multipoint quantitative-trait linkage analysis in general pedigrees. *American Journal of Human Genetics, 62,* 1198–1211.

Amos, C. I., & Elston, R. C. (1989). Robust methods for the detection of genetic linkage for quantitative data from pedigrees. *Genetic Epidemiology, 6,* 349–360.

Bertelsen, A., Harvald, B., & Hauge, M. A. (1977). A Danish twin study of manic-depressive disorders. *British Journal of Psychiatry, 130,* 330–351.

Blackwelder, W. C., & Elston, R. C. (1982). Power and robustness of sib-pair linkage tests and extension to larger sibships. *Common Statistical Theory and Methods, 11,* 449–484.

Botstein, D., White, R. L., Skolnick, M. H., & Davies, R. W. (1980). Construction of a genetic linkage map in man using restriction fragment length polymorphisms. *American Journal of Human Genetics, 32,* 314–331.

Bouchard, T. J., & Propping, P. (1993). *Twins as a tool of behavioral genetics.* Chichester, England: Wiley.

Caldarone, B., Saavedra, C., Tartaglia, K., Wehner, J. M., Dudek, B. C., & Flaherty, L. (1997). Quantitative trait loci analysis affecting contextual conditioning in mice. *Nature Genetics, 17,* 335–337.

Carey, G., & Williamson, J. (1991). Linkage analysis of quantitative traits: Increased power by using selected samples. *American Journal of Human Genetics, 49,* 786–796.

Chee, M., Yang, R., Hubbell, E., Berno, A., Huang, X. C., Stern, D., Winkler, J., Lockhart, D. J., Morris, M. S., & Fodor, S. P. A. (1996). Accessing genetic information with high-density DNA arrays. *Science, 274,* 610–614.

Cleves, M. A., Olson, J. M., & Jacobs, K. B. (1997). Exact transmission-disequilibrium tests with multiallelic markers. *Genetic Epidemiology, 14,* 337–347.

Collins, F. S., Guyer, M. S., & Chakravarti, A. (1997). Variations on a theme: Cataloging human DNA sequence variation. *Science, 278,* 1580–1581.

Cook, E. H., Stein, M. A., Krasowski, M. D., Cox, N. J., Olkon, D. M., Kieffer, J. E., & Leventhal, B. L. (1995). Association of attention-deficit disorder and the dopamine transporter gene. *American Journal of Human Genetics, 56,* 993–998.

DeFries, J. C., & Fulker, D. W. (1985). Multiple regression analysis of twin data. *Behavior Genetics, 15,* 467–473.

DeRisi, J., Penland, L., Brown, P. O., Bittner, M. L., Meltzer, P. S., Ray, M., Chen, Y., Su, Y. A., & Trent, J. M. (1996). Use of a DNA microarray to analyze gene expression patterns in human cancer. *Nature Genetics, 14,* 457–460.

Eaves, L., & Meyer, J. (1994). Locating human quantitative trait loci: Guidelines for the selection of sibling pairs for genotyping. *Behavior Genetics, 24,* 443–455.

Eaves, L. J. (1984). The resolution of genotype x environment interaction in segregation analysis of nuclear families. *Genetic Epidemiology, 1,* 215–228.

Elston, R. C., & Stewart, J. (1971). A general model for the analysis of pedigree data. *Human Heredity, 21,* 523–542.

Ewens, W. J., & Spielman, R. S. (1995). The transmission/disequilibrium test: History, subdivision, and admixture. *American Journal of Human Genetics, 57,* 455–464.

Falconer, D. S. (1965). The inheritance of liability to certain diseases, estimated from the incidence among relatives. *Annals of Human Genetics, 29,* 51–76.

Falconer, D. S. (1967). The inheritance of liability to certain diseases with variable age of onset, with particular reference to diabetes mellitus. *Annals of Human Genetics, 31,* 1–20.

Falconer, D. S. (1989). *Introduction to quantitative genetics* (3rd ed.). New York: Wiley.

Falk, C. T., & Rubinstein, P. (1987). Haplotype relative risks: An easy reliable way to construct a proper control sample for risk calculations. *Annals of Human Genetics, 51,* 227–233.

Fields, C., Adams, M. D., White, O., & Venter, J. C. (1994). How many genes in the human genome? *Nature Genetics, 7,* 345–346.

Fodor, S. P. A. (1997). Massively parallel genomics. *Science, 277,* 393–395.

Galton, F. (1865). Hereditary talent and character. *McMillan's Magazine, 12,* 157.

Gelernter, J., Goldman, D., & Risch, N. J. (1993). The A1 allele at the D_2 dopamine receptor gene and alcoholism: A reappraisal. *Journal of the American Medical Association, 269,* 1673–1677.

Gottesman, I. I. (1994). Complications to the complex inheritance of schizophrenia. *Clinical Genetics, 46,* 116–123.

Gottesman, I. I. (1997). Twins: En route to QTLs for cognition. *Science, 276,* 1522–1523.

Gu, C., & Rao, D. C. (1997a). A linkage strategy for detection of human quantitative-trait loci: I. Generalized relative risk ratios and power of sib pairs with extreme trait values. *American Journal of Human Genetics, 61,* 200–210.

Gu, C., & Rao, D. C. (1997b). A linkage strategy for detection of human quantitative-trait loci: II. Optimization of study designs based on extreme sib pairs and generalized relative risk ratios. *American Journal of Human Genetics, 61,* 211–222.

Guo, S.-W., & Thompson, E. A. (1992). A Monte Carlo method for combined segregation and linkage analysis. *American Journal of Human Genetics, 51,* 1111–1126.

Hacia, J. G., Brody, L. C., Chee, M. S., Fodor, S. P. A., & Collins, F. S. (1996). Detection of heterozygous mutations in *BRCA1* using high density oligonucleotide arrays and two-color fluorescence analysis. *Nature Genetics, 14,* 441–447.

Haseman, J. K., & Elston, R. C. (1972). The investigation of linkage between a quantitative trait and a marker locus. *Behavior Genetics, 2,* 3–19.

Hasstedt, S. J. (1989). *PAP—Pedigree analysis package, revision 3.0.* Salt Lake City: University of Utah Med Center/Department of Human Genetics.

Hauser, E. R., Boehnke, M., Guo, S.-W., & Risch, N. J. (1996). Affected-sib-pair interval mapping and exclusion for complex genetic traits: Sampling considerations. *Genetic Epidemiology, 13,* 117–137.

Hodge, S. E. (1993). Linkage analysis versus association analysis: Distinguishing between two models that explain disease-marker associations. *American Journal of Human Genetics, 53,* 367–384.

Joreskog, K. G., & Sorbom, D. (1989). *LISREL 7. A guide to the program and applications* (2nd ed.). Chicago: SPSS.

Kendler, K. S. (1995). Genetic epidemiology in psychiatry: Taking both genes and environment seriously. *Archives of General Psychiatry, 52,* 895–899.

Kendler, K. S., & Gruenberg, A. M. (1984). An independent analysis of the Danish adoption study of schizophrenia: VI. The relationship between psychiatric disorders as defined by *DSM-III* in the relatives and adoptees. *Archives of General Psychiatry, 41,* 555–564.

Kendler, K. S., Gruenberg, A. M., & Kinney, D. K. (1994). Independent diagnoses of adoptees and relatives as defined by *DSM-III* in the provincial and national samples of the Danish adoption study of schizophrenia. *Archives of General Psychiatry, 51,* 456–468.

Kendler, K. S., Gruenberg, A. M., & Strauss, J. S. (1981a). An independent analysis of the Copenhagen sample of the Danish adoption study of schizophrenia: II. The relationship between schizotypal personality disorder and schizophrenia. *Archives of General Psychiatry, 38,* 982–984.

Kendler, K. S., Gruenberg, A. M., & Strauss, J. S. (1981b). An independent analysis of the Copenhagen sample of the Danish adoption study of schizophrenia: III. The relationship between paranoid psychosis (delusional disorder) and the schizophrenia spectrum disorders. *Archives of General Psychiatry, 38,* 985–987.

Kendler, K. S., McGuire, M., Gruenberg, A., O'Hare, A., Spellman, M., & Walsh, D. (1993a). The Roscommon family study: I. Methods, diagnosis of probands, and risk of schizophrenia in relatives. *Archives of General Psychiatry, 50,* 527–540.

Kendler, K. S., McGuire, M., Gruenberg, A., Spellman, M., O'Hare, A., & Walsh, D. (1993b). The Roscommon family study: II. The risk of nonschizophrenic nonaffective psychoses in relatives. *Archives of General Psychiatry, 50,* 645–652.

Kendler, K. S., McGuire, M., Gruenberg, A., O'Hare, A., Spellman, M., & Walsh, D. (1993c). The Roscommon family study: III. Schizophrenia-related personality disorders in relatives. *Archives of General Psychiatry, 50,* 781–788.

Kendler, K. S., O'Neill, F. A., Burke, J., Murphy, B., Duke, F., Straub, R. E., Shinkwin, R., Ni Nuallain, M., MacLean, C. J., & Walsh, D. (1996). Irish study of high-density schizophrenia families: Field methods and power to detect linkage. *American Journal of Medical Genetics, 67,* 179–190.

Kety, S. S. (1987). The significance of genetic factors in the etiology of schizophrenia: Results from the National Study of Adoptees in Denmark. *Journal of Psychiatric Research, 21,* 423–429.

Kety, S. S., & Ingraham, L. J. (1992). Genetic transmission and improved diagnosis of schizophrenia from pedigrees of adoptees. *Journal of Psychiatric Research, 26,* 247–255.

Kety, S. S., Rosenthal, D., Wender, P. H., & Schulsinger, F. (1968). The types of prevalence of mental illness in the biological and adoptive families of adopted schizophrenics. In

D. Rosenthal & S. S. Kety (Eds.), *The transmission of schizophrenia* (pp. 345–362). Oxford, England: Pergamon Press.

Kety, S. S., Wender, P. H., Jacobsen, B., Ingraham, L. J., Jansson, L., Faber, B., & Kinney, D. K. (1994). Mental illness in the biological and adoptive relatives of schizophrenic adoptees. Replication of the Copenhagen study in the rest of Denmark. *Archives of General Psychiatry, 51,* 442–455.

Konigsberg, L. W., Blangero, J., Kammerer, C. M., & Mott, G. E. (1991). Mixed model segregation analysis of LDL-C concentration with genotype-covariate interaction. *Genetic Epidemiology, 8,* 69–80.

Kruglyak, L., Daly, M. J., Reeve-Daly, M. P., & Lander, E. S. (1996). Parametric and nonparametric linkage analysis: A unified multipoint approach. *American Journal of Human Genetics, 58,* 1347–1363.

Kruglyak, L., & Lander, E. S. (1995a). Complete multipoint sib-pair analysis of qualitative and quantitative traits. *American Journal of Human Genetics, 57,* 439–454.

Kruglyak, L., & Lander, E. S. (1995b). High-resolution genetic mapping of complex traits. *American Journal of Human Genetics, 56,* 1212–1223.

LaBar, K. S., LeDoux, J. E., Spencer, D., & Phelps, E. A. (1995). Impaired fear conditioning follows unilateral temporal lobectomy in humans. *Journal of Neuroscience, 15,* 6846–6855.

Lalouel, J. M., Rao, D. C., Morton, N. E., & Elston, R. C. (1983). A unified model for complex segregation analysis. *American Journal of Human Genetics, 35,* 816–826.

Lander, E. S. (1996). The new genomics: Global views of biology. *Science, 274,* 536–539.

Lander, E. S., & Green, P. (1987). Construction of multilocus genetic maps in humans. *Proceedings of the National Academy of Sciences of the USA, 84,* 2363–2367.

Lander, E. S., & Kruglyak, L. (1995). Genetic dissection of complex traits: Guidelines for interpreting and reporting linkage results. *Nature Genetics, 11,* 241–247.

Lander, E. S., & Schork, N. J. (1994). Genetic dissection of complex traits. *Science, 265,* 2037–2048.

Lathrop, G. M., Lalouel, J. M., & White, R. L. (1986). Construction of human linkage maps: Likelihood calculations for multipoint analysis. *Biometrics, 3,* 39–52.

LeDoux, J. E. (1992). Brain mechanisms of emotion and emotional learning. *Current Opinions in Neurobiology, 2,* 191–197.

Lijam, N., Paylor, R., McDonald, M. P., Crawley, J. N., Deng, C.-X., Herrup, K., Stevens, K. E., Maccaferri, G., McBain, C. J., Sussman, D. J., & Wynshaw-Boris, A. (1997). Social interaction and sensorimotor gating abnormalities in mice lacking *Dvl1. Cell, 90,* 895–905.

Lockhart, D. J., Dong, H., Byrne, M. C., Follettie, M. T., Gallo, M. V., Chee, M. S., Mittmann, M., Wang, C., Kobayashi, M., Horton, H., & Brown, E. L. (1996). Expression monitoring by hybridization to high-density oligonucleotide arrays. *Nature Biotechnology, 14,* 1675–1680.

McGue, M., Gottesman, I. I., & Rao, D. C. (1983). The transmission of schizophrenia under a multifactorial threshold model. *American Journal of Human Genetics, 35,* 1161–1178.

McGue, M., Gottesman, I. I., & Rao, D. C. (1985). Resolving genetic models for the transmission of schizophrenia. *Genetic Epidemiology, 2,* 99–110.

McGue, M., Gottesman, I. I., & Rao, D. C. (1986). The analysis of schizophrenia family data. *Behavior Genetics, 16,* 75–87.

McGuffin, P., Owen, M. J., O'Donovan, M. C., Thapar, A., & Gottesman, I. I. (1994). *Seminars in psychiatric genetics.* London, England: Royal College of Psychiatrists.

Mendel, G. (1865). Experiments in plant hybridization. In A. J. Peters (Ed.), *Classical papers in genetics.* Englewood Cliffs, NJ: Prentice-Hall.

Moldin, S. O. (1997a). Detection and replication of linkage to a complex human disease. *Genetic Epidemiology, 14,* 1023–1028.

Moldin, S. O. (1997b). The maddening hunt for madness genes. *Nature Genetics, 17,* 127–129.

Moldin, S. O., & Gottesman, I. I. (1997). Genes, experience, and chance in schizophrenia: Positioning for the 21st century. *Schizophrenia Bulletin, 23,* 547–561.

Moldin, S. O., & Van Eerdewegh, P. (1995). Multivariate genetic analysis of oligogenic disease. *Genetic Epidemiology, 12,* 801–806.

Morton, N. E. (1955). Sequential tests for the detection of linkage. *American Journal of Human Genetics, 7,* 277–318.

Morton, N. E., & MacLean, C. J. (1974). Analysis of family resemblance: III. Complex segregation of quantitative traits. *American Journal of Human Genetics, 26,* 489–503.

Morton, N. E., Rao, D. C., & Lalouel, J. M. (1983). *Methods in genetic epidemiology.* New York: Karger.

Neale, M. C. (1994). *MX: Statistical modeling.* Richmond: Department of Psychiatry, Medical College of Virginia/Virginia Commonwealth University.

Neale, M. C., & Cardon, L. R. (1992). *Methodology for genetic studies of twins and families.* Norwell: Kluwer Academic.

O'Connell, J. R., & Weeks, D. E. (1995). The VITESSE algorithm for rapid exact multilocus linkage via genotype set-recoding and fuzzy inheritance. *Nature Genetics, 11,* 402–408.

Ott, J. (1991). *Analysis of human genetic linkage* (Rev. ed.). Baltimore: John Hopkins University.

Plomin, R., Owen, M. J., & McGuffin, P. (1994). The genetic basis of complex human behaviors. *Science, 264,* 1733–1739.

Ramakrishnan, V., Meyer, J. M., Goldberg, J., & Henderson, W. G. (1996). Univariate analysis of dichotomous or ordinal data from twin pairs: A simulation study comparing structural equation modeling and logistic regression. *Genetic Epidemiology, 13,* 79–90.

Risch, N., & Botstein, D. (1996). A manic depressive history. *Nature Genetics, 12,* 351–353.

Risch, N. J. (1990a). Genetic linkage and complex diseases, with special reference to psychiatric disorders. *Genetic Epidemiology, 7,* 3–16.

Risch, N. J. (1990b). Linkage strategies for genetically complex traits: I. Multilocus models. *American Journal of Human Genetics, 46,* 222–228.

Risch, N. J. (1991). A note on multiple testing procedures in linkage analysis. *American Journal of Human Genetics, 48,* 1058–1064.

Risch, N. J. (1993). Exclusion mapping for complex diseases. *American Journal of Human Genetics, 53,* A185.

Risch, N. J., Ghosh, S., & Todd, J. A. (1993). Statistical evaluation of multiple-locus linkage data in experimental species and its relevance to human studies: Application to nonobese diabetic (NOD) mouse and human insulin-dependent diabetes mellitus (IDDM). *American Journal of Human Genetics, 53,* 702–714.

Risch, N. J., & Merikangas, K. (1996). The future of genetic studies of complex human diseases. *Science, 273,* 1516–1517.

Risch, N. J., & Zhang, H. (1995). Extreme discordant sib pairs for mapping quantitative trait loci in humans. *Science, 268,* 1584–1589.

Risch, N. J., & Zhang, H. (1996). Mapping quantitative trait loci with extreme discordant sib pairs: Sampling considerations. *American Journal of Human Genetics, 58,* 836–843.

Rowen, L., Mahairas, G., & Hood, L. (1997). Sequencing the human genome. *Science, 278,* 605–607.

SAGE. (1994). *Statistical analysis for genetic epidemiology.* Cleveland, OH: Department of Epidemiology and Biostatistics, Case Western University.

Schuler, G. D., Boguski, M. S., Stewart, E. A., Stein, L. D., Gyapay, G., Rice, K., White, R. E., Rodriguez-Tome, P., Aggarwal, A., Bajorek, E., Bentolila, S., Birren, B. B., Butler, A., Castle, A. B., Chiannilkulchai, N., Chu, A., Clee, C., Cowles, S., Day, P. J. R., Dibling, T., Drouot, N., Dunham, I., Duprat, S., East, C., Edwards, C., Fan, J.-B., Fang, N., Fizames, C., Garrett, C., Green, L., Hadley, D., Harris, M., Harrison, P., Brady, S., Hicks, A., Holloway, E., Hui, L., Hussain, S., Louis-Dit-Sully, C., Ma, J., MacGilvery,

A., Mader, I., Maratukulam, A., Matise, T. C., McKusick, K. B., Morissette, J., Mungall, A., Muselet, D., Nusbaum, H. C., Page, D. C., Peck, A., Perkins, S., Piercy, M., Qin, F., Quackenbush, J., Ranby, S., Reif, T., Rozen, S., Sanders, C., She, X., Silva, J., Slonim, D. K., Soderland, C., Sun, W.-L., Tabar, P., Thangarajah, T., Vega-Czarny, N., Vollrath, D., Voyticky, S., Wilmer, T., Wu, X., Adams, M. D., Auffray, C., Walter, N. A. R., Brandon, R., Dehejia, A., Goodfellow, P. N., Houlgatte, R., Hudson, J. R., Ide, S. E., Iorio, K. R., Lee, W. Y., Seki, N., Nagase, T., Ishikawa, K., Nomura, N., Phillips, C., Polymeropoulos, M. H., Sandusky, M., Schmitt, K., Berry, R., Swanson, K., Torres, R., Venter, J. C., Sikela, J. M., Beckmann, J. S., Weissenbach, J., Myers, R. M., Cox, D. R., James, M. R., Bentley, D., Deloukas, P., Lander, E. S., & Hudson, T. J. (1996). A gene map of the human genome. *Science, 274,* 540–546.

Sham, P. C., Walters, E. E., Neale, M. C., Heath, A. C., MacLean, C. J., & Kendler, K. S. (1994). Logistic regression analysis of twin data: Estimation of parameters of the multifactorial liability-threshold model. *Behavior Genetics, 24,* 229–238.

Silver, L. M. (1995). *Mouse genetics: Concepts and applications.* New York: Oxford University Press.

Southern, E. M. (1975). Detection of specific sequences among DNA fragments separated by gel electrophoresis. *Journal of Molecular Biology, 98,* 503–517.

Spielman, R. S., & Ewens, W. J. (1996). The TDT and other family-based tests for linkage disequilibrium and association. *American Journal of Human Genetics, 59,* 983–989.

Spielman, R. S., & Ewens, W. J. (1998). A sibship test for linkage in the presence of association: The sib transmission/disequilbrium test. *American Journal of Human Genetics, 62,* 450–458.

Spielman, R. S., McGinnis, R. E., & Ewens, W. J. (1993). Transmission test for linkage disequilibrium: The insulin gene region and insulin-dependent diabetes mellitus (IDDM). *American Journal of Human Genetics, 52,* 506–516.

Thompson, E. A. (1994a). Monte Carlo likelihood in the genetic mapping of complex traits. *Philosophical Transactions of the Royal Society of London, Series B, 344,* 345–351.

Thompson, E. A. (1994b). Monte Carlo likelihood in genetic mapping. *Statistics in Science, 9,* 355–366.

Tiret, L., Abel, L., & Rakotovao, R. (1993). Effect of ignoring genotype-environment interaction on segregation analysis of quantitative traits. *Genetic Epidemiology, 10,* 581–586.

Vogel, F., & Motulsky, A. G. (1997). *Human genetics: Problems and approaches.* New York: Springer-Verlag.

Wade, N. (1998, May 10). Scientist's plan: Map all DNA within three years. *New York Times,* pp. 1, 20.

Wang, D., Sapolsky, R., Spencer, J., Rioux, J., Kruglyak, L., Hubbell, E., Ghandour, G., Hawkins, T., Hudson, T., Lipshutz, R., & Lander, E. S. (1996). Toward a third generation genetic map of the human genome based on bi-allelic polymorphisms. *American Journal of Human Genetics, 59,* A3.

Wang, D., Fan, J.-B., Siao, C.-J., Berno, A., Young, P., Sapolsky, R., Ghandour, G., Perkins, N., Winchester, E., Spencer, J., Kruglyak, L., Stein, L., Hsie, L., Topaloglou, T., Hubbell, E., Robinson, E., Mittman, M., Morris, M. S., Shen, N., Kilburn, D., Rioux, J., Nusbaum, C., Rozen, S., Hudson, T. J., Lipshutz, R., Chee, M., & Lander, E. S. (1998). Large-scale identification, mapping, and genotyping of single-nucleotide polymorphisms in the human genome. *Science, 280,* 1077–1082.

Weeks, D. E., & Lathrop, G. M. (1995). Polygenic disease: Methods for mapping complex disease traits. *Trends in Genetics, 11,* 513–519.

Wehner, J. M., Radcliffe, R. A., Rosmann, S. T., Christensen, S. C., Rasmussen, D. L., Fulker, D. W., & Wiles, M. (1997). Quantitative trait locus analysis of contextual fear conditioning in mice. *Nature Genetics, 17,* 331–334.

Chapter 23

Focus Chapter

RESEARCH METHODS IN THE STUDY OF SEXUAL BEHAVIOR

Janet S. St. Lawrence, Ph.D., and Mary McFarlane, Ph.D.

Few areas of behavioral research have been so neglected as the study of human sexuality (Parker, 1994). Before the emergence of the HIV/AIDS epidemic, for nearly fifty years, sex research was marginalized and given a low priority for research funding. Very few centers conducted research on sexual behavior, and this absence of a research community seriously hampered the potential to respond to a new epidemic linked to sexual behavior (Gagnon, 1988; Turner, Miller, & Moses, 1989). The AIDS crisis raised awareness of the need for better understanding of sexual behavior and increased funding became available for studies evaluating the relationships between sexual behavior and HIV transmission.

Given the serious limits of available information, the early research quantified sexual attitudes and behaviors in different communities at risk for HIV infection. Behavioral data began to accumulate about numbers of sex partners, methods of partner selection, condom use patterns, and attitudes toward prevention. These early studies documented the frequencies of behaviors linked to HIV infection and improved our understanding of sexual dynamics in different groups of people. However, most of these surveys provided little guidance into the myriad scientific and social issues associated with developing effective interventions (Parker, 1994). One consistent finding documented the absence of behavior change in response to information alone and, in places where behavior change appeared, normative social supports for safer behavior and the absence of AIDS-related discrimination were more important than information provision in stimulating behavior change (Kippax, Connell, Dowsett, & Crawford, 1993).

Sexual research must now move beyond surveys of attitudes and practices to examine the contexts that shape sexual activities as well as the interpersonal, social, cultural, political, and economic contexts in which behaviors occur and become meaningful. Thus, social and behavioral research in human sexual behavior is now emphasizing research methods and theoretical frameworks that will lead to a better understanding of the relationships between sexually transmitted diseases (STDs) and sexual behavior (Boulton, 1993; Gagnon & Parker, 1994). The past few decades have brought an increased understanding of human sexuality and this research is being assimilated into innovative new approaches for the treatment of sexual dysfunctions, prevention of STDs, and prevention initiatives to reach individuals, couples, communities, and the general population.

There are different kinds of sex research studies, and their techniques vary in terms of the (a) method of outcome measurement (i.e., individual's self-reports of sexual behavior, direct observation of sexual behavior, or laboratory measures to corroborate self report); (b) sample size (i.e., whether large numbers of people are surveyed or the research targets a smaller number or is limited to a single individual); (c) research setting (i.e., whether the studies are conducted in an experimental setting or in the field); and (d) whether sexual behaviors are studied as they occur or some attempt is made to modify behavior using experimental methodologies.

It is important for researchers to have some knowledge of the techniques that are used in sexual research and of their limitations. This knowledge can help to evaluate studies that are cited as evidence for various conclusions and to decide whether to accept the conclusions that are drawn. Even more important, an understanding of methodological issues will help to plan and evaluate future research. In this chapter, we briefly review the history of research efforts in human sexuality, discuss methodological issues that arise in sex research, and apply these methodological choices to develop an intervention study of sexual behavior change.

METHODOLOGICAL ISSUES IN CONDUCTING RESEARCH ON HUMAN SEXUALITY

Sampling Issues

One of the first steps before beginning research on sexual behavior is to identify the *population* that will be studied. Will the population consist of all adults in the United States, of bisexual men, of individuals diagnosed with an STD, or of some other population? When the research question addresses a given population, it is usually impractical for the researcher to measure the behavior of the entire population, so a *sample* is selected to represent the population of interest.

Selecting a sample is the point when thorny issues first arise. If the sample is to be random (a representative sample from the entire population) and if it is a reasonably large sample, then the results can be generalized back to the population of interest. For example, if we are interested in learning at what age adolescents become sexually active, then by randomly selecting 1 out of every 100 adolescents in the United States, the results will probably reflect the behavior of all adolescents across the country. To illustrate the problems, if our adolescent sample includes only teenagers whose parents agree to let them participate in a sexual behavior study, then the results may or may not be representative of all adolescents.

As discussed by O'Leary, DiClemente, and Aral (1997), the most scientifically rigorous method of sampling the target population is *probability sampling*, in which each member of the target population is assigned some probability of being invited to participate in the study. In the simplest case, each member of the target population has an equal chance of being invited. In a more realistic scenario, we might imagine that younger adolescents are less likely to participate in a study on sexual behavior; therefore, we would invite a larger number of young adolescents so as to achieve an appropriate and representative sample size. In this case, the probability of inviting a young adolescent to participate would be higher than the probability of inviting an older adolescent to join the study. An alternative to probability sampling is *stratified sampling*, in which we gather larger or smaller samples of particular subgroups of the population. For example, the percentage of injecting drug users may be small, but we may choose this group to comprise one-third of a sample. The motivation for stratification in this case is the elevated risk for STD/HIV of injecting drug users.

Though probability sampling and stratified sampling are ideal sampling methods, it is probably unrealistic to assume that such a sample can be recruited for an STD/HIV behavioral intervention study. Potential participants will only agree to take part in a study if they are motivated by a perceived risk of or interest in STD/HIV, a desire to earn the promised incentives or to be with friends who have already volunteered, or an altruistic desire to make a contribution to science. Whatever their motivation, those who agree to participate may be different in some way from those who do not agree to participate. Researchers can only hope that the factors that set these individuals apart do not affect the outcomes of the study. These factors in participants and nonparticipants can also be measured to clarify the differences between the population to which the research can make generalizations and the general population.

Other methods of accessing target populations for STD/HIV behavioral intervention studies include venue sampling, snowball sampling, and convenience sampling. In the case of *venue sampling*, researchers travel to locations where the members of the target population can be found. In an adolescent study, for example, the researchers may attempt to access members of the target population at a school, a mall, a public basketball court or athletic field, and a youth center. When using venue sampling, it is critical to note the location from which each individual was recruited, so that we can later evaluate whether adolescents recruited from a school are different in some interesting way than adolescents recruited from a mall. In the case of *snowball sampling*, participants who have enrolled in the study are encouraged to recruit others or to provide names of friends who may be interested in participating so that the researchers may approach them about participating in the study. Thus, each participant contributes not only himself or herself to the study, but also provides a point of entry into his or her social network. A danger of snowball sampling is that it is nonrandom: Participants help to recruit their friends and their friends' friends, such that a particularly homogeneous sample may result. Researchers who engage in snowball sampling may need to take extra precautions to ensure that the sample is representative of the target population. Finally, in *convenience sampling*, researchers follow a take-whomever-is-available approach. For example, in a study of adolescents and condom use, researchers may choose to interview only those adolescents who happen to be in an adolescent health clinic during a particular week. This sampling method is clearly less than optimal if the results are to generalize to the population of adolescents. However, many studies have utilized this sampling method because it is financially affordable and, as the term implies, convenient.

In most cases, sampling proceeds through three phases. First, the researcher identifies the population of interest and, second, contacts people from that population to participate in the research. The strategies for obtaining samples are fairly well developed and do not pose a problem for researchers, provided that they actually use them. A more difficult problem, however, arises in the third stage, when the researcher is faced with actually convincing people who were identified for the sample to participate. If individuals refuse to participate, and refusals can be common when people are contacted to participate in sex research, then the researcher's probability sample is tainted. This poses the problem of *nonresponse* or *refusal bias*. Essentially, the researcher is left with a sample of individuals who volunteered to participate in the research, thus introducing a problem called *volunteer bias*.

The problem of nonresponse would not be serious if those who refuse to participate are identical in their sexual behavior to those who agree to participate. But this is not usually the case. Instead, those who refuse to participate are likely to differ in some way from the participants. This leads to a *biased sample*. People who agree to participate in sex research, by and large, tend to be more liberal and more sexually experienced than those who refuse to participate (Rosen et al., 1995).

Measurement Issues

Reliability of Self-Reported Sexual Behavior

It is relatively rare for researchers to directly observe and measure the sexual behavior of their participants. Instead, most researchers rely on respondents' self-reported sexual behavior, which raises questions as to how accurately people report their own sexual behavior. There are a number of reasons to suspect inconsistencies between what people report and what they actually do in their private lives. For example, concerns about privacy, embarrassment, or fear of reprisals can lead people to conceal their true sexual behavior. Some may even embellish their actual behavior by overrepresenting the truth. Even people who are highly motivated to provide truthful answers may have inaccurate memories that affect their self-reported behaviors.

Test-Retest Reliability Researchers have assessed the stability of self-reported sexual behavior in a variety of populations: gay men (McLaws et al., 1990), heterosexual adults (Kauth et al., 1991), and adolescents (McFarlane & St. Lawrence, 1997). Test-retest correlations have ranged from 0.3 to 0.9 across different sexual behaviors for gay men and heterosexual adults, making it easier for them to recall specific instances. Adolescents had higher test-retest correlations, perhaps because they have less sexual experience and fewer sexual encounters than adults. Generally, reliability tends to be higher for infrequent practices than for more frequent practices (McLaws et al., 1990). The wide range in retest correlations, however, underscores the danger of assuming that high reliability for one sexual behavior necessarily means that other sexual behaviors will have the same consistency in self-reported data. Generally, reliability is higher for incidence questions (i.e., "Have you ever . . . ?") than for frequency items ("How often do you . . . ?") and for short time periods (a month) versus longer durations (a year). Thus, a researcher can use categorical or dichotomous items rather than measuring frequency to increase reliability, but only at the expense of the specificity provided by interval-level data.

Intentional Distortion   If you were interviewing people about sexual behavior and a 40-year-old man told you he had never masturbated, would you believe him or would you wonder whether he was uncomfortable admitting it? If an elderly woman told you that she and her husband had intercourse three times a day, would you believe her or would you speculate that she might be overstating? For a variety of reasons, participants in sexual research may give self-reports that distort reality. Such misrepresentations may either exaggerate or underreport actual behavior. Unfortunately, we usually do not know whether the individual is embellishing or minimizing his or her sexual activity. Distortion is a fundamental problem when relying on self-report data. One strategy that has been found to encourage honest reporting is to carefully protect the confidentiality and anonymity of the participant. But even if all respondents attempted to be completely truthful, two other factors might still contaminate their self-reports: inaccurate recall and estimation errors.

Inaccurate Recall   Some of the questions in surveys of sexual behavior ask people to recall their sexual behavior for literally years in the past. For example, for many years, our knowledge of children's sexual behavior was based on a study by Alfred Kinsey in which adults were asked about their sexual behavior when they were children. When, for example, a 50-year-old man is asked how often he masturbated when he was 15, he may not be able to recall this information accurately. Several recent studies suggest that a better alternative is to ask people about their current sexual behavior using a retrospective recall period of no more than a few months (Kauth, St. Lawrence, & Kelly, 1991; McFarlane & St. Lawrence, 1997).

Estimation   Another source of inaccuracy in self-report data is when people try to estimate behaviors or events that they probably cannot calculate very precisely. For example, one question from the Kinsey survey asked people how long they spent in foreplay. It is difficult to estimate time under any circumstance, and even more difficult when the person is engaged in an absorbing activity. The point is that sometimes people are asked to estimate behaviors that probably result in inaccurate reports because they make unwitting errors as they estimate their response.

Validity of Self-Reported Sexual Behavior

Several studies have evaluated the validity of self-reported sexual behavior or used corroborative strategies such as diaries or partner reports to validate self-reports (cf. Catania, Gibson, Chitwood, et al., 1990). Strategies for validating self-report have occasionally relied on biological markers (e.g., Udry & Morris, 1967), but this can be prohibitively expensive in large-population-based surveys. Nonetheless, there is a growing body of research that supports the validity of people's self-reports of sexual behavior based on corroborative measures of STDs or HIV seroconversion (for reviews, see Catania, Dolcini, & Coates, 1992; Doll et al., 1994). Occasionally, researchers have collected self-reports of STDs in an effort to validate self-reports of sexual behavior (Laumann, Gagnon, Michael, & Michaels, 1994), which might be a reasonable strategy if people accurately report their past STDs. Other research calls into question even the validity of self-reported STDs (Siegel et al., 1992).

When researchers have studied couples in which one partner was infected with HIV and the other was not, they generally have found that new infections in the previously uninfected partner were consistent with the information he or she provided about condom use (cf. Allen et al., 1992; Saracco et al., 1993). Although these types of studies suggest that self-reports of condom use were consistent with biological outcomes, they cannot be generalized to other populations for two reasons. First, these couples may have been more motivated to provide accurate information; second, because they were interviewed at regular intervals, their recall may have improved as a result of the frequent contact. Furthermore, the frequent contact with sex researchers may have motivated participants to change their behavior.

Other strategies have also been used, such as behavioral diaries (McLaws, Oldenberg, Ross, & Cooper, 1990), sophisticated statistical methods that adjust self-report of sensitive behaviors (Zimmerman & Langer, 1995), and correlating partners' reports of their sexual behavior (Coates et al., 1988; Kinsey, Pomeroy, & Martin, 1948). Although each of these corroborative methods strengthens our confidence in self-reported behavior, they are also subject to error, and no "gold standard" for collecting information about naturally occurring sexual behavior outside of laboratory settings currently exists.

Psychophysiological Measurement

Direct assessment of sexual behavior is obviously problematic because of the very nature of a sexual interaction. The places where naturally occurring behavior takes place are most often those that cannot be directly observed or monitored. Indeed, the cultural prohibitions against doing so preclude attempting such assessments. Even if it were possible to do so, awareness of being monitored would probably change behavior to such an extent that it might bear little resemblance to its normal and usual occurrences. Ordinarily, when behaviors cannot be observed directly in the natural environment, contrived situations are devised to assess the nature and strength of a given behavior within a more convenient setting for the research. However, the sensitivity of sexual behavior makes assessment, even in a contrived laboratory situation, difficult.

Measures of penile erection are one of the measures employed in assessment of sexual arousal. Other measures, such as galvanic skills response, cardiac rate, respiration, and pupil size have also been used as emotional correlates of sexual arousal. Two penile transducer devices have been used to measure penile circumference. The first is a mercury-filled elastic tube that encircles the penis. As penile tumescence occurs, the elastic tubing lengthens and electrical resistance of the mercury column increases. These changes can then be recorded. A second widely used device to measure penile circumference is a thin, metal ringlike device open at one end that is placed around the penis, forming a semicircle. At the base of the ring are strain gauges. During an erection, the rings separate, which causes bending of the strain gauge, producing increased electrical output. The device is easily calibrated and demonstrates a remarkably linear output over the full range of circumference changes in penile tumescence. One disadvantage of the strain gauge is that it is more subject to movement artifact, although this is usually readily identified on the resulting printout. Physiological measures of sexual functioning in females have been developed, but are rarely available or used outside of highly specialized research centers.

Instrumentation Issues

Methods of Data Collection

Three methods of data collection are used commonly in sexual research to collect self-reported behavior. In the first, interviewers question people directly about their sexual behavior face-to-face or over the telephone. In the second method, people are given a questionnaire or diary to complete and return. A third method involves gathering information through a computer-administered assessment. Each of these methods has some advantages and some disadvantages, and it is unclear whether any one method offers a distinct advantage over any other for data collection. The advantage of a personal interview is that the interviewer can establish rapport and trust with the participant and it is hoped that this facilitates honest reporting. An interviewer can also vary the sequence of the questions based on the person's responses. It is difficult to incorporate the same flexibility into a self-administered questionnaire. On the other hand, interviews are a time- and cost-intensive method of data collection.

Questionnaires are more economical because they do not require paying interviewers for the many hours that are necessary when participants are interviewed individually. When people are not required to put any identifying information on the questionnaire, they feel more reassured that their confidentiality is protected and may respond more honestly than in a face-to-face interview. Responses to questionnaires are also less subject to being influenced by characteristics of the interviewer such as the interviewer's personality or an inadvertent facial grimace when a particular behavior is mentioned. However, questionnaires are also dependent on the literacy of the respondent, who has to read, understand, and respond to the questions.

More recently, computers have been used for data collection, sometimes with earphones so the respondent can hear the questions in privacy and enter his or her responses directly into the computer. This offers several advantages: the individual enters answers unobserved, the program can use branching strategies that simulate an oral interview by omitting or including items based on earlier responses, and the information is automatically entered into a data file, eliminating the cost and time of having staff code and enter the data for later analysis. Even this method is not foolproof, however, because individuals can still be inaccurate and equipment malfunctions can occur, losing valuable data. In addition, not everyone reacts positively to such impersonal data collection and some people are not comfortable using computers.

Interviewer Variables

Extraneous factors can also influence data collected in sexual behavior research. Interviews on sexual behavior may be particularly sensitive to interviewer effects. For example, people may be more comfortable reporting to an interviewer of the same gender or ethnicity or age. Thus, the gender, ethnicity, or age of the interviewer could influence the answers that are given. Generally, studies of interviewer effects have found little effect from interviewers' sexual orientation or age on responses to sexual questions (Darrow et al., 1986), although gender differences have been found (Darrow et al., 1986; Catania, Gibson, Chitwood, et al., 1990). People tend to report more information to female interviewers, women are more influenced by interviewer gender differences, and women tend to disclose more personal details than men. Overall, however, the literature on interviewer variables does not provide much in the way of definitive guidance for researchers.

SURVEY RESEARCH

Surveys are one of the most common methods for conducting research on human sexual behavior. In the major sex surveys, data are collected from a large sample of people. To illustrate the use of survey research, we describe some of the best-known surveys, pointing out both their strengths and their weaknesses. Certainly, the best known of these studies were those conducted by Kinsey and his colleagues in the 1940s.

The Kinsey Studies of Human Sexual Behavior

Alfred Kinsey and his colleagues, Wardell Pomeroy and Clyde Martin, published *Sexual Behavior in the Human Male* in 1948, followed by publication of *Sexual Behavior in the Human Female* (Kinsey, Pomeroy, Martin, & Gebhard, 1953). These two books are known as the Kinsey reports. More than 5,000 males and females were interviewed for each volume.

The Kinsey reports have been criticized on a number of fronts based on questions about their sampling, interviewing, and accuracy of the results. Even though some African Americans were interviewed, only interviews with Caucasians were included in the resulting publications. These interviews were conducted over more than 10 years, from 1938 to 1949, although the largest number of interviews were conducted between 1943 and 1946. At the outset, Kinsey was inattentive to sampling issues. His goal was to collect sex histories on as many people as possible. He began by conducting interviews on the university campus and later moved on to continue interviewing in large cities. After the research was underway, he became more concerned with sampling and developed a strategy he called "100% sampling." Using this method, he would contact a group, obtain its support, and then try to get each of its members to give a sexual history. After getting the group's endorsement, he counted on peer pressure to ensure that all of its members would participate. Unfortunately, the groups were not chosen randomly. Among the groups from which his "100%" samples were obtained were 2 sororities, 9 fraternities, and 13 professional groups. Almost one-fourth of the interviews in the Kinsey reports came from these 100% samples. In the 1953 book, Kinsey indicated that he deliberately chose not to use probability sampling because of the problem associated with nonresponse bias. This is a legitimate point, but the end result is that we have no information on how representative the sample was and considerable information indicating it was not (for example, the exclusion of minorities). Kinsey attempted to statistically adjust for sampling inadequacies so that the sample would correspond with the U.S. census, but this did not deflect criticism about the sampling methods.

Kinsey's sampling methods were, without question, scientifically dubious, but the procedures that he used for interviewing remain highly regarded today. The interviewers were trained to establish rapport with the people they interviewed and to treat all responses matter-of-factly. They were also adept at posing questions in language that was easy to understand and the questions were worded to facilitate reporting sensitive behaviors. For example, interviewers did not ask "Have you ever masturbated?" Instead they asked "At what age did you begin masturbating?" They also took careful steps to ensure that the interview responses would remain anonymous.

One notable strength of the Kinsey reports, given the fact that they were conducted more than 50 years ago, is the extent to which Kinsey attempted to evaluate the reliability of the interview data. For a portion of the sample, interviews were repeated more than a year later and correlations between the two interviews were computed to estimate the test-retest reliability of their data. They found a high degree of agreement between the two interviews on all of their measures, suggesting that the self-reports were highly consistent. Another method they used to check for accuracy was to interview a husband and a wife independently and evaluate the extent to which their answers corresponded. The highest correlations between spouses was on objective facts such as the number of years they had been married or how long after the marriage their first child was born. The lowest correlation (about .50) was between husband's and wife's estimates of the average frequency with which they had intercourse early in their marriage. Thus, it appears that the Kinsey self-report data varied from being fairly accurate on subjective items such as the reported frequencies of sexual behavior to highly accurate on items such as vital statistics. When all is said and done, it is possible that the Kinsey data are very accurate—or very inaccurate. There is simply no way of knowing.

The Hunt Survey

After the Kinsey survey, several decades passed before another large-scale attempt to survey Americans about sexual behavior. In the early 1970s, the Playboy Foundation commissioned a sex survey to collect updated information about sexual behavior and compare the data against Kinsey's results 30 years before, using more rigorous sampling procedures. The results were serialized in *Playboy* magazine and later published as *Sexual Behavior in the 1970s* by Morton Hunt (1974).

An independent research organization was commissioned to develop the sampling plan, design the questionnaire, and collect the data. They chose 24 cities across the United States and randomly selected names from the telephone books in each city, called these people, and asked them to participate anonymously in a panel discussion of trends in American sexual behavior. Of those contacted, only 20% actually came to the panel discussions. One ethical issue should certainly be identified regarding the Hunt study: Subjects were not told at the time they were recruited that they would be asked to fill out a questionnaire about their own sexual behavior after the panel discussion!

According to Hunt, the sample closely paralleled the American population in gender, race, marital status, age, education, occupation, and urban-rural background. However, because the sample was obtained from telephone books, people such as the homeless or those in institutions (such as prisons, mental hospitals, and colleges) were excluded. In addition, because 80% of the probability sample did not participate, differences might have existed between the 20% who agreed to participate and the 80% who did not. Unlike Kinsey, who used face-to-face interviews, Hunt used questionnaires supplemented by a small number of face-to-face interviews.

After the Hunt survey, research on sexual behavior languished for almost two decades until renewed interest in human sexuality research was stimulated by the appearance of AIDS, although there were some intermittent small studies that tended to have selected, limited populations and/or focus on narrow questions such as age of sexual debut. For the most part, these studies asked relatively few questions about sexual behaviors, focusing instead on social issues and problems associated with sex, such as contraception or premarital sex. No comprehensive survey of Americans' sexual behavior would recur until the 1990s.

The Laumann Survey

The appearance of AIDS in the early 1980s caught public health, medicine, and social science poorly informed about sexual behavior, and it rapidly became apparent that scientific progress in controlling this new disease was hampered by the lack of any recent, scientifically sound, population-based knowledge about sexual behavior. In response, a number of federal agencies—including the Centers for Disease Control and Prevention (CDC), the National Center for Health Statistics (NCHS), the National Institute of Child Health and Human Development (NICHHD), the National Institute on Aging (NIA), and the National Institute of Mental Health (NIMH)—pooled financial resources to support a population-based study. After the prestigious Institute of Medicine issued a national report decrying the lack of knowledge about sexual behavior, the NICHHD issued a request for proposals to conduct a population-based survey in 1987. A proposal to conduct such a survey was submitted by Edward Laumann and his colleagues at the University of Chicago and was favorably reviewed by both government and nongovernment scientists, but encountered massive political struggles. As a result of its political sensitivity and the ensuing controversy, federal funding to conduct the research was withheld by Congress. In fact, Congressional legislation well into the mid-1990s explicitly prohibited federal agencies from funding this national survey. After it was clear that the planned large-scale national survey was doomed, the scientists who submitted the original proposal assembled a variety of private funding sources and carried out a more modest version of their proposed study (Laumann et al., 1994) that remains one of our best available sources of information about self-reported human sexual behavior.

LABORATORY RESEARCH USING DIRECT OBSERVATIONS

One alternative to using self-report data is to directly observe sexual behavior in a laboratory setting. Direct observations overcome many of the problems of self-report. The classic example of this approach is Masters and Johnson's laboratory research on the physiology of the human sexual response cycle (Masters & Johnson, 1966, 1979). When William Masters first began his research into the physiology of sexual response in the mid-1950s, no one had ever attempted to study human sexual behavior in a laboratory. As a result, Masters was faced with developing from scratch all of the needed research strategies. He started by interviewing men and women who worked as prostitutes and acquired instrumentation for his laboratory such as an electrocardiograph to measure

594 Areas of Clinical Research: Psychopathology and Health

heart rate over the sexual cycle, an electromyograph to measure muscular contractions, and a pH meter to measure the acidity of the vagina during a sexual response cycle. Prostitutes helped "dry run" the apparatus, but Masters recognized that they would not be satisfactory participants for his research. Masters's first breakthrough occurred when he decided it was possible to recruit research participants from the general population to engage in sexual behavior in a laboratory setting where their behavior and physiological responses would be carefully observed, measured, and recorded. This approach had never been used; even Kinsey went no further than obtaining people's verbal reports of their sexual behavior.

Certainly the people Masters and Johnson studied were not a random sample from the U.S. population. In fact, we might imagine that people who would volunteer for such research might be quite different from the general population. The description of the sample does indicate that they were more educated than the general population and predominantly White. The sample also omitted people who were not sexually experienced or who were unwilling to have their sexual behavior studied in the laboratory, so Masters and Johnson's results would not generalize to such people.

Masters and Johnson were not particularly concerned with sampling, because they assumed the physiological processes they were studying were essentially the same in all people. Whether this is true remains to be seen, but it does not appear to be an unreasonable assumption. Regardless, their inattention to sampling meant that Masters and Johnson could not generalize the results from their research. For example, they could not say that x% of all women have multiple orgasms because any percentages they calculated would describe only their subjects and not the general population. In defense of their inattention to sampling, even if Masters and Johnson had tried to recruit a probability sample, they almost certainly would have encountered very high refusal rates that would have ruined the probability sample.

In the laboratory, physiological responses of the subjects were recorded during sexual intercourse, masturbation, and "artificial coitus" using an artificial penis that contained a recording apparatus that made it possible to observe females' vaginal sexual responses. Several years later, Masters and Johnson conducted a similar study of homosexual behavior (Masters & Johnson, 1979), this time using gay men and lesbian women volunteers. This second study was essentially the same as their 1966 study; only the sexual orientation of the sample was different.

Measures such as those used by Masters and Johnson avoid entirely the problems of distortion in self-reports, but they also measure different constructs. It would not be possible, for example, from this research to conclude how frequently a subject masturbated. Instead, they measured how the body responds to sexual stimulation with a level of accuracy and detail that is impossible to obtain from self-report. However, even laboratory studies have their detractors. One criticism that was raised is whether people respond the same sexually in the laboratory when they know they are being studied as they would in the privacy of their own homes. Another problem is that Masters and Johnson's results have not been replicated (i.e., independently confirmed) by other researchers. Although scientists tend to believe that Masters and Johnson's results are valid, the data still need to be corroborated by other research.

Masters and Johnson are to be credited with paying careful attention to the ethical implications of their research. For example, they were careful to observe the principle of informed consent. All volunteers were given detailed explanations of what would be required during the research and they were given ample opportunity to withdraw at every stage of the research. They also eliminated from the pool of volunteers anyone who seemed anxious or distressed during the initial interview. In addition, recognizing that participation in such novel research could have unanticipated consequences, Masters and Johnson continued to contact their subjects at five-year intervals long after the research ended.

In summary, direct observation of sexual behavior as performed by Masters and Johnson has some advantages as well as some disadvantages. Such research avoids the problems of self-report and is able to answer much more detailed physiological questions than self-report ever could. On the other hand, such research is costly and time consuming, making large samples prohibitively expensive. In addition, high refusal rates are probably unavoidable, making probability sampling impossible.

PARTICIPANT-OBSERVATION RESEARCH METHODS

Another research method used by anthropologists and sociologists is the participant-observation technique. Using this type of research, the scientist actually becomes a part of the group being studied and makes observations from "inside" the group or community. The researcher may combine direct observations of sexual behavior with interview data. Examples of this type of research are two classic studies of sexual behavior, a study of gay men engaging in sex in public places such as rest rooms (Humphreys, 1970), and of swinging couples (Bartell, 1970). We will (briefly) describe Humphreys's study of the "tearoom trade" to illustrate participant-observation research. Humphreys acted as a lookout while men engaged in homosexual acts in public rest rooms. His role was to sound a warning if police or unexpected others appeared. This allowed Humphreys to directly observe the sexual behavior. In addition, he recorded the license plate numbers of the men, traced them, and later interviewed them in their homes. Humphreys collected a wealth of information during the study, but he also violated most of the ethical principles that govern behavioral research today. He had no informed consent from the subjects, who were never even aware that they were participating in research. Thus, Humphreys's study has been very controversial and it is unlikely that any researcher today would be allowed to conduct such a study.

EXPERIMENTAL SEX RESEARCH

All of the studies discussed up to this point have one thing in common: They were all cross-sectional studies of sexual behavior as it occurred naturally using either self-reports or direct observations. The data collected from such studies are correlational in nature. At best, they can tell us that certain factors are related to one another, but they cannot tell us what causes various aspects of sexual behavior. An alternative is to conduct experimental research that allows us to determine what caused behavior. According to the technical definition of an experiment, one factor must be manipulated while all other factors are held constant. If groups were comparable before the experiment, then any differences among the groups who received different treatments can be attributed to that factor. Most experimental research has been conducted in the laboratory, although researchers are now beginning to evaluate interventions conducted with groups and even communities.

As one example of an experimental study, we might consider a classic study of male/female differences in sexual arousal after reading erotic stories that was conducted by Schmidt, Sigusch, and Schafer (1973). They recruited an equal number of male and female college students who, in the course of the experiment, read erotic stories. Half read stories in which the characters were very affectionate with one another, and the balance read stories in which the affection was missing. Immediately after reading a story, participants rated how sexually arousing it had been (note that this study used self-report). The stories that included affection were rated as significantly more arousing than stories without affection. Thus, the experimenters concluded that affection between characters in an erotic story *causes* people to become more aroused.

Experimental research on human sexual behavior permits us to make much more powerful statements about causes. Experimental studies also, at times, circumvent the problems of memory that plague survey research, although even experimental research often relies on self-reports. Experimental research also is more time-consuming and costly; therefore, it can generally be done only with relatively small samples of subjects.

APPLYING SCIENTIFIC METHODS IN SEXUAL RESEARCH: HYPOTHETICAL RESEARCH PROJECT

We have discussed methodological issues that confront researchers interested in studying human sexual behavior. We will now use these same scientific issues to create a hypothetical research project and walk through the project from start to finish, emphasizing the decisions that arise at each phase of the research. This example is not based on any particular project, but reflects experience accumulated over a variety of projects.

The goal of our hypothetical project will be to develop, implement, and evaluate an intervention to increase sexually active adolescents' use of condoms for prevention of STDs and teen pregnancy. We begin with a brief review of ethical concerns in sexuality research, then prepare a formative research phase, in which we refine our research goals and chart the course of the project. Following the formative phase, we prepare the implementation phase, during which the intervention is developed and tested in the field. Finally, we create our strategy for the evaluation plan. It is important to realize that any scientific problems left unsolved during any phase will affect later stages of the project.

Ethical Considerations

The planning phase will also necessitate attention to the ethical issues inherent in research inquiry. The planning, implementation, and evaluation of any study involving human participants must proceed under strict ethical conditions, particularly when it is addressing human sexual behavior, STDs, or HIV/AIDS research, which has already been tainted by the Tuskegee Syphilis Study (Jones, 1981), in which medical treatment was withheld after an effective treatment became available. In addition to the issues raised by the Tuskegee Syphilis Study, several STD/HIV-related studies raised public discussions over the advisability of withholding treatment from "control groups" of infected persons (Kaiser, 1997). These studies contributed to a mistrust of investigators on the part of potential research participants. Current ethical guidelines are identified in "The Belmont Report" (1978). Privacy and confidentiality are of utmost importance to participants in AIDS research, who may fear that their participation could result in negative consequences such as reprisal, stigmatization, or ostracism.

Conformity to the ethical guidelines discussed above must be approved by an Institutional Review Board (IRB) before any project can commence. The IRB, in turn, must have been approved by the federal Office for Protection from Research Risk (OPRR). If this latter approval is not in place, then the project itself must be reviewed by the OPRR if the project is being funded by any federal agency. These ethical guidelines are in place for the protection of both the researcher and the participant. For further consideration of ethical issues in STD/HIV research, see Coyle, Boruch, and Turner (1991), Melton and Gray (1988), and Melton (1989).

Formative Research

Recall that the goal of our hypothetical project is to increase sexually active adolescents' condom use for the prevention of STD/HIV. Literature reviews are invariably the starting point for most research. However, in the case of sexual behavior research, the complexity is greater than usual because the relevant literature is published across different disciplines. Journal articles about sexual behavior research and STD/HIV interventions will appear in biomedical, epidemiology, public health, anthropology, sociology, psychology, and many other types of journals. These multidisciplinary perspectives must be fully reviewed so that the researcher understands the historical, medical, individual, community, and societal issues to be considered when carrying out sexual behavior research.

Choosing a Population

The literature review should begin to answer several questions. For example, according to current information from national surveys, in what groups of adolescents is condom use already prevalent? Even more important, in what adolescent populations is condom use *not* prevalent? In what populations is condom use likely to have the greatest impact in reducing disease transmission? Are these populations defined by age, race, education, family income, work status, type of sex partners, or behavioral factors? Are these populations present and accessible in the investigator's community? What interventions already have been attempted with these groups? Which interventions, if any, succeeded? Answers to these questions will help us to clarify which population(s) should be included in our study. The choice of a population to be studied is especially important in STD/HIV prevention research, because past research has generally concentrated on very specific populations, such as men who have sex with men, adolescents, injecting drug users, and women who trade sex for food or drugs. Interventions that work in one of these groups are not necessarily successful in another (Doll, 1996; Kalton, 1993). One reason for this lack of generalizability is that each population tends to engage in a different set of risky behaviors. Because of these populations' behavioral differences, interventions targeted at injecting drug users probably need to be different from interventions targeted at adolescents. Thus, when identifying a population for our project, we must keep in mind to what population we wish to generalize this research.

Selecting a Theoretical Framework

Once the population has been selected, the next step is to identify the theoretical model that will drive the STD/HIV behavioral research. Relevant theories may include the Health Belief Model (Rosenstock, 1974), the Theory of Reasoned Action (Azjen & Fishbein, 1977), Social Cognitive Theory (Bandura, 1994), the Transtheoretical Model (Prochaska, Redding, Harlow, Rossi, & Yelicer, 1994), the AIDS Risk Reduction Model (Catania, Kegeles, & Coates, 1990), and the Information-Motivation-Behavior model (Fisher & Fisher, 1992). The theoretical background will lay the groundwork for design and delivery of the intervention, as well as influence the evaluation plan. Another important aspect of the literature review will be the search for theory-relevant measures that have previously been successful, preferably in the population we have chosen.

Formative Research

During the formative research phase, time and energy is devoted to learning more about the cultural context of sexual behavior, as well as the nature and prevalence of sexual acts, knowledge, attitudes, and perceptions about sexuality and AIDS, and knowledge, attitudes, and beliefs about condoms in the target population. This is usually accomplished through qualitative methods such as in-depth focus groups, interviews (McCracken, 1988), and quantitative surveys. These qualitative and quantitative methods yield different information (Bauman & Adair, 1992; Michaels, 1996), and researchers who limit themselves to using only one of these two methods will inevitably lack some valuable information regarding the target population.

In our hypothetical example, suppose we choose to study adolescent males in small cities. We may want to hold several focus groups to discuss the cultural context of sexual behavior. For example, we may convene a focus group of minority adolescents who are attending school, as well as a focus group of demographically similar adolescents who do not attend school. This ensures that we hear the opinions of those adolescents who have received health-related messages through the school system, as well as the opinions of those who have not. We should certainly engage in discussions with community leaders who hold some stake in the future of our target population; for example, we may want to hold focus groups of parents, teachers, counselors, and members of the local religious organizations. These focus groups provide useful information, but also offer an opportunity for the researchers to establish credibility and gain support in the community.

During a focus group, individuals from the target population gather in a private area, free from interruptions or the gaze of curious passersby, to discuss their opinions regarding several issues put forth by the organizer (Morgan, 1988a). The group leader's role is to guide discussion, clarify responses, and elicit information, while carefully avoiding any influence on the specific opinions that are expressed (Bernard, 1994). The role of the leader is demanding; he or she must ensure that the participants are allowed to freely express themselves, while also pacing the discussion so the appropriate topics are each discussed in detail. This requires the leader to smoothly guide conversation from topic to topic without interrupting the conversational flow or interfering with the participants' freedom of self-expression. Every attempt should be made to match the leader's personal characteristics with those of the focus group participants; for example, the leader should match the participants in race, gender, and age where feasible (Warren & Rasmussen, 1977). It has been suggested that leaders whose demographics match those of the participants may be more credible and create more of a sense of acceptance and belonging than unmatched leaders. However, there is some literature to suggest that this matching may not make much difference (e.g., Darrow et al., 1986). It is also important to select members of the focus group who will be able to freely discuss issues with one another; for example, adolescent females may be less willing to discuss sensitive topics if adolescent males are in the room. In general, the constituents of the focus group must be selected in such a way that the likelihood of open and free discussion will be maximized. Focus group methods are well summarized by Morgan (1988a, 1988b), Frey and Fontana (1991), and Goldman and McDonald (1987).

After identifying who will be involved in the focus groups, we need to prepare a list of the topics for the discussion. This list will form the outline that will be followed by the group leaders in facilitating discussion (Zeller, 1993). A group is not likely to stay on task for more than two hours, so the list of discussion topics should be streamlined to address the most essential topics. That is, we should concentrate on eliciting domains of greatest interest for our future research and intervention plan. For example, once our focus group of adolescent males is comfortable, the group leader might introduce discussion about some of the following issues: (a) attitudes and perceptions of peers' sexual activity; (b) whether sexual activity is positively or negatively valued among peers, parents, and other members of the social network; (c) types of sexual acts (vaginal, oral, anal) and sexual partners (casual, steady) and the meanings attached to different behaviors; (d) knowledge about STD/HIV, its transmission mechanisms, and prevention options; (e) reasons why adolescents do or do not use condoms; (f) the types of messages presented to adolescents by parents, peers, and others regarding safe sex and sexual behavior in general and how these messages are perceived; (g) what kinds of situations they've experienced that presented some risk and was hard for them to handle; and (h) their ideas about what kinds of safe-sex programs might be offered in the community to increase condom use by sexually active adolescents.

Though this list of issues is not exhaustive, the discussions will add to the knowledge gained from the literature review regarding the target population. We may find in the focus groups members of the community who are willing and able to reach adolescents and have an interest in teaching condom skills to them. We may learn during the focus groups that adolescents are fairly knowledgeable about sex but not about condoms. Or we may find out that the adolescents who are sexually active want to protect themselves but find it hard to refuse unwanted invitations or to negotiate condom use with their partners. Furthermore, the discussion will allow us to listen to the local "sexual dialect," the words and phrases most commonly used to describe sexual acts, partners, preferences, and norms (Bauman & Adair, 1992; DiMauro, 1995). Beyond the obvious benefits of convening a focus group is the valuable experience gained by observing members of the target population in discussions. Through these observations, the focus group leader can gather impressions regarding sensitivity to discussions about sex, willingness to participate in research efforts, perceptions of community norms, and much more. In turn, focus group participants who are satisfied that the researcher will use their opinions and ideas may be more likely to endorse the project in their community.

Individual Interviews

If the value of a focus group stems from the researcher's ability to gather information from open discussion of research-related issues, then the value of an individual interview is gathering in-depth personal opinions that may not be discussed openly in a group setting (McCracken, 1988). Individual interviews make it possible to elicit more detailed information (Kotarba, 1980). For example, youth group leaders, peers, gang members, and other influential members of the community or target population may provide detailed, but different, descriptions of the barriers and facilitators to condom use for local adolescents. Furthermore, individual interviews with parents, teachers, and other influential adults also help researchers gain a more thorough understanding of the community's readiness for or resistance to interventions aimed at increasing adolescents' condom use. Additionally, it is helpful to conduct in-depth interviews with youth so as to understand in greater depth some of the issues that arose during focus-group sessions. During these interviews, an enterprising researcher will discover roadblocks to implementing condom-use intervention, members of the community who can help to eliminate the roadblocks, and methods of intervening with this population in a credible, effective, and sensitive manner.

In our hypothetical project, we may learn during the focus groups that parents are unwilling to allow their children to learn condom skills because they fear that their children will become sexually active if they do so. In-depth interviews with these and other parents will identify this barrier and help the researchers discover possible methods of addressing the parents' fears. Thus, in-depth individual interviews can help reveal significant barriers to research as well as innovative solutions to removing those barriers as researchers learn more information about the sexual culture of the population.

There are a few important points to consider during interviews. These points are explored in depth in Gorden (1992). First, the interviewer must be someone with whom interviewees are comfortable expressing themselves about personal and sensitive topics. This involves more than simply matching or contrasting interviewers to interviewees in race and gender. Interviewers are faced with the need to establish rapport, allowing interviewees to relax and feel comfortable before delving into personal topics. Second, the interview should take place in a location that lends itself to private conversation without interruptions or onlookers. Third, interviewers should be careful not to interject their own knowledge, attitudes, perceptions, values, and judgments into the conversation (Brenner, 1985). The interviewer should listen attentively and ask for clarifications when necessary, but should not attempt to influence the interviewee. Finally, the interviewer must be skilled in making detailed notes while listening intently to the interviewee (Patton, 1987). The notes serve as a summary of the entire interview and must be legible, descriptive, and comprehensible; another investigator should be able to reconstruct the tone and content of the interview solely from the notes if the need arises. These notes are of utmost importance, even when a tape recorder is used, because interviewers may forget to record parts of the interview, fail to flip the cassette at the appropriate time, or be unable to understand part of the discussion when listening to a tape. In short, the interviewer is the primary instrument for eliciting and recording data from an interview and, as such, he or she must perform in an objective, effective, and reliable manner (Cassell, 1977).

Quantitative Surveys

Focus groups and individual interviews provide in-depth information about the research topic and about the target population. In the case of our research on condom use in adolescents, we now have information regarding sexual activity in our population, social norms regarding sex, condoms, and STD/HIV, barriers and facilitators affecting condom use in our population, the structure of the social network surrounding the adolescents, and ideas for an intervention in this population. This knowledge, however, is based on a set of interviews with a relatively small number of people. The next phase in our research will help us determine the pervasiveness of the issues identified from the focus groups and interviews. We also may want to identify some of the possible predictors and correlates of the issues that arose. To identify these relationships among the issues in the population, we must gather information from a larger number of population members. The mechanism by which we will accomplish this is the *quantitative survey*.

Developing a survey instrument to study issues related to sexuality is tricky science. Though some surveys of STD/HIV knowledge, attitudes, and behaviors exist (e.g., Catania, Coates, et al., 1992), researchers usually find it necessary to either adjust current instruments or create entirely new ones to suit their research projects. This is because, as we discussed before, so much of the research focusing on sexuality and STD/HIV is highly population-specific, and the instruments that are appropriate for one population are often inappropriate in another. In this section, we review some of the threats to the usefulness of quantitative surveys, including issues related to literacy, cultural appropriateness, selection bias, response bias, recall bias, instrument length, order effects, and effects associated with the method of administering the instrument. Excellent reviews of these methodological issues are available in Catania, Binson, Vander Straten, and Stone (1995), Catania, Gibson, Chitwood, et al. (1990), and Ostrow and Kessler (1993).

In our hypothetical research project, based on the information we accumulated from the literature review, the focus groups, and the individual interviews, let's assume that we have decided that the intervention will focus on adolescent males. This means that literacy requirements and cultural appropriateness of our survey must be considered carefully. It is all too easy to assume that students in the tenth grade read at a tenth-grade level; however, this assumption is frequently untenable. To calibrate our survey to our population's reading level, we may either use current knowledge of the reading level in our population or test a sample of the population to determine the appropriate reading level for the survey. If the reading level of the population is low, we may need to consider administering the survey in a manner that does not require the respondent to read the questions. For example, we might hire an interviewer to administer the survey or we might administer the survey over the telephone.

Once the reading level has been determined, we must ensure that the language in our survey is culturally appropriate. For example, in a Hispanic population, we may be tempted to simply translate the instrument into Spanish and believe that we have culturally adapted the survey. However, this strategy is inadequate because different Spanish speakers (e.g., Dominicans, Puerto Ricans, Mexicans, Colombians) use different words to express similar concepts (Carballo-Dieguez, 1996). Culturally appropriate terminology should be gleaned from the focus groups and then used in the quantitative survey. At the same time, every effort should be made to avoid condescension when using culturally appropriate jargon.

In developing our quantitative survey, we also have to bear in mind that the length of the instrument can be inversely related to the quality of data we collect. Long, repetitive questionnaires quickly lead to boredom, distraction, and fatigue in the respondents, discouraging them from completing the entire survey. Thus, although we may want to gather a tremendous amount of information, some prioritization is necessary. In most populations, brief and focused questionnaires are likely to yield higher-quality data than long questionnaires with no clear focus.

Along the same lines, it is also necessary to think in advance about the order of the questions on the survey. For example, in our survey of adolescents, we should begin with a few introductory questions regarding demographics or other "safe" topics, rather than immediately asking about sensitive topics such as number of sex partners. The sensitive questions can be introduced after the respondent is comfortable with the questionnaire format. In-depth descriptions of issues related to the order of questions on a survey are available in Bradbum and Sudman (1983) and Catania, McDermott, and Pollack (1986). Furthermore, items on the questionnaire should follow a smooth, logical format. One of the authors once reviewed a survey instrument in which a question about experiences with rape preceded a question about the death of house pets. The abrupt switch from a question about rape to a question about house pets represents a terrible flow of questions in a survey of sensitive topics.

Throughout the questionnaire's construction, we must always consider the types of questions we are asking and whether we are asking them in a manner that is understandable and answerable for the target population, trying to control for recall and response biases. Consider the following survey item: "In the last three months, I had vaginal sex ____ times with ____ partners." This question requires the respondent to think back over the last three months, count the number of acts of vaginal sex, and count the number of vaginal sex partners. If the respondent cannot remember the entire time period, he or she may simply recall the prior month, then multiply the number of acts by three to estimate the prior three months. The respondent may fail to recall several acts or may under- or overestimate the number of acts during the recall period, resulting in *recall bias* (Bajos, Spira, Ducot, Leridon, & Riandey, 1991; Catania, Gibson, Chitwood, et al., 1990; Dolcini et al., 1993; McQueen et al., 1989; Morris, 1993; Smith, 1992). Recall bias can be reduced by keeping the recall period short and by ensuring that the recall period is meaningful to the members of the target population. For example, in the case of the adolescent population, three months may be a meaningless time period (Capaldi, 1996); however, "since school started," or "over the summer," or "since the winter holidays" may have more meaning.

Even if a respondent recalls the number of sex acts and sex partners, he or she may be reluctant to share that information. For example, one adolescent male may fear reprisal if anyone finds out, so he may not respond to our question about vaginal sex at all. Another adolescent could exaggerate his sexual activity in an effort to appear mature and "manly." Finally, adolescents may admit to being sexually active but may not be as willing to admit to the actual number of partners or number of sexual acts during the recall period. All of these scenarios represent different sources of response bias. One way to reduce response bias is to assure the participants that their responses will be confidential; thus, there is no need to hide the truth for fear of reprisal and no need to brag about sexual activity to enhance a sexual image. Despite these assurances, it is unlikely that we will ever be completely free of response bias in survey research. The best way to deal with response bias in large-scale surveys is to attempt to measure its effects on our results. Methods for controlling response bias and other kinds of measurement error are well described by Catania and his colleagues in several publications (e.g., 1990, 1993, 1995).

After the survey instrument is constructed, we must consider how it should be administered for our target population. Obvious options are to use a self-administered questionnaire, with or without an interviewer present in the room; a face-to-face, interviewer-administered questionnaire; a questionnaire administered over the phone by an interviewer; diary records; or a computer-assisted interview (either in person or over the telephone) in which the respondent presses buttons to choose responses. Each of these methods has its advantages and disadvantages with respect to measurement errors, respondents' perceptions of the study, and respondents' perceptions of anonymity and privacy (Catania et al., 1995). For example, computer-assisted telephone interviewing provides a uniform presentation of the questions in an anonymous format; however, some respondents may be put off by this impersonal approach.

In the case of adolescents, several characteristics of the population may influence the decision regarding which mode of administration to use. Because of the adolescents' literacy level and comfort with questionnaires, the self-administered, paper-and-pencil method may not be appropriate. By the same token, telephone interviews with adolescents can be a problem, because it is difficult to ensure parental consent for the adolescent's participation over the phone. Because of these restrictions, we will decide for this example that the most effective mode of administration will be an interview. One method that has proven successful involves the projection of the survey questions onto a large screen. The interviewer reads the questions to the adolescents, who mark their responses to the questions on their own sheets of paper. This method has the advantage of circumventing literacy problems while allowing the adolescents to respond to the questions without voicing their answers to an interviewer. Each population will have special, but different, requirements and preferences that must be considered when choosing the method of administration.

After constructing a survey and deciding on a method for its administration, the instrument should be pilot-tested with a small sample from our target population. During the pilot-testing, the questionnaires are administered in exactly the manner in which we anticipate administering it during the actual survey. After the pilot test is finished, however, we may ask the respondents to provide us with detailed critiques of our instruments. Was the questionnaire too long? Did the questions make sense? Was the language and terminology appropriate? Were any questions hard to answer? Was anything offensive? What could make the questionnaire better? Are there any questions that we should ask that we didn't? Are members of the target population likely to be willing to respond to a questionnaire like this? This information is extremely helpful in refining the instrument. In fact, pilot-testing is such an important enterprise that Cannell and colleagues (Cannell, Oksenberg, Kalton, Bischoping, & Fowler, 1989; Oksenberg, Cannell, & Kalton, 1991) developed a pilot-testing system. Using this system, researchers are able to obtain critiques of survey items and can readily pinpoint and address problems.

As we pilot-test, we may begin to detect potential problems with *selection bias*. Selection bias arises when a true random sample of the population is difficult or impossible to attain (Catania, Gibson, Chitwood, et al., 1990; Catania, Gibson, Marin, et al., 1990, 1993). In our research with adolescents and condom use, we may find that adolescents who are not sexually active are not interested in participating. We also may find that males are more likely to refuse to participate than females, or that older adolescents are more willing to participate than their younger counterparts. Perhaps willingness to participate varies with other demographic variables such as race, education, or parents' marital status. Although we cannot always pinpoint the exact reason for selection bias, we can attempt to measure and correct for it (see Catania et al., 1993). This is accomplished by careful recording of demographics and/or other pertinent information from both participants and nonparticipants. These data should be carefully monitored to examine the possible trends in refusals throughout the recruitment process. When a trend in refusal rates has been established during the pilot-testing, it is necessary to correct it in the larger survey by oversampling the underrepresented groups (see the section on sampling). If the trend is not corrected in this way, we will be able to generalize only to the population that our sample represents rather than to the larger population of adolescent males. Therefore, it is in our best interest to carefully monitor recruitment and to correct any refusal trends with targeted sampling.

After the pilot test of our survey instrument, the next step is to obtain a larger representative sample from the target population and administer the questionnaire. The quantitative phase in formative research usually provides a wealth of information; in this example, such information could add to our understanding about adolescents' condom use, sexual behavior, knowledge, attitudes, and beliefs about STD/HIV. Furthermore, because of the larger number of respondents in the survey, we should be able to identify relationships among the variables. This, in turn, can guide the development of an intervention to increase the use of condoms in the target population. For example, we may find that condom use is quite high in members of the population who have access to free condoms, who know how to use condoms, and who have learned about STD/HIV prevention. Conversely, we may find that condom use is very low in adolescents who cannot freely acquire condoms, who have limited experience in using them, or who consider themselves at very low risk for STD/HIV. Of course, we know that the correlation among these variables does not imply that one variable causes another. However, the result of our survey and our knowledge of theoretical models may help us to develop an intervention in which adolescents are shown how to acquire and use a condom correctly and learn about their risk of STD/HIV, as well as acquire the behavioral skills to negotiate condom use successfully with a prospective partner or to refuse a sexual invitation if it is unwanted.

In the preceding subsections, we discussed the role of formative research, beginning with qualitative focus groups and interviews and ending with a quantitative survey of a representative sample from our target population. In the qualitative phase, we used focus groups and interviews to define the domains of interest for our survey and intervention. In the quantitative phase, we gathered more information in each of the domains of interest from a larger sample and then used this data set to examine relationships among access to condoms, condom use, ability to refuse a sexual invitation, comfort and skill negotiating condom use with a prospective partner, and knowledge of STD/HIV risk. Finally, we are ready to use our knowledge about these relationships to formulate our intervention, which we describe in the next section.

Intervention

Choosing Outcomes

We have decided to have an intervention that is designed to (a) help adolescents acquire condoms, (b) train adolescents in correct condom use, (c) educate adolescents regarding their risk for STD/HIV, and (d) train them in the behavioral competencies needed to negotiate condom use with a partner or to refuse a sexual invitation. How will we decide whether we have completed these tasks successfully? We must clearly define in advance which specific behaviors we would like our intervention to change and how we intend to measure these behaviors. If we fail to define these behaviors and measures clearly, we will have no basis for claiming that our intervention worked for our target population. Choosing the appropriate measures, or outcomes, will be our next order of business.

One of our goals is to educate adolescents about where they can acquire condoms, so one straightforward way to evaluate our outcome would be to ask adolescents at preintervention, "Where can you get free condoms? Where can you buy condoms?" After the intervention, we can ask these questions a second time. The extent to which the adolescents learned their condom-acquisition options should be reflected in the difference between the intervention participants' responses at preintervention and their responses after the intervention.

Our second task is to enable adolescents to use condoms correctly if or when they are sexually active. The outcome we seek to evaluate, then, is correct condom use. This may seem a bit tricky to measure, but in fact, this goal can be accomplished by having a demonstration on penile models. At preintervention, the adolescents are asked to place a condom on the model penis and an interviewer rates the adolescent on each component of the task that is completed correctly. After the intervention, the adolescent performs the task again, and the interviewer again rates the adolescent on each step. The extent to which the adolescent has learned correct condom use will be reflected by the difference between the preintervention and postintervention ratings on the condom application task. If we randomly assigned youth to an intervention or control intervention, then changes on this measure should be apparent only for the intervention group after the intervention ends.

Another skill we defined involves social competencies, the skills to refuse an unwanted initiation and to successfully negotiate condom use with a potential partner if the youth is going to have sex. The acquisition of such skill competencies can be measured by using role-play vignettes, constructed from the information we acquired in the focus groups and in-depth interviews to ensure the role-play scripts have ecological validity for our sample. There is an extensive literature on measuring social skills, and researchers usually measure specific behavioral components (i.e., acknowledging the partner's wish, stating a clear and specific refusal) and an overall rating that reflects judges' evaluations of the individual's skill in handling the situation. Role-play assessments can be audio- or videorecorded and then rated by trained research assistants at a later time. It is necessary, of course, to keep the raters "blind" (unaware of the experimental condition or the timing of the assessment) and to train them carefully in the rating procedures. Usually, two raters will overlap on some proportion of the tapes so the researcher can evaluate the extent to which raters agree, usually required to be a minimum of 80% agreement to indicate that the skills can be evaluated reliably. On these measures, too, we would expect to see changes between the participants' responses at preintervention and those after the intervention for those who were in the experimental intervention.

Finally, we want to evaluate whether the adolescents are more accurate in assessing their own risk of STD/HIV after the intervention. In this case, we must carefully define what we mean by risk appraisal. For our study, we will declare that the adolescents must know the behaviors that transmit STD/HIV, be able to list each risk behavior in which they have engaged, and be able to correctly recognize the risk associated with their behavior. At preintervention and postintervention, we could decide to measure knowledge of STD/HIV risk factors, self-reported frequency of behaviors, and self-evaluation of STD/HIV risk. We will then judge the accuracy of their self-evaluations by examining the risk behaviors of each individual, establishing our own assessment of that individual's risk, and comparing our assessment with that of the respondent. A change in accuracy of perceived risk will be reflected in the difference between preintervention and postintervention accuracy scores.

Biomedical Outcomes

In most STD/HIV intervention studies, discussion about measuring biomedical outcomes inevitably arises. The reason for measuring biomedical outcomes is the fact that we are teaching behavioral strategies to the target population, with the ultimate goal of reducing disease transmission. Therefore, it makes sense to measure the incidence of disease in the population before and after the intervention, as well as measuring the cognitive and behavioral outcomes discussed above. Another argument in favor of measuring biomedical outcomes refers to the fact that biomedical outcomes can be used to validate the behavioral measures, although neither method offers "perfect' measurement. However, when all of the measurement domains produce similar findings, our confidence in the study's results is increased. In the case of our study of STD/HIV prevention in adolescents, a biomedical outcome could be the number of new infections of STD or HIV diagnosed during the study period or through the follow-up period after the intervention ends. At the end of the study, the number of new infections in the intervention group can be compared to the number of new infections in the control group. One caution, however, should be noted: The use of biomedical outcomes generally requires greatly increased sample sizes to attain adequate statistical power.

Intervention Format

Now that we have decided on the variables we will measure, we must decide how we will intervene and teach the skills we designated as our goals. In this example, we might implement an intervention involving small media (e.g., role model stories), interactive discussions, and skill practice to provide the communication skills adolescents need to be able to refuse unwanted sexual initiations or to negotiate condom use if they are going to have sex; demonstrations combined with practice accessing and using condoms correctly; and information about STD/HIV prevention. In this particular study, we probably would not, for example, use mass media such as radio and television because we cannot guarantee the intervention would reach only the intervention group and not the control group. We will focus our remaining discussion on methodological issues specifically related to implementing interventions in populations at risk for STD/HIV. For references to specific STD/HIV interventions, see Bond (1992).

An issue central to the implementation of STD/HIV interventions is to decide the length and format of each session and the number of sessions that will be necessary. Do we want to hold individual sessions or group sessions? In the case of our adolescents, we may want to lean toward group sessions because we will at some point ask them to practice putting a condom on a model penis and we will have them role-playing to practice the social competency skills for refusal and partner negotiation. Another advantage of using small group is that the participants can role-play practice together, observe and learn from one another, and begin to create peer support networks favoring prevention.

Should we try to educate our participants about all topics in one session or should we hold more than one session? This issue is constantly debated, because in some populations, the benefits of multiple sessions are counterbalanced by the difficulty of convincing participants to return. Attrition rates for multiple-session interventions range from 8.5% to over 50% (Kalichman, Carey, & Johnson, 1996), implying that we will need to recruit an additional number of people in each group to retain a sufficient sample size for statistical analysis and that we will have to develop time-intensive procedures to promote retention. However, in our review of the literature we will have learned that the most effective interventions for adolescents averaged 14 hours of contact time; thus, we will choose a multisession intervention.

Incentives

Do we intend to offer our participants some sort of incentive to help with retention? Often, research participants are given cash, grocery store gift certificates, transportation tokens, medical care, or other forms of compensation for their time and effort. Some incentives are more or less appropriate for different populations; for example, some researchers who study drug-using populations prefer to provide incentives other than cash, because a monetary incentive could be exchanged for drugs. In some cities, populations at high risk for disease have been so often studied that individuals are well aware of the chance to make money from researchers, and the presence of multiple research studies accessing the same target population can create competition between researchers

(Morrow, 1996). Decisions regarding the appropriate incentives to offer, then, must include a consideration of the amount of time a participant must devote to the study, the amount of money or effort it takes to travel to the study location, the level of effort and attention required from the participant during the sessions, the needs of the participants, and the culture surrounding research in the target population.

An additional decision regarding incentives involves a decision when to provide them to the participants. For example, in a study with more than one assessment, providing all of the incentives at the end of the preintervention session is, of course, a bad idea, because it is unlikely the participants will return for another session if they are paid before the fact. On the other hand, it may be inadvisable to withhold the incentives until the end of the last session, because participants may begin to disbelieve that the incentives will ever appear. One strategy that has helped to sustain high attendance rates is to award the incentive than an absent participant would have received and divide it among the individuals who are present (St. Lawrence, 1981).

Monitoring Maintenance

After our intervention is completed, how many times should we reassess the adolescents' skills in condom use, refusal, and partner negotiation; knowledge of STD/HIV prevention; and ability to self-evaluate risk for acquiring STD/HIV? Certainly, we will want to have assessments at preintervention and again after the intervention to evaluate whether there is any immediate outcome from our program. We may decide to conduct the skills assessments on condom use, refusal, and negotiation only before and after the intervention to evaluate whether, in fact, participants in the experimental intervention actually acquired the skills that we wanted to teach. In addition, we will want to know whether any behavior change produced by our intervention are sustained as time passes. In much of the literature, the length of follow-up periods tends to be rather short; three months appears to be about the usual length of follow-up (cf. Jemmott, Jemmott, & Fong, 1992). Only a few researchers have extended the follow-up period for as long as a full year (St. Lawrence et al., 1995). To decide the length of the follow-up period and the number of reassessments, we should consider some of the following questions: How long do we expect the effects of the intervention to last? How often should reassessments occur such that the behavior changes can be captured without influencing results or causing our participants undue burden? At what point is it no longer feasible to access this population? In the case of our adolescent study, we will choose to reassess the sexual behavior and disease outcomes at three-month intervals after the intervention. These repeated measurements will allow us to examine the effects of the intervention over a long period of time but will not be overly frequent.

Now that our intervention plan is beginning to take shape, we still have some important decisions to make involving randomization, the control group, and assurance that the group leaders adhere to the experimental protocol.

Randomization

We must decide on a strategy for randomizing the participants to a treatment or non-treatment control condition. Some studies do not employ randomized designs, instead opting for quasi-experimental designs (Kessler, 1993; see Kazdin, this volume). We will focus on studies in which participants are randomly assigned to conditions, as this is preferable in experimental research. In these studies, we may choose to employ a purely random process such as a coin toss; that is, for each participant enrolled in the study, we flip a coin to determine which experimental condition will be assigned. In some studies, this method will prove very difficult. For example, suppose we are planning to perform group sessions with our adolescents. We might recruit adolescents from classrooms, athletic events, youth centers, or other group settings; therefore, it would be most convenient to randomize everyone in a particular location to the same condition, so that we need only perform one intervention at each place. This technique, called randomization by clusters, is scientifically sound but will raise the necessary sample size for the study. This is because the appropriate unit of statistical analysis is always the same as the unit of randomization, which is now the recruitment site rather than the individual. Thus, statistical analysis must account for the similarity of individuals within clusters. Although this method of randomization may be more convenient for the investigators, the additional sample size requirements and the complications introduced into the statistical analysis must be taken into consideration.

Any discussion of randomization must include a caution about guarding against the breakdown of randomization. Randomization can be impeded in any number of ways, although we present only two here. In one situation, an investigator may feel a moral obligation to provide any sexually active individuals with a safer-sex, STD/HIV-prevention intervention. This investigator runs a serious risk of confounding the study results by providing the intervention only to a sample of highly at-risk individuals and assigning all individuals at lesser risk to a control condition. As a result, the groups are not comparable. This situation can be avoided if the investigator agrees that the control group will be provided the same intervention once the scientific study has been completed. In a second situation, individuals from the intervention group may complicate, or *confound,* randomization by sharing intervention materials with friends who are in the control group. This scenario is easy to envision if the sample has been amassed by snowball sampling and individuals are randomized into different groups. The breakdown of randomization brings serious threats to the validity of the study and so should be carefully addressed. Usually, this is done by preliminary statistical analyses that check to ensure the groups were equivalent before the experimental intervention was delivered.

Activities of the Comparison (Control) Group

In the example of our adolescent study, suppose we decided to provide individual intervention sessions to adolescents in the treatment group, but no sessions at all to adolescents in the control group. Should any aspect of the adolescents' knowledge, attitudes, perceptions, or behaviors change, we would want to attribute these changes to the intervention, but it is also possible that they might have been due to the simple fact that the adolescents in the intervention received attention and instruction, whereas those in the control group did not. To eliminate this confound, the control group can receive similar levels of attention and instruction, but in an intervention that is unrelated to condom-use, refusal and negotiation skills or self-assessment of risk. We may provide the control group with other forms of health or safety instruction in a format similar to that of the intervention being provided to the treatment group but with unrelated content. Should ethical concern require that the control group eventually be provided with the intervention being given to the treatment group, this can be accomplished after the study is complete.

As we have illustrated in this section, the decisions to be made before the research even begins are many. An equal challenge for the researchers involves remembering each decision and adhering to it throughout the study. Though this may appear trivial at the outset, scientific research is dynamic: Researchers and interviewers are constantly embarking upon simultaneous new studies, sometimes leaving studies altogether, to be replaced with researchers who were not involved in the original decision-making processes. The only way to ensure proper adherence to study protocol is to carefully record each experience and methodological decision in a study manual. This manual should be updated each time a new decision is made or a new study component is added, and should be rigorously followed by each member of the research team. Any deviations from protocol should also be carefully noted so that the evaluation of the study takes into account all eventualities.

Evaluation

The goal of evaluating an intervention is to summarize its efficacy, feasibility, cost-effectiveness, acceptability, potential for being adopted by other agencies and programs, generalizability, and merit in terms of future research for the prevention of STD/HIV. As stated by the National Research Council (1989), evaluating an STD/HIV behavioral intervention program involves answering "several key questions":

1. What were the objectives of the intervention?
2. How was the intervention designed to be conducted?
3. How was the intervention actually conducted?
   Who participated? [And who did not?]
   Were there any unexpected problems?
   What parts of the program were easier to conduct than was anticipated?
   What parts were more difficult to conduct than was anticipated?
4. What outcomes were observed, and how were they measured?
5. What were the results of the intervention? (p. 318)

To the extent that the research was rigorously conducted and documented at all stages, the evaluation is fairly straightforward.

CONCLUSION

This chapter reviewed some of the major methodological issues that arise in sex research and used the information to illustrate the process researchers follow in designing and delivering an intervention study. The goal was to help readers develop skills for understanding and evaluating sex research.

Ideally, research on human sexual behavior should employ random sampling or probability sampling, although this can be a problem because many people will refuse to participate in sex research. Large quantitative surveys generally rely on self-report, which may be inaccurate due to purposeful distortion, memory lapses, or inability to estimate or recall the information. Direct observation would avoid these problems but lead to an even more restricted sample of subjects and is not appropriate for many questions of interest. Direct observation also answers different questions from those answered by surveys and raises complicated ethical issues. In all behavioral research, the ethical principles of informed consent and protection from harm are a basic and unalterable necessity, although, as we saw, historically some sex researchers were remiss in attending to ethical considerations.

The major sex surveys reviewed included Kinsey's interview study during the 1940s, Hunt's study in 1974, and Laumann's survey of sexual practices in the United States in the 1990s. Although other specialized or smaller surveys were done over the years, the samples in those studies did not allow for any general conclusions. The goal of experimental research is to be able to determine what factors cause different aspects of human sexual functioning. In the latter part of this chapter, we used the methodological issues that arise to design, from start to finish, a programmatic research project to effect adolescents' use of condoms during sexual activity.

REFERENCES

Ajzen, I., & Fishbein, M. (1977). Attitude-behavior relations: A theoretical analysis and review of empirical research. *Psychological Bulletin, 84,* 888–918.

Allen, S., Tice, J., De Perre, P. V., Serufilira, A., Hudes, E., Nsengumuremi, F., Bogaerts, J., Lindan, C., & Hulley, S. (1992). Effect of serotesting with counseling on condom use and seroconversion among HIV discordant couples in Africa. *British Medical Journal, 304,* 1605–1609.

Bajos, N., Spira, A., Ducot, B., Leridon, H., & Riandey, B. (1991, June). *Sexual behavior in France: Feasibility study.* Paper presented at the VIIth International Conference on AIDS, Florence, Italy.

Bandura, A. (1994). Social cognitive theory and exercise of control over HIV infection. In R. J. DiClemente & J. L. Peterson (Eds.), *Preventing AIDS: Theories and methods of behavioral interventions.* New York: Plenum Press.

Bartell, G. D. (1970). Group sex among the mid-Americans. *Journal of Sex Research, 6,* 113–130.

Bauman, L. J., & Adair, E. G. (1992). The use of ethnographic interviewing to inform questionnaire construction. *Health Education, 19,* 9–23.

Bernard, H. R. (1994). *Research methods in anthropology: Qualitative and quantitative approaches.* Walnut Creek, CA: AltaMira Press.

Bond, L. (1992). *A portfolio of AIDS/STD behavioral interventions and research.* Washington, DC: Pan American Health Organization.

Boulton, M. (1993). Methodological issues in HIV/AIDS social research: Recent debates, recent developments. *AIDS, 7,* 249–255.

Bradbum, N., & Sudman, S. (1983). *Asking questions: A practical guide to questionnaire design.* San Francisco: Jossey-Bass.

Brenner, M. (1985). Intensive interviewing. In M. Brenner, J. Brown, & D. Canter (Eds.), *The research interview: Uses and approaches.* London: Academic Press.

Cannell, C., Oksenberg, L., Kalton, G., Bischoping, K., & Fowler, F. (1989). *New techniques for pretesting survey questions* (NCHSR #HS05616). Ann Arbor: University of Michigan Survey Research Center.

Capaldi, D. M. (1996). The reliability of retrospective report for timing first sexual intercourse for adolescent males. *Journal of Adolescent Research, 11,* 375–387.

Carballo-Dieguez, A. (1996, April 26–28). *Sexual research with Latino men who have sex with men: Methodological issues.* Discussion paper presented at the workshop: Researching sexual behavior: Methodological issues, Bloomington, Indiana.

Cassell, J. (1977). The relationship of observer to observed in peer group research. *Human Organization, 36,* 412-416.

Catania, J. A., Binson, D., Van der Straten, A., & Stone, V. (1995). Methodological research on sexual behavior in the AIDS era. *Annual Review of Sex Research, 6,* 77–125.

Catania, J. A., Coates, T. J., Stall, R. D., Turner, H., Peterson, J., Hearst, N., Dolcini, M., Hudes, E., Gagnon, J., Wiley, J., & Groves, R. (1992). Prevalence of AIDS-related risk factors and condom use in the United States. *Science, 258,* 1101–1106.

Catania, J. A., Dolcini, M. M., & Coates, T. J. (1992). Catania and colleagues respond. *American Journal of Public Health, 82,* 1564–1565.

Catania, J. A., Gibson, D., Chitwood, D., & Coates, T. J. (1990). Methodological problems in AIDS behavioral research: Influences on measurement error and participation bias in studies of sexual behavior. *Psychological Bulletin, 108,* 339–362.

Catania, J. A., Gibson, D., Marin, B., Coates, T. J., & Greenblatt, R. (1990). Response bias in assessing sexual behaviors relevant to HIV transmission. *Evaluation and Program Planning, 11,* 19–29.

Catania, J. A., Kegeles, S. M., & Coates, T. J. (1990). Towards an understanding of risk behavior: An AIDS risk reduction model (ARRM). *Health Education Quarterly, 17,* 53–72.

Catania, J. A., McDermott, L., & Pollack, L. (1986). Questionnaire response bias and face-to-face interview sample bias in sexuality research. *Journal of Sex Research, 22,* 52–72.

Catania, J. A., Turner, H., Pierce, R., Golden, E., Stocking, C., Binson, D., & Mast, K. (1993). Response bias in surveys of AIDS-related sexual behavior. In D. G. Ostrow & R. C. Kessler (Eds.), *Methodological issues in AIDS behavioral research.* New York: Plenum Press.

Coates, R., Soskolne, C., Calzavara, L., Read, S., Fanning, M., Shaphard, F., Klein, M., & Johnson, J. (1988). Validity of sexual contacts of men with AIDS or an AIDS-related condition. *American Journal of Epidemiology, 128,* 719–728.

Coyle, S., Boruch, R. F., & Turner, C. (1991). *Evaluation of AIDS prevention programs.* Washington, DC: National Academy Press.

Darrow, W., Jaffe, H., Thomas, P., Haverkos, H., Rogers, M., Guinan, M., Auerbach, D., Spira, T., & Curran, J. (1986). Sex of interviewer, place of interview, and responses of homosexual men to sensitive questions. *Archives of Sexual Behavior, 15,* 79–88.

DeLamater, J. (1974). Methodological issues in the study of premarital sexuality. *Sociological Methods Research, 2,* 30–61.

DeLamater, J., & MacCorquodale, P. (1975). The effects of interview schedule variations on reported sexual behavior. *Sociological Methods Research, 4,* 215–236.

DiMauro, D. (1995). *Sexuality research in the United States: An assessment of the social and behavioral sciences.* New York: The Sexuality Research Assessment Project.

Dolcini, M. M., Catania, J. A., Coates, T. J., Stall, R., Hudes, E. S., Gagnon, J. H., & Pollack, L. M. (1993). Demographic characteristics of heterosexuals with multiple partners: The national AIDS behavioral surveys (NABS). *Family Planning Perspectives, 25,* 208–214.

Doll, L. S. (1996, April 26–28). *Methodological issues in research on bisexual men and women and lesbians.* Discussion paper presented at the workshop: Researching sexual behavior: Methodological issues, Bloomington, Indiana.

Doll, L. S., Harrison, J. S., Frey, R. L., McKiman, D., Bartholow, B. N., Douglas, J. M., Joy, D., Bolan, G., & Doetsch, J. (1994). Failure to disclose HIV risk among gay and bisexual men attending sexually transmitted disease clinics. *American Journal of Preventive Medicine, 10,* 125–129.

Fisher, J. D., & Fisher, W. A. (1992). Changing AIDS-risk behavior. *Psychological Bulletin, 111,* 455–474.

Frey, J. H., & Fontana, A. (1991). The group interview in social research. *Social Science Journal, 28,* 175–187.

Gagnon, J. H. (1988). Sex research and sexual conduct in the era of AIDS. *Journal of Acquired Immune Deficiency Syndrome, 1,* 593–601.

Gagnon, J. H., & Parker, R. G. (1994). *Conceiving sexuality: Approaches to sex research in a postmodern world.* New York and London: Routledge.

Goldman, A. E., & McDonald, S. S. (1987). *The group depth interview: Principles and practice.* Englewood Cliffs, NJ: Prentice-Hall.

Gorden, R. (1992). *Basic interviewing skills.* Itasca, IL: Peacock.

Humphreys, L. (1970). *Tearoom trade: Impersonal sex in public places.* Chicago: Aldine.

Hunt, M. (1974). *Sexual behavior in the 1970s.* Chicago: Playboy Press.

Jemmott, J. B., Jemmott, L. S., & Fong, G. T. (1992). Reductions in HIV risk-associated sexual behaviors among Black male adolescents: Effects of an AIDS prevention intervention. *American Journal of Public Health, 82,* 372–377.

Jones, J. (1981). *Bad blood: The Tuskegee syphilis experiment.* New York: Free Press.

Kaiser, J. (Ed.). (1997). Bangkok study adds fuel to AIDS ethics debate. *Science, 278,* 1553.

Kalichman, S. C., Carey, M. P., & Johnson, B. T. (1996). Prevention of sexually transmitted HIV infection: A meta-analytic review of the behavioral outcome literature. *Annals of Behavioral Medicine, 18,* 6–13.

Kalton, G. (1993). Sampling considerations in research on HIV risk and illness. In D. G. Ostrow & R. C. Kessler (Eds.), *Methodological issues in AIDS behavioral research.* New York: Plenum Press.

Kauth, M., St. Lawrence, J. S., & Kelly, J. A. (1991). Reliability of retrospective assessments of sexual HIV risk behavior: A comparison of biweekly, three-month, and twelve-month self-reports. *AIDS Education and Prevention, 3,* 207–214.

Kessler, R. C. (1993). Quasi-experimental designs in AIDS psychosocial research. In D. G. Ostrow & R. C. Kessler (Eds.), *Methodological issues in AIDS behavioral research.* New York: Plenum Press.

Kinsey, A. C., Pomeroy, W. B., & Martin, C. E. (1948). *Sexual behavior in the human male.* Philadelphia: Saunders.

Kinsey, A. C., Pomeroy, W. B., Martin, C. E., & Gebhard, P. H. (1953). *Sexual behavior in the human female.* Philadelphia: Saunders.

Kippax, S., Connell, R. W., Dowsett, G. W., & Crawford, J. (1993). *Sustaining safe sex.* London: Falmer Press.

Kotarba, J. A. (1980). Discovering amorphous social experience: The case of chronic pain. In W. B. Shaffir, R. A. Stebbins, & A. Turowetz (Eds.), *Fieldwork experience: Qualitative approaches to social research.* New York: St. Martin's Press.

Laumann, E. O., Gagnon, J. H., Michael, R. T., & Michaels, S. (1994). *The social organization of sexuality: Sexual practices in the United States.* Chicago: University of Chicago Press.

Masters, W. H., & Johnson, V. (1966). *Human sexual response.* Boston: Little, Brown.

Masters, W. H., & Johnson, V. (1979). *Homosexuality in perspective.* Boston: Little, Brown.

McCracken, G. (1988). *The long interview.* Newbury Park, CA: Sage.

McFarlane, M., & St. Lawrence, J. S. (1997). *Adolescents' recall of sexual behavior: Consistency of self-report and the effect of variations in recall duration.* Under editorial review.

McLaws, M. L., Oldenburg, B., Ross, M. W., & Cooper, D. A. (1990). Sexual behavior in AIDS-related research: Reliability and validity of recall and diary measures. *Journal of Sex Research, 27,* 265–281.

McQueen, D., Gorst, T., Nisbet, L., Robertson, B., Smith, R., & Uitenbroek, D. (1989). *A study of lifestyle and health (Interim Report No. 1).* Edinburgh, England: University of Edinburgh Research Unit in Health and Behavioral Change.

Melton, G. B. (1989). Ethical and legal issues in research and intervention. *Journal of Adolescent Health Care, 10,* 36S–44S.

Melton, G. B., & Gray, J. N. (1988). Ethical dilemmas in AIDS research: Individual policy and public health. *American Psychologist, 43,* 60–64.

Michaels, S. (1996, April 26–28). *Integrating quantitative and qualitative methods in the study of sexuality.* Discussion paper presented at the workshop: Researching sexual behavior: Methodological issues, Bloomington, Indiana.

Morgan, D. L. (1988a). *Focus groups as qualitative research.* Beverly Hills, CA: Sage.

Morgan, D. L. (1988b). *Successful focus groups.* Beverly Hills, CA: Sage.

Morris, M. (1993). Telling tales explain the discrepancy in sexual partner reports. *Nature, 365,* 437–440.

Morrow, D. J. (1996, September 29). Swallowing bitter pills for pay: Trials of human guinea pigs. *The New York Times,* 3–1, 3–10.

National Research Council. (1989). *AIDS: Sexual behavior and intravenous drug use.* Washington, DC: National Academy Press.

Oksenberg, L., Cannell, C., & Kalton, G. (1991). New strategies for pretesting survey questions. *Journal of Official Statistics, 7,* 349–365.

O'Leary, A., DiClemente, R. J., & Aral, S. O. (1997). Reflections on the design and reporting of HIV/AIDS behavioral intervention research. *AIDS Education and Prevention, 9*(Suppl. A), 1–14.

Ostrow, D. G., & Kessler, R. C. (Eds.). (1993). *Methodological issues in AIDS behavioral research.* New York: Plenum Press.

Parker, R. G. (1994). Sexual cultures, HIV transmission, and AIDS prevention. *AIDS, 8,* 309–314.

Patton, M. Q. (1987). *How to use qualitative methods in evaluation.* Newbury Park, CA: Sage.

Prochaska, J. O., Redding, C. A., Harlow, L. L., Rossi, J. S., & Velicer, W. F. (1994). The transtheoretical model of change and HIV prevention: A review. *Health Education Quarterly, 21,* 471–486.

Rodgers, J. (1982). The rescission of behaviors: Inconsistent responses in adolescent sexuality data. *Social Science Research, II,* 280–296.

Rosen, R. C., Davis, C. M., & Ruppel, H. J. (Eds.). (1995). *Annual review of sex research: An integrative and interdisciplinary review* (Vol. 6). Mt. Vernon, IA: Society for the Scientific Study of Sexuality.

Rosenstock, I. (1974). The health belief model and preventive health behavior. *Health Education Monographs, 2,* 328–335.

Saracco, A., Musicco, M., Nicolosi, A., Angarana, G., Arici, C., Gavazzeni, G., Costigliola, P., Gapa, S., Gervasoni, C., & Luzzati, R. (1993). Man-to-woman sexual transmission of HIV: A longitudinal study of 343 steady partners of infected men. *Journal of Acquired Immune Deficiency Syndrome, 6,*497–502.

Schmidt, G., Sigusch, V., & Schafer, S. (1973). Responses to reading erotic stories: Male-female differences. *Archives of Sexual Behavior, 2,* 181–199.

Siegel, D., Golden, E., Washington, A., Morse, S., Fullilove, M., Catania, J., Marin, B., & Hulley, S. (1992). Prevalence and correlates of herpes simplex infections: The population-based AMEN study. *Journal of the American Medical Association, 286,* 1702–1708.

Smith, T. W. (1992). A methodological analysis of the sexual behavior questions on the general social surveys. *Journal of Official Statistics, 8,* 309–325.

St. Lawrence, J. S. (1981). Efficacy of a money deposit contingency on clinical outpatients' attendance and participation in assertive training. *Journal of Behavior Therapy and Experimental Psychiatry. 12,* 237–240.

St. Lawrence, J. S., Brasfield, T. L., Jefferson, K. W., Allcyne, E., O'Bannon, R. E., & Shirley, A. (1995). Cognitive-behavioral intervention to reduce African American adolescents' risk for HIV infection. *Journal of Consulting and Clinical Psychology, 63,* 221–237.

Taylor, S. J., & Bogdan, R. (1984). *Introduction to qualitative research methods: The search for meanings.* New York: Wiley.

The Belmont report: Ethical principles and guidelines for the protection of human subjects of research. (1978). DHEW Publication No. [OS] 78-0012. Washington, DC: Department of Health, Education and Welfare.

Turner, C. F., Miller, H. G., & Moses, L. E. (1989). *AIDS: Sexual behavior and intravenous drug use.* Washington, DC: National Academy Press.

Udry, J., & Morris, N. (1967). A method for validation of reported sexual data. *Journal of Marriage and the Family, 29,* 442–446.

Warren, C. A. B., & Rasmussen, P. K. (1977). Sex and gender in field research. *Urban Life, 6,* 349–370.

Zeller, R. A. (1993). Combining qualitative and quantitative techniques to develop culturally sensitive measures. In D. G. Ostrow & R. C. Kessler (Eds.), *Methodological issues in AIDS behavioral research.* New York: Plenum Press.

Zimmerman, R. S., & Langer, L. M. (1995). Improving prevalence estimates of sensitive behaviors: The randomized lists technique and self-reported honesty. *Journal of Sex Research, 32,* 107–117.

PART FIVE

SPECIAL POPULATIONS

Chapter 24 —————————————————————————

Focus Chapter

RESEARCH METHODS WITH CHILDREN

JAN L. CULBERTSON, PH.D.

Over the past 40 years, research trends, paradigms, and methodology focused on psychological issues with children have evolved rapidly. Since the early 1960s, the field of clinical child psychology has been shaped by the research that has framed and explored the pertinent questions of its era. Social influences and changes in the broader health care field have challenged the efficacy of our clinical practices and driven our research to new heights.

The field of clinical child psychology is very broadly defined to encompass the training, research, and clinical practice aspects of psychological assessment and intervention, normal development processes, psychopathology, and the prevention of mental health problems. Research in clinical child psychology is integrative, involving applications in various contexts and service settings (including families, schools, community agencies, child protective services, juvenile justice agencies, hospitals, etc.); collaboration with other professional disciplines (such as social work, law, medicine); encompassing diversity issues (ethnic, cultural, and gender); and incorporating research paradigms from developmental psychology, neuropsychology, biological psychology, adult clinical psychology, and community psychology, to name a few. The field extends this broad scope to encompass scholarly contributions to advocacy and policy development affecting children, adolescents, and families. Given such a breadth and diversity of clinical issues, it is no wonder that the nature of research has changed dramatically over the years. This chapter reviews briefly the historical trends in clinical child psychology research, the methodological and research challenges that are commonly faced by researchers, and current and future trends in clinical child research.

HISTORICAL TRENDS IN CLINICAL CHILD RESEARCH

Although research in developmental psychology has a history dating from the early 1900s, research in applied or clinical child psychology has emerged over the past 30 to 40 years. The formation in 1962 of a Section of Clinical Child Psychology within the Division of Clinical Psychology (Division 12) of the American Psychological Association

I would like to thank Valerie N. Hartman and Ginger King for their invaluable assistance in research for this chapter.

(APA) provided the impetus for practitioners and researchers interested in children to come together professionally and begin charting the course of the new subspecialty. In the early years, concerns about the relevance of traditional research paradigms within developmental psychology were raised (Sears, 1975), and there was a plea for child researchers to become more involved with socially relevant issues and practical applications (Hetherington, 1998). By 1971, the Section established its first journal—the *Journal of Clinical Child Psychology*.

The earliest published articles in the journal were brief, generally nonreferenced, and often centered around a topical theme (see Routh, 1994). Many of the articles advocated for changes in policies or laws affecting children, including ending corporal punishment in the schools, better educational services for children who were mentally retarded, eradication of child abuse, and similar themes. A policy of editorial and peer review of all submissions was not instituted until the late 1970s, but thereafter, the journal had a growing emphasis on increasing the methodological rigor and scholarly contributions of the articles.

Routh, Patton, and Sanfilippo (1991) surveyed the changing trends in clinical child psychology research over an 18-year period from 1971 to 1989 by examining characteristics of articles published in the *Journal of Clinical Child Psychology*. They found that over the course of the journal's history, the mean percentages of articles reflecting original research increased from 9.53% to over 90% by 1989. During that time, the percentage of first authors affiliated with colleges and universities rose from 37% to 82.5%. Articles devoted to the professional practice of clinical child psychology were highest during the 1978–1982 period (about 33%), but thereafter declined to 0.33% of the total articles published. In an effort to support the journal's mission of publishing articles devoted to child advocacy and policy, a special issue was published (Vol. 20, No. 1) including scholarly policy analyses and data-based original research articles addressing various aspects of policy relating to children and youth.

Culbertson (1996) later surveyed the nature of articles published in the *Journal of Clinical Child Psychology* during the five-year period of 1992–1996, and noted an increased focus on articles devoted to research design and methodology compared to previous eras. A special issue of the journal (1995, Vol. 24, No. 2) was devoted to methodological issues in clinical child psychology research, and another special section (1994, Vol. 23, No. 2) discussed special methodological considerations regarding research that is conducted in nonmental health environments (such as schools, primary health care settings, and the juvenile justice system). The topics of articles published during the early 1990s reflected the social issues of the time (e.g., child maltreatment, ethnic and cultural issues), but emerging areas of research in social competence and the effects of stress on the coping responses of children were also apparent. The breadth of topics under study was matched by increased methodological rigor, as reflected in increasingly diverse and complex designs, use of multivariate statistics to analyze multiple dependent and independent variables simultaneously, use of multimethod designs, and more sensitive consideration of the context in which the research question was conceptualized.

The trends in research topics and methodology in the latter part of the 1990s reflect the growing demand for empirically supported psychosocial interventions for children (Kazdin & Kendall, 1998; Lonigan, Elbert, & Johnson, 1998), exploration of developmental influences on the emergence of psychopathology (Campbell, 1996), and emerging models for developmentally based, integrated psychotherapy with children (Russ, 1998). Continuation of these strides in clinical child research, building on past successes and learning from past mistakes, will undoubtedly lead to more generalizable and clinically useful information derived from our research efforts.

METHODOLOGICAL ISSUES COMMONLY ENCOUNTERED IN CLINICAL CHILD RESEARCH

Research with children creates unique methodological challenges, including developmental issues related to maturation, contextual influences of the child's environment, and dependence upon informants to provide relevant clinical information.

Developmental Influences

Developmental Variation and Discontinuities

Research with children requires an understanding of the range of normal behavior and the major developmental transitions that influence children's behavior at each age. Development generally occurs in a discontinuous rather than a continuous fashion, so that one skill may surge ahead while another skill matures at a slower rate for a period of time. This pattern of developmental discontinuity makes it difficult for researchers to establish strict age guidelines for measuring a specific developmental skill. For example, transitions in cognitive development from the concrete operations to formal operations periods can influence children's processing of information and the reasoning abilities they bring to emotional and behavioral functioning during treatment. Developmental transitions in social/emotional maturation provide a context for interpreting certain behaviors as normal or abnormal (e.g., oppositional and defiant behavior is typical in toddlers as they negotiate the struggle toward greater independence, but this behavior typically is under better self-control by age 6 years). Similar developmental transitions in attention and activity level, regulation and modulation of emotions, development of empathy, and preference for individual vs. interactive modes of play can influence the processes and outcome variables under study in child research. Individual differences in temperament also create wide variations in normal behavior, ranging from inhibited to flexible to outgoing to irritable and demanding. It is important for researchers to avoid misinterpreting these normal temperamental variations as possible indicators of dysfunction. Children do not make developmental transitions at fixed ages, and researchers must consider the individual variations in emergence of each developmental skill when planning the age range of the population under study. This suggests that subject selection may be based at times on children's functional abilities or their developmental acquisition of certain skills rather than strict chronological age guidelines.

Researchers who are aware of these important developmental influences on behavior can design research that addresses or incorporates controls for many of these variables to avoid confounding the outcomes. For example, longitudinal designs that use the child as his or her own control can be helpful in understanding the relationship between various risk factors and developmental outcome. Including quality assessment of each child's developmental status at the outset of the research can help to establish more homogeneous subject populations, or conversely, describe more accurately how the subject groups differ.

Equivalence of Measurement

The equivalence of measures across ages must also be considered in child research. The same construct may have to be measured differently at different ages. For example, the construct of self-control in preschoolers (e.g., waiting one's turn to play with a toy rather than grabbing the toy from a peer's hands) or fourth graders (e.g., not interrupting in class) would be assessed differently than self-control in twelfth graders (e.g., refraining from alcohol abuse). Yet, changes in measurement methods over time can compromise the internal validity of research (i.e., the degree to which change in functioning can be attributed to experimental variables) and can affect the analyses and conclusions. Black and Holden (1995) suggest that problems with measurement change can be eliminated if one chooses a narrow age cohort or uses measures that are not age-dependent. The problem can be minimized if one uses multiple measures for important constructs, and whenever possible, chooses those that span a broad age range.

Longitudinal Research Paradigms

Longitudinal research designs are often used to investigate children's development. These designs involve examining the long-term effects of some event (e.g., inadequate nutrition or maternal neglect during the first year of life) or intervention (providing early educational stimulation and enrichment) on specific outcome variables. Longitudinal designs allow the researcher to collect information from participants using a set of measures repeated at multiple time periods; this approach minimizes error variance and often allows the detection of small behavior changes (Black & Holden, 1995). These designs also allow one to investigate intra-individual change, evaluate the variables associated with onset of dysfunction over time, and assess multiple outcome options.

According to Black and Holden (1995), disadvantages of longitudinal designs are often tied to the length of time over which the research is conducted and the host of intervening variables that can potentially affect outcome. Collection of data over a long period of time may lead to outdating of procedures and measures, interference from natural influences in the environment or society that may impact all or part of the cohort under study, and subject attrition (i.e., leaving the study before it is completed). Attrition of participants increases the probability of Type II experimental error (i.e., finding no difference when actual differences are present) and affects the generalizability of the findings, especially if one type of participant tends to drop out at a higher rate than other types (Black & Holden, 1995). For instance, assume one is studying the relative effects of two types of early interventions with high-risk parents—one intervention involving supportive visits from a paraprofessional and the other involving parent training on specific skills for stimulating the development of their newborn. Assume an overall 35% drop-out rate of parents in the study, but the drop-out group is disproportionately comprised of parents from lower socioeconomic strata (SES) compared to those who remain in the study (who were middle SES). At the conclusion of the study, it would be difficult to ascertain whether the outcome of better parenting skills in the middle SES group of parents was attributable to the nature of the intervention, the fact that more of them completed the study rather than dropped out, or statistical power issues related to a smaller sample size at the conclusion of the study.

In longitudinal designs, the possibility of staff attrition is heightened compared to studies with briefer data collection periods. Loss of staff can undermine the assessment of critical process variables if the relationship between staff and participants is a central part of the design (Black & Holden, 1995). Efforts to retain staff through frequent de-briefing, supervision, and feedback are useful. Working with certain populations is stressful, and researchers need to address the professional needs of staff in a sensitive manner to facilitate their ongoing commitment to the study. If staff attrition occurs, the integrity of the research can be maintained by assuring that there are clearly defined and described procedures along with careful education and supervision of replacement staff.

Contextual Influences

The design and interpretation of child research is often dependent on a variety of contextual factors in the child's environment that can influence behavior. Primary among these is familial influences, but also the contexts of peer groups, school environment, socioeconomic status, health status, and cultural factors are important contextual variables. Family influences have been implicated in many lines of research, such as research examining the long-term adjustment of children with co-morbid attention deficit hyperactivity disorder (ADHD) and aggression (cf, Barkley, 1998). Children with this co-morbidity often have a poorer prognosis than children without co-morbid ADHD, but they also tend to have fathers with such psychopathology as antisocial personality disorder and increased problems controlling aggressive and violent behavior. Conversely, research examining children's resilience in the face of adversity (such as poverty and lack of enrichment opportunities) often reveals that family support variables are influential in achieving positive outcomes. Depending upon the nature of the outcome variables being studied, researchers might be interested in family variables such as marital status (single, married, divorced), ongoing marital conflict, birth order of the target child, presence or absence of parental psychopathology, educational or literacy level of parents, family communication patterns, and ways in which emotions are expressed in the family system.

Contextual variables related to school settings often have direct effects on child behavior. For example, research investigating the relative amount of disruptive classroom behavior in children with ADHD versus those without ADHD may find that the results vary as a function of the amount of structure inherent in the classroom routine, the freedom of children to move about versus having to remain seated for long periods, organization of the teacher, or willingness of the teacher to provide reminders and praise for the child's on-task behavior.

Cultural factors often influence the constructs being measured in child research and the clinical utility of the outcome. For example, in the area of parent training, understanding cultural differences in the degree of permissiveness vs. strictness related to child discipline, the way emotions are expressed within the cultural group, the perceived role of parents vs. other members of the family in providing discipline, the amount of respect for elders inherent within the cultural group, or parental attitudes toward corporal punishment may influence the design and outcomes of research.

Moderating and Mediating Factors

The potential influence of moderating and mediating factors on research outcomes has received considerable attention in recent years (cf, Baron & Kenny, 1986; Holmbeck, 1997). Moderator variables refer to factors—such as socioeconomic status, or cultural beliefs and practices—that can alter the relationship between predictor and outcome variables and thus distort the interpretation of the findings (Baron & Kenny, 1986). For instance, early investigations of the impact of biological risk (such as premature birth) on developmental outcome of infants consistently revealed that socioeconomic variables were strongly associated with outcome, and often accounted for greater variance than the degree of biological risk associated with gestational age and birth weight.

Mediator variables influence the link between antecedent and outcome variables through certain psychological processes (Baron & Kenny, 1986). For example, treatment outcome with children can be affected by mediating factors within the family that lead to attrition, such as parents who have significant psychopathology or who are experiencing multiple sources of stress (Kazdin, Mazurick, & Bass, 1993). Often multivariate data analysis strategies are used to evaluate the relative contribution of mediating and moderating factors as they relate to outcome. It is important for the researcher to be aware of these potential factors and consider their possible influences upon outcome in each research design.

Dependence on Multiple Sources of Information

Research with children often depend on multiple informants other than only the child for information related to critical variables under study. Sources of information may include mother, father, teacher, peer, and sibling in addition to the child, and methods may range from age-normed behavioral rating scales to structured interviews. Problems arise when there is lack of agreement among various sources of information, and the researcher must decide on which source to weight more heavily than another in arriving at diagnostic consensus. Some researchers argue that weighting should depend on symptom type, as children are considered the best reporters of their own internalizing symptoms (Herjanic & Reich, 1982). Others argue that all sources of information should be weighted equally (Piacentini, Cohen, & Cohen, 1992).

When discrepancies arise between parent-child or mother-father reports, it is important to consider the possible explanations for these discrepancies. Perception of a given informant may depend on the sphere of information available to the informant; differences in perspective that are driven by age and sex of the child, or age, sex, and psychiatric status of the adult informant; different thresholds for tolerance of symptomatology; and the context in which the observations are made (Tarullo, Richardson, Radke-Yarrow, & Martinez, 1995). There also are decisions to be made about the degree of agreement necessary to constitute agreement (e.g., of three informants, should all three agree or is it sufficient that only two of three agree on the diagnostic symptoms?). Research suggests that interrater agreement often depends on the nature of the child's problems, in that parental agreement is usually higher with externalizing than internalizing behaviors (Tarullo et al., 1995). One research team reported that children are more likely to report internalizing symptoms such as fears, anxieties, psychotic symptoms, and covert antisocial behaviors than their parents (Edelbrock, Costello,

Dulcan, Conover, & Kalas, 1986). Researchers thus will need to determine which informant is likely to provide most valid information depending on the nature of the symptoms or diagnoses under study. Use of multiple sources of information, though it necessitates decisions about how to weight results if there are discrepancies, often will increase the likelihood of a valid assessment.

CURRENT ISSUES IN CLINICAL CHILD RESEARCH

Treatment Outcome Research

One of the primary driving forces in clinical child psychology in recent years relates to providing empirical documentation of the effectiveness of psychological interventions with children. Diminishing health care resources and rationing of mental health care by large health maintenance organizations has led to a greater impetus for research support of treatments that work. There are at least four broad-based meta-analytic reviews of the treatment outcome literature with children—and these reviews have collectively examined over 300 outcome studies conducted between 1952 and 1993 involving children between the ages of 2 and 18 (Casey & Berman, 1985; Kazdin, Bass, Ayers, & Rodgers, 1990; Weisz, Weiss, Alicke, & Klotz, 1987; Weisz, Weiss, Han, Granger, & Morton, 1995). The findings of these meta-analyses provide support for the general effectiveness of psychological treatments with children, indicating that a typical child involved in an intervention group scores higher on outcome measures than do 76% to 81% of children in a control group (Lonigan et al., 1998). However, these meta-analyses provide only general support of treatment effectiveness and fail to indicate what specific types of intervention are effective for particular problems (Lonigan et al., 1998).

As the field of clinical child psychology strives to identify empirically supported interventions, there is debate about many aspects of the issues. For instance, what degree of evidentiary support should be required for demonstrating that certain interventions are of value for specific problems (VandenBos, 1996)? Should the field defer to outside pressures from managed care, governmental agencies, and professional organizations to develop practice standards based on the research (Munoz, Hollon, McGrath, Rehm, & VandenBos, 1994)? How relevant is the outcome research to the real world of clinical practice, where some suggest there is greater variability in patient motivation, symptoms of psychopathology, therapist training and experience, adherence to carefully scripted treatment protocols, and influences from third-party reimbursement sources to abbreviate the course of treatment (Lonigan et al., 1998; Weisz, Donenberg, Han, & Weiss, 1995). Many authors have documented the differences between clinical trials research and actual clinical practice (e.g., Goldfried & Wolfe, 1996; Kazdin, 1995, 1997; Seligman, 1995), noting that clinical trials research often is conducted with nonreferred children, and children without comorbid disorders, who are treated for a fixed period of time, often by persons in training. These discrepancies with the parameters of typical clinical practice raise important issues about the generalizability and transportability (Kendall & Southam-Gerow, 1995) of research findings.

Treatment outcome research is still at a relatively early stage in relation to the range of clinical disorders, patient characteristics, and types of research questions that have been addressed to date (Kazdin, 1995). Therefore, a number of authors have addressed the methodological limitations in current research and provided suggestions for improving and expanding treatment outcome research in the future (Kazdin, 1995, 1997; Kazdin & Kendall, 1998; Kendall et al., this volume; Peterson & Bell-Dolan, 1995; Weisz & Hawley, 1998). The sections that follow discuss current methodological issues and suggestions for improving the quality of outcome research to achieve the goal of supporting progress in the field.

Conceptualization of Clinical Dysfunction

The aggregate of current treatment outcome studies is limited in terms of the specific disorders under study (e.g., moving beyond broad categorizations of "internalizing" or "externalizing" disorders to study of the specific disorders that comprise the categories), and also in terms of the conceptualization of each disorder under study (Kazdin & Kendall, 1998). Kazdin and Kendall (1998) make a strong case for improved conceptualization of the factors that lead to the pattern of functioning that we want to change, including factors related to onset, maintenance, termination, and recurrence of the problem and factors that help to characterize more clearly the specific problem under study. They also urge direct testing of the processes hypothesized to be implicated in the clinical problem (e.g., considering whether cognitive, family, or biological processes may play a pivotal role in onset, maintenance, or escalation of the pattern of functioning). It is through efforts to test processes related to the dysfunction that researchers are likely to identify the various subtypes of a given disorder, the multiple paths leading to a similar onset or pattern of dysfunction, and key moderators that may alter the risk factors associated with development of the disorder (Kazdin & Kendall, 1998). Related issues include the importance of characterizing the nature of the symptoms (e.g., severity, intensity, frequency, chronicity) and addressing the prevalence of co-morbidity in clinical populations, where two or more disorders co-occur (Kazdin, 1995). Most existing outcome research strives for patient homogeneity along these characteristics, and attempts to exclude patients with co-morbidity. But treatment for a given problem may vary in effectiveness depending upon the number, type, and severity of other symptoms or disorders that are present (Kazdin, 1995).

Conceptualization and Specification of Treatment

Conceptualization of the processes and mechanisms that are presumed to underlie therapeutic change is fundamental to treatment outcome research. These processes, whether they be psychodynamic, familial, or cognitive, may be assessed directly and even compared within the same study (Kendall & Flannery-Schroeder, 1998). Often the processes under study are those considered to be involved in the problem or disorder being treated, and their direct assessment can shed light on their contributions to the disorder (Kazdin & Kendall, 1998).

It is helpful if the parameters of treatment are varied and evaluated systematically in the study of treatment outcome. Parameters such as intensity (the amount of treatment within a given time frame or an enhanced version of the treatment) and duration (how long treatment is administered over time) are important to consider in research design (Kazdin, 1995). The restrictiveness of the intervention, or the degree to which constraints are placed upon individuals as part of treatment, is important to consider. Whether the treatment is implemented daily as part of a residential or day hospital setting, or whether it is provided in an outpatient setting for 1 hour per week, can influence the outcome parameters.

Specific description of treatment, often in the form of a manual that details specific content and procedures, is essential to clear understanding of precisely what was done and to replication in research and clinical practice (Kazdin & Kendall, 1998). Although there is some debate about the generalizability of treatments that hold to strict regimes (Strupp & Anderson, 1997; Weisz & Hawley, 1998), there is currently no better alternative to specification and documentation of the critical aspects of intervention (Kazdin & Kendall, 1998). Problems in generalization occur often because statements about the efficacy of treatments are based on those individuals who successfully complete all components of a treatment plan, in contrast to most real world therapy environments where therapy attrition (or dropout) often occurs early in treatment, and without notice, so that only a portion of the planned treatment regime could be completed (Weisz & Hawley, 1998). Research information is lacking about the efficacy of completing only portions of the treatment plan, and, more importantly, which portions of the plan are essential to a good outcome.

Direct tests of treatment outcome and processes are central to demonstrating that change has occurred and that the treatment is responsible for the change. A variety of treatment tests—through open or uncontrolled studies, single-case designs, and randomized clinical trials—can provide evidence of such change (Kazdin & Kendall, 1998). Expanding the study of various treatment techniques is essential because most techniques have not been studied systematically. Approximately half of all outcome studies involve behavioral or cognitive-behavioral treatment (Kazdin et al., 1990), and many other approaches commonly used in child psychotherapy have little empirical support (Barrnett, Docherty, & Frommelt, 1991). For example, additional research with psychodynamic psychotherapy, family therapy, and developmentally based psychotherapies is needed. Finally, research examining whether treatment parameters actually affect those processes that are considered to be critical to the treatment model is important. Both moderating and mediating factors, as discussed earlier in this chapter, might produce, facilitate, or mediate change. These factors include things such as relationship, alliance, and bonding between the child (or parent) and therapist (Holmbeck, 1997). The conditions for effective application of treatment and the moderators that influence the efficacy and effectiveness of treatment, are also important to consider. These may include parental psychopathology, socioeconomic disadvantage, severity of symptomatology, or parent stress, which are contextual influences that affect both the development of clinical disorders and the likelihood that treatment processes will be altered in the course of treatment.

Assessment of Treatment Outcome

Kazdin and Kendall (1998) suggest attention to a variety of parameters that provide information regarding efficacy and effectiveness of treatment outcome. Within the context of child functioning, researchers are admonished to look beyond symptom reduction to variables such as whether the extent of everyday functional impairment is reduced and whether there are improvements in the child's prosocial competence, academic functioning, and peer relationships/social functioning. Within the domain of parental and family functioning, assessment measures such as the extent of psychopathology or dysfunction are important, but other risk and resilience factors should be examined also. These may include contextual influences such as stress and quality of life, or adaptive factors such as social support from family and friends. Also important is inclusion of measures of social impact—for instance, the consequences that treatment may have on various systems (such as school activities, truancy, avoidance of detention), use of services, and the monetary cost-benefits of treatment.

The timing of outcome assessment is limited in current treatment outcome research, with most studies reporting limited or no follow-up data (Weisz, Weiss, et al., 1995). As Kazdin and Kendall (1998) point out, conclusions about the efficacy and effectiveness of treatment relative to no-treatment, or about the relative efficacy of two or more treatments, can vary at posttreatment and at follow-up. Obtaining this essential follow-up data can help distinguish between treatments that have positive short-term effects (at the time of treatment termination) versus those with positive long-term effects (assessed at varying stages of follow-up). Finally, the clinical significance of outcomes obtained with treatment must be considered. Merely demonstrating statistically significant improved scores on behavioral rating scales at outcome may not translate to significant and meaningful functional improvements in the child's life. Assessing for each child the aspect of functioning that is most salient to the presenting concerns and reasons for treatment would be a more sensitive measure of the clinical significance of treatment.

In general, Kazdin and Kendall (1998) suggest that a new generation of treatment outcome research is needed to expand on the conceptual basis for both the clinical dysfunction and the treatment parameters under study, add breadth to the clinical populations being treated, and strive to increase the clinical relevance of the treatments to the settings and conditions under which therapy is typically conducted.

RESEARCH IN NONMENTAL HEALTH SERVICE SETTINGS

Most children who receive mental health services through the public sector do so in settings other than traditional practice or mental health treatment facilities (Hoagwood, 1994). Examples include the public schools, juvenile justice system, child welfare and foster care system, and the primary health care system. Although there is little reliable data that estimates the number of children with mental health disorders in these various settings, it is known that the majority of youth in the juvenile justice system carry diagnoses of disruptive behavior disorders (Hoagwood, 1994), and some investigators report that as many as 25% of children in primary health care settings have significant behavioral or emotional adjustment problems (Finney, Riley, & Cataldo, 1991). The reports of child abuse and neglect over the past two decades have risen dramatically to over 3 million (U.S. Advisory Board on Child Abuse & Neglect, 1995), and children within the child protective services system are often in need of mental health services. Current psychotherapy outcome research with children has focused mainly on populations who access the more traditional settings for treatment, and who may possess characteristics that are more amenable to treatment success (such as middle socioeconomic status, majority culture, parents who are able to work in the best interests of their children). In contrast, many children treated in the public sector are likely to have briefer treatment encounters, drop out before treatment is completed, have cultural and ethnic differences that influence their response to traditional therapeutic methods, and have parents with multiple stresses that compromise their ability to participate in and support the therapeutic process. Thus, examining the methodological challenges to conducting research in these various sectors is important for addressing the unmet need for effective mental health services.

Threats to Internal Validity

Hoagwood (1994) examined the various threats to internal, external, and construct validity imposed by three service systems—school, primary health care, and juvenile justice systems. She described internal validity as the degree to which changes in the child's functioning can be attributed to experimental intervention. The threats to internal validity include attrition, random assignment, sample selection, and selection of control groups, to name a few. Attrition is often found in primary care systems due to managed care health provisions and increased family mobility in populations who are socioeconomically disadvantaged. In the juvenile justice system, attrition often is due to court orders, where loss of subjects in certain treatment conditions can seriously interfere with generalization of results (Hoagwood, 1994). Although attrition in school populations is not as bad, it is more of a threat in urban school districts among disadvantaged and sometimes homeless populations. One possible solution to the naturally occurring attrition is to delay random assignment as long as possible—at least until after pretest data have been collected. Although attrition prior to random assignment will affect external validity, attrition following randomization tends to affect internal validity (Bickman, 1992).

Randomization is one of the strongest methods for controlling threats to internal validity, but it is often difficult to implement in nonmental health settings (Hoagwood, 1994). For example, in the juvenile justice system youth are often assigned to a particular intervention on the basis of a court order or other legal and political factors. Direct service providers (such as caseworkers, teachers, probation officers) in many public sector settings view randomization with suspicion, because they are concerned that some children may be denied needed treatment for a period of time, or because it disrupts the operation of the agency (Metcalf & Thornton, 1992). Often this threat to internal validity can be addressed through comparing a new treatment to an already existing treatment approach, or planning with the direct service provider in advance the conditions under which a youth might be transferred from a control to an experimental group (Bickman, 1992). The latter situation might occur when a control group youth is on a waiting list for services, but suddenly has an escalation in symptoms that necessitates moving him or her immediately into a treatment group. To assure that there is some standard, and agreed-upon, basis for this decision can prevent unsubstantiated moves that are inconsistent with the parameters of the study.

Selection of experimental and control groups also poses threats to internal validity. Problems of co-morbidity in samples can increase the complexity of pretesting and the need for more experienced clinicians who can ensure greater diagnostic reliability (Hoagwood, 1994). Within school settings, some diagnostic services are available to assist with assessment of co-morbidity, but this issue must be addressed in experimental design in other settings for which services are not available. Selection of appropriate comparison groups is particularly difficult in the juvenile justice system, where research participants are often placed in restrictive environments for which there are few other comparisons. In school and primary health care settings, developing equivalency of intervention and comparison groups and maintaining them over the course of the treatment is critical to maintaining internal validity as well. Both treatment integrity and rater and subject blindness are also important to the process, though sometimes difficult to carry out in settings such as the primary health care setting where investigators often know the status of their participants (Hoagwood, 1994).

Threats to External Validity

External validity refers to the extent to which research results can be generalized to other populations or settings (Hoagwood, 1994). Threats to external validity are often seen in the heterogeneity of sample characteristics, which is complicated by problems with standardized assessment instruments and presence of co-morbid disorders. Also, contextual factors may have great influence on maintaining treatment outcomes, particularly in the juvenile justice system (Quay, 1987).

Treatments for delinquent youth may be effective while the youth remains in the juvenile justice setting, but may not be maintained after they are returned to the community because of interference from contextual factors (such as violence in the home, or inability of the parents to support the therapeutic gains obtained in the juvenile justice setting). Children who are treated in residential settings for severe emotional disorders may maintain treatment outcomes better if their home, school, and community supports are available upon discharge (Hoagwood & Cunningham, 1992). Finally, bias in making referrals for the proposed research poses a threat to external validity when basic assumptions about random assignment of subjects cannot be made. An example that has been discussed often in the ADHD literature suggests that teachers may be prone to refer boys for evaluation of ADHD and treatment more often than girls because of a bias in perception that boys are more disruptive and more likely to get in trouble than girls. Such biases can also reduce the statistical power of the research, and can threaten the generalizability of findings to at-risk populations (Hoagwood, 1994).

Threats to Construct Validity

Construct validity involves the extent to which a particular construct being assessed accurately measures the theoretical construct under question (Hoagwood 1994). Threats to construct validity in non-mental health service system research often relate to problems in accurate assessment and differential diagnosis of mental health problems under study. In the United States, there are no systematic screening procedures for use in primary health care settings and often there are concerns about stigmatizing young children with disorder diagnoses (Kelleher & Long, 1994). This may lead to a delay or failure to detect disorders in young children. In school and other settings involving children, parents and teachers must be relied upon as informants about primary mental health characteristics under study. The reliability of informant reports, as discussed in the previous section, is an important new area of research that will support the construct validity of research with children.

Finally, there are many gaps in our knowledge of normative developmental processes, parenting, and family systems issues in ethnic, racial, and cultural minority groups. Until this basic normative research is conducted, the theoretical constructs underlying much of our research with minority populations is suspect. Also, it follows that the availability of assessment instruments and treatment approaches that are ethnically and culturally valid is an ongoing problem and represents one of the areas most in need of research attention (Hoagwood, 1994). These issues become much more problematic in public sector mental health service systems (such as juvenile justice), where minority children and youth are vastly overrepresented.

In summary, service system research is an emerging area in clinical child psychology that promises to increase the relevance and practical application of our knowledge about assessment and intervention with children. Although more complex with regard to methodological challenges, this area of research, and the growing body of information that helps to deal with the challenges, should prove to be useful in bridging the gap between laboratory-based clinical outcome research and the real world in which clinicians must search for the most effective treatments under conditions that are not always conducive to methodological rigor.

FUTURE DIRECTIONS IN CLINICAL CHILD RESEARCH

The future of clinical child research will likely be more demanding than the past because researchers are being held to higher standards—standards that are founded on the prior generation of research with all its lessons. Increasingly, there is a trend to blend theoretical positions and ask more complex research questions about the interactions among variables that affect the development of psychopathology and its treatment. Increasingly, we are being held to higher standards of efficacy and effectiveness by a public who is more sophisticated as consumers of mental health services. Finally, the challenges of underserved children and youth with mental health problems, especially those from minority and economically disadvantaged populations, pose more complex research questions about how to conduct methodologically sound studies that have relevance to the community settings and service systems in which these children seek help. The rich history of clinical child research has served us well, and has provided an exciting impetus for the next generation of research.

REFERENCES

Barkley, R. A. (1998). *Attention deficit hyperactivity disorder.* New York: Guilford Press.

Baron, R. M., & Kenny, D. A. (1986). The moderator-mediator variable distinction in social psychological research: Conceptual, strategic, and statistical considerations. *Journal of Personality and Social Psychology, 51,* 1173–1182.

Barrnett, R. J., Docherty, J. P., & Frommelt, G. M. (1991). A review of psychotherapy research since 1963. *Journal of the American Academy of Child and Adolescent Psychiatry, 30,* 1–14.

Bickman, L. (1992). Designing outcome evaluations for children's mental health services: Improving internal validity. In L. Bickman & D. J. Rog (Eds.), *Evaluating mental health services for children* (pp. 57–68). San Francisco: Jossey-Bass.

Black, M. M., & Holden, E. W. (1995). Longitudinal intervention research in children's health and development. *Journal of Clinical Child Psychology, 24,* 163–172.

Campbell, S. B. (1996). Introduction to the special section—young children at risk for psychopathology: Developmental and family perspectives. *Journal of Clinical Child Psychology, 25,* 372–375.

Casey, R. J., & Berman, J. S. (1985). The outcome of psychotherapy with children. *Psychological Bulletin, 98,* 388–400.

Culbertson, J. L. (1996). Editorial. *Journal of Clinical Child Psychology, 25,* 370–371.

Edelbrock, C., Costello, A. J., Dulcan, M. K., Conover, N. C., & Kalas, R. (1986). Parent-child agreement on child psychiatric symptoms assessed via structured interview. *Journal of Child Psychology and Psychiatry, 27,* 181–190.

Finney, J. W., Riley, A. W., & Cataldo, M. F. (1991). Psychology in primary health care: Effects of brief targeted therapy on children's medical care utilization. *Journal of Pediatric Psychology, 16,* 447–461.

Goldfried, M. R., & Wolfe, B. E. (1996). Psychotherapy practice and research: Repairing a strained relationship. *American Psychologist, 51,* 1007–1016.

Herjanic, B., & Reich, W. (1982). Development of a structured psychiatric interview for children: Agreement between child and parent on individual symptoms. *Journal of Abnormal Child Psychology, 10,* 307–324.

Hetherington, E. M. (1998). Relevant issues in developmental science: Introduction to the special issue. *American Psychologist, 53,* 93–94.

Hoagwood, K. (1994). Issues in designing and implementing studies in non-mental health care sectors. *Journal of Clinical Child Psychology, 23,* 114–120.

Hoagwood, K., & Cunningham, M. (1992). Outcomes of children in residential placement for educational purposes. *Journal of Child and Family Studies, 2,* 129–140.

Holmbeck, G. N. (1997). Toward terminological, conceptual, and statistical clarity in the study of mediators and moderators: Examples from the child-clinical and pediatric psychology literatures. *Journal of Consulting and Clinical Psychology, 65,* 599–610.

Kazdin, A. E. (1995). Scope of child and adolescent psychotherapy research: Limited sampling of dysfunctions, treatments, and client characteristics. *Journal of Clinical Child Psychology, 24,* 125–140.

Kazdin, A. E. (1997). A model for developing effective treatments: Progression and interplay of theory, research, and practice. *Journal of Clinical Child Psychology, 26,* 114–129.

Kazdin, A. E., Bass, D., Ayers, W. A., & Rodgers, A. (1990). Empirical and clinical focus of child and adolescent psychotherapy research. *Journal of Consulting and Clinical Psychology, 58,* 729–740.

Kazdin, A. E., & Kendall, P. C. (1998). Current progress and future plans for developing effective treatments: Comments and perspectives. *Journal of Clinical Child Psychology, 27,* 217–226.

Kazdin, A. E., Mazurick, J. L., & Bass, D. (1993). Risk for attrition in treatment of antisocial children and families. *Journal of Clinical Child Psychology, 22,* 2–16.

Kelleher, K., & Long, N. (1994). Barriers and new directions in mental health services research in the primary care setting. *Journal of Clinical Child Psychology, 23,* 133–142.

Kendall, P. C., & Flannery-Schroeder, E. (1998). Methodological issues in treatment research for anxiety disorders in youth. *Journal of Abnormal Child Psychology, 26,* 27–38.

Kendall, P. C., & Southam-Gerow, M. (1995). Issues in the transportability of treatment: The case of anxiety disorders in youth. *Journal of Consulting and Clinical Psychology, 63,* 702–708.

Lonigan, C. J., Elbert, J. C., & Johnson, S. B. (1998). Empirically supported psychosocial interventions for children: An overview. *Journal of Clinical Child Psychology, 27,* 138–145.

Metcalf, C. E., & Thornton, C. (1992). Random assignment. *Children and Youth Services Review, 14,* 145–156.

Munoz, R. F., Hollon, S. D., McGrath, E., Rehm, L. P., & VandenBos, G. R. (1994). On the AHCPR depression in primary care guidelines: Further considerations for practitioners. *American Psychologist, 49,* 42–61.

Peterson, L., & Bell-Dolan, D. (1995). Treatment outcome research in child psychology: Realistic coping with the "Ten Commandments" of methodology. *Journal of Clinical Child Psychology, 24,* 149–162.

Piacentini, J. C., Cohen, P., & Cohen, J. (1992). Combining discrepant diagnostic information from multiple sources: Are complex algorithms better than simple ones? *Journal of Abnormal Child Psychology, 20,* 51–63.

Quay, H. C. (1987). Institutional treatment. In H. C. Quay (Ed.), *Handbook of juvenile delinquency* (pp. 244–265). New York: Wiley.

Routh, D. K. (1994). *Clinical psychology since 1917: Science, practice, and organization* (pp. 44–46). New York: Plenum Press.

Routh, D. K., Patton, L., & Sanfilippo, M. D. (1991). Celebrating 20 years of the *Journal of Clinical Child Psychology:* From child advocacy to scientific research and back again. *Journal of Clinical Child Psychology, 20,* 2–6.

Russ, S. W. (1998). Special section on developmentally based integrated psychotherapy with children: Emerging models. *Journal of Clinical Child Psychology, 27,* 2–3.

Sears, R. R. (1975). Your ancients revisited: A history of child development. In E. M. Hetherington (Ed.), *Review of child development research* (Vol. 5, pp. 1–73). Chicago: University of Chicago Press.

Seligman, M. E. P. (1995). The effectiveness of psychotherapy: The Consumer Reports Study. *American Psychologist, 50,* 965–974.

Strupp, H. H., & Anderson, T. (1997). On the limitations of therapy manuals. *Clinical Psychology: Science and Practice, 14,* 76–82.

Tarullo, L. B., Richardson, D. T., Radke-Yarrow, M., & Martinez, P. E. (1995). Multiple sources in child diagnosis: Parent-child concordance in affectively ill and well families. *Journal of Clinical Child Psychology, 24,* 173–183.

U.S. Advisory Board on Child Abuse and Neglect. (1995). *A nation's shame: Fatal child abuse and neglect in the United States.* Washington, DC: National Clearinghouse on Child Abuse and Neglect.

VandenBos, G. R. (1996). Outcome assessment of psychotherapy [Special issue]. *American Psychologist, 51,* 1005–1079.

Weisz, J. R., Donenberg, G. R., Han, S. S., & Weiss, B. (1995). Bridging the gap between laboratory and clinic in child and adolescent psychotherapy. *Journal of Consulting and Clinical Psychology, 63,* 688–701.

Weisz, J. R., & Hawley, K. M. (1998). Finding, evaluating, refining, and applying empirically supported treatments for children and adolescents. *Journal of Clinical Child Psychology, 27,* 206–216.

Weisz, J. R., Weiss, B., Alicke, M. D., & Klotz, M. L. (1987). Effectiveness of psychotherapy with children and adolescents: A meta-analysis for clinicians. *Journal of Consulting and Clinical Psychology, 55,* 542–549.

Weisz, J. R., Weiss, B., Han, S. S., Granger, D. A., & Morton, T. (1995). Effects of psychotherapy with children and adolescents revisited: A meta-analysis of treatment outcome studies. *Psychological Bulletin, 117,* 450–468.

Chapter 25 ─────────────────────────

Focus Chapter

RESEARCH METHODS WITH ADOLESCENTS

Grayson N. Holmbeck, Ph.D., and Wendy E. Shapera, M.S.

Both the quantity and quality of research on adolescents have increased dramatically over the past 30 years. The first peer-review journal devoted exclusively to the study of adolescents was published in 1966 *(Adolescence),* with several journals following *(Journal of Youth and Adolescence* in 1972; *Journal of Early Adolescence* in 1981; *Journal of Adolescent Research* in 1986; *Journal of Research on Adolescence* in 1991). Special issues of other journals (e.g., *Child Development* in 1982; *American Psychologist* in 1993; *Psychotherapy* in 1995; *Developmental Psychology* in 1996) have been devoted to disseminating findings from research on adolescents. The Society for Research on Adolescence had its first biennial conference in 1984. Moreover, handbooks covering adolescent development (Adelson, 1980; Feldman & Elliott, 1990; Lerner, Petersen, & Brooks-Gunn, 1991; Van Hasselt & Hersen, 1987) and clinical issues during adolescence (Lerner et al., 1991; Tolan & Cohler, 1993; Van Hasselt & Hersen, 1995; Weiner, 1992) have appeared. Finally, and for the first time, a chapter devoted exclusively to "adolescent development" (Grotevant, 1997) has been included in the most recent version of the *Handbook of Child Psychology.* Thus, the field of adolescent research has matured to the point where it is now possible to discuss research methods that apply specifically to the study of children during the second decade of life.

In this chapter, we first ask the question: Why study adolescents? Second, we present the results of a literature search that provide a systematic overview of the types of clinical research on adolescents (i.e., the populations studied and the research methods and designs employed) that have appeared recently in the primary clinical and developmental psychology journals. Third, we present an overview of the types of constructs that have been of interest to researchers who study adolescents. In this section, a developmental framework for understanding and researching adolescent adaptation and adjustment is presented. Finally, relevant methodological strategies and issues that have emerged in this field are reviewed.

Completion of this manuscript was supported by NIMH (#R01-MH50423), Social and Behavioral Sciences Research Grants 12-FY93-0621, 12-FY95-0496, and 12-FY97-0270 from the March of Dimes Birth Defects Foundation, and a paid leave from Loyola University of Chicago. Correspondence regarding this chapter should be sent to: Grayson N. Holmbeck, Loyola University of Chicago, Department of Psychology, 6525 N. Sheridan Rd., Chicago IL 60626 (gholmbe@orion.it.luc.edu.).

WHY STUDY ADOLESCENTS?

Adolescence is a transitional period between childhood and adulthood that is characterized by a host of dramatic biological, psychological, and social role changes. In fact, it is safe to say that adolescence, as a developmental period, includes more changes than any other stage of life except infancy (Feldman & Elliott, 1990). Moreover, there are two transition points during this single developmental period: the transition to early adolescence from childhood and the transition to adulthood from late adolescence (Steinberg, 1996).

Given the multitude of such changes, it is not surprising that there are also significant changes in the types and frequency of psychological disorders that are manifested during adolescence (as compared to childhood; Rutter, 1980). For some adolescents, it is a period of adaptation and improved mental health, but for others it is a period of maladaptation and increasing levels of psychopathology. In keeping with this developmental psychopathology perspective, many scholars have attempted to identify risk and protective processes that are predictive of such individual differences in developmental pathways (Cicchetti & Toth, 1996; Rolf, Masten, Cicchetti, Nuechterlein, & Weintraub, 1990; see Cicchetti & Rogosch, this volume). A protective factor may enhance the psychosocial well-being of a well-adjusted adolescent or protect children at risk for maladjustment from exhibiting increasing levels of problem behaviors. Similarly, exposure to risk factors may make a well-adjusted child more vulnerable to psychosocial maladjustment or exacerbate the level of maladjustment already present in an at-risk child (Rutter, 1990).

Protective and vulnerability processes may have their greatest impact during life transitions or periods of dramatic developmental change (Rutter, 1990). As noted above, adolescence is one such period when an individual's developmental trajectory is likely to be dramatically altered by exposure to protective or risk factors. Some have argued that "the transitional nature and disequilibrium of adolescence represents an opportune period for intervention, as times of developmental change may result in a greater receptivity to intervention" (Cicchetti & Toth, 1996, p. xiii). Given that *change* is the defining feature of adolescence and given the opportunities for having a positive impact on a system that is in a state of flux, many scholars have begun to focus their sights on this critical period of development.

OVERVIEW OF RECENT RESEARCH ON ADOLESCENTS

To get a better idea of the types of research that have been done recently on the adolescent period, we conducted a hand-search of all articles published from 1992 to 1997 (inclusive) in the following nine clinical and developmental journals (ns refer to the number of articles selected from each journal): *Journal of Consulting and Clinical Psychology* ($n = 64$), *Journal of Child Clinical Psychology* ($n = 54$), *Behavior Therapy* ($n = 10$), *Journal of Abnormal Psychology* ($n = 37$), *Child Development* ($n = 73$), *Developmental Psychology* ($n = 46$), *Development and Psychopathology* ($n = 64$), *Journal of Research on Adolescence* ($n = 81$), and *Journal of Family Psychology* ($n = 36$). Although this set of journals obviously does not include all articles published

Table 25.1.   Review of adolescent research published from 1992 to 1997 in 9 journals
(n = 465 articles)

Dimensions and Subcategories	n of Studies	Percentage of Total Articles
Age of Participants		
"Adolescents"	135	29
Early adolescence	113	24
Early/middle adolescence	108	23
Middle adolescence	41	9
Middle/late adolescence	35	7
Late adolescence	33	7
Type of Study		
Correlational/prediction	374	80
Group differences	35	7
Treatment outcome	32	7
Measure construction	24	5
Type of Data		
Questionnaire	361	69
Unknown (based on abstract)	59	11
Observational	51	10
Interview	25	5
Record review (e.g., medical)	15	3
Psychological tests	8	2
Biological	5	1
Longitudinal?		
No	264	57
Yes	201	43
Predictors		
Family relationships/attachment	137	20
Demographics	120	18
Individual psychopathology (e.g., group differences)	98	14
Personality/temperament/coping/self-esteem/intelligence	96	14
Peer relationships	55	8
Therapeutic intervention	35	5
Biological/sexual behavior	30	4
Victimization/trauma	28	4
Parental psychopathology	27	4
Social support	23	3
School transition/failure	16	2
Medical illness/prematurity	14	2
Outcomes		
Individual psychopathology/behavior problems	315	53
Adaptive outcomes (e.g., competence)	74	12
School failure/dropout	49	8
Family environment	44	7
Sexual behavior	30	5
Peer relations/rejection	30	5
Cognitions/attributions	16	3

Table 25.1.   *(continued)*

Dimensions and Subcategories	*n* of Studies	Percentage of Total Articles
Treatment adherence	16	3
Physical health/pain	12	2
Victimization/abuse	8	1

Note: The *n*s for type of data, predictors, and outcomes were 524, 679, and 594, respectively, owing to multiple types of data/predictors/outcomes for some studies. Early, middle, and late adolescence are defined with respect to the following age ranges: 11–14, 15–18, and 19–21, respectively (Steinberg, 1996). Percentages may not add up to 100% due to rounding. Demographics include age, grade, gender, socioeconomic status, family structure, maternal age, and ethnicity.

on this topic, these journals are high-quality publications that represent the major areas of adolescent research (i.e., clinical psychology, developmental psychology, and family psychology). The search was conducted by reading abstracts from all manuscripts involving adolescents as the primary participants that appeared in these journals from 1992 to 1997 and selecting those that focused on clinical issues (either because they examined clinically relevant adjustment predictors and/or outcomes or because they were treatment-outcome or prevention studies). Each selected abstract was coded for the following information (when relevant): (a) name of journal, (b) age of participants (early, middle, late adolescence), (c) type of study (e.g., correlational/prediction, group differences, treatment outcome, and measure validation), (d) type of data (e.g., questionnaire, observational, biological, record review, standardized psychological tests, interview), (e) whether the study was longitudinal (yes/no), (f) predictors, (g) outcomes, and (h) statistical methods (e.g., regression, correlation, factor analysis, path analysis, latent growth curve analyses). An overview of the research literature review (465 articles) is provided in Table 25.1. Statistical methods are not included in this table because the types of statistical analyses employed were not mentioned in the majority (77%) of selected abstracts.

What types of research are currently being conducted? Based on the data in Table 25.1, it appears that researchers prefer to study young adolescents (e.g., those in junior high school) over older adolescents (those who are beyond high school age), although this may reflect a bias in our selection of journals for review. Although the bulk of the research that was published between 1992 and 1997 was correlational in nature (80%) and involved the use of questionnaire data (69%), a sizable minority (43%) of the research was longitudinal. A substantial portion of the research involved family and demographic variables as predictors and individual adjustment/psychopathology variables as outcomes. There were few treatment-outcome studies involving adolescent participants during the period of this review (*n* = 32 or 7%; see Table 25.1). Moreover, relatively few investigators employed observational or interview methodologies or examined social systems other than the family (e.g., peer relationships/peer rejection). Simply put, although it appears that there are several research areas that have matured considerably over the past two or three decades (e.g., associations between family relationships and adjustment outcomes during adolescence), there are a number of areas and methodologies that have received much less attention.

CONSTRUCTS OF INTEREST IN RESEARCH ON ADOLESCENCE

An additional implication of the data in Table 25.1 is that there are numerous social and intrapersonal domains as well as psychosocial outcomes that have been studied by investigators interested in the adolescent period. Thus, we review a developmental framework for understanding and researching adolescent adaptation and adjustment (Figure 25.1). We believe that an appreciation for the rapid developmental changes of adolescence and the contexts of such development will aid the researcher in conducting high-quality, developmentally relevant research on adolescents. This framework summarizes the major constructs that have been studied by researchers in this field and is based on earlier models presented by Hill (1980, 1983), Holmbeck (1994, 1996; Holmbeck & Kendall, 1991; Holmbeck & Updegrove, 1995), Steinberg (1996), and Grotevant (1997). See these references for more complete descriptions of the constructs reviewed (a thorough review of the constructs is beyond the scope of this methodology chapter). Each of the components of the model will be reviewed in turn and relevant research issues and state-of-the-art measurement strategies will be described.

The model presented here is biopsychosocial in nature, insofar as it emphasizes the biological, psychological, and social changes of the adolescent developmental period

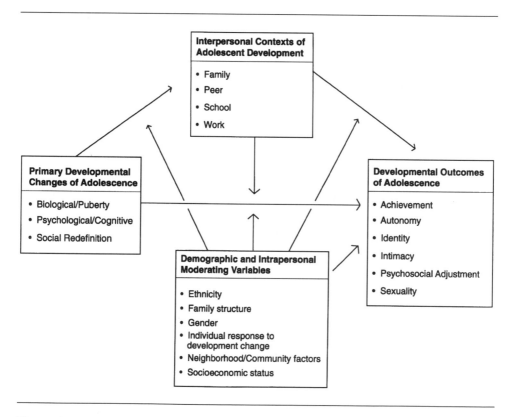

Figure 25.1. A developmental-contextual framework for understanding and researching adolescent adaptation and adjustment. (Arrows directed toward midpoints of other arrows are considered moderated effects.)

(see Figure 25.1). In addition to this focus on intraindividual development, we have also attempted to incorporate more recent discoveries from studies of contextual effects during adolescence. For example, recent research has gone beyond asking whether family variables are associated with adolescent adjustment outcomes and now attempts to isolate those contexts or circumstances in which such associations are most pronounced. In short, this model is both developmental and contextual (Steinberg, 1995). Despite our attempt to be comprehensive, however, investigators typically do not examine all components of this type of model in a single study; rather, specific connections among components are usually investigated in separate studies.

AN OVERVIEW OF THE FRAMEWORK

At the most general level, the framework presented in Figure 25.1 indicates that the primary developmental changes of adolescence have an impact on the developmental outcomes of adolescence via the interpersonal contexts in which adolescents develop. In other words, the developmental changes of adolescence have an impact on the behaviors of significant others which, in turn, influence the ways adolescents resolve the major issues of adolescence, namely, autonomy, sexuality, identity, and so on.

For example, suppose that a young preadolescent girl begins to physically mature much earlier than her age-mates. Such early maturity will likely impact on her peer relationships, insofar as early maturing girls are more likely to date and initiate sexual behaviors at an earlier age than are girls who mature on time (Magnusson, Stattin, & Allen, 1985). Such impacts on male peers may influence her own self-perceptions in the areas of identity and sexuality. In this way, the behaviors of peers in response to the girl's early maturity could be said to *mediate* associations between pubertal change and sexual outcomes (and therefore account, at least in part, for these significant associations). We use the term mediation because of the proposed A→B→C relationship inherent in this example, whereby B is hypothesized to mediate associations between A and C (see Baron & Kenny, 1986; Holmbeck, 1997, for a more thorough explanation of mediated effects).

Such causal and mediational influences may vary depending on the demographic and intrapersonal context in which they occur (see Figure 25.1). Specifically, associations between the primary developmental changes and the developmental outcomes may be *moderated* by demographic variables such as ethnicity, gender, socioeconomic status, and the like. We use the term moderated because it is expected that associations between the primary changes and developmental outcomes may *differ* depending on the demographic status of the individual (see Baron & Kenny, 1986; Holmbeck, 1997, for a more thorough explanation of moderated effects). For example, if associations between pubertal change and certain sexual outcomes held *only* for girls, we could infer that gender moderates such associations. In addition to serving a mediational role as described above, the interpersonal contexts (i.e., family, peer, school, and work contexts) can also serve a moderational role in the association between the primary changes and the developmental outcomes. For example, early maturity may lead to poor adjustment outcomes *only* when families react to early pubertal development in certain ways (e.g., with increased restrictiveness and supervision); in this example, familial reactions to puberty moderate associations between pubertal development and adjustment outcome.

Primary Developmental Changes of Adolescence

Upon further examination of the framework in Figure 25.1, it can be seen that there are three types of primary developmental changes that occur during adolescence: biological/pubertal, psychological/cognitive, and social role changes. They are viewed as "primary" because (a) they are universal across culture, and (b) they occur temporally prior to the developmental outcomes of adolescence (i.e., changes in autonomy, identity, sexuality, etc.). Despite the universality and intensity of these changes, there has unfortunately been a decided lack of attention to developmental issues in the adolescent clinical literature, as is clear upon examination of the literature review data in Table 25.1 (Holmbeck & Kendall, 1991; Holmbeck & Updegrove, 1995; Kendall & Holmbeck, 1991; Kendall & Williams, 1986; Tolan & Cohler, 1993).

Biological/Pubertal Changes

With respect to the biological/pubertal changes of adolescence, changes in body proportions, facial characteristics, voice, body hair, strength, and coordination are found in males and changes in body proportions, body hair, breast growth, and menarcheal status are found in girls (Tanner, 1962). Crucial to the understanding of this process is the knowledge that the peak of pubertal development occurs two years *earlier* in the modal female than in the modal male. *Intra*individual variation is evident with respect to the differential onset of the various pubertal changes (e.g., the beginning of breast development typically occurs prior to menarche for girls). Moreover, there is *inter*individual variation in the time of onset, duration, and termination of the pubertal cycle (Brooks-Gunn & Reiter, 1990), and these differences have social consequences. Thus, it is possible, for example, that two 14-year-old boys may be at very different stages of pubertal development, such that one boy has not yet begun pubertal changes and the other boy has experienced nearly all pubertal events, with the latter possibly being favored over the former for involvement in athletic activities, dating, and social events. Finally, research also suggests that both *pubertal status* (an individual's placement in the sequence of predictable pubertal changes) and *pubertal timing* (timing of changes relative to one's age peers) have an impact on the quality of family relationships and certain indicators of psychosocial adjustment (Alsaker, 1995; Buchanan, Eccles, & Becker, 1992; Holmbeck & Hill, 1991; Paikoff & Brooks-Gunn, 1991; Petersen, 1988). In studies such as these, pubertal timing, pubertal status, and age may be confounded. Thus, when testing the effects of one of these three maturational variables, appropriate methodological and/or statistical controls for the remaining variables should be instituted (Steinberg, 1987). Both self-report and physician-report measures (which can include either Likert scale or Tanner schematic drawings) have been developed that capture the complexity of the puberty construct (see Buchanan, 1991, for a review). In addition, hormone-behavior studies can be conducted by using radioimmunoassays of blood samples and examining associations between hormone levels and behavioral outcomes (e.g., Nottelmann, Inoff-Germain, Susman, & Chrousos, 1990).

Psychological/Cognitive Changes

Although efforts have been made at taking cognitive development into account when designing treatments (e.g., Guerra, 1993; Kendall, 1984; Kendall, Lerner, & Craighead,

1984; Shirk, 1988), few investigators have taken such development into account when conducting clinical research (for one exception, see Schleser, Cohen, Meyers, & Rodick, 1984). Though less overtly observable, cognitive changes in adolescence are probably as dramatic as the physical changes (Gordon, 1988; Keating, 1990). Piaget (1970) is credited with the identification of adolescence as the period of formal operational thinking where adult-level reasoning can take place. Adolescents who have achieved such thinking abilities are able to think more complexly, abstractly, and hypothetically. They are able to explore several possibilities when making decisions, and many adolescents are able to think realistically about the future.

Also of interest here are the child's socially relevant cognitions, such as one's understanding of significant others and their behaviors (i.e., social cognition; Dodge & Coie, 1987; Flavell & Ross, 1981; Overton, 1983; Shantz, 1983). Healthy developmental outcomes during adolescence are dependent on the adolescent acquiring the following: role-taking and empathy skills, social information-processing skills, and prosocial behavior skills (Guerra, 1993). All of these cognitive variables have implications for level of adjustment outcomes (e.g., aggression; Dodge, Price, Bachorowski, & Newman, 1990).

Measurement of cognitive development is achieved with a variety of methods ranging from Piagetian problem-solving tasks (e.g., Gray & Hudson, 1984; Ward & Overton, 1990) to semistructured social-cognition interviews (Selman, 1980). Given the likelihood that the degree of cognitive development varies across content domains, it may be most productive to utilize domain-specific assessment techniques. For example, suppose one is interested in associations between adolescent cognitive development and use of contraception in sexual encounters. In such a study, it may be preferable to assess the sophistication of adolescents' cognitive understanding of sexual risk rather than assessing general cognitive developmental changes with Piagetian problem-solving tasks (Holmbeck, Crossman, Wandrei, & Gasiewski, 1994). Measures of cognitive development within the domain of interest are more likely to yield significant associations with outcomes from the same domain.

Social Role Changes

Finally, and with respect to social redefinition, a variety of changes in the social status of children occur during adolescence (Hill, 1980). Although such social redefinition is universal, the specific changes vary greatly across culture. Steinberg (1996) cites changes across four domains: interpersonal, political, economic, and legal.

The ability of the adolescent to adapt to these changes in social status as well as manage the transition to adulthood has prompted many investigators to examine the late adolescent transition period. Specifically, research efforts have focused on identifying predictors that differentiate between those who have difficulty managing this transition and those who experience relatively smooth transitions (Steinberg, 1996). Longitudinal studies are preferred in this area because such designs allow one to determine factors that *predate* a problematic transition (e.g., difficulty leaving home to live independently) versus those that are the *result* of a difficult transition (e.g., Stattin & Magnusson, 1994).

In summary, we see that there are three types of primary developmental changes of adolescence that "start the ball rolling" during this developmental period. All of these developmental milestones and tasks have implications for adaptation and adjustment, as indicated in Figure 25.1. Despite their "primary" status, it is rare that such developmental changes are taken into account in clinical research (Table 25.1). We now turn to the interpersonal contexts of adolescence.

Interpersonal Contexts of Adolescent Development

In this section, we review the following contexts within the interpersonal portion of the framework: family, peers, school, and work.

Family Context

As can be seen in Table 25.1, the familial context is one of the most commonly studied predictors of adolescent adjustment problems. Scholars who have written about adolescence from a psychoanalytic perspective have viewed the adolescent developmental period as a time of storm and stress when extreme levels of conflict with parents result in a reorientation toward peers (Freud, 1958). Interestingly, recent research involving representative samples of adolescents has *not* supported these early storm-and-stress notions (Holmbeck, 1996; Laursen & Collins, 1994; Steinberg, 1990). On the other hand, it does appear that adolescence is a time of transformation in family relationships and that there is a moderate increase in conflict, particularly over rather mundane issues (Collins, 1990; Holmbeck, 1996; Paikoff & Brooks-Gunn, 1991; Steinberg, 1990). In fact, some have argued that the conflicts that arise during the transition to adolescence may serve an adaptive role (Cooper, 1988; Holmbeck, 1996; Holmbeck & Hill, 1991).

One of the major tasks for parents during this developmental period is to be responsive to adolescents' needs for increasing responsibility and decision-making power in the family, while *at the same time* maintaining a high level of cohesiveness in the family environment (Smetana, 1988). Parents who lack flexibility and adaptability during this developmental period, particularly in areas of strictness and decision making, tend to have offspring with less adaptive outcomes (Fuligni & Eccles, 1993; Holmbeck, Paikoff, & Brooks-Gunn, 1995; Kidwell, Fischer, Dunham, & Baranowski, 1983).

The major family constructs that have been of interest to researchers who study adolescents are as follows (see Holmbeck et al., 1995, for a review): parent-adolescent conflict, attachment between parent and adolescent, parenting styles and practices (including the degree of parental control and the quality of parental affect toward the child), parental monitoring and supervision, parental discipline techniques, parenting behaviors that promote autonomy and relatedness, parent-adolescent collaborative problem solving, and the quality of the marital relationship (in two-parent families). The manner in which these constructs are assessed varies. Both questionnaire methods (adolescent report and parent report) and observational coding systems are available for most of these constructs (see Cone, this volume, for a discussion of observational methodology). In many studies that focus on family relationships, both questionnaire and observational data are employed. Interestingly, associations across method or across respondent are typically moderate to low (e.g., Hayden et al., 1998; Melby, Conger, Ge, & Warner, 1995).

A recent development in the clinical and developmental literatures involves the assessment of older adolescents' working models of attachment (an assessment technique that yields attachment categories that are analogous to those that are coded in studies of infants using the Strange Situation paradigm; Ainsworth, Blehar, Waters, & Wall, 1978). To conduct this assessment, an interview technique (AAI, Adult Attachment Interview; George, Kaplan, & Main, 1984) is used; this instrument assesses the individual's organization of memories of significant attachment relationships. Based on coding (e.g., a useful Q-sort technique for rating the transcriptions of these interviews has been developed; Kobak, Cole, Ferenz-Gillies, Fleming, & Gamble, 1993), individuals can be classified into one of the following categories: secure-autonomous, insecure dismissing, insecure-preoccupied, and insecure-unresolved. In a special issue of the *Journal of Consulting and Clinical Psychology,* several studies that included adolescents as participants demonstrated strong associations between classifications on the AAI and psychopathology outcomes (Adam, Sheldon-Keller, & West, 1996; Allen, Hauser, & Borman-Spurrell, 1996; Cole-Detke & Kobak, 1996; Rosenstein & Horowitz, 1996).

Peer Context

One of the most robust predictors of psychological difficulties during adulthood (e.g., dropping out of school, criminality) is poor peer relationships during childhood and adolescence (e.g., associations with antisocial peers, engaging in peer victimization and bullying; Parker & Asher, 1987; Schwartz, Dodge, & Coie, 1993). Most now agree that child and adolescent peer relationships are necessities and not luxuries and that these relationships can have positive effects on adjustment as well as on cognitive, social-cognitive, sex role, and moral development (Berndt & Savin-Williams, 1993; Parker & Asher, 1987). Peer relationships during childhood and adolescence also appear to evolve through a series of developmental stages (e.g., Berndt, 1983; Brown, 1990; Selman, 1981).

Recently, investigators have been quite creative in examining the ever-changing landscape of adolescent peer relationships. For example, Hogue and Steinberg (1995) examined *selection effects* (i.e., the tendency for people to choose friends who are similar to them on various attributes) and *socialization effects* (i.e., the tendency for friends to become more alike over time) in a longitudinal study of adolescent peer groups ("cliques") with respect to the implications that such effects have for increases in internalizing symptoms. Their methodology involved having participants state the names of five close friends. Because they were studying all children in the school, the friends were also participants in the study. In this way, they were able to examine change in individuals as well as change in groups of friends so as to differentiate between socialization and selection effects. In studies of larger reputation-based groups of adolescents ("crowds," e.g., jocks, druggies), Brown (1990) has documented the importance of examining more general peer reputations and the effects of such reputations on psychosocial outcomes. School-specific crowds are defined by first identifying adolescent social milieu "experts" (with the help of school administrators) and asking these adolescent experts to identify the crowd membership of all of their classmates.

Finally, sociometric techniques that were originally developed for use with younger children (Coie & Dodge, 1983) have recently been employed with adolescent samples (e.g., Parkhurst & Asher, 1992). Such techniques are based on peer nominations whereby students identify other students whom they like the best, students whom they like the least, students who fight a lot, and so on. Based on these nominations, students are classified as popular, average, rejected, neglected, or controversial. Although these techniques have been criticized on conceptual, empirical, and ethical grounds (e.g., Bukowski & Hoza, 1989), they show great promise for the study of peer relations during adolescence.

School Context

Scholars have argued that we should be interested not only in the impact of school on cognition and achievement, but that we also should examine how school is an important environment for the development of one's personality, values, and social relationships (Entwisle, 1990; Trickett & Schmid, 1993). With increasing age, children are exposed to more complex school environments (Minuchin & Shapiro, 1983). Movement between schools (such as between an elementary school and a junior high school) can be viewed as a stressor, with multiple school transitions producing more deleterious effects (Petersen & Hamburg, 1986; Simmons & Blyth, 1987; see Felner, Ginter, & Primavera, 1982, for an example of a prevention intervention that targets stressors during school transitions).

As is the case with school transitions, the school environment also impacts on adolescent development. Philosophies of education, teacher expectations, curriculum characteristics, and interactions between teacher and student have been found to be related to a variety of child and adolescent adjustment outcomes (Minuchin & Shapiro, 1983; Roeser & Eccles, 1998; Rutter, Maughan, Mortimore, & Ouston, 1979). Also, the high rate of dropouts in some school districts indicates that the school environment and student needs have not been well matched (Eccles et al., 1993).

In studies of schools, an important research issue involves the "level of analysis." Specifically, the school district, the school, the classroom, or the student could all represent levels of analysis. For example, in Perry et al.'s (1996) evaluation of the Project Northland communitywide prevention program for alcohol use during early adolescence, 24 school districts were randomly assigned to intervention or control conditions (see Spoth, Redmond, & Shin, 1998, for a similar example). In this case, the total N is 24 across groups when conducting intervention versus control analyses (rather than 2,351, which represented the number of students in the study). For other analyses (e.g., family predictors of individual differences in alcohol use), the N would be 2,351. A relatively new statistical technique (HLM, hierarchical linear modeling; Bryk & Raudenbush, 1992) is useful in examining multilevel data such as that just described (see Farrell, this volume).

Work Context

Although more than 80% of all high school students in this country work before they graduate (Steinberg, 1996) and many government agencies have recommended that adolescents work, little research has been done on the effects of such work on adolescent development and the adolescents' relationships with significant others (Greenberger & Steinberg, 1986; Lewko, 1987). Based on the research that has been done (Greenberger & Steinberg, 1986), it seems clear that the work environment has both positive *and* negative effects on adolescent development. Although adolescents who work tend to develop an increased sense of self-reliance, they are also more likely to (a) develop cynical attitudes about work, (b) spend less time with their families and peers, (c) be less involved in school, (d) abuse drugs or commit delinquent acts, and (e) have less time for self-exploration and identity development.

Despite the importance of these findings, a number of research questions remain unanswered. For example, it is not clear whether the impact on adolescent development differs for work conducted inside the home (such as participating in a family-run business) versus work conducted outside the home. Also, does the impact differ for work that is conducted due to financial need (either for self or family) versus work conducted to earn discretionary funds? Finally, an issue that is attracting increased empirical attention is the problem of youth unemployment in 18- to 21-year-olds (particularly among adolescents who have dropped out of high school; Steinberg, 1996).

Developmental Outcomes of Adolescence

In this section, the following developmental outcome constructs are reviewed (Figure 25.1): achievement, autonomy, identity, intimacy, psychosocial adjustment, and sexuality. Given that the focus of this chapter is on research issues in clinical psychology, the section on psychosocial adjustment is emphasized.

Achievement

Decisions made during one's adolescence can have serious consequences for one's future education and career (Henderson & Dweck, 1990). Such decisions present the adolescent with new opportunities but also limit the range of possible employment and educational options available in the future. Given the complexity of achievement decisions, adolescents who experience advances in cognitive abilities (i.e., the ability to employ future-oriented thinking, abstract reasoning, hypothetical thinking) will be at an advantage when they begin to make education- and career-related decisions. With respect to measurement, a host of instruments are available, including measures of school grades, academic motivation, and the value a child places on education (Roeser & Eccles, 1998).

Autonomy

Autonomy is a multidimensional construct insofar as there is more than one type of adolescent autonomy (Douvan & Adelson, 1966; Hill & Holmbeck, 1986; Steinberg, 1990). Emotional autonomy is the capacity to relinquish childlike dependencies on parents (Fuhrman & Holmbeck, 1995; Lamborn & Steinberg, 1993; Ryan & Lynch, 1989; Steinberg & Silverberg, 1986). Adolescents increasingly come to de-idealize their parents, see them as "people" rather than simply as parenting figures, and be less dependent on them for immediate emotional support.

When adolescents are behaviorally autonomous, they have the capacity to make their own decisions, to be less influenced by others, and to be more self-governing and self-reliant (Steinberg, 1990). Susceptibility to peer pressure increases to a peak in early adolescence, due in part to an increase in peer pressure prior to early adolescence and an accompanying decrease in susceptibility to parental pressure.

The following autonomy-related issues become relevant during the adolescent period: (a) the degree to which the adolescent is responsible in managing the level of autonomy he or she has been granted, (b) whether parent and adolescent have realistic expectations for the level of autonomy that should be granted in the future, (c) the degree to which there is a discrepancy between how much autonomy the parent is willing to grant and the amount of autonomy the adolescent is able to manage (Holmbeck & O'Donnell, 1991), (d) the parents' responses to their child's attempts to be autonomous (i.e., do they have the ability to foster healthy levels of autonomy in their offspring?), and (e) the degree of flexibility demonstrated by parents in changing their parenting around autonomy issues (Holmbeck et al., 1995). Measures of emotional and behavioral autonomy are available (Fuhrman & Holmbeck, 1995; Holmbeck & O'Donnell, 1991). Discrepancies between parental and adolescent perceptions can be examined with these measures and used as predictors of psychosocial adjustment outcomes (e.g., Holmbeck & O'Donnell, 1991).

Identity

Adolescents develop an identity through role explorations and role commitments (Erikson, 1968; Harter, 1990). One's identity is multidimensional and includes self-perceptions and commitments across a number of domains, including occupational, academic, religious, interpersonal, sexual, and political. Questionnaire- and interview-based research (e.g., Bennion & Adams, 1986; Marcia, 1966) in the area of identity development has isolated at least four identity statuses that are defined with respect to two dimensions: commitment and exploration. These identity statuses are: identity moratorium (exploration with no commitment), identity foreclosure (commitment with no exploration), identity diffusion (no commitment and no systematic exploration), and identity achievement (commitment after extensive exploration). A given adolescent's status can change over time, reflecting increased maturation and development or, alternatively, regression to some less adaptive identity status. Perhaps most important, an adolescent's identity status can also vary depending on the domain under consideration (e.g., academic vs. interpersonal; Bennion & Adams, 1986). Additional components of identity that are often assessed in studies of adolescents are self-concept, self-esteem, ethnic identity, and sex role development (Steinberg, 1996). Developmentally appropriate measures of self-concept have been developed by Harter (1988; see discussion that follows).

Intimacy

It is not until adolescence that one's friendships have the potential to become intimate (Savin-Williams & Berndt, 1990). An intimate relationship is characterized by trust, mutual self-disclosure, a sense of loyalty, and helpfulness. Girls' same-sex relationships are described as more intimate than are boys' same-sex relationships. Having intimate friendships is adaptive; adolescents with such friendships are more likely to have positive adjustment outcomes. Some scholars have proposed that friendships change during the adolescent period because of accompanying social-cognitive changes (Figure 25.1). The capacity to exhibit empathy and take multiple perspectives in social encounters makes it more likely that friendships will become more mature, complex, and intimate.

Psychosocial Adjustment

A host of psychosocial adjustment outcomes have been of interest to researchers who study the adolescent period. Handbooks on the topic typically have chapters on the following diagnostic categories (e.g., Tolan & Cohler, 1993; Van Hasselt & Hersen, 1995; Weiner, 1992): depression and anxiety disorders, suicidal behavior, conduct disorders and delinquency, substance use disorders, eating disorders (anorexia and bulimia), schizophrenia, and academic underachievement. Most recent studies typically focus on a single outcome (e.g., delinquency), given that the predictors for each type of outcome tend to vary and because the outcomes themselves tend to be multidimensional (Tolan & Cohler, 1993). Psychopathology can be assessed with self-, parent, and/or teacher report on questionnaires or with adolescent report in diagnostic clinical interviews (e.g., DICA, Diagnostic Interview for Children and Adolescents; Reich, Shayka, & Taibleson, 1991).

As noted earlier, there are dramatic changes in the rates of psychiatric disorders during the adolescent period (e.g., increases in rates of schizophrenia, decreases in rates of enuresis), with some disorders becoming major psychiatric problems for the first time during this developmental period (e.g., eating disorders; Rutter, 1980). The features of certain childhood disorders change as the child moves into the adolescent years (e.g., attention-deficit/hyperactivity disorder) and there are also dramatic gender differences for some disorders during adolescence (e.g., depression; Nolen-Hoeksema, 1994). As will be discussed later, many scholars have become interested in predictors of rates of change in disorders. For example, one might ask: Why do depression scores increase rapidly over time for some adolescents but not for others? To answer questions such as this, longitudinal studies with appropriate data analytic techniques are needed (see below; also see Cicchetti & Rogosch, this volume, for a developmental psychopathology perspective on such questions).

Although investigators tend to examine single outcomes, the various problem behaviors of adolescence tend to be intercorrelated, insofar as they tend to co-occur within the same individuals. One clustering scheme suggests that there are two broadband categories of psychopathology (Achenbach, 1982, 1985): *internalizing* problems (i.e., disorders that represent problems within the self such as depression, anxiety, somatic complaints, and social withdrawal) and *externalizing* problems (i.e., disorders that represent conflicts with the external environment such as delinquency, aggression, and other self-control difficulties).

Alternatively, Jessor and colleagues (Jessor, Donovan, & Costa, 1991; Jessor & Jessor, 1977) have proposed that there is a "problem behavior syndrome" that characterizes some adolescents, such that there tend to be high intercorrelations among several types of problem behavior (e.g., drug use, sexual intercourse, drinking, and aggression). According to problem behavior theory, such behaviors develop as a function of the same etiological factors and, therefore, tend to co-occur in the same individuals (findings that have been replicated in other laboratories; e.g., Farrell, Danish, & Howard, 1992).

Sexuality

Most children have mixed reactions to becoming a sexually mature adolescent. Parents also have conflicting reactions to such increasing maturity. Despite the importance of this topic, we know very little about normal adolescent sexuality, primarily due to the difficulty in conducting studies on this topic (Katchadourian, 1990). There are a host of factors that are associated with the onset and maintenance of sexual behaviors. Pubertal changes of adolescence have both direct (hormonal) and indirect (social stimulus) effects on sexual behaviors. Ethnic and religious differences in the onset of sexuality also exist. Finally, personality characteristics (e.g., the development of a sexual identity) and social factors (e.g., parent and peer influences) also serve as antecedents to early onset of adolescent sexual behaviors (Figure 25.1). The increasing rates of sexually transmitted diseases among adolescents and the fact that many young adults with AIDS (acquired immune deficiency syndrome) probably became infected as adolescents would suggest that adolescent sexuality is deserving of considerable attention from mental health practitioners working with adolescents (see St. Lawrence & McFarlane, this volume). With respect to assessment of sexual behaviors, several techniques have been developed to increase the credibility of adolescent reports (see below).

METHODOLOGICAL STRATEGIES AND ISSUES

Having discussed the major constructs that have been of interest to researchers who study adolescents, we now turn to a discussion of major methodological strategies that are commonly employed in studies of adolescents. This discussion, though not exhaustive, reviews the issues and decisions that confront researchers in this area. Other chapters in this handbook also review techniques that are relevant to the study of adolescents (see chapters by Cicchetti & Rogosch, Culbertson, Farrell, Jacob, Kazdin, and Tolan, this volume).

Many researchers who study this period of development are interested in identifying factors that exacerbate levels of maladaptation, factors (including treatment interventions; see Kendall, Flannery-Schroeder, & Ford, this volume) that decrease current levels of problem behaviors, and factors that protect individuals from increasing levels of maladaptation in the future (e.g., see Boyd, Howard, & Zucker, 1994, for a collection of studies on the prevention of alcohol abuse among adolescents; also see Tolan, this volume). The most informative research on adolescents is theory-based, insofar as the investigator has proposed testable hypotheses based on theory and uses a research design that will generate interpretable findings and clear answers to important theory-driven research questions.

The following methodological strategies and issues are discussed in this section: longitudinal studies, mediators and moderators, the use of multiple reporters and multiple methods, using developmentally relevant measures, innovative data collection strategies, and the validity of adolescent self-reports.

Longitudinal Studies

Although longitudinal designs are potentially informative regardless of the age of the participants (see Cicchetti & Rogosch, this volume), such designs are particularly informative when they focus on periods of rapid developmental change, such as the adolescent period of development (Grotevant, 1997). Change is the defining feature of adolescence, and a failure to study change during this period would be to ignore a critical characteristic of the population under investigation.

A review of all possible longitudinal designs is beyond the scope of this chapter (see Cicchetti & Rogosch, this volume), but the study of developmental trajectories is particularly relevant to the examination of adjustment outcomes in adolescents. Specifically, the notion here is that adolescents can progress along different developmental pathways and that, once on a particular pathway, events can alter the trajectory of a pathway in a maladaptive or adaptive direction (Rutter, 1990). Developmental trajectories can be adaptively or maladaptively stable with little or no slope (indicating that the individual demonstrates stability of positive outcomes or stability of negative outcomes over time), have positive or negative slopes (indicating increases or decreases, respectively, in adjustment over time), or be curvilinear (indicating that the individual has experienced a dramatic shift in his or her trajectory over time; Compas, Hinden, & Gerhardt, 1995; Schulenberg, Wadsworth, O'Malley, Bachman, & Johnston, 1996). An advantage of this strategy is that it isolates patterns of change as an individual differences variable. This strategy differs from a more variable-centered approach, where variable associations are reported for a sample as a whole; such a strategy focuses on average change across a sample of individuals and, therefore, may not capture the nature of change that occurs for various subsets of a sample (Schulenberg et al., 1996).

How does one study such trajectories? Of course, longitudinal data are needed. Ideally, one would have at least three data collections over time (to demonstrate or rule out the presence of curvilinear trends and to meet the requirements of certain statistical techniques). Slopes of growth trajectories can be estimated for *each* individual in the sample, and these slopes can be employed as outcome variables in subsequent data analyses (see chapters by Farrell and Tolan, this volume). Both the level of the trajectory (at any sampling point) and the slope become individual differences variables that can be predicted with other variables. Moreover, with such analyses, associations between change in (i.e., the slope of) one variable and change in (i.e., the slope of) another variable can also be examined. For example, one could examine whether increases over time in life events during the transition to adolescence are associated with concurrent (or future) increases in depression. For reviews of statistical strategies, see discussions of latent growth curve modeling and hierarchical linear modeling (Bryk & Raudenbush, 1992; Duncan & Duncan, 1995; Willet & Sayer, 1994; see Colder, Chassin, Stice, & Curran, 1997; Duncan, Duncan, & Hops, 1996, for empirical examples).

An alternative to this growth curve approach is to identify longitudinal subtypes within one's sample and use standard multivariate techniques (multivariate analysis of variance [MANOVA], logistic regression, discriminant analysis) to identify predictors of longitudinal subtype membership. In an example of this latter strategy, Schulenberg et al. (1996) isolated five subtypes of longitudinal binge drinking trajectories and found different risk factors for these different trajectory subtypes.

Another useful design is to examine adolescent outcomes as the end point of a longitudinal study beginning in childhood. For example, Henry, Caspi, Moffitt, and Silva (1996) examined factors in early childhood (age 3) that predicted conviction status (i.e., not convicted, convicted for nonviolent offenses, convicted for violent offenses) at age 18. Family factors and early childhood temperament discriminated between conviction status groups 15 years later. Alternatively, adolescent predictors can be used as the starting point in a longitudinal design with outcomes in adulthood (e.g., Allen, Hauser, Bell, Boykin, & Tate, 1996). These types of studies also raise another important issue in the study of adolescents, namely, the ideal starting point for longitudinal studies. If one is interested in examining the transition to adolescence, it is probably best to begin the study prior to the onset of adolescence (e.g., one can begin studying 8- or 9-year-olds, prior to the onset of pubertal change). Alternatively, if one is interested in the transition to adulthood, a study that begins with participants in high school may be optimal.

Moderators and Mediators

Many researchers have become interested in the *why* of development (Grotevant, 1997; Holmbeck, 1996) and have examined mediators and moderators of associations between predictors and adolescent adjustment outcomes (see Baron & Kenny, 1986; Holmbeck, 1997, for a discussion of moderated and mediated effects and the statistics used to test each type of effect; also see Figure 25.1 for examples of both types of effects).

With respect to mediated effects, numerous past studies have found a strong positive association between high levels of marital conflict and child and adolescent adjustment problems. More recently, investigators have begun to ask why these two variables are associated, positing that variables such as changes in parenting behaviors and children's emotional security may mediate such relations (e.g., Davies & Cummings, 1998). It has been suggested, for example, that high levels of marital conflict produce negative changes in the quality of parenting to which the child is exposed, which, in turn, produce increases in adolescent adjustment problems (Fauber, Forehand, Thomas, & Wierson, 1990).

With respect to moderated effects, investigators have become interested in the degree to which there are interactions between developmental (e.g., biological and cognitive development) and other independent variables (e.g., family and peer variables or demographic variables) in predicting level of problem behaviors. For example, Molina and Chassin (1996) asked the following question: Does ethnicity moderate associations between puberty and parent-child relationships, such that associations between puberty and parent-child relationships vary as a function of ethnicity? In a study that addressed a different research question, Cauffman and Steinberg (1996) found that there was an interaction between menarcheal status (a biological predictor in adolescent girls; Figure 25.1) and dating status (an interpersonal/social predictor involving peers; Figure 25.1) in predicting degree of dieting and disordered eating patterns (a developmental outcome; see Swarr & Richards, 1996, for a similar example). An example of a moderated relationship can also be drawn from the marital conflict literature. Specifically, researchers have become interested in adolescent's cognitive appraisals of marital conflict and the degree to which certain types of appraisals *buffer* the child from the effects of marital conflict (e.g., Grych & Fincham, 1990).

The Use of Multiple Reporters and Multiple Methods

There are numerous advantages to using multiple informant data. One can combine data across reporters into composites (provided these data are significantly associated; Achenbach, McConaughy, & Howell, 1987) to yield multirespondent, multisetting data. (The data become multisetting if one employs parent report *and* teacher report data, for example.) Ideally, one can use measurement modeling procedures (i.e., confirmatory factor analysis with structural equation modeling statistical software) to develop constructs where measurement error is eliminated (see Ge, Best, Conger, & Simons, 1996, for an example). Alternatively, if one only employs self-report data, one cannot rule out common method variance explanations for the findings (i.e., it may be that high correlations between variables have emerged because of response biases rather than because of actual associations between the constructs studied).

Similarly, it is useful to use multiple methods to assess each of the constructs of interest. For example, in studies of family relationships (e.g., Gonzales, Cauce, & Mason, 1996; Hayden et al., 1998), one might employ adolescent report data on parental behavior, parent report data on parental behavior, and observer report data on parental behavior (see Melby et al., 1995, for an example involving self-, spouse-, and observer-reported marital behavior in families of adolescents). Although these multi-method data are not typically highly associated (as discussed earlier), careful measurement can yield moderate and significant associations (Gonzales et al., 1996; Melby et al., 1995). On the other hand, it is worth noting that a single perspective may be useful if that perspective is of primary interest, even if it is not related to the perceptions of others (e.g., adolescent perceptions of parenting behaviors).

Interestingly, the demographic match or mismatch between raters of observed data and the participants in the study have an impact on the degree of agreement between raters and participants. In perhaps the most elegant demonstration of this phenomenon, Gonzales et al. (1996) found that parent and child report ratings from African American mothers and their adolescent offspring were more highly associated with observational ratings done by African American coders than they were with ratings done by non-African American coders.

Using Developmentally Relevant Measures

When selecting measures to use in one's research with adolescents, it is critical that one consider the developmental relevance of the constructs assessed by a measure. For example, developmentally relevant observational coding systems are available for coding parent-adolescent observational data (e.g., Allen et al., 1994). Allen and his colleagues employ parent-adolescent conflict tasks (which are themselves developmentally relevant) and then code the tasks for parental behaviors that inhibit and promote adolescent autonomy development. As noted earlier, autonomy is a developmentally relevant construct.

When using questionnaires, it is important that one examine the developmental relevance of individual questionnaire items, even when using established measurement techniques. For example, an item such as "Who decides when you do your homework— you or your parent?" may be appropriate for young adolescents but would probably not be appropriate when studying a late adolescent college sample.

An additional issue concerns the choice of constructs to study. When one studies families, for example, there are literally hundreds of potential family constructs to examine (even after one has isolated the pool of developmentally relevant constructs). Again, the choice of measures should be based on the hypotheses under investigation and the theory being tested. If one has a theory and a set of hypotheses and is still unable to decide on family constructs to study, then it is possible that one's hypotheses and/or theory are not specific enough. Alternatively, if one is attempting to select from a set of measures that all purportedly measure the same construct, then psychometric factors should be considered (see Haynes, Nelson, & Blaine, this volume).

One example of a developmentally appropriate questionnaire that has been developed recently is the Minnesota Multiphasic Personality Inventory-Adolescent (MMPI-A; Butcher et al., 1992; see Butcher, this volume), a downward extension of the MMPI-2 that was developed specifically for use with adolescents in clinical and research settings. The MMPI-A was developed because (a) many of the items of the MMPI and MMPI-2 were inappropriate for adolescent respondents, (b) national ethnically representative norms were not available, (c) a number of scales from the adult version were not relevant to adolescents, and (d) new scales that were developmentally relevant to adolescents could be developed (Archer, 1992; Weed, Butcher, & Williams, 1994). In fact, the MMPI-A includes several content and supplementary scales that are not included on the MMPI-2 (i.e., Alienation, Conduct Problems, Low Aspirations, School Problems, Immaturity, Alcohol/Drug Problems Proneness scale, and Alcohol/Drug Problems Acknowledgment scale). The measure is useful with ethnic minorities (Negy, Leal-Puente, Trainor, & Carlson, 1997) and includes a number of validity scales that are useful in detecting random responding and nonvalid protocols (e.g., Baer, Ballenger, Berry, & Wetter, 1997).

An upward extension of the Self-Perception Profile for Children (Harter, 1985) has been developed for use with adolescents (the Self-Perception Profile for Adolescents; Harter, 1988). As with the MMPI-A, a number of subscales were added to previous versions of the Self-Perception Profile to make it relevant for adolescent respondents. Specifically, Job Competence, Romantic Appeal, and Close Friendships are subscales that were added to the child version of this measure (the other subscales are virtually identical to those included on the child version).

Innovative Data Collection Strategies

Given the age of adolescents (as compared to younger children), one can take advantage of adolescents' advanced reasoning skills and employ more sophisticated, and perhaps more valid, self-report techniques. One such methodology, the Experience Sampling Method (ESM; also known as the "beeper" method), requires adolescents to carry pagers and respond to random signals (e.g., 7–8 per day) with reports of where they are, who they are with, what they are doing, and what they are feeling, as well as other reports of subjective experience (e.g., Larson, Richards, Moneta, Holmbeck, & Duckett, 1996). With this methodology, one is able to avoid some of the problems inherent in long-term retrospective self-report strategies. The daily phone call methodology is an analogous strategy that has been employed with parents and also may have utility with adolescent respondents (e.g., Quittner & Opipari, 1994).

Another strategy involving observational data is the video-recall technique (Gottman & Levenson, 1985; Powers, Welsh, & Wright, 1994). With this method, parents and adolescents serve as raters of their own videotaped behavior. Specifically, after engaging in a task together, parents and adolescents are asked to view the tape and make ratings of their own behavior and then of the other family members' behavior. The constructs assessed can vary depending on the research questions, but this methodology has the potential to provide useful information on an individual's reported subjective state (as well as the individual's perceptions of the other family members' subjective state) during observed interaction. Such methods have also been applied to adolescent dating dyads (Welsh, Vickerman, Kawaguchi, & Rostosky, 1998).

The Validity of Adolescent Self-Reports

Although concern over the validity of self-reports is an issue in any study, these concerns are particularly relevant in studies where alternative or additional reporting methods are not available or are not easily obtained. Those who conduct research with adolescents need to be aware that there is a tendency for some adolescents to provide nonvalid responses. One benefit of the MMPI-A (see earlier discussion; Butcher et al., 1992) is that it includes several subscales that were designed to detect various nonvalid response styles (e.g., response inconsistencies, random responding, "fake good" and "fake bad" presentations).

One area of adolescent self-report that has been scrutinized is the reporting of drug use and sexual behaviors. Fortunately, methods of identifying adolescents who are providing nonvalid drug data are available (Farrell, Danish, & Howard, 1991). For example, subjects may be asked to report their use of various drugs; included within the list of drugs is a fictitious drug. It could be assumed that adolescents who report using such fictitious drugs may be exaggerating their use of other drugs or that they may not be attending properly to the questions posed (Farrell et al., 1991). With respect to reports of sexuality (also see St. Lawrence & McFarlane, this volume), methods have been developed to increase the validity of self-report data. In one study, Paikoff et al. (1997) employed one-on-one same-gender interviews of adolescent respondents whereby questions of increasing sexual involvement were asked until the respondent reported that they had not engaged in a behavior. At this point, the interview was terminated. This strategy is preferable to a checklist strategy, which may lead to overreporting (or perhaps underreporting) and embarrassment. Some investigators have also employed audiotape administration of sexuality interviews to reduce adolescents' embarrassment over having to report sexual behaviors to an interviewer.

CONCLUSION

The purpose of this chapter was to provide an overview of research methodologies that have been used in the study of adolescents. A search of the recent literature revealed that there are many important areas of research that have been neglected. For example, there have been relatively few treatment-outcomes studies where adolescents are participants. Moreover, more research on the effects of peer relationships on adolescent adjustment is needed, as is research that combines developmental and contextual variables within a longitudinal framework (Steinberg, 1995). A developmental-contextual framework for the study of adolescents was presented, as was a description of each of the components of this model. Measurement issues related to these components were also discussed. Finally, an overview of several issues that should be considered when designing research on adolescents was presented. Clearly, research on adolescents has important prevention and policy implications—attention to research design and other methodological issues is critical if we are to begin to develop interventions that serve a protective and developmentally facilitative function for children in the second decade of life.

REFERENCES

Achenbach, T. M. (1982). *Developmental psychopathology* (2nd ed.). New York: Wiley.

Achenbach, T. M. (1985). *Assessment and taxonomy of child and adolescent psychopathology* (Vol. 3). Beverly Hills, CA: Sage.

Achenbach, T. M., McConaughy, S. H., & Howell, C. T. (1987). Child/adolescent behavioral and emotional problems: Implications of cross-informant correlations for situational specificity. *Psychological Bulletin, 101,* 213–232.

Adam, K. S., Sheldon-Keller, A. E., & West, M. (1996). Attachment organization and history of suicidal behavior in clinical adolescents. *Journal of Consulting and Clinical Psychology, 64,* 264–272.

Adelson, J. (1980). *Handbook of adolescent psychology.* New York: Wiley.

Ainsworth, M. D. S., Blehar, M. C., Waters, E., & Wall, S. (1978). *Patterns of attachment: A psychological study of the Strange Situation.* Hillsdale, NJ: Erlbaum.

Allen, J. P., Hauser, S. T., Bell, K. L., Boykin, K. A., & Tate, D. C. (1994). *Autonomy and relatedness coding system manual (Version 2.0).* (Unpublished coding manual.) Charlottesville: University of Virginia.

Allen, J. P., Hauser, S. T., & Borman-Spurrell, E. (1996). Attachment theory as a framework for understanding sequelae of severe adolescent psychopathology: An 11-year follow-up study. *Journal of Consulting and Clinical Psychology, 64,* 254–263.

Alsaker, F. D. (1995). Timing or puberty and reactions to pubertal changes. In M. Rutter (Ed.), *Psychosocial disturbances in young people: Challenges for prevention* (pp. 37–82). New York: Cambridge University Press.

Archer, R. P. (1992). *MMPI-A: Assessing adolescent psychopathology.* Hillsdale, NJ: Erlbaum.

Baer, R. A., Ballenger, J., Berry, D. T. R., & Wetter, M. W. (1997). Detection of random responding on the MMPI-A. *Journal of Personality Assessment, 68,* 139–151.

Baron, R. M., & Kenny, D. A. (1986). The moderator-mediator variable distinction in social psychological research: Conceptual, strategic, and statistical considerations. *Journal of Personality and Social Psychology, 51,* 1173–1182.

Bennion, L. D., & Adams, G. R. (1986). A revision of the Extended Version of the Objective Measure of Ego Identity Status: An identity instrument for use with late adolescents. *Journal of Adolescent Research, 1,* 183–198.

Berndt, T. J. (1983). Social cognition, social behavior, and children's friendships. In E. T. Higgins, D. N. Ruble, & W. W. Hartup (Eds.), *Social cognition and social development: A sociocultural perspective* (pp. 158–189). New York: Cambridge University Press.

Berndt, T. J., & Savin-Williams, R. C. (1993). Peer relations and friendships. In P. H. Tolan & B. J. Cohler (Eds.), *Handbook of clinical research and practice with adolescents* (pp. 203–220). New York: Wiley.

Boyd, G. M., Howard, J., & Zucker, R. A. (1994). Preventing alcohol abuse among adolescents: Preintervention and intervention research [Special issue]. *Journal of Research on Adolescence, 4.*

Brooks-Gunn, J., & Reiter, E. O. (1990). The role of pubertal processes. In S. S. Feldman & G. R. Elliott (Eds.), *At the threshold: The developing adolescent* (pp. 16–53). Cambridge, MA: Harvard University Press.

Brown, B. B. (1990). Peer groups and peer cultures. In S. S. Feldman & G. R. Elliott (Eds.), *At the threshold: The developing adolescent* (pp. 171–196). Cambridge, MA: Harvard University Press.

Bryk, A. S., & Raudenbush, S. W. (1992). *Hierarchical linear modeling.* Thousand Oaks, CA: Sage.

Buchanan, C. M. (1991). Assessment of pubertal development. In R. M. Lerner, A. C. Petersen, & J. Brooks-Gunn (Eds.), *Encyclopedia of adolescence* (Vol. 2, pp. 875–883). New York: Garland.

Buchanan, C. M., Eccles, J. S., & Becker, J. B. (1992). Are adolescents the victims of raging hormones? Evidence for activational effects of hormones on moods and behavior at adolescence. *Psychological Bulletin, 111,* 62–107.

Bukowski, W. M., & Hoza, B. (1989). Popularity and friendship: Issues in theory, measurement, and outcome. In T. J. Berndt & G. W. Ladd (Eds.), *Peer relationships in child development* (pp. 15–45). New York: Wiley.

Butcher, J. N., Williams, C. L., Graham, J. R., Archer, R. P., Tellegen, A., Ben-Porath, Y. S., & Kaemmer, B. (1992). *MMPI-A (Minnesota Multiphasic Personality Inventory-Adolescent): Manual for administration, scoring, and interpretation.* Minneapolis: University of Minnesota Press.

Cauffman, E., & Steinberg, L. (1996). Interactive effects of menarcheal status and dating on dieting and disordered eating among adolescent girls. *Developmental Psychology, 32,* 631–635.

Cicchetti, D., & Toth, S. L. (Eds.). (1996). *Adolescence: Opportunities and challenges* (Vol. 7: Rochester Symposium on Developmental Psychopathology). Rochester, NY: University of Rochester Press.

Coie, J. D., & Dodge, K. A. (1983). Continuities and changes in children's social status: A five-year longitudinal study. *Merrill-Palmer Quarterly, 29,* 261–281.

Colder, C. R., Chassin, L., Stice, E. M., & Curran, P. J. (1997). Alcohol expectancies as potential mediators of parent alcoholism effects on the development of adolescent heavy drinking. *Journal of Research on Adolescence, 7,* 349–374.

Cole-Detke, H., & Kobak, R. (1996). Attachment processes in eating disorder and depression. *Journal of Consulting and Clinical Psychology, 64,* 282–290.

Collins, W. A. (1990). Parent-child relationships in the transition to adolescence: Continuity and change in interaction, affect, and cognition. In R. Montemayor, G. Adams, & T. Gullotta (Eds.), *Advances in adolescent development: From childhood to adolescence: A transitional period?* (Vol. 2, pp. 85–106). Beverly Hills, CA: Sage.

Compas, B. E., Hinden, B. R., & Gerhardt, C. A. (1995). Adolescent development: Pathways and processes of risk and resilience. *Annual Review of Psychology, 46,* 265–293.

Cooper, C. R. (1988). Commentary: The role of conflict in adolescent-parent relationships. In M. R. Gunnar & W. A. Collins (Eds.), *21st Minnesota symposium on child psychology* (pp. 181–187. Hillsdale, NJ: Erlbaum.

Davies, P. T., & Cummings, E. M. (1998). Exploring children's emotional security as a mediator of the link between marital relations and child adjustment. *Child Development, 69,* 124–139.

Dodge, K. A., & Coie, J. D. (1987). Social information-processing factors in reactive and proactive aggression in children's peer groups. *Journal of Personality and Social Psychology, 53,* 389–409.

Dodge, K. A., Price, J. M., Bachorowski, J., & Newman, J. P. (1990). Hostile attributional biases in severely aggressive adolescents. *Journal of Abnormal Psychology, 99,* 385–392.

Douvan, E., & Adelson, J. (1966). *The adolescent experience.* New York: Wiley.

Duncan, T. E., & Duncan, S. C. (1995). Modeling the processes of development via latent variable growth curve methodology. *Structural Equation Modeling, 2,* 187–213.

Duncan, T. E., Duncan, S. C., & Hops, H. (1996). The role of parents and older siblings in pre-dicting adolescent substance use: Modeling development via structural equation latent growth methodology. *Journal of Family Psychology, 10,* 158–172.

Eccles, J. S., Midgley, C., Wigfield, A., Buchanan, C. M., Reuman, D., Flanagan, C., & MacIver, D. (1993). Development during adolescence: The impact of stage-environment fit in young adolescents' experiences in schools and in families. *American Psychologist, 48,* 90–101.

Entwisle, D. R. (1990). Schools and the adolescent. In S. S. Feldman & G. R. Elliott (Eds.), *At the threshold: The developing adolescent* (pp. 197–224). Cambridge, MA: Harvard University Press.

Erikson, E. (1968). *Identity: Youth and crisis.* New York: Norton.

Farrell, A. D., Danish, S. J., & Howard, C. W. (1991). Evaluation of data screening methods in surveys of adolescents' drug use. *Psychological Assessment, 3,* 295–298.

Farrell, A. D., Danish, S. J., & Howard, C. W. (1992). Relationship between drug use and other problem behaviors in urban adolescents. *Journal of Consulting and Clinical Psychology, 60,* 705–712.

Fauber, R., Forehand, R., Thomas, A. M., & Wierson, M. (1990). A mediational model of the impact of marital conflict on adolescent adjustment in intact and divorced families: The role of disrupted parenting. *Child Development, 61,* 1112–1123.

Feldman, S. S., & Elliott, G. R. (Eds.). (1990). *At the threshold: The developing adolescent.* Cambridge, MA: Harvard University Press.

Felner, R. D., Ginter, M., & Primavera, J. (1982). Primary prevention during school transitions: Social support and environmental structure. *American Journal of Community Psychology, 10,* 277–290.

Flavell, J. H., & Ross, L. (1981). *Social cognitive development: Frontiers and possible futures.* New York: Cambridge University Press.

Freud, A. (1958). Adolescence. *Psychoanalytic Study of the Child, 13,* 231–258.

Fuhrman, T., & Holmbeck, G. N. (1995). A contextual-moderator analysis of emotional auton-omy and adjustment in adolescence. *Child Development, 66,* 793–811.

Fuligni, A. J., & Eccles, J. S. (1993). Perceived parent-child relationships and early adoles-cents' orientation toward peers. *Developmental Psychology, 29,* 622–632.

Ge, X., Best, K. M., Conger, R. D., & Simons, R. L. (1996). Parenting behaviors and the oc-currence and co-occurrence of adolescent depressive symptoms and conduct problems. *Developmental Psychology, 32,* 717–731.

George, C., Kaplan, N., & Main, M. (1984). *Attachment interview for adults.* Unpublished man-uscript, University of California, Berkeley.

Gonzales, N. A., Cauce, A. M., & Mason, C. A. (1996). Interobserver agreement in the assess-ment of parental behavior and parent-adolescent conflict: African American mothers, daughters, and independent observers. *Child Development, 67,* 1483–1498.

Gordon, D. E. (1988). Formal operations and interpersonal and affective disturbances in ado-lescents. In E. D. Nannis & P. A. Cowan (Eds.), *Developmental psychopathology and its treatment* (No. 39, pp. 51–74). San Francisco: Jossey-Bass.

Gottman, J. M., & Levenson, R. W. (1985). A valid procedure for obtaining self-report of af-fect in marital interaction. *Journal of Consulting and Clinical Psychology, 53,* 156–160.

Gray, W. M., & Hudson, L. M. (1984). Formal operations and the imaginary audience. *Devel-opmental Psychology, 20,* 619–627.

Greenberger, E., & Steinberg, L. (1986). *When teenagers work: The psychological and social costs of adolescent employment.* New York: Basic Books.

Grotevant, H. D. (1997). Adolescent development in family contexts. In W. Damon (Ed.), *Handbook of child psychology* (Vol. 3, pp. 1097–1149). New York: Wiley.

Grych, J. H., & Fincham, F. D. (1990). Marital conflict and children's adjustment: A cognitive-contextual framework. *Psychological Bulletin, 108,* 267–290.

Guerra, N. G. (1993). Cognitive development. In P. H. Tolan & B. J. Cohler (Eds.), *Handbook of clinical research and practice with adolescents* (pp. 45–62). New York: Wiley.

Harter, S. (1985). *Manual for the self-perception profile for children.* Unpublished manual. Denver, CO: University of Denver.

Harter, S. (1988). *Manual for the self-perception profile for adolescents.* Unpublished manual. Denver, CO: University of Denver.

Harter, S. (1990). Self and identity development. In S. S. Feldman & G. R. Elliott (Eds.), *At the threshold: The developing adolescent* (pp. 352–387). Cambridge, MA: Harvard University Press.

Hayden, L. C., Schiller, M., Dickstein, S., Seifer, R., Sameroff, A., Miller, I., Keitner, G., & Rasmussen, S. (1998). Levels of family assessment: I. Family, marital, and parent-child interaction. *Journal of Family Psychology, 12,* 7–22.

Henderson, V. L., & Dweck, C. S. (1990). Motivation and achievement. In S. S. Feldman & G. R. Elliott (Eds.), *At the threshold: The developing adolescent* (pp. 308–329). Cambridge, MA: Harvard University Press.

Henry, B., Caspi, A., Moffitt, T. E., & Silva, P. A. (1996). Temperamental and familial predictors of violent and nonviolent criminal convictions: Age 3 to age 18. *Developmental Psychology, 32,* 614–623.

Hill, J. P. (1980). *Understanding early adolescence: A framework.* Carrboro, NC: Center for Early Adolescence.

Hill, J. P. (1983). Early adolescence: A framework. *Journal of Early Adolescence, 3,* 1–21.

Hill, J. P., & Holmbeck, G. N. (1986). Attachment and autonomy during adolescence. In G. J. Whitehurst (Ed.), *Annals of child development* (Vol. 3, pp. 145–189). Greenwich, CT: JAI Press.

Hogue, A., & Steinberg, L. (1995). Homophily of internalized distress in adolescent peer groups. *Developmental Psychology, 31,* 897–906.

Holmbeck, G. N. (1994). Adolescence. In V. S. Ramachandran (Ed.), *Encyclopedia of human behavior* (Vol.1, pp. 17–28). Orlando, FL: Academic Press.

Holmbeck, G. N. (1996). A model of family relational transformations during the transition to adolescence: Parent-adolescent conflict and adaptation. In J. A. Graber, J. Brooks-Gunn, & A. C. Petersen (Eds.), *Transitions through adolescence: Interpersonal domains and context* (pp. 167–199). Mahwah, NJ: Erlbaum.

Holmbeck, G. N. (1997). Toward terminological, conceptual, and statistical clarity in the study of mediators and moderators: Examples from the child-clinical and pediatric psychology literatures. *Journal of Consulting and Clinical Psychology, 65,* 599–610.

Holmbeck, G. N., Crossman, R. E., Wandrei, M. L., & Gasiewski, E. (1994). Cognitive development, egocentrism, self-esteem, and adolescent contraceptive knowledge, attitudes, and behavior. *Journal of Youth and Adolescence, 23,* 169–193.

Holmbeck, G. N., & Hill, J. P. (1991). Conflictive engagement, positive affect, and menarche in families with seventh-grade girls. *Child Development, 62,* 1030–1048.

Holmbeck, G. N., & Kendall, P. C. (1991). Clinical-childhood-developmental interface: Implications for treatment. In P. R. Martin (Ed.), *Handbook of behavior therapy and psychological science: An integrative approach* (pp. 73–99). New York: Pergamon Press.

Holmbeck, G. N., & O'Donnell, K. (1991). Discrepancies between perceptions of decision-making and behavioral autonomy. In R. L. Paikoff (Ed.), *Shared views in the family during adolescence: New directions for development* (No. 51, pp. 51–69). San Francisco: Jossey-Bass.

Holmbeck, G. N., Paikoff, R. L., & Brooks-Gunn, J. (1995). Parenting adolescents. In M. Bornstein (Ed.), *Handbook of parenting* (Vol. 1, pp. 91–118). Hillsdale, NJ: Erlbaum.

Holmbeck, G. N., & Updegrove, A. L. (1995). Clinical-developmental interface: Implications of developmental research for adolescent psychotherapy. *Psychotherapy, 32,* 16–33.

Jessor, R., Donovan, J. E., & Costa, F. M. (1991). *Beyond adolescence: Problem behavior and young adult development.* New York: Cambridge University Press.

Jessor, R., & Jessor, S. L. (1977). *Problem behavior and psychosocial development: A longitudinal study of youth.* New York: Academic Press.

Katchadourian, H. (1990). Sexuality. In S. S. Feldman & G. R. Elliott (Eds.), *At the threshold: The developing adolescent* (pp. 330–351). Cambridge, MA: Harvard University Press.

Keating, D. P. (1990). Adolescent thinking. In S. S. Feldman & G. R. Elliott (Eds.), *At the threshold: The developing adolescent* (pp. 54–89). Cambridge, MA: Harvard University Press.

Kendall, P. C. (1984). Social cognition and problem solving: A developmental and child-clinical interface. In B. Gholson & T. L. Rosenthal (Eds.), *Applications of cognitive-developmental theory* (pp. 115–148). New York: Academic Press.

Kendall, P. C., & Holmbeck, G. N. (1991). Psychotherapeutic interventions for adolescents. In R. M. Lerner, A. C. Petersen, & J. Brooks-Gunn (Eds.), *Encyclopedia of adolescence* (pp. 866–874). New York: Pergamon Press.

Kendall, P. C., Lerner, R. M., & Craighead, W. E. (1984). Human development and intervention in childhood psychopathology. *Child Development, 55,* 71–82.

Kendall, P. C., & Williams, C. L. (1986). Therapy with adolescents: Treating the "Marginal Man." *Behavior Therapy, 17,* 522–537.

Kidwell, J., Fischer, J. L., Dunham, R. M., & Baranowski, M. (1983). Parents and adolescents: Push and pull of change. In H. I. McCubbin & C. R. Figley (Eds.), *Stress and the family: Vol. I. Coping with normative transitions* (pp. 74–89). New York: Brunner/Mazel.

Kobak, R., Cole, H., Ferenz-Gillies, R., Fleming, W., & Gamble, W. (1993). Attachment and emotion regulation during mother-teen problem-solving: A control theory analysis. *Child Development, 64,* 231–245.

Lamborn, S. D., & Steinberg, L. (1993). Emotional autonomy redux: Revisiting Ryan and Lynch. *Child Development, 64,* 483–499.

Larson, R. W., Richards, M. H., Moneta, G., Holmbeck, G., & Duckett, E. (1996). Changes in adolescents' daily interactions with their families from ages 10 to 18: Disengagement and transformation. *Developmental Psychology, 32,* 744–754.

Laursen, B., & Collins, W. A. (1994). Interpersonal conflict during adolescence. *Psychological Bulletin, 115,* 197–209.

Lerner, R. M., Petersen, A. C., & Brooks-Gunn, J. (1991). *Encyclopedia of adolescence* (Vols. 1 & 2). New York: Garland.

Lewko, J. H. (Ed.). (1987). *How children and adolescents view the world of work* (No. 35, New Directions for Child Development). San Francisco: Jossey-Bass.

Magnusson, D., Stattin, H., & Allen, V. L. (1985). A longitudinal study of some adjustment processes from mid-adolescence to adulthood. *Journal of Youth and Adolescence, 14,* 267–283.

Main, M., Kaplan, N., & Cassidy, J. (1985). Security in infancy, childhood, and adulthood: A move to the level of representation. In I. Bretherton & E. Waters (Eds.), Growing points of attachment theory and research (pp. 66–106). *Monographs of the Society for Research on Child Development, 50*(1–2, Serial No. 209).

Marcia, J. E. (1966). Development and validation of ego identity status. *Journal of Personality and Social Psychology, 3,* 551–558.

Melby, J. N., Conger, R. D., Ge, X., & Warner, T. D. (1995). The use of structural equation modeling in assessing the quality of marital observations. *Journal of Family Psychology, 9,* 280–293.

Minuchin, P. P., & Shapiro, E. K. (1983). The school as a context for social development. In E. M. Hetherington (Vol. Ed.) & P. H. Mussen (Ed.), *Handbook of child psychology* (Vol. 4, pp. 197–274). New York: Wiley.

Molina, B. S. G., & Chassin, L. (1996). The parent-adolescent relationship at puberty: Hispanic ethnicity and parent alcoholism as moderators. *Developmental Psychology, 32,* 675–686.

Negy, C., Leal-Puente, L., Trainor, D. J., & Carlson, R. (1997). Mexican-American adolescents' performance on the MMPI-A. *Journal of Personality Assessment, 69,* 205–214.

Nolen-Hoeksema, S. (1994). An interactive model for the emergence of gender differences in depression in adolescence. *Journal of Research on Adolescence, 4,* 519–534.

Nottelmann, E. D., Inoff-Germain, G., Susman, E. J., & Chrousos, G. P. (1990). Hormones and behavior at puberty. In J. Bancroft & J. M. Reinisch (Eds.), *Adolescence and puberty* (pp. 88–123). New York: Oxford University Press.

Overton, W. F. (Ed.). (1983). *The relationship between social and cognitive development.* Hillsdale, NJ: Erlbaum.

Paikoff, R. L., & Brooks-Gunn, J. (1991). Do parent-child relationships change during puberty? *Psychological Bulletin, 110,* 47–66.

Paikoff, R. L., Parfenoff, S. H., Williams, S. A., McCormick, A., Greenwood, G. L., & Holmbeck, G. N. (1997). Parenting, parent-child relationships, and sexual possibility situations among urban African American preadolescents: Preliminary findings and implications for HIV prevention. *Journal of Family Psychology, 11,* 11–22.

Parker, J. G., & Asher, S. R. (1987). Peer relations and later personal adjustment: Are low-accepted children at risk? *Psychological Bulletin, 102,* 357–389.

Parkhurst, J. T., & Asher, S. R. (1992). Peer rejection in middle school: Subgroup differences in behavior, loneliness, and interpersonal concerns. *Developmental Psychology, 28,* 231–241.

Perry, C. L., Williams, C. L., Veblen-Mortenson, S., Toomey, T. L., Komro, K. A., Anstine, P. S., McGovern, P. G., Finnegan, J. R., Forster, J. L., Wagenaar, A. C., & Wolfson, M. (1996). Project Northland: Outcomes of a community-wide alcohol use prevention program during early adolescence. *American Journal of Public Health, 86,* 956–965.

Petersen, A. C. (1988). Adolescent development. In M. R. Rosenzweig & L. W. Porter (Eds.), *Annual review of psychology* (Vol. 39, pp. 583–608). Palo Alto, CA: Annual Reviews.

Petersen, A. C., & Hamburg, B. A. (1986). Adolescence: A developmental approach to problems and psychopathology. *Behavior Therapy, 17,* 480–499.

Piaget, J. (1970). Piaget's theory. In P. H. Mussen (Ed.), *Manual of child psychology* (3rd ed., pp. 703–732). New York: Wiley.

Powers, S. I., Welsh, D. P., & Wright, V. (1994). Adolescents' affective experience of family behaviors: The role of subjective understanding. *Journal of Research on Adolescence, 4,* 585–600.

Quittner, A. L., & Opipari, L. C. (1994). Differential treatment of siblings: Interview and diary analyses comparing two family contexts. *Child Development, 65,* 800–814.

Reich, W., Shayka, J. J., & Taibleson, C. (1991). *Diagnostic interview for children and adolescents (DICA-R-A; Adolescent version).* Unpublished interview, Washington University.

Roeser, R. W., & Eccles, J. S. (1998). Adolescents' perceptions of middle school: Relation to longitudinal changes in academic and psychological adjustment. *Journal of Research on Adolescence, 8,* 123–158.

Rolf, J., Masten, A. S., Cicchetti, D., Nuechterlein, K. H., & Weintraub, S. (1990). *Risk and protective factors in the development of psychopathology.* New York: Cambridge University Press.

Rosenstein, D. S., & Horowitz, H. A. (1996). Adolescent attachment and psychopathology. *Journal of Consulting and Clinical Psychology, 64,* 244–253.

Rutter, M. (1980). *Changing youth in a changing society: Patterns of adolescent development and disorder.* Cambridge, MA: Harvard University Press.

Rutter, M. (1990). Psychosocial resilience and protective mechanisms. In J. Rolf, A. S. Masten, D. Cicchetti, K. H. Nuechterlein, & S. Weintraub (Eds.), *Risk and protective factors in the development of psychopathology* (pp. 181–214). New York: Cambridge University Press.

Rutter, M., Maughan, B., Mortimore, P., & Ouston, J. (1979). *Fifteen thousand hours: Secondary schools and their effects on children.* Cambridge, MA: Harvard University Press.

Ryan, R., & Lynch, J. (1989). Emotional autonomy versus detachment: Revisiting the vicissitudes of adolescence and young adulthood. *Child Development, 60,* 340–356.

Savin-Williams, R. C., & Berndt, T. J. (1990). Friendship and peer relations. In S. S. Feldman & G. R. Elliott (Eds.), *At the threshold: The developing adolescent* (pp. 277–307). Cambridge, MA: Harvard University Press.

Schleser, R., Cohen, R., Meyers, A., & Rodick, J. D. (1984). The effects of cognitive level and training procedures on the generalization of self-instructions. *Cognitive Therapy and Research, 8,* 187–200.

Schulenberg, J., Wadsworth, K. N., O'Malley, P. M., Bachman, J. G., & Johnston, L. D. (1996). Adolescent risk factors for binge drinking during the transition to young adulthood: Variable- and pattern-centered approaches to change. *Developmental Psychology, 32,* 659–674.

Schwartz, D., Dodge, K. A., & Coie, J. D. (1993). The emergence of chronic peer victimization in boys' play groups. *Child Development, 64,* 1755–1772.

Selman, R. L. (1980). *The growth of interpersonal understanding.* New York: Academic Press.

Selman, R. L. (1981). The child as a friendship philosopher. In S. R. Asher & J. M. Gottman (Eds.), *The development of children's friendships* (pp. 242–272). New York: Cambridge University Press.

Shantz, C. U. (1983). Social cognition. In J. H. Flavell & E. M. Markman (Vol. Eds.) & P. H. Mussen (Ed.), *Handbook of child psychology* (Vol. 3, pp. 495–555). New York: Wiley.

Shirk, S. R. (Ed.). (1988). *Cognitive development and child psychotherapy.* New York: Plenum Press.

Simmons, R. G., & Blyth, D. A. (1987). *Moving into adolescence: The impact of pubertal change and school context.* New York: Aldine de Gruyter.

Smetana, J. G. (1988). Concepts of self and social convention: Adolescents' and parents' reasoning about hypothetical and actual family conflicts. In M. R. Gunnar & W. A. Collins (Eds.), *Development during the transition to adolescence: Minnesota Symposia on Child Psychology* (Vol. 21, pp. 79–122). Hillsdale, NJ: Erlbaum.

Spoth, R., Redmond, C., & Shin, C. (1998). Direct and indirect latent-variable parenting outcomes of two universal family-focused prevention interventions: Extending a public health-oriented research base. *Journal of Consulting and Clinical Psychology, 66,* 385–399.

Stattin, H., & Magnusson, D. (1994). *Behavioral and interpersonal antecedents behind the age at leaving home, and the future consequences for parent-child relations.* Paper presented at the biennial meetings of the Society for Research on Adolescence, San Diego.

Steinberg, L. (1987). Impact of puberty on family relations: Effects of pubertal status and pubertal timing. *Developmental Psychology, 23,* 451–460.

Steinberg, L. (1990). Interdependence in the family: Autonomy, conflict, and harmony in the parent-adolescent relationship. In S. S. Feldman & G. L. Elliott (Eds.), *At the threshold: The developing adolescent* (pp. 255–276). Cambridge, MA: Harvard University Press.

Steinberg, L. (1995). Commentary: On developmental pathways and social contexts in adolescence. In L. J. Crockett & A. S. Crouter (Eds.), *Pathways through adolescence: Individual development in relation to social contexts* (pp. 245–253). Mahwah, NJ: Erlbaum.

Steinberg, L. (1996). *Adolescence* (4th ed.). New York: McGraw-Hill.

Steinberg, L. D., & Silverberg, S. B. (1986). The vicissitudes of autonomy in early adolescence. *Child Development, 57,* 841–852.

Swarr, A. E., & Richards, M. H. (1996). Longitudinal effects of adolescent girls' pubertal development, perceptions of pubertal timing, and parental relations on eating problems. *Developmental Psychology, 32,* 636–646.

Tanner, J. (1962). *Growth at adolescence* (2nd ed.). Springfield, IL: Thomas.

Tolan, P. H., & Cohler, B. J. (1993). *Handbook of clinical research and practice with adolescents.* New York: Wiley.

Trickett, E. J., & Schmid, J. D. (1993). The school as a social context. In P. H. Tolan & B. J. Cohler (Eds.), *Handbook of clinical research and practice with adolescents* (pp. 173–202). New York: Wiley.

Van Hasselt, V. B., & Hersen, M. (Eds.). (1987). *Handbook of adolescent psychology.* New York: Pergamon Press.

Van Hasselt, V. B., & Hersen, M. (Eds.). (1995). *Handbook of adolescent psychopathology.* New York: Lexington Books.

Ward, S., & Overton, W. (1990). Semantic familiarity, relevance, and the development of deductive reasoning. *Developmental Psychology, 26,* 488–493.

Weed, N. C., Butcher, J. N., & Williams, C. L. (1994). Development of MMPI-A alcohol/drug problem scales. *Journal of Studies in Alcohol, 55,* 296–302.

Weiner, I. B. (1992). *Psychological disturbance in adolescence* (2nd ed.). New York: Wiley.

Welsh, D. P., Vickerman, R., Kawaguchi, M. C., & Rostosky, S. S. (1998). *Discrepancies in adolescent romantic couples' and observers' perceptions of couple interaction and their relationship to mental health.* Manuscript submitted for publication.

Willet, J. B., & Sayer, A. G. (1994). Using covariance structure analysis to detect correlates and predictors of individual change over time. *Psychological Bulletin, 116,* 363–381.

Chapter 26

Focus Chapter

RESEARCH METHODS WITH OLDER ADULTS

Bruce Rybarczyk, Ph.D., and Martita Lopez, Ph.D.

As recently as the 1800s, the average age of death was about 35 years, and even early this century most people died before they reached age 50. Currently, the average life span is about 75 years, and older adults make up 13% of the U.S. population. By the year 2030, that percentage is expected to jump to 30% of the general population. This dramatic shift toward an older population will necessitate a commensurate increase on the part of psychologists in the study and treatment of older adults.

The past 50 years have seen the birth of the specialty in psychology referred to as geropsychology, as well as the equivalent specialty in clinical psychology referred to as clinical geropsychology. Initial interest in clinical geropsychology was focused on dementia and Alzheimer's disease primarily (Niederehe, Cooley, & Teri, 1995), but the field has gradually broadened to include a much wider array of clinical issues (see Hersen & Van Hasselt, 1996; Woods, 1996). The first American Psychological Association (APA) journal addressing geropsychology, *Psychology and Aging,* did not appear until 1986, and the first journal focusing exclusively on clinical geropsychology, the *Journal of Clinical Geropsychology,* was inaugurated in 1995. This belated interest in later adulthood has been gaining momentum, with APA creating a Continuing Committee on Aging and recognizing geropsychology as an area of proficiency in 1998.

Unfortunately, only a relatively small number of health care professionals and scientists have been entering the field of aging. Numerous explanations for this age bias in career choice have been offered, including a wider culture that devalues older adults, fears about our own aging process, a belief that the health problems of older adults are overwhelming and irreversible, and a lack of exposure to positive views of older adults in training programs (Quinn, 1987). The study of late adulthood has not been a priority within the field of psychology until recently. Freudian and neo-Freudian developmental theories that predominated over the first half of the century (Erikson notwithstanding) held that personality was largely determined during childhood and adolescence. Old age was often viewed as a time of rigid or even regressed psychological functioning. Nonetheless, as the field matures, the number of graduate students receiving training in geropsychology is slowly growing (Haley & Gatz, 1995).

Two distinct lines of research have moved the field of geropsychology forward: scientific gerontology and research in mental health and aging (Knight, 1996). Scientific gerontology has addressed issues about *normal* aging through large-scale cross-sectional and longitudinal studies, such as how personality changes or remains stable with age, what constitutes healthy aging, and how older adults cope with stress differently than younger adults. Methodological advances in the 1970s were paralleled by the development of the life span approach to psychological research on aging (see Staudinger, Marsiske, & Baltes, 1995, for a complete description). As a result of the life span approach, "the conception of later life emerged as more continuous with early adulthood and middle-age than had been thought before" (Knight, Santos, Teri, & Lawton, 1995, p. 3). On a broader level, these studies have been highly instrumental in debunking numerous negative stereotypes about aging and creating a much more balanced picture that includes the strengths and diversity found among older adults.

The mental health and aging line of research has been more limited, with most progress occurring in the past 15 years (Niederehe et al., 1995). Much of this research has been conducted in clinical settings such as Veterans Administration hospitals, nursing homes, and university medical centers. These researchers have focused on diagnostic and treatment issues with dementia, late life depression, and other psychiatric disorders of late life. Caregiver stress and caregiver interventions have also been prime areas of research. Fortunately, the pace of mental health and aging research has picked up considerably in recent years. For example, the 1991 National Institutes of Health (NIH) consensus panel statement on diagnosis and treatment of depression in late life was updated in 1997 (Lebowitz et al., 1997) to accommodate the numerous new findings obtained in the interim period. Clinical psychologists have only recently begun to make substantial research contributions to the study of mental health and aging (Niederehe et al., 1995).

Much important research still needs to be conducted. We need to expand our knowledge base about both normal and "optimal" aging, to further elucidate the unique manifestations of psychopathology in later life, to understand how psychopathology interacts with physical health in older adults, to test a range of clinical interventions that have been empirically validated with younger adults only, to develop new age-appropriate interventions where necessary, and to develop innovative clinical services that are both accessible and acceptable to older adults (Logsdon, 1995). Accordingly, an overarching objective of this chapter is to call on psychology students and investigators to take part in these research goals. Even for those who do not choose to specialize in geropsychology, these empirical questions can be incorporated into one of the more commonly chosen specialty areas in which there is significant overlap (e.g., health psychology, rehabilitation psychology, neuropsychology).

Given the goals of this book and the limitations of space, we will focus on reviewing the research issues that advanced graduate students and investigators need to grasp in order to interpret and conduct research with older adults. These topics will include age as a research variable, the common research methodologies used in geropsychology, choosing a representative sample, participant recruitment, assessment issues, and future directions in geropsychology research. We use examples to illustrate these issues from both the normal and abnormal aging research traditions.

AGE AS A RESEARCH VARIABLE

A basic question that must always be addressed in psychological research on aging is the definition of age as a variable. Because the experimenter cannot manipulate levels of age, it resembles other demographic participant variables such as gender, occupation, and level of education. Certain dependent variables are expected to vary with age, but changes in these variables, for example, health status and social support, depend on how age is defined. Age can be defined in many ways, including chronologically, psychologically, socially, biologically, and physically. Every person is a different "age" on each of these dimensions, and chronological age alone means little other than the passage of time since the individual was born. Two 75-year-old people can be vastly different in terms of their psychological status, for example, in terms of life satisfaction, activity, and view of how much time is left in life. These issues are similar to those faced in the study of adolescents, where pubertal status and pubertal timing differ greatly among individuals of the same chronological age (see Culbertson and Holmbeck and Shapera chapters, this volume). One fundamental principle in geropsychology is the increasing heterogeneity of people as they age, with the result that older adults differ more widely from each other in various physical and psychological domains (e.g., cognitive functioning) than do younger adults (Zeiss & Steffen, 1996).

Specific dimensions of age, and how they are measured, should be included in studies of older adults, and investigators should not automatically equate chronological age with other participant variables. Often, chronological age will not be the most important "age" to consider. Several commonly studied psychosocial stages that are not universal and only roughly age-dependent include moving into retirement, becoming the caregiver of a spouse, and spousal bereavement. Another nonchronological age category that is used in gerontology literature is the *frail elderly*, which refers to the stage in the life cycle when physical impairments necessitate a dependency on others for daily care. Geropsychology still needs to advance to the point of developing theoretically based measures of developmental age similar to those used in child and adolescent developmental research (see Culbertson and Holmbeck and Shapera chapters, this volume). Notable exceptions in gerontology research are two measures of the degree of resolution of Erikson's final psychosocial stages (Hawley, 1985; Walasky, Whitbourne, & Nehrke, 1984) and Gutmann's (1987) standardized use of the Thematic Apperception Test (TAT) to score individuals on their achievement of a hypothesized gender-identity shift after midlife.

A related notion is that of "subjective age," which refers to how old a person feels. Older adults typically report that their subjective age is younger than their chronological age, even when their health status is declining. This variable has been shown to correlate highly with a variety of measures of psychological adjustment and be predictive of morbidity and mortality (Mossey, 1995). Another subjective measure of age that has been tested in some recent innovative research is how many years individuals believe they have remaining in their lives (Carstensen, 1995). This variable was shown to be predictive of selection of social partners, with individuals who perceive less future time choosing to affiliate with family members and those perceiving more future time choosing unfamiliar persons who provide an opportunity for future connections and/or the acquisition of new information. When asked why they made this latter choice, older persons often explicitly reported that they had no time to waste and had to be careful about their choices (Fredrickson & Carstensen, 1990).

It is also important to define the term "older adults." Traditionally, older adults have been thought of as persons 60 years old and above. However, because the age span of interest to researchers now approaches 100 years, it is increasingly necessary to divide older adults into different subgroups. One common way to do this is to partition older adults into the "young-old," or those 55–75 years of age, and the "old-old," those over age 75. The "oldest-old," those over age 85, are also an important population to study, as they are the fastest growing age group in the United States. The field of psychology and aging currently knows very little about this age group (Niederehe et al., 1995).

An additional basic issue in research with older adults is the necessity of including age, however it is defined, in the research design and analyzing the data for its effect. Too often, age is controlled for in the design either by matching or by specific data analyses. When this occurs and age is not related to outcome measures, important information on the interaction of age and other independent variables is lost. Even in the realm of outcome research, post hoc analyses and meta-analyses examining the moderating effect of age can be illuminating. For example, a meta-analysis of behavioral treatments for tension headaches showed a significant negative relationship ($r = -.63$) between mean improvement after treatment and the average age of patients in a study (Holroyd & Penzien, 1986). Age was the most important subject variable and accounted for a full 40% of outcome variance. This finding suggests that tension headaches have a different etiology in older adults and interventions need to be designed accordingly.

RESEARCH DESIGNS IN GEROPSYCHOLOGY

The time-dependent concepts of age, cohort, and historical period all must be considered to understand research designs in the psychology of aging. *Age* as a variable was discussed in the previous section, with emphasis placed on the notion that chronological age cannot be assumed to refer to specific levels or types of physical, biological, social, or psychological functioning. However, in the gerontology literature, age as a variable is usually explicitly or implicitly referring to changes caused by *maturation,* or *ontogenic* development (i.e., coming from within).

Age, or birth, *cohort* is a term that refers to a group of people born during the same time period. It is different from a generation, in that researchers set the time span wherever they desire. These cohort groups share the same historical perspective, including developmental stressors, issues, and conflicts, at equivalent points in the maturation sequence. For example, Baby Boomers were coming of age during the turbulent decades of the 1960s and 1970s, which included the Vietnam War, the rise of the drug culture, the loosening of social rules concerning sexual behavior, and Watergate. The way this cohort entered adulthood was significantly influenced by these historical events.

The importance of considering cohort effects is illustrated in the body of research attempting to answer the question of whether older adults are more vulnerable to depression than other age groups. This research has led to the widely accepted conclusion that older adults may exhibit higher levels of depressive symptoms (e.g., dysphoria) but are not more vulnerable to major depression or dysthymia (Blazer, 1997). However, until recently, researchers examining psychopathology in older adults largely ignored the question of whether the prevalence rates being studied were age- or cohort-based. Two recent retrospective studies show that rates of major depression appear to have increased over this century, with successive birth cohorts showing increased lifetime risks and earlier ages of onset (Lewinsohn, Rohde, Seeley, & Fischer, 1993; Warshaw, Klerman, & Lavori, 1991). This increased risk of depression is most apparent in cohorts born after World War II (Warshaw et al., 1991). Even the well-known gender gap finding that women are more likely to experience major depression than men is narrowing, due to a recent increase in risk of depression among young men (Warshaw et al., 1991).

Historical period refers to the social time at the point when the data are being collected. This variable, also known as *time of measurement,* influences all members of a population, regardless of cohort membership, living through a given historical period. For example, presumably due to historical factors, there was an increase in the rates of depression for all age groups between 1960 and 1975 (Warshaw et al., 1991). Another example cited by Whitbourne (1996) is that any age group tested in the 1990s may have higher intelligence test scores than a comparable group of adults tested in the 1970s due to the "information explosion" that has paralleled the growth of high-technology communication. Historical events such as wars, economic depressions, and epidemics also influence a whole population, including most or all cohorts, at about the same time.

It may be obvious by now that age, cohort, and historical period are time-related interdependent concepts that cannot be varied independently. It is not possible to draw valid conclusions about any one of these concepts without considering the effects of at least one of the others because of their common basis on calendar time. For example, an individual who was tested in 1995 (time of measurement) and born in 1930 (cohort) would have to be 65 years old (age) at the time of testing. This interdependence has prompted the development of various experimental designs to distinguish the effects of these concepts so that an individual's aging can be differentiated from the effects of other variables. For more complete discussions of this complex issue, see Adam (1978) and Schroots and Birren (1988).

Studies of aging often focus on change over time. Three different time-associated experimental designs help researchers find the answers they seek regarding age-associated change: longitudinal, cross-sectional, and sequential designs. These designs address the interdependence of age, cohort, and historical period in different ways.

Longitudinal Designs

In longitudinal designs, the same individuals are studied at different points in their lives. These individuals are measured repeatedly over an extended period of time and compared with themselves (Figure 26.1). In addition, sometimes shorter periods can lead to important longitudinal results. For example, the MacArthur Studies of Successful Aging examined an older cohort, age 70–79 years, of high-functioning men and women in 1988 and again 2.5 years later. The results showed that moderate and/or strenuous exercise activity and greater frequency of emotional social support predicted physical performance, after controlling for known sociodemographic and health status predictors (Seeman et al., 1995).

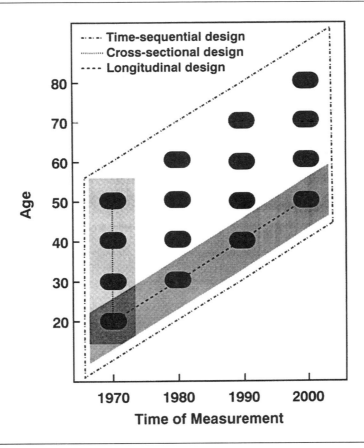

Figure 26.1. Cross-sectional, longitudinal, and time-sequential research designs.

Longitudinal designs are appealing to researchers for a number of reasons, the obvious one being that aging processes can be observed directly across time. At the end of the time period, the researcher can describe changes among older adults on a particular set of variables. Furthermore, depending on the goals of the study, participants may not have to be sorted out and carefully matched because they are compared to themselves. Unfortunately, longitudinal designs also have drawbacks. Selective dropout may occur, as those who are the most cooperative, healthy, and stable tend to stay in the study longer than others. Thus, those who remain are no longer fully representative of the original sample. If the study lasts long enough, the size of the sample may dwindle to the point where it is nearly impossible to adequately analyze the data. Another problem concerns the repeated testing of the same participants. These individuals gain familiarity with the test measures and may improve their scores as a result. Participant attrition, due to mortality, illness, or dropout, and practice effects are the two most common problems that plague researchers using longitudinal designs.

Another difficulty with longitudinal designs has to do with the time commitment required of both researchers and participants. These designs, which may last decades, require a great deal of time and resources, and publication of results may have to be delayed much longer than is standard in most research settings. Furthermore, over the lengthy course of the study, the original researcher may change jobs or retire, thus necessitating a replacement investigator.

When the study covers decades, the problem of outdated assessment measures often occurs. Those constructs that were of interest during one period often do not withstand the test of time and may be outdated when the next wave of assessment occurs. Researchers must decide whether to add new measures, thus losing continuity, or to preserve continuity and try to get as much useful information from the old measures as possible.

Finally, researchers using longitudinal designs must grapple with a fundamental drawback inherent in the design, that is, the confounding of the effects of personal age and the effects of historical period (Whitbourne, 1996). The only information that can be gleaned is on changes over time within a group of people.

Cross-Sectional Designs

In cross-sectional designs, a sample of individuals of one age is observed or measured and compared with one or more samples of individuals of other ages (Figure 26.1). These designs are most useful when the focus of a study is on difference. For example, a high percentage of published research on age and cognition is conducted with cross-sectional designs. Most of these studies use the extreme-age-groups design, in which a group of young adults, often college students, is compared with a group of older adults, thus maximizing potential differences.

Cross-sectional designs have several advantages, chief among them the fact that the cross-sectional method is highly efficient. Studies using these designs can be conducted more quickly than studies using longitudinal designs, and they are far more manageable.

Differences between groups in cross-sectional studies are assumed to reflect their differences in age, not other factors related to the selection of participants such as educational level or health status. The threat that these extraneous factors pose to the validity of the findings has been called the Achilles' heel of cross-sectional studies (Hertzog, 1996). Hertzog describes this as the largest single design problem in gerontological research and defines the problem as the extent to which the internal validity threat of selection (e.g., health status) represents a rival explanation for observed group differences. Unfortunately, there are many published studies in aging that suffer from selection effects, particularly those published in the 1960s and 1970s. Selection effects can create or mask cross-sectional age differences. Attrition is another hidden issue for cross-sectional designs, in that those individuals who survive to older age are those who are healthier and have avoided accidents. The older sample obtained, therefore, may not be comparable to the younger sample.

Another issue concerns the age range and number of the groups being measured. The age range of the groups being studied should be relatively small and equivalent across groups. Too often researchers broaden the acceptable age range for their older adult participants, for example, ages 65–80 years, for practical reasons having to do with ease of recruiting participants. The drawback of this approach is the dissimilarity among individuals in this broad age range (i.e., a 65-year-old often has more developmental similarity with a 45-year-old than with an 85-year-old), making accurate conclusions about any data obtained much more difficult. The problem is intensified when a broader age range is used for older adults than for the younger comparison group, which is often the case. A better approach is to use the same small age range for each age group measured. All other things being equal, it is also preferable to have three or more age groups rather than two, so that researchers can draw conclusions from their data with more confidence (Whitbourne, 1996). A third age group also permits the examination of curvilinear effects.

Another potential limitation of cross-sectional studies is the issue of measurement equivalence across age levels. Measures must be reliable and valid with all participants assessed, younger and older, and investigators must actively ensure that this is the case. A final limitation is the inability of cross-sectional designs to shed light on growth trends, or age changes. These designs allow the investigator to make conclusions only regarding age differences, that is, that one group is higher or lower than another on the variable being measured.

One variation of the cross-sectional design that gives a researcher more confidence in making assertions about age effect findings is cross-cultural replication. If it can be shown that the same age differences are found in another culture, particularly in non-Western and nonindustrialized cultures, then cohort effects as an alternative to maturation can be considered less plausible. For example, after finding similar cross-sectional age differences in TAT stories among men in American, Mayan Indian, and nomadic Galilean and Druze cultures, Gutmann was able to theorize that this represented a universal developmental shift in males toward integration of a more stereotypically feminine orientation to the world (see Gutmann, 1987, for summary of research).

Sequential Designs

In response to the inadequacies of longitudinal and cross-sectional designs, Schaie (1965) developed a *sequential* strategy that took into account age, cohort, and historical period as separate indices. This strategy involved a combination of cross-sectional and longitudinal designs. Individuals of several different ages are measured repeatedly over an extended period of time. Schaie described several variations of the sequential design strategy, including cohort-sequential, time-sequential, and cross-sequential. Each variation takes two of the three factors of age, cohort, and historical period into account.

Using the time-sequential method, a given set of age levels is measured at each of several times of measurement. The accompanying assumption is that change is related to age and/or historical period, but not to cohort. Figure 26.1 provides an illustration of a time-sequential design. In cohort-sequential designs, several cohorts are observed across the same age interval or levels, though at different times of measurement (i.e., one or more replications of a longitudinal design). The assumption is that change is related to age and/or cohort, but not to historical period. The cross-sequential approach involves assessing several cohorts for the same set of times of measurement, though at different ages (i.e., one or more replications of a cross-sectional design). Here it is assumed that change is related to cohort and/or historical period, but not age. Figure 26.2 provides an illustration of cohort-sequential and cross-sequential designs.

The well-known Seattle Longitudinal Study is an example of the cohort-sequential design. In this study, which started in 1958, 500 participants were randomly sampled and

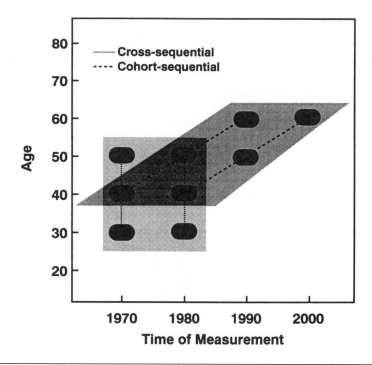

Figure 26.2. Cross-sequential and cohort-sequential designs.

equally distributed by sex and age across the range from 20 to 70 years from the approximately 18,000 individuals who were then members of a health maintenance organization in the Pacific Northwest (e.g., Schaie, Maitland, Willis, & Intrieri, 1998). The
survivors of the original sample were retested and additional panels were added in
seven-year intervals, so that there have now been six cycles of testing completed. The
sample was divided into six age cohorts. One important result of this study has been a
complete rethinking of the common myth that adults become more psychologically rigid,
or inflexible, as they age. This finding had been supported by previous cross-sectional
research. Data from the Seattle Longitudinal Study demonstrated that successive cohorts of participants became more flexible and that individual decreases in flexibility
were far smaller than had been thought previously (Schaie & Willis, 1991).

Schaie (1965) asserted that the systematic application of sequential methods and assumptions allows the identification of the sources of change in behavior. The limitations
of Schaie's sequential designs have been thoroughly described by Baltes (1968) and others (e.g., Nesselroade & Labouvie, 1985). Many of these limitations are based on the
fact that age, cohort, and historical period are all interdependent, so that once you set
two of these variables, the third is automatically determined. As a result, interpretations
of data from these studies are open to alternative explanations. Nesselroade and Labouvie argue that the increased efforts and costs associated with sequential strategies are
justified only under two conditions: (a) when sampling procedures are rigorous and
sample sizes are large enough to ensure adequate internal validity for drawing conclusions about cohort differences, and (b) when the set of measured variables includes

empirical indicators of maturational and environmental factors, thereby making the results amenable to more explicit forms of causal modeling.

Despite their limitations, sequential methods offer the advantages of allowing both longitudinal and cross-sectional comparisons of participants' performance, and they permit researchers to measure the existence of cohort effects. The replication involved in a sequential design also strengthens the conclusions that can be drawn by the investigator. Practical liabilities of sequential designs include their higher expense and the longer time period required to collect the data. In addition, they may suffer from some of the problems of both cross-sectional and longitudinal designs.

Multivariate Research

Multivariate methods, such as multiple regression and structural equation modeling, have become increasingly prevalent in geropsychology research and provide opportunities to test hypotheses that are not possible with other designs. One key advantage of multivariate analyses is that they allow for the examination of age as a continuous variable, so the same study can include individuals from a wide range of ages. One problem is that these studies often assume that the age effects are linear and gradual (e.g., decreased psychomotor speed) when some changes may in fact be curvilinear or rapid in onset.

Multivariate statistical methods are crucial for teasing apart the subtle and often reciprocal interrelations among psychological, social, and physical variables in older adults. As Hartke (1991) notes, "physical and mental systems become more interdependent and reactive to each other with increasing age" (p. 4). Katz (1995) makes the similar observation that late life psychological disorders are notable for "their substantial impact on well-being, quality of life, self-care, health care utilization, morbidity and mortality; their effects on family caregivers; and their occurrence within the context of general medical problems of late life" (p. 257).

An example of a geropsychology study using multiple regression to assess whether several *biopsychosocial* variables predicted recovery from illness was conducted by Nanna and colleagues (Nanna, Lichtenberg, Buda-Abela, & Barth, 1997). Participants consisted of 423 medical rehabilitation inpatients between the ages of 60 and 99 with a variety of medical conditions (e.g., stroke, amputation, joint replacements). Measures of depression and cognition at admission accounted for 7% of unique variance of a discharge measure of self-care abilities (Activities of Daily Living; ADL). These two variables were entered into a regression equation after admission level of ADL, a series of demographic variables, and the number of existing medical conditions. These results supported the belief that timely assessment and treatment of psychological conditions should be an essential component of any older adult medical rehabilitation service.

Mutran and colleagues (Mutran, Reitzes, Mossey, & Fernandez, 1995) provided an example of a study using structural equation modeling (see Farrell, this volume) to assess the causal relationships among biopsychosocial variables. They examined the relationship among social support, depression, and recovery of walking ability following hip fracture over three time points during a six-month period. The analyses showed that Time 1 inadequacy of social support and depression resulted in less improvement in walking ability at Time 2 (two months postfracture). However, the flow of causal influence was in the reverse direction at six months, with limited walking ability lead-ing to increased levels of depression. In this case, knowing the direction of causal influ-ence was critical to being able to make recommendations about when to provide psychological interventions for hip fracture patients.

CHOOSING A REPRESENTATIVE SAMPLE

Once a researcher has decided on a methodology, the next question to be addressed is how to select a representative sample. As noted above, the modal geropsychological study is cross-sectional. Older participants are usually compared to college students (in cognitive aging studies) or middle-aged samples (in coping or depression studies). The researchers usually narrow their sample of older adults to "community-dwelling" participants, excluding only approximately 5% of the over-65 population who reside in nursing homes. Beyond that, more meticulous researchers often employ a self-report measure of health to exclude participants with significant medical illnesses. They may also include a brief cognitive screening measure to certify that all participants have cognitive functioning "within normal limits."

Although these are the most common measures taken to define a sample, they raise several questions regarding generalizability, or external validity, that are not often ad-dressed. The approach of using community-dwelling elderly is usually an unstated and cursory attempt to screen out participants who have substantial *secondary aging* (age changes related to medical illness or disease). This approach, as Birren and Cunning-ham (1985) note, "cheerfully ignores the high prevalence of chronic diseases even in the community-dwelling elderly" (p. 21). To truly screen out individuals who have *any* age-related diseases that have an impact on cognition, for example, one would need to elim-inate a very large percentage of potential participants. One study (Howieson, Holm, Kaye, Oken, & Howieson, 1993) assessed neuropsychologic functioning of the "opti-mally healthy oldest-old (age 85+)" (p. 1882). The investigators eliminated participants who met any of the following extensive criteria: any medical condition shown to affect brain functioning, history or evidence from medical examination of a neurologic illness, risk factors for vascular disease, any loss of consciousness that lasted longer than five minutes, present or past alcoholism or drug abuse, major psychiatric disorders, a score on the Geriatric Depression Scale greater than 10 (mild depression), or use of a med-ication that might impair cognition. Obtaining this "pure" sample required expensive and time-consuming screening, including a medical exam and medical record review, that ultimately eliminated 85% of their potential participants.

Most researchers do not have the luxury of using such strict exclusion criteria to eliminate secondary aging factors. More important, even if a researcher can success-fully eliminate participants with medical conditions that may affect the variables being studied (e.g., depression, cognition, self-esteem), serious questions can be raised about the generalizability of the findings. Although the results may say something about the effects of *primary aging* (normal age-graded changes) alone on the variables in ques-tion, they do not answer questions about the *usual* aging process. Taking this point even further, one could make a case against studies using only community-based participants because they exclude the appropriate percentage of nursing home residents (i.e., 5% of adults over age 65) necessary for it to qualify as a truly representative sample.

The practice of excluding older adults with chronic illness in geropsychological intervention studies has had important consequences for clinicians. In recent years, a sufficient number of psychotherapy outcome studies have been conducted with older adults to allow for meta-analyses of these results (Engels & Vemey, 1997; Scogin & McElreath, 1994). The body of research is compelling in terms of demonstrating that psychotherapy is as effective in alleviating depression in older adults as in younger adults. However, researchers have targeted depressed older adults with good physical health. Unfortunately, older adults with physical illness are approximately 2.5 times more likely to be depressed than their healthy age peers (Rapp, Parisi, Walsh, & Wallace, 1988). Furthermore, researchers have excluded other groups who are at risk for depression, including nursing home residents, minorities, the old-old, and those with even minor levels of cognitive impairment.

Intervention studies with medically ill older adults have been made more plausible by numerous suggestions regarding how to modify psychotherapy for depressed older adults with physical or cognitive impairments and/or fatigue (e.g., shorter sessions, telephone therapy, written instruction; see Rybarczyk et al., 1992). The same problem is present in the literature demonstrating the efficacy of behavioral treatments for geriatric insomnia (see Morin, 1993, for review). No studies have included older adults with the highest rates of insomnia: older adults with chronic illness.

One variable that is crucial to defining a sample of older adults is the ethnic and racial composition of the group. Many gerontologists have observed that ethnic and race identity are stronger for older adults relative to younger adults. When a younger comparison group is involved, the investigator should try to minimize the impact of this variable, which is important but independent of age effects. One approach to this is to recruit participants in different age groups from the same organization (e.g., place of worship), neighborhood, or family. This latter approach was employed in a recent study by Levin, Markides, and Ray (1996), who examined the relationship between religious attendance and psychological well-being in three generations within the same families of Mexican Americans.

A great deal of care needs to be taken when attempting to "match" older and younger adult samples on education, cognitive functioning, and occupation. Younger cohorts are far more likely to have gone to college than older adults who grew up during the pre-WWII era. Hence, a college graduate in his or her seventies is likely to be more exceptional in terms of intelligence, achievement, and social privilege than a 40-year-old college graduate. This problem is inherent in a common research design that involves comparisons between current university students and alumni. Occupation as a matching variable in cognitive studies also has a limitation because of a greater level of attrition, via early retirement or changing to a less demanding career, among less competent individuals in the older group (Salthouse, 1990).

PARTICIPANT RECRUITMENT

Researchers who study psychopathology and mental health treatment among older adults are quick to point out that one of the major challenges in this field is the recruitment and retention of participants. This challenge is related to the fact that older adults are both poorly informed about depression and its treatment (Silverstein, 1984) and reluctant to seek services (Waxman, Carner, & Klein, 1984). To complete a series of well-known studies of cognitive-behavioral therapy for geriatric depression, the researchers had to apply a "considerable amount of time and energy" and creativity toward recruitment (Thompson & Gallagher, 1986). In addition to sending notices to health professionals and using TV, radio, and newspaper advertising, they distributed educational flyers and conducted numerous talks at mental health centers, senior centers, and senior apartments. The strategy was to educate the public about the nature of geriatric depression and to obtain self-referrals at the same time.

These challenges in recruitment for psychopathology studies are balanced by the fact that studies examining "normal" elderly are usually easier to recruit for than those involving younger adults. The incentives for research participation among older adults are often much different from those used with younger adults (i.e., financial reward, course credit). When older adults are retired and have more discretionary time, they frequently are willing to participate for social or altruistic reasons. Hence, clubs, places of worship, and volunteer organizations are among the most common sources of recruitment of older adult participants. One of the most extraordinary longitudinal studies of aging and Alzheimer's disease, currently ongoing, involves 678 Catholic nuns who agreed to undergo extensive diagnostic testing and subsequent postmortem autopsies (Snowdon et al., 1996). A drawback of this selection approach is the fact that these volunteer groups are likely to be somewhat different from the general population of older adults.

When studying the frail elderly, researchers need to address an additional set of issues. First, to gain access to these individuals, the researcher often has to enlist the support of a "gatekeeper" (Carp, 1986). Examples include spouses, family members, physicians, nurses, nursing home administrators, and senior center directors. These individuals have their own agendas that must be understood as well as "turf" that needs to be respected. Often, these individuals must be informed about the hypotheses and educated about the importance of research in the field of gerontology. It must be emphasized from the outset, however, that the answers given by participants will be kept fully confidential. Gatekeepers often will try to make a case for why they need to know participants' responses (e.g., "It will help me take better care of them"). Second, due to the institutional environment that these participants often reside in, it is difficult to secure privacy. Nonetheless, great pains should be taken to accomplish this because of the high likelihood that the presence of others will contaminate the data. Ethical issues surrounding consent are also much more complex among the frail elderly. For example, family members need to give consent when an elderly person does not comprehend the details of the study. Finally, the risk of treating frail elderly participants in ways that may be perceived as condescending is greater than with healthy elderly participants.

ASSESSMENT ISSUES

Choosing measurement instruments is another area where special considerations are warranted when studying older adults. First and foremost is the need to minimize normative age-related changes in cognitive functioning that undermine test reliability, such as increased cognitive fatigue and decreased attention span. These issues are more pronounced among the frail elderly, who frequently have sensory impairments and medical illnesses that affect stamina. Even older adults without significant cognitive changes tend to expend more energy on paper-and-pencil tests due to increased cautiousness and performance anxiety in older adults combined with limited cohort experience with current testing formats (Edelstein, Staats, Kalish, & Northrop, 1996).

Fortunately, numerous approaches have been developed to minimize these threats to reliability. Brief instruments with easy answer formats (e.g., dichotomous) and brief forms of lengthier instruments are available and should be used with older adults. Even single-item measures can be valid (e.g., self-rated health; see Mossey, 1995, for discussion). Other solutions for reducing the error associated with poorer concentration include oral administration of tests, using larger-print questionnaires, providing frequent rests, and giving questionnaires over the telephone so as to minimize fatigue associated with transportation and adaptation to a novel environment. Telephone assessment of memory in older adults has been shown to be comparable to in-person assessment (Carpenter, Strauss, & Ball, 1995). Oral administration of tests has the added benefit of reducing nonresponses and "don't know" answers frequently encountered in paper-and-pencil testing of the elderly (Carp, 1986).

There are also validity issues that need to be considered when choosing measurements. Many instruments have not been validated separately for older adults. This issue is salient when measuring one of the numerous variables that take on different characteristics with advancing age, such as social support and depression. Depression, for example, has been shown to have a different constellation of symptoms in later life (e.g., less sadness; Newmann, 1989) and to have symptoms that are confounded with normative age-related changes (e.g., decreased memory, poorer quality of sleep). This has led to the development and subsequent popular usage of the Geriatric Depression Scale (Yesavage, Brink, Rose, & Leirer, 1983). Scales have also been designed to measure depression in specific medical populations, so that confounding variables can be further minimized (Koenig, Cohen, Blazer, Meador, & Westlund, 1992; Rybarczyk, Winemiller, Lazarus, Haut, & Hartman, 1996). When measures do have age-adjusted norms, they need to be used cautiously if they were based on a select group of healthy older adults.

Due to the increased biopsychosocial interactions that are characteristic of older adults, geropsychological research usually includes more measures than research conducted with younger participants. When using self-report, this can exacerbate the age-related problems with stamina. However, there are numerous valid and reliable behavioral medicine measures that do not rely on self-report, such as weight gain or loss, blood pressure, measures of lung capacity, actigraphy measures of sleep, spouse ratings of behavior or adjustment, and health care provider ratings of health and adjustment. In a study of older adults with amputations, single-item adjustment ratings by the individual's prosthetist (professionals who construct and fit artificial limbs) proved to be highly correlated with self-report of depressive symptoms (Rybarczyk, Nyenhuis, Nicholas, Cash, & Kaiser, 1995). There are also extensive opportunities for using alternative sources of data, such as medical chart information and records of health care utilization or use of prescription medications. In studies of psychosocial interventions for medical patients, these types of variables also provide the opportunity to assess the cost-benefit ratio, which is a critical issue for policymakers.

FUTURE DIRECTIONS

As noted above, there remains a critical need to increase research in the area of clinical geropsychology. A number of high-priority research areas have been identified by leaders in this field (e.g., Lebowitz et al., 1997; Logsdon, 1995; Niederehe et al., 1995), including elucidating the precise interplay between mental health and physical health; differential diagnosis between normal cognitive aging and early presentations of dementia; the efficacy of psychological interventions with medically ill older adults; and the comparative efficacy of different psychosocial interventions, prevention interventions, and interventions aimed at the oldest old. An additional key goal is to understand how the increasing ethnic and racial diversity of older adults changes the earlier mental health findings that were based on nonminority populations (Niederehe et al., 1995). Estimates predict that the percentage of elderly who are minorities will grow from 13% in 1985 to 21% in 2020 to 30% in 2050 (Harper & Alexander, 1990).

There is also a need for continued research aimed at closing the large gap between the mental health needs and the service utilization of older adults. These studies would include preliminary investigations of new methods of mental health service delivery (e.g., home-based programs), cost-effective interventions (e.g., telephone, peer counseling, or group programs), and interventions integrated into the context of primary care. Lichtenberg and colleagues (Lichtenberg, Kimbarow, Mackinnon, Morris, & Bush, 1995), for example, recently demonstrated that occupational therapists can be effective in administering cognitive-behavioral interventions for depression in the context of other rehabilitation activities. Another study (Rybarczyk, DeMarco, DeLaCruz, & Lapidos, in press) showed that classroom and "home course" coping skills training programs for older adults with chronic illness can enhance overall quality of life.

As Gutmann notes (1992), our development of larger theories on aging needs to keep pace with our methodological sophistication. One promising new theoretical area is the integration of the life span theoretical approach with the field of developmental psychopathology (see Staudinger et al., 1995). This perspective would combine research in the areas of reserve capacity (i.e., an individual's potential for change and growth) with research in the resilience found in older adults (i.e., the ability to maintain and regain adequate levels of functioning in the face of risks and losses). Staudinger and colleagues argue that this combined approach would lead to a greater understanding of how resilience can be enhanced by age-appropriate interventions and environments. For example, interventions should be designed to capitalize on areas where there is a greater degree of reserve capacity.

One of the most exciting aspects of geropsychology is that investigators have an opportunity to conduct studies that provide critical information to clinicians and policymakers. For example, a widely cited study by Rodin and Langer in 1977 influenced policy in a range of institutional settings for older adults. The study showed that a group of 47 nursing home residents who lived on a unit where they were encouraged to take greater personal responsibility for their environment had higher nurse ratings of adjustment, fewer illnesses, and decreased mortality compared to a matched control group. Another important study by Clark (1992) with 73 older male suicide victims contradicted the myth that elderly suicides were most common among socially isolated individuals and those with terminal illnesses. In postmortem interviews with family and friends, it was determined that individuals who committed suicide were highly likely to have had an undiagnosed clinical depression. Accordingly, these individuals were not capable of "rational suicide." These data were widely used in the public debate to argue against the notion that older adults should be given routine legal access to physician-assisted suicide.

We hope that potential investigators will be inspired by the research and methodological issues outlined in this chapter. The opportunities to make an impact on the field are abundant. Unfortunately, the number of graduate psychology students who receive specialized course work and/or training in geropsychology remains inadequate to address the needs of this underserved and rapidly expanding segment of our population (Gatz & Finkel, 1995). More opportunities, mentors, and financial incentives need to be provided in graduate training programs to attract the required researchers and clinicians into the field. Students need to be attracted to the field by being taught that older adults are *interesting* rather than merely *needy* (Haley & Gatz, 1995). It may not be an exaggeration to say that the quality of life for millions of older Americans in the next century will partly depend on how many young investigators answer the call.

REFERENCES

Adam, J. (1978). Sequential strategies and the separation of age, cohort, and time-of-measurement contributions to developmental data. *Psychological Bulletin, 85,* 1309–1316.

Baltes, P. B. (1968). Longitudinal and cross-sectional sequences in the study of age and generation effects. *Human Development, 11,* 145–171.

Birren, J. E., & Cunningham, W. R. (1985). Research on the psychology of aging: Principles, concepts and theory. In J. E. Birren & K. W. Schaie (Eds.), *Handbook of the psychology of aging* (2nd ed., pp. 3–30). New York: Van Nostrand-Reinhold.

Blazer, D. G. (1997). Depression in the elderly: Myths and misconceptions. *Psychiatric Clinics of North America, 20*(1), 111–120.

Carp, F. M. (1986). Maximizing data quality in community studies of older people. In M. P. Lawton & A. R. Herzog (Eds.), *Special research methods for gerontology* (pp. 93–122). Amityville, NY: Bayview.

Carpenter, B. D., Strauss, M. E., & Ball, A. M. (1995). Telephone assessment of memory in the elderly. *Journal of Clinical Geropsychology, 1,* 107–117.

Carstensen, L. L. (1995). Evidence for a life-span theory of socioemotional selectivity. *Current Directions in Psychological Science, 4,* 151–156.

Clark, D. C. (1992). "Rational" suicide and people with terminal conditions or disabilities. *Issues in Law and Medicine, 8*(2), 147–166.

Edelstein, B., Staats, N., Kalish, K. D., & Northrop, L. E. (1996). Assessment of older adults. In M. Hersen & V. B. Van Hasselt (Eds.), *Psychological treatment of older adults* (pp. 35-68). New York: Plenum Press.

Engels, G. I., & Vermey, M. (1997). Efficacy of nonmedical treatments of depression in elders: A quantitative analysis. *Journal of Clinical Geropsychology, 3,* 17–35.

Fredrickson, B. L., & Carstensen, L. L. (1990). Choosing social partners: How old age and anticipated endings makes people more selective. *Psychology and Aging, 5,* 163–171.

Gatz, M., & Finkel, S. I. (1995). Education and training of mental health service providers. In M. Gatz (Ed.), *Emerging issues in mental health and aging* (pp. 282–302). Washington, DC: American Psychological Association.

Gutmann, D. (1987). *Reclaimed powers.* New York: Basic Books.

Gutmann, D. (1992). The disappearing geropsychologist. *Center on Aging Newsletter, 6*(3), 1–3.

Haley, W. E., & Gatz, M. (1995). Doctoral training and methods for attracting students to work in clinical geropsychology. In B. G. Knight, L. Teri, P. Wohlford, & J. Santos (Eds.), *Mental health services for older adults: Implications for training and practice in geropsychology* (pp. 113–118). Washington, DC: American Psychological Association.

Harper, M. S., & Alexander, C. D. (1990). Profile of the black elderly. In M. S. Harper (Ed.), *Minority aging: Essential curricula content for selected health and allied health professionals* (DHHS Publication No. HRS P-DV-90-4). Washington, DC: U.S. Government Printing Office.

Hartke, R. J. (1991). Introduction. In R. J. Hartke (Ed.), *Psychological aspects of geriatric rehabilitation.* Gaithersburg, MD: Aspen.

Hawley, G. A. (1985). Construction and validation of an Eriksonian measure of psychosocial development [Abstract]. *Dissertation Abstracts International, 45*(9-A), 2804.

Hersen, M., & Van Hasselt, V. B. (Eds.). (1996). *Psychological treatment of older adults.* New York: Plenum Press.

Hertzog, C. (1996). Research designs in aging and cognition. In J. E. Birren & K. W. Schaie (Eds.), *Handbook of the psychology of aging* (4th ed.). San Diego, CA: Academic Press.

Holroyd, K. A., & Penzien, D. B. (1986). Client variables and the treatment of recurrent tension headaches: A Meta-analytic review. *Journal of Behavioral Medicine, 9*(6), 515–535.

Howieson, D. B., Holm, M. A., Kaye, J. A., Oken, B. S., & Howieson, J. (1993). Neurologic function in the optimally healthy oldest old: Neuropsychological evaluation. *Neurology, 43,* 1882–1886.

Katz, I. R. (1995). Infrastructure requirements for research in late-life mental disorders. In M. Gatz (Ed.), *Emerging issues in mental health and aging* (pp. 256–281). Washington, DC: American Psychological Association.

Knight, B. G. (1996). Psychodynamic therapy with older adults: Lessons from scientific gerontology. In R. T. Woods (Ed.), *Handbook of the clinical psychology of aging* (pp. 545–560). New York: Wiley.

Knight, B. G., Santos, J., Teri, L., & Lawton, M. P. (1995). The development of training in clinical geropsychology. In B. G. Knight, L. Teri, P. Wohlford, & J. Santos (Eds.), *Mental health services for older adults: Implications for training and practice in geropsychology* (pp. 1–8). Washington, DC: American Psychological Association.

Koenig, H. G., Cohen, H. J., Blazer, D. G., Meador, K. G., & Westlund, R. (1992). A brief depression scale for use in the medically ill. *International Journal of Psychiatry in Medicine, 22*(2), 183–195.

Lebowitz, B. D., Pearson, J. L., Schneider, L. S., Reynolds, C. F., Alexopoulos, G. S., Bruce, M. L., Conwell, Y., Katz, I. R., Meyers, B. S., Morrison, M. F., Mossey, J., Niederehe, G., & Parmelee, P. (1997). Diagnosis and treatment of depression in late life: Consensus statement update. *Journal of the American Medical Association, 278,* 186–1190.

Levin, J. S., Markides, K. S., & Ray, L. A. (1996). Religious attendance and psychological well-being in Mexican Americans: A panel analysis of three-generations data. *The Gerontologist, 36,* 454–463.

Lewinsohn, P. M., Rohde, P., Seeley, J. R., & Fischer, S. A. (1993). Age-cohort changes in the lifetime occurrence of depression and other mental disorders. *Journal of Abnormal Psychology, 102,* 110–120.

Lichtenberg, P. A., Kimbarow, M. L., Mackinnon, D., Morris, P. A., & Bush, J. V. (1995). An interdisciplinary behavioral treatment program for depressed geriatric rehabilitation. *The Gerontologist, 35,* 688–690.

Logsdon, R. G. (1995). Psychopathology and treatment: Curriculum and research needs. In B. G. Knight, L. Teri, P. Wohlford, & J. Santos (Eds.), *Mental health services for older adults: Implications for training and practice in geropsychology* (pp. 41–51). Washington, DC: American Psychological Association.

Morin, C. (1993). *Insomnia: Psychological assessment and management.* New York: Guilford Press.

Mossey, J. M. (1995). Importance of self-perceptions for health status among older persons. In M. Gatz (Ed.), *Emerging issues in mental health and aging* (pp. 124–162). Washington, DC: American Psychological Association.

Mutran, E. J., Reitzes, D. C., Mossey, J., & Fernandez, M. E. (1995). Social support, depression, and recovery of walking ability following hip fracture surgery. *Journal of Gerontology: Social Sciences, 50B,* S354–361.

Nanna, M. J., Lichtenberg, P. A., Buda-Abela, M., & Barth, J. T. (1997). The role of cognition and depression in predicting functional outcome in geriatric medical rehabilitation patients. *Journal of Applied Gerontology, 16*(1), 120–132.

Nesselroade, J. R., & Labouvie, E. W. (1985). Experimental design in research on aging. In J. E. Birren & K. W. Schaie (Eds.), *Handbook of the psychology of aging* (2nd ed., pp. 35–60). New York: Van Nostrand-Reinhold.

Newmann, J. P. (1989). Aging and depression. *Psychology and Aging, 4,* 150–165.

Niederehe, G., Cooley, S. G., & Teri, L. (1995). Research and training in clinical geropsychology: Advances and current opportunities. *Clinical Psychologist, 48,* 37–44.

Quinn, J. L. (1987). Attitudes of professionals toward the aged. In G. L. Maddox (Ed.), *The encyclopedia of aging* (pp. 45–47). New York: Springer.

Rapp, S., Parisi, S. A., Walsh, D. A., & Wallace, C. E. (1988). Detecting depression in elderly medical inpatients. *Journal of Consulting and Clinical Psychology, 56,* 509–513.

Rodin, J., & Langer, E. J. (1977). Long-term effects of a control relevant intervention with the institutionalized aged. *Journal of Personality and Social Psychology, 35,* 897–902.

Rybarczyk, B. D., DeMarco, G., DeLaCruz, M., & Lapidos, S. (in press). Comparing mind/body wellness interventions for older adults with chronic illness: Classroom vs. home instruction. *Behavioral Medicine.*

Rybarczyk, B. D., Gallagher-Thompson, D., Rodman, J., Zeiss, A., Gantz, F., & Yesavage, J. (1992). Applying cognitive-behavioral psychotherapy to the chronically ill elderly: Treatment issues and case illustration. *International Psychogeriatrics, 4*(1), 127–140.

Rybarczyk, B. D., Nyenhuis, D. L., Nicholas, J. J., Cash, S. M., & Kaiser, J. (1995). Body image, perceived social stigma and the prediction of psychosocial adjustment to leg amputation. *Rehabilitation Psychology, 16,* 113–129.

Rybarczyk, B. D., Winemiller, D. R., Lazarus, L., Haut, A., & Hartman, C. (1996). Validation of a depression screening measure for stroke inpatients. *American Journal of Geriatric Psychiatry, 4,* 131–139.

Salthouse, T. A. (1990). Cognitive competence and expertise in aging. In J. E. Birren & K. W. Schaie (Eds.), *Handbook of the psychology of aging* (3rd ed.). San Diego, CA: Academic Press.

Schaie, K. W. (1965). A general model for the study of developmental change. *Psychological Bulletin, 64,* 92–107.

Schaie, K. W., Maitland, S. B., Willis, S. L., & Intrieri, R. C. (1998). Longitudinal invariance of adult psychometric ability factor structures across 7 years. *Psychology and Aging, 13,* 8–20.

Schaie, K. W., & Willis, S. L. (1991). Adult personality and psychomotor performance: Cross-sectional and longitudinal analyses. *Journal of Gerontology: Psychological Sciences, 46,* P275–284.

Schroots, J. J. F., & Birren, J. E. (1988). The nature of time: Implications for research on aging. *Comprehensive Gerontology, C, 2,* 1–29.

Scogin, F., & McElreath, L. (1994). Efficacy for psychosocial treatments for geriatric depression: A quantitative review. *Journal of Consulting and Clinical Psychology, 62,* 69–74.

Seeman, T. E., Berkman, L. F., Charpentier, P. A., Blazer, D. G., Albert, M. S., & Tinetti, M. E. (1995). Behavioral and psychosocial predictors of physical performance: McArthur studies of successful aging. *Journal of Gerontology: Medical Sciences, 50A,* M177–M183.

Silverstein, W. M. (1984). Informing the elderly about public services: The relationship between sources of knowledge and service utilization. *The Gerontologist, 24,* 37–40.

Snowdon, D. A., Kemper, S. J., Mortimer, J. A., Greiner, L. H., Wekstein, D. R., & Markesbery, W. R. (1996). Linguistic ability in early life and cognitive function and Alzheimer's disease in late life: Findings from the Nun study. *Journal of the American Medical Association, 275*(7), 528–532.

Staudinger, U. M., Marsiske, M., & Baltes, P. B. (1995). Resilience and reserve capacity in later adulthood: Potentials and limits of development across the life span. In D. Cicchetti & C. J. Cohen (Eds.), *Developmental psychopathology handbook* (Vol. 2, pp. 801–847). New York: Wiley.

Thompson, L. W., & Gallagher, D. (1986). Psychotherapy for late-life depression. *Generations, 10*(3), 38–44.

Walasky, M., Whitbourne, S. K., & Nehrke, M. F. (1984). Construction and validation of an ego integrity status interview. *International Journal of Aging and Human Development, 18,* 61–72.

Warshaw, M. G., Klerman, G. L., & Lavori, P. W. (1991). The use of conditional probabilities to examine age-period-cohort data: Further evidence for a period effect in major depressive disorder. *Journal of Affective Disorder, 23,* 119–129.

Waxman, H. M., Carner, E. A., & Klein, M. (1984). Underutilization of mental health professionals by community elderly. *The Gerontologist, 24,* 23–30.

Whitbourne, S. K. (1996). *The aging individual: Physical and psychological perspectives.* New York: Springer.

Woods, R. T. (Ed.). (1996). *Handbook of the clinical psychology of aging.* New York: Wiley.

Yesavage, J. A., Brink, T. L., Rose, T. L., & Leirer, V. O. (1983). Development and validation of a geriatric depression screening scale: A preliminary report. *Journal of Psychiatric Research, 17,* 37–49.

Zeiss, A., & Steffen, A. (1996). Behavioral and cognitive-behavioral treatments: An overview of social learning. In S. H. Zarit & B. G. Knight (Eds.), *A guide to psychotherapy and aging* (pp. 35–60). Washington, DC: American Psychological Association.

Chapter 27

Focus Chapter

RESEARCH METHODS WITH COUPLES

KATHLEEN A. ELDRIDGE, M.A., ERIKA LAWRENCE, M.A., and ANDREW CHRISTENSEN, PH.D.

Research on close relationships has grown rapidly in recent years. With this growth, investigators have expanded and refined the methodology used to conduct research on couples. In this chapter, we address four common methodological issues as they relate to couples research: sampling, design, measurement, and data analysis. Although not an exhaustive review of these four areas, we focus on what we believe are the most important methodological concerns and exciting advances currently taking place in the field of couples research.

Much of our chapter relates to two broad categories of inquiry in couples research: How do couples function?, a question asked by investigators conducting basic research on marriage, and How can we help couples function better?, a question asked by those conducting applied research on intervention or prevention.

SAMPLING

Investigators can control the sample they obtain in two ways: by setting eligibility criteria and by choosing recruitment methods. These decisions influence the characteristics of the sample, the results of the study, and the generalizability of those results. As a whole, the field of couples research has been hindered by the limited nature of the samples studied. A recent meta-analysis of longitudinal studies on marriage demonstrates that most of these studies sampled middle-class Caucasians (Karney & Bradbury, 1995). Further, most samples have consisted of heterosexual married couples, suggesting that much of what research has taught us about marriage may not apply to other types of intimate relationships. Fortunately, recent investigations of communication in couples have compared heterosexual, gay, and lesbian partners and found important differences among these samples (see Julien, Arellano, & Turgeon, 1997; see also the chapter by Sue, Kurasaki, & Srinivasan, this volume, for information about diverse samples in clinical research). The inclusion of such nontraditional samples in couples research is necessary to broaden the generalizability and applicability of findings.

Eligibility Criteria

To generate an appropriate sample for a given research question, investigators choose couples that meet specific inclusion and exclusion criteria. If the criteria create a homogeneous sample, then the resulting data may contain little error variance, which increases the likelihood of finding statistically significant effects. However, the more homogeneous the population, the less generalizable the results are to couples with different characteristics. For example, Christensen (1996) and Jacobson (1996) require that couples meet several inclusion and exclusion criteria to be eligible for their multisite clinical trial of couples therapy, such as scoring within a specified distressed but nonviolent range on questionnaires. Further, couples are excluded if either partner is currently in psychotherapy (which would confound the effects of couples therapy) or meets *Diagnostic and Statistical Manual of Mental Disorders,* 4th edition *(DSM-IV)* criteria for certain disorders, such as substance dependence (which could make treatment progress difficult). These specifications create a homogeneous and perhaps treatable sample, but may not accurately represent the couples who seek treatment in community clinics and private practices. The investigator's dilemma can be summarized as follows: "The utility of increasing subject homogeneity must be weighed against this ever-diminishing generalizability" (Whisman, Jacobson, Fruzzetti, & Waltz, 1989, p. 180).

The investigator chooses eligibility criteria based on knowledge gained from previous research, common sense, and practical constraints. For example, Christensen (1996) and Jacobson (1996) decided to exclude violent couples from their marital therapy outcome study based on data that suggest couples therapy may be inappropriate for severe forms of domestic violence (Margolin & Burman, 1993). A couples format for intervention may send the message that the victim is responsible for the violence. Further, couples therapy exposes serious conflicts in the relationship and therefore may place the victim at risk for further violence (Holtzworth-Munroe, Beatty, & Anglin, 1995; Margolin & Burman, 1993). Bradbury (Davila, Bradbury, & Fincham, in press; Sullivan & Bradbury, 1997) allowed only newlyweds in their first marriage to participate in his longitudinal investigation of couples and family development because these couples presumably have different characteristics than those who have been married before. In addition, for practical reasons, these three researchers recruited only English-speaking couples with at least a tenth-grade education to ensure that they would be able to accurately fill out questionnaires.

Recruitment Methods

The second way investigators generate an appropriate sample is by choosing a recruitment strategy. The best but most expensive way to recruit couples is through random sampling of the population of interest. For example, Straus and Gelles (1992) conducted two national surveys of family violence through probability sampling of areas and random digit dialing of households in those areas. Because of these procedures, they were able to generalize their results to the entire U.S. population of persons who have telephones. However, their only means of data collection was a telephone interview.

Because of the high cost of random sampling procedures and the limited assessment methods they can incorporate, most couples researchers recruit participants through public announcements and advertisements. However, because it is difficult to collect data from couples not responding to these solicitations, investigators cannot determine how their obtained sample of responders differs from the population of couples to which they wish to generalize their results. Rosenthal and Rosnow (1975) reviewed the existing research on differences between those who volunteer for psychological studies and those who do not, and reported that volunteers tend to earn higher incomes and be more educated, sociable, and motivated to seek approval than those not volunteering. Presumably, their findings apply to couples as well as to individual volunteers.

A popular method used to recruit maritally distressed couples is sampling from couples seeking treatment. For example, Vivian and her colleagues (Langhinrichsen-Rohling & Vivian, 1994) recruited a distressed sample by collecting data from 112 couples seeking treatment at a marital therapy clinic. Because these investigators included every couple that came to the clinic within a specified time, without imposing any additional inclusion or exclusion criteria, their sample can be considered more representative of couples seeking treatment than a sample obtained after imposing additional criteria.

In applied research, the method of recruitment affects not only the sample obtained, but can also affect the outcomes produced by the interventions. Pearlman, Zweben, and Li (1989) found that couples recruited for alcohol treatment research through newspaper and radio advertisements were older and had higher educational, occupational, and financial statuses than couples recruited through clinic referrals. The couples recruited through advertisements also reported more stable and satisfying marriages and more pretreatment drinking but less adverse consequences of drinking than clinic clients. Even though there was no difference in drinking behaviors or marital outcome between the two groups at posttreatment, clinic clients were more likely to have sustained positive changes in drinking behaviors at a six-month follow-up than clients recruited though advertisements (Pearlman et al., 1989).

A more dramatic example of how recruitment can affect findings is evident in the field of domestic violence, where feminist and family violence researchers often disagree about the severity, cause, and associated fear, injury, and psychological impact of physical aggression. Johnson (1995) has suggested that these two groups are obtaining discrepant results because they use different sampling techniques and therefore study two different populations. He asserts that most feminist researchers recruit women from shelters, emergency rooms, and criminal courts, whereas family violence researchers often use random samples from the community, student samples, or respondents to advertisements. As a result of these different recruitment strategies, the former group is presumably investigating more severe forms of violence than is the latter and consequently reaches different conclusions regarding the phenomenon of domestic violence.

The importance of recruitment strategy is also highlighted in prevention research. There is evidence that some samples recruited for preventive treatment show little need for that intervention. Sullivan and Bradbury (1997) demonstrated that newlyweds who participated in premarital divorce-prevention programs were not at high risk for marital discord. In fact, some men who did participate in premarital programs were at lower risk than those who did not, in that they were older and had higher incomes, higher relationship satisfaction, less relationship aggression, and less neuroticism. These investigators concluded that specialized recruitment methods will be necessary to make the availability of premarital programs widely known and participation in them greater for couples at high risk for marital distress.

Unfortunately, there is little published research on how recruitment techniques influence the sample of couples obtained and how this sample may differ from the population of couples to which the investigator intends to generalize. However, there have been recent attempts to fill this void in the literature. Bradbury (Davila et al., in press; Sullivan & Bradbury, 1997) used two different methods to recruit two newlywed samples: newspaper announcements and mass mailings to couples filing for marriage licenses. In addition to documenting a low response rate with both methods, Bradbury and colleagues found that the method of recruitment heavily influenced the characteristics of the sample. Specifically, newlyweds recruited through newspaper advertisements reported more characteristics associated with higher risk for marital distress and dissolution, such as younger age, lower income, lower marital satisfaction, and more depression, than the newlyweds recruited through the mailed invitations (Karney et al., 1995). Further, the couples who responded to the mailed invitations were significantly different from those who did not respond in that they were less traditional and of higher educational and occupational status (Karney et al., 1995).

Specifying how different recruitment methods elicit particular subgroups of couples is necessary if researchers are to compare findings, choose appropriate eligibility criteria, select appropriate recruitment methods, and understand how their samples differ from the larger population of couples.

Collecting Data from One vs. Both Partners

Partners vary in their view of their relationship, for example, in their perception of subjective states such as marital satisfaction (Snyder, Wills, & Keiser, 1981) and their report of observable behaviors such as the occurrence of domestic violence (Jouriles & O'Leary, 1985; Langhinrichsen-Rohling & Vivian, 1994; O'Leary & Arias, 1984; Szinovacz, 1983), drinking behavior (McGrady, Paolino, & Longabaugh, 1978), and couple activities (Christensen & Nies, 1980; Jacobson & Moore, 1981). Therefore, an important decision unique to couples research is whether sampling should include one or both partners. Several researchers have noted the importance of involving both partners in studies on couples rather than basing results on just one mate (Acitelli, 1997; Baucom, 1983; Whisman et al., 1989).

Attridge, Berscheid, and Simpson (1995) investigated this question empirically by evaluating whether longitudinal predictions of relationship stability were enhanced by assessing both partners rather than just one. They found that assessments of both members in the relationship improved predictions of stability, but the improvement over one-partner predictions was small. Further, females' assessments were no more predictive of relationship stability than males' assessments, but assessments from the less committed partner were significantly more predictive than measures from the more committed partner (Attridge et al., 1995). This suggests that assessments of both partners may not always be necessary, and one gender may not provide better information than the other. Therefore, investigators should determine whom to recruit (or whose data to use if both partners' data are available) based on the scientific objectives of their particular research and empirical data on whose reports are more scientifically useful for the question under study.

Including both partners in couples research creates unique sampling challenges. In evaluating the characteristics of couples volunteering to participate in relationship research, Hill and colleagues (Hill, Rubin, Peplau, & Willard, 1979) found that, when mailed a questionnaire about relationships, a higher percentage of women than men completed and returned the questionnaire. In addition, a higher percentage of men than women indicated on their questionnaire that their partner may be interested in participating in further aspects of the research, and a higher percentage of these men than women were actually successful in eliciting their mates' participation in further aspects of the research. Moreover, women were more likely to participate regardless of the status of their relationship, whereas men were more likely to participate if they were married than if they were dating or their relationship had dissolved (Hill et al., 1979). These findings illustrate that heterosexual women may be more easily engaged in couples research than their partners and that obtaining data from both mates, although more methodologically sound than recruiting one, may be more challenging.

Obtaining data from both partners also creates a unique statistical challenge when deciding whether to analyze partners' data independently or in combination. One option is to test each hypothesis separately for men and women and report the results independently. A second approach is to enter both partners' data into the analyses but preserve the information about the couple as a unit (e.g., by treating husbands and wives as repeated measures of a couple factor). This method typically increases the power of the study and may account for more of the variance relative to independent analyses. Further, using data from both partners allows the examiner to get a better view of the couple. A third strategy is to average both partners' reports, which is the best measure of their joint perception. However, this latter strategy may disguise important individual information and differences between partners. A final option is to create a discrepancy score reflecting the difference between partners' reports, as the discrepancy between partners may be a stronger predictor of other variables than their individual scores.

RESEARCH DESIGN

There are three major types of design to consider in this area of research: passive observational, quasi-experimental, and true experimental designs (Cook & Campbell, 1979). In a true experimental design, there is both manipulation of an independent variable and random assignment of participants to conditions. In a quasi-experimental design, there is manipulation of an independent variable but no random assignment to conditions. In a passive observational design, there is neither manipulation nor random assignment.

Passive Observational Designs

Because we cannot manipulate which individuals begin or maintain relationships, or randomly assign couples to conflicting or satisfying relationships, passive observational designs, such as cross-sectional and longitudinal investigations, are the most commonly employed designs in couples research.

Cross-Sectional Studies

Historically, much couples research has been conducted by dividing couples into categorical groups and evaluating the differences between them. For example, much of the literature consists of comparisons between satisfied and distressed couples and between violent and nonviolent couples. Other researchers have focused on the factors that are correlated with relationship satisfaction (the most commonly employed criterion variable in couples research) or with physical aggression. Recently, however, more sophisticated comparisons of couples have been developed. Rather than simply comparing clinic couples in treatment to community couples, Christensen and Shenk (1991) compared community, clinic, and divorcing couples. Others have eschewed the simple violent versus nonviolent comparisons in favor of a more sophisticated comparison among couples that separates the correlates of violence from those of marital distress, such as a comparison among distressed-violent, distressed-nonviolent, nondistressed-violent, and nondistressed-nonviolent couples (Lawrence & Bradbury, 1998). All of these designs are limited in their ability to explicate the cause of a phenomenon, because variables other than those being compared—the proverbial third variable problem—may account for the phenomenon.

Longitudinal Studies

In contrast to the one-time snapshot of relationships provided by cross-sectional designs, longitudinal designs can reveal the sequence of events in, or the natural course of, relationships over time. Intimate relationships, particularly marriage, are by definition longitudinal in nature; couples usually vow to be together for life. A relationship is therefore a process over time rather than a singular event, which makes longitudinal designs more appropriate for most empirical questions about couples. However, longitudinal research presents the practical challenge of retaining couples in the study for more than a one-time assessment. In addition, there are a number of methodological issues that must be addressed.

Duration of Longitudinal Research   We typically think of a longitudinal study as lasting months or years. However, studies over shorter time frames have also been conducted. For example, Margolin, Christensen, and John (1996) examined whether the occurrence of parent-child conflict and sibling conflict were dependent on a marital conflict preceding them. To answer this question, they examined families three times daily over a two-week period. Similarly, Repetti (1993) assessed male air traffic controllers for three consecutive days to better understand the association between the man's level of stress and the subsequent support he received from his partner on a daily basis.

When to Start Longitudinal Research   Longitudinal researchers vary in the point of the relationship at which they begin to examine couples. Most of the literature has been based on couples in established marriages. For example, Gottman and Krokoff (1989) conducted a three-year longitudinal study on 25 couples who had been married an average of 24 years. They examined the extent to which spouses' positive and negative affect during high-conflict discussions predicted their subsequent marital satisfaction.

However, there are several problems with examining couples in established marriages. First, the research excludes many marriages that end in divorce soon after the wedding. About half of all marriages end in separation or divorce, most within the first few years of marriage (Bumpass, 1990). A sample of participants who have been married an average of 24 years is missing a substantial number of couples who divorced well before the 24-year mark. Second, we do not know the developmental course of these marriages, information that presumably would make their current state, such as their level of affect and marital satisfaction, more understandable. Third, couples in established marriages may be at markedly different points in the marital life cycle. For example, spouses' mean age in the Gottman and Krokoff (1989) study was 45 years. Therefore, this study may represent some couples who are seeing their grown children leave home and some couples who are still tending to young children because they had children later in life.

To avoid some of these methodological problems, many researchers have begun to examine couples earlier in their relationships and at a particular definable point in their relationships. For example, Bradbury (Davila et al., in press; Sullivan & Bradbury, 1997) examined couples soon after their wedding, allowing him to study marriages from a point at which spouses are still satisfied in their relationships. However, even beginning a study at the onset of marriage hinders us from examining the initial stages of the relationship before marriage. In an effort to capture the entire relationship from its onset, Hill and Peplau (1998) assessed 231 dating couples when they were in college and followed them for 15 years. Similarly, Kelly and Conley (1987) examined 278 engaged couples in the 1930s and conducted a follow-up study 50 years later.

Frequency of Assessments   A final issue in the design of longitudinal research is when to assess couples. Will we catch the interesting phenomena of relationships if we assess couples annually? Would biannual assessments provide richer information? Or should couples be contacted every two weeks to catch all life events and changes in the relationship? Yet another possibility is to plan assessments around specific life events instead of by time periods. The more common approach to date has been to examine couples based on time, such as by conducting assessments of couples yearly. Others, however, have planned assessments around major events, such as childbirth, without regard to time frame. Christensen (1998) has argued for longitudinal designs that emphasize events over the mere passage of time. For example, he suggests that couples who are experiencing the same major event such as the birth of a child are more likely to be similar than couples who, for example, have been married two years, some of whom have children and others do not. An ideal approach would be to combine these methodologies by examining couples from the onset of their relationship and assessing them both over time and around specific events. For example, a study might examine couples from the point at which the couple starts dating or gets married and obtain assessment data every few months over several years. Simultaneously, however, it would be useful to design unique assessment batteries for couples during specific relationship events, such as the transition to parenthood. Such techniques would demand a great deal practically from participating couples, but presumably would provide the greatest understanding of the developmental course of intimate relationships.

Quasi-Experimental Designs

In quasi-experimental designs, investigators manipulate the levels of an independent variable but do not randomly assign subjects to different conditions. Although not commonly used in couples research, Markman and colleagues (e.g., Markman, Floyd, Stanley, & Storaasli, 1988; Markman, Renick, Floyd, Stanley, & Clements, 1993) have conducted a series of treatment outcome studies using quasi-experimental designs. In these studies, premarital couples were recruited to participate in a program designed to prevent marital distress. Couples who agreed to participate received the prevention program and couples who declined were placed in the no-treatment control group. In this example, a manipulation was conducted (the prevention program), but couples chose whether or not to participate in the program rather than being randomly assigned to participation or nonparticipation.

Experimental Designs

Treatment Studies

Experimental treatment outcome designs have been widely used in couples research to determine the influence of intervention on relationships (see Baucom, Shoham, Mueser, Daiuto, & Stickle, 1998; Christensen & Heavey, in press; Kendall, Flannery-Schroeder, & Ford, this volume). The majority of these investigations, which are often called clinical trials, have involved behavioral marital therapy. Initially, researchers compared this behavioral treatment to control conditions of couples waiting for treatment. Since then, researchers have examined other approaches to couples therapy, such as cognitive behavioral and insight oriented treatments.

Virtually all of the research on couples therapy is efficacy research, which means that it is research conducted with the highest priority given to internal validity. Typically, these studies are conducted in a research setting (usually a hospital or university) and assess the effect of manualized, supervised, controlled treatment on couples that have met specific eligibility criteria and have been randomly assigned to a treatment condition. Therapists are specially trained in the treatment conditions, and their adherence in delivering the treatments is assessed. The advantage of efficacy research is that causal inferences can be made regarding the outcomes of treatment. The disadvantage is that the results may not be generalizable to the larger population of distressed couples or to treatments delivered under less stringent conditions.

In contrast to efficacy research, effectiveness research investigates the effects of clinic-based treatments that are implemented to often unselected couples seeking therapy in that setting. The disadvantage of most effectiveness research is the lack of random assignment and lack of control over treatment, which prevents causal inferences from being made. However, the results are often more generalizable to couples seeking treatment and to ordinary clinicians delivering those treatments. Very little effectiveness research has been conducted in the field of couples therapy, but one recent investigation in Germany indicated that the therapy delivered in research settings may be more successful at reducing marital distress than the treatment offered in community clinics and private practices (Hahlweg & Klann, 1997).

Recently, Seligman (1995) suggested a greater focus on effectiveness research over efficacy research. However, his suggestions were met with criticism by many, who complained of the methodological inadequacy of effectiveness research. Jacobson and Christensen (1996) suggested that the methodological rigor of clinical trials could be incorporated into effectiveness contexts. Randomized assignment of clients to treatments could be done in clinics as well as in research laboratories; treatment manuals could describe flexible therapy rather than restricting therapists to rigid protocols. As an example, Jacobson and his colleagues (Jacobson et al., 1989) compared a research-structured to a clinically flexible version of behavioral marital therapy. Although both performed similarly on outcome measures at posttreatment, the clinically flexible version led to greater maintenance of treatment gains over time.

We would recommend that outcome researchers begin a program of research with efficacy studies. When an approach receives some empirical validation, then the transportability of this treatment into clinical settings can be tested using the clinical trial methodology. For example, Christensen and Heavey (in press) describe a program of research by Markman and Stanley that is evaluating the transportability of a well-researched premarital divorce prevention program, the Premarital Relationship Enhancement Program (PREP), to churches, the most common site where couples seek premarital counseling. In their study, couples are randomly assigned to one of three conditions: (a) PREP delivered by the research team, (b) PREP delivered by clergy and lay leaders trained by the research team, or (c) the church's typical premarital training program.

Other Experimental Studies

Experimental manipulations have also been implemented in basic research on couples. For example, in studying conflict, investigators have usually asked couples to choose a common area of disagreement to discuss and then have observed the subsequent interaction. Recently, Christensen, Heavey, and colleagues (Christensen & Heavey, 1990; Heavey, Layne, & Christensen, 1993) introduced an experimental design into these discussions by manipulating topic selection by the husband or wife. Because the nature of the interaction was influenced by whose topic was discussed, this manipulation led to a more comprehensive understanding of the behaviors exhibited during problem-solving discussions.

Partners' cognition has also been experimentally manipulated to examine the association between causal attributions and marital satisfaction. In one study, Fincham and Bradbury (1988) instructed 32 spouses to read negative descriptions of themselves written by their partners. In all cases, the experimenters requested negative descriptions. However, only half of the spouses reading these descriptions were told that the descriptions were written at the experimenter's request, thus providing an external cause for the negative statements. The other half were not provided with this information and therefore were left to assume that their partners chose to write negative descriptions of them. Spouses then listed their thoughts prompted by the descriptions and engaged in five-minute discussions with their partners. Manipulating the cause spouses attributed to their partner's negative descriptions affected their own behavior and their cognition toward their partners.

Finally, Cummings and colleagues (Cummings, Iannotti, & Zahn-Waxler, 1985) conducted a series of laboratory studies in which they manipulated the type of discussion between adults that was witnessed by children to determine the effect adult conflict has on children. One group of 2-year-olds witnessed a series of three discussions between adults: a friendly exchange, an angry exchange, and the resolution of the angry exchange. A control group of 2-year-olds was exposed to three emotionally neutral interactions between adults. Using behavioral observation, Cummings and colleagues measured the amount of aggression the children exhibited toward each other after witnessing each of these interactions. They found that aggression increased after exposure to the angry exchange and declined after the resolution exchange. Children in the control group did not differ in aggression over time. These results were replicated in a follow-up study of these children three years later (Cummings, 1987).

MEASUREMENT

The most important decisions in measurement regard which constructs to assess and the mode of assessment to use. The focus of the research often determines the best approach to these issues. Yet, current debates question the traditional answers to these inquiries.

Current Issues in What to Measure

Defining Outcome

For treatment studies as well as basic research on marriage, an important measurement decision is how to define outcome. Typically, investigators consider the primary indicators of outcome to be relationship satisfaction and stability. Relationship dissolution and divorce have been considered negative outcomes in basic research and treatment failures in applied research. Yet, individual functioning may improve as a result of separation or divorce, and, in this sense, relationship dissolution could be a positive outcome. Conversely, if relationship maintenance comes at the expense of individual well-being, stability is not a good outcome. Some premarital programs designed to prevent marital distress have couples reevaluate their decision to marry in the belief that some couples may wisely choose to separate (Bagarozzi & Rauen, 1981). For these reasons, Christensen and Heavey (in press) stress the importance of assessing individual functioning in addition to relationship satisfaction and stability. They also argue for assessing child outcomes in couples who have children. Furthermore, they suggest continued assessment of individuals even after a separation or divorce. Even if one treatment is no better than another in preventing separation or divorce, one may be more effective in promoting a healthy transition out of the current relationship. Similarly, even if a couple gets divorced in a longitudinal study of marriage, they may learn from the experience and go on to a better relationship. In their clinical trial, Christensen (1996) and Jacobson (1996) have incorporated several measures of individual and child functioning as well as measures of marital functioning. With these data, they can determine how the individual, child, and marriage are affected by marital therapy.

Type of Communication

The behavioral model of marriage led to numerous investigations of problem solving in couples. Couples' videotaped attempts to resolve problems are coded using a variety of systems, such as the Couples Interaction Scoring System (CISS; Gottman, 1979; Krokoff, Gottman, & Hass, 1989) and the Marital Interaction Coding System (MICS; Weiss & Summers, 1983), which rate verbal and nonverbal behavior, and the Specific Affect Coding System (SPAFF; Gottman & Krokoff, 1989), which rates affect by considering verbal and nonverbal indicators of emotion. The research on problem solving indicates that specific aspects of couples' communication around conflict are associated with, and predictive of, marital satisfaction and stability (e.g., Weiss & Heyman, 1997). However, recent research has demonstrated that skills in providing and receiving support may also influence marital functioning (e.g., Cutrona & Suhr, 1994; Julien & Markman, 1991) and therefore may provide separate predictive information beyond that provided by problem-solving ability (Pasch & Bradbury, 1998; Pasch, Bradbury, & Sullivan, 1997).

Physical Health

Relationship satisfaction and communication are variables with a long history in couples research. Recently, health-related variables have become a fascinating addition to this field. Investigators have noted a general association between marital dissatisfaction and health problems (Burman & Margolin, 1992). In addition, the possible causal effects of health problems on marital quality have been examined, as well as the influence of relationship quality on response to illness (Schmaling & Sher, 1997).

Researchers have investigated the specific relationship between marital quality and physiological reactions. For example, Levenson and Gottman (1983, 1985) conducted a longitudinal study to determine the causal relationship between physiological arousal and marital satisfaction. They found that more physiological arousal during marital conflicts predicted greater decline in marital satisfaction over the following three years, and that 60% of the variance in marital satisfaction was accounted for with measures of physiological interrelatedness between couples. Kiecolt-Glaser et al. (1988) demonstrated that separated or divorced males had poorer scores on immunity indices than married males. In addition, among married men, those with poorer marital quality were inferior on immunological measures. Furthermore, in a longitudinal investigation, married couples exhibiting negative or hostile behaviors during discussion of a marital problem demonstrated greater negative immunological changes over the subsequent 24 hours relative to couples exhibiting less negativity or hostility in their discussions (Kiecolt-Glaser, Malarkey, Chee, & Newton, 1993).

Taking these findings into consideration, Schmaling and Sher (1997) proposed a cyclical model for conceptualizing the association between distressed intimate relationships and poor health, which suggests that negative behaviors in a relationship create emotional "pathogens," which foster illness vulnerability, morbidity/illness behavior, dysfunctional responses, and further negative relationship behaviors.

Mode of Assessment

Several investigators have written about the relative utility of using self-report, interview, and behavior observation methods to assess couples (see Jacob, 1987; see also the chapters by Butcher and by Cone, this volume, for more on self-report, objective, and observational assessment). Instead, we focus on two current issues: how to assess marital satisfaction, and how to assess domestic violence.

Marital Satisfaction

For some time, researchers used the terms marital satisfaction and marital adjustment interchangeably. Self-report questionnaires such as the Marital Adjustment Test (MAT;

Locke & Wallace, 1959), Dyadic Adjustment Scale (DAS; Spanier, 1976, 1979; Spanier & Thompson, 1982), and Marital Satisfaction Inventory (MSI; Snyder, 1979; Snyder, Trull, & Wills, 1987) were used to measure these constructs. More recently, researchers have begun differentiating marital satisfaction and marital adjustment, defining marital satisfaction as a global sentiment about the marriage and marital adjustment as both behaviors and evaluative emotions.

Heyman, Sayers, and Bellack (1994) explain that measures such as the DAS were created based on psychometrics rather than theory. As such, the DAS successfully discriminates distressed from nondistressed couples. However, Norton (1983) clarifies that the DAS combines ratings of the interaction between partners (behaviors) with subjective feelings about the relationship (sentiments). This combination causes inflated correlations between marital satisfaction as measured by the DAS and other variables of interest, such as communication behaviors, because the DAS contains behavioral items (Norton, 1983).

Currently, some investigators consider the DAS a multifactorial measure of marital adjustment that assesses both agreement between partners and their relationship satisfaction (Eddy, Heyman, & Weiss, 1991; Heyman et al., 1994), whereas others define it as a unidimensional measure of marital satisfaction (Kazak, Jarmas, & Snitzer, 1988; Sharpley & Cross, 1982). Because adjustment and satisfaction are highly correlated, in some cases the difference between them is unimportant. The distinction is essential, however, when investigators are examining the impact of behavior on satisfaction. If the goal is to obtain a correlation between behavior and satisfaction, pure measures of both constructs are required to prevent unrealistically high correlations that are an artifact of overlap in the measures. For example, if one examines the relationship between affection and satisfaction, using the DAS as a measure of satisfaction would create an inflated correlation because there are items on the DAS measuring affectionate behavior. Hence, when accurate correlations between behavior and relationship satisfaction are desired, researchers should use pure measures of satisfaction rather than measures of marital adjustment such as the DAS.

Domestic Violence

Couples' reports of domestic violence are often incongruent, perhaps more so than other spouse reports because of the punitive action and social stigma associated with its occurrence. As we stated earlier in the chapter, it is often necessary to get both partners' reports because frequently they vary. However, it is also possible that certain modes of collecting data lead to either greater consistency or greater accuracy. Investigators in the area of domestic violence have begun determining how mode of measurement influences responses. For example, Lawrence, Heyman, and O'Leary (1995) assessed the presence of aggression in 50 severely distressed couples using telephone and written administrations of the Conflict Tactics Scales (CTS; Straus, 1979). Interestingly, they found that both husbands' and wives' reports of physical aggression were consistent across telephone interview and questionnaire assessments, so different modes of assessment elicited comparable reports. However, across spouses, reports of husband-to-wife aggression were significantly less consistent than reports of wife-to-husband aggression, with wives reporting significantly more husband-to-wife aggression than did husbands. Investigations such as this one are necessary to enable researchers to make informed decisions about how to assess couples. In this case, investigators will need to assess both partners to get the most accurate reports (Jouriles & O'Leary, 1985; Lawrence et al., 1995) and assess the wife if constrained to evaluating only one partner.

DATA ANALYSIS

Historically, statistical techniques such as analyses of variance (ANOVAs), multivariate analyses of variance (MANOVAs), multiple regression, and bivariate correlations have been used in the analysis of couples data. Although these approaches continue to be valuable, there is a series of new techniques being explored in couples research. In this section, we provide an overview of four relatively new ways to analyze multiple-wave longitudinal and outcome data on intimate relationships: growth curve analyses, survival analyses, sequential analyses, and regressed change analyses.

Growth Curve Analyses

Growth curve analyses differ from existing analyses in that they allow an examination of *continuous* change in relationships. When analyzing a sample containing at least three data points, these unique analyses provide information on how individual partners (or couples) change over time, where they are initially on the variable in question, and how much they vary from the rest of the sample (e.g., Karney & Bradbury, 1997).

There are several advantages to growth curve modeling. First, initial levels of the variable in question are not only included in the analyses but examined as unique information, rather than being omitted or covaried out of analyses. Second, individual variability in couples' trajectories are examined rather than collapsing across the sample. Third, curvilinear trends can be examined using this approach. Fourth, growth curve analyses are more flexible than previous statistical techniques. Individual parameters are estimated rather than group differences, so data can be analyzed even if they were gathered at different times or if the duration between data points is not exactly the same for each couple. Further, couples' data can be analyzed even if partners did not provide data at one of the time points.

Survival Analyses

Researchers have traditionally analyzed relationship outcomes, such as marital status (together or separated) or marital quality (level of satisfaction), using correlational or chi-square analyses. However, correlations simply provide the degree of association between the predictor and criterion variables at the end of the study, and do not indicate when the outcome variable, such as separation, is likely to occur. Similarly, chi-square analyses generate a dichotomous criterion variable and do not take into account when couples are likely to become maritally distressed. In contrast, survival analyses (Singer & Willett, 1991) provide a unique way to analyze relationship outcomes using longitudinal data. They allow for an examination of *when* specific types of couples are at risk rather than simply indicating whether or not couples yield a certain outcome.

Generating survival curves has several advantages. First, different types of couples may be compared to determine whether one type is at risk for distress or dissolution earlier than another type. Second, theoretical models may be tested using survival analyses. Third, these analyses are flexible enough to adjust for data collected at different times, as long as the interval between time points remains constant, because each individual spouse's (or couples') survival at each time point is analyzed. Fourth, survival analyses can be adjusted to include couples who may not have provided data at certain time points during the overall assessment period.

Sequential Analyses

In contrast to growth curve and survival analyses, sequential analyses have been used in couples research since 1979, when Gottman and colleagues (e.g., Bakeman & Gottman, 1986; Gottman, 1979) first discussed the usefulness of sequential analyses in understanding couples' interactions. Also known as lag time analyses, sequential analyses are particularly useful in determining the *order* as well as the associations among variables, such as whether the occurrence of one behavior is dependent on the occurrence of another. Time intervals may be measured in hours, days, weeks, or even months. Researchers analyze each time lag to determine whether the occurrence of one event follows and is dependent upon the occurrence of another event.

For example, Margolin and colleagues (e.g., Margolin, John, & O'Brien, 1989; Margolin & Wampold, 1981) have used sequential analyses to examine interactions among couples and family members. Margolin et al. (1996) measured four interactions: marital tension, parent-child tension, sibling tension, and family tension (both parents and at least one child) at three time points: morning, afternoon, and evening. They analyzed the *sequence* of these interactions to determine whether tension between some of these family members was dependent upon tension between others.

Regressed Change Score Analyses

There has been a debate in the past decade about how to analyze longitudinal change (e.g., Gottman & Krokoff, 1990; Smith, Vivian, & O'Leary, 1991; Woody & Costanzo, 1990). One way is to compute *raw change scores,* in which the difference between a variable at Time 1 and Time 2 is calculated, and the raw difference score is correlated with another variable of interest (e.g., Gottman & Krokoff, 1989). A second approach is to develop a model with regressed change by computing partial correlations of the residuals of Time 2 scores with Time 1 scores removed. This is known as the *regressed change* approach. Although regressed change scores have been considered a useful alternative to raw change scores in couples research (e.g., Woody & Costanzo, 1990), Gill, Christensen, and Fincham (in press) found little difference between the two techniques. Researchers should probably use both methods to determine if they lead to similar results.

CONCLUSION AND IMPLICATIONS

Our selective overview of couples research focused on recent controversies and advances. In doing so, two themes have emerged. The first is that the scope of couples research has expanded tremendously. For example, investigators are exploring new variables such as health and social support. In addition, they are widening their assessments beyond the standard relationship factors to include measures of individual functioning. Further, longitudinal researchers have broadened our understanding of couples beyond that provided by cross-sectional designs.

The second emerging theme is that couples research is being conducted with greater precision. Longitudinal assessments can either be conducted around time points or around important events. Researchers have begun delineating their sampling strategies and how these methods affect the sample and results obtained. Data analyses that provide a more exact indication of change over time that is distinct from initial and end state are now being utilized.

Fortunately, the expanding scope of couples research has not hindered advancement in precision. Because of this dual progression, couples researchers now have many options and decisions to make in conducting their research. This flexibility makes conducting research on couples an exciting and intellectually stimulating experience with the potential to produce accurate, reliable, and valid findings.

REFERENCES

Acitelli, L. K. (1997). Sampling couples to understand them: Mixing the theoretical with the practical. *Journal of Social and Personal Relationships, 14,* 243–261.

Attridge, M., Berscheid, E., & Simpson, J. A. (1995). Predicting relationship stability from both partners versus one. *Journal of Personality and Social Psychology, 69*(2), 254–268.

Bagarozzi, D. A., & Rauen, P. (1981). Premarital counseling: Appraisal and status. *American Journal of Family Therapy, 9,* 13–30.

Bakeman, R., & Gottman, J. M. (1986). *Observing interaction: An introduction to sequential analyses.* New York: Cambridge University Press.

Baucom, D. H. (1983). Conceptual and psychometric issues in evaluating the effectiveness of behavioral marital therapy. *Advances in Family Intervention, Assessment and Theory, 3,* 91–117.

Baucom, D. H., Shoham, V., Mueser, K. T., Daiuto, A. D., & Stickle, T. R. (1998). Empirically supported couple and family interventions for marital distress and adult mental health problems. *Journal of Consulting and Clinical Psychology, 66*(1), 53–88.

Bumpass, L. L. (1990). What's happening to the family? Interactions between demographic and institutional change. *Demography, 27,* 483–498.

Burman, B., & Margolin, G. (1992). Analysis of the association between marital relationships and health problems: An interactional perspective. *Psychological Bulletin, 112,* 39–63.

Chambless, D. L., Sanderson, W. C., Shoham, V., Johnson, S. B., Pope, K. S., Crits-Christoph, P., Baker, M., Johnson, B., Woody, S. R., Sue, S., Beutler, L., Williams, D. A., & McCurry, S. (1996). An update on empirically validated therapies. *Clinical Psychologist, 49,* 5–18.

Christensen, A. (1996). *Acceptance and change in marital therapy.* Unpublished grant proposal funded by National Institute of Mental Health (R10-MH56223), University of California, Los Angeles.

Christensen, A. (1998). On intervention and relationship events: A marital therapist looks at longitudinal research on marriage. In T. N. Bradbury (Ed.), *The developmental course of marital dysfunction* (pp. 377–392). New York: Cambridge University Press.

Christensen, A., & Heavey, C. L. (1990). Gender and social structure in the demand/withdraw pattern of marital conflict. *Journal of Personality and Social Psychology, 59,* 73–81.

Christensen, A., & Heavey, C. L. (in press). Interventions for couples. *Annual Review of Psychology.*

Christensen, A., & Nies, D. C. (1980). The spouse observation checklist: Empirical analysis and critique. *American Journal of Family Therapy, 8,* 69.

Christensen, A., & Shenk, J. L. (1991). Communication, conflict, and psychological distance in nondistressed, clinic, and divorcing couples. *Journal of Consulting and Clinical Psychology, 59*(3), 458–463.

Christensen, A., Sullaway, M., & King, C. E. (1983). Systematic error in behavioral reports of dyadic interaction: Egocentric bias and content effects. *Behavioral Assessment, 5,* 129–140.

Cook, T. D., & Campbell, D. T. (1979). *Quasi-experimentation: Design and analysis issues for field settings.* Boston: Houghton Mifflin.

Cummings, E. M. (1987). Coping with background anger in early childhood. *Child Development, 58,* 976–984.

Cummings, E. M., Iannotti, R. J., & Zahn-Waxler, C. (1985). The influence of conflict between adults on the emotions and aggression of young children. *Developmental Psychology, 21,* 495–507.

Cutrona, C. E., & Suhr, J. A. (1994). Social support communication in the context of marriage: An analysis of couples' supportive interactions. In B. R. Burleson, T. L. Albrecht, & I. G. Sarason (Eds.), *Communication of social support: Messages, interactions, relationships, and community* (pp. 113–135). Thousand Oaks, CA: Sage.

Davila, J., Bradbury, T. N., & Fincham, F. (in press). Negative affectivity as a mediator of the association between adult attachment and marital satisfaction. *Personal Relationships.*

Eddy, J. M., Heyman, R. E., & Weiss, R. L. (1991). An empirical evaluation of the Dyadic adjustment scale: Exploring the differences between marital "satisfaction" and "adjustment." *Behavioral Assessment, 13,* 199–220.

Elwood, R. W., & Jacobson, N. S. (1982). Spouses' agreement in reporting their behavioral interactions: A clinical replication. *Journal of Consulting & Clinical Psychology, 50,* 783–784.

Fincham, F. D., & Bradbury, T. N. (1988). The impact of attributions in marriage: An experimental analysis. *Journal of Social & Clinical Psychology, 7*(2/3), 147–162.

Gill, D. S., Christensen, A., & Fincham, F. D. (in press). Predicting marital satisfaction from behavior: Do all roads really lead to Rome? *Personal Relationships.*

Gottman, J. M. (1979). *Marital interaction: Experimental investigations.* New York: Academic Press.

Gottman, J. M., & Krokoff, L. J. (1989). Marital interaction and satisfaction: A longitudinal view. *Journal of Consulting and Clinical Psychology, 57*(1), 47–52.

Gottman, J. M., & Krokoff, L. J. (1990). Complex statistics are not always clearer than simple statistics: A reply to Woody and Costanzo. *Journal of Consulting & Clinical Psychology, 58,* 502–505.

Hahlweg, K., & Klann, N. (1997). The effectiveness of marital counseling in Germany: A contribution to health services research. *Journal of Family Psychology, 11,* 410–421.

Hahlweg, K., & Markman, H. J. (1988). Effectiveness of behavioral marital therapy: Empirical status of behavioral techniques in preventing and alleviating marital distress. *Journal of Consulting and Clinical Psychology, 56,* 440–447.

Heavey, C. L., Layne, C., & Christensen, A. (1993). Gender and conflict structure in marital interaction: A replication and extension. *Journal of Consulting and Clinical Psychology, 61*(1), 16–27.

Heyman, R. E., Sayers, S. L., & Bellack, A. S. (1994). Global marital satisfaction versus marital adjustment: An empirical comparison of three measures. *Journal of Family Psychology, 8,* 432–446.

Hill, C. T., & Peplau, L. A. (1998). Premarital predictors of relationship outcomes: A 15-year follow-up of the Boston couples study. In T. N. Bradbury (Ed.), *The developmental course of marital dysfunction* (pp. 237–278). New York: Cambridge University Press.

Hill, C. T., Rubin, Z., Peplau, L. A., & Willard, S. G. (1979). The volunteer couple: Sex differences, couple commitment, and participation in research on interpersonal relationships. *Social Psychology Quarterly, 42,* 415–420.

Holtzworth-Munroe, A., Beatty, S. B., & Anglin, K. (1995). The assessment and treatment of marital violence: An introduction for the marital therapist. In N. S. Jacobson & A. S. Gurman (Eds.), *Clinical handbook of couple therapy* (2nd ed., pp. 317–339). New York: Guilford Press.

Jacob, E. (1987). Qualitative research traditions: A review. *Review of Educational Research, 57,* 1–50.

Jacobson, N. S. (1996). *Acceptance and change in marital therapy.* Unpublished grant proposal funded by National Institute of Mental Health (R10-MH56223), University of Washington.

Jacobson, N. S., & Christensen, A. (1996). Studying the effectiveness of psychotherapy: How well can clinical trials do the job? *American Psychologist, 51,* 1031–1039.

Jacobson, N. S., & Moore, D. (1981). Spouses as observers of the events in their relationship. *Journal of Consulting and Clinical Psychology, 49,* 269–277.

Jacobson, N. S., Schmaling, K. B., Holtzworth-Munroe, A., Katt, J. L., Wood, L. F., & Follette, V. M. (1989). Research-structured vs. clinically flexible versions of social learning-based marital therapy. *Behavior Research and Therapy, 27,* 173–180.

Johnson, M. P. (1995). Patriarchal terrorism and common couple violence: Two forms of violence against women. *Journal of Marriage and the Family, 57,* 283–294.

Jouriles, E. N., & O'Leary, K. D. (1985). Interspousal reliability of reports of marital violence. *Journal of Consulting and Clinical Psychology, 53,* 419–421.

Julien, D., Arellano, C., & Turgeon, L. (1997). Gender issues in heterosexual, gay, and lesbian couples. In W. K. Halford & H. J. Markman (Eds.), *Clinical handbook of marriage and couples interventions* (pp. 107–127). New York: Wiley.

Julien, D., & Markman, H. J. (1991). Social support and social networks as determinants of individual and marital outcomes. *Journal of Social and Personal Relationships, 8,* 549–568.

Karney, B. R., & Bradbury, T. N. (1995). The longitudinal course of marital quality and stability: A review of theory, method, and research. *Psychological Bulletin, 118,* 3–34.

Karney, B. R., & Bradbury, T. N. (1997). Assessing longitudinal change in marriage: An introduction to the analysis of growth curves. *Journal of Marriage and the Family, 57,* 1091–1108.

Karney, B. R., Davila, J., Cohan, C. L., Sullivan, K. T., Johnson, M. D., & Bradbury, T. N. (1995). An empirical investigation of sampling strategies. *Journal of Marriage and the Family, 57,* 909–920.

Kazak, A. E., Jarmas, A., & Snitzer, L. (1988). The assessment of marital satisfaction: An evaluation of the Dyadic adjustment scale. *Journal of Family Psychology, 2,* 82–91.

Kelly, E. L., & Conley, J. J. (1987). Personality and compatibility: A prospective analysis of marital stability and marital satisfaction. *Journal of Personality and Social Psychology, 52*(1), 27–40.

Kiecolt-Glaser, J. K., Kennedy, S., Malkoff, S., Fisher, L., Speicher, C. E., & Glaser, R. (1988). Marital discord and immunity in males. *Psychosomatic Medicine, 50,* 213–229.

Kiecolt-Glaser, J. K., Malarkey, W. B., Chee, M., & Newton, T. (1993). Negative behavior during marital conflict is associated with immunological down-regulation. *Psychosomatic Medicine, 55,* 395–409.

Krokoff, L. J., Gottman, J. M., & Hass, S. D. (1989). Validation of a global rapid couples interaction scoring system: Coding marital interaction [Special issue]. *Behavioral Assessment, 11,* 65–79.

Langhinrichsen-Rohling, J., & Vivian, D. (1994). The correlates of spouses' incongruent reports of marital aggression. *Journal of Family Violence, 9,* 265–283.

Lawrence, E., & Bradbury, T. N. (1998). *Interspousal aggression and marital dysfunction: A longitudinal analysis.* Manuscript submitted for publication.

Lawrence, E., Heyman, R. E., & O'Leary, K. D. (1995). Correspondence between telephone and written assessments of physical aggression in marriage. *Behavior Therapy, 26,* 671–680.

Levenson, R. W., & Gottman, J. M. (1983). Marital interaction: Physiological linkage and affective exchange. *Journal of Personality & Social Psychology, 45,* 587–597.

Levenson, R. W., & Gottman, J. M. (1985). Physiological and affective predictors of change in relationship satisfaction. *Journal of Personality & Social Psychology, 49,* 85–94.

Locke, H. J., & Wallace, K. M. (1959). Short marital adjustment and prediction tests: Their reliability and validity. *Marriage and Family Living, 21,* 251–255.

Margolin, G., & Burman, B. (1993). Wife abuse versus marital violence: Different terminologies, explanations, and solutions. *Clinical Psychology Review, 13,* 59–73.

Margolin, G., Christensen, A., & John, R. S. (1996). The continuance and spillover of everyday tensions in distressed and nondistressed families. *Journal of Family Psychology, 10*(3), 304–321.

Margolin, G., John, R. S., & O'Brien, M. (1989). Sequential affective patterns as a function of marital conflict style. *Journal of Social and Clinical Psychology, 8*(1), 45–61.

Margolin, G., & Wampold, B. E. (1981). Sequential analysis of conflict and accord in distressed and nondistressed marital partners. *Journal of Consulting and Clinical Psychology, 49*(4), 554–567.

Markman, H. J., Floyd, F. J., Stanley, S. M., & Storaasli, R. D. (1988). Prevention of marital distress: A longitudinal investigation. *Journal of Consulting and Clinical Psychology, 56*(2), 210–217.

Markman, H. J., Renick, M. J., Floyd, F. J., Stanley, S. M., & Clements, M. (1993). Preventing marital distress through communication and conflict management training: A 4- and 5-year follow-up. *Journal of Consulting and Clinical Psychology, 61*(1), 70–77.

McGrady, B. S., Paolino, T. J., & Longabaugh, R. (1978). Correspondence between reports of problem drinkers and spouses on drinking behavior and impairment. *Journal of Studies on Alcohol, 39,* 1252–1257.

Norton, R. (1983). Measuring marital quality: A critical look at the dependent variable. *Journal of Marriage and the Family, 45,* 141–151.

O'Leary, K. D., & Arias, I. (1984). Assessing agreement of reports of spouse abuse. In G. T. Hotaling, D. Finkelhor, J. T. Kilpatrick, & M. A. Straus (Eds.), *New dimensions in family violence research* (pp. 218–227). Newbury Park, CA: Sage.

Pasch, L. A., & Bradbury, T. N. (1998). Social support, conflict, and the development of marital dysfunction. *Journal of Consulting and Clinical Psychology, 66,* 219–230.

Pasch, L. A., Bradbury, T. N., & Sullivan, K. T. (1997). Social support in marriage: An analysis of intraindividual and interpersonal components. In G. R. Peirce, B. Lakey, I. G. Sarason, & B. R. Sarason (Eds.), *Sourcebook of social support and personality* (pp. 229–256). New York: Plenum Press.

Pearlman, S., Zweben, A., & Li, S. (1989). The comparability of solicited versus clinic subjects in alcohol treatment research. *British Journal of Addiction, 84,* 523–532.

Renne, K. S. (1970). Correlates of dissatisfaction in marriage. *Journal of Marriage and the Family, 32,* 54–67.

Repetti, R. L. (1993). Short-term effects of occupational stressors on daily mood and health complaints. *Health Psychology, 12*(2), 125–131.

Rosenthal, R., & Rosnow, R. L. (1975). *The volunteer subject.* New York: Wiley.

Schmaling, K. B., & Sher, T. G. (1997). Physical health and relationships. In W. K. Halford & H. J. Markman (Eds.), *Clinical handbook of marriage and couples interventions* (pp. 323–345). New York: Wiley.

Seligman, M. E. P. (1995). The effectiveness of psychotherapy: The Consumer Reports study. *American Psychologist, 50,* 965–974.

Sharpley, C., & Cross, D. (1982). A psychometric evaluation of the Spanier Dyadic adjustment scale. *Journal of Marriage and the Family, 44,* 739–741.

Singer, J. D., & Willctt, J. B. (1991). Modeling the days of our lives: Using survival analysis when designing and analyzing longitudinal studies of duration and the timing of events. *Psychological Bulletin, 110,* 268–290.

Smith, D. A., Vivian, D., & O'Leary, K. D. (1991). The misnomer proposition: A critical reappraisal of the longitudinal status of "negativity" in marital communication. *Behavioral Assessment, 13,* 7–24.

Snyder, D. K. (1979). *Marital satisfaction inventory: Administration booklet.* Los Angeles: Western Psychological Services.

Snyder, D. K., Trull, T. J., & Wills, R. M. (1987). Convergent validity of observational and self-report measures of marital interaction. *Journal of Sex and Marital Therapy, 13,* 224–236.

Snyder, D. K., Wills, R. M., & Keiser, T. W. (1981). Empirical validation of the marital satisfaction inventory: An actuarial approach. *Journal of Consulting & Clinical Psychology, 49,* 262–268.

Spanier, G. B. (1976). Measuring dyadic adjustment: New scales for assessing the quality of marriage and similar dyads. *Journal of Marriage and the Family, 38,* 15–28.

Spanier, G. B. (1979). The measurement of marital quality. *Journal of Sex and Marital Therapy, 5,* 288–300.

Spanier, G. B., & Thompson, L. (1982). A confirmatory analysis of the dyadic adjustment scale. *Journal of Marriage and the Family, 44,* 731–738.

Straus, M. A. (1979). Measuring intrafamily conflict and violence: The conflict tactics (CT) scales. *Journal of Marriage and the Family, 41,* 75–88.

Straus, M. A., & Gelles, R. J. (Eds.). (1992). *Physical violence in American families: Risk factors and adaptations to violence in 8,145 families.* New Brunswick, NJ: Transaction.

Sullivan, K. T., & Bradbury, T. N. (1997). Are premarital prevention programs reaching couples at risk for marital dysfunction? *Journal of Consulting and Clinical Psychology, 65,* 24–30.

Szinovacz, M. E. (1983). Using couple data as a methodological tool: The case of marital violence. *Journal of Marriage and the Family, 45,* 633–644.

Task Force on Promotion and Dissemination of Psychological Procedures. (1995). Training in and dissemination of empirically-validated psychological treatments: Report and recommendations. *The Clinical Psychologist, 48,* 3–23.

Weiss, R. L., & Heyman, R. E. (1997). A clinical-research overview of couples interactions. In W. K. Halford & H. J. Markman (Eds.), *Clinical handbook of marriage and couples interventions* (pp. 13–41). New York: Wiley.

Weiss, R. L., & Summers, K. J. (1983). Marital interaction coding system-III. In E. Filsinger (Ed.), *Marriage and family assessment* (pp. 85–115). Beverly Hills, CA: Sage.

Whisman, M. A., Jacobson, N. S., Fruzzetti, A. E., & Waltz, J. A. (1989). Methodological issues in marital therapy. *Advanced Behavior Research and Therapy, 11,* 175–189.

Woody, E. Z., & Costanzo, P. R. (1990). Does marital agony precede marital ecstasy? A comment on Gottman and Krokoff's "Marital interaction and satisfaction: A longitudinal view." *Journal of Consulting and Clinical Psychology, 58*(4), 499–501.

Chapter 28

Focus Chapter

RESEARCH METHODS WITH FAMILIES

THEODORE JACOB, PH.D., RUTH ANN SEILHAMER, PH.D., and MIRIAM L. JACOB, M.S.W.

The field of family studies includes a wide range of research activities conducted by behavioral and social scientists from both basic and applied disciplines as well as from interdisciplinary programs of study. Of special importance to the realm of clinical psychology, research of the past three decades has repeatedly implicated the family in the etiology, course, treatment, and prevention of most psychopathological disorders. Equally important, there is increasing recognition that family influences play a key role in a range of major social problems, which, although not achieving psychiatric status, are critical to the physical and psychological welfare of millions (e.g., divorce, spouse and child abuse, rape, inadequate learning environments for children, and the multitude of maladaptations often associated with socialization processes among special needs populations). Finally, studies of normative family transitions—marriage, childbirth, aging, and death of a spouse/parent—continue to be supported in the anticipation that stronger theories and more adequate databases will clarify and enrich our understanding of development gone astray. Regardless of disciplinary identification, theoretical orientation, or substantive focus, all family researchers must ultimately select, revise, or develop measurement procedures that operationalize the family constructs they wish to investigate.

In pursuing this goal, the researcher soon encounters a tremendous number of instrument choices spanning a range of constructs and applications, what L'Abate (1994) has called an "embarrassment of riches." Because the authors cannot distill and analyze this large body of work in this brief chapter, the reader is encouraged to examine the following references to this literature for detailed presentations of the development and psychometric properties of specific instruments, for an appreciation of the diversity and breadth of family assessment methods, and for further discussion of the complex methodological issues in family assessment research (Boss, Doherty, LaRossa, Schum, & Steinmetz, 1993; Bray, 1995; Brody & Sigel, 1990; Christensen & Arrington, 1987; Conoley & Werth, 1995; Copeland & White, 1991; Draper & Marcos, 1990; Fredman & Sherman, 1987; Gottman, 1987; Grotevant & Carlson, 1989; Huston & Robins, 1982; Jacob & Tennenbaum, 1988; Jacob, Tennenbaum, & Krahn, 1987; Karpel & Strauss, 1983; L'Abate, 1994; L'Abate & Bagarozzi, 1993;

Research for this chapter was supported by NIAAA Grant No. 08098AA from the National Institute on Alcohol Abuse and Alcoholism and by a Research Career Scientist Award from the V.A. Palo Alto Health Care System awarded to the first author.

Margolin, 1987; Markman & Notarius, 1987; Robins, 1990; Sawin & Harrigan, 1995; Sigel & Brody, 1990; Skinner, 1987; Touliatos, Perlmutter, & Straus, 1990).

The focus of the present chapter is twofold. First, a general schema for classifying family assessment procedures is presented, including examples and references to particular instruments that represent different aspects of this domain. Second, a selective analysis of methodological problems associated with the field of family assessment is presented, providing the reader with an appreciation of key methodological issues and areas in need of further study.

CLASSIFYING FAMILY ASSESSMENT PROCEDURES

In the context of describing family assessment procedures, three organizing dimensions are particularly helpful: (a) the source from which information is obtained, (b) the family unit that is the focus of assessment, and (c) the major constructs that the instrument attempts to measure.

Data Source

The major distinction regarding data source involves instruments based on the self-reports of family members versus instruments based on the direct observation of families during actual interactions. Common to all variants of the self-report approach is the requirement that the informant be asked for his or her perceptions of family events—perceptions that can relate to individuals, relationships, the family in general, or to links between the family and extrafamilial influences. There are many advantages of the self-report strategy, including the strong face validity that is associated with test items; ease of administration and scoring; test developments based on large representative samples to which individual assessments can be generalized; and access to family data that cannot be reasonably obtained by other procedures (e.g., the nature of sexual interactions and members' expressed satisfaction/happiness with different aspects of family life). Observational procedures, on the other hand, provide direct access to the actual interactions of family members. Under the best of circumstances, such procedures provide highly detailed information regarding streams of behavior that characterize the family in operation as well as precise information regarding the family's response, solution, or performance on objective tasks and problems. Given such data, specific coding systems can be applied to these interactions, allowing for detailed descriptions of family processes and patterns of interaction.

Within each of these major data sources, one can find important subgroups of instruments. Self-report procedures, for example, include objective tests such as the Family Environment Scale (FES; Moos & Moos, 1981) and the Family Assessment Measure (FAM; Skinner, Steinhauer, & Santa-Barbara, 1982) that tap various aspects of family functioning. Examples of structured interviews are the McMaster Structured Interview of Family Functioning (McSIFF; see Epstein, Bishop, Ryan, Miller, & Keitner, 1993), the Camberwell Family Interview Schedule (CFIS; Vaughn & Leff, 1976) and the UCLA Parent Interview (Valone, Norton, Goldstein, & Doane, 1983) for assessing expressed emotion, and the Family Ritual Interview developed by Wolin and his colleagues to investigate the preservation of rituals in families of alcoholics (Wolin, Bennett, & Noonan, 1979; Wolin, Bennett, Noonan, & Teitelbaum, 1980). Other instruments are behaviorally focused, such as the marital and parental versions of the Areas of Change Questionnaire (ACQ; Jacob & Seilhamer, 1985; Weiss, Hops, & Patterson, 1973), Child Report of Parent Behavior Inventory (CRPBI; Schaefer, 1965), and the Quality of Relationships Inventory (QRI; Pierce, Sarason, & Sarason, 1991).

Instruments in the observational grouping can be further subdivided into laboratory analogues and naturalistic observations. One type of laboratory procedure involves the use of structured tasks or games that yield outcome measures based on the family's performance (Ferreira & Winter, 1966; Reiss & Klein, 1987). For example, the Revealed Differences Technique (Strodtbeck, 1951, 1958) requires family members to derive a joint ranking from previously ranked individual choices for a variety of questions about family activities and functions; the relative predominance of one member's individual choices and influence on the joint ranking provides an assessment of power in family decision making. A second laboratory procedure involves the assessment of actual interactions among family members using personally relevant topics that are generated from previously completed questionnaires (e.g., Jacob, Seilhamer, & Rushe, 1989) or previously identified conflict areas (e.g., Gottman et al., 1995). These discussions, often videotaped or audiotaped to provide a permanent record, are then assessed by various means: detailed, multicomponent coding systems that preserve the ordering of behavior over time; ratings of the total interaction along general/global dimensions of interest; and the recording of members' psychophysiological or physical responses during the ongoing interactions (Gottman et al., 1995; Weiss & Summers, 1983).

In contrast with these laboratory-based procedures, naturalistic observations involve the observation and assessment of family interaction in the home setting. Methods for collecting data in natural contexts include audiotaping and videotaping that can be subjected to detailed coding systems or to more global ratings (Jacob, Tennenbaum, Bargiel, & Seilhamer, 1995; Weiss & Summers, 1983). In an innovative approach to assessing individual understanding of interpersonal events, Powers, Welsh, and Wright (1994) used a "video-recall" method whereby they videotaped parents and adolescents in their home discussing specific relationship issues and then had the family members rate the interactions while viewing them in the university laboratory a few days later. Other researchers have used daily diaries (Quittner & Opipari, 1994) or beepers to signal family members to record details of current daily events (Larson & Richards, 1994); these observations, as recorded by family participants, provide samples of day-to-day family experiences.

The relative advantages and liabilities of self-report and observational methods have been much discussed in many areas of social science. The last section of this paper presents a more detailed consideration of the strengths, limitations, and future needs of these methodological approaches as they apply to the field of family research.

Unit of Assessment

In the measurement of family processes, the assessment focus can involve individuals, relationships between two (dyads) or more members, the whole family, or the interface between the family and extrafamilial environment.

Individual assessments have involved traditional tests of personality or psychopathology, including both objective or projective procedures—instruments that can provide important data regarding the psychiatric and psychosocial status of the individual members. In addition, probably due to the lack of available whole-family measures, some early researchers used individual assessment data to derive family-level variables; for example, the measurement of communication deviance is based on analysis of each parent's individual Rorschach responses (Singer & Wynne, 1966).

The second level of assessment focuses on descriptions of the marital, parent-child, and child-sibling relationships. In contrast with the assessment of individuals, relationship assessments provide information about dyadic status and functioning, whether determined from an individual's reports regarding the relationship or from an observer's coding of an ongoing interaction between two family members. By far the most extensive group of dyadic assessment measures has concerned marital relationships (Johnson, 1995; Spanier & Thompson, 1982), whereas procedures for assessing parent-child and child-sibling relationships have been fewer and more limited in scope.

The next level of assessment is that of the whole family whereby test scores, ratings, or performance variables are intended to characterize the family in general or as a totality. Again, assessments of this unit can be obtained via self-report procedures (i.e., an individual's perceptions/descriptions of his or her family), laboratory outcome procedures (i.e., the family's performance on a structured task), or process and content codings obtained from laboratory or naturalistic observation of interactions among family members. Examples of projective methods that address the family as a unit are conjoint family drawings (Bing, 1970; Oster & Gould, 1987) and a consensus version of the Thematic Apperception Test (Fredman & Sherman, 1987).

Finally, there are several assessment procedures that provide information about extrafamilial variables and their impact on family functioning. Measures of social support and social networks (Anderson, 1982), for example, are based on the recognition that the family system can vary in its permeability and, in turn, the degree to which extrafamilial systems can impact on the family unit. In discussing the family's adjustment to crises and stress, Buehler (1990) comments on the importance of evaluating the availability and the efficacy of family system resources. Instrument development in this area has focused largely on family adaptation and utilization of extrafamilial resources associated with specific stressors, such as chronic illness, divorce, or death (see Brody & Sigel, 1990; Buehler, 1990; Conoley & Werth, 1995; Walsh, 1993). Examples of instruments that evaluate community and extended family supports are the Feetham Family Functioning Survey (FFFS; Roberts & Feetham, 1982) and the Family Inventory of Resources for Management (FIRM; McCubbin & Comeau, 1987).

Constructs Assessed

How one conceptualizes and examines the relationship between family influences and childhood or adult disorders will vary in relation to one's theoretical model, study objective, and psychopathology under consideration. First, the family's role in psychopathology is often seen to vary as a function of the particular theoretical or clinical-theoretical model one selects. For some family researchers, global, systemwide variables (often referred to as family environmental influences) assume primary importance, whereas other investigators emphasize highly circumscribed behaviors and specific responses as key variables. Second, different study objectives will dictate the selection of those family variables most germane to the investigative focus. Interests in etiology, for example, may direct attention toward one level or type of family influence which may not be as relevant to studies of course and maintenance or to efforts aimed at developing effective programs of intervention or prevention. Finally, the particular psychopathology of interest will direct attention toward some family variables rather than others. Interests in the cognitive dysfunctions of schizophrenia, for example, led Goldstein and Wynne (Doane et al., 1982; J. Lewis, Rodnick, & Goldstein, 1981) to assessments of communication deviance, a family variable that is probably less relevant to psychopathologies in which behavioral and affective disturbances, rather than cognitive deficits, are the primary features of the disorder.

In light of these considerations, together with the fluid and developing nature of family theory, research, and treatment, it is clear that no single family variable or family model can guarantee immediate and profound insights if selected to guide research efforts in adult or childhood disorders. At the same time, theoretical and empirical efforts of the past four decades—involving the fields of family sociology, childhood development, systems/communication theory, and social learning theory—do offer a rich and, in some cases, compelling matrix of family variables and models that deserve the serious consideration of clinical psychology researchers.

Survey of the family studies and child development literatures reveals several sets of constructs that seem most relevant to understanding the family-psychopathology complex. Furthermore, this relatively small matrix of influences appears to capture most of the past and current thinking regarding the family's potential roles in disorders of childhood and adulthood. Four sets of constructs are selected here: affect, control, communication, and family systems properties. Theoretically, each of these processes can be assessed in regard to the interaction of family dyads (marital, mother-child, father-child, child-sibling), triads, or the entire family, although certain constructs (processes) have been discussed most extensively in regard to certain family subgroups with much less attention directed toward other family groupings.

Affect

The primacy of the affective bond as a determinant of relationship satisfaction and individual outcome has been emphasized across a broad range of disciplines and types of interpersonal relationships. From early studies of infant attachment (Ainsworth, Blehar, Waters, & Wall, 1978) and group process (Parsons & Bales, 1955; Steinhauer, 1987) to investigations of marital dissatisfaction (R. Lewis & Spanier, 1979; Weiss, 1981) and patterns of childhood socialization (Rollins & Thomas, 1979), the importance of a supportive and nurturant affective relationship has been repeatedly underscored. Clearly, the affective relationships characterizing the parent-child and marital dyads has received most emphasis by theorists and clinicians, although various researchers have suggested that this "feeling" dimension—the ties that bind—can and should be assessed in regard to the family in general (Moos & Moos, 1976; Olson, Sprenkle, & Russell, 1979). Additionally, assessment of the affective nature of child-sibling relationships, often expressed in caretaking, alliances, and other supportive behaviors, is receiving more attention (Brody & Stoneman, 1990; Schicke, 1995) . Also, in contrast to examining the affective quality of family relationships at the dyadic level, some researchers are looking at the role of intraindividual affective states in the interpretation, reactivity, expected outcome, and recall of family interactional events, particularly conflict (Davies & Cummings, 1995).

Control

As with the affective dimension, interpersonal influence has been of major importance in conceptualizations of a wide range of relationships (Foa & Foa, 1974; Leary, 1957). In studies of adult relationships—in particular, the marital dyad—various terms have been used to describe this dimension, the most common descriptors being power, influence, and dominance (Hadley & Jacob, 1976). In studies of relationships involving members of unequal status—namely, the parent-child dyad—the literature has focused on strategies, techniques, and styles of parenting behavior with an overriding interest in those processes by which parents attempt to control and shape the behavior of their offspring during early childhood and adolescence (Rollins & Thomas, 1979). Similar to assessments of affect, the measurement of influence and control strategies at a general family level or with regard to parent-child or marital dyads has received most attention (Moos & Moos, 1976; Olson et al., 1979; Shehan & Lee, 1990), whereas the assessment of dominance structures in child-sibling relationships has received minimal attention.

Communication

The term communication can be defined so broadly as to almost be interchangeable with interpersonal behavior. In the family literature of relevance to psychopathology, however, several meanings can be identified, each of which is related to a particular model linking patterns of family communication with offspring status.

First, there has been continued interests in relating certain types of communication distortions to the development and perpetuation of cognitive disorder in children. Most important, this line of theory and research began during the early 1950s with the appearance of several family theories of schizophrenia (Mishler & Waxler, 1965). All of these models emphasized the unique patterns of communication that characterize these families and the role of communication distortion in the subsequent development of the child's cognitive disturbances. During the next 30 years, key concepts from these early efforts—in particular, the notions of double bind, transactional thought disorder, and more recently, communication deviance—guided several research programs aimed at identifying, prospectively, those patterns of family communication that predict severe psychiatric disorder as the offspring enter late adolescence and early adulthood (J. Lewis et al., 1981).

Although originally related to schizophrenia, investigators soon broadened the meaning of double bind communication, integrated it into a rapidly developing literature on nonverbal communication, and began various studies of family communication with disturbed but nonpsychotic samples (see review by Jacob & Lessin, 1982). These developments prompted considerable interest in exploring the relationship between verbal and nonverbal communication channels. Within this area, a particular focus has involved the conditions under which channel inconsistency (i.e., nonredundant information) emerges and the impact of such inconsistent messages on receivers.

A third focus on family communication has involved studies of family problem solving in dysfunctional family units and the development of treatment programs aimed at enhancing those communication skills thought to be most relevant to the effective and satisfactory resolution of conflict (Gottman, Notarius, Gonso, & Markman, 1976; Olson, Russell, & Sprenkle, 1980; Thomas, 1977). In large part, this direction of research and practice has been stimulated by the efforts of family researchers most closely identified with social learning theory (Vincent, 1980).

Systems Properties

This set of constructs derives most directly from the application of systems concepts to the family unit. Bateson's early collaboration with Jackson, Haley, and Weakland (1956) during the early 1950s provided the major foundation and stimulus for this clinical-theoretical framework, which, in turn, generated a variety of provocative and highly influential models of family psychopathology and treatment. In contrast with the other major constructs, attention is here directed toward general properties and principles of family systems that characterize relationships within the family, as well as between the family and extrafamilial systems that influence family functioning. As with the other constructs, these system properties can be related to the etiology, impact, and modification of various forms of psychopathology. Included in this domain of processes would be such characteristics as system flexibility and adaptability, the family's ability to change patterns of control and affect expression in response to changing needs of members and situational stresses imposed on the family (Olson et al., 1979). Related processes such as boundary permeability, subsystem relationships, and alliance structures (Minuchin, 1974) have also been emphasized in the application of systems perspectives to the diagnosis and treatment of family dysfunction. Vuchinich, Emery, and Cassidy (1988) based an observational study of third-party intervention in dyadic interactions on the contention that additional family members often become involved in what begins as a dyadic conflict. In their observations of videotaped dinners in the home, they found specific effects for child gender (girls are more likely to intervene than boys), parents' behavior (they are usually on opposing sides), and role ascriptions (fathers use authority, mothers use mediation, children use distraction). This observational study is an example of an effort to examine family systemic phenomena, such as triangulation, alliances, and scapegoating. Other theorists have highlighted the family's use of time and space as well as amount of interaction that occurs within different family subsystems as relevant to understanding the nature of functional versus dysfunctional family systems (Kantor & Lehr, 1975; Steinglass, 1979). Finally, the family's dealing with extrafamilial systems, including the impact of social networks, extended family relationships, and community agencies, has been thought of as an important interface that should be understood to appreciate fully the internal workings of the family system itself.

LIMITATIONS AND FUTURE RESEARCH DIRECTIONS

As can be gleaned from the foregoing overview, the family assessment domain is characterized by a great diversity of instruments that span a range of constructs, assessment foci, data sources, target populations, and applications. Although our evaluation of the field is generally positive and optimistic, it is tempered by the recognition that much work remains to be done. Whereas some writers encourage a "moratorium" on the development of new instruments and more attention to demonstrating the psychometric rigor of existing family measures (L'Abate & Bagarozzi, 1993), societal changes have suggested new areas of concern that require new types of measurement procedures. For example, existing assessment measures may not adequately address special issues related to dual-career families, divorce, single parenting, stepparent families, lesbian and gay families, the cultural differences of minority populations, homeless families, or the impact of chronic illness on individual family members and systemic family functioning. Additionally, medical advances have increased longevity, which in turn has increased the number of living generational levels and family stresses related to the care of the elderly. The reader is referred to recent reviews that include further discussion and abstracts of instruments for special needs populations (see Buehler, 1990; Conoley & Werth, 1995). In the remainder of this chapter, we discuss major issues and difficulties that characterize the extant family assessment with the aim of encouraging rigorous and programmatic research concerned with the development, refinement, and validation of family assessment procedures (see Table 28.1).

Table 28.1. Future research directions

Research Topic	Questions in Need of Answers
Instrument dimensionality	How many dimensions best characterize report-based and observation-based measures of family functioning? Is instrument dimensionality similar across different family subsystems?
Correspondence across different family members	To what degree do different family members describe family functioning in a similar fashion? Does correspondence across different family members vary as a function of family subsystem assessed?
Correspondence across different family subsystems	To what degree is there similarity in the description of different family subsystems? Under what conditions are cross-system similarities maximized?
Correspondence across different methods	Is there convergent and discriminate validity of key family constructs assessed by different methods? Does correspondence across methods vary in relation to construct assessed and subsystem assessed?
Undeveloped assessment targets and concepts	How can key family systems concepts be operationalized and measured? What methods appear best suited for describing such complex processes? Can such constructs be differentiated from the general family dimensions of affect, engagement, and control?

General Limitations of Report and Observational Methods

Self-report procedures are not only convenient and relatively inexpensive, but allow for the possibility of large-sample, normative data to which individual protocols can be related. Most important, only self-report procedures can capture members' cognitions and attributions about relationships and events—data that are increasingly viewed as essential to the goals of understanding and predicting family processes and outcomes (Davies & Cummings, 1995; Robinson & Jacobson, 1987). On the other hand, self-report procedures are, in the end, an individual's perceptions of self and other—perceptions that can be inaccurate, biased, and at times serious distortions of what other observers might conclude about the individuals and relationships in question. Furthermore, the researcher must reconcile the inevitable inconsistencies that are found in reports from different family members. Finally, most self-report data provide little in the way of the fine-grained details of moment-to-moment, day-to-day interactions among family members, data that are of great importance to researchers interested in the analysis of actual family processes.

In contrast with self-report procedures, observational procedures inform us most directly about actual interchanges among family members. If recorded, coded, and analyzed carefully and creatively, such data provide a critical foundation for an empirically based theory of family interaction and its links with disorders of children and adults. Notwithstanding these attributes, direct observation strategies involving the use of complex coding procedures are costly and labor-intensive, requiring a significant commitment of time and resources to collect, collate, and analyze complex interaction data. Furthermore, there are methodological issues of continuing concern involving this approach, including subject reactivity and the meaningfulness of highly specific behavioral codes as indices of the larger dimensions and constructs of relevance to family theory and therapy.

The unique features and methodological limitations of self-report and observational procedures have been the subjects of many publications in the family research literature. From our view, it would be a mistake to conclude that one method is *generally* more valuable, useful, or defensible than another in family studies of psychopathology. Instead, we suggest that both strategies are necessary for a full understanding of so complex a process as family interaction and psychopathology. Rather than debate the relative merits and limitations of each approach, a more fruitful strategy would be to determine what understanding of which problems can be achieved with which methodology.

Instrument Dimensionality

Family assessment instruments often include a variety of subscales (codes, rating scales) purporting to assess particular concepts of general or specific relevance to the theoretical model on which the instrument is based. However, in many instances—and this point is particularly relevant to self-report methods—a convincing case has not been made for the statistical independence of the component scales (e.g., Fowler, 1981, 1982; Skinner, Steinhauer, & Santa-Barbara, 1983; Waldron, Sabatelli, & Anderson, 1990). It may not be possible for individuals to differentiate facets of relationships as clearly and subtly as theory suggests or as other methods are able to do, especially when self-reports focus on intimate, emotionally charged relationships in which the respondent is a participant. In reality, relationships may be most clearly and parsimoniously differentiated along but two or three dimensions, a conclusion that has received considerable support from a range of theory and research in the domain of interpersonal processes (Benjamin, 1974; Foa & Foa, 1974; Kiesler, 1983; Leary, 1957; Olson, 1993; Wiggins & Broughton, 1985). A more recent assessment of whole-family report procedures (Gondoli & Jacob, 1993) supports this conclusion, indicating that score variance is best captured by three general factors (affect, control, and activity) rather than by the many dimensions that these instruments purport to measure. Likewise, intricate coding systems designed for observational data may yield a limited number of meaningful, independent factors. Several researchers (Bell & Bell, 1989; Chamberlain & Bank, 1989) have encouraged an integration or convergence of "micro" (i.e., more molecular) approaches that claim greater objectivity and "macro" (i.e., more global) approaches that claim greater interpretability.

Cross-Member Correspondence

Having clarified the dimensionality of particular instruments, the assessment of correspondence becomes the critical next step. The least complex example of this issue is found in the assessment of different members' reports of the same relationship.

The study of correspondence across different members' reports has a long history in family studies as well as the broader social science literature (Cook & Goldstein, 1993; Feldman, Wentzel, & Gehring, 1989; Surra & Ridley, 1991). Although early work on this topic indicated low to moderate correlations between different informants, many of these studies were small-scale efforts of questionable quality. Recent work in this area, however, has offered stronger designs and statistical analyses and, in turn, has provided a clearer and more encouraging picture than that discerned from earlier studies. Cook and Goldstein (1993), for example, examined the correspondence among three members' reports (mother, father, child) on the same dyadic relationships (mother to child negativity, and father to child negativity). Through a latent variable approach, the investigators were able to determine the degree to which each member's reports represented a "unique perspective" versus a common perspective shared by that of other family members. Most important, each member's ratings were found to contain a significant "true score" component—variance that is explained/caused by the construct under investigation. In addition, the ratings of the adolescent child (but not those of mother or father) evidenced a systematic rater effect; that is, the adolescent's rating of father-child negativity and mother-child negativity were correlated "independent of mother's and father's actual negativity." Finally, notwithstanding the significance of this finding, the correlations were modest, lending support to the discriminant validity of the ratings. In sum, these data suggest that different family members are, to a significant degree, reporting on the same reality; that specifying family subsystems should be incorporated into future research designs because findings relevant to one subsystem may not generalize to a different subsystem; and that a latent variable approach can add significant clarity and power to analyses of correspondence among reporters.

Cross-Method Correspondence

Discrepancies that occur when different members' reports are compared on the same instrument represent one, and probably the least complex, example of measurement correspondence. As other instruments or methods are introduced, however, comparisons become increasingly complicated. Viewed along a continuum, it is clear that some comparisons are more complex than others because of variations in the specific instrument, general type of instrument, member providing data, and concept assessed. Stated otherwise, comparisons involving two family assessment procedures can reflect differences between data sources, between instruments, between methods, between concepts, or any combination of these conditions.

In general, empirical studies of cross-method correspondence among family assessment procedures have been limited and nonsystematic in design. One of the few exceptions to this conclusion has involved the study of "family power" carried out over the past two decades, although even this literature cannot be considered entirely adequate (for early reviews, see Hadley & Jacob, 1973, 1976). Two studies examined the correspondence between marital assessment procedures based on report, observational, and quasi-observational methods, with one analysis yielding little evidence for cross-method correspondence (Margolin, 1978) and the other providing substantial support for correspondence across methods (Stein, Girodo, & Dotzenroth, 1982). Most relevant to family (versus marital) assessment procedures, Reiss and his colleagues published two studies comparing the correspondence between the Card Sort Procedure and two report instruments, the FES (Oliveri & Reiss, 1984) and the Family Adaptability and Cohesion Scales (FACES; Sigafoos, Reiss, Rich, & Douglas, 1985). In both analyses, there was little, if any, support for correspondence across methods.

Clearly, cross-method comparisons become increasingly difficult as the differences between assessment procedures increases. Various analyses of this issue have appeared in the family and general behavioral science literature during the past two decades (Baucom & Sayers, 1989; Huston & Robins, 1982; Olson, 1977; Surra & Ridley, 1991). Several investigators have examined individual differences and relationship variables that can affect correspondence between reports and observations (e.g., Bradbury & Fincham, 1990; Jacobson, 1985; Oliveri & Reiss, 1984; Sigafoos et al., 1985), whereas others have offered innovative laboratory-based analyses of "insider-outsider" differences (Margolin, Hattem, John, & Yost, 1985; Notarius, Benson, Sloane, Vanzetti, & Hornyak, 1989). To aid selection of measures for research or clinical application, L'Abate and Bagarozzi (1993) present an "insider's-outsider's" scale for rating the utility of a given instrument or assessment procedure. Many of these inquiries can provide important guidance for further investigations of method correspondence.

Underdeveloped Assessment Targets and Concepts

Given the multicomponent nature of family structure and the impact of each subsystem on another, on individual family members, and on the family as a totality, it is necessary to develop reliable and valid procedures for the description of all family components (individual, dyadic, triadic, or whole family units). There is a relative abundance of useful procedures for the assessment of the whole family, particularly self-report instruments, whereas assessment methods for other family subgroups are less developed.

In particular, the assessment of sibling relationships (especially among preadolescent and adolescent children) is an area of both concern and relative neglect (Bank & Kahn, 1982; Lamb & Sutton-Smith, 1982). A notable exception is Furman's Sibling Relationship Questionnaire (SRQ; Furman & Buhrmester, 1985a, 1985b). Based on a very different methodology, a quasi-observational procedure, Seilhamer's (1983) modification of the Spouse Observation Checklist (SOC; Weiss et al., 1973) for the assessment of sibling relationships, the Sibling Observation Schedule (SOS) shows considerable promise as a relatively objective, behaviorally specific cataloguing procedure, whereby important day-to-day events (both negative and positive) transpiring in sibling relationships can be collected. Both the SRQ and the SOS have negotiated only the early stages of test development, and their ultimate value as useful instruments depends on the considerable amount of psychometric and application experiences that lie ahead.

A second area in which there is surprising scarcity of psychometrically sound, well-researched instruments involves reports of parent-child relationships. Our 1988 book (Jacob & Tennenbaum, 1988) reviewed parent-child self-report measures and found a rather small set of procedures varying considerably in terms of established psychometric foundations, indicating the absence of programmatic effort directed toward such developments, notwithstanding the key role that parent-child relationships have played in theories of the etiology, course, outcome, and treatment of childhood disorders. The most recent and welcome addition to this domain is the Alabama Parenting Questionnaire (APQ; Shelton, Frick, & Wootton, 1996). Also, an increasing interest in relationships between parents and their adult children is reflected in the development of instruments addressing this developmental phase of family life, such as the Adult Parenting Burdens (Windle, 1995), the Quality of Relationships Inventory (Pierce et al., 1991), and the Parents as Facilitators of Independence, a subscale of Kenny's (1995) Attachment Questionnaire. In contrast to self-report measures, a plethora of laboratory and naturalistic observation coding systems for describing family and, more particularly, parent-child interaction have been carefully developed and widely applied since the mid-1960s.

Finally, instruments specifically designed for the assessment of systems properties, although sometimes found within the literature, are relatively few in number, still at an early stage of development, and do not include various key constructs and relationships relevant to this focus. For examples of instruments that have attempted to address family system properties, see Steinglass (1981), Rosman (1985), and Perosa, Hansen, and Perosa (1981).

Need for Additional Assessment Methods

Notwithstanding the considerable range of available family assessment procedures, each major grouping is, nevertheless, characterized by significant practical limitations and/or difficulties in providing compelling demonstrations for instrument validity. Several promising methods—viewed as additions rather than replacements—can be identified, one of which deserves special notice. Specifically, there is a developing set of quasi-observational techniques (the prototype being Weiss's [Weiss & Perry, 1979] SOC). Although representing members' reports or perceptions of self, other, and associated interactions, the strength of these techniques resides in the potential for collecting objective information on contemporary patterns of interchange among family members. Weiss's term, *quasi-observational,* was intended to capture a point along a continuum ranging from global self-reports of a retrospective nature to detailed codings (observations) of current family interactions as rated by highly trained ("stranger") observers. In contrast with the former, quasi-observational procedures emphasize more molecular and contemporary behaviors of specific relevance to relationship processes, and differ from the latter in terms of utilizing a participant-observer format, which allows access to events and interactions that outsiders would not be able to "see." Beyond these characteristics, quasi-observational data methods are still relatively inexpensive to obtain, allowing for the collection of large data sets to which powerful multivariate data analytic procedures can be applied. Although not without limitations and methodological difficulties of their own (e.g., potential reactivity effects and reconciliation of intermember differences in resultant observations), their uniqueness and potential significance certainly encourage continued examination, refinement, and validation of these procedures.

CONCLUSION

The great expansion of interest in families over the past three decades has generated a wide array of conceptual models and assessment methods for probing various family characteristics, as well as for understanding families in the context of larger cultural and social structures. The selection of a procedure for evaluating families, either for research or clinical purposes, involves several key tasks that must be addressed.

The first task is to clearly identify the constructs or aspects of family functioning that are the investigative focus or clinical concern; in other words, selection of methods should be driven by a theoretical model. The second step involves determining if such constructs are adequately assessed by self-report methods or observational methods or both. As described above, there are many handbooks and reviews that catalogue and describe the psychometric properties of existing measures (often according to constructs of interest or levels of family subsystems). Ultimately, instrument selection should be guided by an awareness of the strengths and limitations of self-report and observational procedures and the degree of redundancy, correspondence, and convergent validity that cross-method assessments exhibit. The third decision involves pragmatics: issues regarding cost, time, ease of administration, which family members are available to serve as data sources, how applicable an instrument is for various family members and various family cultures, and how information from different family members may vary for any given instrument. In the final selection, the clinician/researcher must interpret emergent findings in light of the conceptual and psychometric limitations of the selected methods. To the extent that instruments are not well grounded in theory or not well established psychometrically, interpretations will be more tentative and results will be less generalizable.

Although considerable progress has been made in the family assessment arena, much work remains to be done in clarifying and strengthening the theoretical and psychometric foundations of the field. Research is needed that addresses questions of correspondence across family members, family subsystems, and methods, and that provides a better understanding of how key family constructs can be meaningfully and efficiently operationalized. In addition to clarifying the family's role in the emergence and maintenance of disordered behavior, there is a need to better understand family processes in nontraditional structures and family adaptability in the context of an ever-changing array of societal stressors. Our understanding of such issues will most certainly depend on the quality of the instruments that we have developed and validated.

REFERENCES

Ainsworth, M. D. S., Blehar, M. C., Waters, E., & Wall, S. (1978). *Patterns of attachment: A psychological study of the strange situation.* Hillsdale, NJ: Erlbaum.

Anderson, C. (1982). The community connection: The impact of social networks on family and individual functioning. In F. Walsh (Ed.), *Normal family processes* (1st ed., pp. 425–445). New York: Guilford Press.

Bank, S., & Kahn, M. D. (1982). *The sibling bond.* New York: Basic Books.

Bateson, G., Jackson, D., Haley, J., & Weakland, J. (1956). Toward a theory of schizophrenia. *Behavioral Science, 1,* 251–264.

Baucom, D., & Sayers, S. (1989). The behavioral observation of couples: Where have we lagged and what is the next step in the sequence? *Behavioral Assessment, 11,* 149–159.

Bell, D. C., & Bell, L. G. (1989). Micro and macro measurement of family systems concepts. *Journal of Family Psychology, 3*(2), 137–157.

Benjamin, L. S. (1974). Structural analysis of social behavior. *Psychological Review, 81,* 392–425.

Bing, E. (1970). The conjoint family drawing. *Family Process, 9,* 173–194.

Boss, P. G., Doherty, R., LaRossa, R., Schum, W. R., & Steinmetz, S. K. (Eds.). (1993). *Sourcebook of family theory and methodology: A contextual approach.* New York: Plenum Press.

Bradbury, T. N., & Fincham, F. (1990). Attributions in marriage: Review and critique. *Psychological Bulletin, 107,* 3–33.

Bray, J. H. (Ed.). (1995). Methodological advances in family psychology: Special section. *Journal of Family Psychology, 9*(2), 107–185.

Brody, G. H., & Sigel, I. E. (Eds.). (1990). *Methods of family research: Biographies of research projects: Vol. II. Clinical populations.* Hillsdale, NJ: Erlbaum.

Brody, G. H., & Stoneman, Z. (1990). Sibling relationships. In I. E. Sigel & G. H. Brody (Eds.), *Methods of family research: Biographies of research projects: Vol. I. Normal families* (pp. 189–212). Hillsdale, NJ: Erlbaum.

Buehler, C. (1990). Adjustment. In J. Touliatos, B. F. Perlmutter, & M. A. Straus (Eds.), *Handbook of family measurement techniques* (pp. 493–516). Newbury Park, CA: Sage.

Chamberlain, P., & Bank, L. (1989). Toward an integration of macro and micro measurement systems for the researcher and the clinician. *Journal of Family Psychology, 3*(2), 199–205.

Christensen, A., & Arrington, A. (1987). Research issues and strategies. In T. Jacob (Ed.), *Family interaction and psychopathology: Theories, methods, and findings* (pp. 259–296). New York: Plenum Press.

Conoley, J. C., & Werth, E. B. (Eds.). (1995). *Family assessment.* Lincoln: Buros Institute of Mental Measurements, University of Nebraska-Lincoln.

Cook, W., & Goldstein, M. (1993). Multiple perspectives on family relationships: A latent variable model. *Child Development, 64,* 1377–1388.

Copeland, A. P., & White, K. M. (1991). *Studying families.* Newbury Park, CA: Sage.

Davies, P. T., & Cummings, E. M. (1995). Children's emotions as organizers of their reactions to interadult anger: A functionalist perspective, *31*(4), 677–684.

Doane, J., Jones, J. E., Fisher, L., Ritzler, B., Singer, M. T., & Wynne, L. C. (1982). Parental communication deviance as a predictor of competence in children at risk for adult psychiatric disorder. *Family Process, 21,* 211–223.

Draper, T. W., & Marcos, A. C. (Eds.). (1990). *Family variables: Conceptualization, measurement, and use.* Newbury Park, CA: Sage.

Epstein, N. B., Bishop, D. S., Ryan, C., Miller, I., & Keitner, G. (1993). The McMaster model: View of healthy family functioning. In N. Walsh (Ed.), *Normal family processes* (2nd ed., pp. 138–160). New York: Guilford Press.

Feldman, S., Wentzel, K., & Gehring, T. (1989). A comparison of views about family cohesion and power. *Journal of Family Psychology, 3,* 39–60.

Ferreira, A. J., & Winter, W. D. (1966). Stability of interactional variables in family decision-making. *Archives of General Psychiatry, 14,* 352–355.

Foa, V., & Foa, E. (1974). *Societal structures of the mind.* Springfield, IL: Thomas.

Fowler, P. C. (1981). Maximum likelihood factor structure of the family environment scale. *Journal of Clinical Psychology, 37,* 160–164.

Fowler, P. C. (1982). Factor structure of the family environment scale: Effects of social desirability. *Journal of Clinical Psychology, 38,* 285–292.

Fredman, N., & Sherman, R. (1987). *Handbook of measurements for marriage and family therapy.* New York: Brunner/Mazel.

Furman, W., & Buhrmester, D. (1985a). Children's perceptions of the personal relationships in their social networks. *Developmental Psychology, 21,* 1016–1024.

Furman, W., & Buhrmester, D. (1985b). Children's perceptions of the qualities of sibling relationships. *Child Development, 56,* 448–461.

Gondoli, D., & Jacob, T. (1993). Factor structure within and across three family assessment procedures. *Journal of Family Psychology, 6,* 278–289.

Gottman, J. M. (1987). The sequential analysis of family interactions. In T. Jacob (Ed.), *Family interaction and psychopathology: Theories, methods, and findings* (pp. 453–478). New York: Plenum Press.

Gottman, J. M., Jacobson, N. S., Rushe, R. H., Shortt, J. W., Babcock, J., La Taillade, J. J., & Waltz, J. (1995). The relationship between heart rate reactivity, emotionally aggressive behavior, and general violence in batterers. *9*(3), 227–248.

Gottman, J. M., Notarius, C., Gonso, J., & Markman, H. (1976). *A couple's guide to communication.* Champaign, IL: Research Press.

Grotevant, H., & Carlson, C. (1989). *Family assessment.* New York: Guilford Press.

Hadley, T. R., & Jacob, T. (1973). Relationship among measure of family power. *Journal of Personality and Social Psychology, 27,* 6–12.

Hadley, T. R., & Jacob, T. (1976). The measurement of family power: A methodological study. *Sociometry, 39,* 384–395.

Huston, T. L., & Robins, E. (1982). Conceptual and methodological issues in studying close relationships. *Journal of Marriage and the Family, 44,* 901–925.

Jacob, T., & Lessin, S. (1982). Inconsistent communication in family interaction. *Clinical Psychology Review, 2,* 295–309.

Jacob, T., & Seilhamer, R. A. (1985). Adaptation of the areas of change questionnaire for parent-child relationship assessment. *American Journal of Family Therapy, 13,* 28–38.

Jacob, T., Seilhamer, R. A., & Rushe, R. (1989). Alcoholism and family interaction: An experimental paradigm. *American Journal of Drug and Alcohol Abuse, 15*(1), 73–91.

Jacob, T., & Tennenbaum, D. L. (Eds.). (1988). *Family assessment: Rationale, methods, and future directions.* New York: Plenum Press.

Jacob, T., Tennenbaum, D., Bargiel, K., & Seilhamer, R. A. (1995). Family interaction in the home: Development of a new coding system. *Behavior Modification, 19,* 147–169.

Jacob, T., Tennenbaum, D. L., & Krahn, G. (1987). Factors influencing the reliability and validity of observation data. In T. Jacob (Ed.), *Family interaction and psychopathology: Theories, methods, and findings* (pp. 297–328). New York: Plenum Press.

Jacobson, N. (1985). The role of observational measures in behavior therapy outcome research. *Behavioral Assessment, 7,* 297–308.

Johnson, D. R. (1995). Assessing marital quality in longitudinal and life course studies. In J. C. Conoley & E. B. Werth (Eds.), *Family assessment* (pp. 155–202). Lincoln: Buros Institute of Mental Measurements, University of Nebraska-Lincoln.

Kantor, D., & Lehr, W. (1975). *Inside the family.* San Francisco: Jossey-Bass.

Karpel, M. A., & Strauss, E. S. (1983). *Family evaluation.* New York: Gardner Press.

Kenny, M. (1995). *The parental attachment questionnaire.* Unpublished manuscript.

Kiesler, D. J. (1983). The 1982 interpersonal circle: A taxonomy for complementarity in human transactions. *Psychological Review, 90,* 185–214.

L'Abate, L. (1994). *Family evaluation: A psychological approach.* Thousand Oaks, CA: Sage.

L'Abate, L., & Bagarozzi, D. A. (1993). *Sourcebook of marriage and family evaluation.* New York: Brunner/Mazel.

Lamb, M. E., & Sutton-Smith, B. (1982). *Sibling relationships: Their nature and significance across the life span.* Hillsdale, NJ: Erlbaum.

Larson, R., & Richards, M. H., (1994). *Divergent realities: The emotional lives of mothers, fathers, and adolescents.* New York: Basic Books.

Leary, T. (1957). *Interpersonal diagnosis of personality.* New York: Ronald Press.

Lewis, J. M., Rodnick, E. H., & Goldstein, M. J. (1981). Intrafamilial interactive behavior, parental communication deviance and risk for schizophrenics. *Journal of Abnormal Behavior, 90,* 448–457.

Lewis, R. A., & Spanier, G. B. (1979). Theorizing about the quality and stability of marriage. In W. R. Burr, R. Hill, F. I. Nye, & I. L. Reiss (Eds.), *Contemporary theories about the family* (Vol. 1, pp. 268–294). New York: Free Press.

Margolin, G. (1978). Relationships among marital assessment procedures: A correlational study. *Journal of Consulting and Clinical Psychology, 46,* 1556–1558.

Margolin, G. (1987). Participant observation procedures in marital and family assessment. In T. Jacob (Ed.), *Family interaction and psychopathology: Theories, methods, and finding* (pp. 391–426). New York: Plenum Press.

Margolin, G., Hattem, D., John, R. S., & Yost, K. (1985). Perceptual agreement between spouses and outside observers when coding themselves and stranger dyad. *Behavioral Assessment, 7,* 235–247.

Markman, H. J., & Notarius, C. I. (1987). Coding marital and family interaction: Current status. In T. Jacob (Ed.), *Family interaction and psychopathology: Theories, methods, and findings* (pp. 329–390). New York: Plenum Press.

McCubbin, H. I., & Comeau, J. (1987). FIRM: Family inventory of resources for management. In H. I. McCubbin & A. I. Thompson (Eds.), *Family assessment inventories for research and practice* (pp. 145–160). Madison: University of Wisconsin-Madison, Family Stress Coping and Health Project.

Minuchin, S. (1974). *Families and family therapy.* Cambridge, MA: Harvard University Press.

Mishler, E. G., & Waxler, N. E. (1965). Family interaction processes and schizophrenia: A review of current theories. *Merrill-Palmer Quarterly of Behavior and Development, 11,* 269–315.

Moos, R. H., & Moos, B. S. (1976). A typology of family social environments. *Family Process, 15,* 357–371.

Moos, R. H., & Moos, B. S. (1981). *Family environment scale: Manual.* Palo Alto, CA: Consulting Psychologists Press.

Notarius, C., Benson, P., Sloane, O., Vanzetti, N., & Hornyak, L. (1989). Exploring the interface between perception and behavior: An analysis of marital interaction in distressed and nondistressed couples. *Behavioral Assessment, 11,* 39–64.

Oliveri, M. E., & Reiss, D. (1984). Family concepts and their measurement: Things are seldom what they seem. *Family Process, 23,* 33–48.

Olson, D. H. (1977). Insiders' and outsiders' views on relationships: Research studies. In G. Levinger & H. L. Raush (Eds.), *Close relationships: Perspectives on the meaning of intimacy* (pp. 115–135). Amherst: University of Massachusetts Press.

Olson, D. H. (1993). Circumplex model of marital and family systems. In F. Walsh (Ed.), *Normal family processes* (pp. 104–137). New York: Guilford Press.

Olson, D. H., Russell, C. S., & Sprenkle, D. H. (1980). Circumplex model of marital and family systems: II. Empirical studies and clinical intervention. In J. Vincent (Ed.), *Advances in family intervention assessment and theory* (Vol. 1, pp. 129–180). Greenwich, CT: JAI Press.

Olson, D. H., Sprenkle, D. H., & Russell, C. S. (1979). Circumplex model of marital and family systems: I. Cohesion and adaptability dimensions, family types, and clinical applications. *Family Process, 18,* 3–28.

Oster, G. D., & Gould, P. (1987). *Using drawings in assessment and therapy: A guide for mental health professionals.* New York: Brunner/Mazel.

Parsons, T., & Bales, R. E. (1955). *Family, socialization and interaction process.* New York: Free Press.

Perosa, L., Hansen, J., & Perosa, S. (1981). Development of the structural family interaction scale. *Family Therapy, 8,* 77–90.

Pierce, G. R., Sarason, I. G., & Sarason, B. R. (1991). General and relationship-based perceptions of social support: Are two constructs better than one? *Journal of Personality and Social Psychology, 61,* 1028–1039.

Powers, S. I., Welsh, D. P., & Wright, V. (1994). Adolescents' affective experience of family behaviors: The role of subjective understanding. *Journal of Research on Adolescence, 4*(4), 585–600.

Quittner, A. L., & Opipari, L. C. (1994). Differential treatment of siblings: Interview and diary analyses comparing two family contexts. *Child Development, 65,* 800–814.

Reiss, D., & Klein, D. (1987). Paradigm and pathogenesis: A family-centered approach to problems of etiology and treatment of psychiatric disorders. In T. Jacob (Ed.), *Family interaction and psychopathology: Theories, methods, and findings* (pp. 203–255). New York: Plenum Press.

Roberts, C. S., & Feetham, S. L. (1982). Assessing family functioning across three areas of relationships. *Nursing Research, 3,* 231–235.

Robins, E. (1990). The study of interdependence in marriage. In F. Fincham & T. Bradbury (Eds.), *The psychology of marriage* (pp. 59–86). New York: Guilford Press.

Robinson, E. A., & Jacobson, N. S. (1987). Social learning theory and family psychopathology: A Kantian model in behaviorism? In T. Jacob (Ed.), *Family interaction and psychopathology: Theories, methods, and findings* (pp. 117–162). New York: Plenum Press.

Rollins, B. C., & Thomas, D. L. (1979). Parental support, power, and control techniques in the socialization of children. In W. R. Burr, R. Hill, F. I. Nye, & I. L. Reiss (Eds.), *Contemporary theories about the family* (pp. 317–364). New York: Free Press.

Rosman, B. L. (1985). *The Philadelphia child guidance clinic family task and scoring manual.* Unpublished manuscript.

Sawin, K. J., & Harrigan, M. P. (1995). *Measures of family functioning for research and practice.* New York: Springer.

Schaefer, E. S. (1965). Child report of parent behavior. *Child Development, 36,* 413–423.

Schicke, M. C. (1995). Sibling relationships. In J. C. Conoley & E. B.Werth (Eds.), *Family assessment* (pp. 131–154). Lincoln: Buros Institute of Mental Measurements, University of Nebraska-Lincoln.

Seilhamer, R. (1983). *The sibling observation schedule: An instrument for the assessment of sibling relationships.* Unpublished master's thesis, University of Pittsburgh, Pittsburgh.

Shehan, C. L., & Lee, G. R. (1990). Roles and power. In J. Touliatos, B. F. Perlmutter, & M. A. Straus (Eds.), *Handbook of family measurement techniques* (pp. 420–492). Newbury Park, NJ: Sage.

Shelton, K. K., Frick, P. J., & Wootton, J. (1996). Assessment of parenting practices in families of elementary school-age children. *Journal of Clinical Child Psychology, 25,* 317–329.

Sigafoos, A., Reiss, D., Rich, J., & Douglas, E. (1985). Pragmatics in the measurement of family functioning. *Family Process, 24,* 189–203.

Sigel, I. E., & Brody, G. H. (Eds.). (1990). *Methods of family research: Biographies of research projects: Vol. I. Normal families.* Hillsdale, NJ: Erlbaum.

Singer, M. T., & Wynne, L. (1966). Principles for scoring communication defects and deviances in parents of schizophrenics: Rorschach and TAT scoring manuals. *Psychiatry, 25,* 260–288.

Skinner, H. A. (1987). Self-report instruments for family assessment. In T. Jacob (Ed.), *Family interaction and psychopathology: Theories, methods, and finding* (pp. 427–452). New York: Plenum Press.

Skinner, H. A., Steinhauer, P., & Santa-Barbara, J. (1982). *Family assessment measure.* Toronto, Ontario Canada: Addiction Research Foundation.

Skinner, H. A., Steinhauer, P. D., & Santa-Barbara, J. (1983). The family assessment measure. *Canadian Journal of Community Mental Health, 2,* 91–105.

Spanier, G. B., & Thompson, L. (1982). A confirmatory analysis of the Dyadic adjustment scale. *Journal of Marriage and the Family, 44,* 731–738.

Stein, S. J., Girodo, M., & Dotzenroth, S. (1982). The interrelationships and reliability of a multilevel behavior-based assessment package for distressed couples. *Journal of Behavioral Assessment, 4,* 343–360.

Steinglass, P. (1979). The home observation assessment method (HOAM): Real-time naturalistic observation of families in their homes. *Family Process, 18,* 337–354.

Steinglass, P. (1981). The alcoholic family at home: Patterns of interaction in dry, wet, and transitional stages of alcoholism. *Archives of General Psychiatry, 38,* 578–584.

Steinhauer, P. D. (1987). The family as a small group: The process model of family functioning. In T. Jacob (Ed.), *Family interaction and psychopathology: Theories, methods, and findings* (pp. 67–115). New York: Plenum Press.

Strodtbeck, F. L. (1951). Husband-wife interaction over revealed differences. *American Sociological Review, 16,* 468–473.

Strodtbeck, F. L. (1958). Family interaction, values and achievement. In A. L. Baldwin, D. C. McClelland, V. Bronfenbrenner, & F. L. Strodtbeck (Eds.), *Talent and society.* Princeton, NJ: Van Nostrand.

Surra, C., & Ridley, C. (1991). Multiple perspectives on interaction: Participants, peers, and observers. In B. Montgomery & S. Duck (Eds.), *Studying interpersonal interaction* (pp. 33–55). New York: Guilford Press.

Thomas, E. J. (1977). *Marital communication and decision making: Analysis, assessment, and change.* New York: Free Press.

Touliatos, J., Perlmutter, B. F., & Straus, M. A. (Eds.). (1990). *Handbook of family measurement techniques.* Newbury Park, CA: Sage.

Valone, K., Norton, J. P., Goldstein, M. J., & Doane, J. A. (1983). Parental expressed emotion and affective style in an adolescent sample at risk for schizophrenia spectrum disorder. *Journal of Abnormal Psychology, 92,* 399–407.

Vaughn, C. E., & Leff, J. P. (1976). The measurement of expressed emotion in the families of psychiatric patients. *British Journal of Social and Clinical Psychology, 15,* 157–165.

Vincent, J. (1980). The empirical-clinical study of families: Social learning theory as a point of departure. In J. Vincent (Ed.), *Advances in family intervention assessment and theory* (Vol. 1, pp. 1–28). Greenwich, CT: JAI Press.

Vuchinich, S., Emery, R. E., & Cassidy, J. (1988). Family members as third parties in dyadic family conflict: Strategies, alliances, and outcomes. *Child Development, 59,* 1293–1302.

Waldron, R., Sabatelli, R., & Anderson, S. (1990). An examination of the factor structure of the family environment scale. *American Journal of Family Therapy, 18,* 256–272.

Walsh, F. (Ed.). (1993). *Normal family processes.* New York: Guilford Press.

Weiss, R. L. (1981). Strategic behavioral marital therapy: Toward a model for assessment and intervention. In J. P. Vincent (Ed.), *Advances in family intervention, assessment and theory* (Vol. 1, pp. 229–271). Greenwich, CT: JAI Press.

Weiss, R. L., Hops, H., & Patterson, G. R. (1973). A framework for conceptualizing marital conflict: A technology for altering it, some data for evaluating it. In R. W. Clark & L. A. Hamerlynck (Eds.), *Critical issues in research and practice: Proceedings of the Fourth Banff International Conference on Behavior Modification* (pp. 309–342). Champaign, IL: Research Press.

Weiss, R. L., & Perry, B. A. (1979). *Assessment and treatment of marital dysfunction.* Eugene: Oregon Marital Studies Program.

Weiss, R. L., & Summers, K. J. (1983). The marital interaction coding system–III. In E. Filsinger (Ed.), *Marriage and family assessment: A sourcebook for family therapy.* Beverly Hills, CA: Sage.

Wiggins, J. S., & Broughton, R. (1985). The interpersonal circle: A structural model for the integration of personality research. *Perspectives in Personality, 1,* 1–47.

Windle, M. (1995). *The parental burdens questionnaire (PBQ).* Unpublished manuscript. Buffalo, NY: Research Institute on Addictions.

Wolin, S. J., Bennett, L. A., & Noonan, D. L. (1979). Family rituals and the recurrence of alcoholism over generations. *American Journal of Psychiatry, 136,* 589–593.

Wolin, S. J., Bennett, L. A., Noonan, D. L., & Teitelbaum, M. A. (1980). Disrupted family rituals: A factor in the intergenerational transmission of alcoholism. *Journal of Studies on Alcohol, 43,* 199–214.

Langer, E. J., 676
Langer, L. M., 589
Langhinrichsen-Rohling, J., 683, 684
Lanyon, R. I., 165
Lapidos, S., 676
LaPorte, R., 547
LaRocca, N. G., 241, 242
LaRossa, R., 700
Larsen, L., 165
Larson, D. B., 554
Larson, L., 228, 355
Larson, R., 213, 702
Larsson, B., 544
Last, C. G., 318, 320
La Taillade, J. J., 702
Lathrop, G. M., 565, 574, 575
Laumann, E. O., 588, 593
Laumann-Billings, L., 446
Laursen, B., 642
Lavigne, J. V., 538, 554
Lavori, P., 486, 666
Lawrence, E., 686, 692, 693
Lawton, M. P., 663
Layne, C., 689
Lazarus, A. A., 344
Lazarus, L., 675
Lazarus, R. S., 259
Le, J., 270
Leal-Puente, L., 652
Leary, T., 375, 709
Leber, B. D., 191, 210, 211
Leber, W. R., 109, 308, 365, 370
Lebowitz, B. D., 663, 676
LeDoux, J. E., 257, 571
Lee, G. R., 705
Lee, H. B., 145
Lee, W. Y., 563, 564
Leff, J., 447
Lehr, W., 706
Leirer, V. O., 675
Leitenberg, H., 356, 502, 520, 521, 526
Lemanek, K. L., 537, 539, 541, 542, 545, 546, 547, 548, 550
Lemeshow, S., 540
Lemmon, G. R., 89
Lennox, R., 138
Lenzenweger, M. F., 235, 491
Leon, A. S., 503, 522, 525, 526
Leonard, B., 198
Lepper, M. R., 49
Lerew, D. R., 467, 478, 487
Leridon, H., 602
Lerman, C., 506, 527
Lerner, R., 438, 640, 641
Lesanics, D., 548
Lesperance, F., 513
Lessin, S., 705
Lester, D., 375
Letarte, H., 336
Levenson, R. W., 189, 211, 254, 258, 469, 652, 691
Leventhal, B. L., 570
Leverich, G., 435
Levin, H. S., 246
Levin, J. S., 673
Levin, L., 190
Levy, D. L., 235
Levy, K., 227, 233

Lewinsohn, P. M., 6, 487, 666
Lewis, A., 560
Lewis, C. M., 365
Lewis, J. M., 704, 705
Lewis, R. A., 704
Lewko, J. H., 644
Lezak, M., 241
Li, S., 683
Liang, K. Y., 540
Liao, J., 404, 406, 408, 409, 412
Lichtenberg, P. A., 671, 676
Lichtenstein, E., 505, 507, 532
Lieberman, A., 347
Lietaer, G., 378
Lifton, N., 233
Light, R. J., 419
Lijam, N., 571
Likosky, W., 523
Lilly, M. A., 246
Lim, J., 171
Limon, J., 518
Lin, K., 20
Lindan, C., 589
Linden, W., 520, 525
Lindholm, K. J., 56, 58
Lindsay, R. L., 39
Lindsley, C. B., 548
Lindzey, G., 168
Link, B. G., 486, 490
Linn, R. L., 126, 128, 291
Lipman, A. J., 482, 483, 484
Lipman, E. L., 23
Lipsey, M. W., 355, 364, 419, 420, 421, 425, 426, 427
Lipshutz, R., 577
Little, R. J., 76, 404, 405, 406, 407, 408, 415, 508
Livanou, M., 349
Llewelyn, S. P., 371, 372, 382, 391
Locke, H. J., 692
Lockhart, D. J., 576
Loeber, R., 454, 548
Loehlin, J. C., 247
Loevinger, J., 158, 227, 232, 233
Loftus, E. F., 505
Loftus, G. R., 73, 97
Logsdon, R. G., 663, 676
Lohr, N., 228
London, P., 367
Long, B., 404, 407, 408, 410, 415
Long, J. S., 87
Long, N., 553, 630
Longabaugh, R., 684
Longoria, N., 197, 207, 214
Lonigan, C. J., 542, 620, 625
Loosen, P. T., 256, 258
Lopez, M., 340
Lopez, S. R., 346, 347
Lorion, R. P., 404, 405, 406, 407, 408, 415
Lösel, F., 421, 424, 426
Louis-Dit-Sully, C., 563, 564
Lovallo, W., 510, 516, 517
Lowe, C. F., 318
Lowe, L., 62
Lowe, M. J., 270
Lowell, 349
Lowery, A., 370
Loweser, J. D., 502, 521, 526

Luborsky, L., 354, 364, 367, 369, 372, 373, 376, 378, 379
Lubowsky, J., 269
Lucio, E., 167
Lucio, G. E., 170
Luck, S. J., 260
Luckey, D., 449
Ludlow, L. H., 279
Lueger, R., 342
Lumley, V., 209
Lundberg, G. D., 113
Luria, A. R., 246
Luthar, S. S., 23, 441
Lutz, W., 96, 110
Lutzenberger, W., 268
Luzzati, R., 589
Lykken, D. T., 261, 263
Lynch, J., 503, 645
Lynch, M., 440, 455
Lyons, L. C., 17
Lytton, H., 193

Ma, J., 563, 564
Maccaferri, G., 571
MacCallum, R. C., 88, 518
MacCorquodale, P., 612
MacGilvery, A., 563, 564
Machado, P. P., 379
Machon, R. A., 469
MacIver, D., 644
Mack, D., 282
MacKinnon, D. P., 406, 415, 676
MacLean, C., 467, 568, 573, 577
Macmillan, III, F. W., 258
Maddux, J. E., 541
Mader, I., 563, 564
Madigan, S., 541
Madill, A., 392
Maerov, S. L., 194, 198, 212
Magnusson, D., 435, 451, 459, 639, 641
Mahairas, G., 563, 564
Maher, B. A., 118
Mahrer, A. R., 367, 368
Maier, W., 289
Main, D., 506
Main, M., 227, 438, 643, 658
Maitland, S. B., 670
Malamood, H. S., 526
Malan, J., 491
Malarkey, W., 255, 691
Malenfant, J., 317
Malinak, J., 420
Maling, M., 342
Malkoff, S., 691
Mallinckrodt, B., 379, 380
Mandler, G., 225
Manis, M., 230, 234, 256
Manke, F., 128
Mann, B. J., 197, 210
Mann, J. J., 109
Mann, T., 38
Manne, S., 524
Manuck, S., 511, 517
Marascuilo, L. A., 323, 325
Maratukulam, A., 563, 564
March, J., 344
Marcia, A., 116
Marcia, J. E., 646
Marco, C., 524

SUBJECT INDEX

in interpersonal behavior (circumplex models),
    375–376
in semantic content, 372–373
Client-level responsiveness: aptitude-treatment
    interactions, 384–385
Clinical research, 3–30
    design strategies, 13–19
    goals, 4–9, 26–27
    guiding questions/concepts, 4–8
    vs. practice, 297
    special challenges, 19–26
    theory, importance of, 8–9
    validity, and threats to, 9–13
Clinical research, assessment:
    item response theory (IRT), 276–294
    neuropsychological and intellectual assessment,
        241–250
    observational methods, 183–223
    personality research/assessment, 155–182
    projective methods, 224–240
    psychometric issues, 125–154
    psychophysiological research, 251–275
Clinical research, general issues:
    ethical perspectives, 31–53
    ethnicity, gender, and cross-cultural issues, 54–71
    overview, 3–30
    publishing findings, and scientific objectivity,
        107–121
    statistical methods, 72–106
Clinical research, psychopathology and health:
    adult health psychology, 499–536
    adult psychopathology, 466–498
    behavioral genetics, 562–583
    developmental psychopathology, 433–465
    pediatric psychology, 537–561
    sexual behavior, 584–615
Clinical research, special populations:
    adolescents, 634–661
    children, 619–633
    couples, 681–699
    families, 700–718
    older adults, 662–680
Clinical research, treatment:
    community-based treatment and prevention, 403–418
    meta-analytic research methods, 419–429
    therapy outcome research methods, 330–363
    time-series (single-subject) designs, 297–329
    treatment process research methods, 364–402
Clinical significance, 350–352
Clinical utility. See Utility, clinical
Cluster and pattern approaches, 456–457
Coding studies, meta-analysis, 425
Cognitive-behavioral therapy, 368, 674
Cognitive deficits, 252
Cognitive development, measuring (adolescence), 641
Cognitive style of client and treatment differences,
    374–375
Cognitive therapy (CT), 312, 313, 316
Cohort, 665
Cohort effect, 18
Cohort-sequential designs, 446, 669
Collaborative Study Psychotherapy Rating Scale—
    Version 6 (CSPRS), 370
Communication, assessing (family research), 705–706
Community-based treatment and prevention, 403–418
    assumptions about samples and sampling, 405–407
    developmental/longitudinal perspective, centrality of,
        407–409
    differentiating types of prevention, 406–407
    epidemiological vs. random sampling, 405–406

expansion to developmental-ecological model,
    408–409
intervention as interaction with development, 409
measuring prevention outcome effects, 410–414
multilevel influences on development and
    intervention, 409
specifying processes of effects, 414–415
Co-morbidity, clinical child research, 626, 629–630
Comprehensive Process Analysis technique (CPA), 371,
    372
Computers/technology, 72–73, 214, 241, 424, 573,
    576–577, 590, 603
Concurrent validity (personality assessment), 174–175
Conditionality, 127
Confabulation, 243
Confidence intervals (CIs), 26, 98
Confidentiality, 44, 47–48, 51, 64
Configurational frequency analysis (CFA), 456, 457
Confirmatory factor analysis, 80, 128, 132, 145,
    650–651
Conflict of interest, and selective publication, 116–117,
    118
Conflict Tactics Scales (CTS), 692
Consent, informed, 20, 38–41, 50, 64, 595
Consequential validity, 132
Constructs and their interpretation, 22–24
Construct validity. See Validity, construct
Content validity. See Validity, content
Contextual influences, 440–441, 623
Continuity vs. discontinuity of disorder, 491–492
Continuous flow model of affective expressivity, 259
Continuous vs. categorical approaches, 453–455
Control, assessing (family research), 705
Control groups, 46, 86, 113, 335–339, 387, 478–479,
    609–610
    random assignment, 339–340
Convenience, samples of, 20, 475, 586
Convergent validity, 128, 129, 131
Copyright laws, 117
Core conflictual relationship theme (CCRT), 372,
    373–374, 376
Correlation, 4, 5, 8
    intraclass (scorer reliability), 204–205
Correlational designs, 474, 481–484, 524
Correlational procedures (scorer reliability), 203–204
Cost benefit analysis, 41–44
Cost-effectiveness evaluations, 139, 140
Counterdemand expectancy control, 336, 339
Couples, research methods with, 681–699
    assessment, mode of, 691–693
    collecting data from one vs. both partners, 684–685
    communication, type of, 690–691
    cross-sectional studies, 685–686
    data analysis, 693–694
    domestic violence, 692–693
    experimental designs, 688–690
    longitudinal studies, 686–687
    marital satisfaction, 691–692
    measurement, 690–693
    outcome, defining, 690
    passive observations, 685–687
    physical health, 691
    quasi-experimental designs, 687–688
    research designs, 685–690
    sampling, 681
    treatment studies, 688–689
Couples Interaction Scoring System (CISS), 690
CPA. See Comprehensive Process Analysis technique
    (CPA)
Criterion-referenced validity, 129

Item response theory (IRT), 132, 137, 148–149, 151,
    160–161, 177, 276–294
  basics, 276–277
  and construct validity (in test development), 277–284
  and personality assessment scales, 160–161
  and reliability (maximizing, in test development),
    284–291
Item-total correlations, 138
ITSACORR, 324–325
IVS. See Irrational Values Scale (IVS)

Juvenile justice system, 628–631

Kappa, 83, 202–203, 208, 376
Kinsey studies, 591–592
K-SADS. See Schedule for Affective Disorders and
    Schizophrenia—Child version (K-SADS)

Laboratory research:
  vs. applied, 16–17
  using direct observations, 593–595
Language, 56, 59–63, 168, 169, 173, 177, 286, 372–373,
    538
Latent class models, 281
Latent growth curve modeling, 457
Latent trait, 145, 161, 201
Latent transition analysis, 85
Laumann survey, 593
LEDS. See Life Events and Difficulties Schedule
    (LEDS)
Lie detection, 256
Lie scale, 163, 165
LIFE. See Living in Familial Environments (LIFE)
Life Events and Difficulties Schedule (LEDS), 490
Life span framework, 435
Likert, 132, 158, 288, 290, 375
Linear discriminant analysis, 83, 87
Linear logistic latent trait model (LLTM), 279
Linear models, 82
  hierarchical, 84, 545, 644
Linear research, 66, 67
Linear regression, 458
Linkage analysis, 564, 573–575
  allele-sharing methods, 575
  parametric methods, 574–575
LISREL (computer package), 573
Living in Familial Environments (LIFE), 210
LLTM. See Linear logistic latent trait model (LLTM)
Local dependence, 132
Lod score, 574, 576
Logistic regression, 83, 87
Longitudinal designs, 18–19, 407–409, 415, 482–484,
    525, 544–545, 622–623, 648–650, 666–668,
    686–687
  adolescence, 648–650
  assessment frequency, 687
  clinical child research, 622–623
  couples, 686–687
  high-risk studies, 484
  older adults, 666–668
  pediatric psychology, 544–545
  prospective studies, 483–484
  remitted disorder studies, 482–483
  retrospective and follow-back studies, 482

Maintenance, monitoring (study of sexual behavior), 608
Malingering. See Response distortion
Managed care, 542, 553, 625, 670. See also Funding
Manipulation check, 344, 474
MANOVA (multivariate analysis of variance), 649, 693

Manual-based treatments, 344
Marital Adjustment Test (MAT), 691
Marital counseling. See Couples, research methods with
Marital Interaction Coding System (MICS), 190, 690
Marital Satisfaction Inventory (MSI), 692
Marital Satisfaction Time Lines, 189
Marlowe-Crowne Inventory, 256
Marriage. See Couples, research methods with
MAT. See Marital Adjustment Test (MAT)
McMaster Structured Interview of Family Functioning
    (McSIFF), 701
McSIFF. See McMaster Structured Interview of Family
    Functioning (McSIFF)
Mean effects, 420–421
Measurement issues. See also Psychometric issues
  continuous vs. categorical approaches, 453–455
  couples research, 690–693
  developmental psychopathology, 453–455
  domains, 112
  geropsychology, 674–675
  health psychology research, 500–501
  measurement equivalence, 455
  pediatric psychology, 547–551
  sex research, 587–589
  treatment research, 347–353
Measurement model, fit of, to data, 78–81
  example of (Figure 4.1), 79
Mechanisms, 7
Mediational models, 415, 518–519
Mediators, 5, 7, 352–353, 471–472, 540–541, 543–544,
    624, 639
Medical conditions. See Physical health/illness
Meta-analysis, 26, 99, 100, 235, 353–356, 419–429
  coding studies, 425
  defining, 420
  hypotheses, specific, 422
  judging mean effects, 420–421
  number of studies needed, 422–423
  publication bias, 424–425
  representativeness of studies, 423–425
  rival explanations, ruling out, 425–427
  steps in, 421–427
Meta-classification, 365–366
MICS. See Marital Interaction Coding System (MICS)
Midtown Questionnaire, 67
Millan Clinical Multiaxial Inventory (MCMI-III), 172
Minnesota Multiphasic Personality Inventory (MMPI),
    146, 159, 162, 163, 164, 165, 166, 167, 169, 171,
    172, 173, 175, 228, 279, 373, 375, 379
  Depression Scale, 522
  MMPI-2, 62, 161, 162, 164, 165, 167, 169, 170, 172,
    173, 175, 176, 177, 229, 235, 652
  MMPI-A (Minnesota Multiphasic Personality
    Inventory-Adolescent), 652, 653
  Restandardization Committee, 167
Minorities. See Ethnicity/gender/cultural issues in
    clinical research
Minors, obtaining informed consent for, 40, 209
MIRA (computer program), 283, 284
Missing data, 73, 74, 75–77, 113, 425
MMPI. See Minnesota Multiphasic Personality
    Inventory (MMPI)
Moderators, 5, 6, 9, 17, 93–95, 96, 352–353, 471–472,
    540–541, 543, 624, 639, 650
Molar vs. molecular behavior category, 196–197
Molecular biology, 571
Molecular genetics, 562
Momentary time sampling, 186
MSI. See Marital Satisfaction Inventory (MSI)
Multifinality, 438, 439